W9-CJZ-924

Mass Media Law and Regulation

43 95

5TH EDITION

Mass Media Law and Regulation

WILLIAM E. FRANCOIS
EMERITUS PROFESSOR OF JOURNALISM
DRAKE UNIVERSITY

IOWA STATE UNIVERSITY PRESS / AMES

KF
2750
.F7
1990

WILLIAM E. FRANCOIS is an emeritus professor of journalism, Drake University, where he taught from 1969–1984 before taking early retirement. He began his teaching career at Marshall University in 1959 after working on daily newspapers for ten years as a reporter and editor. He currently is teaching at the University of North Florida in Jacksonville. A Fulbright Distinguished Lecturer at Seoul National University in 1988, Dr. Francois also was a distinguished visiting consultant in mass communications at American University in Cairo, Egypt, for two years. He has given U.S. Information Agency-sponsored lectures in many parts of the world. Among honors received were American Bar Association Certificates of Merit in 1972 and 1973 in recognition of "a distinguished contribution to public understanding of the American system of law and justice." The certificates resulted from columns he wrote for *Writer's Digest* magazine titled "Law and the Writer."

© 1990 William E. Francois
Earlier copyright © 1975, 1978, 1982, by John Wiley & Sons, and 1986 by Macmillan Publishing Company

Fifth edition, 1990

All rights reserved

Manufactured in the United States of America
♾ This book is printed on acid-free paper.

No part of this book may be reproduced in any form or by any electronic or mechanical means, including information storage and retrieval systems, without written permission from the publisher, except for brief passages quoted in a review.

Authorization to photocopy items for internal or personal use, or the internal or personal use of specific clients, is granted by Iowa State University Press, provided that the base fee of $.10 per copy is paid directly to the Copyright Clearance Center, 27 Congress Street, Salem, MA 01970. For those organizations that have been granted a photocopy license by CCC, a separate system of payment has been arranged. The fee code for users of the Transactional Reporting Service is 0–8138-0968–1/90 $.10.

Library of Congress Cataloging-in-Publication Data

Francois, William E.
    Mass media law and regulation / William E. Francois.—5th ed.
        p. cm.
    ISBN 0–8138–0968–1 (alk. paper)
        1. Press law—United States. 2. Mass media—Law and legislation—United States. I. Title.
    KF2750.F7 1990
    343.73′099—dc20
    [347.30399]   89–77432

CANISIUS COLLEGE LIBRARY
BUFFALO, N. Y.

TO IRENE

CONTENTS

PREFACE

Mass Media Law and Regulation is written for journalism students by a journalist in the hope that it will be readable and enlightening—a textbook that newcomers to the complex field of mass media law can use without foreboding. Toward this end the minutiae of legal technicalities—important, no doubt, to law school students—frequently have been omitted or have received only brief attention. If, in the main, this has helped to give greater emphasis to the principal ideas, issues, and cases affecting the media, then the shortcomings caused by such omissions may be tolerable.

To those readers who begin a "law book" with the notion that they are entering a realm of quietude or equable monotony, such an idea should be short-lived. Many issues involving the media are explosive because of the "interests" that are in competition. For the most part the Bill of Rights represents consensus of the American people and jurisprudence. An exception is freedom of the press. It, above all others, is still being contested in the public opinion and in the branches of government. Laws are enacted that infringe upon that freedom; courts issue injunctions tantamount to prior restraint of the press; officers of executive branches of government frequently attack the press or contrive to make it impotent. The record will show that the press is not entirely free, nor left untrammeled. Injunctions, subpoenas, the jailing of journalists, "gag" orders, withholding of information, and White House "enemies" lists have had the effect, intentionally or otherwise, of inhibiting or cowing segments of the Fourth Estate. No other Bill of Rights guarantee is so hotly contested nor so transparently violated as the "First" freedom.

But the smoke of battle has not blown in one direction only. A momentous decision in 1964 helped to strengthen the backbone of timorous journalists who might otherwise refrain from publishing critical reports about government officials or public figures; a federal Freedom of Information Act, imperfect though it is, came into existence in 1967, and open-meeting and open-record laws have been enacted by all state governments.

Such issues and concerns are a part of this book. Many

others also are recorded. However, communication law is dynamic, requiring periodic revision of a textbook about such law.

This fifth edition includes a substantial number of new developments not included in earlier editions. Here are some "samplings":

In Chapter 1, Professor Leonard Levy has modified his views about the extent of press freedom in early America. Chapter 2 includes information on Supreme Court appointments by President Reagan, including new Chief Justice William Rehnquist and Associate Justices Antonin Scalia and Anthony M. Kennedy. Only Justices Brennan and Marshall remain as the "old guard" liberals, and both are in their 80s. Further, President George Bush is likely to continue the Reagan practice of appointing "conservatives" to fill federal court vacancies.

In Chapter 3, a Supreme Court decision in 1988 gives public school officials considerable voice in what can or cannot be published in high school newspapers. The Court also has answered an earlier question by stating that information is property, thus equating the theft of information with the theft of property.

Whenever public officials or public figures sue the news media, they must show actual malice by "clear and convincing" evidence, as Chapter 5 points out. And in Chapter 6, the public interest/public concern test regains some vitality in cases decided by the U.S. Supreme Court. In addition, private figure plaintiffs must show falsity whenever the matter complained of is of public concern.

The list of new developments goes on and on, including the Federal Communications Commission repeal of the Fairness Doctrine in 1987.

These developments are some of the reasons why this new edition is necessary. But publication of a revised edition does not mean that students can "rest easy." If they want to stay up to date with current developments, they should acquire the habit, if they have not already done so, of regularly reading *Editor & Publisher, Advertising Age,* and *Broadcasting,* plus publications that deal exclusively with media law developments, such as *Media Law Reporter* or *The NEWS Media & The LAW.* In fact, *Media Law Reporter* and *The U.S. Law Week,* which are copyrighted by the Bureau of National Affairs, Inc., in Washington, D.C., have been frequent sources of information for this book.

I close now with a "confession" of my bias and perspective in regard to press-freedom issues. First, I am a journalist-turned-teacher who still thrills to the words of the late Supreme Court Justice Hugo L. Black and his unequivocal championing of First Amendment freedoms. Second, however, I have tried to present various viewpoints concerning major issues with the objective of providing balance among competing ideas, thereby lessening the impact of any bias. The reader will judge the success of this effort.

TABLE OF CASES

For the most complete information on a case, readers should first look at the page or pages referred to by italicized page numbers whenever there is more than one reference. Except in a few instances, court cases which involved the United States, a state or a federal agency are indexed so that if the name of the case, for example, is *U.S. v. Caldwell,* it will be listed Caldwell (U.S. v. _____). Any case adjudicated by the Federal Communications Commission (FCC) or Federal Trade Commission (FTC) will carry the parenthetical notation of the agency to distinguish it from one adjudicated by the courts. Thus, *KHJ-TV (FCC)* is a case decided by the FCC.

Mass Media Law
and Regulation

Early Press Controls and the First Amendment

HIGHLIGHTS

■ The three principal press controls used in England, beginning in the sixteenth century, were licensing, taxation, and seditious libel (printing criticisms of those in government). Depending on their severity, these were forms of prior restraint of the press; i.e., restraint prior to publication.

■ John Peter Zenger trial in 1735 and *People v. Croswell* (1805) established truth as a defense to seditious libel charges in the U.S.

■ Chafee, Levy, and Berns provide different interpretations concerning reasons for adoption of the First Amendment and the emergence of libertarianism.

■ Blackstonian doctrine, in the mid-1700s, provided one of the earliest definitions of freedom of press; namely, the absence of prior restraint (no restraints prior to publication).

■ *Grosjean v. American Press Co.* led the U.S. Supreme Court in 1936 to declare unconstitutional a Louisiana-enacted discriminatory tax against newspapers.

Through much of history a familiar pattern emerges. Those with political or ecclesiastical power frequently have sought to restrain or prohibit information and ideas intended for the masses. Efforts of the Romans to suppress Christianity were matched by attempts of the Roman Catholic Church and other religious groups to stamp out heresy and blasphemy in the Middle Ages. Monarchs, parading under the banner of divine right of kings, and ecclesiastics sought to restrict or prevent the flow of information critical of state or church.

In Europe, the invention of movable type by Johannes Gutenberg in the mid-1400s eventually resulted in revolutions in education, politics, and economics. Those in authority did not at first recognize the danger to them of the new printing method. When they did, controls of various kinds were instituted. In England, these took three principal forms: licensing, taxation, and seditious libel, the latter making criticism of those in authority a crime. Depending on how these controls were used, or their severity, they are examples of prior restraint of the press.

Licensing in England

The printing press was introduced into England in 1476.[1] One of the earliest efforts to control it took the form of a proclamation by Henry VIII in 1529 that banned certain books odious to him or to the clergy who advised him. The following year a licensing system was begun, and a book seller was hanged for attempting to sell a proscribed book. Licensing of printing did not end until 1697. From 1538, when a full-blown licensing system was instituted on the theory that printing was a state matter and therefore subject to control by the crown, until 1585, various edicts were issued against printers, subjecting them to harsh penalties if they criticized church or government.

Court of Star Chamber

Among the controllers was the infamous Court of the Star Chamber, created by royal edict in 1588. Consisting of high-ranking government members who sat behind closed doors in the "starred chamber" at Westminster, the "court" continued until 1641, issuing decrees and ordering any punishment it deemed proper, except the death sentence.[2] Fines, press seizures, cutting off ears, splitting noses, and imprisonment were penalties meted out by the Star Chamber.

When reference is now made to "star-chambered proceedings," it is to meetings of government officials behind closed doors—the press and public being excluded, as was the case with Court of the Star Chamber proceedings.

Parliament as Censor

The Star Chamber was abolished in 1641, but harassment of printers continued during the Long Parliament (1640–1660) by means of a licensing agency (the Company of Stationers), a Board of Licensers, or by various parliamentary committees. The zealousness of Parliament in controlling the press is demonstrated by this report in Corbett's *Parliamentary History of England* concerning a law passed on June 11, 1643:

> The Liberty of the Press having of late been very grievous to the Parliament, they passed an Ordinance to restrain it, and to strengthen some former Orders made for that purpose.

The most material Clauses are these: "That no Order or Declaration of either house [of Parliament] shall be printed without order of one or both the said houses; nor any other book, pamphlet, paper, . . . shall from henceforth be printed, bound, stitched, or put out to sale, by any person . . . , unless the same be first approved and licenced under the hands of such persons as both, or either, of the said houses shall appoint for licencing of the same; and be entered in the Register Book of the Company of Stationers, according to ancient custom, and the printer thereof to put his name thereto. — The master and wardens of the said company . . . are authorized and required to make diligent search . . . and to seize and carry away such printing presses, letters and other materials, of every such irregular printer, which they find so misemployed; . . . and likewise to make diligent search . . . for such scandalous and unlicenced books, not entered, nor signed with the printer's name as aforesaid, being printed, contrary to this Order; and the same to seize and carry away; . . . and likewise to apprehend all authors, printers, and other persons whatsoever employed in compiling, printing, stitching, binding, publishing and dispersing of the said scandalous, unlicenced, and unwarrantable papers, books, and pamphlets as aforesaid; and all those who shall resist the said parties in searching after them, and bringing them before either of the houses or the committee of examinations, that so they may receive such further punishments as their offences shall demerit; and not to be released until they have given satisfaction to the parties employed in their apprehension . . . not to offend in like sort for the future.[3]

To demands for freedom of press, Parliament responded in 1649 by making seditious publication a crime of treason, punishable by death, and by limiting printing to the confines of London and several other major cities.

With varying intensity, prepublication controls continued until 1695 when Parliament permitted the Regulation of Printing Act to expire. The result was an end to press censorship in England.[4] But printers did not suddenly find themselves free of punishment if convicted of seditious libel or treason. As late as 1794, two printers were tried for treason, but their acquittal marked the end of this fearsome threat against those who published criticisms of those in power.

That printers and authors ignored or circumvented press controls is evidenced by Queen Anne's message to Parliament on January 17, 1712, as reported by Corbett:

Her majesty finds it necessary to observe, how great licence is taken in publishing false and scandalous Libels, such as are a reproach to any government. This evil seems to be grown too strong for the laws now in force; it is therefore recommended to you to find a remedy equal to the mischief.[5]

And the House of Commons responded:

We are very sensible how much the Liberty of the Press is abused, by turning it into such a licentiousness as is a just reproach to the nation; since not only false and scandalous libels are printed and published against your majesty's government, but the most horrid blasphemies against God and religion; and we beg leave humbly to assure your majesty, that we will do our utmost to find out a remedy equal to this mischief, and that may effectually cure it.[6]

Parliament attempted to reimpose a law similar to the one passed in 1643, but for various reasons it failed to gain passage. Instead, a tax was imposed upon the press.

The radical whigs were one reason why Parliament did not act more aggressively to curb the press. The whigs, through pamphlets and the press itself, increasingly in the early 1700s and more stridently called for greater freedom of expression and their views would be echoed in the American colonies in the years leading to the American Revolution.

Taxation in England

In 1712 Parliament passed the first stamp act—a tax on newspapers and pamphlets, on advertising, and on the print paper itself. This "tax on knowledge" was enacted as a means of punishing scandalous and licentious publications, of forcing registration of a growing number of publications (thereby making it easier to control them), and of bolstering the treasury. This means of exerting control continued to plague the British press until abolished in 1855.

Seditious Libel in England

Technically, this "crime" against the state—printing criticisms of those in authority—did not constitute prior restraint, as did licensing, because it occurred *after* publication; but penalties were so severe that the chilling effect on freedom to publish was comparable to prior restraint because printers often were frightened into self-censorship.

Just when the crime of seditious libel began is uncertain. Not only is the common-law origin of seditious libel obscure,[7] but so is the historical development of the defense of truth whenever a printer was accused of such a crime.[8] As early as the thirteenth century it had been a crime to spread rumors about the crown and noblemen, but even then truth could be a defense. Yet in a 1606 case, *De Libellis Famosis,* the Star Chamber refused to allow such a defense.[9] Not until the Fox Libel Act in 1792 did a major change occur—when juries were permitted to decide if in fact libel had occurred. Previously, such a determination had been the prerogative of judges. The only function of juries had been to ascertain if the accused had published the matter complained of. Under the new legislation, juries also were permitted to ignore a judge's instructions and to return whatever verdict they wished.

Although the Fox Libel Act did not end the crime of seditious libel, convictions became more difficult to obtain. In 1793 there were wholesale arrests of printers, a renewed crackdown that prompted Englishman Robert Hall to write a tract, *An Apology for the Freedom of the Press and for General Liberty,* in which he put forth his concept of what the crime of libel should be. Hall argued that only overt acts against the government, not "mere" opinions, should be proscribed adding: "The law hath amply provided against overt acts of sedition and disorder, and to suppress mere opinions by another method than reason and argument, is the height of tyranny."[10]

In the following years, prosecutions steadily decreased, especially after passage of Lord Campbell's Act of 1843 that established truth as a defense in criminal libel cases—long after it had been used as a defense in the American colonies.

Licensing in America

Although newspapers in the colonies generally were not required to be licensed, some of the earliest ones followed English precedent by submitting to censorship. The first continuously published newspaper in America, the Boston *News-Letter* (1704–1776), carried "Published by Authority" under its nameplate, which meant that the colonial governor could disapprove of stories, thereby preventing their publication.[11]

Blackstonian Doctrine. Other colonial newspapers had problems "with authority," but by the mid-1700s the idea of prior restraint being the antithesis of press freedom had gained recognition from one of England's foremost legal authorities, Sir William Blackstone. His view of press freedom would be very influential in America until the late 1800s:

> The liberty of the press is indeed essential to the nature of a free state; but this consists in laying no previous restraints upon publications and not in freedom from censure for criminal matter when published. Every free man has an undoubted right to lay what sentiments he pleases before the public; to forbid this, is to destroy the freedom of the press; but if he publishes what is improper, mischievous or illegal, he must take the consequences of his own temerity.[12]

In recent times, licensing has not been a news media problem. It occasionally has surfaced in the form of city ordinances that require a permit, license, or prior approval of a municipal officer before the "poor people's press"—pamphlets—can be distributed. In one such case, the U.S. Supreme Court held a municipal ordinance invalid which required that the city manager give approval before pamphlets could be distributed. Speaking for the Court, Chief Justice Charles Evans Hughes said of the ordinance: "Whatever the motive which induced its adoption, its character is such that it strikes at the very foundation of the freedom of the press by subjecting it to license and censorship."[13]

Taxation in America

British stamp acts also were applied against colonial printers in America and induced growing resentment. A special Stamp Act of March 1765 aroused intense opposition, and most newspapers refused to pay the tax. Inability or unwillingness to enforce the Act led to its repeal after one year.[14]

Following the Revolutionary War, Massachusetts attempted to impose a tax on newspapers, but public reaction was so great that the law was rescinded before it could be put into effect.[15]

Grosjean Case. The landmark case involving discriminatory tax against newspapers began in 1934 when the Louisiana legislature enacted a two percent tax on the gross receipts of newspapers having circulations larger than 20,000 copies per week. The lawmakers acted at the the behest of Huey Long, a state political power who was feuding with all but one of the 13 largest newspapers in the state. The constitutionality of the statute was challenged, and the U.S. Supreme Court unanimously declared it unconstitutional in *Grosjean v. American Press Co.* (1936). Justice George Sutherland, in giving the Court's opinion, traced the history of such taxation:

> For more than a century prior to the adoption of the [First] Amendment—and, indeed, for many years thereafter—history discloses a persistent effort on the part of the British government to prevent or abridge the free expression of any opinion which seemed to criticize or exhibit in an unfavorable light, however truly, the agencies and operations of government. The struggle between the proponents of measures to that end and those asserting the right of free expression was continuous and unceasing. As early as 1644, John Milton, in an "Appeal for the Liberty of Unlicensed Printing," assailed an act of Parliament which had just been passed providing for censorship of the press previous to publication. He vigorously defended the right of every man to make public his honest views "without previous censure and declared the impossibility of finding any man base enough to accept the office of censor and at the same time good enough to be allowed to perform its duties. The act expired . . . in 1695. It was never renewed; and the liberty of the press thus became . . . merely "a right or liberty to publish without a license what formerly could be published only with one." But mere exemption from previous censorship was soon recognized as too narrow a view of the liberty of the press.
>
> In 1712, in response to a message from Queen Anne . . ., Parliament imposed a tax upon all newspapers and upon advertisements. . . . That the main purpose . . . was to suppress the publication of comments and criticisms objectionable to the Crown does not admit doubt. . . . There followed more than a century of resistance to, and evasion of, the taxes, and of agitation for their repeal. . . .
>
> The framers of the First Amendment were familiar with the English struggle, which then had continued for nearly 80 years and was destined to go on for another 65 years, at the end of which time it culminated in a lasting abandonment of the obnoxious taxes. . . . It is impossible to concede that by the words "freedom of the press" the framers of the amendment intended to adopt merely the narrow view then reflected by the law of England that such freedom consisted only in immunity from previous censorship; for this abuse had then permanently disappeared from the English practice. It is equally impossible to believe that it was not intended to bring within the reach of these words such modes of restraint as were embodied in the . . . taxation already described. . . . [16]

This decision did not rule out nondiscriminatory business taxes against newspapers. As Sutherland pointed out:

> It is not intended by anything we have said to suggest that the owners of newspapers are immune from any of the ordinary forms of taxation for support of the government. But this is not an ordinary form of tax, but one . . . with a long history of hostile misuse against freedom of press.

Similarly, the Supreme Court declared in a 1937 case that the Associated Press was not immune from regulation because it was an agency of the press, saying: "The publisher of a newspaper has no special immunity from the application of general laws. . . . Like others he must pay equitable and nondiscriminatory taxes on his business."[17]

Minnesota Tax Case. A more recent example of a discriminatory tax against some newspapers is afforded by *Minneapolis Star v. Minnesota Commissioner of Revenue* (1983).[18] In an 8–1 decision, the U.S. Supreme Court declared unconstitutional a Minnesota "use tax" imposed in 1971 on the cost of paper and ink products consumed in the production of newspapers, although the first $100,000 worth of paper and ink used annually was exempt from taxation.

In her opinion for the Court, Justice Sandra O'Connor said that *Grosjean* was not controlling because there was no "impermissible or censorial motive on the part of the [Minnesota] legislature" whereas in *Grosjean* there was a perception on the part of the Court "that the state imposed the tax with an intent to penalize a selected group of newspapers."[19]

The Minnesota tax violated the First Amendment not only because it singled out the press, said O'Connor, but also because it targeted a small group of newspapers. The $100,000 exemption, she explained, resulted in only a handful of publishers paying any tax at all, and even fewer paying a significant amount of tax.[20]

Since the raising of revenue was the main interest asserted by the state in enacting the tax, the Court said an alternative means is available for achieving the same interest without raising First Amendment concerns, namely, taxing businesses generally, thereby avoiding the censorial threat implicit in a tax that singles out the press.

The Court's action had the effect of requiring the state to refund the taxes paid by newspapers which, in the case of the *Minneapolis Star and Tribune,* amounted to about one million dollars.

Other Tax Cases

In 1987, the U.S. Supreme Court again invalidated a state law that taxed general-interest magazines but exempted newspapers and religious, professional, trade, and sports publications.[21] The Court ruled that states generally cannot tax some types of publications while exempting others. In that same year, the Colorado Supreme Court decided that Denver's sales tax, as applied to the retail sales of newspapers, was constitutional.[22]

Seditious Libel in America

Zenger Trial. The famous John Peter Zenger case did not change the common-law crime of seditious libel in the United States, but it marked "a milestone in the fight for the right to criticize government," according to Supreme Court Justice William O. Douglas.[23] The trial provided a historically important precedent that truth could be a defense against a seditious libel charge.

Zenger, the publisher of the *New York Weekly Journal,* had printed criticisms of Governor William Cosby. A grand jury refused to indict the publisher and finally the colony's attorney general, at the behest of Cosby, brought seditious libel charges. Zenger was arrested and held in jail for eight months while awaiting trial! But even while he was in jail, he continued to edit the newspaper through the "keyhole" of his jail cell—doing so by means of visits from his wife and sponsors of his newspaper.

During the 1735 trial in New York, Zenger's widely known attorney, Andrew Hamilton of Philadelphia, recounted that there had been only one other previous indictment for seditious libel in the colonies, involving a clergyman who had criticized a government official.[24] Then, to the surprise of the prosecution, Hamilton admitted that Zenger had published the criticisms complained of, an admission tantamount to a plea of guilty in those days since the prosecution only had to show who had published the criticism. But Hamilton turned to the jury and in an eloquent plea argued for the defense of truth. The jury agreed that the criticisms were true and acquitted the defendant.

The Zenger trial was probably the last of its kind conducted before "royal judges," according to Professor Leonard Levy of Claremont Graduate School who indicated that not more than six such prosecutions were tried before these judges during the entire colonial period. As Levy wrote:

> Indeed, the maligned judges were virtually angels of self-restraint when compared with the intolerant public—or when compared with the oppressive governors, who, acting in a quasi-judicial capacity with their councils, were more dreaded and active instruments of suppression than the common-law courts.
>
> The most suppressive body by far, however, was that acclaimed bastion of the people's liberties, the popularly elected assembly. That the law bore down harshly on verbal crimes in colonial America was the result of the inquisitorial propensities of the governors and legislators, which vied with each other in ferreting out slights upon the government. The law of seditious libel was enforced in America primarily by the provincial assemblies, exercising their power to punish alleged "breaches of parliamentary privilege." Needing no grand jury to indict and no petty jury to convict, the assemblies zealously sought to establish the prerogative of being as immune to criticism as the House of Commons they all emulated. An assembly might summon, interrogate, and fix criminal penalties against anyone who had supposedly libeled its members, its proceedings, or the government generally.[25]

There were many such arrests, including one that provoked great controversy in 1770 when Alexander McDougall, a member of the Sons of Liberty, was arrested on a charge of seditious libel against the New York Assembly.[26] The assemblymen were so sure he would be convicted that they turned him over to a common-law court where bail was set, but McDougall refused to post bail and remained a martyr in prison for 10 weeks. Then, with scores of partisans accompanying him, the defendant was taken before a grand jury which indicted him. A trial was set, but before it could begin a star witness died and a series of postponements resulted. Frustrated, the Assembly issued its own warrant and ordered the sergeant-at-arms to bring McDougall before it. He appeared, refused to enter a plea, said he had no attorney, and resisted any attempts at questioning. Soon the legislators fell to quarreling among themselves and finally decided to accept an apology in lieu of further action; but McDougall refused to apologize and was jailed for nearly three months until the legislative session ended and the charges against him were dropped.

FIRST AMENDMENT: CHAFEE, LEVY, BERNS INTERPRETATIONS

Whether the adoption of the First Amendment as part of the Bill of Rights on December 15, 1791, was intended to wipe out the crime of seditious libel sparks debate. Professor Zechariah Chafee, Jr. of Harvard University believed the First Amendment "was written by men . . . who intended to wipe out the common law of sedition, and make further prosecutions for criticism of the government, without any incitement to lawbreaking, forever impossible in the United States. . . . "[27] But Professor Levy contended that the Bill of Rights may only have been "the chance product of political expediency"[28] and that a broad libertarian theory of freedom of speech and press did not emerge in the United States until the Jeffersonians were forced to defend themselves against the Federalist-enacted Sedition Act of 1798.[29]

Constitutional Convention. To understand what Levy meant by "political expediency," it is necessary to go back to the time when the U.S. Constitution was being written. This drafting process was done behind closed doors and required about four months. No official minutes were kept so historians must rely on delegates' recollections of what happened. Levy says that not until three days before the convention ended on September 17, 1787, did anyone there urge that basic freedoms be enumerated in the proposed Constitution. The reason lay not in any diminished belief that certain freedoms belonged to the people, but rather, as expressed by Alexander Hamilton, that the federal government was one of delegated powers, and that powers not given to the government were retained by the people. Hamilton argued that a listing of such rights might be dangerous since any right inadvertently omitted might be deemed not to belong to the people.

Among those who remained unconvinced were Patrick Henry and Thomas Jefferson. Henry urged his state of Virginia not to ratify the Constitution until basic rights were guaranteed by that document. In fact, five states might not have ratified the Constitution if assurances had not been given by James Madison that such guarantees would quickly be forthcoming (the "political expediency" referred to by Levy). Even with such assurances, the states of Virginia, New York, North Carolina, and Rhode Island shied away from giving their approval until after the ninth state—South Carolina—had ratified the Constitution, thereby making it binding on those states that already had done so. The Constitution went into effect in March 1789. Shortly after the First Congress convened in 1789, a number of constitutional amendments were proposed, as promised at the convention by Madison, the "father" of the Constitution. One of them, as drafted by Madison, provided that the people "shall not be deprived or abridged of their right to speak, to write, or to publish their sentiments; and the freedom of the press, as one of the great bulwarks of liberty, shall be inviolable."[30]

But let's back up a bit.

During the War of Independence, 11 of the 13 states adopted state constitutions and nine of them had freedom of press guarantees.[31] The first of the early press clauses was drafted in 1776 for the Virginia Declaration of Rights and read: "That the freedom of the Press is one of the greatest bulwarks of liberty, and can never be restrained but by despotick Governments." Pennsylvania protected both freedom of speech and press, declaring: "That the people have a right to freedom of speech, and of writing, and publishing their sentiments; therefore the freedom of press ought not to be restrained."

Thus, when the states' delegates gathered in 1787 in Philadelphia to draft the federal constitution, freedom of press already was protected in most states.

Whether the Constitution should specifically guarantee certain rights of the people proved a great public issue, more so in the ratification process than at the Constitutional Convention where the issue surfaced during the closing days of the convention.

Virginia, New York, and North Carolina proposed amendments to the federal Constitution aimed at guaranteeing press freedom. For example, Virginia's ratifying convention adopted a proposed amendment in mid-1788 that read: "That the people have a right to freedom of speech, and of writing and publishing their sentiments; that the freedom of the press is one of the greatest bulwarks of liberty and ought not to be violated." This proposal was almost identical to the one submitted by Madison on June 8, 1789, when he proposed 12 amendments to the Constitution during the First Congress. His and other proposals were sent to a select committee of Congress. Not much is known about what happened at the committee sessions, but Madison's press-clause proposal was rewritten as follows: "The freedom of speech and of the press, and the right of the people peaceably to assemble and consult for their common good, and to apply to the Government for the redress of grievances, shall not be infringed."

The House debated the proposed amendments and on August 24, 1789, adopted a resolution to propose them to the states. Senate proceedings were closed to the public so the record there is very sketchy. On September 4, a new version of the proposed press guarantee appeared for consideration in the Senate, namely: "That Congress shall make no law, abridging the freedom of speech, or of the press, or the right of the people peaceably to assemble and consult for their common good, and to petition the government for a redress of grievances."[32] Just why the language, "that Congress shall make no law . . .," was used is unknown. As the author of a law review article wrote:

> It may have been merely editorial, reflecting a desire to state the amendment in active rather than passive voice. Or it may have reflected a determination to make clear that the amendment was to limit only Congress, not the states.[33]

A conference committee resulted and on September 25 the speaker and the vice-president signed a resolution asking President Washington to send 12 proposed amendments to the governors of the states for ratification. By then, the proposed Bill of Rights was the product of three committees and several floor amendments in both houses, and the language of what would become the First Amendment had gone through five versions with the final language being a compromise.[34] At the time, the provision now known as the First Amendment was third on the list submitted to the states. It became first only because Amendments One and Two were not ratified. As the law review author noted:

> If the order of amendments represented their importance to the Founders, then we know that nothing was as important to them as the election (Amendment One) and compensation (Amendment Two) of congressmen.[35]

But then freedom of press or speech was never first on anyone's list, as the article on the origins of the press clause pointed out:

> It was the last right mentioned in the Address to the Inhabitants of Quebec;[36] it was article twelve of the Pennsylvania Declaration of Rights; the sixteenth of twenty amendments proposed by the Virginia Ratifying Convention and the second clause of the fourth proposition in Madison's proposed bill of rights.[37]

Bill of Rights. In all, 10 amendments—called the Bill of Rights—were approved by the states and went into effect on December 15, 1791, including the First Amendment which states: "Congress shall make no law respecting an establishment of religion, or prohibiting the free exercise thereof; or abridging the freedom of speech or of the press; or the right of the people peaceably to assemble, and to petition the government for a redress of grievances."

To guard against the danger envisioned by Hamilton, Madison also proposed what was to become the Ninth Amendment, which reads, in part: "The enumeration in the Constitution, of certain rights, shall not be construed to deny or disparage others retained by the people."

Levy argued that states' rights was the motivating force behind adoption of the First Amendment (hence the words: "*Congress* shall make no law . . . "), and that Madison's pledge to bring forth amendments as quickly as possible—a promise given so delegates would complete work on the Constitution—amounted to political expediency. He holds that broad libertarianism did not emerge until debate began in Congress over enactment of the alien and sedition laws in 1798.

But Professor Walter Berns of the University of Toronto disagreed for the same reason put forth by Levy in arguing that the framers of the First Amendment were not motivated by broad libertarianism, but instead acted out of concern for states' rights. Berns contended that states' rights, not libertarianism, prompted opposition to the 1798 legislation.[38]

Sedition Act of 1798

The Sedition Act provided, in part:

That if any person shall write, print, utter or publish, or shall cause or procure to be written, printed, or uttered or published, or shall knowingly and willingly assist or aid in writing, printing, uttering or publishing any false, scandalous and malicious writing or writings against the government of the United States, or either house of the Congress of the United States, or the President of the United States, with intent to defame the said Government, or either house of the said Congress, or the said President, or to bring them, or to excite against them . . . the hatred of the good people of the United States . . . shall be punished by a fine not exceeding $2,000 and by imprisonment not exceeding two years.

The law was the work of the Federalists who enacted it shortly after a peace treaty was signed with Great Britain. The treaty had angered France, then at war with England, and her supporters in America (the Republicans). The result was the seizure of some American ships by French vessels, a demand for "tribute" to end such seizures, followed by passage of the Alien and Sedition laws that could be used against "vocal" French supporters in the United States. After recounting some of the debate during consideration of the sedition legislation, Berns wrote:

. . . [A]ccording to Leonard Levy, it was only under "the pressure of the Sedition Act . . . [that] writers of the Jeffersonian party were driven to originate so broad a theory of freedom of expression that the concept of seditious libel was, at last, repudiated."[39] Such a theory did not, however, emerge from the debates in the House. Edward Livingston insisted that the bill violated the First Amendment, and Livingston was supported in this view by the next speaker, Nathaniel Macon of North Carolina. But the debates reveal that neither Livingston nor Macon—nor any of their Republican colleagues—adopted a broad "libertarian" understanding of the principle of freedom of expression. The bill "directly violated the letter of the constitution," Macon said. . . . But he then acknowledged that "persons might be prosecuted for a libel under the State Governments," and questioned the necessity of a federal law. In short, he, like his colleagues during the debate . . ., objected to the Sedition bill on constitutional grounds and, more precisely, on states' rights grounds, but he did not argue that such legislation was objectionable in principle. He made this clear later in the debate . . . when he asserted that liberty of the press was sacred and ought to be left where the Constitution had left it: "The states have complete power on the subject, and when Congress legislates, it ought to have confidence in the States. . . ."

Harrison Otis of Massachusetts had taxed the Republicans with inconsistency by quoting state constitutional provisions respecting the rights of free speech and press, then quoting statutes of the same states making libel a criminal offense and punishing licentiousness and sedition. In accusing them of inconsistency, however, he was to some extent missing the thrust of their argument. They were not contending for free speech and press; they were contending for states' rights, for the right of the states to punish seditious libel. The United States for them existed as a form of words, but not as a sovereign nation.[40]

Under attack by critics, Levy modified his views about press freedom in early America. He still believes that the First Amendment was intended to restrain Congress, but not the states, and that the freedom of press clause was aimed at protecting the press from little else but prior restraint. Furthermore, he holds to the idea that the Bill of Rights was, in large measure, a "lucky political accident" (the political expediency idea). But he acknowledges that the book, *Legacy of Suppression,* in which he expressed views contrary to those of Chafee, warrants some criticism.

He wrote in a law review article that the book's most common fault, as pointed out by "knowledgeable reviewers," was its insufficient attention to the actual practices of the press.[41] He continued:

> Those critics were right. In researching *Legacy,* I scanned hundreds of issues of colonial, revolutionary, and early national newspapers looking for discussions of freedom of the press. I found reflected only stunted understandings, but I was oblivious to the fact that after enactment of the Stamp Act, in 1765, American newspapers *practiced* freedom of the press. Their pages screamed out denunciations of public men and measures. . . .
>
> In short, the law threatened repression, but the press conducted itself as if the law of criminal libel hardly mattered. My principal thesis—that neither the American Revolution nor the framers of the First Amendment intended to abolish the common law of seditious libel—remains unchanged. . . .
>
> Nevertheless, the failure of *Legacy* to discuss press practices and their implications is a serious one. Accordingly, I have prepared a new version of the book that so substantially alters its viewpoint on the actual condition of the press that I have abandoned the original title as partly misleading. The revised edition will be entitled *The Emergence of Free Press.*[42]

The revised edition was reviewed by Professor David M. Rabban of the University of Texas Law School.[43] He believes that despite two major concessions (i.e., the press actually enjoyed remarkable freedom, and the framers of the First Amendment intended to protect some publication from criminal liability even after it appeared in print), Levy retains most of his major conclusions as stated in *Legacy of Suppression.* Rabban then states his chief criticism of the revised edition:

> Despite Levy's impressive revisions, *Emergence of a Free Press* suffers from the same fundamental problem as *Legacy of Suppression.* Preoccupied by his "unshakable belief that the concept of seditious libel and freedom of the press are incompatible," Levy is as anachronistic as the twentieth century libertarians he criticizes. Just as Chafee and his followers tried to recreate the past to conform to their modern libertarian ideas, Levy judges the libertarianism of the eighteenth century by a twentieth century standard. As a result, Levy fails to appreciate the extent to which his own evidence reveals substantial legal and theoretical support for freedom of political expression before the Sedition Act of 1798.[44]

The debate continues. What did the leaders of the newly emerged nation intend when they drafted the First Amendment? What do those words mean?

What were the political realities that led to adoption of a free press guarantee and its antithesis, a sedition act? Other viewpoints will be set forth in the next chapter. As for the sedition law, some 25 arrests and 10 convictions resulted until the law was allowed to lapse in 1801 after Jefferson became President and pardoned those still in jail. Congress eventually voted restitution of the fines, although it never appropriated the money to do so. Whether the act was constitutional remained unsettled since that question did not reach the Supreme Court.

At the time of the alien and sedition laws, a common-law crime of seditious libel generally was assumed to exist at the federal level; however, in 1812 a divided Supreme Court held that there was no federal common-law crime of sedition.[45]

Croswell Case

Between the expiration of the sedition law and the Court's opinion in 1812, a remarkable case occurred in New York involving Harry Croswell, editor of the Federalist newspaper, *The Wasp,* and his printed villification of Jefferson. An indictment had been returned charging him with being a "malicious and seditious man." At his trial in 1804, Croswell sought to use truth as a defense, but the trial judge, a Republican, declared that the truth of the printed accusations was irrelevant.[46] Also, the jury was instructed to decide only whether the defendant had printed the alleged libel, not whether the words were seditious.

Croswell was convicted; he appealed, and his principal defense attorney was Alexander Hamilton, the leading Federalist at that time. One of the four state supreme court judges hearing the appeal was James Kent whose subsequent opinion "may be said to constitute the foundation on which American law of freedom of the press was subsequently built,"[47] even though his opinion was not controlling because the court split 2–2, thereby leaving the conviction intact. However, an order for a new trial was never carried out, partly because Hamilton was killed shortly thereafter in a duel with Aaron Burr.

During the state supreme court hearing, Hamilton had argued that denial of truth as a defense stemmed from a polluted source, the Star Chamber. Both he and Judge Kent, in the latter's opinion, carried their arguments beyond Blackstonian doctrine. Hamilton argued that liberty of the press "consisted in publishing with impunity, truth with good motives, and for justifiable ends, whether it related to men or to measures."[48] This was to become basic to the law of libel in most states. Hamilton also argued that a jury should decide the question of intent because a judge might be swayed by allegiance to government.

During the hearing a clash of fundamental doctrines emerged. The chief justice of the state court argued, in his opinion, that "truth may be as dangerous to society as falsehood"[49] and may be destructive of government; whereas Hamilton insisted that truth is "all-important to the liberties of the people [and] an ingredient in the eternal order of things."[50]

From this case emerged the defense of truth when published with good motives and for justifiable ends. New York enacted this concept into law the following year and included it in the state constitution in 1821.[51] More than 125 years later, Justice Robert H. Jackson of the U.S. Supreme Court referred to the

Croswell case as the "leading state case," and said that the provision in the New York Constitution "states the common sense of American criminal libel law."[52]

SUMMARY

Three major controls were exercised over the press in England during a 250-year period beginning in the sixteenth century. They were licensing, taxation, and seditious libel. Of the three, licensing most represents prior restraint, although the fear of punishment for seditious libel could be so great as to constitute self-imposed restraint or self-censorship. Most infamous of the censors was the Court of the Star Chamber that met behind closed doors to decide the fate of printers accused of violating edicts of the time.

In America the Blackstonian doctrine—that liberty of the press consisted of the absence of prior restraint, with the press accountable for any misdeeds *after* publication—had a profound impact on conceptualization and interpretation of the "first freedom." In addition, the trial of John Peter Zenger (1735) and the case of the *People of New York v. Croswell* (1804) were instrumental in establishing the principle that truth was a defense to seditious libel charges.

An attempt to impose a discriminatory tax on newspapers was struck down as unconstitutional in the landmark case of *Grosjean v. American Press Co.* (1936).

The intent of the Founding Fathers concerning press freedom has given rise to different viewpoints. Professor Chafee believed that the First Amendment was written with the intention of wiping out forever the crime of seditious libel.

Although Levy later modified his views, conceding that the press acted as though there were no repressive laws, he still believes that political expediency, not libertarianism (as Chafee believed), accounted for the Bill of Rights being presented to the states for adoption as a means of gaining favorable action on the Constitution itself. Furthermore, Levy contends that the First Amendment was aimed primarily at preventing federal government incursions into the domain of the states, and that broad libertarianism did not emerge until the Jeffersonian Republicans were forced to defend themselves against the Federalist-enacted alien and sedition laws. But Berns is of the opinion that states' rights, not libertarianism, account for Republican opposition to the alien and sedition laws.

Just what the Founding Fathers had in mind concerning freedom of press continues to stir controversy and is the subject of further review in the next chapter.

QUESTIONS IN REVIEW

To help you prepare for an examination on the material covered in this chapter, here are some review questions. After you have answered them, check the answers.

1. If we report that a school board held a "star-chamber" meeting, we mean:

2. What three kinds of controls were imposed on printers in England in the early days of the press?
3. What was seditious libel?
4. Briefly, what is the Blackstonian concept of liberty of press?
5. True or False? *Grosjean v. American Press Co.* made it clear that any tax against newspapers was unconstitutional.
6. The John Peter Zenger trial in 1735 helped to establish what principle in American libel law?
7. Professor Chafee believed that those who wrote the First Amendment were motivated by broad libertarianism. Professor Levy disagreed. Why?
8. How does the concept of states' rights influence interpretation of the First Amendment?
9. The case of Harry Croswell in *People v. Croswell* led the State of New York to do what?
10. Summarize what is protected by the First Amendment.

ANSWERS

1. It met in secret session.
2. Licensing, taxation, seditious libel.
3. Printed criticisms of those in authority.
4. No prior restraint against the press, but the press can be held accountable *after* publication.
5. False. Nondiscriminatory business taxes were permissible. The Louisiana tax was declared unconstitutional because it clearly discriminated against larger newspapers.
6. Truth was a defense to a seditious libel charge.
7. Professor Levy contended that the First Amendment resulted from political expediency — a move to gain delegate support for the U.S. Constitution so it could be submitted to the states for ratification. Broad libertarianism, he argued, did not emerge until the Jeffersonians were forced to defend themselves against the Sedition Act of 1798.
8. The First Amendment states that *Congress* shall make no law abridging freedom of speech, press, religion, and so on. States' righters contended that the states were left free by this prohibition against Congress to deal with the press as they wished.
9. The *Croswell* case led the State of New York to enact a statute establishing truth with good motives for justifiable ends as a defense in a criminal libel case. Later, this defense was incorporated into the state constitution.
10. Congress shall make no law concerning establishment of religion, nor abridge freedom of speech, press, the right of assembly, the right to petition government for redress.

ENDNOTES

1. For detailed history: Frederick S. Siebert, *Freedom of the Press in England 1476–1776* (Urbana, Ill.: University of Illinois Press, 1952).
2. It was this court that gave rise to the expression "star-chamber proceeding," which means public affairs being conducted in secret behind closed doors. To counteract secret meetings by government officials in modern times, many states have enacted "open meeting" laws. See Chapter 9.

3. Corbett, *Parliamentary History of England,* III, pp. 131–32.

4. Zechariah Chafee, Jr., *Free Speech in the United States* (Cambridge, Mass.: Harvard University Press, 1954), p. 18.

5. Corbett, op. cit., note 3, Vol. VI, p. 1063.

6. Ibid., p. 1065.

7. Common law derived from the customs and usages in ancient England. It is now called "case law" and is based, unlike statutory law, on cases decided by judges. Thus, U.S. Supreme Court decisions have the effect of law—case law—even though no legislative body has specifically enacted such law. The kinds of law that affect mass communication are common law, statutory law, constitutional law, plus governmental regulations (administrative law).

8. Siebert, *Freedom of the Press,* pp. 117–18.

9. Ibid., p. 119.

10. Leonard W. Levy, ed., *Freedom of the Press from Zenger to Jefferson* (Indianapolis: Bobbs-Merrill, 1966), pp. lxii–lxiii. Compare absolutist view, Chapter 2.

11. Frank Luther Mott, *American Journalism,* 3d ed. (New York: Macmillan, 1962), pp. 13–14.

12. *Commentaries on the Laws of England,* Book 4, Sections 151–52, published in London in 1769. The Blackstonian concept of press freedom greatly influenced a majority of the U.S. Supreme Court when it ruled in *Near v. Minnesota* (1931) that with few exceptions prior restraint violates the First Amendment. See Chapter 3.

13. Lovell v. City of Griffin, Ga., 303 U.S. 444, 451, 58 S. Ct. 666, 669, 82 L.Ed. 949, 953 (1938).

14. Mott, *American Journalism,* pp. 71–74.

15. Ibid., pp. 143–44.

16. Grosjean v. American Press Co., 297 U.S. 233, 56 S. Ct. 444, 80 L.Ed. 660 (1936).

17. Associated Press v. National Labor Relations Board, 301 U.S. 103, 132–33, 57 S. Ct. 650, 656, 81 L.Ed. 961 (1937).

18. Minneapolis Star v. Minnesota Commissioner of Revenue, 9 *Med.L.Rptr.* 1369, April 19, 1983. Justice Rehnquist dissented and Justice White concurred in part and dissented in part. White agreed that the $100,000 exemption, which limited the tax burden to only a few newspapers, was sufficient reason to invalidate the tax. He did not believe the Court should have gone further when it addressed the question of whether a state may impose a use tax that is not targeted on a small group of papers. That question "could be left for another day," he said (at 1375).

19. Ibid., at 1371.

20. Ibid., at 1376–77.

21. Arkansas Writer's Project, Inc. v. Ragland, *Editor & Publisher,* May 16, 1987, p. 34.

22. 14 *Med.L.Rptr.* 1964, January 5, 1988.

23. William O. Douglas, *The Right of the People* (New York: Doubleday & Company, Inc. 1958), p. 38. Copyright © 1958 by William O. Douglas, reprinted by permission of Doubleday & Company, Inc.

24. Levy, *Freedom of the Press,* p. 57.

25. Ibid., pp. xxxiv–xxxv.

26. Ibid., p. xxxv, note 50.

27. Chafee, *Free Speech in the United States.* p. 21.

28. Leonard Levy, *Legacy of Suppression: Freedom of Speech and Press in Early American History* (Cambridge, Mass.: Harvard University Press, 1960), p. vii.

29. Primarily an eighteenth-century concept, "libertarianism" means liberty for the individual against governmental interference. It derives mainly from the belief that man has certain inherent or natural rights—among them the right to pursue truth. A concomitant of such a right is free speech and press which, according to the theory, help citizens make the wise decisions necessary if self-government is to survive.

30. 1 *Annals of Congress,* p. 434.

31. David A. Anderson, "The Origins of the Press Clause," 30 *UCLA Law Review* 456, 464 (1983), © 1983 by the Regents of the University of California. All rights reserved. Connecticut and Rhode Island operated under their colonial charters and New York and New Jersey did not include freedom of press guarantees in their constitutions.

32. Ibid., p. 481.

33. Ibid. (footnotes omitted).
34. Ibid., p. 476.
35. Ibid., p. 482 (footnotes omitted).
36. On the eve of the War for Independence, the Continental Congress approved a declaration of rights, including one on freedom of press, intended to make allies of the settlers in Quebec.
37. Op. cit, pp. 482–83 (footnotes omitted).
38. Walter Berns, "Freedom of the Press and the Alien and Sedition Laws: A Reappraisal," *The Supreme Court Review* (Chicago: University of Chicago Law School), 1970, pp. 110–11.
39. Leonard Levy, *Legacy of Suppression,* Torchbook ed. (New York: Harper, 1963), pp. 259–60.
40. Berns, "Freedom of the Press," pp. 120–21.
41. Leonard Levy, "The Legacy Reexamined," *Stanford Law Review,* February 1985. © by the Board of Trustees of the Leland Stanford Junior University.
42. Ibid., pp. 768–70 (footnotes omitted).
43. David M. Rabban, "The Ahistorical Historian: Leonard Levy on Freedom of Expression in Early American History," *Stanford Law Review,* February 1985. © by the Board of Trustees of the Leland Stanford Junior University.
44. Ibid., p. 800.
45. U.S. v. Hudson and Goodwin, 7 Cranch 32, 34 (1812). The fact that the Supreme Court in 1812 found no federal common-law crime of sedition did not preclude Congress' passing a law making seditious libel a crime. Also, the protections accorded freedom of press and other freedoms by the Bill of Rights were not binding on the states until the U.S. Supreme Court declared otherwise in Gitlow v. U.S. (1925). See Chapter 2.
46. People v. Croswell, 3 Johns 337 (1804).
47. Berns, "Freedom of the Press," p. 151.
48. Ibid., p. 153.
49. Ibid., p. 155.
50. Ibid., p. 156.
51. Ibid., p. 158. See Chapter 4.
52. Ibid., p. 159. See opinion in Beauharnais v. Illinois, 343 U.S. 250, 295, 297 (1952) and Chapter 5.

2

First Amendment Theory and Practice

HIGHLIGHTS

■ "Marketplace of ideas" concept of the First Amendment is that all ideas (good and bad) should be allowed to compete in the marketplace. Government should not interfere. Justice Oliver Wendell Holmes in 1919 in *Abrams v. U.S.*

■ First Amendment absolutists hold that government is powerless under the First Amendment to control speech or press.

■ Alexander Meiklejohn believes the First Amendment *absolutely* protects "political" speech, that is, speech or press that makes people better citizens.

■ Various tests used by the Supreme Court in deciding speech/press cases include liberty versus license, reasonable tendency, clear and present danger, preferred position for the First Amendment, balancing of competing interests, and speech versus nonspeech.

■ Different views of Free Press Clause of First Amendment have been expressed by Justice Stewart, Chief Justice Burger, and Justice Brennan. Stewart argues that the press is given special protection; Burger contends that the press, as an institution, is no more protected than a pamphleteer or any other individual; and Brennan offers a two-model approach for understanding what is or is not protected by the First Amendment. The "speech" model is based on the idea that communication processes through which citizens exercise their rights of self-government are absolutely protected, as is a citizen's right of self-expression. The press's news dissemination function is included in this model. Brennan's "structural" model would allow balancing of interests. This model encompasses "incidental rights of the press," including the press's newsgathering function.

In 1774 the First Continental Congress issued a declaration aimed at the inhabitants of Quebec, concerning liberty of persons, trial by jury, representative government, and freedom of press. Of the latter, the Congress declared:

> The importance of this consists, besides the advancement of truth, science, morality and arts in general, in its diffusion of liberal sentiment on the administration of government, its ready communication of thoughts between subjects, and its consequential promotion of union among them, whereby oppressive officials are shamed or intimidated into more honorable and just modes of conducting affairs.[1]

And in 1786 Thomas Jefferson, while referring to Shays' Rebellion—during which some 2000 armed farmers marched in protest against high taxes and were disarmed by militia—made this famous comment in the belief that the farmers' action stemmed from ignorance:

> The way to prevent these irregular interpositions of the people, is to give them full information of their affairs through the channels of the public papers, and to contrive that these papers penetrate the whole mass of the people. The basis of our government being the opinion of the people, the very first object should be to keep that right; and were it left to me to decide whether we should have a government without newspapers or newspapers without government, I should not hesitate a moment to prefer the latter.

In terms of people governing themselves, the "father" of the Constitution, James Madison, said:

> Nothing could be more irrational than to give the people power, and to withhold from them information without which power is abused. A people who mean to be their own governors must arm themselves with power which knowledge gives. A popular government without popular information or the means of acquiring it is but a prologue to a farce or a tragedy, or perhaps both.[2]

Jefferson put it more succinctly, saying: "If a nation expects to be both ignorant and free it expects what never was and never will be."

Such sentiment shows the value placed on the press by early governmental leaders, although it should be emphasized that brave words were not always matched by actions. Despite declarations such as those of Madison and Jefferson, disagreement persists as to the Founding Fathers' intent when they wrote the First Amendment and the meaning of its words. Evidence of this is seen in differences of opinion among Supreme Court members as well as in the viewpoints of Chafee, Levy, and Berns. One of the major reasons for disagreement pivots on the issue of federal versus state power; that is, construing the First Amendment as a prohibition against Congress, but not the states, from passing laws abridging freedom of speech/press. Concern over states' rights generated considerable debate throughout the formative period of the Republic. In fact, it was not until the adoption of the Fourteenth Amendment in 1868 and a U.S. Supreme Court decision in 1925 in *Gitlow v. People of New York* that federal constitutional guarantees in the Bill of Rights were extended to include the states.[3]

Before exploring additional conceptions about freedom of press and what the First Amendment means, some comment about the wondrous ways of the law might be helpful. The fact that the law changes, that meanings change, should surprise no one; yet when something as fundamental as the Bill of Rights changes, the result can be perplexity and even dismay. Therefore, the words of Irving R. Kaufman, a U.S. Circuit Court judge who gave the eleventh annual James Madison lecture at New York University Law School, are illuminating:

> The First Amendment is basically aimed at regulating the *process* of exchanging ideas and forming opinions; in a word, at facilitating the freest possible use of channels of communication consistent with public order and safety. However, because the amendment is not directed at creating a structure but at encouraging an ideal process, it is by its nature incapable of precise definition. Consistency with the purpose and the concommitants of the ideal process implies that there will be a continual task of reevaluating the effectiveness of particular structures and particular solutions, not only from generation to generation, but from day to day. Sharp distinctions—you *may* parade; you may *not* picket; speech *is* protected; conduct is *not*—are far easier to apply and understand, but they do not aid in the process of facilitating exchange of messages; they ignore the almost infinite range not only of the media, but of the locations in which they are employed. Hence, when we deal with implementing a process, the best we can hope for are lines of analysis, specifications of important interests and perhaps a few—a very few—tentative groping formulations. [Federal Judge] Learned Hand with his characteristic boldness put it this way: "Law has always been unintelligible because it ought to be in words and words are utterly inadequate to deal with the fantastically multiform occasions which come up in human life." There is an agony, no less severe because it is intellectual rather than physical, in dealing with problems that have no neat resolutions, that defy precision, that mock finality. Yet it is an agony that judges cannot lightly forego. It is born of a deep concern for expanding the horizons of speech. It reflects an abiding faith in the essential wisdom of reaching accommodation through rational discourse.[4]

At the time of the controversy over the inclusion of a Bill of Rights in the Constitution, Alexander Hamilton wrote in one of his *Federalist* papers:

> What is the liberty of the Press? Who can give it any definition which would not leave the utmost latitude for evasion? I hold it to be impracticable; and from this I infer, that its security, whatever fine declarations may be inserted in any constitution respecting it, must altogether depend on public opinion and on the general spirit of the people and of the government.[5]

Recognizing the difficulties inherent in defining the words contained in the First Amendment, and in interpreting events that occurred many years ago, let's nonetheless examine some of the "tentative, groping formulations" that have been used in trying to resolve free-speech/free-press problems.

JUDGE COOLEY'S VIEW

The doctrine stated by Blackstone in the eighteenth century was one of the earliest conceptualizations of freedom of press, namely, that such freedom consisted of no prior restraint against publication. Once publication occurred, there could be state or private action against the publisher. This doctrine exerted considerable influence over interpretations of free-speech/free-press guarantees primarily because there were few court cases involving free speech and free press until the United States' involvement in World War I — an involvement bitterly opposed by some individuals and groups. Several factors account for the relatively few First Amendment cases. Chief among them would be the Western frontier. Dissidents in the more established areas of the United States, including printers and other kinds of newspaper people, could pack up and move westward if they felt there were too many constraints on their freedom. But after the frontier disappeared, this was no longer true. Also, courts were faced with other issues that they believed deserved more attention during the nation-building period.

Some theorists or interpreters of the First Amendment did emerge prior to World War I, among them Judge Thomas M. Cooley. About a century after Blackstone had defined freedom of press under common law, Judge Cooley would argue that there had to be more to the guarantee of free press than just immunity from prior restraint. He wrote:

> The evils to be prevented were not the censorship of the press merely, but any action of the government by means of which it might prevent such free and general discussion of public matters as seems absolutely essential to prepare the people for an intelligent exercise of their rights as citizens.[6]

Cooley did not believe that the press should be absolutely protected. In fact, he believed that publication could result in public or private offenses — the former involving blasphemy, obscenity, or scandalous reports; the latter involving libel.

The more traditional theory looked upon the First Amendment as being media oriented; that is, the guarantee was included in the Bill of Rights to prevent government interference with the press. The reason: to make the Fourth Estate the watchdog of the governors. Contrast this conceptualization with Cooley's view of the First Amendment being citizen oriented; that is, the guarantee of freedom so the press can meet its principal obligation of preparing people for their roles as citizens.

"MARKETPLACE OF IDEAS" CONCEPT

Among the progenitors of the idea that the First Amendment is a means of citizen preparation was Justice Oliver Wendell Holmes, who served on the Supreme Court during and after World War I when dissemination of radical doctrine often led to arrest under criminal anarchy or criminal syndicalism laws. More widely known for his enunciation of the clear and present danger doctrine, discussed later in this chapter, Justice Holmes also expounded the "marketplace of ideas" concept in a 1919 dissenting opinion in *Abrams v. U.S.*[7] In that opinion, he said:

> . . . [T]hat the ultimate good desired is better reached by free trade in ideas—that the best test of truth is the power of the thought to get itself accepted in the competition of the market. . . . That at any rate is the theory of our Constitution. It is an experiment as all life is an experiment.

Compare the "marketplace of ideas" concept with the stirring words of English poet John Milton who argued against licensing of the press in *Areopagitica* (1644). Let truth and falsehood grapple, he wrote. "Who ever knew Truth put to the worse in a free and open encounter?"

Somewhat the same concept lies at the heart of a 1943 decision by a federal court that enjoined the Associated Press from enforcing highly restrictive membership practices and from preventing its 1200 members from communicating news to non-Associated Press members. In a 2–1 decision in that case, Judge Learned Hand wrote:

> However neither exclusively, nor even primarily, are the interests of the newspaper industry conclusive; for that industry serves one of the most vital of all general interests: the dissemination of news from as many different sources, with as many different facets and colors as is possible. That interest is closely akin to, if indeed it is not the same as, the interest protected by the First Amendment; it presupposes that right conclusions are more likely to be gathered out of a multitude of tongues, than any kind of authoritative selection. To many this is, and always will be, folly; but we have staked upon it our all.[8]

Unconvinced, the Associated Press appealed, in part upon the traditional First Amendment ground that the Sherman Antitrust Act, when applied to publishers, constituted an abridgment of press freedom. Justice Hugo L. Black, in giving the Court's opinion that affirmed the lower court's enjoinder, said of the Associated Press claim:

> It would be strange indeed however if the grave concern for freedom of the press which prompted adoption of the First Amendment should be read as a command that the government was without power to protect that freedom. The First Amendment, far from providing an argument against application of the Sherman Act, here provides powerful reasons to the contrary. That Amendment rests on the assumption that the widest possible dissemination of information from diverse and antagonistic

sources is essential to the welfare of the public, that a free press is a condition of a free society. Surely a command that the government itself shall not impede the free flow of ideas does not afford nongovernment combinations a refuge if they impose restraints upon that constitutionally guaranteed freedom.[9]

Here, then, are foundation stones of the First Amendment. They include the negative command — the traditional concept — that government shall not impede the free flow of ideas. There also is a positive aspect that government can and should use its power to ensure a free press toward the goal of providing the widest possible dissemination of information from diverse and antagonistic sources. Clearly, in this decision and in later ones, the First Amendment guarantee is "not for the benefit of the press so much as for the benefit of us all."[10]

FREEDOM FORMULATIONS

Before returning to different viewpoints concerning what the First Amendment should or should not protect let's examine some of the formulations used by the Supreme Court to resolve free-speech/free-press issues. As noted, few such cases reached the Court until World War I brought growing dissent to United States involvement in that war. One reaction to such dissent was passage of the Espionage Act of 1917 which established these offenses:

Whoever, when the United States is at war, shall willfully make or convey false reports or false statements with intent to interfere with the operation or success of the military or naval forces of the United States or to promote the success of its enemies; and whoever, when the United States is at war, shall willfully cause or attempt to cause insubordination, disloyalty, mutiny, or refusal of duty, in the military or naval forces of the United States; or shall willfully obstruct the recruiting or enlistment service of the United States, shall be punished by a fine of not more than $10,000 or imprisonment for not more than 20 years, or both.[11]

Since the original act did not punish disloyal words, and because of narrow court interpretations of "willfully obstruct," Congress amended the law in 1918 by inserting "attempt to obstruct," and by adding these additional offenses:

To say or do anything with intent to obstruct the sale of U.S. bonds; to utter, print, write or publish any disloyal, profane, scurrilous or obscene language, or language intended to cause contempt, scorn, contumely, or disrepute as regards the form of government of the United States, the Constitution, the flag, including advocating, teaching, defending or suggesting the doing of any of these acts.

Those found guilty were liable to $10,000 fine or 20 years in prison, or both.

The original Espionage Act was still on the books when the United States entered World War II, but the 1918 amendment was repealed in 1921. In referring to the World War I era, Professor Chafee said:

Never in the history of our country, since the Alien and Sedition Laws of 1798, has the meaning of free speech been the subject of such sharp controversy as during the years since 1917. Over 1,900 prosecutions and other judicial proceedings during [World War I] . . ., involving speeches, newspaper articles, pamphlets, and books, were followed after the armistice by a widespread legislative consideration of bills punishing the advocacy of extreme radicalism. It is becoming increasingly important to determine the true limits of freedom of expression, so that speakers and writers may know how much they can properly say, and governments may be sure how much they can lawfully and wisely suppress.[12]

The "true limits" will always remain elusive and tentative because of the wide range of media and circumstances. For such reasons, none of the tests used since World War I has been found acceptable for long periods of time. Somewhat in the order of their emergence, these tests include liberty versus license (also referred to as use-abuse or right versus wrong speech/press), clear and present danger, preferred position, balancing, and speech versus nonspeech.[13]

Liberty versus License (Use-Abuse or Right versus Wrong)

Liberty versus license and related formulations prevailed before, during, and shortly after World War I. They required judges to make distinctions between so-called "right" or "good" speech/press, which therefore were protected, and "evil," "licentious," or "bad" speech/press. Among the criteria used in attempting to make such distinctions was the *inherent* or *reasonable tendency* of the speech/press to bring about the feared evil or licentiousness.[14] The inflexibility of such standards as right/wrong or good/evil made them unsatisfactory; as a consequence, different formulas emerged.

Clear and Present Danger

The clear and present danger test was announced in 1919 by Justice Oliver Wendell Holmes in his opinion for a unanimous Court in *Schenck v. U.S.*[15] Charles Schenck, the secretary of the Socialist party, and other party functionaries were convicted of three counts under the Espionage Act, including distribution of circulars that the courts held were intended to obstruct recruitment and to cause insubordination among military personnel. In affirming the convictions, Holmes wrote for the Court:

> We admit that in many places and in ordinary times the defendants in saying all that was said in the circular would have been within their constitutional rights. But the character of every act depends upon the circumstances in which it is done. The most stringent protection of free speech would not protect a man from an injunction against uttering words that may have all the effect of force. The question in every case is whether the words used are used in such circumstances and are of such a nature as to create a clear and present danger that they will bring about the substantive evils that Congress has a right to prevent.

In another case, Holmes cited a different example:

> The First Amendment . . . obviously was not intended to give immunity for every possible use of language . . . We venture to believe that neither Hamilton nor Madi-

son, nor any other competent person then or later, ever supposed that to make criminal the counseling of a murder . . . would be unconstitutional interference with free speech.[16]

Abrams v. U.S. In *Abrams v. U.S.,* a majority of the Court held that the publication and distribution of pamphlets during World War I, which criticized the use of American forces in Russia during the Bolshevik revolution and called for a strike of munitions workers, were not protected by the First Amendment.[17] Justices Holmes and Louis D. Brandeis dissented, in part because they believed there was insufficient evidence that Abrams *intended* to "cripple or hinder the United States in the prosecution of the war."

Concerning the clear and present danger test, Holmes said: "Now nobody can suppose that the surreptitious publishing of a silly leaflet by an unknown man, without more, would present any immediate danger that its opinion would hinder the success of the government arms or have any appreciable tendency to do so."

Holmes in the same opinion also said: "Only the emergency that makes it immediately dangerous to leave the correction of evil counsels to time warrants making any exception to the sweeping command, 'Congress shall make no law abridging the freedom of speech.' "

The clear and present danger test was used sparingly by a majority of the Court during the 1920s, chiefly because there were difficulties in applying the test. For example, who should make the critical determination that the danger existed—administrators, lawmakers, judges? How immediate must the danger be? Must government wait until the moment before its enemies intend to strike? Some of these difficulties are reflected in two important free speech cases.

Gitlow v. People of the State of New York. In *Gitlow v. People of the State of New York,* the U.S. Supreme Court affirmed the conviction of Benjamin Gitlow, a Socialist party member who had distributed a pamphlet in alleged violation of the state's criminal anarchy law.[18] In its 1925 decision, the Court asserted that the state had exercised its police power reasonably and that it was up to the state legislature to determine whether "utterances of a certain kind involve such danger of substantive evil that they may be punished. . . ." If the legislature made a determination that such danger existed, then *reasonable* action could be taken to deal with it. Holmes and Brandeis dissented on the ground that there was no "present danger."

Justice Edward T. Sanford's opinion for the Court was of major significance because federal guarantees in the First Amendment were held applicable to the states via the due process clause of the Fourteenth Amendment. In an earlier case, the Court had said that the Fourteenth Amendment imposed no restrictions on the states concerning freedom of speech or press, but in *Gitlow,* the Court for the first time declared that federal speech/press guarantees cannot be impaired by states; rather, they are applicable in the states through the Fourteenth Amendment.

Whitney v. California. In *Whitney v. California,* Anita Whitney was convicted under a state law that made it unlawful to advocate, teach, aid, or abet the commission of a crime, sabotage, or other unlawful method in order to accomplish a political or industrial ownership change.[19] Her presence at a Communist Labor party convention was held sufficient for conviction. The Supreme Court affirmed the conviction, primarily because the justices believed they should not review questions of fact decided by state courts. Brandeis and Holmes concurred, with Brandeis arguing that when an indefinite standard of constitutionality is being used (such as the clear and present danger test), the courts, and not the legislatures, must decide how near or remote the danger is.

The Holmes test fell into obscurity in the 1930s and was revived in the 1940s. Its use was urged in the call by the Commission on Freedom of the Press for "the repeal of legislation prohibiting expression in favor of revolutionary changes in our institutions where there is no clear and present danger that violence will result from the expression."[20]

Preferred Position

The preferred position contention is based on the belief that the First Amendment has primacy over other rights. In any balancing of rights, the First Amendment must be given preference. The use of preferred position was most notable during the 1940s when both Justices Black and Douglas were sitting on the Court and is clearly evidenced in a 1946 case, *Marsh v. Alabama,* in which the Court concluded:

> When we balance the Constitutional rights of owners of property against those of the people to enjoy freedom of press and religion, as we must here, we remain mindful of the fact that the latter occupy a preferred position. As we have stated before, the right to exercise the liberties safeguarded by the First Amendment "lies at the foundation of free government by free men. . . ."[21]

Supreme Court Justice Benjamin N. Cardoza also referred to the First Amendment as the "preferred" freedom which lies at the core of our democracy. Freedom of expression, he said, is "the matrix, the indispensible condition of nearly every form of freedom."

Balancing of Interests

Although the clear and present danger doctrine still is used occasionally, it has largely been supplanted by other tests since the 1950s, particularly the "balancing of interests" concept. When other rights conflict with the First Amendment — for example, right of privacy, property rights, the right of government to safeguard citizens from various kinds of dangers or evils — then such rights must be balanced and determinations made as to which right shall prevail under given circumstances.

Major criticisms of the balancing test include: it is basically standardless, and it depends heavily on the emphasis given by judges to competing rights.

However, from a positive viewpoint, the balancing test does not "dispose of First Amendment issues through the mechanical application of inflexible formula."[22]

As one scholar pointed out:

> None of the tests that have prevailed at different periods during the history of the Amendment has stood the test of time for more than a decade. Furthermore, it has been asserted that the several tests are not as different from one another as they appear to be on the surface—that the difference between "liberty versus license," "clear and present danger," and the current [early 1960s] "balancing of interests" tests is more semantical than real and that they all involve some sort of "balancing."[23]

Speech versus Nonspeech

During the 1960s and 1970s, several formulations were used which are virtually the same in that they attempt to distinguish between "pure speech" and that which goes "beyond speech" and therefore is more subject to regulation. This "beyond speech" behavior has been given several names in various Supreme Court decisions, including "nonspeech," "speech plus," or "action speech."

The idea that action, not mere expression, could be subject to punishment is not a new one. It was put forth by libertarians prior to the Revolutionary War and found expression as early as 1771 in a pamphlet published in England by the "Father of Candor." Libertarians believed that sedition should be judged solely on the basis of action, not mere words.

Yates v. U.S. An attempt to make a distinction in beyond-speech behavior was evident in the Court's decision in *Yates v. U.S.*[24] This 1957 case virtually ended any further prosecutions under the Alien Registration Act of 1940 (the Smith Act), the first peacetime sedition law enacted by Congress since 1798. What Congress did was to apply part of the 1917 Espionage Act to peacetime situations in part because of the spread of Hitlerism and communism abroad and the fear of disloyalty at home. About 100 persons were fined or imprisoned under the Smith Act until the Court in *Yates* reviewed the convictions of 14 Communist party leaders on charges of advocating the violent overthrow of the government and either reversed the convictions or ordered new trials. In *Yates* Justice John M. Harlan's opinion for the Court hinged largely on making a distinction between "advocacy of forcible overthrow as an abstract doctrine and advocacy of action to that end. . . ." Harlan said the trial judge's instructions to the jury failed to note the "subtlety of these distinctions" between advocacy of doctrine as opposed to advocacy of unlawful action.

U.S. v. O'Brien. Harlan's attempt to distinguish between the two types of advocacy is a precursor of subsequent tests that would be applied. For example, in *U.S. v. O'Brien,* a nonspeech-action formula was used.[25] David P. O'Brien had been convicted of burning his draft card on March 31, 1966, while he and three companions stood on the steps of the South Boston Courthouse and spoke against involvement in the Vietnam War. The test applied by Chief Justice Earl Warren in the Court's 1968 decision was that O'Brien's action in burning the draft card was properly subject to government regulation even though the speech was not.

Amalgamated Food Employees Union Local 590 v. Logan Valley Plaza. A similar dichotomy was used by a majority of the Court in another case decided that same year. In *Logan Valley Plaza,* the Court in a 6–3 split held that a shopping center could not prevent a labor union from picketing a store or union members from distributing handbills on the basis of a claim to private property rights when the property was otherwise open to the public.[26] In a concurring opinion, Justice Douglas described the picketing as "free speech *plus.*" The *plus,* he agreed, was subject to regulation under certain circumstances.

The nonspeech, action-speech, and speech-plus formulations are consistent with a theory of the First Amendment advanced by Professor Thomas I. Emerson of Yale University, who wants a line drawn between expression and action, with the former fully protected under the First Amendment.[27]

The central idea of a system of freedom of expression, writes Emerson, "is that a fundamental distinction must be drawn between conduct which consists of 'expression' and conduct which consists of 'action.' "[28] Expression, he states, must be freely allowed and encouraged, but "action" can be controlled.

Just what constitutes "expressive" conduct as distinct from "action" conduct is not easily defined, nor is the U.S. Supreme Court committed to the idea that expressive conduct always is protected by the First Amendment.

In *Tinker v. Des Moines School District* (1969), the Court upheld the right of students to express their opposition to the Vietnam War by wearing black armbands even though this "conduct" was in violation of school policy. The Court said that the wearing of armbands is "closely akin to 'pure speech.' "[29] But by a 7–2 vote, the Court, in mid-1984, upheld a government ban on sleeping in national parks near the White House, saying that the ban did not violate the free speech rights of those who wanted to camp overnight to demonstrate the plight of the homeless. In overturning the U.S. Court of Appeals, District of Columbia Circuit, which had held 6–5 that the sleep-in was a form of protected expression, Justice Byron R. White said in his opinion for the Court that even if the sleep-in was a form of "expressive conduct," it still was subject to reasonable government regulation.[30] In fact, courts generally have held that speech is subject to "reasonable time, place and manner" regulation without First Amendment rights being violated.

More recently, the Supreme Court upheld the ruling of the Texas Court of Criminal Appeals when it decided that the burning of an American flag in response to the nomination in 1984 of Ronald Reagan to be the Republican party's nominee for President was "expressive conduct" (a means of political protest). The 5–4 ruling in mid-1989 spurred politicians, including President Bush, to call for a constitutional amendment to allow punishment of any "desecration" of the flag.

Difficulties with Speech/Action Dichotomy. As with other freedom formulations, there are difficulties with the pure-speech/action-speech dichotomy. In a

1973 decision, the New Hampshire Supreme Court took note of one difficulty; that is, no test has yet been established for determining when conduct, or action, becomes such an integral part of expression that the one is inseparable from the other.[31] Under such a circumstance, would pure speech fall short of First Amendment protection, or must both expression and action be protected in order to preserve the free speech guarantee? Also, the pure-speech/action-speech test has limited application. It can be applied to the pamphleteer, the soapbox orator, and the parader, but is it applicable to the mass media? In fact many of the cases cited thus far—*Schenck, Gitlow, Abrams, Whitney, Marsh, Yates, O'Brien, Logan Valley*—have involved the use of state power against individuals rather than against the mass media. In the Pentagon Papers cases (Chapter 3), state power was used against the "establishment" press but such instances are far less frequent, though more spectacular, than when the state is pitted against an individual. At the risk of oversimplication, one reason lies in the fact that the mass media, for the most part, are part of the establishment. They have, among their functions, the task of transmitting the values of the dominant societal groups. For the most part the media are less critical of the system because they are part of it; whereas the poor man's press, the underground press, and the alienated soapbox orator usually are opposed to the system. Also, the "establishment" press, particularly the larger organizations, has the resources to fight back against government attempts to restrict press freedom. Not so with the "poor man's press."

Absolutists' View

One group of theorists advocates the utmost protection for the news media. At the forefront were two prominent members of the Supreme Court.

From the time that Justice Black was appointed to the U.S. Supreme Court in 1937, until his death in 1971, and from the time that Douglas took his oath as an associate justice of the Court in 1939, until his retirement in 1975, the absolutists' view of the First Amendment was represented in many Court cases.

The absolutists' position is contained in this statement by Black, repeated on numerous occasions, that the federal government "is without any power whatever under the Constitution to put any type of burden on speech and expression of ideas of any kind." Black would draw the line between speech and illegal conduct—as libertarians would have done in the 1770s. Black agreed that government has the right to put down rebellion, but it would not have the right to still the voices of dissent and rebellion. He would concur with Douglas's view that the First Amendment allows all ideas to be expressed—whether orthodox, popular, offbeat, or repulsive. Douglas said:

> I do not think it permissible to draw lines between the "good" and the "bad" and be true to the constitutional mandate to let all ideas alone. If our Constitution permitted "reasonable" regulation of freedom of expression, as do the constitutions of some nations, we would be in a field where the legislative and the judiciary would have much leeway. But under our charter all regulation or control of expression is barred.

Government does not sit to reveal where the "truth" is. People are left to pick and choose between competing offerings.[32]

Douglas, in a concurring opinion in *Garrison v. State of Louisiana* (see Chapter 3), said "freedom of expression can be suppressed if . . . it is so closely brigaded with illegal action as to be an inseparable part of it. . . . "

The absolutist view never gained the sustained support of a majority of the U.S. Supreme Court. Nor did it draw favorable consideration in the 1947 report of the nongovernmental Commission on Freedom of Press. That report drew vitriolic comment from many media owners and editors principally because of recommendations that the government should facilitate new ventures in the communications industry and that an independent agency should be established to monitor the performance of the press.[33] Although recognizing the importance of freedom of press to society, the commission said such freedom has "to be balanced against other ideals such as the sound training of youth." Absolute freedom of press, the commission declared, is "neither probable nor desirable."[34]

Shortly before his death, Justice Black eloquently expressed his view of why the Founding Fathers gave First Amendment protection to the press. He did so in a separate opinion after joining a majority of the Court in refusing to permit a further ban on publication of a secret government study concerning the United States' involvement in the Vietnam War (see Chapter 3). Justice Black said:

> Madison and the other framers of the First Amendment, able men that they were, wrote in language they earnestly believed could never be misunderstood: "Congress shall make no law . . . abridging the freedom . . . of the press." Both the history and the language of the First Amendment support the view that the press must be left free to publish news, whatever the source, without censorship, injunctions or prior restraints.
>
> In the First Amendment the Founding Fathers gave the free press the protection it must have to fulfill its essential role in our democracy. The press was to serve the governed, not the governors. The Government's power to censor the press was abolished so that the press would remain forever free to censure the Government.[35]

If Black's view of the First Amendment were an accepted fact, our inquiry into mass media law and regulation would be shortened considerably. Such is not the case as evidenced by different free-speech/free-press formulations that have emerged.

MEIKLEJOHN'S INTERPRETATION

The writings and opinions of Black and Douglas advocate protection of all kinds of speech and press, even those that could be labeled "bad" or "seditious," that have no apparent value in preparing people to be better citizens or are obscene.

The late Professor Alexander Meiklejohn, whose views significantly influenced some Supreme Court decisions, argued in 1948 that the First Amendment protects those activities of thought and communication by which citizens carry out the self-governing process. Any thoughts and communication necessary to such a process are *absolutely* protected by the First Amendment, he said.[36]

For Meiklejohn, the central purpose of the First Amendment is "to give to every voting member of the body politic the fullest possible participation in the understanding of those problems with which the citizens of a self-governing society must deal."[37] Therefore, the First Amendment guarantee is "assured only to speech which bears, directly or indirectly, upon issues with which voters have to deal — only, therefore, to the consideration of matters of public interest."[38] Such a limitation — matters of public interest — can be interpreted broadly or narrowly, but obviously not all speech and press would fall within the meaning of that phrase. In essence, what Meiklejohn argued is that all "political" speech should be unconditionally immunized from punishment. Such immunization, he contended, would assure robust, uninhibited debate on matters of public interest.

One of the difficulties with the Meiklejohn "political speech" approach concerns the definition of "political speech." If it is interpreted too narrowly, then other kinds of speech might be endangered. Meiklejohn responded to such criticism by expanding the concept to include speech that pertains to the sciences, the arts, morality — all of which can be related to the self-governing process and the development of citizenship. Therefore, such speech should unconditionally be protected from government interference.

The impact of Meiklejohn's ideas on the Supreme Court is seen in a 1964 landmark case, *New York Times Co. v. Sullivan,* in which Justice William J. Brennan, Jr., in his opinion for the Court, wrote that a libel suit against the newspaper had to be considered "against the background of a profound national commitment to the principle that debate on public issues should be uninhibited, robust, and wide-open. . . ."[39] Similarly, in *Red Lion Broadcasting Co. v. FCC,* Justice White, in an opinion for a unanimous Supreme Court in 1969, said that what was crucial in resolving the case was "the right of the public to receive suitable access to social, political, esthetic, moral, and other ideas and experiences. . . ."[40] It is this right, and not the rights of the broadcaster, that cannot be constitutionally abridged, the Court declared.

Chafee was among those who criticized the "political speech" doctrine. He believed that separating political speech from private speech would be difficult. More than that, he asked the extent to which speech could realistically be protected when courts are asked to defy legislatures. He looked upon the clear and present danger doctrine as at least allowing Congress some leeway in legislating in an area of concern while still imposing limitations upon such legislation.[41] This would not be the case with speech that fell within the reach of the Meiklejohn concept. Arguably many kinds of speech could be classified as "matters of public interest."

DIFFERENT COURTS, DIFFERENT INTERPRETATIONS

Ultimately, of course, the Constitution, including the First Amendment, is what the U.S. Supreme Court says it is, and the Court changes over time. New justices are appointed; older members die or retire. Different interpretations of the Constitution result.

Chief Justice Warren

Earl F. Warren served as Chief Justice from October 5, 1953, until June 23, 1969 — a period regarded by some as one of the most turbulent in Supreme Court history particularly in regard to social issues confronted by the Court. Warren died on July 9, 1974, and at a memoriam a longtime friend, Attorney Edward Bennett Williams, said of him:

> He worried constantly whether in our obsession with security we were developing a lassitude about liberty. . . .
> . . . He feared and said that an alarming number of Americans were prepared to meet the problems of crime, violence, and dissent by the abridgement of freedom. . . .
> The Chief had a total commitment to robust, open, unrestrained debate on public issues — to the right of the press and the people to speak freely on all subjects, to criticize, dissent, petition, assemble, and demonstrate. He recognized no principle to be so universally held as not to be subject to question, to challenge, and to debate. And so too did the Warren Court have a zest for political freedom of the individual. It recognized that informed and reasonable dissent is better for our kind of society than mindless compliance.[42]

Chief Justice Burger

In 1969 President Richard M. Nixon named Warren E. Burger as Chief Justice of the United States to replace Earl Warren, who had retired. Nixon later appointed other members of the Court: Harry A. Blackmun, Lewis F. Powell, Jr., and William H. Rehnquist. In a span of six years, a politically conservative President appointed four of the nine Court members. In 1975 Nixon's successor, President Gerald Ford, appointed John Paul Stevens to replace Douglas who retired after serving on the high court for 36 years — the longest any person has so served.

Then, in 1981 Justice Potter Stewart, who had served nearly 23 years on the Court and who had provided "swing" votes in a number of press cases, announced his retirement effective July 3, 1981. President Ronald Reagan thereupon nominated an Arizona appeals court judge, Sandra O'Connor, as Stewart's replacement. Two months later, O'Connor became the first woman member in the Court's 191-year history.

What once had been considered by many observers to be a "liberal" court now seemed to have swung toward the opposite end of the political spectrum. With the appointment of O'Connor to the bench, the "liberals" on the Court had been reduced to two — Brennan and Thurgood Marshall, although Blackmun later would be included in that grouping. At best, labels such as "liberal" or "conservative" are a poor way to delineate legal, political, and philosophical beliefs, and so it was with the Burger Court—a Court often described as "conservative" on free-speech/free-press and law-and-order issues.

Some of the concerns about the "Burger Court" resulted from a series of decisions in 1978 and 1979 that sparked renewed debate over the Free Press Clause of the First Amendment.

Here is a synopsis of cases which provoked the most concern. A more complete review of these cases is provided in subsequent chapters.

1. In July 1979 a majority of the Court ruled in *Gannett v. DePasquale* that the press and public can be excluded from pre-trial hearings. Whether they also could be excluded from criminal trials was not clearly answered at that time (Chapter 10).
2. Also in July 1979 the Court declined to order a lower court to expedite a review of a judicial order which enjoined *The Progressive* magazine from publishing an article about the H-bomb. This was a classic prior restraint case (Chapter 3).
3. In April 1979 the Court in *Herbert v. Lando* ruled that journalists' thoughts, opinions, and conclusions formed during the editorial process could be the subject of questioning by a libel plaintiff's attorney. Such an inquiry was necessary, said the Court, if the libel plaintiff were to have any hope of showing the requisite "actual malice" on the part of the journalist—a showing necessary to a successful libel action on the part of public officials and public figures (Chapter 5).
4. In November 1978 the Court declined to review a New Jersey court decision that resulted in *New York Times'* reporter Myron Farber spending 40 days in jail and the *Times* being fined $285,000 for contempt of court in connection with a trial judge's order that confidential information, including confidential sources, be divulged to the trial judge. The judge then would decide if the information would be useful to the defense in a murder trial. The reporter refused to obey the order because of a pledge of confidentiality that had been given and because, according to the reporter's attorneys, the First Amendment protected him from forced disclosure (Chapter 11).
5. In June 1978 the Court held that the news media have no more rights than does the public to gain access to public institutions (a prison in this case, *Houchins v. KQED*) (Chapter 11).
6. In May 1978 the Court issued its ruling in *Zurcher v. Stanford Daily* that the First Amendment is no bar to a search of a newspaper office if there is reasonable grounds to believe that criminal evidence may be found on the premises (Chapter 11).

In each of the cases above, First Amendment claims were put forth by the press, but they failed to turn the tide that, according to segments of the Fourth Estate, was running against First Amendment freedoms. For example, the "erosion" of First Amendment rights dominated the 93d annual convention of the

American Newspaper Publishers Association in New York City in April 1979. Association President Allen Neuharth set the tone for the meeting in his keynote address by declaring, "The First Amendment is in trouble. We must take up the fight to rescue it."[43] Professor John Hohenberg in *A Crisis for the American Press* (1979) wrote that the American people and their press are being subjected to the worst repression since the Alien and Sedition Acts of 1798.[44]

Against the backdrop of these and other cases, the debate over the Free Press Clause and the First Amendment continued.

Protection for the Press as an Institution

Justice Stewart, in an address at Yale Law School's sesquicentennial convocation, put forth the thesis that the Free Press Clause extends protection to the press as an institution—that the guarantee created a fourth branch of government—an unofficial one, to be sure, but one that was intended by the Founding Fathers to keep a check on the three official branches. Therefore, certain rights accrue to the press as an institution that otherwise would not exist.

Stewart said:

If the Free Press guarantee meant no more than freedom of expression, it would be a constitutional redundancy. Between 1776 and the drafting of our Constitution, many of the state constitutions contained clauses protecting freedom of the press while at the same time recognizing no general freedom of speech. By including both guarantees in the First Amendment, the Founders quite clearly recognized the distinction between the two.

It is also a mistake to suppose that the only purpose of the constitutional guarantee of a free press is to insure that a newspaper will serve as a neutral forum for debate, a "market place for ideas," a kind of Hyde Park corner for the community. A related theory sees the press as a neutral conduit of information between the people and their elected leaders. These theories, in my view, again give insufficient weight to the institutional autonomy of the press that it was the purpose of the Constitution to guarantee.

In setting up the three branches of the Federal Government, the Founders deliberately created an internally competitive system. As Mr. Justice Brandeis once wrote: "The (Founders') purpose was, not to avoid friction, but, by means of the inevitable friction incident to the distribution of the government powers among three departments, to save the people from autocracy."

The primary purpose of the constitutional guarantee of a free press was a similar one: to create a fourth institution outside the Government as an additional check on the three official branches. . . .

The relevant metaphor, I think, is the metaphor of the Fourth Estate. What Thomas Carlyle wrote about the British Government a century ago has a curiously contemporary ring: "Burke said there were Three Estates in Parliament; but, in the Reporters' Gallery yonder, there sat a Fourth Estate more important by far than they all." It is not a figure of speech or witty saying; it is a literal fact—very momentous to us in these times.

For centuries before our Revolution, the press in England had been licensed, censored, and bedeviled by prosecutions for seditious libel. The British Crown knew that a free press was not just a neutral vehicle for the balanced discussion of diverse ideas. Instead, the free press meant organized, expert scrutiny of government. The press was a conspiracy of the intellect, with the courage of numbers. This formidable check on official power was what the British Crown had feared — and what the American Founders decided to risk.

It is this constitutional understanding, I think, that provides the unifying principle underlying the Supreme Court's recent decisions dealing with the organized press.[45]

In his analysis Stewart pointed out that the press could have been made to function as a public utility or as a neutral marketplace of ideas. But such an idea was not included in the Constitution that the Founders wrote, said Stewart, adding: "Perhaps our liberties might survive without an independent established press. But the Founders doubted it, and, in the year 1974 [in the aftermath of the Watergate scandal], I think we can all be thankful for their doubts."

Stewart's views provide a theoretical framework by which to consider the First Amendment's Free Press Clause; namely, the guarantee was for an institution. The press was given favored status so it could be an unofficial fourth branch of government — a watchdog of government. Followed to its logical conclusion, such a view places the press within the grand design of "checks and balances" and assigns an adversary role to the Fourth Estate in its relationship to government.

Professor Vincent Blasi shares Stewart's view of the Press Clause in putting forth his notion of a checking function of the First Amendment; that is, the free-press guarantee gives the news media the protection they must have to keep government accountable and to reduce the danger of government abuse of its power.[46] Thus, the media provide a check on government power.

Whether history supports Stewart's view is questionable. Professor Don Pember of Washington University, after a five-month study, concluded that there was no evidence to support Stewart's thesis of a special status for the press in the Press Clause.[47] Such a study, however, will not end the dispute. As the author of a law review article wrote:

Whether the Framers of the First Amendment intended an independent role for the press clause is a question not much considered by the disputants in this controversy.[48] Justice Stewart grounded his view on history, but without undertaking any extensive review of the origins of the press clause.[49] Professor Melville B. Nimmer asserted that "(h)istory casts little light on the question here posed. . . . But as we have seen in other constitutional contexts, the original understanding of the Founders is not necessarily controlling."[50] [Journalist Anthony] Lewis reviewed the literature, without pursuing his own historical inquiry, and found "(n)o historian (who) has produced any evidence to support" Justice Stewart's position.[51] [Professor David] Lange briefly examined the eighteenth century literature on press freedom and found the evidence for Stewart's view "not entirely persuasive."[52] He noted that neither the Fourth Estate metaphor nor the press as we know it had yet been conceived when the First Amendment was drafted.[53]

Freedom of Press as an Individual Right: Burger

A different conceptualization of the Press Clause sees freedom of press as an individual right. As pointed out by Chief Justice Burger, a pamphleteer was as much a part of the "press" in the 1700s as were newspapers; the right of an individual to speak or to write his views was of great concern to those who advocated a Bill of Rights, and the first ten amendments to the Constitution, by and large, stress individual rights, not the rights of institutions such as the press.

Burger seemed to go out of his way to disagree with Stewart's interpretation when he wrote a concurring opinion in *First National Bank of Boston v. Bellotti, Attorney General of Massachusetts* (1978).[54] In this case, the Court, by a 5–4 vote, declared unconstitutional a Massachusetts statute which barred business corporations from spending money to influence votes on referenda except when they "materially affect" a corporation's business or assets. In its decision, the Court recognized that corporations have First Amendment rights.

Burger gave two major reasons why he believes the Press Clause does not confer any special right on a "select group" (the press): (1) the Press Clause was included "simply because it [the press] had been more often the object of official restraints" shortly after the invention of the printing press; and (2) there would be the difficulty of knowing which entities would be included in the "institutional press." He went on to say:

> Because the First Amendment was meant to guarantee freedom to express and communicate ideas, I can see no difference between the right of those who seek to disseminate ideas by way of a newspaper and those who give lectures or speeches. . . . "[T]he purpose of the Constitution was not to erect the press into a privileged institution but to protect all persons in their right to print what they will as well as to utter it. '. . . The liberty of the press is no greater and no less . . .' than the liberty of every citizen of the Republic." *Pennekamp v. Florida,* 328 U.S. 331, 364 (1946) (Frankfurter, J., concurring).
>
> In short, the First Amendment does not "belong" to any definable category of persons or entities; it belongs to all who exercise its freedom.[55]

Brennan's Two-Model Approach

Justice Brennan in an address on October 17, 1979, at the dedication of the S.I. Newhouse Center for Law and Justice at Rutgers University, offered two models of the role of the press in society as a means of better understanding the protective nature of the First Amendment. The first is the "speech" model. According to this model, the First Amendment "more or less absolutely" prohibits any government interference with freedom of expression or the press's dissemination of news. Thus, when government has attempted to impose prior restraints on the press, the Supreme Court has firmly rejected such attempts, according to Brennan. In essence, this model sees the First Amendment as forbidding government interference in the communication process by means of which citizens exercise and prepare to exercise their rights of self-government. Thus, the "speech" model protects self-expression *and* the communicative processes through which citizens exercise their rights of self-government.

The second model, which he labeled "structural," focuses on the relationship of the press to the communicative functions required by our democracy. To the extent that the press makes these functions possible, the model also requires First Amendment protection. But this model also requires balancing—balancing the effects of any impositions on the press's newsgathering function against the social interests served by the impositions. Thus, society's interest in law enforcement may outweigh the disadvantages of some impositions on the press. In the newspaper search case, for example, the issue was not a restriction on what the press could say—the dissemination function—but rather "whether special procedures were necessary to protect the press's ability to gather and publish news" as part of the self-governing process. The Court had to weigh whatever First Amendment interests were implicated (such as the press serving the self-governing process) against society's interest in law enforcement. It found in favor of society's interest in law enforcement.

Concerning the *Gannett v. DePasquale* decision, discussed later, and the press's reaction to it, Brennan stressed the view

> . . . [T]hat the impact of the press's quite correct reaction was undercut by the unjustified violence of its previous responses to *Herbert v. Lando* and other such cases involving the structural model of the press. This fact was cogently noted by Anthony Lewis in his column in *The New York Times:*
>
>> The press . . . should forswear absolutes. The reiterated claim of recent years that its freedom has no limits has done the press no good. If the press began recognizing that there are difficult issues, involving more than one interest, it could more effectively criticize the facile simplicities of a *Gannett* decision.[56]
>
> I think Mr. Lewis is correct. And I say this with some urgency, for the integrity of the press must be preserved, not only for cases like *Gannett,* where the press puts forward the claims of the public, but even for cases like *Zurcher,* where the press puts forward its own structural claims. For the application of the First Amendment is far from certain in the as yet uncharted domains foreshadowed by the structural model of the press. The Court needs help in scouting these dim areas in which the shield of the Amendment is put forward not to guard the personal right to speak, but to protect social functions of impersonal dimensions. The press can and must assist the Court in mustering proper legal conclusions from the accumulated experience of the Nation. But the press can be of assistance only if bitterness does not cloud its vision, nor self-righteousness its judgment.[57]

Reaction to Brennan's address varied among press and law experts. For example, Richard M. Schmidt, Jr., general counsel for the American Society of Newspaper Editors, said that although he admired and respected Justice Brennan, he nonetheless thought that the press's reaction to the Court's decisions, noted above, was not unreasonable. He said, "With the fallout from the court's opinions thrusting the press into the litigation arena with increasing frequency, perhaps the press is entitled to a little 'paranoia.' "[58]

Floyd Abrams, a First Amendment lawyer in New York, made these comments:

Justice Brennan is so proven a friend of the First Amendment, as well as the rest of the Bill of Rights, that when he is critical of the press, the press should indeed listen. And think. There is no doubt that some of the reporting, say the *Herbert* case, was sloppy; but so may it be said that some of the judicial writing in *Herbert,* itself, was less than precise—even though judges have a far less demanding deadline than do journalists. . . . The press should, of course, attempt to be more accurate; it should not be less intense in defense of its own abilities.[59]

Lewis, the *New York Times'* columnist mentioned by Brennan, had this to say of the speech:

In general, I thought it was an exceptionally thoughtful and useful speech. I think it may be the beginning of a new look at Supreme Court doctrine relating to the press. . . . I think that if you begin thinking about the cases as representing two different problems, you would be helping the freedom of the press. One problem is when the press has facts and desires to publish them. That's what Justice Brennan calls the free speech model. There, the Supreme Court has said . . . that it is virtually impossible, under our Constitution, to keep the press from publishing what it knows. The second category Brennan calls the structural model, but I would call the incidental rights of the press, since they are things incidental to and useful to the press's duty and right to publish. . . . Justice Brennan . . . urges the press to recognize that there are . . . other interests that have to be raised. . . . He says that the right constitutional solution is to weigh those interests against the needs of the press in each case. I think that is a wise piece of advice because it would often give the press constitutional rights that have not so far been recognized.[60]

Quite a different viewpoint was expressed by Robert White II, publisher of the *Mexico Ledger* in Missouri and member of the American Newspaper Publishers Association Press/Bar Relations Committee. He said:

The First Amendment said "Congress shall make no law . . . abridging freedom of speech, or of the press." It does not define the press, as Justice Brennan does, as having two models, one of which is pure, to be treated like the honor of a woman, and the other, impure, to be treated whatever way pleases elected or appointed government officials—specifically, judges.[61]

A few months after Brennan's address, a former Supreme Court justice, Arthur J. Goldberg, who served during the Warren Court era, began a speech in this way: "Now is the time for all good men to come to the aid of the First Amendment. It is under attack."[62] After reviewing a number of Supreme Court decisions, he made this comment:

When I was on the Supreme Court we handed down an opinion saying that First Amendment freedoms need "breathing space" to survive.

This is an elementary truth and we must be eternally vigilant to ensure that "breathing space" is provided.

But the simple fact is that the First Amendment is being denied adequate "breathing space."[63]

And from Harold Leventhal of the U.S. Court of Appeals for the District of Columbia Circuit came a warning. In a speech to the Associated Press Managing Editors Association on October 16, 1979, Judge Leventhal said that an "intemperate and oversimplified" reaction by the press to certain Supreme Court decisions "runs the serious risk of creating among its constituency the perception that the Court is not to be trusted," and this may result in the "erosion of legitimacy of the Court, and the loss of the media's staunchest ally."[64] He then discussed the trend of the evolving law of the press, based on Justice Powell's pivotal votes in *Branzburg v. Hayes* (Chapter 11), *Zurcher,* and *Gannett.* This trend, said Leventhal, recognizes that the press "has the First Amendment rights of the public, but with a little more, because it has the institutional role of being the eyes and ears of the public."[65]

THEORY INTO PRACTICE

At some point theory must face up to practice, and so it is with freedom of speech and press. Court decisions make it possible to make some generalizations about the First Amendment and what it protects. The following generalizations and cases will be discussed in more detail in subsequent chapters.

1. The First Amendment does not invalidate every incidental burdening of the press that may result from the enforcement of civil or criminal statutes of general applicability.[66] The publisher has no special immunity from the application of general laws. Thus, he or she is not exempt from some antitrust statutes,[67] and the newspaper is subject to nondiscriminatory general taxation.[68]
2. Under certain circumstances, prior restraint of the press is constitutionally permissible, although the government faces a heavy burden of showing justification for such restraint.[69] Prior restraint has judicial approval in instances involving movement of troop transports, location of troops when the nation is at war, protection of the vital security interest of the nation and community, maintenance of community "decency," and protection against words that have all the effect of force.
3. The press cannot with impunity publish everything it wishes. Even when it publishes a matter of public interest, it is subject to liability if it publishes knowing or reckless falsehoods that damage a person's reputation.[70]
4. Even when the press publishes a matter of public interest, it cannot tortiously, or wrongfully, gather information or intrude upon a person's privacy.[71]
5. The use of a person's name or likeness for commercial purposes is actionable if prior permission has not been given.[72]
6. A newspaper or journalist may be punished for contempt of court in appropriate circumstances.[73]

7. It has generally been held that the First Amendment does not guarantee the press a right of special access to information not available to the public generally. The "right to speak and publish does not carry with it the unrestrained right to gather information."[74] However, the Supreme Court has held that both the public and press have a conditional First Amendment right to attend criminal trials.[75]

8. Courts can proscribe extrajudicial statements to the press by witnesses, court officials, law enforcement officers, and others; that is, they can impose restraint upon potential news sources rather than directly upon the press. Direct restraints or gags on the press can be constitutionally imposed only in rare circumstances. Generally, judges must use other means to prevent interference with an accused person's right to a fair trial.[76]

9. False or deceptive commercial speech (advertising) is not protected by the First Amendment;[77] however, truthful commercial speech enjoys such protection with several notable exceptions, including the ban on the advertising of tobacco products on radio and television.

10. Radio and television can be subjected to more government regulation than the print medium because of their special characteristics and because of special conditions applicable only to them.[78]

These generalizations can also be made:

1. Speech which incites imminent lawless action is not protected by the First Amendment.[79]

2. "Fighting words" are outside the protection of the First Amendment because they are so shocking and insulting that harm results; therefore, the state may regulate such speech.[80]

3. Obscenity is not protected by the First Amendment because it has minimal social value and is offensive to contemporary moral standards.[81]

Present Supreme Court

Chief Justice Burger retired in July 1986 after 17 years as Chief Justice to devote more time to help organize the nation's celebration of the 200th anniversary of the Constitution. President Reagan nominated Associate Justice Rehnquist to become Chief Justice, and the Senate, on September 17, 1986, confirmed the nomination by a 65–33 vote. Rehnquist was severely criticized during debate over the nomination. His views of the Constitution and of the Bill of Rights, especially the First Amendment, were characterized by opponents of confirmation as extreme right wing or ultraconservative.

A look at Rehnquist's voting record on First Amendment issues since being named to the Supreme Court by President Nixon in 1971 (and confirmed by a 68–28 vote) showed a consistent pattern of interpreting that amendment in ways quite different from such First Amendment "stalwarts" as Justices Black, Douglas, Brennan, and Marshall. Whether as Chief Justice his voting pattern remains the same will be subjected to considerable scrutiny. Interestingly, he wrote an opinion for a unanimous Supreme Court in 1988 that reversed a $200,000 award to the Rev. Jerry Falwell against *Hustler* magazine—an opinion that could only be construed as "liberal" in various ways, including the precedents cited.[82] Then, several months later, he wrote another opinion for the Court in which the validity of the independent counsel provisions of the Ethics in Government Act was upheld. The law allowed independent prosecutors to be used to prosecute former top Reagan aides accused of wrongdoing and had been opposed by the Reagan administration.

In addition to Rehnquist being named Chief Justice, another "conservative" was named to fill the vacancy created when Rehnquist moved up. Judge Antonin Scalia of the U.S. Court of Appeals for the District of Columbia Circuit was confirmed by the Senate on September 19, 1986. Then Justice Powell sprang a surprise. He announced he would retire in mid-1987. Another federal judge, Anthony M. Kennedy, became the 104th justice on the Supreme Court bench on February 18, 1988. He was President Reagan's third choice to succeed Powell. His first choice, federal Judge Robert Bork, was defeated by a Senate vote, and the second nominee, Judge Douglas Ginsburg, asked that his name be withdrawn after he disclosed that he had smoked marijuana several times while a law school professor.

The new Court lineup left only Brennan and Marshall as the "liberal" wing, with Blackmun sometimes tagged with that label. But at the time of Kennedy's appointment, the "liberal" trio were in their eighties or close to it, although they had given no indication of any plans to retire.

As a consequence of these and other recent changes in the Court's membership, there were gloomy predictions of trouble ahead for the Fourth Estate. During the past few years, a number of Supreme Court decisions favorable to the press had been decided by one-vote margins, and in some of those cases Burger and Powell had lined up on the press's side.

In any event, at the time Kennedy at age 52 joined the Court, the other members and their ages were: Rehnquist, 64; Brennan, 82; Marshall, 80; Blackmun, 79; White, considered a "moderate conservative," 71; Stevens, 68; O'Connor, 58; and Scalia, 52.

Reagan's impact extended beyond the Supreme Court. During his two terms in office he made 375 appointments—or almost half of the 761 sitting federal judges. About 2 percent were black and 8.5 percent were women. Many of the appointees were chosen because of their conservative views on certain issues or because of their ideologies, or both. Thus, long after leaving office, Reagan's influence will be felt in the federal judiciary. And his successor, George Bush, also is expected to have considerable impact on the judiciary, given the ages of the Supreme Court's "liberals" and the 41 federal court vacancies existing when Bush assumed office, including nine at the appellate court level. Additionally, a number of federal judges had held up on plans to retire during the Reagan years in the hope that a Democrat would be elected president in 1988. Faced with at least four more years of a Republican in the White House, they may go ahead with retirement plans.

States as Protectors

As the U.S. Supreme Court steps back or shies away from more "liberal" positions in free-speech/free-press cases or leaves basic issues or concerns unresolved, state courts and legislatures may become more active in protecting certain rights. For example, a 5–4 majority of the U.S. Supreme Court decided in 1972 (with four Nixon appointees joining Justice White) that the owners of a shopping mall could prevent the peaceful distribution of handbills by an anti-Vietnam war group.[83] Whether the decision in *Lloyd Corporation Ltd. v. Tanner* overturned the Court's 1968 ruling in *Amalgamated Food Employees Union Local 590 v. Logan Valley Plaza, Inc.,* mentioned earlier, was in dispute until 1976. That is when a 6–2 majority of the Court declared, in *Hudgens v. National Labor Relations Board,* that the First Amendment only protects free expression from government interference and does not protect pickets in a privately owned shopping center.[84] Justice Marshall, joined by Brennan, wrote a dissenting opinion. He believed that for freedom-of-speech purposes walkways in shopping malls are similar to public parks and sidewalks.

Lloyd Corporation still held up even though the Supreme Court in 1980 affirmed a decision of the California Supreme Court in *Pruneyard Shopping Center v. Robins.*[85] The state court had held that the California Constitution protects "speech and petitioning, reasonably exercised in shopping centers even when the centers are privately owned."[86] The U.S. Supreme Court said that *Lloyd Corporation* does not limit a state that wants to be more expansive in protecting individual liberties.

The California court's action is in keeping with the urgings of Justice Brennan that state judiciaries should maintain the more liberal traditions of the Warren Court. Brennan's view is shared by Justice Stanley Mosk of the California Supreme Court, who said:

> Today a new body of constitutional law is emerging, based not on the Constitution of the United States but on the Constitutions of the several states. Liberal state courts have taken the doctrines of federalism and states' rights, heretofore associated with people like George Wallace, and adapted them to give citizens more rights under their state constitutions rather than to oppress them.

If, as many believe, the U.S. Constitution sets a floor for civil liberties protection, but not a ceiling, then states can, if they wish, become more active in providing greater protection of basic freedoms. In fact, this is what happened after the U.S. Supreme Court, by a 5–3 vote, ruled in *Zurcher v. Stanford Daily* (1978) that police could make an unannounced search of a newsroom when armed with a search warrant, even though the newspaper was an innocent third party. States like California, Illinois, Nebraska, Oregon, Texas, and Washington enacted legislation to provide greater protection to the news media. And so did Congress! Similarly, the states of Connecticut, New Jersey, and Pennsylvania joined California in giving greater protection to speech rights when those rights clash with private property rights. And when the U.S. Supreme Court ruled in 1988 (with Brennan, Marshall, and Blackmun dissenting) that public school officials can regulate the content of school publications and plays if it results from a supervised learning experience (such as a journalism class),[87] the Massachusetts legislature acted. It passed a law declaring that the rights of public school students to freedom of expression shall not be abridged (see Chapter 3). California already had special protection in place for the student press through its State Education Code.

SUMMARY

The "marketplace of ideas" concept, enunciated by Justice Holmes in 1919, has influenced contemporary thought on the meaning and scope of the First Amendment. Under this theory, the First Amendment provides protection so that ideas may freely enter the marketplace where the public can pick and choose. From this kind of competition, it is hoped that truth will emerge.

The Meiklejohn theory also has been a powerful influence in determining what kind of speech should be absolutely protected. Political speech, he said. And within that category he would include speech related to the sciences, the arts, morality — any speech that has anything to do with the self-governing process. Meiklejohn's ideas strongly influenced the U.S. Supreme Court's decision in 1964 that greatly enhanced the news media's protection against libel suits brought by public officials (*New York Times v. Sullivan*).

Meiklejohn stopped short of the absolutists who, like Justice Black, contend that all speech, without exception, should be absolutely protected from government interference. The absolutists have rarely mustered majority support in the Supreme Court which, in its efforts to distinguish protected speech from that which lies outside the ambit of the First Amendment, has resorted to various formulations since the turn of the century. These include liberty versus license, reasonable tendency, clear and present danger, preferred position, balancing, and speech versus nonspeech (or pure speech versus action speech, speech versus speech-plus). Under certain conditions, nonspeech elements are subject to regulations and when pure speech commingles so the two are inseparable, then speech itself may be subject to control.

The uncertainty surrounding the meaning of the First Amendment stems from not having an official record of either the Constitutional Convention, at which the desirability of a Bill of Rights was discussed, or of the First Congress's committees which met in secret and hammered out what ultimately became the first 10 amendments to the Constitution. Were such records kept, we would have a better idea of what the lawmakers intended when, for example, they wrote the Free Press Clause.

Justice Stewart says that the clause extends protection to the press as an institution. Not so, says Chief Justice Burger. The press's First Amendment rights are the same as any citizen's. Justice Brennan put forth a two-model approach as a way of better understanding what is or is not protected by the First Amendment. The "speech" model protects "more or less absolutely" the right of the press to publish information that helps citizens exercise their rights of self-government. The "structural" model also anticipates First Amendment protection when the press is carrying out those functions required by our democracy, but where that is not the case, then the rights claimed by the press have to be balanced against other rights. Judge Leventhal believes the press has the same First Amendment rights as the public, plus a little more because of the institutional role it has as watchdog of government.

With the exception of absolutism, however, a distillation remains no matter which theory or formula is used in explaining the First Amendment; that is, some kinds of speech and press can be controlled or punished under some kinds of conditions.

QUESTIONS IN REVIEW

1. The Fourteenth Amendment and *Gitlow v. State of New York* had what major effect?
2. Prof. Meiklejohn asserted that the First Amendment should unconditionally protect speech and press which relate, directly or indirectly, to certain matters, namely _____. In effect, Meiklejohn urged that _____ speech be fully immunized by the First Amendment.
3. Although Justice Black was an absolutist in regard to First Amendment protection for speech and press, he made a distinction between such speech/press and _____, the latter subject to regulation.
4. The clear and present danger doctrine was enunciated in *Schenck v. U.S.* by _____.
5. What is Justice Holmes's "marketplace of ideas" concept?
6. The burning of a draft card in *U.S. v. O'Brien* was held not to be protected by the First Amendment. Why?
7. Name as many First Amendment formulations as you can recall; for example, liberty versus license, clear and present danger. . . .
8. True or False? Justice Stewart believes that the Press Clause provides protection to the press as an institution.
9. True or False? Chief Justice Burger argues that the press has greater First Amendment protection than citizens because of its function as watchdog of government.
10. True or False? The "speech" model of the First Amendment, as advanced by Justice Brennan, would "more or less absolutely" protect the right of the press to publish information that citizens need to govern themselves.

ANSWERS

1. Extended Bill of Rights guarantees to states.
2. Matters of public interest. Political speech.
3. Unlawful conduct.
4. Justice Oliver Wendell Holmes.
5. The marketplace concept states that the best test of truth is the power of thought to get itself accepted in competition of the marketplace. This idea can be related to poet-writer John Milton who wanted to let truth and falsehood "grapple." Whoever heard of truth being put to the worst, Milton wrote, in such an encounter?

6. The draft-card burning was held to be nonspeech or action speech, as distinct from pure speech. Where protected speech can be separated from illegal action, the speech will be protected, but the action won't.
7. Preferred position, balancing of interests, speech versus nonspeech or speech-plus, and absolutism.
8. True.
9. False.
10. True.

ENDNOTES

1. *Journal of the Continental Congress,* Vol. I, p. 57 (1800 ed.).
2. Alvin E. Austin, "Codes, Documents, Declarations Affecting the Press," (unpublished paper) Department of Journalism, University of North Dakota, August 1964, p. 55.
3. Gitlow v. People of New York, 268 U.S. 652, 45 S.Ct. 625, 69 L.Ed. 1138. As Justice Sanford said for a majority of the Court: "For present purposes we may and do assume that freedom of speech and of the press—which are protected by the First Amendment from abridgment by Congress—are among the fundamental personal rights and 'liberties' protected by the due process clause of the 14th Amendment from impairment by the States."
4. Lecture given by Irving R. Kaufman, March 18, 1970, "The Medium, the Message and the First Amendment," as reprinted in *New York University Law Review,* Vol. 45, No. 4, October 1970, pp. 783–84. Consider, for example, the problems associated with applying the First Amendment to a prison newspaper published by inmates, or the question of freedom of speech/press when applied to students in state or private schools.
5. *The Federalist, by Alexander Hamilton, James Madison and John Jay,* No. 84 by Hamilton, "The Lack of a Bill of Rights," ed. by Benjamin Fletcher Wright (Cambridge, Mass.: Harvard University Press, 1961), p. 535.
6. Thomas M. Cooley, *Constitutional Limitations,* 6th ed. (Boston: Little, Brown and Co., 1890), p. 518.
7. Abrams v. U.S., 250 U.S. 616, 40 S.Ct. 17, 63 L.Ed. 1173.
8. U.S. v. Associated Press, 52 F.Supp. 362, 372 (S.D.N.Y.).
9. Associated Press v. U.S., 326 U.S. 1, 65 S.Ct. 1416, 89 L.Ed. 2013 (1945). Justices Roberts and Murphy dissented, and Justice Jackson took no part in the decision.
10. Time, Inc. v. Hill, 385 U.S. 374, 389, 87 S.Ct. 534, 543, 17 L.Ed.2d 456, 468 (1967).
11. 50 U.S. Code 33.
12. Zechariah Chafee, Jr., *Free Speech in the United States* (Cambridge, Mass.: Harvard University Press, 1954), p. 3.
13. The tests of whether material is obscene or pornographic and therefore not protected by the Constitution are omitted from this chapter but reviewed in detail in Chapter 12. Similarly, the "public interest" formulation, as applied to libel and privacy cases, is reviewed in Chapters 5–7.
14. See Edward G. Hudon, *Freedom of Speech and Press in America* (Washington: Public Affairs Press, 1963), pp. 57, 66–68. In a 1941 decision, the Supreme Court said that neither "inherent tendency" nor "reasonable tendency" was enough to justify a restriction of free expression.
15. Schenck v. U.S., 249 U.S. 47, 52, 39 S.Ct. 247, 249, 63 L.Ed. 470.
16. Frohwerk v. U.S., 249 U.S. 204, 206, 39 S.Ct. 249, 250, 63 L.Ed. 561, 564 (1919).
17. Abrams v. U.S., op. cit., note 7.
18. Gitlow v. People of New York, op. cit., note 3.
19. Whitney v. California, 274 U.S. 357, 47 S.Ct. 641, 71 L.Ed. 1095 (1927).
20. Chafee, *Free Speech in the United States,* op. cit., note 12, p. 801.
21. Marsh v. Alabama, 326 U.S. 501, 509, 66 S.Ct. 276, 280, 90 L.Ed. 265, 270.
22. Notes, "The First Amendment and Regulation of Television News," *Columbia Law Review,* Vol. 72, No. 4, April 1972, pp. 759–60.

23. Hudon, *Freedom of Speech,* op. cit., note 14, pp. 172–73.
24. Yates v. U.S., 354 U.S. 298, 77 S.Ct. 1064, 1 L.Ed.2d 1356.
25. U.S. v. O'Brien, 391 U.S. 367, 88 S.Ct. 1673, 20 L.Ed.2d 672.
26. Amalgamated Food Employees Union Local 590 v. Logan Valley Plaza, Inc., 391 U.S. 308, 88 S.Ct. 1601, 20 L.Ed.2d 603 (1968).
27. Thomas I. Emerson, "Toward a General Theory of the First Amendment," 72 *Yale Law Journal* 877, 917–18 (1963).
28. Emerson, *The System of Free Expression* (New York: Random House, 1970), p. 17.
29. Tinker v. Des Moines School District, 393 U.S. 503, 89 S.Ct. 733 (1969).
30. "Sleep-In Ban Upheld." *New York Times,* July 1, 1984, p. E7.
31. State v. James A. Cline, 305 A.2d 673.
32. Dissenting opinion in Ginzburg v. U.S., 383 U.S. 463, 476, 86 S.Ct. 942, 950, 16 L.Ed. 2d 31, 41 (1966) and Mishkin v. State of New York, 383 U.S. at 491, 86 S.Ct. at 974, 16 L.Ed. 2d at 50.
33. The 13-member commission, which included no journalists (an omission that drew considerable criticism from the Fourth Estate), operated under grants from Time, Inc., and Encyclopedia Britannica, Inc., to the University of Chicago. The commission issued a book-length report entitled *A Free and Responsible Press* and was chaired by Robert M. Hutchins, then chancellor of the University of Chicago, with Professor Chafee as vice chairman. Not until May 1973 did a national watchdog group, the National News Council — originally composed of nine public members and six representatives from the media — emerge under the aegis of a nonprofit research foundation, the Twentieth Century Fund. Largely ignored by the press, the council ceased to exist in December, 1984.
34. Zechariah Chafee, Jr., *Government and Mass Communications* (Hamden, Conn.: Archon Books, 1965), pp. 6, 801–02.
35. The Pentagon Papers cases: New York Times Co. v. U.S. and U.S. v. Washington Post Co., 403 U.S. 713, 91 S.Ct. 2140, 29 L.Ed.2d 822 (1971).
36. Alexander Meiklejohn, "The First Amendment Is an Absolute," 1961 *Supreme Court Review* 245, 255.
37. Alexander Meiklejohn, *Political Freedom: The Constitutional Powers of the People* (New York: Harper & Row Publishers, Inc., 1960), p. 75.
38. Ibid., p. 79. The phrase "matters of public interest" has become the key one in development of both the law of libel and invasion of privacy as these relate to the mass media.
39. New York Times v. Sullivan, 376 U.S. 254, 84 S.Ct. 710, 11 L.Ed.2d 686 (1964). See Chapter 5.
40. See Chapter 14.
41. Chafee, Book Review, 62 *Harvard Law Review* 289, 898 (1949).
42. As reported in *Supreme Court Reporter,* Vol. 94A (St. Paul, Minn.: West Publishing Co., 1975), pp. 21–22.
43. *ANPA Public Affairs Newsletter,* May/June 1979, p. 1.
44. *The QUILL,* April 1979, p. 19.
45. Potter Stewart, address at Yale Law School Sesquicentennial Convocation, November 2, 1974; reported in 26 *Hastings Law Journal* 631 (1975).
46. Vincent Blasi, "The Checking Value in First Amendment Theory," 1977 *American Bar Foundation Research Journal* 523, 561.
47. Donald Pember, *The Bulletin,* published by the American Society of Newspaper Editors, December/January 1979, p. 6.
48. Two of our most prominent First Amendment theorists, Chafee and Emerson, warn us that historical inquiry is futile, either because "the framers had no very clear ideas as to what they meant," see Chafee, Book Review, 62 *Harvard Law Review* 891, 898 (1949), or because it is impossible at this late date to ascertain what they meant, see Emerson, "Colonial Intentions and Current Realities of the First Amendment," 125 *Pennsylvania Law Review* 737 (1977). But First Amendment historian, Leonard Levy, believes it is possible to ascertain what the Framers meant, but tells us it does not matter, that we are not bound by their understanding anyway. See L. Levy, *Legacy of Suppression: Freedom of Speech and Press in Early American History* (Cambridge, Mass.: Harvard University Press, 1960), p. 4.
49. Stewart, op. cit., note 45, at 632–34.

50. Melville B. Nimmer, "Introduction—Is Freedom of the Press a Redundancy: What Does It Add to Freedom of Speech?" 26 *Hastings Law Journal* 639, at 640–41 (1975).

51. Anthony Lewis, "A Preferred Position for Journalism?" 7 *Hofstra Law Review* 595 (1979).

52. David Lange, "The Speech and Press Clauses," 23 *UCLA Law Review* 77 (1975).

53. David A. Anderson, "The Origins of the Press Clause," 30 *UCLA Law Review* 455, at 461–62 (footnotes omitted).

54. 3 *Med.L.Rptr.* 2105, May 9, 1978.

55. Ibid., at 2120.

56. *The New York Times,* July 5, 1979.

57. Dedicatory address at S.I. Newhouse Center for Law and Justice at Rutgers University on October 17, 1979, as reported in *Editor & Publisher,* October 27, 1979, pp. 10+.

58. "Press-law experts split in reaction to Brennan talk," *Presstime,* December 1979, p. 20. Copyright 1979 by the American Newspaper Publishers Association.

59. Ibid.

60. Ibid, pp. 20–21.

61. Ibid., p. 20.

62. Speech given by former Associate Justice Arthur J. Goldberg at a lecture series held in April 1980 at Western Connecticut State College, Danbury, Conn., and reported in *Editor & Publisher,* May 10, 1980, p. 7.

63. Ibid.

64. "News Notes," *Media Law Reporter,* November 6, 1979.

65. Ibid.

66. Combined cases of U.S. v. Caldwell, Branzburg v. Hayes, In the Matter of Paul Pappas, 408 U.S. 665, 92 S.Ct. 2646, 33 L.Ed. 2d 626 (1972), in which Justice White listed many of the limitations on free press contained in the summarization. See Chapter 11.

67. Associated Press v. U.S., op. cit., note 9.

68. Grosjean v. American Press Co., 297 U.S. 233, 56 S.Ct. 444, 80 L.Ed. 660.

69. See Chapter 3.

70. See Chapter 5.

71. See Chapter 7.

72. See Chapter 7.

73. Craig v. Harney, 331 U.S. 367, 377–78, 67 S.Ct. 1249, 1255–56, 91 L.Ed. 1547, 1553 (1947). See Chapter 10.

74. Zemel v. Rusk, 381 U.S. 1, 17, 85 S.Ct. 1271, 1281, 14 L.Ed.2d 179, 190 (1965). See also Chapter 11.

75. See Chapter 11.

76. See Chapter 10.

77. See Chapter 13.

78. See Chapter 14.

79. Brandenburg v. Ohio, 395 U.S. 444, 89 S.Ct. 1827, 23 L.Ed.2d 430 (1969).

80. Chaplinsky v. New Hampshire, 315 U.S. 568, 62 S.Ct. 766, 86 L.Ed. 1031 (1942).

81. Roth v. United States, 354 U.S. 476, 77 S.Ct. 1304, 1 L.Ed.2d 1498 (1957). See Chapter 12.

82. Hustler Magazine v. Falwell, 14 *Med.L.Rptr.* 2881, March 15, 1988. See Chapter 7.

83. Lloyd Corporation Ltd. v. Tanner, 407 U.S. 551, 92 S.Ct. 2219, 33 L.Ed.2d 131.

84. *U.S. Law Week* 1138, March 9, 1976.

85. 447 U.S. 74, 100 S.Ct. 2035 (1980).

86. 23 Cal.3d 899, 592 P.2d 341 (1979).

87. Hazelwood School District v. Kuhlmeier, 14 *Med.L.Rptr.* 2081, February 2, 1988. See Chapter 3.

3

Prior Restraint, Injunctions, Censorship

HIGHLIGHTS

■ *Near v. Minnesota* (1931) and *New York Times Co. v. U.S.* and *U.S. v. Washington Post* (1971), the latter two known as the Pentagon Papers case, resulted in rulings by the U.S. Supreme Court which overturned prior restraints on publication, but the Court made it clear that the First Amendment ban on prior restraint is not absolute.

■ *U.S. v. The Progressive* stemmed from a U.S. District Court judge's injunction against publication of a magazine article giving details of how to build an H-bomb. But after similar information was published elsewhere, the U.S. Justice Department gave up efforts to prevent publication of the article.

■ Numerous instances of prior restraint and press censorship are reported annually, especially involving the student press. And the Supreme Court, in *Hazelwood School District v. Kuhlmeier* (1988), ruled that public school officials can regulate the content of a school publication or play in a reasonable manner if that content results from a supervised learning experience, such as from a journalism class.

Many prior restraint cases involve the attempted publication or distribution of pamphlets, so-called "underground" newspapers and the student press. The established news media generally are not directly involved. This is particularly true of prior restraint cases. On occasion, however, the ghost from an earlier

CANISIUS COLLEGE LIBRARY

period of suppression and oppression returns as a reminder of the potential vulnerability of all segments of the press.

There are two classic prior restraint cases—*Near v. Minnesota* in 1931 and the Pentagon Papers case in 1971. *The Progressive* magazine case in 1979 never ripened into a Supreme Court decision. These three cases began with the issuance of injunctions[1] to halt publication of a newspaper, in the *Near* case; a series of newspaper stories, in the combined cases of *New York Times Co. v. U.S.* and *U.S. v. Washington Post;* and a magazine article about the H-bomb, in *The Progressive* magazine case.

NEAR v. MINNESOTA

The landmark case *Near v. Minnesota* resulted from enactment of a state law, dubbed the Minnesota "Gag Law," which permitted abatement, as a nuisance, of any "malicious, scandalous, and defamatory" publication, or one judged to be obscene, by means of court-issued injunctions. The Hennepin County attorney sought an injunction against the *Saturday Press* and its manager, J.M. Near, claiming the newspaper had published "malicious, scandalous and defamatory" statements about Minneapolis city officials. The lower court judge agreed and permanently enjoined the *Saturday Press,* an action upheld by the state supreme court.

In 1931 the U.S. Supreme Court in a 5–4 decision held the Minnesota law to be in violation of the First Amendment.[2] In his opinion for the Court, Chief Justice Charles E. Hughes cited Justice Holmes' admonition in *Schenck v. U.S.:* "When a nation is at war many things that might be said in time of peace are such a hindrance to its efforts that their utterance will not be endured so long as men fight and that no court could regard them as protected by any constitutional right."

Hughes then enumerated those situations which would permit prior restraint:

> No one would question but that a government might prevent actual obstruction to its recruiting service or the publication of the sailing dates of transports or the number and location of troops. On similar grounds, the primary requirements of decency may be enforced against obscene publications. The security of the community life may be protected against incitement to acts of violence and the overthrow by force of orderly government. The constitutional guaranty of free speech does not "protect a man from an injunction against uttering words that may have all the effect of force." . . . Gompers v. Bucks Stove & Range Co., 221 U.S. 418. . . . These limitations are not applicable here.
>
> . . . As was said by Chief Justice Parker, in Commonwealth v. Blanding, 3 Pick, 304, 313, 15 Am.Dec. 214, with respect to the Constitution of Massachusetts, ". . . The liberty of the press was to be unrestrained, but he who used it was to be responsible in case of its abuse."
>
> The fact that for approximately 150 years there has been almost an entire absence of attempts to impose previous restraints upon publications relating to the

malfeasance of public officers is significant of the deep-seated conviction that such restraints would violate constitutional right. . . .

The importance of this immunity has not lessened.

In a dissenting opinion, Justice Pierce Butler wrote:

The Court quotes Blackstone in support of its condemnation of the statute as imposing a previous restraint upon publication. But the *previous restraints* referred to by him subjected the press to the arbitrary will of an administrative officer. He describes the practice (Book IV, p. 152): "To subject the press to the restrictive power of a licenser, as was formerly done, both before and since the [1688] revolution is to subject all freedom of sentiment to the prejudices of one man, and make him the arbitrary and infallible judge of all controverted points in learning, religion, and government."

Butler did not believe that Blackstone included in his doctrine prior restraints imposed by the *judiciary*. Furthermore, he argued that no one was seeking to place a prior restraint on the *Saturday Press:*

It is fanciful to suggest similarity between the granting or enforcement of the decree authorized by this [Minnesota] statute to prevent *further previous restraint* upon the press by licensers as referred to by Blackstone. . . .

In this case there was previous publication made in the course of the business of regularly producing malicious, scandalous, and defamatory periodicals. . . . There is no question of the power of the state to denounce such transgressions.

But the Chief Justice narrowly prevailed and the precedent was established that there could be prior restraint in only a very few situations: troop movements during wartime, obstruction to recruitment efforts, cases of obscenity, incitement to acts of violence, and overthrow by force of orderly government. And, said Hughes, the freedom from prior restraint does not depend upon the truth of the allegations made against public officials, although he agreed that the media could be held accountable *after* publication.

PENTAGON PAPERS CASE

Forty years passed before another major attempt to block publication of information by newspapers reached the Supreme Court. The famous Pentagon Papers case in 1971 was one of the most dramatic and suspenseful confrontations yet to occur between press and government. It involved multiple injunctions to stop various newspapers from publishing a secret war study; it led to unprecedented speed on the part of the nation's highest tribunal to resolve the constitutional dilemma; and it badly divided the court, thereby leaving a residue of uncertainty in both press and government circles.

The case resulted from a study authorized by Defense Secretary Robert McNamara in 1967 concerning United States involvement in the Vietnam War.

The period 1945–1968 was examined and the results, labeled "top secret," were contained in 47 volumes collectively entitled *History of the United States Decision-Making Process on Vietnam Policy.*

Early in 1971, a copy of the report amounting to some 7000 pages was obtained by Neil Sheehan, a *New York Times* reporter. What followed led to a 1972 Pulitzer Prize award to the newspaper.

A four-month hush-hush project ensued with some 75 *Times* employees being housed in a New York hotel where the massive report was read, discussed, and ultimately digested into a planned 10-article series. The *Times* even brought in a cryptographic expert to help guard against any American codes being compromised by publication.[3]

The first article appeared June 13, 1971. A second was published the following day at which time U.S. Attorney General John Mitchell sought to halt publication because it was "directly prohibited" by the Espionage Act of 1918. Another article appeared before a temporary injunction could be obtained from Judge Murray Gurfein of U.S. District Court for the Southern District of New York. The judge ordered the temporary ban after the government argued that publication would result in "irreparable injury" to the national defense and seriously interfere with the conduct of foreign affairs. Newspaper attorneys contended that the government's attempt to restrain further publication was "classic censorship," and that the injunction, even though temporary, would constitute the first time in the nation's history that a judge had ordered a newspaper not to print something.

The government soon discovered that it would have to cope with more than one newspaper. The *Washington Post* quickly succeeded in obtaining about 4000 copied pages of the study, and after a 12-hour debate among newspaper editors, reporters, and lawyers, the publisher gave the go-ahead to print a condensation beginning in the June 17 main edition.[4] On June 18, the Attorney General asked the *Post* to halt publication, but the newspaper declined to do so. A temporary injunction was sought; but Judge Gerhard Gesell of the District of Columbia, unlike his counterpart in New York, refused to issue such a ban, saying: "What is presented is a raw question of preserving the freedom of the press as it confronts the efforts of the government to impose prior restraint on publication of essentially historical data." He also said government attorneys had failed to show that publication would cause "serious injury to the United States."

On June 19, a three-judge panel of the U.S. Court of Appeals in Washington issued the temporary injunction in a split 2–1 decision and ordered reconsideration by Judge Gesell.

Simultaneously, Judge Gurfein in New York dissolved the temporary injunction and issued his ruling which was based largely on the proposition that prior restraint would be unconstitutional. Major precedents were *Near v. Minnesota* and *Grosjean v. American Press Co.* Both cases provided powerful arguments for the judge, who said:

> Fortunately upon the facts adduced in this case there is no sharp clash such as might have appeared between the vital security interest of the Nation and the compelling

Constitutional doctrine against prior restraint. If there be some embarrassment to the Government in security aspects as remote as the general embarrassment that flows from any security breach, we must learn to live with it. The security of the Nation is not at the ramparts alone. Security also lies in the value of our free institutions. A cantankerous press, an obstinate press, a ubiquitous press must be suffered by those in authority in order to preserve the even greater values of freedom of expression and the right of the people to know.[6]

Although Judge Gurfein decided that no sharp clash existed between the nation's vital security interest and the First Amendment—a judgment later disputed by some U.S. Supreme Court members—the U.S. Court of Appeals (Second Circuit) intervened to prevent further publication so that the issues could be reviewed on appeal. Faced with the prospect of additional delay, the *Times* appealed to the U.S. Supreme Court. Meanwhile, the U.S. Court of Appeals in Washington, D.C., had voted 7–2 to permit the Post to resume publication and so the government appealed that decision to the highest tribunal.

Supreme Court's Decision

On June 25, the Supreme Court voted 5–4 to halt temporarily further publication of any copies of the Pentagon Papers that had become available to various newspapers and wire services. Though temporary, this was the first such ban ever imposed by the highest court in the land. Justices Black, Douglas, Brennan, and Marshall voted against the ban; Chief Justice Burger and Justices Stewart, White, Harlan, and Blackmun favored it.

Oral arguments took place the next day. The U.S. solicitor general argued that publication of additional secret information would affect the lives of Americans fighting in Vietnam and pose a grave and immediate threat to national security. Attorneys for the two newspapers contended the government had made broad claims but offered little proof about the dangers that would result from publication. In an *amicus curiae* (friend of the court) brief filed by the American Civil Liberties Union, the Court was reminded that 19 federal judges had rejected the government's position. The other seven had believed further proceedings were desirable or necessary before reaching a decision. "Not a single federal judge has so far stated his agreement with the Government's claim," the brief noted. "Surely, this is a weighty evidence as to the 'sensitivity' of the documents."[7]

With unprecedented speed—five days from the time of oral arguments until a decision was reached—the Court decided 6–3 to uphold the decisions of the district courts in New York and Washington, thereby permitting resumption of publication of the Pentagon Papers. In the majority were Justices Black, Douglas, Brennan, Marshall (the four who had opposed temporary restraints), Stewart, and White. Opposed were Chief Justice Burger and Justices Harlan and Blackmun; but their dissent should not be construed as support of prior restraints vis-à-vis the facts in these cases. Rather, they indicated that the ban against publication should be continued while "orderly" proceedings were undertaken in the lower courts. The Chief Justice and Blackmun deplored the "frenetic haste" that accompanied their deliberations — five days in these cases, five months in *Near v. Minnesota.*

The brief per curiam[8] decision of the Court (all nine members wrote separate opinions) stated:

> "Any system of prior restraints of expression comes to this Court bearing a heavy presumption against its constitutional validity." *Bantam Books, Inc. v. Sullivan,* 372 U.S. 58, 70 (1963); *See also Near v. Minnesota,* 283 U.S. 697 (1931). The Government "thus carries a heavy burden of showing justification for the enforcement of such a restraint." *Organization for a Better Austin v. Keefe,* 402 U.S. 415, 419 (1971). The District Court for the Southern District of New York . . . and . . . for the District of Columbia . . . held that the Government had not met that burden.
>
> We agree.[9]

Before proceeding to the individual opinions, let's examine two of the precedents cited in the per curiam decision.

Bantam Books (1963). Justice Brennan in *Bantam Books* gave the opinion of the Court which reversed a ruling by the Rhode Island Supreme Court. The state court had upheld the constitutionality of the operations of the state Commission to Encourage Morality in Youth, but reversed a lower court decision that had enjoined various book and magazine distributors from selling, distributing, or displaying publications believed by the commission to be unfit for youths under 18 years of age. For example, the commission notified one distributor of its objections to such publications as *Peyton Place* and *The Bramble Bush* (the latter published by Bantam Books, Inc.), and such magazines as *Playboy* and *Rogue.* The commission threatened action by the state's attorney general if distributors failed to "cooperate."

Justice Brennan wrote, in part:

> What Rhode Island has done, in fact, has been to subject the distributor of publications to a system of prior administrative restraints, since the Commission is not a judicial body and its decisions to list particular publications as objectionable do not follow judicial determinations that such publications may lawfully be banned. Any system of prior restraints of expression comes to this Court bearing a heavy presumption against its constitutional validity. . . . We have tolerated such a system only where it operated under judicial superintendence and assured an almost immediate judicial determination of the validity of restraint. . . . The system at bar includes no such saving feature.

Organization for a Better Austin (OBA). The petitioners, OBA, already had been under a *temporary* injunction for more than three years(!) before the Supreme Court acted.[10] Illinois courts had enjoined OBA from "passing out pamphlets, leaflets or literature of any kind, and from picketing, anywhere in the city of Westchester, Illinois." OBA, through the use of "poor man's press" techniques, had been publicly protesting against alleged "panic peddling" or "blockbusting" activities of a real estate broker in a racially integrated area during September and October 1967. The broker brought an invasion of privacy action and sought to enjoin OBA. The Cook County Circuit Court issued a temporary injunction and, on appeal, this action was affirmed by the Appellate Court of Illinois.

Chief Justice Burger delivered the opinion of the Supreme Court, which reversed the Illinois Appellate Court and ordered the injunction vacated. He wrote:

> The Appellate Court appears to have viewed the alleged activities as coercive and intimidating, rather than informative, and therefore not entitled to First Amendment protection. . . .
>
> It is elementary . . . that in a case of this kind the courts do not concern themselves with the truth or validity of the publication. Under *Near v. Minnesota* . . ., the injunction, so far as it imposes prior restraint on speech and publication, constitutes an impermissible restraint on First Amendment rights. Here, as in that case, the injunction operates not to redress alleged private wrongs, but to suppress, on the basis of previous publications, distribution of literature "of any kind" in a city of 18,000.
>
> This Court has often recognized that the activity of peaceful pamphleteering is a form of communication protected by the First Amendment.
>
> . . . Any prior restraint on expression comes to this Court with a "heavy presumption" against its constitutional validity. *Carroll v. President and Commissioners of Princess Anne,* 393 U.S. 175, 181, 89 S.Ct. 347, 351, 21 L.Ed.2d 325 (1968); *Bantam Books, Inc. v. Sullivan.* . . . Respondent thus carries a heavy burden of showing justification for the imposition of such a restraint. He has not met that burden. No prior decisions support the claim that the interest of an individual in being free from public criticism of his business practices in pamphlets or leaflets warrants use of the injunctive power of a court. Designating the conduct as an invasion of privacy, the apparent basis for the injunction here, is not sufficient to support an injunction against peaceful distribution of informational literature of the nature revealed by this record.

Separate Opinions of Justices

The main Pentagon Papers arguments of the Court members are summarized here. Justice Black's came three months before his death.

Justice Black (Joined by Douglas) Concurring. In part, Black stated:

> Our Government was launched in 1789 with the adoption of the Constitution. The Bill of Rights, including the First Amendment, followed in 1791. Now, for the first time in the 182 years since the founding of the Republic, the Federal courts are asked to hold that the First Amendment does not mean what it says, but rather means that the Government can halt the publication of current news of vital importance to the people of this country.
>
> In seeking injunctions against these newspapers and in its presentation to the Court, the executive branch seems to have forgotten the essential purpose and history of the First Amendment. When the Constitution was adopted, many people strongly opposed it because the document contained no bill of rights to safeguard certain basic freedoms. They especially feared that the new powers granted to a central govern-

ment might be interpreted to permit the government to curtail freedom of religion, press, assembly and speech. In response to an overwhelming public clamor, James Madison offered a series of amendments to satisfy citizens that these great liberties would remain safe and beyond the power of government to abridge. Madison proposed what later became the First Amendment in three parts, two of which proclaimed: "The people shall not be deprived or abridged of their right to speak, to write, or to publish their sentiments; and the freedom of the press, as one of the great bulwarks of liberty, shall be inviolable." The amendments were offered to curtail and restrict the general powers granted to the executive, legislative and judicial branches two years before in the original Constitution. The Bill of Rights changed the original Constitution into a new charter under which no branch of government could abridge the people's freedoms of press, speech, religion and assembly.

Yet the Solicitor General argues and some members of the Court appear to agree that the general powers of the Government adopted in the original Constitution should be interpreted to limit and restrict the specific and emphatic guarantees the Bill of Rights adopted later. I can imagine no greater perversion of history.

Madison and the other framers of the First Amendment, able men that they were, wrote in language they earnestly believed could never be misunderstood: "Congress shall make no law abridging the freedom of the press." Both the history and language of the First Amendment support the view that the press must be left free to publish the news, whatever the source, without censorship, injunctions or prior restraints.

In the First Amendment the Founding Fathers gave the free press the protection it must have to fulfill its essential role in our democracy. The press was to serve the governed, not the governors. The Government's power to censor the press was abolished so that the press would remain forever free to censure the Government.

The press was protected so that it could bare the secrets of government and inform the people. Only a free and unrestrained press can effectively expose deception in government. And paramount among the responsibilities of a free press is the duty to prevent any part of the Government from deceiving the people and sending them off to distant lands to die of foreign fevers and foreign shot and shell.

In my view, quite far from deserving condemnation for their courageous reporting, the *New York Times,* the *Washington Post* and other newspapers should be commended for serving the purpose that the Founding Fathers saw so clearly. In revealing the workings of government that led to the Vietnam war, the newspapers nobly did precisely that which the founders hoped and trusted they would do.

. . . [W]e are asked to hold that despite the First Amendment's emphatic command, the executive branch, the Congress and the judiciary can make laws enjoining publication of current news and abridging freedom of the press in the name of "national security."

. . . The word "security" is a broad, vague generality whose contours should not be invoked to abrogate the fundamental law embodied in the First Amendment. The guarding of military and diplomatic secrets at the expense of informed representative government provides no real security for our Republic.

The framers of the First Amendment, fully aware of both the need to defend a new nation and the abuses of the English and colonial Governments, sought to give this new society strength and security by providing that freedom of speech, press, religion and assembly should not be abridged. This thought was eloquently expressed in 1937 by Mr. Chief Justice Hughes — great man and great Chief Justice that he was — when the Court held a man could not be punished for attending a meeting run by Communists.

The greater the importance of safeguarding the community from incitements to the overthrow of our institutions by force and violence, the more imperative is the need to preserve inviolate the constitutional rights of free speech, free press and free assembly in order to maintain the opportunity for free political discussion to the end that government may be responsive to the will of people and that changes, if desired, may be obtained by peaceful means. Therein lies the security of the Republic, the very foundation of constitutional government.

Justice Douglas (Joined by Black) Concurring. *Near v. Minnesota* refutes the government's contention that it has "inherent powers," in the absence of congressional approval through statute, "to go into court and obtain an injunction to protect national interest." Also, the First Amendment prohibits "the widespread practice of governmental suppression of embarrassing information."

Justice Brennan Concurring. The error from the start was granting any injunctive relief whatsoever. Under the circumstances presented by these cases, the First Amendment "stands as an absolute bar to the imposition of judicial restraints." The only exception would be for the government to prove that the publication would "directly and immediately cause the occurrence of an event kindred to imperiling the safety of a transport already at sea. . . ." Brennan's example of when prior restraint might be constitutionally imposed is very narrowly drawn.

Justice Marshall Concurring. Justice Marshall's opinion is devoted almost exclusively to the concept of separation of powers between the legislative, executive and judicial branches of the federal government. As noted by Douglas, Congress had not specifically made newspaper publication of "secret" government documents a crime, either under the Espionage Act or in related legislation. The issue, therefore, was whether the executive branch had the authority to invoke the jurisdiction of the courts to protect what it believed to be the national interest. Marshall decided that it would be "utterly inconsistent with the concept of separation of power for this Court to use its power of contempt to prevent behavior that Congress specifically has declined to prevent."

Justice Stewart (Joined by White) Concurring. The test is whether the disclosure of any of the secret information will "surely result" in direct, immediate and irreparable damage to the nation or its people. Stewart said he could not be sure of such a result; therefore, the First Amendment permitted only one possible judicial resolution of the issues presented. However, he took note of the government's argument that publication of the material would not be in the national interest; and, in fact, he agreed that this would be so "with respect to some of the documents involved." Any ambivalence on his part, however, was overcome by the test he applied.

Justice White (Joined by Stewart) Concurring. The publication of documents characterized by the government as the "most sensitive and destructive" will do substantial damage to the public interest, White said. In spite of such an unqualified view he nonetheless held that the government "has not satisfied the very heavy burden it must meet to warrant an injunction against publication. However, he did not rule out the possibility that criminal proceedings might be initiated *after* publication.

Chief Justice Burger Dissenting. The lack of facts and "frenetic" haste were laments of the Chief Justice. He would like to have seen the status quo maintained long enough for the lower courts to consider the issues in "judicial calm," and he scolded the Times for not doing what any citizen should do when "stolen property" is found; that is, report the discovery "forthwith" to proper authorities.

Burger also did not rule out the possibility of criminal action being filed after publication. And he made it clear that he did not hold with any absolutist view, saying:

> . . . [T]he First Amendment right . . . is not an absolute, as Justice Holmes so long ago pointed out in his aphorism concerning the right to shout fire in a crowded theater. There are other exceptions, some of which Chief Justice Hughes mentioned by way of example in *Near v. Minnesota*. . . . There are no doubt other exceptions no one has had occasion to describe or discuss.

The Chief Justice's apparent willingness to engraft additional exceptions onto the *Near* prohibition against most forms of prior restraint should be compared with Brennan's obvious reluctance to do so.

Justice Blackmun Dissenting. Justice Blackmun, too, argued against the absolutist view and expressed the fear that the nation already might have been harmed by publication. If so, he wanted the public to know that the responsibility rested with the newspapers.

Justice Harlan (Joined by Burger and Blackmun) Dissenting. Unlike the opinions of Douglas and Marshall, Harlan argued that the judiciary has a narrow role to play once the executive branch has made certain determinations about national security and foreign affairs — two areas in which the President is given broad powers. Harlan also criticized the "frenzied train of events" and raised a number of issues:

- Whether the First Amendment permits the federal courts to enjoin such publication if the stories present a serious threat to national security.
- Whether the mere "threat" to publish is sufficient to justify an injunction.
- Whether the newspapers are entitled to retain and use stolen documents.
- Whether disclosure would, in fact, seriously impair national security.

Such questions would have to be considered in light of the "strong First Amendment policy against prior restraints" and in view of the fact that some dissemination already had occurred. As Harlan said, "These are difficult questions of fact, of law and of judgment; the potential consequences of erroneous decision are enormous."

Discussion

The importance of the Pentagon Papers decision is debatable. Viewed in one way, the outcome was a victory for the press in that prior restraint was dissolved and an old principle vindicated; and yet the press had little to celebrate. First, the press underwent court-imposed restraints for 15 days while the issues were being scrutinized. Second, the per curiam decision by the majority allows the government to try again whenever it thinks it can meet the "heavy burden" to show *justification* for such restraint. Certainly the door is left open for the Attorney General—perhaps at the behest of a chief executive who might be angered by "unfriendly" newspapers—to try again.

Let's assume that another attempt will be made by the federal government to prevent publication of information classified as secret or top secret. What yardstick will be used by the judiciary to determine if there is justification for restraint? Does "irreparable damage" or "substantial damage" to the national or public interest meet the test? Which one, since they arguably are not the same? And are national interest and public interest the same? This latter question is not offered facetiously since the public's right to know is basic to our system of government. The 47 volumes of *history* dealt with the decision-making process by which the United States entered the Vietnam War and became increasingly involved. Surely the public had a right to be informed of these historical developments. Or did it?

The per curiam decision shows that six justices could agree only on an ambivalent statement: a "preferred position" doctrine on the one hand (any prior restraint bears a heavy presumption against its constitutionality), and a "balancing" theory (weighing the justification shown by the government) on the other. If the individual opinions of the majority are examined, there is additional concern about the outcome of future confrontations between press and government. Justices White and Stewart based their positions on government not having met its burden to justify restraint. What about the next time?

In summarizing the result of the Pentagon Papers case, the Twentieth Century Fund's Task Force on Government and the Press said that "while basic issues were posed, basic issues were not resolved." The Task Force, consisting of 12 members drawn mostly from the ranks of journalism (three members were from the legal profession), made this observation:

> The outcome [basic issues were not resolved] should not be considered a criticism of the Supreme Court. There is a good reason to believe that the ends of justice are frequently best served when decisions are made on the narrowest possible grounds, and that sweeping questions of policy are best determined in other areas. But whatever merit there may be in this view, the fact remains that there is as yet no authoritative concept of whether publication boundaries exist."[11]

Related Issues

Other issues generated by the Pentagon Papers case are briefly discussed, but most are beyond the scope of this book.

How "Secret" Are the Secrets?. The question of why 47 volumes of a government study should be classified is a bothersome one. Was the study classified, as some suggest, to prevent embarrassment to high government officials? And if the 47 volumes were so secret, how could someone copy 7000 pages and not be detected, either while in the act of copying them or while transporting the copies or the original to another location?

In commenting on some ludicrous situations that have developed, the Washington bureau chief of *The New York Times* had this to say:

> For practically everything that our government does, plans, thinks, hears, and contemplates in the realms of foreign policy is stamped and treated as secret — and then unraveled by that same government, by the Congress, and by the press in one continuing round of professional and social contacts and cooperative and competitive exchanges of information.
>
> . . . Presidents make "secret" decisions only *t* reveal them for the purpose of frightening an adversary nation, wooing a friendly electorate, protecting their reputations. The military services conduct "secret" research in weaponry only to reveal it for the purpose of enhancing their budgets, appearing superior or inferior to a foreign army, gaining the vote of a congressman or the favor of a contractor."[12]

The issue of the public's right to know versus the bureaucracy's penchant for secrecy drew this comment from Norman Dorsen, general counsel for the American Civil Liberties Union, when he appeared before a congressional committee:

> Given our experience in many thousand cases on these problems, we suggest that any review of the Government's classification system must be based on the constitutional premise that the paramount guarantee of the First Amendment is the public's right to know what the Government is doing, and so long as the information relates to the conduct of government, no matter how embarrassing, deceitful, or dishonest that conduct may be, the people have a right to know about it, and the Congress, no less than the press, has a duty to insure that the public is so informed. . . . [W]e feel that there is a constitutional presumption, not merely a policy presumption, against any system of classification which results in the withholding, from the American public, of information concerning its Government.[13]

Why "Serialize" Publication? A one-time publication of the information would have made unlikely the confrontation which developed. When asked why this was not done, the *New York Times* managing editor said he "did not think it was proper to print it all at once" because the material was hard to digest and there would have been no opportunity "for anybody to comment on it" if published all at one time. In addition, he said he did not believe "in editing or publishing out of fear of what the Government might do."[14]

Endless pages of type are not attractive typographically, but the information would be as easily comprehended in that form as spread through ten different issues. And certainly no one would be compelled to read the entire digest at one sitting, had it been published all at once. Concerning the desire to permit comment, such reasoning is difficult to follow since considerable reaction would be likely one way or the other. Not editing or publishing out of fear of what government might do seems the more solid reason for serializing.

Complexity of the Issues. Support for the dissenting judges' opinions can be found in a case that was decided nearly six months after the Pentagon Papers decision — a case that also demonstrates the complexity of the issues facing the judiciary.

Four of the 47 volumes of the secret study were not available to the *Times* or other newspapers. Believing that the public should know the contents of these remaining volumes, forced-disclosure lawsuits were brought by two members of Congress, Representative John E. Moss of California and Representative Ogden Reid of New York, both leaders in the fight for freedom-of-information legislation, and by Paul Fisher of the Freedom of Information Center. Judge Gesell, who earlier had refused to issue a temporary injunction against the *Post,* ruled that the four volumes were exempt from forced disclosure under the Freedom of Information Act of 1967 (see Chapter 9). In commenting on the difficulty that would confront the judiciary in making decisions on the issues raised by the lawsuits, the judge said:

> The determination of the interests of national defense or foreign policy cannot be made by applying some simple litmus test to a document presented, particularly in a case where good faith is not in issue. The court, with no experience or background in such matters, would require detailed . . . background briefing even to make a tentative judgment. . . .[15]

This case highlights a major problem facing the judiciary when called upon to resolve complex issues involving national defense, foreign affairs, economics, or other complicated matters.

U.S. v. THE PROGRESSIVE

Certainly one of the more complex matters facing society is atomic and hydrogen power and their potential for destroying or saving civilization. Whether certain information about the H-bomb could be made public when weighed against First Amendment issues was the problem that confronted Judge Robert W. Warren of the U.S. District Court for the Western District of Wisconsin. He issued a temporary restraining order in March 1979 against *The Progressive* magazine at Madison, Wisconsin, and free-lance writer Howard Morland, blocking publication of an article, "The H-Bomb Secret: How We Got It, Why We're Telling It." After hearing arguments for and against publication, Judge Warren on March 26 decided to replace the temporary order with a preliminary injunction against publication. He did so after reaching two conclusions: some of the information would likely violate the Atomic Energy Act passed in 1946;[16] and the government had made a showing of the likelihood of "direct, immediate, and irreparable injury" to the nation if the article were published.[17] Such a standard had been suggested by Justice Stewart in the Pentagon Papers case nine years earlier in which he and Justice White became the "swing" votes in the 6–3 per curiam decision.

Author Morland and the magazine's editor, Erwin Knoll, contended that the article was based on publicly available information. In fact, Justice Department attorneys conceded that two documents available to the public at the Los Alamos Scientific Laboratory library contained details on secret devices used to trigger H-bombs. The documents were removed from the library and again classified as secret while the legal battle continued—a battle that ultimately cost the small, rarely profitable magazine nearly $250,000, according to Knoll.[18]

Upon reconsideration, Judge Warren decided on June 15, 1979, not to lift the publication ban. Despite contentions that the H-bomb secret was already known to other scientists and foreign countries, the judge concluded that only the Morland article contained "a comprehensive, accurate and detailed analysis" of three important concepts utilized in construction of the bomb.[19] For this reason, and because of the likely violation of the Atomic Energy Act and the likelihood that publication would cause direct, immediate and irreparable injury to the nation, the judge denied the defendants' motion to vacate the injunction.

Given Judge Warren's refusal to lift the ban, the defendants appealed to the Seventh Circuit U.S. Court of Appeals and subsequently sought a writ of mandamus to force the appellate court to expedite its review. But the U.S. Supreme Court, in a 7–2 per curiam decision on July 2, 1979, denied the motion with Justice White, joined by Brennan, dissenting.[20] The Court turned down petitioners largely on the basis that they had taken nearly three months to prepare their own brief on the merits of the case—a delay that in effect foreclosed on any constitutional right they might have had for an expedited review.

In his dissent, Justice White cites a number of precedent cases, including *New York Times Co. v. U.S.,* in stating:

> It is my view that the Court of Appeals, by declining to hear arguments until the conclusion of its summer recess, has unduly delayed plenary consideration of this case. And I do not agree with my Brothers that the petitioners have forfeited what rights to an early hearing they might otherwise have had. Our cases indicate that the proffered justification for an injunction against publication should be considered and verified or rejected by appellate courts without unnecessary delay.[21]

Next came a series of events in September 1979 which led the Justice Department to abandon further efforts to suppress publication of the article—thus the Supreme Court did not consider the merits of the case. A computer programmer, Charles Hansen, who occasionally wrote about military technology and who was angered by the prior restraint imposed upon *The Progressive,* wrote a long letter about H-bomb technology to a U.S. senator. Excerpts from that letter were published in the *Peninsula Times Tribune* at Palo Alto, California, but the attempted publication of the letter by the University of California student newspaper, *Daily Californian,* at Berkeley, was thwarted by a court-issued injunction. Then, on September 16, 1979, the *Press Connection* at Madison, Wisconsin, published the entire letter, and the *Chicago Tribune* notified the government that it was planning to publish the letter, which it subsequently did. The secret was no longer a secret, according to a Justice Department spokesman, and so further attempts to halt publication about the H-bomb were ended.

Case Differentiated from Pentagon Papers

In deciding as he did, Judge Warren distinguished *The Progressive* case from the 1971 prior restraint of *The New York Times* and *Washington Post.* Defendants had relied in part on this earlier decision in trying to convince the judge to dissolve the temporary restraining order. Instead, the judge made these distinctions between the two cases: (1) The Pentagon Papers involved historical data concerning events three to 20 years prior to attempted publication; (2) no cogent reasons had been advanced by the government in the earlier case as to why the publication affected national security except that publication might cause some embarrassment to the United States; and (3) a specific statute was involved in *The Progressive* case—the Atomic Energy Act, Section 2274 which prohibits anyone from communicating, transmitting or disclosing any restricted data to any person "with reason to believe such data will be utilized to injure the United States or to secure an advantage to any foreign nation."[22] Section 2104 of the Act defines restricted data to mean all data concerning (1) design, manufacture, or utilization of atomic weapons; (2) the production of special nuclear material; or (3) the use of special nuclear material in the production of energy.

The Act, passed at the beginning of the Cold War era, is broadly worded in that information falling within the scope of Section 2104 is automatically classified and must first be declassified before it can be made public. Violators face a 10-year prison term, $10,000 fine, or both.

On one occasion, *Scientific American* was threatened with injunctive action by the Atomic Energy Commission (AEC) if it did not delete what the AEC said was restricted data. The magazine did so. Until *The Progressive case,* most writers and/or publishers followed what came to be standard operating procedure; that is, they would submit stories to the AEC (now the Energy Department) for clearance, otherwise they would have no way of knowing if what they published included any "restricted data." Such a system constitutes censorship.

The Progressive, a "liberal" magazine often critical of government and its policies, had asked Morland to do the article. When it was completed, the magazine sent it to several scientists for comment. One of them sent a portion of the manuscript to the Energy Department, advising the magazine that he had done so. Ultimately the Energy Department told the magazine that a portion of the manuscript contained restricted data, but that the offending information could not be identified because to do so would violate security. However, the Department was willing to rewrite the article as it customarily did with material submitted to it for review. The editor refused, indicating his intention to publish the article, and the government thereupon sought the injunction. At one point prior to issuance of the injunction, Judge Warren hoped that a compromise could be reached as urged by the Federation of American Scientists in an amicus curiae brief. As Warren said:

> This group, with half of America's Nobel laureates in its ranks, urged *The Progressive* to recognize the damage the article could do to both nuclear non-proliferation policies and First Amendment rights. It sees the dangers of the present confrontation and suggests that similar cases can arise in the future involving this or other technologies.
>
> . . . The group suggests that the accommodation of such conflicting interests is not best done in the glare of a judicial spotlight, but that the parties, seemingly at odds can, with effort, satisfy both their interests with a non-legal resolution.
>
> The government seeks only the deletion of certain technical material and, in the Court's opinion, would have an interest in settling this case out of court. On the other hand, the Court believes that *The Progressive* has an obligation to its colleagues in the press and does not really require the objected-to material in order to ventilate its views on government secrecy and the hydrogen bomb.
>
> In this context, the Federation urges that the Court give the parties every last chance to try to resolve the matter out-of-court, so as to simultaneously moot the case and set a desirable precedent for the future.[23]

The Progressive objected to such a procedure, particularly to a government department rewriting the article and so the injunction was issued.

Media Opinion Split

The Progressive case did not engender a desire among editors and publishers to rally around the magazine in its First Amendment fight as had the Pentagon Papers case. Some newspapers and magazines did so, as attested by the more than 20 amici briefs filed on behalf of the defendants, including one by Professor Thomas I. Emerson for *Scientific American* in which he said, in part:

> The rule against prior restraint is inherently incapable of accommodating exceptions. Once an exception has been recognized, all the government has to do is to allege that a certain contemplated publication falls within the exception. The court then issues a restraining order so as to allow the government to present its case. A hearing is held and the court decides whether the matter falls within the exception. Appeals to higher courts follow. This process is itself a system of prior restraint. . . . The scope of the exception is thus determined by the government's claim and the exception has swallowed up the rule.[24]

The *Washington Post* thought the case was a "real First Amendment loser,"[25] and its editor, Ben Bradlee, said at a conference to discuss the case that he supported the magazine "with about as much enthusiasm as I would Larry Flynt and *Hustler*."[26]

The *Los Angeles Times* thought it was the wrong issue, at the wrong time, in the wrong place.[27]

Newsweek's managing editor, Kenneth Auchincloss, said he could not see what public interest was served by disclosing how to build a hydrogen bomb.

The *New York Times, Chicago Tribune, St. Louis Post-Dispatch, Minneapolis Tribune,* and quite a few other newspapers supported the magazine. Most of them took the position that the information already was available to the public, the government was secrecy-minded when it need not be, and that the First Amendment stood as a bar to prior restraint.

In defense of his position, editor Knoll said, in part:

> The information suppressed need not be—and in *The Progressive*'s case is not—government information. Howard Morland never saw a classified document. The government contends that under the Atomic Energy Act, *all* nuclear information, unless it has been specifically declassified, is "data restricted at birth"—that is, classified as soon as it comes into being, even if we originate it.
>
> What we have, in other words, is an Official Secrets Act—and an incredibly broad and sweeping one—that has gone unchallenged since 1946.
>
> . . . Where has the press been all these years?[29]

Issues Left Unresolved

As in the Pentagon Papers case, issues remained unresolved, among them:

1. Are the prior restraint provisions of the Atomic Energy Act overly broad and therefore unconstitutional?
2. Is Justice Stewart's test (a showing by the government that publication would likely produce a "direct, immediate, and irreparable injury" to the nation) the appropriate one to use?
3. Were affidavits from Secretary of State Cyrus Vance, Defense Secretary Harold Brown, and Energy Secretary James R. Schlesinger, plus those from scientists, which took the position that publication would violate the Atomic Energy Act, sufficient to constitute the basis for a judgment that direct, immediate, and irreparable injury would be done to the nation if publication occurred? What about the affidavits from other scientists who said the information in the article already was publicly available? How much weight should have been accorded to them?
4. With Justices Black and Douglas gone from the Court, how would the Supreme Court have voted? Was this, as some lawyers, scientists and editors contended, a "bad" case from a First Amendment standpoint?
5. Can the press, with impunity, ignore judgments of federal government officials that information is classified and proceed to publish that information? Can they be held accountable after publication?
6. Even though a case is made moot by publication of information said to be restricted, should the Supreme Court allow it to terminate in that manner or should it have brought the case up for expedited review (as it did in the Pentagon Papers case)?

There are, of course, ethical considerations that remain unresolved.

Proposed "Official Secrets Act"

Editor Knoll referred to the Atomic Energy Act as an "Official Secrets Act." In 1973 Senate Bill 1 (S. 1), consisting of some 750 pages, was introduced by Senator John McClellan to revise the U.S. Criminal Code. Although the Criminal Code concededly is in need of revision, some of the proposals originally contained in S. 1 would have had a drastic impact on the press, so much so that S. 1 was referred to as the counterpart of the British Official Secrets Act. The British law makes it a crime for any person in government to communicate any official information obtained as a result of his government position to any unauthorized person. It also is an offense for a person to receive such information, or to attempt to get another person to commit an offense under the act. This section is absolute in that it pertains to all information learned by a government employee during the course of employment, regardless of its importance, nature, or original source.[30]

Faced with opposition from civil liberty and journalism organizations, Senator McClellan withdrew some of the controversial sections of the proposed code in 1977.

Congress did not approve the revised code, but a Senate-passed version would have included some provisions designed to protect the press, such as (1) protection from any orders "constitutionally invalid under the First Amendment," and (2) a prohibition against prosecution of a reporter or newspaper for "theft" or "receiving stolen property" if the theft involved government information.

"Stolen Property" Theory of Restraint

In 1969 the *Los Angeles Free Press* was enjoined from continuing with the publication of information about state narcotics agents. The court-issued injunction was condemned by the California Freedom of Information Committee as "almost unheard of" judicial censorship.[31]

The *Free Press* had obtained the names, addresses, and telephone numbers of 80 undercover narcotics agents attached to the California state attorney general's office, and proceeded to publish this information under the following headlines, "There Should Be No Secret Police" and "Know Your Local Nark." The highly confidential roster allegedly had been stolen from the mail room of the attorney general's office in Los Angeles. The case, and the vulnerability of the press to prosecution on the theory that leaked government information is *property,* was reviewed by Professor Everette E. Dennis in a law review article, summarized as follows.[32]

■ *Free Press* editor Arthur G. Kunkin and reporter Gerald R. Applebaum each were indicted on two counts of receiving stolen property under California Penal Code Section 496, part of which states: "Every person who buys or receives any property which had been stolen or which has been obtained in any manner constituting theft or extortion, knowing the property to be so stolen or obtained, or who conceals, withholds or aids in concealing or withholding any such property from the owner, knowing the property to be so stolen or obtained" is liable to criminal prosecution.

■ A clerk in the mail room who gave the list to the *Free Press* was tried separately and convicted on two counts of theft of government records.

■ Kunkin and the reporter were convicted by a jury in Superior Court of Los Angeles County of receiving stolen property. They were fined $1000 and $500 respectively and placed on probation.

■ As the criminal case progressed through the courts, the narcotics agents filed a $15 million civil suit against the newspaper. The *Free Press* settled this suit out of court for $43,000 in 1971. As part of the settlement, Kunkin agreed to print an apology which was run on the paper's front page under the banner headline, "NARCS 43,000 – FREEP 0."

■ On appeal in the criminal case, the California Court of Appeals, Second District, held that Kunkin and Applebaum had *knowingly* received property of value and were liable under Section 496. The court concluded that the stolen roster "fully qualified as property within the meaning" of Section 496.[33] The court stated that photocopies of the roster also would have fallen under the classification of "property," although this was not at issue in this case. Further, it would have made no difference in terms of Section 496 whether or not the roster was physically removed from the office if the information were transmitted by some other means, such as photocopies or memorizing.

On the freedom of press issue, the appellate court reasoned that to find for the defendants on the basis of freedom of press would be the same as legalizing a "thieves' market" for stolen documents.

In a dissenting opinion, Presiding Justice Lester W. Roth raised a number of issues and questions, including the theoretical possibility that every purchaser of the August 8, 1969, issue of the *Free Press* could be prosecuted for receiving stolen property in violation of Section 496. The acceptance of the majority view, he warned, would set up "newsgathering crimes." And although he did not doubt the authority of government to enact criminal laws to protect government secrets, Roth said there was no such law in California because, in his view, documents are not equatable to stolen *goods,* or merchandise. Therefore, the conviction of Kunkin and Applebaum for receiving "stolen goods" was inappropriate.[34]

■ The California Supreme Court unanimously reversed the lower courts because there "was no substantial evidence to support the jury's finding that the defendants knew the roster was stolen."[35] However, in its ruling the court did not reject the lower courts' determination that information was "property" within the meaning of Section 496.

Dennis commented:

The mere possibility that a reporter or news organization might be prosecuted for publication or broadcast of leaked information imposes a severe chilling effect on newsgathering efforts. Although Kunkin and Applebaum in the end escaped punishment, the costs were high and the victory was hollow. Under the pressure from the criminal prosecution, Kunkin settled the civil suit against him for $43,000 and an agreement to publish a front page apology. . . . In addition, the legal fees incurred by Kunkin, amounting to over $100,000 by one account, were enough to seriously jeopardize the operation of the paper.[36]

In reviewing the situation at the federal level, and in particular the Pentagon Papers case, Dennis wrote:

There remains some doubt . . . as to whether the First Amendment prohibits prosecution of the press for property crimes for the publication of leaked information. Despite the lack of authority on this question, however, a majority of the Supreme Court appears to believe that at least in some situations such prosecution would be constitutionally acceptable. Of the six justices who comprised the majority in *New York Times Co. v. United States,* Justice White and Stewart found that "Congress has the power to enact specific and appropriate criminal laws to protect government property and preserve government secrets," and said they would have no problem sustaining criminal convictions under such laws. Justice Marshall also noted that Congress has the power to enact criminal prohibitions against the receipt or purchase of certain documents. Two of the three dissenting justices, Chief Justice Burger and Justice Blackmun . . . agreed with Justice White that penal sanctions would be appropriate. Thus, a majority of the Supreme Court is willing to apply criminal sanctions against the receipt of stolen property to newsmen who knowingly receive stolen documents.[37]

The *Free Press* case shows a different threat to freedom of press, other than prior restraint, if information can be classified as "property." Two recent cases have resolved that question: *Winans et al. v. U.S.* (1987)[38] and *U.S. v. Morison* (1988).[39]

In the *Winans* case, the U.S. Supreme Court unanimously upheld the conviction of former *Wall Street Journal* reporter R. Foster Winans on charges of violating federal wire and mail fraud statutes. Winans was one of two full-time writers of the *Journal*'s "Heard on the Street" column when he began passing information about the contents and timing of yet-to-be-published columns to two stockbrokers. The leaked information was used to trade securities mentioned in the column at a profit shared with Winans. Winans also made six trades for his roommate, David Carpenter, based on information that was to be published in future columns.

The "inside trading" schemes netted the participants $690,000 in profits.

The *Journal* had a conflict-of-interest policy which stated that information obtained by employees in their work is the property of the newspaper's owner, Dow Jones & Co. The policy prohibits employees from trading in the stocks of companies that were the subject of *Journal* articles until two days after the articles appeared.

As Justice White said for the Court, "Both courts below [the trial court and the Second Circuit U.S. Court of Appeals] expressly referred to the *Journal*'s interest in the confidentiality of the contents and timing of the 'Heard' column as a property right . . . and we agree with that conclusion."[40] The intangible nature of information does not make it any less "property," said White. He then quoted from *Cyclopedia of Law of Private Corporations:*

> Confidential information acquired by a corporation in the course and conduct of its business is a species of property to which the corporation has the exclusive right and benefit, and which a court of equity will protect through the injunctive process or other appropriate remedy.[41]

The mail and wire fraud charges were based on the use of telephone lines to transmit *Journal* articles to the newspaper's printing plants and the newspaper being mailed to subscribers.

The Court's decision gives prosecutors and others considerable leeway to go after reporters and others accused of misusing confidential information. There's considerable concern that corporations will use the *Winans* decision to punish unauthorized leaks of information that have nothing to do with insider trading schemes. And the decision could impact heavily on laws governing trade secrets. Furthermore, the mere threat of criminal action against government or private business employees who otherwise would leak information is a considerable deterrent.

Five months after the Court's decision, the Fourth Circuit U.S. Court of Appeals upheld the conviction of a former Navy intelligence analyst, Samuel L. Morison, on charges of espionage and theft of government property that resulted when he provided classified U.S. satellite photos to a magazine, *Jane's Defence Weekly*. The photos showed a Soviet aircraft carrier under construction.

Morison, a civilian employee, was an editor of *Jane's Fighting Ships* and wrote articles for *Jane's Defence Weekly*, both published in Britain. He was sentenced to two years in prison by a U.S. District Court judge.

The Circuit Court ruled that the Espionage Act of 1917 applied to Morison, saying that the law was not limited to "classic spying" in which secret documents are handed to a foreign spy.

This case marked the first U.S. criminal conviction for leaking secret government information to the press. Some U.S. newspapers republished the photographs used in the British publication.

On October 17, 1988, the U.S. Supreme Court denied review.

As one journalism publication editorialized:

> By implication, the Fourth Circuit extended the *Winans* holding so that the government, as well as the private sector, may protect its pure "information" as though it were property. This holding [in *U.S. v. Morison*] might open the door to prosecution of journalists who receive government information orally for theft of government property.[42]

INJUNCTIVE POWER

The *Near,* Pentagon Papers, *The Progressive,* and *Free Press* cases had one thing in common. Each involved the use of the injunctive power of the courts — a power which, in effect, turns the courts into instruments of prior restraint.

The power to issue injunctions or restraining orders dates back to medieval England and the emergence of the concept of "equity." If the law could not protect or compensate a person who had suffered some kind of damage or injury to property, that person could go into a court of equity and seek relief in the form of a judge's order forbidding or commanding that something either be stopped or done.

In the United States, the Judiciary Act of 1789 gave federal judges this power, and most of the states followed suit either by statute or by court decisions. Injunctions have been used to prevent a multiplicity of suits; whenever there would be difficulty in ascertaining compensatory damages, such as in invasion of privacy situations; and when a damage remedy would be meaningless, such as insolvency on the part of a defendant. As a law review article pointed out:

> In some areas, . . . assertions of free speech have prevented neither substitutional nor injunctive relief. The right to privacy, for example, has been protected by injunctions alone. Similarly, no reluctance to enjoin is apparent in the few cases granting relief against false advertising. And trade secrets are generally protected by injunction, although it has been asserted that "the public interest in free access to useful information suggests that, if at all possible, damages should be favored over equitable relief. . . ."
>
> In yet . . . [another] group of cases, however, courts have granted damage relief against commercial disparagement, business defamation, and person defamation, but have refused on free speech grounds, to enjoin the same kinds of conduct, invoking the venerable rule that equity will not enjoin a libel or slander. This maxim enjoys continuing vitality in most American jurisdictions, although long rejected in England. American courts have generally held that injunctive relief against defamation would infringe unduly upon the defendant's and the community's interests in free speech. . . .[43]

Another law review article pointed out:

> . . . [A]s far as injunctions against speech and writing are concerned, the prior restraint doctrine has not even been consistently applied. For there are certain lines of cases, existing side by side with those refusing injunctive relief in the defamation-privacy area, where injunctions against speech and writing have come to be freely granted. These cases, no less than those involving defamation and privacy, constitute prior restraints on expression. Thus, they demonstrate that the sweeping statements . . . that equity will never enjoin expression must be taken with a very large grain of salt indeed.[44]

Injunctive power was evident in the willingness of Illinois courts to enjoin *temporarily* the distribution of leaflets in a community of 18,000 for three years, and in a Rhode Island court's enjoinder against the sale, distribution, or display of certain books and magazines that might fall into the hands of youths. In both instances, these courts were reversed, but not until they had succeeded in imposing unconstitutional prior restraints.

Book and magazine publishers, underground newspapers, film producers and distributors and, to a lesser extent, the "establishment" news media, have been the targets of injunction-seekers. So-called underground newspapers were special targets. In 1966, for example, three such newspapers were hit with enjoinders, including a permanent injunction against *Kiss,* a New York publication specializing in sex.

Many cases involving the use of injunctions against the press took place during the 1960s and 1970s — turbulent years in America because of civil rights and Vietnam war concerns and issues. By comparison, the confrontations between government and the press during the 1980s have been far less numerous and considerably less spectacular.

In addition to the cases already mentioned, here are some other examples of the injunctive power being used as a tool of prior restraint:

Alfred Knopf, Inc. v. William Colby, CIA. In 1972, the federal government obtained a temporary injunction against Victor Marchetti, an agent for the Central Intelligence Agency from 1955–69, prohibiting him from disclosing any information relating to CIA intelligence activities. The order was issued by U.S. District Court Judge Albert V. Bryan, Jr. of the Eastern District of Virginia. The government's position was that Marchetti had agreed in writing not to reveal any information learned during his CIA employment, that he was planning to write a book, and that publication of the book would result in "grave and irreparable injury" to United States' interests. Ultimately the judge converted the temporary injunction into a permanent one. On appeal, the U.S. Court of Appeals affirmed, except that it ruled that only *classified information* could be deleted from the book by the CIA. The U.S. Supreme Court declined to review the case.

Marchetti and John D. Marks, who had worked for the U.S. State Department in matters affecting intelligence gathering, subsequently wrote *The CIA and the Cult of Intelligence.* When the manuscript was completed, it was submitted to the CIA which said that 339 portions of the book had to be deleted (between 15 and 20 percent of the entire manuscript). Joined by the publishing company, Alfred Knopf, Inc., the authors commenced a suit. By the time trial took place in early 1974 before Judge Bryan, the CIA had reduced the number of requested deletions from 339 to 168 — and the book went to press with that many excisions. Each deletion was shown in the published book.

On March 29, 1974, Judge Bryan ruled that only 26 of the 168 disputed deletions pertained to classified information. Thus, the publisher would be free to publish all but those 26 items. However, the judge stayed an order pending an appeal.

All parties appealed. The U.S. Court of Appeals subsequently ruled that there was a presumption of regularity on the part of public officials in classifying government information and in the absence of a showing of proof to the contrary, the government could require deletion of the items solely on the basis that those items were required to be classified.[45] Furthermore, Marchetti effectively relinquished his First Amendment rights concerning disclosure of classified information when he entered into a "secrecy agreement" with CIA. The First Amendment, said the three-judge panel, is no bar to an injunction forbidding such disclosure when the classified information was obtained during the course of working for the CIA. Therefore, in remanding the case to the U.S. District Court, the three-judge panel said that only those items which came to the authors after they had terminated their employment with government agencies could be disclosed.

Ultimately, the CIA permitted another 25 of the missing passages to be printed in whole or in part. Their restoration raised questions as to why they were deleted in the first place. For example, the censors deleted this sentence: "The purpose of this session [of the National Security Council in December, 1969] was to decide what American policy should be toward the governments of southern Africa."

Two words were removed from this sentence: "Henry Kissinger talked about the kind of general posture the United States should maintain toward the _____ _____ and outlined the specific policy options open to the President." The missing words were "white regimes."

There were other equally innocuous words or sentences that succumbed originally to the CIA censor and, when restored, showed that they related to policy matters that, at the time of the book's publication, were already history. Certainly the restored information did not disclose the identity of any CIA agents — a major argument used by the CIA in seeking to prevent publication of information about its activities.

CIA and Frank Snepp. In a case similar to *Knopf, Inc. v. Colby,* a U.S. District Court judge issued an order in 1978 in *U.S. v. Snepp* impounding any profits from the sale of a book, *Decent Interval,* written by former CIA agent Frank W. Snepp III. The order by Judge Oren E. Lewis of Alexandria, Virginia, also enjoined the author from any further violations of a secrecy agreement he had signed with the CIA. The agreement required him to submit to the agency for prepublication review anything that he wrote about the CIA. His breach of the agreement, said the judge, "involves a substantial wrong to the U.S."[46] Anyone who breaches such a trust, continued the judge, "ought not to be permitted to retain his ill-gotten gains."

Snepp's book, published in 1977, criticized the CIA's involvement in Vietnam, particularly during the closing days of the war. The government did not contend that any security secrets were disclosed by the book, but only that Snepp had a "fiduciary duty" to keep silent because of his contract with the CIA. This case probably was the first one in which the government sought restraints on publication when disclosure of classified information was not directly an issue.

On appeal, the Fourth Circuit U.S. Court of Appeals, in a 2–1 panel split, ruled that Snepp had violated the secrecy agreement and that the First Amendment is not violated by the contractual agreement of prior CIA consent to publication.[47] The panel unanimously agreed that an injunction against further breaches of the contract was fully justified; however, it split over Judge Lewis's requirement that the impounded profits be placed in a constructive trust with any profits to go to the government. Two of the appellate judges said that the District Court improperly imposed the trust. But the U.S. Supreme Court in 1980 issued summary judgment upholding the District Court judge's constructive trust requirement. In its 6–3 per curiam decision, the Court also rejected Snepp's claim that the secrecy agreement violated the First Amendment. Such agreements, said the majority, are a "reasonable means" for protecting national security information and the confidentiality "so essential to the effective operation of our foreign intelligence service."[48] The decision upheld the government's power to control the release of certain kinds of information by present and former government employees.

Justice Stevens, joined by Brennan and Marshall, dissented, contending that the Court's decision to dispose of the case summarily was unprecedented. The Court, said Stevens, "seems unaware of the fact that its drastic new remedy has been fashioned to enforce a species of prior restraint on a citizen's right to criticize his government."

Later, in a speech to the American Judicature Society, Stevens resumed his criticism of the Court, saying that its "exercise of lawmaking power" in the *Snepp* case was "totally unnecessary."[49] The Court has shown a "lack of judicial restraint," he said, "in both deciding when to review novel questions and in deciding what questions need review." He noted that *Snepp* was decided by the Court without hearing arguments and by means of a per curiam opinion. The Court "is deciding more cases on the merits without the benefit of full briefing and argument, using the currently fashionable technique of explaining its reasons in a 'per curiam' opinion—a document generally written for the Court by an anonymous member of its ever increasing administrative staff."[50]

In discussing the impact of the *Snepp* decision, the then chairman of the Freedom of Information Committee of the Society of Professional Journalists, Sigma Delta Chi, Bob Lewis, wrote:

> The decision has been interpreted as giving all federal agencies the right to require prepublication clearance of articles from *all* present and former employees—even in the absence of a signed contract. Presidents and Cabinet members could be required to submit their memoirs for government approval. The government may act not only to protect classified data, but also information that has "the appearance of confidentiality."
>
> The decision is a license to censor, to impose secrecy restrictions without a showing of need.
>
> . . . Free press advocates are caught in a Catch 22 on whether Congress should attempt to limit the reach of *Snepp*. If Congress legislates in this area, it would restrict the options of censorship available to federal agencies. At the same time, it would legitimize secrecy agreements, which are, in effect, a prior restraint on publication that should be imposed, if at all, only when there is an immediate and irreparable danger to the national security.

. . . Another problem facing Congress if it attempts to legislate in the secrecy pact area is where to place the authority to appeal. Now it rests with the censoring agency.

Other questions raised by congressional committee hearings:

Should censorship be applied with the same force to former employees as to present employees? Should a statute of limitations be imposed rather than a lifetime ban on writing on intelligence? Should censorship be limited to nonfiction works? Should a distinction be made between writings that compromise intelligence secrets and writings that merely embarrass intelligence agencies?

The Supreme Court's *Snepp* decision has raised more questions than it answered.[51]

President Reagan Issues Directive. Concern over leakage of classified information led President Reagan to issue Executive Order 12356 and a directive, "Safeguarding National Security Information" in March 1983, which required any federal employee with access to top-secret information to submit for review any manuscripts containing intelligence information.[52] Such employees had to sign a lifetime prepublication review contract. This, plus plans to administer lie detector tests to any of the 2.5 million federal employees on short notice should it be deemed necessary, aroused widespread criticism from both in and out of Congress that the White House backed away from such actions.[53]

A year earlier, Congress had passed legislation making it a crime to disclose the identity of U.S. spies even if the information came from public records and even if the disclosure was done accidentally. Journalists are not excluded. Federal employees can be sentenced to 10 years in prison and fined $50,000 for violating the law; nongovernment violators face imprisonment of up to four years and a $15,000 fine.[54] This legislation came about in response to the Philip Agee case.

Agee v. CIA. Philip Agee, another former CIA agent, helped to write two books about CIA activities in which he named people who he said were U.S. spies in Western Europe and Africa. The Justice Department initiated a civil action against him, based on his contract with the CIA, and the U.S. District Court for the District of Columbia ruled in late 1980 in *Agee v. CIA* that a constructive trust over proceeds earned by Agee from the books was not warranted because of unresolved factual questions concerning CIA's motivation in seeking the trust.[55] However, Judge Gesell did issue a permanent injunction against Agee, requiring his full compliance with the secrecy agreement between him and the agency in future activities.

Agee also had his passport revoked by the U.S. State Department – an action upheld by a 7–2 decision of the U.S. Supreme Court in *Haig v. Agee* (1981).[56] The department's regulations authorize revocation for activities abroad that "are causing or are likely to cause serious damage to the national security or foreign policy of the United States." Chief Justice Burger said for the Court that Agee's conduct in foreign countries presented a "serious danger to American officials abroad and serious danger to the national security." Using a speech versus action-speech test, the majority agreed that any restrictions on Agee were not on his speech because, they said, he is free to criticize the government.

Brennan and Marshall dissented.

Floyd Abrams, a lawyer noted for defending media in First Amendment cases, said the *Agee* decision is "very dangerous" because it "could significantly interfere with the right of journalists and the public to travel in circumstances where the government opposes such travel."[57]

The *Snepp* and *Agee* cases highlight a fundamental problem in our society. Broadly stated, a free society must have information, but even a democratic society requires some secrecy, particularly in the area of national security and intelligence gathering. Viewed from the perspective of the CIA director, the concern over divulgence of secret information is great indeed. In a speech to the National Press Club on October 25, 1978, Admiral Stansfield Turner began by saying:

> In the nineteen months that I have been Director of Central Intelligence, I have come into the habit of screening the press clips first thing every morning. I almost hold my breath until I know if today's disclosures include some of our sensitive sources of intelligence. Sometimes it comes out through a leak, sometimes from the forced testimony of one of our officers in court and sometimes from the subpoena of a document or notes. As a result, I have almost come to think of you in the media and we in intelligence as being adversaries.[58]

Admiral Turner then suggested that the intelligence community and the press had somewhat the same problem; namely, protecting sources of information (see Chapter 11 on journalists' claim to a First Amendment privilege to shield confidential sources of information and, in some instances, the information itself).

He concluded his talk by urging mutual respect and a closer working relationship. "A greater degree of communication and perhaps even trust," he said, "will benefit us both and will permit us jointly to serve [the] American people more effectively."[59]

Ironically, Admiral Turner was the person responsible for the civil case against Snepp. He established a Publications Review Board within the CIA to ensure that no secrets were divulged in the writing or speeches of present or former CIA agents. But after he left government service, he wrote a book about the super-secret agency and large portions of it were ordered deleted by the CIA's Publications Review Board. Some chapters were rewritten and negotiations proceeded over other passages.

ABC, Inc. v. Smith Cabinet Manufacturing Co., Inc. In what may have been the first instance of prior restraint against network television news, a manufacturer of baby cribs obtained an injunction against a segment of a planned ABC-TV documentary, "ABC News Close Up—On Fire!" The injunction was issued by an Indiana state court and prohibited the network from showing a 40-second segment depicting a baby crib being burned. The company had claimed that the film segment was libelous and misleading because it condensed a 10-minute test into 40 seconds.

ABC-TV in its telecast of the documentary on November 26, 1973, deleted the crib-burning segment. In its place was a message that the omitted segment was in litigation. Then, on June 14, 1974, an Indiana appeals court ruled in *ABC, Inc. v. Smith Cabinet Manufacturing Co., Inc.* that the injunction was an unconstitutional prior restraint. In so doing the court rejected the manufacturer's argument that radio and television have less First Amendment protection than other media and held that "subject to specified controls the basic concept of freedom of speech and freedom of press apply nonetheless to the broadcasting industry.[60] Furthermore, said the court, truth or falsity has no bearing on a prior restraint issue. The crib manufacturer appealed and the state supreme court stayed the appellate court's order overturning the injunction. Thus, the prior restraint remained in effect. On September 13, 1974, the injunction was lifted after the appeal was dismissed at the request of both parties. On that evening's ABC-TV news, after a prior restraint of 291 days, the burning crib scene was shown.

Nebraska Press Association v. Judge Stuart. On October 22, 1975, a Lincoln County, Nebraska, court judge entered an order prohibiting anyone at the preliminary hearing of an accused murderer from releasing any testimony given, or evidence adduced, at the hearing. The order included representatives of the press who were attending the open-court hearing. Later, another Nebraska court "gagged" the press, specifically forbidding the reporting of five subjects, including the existence or contents of a confession made by the accused. The confession had been introduced in open court at the defendant's arraignment. Not until June 30, 1976, did the U.S. Supreme Court declare the "gag" order to be an unconstitutional prior restraint (see Chapter 10). Even though the press emerged as "winner" in *Nebraska Press Assn. v. Judge Stuart,* the prohibition against prior restraint was not absolute, and the judiciary *in fact* had restrained the press until the U.S. Supreme Court set aside the gag order — a procedure which ordinarily takes considerable time.

60 Minutes Episode. The desire of the judiciary to protect an accused person's right to a fair trial has led to many confrontations between the bench and the press (see Chapters 10 and 11). A somewhat bizarre legal episode pitted a U.S. District Court judge against a *60 Minutes* segment on CBS Television.

The judge, Adrian Duplantier, was to have presided over the trial of seven New Orleans police officers accused of civil rights violations in their investigation into the slaying of a fellow officer. Four blacks were killed during the investigation, but the officer's killer was not found. About three weeks before jury selection was to begin, a *60 Minutes* segment dealing with this event was scheduled to be aired. Duplantier wanted to preview the script after the policemen's defense attorneys claimed the broadcast would violate their clients' fair-trial rights.

Initially, the network's lawyers in New Orleans said they would comply, but after they discussed the matter with network lawyers in New York, they told the judge that they would not provide the script for preview. The judge thereupon held CBS in criminal contempt and ordered it not to air that segment of the program — an order promptly overturned by the Fifth Circuit because it was deemed an unconstitutional prior restraint. The appellate court said that before a trial court can impose a prior restraint, it must determine the nature and extent of the pretrial news coverage; whether other measures would be likely to mitigate the effects of unrestrained pretrial publicity; and how effectively a restraining order would operate to prevent the threatened danger.

With the trial site changed to Dallas, Texas, Duplantier narrowed his order to ban the broadcast only in the Dallas area. This order also was overturned by the Fifth Circuit. Subsequently, Justice White and Chief Justice Burger refused to overturn the Fifth Circuit's decision, and so the *60 Minutes* segment was aired January 16, 1983. As a consequence, Judge Duplantier asked the U.S. attorney to begin criminal contempt proceedings against the network for its failure to submit the script for review. On February 2, in a secret meeting, twelve of the fourteen judges of that federal district (with two judges absent) adopted a resolution calling for the hiring of a private attorney to begin criminal contempt action if the Justice Department decided not to do so. The Justice Department decided not to act, believing there was little chance CBS would be found guilty. So the private attorney was hired.

The contempt case was prosecuted before another U.S. District Court judge, Earl Veron, who acquitted CBS Television, saying the First Amendment prohibited Duplantier from acting as a "reviewing" editor.

An attempted appeal led the U.S. Court of Appeals for the Fifth Circuit to state that it had no jurisdiction because, in part, the private attorney did not represent the United States as required for appellate jurisdiction under the Criminal Appeals Act (18 U.S. Code 3731).

In re Providence Journal Co. Another prior restraint case began on November 13, 1985, when a U.S. District Court judge issued a temporary order prohibiting publication by the *Providence* (R.I.) *Journal* of information gained from FBI files obtained through the Freedom of Information Act. The article was based on illegal FBI wiretaps made in the 1960s of conversations between a reputed organized crime figure, the late Raymond L. S. Patriarca, and his son, Raymond J. The order was issued by Judge Francis J. Boyle after attorneys for Raymond J. Patriarca said they were trying to protect Patriarca's privacy.

The *Journal* published the story on November 14 because it believed the judge's actions violated the First Amendment. The judge later said the order was probably unconstitutional and rescinded it, but Patriarca's attorneys filed a motion seeking a criminal contempt action against the newspaper because it had published the story while the judge's order still was in effect. The judge thereupon found the newspaper and executive editor Charles Hauser guilty of criminal contempt. He fined the newspaper $100,000 and gave Hauser an 18-month suspended jail sentence.

On December 31, 1986, a three-judge panel of the First Circuit U.S. Court of Appeals ruled in *In re Providence Journal Co.* that the newspaper could not be held in criminal contempt for violating a "transparently invalid" prior restraint on pure speech.[61]

The panel cited *Organization for a Better Austin v. Keefe* and *Nebraska Press Association v. Stuart* in reaching its decision, and said:

> The only interest implicated by the newspaper's publication is the son's right to privacy. That publication would be embarrassing or infringe the son's privacy rights is insufficient for issuing a prior restraint. His sole remedy is an action for damages.[62]

After a rehearing *en banc,* the First Circuit, in a per curiam decision, modified, but did not vacate, the panel's opinion so that a publisher, faced with what the publisher believes is an unconstitutional prior restraint, should first make a "good faith effort" to seek emergency appellate relief before defying a court order against publication.[63]

The court said that "it is not asking much, beyond some additional expense and time, to require a publisher, even when it thinks it is the subject of a transparently unconstitutional order of prior restraint, to make a good faith effort to seek emergency relief from the appellate court. If timely access to the appellate court is not available or if timely decision is not forthcoming, the publisher may then proceed to publish and challenge the constitutionality of the order in the contempt proceeding."[64]

The *en banc* court pointed out that the publisher must "concern itself with establishing a record of its good faith effort — that being the price we should pay for the preference of court over party determination of invalidity."

The First Circuit court's ruling was left intact when the U.S. Supreme Court voted 6–2 to reject an attempt to reinstate the contempt charges against the newspaper and its editor.[65] The Court did so on a technicality. It did not decide the substantive issue: Can the press violate a transparently invalid court order not to publish something and escape punishment?

A special prosecutor had been used in the *Journal* contempt of court case and Justice Blackmun, in his opinion for the Court, said the appeal of the First Circuit's ruling should have been filed by the solicitor general, not the special prosecutor.

Concurring were Justices Brennan, White, Marshall, O'Connor, and Scalia. Justice Stevens, joined by Chief Justice Rehnquist, filed a dissenting opinion in which he called for a review of the case and questioned whether Congress intended to give the Justice Department exclusive authority over whether a case is to be appealed to the Supreme Court. Justice Kennedy took no part.

The result in the *Journal* case is similar to one in a case decided by the Fifth Circuit U.S. Court of Appeals following $300 fines imposed by a U.S. District Court judge against two Baton Rouge, Louisiana, newsmen who ignored a judge's order not to publish testimony given during an open court hearing.[66] The Fifth Circuit court ruled that unless there is a *showing* of "transparent invalidity" or "patent frivolity" surrounding a court order, "it must be obeyed until reversed by orderly review or disrobed of authority by delay or frustration in the appellate process, regardless of the ultimate determination of constitutionality, or lack thereof." The court found that the judge's order violated the First Amendment but nevertheless upheld the fines. The U.S. Supreme Court declined to review the Fifth Circuit court's decision.[67]

Frick v. Stevens. No chapter on prior restraint and the use of the injunctive power would be complete without mention of a notable example of a judge's refusal to countenance such censorship. The daughter of a deceased Pennsylvania industrialist sought to enjoin further publication of a book about her father because of unflattering remarks concerning him. In ruling against an injunction, Judge Clinton R. Weidner of the Cumberland County Court of Common Pleas said, in part:

> . . . Miss Helen C. Frick seeks to enjoin publication and distribution of the book, *Pennsylvania: Birthplace of a Nation,* in its present form because she does not believe certain statements about her father. . . . She admits she knows nothing of his business dealings, but claims they must be untrue because of the character of his personal relations with her as his daughter.
>
> By analogy, Miss Frick might as well try to enjoin publication and distribution of the Holy Bible because, being a descendant of Eve, she does not believe Eve gave Adam the forbidden fruit in the Garden of Eden, and because her senses are offended by such a statement about an ancestor of hers.[68]

The judge concluded that there had been no wrong done by the defendant and that the plaintiff, Miss Frick, had suffered no injury. Therefore, there was no remedy at law or in equity that need be applied.

Reverse Actions
Not only have courts ordered the media or journalists *not* to do something, but in rare instances the media have been ordered to do something. In Houston, Texas, a federal judge in May 1980 ordered a state-owned public television station, KUHT, to telecast the film, *Death of a Princess,* after the station decided to cancel the program. The British-made film is a fictionalized version of the execution of a Saudi Arabian princess in 1977 for adultery. The Saudi government had protested the decision by the Public Broadcasting Service to air the program on May 12, 1980, for affiliated stations. Eight stations in Texas canceled the showing, including KUHT, which is located in the heart of Arab-American oil activity. When the film was televised in Great Britain, the Saudi government asked the British government to withdraw its ambassador. Normal diplomatic relations were not restored until several months later.

Judge Gabrielle McDonald ruled that the KUHT decision to cancel was an impermissible intrusion of government into programming decisions. Lawyers for the station appealed quickly, citing potential First Amendment violations. The order was vacated by the U.S. Court of Appeals.

Eventually the *en banc* Fifth Circuit Court of Appeals upheld two public TV stations in their refusal to televise the program. The Alabama and Texas viewers who brought the lawsuits *(Muir v. Alabama Television Commission and Barn-*

stone v. University of Houston) had argued that the public TV stations should be forbidden from canceling programs for political reasons. But the court, consisting of 28 judges (six of whom dissented), believed that the public TV stations are not public forums to which the public has a right of access.

In his opinion for the court, Judge James C. Hill wrote that the "general invitation extended to the public is not to schedule programs, but to watch or decline to watch what is offered."[69] Hill added that when state officials operate a public television station they must necessarily make discriminating choices. However, if there was a "general proscription against political programming," said the judge, this would "clearly be contrary to the licensees' statutory obligations, and would render virtually every programming decision subject to judicial challenge."

This important distinction was made: A state's "exercise of editorial discretion over its own expression" is different, wrote Hill, than if Alabama or Texas sought to prohibit the exhibition of the film by another party.

The dissenters argued that once the plaintiff demonstrates that the government has silenced a message because of its substantive content, the government's decision becomes presumptively unconstitutional.

The Supreme Court declined to review the *en banc* decision.[70]

STUDENT PRESS AND CENSORSHIP

Numerous instances of prior restraint, censorship, dismissal of editors and even entire newspaper or yearbook staffs occur each year at high schools and colleges, both public and private. The Student Press Law Center (SPLC) in Washington, D.C., provides legal assistance and information to student journalists and faculty advisers who experience censorship or other legal problems. It is the only national organization devoted exclusively to protecting the First Amendment rights of high school and college journalists. SPLC reports that each year it learns of more than 300 censorship instances in high schools and colleges around the United States.[71]

The U.S. Supreme Court considered, for the first time, students' rights of expression not connected with religion in *Tinker v. Des Moines Independent Community School District* (1969). The case involved three students who wore black armbands to school to protest United States involvement in the Vietnam war. They were suspended until they chose to return to school without the armbands. An appeals court said school officials had a right to suspend the students because they feared the armbands would create a school disturbance. But the Supreme Court, by a 7–2 vote, overturned the lower court.

Justice Abe Fortas, writing for the majority, said students do not "shed their constitutional rights to freedom of expression at the school house gate. . . ."[72] In the absence of a specific showing of constitutionally valid reasons to regulate their speech, students are entitled to freedom of expression of their views, wrote Fortas. The students' expression could have been prohibited only if it materially and substantially had disrupted the work and discipline of the school.

Justice Black dissented. In his view, schools are not the place for demonstrations, but where students go to learn what the state deems fit to teach. "If the time has come," he wrote, "when pupils of state-supported schools—kindergarten, grammar or high schools—can defy and flout orders of school officials to keep their minds on their own school work, it is the beginning of a new revolutionary era of permissiveness in this country fostered by the judiciary."

Justice Harlan also dissented, arguing that those protesting abridgement of their speech should have to prove that school officials acted from other than legitimate school concerns.

Justices White and Stewart wrote separate, concurring opinions. White said he understood the decision to recognize that expression by means of disruptive conduct is not given the same protection as pure speech, and Stewart believed that in some narrowly limited areas children might be given lesser freedom of expression than adults.

The age/maturity factor mentioned by Stewart has been reflected in a number of court decisions since *Tinker.* The Ninth Circuit U.S. Court of Appeals has ruled (1) secondary students' rights to freedom of speech or expression are not necessarily coextensive with those of adults and may be modified or curtailed by school policies that are reasonably designed "to adjust those rights to the needs of the school environment"[73]; and (2) the "activities of high school students . . . may be more stringently reviewed than the conduct of college students, as the former are 'in a much more adolescent and immature stage of life and less able to screen fact from propaganda.' "[74] The view that students' rights are not necessarily "coextensive with those of adults" was put forth by Justice Stewart in his concurring opinion in *Tinker.*

The theoretical underpinning for *Tinker* is the "marketplace of ideas" concept circumscribed by a kind of "clear and present danger" test as represented in the *Tinker* standard, that is, the "material and substantial interference" in the classroom or school.

The marketplace concept was applied to the school setting by the U.S. Supreme Court in *Keyishian v. Board of Regents* (1967), with the Court supporting the need to expose youngsters "to that robust exchange of ideas which discovers truth 'out of a multitude of tongues, [rather] than through any kind of authoritative selection.' "[76]

The timing of the application of the "material and substantial interference" or disruption test is a problem, as it was with the use of the "clear and present danger" test when applied in First Amendment cases. The Fourth Circuit U.S. Court of Appeals said that public school officials could exercise prior restraint on publications distributed on school premises during school hours "in those special circumstances where they can 'reasonably forecast substantial disruption . . .' on account of such printed material. . . ."[77] Further, the Fourth Circuit held that the rights of secondary school students may be modified or curtailed by school regulations "reasonably designed to adjust these rights to the needs of the school environment."[78]

"State Action" Required

Another distinction needs to be made. Students at private institutions generally are not protected by the Constitution from actions taken by their schools. The reason is that "state action" is not involved as it is when the "state" operates public schools. There are exceptions to this general rule. If, for example, significant state funds are involved (in one case the state contributing 35 percent of the school's total budget), then state action is involved and the Fourteenth Amendment is operative. Also, if the state is involved in the appointment or selection of the trustees, this would constitute state action. Similarly if the state has had a hand in the kind of rules and regulations adopted by the school, this might satisfy the state action requirement. An episode at Baylor University illustrates the dilemma faced by journalism students at a private institution.[79] Briefly, the controversy began with the announcement that a *Playboy* magazine photographer would be coming to Waco, Texas, to photograph Baylor coeds for an issue on "Girls of the Southwest Conference." University President Abner V. McCall said any Baylor coed who appeared nude or seminude in the issue would be subjected to disciplinary action. The student newspaper, *The Lariat,* took the position that the decision was one for the individual student to make, not the president. The upshot was an order from the president to *The Lariat* not to print anything more about the matter and a declaration that he was the publisher and as such could determine the policies of the newspaper.

An editorial followed, saying the ban infringed on the editors' academic freedom. The issue continued to heat up. By the time it was over, the editors had been fired, two journalism faculty members had resigned because of concern over the journalistic principles involved, the newspaper was temporarily shut down, and the controversy had drawn national publicity.

The university president's assertion that he was the publisher of the student newspaper should be contrasted with the views of the Fourth and Fifth Circuit courts, to wit: Even though a student newspaper is totally funded by a public school, is printed with school facilities, and is written during school hours under the supervision of an adviser does not mean that the school, or principal, is the "publisher" of the paper with attendant power of editorial control.[80]

A further comparison of the importance of the public versus private school status (in terms of First Amendment protection) can be made between the outcome at Baylor University and one at the University of Minnesota in which the student newspaper *The Minnesota Daily,* won a First Amendment claim against the Board of Regents, who had voted to replace a compulsory fee system for funding the newspaper with a refundable fee system. The change, according to a three-judge panel of the Eighth Circuit U.S. Court of Appeals in *Stanley v. Magrath* (1983), was motivated in part by the publication of a controversial "humor" issue that satirized Christ, religious groups, public figures, and various ideas and trends to the point that vehement criticism of the newspaper resulted. The regents ultimately voted to offer students the chance to obtain a refund of that part of their fee that went to publications. The panel, citing various precedents, declared that a public university "may not constitutionally take adverse action against a student newspaper, such as withdrawing or reducing the paper's funding, because it disapproves of the content of the paper."[81] It is clear, wrote Judge Richard S. Arnold for the three-judge panel, "that the First Amendment prohibits the Regents from taking adverse action against the *Daily* because the contents of the paper are occasionally blasphemous or vulgar." The court then cited a U.S. Supreme Court decision in *Papish v. University of Missouri Board of Curators* (1973), to wit: offense to good taste, no matter how great, does not justify restriction of speech;[82] and an Eighth Circuit holding that a school board cannot ban films because of religious or ideological content.[83] Interestingly, the three-judge panel held that the Regents must show, by a preponderance of the evidence (a tougher test than the "clear and convincing" evidence test), that it had a constitutionally permissible motive for changing the newspaper funding system.[84] Thus, the burden of proof was placed squarely on the Board of Regents, not on the newspaper editors.

In a footnote, Judge Arnold pointed out that as far as the First Amendment is concerned, the university could choose not to own or support any newspapers, "so long as its motivation is permissible."[85]

Rather than appeal, the university decided to settle out of court. It agreed to pay the newspaper $182,000 for legal fees incurred by the paper during the four-year dispute, and to reinstate the mandatory fee system. Both the university and the newspaper agreed to set up a $20,000 fund for periodic seminars on press freedom and responsibility.[86]

Protected versus Unprotected Speech

As noted in *Tinker,* expression that would materially and substantially interfere with the school or classroom is not constitutionally protected. Similarly, the First Amendment rights of students must yield to the superior interest of the school in seeing that materials that encourage actions which endanger the health or safety of students are not distributed on school property, according to the Fourth Circuit, which upheld a ban on further distribution on school property of an "underground" newspaper that contained an advertisement promoting the sale of a water pipe and paraphernalia used in connection with cocaine.[87] "Obscene" literature, as defined by the Supreme Court (see Chapter 12), can be legally suppressed by school officials, the Fifth and Seventh Circuit courts have ruled,[88] as can libelous expression.[89] And the Supreme Court has ruled that school officials can lawfully ban speech which is "directed to inciting or producing imminent lawless action and is likely to incite or produce such action."[90] Furthermore, school officials can regulate the time, place, and manner of distribution, according to the Seventh Circuit.[91] But that same court struck down as overbroad a rule banning distribution of literature "while classes are being conducted," as it did the following rule: "No student shall distribute in any school any literature that is either by its content or by the manner of distribution itself, productive of, or likely to produce a significant disruption of the normal educational processes, functions or purposes in any of the Indianapolis schools or injury to others."[92]

The Ninth Circuit took this position in a 1982 decision:

> Writers on a high school newspaper do not have an unfettered constitutional right to be free from pre-publication review. In fact, the special characteristics of the high school environment, particularly one involving students in a journalism class that produces a school newspaper, call for supervision and review by school faculty and administrators.[93]

Hazelwood School District v. Kuhlmeier. The Ninth Circuit anticipated by six years a major U.S. Supreme Court decision in *Hazelwood School District v. Kuhlmeier* (1988).[94] By a 5–3 vote, the Court held that public school officials can regulate the content of a school publication or play in any reasonable manner if that publication or play results from a supervised learning experience, such as a journalism class, rather than from an activity that is open to the "indiscriminate use" of students generally. If the latter, then the publication is a "public forum."

The case began in May 1983 when the staff of the *Spectrum,* a newspaper published by a journalism class at Hazelwood East High School in St. Louis, prepared a special two-page section on teenagers' problems. On May 10 the adviser took the page proofs to the school principal for review. The principal objected to two of the stories. One dealt with the pregnancy experiences of three students who had been given fictitious names, and the other detailed the impact of a parental divorce on students. The principal thought that the identity of the three students who had been pregnant might become known and that references to sexual activity and birth control were inappropriate. He also believed that the parents in the divorce article should have been given an opportunity to respond to remarks made about them by their children. He ordered the adviser to delete the two pages containing those articles. The students then filed suit in U.S. District Court seeking an order to require the principal to permit publication of the articles and money damages.

The District Court denied the injunction request in 1985, saying that school officials may impose reasonable restraints on students' speech in activities that are an integral part of the school's educational function. The court termed the principal's concerns legitimate and reasonable.

In upholding the District Court and reversing the Eighth Circuit U.S. Court of Appeals, the Court, in an opinion by Justice White, held "that educators do not offend the First Amendment by exercising editorial control over the style and content of student speech in school-sponsored activities so long as their actions are reasonably related to legitimate pedagogical concerns."[95]

White was joined in his opinion by Chief Justice Rehnquist and Justices Stevens, O'Connor, and Scalia. Justice Brennan wrote a dissenting opinion joined by Justices Marshall and Blackmun.

The Court also held that:

■ The First Amendment rights of students in public schools are not automatically coextensive with the rights of adults in other settings, and must be applied in the light of the special characteristics of the school environment. A school need not tolerate student speech that is inconsistent with its basic educational mission, even though the government could not censor similar speech outside the school.
■ The school newspaper in question could not be characterized as a public forum. The Eighth Circuit had taken a different view.
■ The school principal had acted reasonably in requiring the deletion of certain articles.

In his opinion, Justice White distinguished between the efforts of school officials to silence student speech "that happens to occur on school premises," as in *Tinker v. Des Moines Independent Community School District,* and the authority to control activities that would be seen as bearing the "imprimatur of the school," such as school-sponsored publications and theatrical productions. The Court specifically did not overturn *Tinker.*

In his strongly worded dissent, Brennan wrote: "In my view, the principal . . . violated the First Amendment's prohibitions against censorship of any student expression that neither disrupts classwork nor invades the rights of others, and against any censorship that is not narrowly tailored to serve its purpose."[96]

Following the *Hazelwood* decision, Massachusetts passed a law which has the effect of nullifying that decision in the state. Titled the "Right of Students to Freedom of Expression," it states the essence of the Court's decision in *Tinker,* namely, that the right of students to freedom of expression in the public schools of Massachusetts shall not be abridged—provided that such rights shall not cause any disruption or disorder within the school. The law also includes this protection for school officials: "No expression made by students in the excerise of such rights shall be deemed to be an expression of school policy and no school officials shall be held responsible in any civil or criminal action for any expression made or published by the students."

In California, special protection for students already existed under Section 48907 of the State Education Code. It states that school officials cannot censor a story unless it is "obscene, libelous, slanderous" or advocates "substantial disruption" of the school system.[97] This protection obviously is not as extensive as that provided by Massachusetts.

Other states are considering legislation that would limit the impact of *Hazelwood* on students' rights.

Public Forums

In *Hazelwood,* the Eighth Circuit considered the student newspaper to be a public forum, but the Supreme Court disagreed. Under different circumstances, such as a newspaper produced by students as extracurricular activity, the publication could have been deemed a public forum and therefore protected against censorship by the First Amendment. Once government creates a First Amendment, or public, forum, it cannot arbitrarily or summarily prevent that forum from being used. Student newspapers, sidewalks, parks, private shopping malls under certain circumstances, and so on, may be deemed public forums for First Amendment purposes, and restrictions upon the use of such forums often are unconstitutional. Thus, a portion of a federal statute that was applied to prevent the exercise of free speech on the sidewalks around the U.S. Supreme Court building was ruled unconstitutional by the Court in *U.S. v. Grace* (1983).[98]

The law which applied only to the nation's highest court, stated: "It shall be unlawful to parade, stand or move in processions or assemblages in the Supreme Court building or grounds, or to display therein any flag, banner or device designed or adapted to bring into public notice any party, organization or movement."

The case arose when court security officials warned Mary Grace, who was carrying a placard with the text of the First Amendment on it, that she was violating the law by "parading" on the sidewalk around the building.

The Court, in affirming a 2–1 decision of the District of Columbia Circuit Court,[99] said the sidewalks around the Court are indistinguishable from any others in the nation's capital. They are public forums and should be treated as such, wrote Justice White. However, the Court, in its 7–2 vote, suggested that the law could be applied to restrict demonstrations on Supreme Court grounds to preserve order and decorum.

Justice Marshall, who agreed with the outcome of the case, would have declared the statute unconstitutional on its face, saying that "every citizen has a right to engage in peaceable and orderly expression in a public place so long as the expression is not incompatible with the primary activity of the place in question."

A government body may unknowingly create a limited public forum as demonstrated by the outcome in *San Diego Committee Against Registration and the Draft (CARD) v. Governing Board of the Grossmont Union High School District* (1986).[100]

The Ninth Circuit U.S. Court of Appeals ruled that once a school board opens a high school newspaper to advertising by the general public, including military recruitment ads, it creates a limited public forum from which the board cannot exclude advertisements regarding alternatives to military service.

What happened is that CARD sought to purchase advertising space in five high school student newspapers. The school board rejected the ad, and CARD claimed that its First Amendment rights had been violated.

The Ninth Circuit panel agreed, saying that once the state creates a limited public forum, its ability to impose further constraints on the type of speech permitted is quite restricted. "Although a State is not required to indefinitely retain the open character of the facility," Judge Wallace said for the panel, "as long as it does so it is bound by the same standards as apply in a traditional public forum. Reasonable time, place, and manner regulations are permissible, and a content-based prohibition must be narrowly drawn to effectuate a compelling state interest."[101]

The panel drew its conclusion based on a 1983 U.S. Supreme Court decision in *Perry Education Association v. Perry Local Educators' Association*[102] In that case and in *Cornelius v. NAACP Legal Defense & Educational Fund,*[103] the Supreme Court identified three types of forums to which the public's right of access varies, as do limitations a state may impose on that right.

The first type of forum is one that has long existed by tradition or by government fiat — one devoted to assembly and debate. For a state to enforce a content-based exclusion, it must show that its regulation is necessary to serve a compelling state interest and that it is narrowly drawn to achieve that end.

The second type of forum consists of public property which the state has opened for use by the public as a place for expressive activity. The Constitution, said the Supreme Court, "forbids a state to enforce certain exclusions from a forum generally open to the public even if it was not required to create the forum in the first place. It was this limited public forum that was found applicable in the CARD case.

The third type of forum takes place on public property that is not by tradition or designation a forum for public communication. In addition to time, place and manner regulations, the state may reserve this forum for its intended purposes, communicative or otherwise, as long as the regulation on speech is reasonable.[104]

Time, Place, Manner Restrictions

In the *CARD* case, the Ninth Circuit noted that reasonable time, place and manner regulation of expression is permissible under the First Amendment. The key word is *reasonable*. For example, you may have a right to express your views in public, but that right may be restricted in such a way that you cannot, except on pain of arrest, exercise it at two o'clock in the morning in a public park when aided by a loudspeaker. Similarly, you may not have a right to stand in the middle of a public street to express your views unless you first obtain a permit. However, such regulations must be both reasonable and narrowly drawn, as the Supreme Court pointed out in *Grayned v. City of Rockford:*

> Our cases make clear that in assessing the reasonableness of a regulation we must weigh heavily the fact that communication is involved; the regulation must be narrowly tailored to further the state's legitimate interest. Access to the streets, sidewalks, parks and other similar public places for the purpose of exercising [First Amendment rights] cannot constitutionally be denied broadly.[105]

The California Supreme Court, in upholding a Los Angeles ordinance regulating the size, weight, appearance and placement of newsstands on city sidewalks, nevertheless pointed out that time, place, and manner regulations of First Amendment activity must be carefully and narrowly drawn to avoid arbitrary and unnecessary curtailment of freedom of speech.[106]

When the city of Minneapolis imposed license and license fee requirements on operators of newsstands located on public sidewalks, a state court found such time, place, and manner restrictions unreasonable and arbitrary and declared them unconstitutionally vague and overbroad.[107] The Minneapolis ordinance was distinguishable from Los Angeles' in that it imposed license and fee requirements, and a requirement that the licensee, through liability insurance, hold the city harmless in the event of injury or death caused by the newsstand or its operation. Such requirements constituted prior restraint on the circulation of printed materials, according to the judge.[108]

When a town sought to prevent littering of the streets by prohibiting the distribution of any sort of printed matter, the Supreme Court struck down the ordinance as unconstitutional, saying:

We are of the opinion that the purpose to keep the streets clean and of good appearance is insufficient to justify an ordinance which prohibits a person rightfully on a public street from handing literature to one willing to receive it. Any burden imposed upon the city authorities in cleaning and caring for the streets as an indirect consequence of such distribution results from the constitutional protection of the freedom of speech and press. This constitutional protection does not deprive the city of all power to prevent street littering. There are obvious methods of preventing littering. Among these is the punishment of those who actually throw papers on the streets.[109]

Content Neutrality

Another First Amendment precept mentioned by the Ninth Circuit in *CARD* is "content neutrality." As the Supreme Court put it, "[A]bove all else, the First Amendment means that government has no power to restrict expression because of its message, its ideas, its subject matter, or its content."[110]

Thus, in *U.S. v. O'Brien,*[111] a case involving the burning of a draft card on the steps of a courthouse, the U.S. Supreme Court upheld O'Brien's conviction for burning the draft card even though the Court agreed that government could not suppress or regulate (other than *reasonable* time, place, manner restrictions) the words uttered by the defendant. The three-part analysis used by the Court in determining that the government's draft card regulations did not infringe First Amendment freedom went like this: (1) the regulations furthered a substantial government interest; (2) the government's interest was unrelated to the suppression of free expression; and (3) the restrictions were no greater than essential to the furtherance of the government's interest.

Content neutrality assumes that regulated expression is protected, but this principle does not apply to unprotected speech, such as obscenity. And its usual application is to time, place, and manner restrictions—the idea being that government can't let one group speak while denying the right to other groups that it may dislike.

SUMMARY

The two classic attempts at prior restraint of the press thus far are *Near v. Minnesota* (1931) and Pentagon Papers (1971). In both instances the Supreme Court rejected attempts to impose such restraint although in the Pentagon Papers case the Court itself imposed a temporary restraint on newspapers wishing to publish the classified government report on Vietnam.

In *Near,* the Court held that not all attempts at prior restraint would be unconstitutional. Singled out as examples of what would be constitutionally sanctioned were prior restraints of:

1. Attempts to obstruct armed forces' recruitment
2. Sailing dates of troop transports
3. Number and location of troops

4. Obscenity
5. Speech or press that threatened the security of community life
6. Utterances which have all the effect of force

In the Pentagon Papers case, a Court majority agreed that (1) any system of prior restraint bears a heavy presumption against it being constitutional; and (2) the government must meet a heavy burden of showing justification for such restraint. Beyond this brief statement lay widely divergent views, scattered like seeds of doubt should the government again test the widely held doctrine that prior restraint is the antithesis of freedom of the press.

The Progressive was enjoined from publishing an article on the H-bomb after a U.S. District Court judge decided that some of the information likely would violate secrecy provisions of the Atomic Energy Act and that the government had made a showing of the likelihood of "direct, immediate, and irreparable injury" to the nation if publication occurred. Ultimately the government dropped its efforts to maintain the ban on publication when information about the H-bomb was published by the *Press Connection* and the *Chicago Tribune*.

As with the Pentagon Papers case, some major issues were not resolved. The U.S. Supreme Court did not consider *The Progressive* case on its merits, merely rejecting the magazine's bid for an expedited review.

Prior restraint is not the only threat to freedom of expression. If information can be classified as "property," then a different kind of threat results. This is what happened in *Winans et al. v. U.S.* in which the Supreme Court said unmistakably that information is property. This 1988 decision raises the specter of government and business prosecuting employees, or even journalists, who disclose the information.

Despite the First Amendment, injunctions have been used frequently to restrain the press. *Alfred Knopf, Inc. v. Colby, U.S. v. Snepp, ABC, Inc. v. Smith Cabinet Manufacturing Co., Inc.,* and the *60 Minutes*—Judge Adrian Duplantier confrontation represent the proverbial tip of the iceberg.

One segment of the press is most vulnerable to prior restraint: namely—the student press. But in *Tinker v. Des Moines Independent Community School District* (1969), the U.S. Supreme Court said students have constitutional rights to freedom of expression and that such expression could be prohibited only if it materially and substantially disrupted the work and discipline of the school. Other exceptions to the general prohibition against prior restraint might be for expression that affects the health or safety of students, or if the expression is obscene or libelous.

But in 1988, in the *Hazelwood School District* case, a majority of the Supreme Court justices agreed that *public* school officials can regulate the content of a school publication or play in any reasonable manner if that publication or play resulted from a supervised learning experience. Such a publication or play is not a *public forum*.

Once government creates a forum, it cannot arbitrarily or summarily prevent that forum from operating. Thus, a sidewalk around the Supreme Court building and a student newspaper that accepted military advertisements were deemed to be "forums."

Government regulation of protected expression must be content-neutral. It can't tolerate some kinds of expression in the marketplace but disallow other kinds (with a few exceptions, such as obscene speech or press). It can, however, impose reasonable time, place, and manner restrictions on the exercise of free speech/press. Courts ultimately decide what is reasonable.

Private school students generally do not enjoy First Amendment rights of expression in the school environment except under certain circumstances in which the state becomes involved in the operation of the school. The reason: no "state action" is involved; hence, the constitutional guarantees against *government* interference in the people's right to express themselves are not activated.

QUESTIONS IN REVIEW

1. The landmark decision in *Near v. Minnesota* ruled unconstitutional the prior restraint of the *Saturday Press*. But the Court majority would have permitted such restraint under such circumstances as:_____ .
2. What was a major reason given by U.S. District Court Judge Gerhard Gesell of the District of Columbia for refusing to issue at the outset any injunction against publication of the Pentagon Papers?
3. The per curiam decision of the U.S. Supreme Court in the Pentagon Papers case relied on two principal ideas in refusing to continue the ban against publication. What were they?
4. Justice Brennan said there was an original error in the Pentagon Papers case. In his opinion, what was it?
5. The *Winans* case is important for which reason?
6. In *Tinker v. Des Moines Independent Community School District* (1969), the U.S. Supreme Court held that _____ .
7. Discuss the forum precept and its applicability to the student press. Be sure to include the *Hazelwood School District* decision of the Supreme Court in the discussion.
8. Protected speech is subject to regulation, such as _____ .

ANSWERS

1. To prevent obstruction of recruiting, publication of sailing dates of transports or location and number of troops, obscenity, incitement to violence, and overthrow of orderly government.
2. Information was historical.
3. Any system of prior restraint carries a heavy presumption against its constitutionality; and government carries a heavy burden to show justification for such restraint. It did not do so in the Pentagon Papers case.
4. Granting any injunctive relief whatsoever.
5. Information is property, and if it is "leaked," or used without authority, those who own the "property" can take legal action.

6. Students have constitutional rights to freedom of expression, and such expression can be prohibited only if it materially and substantially disrupts the work and discipline of a school.
7. Once a government unit, such as a school, creates a "forum," it cannot control what is said at or printed in that forum (except in rare instances). It can impose only reasonable time, place, and manner regulations. The exceptions likely would be: (1) obscenity, since obscene works are not protected by the First Amendment (see Chapter 12); (2) expression which would materially and substantially disrupt the work and discipline of a school; (3) libelous works; and (4) expression that would adversely affect the health and safety of students. In *Hazelwood School District,* the Court made it clear that a supervised learning experience is not a forum.
8. Reasonable time, place, and manner restrictions.

ENDNOTES

1. An injunction is a mandatory or prohibitive order issued by a court which either requires a person to do something or to abstain from, or cease doing, something. The injunction may be permanent, as in the *Near* case, or temporary, as in the Pentagon Papers situation.
2. Near v. Minnesota, 283 U.S. 697, 51 S.Ct. 625, 75 L.Ed. 1357.
3. A.M. Rosenthal, "Why We Published," *Columbia Journalism Review,* Vol. 10. No. 3, September/October 1971, p. 19.
4. Ben H. Bagdikian, "What Did We Learn," *Columbia Journalism Review,* Vol. 10, No. 3, September/October 1971, p. 48.
5. See Appendix A for explanation of federal and state court structure and procedures.
6. Opinion reported in *The New York Times,* June 20, 1971, © by the New York Times Company. Reprinted by permission.
7. *U.S. Government Information Policies and Practices — The Pentagon Papers,* Part 3; hearings before the House Subcommittee of the Committee on Government Operations, 92d Congress, Ist Session, June 30–July 7, 1971, p. 839.
8. *Per curiam* means that no identifiable member of the Court wrote the opinion.
9. New York Times v. U.S., and U.S. v. Washington Post Co., 403 U.S. at 714, 91 S.Ct. at 2141, 29 L.Ed.2d at 824–25.
10. Organization for a Better Austin v. Keefe, 402 U.S. 415, 91 S.Ct. 1575, 29 L.Ed.2d 1 (1971).
11. Twentieth Century Fund Task Force, *Press Freedom Under Pressure* (New York: The Twentieth Century Fund, 1972), pp. 39–40.
12. Max Frankel, "The 'State Secrets' Myth," *Columbia Journalism Review,* Vol. 10, No. 3, September/October 1971, pp. 22–23.
13. *U.S. Government Information Policies,* op. cit., note 7, pp. 811–12.
14. Rosenthal, "Why We Published," p. 17.
15. Unreported opinion by District Court Judge Gesell in *Moss v. Melvin Laird, Secretary of Defense,* and *Paul Fisher v. Department of Defense,* decided December 7, 1971. It should be noted that these lawsuits were brought under the Freedom of Information Act (see Chapter 9), which specifically permits the federal government to withhold classified information on national defense and foreign affairs. The Pentagon Papers case concerned prior restraint of publication in that the newspapers already had the information. The complexity may be the same in both cases, but not the issues.
16. 42 U.S.C. 2274(b).
17. U.S. v. The Progressive, 4 Med.L.Rptr. 2377, 2384.
18. *Editor & Publisher,* January 12, 1980. For an in-depth look at the cost of such litigation, see John Soloski and Carolyn Stewart, "The Cost of Prior Restraint: *U.S. v. The Progressive,*" 6 *Communications and the Law* 2, April 1984, pp. 3 + .

19. U.S. v. The Progressive, 5 *Med.L.Rptr.* 2441, 2443, March 18, 1980.
20. Morland v. Sprecher, Judge, U.S. Court of Appeals, supplement to *Media Law Reporter,* July 10, 1979.
21. Ibid.
22. U.S. v. The Progressive, 4 *Med.L.Rptr.* 2377, 2380.
23. Ibid., at 2382.
24. As reported in Robert Friedman, "The United States v. The Progressive," *Columbia Journalism Review,* Vol. XVIII, No. 2, July/August 1979, p. 35.
25. "The Press at Odds," *The QUILL,* June 1979, p. 31.
26. "Worried and Without Friends at Court," *Time,* June 18, 1979, p. 71.
27. "The Press at Odds," *The QUILL,* p. 31.
28. Ibid.
29. Erwin Knoll, "If . . .," *The QUILL,* June 1979, p. 32.
30. For an extensive review of the British Secrets Act, see "Official Secrets Acts, the D-Notice System and the British Press," a paper presented by Professor Albert G. Pickerell at the 1975 convention of the Association for Education in Journalism, Ottawa, Canada, August 17–20, 1975.
31. *FoI Digest,* Vol. 11, No. 3, September/October, 1969, p. 1.
32. Everette E. Dennis, "Leaked Information as Property: Vulnerability of the Press to Criminal Prosecution," *Saint Louis University Law Journal,* Vol. 20, No. 4, 1976, with summarization based on information from pp. 618–20 (footnotes omitted). Copyright © 1976 by Saint Louis University School of Law.
33. People v. Kunkin, 100 Cal. Rptr. 845 (1972).
34. Ibid., p. 868.
35. 107 Cal. Rptr. 184, 192, 507 P.2d 1392, 1400 (1973).
36. Dennis, "Leaked Information," pp. 623–24.
37. Ibid., p. 615.
38. Carpenter, Felis, and Winans v. U.S., 14 *Med.L.Rptr.* 1853, December 1, 1987.
39. U.S. v. Morison, 15 *Med.L.Rptr.* 1369, June 21, 1988.
40. Op. cit., at 1856.
41. W. Fletcher, *Cyclopedia of Law of Private Corporations* (rev. ed., 1986), p. 260 (footnotes omitted).
42. Editorial, "Supreme Court Term Began With a Bang, Ended With a Whimper," *The NEWS Media & The LAW,* Spring, 1988.
43. "Developments in the Law," *Harvard Law Review,* Vol. 78, No. 5, March 1965, p. 996, 1008–9. Copyright 1965 by the Harvard Law Review Association.
44. William O. Bertlesman, "Injunctions Against Speech and Writing: A Re-evaluation," *Kentucky Law Journal,* Vol. 59, No. 2, 1970–71, pp. 324–25.
45. Alfred Knopf, Inc., v. William Colby, CIA director, 509 F.2d 1362 (4th Circuit, 1975). Certiorari denied April 14, 1975 (95 S.Ct. 1555).
46. "News Notes," *Media Law Reporter,* July 18, 1978.
47. 4 *Med.L.Rptr.* 2313, April 10, 1979, 595 F.2d 926.
48. "News Notes," *Media Law Reporter,* March 4, 1980.
49. "News Notes," *Media Law Reporter,* August 17, 1982.
50. Ibid.
51. "Report," by Bob Lewis, in *The QUILL,* June 1980, p. 52.
52. *FoI Digest,* September/October, 1983, p. 1.
53. *Editor & Publisher,* February 18, 1984, p. 9.
54. See Chapter 9 for more details.
55. Agee v. CIA, 6 *Med.L.Rptr.* 2006, November 4, 1980.
56. Haig v. Agee, 7 *Med.L.Rptr.* 1545, July 21, 1981.
57. "News Notes," *Media Law Reporter,* August 18, 1981.
58. Address by Admiral Stansfield Turner, "Protecting Secrets in a Free Society," delivered to the National Press Club in Washington, D.C., on October 25, 1978.
59. Ibid.

60. Reporters Committee for Freedom of the Press, Washington, D.C., *Press Censorship Newsletter,* No. 6, December/January 1974–75, p. 7.

61. In re Providence Journal Co., 55 *U.S. Law Week* 2377, January 20, 1987.

62. Ibid.

63. "News Notes," *Media Law Reporter,* May 26, 1987.

64. Ibid.

65. *Editor & Publisher,* May 7, 1988, p. 13.

66. U.S. v. Dickinson, 465 F.2d 496 (1972).

67. Dickinson v. U.S., 94 S.Ct. 270 (1973).

68. Frick v. Stevens, 43 D C 2d 6; also *FoI Digest,* Vol. 8, No. 7, May/June, 1967.

69. "News Notes," *Media Law Reporter,* October 26, 1982.

70. "News Notes," *Media Law Reporter,* March 15, 1983.

71. Vanessa Orlando, "Censorship Runs Rampant," SPLC *Report,* Spring, 1980, p. 10.

72. Tinker v. Des Moines Independent Community School District, 393 U.S. 503, 506, 89 S.Ct. 733, 736, 21 L.Ed.2d 731 (1969).

73. Nicholson v. Board of Education Torrance Unified School District, 682 F.2d 858, 863 (9th Circuit, 1982), citing Williams v. Spencer, 622 F.2d 1200, 1205 (4th Circuit, 1980).

74. Ibid., note 4 at 863, citing Schwartz v. Schuker, 298 F. Supp. 238, 242 (Eastern District of New York, 1969).

75. Tinker, op cit., note 72, 393 U.S. at 515, 89 S.Ct. at 741.

76. Keyishian v. Board of Regents, 385 U.S. 589, 603, 87 S.Ct. 675, 683, 17 L.Ed.2d 629 (1967).

77. Williams v. Spencer, 622 F.2d 1200, 1206 (1980), citing Quarterman v. Byrd, 453 F.2d 54, 58 (4th Circuit, 1971).

78. Ibid., Quarterman, at 58.

79. For a review of the situation at Baylor University, see "Blowup at Baylor," written by Melissa Millecam, Juan Ramon Palomo, and Charles Long, in *The QUILL,* May 1980, pp. 23+.

80. Joyner v. Whiting, 477 F.2d 456 (4th Circuit, 1973); and Bazaar v. Fortune, 476 F.2d 507 (5th Circuit, 1973), as reported in Michael D. Simpson, "Constitutional Standards for Student Publication Guidelines," Student Press Law Center *Report,* Winter 1978–79, p. 30.

81. Stanley v. Magrath, 9 *Med.L.Rptr.* 2352, 2354 (8th Circuit, 1983). Also cited were Joyner v. Whiting, 477 F.2d 456, 460 (4th Circuit, 1973); and Antonelli v. Hammond, 308 F.Supp. 1329, 1337–38 (District of Massachusetts, 1970).

82. Papish v. University of Missouri Board of Curators, 410 U.S. 667, 670 (1973), in which the Court invalidated a student's expulsion that was motivated by disapproval of the content of a newspaper the student distributed on campus.

83. Pratt v. Independent School District No. 381, 670 F.2d 771, 773 (8th Circuit, 1982).

84. Stanley, op. cit., note 81, at 2355–56.

85. Ibid., note 6 at 2355.

86. "Minnesota Student Paper Wins Dispute with University's Regents," *FoI Digest,* March/April, 1984, p. 6.

87. Williams v. Spencer, 622 F.2d 1200 (4th Circuit, 1980).

88. Shanley v. Northeast Independent School District, 462 F.2d 960 (5th Circuit, 1972); and Jacobs v. Board of School Community, 490 F.2d 601 (7th Circuit, 1973) dismissed as moot, 420 U.S. 128 (1975).

89. Ibid., Shanley, and Fujishima v. Board of Education, 460 F.2d 1355 (7th Circuit, 1972).

90. Brandenburg v. Ohio, 395 U.S. 444, 89 S.Ct. 1827 (1969).

91. Fujishima, op. cit., note 89.

92. Jacobs, op. cit., note 88. For a more complete review of protection for the scholastic press, see Michael D. Simpson, "Constitutional Standards for Student Publication Guidelines," SPLC *Report,* Winter 1978–79, pp. 30+.

93. Nicholson, op. cit., note 73, at 863.

94. 14 *Med.L.Rptr.* 2081, February 2, 1988.

95. Ibid., at 2087.

96. Ibid., at 2089.

97. *Editor & Publisher,* February 6, 1988, p. 17.

98. U.S. v. Grace, 103 S.Ct. 1702, 75 L.Ed. 2d 632 (1983).
99. 665 F.2d 1193 (1981).
100. 55 *U.S. Law Week* 2007, July 1, 1986.
101. Ibid.
102. 460 U.S. 37, 51 *U.S. Law Week* 4165.
103. 53 *U.S. Law Week* 5116.
104. Op. cit., 55 *U.S. Law Week* 2007–08.
105. Grayned v. City of Rockford, 408 U.S. 104, 117.
106. Kash Enterprises, Inc. v. City of Los Angeles, 138 Cal. Rptr. 53, 2 *Med.L.Rptr.* 1716 (1977).
107. Minnesota Newspaper Association v. Minneapolis, 9 *Med.L.Rptr.* 2116, September 27, 1983 (District Court, 4th Judicial District).
108. Ibid., at 2126.
109. Schneider v. State (Town of Irvington), 308 U.S. 147, 60 S.Ct. 146 (1939).
110. Police Department v. Mosley, 408 U.S. 92, 95 (1972).
111. 391 U.S. 367, 88 S.Ct. 1673, 20 L.Ed.2d 672 (1968). See Chapter 2.

4

Libel

HIGHLIGHTS

◼ Definitions of libel and slander.

◼ Libel per se (libelous on the face of it).

◼ Libel per quod (libelous because of extrinsic factors, special circumstances, innuendo).

◼ Publication, identification, defamation, fault, actual injury, and lack of privilege must be present for a libel lawsuit by a private person to succeed.

◼ Headline and story ordinarily are considered together in establishing whether a defamation has occurred, but there are cases where the headline alone was sufficient for a successful libel action.

◼ Groups can be libeled. As the group gets larger, the chances of a successful libel action diminish.

◼ Corporations, like individuals, can recover damages for libel.

◼ Defenses against a libel lawsuit are truth, privilege, and fair comment and criticism.

◼ Types of damages that can be awarded in a successful libel lawsuit are general or compensatory, special, and punitive or exemplary.

◼ Many states bar the award of punitive damages if a defendant prints a retraction; but such a retraction generally does not preclude the recovery of general and/or special damages.

Previous chapters examined the struggle for freedom of press and the emergence of constitutional safeguards, but the news media can be held accountable after publication. Any examination of accountability should start with libel and proceed to invasion of privacy since these two torts, or wrongs, in the civil law have been the principal dangers confronting the news media once publication or broadcast occurs. Although such dangers have been reduced as the result of U.S. Supreme Court decisions, they have not been eliminated; hence the need to examine applicable law.

KINDS OF LAW

The law is a set of rules by which citizens regulate their conduct in relation to each other and to the state. But there are different kinds of law—common law, case law, statutory law, constitutional law, and regulatory law. They all have a bearing on libel.

"Common law" derives from the English legal system. When that system first began to take shape, judges were appointed to administer the "law and custom of the realm." Consequently, they established rules based on general customs and such rules became "common law" as contrasted with particular or special "law," such as canon or ecclesiastical law. Common law is frequently referred to as judge-made law.

"Case law" results from decisions by courts in leading cases and, like common law, develops over time. As mentioned earlier, there is an oft-repeated expression that the law is what the U.S. Supreme Court says it is. In every case decided by the Supreme Court—and by other courts, for that matter—the law is what that particular court says it is in that particular case. The end result is case law. It is from case law that precedents are derived (cases used to help judges decide future cases of a similar type). And from this comes the "doctrine of stare decisis" (to stand by decisions) which holds that once a court has laid down a principle of law as applicable to a certain set of facts, the court will adhere to that principle and apply it to future cases in which the facts are substantially the same.

"Statutory law" results from enactments by legislative bodies. There are no federal statutes dealing with libel, but there are many state laws related to libel.

"Constitutional law" derives from court interpretations of federal and state constitutions. For example, the First Amendment was applied to libel law for the first time in 1964. Until then, the development of libel law had been within the province of the various states on the theory that false and defamatory words were not deserving of First Amendment protection because the public derived nothing of value from such "speech."

Another important distinction in law is between its two main branches, criminal and civil. "Criminal law" involves prosecution and punishment by the state. "Civil law" pertains to injury done to a person (or corporation) who, because of that injury, is entitled to recover compensation or damages from the party that caused the injury. Criminal law deals with offenses against the state or community; civil law concerns private claims and private wrongs that may or may not be crimes.

"Criminal libel" (word crimes) will be examined more fully in Chapter 5.

Civil law includes such matters as breaches of contract, torts (civil wrongs for which damages are recoverable, such as for defamation, trespass, or cases of alleged negligence), property relationships (such as bankruptcies, real estate transactions, administration of estates), and matrimonial matters (divorce, separation, child custody).

Defamation

Briefly, a defamation, by words, pictures, or drawings, defames or injures a person's good name or repuation. If the words are written or published, the defamation is called "libel." If the words are spoken, the defamation is called "slander" (oral defamation as contrasted with written or printed defamation). Because the written word is more permanent, libel historically has been considered the more serious of the two torts.

Slander and libel are rooted in the common law of England and go back to the time when swords were drawn to defend good names and reputations. In part the common law of slander and libel developed to halt such violence.

Slander

Records of feudal courts in England show that slander generally was recognized as a cause of action as far back as the thirteenth century, although it frequently was supplementary to charges of trespass or other offenses against good order. As the feudal courts disappeared, jurisdiction in slander cases passed to ecclesiastical courts. Not until 1536 is an action for defamation found in the King's Courts, although the jurisdiction of the ecclesiastical tribunals lingered until 1855 when they were abolished by the Ecclesiastical Court Act. From the mid-1500s on, such actions more and more frequently ended up in the King's Courts (courts established by the king or queen to deal with civil and criminal matters). The reason: Damages were found to be a more useful and attractive remedy than ecclesiastical pains, and during the reigns of Elizabeth I, James I, and Charles I there was an "extraordinary flood" of such litigation.

Slander generally is not actionable per se. Instead, special damages must be alleged and proved. But several kinds of slander were identified in English common law as more serious than others and these were held to be actionable per se, meaning no proof of special damages was required. These are: (1) imputations of a crime; (2) statements injurious to one's trade, business, or occupation; or (3) statements that someone has a loathsome disease. Most American jurisdictions have added a fourth exception; that is, saying that a woman is unchaste.[1] Once the plaintiff has shown special damages, then general damages may be recovered, but in Louisiana and Washington, any defamation is actionable without proof of special damage.

Our interest in slander stems from its relationship to broadcasting. Are words communicated via radio and television to be treated as slander or libel?

Broadcasters would prefer the law of slander principally because of the requirement that special damages must be proved in all but slander per se cases. Also, no general damages can be awarded until such proof is forthcoming. Generally, however, the law of libel is applied. The reason: Allegedly defamatory words usually are read from a script, which is written. As the Georgia Supreme Court said, the reading aloud of a written defamation to any other person constitutes libel.[2] However, the word "defamacast" has been used to represent a hybrid of the law of slander and libel.[3]

Libel

A number of statutes were enacted in England that greatly influenced libel law developments there. The most noteworthy were:

1. *Fox Libel Act of 1792*. This Act gave juries the power to return verdicts in libel cases where previously such decisions were the prerogative of judges.
2. *Lord Campbell's Act of 1843*. This Act provided that an apology, fairly given, could mitigate damages in defamation actions. It also established truth as a defense in criminal libel cases—long after such a defense had been established in the United States.
3. *Newspaper Libel Act of 1881*. Newspapers were given the privilege of printing fair, accurate, and nonmalicious reports of proceedings at public meetings which, even though defamatory, could not result in successful libel actions.
4. *Law of Libel Amendment Act in 1888*. The privilege accorded in the Act of 1881 was extended to fair and accurate reports of judicial proceedings.

LAW OF DEFAMATION

In the United States, development of defamation law occurred at the state level until the landmark decision of the U.S. Supreme Court in *New York Times v. Sullivan*. Prior to this 1964 case, state laws governed libel actions. Thus, there are 51 different jurisdictions, the 50 states and the District of Columbia, that deal with libel and slander.

Definitions of Libel

As previously noted, a "libel" is a printed or written defamation. In Latin, "defamation" means "to spread a bad report about someone." A libel is a printed defamation that injures a person's good name or reputation. That is the main thrust or injury of a libel. But the definition is by no means complete. To make it so requires examination of the law in each of the states and the District of Columbia. Fortunately, the laws have much in common so, from a few states, we can glean the general characteristics of libel in other jurisdictions.

The California Civil Code (§45) defines libel as a

false and unprivileged publication by writing, printing, picture. effigy. or other fixed representation to the eye. which exposes any person to hatred, contempt, ridicule, or obloquy, or which causes'him to be shunned or avoided, or which has a tendency to injure him in his occupation.

New York defines libel as

words which tend to expose one to public hatred, shame, obloquy, contumely, odium, contempt, ridicule, aversion, ostracism, degradation or disgrace, or to induce an evil opinion of one in the minds of right-thinking persons, and to deprive one of their confidence and friendly intercourse in society.[4]

In Ohio, libel is a false and malicious publication made with intent to injure a person's reputation or expose him to public hatred, contempt, ridicule, shame, or disgrace, or to affect him adversely in his trade or profession.[5]

Oregon defines a defamatory communication as one which subjects a person to hatred, contempt, or ridicule, or tends to diminish the esteem, respect, goodwill or confidence in which that person is held, or to excite adverse, derogatory or unpleasant feelings or opinions against that person.[6]

The Pennsylvania definition of libel is: a maliciously written or printed publication which tends to blacken a person's reputation or expose him to public hatred, contempt, or ridicule, or which injures him in his business or profession.[7]

A Texas statute defines libel as

a defamation expressed in printing or writing, or by signs and pictures, or drawings tending to blacken the memory of the dead, or tending to injure the reputation of one who is alive, and thereby expose him to public hatred, contempt or ridicule, or financial injury, or to impeach the honesty, integrity, or virtue, or reputation of any one, or to publish the natural defects of any one and thereby expose such person to public hatred, ridicule, or financial injury.[8]

And in Wisconsin, a communication is defamatory if it is capable of a meaning which tends to harm the reputation of a person such as to lower that person in the estimation of the community or to deter third persons from associating or dealing with him.[9]

Note that the word "malicious" or "maliciously" is used in the Ohio and Pennsylvania definitions. The concept of malice is a legal boobytrap because malice is definable in various ways. For example, the common-law definition of malice, which is generally required under state tort law to support an award of punitive damages (discussed later), concentrates on the defendant's attitude toward the plaintiff and is shown by ill will, evil or corrupt motive, intention to injure, hatred, enmity, hostility, or spite. This common-law malice was sometimes called actual malice. But commencing with the Supreme Court's decision in *Times-Sullivan,* the meaning of actual malice for First Amendment purposes has been defined as knowingly publishing falsehoods or reckless disregard of the truth (a shift to the defendant's attitude toward falsity of the matter published rather than the defendant's attitude toward the plaintiff).[10]

There are other kinds of malice, too.

- *Malice in fact.* This is a wrongful act done intentionally without just cause or excuse.
- *Presumed malice or malice in law.* Under state libel law, malice often is presumed merely upon proof of publication of defamatory matter. Presumed malice arose out of the difficulty of proving what was in the defendant's mind at the time defamatory matter was published. Under presumed malice, it makes no difference what the publisher or reporter intended; a defamatory falsehood resulted, therefore, malice is presumed.
- *Express malice.* This kind of malice is similar to, or the same as, common law "actual malice" and involves ill will, revenge, or other bad or corrupt motive on the part of defendant.

Libel Per Se, Libel Per Quod

In most states, two kinds of libel are cognizable: libel *per se* and libel *per quod.*

"Libel per se" means libel on the face of it; that is, the words clearly are defamatory. "Libel per quod" means that the defamation is not apparent from the words themselves; instead, the words generally require extrinsic facts or knowledge before the defamation becomes apparent. For example, there is nothing wrong with publishing a brief news item that a Mrs. Barbara Jones gave birth to an eight-pound boy. She's married. Everything on the surface seems all right. But if this Mrs. Jones has been married only three weeks, and if, because of a hospital mixup in identification, this Mrs. Jones is not the one who gave birth to the boy (another Mrs. Barbara Jones did), then the news report may have injured her.

Several jurisdictions require that special damages (out-of-pocket losses) be proved for libel per quod except where the libel falls into one of the four slander per se areas.

A considerable debate concerning libel per quod has taken place with the American Law Institute's *Restatement (Second) of Torts* (1977) rejecting any notion of libel per quod.[11] Vermont courts have not recognized libel per quod, but the state's supreme court in 1983, in seeking to end confusion resulting from the use of libel per se, libel per quod, and slander per se terminology, urged the use of these terms: "libel as a matter of law" and "slander as a matter of law."[12] Both terms would refer to situations where the court, rather than the jury, has determined that a libel or a slander has, in fact, occurred. Thus, libel per se is "libel on the face of it" after a court has so declared. When a court cannot make such a determination, the question is referred to a jury. As the Court said:

> Vermont's reported decisions do not recognize libel per quod, and we adhere to the wisdom of that course today. We hold that libel, whether defamatory on the face of the writing alone or with the aid of extrinsic evidence, is actionable per se.[13]

Libel Per Se. Under Georgia law, libel per se is a publication which charges that a person is guilty of a crime, or is dishonest or immoral. To be actionable, the statement must be false and malicious, but the malice is inferred from the nature of the defamation.[14] In Ohio, a publication that exposes or reflects on the character of a person and subjects that person to ridicule, hatred, or contempt, or affects him injuriously in his business, trade, or profession is libelous per se.[15] And in New York, where the definition is similar to that of Ohio, a writing is libelous per se if it tends to expose a person to hatred, contempt, or aversion, or to induce an evil opinion of him in the community, or tends to injure him in his professional capacity.[16]

Certain words are defamatory on their face. To falsely identify a person as a communist is libelous per se in Arizona, California, Connecticut, Hawaii, Illinois, Mississippi, New York, Ohio, Pennsylvania, and probably in most other jurisdictions.[17] This has been the case since the Cold War. But when the United States and Russia were allies during World War II, the identification of a person as a communist was not libelous in several cases reported at the time. And if relationships between Russia and the United States continue to improve, as they have under Soviet leader Mikhail Gorbachev's policy of more openness, the sting of being identified falsely as a communist may be removed. Even President Reagan no longer believes that Russia is the "evil empire," as he once said.

To falsely impute criminal conduct, dishonesty, unchastity, immorality, or to make similar characterizations, constitutes libel per se. To falsely write that a person is a homosexual or a lesbian probably is libelous per se in most jurisdictions, although the sting of the words—and therefore their defamatory potential—changes over time and is influenced by place and circumstance. There are, of course, many other words that can be added to the libel per se list—blackmailer, embezzler, swindler, murderer, traitor, leper, and so on.

"Innocent Construction" Rule. When written words are not actionable "on their face," or when their real meaning may be found only by reference to circumstances, it will be up to a jury to determine if the words are libelous. Because of ambiguity, innuendo, allusion, irony, satire, or figure of speech, it may be difficult to determine the true meaning behind them.

For example, the word "fix" has many meanings. When used in connection with a traffic ticket, it could be libelous on its face because of the imputation of crookedness. It could also be construed to mean "void" as to void a parking ticket in a legal manner. This latter meaning would not serve as a basis for a successful libel action.

Innuendo might be illustrated by the use of the word "friend." A plaintiff contended unsuccessfully that the use of such a word was intended to mean, and was understood by the general public to mean, that the plaintiff and a woman—his "friend"—were engaging in an illicit love affair.[18]

Just how should potentially damaging words be interpreted, and by whom? The rules vary.

Many jurisdictions adhere to what is called the "innocent construction" rule; that is, if language is capable of innocent construction, then it is nondefamatory[19]

In New York and California, as in most states, the words alleged to be defamatory must be given their natural meaning and courts are not to strain to interpret them in their mildest and most inoffensive form. In Hawaii, as elsewhere, the state supreme court has said that if the defamatory words are susceptible of both an innocent and a defamatory meaning, a jury should determine the sense in which the words are understood.[20]

Defamation, Publication, Identification, Negligence or Greater Fault, Actual Injury, Lack of Privilege

Printed words that are false and defamatory are libelous, but for a private person (unlike a public official or public figure (see Chapter 6)) to succeed with a defamation lawsuit, five other elements also are necessary. Let's look at these elements:

Defamation and falsity. the printed statement must be false and defamatory (not all false statements are defamatory). Falsity is always associated with the element of defamation because all states permit the defense of truth to libel or slander actions, a defense which will be examined shortly. Thus, to defame someone is to injure that person's reputation by calumny, by lying.

Publication. In civil libel law, "publication" means communication of the defamatory matter to a third person. In this regard every republication of a libel becomes a separate libel on the theory that each tale-bearer is as blameworthy as the tale-maker. And the fact that plaintiff may have ignored an earlier defamatory statement is no defense to an action provided the statute of limitations (explained later) has not run out.

A case involving the *Alton* (Illinois) *Telegraph* emphasizes the fact that the word "publication" goes beyond the usual meaning of that word. The newspaper was hit with a $9.2 million judgment even though it never published a word pertaining to the incident that prompted the lawsuit.

A real estate developer, James Green, his construction company, and other plaintiffs brought libel actions against the newspaper and two of its reporters. The suits arose from a confidential memorandum sent in 1969 to a prosecuting attorney in the U.S. Justice Department by two *Telegraph* reporters asking for help in verifying information about alleged organized crime activities in Alton. The Justice Department never responded to the memorandum and nothing about the matter was ever published in the newspaper, but the Justice Department did contact the Federal Home Loan Bank Board and suggest an investigation by that Board in connection with a loan being requested by Green. One result was that an Alton bank voluntarily adopted certain credit restrictions which led to a denial of future loans to Green and his company. Green contended successfully that the memo resulted in his loss of credit with the local bank and the eventual loss of some building projects. In June 1980 an Illinois Circuit Court jury awarded him and other plaintiffs $6.7 million compensatory and $2.5 million punitive damages.[21] The *Telegraph* appealed, but the Illinois Appellate Court for the Fifth District ruled in 1982 that it lacked jurisdiction.[22] The court pointed out that under a state supreme court rule, an appellant may obtain a stay of enforcement of the judgment by posting an appeal bond with the court, but the *Tele-*

graph was unable to post such a bond because of the size of the judgment against it. It therefore filed a bankruptcy petition "as the sole remaining means of preserving . . . [the newspaper's] assets and business while pursuing its right to appeal."[23]

The *Telegraph* came out of bankruptcy in 1983 after the Bankruptcy Court brought about a settlement of $50,000 with the estate of the last remaining libel plaintiff.[24] Earlier, Green had agreed to settle for $1.4 million, and his company, for one dollar. The money for the settlement came primarily from the newspaper's "umbrella" insurance carriers, which put up $1 million. The newspaper had to borrow the rest.[25]

Theoretically, everyone connected with the publication or distribution of a libel can be sued, including printers and newspaper carriers. In practice, defamation suits usually are limited to those who have played an active or conscious role. Such persons must have been more than innocent "tools." For example, A U.S. District Court ruled in 1975 that the *Washington Post* did not have to independently verify facts in an allegedly defamatory column. For this reason the court granted the newspaper's motion to dismiss the suit against it, but declined to do the same for Jack Anderson whose syndicated "Washington Merry-Go-Round" column had contained the allegedly defamatory items that resulted in the lawsuit.[26]

In addition to the writer of the allegedly defamatory report being named as defendant, the corporate entity and the publisher or station owner usually will be named in the lawsuit under the doctrine of respondeat superior, that is, publishers or station owners are liable for the acts of their employees.[27]

Identification. Another requirement for a successful libel action is "identification." Only an identifiable person can suffer injury to reputation. This does not mean that identification succeeds only when a person's name is used. Partial or incomplete identification may be sufficient to meet this requirement. Thus, if someone wrote a defamatory statement about a 17-year-old redhaired girl who lived on West Fifth Avenue—and identified her in just that way—but the report did not include the girl's name or specific address, this would be sufficient to constitute identification if there were only one such girl residing on West Fifth Avenue. If there were two such girls, both would be libeled. Generally, a person who is not named in the defamatory matter must establish that the publication was defamatory to him or her.[28]

If an individual is a member of a group that has been defamed, the size of the group will determine if the individual can succeed with a defamation suit. The larger the group the less likelihood the individual can meet the requirement of identification. A member of a political party, a race of people, or other large group will not be able to show identification. However, if the words provoke the anger of the group, such that violence is likely, the state might step in and file a criminal libel action (discussed in Chapter 5).

The question remains: How large must the group be before the danger of a successful *civil* lawsuit disappears? Let's examine some cases for the answer.

A member of the 1956 championship Oklahoma University football team successfully sued the publishers of *True* magazine for $75,000 in actual damages following publication of an article, "The Pill That Can Kill Sports." In that article, *True* had implied that the team had used a stimulative drug. Although unidentified in the article, the plaintiff sued. The Oklahoma Supreme Court, in *Fawcett Publications v. Morris,* affirmed the trial court's directed verdict for the plaintiff and, in so doing, said that the article libeled every member of the 60-man team, even though they, like the plaintiff, had not been individually identified.[29]

In a 1975 case, *Webb v. Sessions,* a Texas Court of Civil Appeals affirmed summary judgment for the defendant *Dallas Morning News* which had published these words: "Special Prosecutor Whitley Sessions described petty thievery as 'a way of life' in the Dallas County Sheriff's Office. . . ." The appellate court said a group or class of 740 persons (the number employed in the sheriff's office at that time) was too large for any member thereof to recover for defamation.[30]

In *Arcand v. Evening Call Publishing Co.* (1977), the First Circuit U.S. Court of Appeals ruled that a defamatory statement aimed at only one unidentified member of a 21-member police force did not give rise to a cause of action for libel on behalf of all members of the police force. To predicate liability "to all members of a group on such an associational attitude would chill communication to the marrow," said the court.[31]

In 1980, a U.S. District Court judge in Michigan dismissed a $300 million libel and slander lawsuit against CBS brought by Michigan United Conservation Clubs. The lawsuit stemmed from a CBS News documentary, "The Guns of Autumn," telecast on September 5, 1975. The lawsuit claimed that about a million Michigan hunters were held up to ridicule by the documentary. The judge ruled that there were too many hunters for the plaintiffs to be able to prove that the telecast referred to them individually.

The exact size of the group or class at which defamatory matter ceases to "point" to a specific individual is both conjectural and uncertain. There remains an element of risk until the group becomes large. Generally, the smaller the group, the greater the risk of identification. But even with smaller groups, as California courts have noted, the publication must defame an ascertainable person and apply with certainty to that person.[32]

Negligence or Greater Fault. The U.S. Supreme Court, in a 1974 decision in *Gertz v. Robert Welch, Inc.* (a case reviewed in Chapter 6), declared that a state cannot impose liability on a media defendant if there's been no fault on the part of the media defendant.[33] Negligence, however, can constitute that fault, as most state supreme courts have declared since the *Gertz* ruling.

Actual Injury. In *Gertz,* the Supreme Court also stipulated that in private person defamation lawsuits against public news media, the state can permit recovery only for "actual injury," which includes not only out-of-pocket losses, but also impairment of reputation and standing in the community, mental anguish and suffering, or personal humiliation.

Gertz drastically altered the law of defamation by doing away with one of the underlying principles of common law; namely, the presumption of injury to reputation upon a showing of defamation per se. As a result of *Gertz,* damages may not be recovered, absent a showing of actual malice on the part of a media defendant (a concept explained in the next chapter), unless there is proof of actual injury.

The *Gertz*-imposed change in defamation law blocks the giving of "gratuitous awards of money damages far in excess of any actual injury"—awards which would have the effect of chilling First Amendment freedoms.[34] As the Supreme Court stated:

> The largely uncontrolled discretion of juries to award damages where there is no loss unnecessarily compounds the potential of any system of liability for defamatory falsehood to inhibit the vigorous exercise of First Amendment freedoms. Additionally, the doctrine of presumed damages invites juries to punish unpopular opinion rather than to compensate individuals for injury sustained by the publication of a false fact.[35]

Lack of Privilege. The sixth element necessary to a successul libel action by a private person is lack of privilege on the part of the news media to publish something that is defamatory about an identifiable person. As will be shown later, the news media have a qualified privilege to publish fair and accurate reports about public and official governmental proceedings—for instance, about the legislature or the judiciary—which, though defamatory, nonetheless are protected under law. The qualification is that the reports must be fair and accurate.

If a person is defamed, for example, by a legislator on the floor of Congress or in a statehouse official proceeding, and the news media fairly and accurately report what the legislator said, the defamed party cannot successfully sue the news media.

The reason for allowing such privileges, both for the legislator and for the news media, is to facilitate the flow of information to the public even at the risk of an innocent person's good name being injured. The privilege may flow out of the federal or state constitutions, statutory law, or common law.

Defamatory Headlines

The general rule is that the headline and the story, or the entire broadcast news item, must be considered as one unit in determining whether the words complained of are defamatory. This was the rule in a South Carolina case when a headline erroneously reported a woman's death, although the last paragraph of the story stated that the woman was in serious condition.[36] However, there are exceptions to the rule.

The West Virginia Supreme Court of Appeals had this to say in *Sprouse v. Clay Communications, Inc.:*

> Generally where the headline is of normal size and does not lead to a conclusion totally unsupported in the body of the story, both headline and story should be considered together for their total impression. However, where oversized headlines are

published which reasonably lead the average reader to an entirely different conclusion than the facts recited in the body of the story, and where the plaintiff can demonstrate that it was the intent of the publisher to use such misleading headlines to create a false impression on the normal reader, the headlines may be considered separately with regard to whether a known falsehood was published.[37]

Concerning broadcasting, the general rule is that the broadcast should be considered as a whole in determining whether it would convey to an ordinary listener a defamatory meaning.[38]

Corporation Libel

A corporation or business, like an individual, may recover damages for loss of business or credit caused by a libel. To allege, for example, that a restaurant is a rendezvous for illegal traffickers in drugs is defamatory per se and the owners may bring suit.

Financial institutions, such as banks, generally fall into a special category insofar as false reports are concerned because of the fear of undermining public confidence in them. Such reports usually are dealt with under a state's criminal law. For example, Section 528.89 of the Iowa Code states:

> Whoever maliciously or with intent to deceive makes, publishes, utters, repeats, or circulates any false report concerning any bank or trust company which imputes, or tends to impute, insolvency or unsound financial condition or financial embarrassment, . . . shall be guilty of a felony and shall be fined not more than $5,000 or imprisonment not more than five years in the penitentiary or by punishment by both such fine and imprisonment.

Trade, Property Libel

Laws exist to protect against disparagement of products and property. In some jurisdictions, such laws are called "slander of goods" or "slander of title."

In suits for disparagement, plaintiffs must show actual or implied malice and special damages. In a classic case, a manufacturer brought suit when the usefulness of battery additives was questioned, but he was unable to show special damages and therefore could not collect any damages.[39] An important distinction should be emphasized. A product can be disparaged, even to the point of saying that it is worthless, and such disparagement would not constitute a libel of the manufacturer. However, a communicator must be on guard not to defame a manufacturer when embarking on criticism of the manufacturer's product(s).

Defenses to Libel Lawsuits

The news media publish or broadcast stories every day that are defamatory but which do not result in libel actions, let alone successful ones. The reason lies in the defenses traditionally permitted by all states — truth, qualified privilege, and fair comment and criticism.

Truth

Truth, also called justification, is a complete defense, but in more than half the states there is an additional requirement: truth with good motives and for justifiable ends.

This defense goes back to the John Peter Zenger trial in 1735 and to the *Croswell* case in 1804 in which Alexander Hamilton and Judge Kent argued for a defense of truth with good motives and for justifiable ends. New York subsequently amended its constitution to allow such a defense. Other jurisdictions that permit a similar defense are

Alaska	Hawaii	Kansas
Arizona	Idaho	Louisiana
California	Illinois	Massachusetts
Florida	Iowa	Michigan
Minnesota	Ohio	Utah
Mississippi	Oklahoma	Washington
Montana	Oregon	Wisconsin
Nevada	Rhode Island	Wyoming
New Jersey	South Dakota	District of Columbia
North Dakota		

Truth alone is a complete defense in Colorado, Indiana, Missouri, Nebraska, New Mexico, North Carolina, South Carolina, and Vermont.

Alabama, Delaware, Kentucky, Maine, New Hampshire, Pennsylvania, Tennessee, and Texas allow the defense of truth more readily when official conduct of public officials is involved.

The states of Arkansas, Georgia, Maryland, and Virginia have constitutional or statutory provisions under which truth may be introduced, but whether this is a complete defense is unclear. West Virginia has no authority on this point.[40]

Prior to a U.S. Supreme Court decision in 1986, the burden of proving truth fell upon the defendant media whenever they were sued by private individuals. The truth had to be provable in court. Hearsay would not do. Generally, it was not necessary to prove that every word was true because minor inaccuracies would not destroy the defense. For example, in Wisconsin the statement only had to be "substantially true."[41] In Illinois, just the "gist or the sting of the defamatory imputation" had to be shown as true.[42]

But the Supreme Court, in *Philadelphia Newspapers v. Hepps* (1986) (discussed in Chapter 6) shifted the burden when it ruled that private persons had to show that the libelous statments were false. Since 1964 public officials have had to show that libelous statements were knowingly false or in reckless disregard of the truth, and public figures have had to do the same since 1967. The cases that brought about these changes are discussed in the next chapter.

Absolute Privilege

Absolute privilege is conferred by statute, constitution, or by judicial interpretation on certain public officials and on some kinds of public documents or records. The theory behind such immunity was spelled out by the U.S. Supreme Court in a 5–4 decision in *Barr v. Matteo*.[43] The rule laid down in that 1959 case was that executive branch officers of the federal government, when acting within the scope of their discretionary duties, were absolutely protected from libel and slander suits. Such a privilege, said the Court majority, shields responsible government officers "against the harassment and inevitable hazards of vindictive or ill-founded damage suits brought on account of action taken in the exercise of their official responsibilities. Among the dissenters was Chief Justice Warren who did so partly on the ground that the privilege should be restricted to Cabinet-rank officers or possibly to those appointed by, and therefore responsible to, the President.

The sweeping nature of *Barr* was placed in doubt by lower court decisions and the mustering of only a bare majority of the Supreme Court justices. Then in 1978 the Court, again by a 5–4 vote, virtually eliminated absolute immunity for federal executive officers in connection with their official duties. In *Butz v. Economou,* the Court ruled that top federal executive officers, perhaps even including the President, have no absolute immunity from being sued if they *deliberately* violate a citizen's constitutional rights.[44] Instead, they have a qualified immunity which shields them if they act in "good faith" and on "reasonable grounds."

Justice White wrote the Court's opinion and said that the extension of absolute immunity to all federal executive officers "would seriously erode the protection provided by basic constitutional guarantees." Justices Brennan, Marshall, Blackmun, and Powell agreed. The dissenters, joining Justice Rehnquist's opinion, said the ruling has the potential for "disruption of government" and that it virtually strips federal officials of any immunity in carrying out their duties. In citing a steady increase in lawsuits against federal officials, Rehnquist said, "It simply defies logic and common experience to suggest that officials will not have this in the back of their minds when considering what official course to pursue." They will become timid.

The majority pointed out that absolute immunity protects officials whose special functions require it, such as administrative law judges, hearing examiners, and agency attorneys who present evidence at hearings.

Absolute Immunity for Judges. Three months prior to its decision in *Butz,* the Court, by a 6–3 vote, upheld the doctrine of judicial immunity from civil actions. In *Stump v. Sparkman,*[45] the majority cited an 1872 case in which it was held that "judges of courts of general jurisdiction are not liable to civil action for their judicial acts, even when such acts are in excess of their jurisdiction, and are alleged to have been done maliciously or corruptly."[46]

Immunity for Legislators. The Court in 1979 held that a U.S. Congress member's newsletters and press releases fall outside the immunity afforded by the

Speech and Debate Clause of the Constitution (Article I, Section 6). This constitutional provision absolutely protects members of Congress while carrying out their official duties on the floor of Congress or in committees. Whether the immunity extends to everything a congressman says or does was partially answered in the *Hutchinson v. Proxmire* decision.[47] Chief Justice Burger gave the opinion of the Court which reversed a Seventh Circuit U.S. Court of Appeals' panel ruling that Senator William Proximire's press release and newsletter were part of the "informing function" of Congress and therefore protected by the Speech and Debate Clause.

With only full dissent by Justice Brennan and partial dissent by Stewart, Burger stated the Court's view by reaffirming the principle in *Doe v. McMillan* (1973), namely:

> A member of Congress may not with impunity publish a libel from the speaker's stand in his home district, and clearly the Speech and Debate Clause would not protect such an act even though the libel was read from an official committee report. The reason is that republishing a libel under such circumstances is not an essential part of the legislative process and is not part of that deliberate process "by which Members participate in committee and house proceedings."[48]

Neither the newsletter nor the press release was essential to the deliberations of the Senate and neither was part of the deliberative process (such as committee hearings held in the capitol or elsewhere), said the Chief Justice.

The *Hutchinson* case began with Proxmire's award of a "Golden Fleece" to the federal agency that sponsored research by Dr. Ronald Hutchinson, a research behavioral scientist at Kalamazoo, Michigan, to determine, according to Proxmire, why rats, monkeys, and humans bite and clench their jaws. The senator had begun his much publicized Golden Fleece "awards" in 1975 — awards that mocked what Proxmire believed were examples of ridiculous or excessive spending by the federal government.

In a speech, he ridiculed the grant to Hutchinson — a speech published in the *Congressional Record*. Since the speech in Congress and its publication in the *Record* were privileged, no successful lawsuit could have resulted. But Proxmire referred to the award in newsletters and in a television interview.

The Court remanded the case for further proceedings and ultimately the senator paid Hutchinson $10,000 in an out-of-court settlement and billed taxpayers for his $124,351 in legal costs.

In a more recent case, *Sundquist v. Chastain* (1987), the U.S. Court of Appeals for the District of Columbia Circuit ruled that a congressman's letter to the executive branch was not protected by the Speech and Debate Clause in the Constitution.[49] The Circuit Court panel decided that Congressman Sundquist (Republican-Tennessee) was not immuned from a libel suit that resulted from a 1985 letter sent by Sundquist on official stationery to the then attorney general, William French Smith. The letter made some accusations against a Memphis attorney who had defended indigent parents jailed for failure to make court-ordered child-support payments.

Under the Speech and Debate Clause, said the Circuit Court panel, tort immunity for members of Congress extends only to the "requirements of their legislative responsibilities."

A coalition of media organizations supported Sundquist's assertion of a qualified privilege. In an amicus brief filed with the U.S. Supreme Court, the group had said that if the decision were allowed to stand, the press would lose an important source of commentary on issues of public concern, since lack of immunity would discourage members of Congress from communicating their views to the press and to their constituents, until their risk of liability had been assessed.[50] Further, the press relies substantially on members of Congress and their staffs for insights into the operations of government, and the "muffling — even slightly — of this vital source of information deprives the electorate and the press of information about the way government functions and the ways its elected and appointed officials operate."[51]

The U.S. Supreme Court denied certiorari.[52]

Qualified Privilege

What is the significance of absolute privilege to journalists? If a journalist gives a "fair" and "accurate" report of something that is absolutely privileged — "fair, accurate, and nonmalicious" being the qualifying requirements — then the journalist cannot be successfully sued even if the absolutely privileged report is defamatory. What this means is that a member of Congress might make a defamatory statement about someone during a speech on the floor of Congress or during a committee hearing, or a witness at a trial might make such a statement which, if published in a newspaper or broadcast, would be libelous per se. But if the journalist gives a fair and accurate report of what was said, then the report is protected against defamation suits.

In Illinois, as in many other states, the privilege exists to report government proceedings provded that any such report (1) is accurate and complete, or a fair abridgement of the proceeding, and (2) is not the result of malice (that is, made soley for the purpose of causing harm to the person defamed).[53] Also, any mistake in the report must be the result of the official proceeding rather than the reporter's interpretation or carelessness.

The presence of malice may offset the privilege. "Malice" often is defined as publishing a report solely for the purpose of causing harm to the person defamed. But the Kansas Supreme Court has defined a qualifiedly privileged publication as one made without actual malice.[54] "Actual malice" is defined by the Kansas Court as publication of a defamatory statement with knowledge that the statement is false or with reckless disregard of whether it is false or not.

In California, the state's Civil Code, Section 47, subdivision 4, has been interpreted as providing an absolute privilege to publish or broadcast a fair and true report of judicial, legislative, or other public official proceedings, or of anything said in the course thereof.[55] As a California appellate court stated in 1984, the privilege is "an absolute one ever since the Legislature in 1945 deleted the qualifying requirement that such privileged publications be made 'without malice.' "[56]

Note that the privilege in California is accorded to reports of *public* proceedings. But in a diversity action (a citizen of one state suing a publication in another state), the Second Circuit U.S. Court of Appeals held that Callifornia's Civil Code Section 47(4) applies to reports concerning *secret* grand jury proceedings.[57] In 1956 New York amended its privilege statute to delete the word "public," so that even news media reports of secret proceedings are protected in that state.

The qualified privilege defense generally is not available to the news media if they report on records or proceedings which are required by law to be kept sealed or secret. Proceedings or documents relating to juvenile delinquents, the identity of rape victims, grand jury proceedings, or morality cases might by law be closed or sealed to the public. Therefore any report of such incidents generally would not be qualifiedly privileged. Pleadings filed by attorneys with the clerk of court are privileged in some states (e.g., California, George, Kentucky, Nevada, New York, Ohio, Pennsylvania, South Carolina, Washington, Wyoming, and the District of Columbia), but not privileged in others because they are mere allegations at that stage of litigation. As such, the allegations may never reach the trial stage because the lawsuit could be dropped.

Must Reporter Personally Check Records?. Journalists often rely on public officials, such as police or prosecutors, to provide the gist of information contained in public records (warrants for arrest, indictments, etc.). Ideally, journalists should examine these public documents, but realistically, they often lack the time. Hence, they depend on someone else to provide such information. As long as both parties supply information accurately and fairly there is no problem. But the South Carolina Supreme Court ruled, in a 3–2 decision, that reporters must check public records themselves to make sure the information is correct.[58] The court reinstated a $35,000 judgment for a man who said a newspaper story erroneously reported he had pleaded guilty to a charge of pirating recording tapes.

The newspaper, the *Myrtle Beach Sun News,* had claimed a common-law privilege to publish information obtained from a public official and that only a showing of actual malice could overcome the privilege. Furthermore, said the newspaper, it was customary procedure for out-of-town newspapers to telephone the U.S. attorney's office for information about criminal proceedings in federal courts. In this instance, the public records were more than 70 miles away!

A jury had awarded the plaintiff $35,000 in damages, but the trial judge overturned the verdict on the ground that there was insufficient evidence to find the newspaper at fault. The Supreme Court, however, said there was sufficient evidence to conclude that the article resulted from incorrect reporting, not misinformation. According to the court, the reporter's failure to check the public records himself departed from accepted journalistic standards.

Because a jury could have found that the reporter inaccurately recorded the information given by the prosecutor, the privilege to report on judicial proceedings is no justification for setting aside the verdict, said the court. The news media are not privileged to report inaccurately. The court also noted that no deadline pressure was involved because the story was not published until six days after pleas were entered by two defendants.

Commenting on the decision, a lawyer for the North Carolina Press Association called it "alarming." To what extent can a journalist rely on public officials for information from public records or judicial proceedings, he asked. "Examine the judicial records or suffer the consequences," he concluded.[59]

Crime Reporting. From a legal standpoint, one of the most dangerous areas of journalism is crime reporting. Reports about identifiable people involved in crime are libelous per se. Prior to 1964, a newspaper often had to rely on qualified privilege if a lawsuit developed. But who or what is privileged on the police beat? The answers are not always easy to come by, hence the need on appropriate occasions to consult with company attorneys.

Warrants for arrest, indictments, and official documents of that type are absolutely privileged. The press has a qualified privilege to report such information. But what about a statement from a public information officer in the police department? The legal status of such a statement is not always clear. Some states, such as Georgia and New Jersey, have laws providing that official statements by police department heads are privileged. Some states extend the privilege to statements made by law enforcement officers in connection with preliminary investigations. In Louisiana, courts have held that the news media were not at fault, and hence not liable, when they relied on information furnished by police public relations officials. In two such cases, these officials falsely reported that an identifiable person had been arrested.[60] The false information was duly published, but the newspapers were held not to be liable.

In Maryland, the Court of Special Appeals ruled in 1984 that a newspaper column item was privileged even though it mistakenly reported that a man was arrested for forgery when in fact he was the victim of forgery.[61] The court said the item was based on an official police department press release that had confused the names of victim and arrestee. However, the court added this warning note:

> We take significant notice of the fact that in this case we are not dealing with some unofficial version of events furnished by a policeman at a crime scene, with some unattributed "leak" or offhand prediction, with some characterization or interpretation of events by a prosecutor in a courtroom corridor, but rather with the authorized release of important information through an established and official channel.[62]

The journalistic rule that emerges from the above cases and situations is that press reports are privileged if they fairly and accurately report information of official action provided by authorized government officials or public records, even if that information is incorrect. It may not be necessary to identify the official source,[63] but doing so is advisable. Although the South Carolina Supreme Court's decision in the *Myrtle Beach Sun News* case seems at odds with this "rule," it should be pointed out that the court believed the inaccuracy resulted from incorrect reporting, not from misinformation provided by an official or authorized source (U.S. attorney's office).

Police blotters or daily logs are absolutely privileged in some states, but most states do not accord such protection to this type of record, reserving it instead for warrants of arrest. Therefore, it may be dangerous to rely on the "blotter" or daily log, although many police reporters do so without bothering to verify the information, say, against a warrant.

Court Reporting. The official proceedings and documents pertaining to public court sessions or records are absolutely privileged. Testimony stricken from the record is not accorded such a privilege.

In *Cox Broadcasting Inc. v. Cohn* (1975), the U.S. Supreme Court ruled that a state—in this case Georgia—could not impose sanctions on the press for publishing information released to the public in official court records open to public inspection.[64] At issue was the publicizing of a rape victim's name in defiance of a state law (see Chapter 7).

Because there are gray areas in knowing if statements or actions of federal, state, and local executive officers are absolutely privileged, or when legislators at various levels of government shed the protective umbrella of absolute immunity, the news media often are compelled to consult attorneys for opinions or to rely on other defenses in the event of lawsuits.

Fair Comment and Criticism

Another defense permitted under state law is fair comment and criticism. It is intended to encourage news media to report and comment on matters of public interest, but the difficulty of using such a defense stems from its inexactness. What is fair comment? When does comment go beyond fairness? What is in the public interest?

Addie Cherry v. Des Moines Leader. A famous case involving such a defense occurred in 1901 when a trio of entertainers, known as the Cherry sisters, filed a libel action against the *Des Moines Leader* which had reprinted a review written by Billy Hamilton of the *Odebolt Chronicle.* Hamilton had written:

> Effie is an old jade of 50 summers, Jessie a frisky filly of 40, and Addie, the flower of the family, a capering monstrosity of 35. Their long skinny arms, equipped with talons at the extremities, swung mechanically, and anon waved frantically at the suffering audience. The mouths of their rancid features opened like caverns and sounds like the wailing of damned souls issued therefrom. They pranced around the stage . . . strange creatures with painted faces and hideous mien. Effie is spavined, Addie is stringhalt and Jessie, the only one who showed her stockings, has legs with calves as classic in their outlines as the curves of a broomhandle.

After viewing the sisters' performance, the Polk County District Court judge directed a verdict for the newspaper. On appeal, the Iowa Supreme Court held:

> . . . [T]he editor of a newspaper has the right, if not the duty, of publishing, for the information of the public, fair and reasonable comments, however severe in terms, upon anything which is made by its owner a subject of public exhibition, as upon any other *matter of public interest,* and such publication falls within the class of privileged communication for which no action will lie without proof of *actual malice* (personal spite or ill will or culpable recklessness or negligence). Surely, if one makes himself ridiculous in his public appearances, he may be ridiculed by those whose duty or right it is to inform the public regarding the character of the performance. . . .[65] [Italics added.]

The italicized language anticipated by many years key words that would be used by the U.S. Supreme Court to strengthen press freedom against libel lawsuits.

The defense of fair comment and criticism is a way of balancing the competing interests between a democratic society that values freedom of discussion and a person's right to his or her good name and reputation. Fair comment and criticism is derived from the common law and represents a qualified privilege; that is, the publication or broadcast complained of is not actionable, according to Illinois courts, if: (1) it is an opinion; (2) it relates not to an individual but to his acts; (3) it is fair in the sense that the reader can see a factual basis for comment and draw his own conclusion; and (4) it relates to a matter of public interest.[66] Most jurisdictions also would add the condition that the comments be reasonable, as in the Cherry sisters case. Also, most courts require that the comments represent the actual opinion of the communicator and not be made for the sole purpose of causing harm to another (common-law "malice").[67] Furthermore, the underlying facts which give rise to the opinion must either be true as stated or generally known to be true. Generally, if the facts are set forth and the comment follows, such comment is characterized as pure opinion (see Chapter 6 for "pure opinion" privilege). However, where the opinion implies the existence of unstated facts, the result may be a mixed opinion, and the determination of a "mixed opinion" as privileged or not ordinarily is a question of law (to be resolved by a judge, not a jury). Whether the subject is a matter of public interest also is a question of law. Should a judge decide that a publication is not a matter of public interest (in some jurisdictions, *legitimate* public interest is the requirement), then the media defendant's only defense is truth. Should the contrary judgment be made, then the plaintiff can defeat the privilege by a showing of malice, that the defendant did not believe in the truth of the criticism, or (in some jurisdictions) that the criticism was unreasonable.

Clearly, there are problems with using the defense of fair comment and criticism. They include: (1) the danger of intruding into a person's private life by means of criticism which goes beyond comment on something that has been offered for public comment; (2) misrepresenting the facts or basing comment on false information; (3) being unreasonably intemperate or vehement in the criticism; and (4) commenting on something that is not a matter of public interest (whether legitimate or not). Also, criticism which imputes dishonest, corrupt, or criminal motives generally is not privileged.

For these reasons, the common-law defense of fair comment and criticism is an uncertain one, but developments since 1964 have taken away much of the need for using this defense. These developments, which are reviewed in the next two chapters, led to the extension of First Amendment protection to pure opinion without all of the qualifications required by the common-law defense of fair comment and criticism.

Damages

If the media are unsuccessful in defending against lawsuits, three kinds of damages can be awarded:

1. General or compensatory. Damage for the loss of reputation, shame, or hurt feelings. Under common law, no proof of damage is necessary once the fact of the defamation is established. In other words, damage is presumed. There is an obvious difficulty in connection with this kind of damage award: How much is a person's good name worth? What kind of price tag attaches to shame and embarrassment?

2. *Special.* Tangible damage, such as loss of job, clientele, or business. The California Civil Code, Section 48(a), subsection 4(b), defines it as "all damages which plaintiff alleges and proves that he has suffered in respect to his property, business, trade, profession or occupation, including such amounts of money as the plaintiff alleges and proves he has expended as a result of the alleged libel. . . ."

3. *Punitive or exemplary.* Damage for gross carelessness or malice. California Code, Section 48(a), subsection 4(d), says exemplary damages "are damages which may in the discretion of the court or jury be recovered in addition to general and special damages for the sake of example and by way of punishing a defendant who has made the publication or broadcast with actual malice. . . ."

As an Illinois appellate court explained it, the two purposes of punitive damages are: (1) to punish for prior conduct and prevent future misconduct, and (2) to proportion the punitive or deterrent aspect of exemplary damages to the means of the offender. In this latter connection, evidence of the defendant's net worth may be relevant and admissible as it relates to the issue of punitive damages. The jury, said the court, would need this information to assess an award which would adequately punish a defendant.[68]

Because punitive damages can constitute the largest monetary award to successful libel plaintiffs, and because such large awards are likely to have a chilling effect on First Amendment freedoms, a number of states have taken steps to reduce or eliminate such awards. Massachusetts has long forbidden such awards. And a New Hampshire statute prohibits these awards unless otherwise provided by law. That state's libel law does not specifically provide for punitive damages.

Georgia's law prohibits the recovery of punitive damages by a libel plaintiff if the defendant can show that the challenged statement was published without malice, was conspicuously corrected within seven days of the plaintiff's written demand, or the challenged information was repudiated in an editorial. A plaintiff who does not request a retraction cannot collect punitive damages.

In Florida, a plaintiff cannot ask punitive damages without making a preliminary showing that they are deserved. In addition, the plaintiff must prove that the defendant's actions were wanton, willful, or gross, and the total amount of punitive damages that can be awarded may not exceed three times the award of compensatory damages.

An Oklahoma statute requires that before a case goes to the jury, a trial judge must determine whether the evidence clearly and convincingly shows that the defendant is guilty of reckless or wanton misconduct, fraud, or malice. If so, the jury then may award punitive damages in any amount. If not, then punitive damages are limited to an amount equal to the compensatory damages awarded.

Alaska's law restricts the award of punitive damages to civil actions where the evidence clearly and convincingly supports such an award.

Minnesota allows a plaintiff to ask for punitive damages only after proving at a formal hearing a clear factual basis for the request. But the law does not place a limit on the amount of punitive damages that can be awarded.

Under New York law, damages fall into two categories, compensatory and punitive. Under compensatory are three subcategories: nominal, general, and special damages. The law presumes some damage to reputation from the defamation, but the award can be nominal. Thus in some widely publicized libel cases, nominal damages of $1 have been awarded.

Reynolds v. Pegler. One of the more noteworthy cases involved two widely known journalists, Hearst columnist Westbrook Pegler and columnist-war correspondent Quentin Reynolds. Pegler's attack upon Reynolds followed the death of Reynolds' long-time friend and fellow journalist, Heywood Broun, who had been the principal organizer of the Newspaper Guild for editorial workers in the 1930s. In a column published on November 29, 1949, Pegler wrote that Reynolds, while riding to the graveside services for Broun, proposed marriage to Broun's widow, that Reynolds was a war profiteer, a "four-flusher" with an "artificial reputation as a brave war correspondent in the London blitz", and that he was one of the "'let's you and him fight' school of heroes. . . ."[69] The U.S. Court of Appeals affirmed the award to Reynolds of $1 nominal damages, plus $100,000 in punitive damages against Pegler personally, $50,000 against the Hearst Corporation, and $25,000 against a newspaper which published the column.

Goldwater v. Ginzburg. In another libel case of unusual interest, U.S. Senator Barry Goldwater successfully sued Ralph Ginzburg and his magazine, *Fact,* for publication of defamatory matter in a special issue of the magazine just before the 1964 presidential election entitled "The Unconscious of a Conservative: A Special Issue on the Mind of Barry Goldwater." The thrust of the two main articles about the 1964 Republican party presidential nominee, according to a summation of the articles by Justice Black in a dissenting opinion, was that Goldwater "had a severely paranoid personality and was psychologically unfit for the high office to which he aspired."[70] The articles, continued Black, "attempted to support the thesis that Senator Goldwater was mentally ill by citing allegedly factual incidents from his public and private life and by reporting the results of a 'poll' of 12,356 psychiatrists. . . ."

Such reckless falsity was punished by an award of $1 in compensatory damage, $25,000 in punitive damages against Ginzburg, and $50,000 in punitive damages against the magazine.

Retraction Statutes

One way to lessen the danger of an award of punitive damages is to print a retraction or correction if a mistake is made. In some states — and California law is very favorable in this regard — publication of a retraction will prevent recovery of all but special damages (and special damages may be hard to prove). A retraction honestly given shows that there was no malice on the part of publication. Evidence of such retraction also becomes a partial or compete defense to punitive damages in Georgia, Maine, Massachusetts, Texas, Virginia, and West Virginia. In 18 states plaintiff may receive general and special but not punitive damages if a full and fair retraction is published upon notice by the plaintiff of the allegedly defamatory statement, provided there is no malice in fact on the part of the publisher. The states include:

Alabama	Kentucky	North Dakota
Connecticut	Michigan	Oklahoma
Florida	Mississippi	South Dakota
Georgia	Montana	Tennessee
Indiana	New Jersey	Utah
Iowa	North Carolina	Wisconsin

In Minnesota and Oregon, publishers are relieved of all but special damages if they print a full and fair retraction in as conspicuous a place as the original charge. In California, Nebraska, and Nevada, no apology or explanation is required — only a correction of the facts — in order to limit recovery to special damage.[71]

Special retraction or correction statues include:

1. *The California Civil Code* (§ *48a(1)*) requires a plaintiff to serve notice and demand for correction within 20 days after knowledge of publication or broadcast. If such notice and demand are given and if a correction does not follow, then a plaintiff, if successful in the libel action, may recover more than special damages.

2. *The Florida Code (770.02 F.S.A.)* permits recovery of only actual damage (general and/or special) if a "fair correction, apology and retraction" is published within 10 days after the affected media are notified in writing of the error(s). The correction-apology-retraction must be published in the same or corresponding editions of the newspaper or periodical in which the libelous matter appeared, and in as conspicuous a place and comparable type as the allegedly libelous article.

Section 770.01 requires a complainant to give a media organization five days' prior notice for the purpose of allowing an apology or retraction before an action for defamation may commence.

3. *The Iowa Code (§ 659.2)* refers to an "innocent" mistake. If such a mistake is made, the plaintiff can recover no more than actual damage unless a retraction is demanded and refused.
4. *The Wisconsin Statutes (§895.05(2))* provides that a reasonable opportunity (seven days) must be given to allow for a correction, and further:

A correction, timely published, without comment, in a position and type as prominent as the alleged libel, shall constitue a defense against the recovery of any damages except actual damages, as well as being competent and material in mitigation of actual damages to the extent the correction published does so mitigate them.

The constitutionality of retraction statutes has been placed in some uncertainty by the action of courts in Montana, Arizona, Kansas, and Ohio.

The Montana retraction statute imposed a demand for retraction as a prerequisite to a libel action (as do a number of other state retraction laws) and was struck down as unconstitutional by the state supreme court in *Madison v. Yunker* (1978).[72] A $102,000 libel action against the University of Montana student newspaper, the *Montana Kaimin,* which had referred to a university employee as a "congenital liar" and an "incompetent," had been dismissed by the trial court because the plaintiff had failed to comply with the statute by not giving those "alleged to be responsible or liable for the publication a reasonable opportunity to correct the libelous or defamatory matter." The state supreme court said that since the state constitution requires that a remedy be afforded for every injury to character, a retraction requirement is in "direct derogation" of that provision. The legislature is powerless to require otherwise, said the court.

Ohio's 50-year-old retraction law was challenged by the *Akron Beacon Journal* because of a provision which imposed criminal liability on a newspaper that failed to publish a retraction on demand of any person who claimed injury from publication of false information.[73] The Summit County prosecutor supported the challenge even though he was one of the defendants in the newspaper's suit.

The statute directed prosecuting attorneys to investigate any failure to print a retraction, and if it was found that a demand was made but not met, a newspaper became liable for a fine of up to $1000.

The challenge resulted after a demand for a retraction was refused by the *Beacon Journal*. The person then filed a complaint with the Summit County prosecutor. In response, the newspaper asked the county Court of Common Pleas to declare the statute unconstitutional because, according to the paper, it violated the newspaper's First Amendment right to be free of government interference in its editorial policy. The prosecutor, in joining the newspaper's challenge, said the statute was unconstitutional because it exacted a penalty against newspapers which have exercised their constitutional right to determine their own content.[74] In 1984 the common pleas court declared the law unconstitutional and no appeal was made.

Another situation concerning retraction laws is evidenced by the successful lawsuit of actress Carol Burnett against the weekly tabloid, the *National Enquirer*. Burnett sued the tabloid after it published this gossip column item on March 2, 1976.

> In a Washington restaurant, a boisterous Carol Burnett had a loud argument with another diner, Henry Kissinger. Then she traipsed around the place offering everyone a bit of her dessert. But Carol really raised eyebrows when she accidentally knocked a glass of wine over one diner and started giggling instead of apologizing. The guy wasn't amused and "accidently" spilled a glass of water over Carol's dress.

Burnett demanded a retraction and the *Enquirer* published this statement in its gossip column on April 8, 1976: "We understand these events did not occur and we are sorry for any embarrassment our reports may have caused Miss Burnett."

Burnett asked for $10 million in damages, but the tabloid's attorneys sought to invoke the California retraction statute's limitation of awards to special damages. However, the California courts decided that the *Enquirer* was not entitled to such protection because it is more like a magazine than a newspaper and the statute—like those in some other states[75]—is lmited to newspapers and broadcast stations. The reason given for omitting magazines is that they do not print the timely news that readers expect to find in newspapers and, therefore, they cannot be classified as "newspapers." They also have more time to check the accuracy of stories.

The jury awarded the actress $300,000 in compensatory and $1.3 million in punitive damages, but the trial judge reduced these awards to $50,000 and $750,000, respectively. A state appeals court affirmed the judgment, but ordered punitive damages cut to $150,0000 unless Burnett elected to undergo a new trial. She accepted the reduced award.[76]

In 1986 the Arizona Supreme Court struck down as unconstitutional the state's retraction statute that had limited libel plaintiffs to recovery of special damages if an adequate retraction was published. The court, in *Boswell v. Phoenix Newspapers,* said that the state constitution provides that a right of action to recover damages for injury shall not be abrogated.[77] The U.S. Supreme Court denied review.[78]

A statute similar to Arizona's also was invalidated in Kansas,[79] but in Minnesota, North Carolina, North Dakota, and Oregon, retraction statutes were upheld.[80]

Issue of Jurisdiction

The *National Enquirer* also figured prominently in a case involving the issue of jurisdition. Usually the state with the most significant relationship to an alleged libel supplies the substantive law, and that is usually the state where the plaintiff lives (if the libel was published in that state), since that is where the plaintiff is presumed to have been most injured.[81] The distribution of each and every copy of a libelous publication in any or all of the states constitutes a separate tort in each of those states and hypothetically could lead to a multitude of libel lawsuits in whatever states the libelous copies were circulated. To prevent such a burden on the judicial system and to prevent litigation expenses that would flow from such actions, the "single publication" rule has been adopted. As summarized in the *Restatement* (*Second*) *of Torts,* the rule is:

> As to any single publication, (1) only one action for damages can be maintained; (b) all damages suffered in all jurisdictions can be recovered in the one action; and (c) a judgment for or against the plaintiff upon the merits of any action for damages bars any other action for damages between the same parties in all jurisdictions.[82]

In deciding the apropriate forum for the lawsuit, factors other than the plaintiff's domicile are considered, such as: (1) the state where the plaintiff's principal activity takes place to which the alleged defamation relates; (2) the state where the plaintiff in fact suffered greatest harm; (3) the state where the publisher is domiciled or incorporated; (4) the state where the defendant's main publishing office is located' (5) the state of principal circulation; (6) the place where the alleged defamation emanated; (7) the state where the libel was first seen; and (8) the law of the several states which might be applied.[83]

All states have long-arm statutes by means of which they can exert jurisdiction over an out-of-state act which causes injury within the state. For example, a California newspaper publishing a story datelined in Wyoming and reporting organized crime allegedly flourishing there was subject to Wyoming jurisdiction; a New York newspaper was subject to suit in Connecticut for libel against a Connecticut resident; and foreign nationals living in the District of Columbia could sue a New York publisher under the District of Columbia long-arm statute.

The *National Enquirer,* based in Lantanna, Florida, and sold in supermarkets nationwide, carried an article in the October 9, 1979, issue under the headline "Husband's Bizarre Behavior Is Driving Shirley Jones to Drink." The actress, and her husband, Marty Ingels, brought a $20 million lawsuit against the tabloid, its editor, Ian Calder, and a reporter, John South. The tabloid did not contest the jurisdiction of California courts, but Calder and Smith did. They moved to quash the service of process on them on the basis that California lacked jurisdiction. The California Superior Court granted the motion because of the "chilling effect" on the First Amendment rights of reporters and editors if they are required to appear in remote jurisdictions to answer for their work (the reporter having used the telephone in Florida to obtain information from California sources). The California Court of Appeal reversed, stating that California had jurisdiction because the publication and its personnel intended to cause tortious injury in California. The U.S. Supreme Court unanimously affirmed the judgment of the Court of Appeal.[84]

Justice William Rehnquist, in writing the Court's opinion in *Calder v. Jones* (*1984*) made these points:

- Of the *Enquirer's* total weekly circulation of 5,292,200 on September 18, 1979, 604,431 copies were sold in California—twice the number in the state with the next highest circulation (New York, 316,911 copies).
- The Due Process Clause of the Fourteenth Amendment permits personal jurisdiction over a defendant in any state with which the defendant has "certain minimum contacts . . . such that the maintenance of the suit does not offend 'traditional notions of fair play and substantial justice.'"[85]
- The allegedly libelous story concerned the California activities of a California resident. It impugned the professionalism of an entertainer whose career was centered in California. The article was drawn from California sources, and the brunt of the harm, in terms of both the actress' emotional distress and the injury to her professional reputation, was suffered in Callifornia. Jurisdiction over the editor and reporter is therefore proper in California based on the "effects" of their Florida conduct in California. An individual injured in California need not go to Florida to seek redress from persons who, though remaining in Florida, knowingly caused the injury in California.
- The First Amendment does not enter into the jurisdictional analysis because any potential chill on protected First Amendment activity would be taken into account by constitutional limitations on the substantive law governing such suits. Jurisdictional questions involve procedural law.

The lawsuit against the *Enquirer* was settled out of court with the tabloid agreeing to publish a retraction and to pay an undisclosed sum to the actress and her husband.[86] According to Ingels, the agreement gave him and his wife the right to republish the retraction "anywhere and forever." They planned to republish the retraction in several major newspapers in the United States and in two entertainment industry newspapers.

Of the Supreme Court's decision, the director of the Reporters Committee for Freedom of the Press, Jack Landau, said it "forces a reporter to travel across the country to defend himself, to put his own assets on the line."[87] To which Jones' attorney, Paul Ablon, responded:

National publications already are spending lots of money sending reporters to cover stories in distant places. Why shouldn't they spend money to have to defend themselves and those reporters?[88]

In another case decided by the U.S. Supreme Court on the same day that the *Calder* decision was announced, the Court unanimously ruled that the regular circulation of a magazine within New Hampshire is sufficient to support that state's exercise of jurisdiction over a nationally circulated magazine, *Hustler,* by a New York resident. *Hustler,* which at the time sold between 10,000 to 15,000 copies monthly in New Hampshire, is published by an Ohio corporation whose principal place of business is California.

Kathy Keeton, described in court papers as the common-law wife of Penthouse publisher Bob Guccione, filed the diversity action in New Hampshire because it was the only state where the suit would not have been time-barred.[89] New Hampshire has a six-year statute of limitation on the filing of such lawsuits whereas most states place time limits of one, two or three years for the commencement of tort actions after publication.

In giving the Court's opinion in *Keeton v. Hustler Magazine, Inc.,* Justice Rehnquist wrote that *Hustler* has "continuously and deliberately exploited the New Hampshire market," therefore "it must reasonably anticipate being haled into court there in a libel action." New Hampshire has an interest in a nonresident's libel action, said Rehnquist, since "false statements of fact harm both the subject of the falsehood and the readers of the statement." Thus, New Hampshire may employ its libel laws "to discourage the deception of its citizens."[90]

By its action, the Court reversed a decision of the First Circuit U.S. Court of Appeals which had upheld a U.S. District Court ruling that the lawsuit was barred by the Due Process Clause of the Fourteenth Amendment. The First Circuit had ruled that it would be unfair for New Hampshire to assert jurisdiction over *Hustler* since that state would have only minimal interest in awarding damages to a nonresident for injuries that occur largely outside New Hampshire.

In response, Rehnquist wrote that "it is undoubtedly true that the bulk of the harm" done to plaintiff occurred outside New Hampshire. "But that will be true in almost every libel action brought somewhere other than the plaintiff's domicile. There is no justification for restricting libel actions to the plaintiff's home forum."[91]

Statute of Limitations

A statute of limitations imposes a deadline on a plaintiff to bring a tort action within a certain period of time. The time period usually commences with the publication or broadcast of the information in question. In Kathy Keeton's case, she first attempted to bring her libel action in Ohio, but found it barred by the state's statute of limitation. Her invasion of privacy lawsuit against the magazine was dismissed, being barred by New York's statute of limitations. Hence, she turned to New Hampshire for relief.[92]

The purpose of such statutes is to prevent lawsuits long after publication when it would be much more difficult to defend against such lawsuits because of reporters' notes, for example, having been discarded.

Among others, California, Maryland, Mississippi, New Jersey, and Virginia have one-year statutes of limitations; Iowa falls into a group of states having a two-year limitation, and a number of states fix three years as the limitation. New Hampshire is in a class by itself.

"Libel Proof" Persons?

From time to time controversy arises concerning the likelihood of someone becoming "libel proof" by virtue of infamous deeds. The Second Circuit U.S. Court of Appeals said in a 1976 case that the doctrine of "libel proof" defendants is a limited and narrow one, meaning that a person may be libel proof in some respect, but not in others.[93] That same court ruled a year earlier that a prison convict was "so unlikley by virtue of his life as a criminal to be able to recover anything other than nominal damages as to warrant dismissal of the case, involving as it does First Amendment considerations."[94] As a matter of law, the court considered the prisoner to be libel proof. Thus, some people do fall into such a classification for all practical purposes.

Both the Alabama and Massachusetts Supreme Courts have ruled that there are instances when a person becomes libel proof. An habitual criminal falls into that category, said the Alabama court.[95] The Massachusetts court said the legal doctrine that treats some people as libel proof "might apply to an habitual criminal or to a criminal notorious for one criminal act."[96]

Penthouse magazine publisher Robert Guccione had a judgment of $1.6 million in punitive damages against *Hustler* magazine reversed by the Second Circuit U.S. Court of Appeals.[97] The court ruled that a statement accusing Guccione of adultery was substantially true and that Guccione was libel proof with respect to an adultery charge. The court said that it was not tenable to maintain "that Guiccione, though libel-proof as to adultery from 1966 to 1979, somehow succeeded in restoring his reputation during the four years prior to the *Hustler* statement."[98]

The average reader, said the court, "would understand that term (adulterer) to include a man who unabashedly committed adultery for 13 of the last 17 years and whose adulterous behavior ended only because his wife ultimately divorced him."[99]

SUMMARY

Defamation means to spread a bad report about someone. If this is done in writing, it is called libel. If done orally, the defamation is called slander. Libel and slander are rooted in the common law of England and arose from the need to defend good name and reputation without resorting to violence. Slander cases were recorded in feudal courts in the thirteenth century, then were handled by ecclesiastical tribunals, and ultimately the King's Court assumed jurisdiction in the 1500s.

As for libel, the Court of the Star Chamber was the center for criminal prosecutions. The practice of this court in awarding damages to an injured party led to the idea that libel might also be treated as a civil offense.

Until 1964, the law of libel in the United States developed at the state level. Thus, to understand its vagaries, state law had to be studied. This is still necessary, but the application of the First Amendment to state law has had the effect of reducing the danger of honest mistakes, particularly if those mistakes are in stories about public officials or public figures (see Chapter 5).

There are two types of libel — per se and per quod. Libel per se means libel on the face of it; libel per quod requires extrinsic facts or circumstances for the defamation to become apparent.

Six elements are necessary for a successful action by a private person (but not a public official or public figure) in libel per se or slander per se cases; these are: (1) false and defamatory statement; (2) publication; (3) identification; (4) negligence on the part of the media or greater fault; (5) actual injury; and (6) lack of privilege. Generally, the larger the group the greater the difficulty of establishing identification. Ordinarily the headline and story, or the entire broadcast item, are considered in deciding if the report is defamatory.

When a libel or slander action results, the media may use three common-law defenses: truth, qualified privilege, fair comment and criticism. In more than half the states, the defense of truth requires good motives for justifiable ends.

Qualified privilege for journalists means that they must give a fair and accurate — and nonmalicious — report of an official government proceeding or document. Usually the proceeding or document must be public for the privilege to apply.

This qualified or conditional privilege flows most readily out of absolutely privileged situations. In *Butz* (1978), the Supreme Court by a bare majority ruled that top federal executive officers have only a qualified immunity. This immunity shields them when they act in "good faith" and on "reasonable grounds." What this decision does to the press's qualified privilege to report the actions and statements of top federal executives is not entirely clear, but probably very little real loss of protection for the press has occurred.

Given the Court decision against Senator Proxmire and Representative Sundquist — in which a newsletter and a letter to the U.S. attorney general were deemed not to be protected by the Speech and Debate Clause — the probability is that information is less likely to become available to the press and public by such means, but can still be made available through "privileged" channels, such as by speeches on the floor of Congress or through publication in the *Congressional Record*. Similar precautions can be taken by state legislators.

Absolute privilege extends to the official and public proceedings and actions of the judicial and legislative branches, at both the federal and state levels, and probably to most legislative and judicial bodies. But journalists need to inform themselves of the qualified privileges they enjoy in their own state by studying appropriate court decisions and pertinent laws, and by discussions with legal counsel.

Fortunately, from the media standpoint, ascertaining the applicability of the common-law conditional privilege to news media reports no longer is crucial to media defenses under certain circumstances. Developments in constitutional law, resulting in a "conditional constitutional privilege," have helped to lessen the consequences of erroneously assuming that a common-law privilege applies. Chapters 5 and 6 will detail these developments.

If a plaintiff is successful in a libel action, three types of damages may be awarded: general or compensatory, special, and punitive or exemplary. In a number of states, publication of a retraction/correction will limit recovery to actual damages or to special damages.

Retraction statutes vary in length. Some states, like California and New York, have one-year limitations on bringing tort action; most have two- or three-year limitations. New Hampshire's six-year limitation is the longest one. In California, as the *National Enquirer* discovered to its sorrow after Carol Burnett sued the tabloid, magazines are not covered by the retraction law.

In cases involving jurisdiction, the U.S. Supreme Court has taken the position that the Fourteenth Amendment permits jurisdiction over a defendant in any state in which the defendant has certain minimum contacts (*Calder v. Jones* (1984)), and that a defendant who continuously and deliberately exploits a market (e.g., New Hampshire) can expect to be haled into court there (*Keeton v. Hustler Magazine* (1984)). Why? Because a state may use its libel laws not only to redress harm to the subject of the falsehood but also to discourage "the deception of its citizens."

QUESTIONS IN REVIEW

1. Define "libel."
2. There are two kinds of libel. Name them and tell what each one means.
3. Certain conditions must be met by a private person plaintiff before a successful libel action can result. What are the conditions?
4. Name the three common-law defenses to a libel suit permitted in each of the states.
5. Calling a person a communist or accusing a person of criminal conduct or dishonesty would constitute what kind of libel?
6. True or False: There is no clear-cut rule as to whether a headline by itself can result in a successful libel action.
7. True or False: Most likely, an individual in a libeled group numbering about 700 would be unable to establish identification.
8. All states accord journalists a qualified or conditional privilege to report on most official government proceedings. What is the condition or qualification?
9. Certain documents or records are absolutely privileged. Name three.
10. Three kinds of damage can be awarded in libel actions. Name them.
11. Generally, publication of a retraction/correction will preclude the award of what kind of damage?
12. Which case demonstrates that a resident of New York can sue a nationally circulated magazine, owned by an Ohio corporation whose principal place of business is California, in New Hampshire?
13. Why could entertainer Carol Burnett collect punitive damages from the National Enquirer even though the Enquirer published a retraction and the forum state's (California's) retraction law precluded such recovery upon publication of a retraction?

ANSWERS

1. Libel is a printed defamation which injures a person's good name or reputation, which causes that person to be shunned by friends and neighbors, which damages that person in his business, profession, calling, or office, or which attributes to that person

some loathsome disease. (You may have included other elements, too, from the various state libel laws.)

2. Libel per se is libel on the face of it. Libel per quod is libel because of special circumstances or extrinsic facts.
3. Defamation (including falsity), publication, identification, negligence or greater fault, actual injury, and lack of a privilege for the defendant media.
4. Truth, qualified privilege, fair comment/criticism. More than half the states append an additional requirement to the defense of truth: truth with good motives for justifiable ends.
5. Libel per se.
6. True.
7. True
8. That such reports be fair and accurate and that they not result from malice.
9. Your list might have included: warrant for arrest, indictment, Congressional Record, and the record of what happened at a public trial.
10. General or compensatory (for injury to good name and reputation), special (for actual loss, such as loss of job, clientele, etc.), and punitive or exemplary (to punish for carelessness and to warn others not to commit such "sins").
11. Punitive.
12. *Keeton v. Hustler Magazine, Inc.* (1984).
13. Because the *Enquirer* was classified as a magazine and magazines are not included in California's retraction statute.

ENDNOTES

1. As noted in the Vermont Supreme Court's review of the law of defamation in Lent v. Huntoon, 9 *Med.L.Rptr.* 2547, 2549, December 20, 1983.
2. Garren v. Southland Corp., 221 S.E.2d 571 (1976).
3. See, for example, American Broadcasting-Paramount Theatres, Inc. v. Simpson, 126 S.E.2d 873 (1962). For examples of the law of libel being applied to broadcasters, see Summit Hotel Co. v. NBC, 8 A.2d 302 (1939); and Hartman v. Winchell, 296 N.Y. 296, 73 N.E.2d 20 (1947).
4. Kimmerle v. New York Evening Journal, 262 N.Y. 99, 186 N.E. 217 (1933).
5. Maloney & Sons, Inc. v. E.W. Scripps Co., 334 N.E.2d 494, 497 (1974).
6. Farnsworth v. Hyde, 512 P.2d 1003 (1973).
7. Burke v. Triangle Publications, Inc., 302 A.2d 408, 410 (1973).
8. Article 5430, V.A.C.S., Acts 1901.
9. DiMiceli v. Klieger, 206 N.W.2d 184, 186–87(1973).
10. Carson v. Allied News Co., 529 F.2d 206 (7th Circuit, 1976).
11. As noted by Vermont Supreme Court in Lent v. Huntoon, 9 *Med.L.Rptr.* 2547, 2550, December 20, 1983.
12. Ibid.
13. Ibid.
14. Rosanova v. Playboy Enterprises, Inc., 411 F.Supp. 440 (D.C. Ga., 1976).
15. Smith v. Huntington Publishing Co., 410 F.Supp. 1270 (1976).
16. Buckley v. Littell, 394 F.Supp. 918, 941 (S.D.N.Y., 1975).
17. Cahill v. Hawaiian Paradise Park Corp., 543 P.2d 1356 (Hawaii Supreme Court, 1975).
18. Heaphy v. Westchester Rockland Newspapers, Inc., 367 N.Y.S.2d 521 (Supreme Court, Appellate Division, 1975).
19. Smith v. Huntington Publishing Co., op. cit., note 15; and Kilbane v. Sabonjian, 347 N.E.2d 757 (Illinois Appellate Court, 1976).
20. Cahill v. Hawaiian Paradise Park Corp., op. cit., note 17.

21. Green v. Alton (Ill.) Telegraph, 8 *Med.L.Rptr.* 1345, May 4, 1982.
22. Ibid.
23. Ibid., at 1350.
24. *Editor & Publisher,* September 10, 1983, p. 17.
25. *Editor & Publisher,* June 19, 1982, p. 16.
26. Carey v. Hume, 390 F.Supp. 1026 (District of Columbia, 1975).
27. Sprouse v. Clay Communications, Inc., 211 S.E.2d 674, 690 (West Virginia Supreme Court of Appeals, 1975).
28. Colucci v. Chicago Crime Commission, 334 N.E.2d 461 (Illinois Appellate Court, 1975).
29. Fawcett Publications, Inc. v. Morris, 377 P.2d 42 (1962); cert. denied, 376 U.S. 512 (1963).
30. Webb v. Sessions, 531 S.W.2d 211.
31. "News Notes," *Media Law Reporter,* January 31, 1978.
32. Noral v. Hearst Publications, 40 Cal. App. 2d 348, 350, 104 P.2d 860, 862 (1940); Barger v. Playboy Enterprises, 10 *Med.L.Rptr.* 1527, 1528 (9th Circuit U.S. Court of Appeals, 1984).
33. Gertz v. Robert Welch, Inc., 418 U.S. 323, 94 S.Ct. 2997, 41 L.Ed.2d 789 (1974).
34. Ibid., at 349.
35. Ibid.
36. Ross v. Columbia Newspapers, Inc., 221 S.E.2d 770 (South Carolina Supreme Court, 1976).
37. Sprouse v. Clay Publications, Inc., op. cit., note 27, at 686. The Supreme Court declined to review the case.
38. Cahill v. Hawaiian Paradise Park, op. cit., note 17, at 1361.
39. National Dynamics Corp. v. Petersen Publishing Co., 185 F.Supp. 573 (Southern District of New York, 1960).
40. The listing of those states allowing the defense of truth was by the U.S. Supreme Court in Garrison v. State of Louisiana, 95 S.Ct. 209, 214 (n. 7) (1964).
41. DeMiceli v. Klieger, op. cit., note 9.
42. Mitchell v. Peoria Journal-Star, 221 N.E.2d 516 (1966).
43. Barr v. Matteo, 360 U.S. 564, 79 S.Ct. 1335, 3 L.Ed. 1434.
44. Butz v. Economou, 438 U.S. 478, 57 L.Ed.2d 895, 98 S. Ct. 2894 (1978).
45. Stump v. Sparkman, 98 S.Ct. 1099 (1978).
46. Bradley v. Fisher, 12 Wall. 335.
47. Hutchinson v. Proxmire., Supplement to 5 *Med.L.Rptr.* 5, July 3, 1979.
48. Doe v. McMillan, 412 U.S. 306, 314–15.
49. Sunquist v. Chastain, 833 F.2d 311. Judge Abner Mikva dissented.
50. "News Notes," *Media Law Reporter,* June 14, 1988.
51. Ibid.
52. 108 S.Ct. 2914 (1988). Justices White, Blackmun, and O'Connor would have granted certiorari.
53. Colucci v. Chicago Crime Commission, op. cit., note 28, 470–71.
54. Gobin v. Globe Publishing Co., 531 P.2d 76, 79 (1975).
55. Green v. Cortez, 10 *Med.L.Rptr.* 1316 (Court of Appeal, Ist Appellate District, 1984).
56. Ibid., at 1318.
57. Reeves v. ABC, 9 *Med.L.Rptr.* 2289 (2d Circuit, 1983), November 1, 1983.
58. Jones v. Sun Publishing Co., 292 S.E.2d 23, 8 *Med.L.Rptr.* 1388.
59. *The NEWS Media & The LAW,* March 30, 1982, p. 24.
60. Wilson v. Capital City Press, 315 So.2d 393 (3rd Circuit Court of Appeal, 1975), and LeBoeuf v. Times Picayune Publishing Corp., 327 So.2d 430 (4th Circuit Court of Appeal, 1976).
61. Steer v. Lexleon, 10 *Med.L.Rptr.* 1582, May 8, 1984.
62. Ibid., at 1584.
63. See, e.g., D'Alfonso v. A.S. Abell Company (District Court, Maryland), 10 *Med.L.Rptr.* 1663, May 22, 1984.
64. Cox Broadcasting v. Cohn, 95 S.Ct. 1029. Justice Rehnquist dissented on jurisdictional grounds.
65. Addie Cherry v. Des Moines Leader, 114 Iowa 298, 299–300, 304.
66. These four elements constitute the common-law defense in Illinois, as stated in Farnsworth v. Tribune Co., 43 Ill. 2d 286 (1969).
67. See *Restatement (Second) of Torts,* §606(1)(b)(c).

68. Fopay v. Noveroske, 334 N.E.2d 79 (Illinois Appellate Court, 5th District, 1975).

69. Reynolds v. Pegler, 223 F.2d 429, (2d Circuit, 1955); cert. denied, 76 S.Ct. 80 (1955).

70. Goldwater v. Ginzburg, 414 F.2d 324 (2d Circuit, 1969); cert. denied, 396 U.S. 1049, 90 S.Ct. 701, 24 L.Ed.2d 695 (1970).

71. Listing of states by type of statute in a paper by Donna Lee Dickerson, "Retraction Statutes v. Actual Malice: A Question of Evidence," presented at the convention of the Association for Education in Journalism in August 1975, Ottawa, Canada, pp. 3–4.

72. "News Notes," *Media Law Reporter,* September 19, 1978.

73. "Retraction Law Constitutionality Tested by Paper," *The NEWS Media & The LAW,* January/February 1984, p. 39.

74. Compare these arguments with the view of the U.S. Supreme Court in such media-access cases as Miami Herald v. Tornillo, 418 U.S. 241 (1974), in which the Court made it clear that there can be no forced access to the pages of a newspaper.

75. At least 10 states have laws like California's in limiting retraction statutes to "newspapers." They are: Idaho, Indiana, Iowa, Kentucky, Minnesota, Mississippi, Nevada, North Dakota, South Dakota, and Utah.

76. "News Notes," *Media Law Reporter,* October 19, 1983 (California Court of Appeals, 2d District). The state supreme court denied review and the U.S. Supreme Court dismissed an appeal for want of jurisdiction. "News Notes," *Media Law Reporter,* February 28, 1984.

77. 13 *Med.L.Rptr.* 1785, Dec. 4, 1986.

78. "News Notes," *Media Law Reporter,* May 5, 1987.

79. Hanson v. Krehbiel, 68 Kan. 670, 75 P. 1041 (1904).

80. Allen v. Pioneer Press, 40 Minn. 117, 41 N.W. 936 (1889); Osborn v. Leach, 135 N.C. 628, 47 S.E. 811 (1904); Meyerle v. Pioneer Pub. Co., 45 N.D. 568, 178 N.W. 792 (1920); and Davidson v. Rogers, 281 Ore. 219, 574 P.2d 24 (1978).

81. *Restatement (Second) of Conflict of Laws* § 150(2) (1977).

82. *Restatement (Second) of Torts* § 577A(4)(1977).

83. As listed by U.S. District Court Judge Irving Kaufman in Palmisano v. News Syndicate Co., Inc., 130 F. Supp. 17, 19 and n. 2 (Southern District of New York, 1955).

84. Calder v. Jones, 10 *Med.L.Rptr.* 1401, April 3, 1984.

85. Ibid., at 1403, citing Miliken v. Meyer, 311 U.S. 457, 463, and International Shoe Co. v. Washington, 326 U.S. 310, 316 (1945).

86. "News Notes," *Media Law Reporter,* May 8, 1984.

87. "Court Allows Libel Suits Anyplace Periodical Is Sold," *San Francisco Chronicle,* March 21, 1984, p. 10.

88. Ibid.

89. "News Notes," *Media Law Reporter,* March 27, 1984.

90. Keeton v. Hustler, 10 *Med.L.Rptr.* 1405, 1406, 1408, April 3, 1984.

91. Ibid., at 1410.

92. Ibid., at 1406, n. 1.

93. Buckley v. Littell, 539 F.2d 882.

94. Cardillo. v. Doubleday & Co., Inc., 518 F.2d 638.

95. Cofield v. Advertiser Company, 12 *Med.L.Rptr.* 2039, May 13, 1986.

96. *Editor & Publisher,* June 8, 1986, p. 88.

97. "News Notes," *Media Law Reporter,* September 16, 1986.

98. Ibid.

99. Ibid.

5

First Amendment and Libel

HIGHLIGHTS

■ *New York Times v. Sullivan* (1964) resulted in the U.S. Supreme Court, for the first time, setting forth a First Amendment qualified privilege for the news media to publish defamatory information about public officials. Previously, state libel laws, not the First Amendment, had been controlling.

The qualification is this: That the media not knowingly publish falsehoods about public officials or recklessly disregard the truth. The effect of this "actual malice" rule has been to reduce markedly media vulnerability to public officials' libel lawsuits.

■ *Curtis Publishing Co. v. Butts* and *Associated Press v. Walker* (1967) led the Supreme Court, in effect, to extend the *Times-Sullivan* "actual malice" rule to public figures.

■ *St. Amant v. Thompson* (1968) resulted in the Supreme Court defining the "reckless disregard" portion of the *Times-Sullivan* "actual malice" test as publishing something with serious doubts as to its truth. Earlier, the Court, in *Garrison v. Louisiana* (1964), said that "actual malice" involves the making of false statements with a high degree of awareness of their falsity.

■ *Hutchinson v. Proxmire* (1979) points to one of the problem areas in the *Times-Sullivan* ruling, namely, that not all government employees are public officials within the actual malice rule.

■ *Herbert v. Lando* (1979) allows a libel plaintiff to penetrate into the editorial process—into a journalist's mind—in an effort to show "actual malice"—a decision sharply criticized by the news media.

■ *Anderson v. Liberty Lobby* (1986) makes it more difficult for libel plaintiffs to prove "actual malice." They must do so by "clear and convincing" evidence.

In 1964, the U.S. Supreme Court drastically altered the law of libel as it pertains to public officials. A First Amendment qualified privilege was forged for the news media as an alternative and much stronger defense to the ones allowed under state laws. The traditional defenses of truth, qualified privilege, and fair comment/fair criticism still remain. However the First Amendent defense is more protective in that it allows the press to safely publish stories and comment about public officials as long as the stories and comments do not contain knowing or reckless falsehoods. This protection later was extended to stories and comment about public figures.

NEW YORK TIMES v. SULLIVAN

To fully grasp the significance of the Supreme Court's unanimous decision in *New York Times v. Sullivan,* consider this fact:[1] For nearly 200 years, the development of libel law in the United States had been the exclusive domain of the separate states on the theory that the First Amendment did not protect false and defamatory speech because there was no value in such speech. *Times-Sullivan* momentously changed this.

Times-Sullivan stemmed from civil rights demonstrations in the South. On March 29, 1960, a full-page advertisement was published in *The New York Times,* cosponsored by 64 prominent persons. The advertisement listed some grievances against Montgomery, Alabama, police and several of the statements were erroneous. L. B. Sullivan, one of three city commissioners at the time, brought suit even though he was not identified by name in the advertisement. He contended that false statements concerning the Montgomery police defamed him because he had supervisory power over the police. When the case went to the jury in Alabama, the judge instructed the jurors that the false statements were libelous per se. The result was a damage award of $500,000! On appeal, the Alabama Supreme Court upheld the lower court. The *Times,* already sued for $2,500,000 by the two other city commissioners and by the state governor, appealed and the stage was set for the historic Supreme Court action.

Significantly, the nation's highest tribunal easily could have sidestepped this case. It was a civil lawsuit between private parties. Government was not pitted against a newspaper. Also, the entire tradition of libel law up to that time was against interference by a federal court. Finally, the libelous words were contained in an advertisement and "commercial expression" generally did not at that time have the full protection of the First Amendment if, indeed, it had any at all. For all these reasons, plus the emotionalism attached to the civil rights struggle, the Court could have ducked *Times-Sullivan*. It chose not to and the result has been a chain reaction of decisions that greatly strengthened the freedom of the press to report on matters affecting the public (the "public interest" requirement).

The landmark decision was written by Justice Brennan and it reversed the award of damages. All nine Court members agreed that damages should not have been awarded and that greater protection was needed by the news media against libel suits brought by public officials. In fact, three of the justices argued that Brennan's opinion for the Court did not go far enough in insulating the press from the dangers of libel.

Actual Malice Rule

What emerged from this case was the *Times-Sullivan* "actual malice" rule which states that a public official can succeed with a libel action only if he or she can show that a "defamatory falsehood relating to official conduct . . . was made with 'actual malice' — that is, with knowledge that it was false or with reckless disregard of whether it was false or not."

Three Obstacles Overcome. In his opinion, Justice Brennan first had to dispose of basic arguments against the Court even considering the case. He responded:

> We may dispose at the outset of two grounds asserted to insulate the judgment of the Alabama courts from constitutional scrutiny. The first is the proposition relied on by the State Supreme Court — that "the Fourteenth Amendment is directed against state actions and not private actions." That proposition has no application to this case. Although this is a civil lawsuit between private parties, the Alabama courts have applied a state rule of law . . . to impose invalid restrictions on their constitutional freedoms of speech and press. It matters not that the law has been applied in a civil action and that it is common law only, though supplemented by statute. . . . The test is not the form in which the state power has been applied but . . . whether such power has in fact been exercised.

As for an advertisement not being protected by the Constitution, Brennan said:

> The publication here was not a "commercial" advertisement. . . . It communicated information, expressed opinion, recited grievances, protested claimed abuses, and sought financial support on behalf of a movement whose existence and objectives are matters of the highest *public interest and concern* [italics added]. . . . That the *Times* was paid for publishing the advertisement is as immaterial in this connection as is the fact that newspapers and books are sold. . . . Any other conclusion would discourage newspapers from carrying "editorial advertisements" of this type, and so might shut off an important outlet for the promulgation of information and ideas by persons who do not themselves have access to publishing facilities — who wish to exercise their freedom of speech even though they are not members of the press. . . . The effect would be to shackle the First Amendment in its attempt to secure "the widest possible dissemination of information from diverse and antagonistic sources. . . ." To avoid placing such a handicap upon the freedoms of expression, we hold that

if the allegedly libelous statements would otherwise be constitutionally protected from the present judgment, they do not forfeit that protection because they were published in the form of a paid advertisement.

A more difficult obstacle for the Court to overcome was the "principle" that publication of defamatory words meant loss of First Amendment protection. Since the advertisement contained defamatory falsehoods, how could the Court impose First Amendment protection? Justice Brennan wrote with great forcefulness:

> . . . [W]e are compelled by neither precedent nor policy to give any more weight to the epithet "libel" than we have to other "mere labels" of state law. . . . Like insurrection, contempt, advocacy of unlawful acts, breach of the peace, obscenity, . . . and the various other formulae for the repression of expression that have been challenged in this Court, libel can claim no talismanic immunity from constitutional limitations. It must be measured by standards that satisfy the First Amendment.

Foremost among the command of that amendment, which clearly is given a "preferred position" in this case, is the need for freedom of expression for public questions and issues in order to facilitate public discussion. Such public discussion is basic to the American system of government and must not be stifled (the Meiklejohn concept). Brennan thereupon applied the rhetoric of broad libertarianism and the marketplace concept by saying:

> Thus we consider this case against the background of a profound national commitment to the principle that debate on public issues should be uninhibited, robust, and wide-open, and that it may well include vehement, caustic, and sometimes unpleasantly sharp attacks on government and public officials.

Such wide-open debate, said Brennan, inevitably will result in false or erroneous expression, but even that kind of speech or press must be protected if freedoms of expression are to have the "breathing space" they need to survive. Therefore, any rule that compels a critic of official conduct to guarantee the truth of all factual assertions—and to do so on pain of libel judgments virtually unlimited in amount—leads to self-censorship. Such censorship is inconsistent with the First Amendment. By such logic, Brennan reached the point where he stated the new standard that emerged from this case:

> The constitutional guarantees require, we think, a federal rule that prohibits a public official from recovering damages for a defamatory falsehood relating to his official conduct unless he proves that the statement was made with "actual malice"—that is, with knowledge that it was false or with reckless disregard of whether it was false or not.

What this malice rule established is a conditional or qualified federal constitutional privilege, to wit: the press can vehemently, caustically, and even *falsely* comment on the public conduct of public officials. The condition is that any falsehoods not result from actual malice, that is, knowingly publishing false-hoods or recklessly disregarding the truth. The significance of this First Amend-ment protection, compared with the pre-1964 defenses of truth and fair com-ment/fair criticism, as permitted under state laws, is far-reaching.

Separate Concurring Opinions

In separate but concurring opinions, Justices Black (joined by Douglas) and Arthur Goldberg argued for an absolute, unconditional privilege to criticize—even falsely—public officials as part of the unqualified right of the people, and therefore of the press, to discuss public affairs with complete immunity. Such a privilege is comparable to the Meiklejohn concept; that is, that "political speech" should be absolutely protected by the First Amendment. However, the majority of the Court limited the privilege to the discussion of the official conduct of public officials provided that such discussion was not the result of "actual mal-ice."

Unlike Black and Douglas, Goldberg believed that protection should remain for the private side of a public official's life, as did Brennan and those who sided with his opinion. But making a distinction between the public and private lives of officials obviously poses problems. At what point does a public official regain the protection of privacy?

Times-Sullivan also produced other uncertainties, among them:

1. Are all public officials included in the conditional privilege? If not, who would be excluded? Police officers and firefighters? Custodians?
2. Are prominent persons who move in and out of government as consult-ants to be treated as public officials?
3. At what point do defamatory falsehoods become "reckless disregard" of the truth?

Subsequent court rulings have come to grips with such questions, but defini-tive answers are elusive. For example, in a mid-1979 decision of the U.S. Su-preme Court in *Hutchinson v. Proxmire,* reviewed previously, a behavioral scien-tist who was research director at a Michigan state mental hospital and had received more than $500,000 in federal research grants, was termed a private individual, not a public figure or a public official.

A U.S. District Court, in granting summary judgment to U.S. Senator Wil-liam Proxmire (who had made defamatory remarks about the type of research being done by the plaintiff with the aid of taxpayers' money), had classified the scientist as a public official, but the U.S. Court of Appeals for the Seventh Circuit, in affirming the lower court's decision, did not decide whether Hutchin-son was or was not a public official. Neither did Chief Justice Burger, in his opinion for the Court which reversed the lower court on the ground that Senator Proxmire did not have absolute immunity from lawsuits under the Speech and Debate Clause of the Constitution. The Court did declare that Hutchinson was a private individual (for reasons discussed in Chapter 6).

Although the Court did not express an opinion on the issue of the "public official" status of Hutchinson, Burger pointed out in a footnote that the Court has not provided precise boundaries for a category of "public officials"; but it does not, he said, include all public employees.[2]

The Court has said that the "public official" designation applies "at the very least to those among the hierarchy of government employees who have, or appear to the public to have, substantial responsibility for or control over the conduct of government affairs."[3] But the Court has not reserved the "public official" designation for high-level public officers alone. Cases before the Court show that such a designation was appropriate for a deputy chief of detectives, a deputy sheriff, an elected clerk of county courts, a county attorney,[4] and possibly for any candidate for public office, at least during the course of an election campaign.[5] Thus, the Texas Supreme Court held that a county surveyor was a public official because he was an elected official even though he was not paid a salary. However, that same person was not a public official when performing private consultation work for the county in which he held public office.[6]

Also, an official court reporter for a Texas district court and a patrolman were held not to be public officials, the latter because he "did not exercise general influence on government affairs."[7] Clearly, there are pitfalls in trying to determine who is or who is not a public official when such a person is not high ranking, does not have substantial responsibility for or control over the conduct of government affairs, or is not an elected official.

CRIMINAL LAW

Times-Sullivan had an important impact on criminal libel laws of the various states. Before turning to specific cases, a review of the "justification" for such laws and the distinctions between criminal and civil libel laws should be helpful.

Criminal libel law developed to halt or punish those who uttered words that might provoke riots, mob violence, or other breaches of the public peace. The theory behind such law is that the state has the responsibility of maintaining public peace and order. Thus, the truth of a criminal libel was immaterial (except for seditious libel) because even truthful words could provoke public disorders. For this same reason, publication to a third person is not a necessary condition, as it is in civil libel, because communication of the libel to the libeled person might provoke him to violence. Similarly, under civil libel law a dead person cannot be defamed, but such a defamation is a crime in many states because the survivors of the deceased might be provoked to violent acts against the libeler. Thus, Iowa's criminal libel statute (repealed January 1, 1978) had stated:

> A libel is a malicious defamation of a person, made public by any printing, writing, sign, picture, representation, or effigy, tending to provoke him to wrath or expose him to public hatred, contempt, or ridicule, or to deprive him of the benefits of public confidence and social intercourse; or any malicious defamation made public as aforesaid, designed to blacken and vilify the memory of one who is dead, and tending to scandalize or provoke his surviving relatives or friends.

The penalty for such a crime was imprisonment in a county jail for not more than one year or a fine of not more than $1000.

Because malice has been difficult to define and because it usually requires intent, there have been few criminal libel prosecutions.

Illinois Case. One pre-*Times-Sullivan* case occurred under an Illinois statute enacted in 1949 that made it a crime to disseminate or exhibit in a public place anything which "portrays depravity, criminality, unchastity, or lack of virtue of a class of citizens of any race, color, creed or religion." Under this statute, a Chicagoan was accused of distributing racist literature. He was convicted and the U.S. Supreme Court, by a 5–4 decision in 1952, upheld the conviction. In giving the Court's opinion in *Beauharnais v. Illinois,* Justice Felix Frankfurter said that the legislature's action was a reasonable way "to curb false and malicious defamation of racial and religious groups."[8] Justices Black and Douglas were among the dissenters, arguing that no group should be protected at the expense of free speech.

Twelve years later, in *Times-Sullivan,* Justice Brennan seemed to go out of his way to stress that the stifling of Beauharnais' freedom was an exception to the usual rule that freedom of speech and press should prevail. Brennan wrote:

> In *Beauharnais v. Illinois,* . . . the Court sustained an Illinois criminal libel statute as applied to a publication held to be both defamatory of a racial group and "liable to cause violence and disorder." But the Court was careful to note that it "retains and exercises authority to nullify action which encroaches on the freedom of utterance under the guise of punishing libel. . . ."[9]

In 1984, in a nonmedia case, the Illinois Supreme Court ruled that the criminal libel statute was constitutional but said that its decision might have been different if political speech had been involved.[10]

Louisiana Law Unconstitutional: *Garrison v. Louisiana.* Almost before the ink was dry on the *Times-Sullivan* opinion, the Supreme Court nullified a criminal libel action against Jim Garrison, district attorney of Orleans Parish in Louisiana, by declaring the Louisiana criminal libel law unconstitutional.

The flamboyant Garrison had been involved in a dispute with eight judges of the Criminal District Court of Orleans Parish when he called a press conference and made disparaging comments about the judges' conduct. As a result he was tried and convicted under Louisiana's criminal defamation statute. The state's supreme court rejected Garrison's contention that the statute unconstitutionally abridged his freedom of speech, and Garrison appealed. The U.S. Supreme Court reversed the conviction and, in an opinion by Brennan, held that the *Times-Sullivan* rule also limited state power to impose criminal sanctions for criticism of the official conduct of public officials.[11] As Brennan wrote, "Where criticism of public officials is concerned, we see no merit in the argument that criminal libel statutes serve interests distinct from those secured by civil libel laws, and therefore should not be subject to the same limitation."[12]

The Court looked favorably on a proposed draft of the Model Penal Code of the American Law Institute that recommended narrowly drawn statutes designed to reach words tending to cause a breach of the peace, such as the statute sustained in *Chaplinsky v. New Hampshire,*[13] or designed to reach speech, such as group vilification, "especially likely to lead to public disorders," such as the statute sustained in *Beauharnais.*[14] In *Chaplinsky,* the Supreme Court had refused constitutional protection for words that by their very utterance, provoke violence or tend to provoke an immediate breach of the peace.

In *Garrison,* the Supreme Court made two other statements that would influence future criminal and civil libel lawsuits pertaining to public officials:

1. "Only those false statements made with a high degree of awareness of their falsity demanded by *New York Times* may be the subject of either civil or criminal sanction."
2. *Times-Sullivan* was not limited to matters relating solely to the official conduct of the public official, but also extended to "anything which might touch on an official's fitness for office. . . . "

Thus, by defining "actual malice" in terms of a high degree of awareness of falsity, the Court dampened the likelihood that successful civil libel actions could be brought by public officials based on "innocent" or "good faith" falsity, that is, an unawareness on the part of the defendant that the words were false. Secondly, the Court made it possible, although still dangerous, for the news media to go beyond the "public side" of a public official's life without risking the loss of the protection of the "actual malice" rule. Anything that "might touch on an official's fitness for office" becomes fair game for the media provided they do not publish falsehoods with a "high degree of awareness of falsity."

The protective scope of such language would be applied in many subsequent libel cases.

Arkansas Statute Unconstitutional. The U.S. Supreme Court's rulings in *Times-Sullivan* and *Garrison* were the bases for an Arkansas Supreme Court's declaration in 1975 that the state's criminal libel statute was unconstitutional. In so doing it reversed the conviction of Joseph Weston, editor of the weekly *Sharp Citizen* of Cave City, Arkansas, who had been fined $4,000 and sentenced to three months' imprisonment.

The state's criminal statute provided that, in all prosecutions for libel, truth "may be given in evidence of justification," but the Arkansas Supreme Court said that this "falls short of the *New York Times* rules which 'absolutely prohibits punishment for truthful criticism.' *Garrison v. Louisiana,* 379 U.S. 64, 78; 85 S.Ct. 209, 217." Under the rule laid down in *Garrison,* said the Arkansas court, "truth is a defense even when the offending publication is not made 'with good motives and for justifiable ends' as provided in Article 2, Section 6, of the Arkansas Constitution."[15]

The Arkansas Supreme Court also said that the statute failed to prohibit punishment for false statements regarding public officials except when made with knowing falsity or reckless disregard of whether the statements were true or false.

A similar result had been reached in Pennsylvania three years earlier,[16] and would be reached in California in 1976 in a case resulting from publication of a picture of actress Angie Dickinson's head superimposed on a nude woman's body.[17] Other states, such as Iowa, also would conclude that their criminal libel statutes did not meet the *Garrison* requirements. But as the California Second District Court of Appeal pointed out in the Dickinson case, *Garrison* "does not appear to eliminate absolutely criminal libel legislation but merely declares the need for appropriate restraints on such legislation. . . ." Minimally, those restraints include the allowance of truth without qualification as a complete defense to a criminal libel charge (Iowa's statute had allowed the defense of truth *with good motives for justifiable ends*), and provision for a test consisting of knowing falsity or reckless disregard of the truth in connection with criticism of public officials.[18]

The fact that criminal prosecution for libel is not entirely foreclosed is seen in Justice Rehnquist's opinion in *Keeton v. Hustler* (1984), discussed previously, in which he mentioned New Hampshire's statute that makes it a misdemeanor for anyone to "purposely communicate to any person, orally or in writing, any information which he knows to be false and knows will tend to expose any other living person to public hatred, contempt or ridicule.[19]

A New York Attorney, Victor Kovner, said Rehnquist had "cited with approval" the New Hampshire criminal libel statute, and added:

> Most of us who practice in this field thought that criminal defamation and criminal libel had left the scene and been gone for many years. Yet, in the wake of this decision, I think we may be seeing criminal prosecutions for libel in the future.[20]

South Carolina Editor Jailed. The truth of the prediction can be seen in the indictment of a South Carolina weekly newspaper editor, Jim Fitts of the *Voice* in Kingstree, in 1988 on two counts of malicious intent to distribute, circulate, and publish false statements. He earlier had been arrested after two state legislators signed complaints that they had been criminally libeled.[21] The editor spent a weekend in jail after a local magistrate imposed a surety bond of $40,000, later changed to a $30,000 personal recognizance bond.

The legislators subsequently asked that the charges be dropped because of all the negative publicity the indictment had brought to Williamsburg County, and this was done.

South Carolina's criminal libel statute was enacted in 1912 and defines the crime of slander and libel as uttering, circulating, or publishing any false statement with malicious intent which injures another's character. It is a misdemeanor punishable by a fine of up to $5,000 or imprisonment for not more than one year, or both.

South Carolina is one of 24 states, plus the District of Columbia, which have such statutes.

TIMES-SULLIVAN EXTENDED TO PUBLIC FIGURES

Another very important change in civil libel law resulted from two cases decided at the same time by the U.S. Supreme Court—*Curtis Publishing Co. v. Butts* and *Associated Press v. Walker* (1967).[22]

Butts Case

The *Butts* case involved a $5 million libel suit filed by Wally Butts, University of Georgia athletic director, following publication of an article, "The Story of a College Football Fix," in the March 23, 1963, issue of *Saturday Evening Post*. The article accused Butts of giving football secrets to Bear Bryant, University of Alabama football coach. Bryant also filed suit for $5 million damages and, following the decision in the Butts case, received an out-of-court settlement reportedly totaling $300,000.

Butts was awarded $60,000 in special damages and $400,000 in punitive damages following a trial at which Curtis Publishing Co. attorneys had to rely on the only defense available to them at the time—truth. Unable to prove the accusations, the company appealed the award of damages. By a 5–4 vote, the U.S. Supreme Court upheld the award of damages (Justices Black, Douglas, Brennan, and White dissenting).

Walker Case

The companion case involved Edwin Walker, a former U.S. Army major general who had involved himself in demonstrations during a Negro's attempt to enroll in the University of Mississippi. A Texas jury awarded Walker, then a candidate for public office, $500,000 in general damages and $300,000 in punitive damages based on inaccuracies in an Associated Press story about Walker's activities during the demonstration. The trial judge ruled there was no evidence of malice on the part of Associated Press and eliminated the punitive damages. The action was upheld by the Texas Supreme Court, but the U.S. Supreme Court reversed any award of damages.

In connection with both cases, Justice Harlan, joined by three other Court members, urged a standard of liability slightly different than the *Times-Sullivan* standard. Harlan wrote:

> . . . [The] similarities and differences between libel actions involving persons who are public officials and libel actions involving those circumstanced as were Butts and Walker . . . lead us to the conclusion that libel actions of the present kind cannot be left entirely to state libel laws, unlimited by any over-riding constitutional safeguards, but that the rigorous federal requirements of *New York Times* are not the only appropriate accommodation of the conflicting interests at stake. We consider and would hold that a "public figure" who is not a public official may also recover damages for a defamatory falsehood whose substance makes substantial danger to reputation apparent, on a showing of highly unreasonable conduct constituting an *extreme departure from the standards of investigation ordinarily adhered to by responsible publishers.* [Italics added.]

After proposing the extreme departure test, Harlan proceeded to make a distinction between "hot news" and other kinds of news, the latter requiring more diligence on the part of journalists:

> The evidence showed that the Butts story was in no sense "hot news" and the editors of the magazine recognized the need for a thorough investigation of the serious charges. Elementary precautions were, nevertheless, ignored. . . .
>
> *The Saturday Evening Post* was anxious to change its image by instituting a policy of "sophisticated muckraking," and the pressure to produce a successful exposé might have induced a stretching of standards. In short, the evidence is ample to support a finding of highly unreasonable conduct constituting an extreme departure from the standards of investigation and reporting ordinarily adhered to by responsible publishers.

In distinguishing the *Butts* case from *Walker,* Harlan wrote:

> In contrast to the *Butts* article, the dispatch which concerns us in *Walker* was news which required immediate dissemination. . . . Considering the necessity for rapid dissemination, nothing in this series of events gives the slightest hint of a severe departure from accepted publishing standards.

Chief Justice Warren, although concurring in the results in both cases, disagreed with the reasons put forth in Harlan's plurality opinion. Warren's views, which drew support from Black, Douglas, Brennan, and White, became the majority position of the Court and extended the *Times* standard to public figures. As the Chief Justice wrote:

> To me, differentiation between "public figures" and "public officials" and adoption of separate standards of proof for each have no basis in law, logic, or First Amendment policy. Increasingly in this country, the distinctions between government and private sectors are blurred.

Justice Black, joined by Douglas, wrote an opinion in which he dissented to the results reached in the *Butts* case, but concurred in the *Walker* case results. He supported the Chief Justice's reasons for extending the *Times* standard to public figure libel cases, but only for the purpose of establishing a majority position for the Court. He and Douglas preferred an absolute First Amendment privilege for the news media, not a conditional one.

Brennan, joined by White, dissented in a separate opinion to the results reached in the *Butts* case. He thought the case should be remanded because of improper jury instructions. However, he believed the *Saturday Evening Post* article was in reckless disregard of the truth. Both justices associated themselves with the reasoning put forth in Warren's opinion for extending the *Times* standard to public figures.

In discussing Harlan's views, the Chief Justice said that an extreme departure standard implies consensus concerning "accepted publishing standards." Even if consensus exists, a further difficulty results when the "hot news" criterion is applied. Just why the First Amendment should be more protective of "hot news" than "cold news" was not altogether clear. If such a standard were to gain widespread use, then one might ask if any magazine, including news magazines, could qualify for the conditional constitutional protection against libel suits.

In a 1971 invasion of privacy suit involving a monthly magazine,[23] the California Supreme Court decided that "hot news" items of possible immediate public concern or interest are "particularly deserving of First Amendment protection." However, the identification of someone involved in a crime some years past, even though such identification is a matter of police record and therefore seemingly privileged under state libel laws, may not be so deserving. In reversing a lower court, the state tribunal did not rule on the merits of the case but allowed further consideration of the invasion of privacy claim. In so doing, the court tacked onto the *Times* standard such codicils as "hot news," recency of events, and a concept of "newsworthiness" which included the "social value" of published facts. It is precisely because of such complicating factors that Justice Black argued in *Times-Sullivan* for an absolute privilege to discuss public affairs. Without question, the magazine article that prompted the California case would fall within a definition of public affairs since it dealt with the crime of truck hijacking.

MALICE RULE AND PRIVATE INDIVIDUALS: THE PUBLIC CONCERN TEST

What began in 1964 as a rule or standard applied to public officials—and then to public figures in 1967—seemed to undergo significant change in mid-1971 when a plurality of the U.S. Supreme Court (Justices Brennan, Blackmun, and Chief Justice Burger) said that the conditional First Amendment privilege should encompass all persons, public and private, who become involved in events of "public or general concern." Justices Black and White concurred in the results but filed separate opinions. Justices Harlan, Marshall, and Stewart dissented. Douglas took no part. If he had, the split would have been 6–3 to affirm a U.S. Court of Appeals that reversed a sizable damage award made to private citizen Rosenbloom in *Rosenbloom v. Metromedia.*[24]

The events leading to this case began in 1963 when Philadelphia police arrested a number of distributors of allegedly obscene magazines and books, among them George A. Rosenbloom. Three days later, police searched his home and a building he rented, seized magazines and books, and filed a second charge against him. The Metromedia-owned radio station, WIP, broadcast substantially the same news item twice—that police had confiscated 3000 obscene books from Rosenbloom. No qualifying word, such as *allegedly* obscene books, was used.

Rosenbloom was acquitted after the trial judge declared that the nudist magazines distributed by the defendant were not obscene. Thus, WIP could not succeed with a defense of truth, nor could it convince a jury that qualified privilege (a police officer's statement made to the press) protected the broadcast. The district court judge added to WIP's plight by informing the jurors that if they found the publication to be untrue, punitive damages could be awarded. The result was an award of $25,000 in general damages and $725,000 in punitive damages, although the trial judge reduced the latter to $250,000.

Metromedia appealed and it was the position taken by the U.S. Court of Appeals (Third Circuit) which Justice Brennan adopted in his plurality opinion. The appellate court had concluded that "the fact that the plaintiff was not a public figure cannot be accorded decisive significance if the recognized important guarantees of the First Amendment are to be adequately implemented." The appellate court had reversed the decision of the trial court after applying the *Times* standard, to this "private person" defamation case.

Brennan wrote:

> Although the limitations upon civil libel actions, first held in *New York Times* to be required by the First Amendment, were applied in that case in the context of defamatory falsehoods about the official conduct of a public official, later decisions have disclosed the artificiality, in terms of the public's interest, of a simple distinction between "public" and "private" individuals or institutions.

This crucial distinction then was made by Brennan:

> If a matter is a subject of public or general interest, it cannot suddenly become less so merely because a private individual is involved, or because in some sense the individual did not "voluntarily" choose to become involved.
>   . . . [W]e think the time has come forthrightly to announce that the determinant whether the First Amendment applies to state libel actions is whether the utterance involved concerns an issue of public or general concern, albeit leaving the delineation of the reach of that term to future cases.

Perhaps from some misgiving about the broad reach of the language being used, Brennan added this suggestion to lawmakers:

> If the States fear that private citizens will not be able to respond adequately to publicity involving them, the solution lies in the direction of ensuring their ability to respond, rather than in stifling public discussion of matters of public concern.

Just what Brennan had in mind here is not clear. Retraction or correction statutes exist, or could be enacted, to *encourage* the media to correct misinformation by limiting recovery of damages whenever a correction is published. If Brennan had in mind a right of access statute that under certain conditions would *require* the media to print or broadcast something from certain individuals, it is hard to see how such a law could pass First Amendment scrutiny — particularly a law which required access to the print medium. Indeed, several years after Brennan made this statement the Supreme Court struck down as unconstitutional a Florida law that mandated a *limited* right of reply for a candidate for public office who had been criticized by a newspaper (see Chapter 15).

Brennan's opinion concluded with a restatement of the *Times* rule as applied to private citizens:

> Our independent analysis of the record leads us to agree with the Court of Appeals that none of the proofs, considered either singly or cumulatively, satisfies the constitutional standard with the convincing clarity necessary to raise a jury question whether the defamatory falsehoods were broadcast with knowledge that they were false or with reckless disregard of whether they were false or not.

Although agreeing with the plurality opinion result, Justice Black wrote a separate opinion in which he again urged the Court to abandon the conditional privilege in favor of an absolute one. This absolutist view subsequently drew support from Professor Thomas I. Emerson of Yale University Law School, a First Amendment scholar who said during an interview:

> I think that even the "actual malice" restriction is too broad; I agree with Justices Black and Douglas that leaving the issue of malice up to a jury reopens the whole question and deprives the press of a great deal of protection which it otherwise would have. Nevertheless, as applied so far the rule has been a major protection. Even the newest Supreme Court appointees [Burger and Blackmun] went along in extending the *Times* doctrine to public issues.[25]

In his dissenting opinion, Justice Harlan shared some of Justice White's concerns, saying:

> I, too, think that when dealing with private libel, the States should be free to define for themselves the applicable standard of care so long as they do not impose liability without fault; that a showing of actual damage should be a requisite to recovery for libel. . . .

It was Harlan's view which a majority of the Supreme Court would adopt in a 1974 decision that has had far-reaching consequences. Before turning to that case, however, the potential significance of the Brennan plurality opinion should be summarized—*potential* because this was not a majority holding by the Court. If it had become so, and there were signs that it might, then the conditional constitutional privilege would have shifted from the kind of people involved to whether news reports concerned "matters of public or general concern." This key phrase was used as long ago as 1890 in a law review article that has been credited with stimulating much of the development of the law of privacy in the United States. The authors of that article would have excluded from the right of privacy matters of "public or general interest" (see Chapter 7). Therefore, with the 1971 plurality opinion, the phrase "public or general interest" or "public or general concern" became the hinge for connecting the First Amendment to libel and privacy laws as they apply to the news media.

Prior to *Rosenbloom,* a number of lower courts had anticipated the Brennan opinion and the movement toward the public interest test. For example, the Court in *Rosenbloom* upheld the Third Circuit's application of a "public interest" test. But the Fifth Circuit also had anticipated the plurality opinion in a number of pre-*Rosenbloom* decisions.[26] Some legal commentators also had predicted that the nature of the event would replace the pre-*Rosenbloom* emphasis given to the status of the participants in the event.[27]

Although journalists might have wished that absolute immunity from defamation suits was what the future held in store, some judges and lawyers sharply disagreed on the significance of the *Rosenbloom* plurality opinion. For example, Judge Barnes of the Maryland Court of Appeals wrote, in a 1972 dissenting opinion:

> In the first place, *Rosenbloom* does not *hold* anything. There is no majority opinion. There is a *plurality* opinion. . . . If one considers the concurring opinion of Mr. Justice Black—who concurred *in the judgment* . . . —to be an oblique ratification of the new Brennan view, even here there would be the concurrence of only four justices and not the necessary five for a *holding* by the Supreme Court. The Brennan view . . . has not become a new federal rule broadening *New York Times* and *Curtis Publishing Co.*[28]

Until 1974 Judge Barnes was in the minority as more and more courts applied the *Rosenbloom* plurality opinion. But in that year the U.S. Supreme Court reached a decision in *Gertz v. Welch, Inc.* that returned the development of libel law back to the states insofar as private figures were involved. *Gertz* and its ramifications will be reviewed in the next chapter, but first, let's look more closely at the "actual malice" rule, specifically, the definition and proof of "actual malice."

Definitions and Proof of "Actual Malice"

Before turning to the 1974 U.S. Supreme Court decision that reversed the trend toward applying a conditional constitutional privilege to reports of matters of public interest, regardless of the type of individual involved, one other case, which strengthened the "actual malice" rule, should be singled out. In *Garrison,* the U.S. Supreme Court ruled that "actual malice" involved the making of false statements with a high degree of awareness on the part of the defendant of their probable falsity. In a 1968 case, *St. Amant v. Thompson,*[29] the Supreme Court held that a plaintiff had to show that the defendant entertained serious doubts as to the truth of the statement. As Justice White said for the Court:

> These cases [*New York Times, Garrison,* and *Curtis Publishing Co. v. Butts*] are clear that reckless conduct is not measured by whether a reasonably prudent man would have published or would have investigated before publishing. There must be sufficient evidence to permit the conclusion that the defendant in fact entertained serious doubts as to the truth of his publication. Publishing with such doubts shows reckless disregard for truth or falsity and demonstrates actual malice.[30]

It is important to note that *Garrison's* "high degree of awareness" and *St. Amant's* "serious doubts as to the truth" requirements concern the defendant's state of mind and are not part of an objective test, such as the one suggested by Justice Harlan in *Curtis Publishing Co.* and *Walker;* namely, a "severe departure from accepted publishing standards." The U.S. Supreme Court in a 1979 case, *Herbert v. Lando,* said it is essential for a plaintiff who wishes to prove "actual malice" to focus "on the conduct and state of mind of the defendant."[31] Although a publisher does not have an absolute duty to investigate the truth of defamatory statements, as noted in *St Amant,* a Seventh Circuit court panel said a publisher nonetheless cannot "feign ignorance or profess good faith when there are clear indications present which bring into question the truth or falsity of defamatory statements."[32] The panel again cited *St. Amant,* adding emphasis to some of the words in pointing out that a publisher cannot:

> . . . automatically insure a favorable verdict by testifying that he published with a belief that the statements were true. The finder of fact must determine whether the publication was indeed made in good faith. Professions of good faith will be unlikely to prove persuasive, . . . when the publisher's allegations are so inherently improbable that only a reckless man would have put them in circulation. Likewise, recklessness may be found *where there are obvious reasons to doubt the veracity of the informant or the accuracy of his reports.*[33]

In *St. Amant,* the Supreme Court gave two examples of what would constitute reckless disregard: (1) a situation in which a journalist had obvious reasons to doubt the veracity of an informant or the accuracy of his reports; and (2) a defamatory story based on an unverified anonymous telephone call.

Herbert v. Lando (1979). This is the case in which Chief Justice Burger said that a plaintiff who wishes to prove "actual malice" must focus on the conduct and the state of mind of the defendant. How does a plaintiff's attorney discover the defendant's state of mind vis-à-vis knowledge of falsity of a published statement? One way is through a procedure known as discovery. Federal Rules of Civil Procedure 26(b) permits discovery of any matter "relevant to the subject matter involved" in a pending action if it would either be admissible in evidence or "appears reasonably calculated to lead to the discovery of admissible evidence."

Discovery proceedings can be utilized by both plaintiff and defendant, and the process can last for weeks or months.

Sharp criticism from the news media came after *Herbert v. Lando* (1979), in which the U.S. Supreme Court allowed plaintiff's discovery efforts to probe into the editorial process involved in the production of a CBS News program and into the thoughts of the program's producer.[34]

The libel action resulted from a report on the CBS program, "The Selling of Colonel Herbert," produced and edited by Barry Lando and narrated by Mike Wallace as part of a *60 Minutes* segment. The program was aired February 4, 1973, and raised questions about the truth of accusations by Anthony Herbert, a lieutenant colonel during the Vietnam War, that his superior officers had covered up atrocities. Herbert said he was relieved of his command for making, and persisting with, such charges.

Lando not only produced the CBS program but subsequently wrote an article for *Atlantic Monthly* in which he detailed his findings about Colonel Herbert. Herbert sued Lando, Wallace, CBS, and *Atlantic Monthly* for defamation, claiming that the program and article falsely and maliciously portrayed him as a liar and a person who had made war-crimes charges to explain his relief from command. Herbert's attorneys then initiated the discovery process, interrogating Lando on 26 separate occasions. The deposition of Lando alone lasted intermittently for over a year, according to Justice Stewart, and filled 2903 pages of transcript. But Lando refused to answer questions concerning what he called the editorial process, claiming a First Amendment privilege not to have to divulge this type of information. U.S. District Court Judge Charles Haight, in New York, held that Lando had to answer the questions. A Second Circuit U.S. Court of Appeals panel, in a 2–1 split decision, reversed, declaring that such an "inquisition" would chill the journalist's thought process. The U.S. Supreme Court reversed by a 6–3 vote (one of the dissenting votes being a partial dissent by Brennan) and remanded the case to the lower courts.

Segments of the press reacted with shock and dismay when the Court's decision was announced. The editor of the *Chicago Sun-Times,* Ralph Otwell, said: "Going into the thought process of a reporter and all the subjective judgments he is forced . . . to make is a George Orwellian invasion of the mind." Richard Schmidt, general counsel for the American Society of Newspaper Editors, said the decision would fall particularly hard on small newspapers, magazines, and radio stations "that can ill afford the costs of defending such actions." Justice Marshall publicly criticized the decision at a meeting of the Second Circuit-Judicial Conference. Editorial autonomy, he said, must be protected to ensure public exposure to a wide range of information and insights. In his dissent, he feared the potential for harassment of defendants. In response, White said U.S. District Courts have the power, under Rule 26(c), to restrict discovery where "justice requires protection for a party or person from annoyance, embarrassment, oppression, or undue burden or expense. . . ."

The Second Circuit relied on U.S. Supreme Court decisions in *Miami Herald Publishing Co. v. Tornillo* (1974) and *Columbia Broadcasting System v. Democratic National Committee* (1973) (see Chapter 15) in stating that the editorial process is protected. But Justice White, in giving the Court's opinion in *Herbert,* said that in those two cases the Court invalidated *government efforts* to preempt editorial decisions by requiring publication of specified material whether the editors wanted to or not. But the holdings in those two cases, said White, "neither expressly nor impliedly suggest that the editorial process is immune from any inquiry whatsoever."

White said that an absolute privilege for the editorial process "is not required, authorized or presaged by our prior cases, and would substantially enhance the burden of proving actual malice," contrary to the expectations of *Times-Sullivan, Curtis Publishing Co. v. Butts,* and similar decisions.

The Court, in rejecting an evidentiary privilege for the editorial process, pointed out that such privileges are not favored and that even those rooted in the Constitution must give way under proper circumstances. White cited the Court's decision in *U.S. v. Nixon* (1974) (see Chapter 9) in which the President was compelled to turn over materials subpoenaed for a judicial proceeding even though he had claimed an absolute privilege against having to do so. The President's powerful interest in confidentiality between himself and his advisers had to yield to the need for evidence.

In commenting on the Court's unanimous decision in *Nixon,* Attorney Floyd Abrams noted the decision that forced President Nixon to turn over, under subpoena, Watergate-related tapes which ultimately led to Nixon's downfall might also have an impact on journalists who sought to avoid compliance with subpoenas. "It would be an ultimate and truly supreme irony," he said in 1974, "if the final gift of the Nixon administration to the press were a decision which, while striking a dagger into the heart of the President, struck through the President and reached the press as well."[35] The *Herbert* decision is a testimonial to that "supreme irony."

In 1986, a three-judge panel of the Second Circuit U.S. Court of Appeals ordered dismissal of Herbert's suit, saying that Herbert had no grounds for the suit.

The *Herbert* decision was cited by a California Superior Court judge, George M. Dell, in ordering reporters for *Penthouse* magazine to disclose confidential sources in connection with a libel action brought by Rancho La Costa, Inc.[36] Judge Dell said *Herbert* "rules out a 'source' privilege just as it does an 'editorial process' privilege." The California Supreme Court refused in 1980 to hear an appeal from the disclosure order.

Clear and Convincing Evidence Required. In *Times-Sullivan* and again in *Rosenbloom,* Justice Brennan indicated that proof of actual malice had to be established by "convincing proof"—a phrase subsequently used by quite a few courts in connection with decisions regarding actual malice. "Clear and convincing" proof requires more than a preponderance of the evidence, said a U.S. Court of Appeals in 1975.[37] Similarly, the Massachusetts Supreme Judicial Court ruled that in any case in which plaintiff must show actual malice, plaintiff must establish such proof by "clear and convincing" evidence, not by the more easily demonstrated "fair preponderance of the evidence."[38]

Then, in 1986, the Supreme Court, in a 6–3 decision in *Anderson v. Liberty Lobby,* ruled that a trial judge must decide that a reasonable jury could find the news media defendant guilty of actual malice by "clear and convincing evidence" before bringing libel suits by public officials and public figures to trial.[39]

Attorney Floyd Abrams hailed the decision as one of the more important libel rulings of the past decade. "It should make it possible," he said, "to rid the courts of weak, unpersuasive and implausible libel claims which waste enormous sums of money and enormous amounts of time. And it should relieve journalists of the burden of participating in trials about cases that never should have been brought in the first place."[40]

The plaintiffs, Willis Carto, founder of Liberty Lobby, and Liberty Lobby itself, had charged that three stories published in 1981 in columnist Jack Anderson's magazine, *The Investigator,* defamed them. In those stories they were accused of being neo-Nazi, fascist, racist, and anti-Semitic. The U.S. District Court for the District of Columbia found that the plaintiffs were public figures and granted the defendants' motion for summary judgment. The U.S. Court of Appeals for the District of Columbia Circuit, concerned about requiring plaintiffs having to try their entire case on pretrial evidence, reversed, holding that the "clear and convincing proof" standard was not applicable to summary judgment motions and that a jury could reasonably find that nine of the thirty allegations were false, defamatory, and had been made with actual malice[41]

In his opinion for the Court, Justice White emphasized that the Court's ruling did not denigrate the jury's role, nor did it authorize trial by affadavits. Issues of credibility, weight of evidence, and legitimate inferences rest with the jury, said White, and trial courts should act with caution in granting summary judgment. But where a factual dispute exists over actual malice, the appropriate summary judgment question will be whether the evidence in the record could support a reasonable jury finding that the plaintiff had shown actual malice by clear and convincing evidence.

Brennan dissented, saying that the Court had failed to explain how a judge could properly assess what a fair-minded jury could reasonably decide. Also, he believed that the "clear and convincing evidence" requirement is for a jury to decide, not a judge.[42]

Rehnquist, joined by Burger, also dissented in part because he believed that the majority failed to apply the new rule to the facts of the case.[43]

Defamacasts and the "Actual Malice" Test

Some communication law problems apply only to radio and television. For example, Section 315 of the Communications Act of 1934 requires a station to provide equal time to candidates under certain conditions. Utilizing the equal time requirement, a candidate for U.S. Senate once claimed that the Farmers Educational and Cooperative Union of America (FECUA) was conspiring to establish "a Communist Farmers Union Soviet . . . in North Dakota." The cooperative sued the candidate and the radio station, WDAY, but the U.S. Supreme Court said in its 1959 ruling that since the station did not have the power to censor the speeches of political candidates, it could not be held liable for what the politician said. If the station were held liable, said the Court, it might be excessively cautious and edit out "legitimate presentation under the guise of lawful censorship."[44] Congress had no such intention when it wrote Section 315, the Court declared.

Even if a station were to have the power to censor a script, it would be powerless to prevent an extemporaneous remark that might be defamatory except in those instances when programs were aired on a delayed-broadcasting basis. For this reason, a Pennsylvania court ruled that a broadcasting company which leases its time and facilities "is not liable for an interjected defamatory remark where it appears that it exercised due care in the selection of the lessee, and, having inspected and edited the script, had no reason to believe an extemporaneous remark would be made." But if a station's employee or agent makes the defamatory remark, the station is liable absent a suitable defense.[45]

As for call-in talk shows, during which stations encourage the listening public to express opinions on various subjects via the station's facilities, such programs, according to a Louisiana appellate court, require licensees and their employees to exercise control by means of delayed-broadcast technique.[46] In these instances, said the court, Congress has not required the licensee to allow the use of his facilities; consequently, the licensee is responsible for whatever is said unless otherwise protected.

The "otherwise protected" defense figured in a Utah case in which the state supreme court affirmed a lower court's award of summary judgment for the defendant radio station in *Denman v. Star Broadcasting Co.*[47] During a call-in talk show, which used the safeguard of a seven-second delay after the words were spoken until they were broadcast, "an unknown male phonomaniac called in and began berating plaintiff's qualifications for [public] office, vaguely attributing such imperfection to some sort of deficiency in business acumen," according to Justice F. Henry Henriod, who delivered the court's opinion. However, the words were of such a nature that an official of KSXX in Salt Lake City felt obliged almost immediately after the broadcast to make a public apology. But as Justice A. H. Ellett pointed out in his dissenting opinion, an apology made after a defamatory remark is no defense to the cause of action, although it might affect the award of damages. The majority, however, held that the talk show dialogue was not "mouthed with malice" (*Times-Sullivan* actual malice) and that the station was protected under Title 45–2–5, Utah Code Annotated 1953, which reads:

> No person, firm, or corporation owning or operating a radio or television broadcasting station or network of stations shall be liable under the laws of libel, slander or defamation on account of having made its broadcasting facilities or network available to any person, whether a candidate for public office or any other person, or on account of having originated or broadcast a program for discussion of controversial or any other subjects, in the absence of proof of actual malice on the part of such owner or operator. In no event, however, shall any such owner or operator be held liable for any damages for any defamatory statement uttered over the facilities of such station or network by or on behalf of any candidate for public office.

Adams v. Frontier Broadcasting Co. *Times-Sullivan* and its commitment to "uninhibited, robust, and wide-open debate" were touchstones for the Wyoming Supreme Court when it affirmed in late 1976 a trial court's summary judgment for the broadcast station in *Adams v. Frontier Broadcasting Co.*[48] The circumstances were similar to *Denman* in that an unknown person telephoned Frontier's radio program, "Cheyanne Today," on station KFBC, and said she wished to read a prepared statement. The caller thereupon stated that a Wyoming businessman, who also was active as a candidate for public office, "had been discharged as Insurance Commissioner for dishonesty."[49] The businessman filed a defamation suit based in part on the "careless, negligent and wrongful conduct of defendant in failure to monitor, control, maintain and supervise the use of its facilities during the program," specifically because the station failed to use a "tape delay system." An electronic delay system was available to Frontier on the date of the broadcast, but it was not used in connection with the talk show.

Ogden Bus Lines v. KSL, Inc. What about an alleged defamatory broadcast which does not involve a public official or a candidate? The Utah Supreme Court in 1976 considered such a situation in *Ogden Bus Lines v. KSL, Inc.*[50] and said that actual malice need not be shown. But if the broadcast item concerned a matter of public interest or concern, then the Utah court said the report was qualifiedly privileged — a privilege that only could be destroyed by malice. However, this kind of malice was defined as "simply an improper motive such as a desire to do harm or that the defendant did not honestly believe his statements to be true or that the publication was excessive."

Times-Sullivan: 20 Years Later

Before looking at some additional cases that involved public officials or public figures, an assessment of the *Times-Sullivan* decision 20 years afterward was made at a 1984 conference on "Libel Law Under the Constitution."

Attorney Floyd Abrams of New York City told the conference that *Times-Sullivan* "is one of the most far-reaching, extraordinary, and beautiful decisions in American history."[51] He pointed out that the decision (1) established the actual malice standard applicable to libel actions brought by public officials and public figures, (2) held as unconstitutional the traditional common-law burden of proof, (3) ruled that criticism of government lies at the heart of the First Amendment, and thereby, for the first time (4) held the Alien and Sedition Act of 1798 unconstitutional, and (5) decided there could be no presumed damages in libel actions (the latter made clear in *Gertz v. Welch, Inc.* (see Chapter 6)).

The attorney who represented commissioner Sullivan in his libel lawsuit, M. Roland Nachman, Jr. of Montgomery, Alabama, told the conference that he was "staggered" when the Court handed down its decision. "I thought that the only way I could lose would be for the Court to change 100 years of libel law, and that's what it did." He believes that extrinsic circumstances made a hard case for his client, such as the size of the damage award and the number of libel actions pending against the *Times* from that one advertisement.

The local counsel for the *Times* at that 1964 case was Eric Embrey, a justice of the Alabama Supreme Court at the time of the conference. He believes that if Sullivan had sued for $50,000, the case never would have gotten to the Supreme Court.[52]

Additional Public Official, Public Figure Cases

The application of the First Amendment to libel law and the resultant "actual malice" requirement has been crucial to the outcome of a number of libel cases as several of the following cases show. But some of these cases also show that the media are still vulnerable.

Pat Montandon v. Triangle Publications, Inc. A jury verdict favoring plaintiff against Triangle Publications, Inc., publisher of *TV Guide,* to the tune of $150,000 compensatory damage and $1000 punitive damage, was affirmed by the California Court of Appeal (First Division) in 1975.[53] The U.S. Supreme Court let the judgment stand by not reviewing the case. The case stemmed from the following publicity release sent to the media:

FRIDAY, SEPTEMBER 20TH, 10:30 PM., "Pat Michaels Show," "From Party-Girl to Call-Girl?" How far can the "party-girl" go until she becomes a "call-girl" is discussed with TV personality Pat Montandon, author, ("How to be a Party-Girl") and a masked anonymous prostitute.

TV Guide published the following:

10:30 (2) Pat Michaels-Discussion (Color) "From Party Girl to Call Girl." Scheduled guest: TV personality Pat Montandon and author of "How to Be a Party-Girl."

The appellate court agreed that Miss Montandon was a public figure, and Justice Bray said for the majority:

The action by the *TV Guide* staff showed a reckless disregard of whether the statement published was true or false, because the staff was aware that the true facts, as stated in the press release, were that Pat Montandon was not a call girl but would be appearing on a show with a call girl; and a staff decision was made to leave out the crucial facts in rewriting the release, thereby implying that plaintiff was a call girl. This is proof of convincing clarity to support the jury's verdict that the article was published not in good faith, but with actual malice.[54]

Hearst Corporation and the Synanon Foundation. The Hearst Corporation agreed to pay the Synanon Foundation in California, and its founder and one other plaintiff, $600,000 to settle a $32 million libel action filed in 1972. The foundation received $300,000 and the remainder went to the founder and to a resident of the self-help organization which specializes in residential treatment of juvenile delinquents, drug addicts, and other "character-disoriented" persons. Included in the settlement, approved by the San Francisco Superior Court in 1976, was a printed apology in the defendant newspaper, the *San Francisco Examiner,* to the foundation and its founder. The $600,000 is believed the largest amount ever paid to settle such a suit.

Plaintiffs brought their action for libel against the *Examiner,* the corporate owner, the president, editors, reporters, and an informant, after publication of two articles, including one headlined "Synanon: 'Racket of the Century.' " The first purported to be a first-person account of a former resident's experiences while undergoing treatment at the self-help organization. In the "as told to" article, allegations were made as "facts" that the nonprofit foundation had abandoned its charitable function and was being used by the founder for self-aggrandizement, that the foundation was engaged in fraudulent fund-raising activities, and that residents were being deprived of their property and harassed.

$475,000 Out-of-Court Settlement. Donald Widener, a documentary film producer falsely accused of surreptitiously taping and dubbing comments during a filmed interview for a documentary, received in 1979 a $475,000 out-of-court settlement of his libel action.[55] An earlier trial had resulted in Widener being awarded $750,000 in compensatory, and $7 million in punitive, damages, but that award was overturned by the trial judge. A California Court of Appeal, however, ruled there was ample evidence for a finding of actual malice and reversed the trial judge. The settlement came during pretrial motions for a new trial. A law school professor believed the settlement was the largest ever for an *individual*.[56]

Widener had produced a documentary on nuclear energy, *Powers That Be,* for KNBC-TV, Los Angeles, in 1971. An engineer for Pacific Gas & Electric (PG&E) was interviewed and later wrote a letter contending the program was "replete with half-truths, innuendos and worse." This letter was reviewed by PG&E officials, who sent it to KNBC with a covering letter in which Widener's use of the interview material was described as "chicanerous." The FCC and some congressmen also received copies of the letter.

Sharon v. Time, Inc. This 1985 case involved a $50 million libel lawsuit against *Time* magazine brought by former Israeli defense minister Ariel Sharon. The lawsuit resulted from a paragraph which stated that Sharon, while defense minister, had discussed with Lebanese Phalangist leaders "the need to avenge the assassination" of the president-elect of Lebanon, Bashir Gemayel. As the plaintiff's attorney told a U.S. District Court jury in New York, the article "put the stamp of mass murderer" on his client because shortly after the reputed discussion supposedly took place, Phalangist troops massacred 700 Palestinian refugees in two West Beirut camps. *Time* said it had relied on secret Israeli government documents, but the main government document, produced during the trial, did not support the magazine's contention.

After more than 80 hours of deliberation, the jury of four women and two men reached these conclusions:

1. The paragraph complained of was false.
2. It defamed Sharon.
3. It did not result from actual malice.

Thus, Sharon won on two of his contentions, but lost on the pivotal third and therefore did not collect any damages. However, *Time* did not escape unscathed. Both parties spent an estimated $3 million for trial costs, and after the verdict, the jury issued a statement in which it said:

> Certain *Time* employees, particularly correspondent David Halevy (who provided the material that led to the disputed paragraph) acted carelessly and negligently in reporting and verifying information that ultimately found its way into the published paragraph in this case.

Sharon did better when he brought a similar suit—this one for $250,000 in damages—against *Time* in an Israeli court. The suit was dismissed in 1986 after the court approved a compromise settlement that involved a Time, Inc., agreement to contribute to Sharon's legal expenses (the amount was not divulged) and to file a statement expressing regret.[57] *Time* admitted that the matter of revenge was not discussed by Sharon and no such statement was contained in an Israeli commission report of the massacre.

Westmoreland v. CBS.

Westmoreland v. CBS. In a documentary, "The Uncounted Enemy: A Vietnam Deception," aired January 23, 1982, CBS accused retired Army General William C. Westmoreland of suppressing U.S. intelligence reports that purportedly showed enemy troop strength higher than previously reported.

Westmoreland filed a $120 million defamation lawsuit against the network and three other defendants.

According to the documentary, Westmoreland underestimated enemy troop strength to make it appear that his forces were winning a war of attrition and because reports of higher enemy strength would be "politically unacceptable," as one witness said during the eight-week trial in a New York federal court in 1985. That trial ended abruptly when Westmoreland agreed to dismissal of his lawsuit. Trial costs for both parties at the time of dismissal were estimated as high as $9 million!

A joint statement was issued with both parties claiming victory. CBS stuck by its documentary and offered no apology or retraction. Westmoreland said he had succeeded in clearing his name, presumably as a result of the publicizing of his case at the bar of public opinion. But it was clear that testimony by several CBS defense witnesses who were former high-ranking intelligence officers during the Vietnam War had made it extremely unlikely that Westmoreland could have shown actual malice on the part of the network and the other defendants. Indeed, the testimony of these former Westmoreland aides made another CBS defense—truth—seem rather strong.

Tavoulareas v. Washington Post. In 1987, the *en banc* U.S. Court of Appeals for the District of Columbia Circuit voted 7–1 to reverse a 2–1 panel decision by the same court that had reinstated a $2 million libel judgment against the *Washington Post*.[58]

The suit was brought by William P. Tavoulareas, president of Mobil Oil Corporation, after publication of a story in 1979 that accused Tavoulareas of setting up his son in a multimillion dollar shipping business that operated Mobil-owned ships under exclusive, no-bid contracts. Tavoulareas sued, claiming that he was defamed by the story's implication that he had misused Mobil's assets to benefit his son.

In 1982, a U.S. District Court jury found that the *Post* had libeled the elder Tavoulareas and awarded him compensatory and punitive damages totaling $2.05 million. But in 1983, District Court Judge Oliver Gasch threw out the verdict and his decision was appealed to the District of Columbia Circuit Court. A three-judge panel voted 2–1 to reinstate the jury's verdict. The judges favoring reinstatement were George MacKinnon and Antonin Scalia. They said the *Post's* reporter knowingly adopted an adversarial stance toward Tavoulareas and that the newspaper encouraged "hard-hitting investigative journalism." These factors suggested to the two judges that any errors in the stories arose from a reckless disregard for the truth. But the *en banc* court, with only McKinnon dissenting (Scalia having by then taken a seat on the Supreme Court bench), said the *Post's* story was substantially true and that Tavoulareas, as a limited public figure, had not met his obligation to show actual malice by clear and convincing proof.[59]

The court noted that Tavoulareas relied heavily on unpublished, internal *Post* memoranda in his attempt to prove actual malice.

"This will not do," wrote senior Judge J. Skelly Wright and Judge Kenneth W. Starr. "Nothing in law or common sense supports saddling a libel defendant with civil liability for a defamatory implication nowhere to be found in the published article itself." Furthermore, said the court, "an adversarial stance is fully consistent with professional investigative reporting. . . . An adversarial stance is certainly not indicative of actual malice . . . where, as here, the reporter conducted a detailed investigation and wrote a story that is substantially true."[60]

The U.S. Supreme Court decided in 1987 not to review the case.

Newton v. NBC. In 1986, a federal jury in Las Vegas, Nevada, awarded entertainer Wayne Newton $19.2 million in libel damages against NBC and others for three reports about Newton that appeared on the television network's "Nightly News" in 1980 and 1981. The reports linked Newton to organized crime figures. The $19.2 million included $5 million in punitive damages, $5 million for injury to reputation, $7.9 million for loss of income, $1.1 million for loss of future income, and $225,000 for physical and mental suffering.

Judge M. D. Crocker upheld the punitive damage award, but overturned the $13.2 million compensatory damages award saying that the evidence supported an award of only $275,000 including the $225,000 for physical and mental suffering.[61] The judge gave Newton until February 1989 to accept the reduced amount or face a new trial on the monetary award.[62] Newton accepted the reduced amount ($6 million, including interest). NBC is appealing.

Concerning the punitive damages award, Judge Crocker said the award is supported by the evidence, and "since NBC has a net worth of $2 billion, the award was not so excessive as to shock the conscience of the court."[63]

Zerangue v. TSP Newspapers (1987). The Fifth Circuit U.S. Court of Appeals ruled in this case that a newspaper's publication of erroneous information less than a month after it had published the same erroneous information raised a jury issue as to actual malice.[64] The erroneous information was twice published in the *Daily World* of St. Landry Parish, La. And both times the newspaper published retractions.

The court said that a publisher has "clear First Amendment protection from liability for the first nonmalicious publication of an erroneous story. However, once the publisher knows that the story is erroneous—as in the instant case—the argument for weighting the scales on the side of First Amendment interests becomes less compelling."[65]

Varanese v. Gail (1987). The Ohio Supreme Court defined actual malice for the first time in the context of advertising when it ruled in this case that a newspaper defendant was not responsible for information published in political advertisements unless "it knew that the ad was false before publication, or where the ad is so inherently improbable on its face, that the defendant must have realized the ad was probably false."[66] Actual malice, said the court in its 6–1 decision, cannot be inferred from evidence of personal spite, ill will, or deliberate intention to injure because the defendant's motives for publishing are irrelevant.

The case resulted from a political advertisement published by the *Geauga Times Leader* that accused a county treasurer of malfeasance in office and of favoring the elimination of services for veterans and the elderly. Footnotes to the allegations in the ad cited the *Times Leader* as the source. The treasurer filed a libel action against the newspaper and in 1985 a Common Pleas Court judge granted summary judgment for the newspaper. An appellate court reinstated the libel case, ruling that a jury could reasonably infer that the newspaper lacked good faith by "sitting back, playing dumb, and claiming reliance on the integrity of the Republican leaders who submitted the ad . . . for publication." The three-judge panel said that the trial court record contained evidence from which a jury could find actual malice with convincing clarity. An appeal then was taken to the state's highest court.

SUMMARY

In *New York Times Co. v. Sullivan* (1964), the U.S. Supreme Court for the first time extended First Amendment protection to libelous words when those words related to the official conduct of a public official. This was a conditional constitutional privilege, the condition being that the defamatory words did not result from "actual malice." And actual malice was defined as knowingly publishing falsehoods or reckless disregard of the truth.

The Court had to overcome obstacles to even consider the case because libel, until then, had been exclusively the province of state law. To the argument that no "state action" was involved in the purely private defamation suit (as would have been the case in a criminal libel action), Justice Brennan replied that the state by law had made it possible for the libel suit to be brought in the first instance. As for the argument that the defamatory words were contained in an advertisement and that historically commercial speech had not enjoyed First Amendment protection, Brennan responded that this was not commercial advertising in the usual sense; rather, it communicated information, expressed opinion, recited grievances on matters of highest public interest and therefore warranted inclusion within the protection of the First Amendment which attempts to secure "the widest possible dissemination of information from diverse and antagonistic sources." As for the contention that libel had always been a state matter lying beyond the reach of the First Amendment — on the theory that false speech ought not be protected — Brennan brusquely swept such an argument aside. He termed the word "libel" a mere label which could not be used to repress speech dealing with public questions and issues. Furthermore, in wide-open debate of the type envisioned as protected by the First Amendment, some falsity was inevitable. Therefore, even some false speech must be protected if freedoms of expression are to have the "breathing space" they need to survive.

Times-Sullivan was applied to a criminal libel statute in *Garrison v. State of Louisiana* (1964). The Louisiana law was declared unconstitutional. In the process, the U.S. Supreme Court declared that only those statements about public officials which are made with a "high degree of awareness of their falsity" can be subjected to sanctions by either criminal or civil libel laws. Thus, a state law which stipulated that *only* truth with good motives and for justifiable ends could be used as a defense in a criminal libel case clearly was unconstitutional.

Garrison also extended the protection of the actual malice rule to any speech which "might touch on an official's fitness for office." Thus, the media could report on matters which went beyond the obvious public side of a public official's life.

The *Garrison* ruling that "high degree of awareness of falsity" defined "actual malice" was expanded in a civil libel action, *St. Amant v. Thompson* (1968), such that evidence was required to show that the defendant entertained serious doubts about the truth of his publication. Absent such proof, which had to be established by "clear and convincing" evidence, as the Supreme Court ruled in *Anderson v. Liberty Lobby* (1986), there can be no finding of actual malice. But the Supreme Court also allowed libel plaintiffs to penetrate the editorial process and the minds of journalists in order to make it possible for them to show actual malice, doing so in *Herbert v. Lando* (1979).

The "actual malice" rule was extended to include reports about "public figures," commencing with the Supreme Court's decision in 1967 in the combined cases of *Curtis Publishing Co. v. Butts* and *Associated Press v. Walker.* Then, in 1971, a plurality opinion of the Supreme Court in *Rosenbloom v. Metromedia* changed the thrust of the constitutional protection from the type of individual involved to whether the "utterance" concerned an issue of public or general concern. Just what that meant was to be decided by future cases. For the next three years, various courts went about the task of delineating the meaning of that term. Such efforts came to a grinding halt in 1974 when a majority of the U.S. Supreme Court fashioned new parameters within which libel suits by "private individuals" were to be decided. However, the actual malice rule still retains its vitality insofar as libel suits by public officials and public figures are concerned.

There are problems. They include knowing when someone is or is not a public official or public figure (a difficulty to be examined more fully in Chapter 6), defining — especially in a "hot news" situation — what "actual malice" consists of, and knowing when a matter being reported is or is not of public interest (and some jurisdictions require that the reports be of *legitimate* public interest for the *Times-Sullivan* privilege to apply).

The establishment of actual malice by "clear and convincing proof" requires a plaintiff to focus on the defendant's state of mind or conduct. A number of cases now provide examples of knowing falsity or reckless disregard of the truth.

QUESTIONS IN REVIEW

1. Why is *Times-Sullivan* a landmark decision of the U.S. Supreme Court?
2. What is the "actual malice" rule or standard as stated in *Times-Sullivan*?
3. How did the Supreme Court in *Garrison v. Louisiana* define the meaning of "reckless disregard"?
4. What was the Court's definition of reckless disregard in *St. Amant v. Thompson*?
5. What is the significance of *Curtis Publishing Co. v. Butts* (1967)?
6. Why was the Louisiana criminal libel statute found to be unconstitutional?
7. If the *Rosenbloom* rationale had survived (as part of a plurality opinion of the U.S. Supreme Court), how would the conditional constitutional privilege enunciated in *Times-Sullivan* have changed?
8. *Herbert v. Lando* (1979) was sharply criticized by the news media. Why?
9. *Anderson v. Liberty Lobby* (1986) requires what kind of proof of actual malice?

ANSWERS

1. Because it extended for the first time a conditional First Amendment privilege (constitutional privilege) to false and defamatory speech.
2. A public official must show that a defamatory falsehood relating to his official conduct was made with knowledge that it was false or with reckless disregard of whether it was false. Note that under *Times-Sullivan* the burden of proof is shifted to the plaintiff whereas under state libel law the news media had the burden of proving the truth of what was broadcast or printed.
3. False statements must be made with a high degree of awareness as to their falsity.
4. That the defendant entertained serious doubts as to the truth of what was published or uttered.
5. The conditional constitutional privilege was extended to reports about "public figures."
6. Because the statute permitted only the defense of truth with good motives and for justifiable ends — but *Times-Sullivan* interpreted the First Amendment as protecting falsity about public officials and their conduct up to the point of reckless disregard of the truth or knowing falsity.
7. The protection afforded would no longer have been based on the type of individual involved (such as a public official) but on the nature of the reports; that is, whether such reports concerned matters of public interest or general public concern.
8. Because it allows libel plaintiffs to penetrate into the editorial process or into the mind of a journalist.
9. Clear and convincing evidence.

ENDNOTES

1. New York Times v. Sullivan, 376 U.S. 254, 84 S.Ct. 710, 11 L.Ed.2d 686.
2. Hutchinson v. Proxmire, 5 *Med.L.Rptr.* 1279, July 31, 1979. See n. 8 in opinion.
3. Rosenblatt v. Baer, 381 U.S. 75, 1 *Med.L.Rptr.* 1558 (1966).
4. See case citations in Foster v. Laredo Newspapers, Inc., 541 S.W.2d 809, 814 (Texas Supreme Court, 1976).
5. Ibid.
6. Ibid.
7. Houston Chronicle v. Stewart, 9 *Med.L.Rptr.* 2318 (Texas Court of Appeals, 1983); Himango v. Prime Time Broadcasting, 10 *Med.L.Rptr.* 1724 (Washington Court of Appeals, 1984).
8. Beauharnais v. Illinois, 343 U.S. 250, 72 S.Ct. 725, 96 L.Ed. 919.
9. New York Times v. Sullivan, *op. cit.,* 376 U.S. at 268, 84 S.Ct. at 719–20, 11 L.Ed.2d at 699.
10. People v. Heinrich, 104 Ill.2d 137, 470 N.E.2d 966 (1984); appeal dismissed, 471 U.S. 101 (1985).
11. Garrison v. State of Louisiana, 379 U.S. 64, 85 S.Ct. 209, 13 L.Ed.2d 125 (1964). Black, Douglas, and Goldberg wrote separate but concurring opinions.
12. Ibid., 85 S.Ct. at 212–13.
13. Chaplinsky v. New Hampshire, 315 U.S. 568, 62 S.Ct. 766, 86 L.Ed. 1031 (1942).
14. Garrison v. Louisiana, op. cit., note 11, 85 S.Ct. at 213.
15. Weston v. State of Arkansas, 528 S.W.2d 412, 258 Ark. 707, 712.
16. Commonwealth v. Armao, 286 A.2d 626 (Pennsylvania Supreme Court, 1972).
17. Pat Eberle v. Municipal Court of Los Angeles, 127 Cal. Rptr. 594 (1976). Justice Mosk dissented; Justices Wood and Lillie concurred in the opinion written by Justice Hanson.
18. Ibid., at 600.
19. Keeton v. Hustler Magazine, Inc., 10 *Med.L.Rptr.* 1405, 1408, n. 6, April 3, 1984. The statute is N.H.R.S.A. § 644:11(A).
20. "News Notes," *Media Law Reporter,* April 3, 1984.
21. *The NEWS Media & The LAW,* Summer 1988, pp. 3–4.
22. Curtis Publishing Co. v. Butts, and Associated Press v. Walker, 388 U.S. 130, 87 S.Ct. 1975, 18 L.Ed.2d 1094.
23. Briscoe v. Readers Digest, 93 Cal. Rptr. 866, 483 P.2d 34. See also Chapter 7.
24. Rosenbloom v. Metromedia, 403 U.S. 29, 91 S.Ct. 1811, 29 L.Ed.2d 296. Also, see Appendix A, plurality and majority opinions of Supreme Court.
25. "Where We Stand: A Legal View," reprinted from *Columbia Journalism Review,* September/October 1971, p. 39.
26. Time, Inc. v. McLaney, 406 F.2d 565, 573 (1969), cert. denied; Bon Air Hotel, Inc. v. Time, Inc., 426 F.2d 858, 861(1970); and Dacey v. Florida Bar, Inc., 427 F.2d 1292, 1295 (1970).
27. See for example, Kalven, *"The New York Times* Case: A Note on 'The Central Meaning of the First Amendment,' " 1964 *Supreme Court Review* 191, 221; and "The Scope of First Amendment Protection for Good-Faith Defamatory Error," 75 *Yale Law Journal* 642, 644–45 (1966).
28. Harnish v. Herald-Mail Co., Inc., 286 A.2d 146, 153.
29. St. Amant v. Thompson, 390 U.S. 727, 88 S.Ct. 1323, 20 L.Ed.2d 262 (1968).
30. Ibid., 390 U.S. at 731, 88 S.Ct. at 1325.
31. Herbert v. Lando, 441 U.S. 153, 160, 4 *Med.L.Rptr.* 2575 (1979).
32. Gertz v. Welch, Inc., 8 *Med.L.Rptr.* 1760, 1776 (1982), July 27, 1982.
33. Ibid.
34. Op. cit., n. 31.
35. Floyd Abrams, in a monograph published by the American Bar Association's Section of Criminal Justice, *The Future of "Newsmen's Privilege": The Whither and Whether of Disclosure for Newspersons* (Washington, D.C.: 1975), p. 8. Reprinted by permission.
36. "News Notes," *Media Law Reporter,* May 20, 1980.
37. Vanenburg v. Newsweek, 507 F.2d 1024 (5th Circuit).
38. Stone v. Essex County Newspapers, Inc., 330 N.E.2d 161, 164 (1975).
39. "News Notes," *Media Law Reporter,* December 10, 1985, 54 *U.S. Law Week* 4755.

40. *Des Moines* (Iowa) *Register,* June 26, 1986, p. 1A.
41. 746 F.2d 1563, 11 *Med.L.Rptr.* 1001.
42. *The NEWS Media & The LAW,* Summer 1986, pp. 12–13.
43. Ibid., p. 13.
44. Farmers Educational and Cooperative Union of America v. WDAY Inc., 360 U.S. 525, 79 S.Ct. 1302, 3 L.Ed.2d 1407.
45. Summit Hotel v. NBC, 8 A.2d 302, 312.
46. Snowden v. Pearl River Broadcasting Corp., 251 So.2d 405 (Louisiana Appeal Court, 1971).
47. Denman v. Star Broadcasting Co., 497 P.2d 1378 (1972).
48. Adams v. Frontier Broadcasting Co., 2 *Med.L.Rptr.* 1166 (1976).
49. Ibid., at 1167.
50. Ogden Bus Lines v. KSL, Inc., 551 P.2d 222.
51. "News Notes," *Media Law Reporter,* April 24, 1984. The conference was sponsored by the American Bar Association's Forum Committee on Communications Law, the American Newspaper Publishers Association, and the American Society of Newspaper Editors.
52. Ibid.
53. Pat Montandon v. Triangle Publications, Inc., 45 Cal. App.3d 938, 120 Cal. Rptr. 186.
54. Ibid., at 944.
55. "News Notes," *Media Law Reporter,* January 23, 1979.
56. *Editor & Publisher,* January 20, 1979, p. 48.
57. "News Notes," *Media Law Reporter,* February 4, 1986.
58. *Editor & Publisher,* March 21, 1987, p. 15.
59. 55 *U.S. Law Week* 2503, March 24, 1987, and 13 *Med.L.Rptr.* 2377, May 26, 1987.
60. Op. cit., n. 58.
61. "News Notes," *Media Law Reporter,* December 1, 1987.
62. "News Notes," *Media Law Reporter,* February 9, 1988.
63. Op. cit., n. 61.
64. "News Notes," *Media Law Reporter,* May 5, 1987.
65. Ibid.
66. *The NEWS Media & The LAW,* Spring 1988, pp. 9–10, 35 Ohio St. 3d 78, 518 N.E.2d 1117 (1987).

6

Private Individuals, Libel, and Media Vulnerability

HIGHLIGHTS

■ In *Gertz v. Welch, Inc.* (1974), the Supreme Court returned the development of libel law back to the states whenever a "private individual" is involved. In effect, states can impose any standard of care they choose so long as they do not impose liability without fault. And the award of any "punitive" damage must be based on "actual malice," as defined in *Times-Sullivan*.

   Gertz and subsequent cases make it clear that private persons must voluntarily thrust themselves into the public limelight or public controversy to become public figures. As the Court said in *Wolston v. Reader's Digest Association* (1979), a private individual is not automatically transformed into a public figure just by becoming involved in a matter that attracts public attention. "Newsworthiness" alone is not the test of public figure status.

■ Different standards of care have been adopted by the states since *Gertz,* but most have opted for an "ordinary negligence" standard.

■ The public interest/public concern test regained vitality in *Dun & Bradstreet v. Greenmoss Builders, Inc.* (1985) and *Philadelphia Newspapers v. Hepps* (1986). A matter of private concern does not warrant the protection afforded by *Gertz,* said a divided Court in *Dun & Bradstreet;* and private figure libel plaintiffs must demonstrate falsity if the alleged defamatory statements involve matters of public concern.

■ In *Bose Corporation v. Consumers Union* (1984), the Supreme
Court held that federal appellate judges must independently review
both the facts and the law in appropriate cases to determine if actual malice has been established with convincing clarity. The decision is important because trial court verdicts often go against media
defendants.

■ Concern has been allayed somewhat by *Anderson v. Liberty Lobby*
(1986) and subsequent developments such that summary judgment
remains available to the news media in defamation action.

Just as it appeared that the *Rosenbloom* plurality opinion was taking hold in
various jurisdictions, a majority of the U.S. Supreme Court decided to make the
news media more vulnerable to libel suits by *private individuals* if the states so
desired. During the interval between *Rosenbloom* and the Supreme Court's decision in *Gertz v. Robert Welch, Inc.* (1974),[1] at least 17 states and several U.S.
Courts of Appeals adopted the *Rosenbloom* plurality opinion as governing libel
actions filed by any type of individual.[2]

The extent to which *Rosenbloom* might have insulated the press from libel
suits is illustrated by the views of Chief U.S. District Court Judge Raymond
Pettine who, just prior to *Gertz,* dismissed a $5 million libel suit against the
Providence Journal Co. in Rhode Island. Pettine said of *Rosenbloom* that it
"may well have the practical effect of affirming the total immunity theory for the
news media."[3] He continued, "After all, what incident covered by the news media
is not or does not become an event of public interest? . . . Indeed, why is a court
better equipped than the professional media to define the parameters of what
events involve public or general interest?"

The press relished such a result. Then came the *Gertz* case.

GERTZ v. WELCH, INC. (1984)

This case indirectly stemmed from the 1968 slaying of a Chicago youth by a
policeman, Richard Nuccio, who later was convicted of second-degree murder.
The family of the slain youth retained Attorney Elmer Gertz to represent them in
civil litigation against Nuccio.

The John Birch Society's monthly magazine, *American Opinion,* commis-
sioned a freelance writer to do an article which appeared in the March 1969 issue.
In that article, Gertz was accused of having a criminal record, of being a "Communist-fronter," and of being the "architect" of a "frame-up" of the Chicago
policeman. He brought a defamation suit against Robert Welch, Inc., the magazine's publisher. A U.S. District Court judge ruled that the article was libelous
per se and a jury awarded Gertz $50,000 in damages. But the judge (prior to the
Supreme Court's *Rosenbloom* decision) reconsidered the applicability of the "ac-

tual malice" test to a defamation suit brought by a private citizen and decided that Gertz would have to show "actual malice" in accordance with the *New York Times* standard. The judge thereupon entered a judgment for Welch, and the Seventh Circuit Court of Appeals sustained the district judge's action. Gertz appealed.

Justice Powell delivered the Court's opinion which drew concurrence from Justices Marshall, Stewart, Blackmun, and Rehnquist. Justice White would have gone further than the majority in returning the development of libel law as it pertains to private citizens to the states where, he contended, it rightfully belongs. Chief Justice Burger and Justices Brennan and Douglas dissented.

Powell began his opinion for the Court in this way: "This Court has struggled for nearly a decade to define the proper accommodation between the law of defamation and the freedoms of speech and press protected by the First Amendment. With this decision we return to that effort. . . ."

In reviewing *Rosenbloom,* Powell pointed to the five separate opinions from among the eight justices who participated (Douglas did not) and said that none of the opinions had commanded more than three votes. He then gave this rationale for leaving the conditional constitutional privilege intact insofar as public officials and public figures are concerned, but rejecting such a privilege in connection with private individuals: Public officials and public figures have greater access to mass media channels to counteract false statements about them (the self-help theory), therefore, they need less libel law protection. But private persons are more vulnerable to injury. The state's interest in protecting such persons therefore is correspondingly greater. Further, those who run for office or who become public figures voluntarily expose themselves to an increased risk of injury from defamatory falsehoods. Thus, private citizens not only are more vulnerable to injury than are public officials and public figures, they are more deserving in terms of recovery of damages.

Concerning private individuals, Powell declared for the Court that states may define for themselves appropriate standards of liability for publishers and broadcasters as long as they do not impose "liability without fault." The same idea was put forth by Harlan in his *Rosenbloom* dissent. The majority also tacked on three other requirements.

1. A state cannot adopt a standard which permits liability for a mere factual misstatement; rather, the substance of the defamatory statement must warn a "reasonably prudent editor or broadcaster" of its defamatory potential. Phrased another way, such a statement must make "substantial danger to reputation apparent."
2. A state can permit recovery of damages only for "actual injury." However, "actual injury," according to Powell, includes not only out-of-pocket losses, but also impairment of reputation and standing in the community, personal humiliation, and mental anguish and suffering.
3. Punitive damages — which, from a publisher's standpoint, often have been the most fearsome aspect of libel suits since they are awarded not for actual injury but to punish a publisher for carelessness — can be

awarded only on a showing of actual malice (as defined in *Times-Sullivan*).

Justice Powell concluded by saying that since the *Gertz* jury had been allowed to impose liability without proof of fault and presume damages without proof of injury, a new trial was necessary. Therefore, the Court reversed the lower courts and remanded the case for further proceedings in accordance with the Court's decision.

Dissenting Opinions

In a strongly worded dissenting opinion, Justice White said that proving a defendant's culpability beyond the act of publishing the defamatory material places a heavy burden on the person bringing the suit. If the plaintiff succeeds in proving intentional or reckless falsehoods, or negligence, on the part of the publisher, then he must prove actual injury.

"Plainly," said White, "with the additional burden on the plaintiff of proving negligence or other fault, it will be exceedingly difficult, perhaps impossible, for . . . the plaintiff to vindicate his reputation interest by securing a judgment for nominal damages. . . ." Furthermore, he said, the states now must struggle to discern the meaning of such ill-defined concepts as "liability without fault" and to fashion novel rules for recovery of damages.

The Chief Justice's principal reason for dissent concerned the apparent reinstitution of a negligence standard for punishing defamatory falsehoods about private persons. Burger said he did not know the parameters of a "negligence" test, but he agreed with Justices Brennan and Douglas that such a test would inhibit some editors. He did, however, agree with Justice White that the orderly development of libel law, insofar as private figures are concerned, would best take place in the states.

Justice Brennan, adhering to his views in *Rosenbloom,* argued that the *Gertz* decision would result in self-censorship on the part of editors and writers, contrary to the command of the First Amendment that debate on public issues be uninhibited, robust, and wide open. Further, he contended that the concept of a "private figure" was difficult to operationalize since all persons are, to some degree, "public" figures. Brennan also raised the spectre of juries punishing the news media for expressing unpopular views despite the majority's caveat that there could be no liability without fault and no recovery of damages (absent "actual malice") without actual injury.

Justice Douglas warned:

It matters little whether the standard be articulated as "malice" or "reckless disregard of the truth" or "negligence," for jury determinations by any of those criteria are virtually unreviewable. [But see *Bose Corporation v. Consumers Union,* discussed later, decided 10 years after *Gertz*]. . . . The standard announced today leaves the States free to "define for themselves the appropriate standard of liability for a publisher or broadcaster" in the circumstances of this case. This, of course, leaves the simple negligence standard as an option, with the jury free to impose damages upon a finding that the publisher failed to act as "a reasonable man." With such continued erosion of First Amendment protection, I fear that it may well be the reasonable man who refrains from speaking.

Who Is or Is Not a Public Figure?

In *Gertz,* the court narrowed the "public figure" category and enlarged that class of people known as "private figures." As Powell said for the Court:

> Hypothetically it may be possible for someone to become a public figure through no purposeful action of his own, but the instances of truly involuntary public figures must be exceedingly rare. For the most part those who attain this status have assumed roles of special prominence in the affairs of society. Some occupy positions of such persuasive power and influence that they are deemed public figures for all purposes. More commonly, those classed as public figures have thrust themselves to the forefront of particular public controversies in order to influence the resolution of the issues involved. In either event, they invite attention and comment.

Thus, those who are not public officials or who have not taken "purposeful action" to thrust themselves into the public limelight, or otherwise involve themselves in public issues, remain private figures who (1) on a showing of liability because of fault, and (2) a showing of actual injury, can recover for defamatory falsehoods if state law permits. Further, a showing of actual malice can result in the award of punitive damages.

Despite such safeguards for the media, the Court's pullback from *Rosenbloom* is a costly one for the media as shown by what ultimately happened in the *Gertz* case. After remand, it took eight years for the case to be retried. In 1981 a jury awarded Gertz $100,000 in compensatory damages and $300,000 in punitive damages. On appeal, a three-judge panel of the Seventh Circuit U.S. Court of Appeals affirmed the award[4] and the U.S. Supreme Court in 1983 declined to review,[5] thereby ending litigation begun in 1969!

The dilemma posed by the *Gertz* case—who is or is not a public figure—continues to perplex the news media and others for, as Brennan noted in his dissenting opinion, the concept of "private figure" is difficult to operationalize. A Supreme Court case in 1976 pointed up this difficulty of making the public/private figure distinction.

Time, Inc. v. Firestone. The *Firestone* libel case began with the publication in December 1967 of the following item in the "Milestones" section of *Time* magazine:

> DIVORCED. By Russell A. Firestone Jr., 41, heir to the tire fortune; Mary Alice Sullivan Firestone, 32, his third wife; a onetime Palm Beach schoolteacher; on grounds of extreme cruelty and adultery; after six years of marriage, one son; in West Palm Beach, Fla. The 17-month intermittent trial produced enough testimony of extramarital adventures on both sides, said the judge, "to make Dr. Freud's hair curl."

As it turned out, the divorce was not granted on the ground of adultery, but rather because the parties were not "domesticated," which, according to Justice Marshall in his dissenting opinion, was not a statutory ground for divorce in Florida.[6]

Ms. Firestone had requested a retraction, a prerequisite under Florida law if a libel lawsuit is to be brought. The magazine refused; the suit was filed, and *Time* won at the lower court level. But that decision was overturned by the state supreme court in 1972 on the ground that the news item was not an event of "great public interest," or did not relate to matters of public or general concern.[7] The case was returned to the lower court to be tried in accordance with Florida's common law on libel. At the time, the state supreme court made a distinction between the public being "titillated or intrigued" by the divorce trial and "real public or general *concern.*" The divorce unquestionably was newsworthy, said the court, but not of real public concern.

Following the trial, Ms. Firestone was awarded $100,000 in damages, which the state's Fourth Circuit Court of Appeals overturned, in part, said the court, because *Time* had fairly reported the final judgment and because the plaintiff had not established any recoverable damages.[8] The state supreme court, in a 5–3 opinion given a few months after *Gertz,* ordered reinstatement of the damages on the basis that the erroneous report of adultery was clear and convincing evidence of negligence.[9] It was *Time*'s turn to appeal.

A majority of the U.S. Supreme Court concluded that Ms. Firestone was a private individual and, therefore, Florida libel law (a negligence test when defamation suits are brought by private persons) should apply. However, the Court remanded the case for a finding of fault, as required by *Gertz.* This action astonished two concurring Justices (Powell and Stewart) because, in their judgment, the Florida Supreme Court already had made such a determination.

Time, Inc., had contended that Ms. Firestone was a public figure and that the "Milestones" item constituted a report of judicial proceeding that deserved the protection of the actual malice standard.

In his opinion for the majority, Justice Rehnquist rejected these arguments. Citing *Gertz* and the requirement that public figures are those who have thrust themselves into the forefront of public controversies, Rehnquist said:

> Respondent [Ms. Firestone] did not assume any role of especial prominence in the affairs of society, other than perhaps Palm Beach society, and she did not thrust herself to the forefront of any particular public controversy. . . .
>
> Petitioner contends that because the Firestone divorce was characterized by the Florida Supreme Court as a "cause cèlèbre," it must have been a public controversy and respondent must be considered a public figure. But in so doing petitioner seeks to equate "public controversy" with all controversies of interest to the public. Were we to accept this reasoning, we would reinstate the doctrine advanced in the plurality opinion in *Rosenbloom* . . . which concluded that the *New York Times* privilege should be extended to falsehoods defamatory of private persons whenever the statements concern matters of general or public interest. In *Gertz,* however, the Court repudiated this position. . . .
>
> Dissolution of a marriage through judicial proceedings is not the sort of "public

controversy" referred to in *Gertz,* even though the marital difficulties of extremely wealthy individuals may be of interest to some portion of the reading public. Nor did respondent freely choose to publicize issues as to the propriety of her married life. She was compelled to go to court by the State in order to obtain legal release from the bonds of matrimony. . . . . Her actions, both in instituting the litigation and in its conduct, were quite different from those of General Walker [*AP v. Walker*]. . . . She assumed no "special prominence in the resolution of public questions." Gertz, 418 U.S., at 351, 94 S.Ct., at 3013. We hold respondent was not a "public figure" for the purpose of determining the constitutional protection afforded petitioner's report of the factual and legal basis for the divorce.[10]

In rejecting a blanket privilege for reports of judicial proceedings, as claimed by *Time,* Rehnquist said:

> The details of many, if not most, courtroom battles would add almost nothing towards advancing the uninhibited debate on public issues thought to provide principal support for the decision in *New York Times.* . . . And while participants in some litigation may be legitimate "public figures," either generally or for the limited purpose of that litigation, the majority will more likely resemble respondent, drawn into a public forum largely against their will in order to attempt to obtain the only redress available to them or to defend themselves against actions brought by the State or by others. There appears little reason why these individuals should substantially forfeit that degree of protection which the law of defamation would otherwise afford them simply by virtue of their being drawn into a courtroom. The public interest in accurate reports of judicial proceedings is substantially protected by *Cox Broadcasting Co.*[11]

Inaccurate and defamatory reports about private individuals deserve no First Amendment protection, said Rehnquist, adding that *Gertz* provides "an adequate safeguard for the constitutionally protected interests of the press and affords it a tolerable margin for error by requiring some type of fault."

As for the ambiguities in the divorce decree itself, Rehnquist dealt another blow to *Time* by stating,

> Petitioner may well argue that the meaning of the trial court's decree was unclear, but this does not license it to choose from among several conceivable interpretations the one most damaging to respondent. Having chosen to follow this tack, petitioner must be able to establish not merely that the item reported was a conceivable or plausible interpretation of the decree, but that the item was factually correct.

Since *Gertz* established that there must be evidence of some fault on the part of a publisher, and since there was no such finding by the trial judge or jury, the case was remanded.

Justice Powell (joined by Justice Stewart) concurred "on the basic principles involved" in what he termed "this bizarre case," and he did so "in order to avoid the appearance of fragmentation of the Court on the basic principles involved. . . ."

Powell did not specify whether he believed that Ms. Firestone was a private figure. Presumably he and Stewart agreed with Rehnquist, Blackmun, and Chief Justice Burger because this was a basic issue in *Firestone*. Rather, he confined his opinion to the question of fault on the part of *Time*. "There is no recognition in the opinion by Rehnquist of the ambiguity of the divorce decree and no discussion of any of the efforts made by *Time* to verify the accuracy of its news report," he wrote. "Nor was there any weighing of the evidence to determine whether there was actionable negligence by *Time* under the *Gertz* standard."

Powell's opinion reads as though he already had reached a conclusion concerning the requisite fault necessary for a finding against *Time*. He wrote, in part, ". . . [T]he decision of the [divorce court] may have been sufficiently ambiguous to have caused reasonably prudent newsmen to read it as granting divorce on the ground of adultery," and "there was substantial evidence supportive of *Time*'s defense that it was not guilty of actionable negligence."[12]

Dissenting Opinions

Brennan, adhering to his views in *Rosenbloom,* dissented, saying what was at stake in *Firestone* "is the ability of the press to report to the citizenry the events transpiring in the nation's judiciary systems." He warned that "error in reporting and debate concerning the judicial process is inevitable" because of the law's complexity, and that any standard—such as the one laid down in *Firestone*—"which would require strict accuracy in reporting legal events factually or in commenting upon them in the press would be an impossible one."[13] To prevent self-censorship, Brennan said the *New York Times* standard should apply to the reporting of *public* judicial affairs.

Justice White also dissented, arguing that *Gertz* was not applicable to this case because the defamatory report had been published in December 1967, long before *Gertz;* therefore, state libel law applied. However, White left no doubt that he believed that any requisite fault had been properly found by the Florida courts.[14]

Marshall also dissented, in part because he believed Ms. Firestone to be a public figure and, alternatively, because there was insufficient basis for a finding of fault under *Gertz*. "The choice of one of several rational interpretations of an ambiguous document, without more, is insufficient to support a finding of fault under *Gertz*," he wrote.[15] Furthermore, he said the Court's disposition of the case is "baffling." As he pointed out, the Florida Supreme Court had termed *Time*'s report a "flagrant example of 'journalistic negligence,'" yet at least three of the members of the Court (Rehnquist, Blackmun, and Burger) apparently were unwilling to read that statement as a conscious determination of fault. If that is not a determination of fault, asked Marshall, what is? It is a determination that is "wholly unsupportable" by facts, he added.

Whether there was the requisite fault will never be known. In 1978, at the time attorneys were discussing arrangements for a new trial, a notice of dismissal of the case was filed. After 10 years of litigation, Mrs. John Asher, the former Ms. Firestone, decided to drop her libel action against *Time* because, according to her attorneys, she believed that she "was completely vindicated by the jury verdict seven and a half years ago."[16]

Firestone and *Gertz* hinged, in large measure, on whether the plaintiffs were private figures, or whether they voluntarily became involved in the events that led to the media reports. Ms. Firestone was compelled by the state to go to court to obtain a divorce; hence, her action was involuntary. Clearly, such a test greatly expands that class of people labeled "private" individuals and contracts that group called "public figures."

Since *Gertz,* various courts have declared the following to be "private persons": the owner of an auto repair business who was falsely reported to have pleaded guilty to a charge of cruelty to animals;[17] a New York restaurant;[18] the wife and son of a police officer, but not the police officer;[19] a sports writer for the *Chicago Tribune* in the circumstances of a memorandum being posted in the sports department by an editor;[20] an automobile dealer;[21] a woman who denied being famed aviatrix Amelia Earhart (although the court said she would be classified as a public figure if she were Amelia Earhart);[22] a high corporation executive with Gulf and Western Industries;[23] a wrecking company;[24] and an advertising agency executive,[25] to name a few.

Wolston v. Reader's Digest Association. This case, decided by the Supreme Court in 1979, emphasizes the limited circumstances that must exist before a person becomes a public figure.[26] The Court, with dissent only from Justice Brennan, reversed the District of Columbia U.S. Court of Appeals' decision upholding a lower court's determination that the petitioner, Ilya Wolston, was a public figure. Not so, said Justice Rehnquist in his opinion for the Court.

A book written by John Barron, *KGB: The Secret Work of Soviet Agents,* was published in 1974 by Reader's Digest Association. One of the passages in the book incorrectly reported that Wolston was among a number of Soviet agents in the U.S. He sued the author and Reader's Digest Association. The U.S. District Court granted summary judgment to defendants, holding that Wolston was a public figure and that the false statement about Wolston did not constitute actual malice. The intermediate appellate court affirmed.

Wolston actually had been held in contempt of court for refusing to go before a grand jury, pleaded guilty, was handed a one-year suspended sentence and placed on probation conditioned on his cooperation with the grand jury investigation of Soviet espionage. There was a flurry of publicity about these events in mid-1958. As Rehnquist noted, after this publicity subsided Wolston "succeeded for the most part in returning to the private life he had led prior to the issuance of the grand jury subpoena."

Rehnquist disagreed with the lower courts and respondents that, by failing to appear before the grand jury and because of the contempt citation, Wolston "voluntarily thrust" or "injected" himself into the forefront of the public controversy surrounding the investigation of Soviet espionage in the U.S. As Rehnquist put it, "It would be more accurate to say that petitioner was dragged unwillingly into the controversy. The government pursued him in its investigaton." He added that the mere fact that Wolston chose not to appear before the grand jury, knowing that his action might be attended by publicity, was not decisive on the question of public figure status.

Although petitioner's actions were "newsworthy," Rehnquist said that did not make him a public figure. He added:

> A private individual is not automatically transformed into a public figure just by becoming involved in or associated with a matter that attracts public attention. To accept such reasoning would in effect reestablish the doctrine advanced by the plurality opinion in *Rosenbloom v. Metromedia*. . . . We repudiated this proposition in *Gertz* and *Firestone*, however, and we reject it again today. A libel defendant must show more than newsworthiness to justify application of the demanding burden of *New York Times*.

Rehnquist said that Wolston assumed no "special prominence in the resolution of public questions"—a quote from *Gertz*.[27] His failure to respond to the subpoena appeared to be caused by poor health. He communicated his desire to testify and, said Rehnquist, when that offer was rejected, he passively accepted punishment. "In short," Rehnquist declared, "we find no basis whatsoever for concluding that petitioner relinquished, to any degree, his interest in the protection of his own name." He continued:

> This reasoning leads us to reject the further contention of respondents that any person who engages in criminal conduct automatically becomes a public figure for purposes of comment on a limited range of issues relating to his conviction. . . .

To hold otherwise, said Rehnquist, would "create an 'open season' for all who sought to defame persons convicted of a crime."

Blackmun, with Marshall joining, concurred in the results (that Wolston was not a public figure), but he had trouble with the "sweep" of Rehnquist's opinion which, Blackmun wrote, "seems to hold . . . that a person becomes a limited-issue public figure only if he literally or figuratively 'mounts a rostrum' to advocate a particular view." He argued that there was no need to adopt so restrictive a definition of public figure on the facts then before the Court.

Brennan agreed with the district court's determination that Wolston was a public figure for the limited purpose of comment in connection with the espionage investigation. But he disagreed with the trial court in granting summary judgment to the author and publisher, saying instead that he thought there was a genuine issue of fact concerning the existence of actual malice.

The importance of *Wolston* is that it reemphasizes how large is that group known as private persons and, correspondingly, how small, by the Court's definitions, is that group called public figures. Mere involvement in courtroom situations or in news events some years earlier does not automatically mean that a person is a public figure.

Hutchinson v. Proxmire. On the same day the Court announced its decision in *Wolston*, it made public its decision in *Hutchinson*.[28] As discussed in the preceding chapter, the Court decided that Senator William Proxmire did not have absolute immunity for his press releases and newsletters concerning a Golden Fleece Award in connection with a grant made to a behavioral researcher.

In Chief Justice Burger's opinion for the Court, which drew dissent only from Justice Brennan, the researcher, Ronald Hutchinson, was found not to be a public figure, contrary to determinations made by lower courts. Those courts reached such a conclusion because of Hutchinson's successful application for federal funds and reports in local newspapers of the federal grant; and because of his access to the media, as demonstrated by his response to the announcement of the Golden Fleece Award. "Neither of those factors," wrote Burger, "demonstrates that Hutchinson was a public figure prior to the controversy engendered by the Golden Fleece Award; his access, such as it was, came after the alleged libel." Burger continued:

> . . . Clearly those charged with defamation cannot, by their own conduct, create their own defense by making the claimant a public figure. See *Wolston.* . . .
>
> Hutchinson did not thrust himself or his views into public controversy to influence others. Respondents have not identified such a particular controversy; at most, they point to concern about general public expenditures. But that concern is shared by most and relates to most public expenditures; it is not sufficient to make Hutchinson a public figure. If it were, everyone who received or benefited from the myriad public grants for research could be classified as a public figure—a conclusion that our previous opinions have rejected. . . .
>
> Moreover, Hutchinson at no time assumed any role of public prominence in the broad question of concern about expenditures. Neither his application for federal grants nor his publications in professional journals can be said to have invited that degree of public attention and comment on his receipt of federal grants essential to meet the public figure level. . . .
>
> Finally, we cannot agree that Hutchinson had such access to the media that he should be classified as a public figure. Hutchinson's access was limited to responding to the announcement of the Golden Fleece Award. He did not have the regular and continuing access to the media that is one of the accouterments of having become a public figure.

The *Hutchinson* decision sheds additional light on factors to be considered in deciding who is or is not a public figure. In connection with the self-help theory, Burger made it clear that Hutchinson's response to Senator Proxmire's announcement of the Golden Fleece Award did not meet the test of access to the media. Such access must be "regular and continuing," said Burger. Furthermore, libel defendants cannot create their own defense by making defamatory comments and then citing the ensuing controversy in order to claim that the defamed person is a public figure.

Public Figure Test

Gertz, Firestone, Wolston, and *Hutchinson* led a federal Circuit Court to announce an objective "public figure" test.

"Newsworthiness alone will not suffice," said the U.S. Court of Appeals for the District of Columbia Circuit Court in *Waldbaum v. Fairchild Publications* (1980).[29] In its opinion, the court put forth a test for determining who is a public figure. The test applies only to cases within the jurisdiction of the District of Columbia Circuit Court unless adopted by other jurisdictions.

According to Judge Edward Tamm, who gave the court's opinion, a libel plaintiff is a limited-issue public figure "if he is attempting to have, or realistically can be expected to have, a major impact on the resolution of a specific dispute that has foreseeable and substantial ramifications for persons beyond its immediate significance."

So saying, the court found Eric Waldbaum, former president of Greenbelt Consumer Services, Inc., a consumer cooperative, to be a public figure for the limited purpose of comment on Greenbelt's innovative policies such as unit pricing and open dating. Waldbaum had sued Fairchild Publications, Inc., because of an article in *Supermarket News* that reported on his ouster as Greenbelt president and that stated that Greenbelt had been losing money and retrenching.

In providing an objective test, Tamm said that a court, analyzing whether a plaintiff is a public figure, must look at the facts, taken as a whole, "through the eyes of a reasonable person." "This objective approach," he said, "should enable both the press and the individual in question to assess the individual's status, in advance, against the same yardstick."

The first step is to determine whether a plaintiff is a public figure for all purposes, Tamm said, adding:

> A person can be a general public figure only if he is a "celebrity"—his name a "household word"—whose ideas and actions the public in fact follows with great interest. As a general rule, a person who meets this test has access to the media if defamed [self-help theory]. In general, too, the person has assumed the risk that public exposure might lead to misstatements about him.

If a person is not a general-purpose public figure, the first step in determining the applicability of the limited-issue public figure definition is to "isolate the public controversy," Tamm said. "Courts must exercise care in deciding what is a public controversy. Newsworthiness alone will not suffice." A public controversy must be a real dispute, the outcome of which affects the general public or some segment of it in an appreciable way.

Tamm continued:

> Once the court has defined the controversy, it must analyze the plaintiff's role in it. Trivial or tangential participation is not enough. [The plaintiff] either must have been purposely trying to influence the outcome or could realistically have been expected, because of his position in the controversy, to have an impact on its resolution.

Finally, said Tamm, "the alleged defamation must have been germane to the plaintiff's participation in the controversy." The test is "whether a reasonable person would have concluded that this individual would play or was seeking to play a major role in determining the outcome of the controversy and whether the alleged defamation is related to that controversy."

The public/private figure sword cuts both ways. A person classified as a public figure will find it much more difficult to win a libel action.

The following cases came after the *Gertz* decision:

Buchanan v. Associated Press (1975). In this case, U.S. District Court Judge Thomas Flannery issued summary judgment for AP in a $12 million libel suit filed by Henry Buchanan, a certified public accountant whose firm was alleged, according to an AP report, to have converted campaign checks into cash and turned them back to the Committee to Reelect the President [Nixon].[30] The court said that a person like Buchanan can become a public figure "for a limited range of issues." Campaign financing was a matter of great public concern, said the court, adding that Buchanan's involvement in a matter of "intense public interest" was voluntary. Therefore, he was a public figure and would have to prove actual malice which, in the opinion of the judge, he would be unable to do.

Rosanova Case (1976). Chief Judge Alexander A. Lawrence of the U.S. District Court in the Southern District of Georgia granted summary judgment to defendant in *Rosanova v. Playboy Enterprises, Inc.,* but only after agonizing over the difficulty of distinguishing between public figures and private individuals.[31] *Playboy* magazine had identified Louis F. Rosanova as a California "mobster" in a July 1974 article entitled "Playboy's History of Organized Crime." Although the plaintiff had been the subject of government investigations and criminal prosecutions, he had never been convicted of a crime, although he conceded that "rap sheets" were kept on him by the FBI and by several states.

Prior to declaring Rosanova a public figure, Judge Lawrence asked, "How and where do we draw a line between public figures and private individuals? They are nebulous concepts. Defining public figures is much like trying to nail a jellyfish to the wall." He added:

> The term "public figures" has been defined as "those persons" who, though not public officials, are "involved in issues in which the public has a justified and important interest." Such figures are, of course, numerous and "include artists, athletes, business people, dilettantes, anyone who is famous or infamous because of who he is or what he has done." *Cepeda v. Cowles Magazines and Broadcasting, Inc.,* 392 F.2d 417, 419 (9th Circuit, 1968), cert. den. 393 U.S. 840, 89 S.Ct. 117, 21 L.Ed.2d 110.[32]

Judge Lawrence used the language of *Gertz* and *Firestone* when he concluded: "The evidence reflects that Mr. Rosanova *voluntarily engaged* in a course that was bound to invite attention and comment. His status as a 'public figure' for the purpose of this case did not result merely from unfavorable publicity concerning himself." (Emphasis added.)

In the light of *Wolston* and *Hutchinson,* would Rosanova still fall into the public figure category?

Meeropol Case (1974). In *Michael and Robert Meeropol v. Louis Nizer and Doubleday & Co., Inc.,*[33] the plaintiffs sought $1 million in damages for alleged defamation and invasion of privacy, but Judge Harold R. Tyler, Jr. of U.S. District Court for the Southern District of New York entered summary judgment in 1974 for defendants.

The plaintiffs are the natural children of Julius and Ethel Rosenberg who were executed in 1953 for conspiring to transmit atomic bomb information to Russia. Nizer wrote a book, *The Implosion Conspiracy,* about the trial and subsequent events. The Meeropols claimed the book contained false and fictitious statements made in reckless disregard of the truth.

Judge Tyler ruled that even though 20 years had elapsed since the Rosenbergs were executed, the children still were public figures because, said the judge in quoting from *Gertz,* they had "assumed roles of especial prominence in the affairs of society" and had invited attention and comment. Furthermore, the drama of the trial still was being portrayed in TV documentaries and in newspaper articles at the time the lawsuit was under consideration. As public figures, said the judge, the Meeropols had access to communication channels to correct any errors which might have occurred. Thus, they could have minimized any adverse impact on their reputation had they chosen to do so.

Given what Justice Rehnquist said about "regular and continuing access to the media" being part of the public figure test, would the Meeropols fall short of having that kind of access? Using the hindsight afforded by *Hutchinson,* one might also ask if the media did not help to create a defense by means of documentaries on TV and newspaper articles—publicity long after the occurrence of the major news event (the trial of the Rosenbergs).

Other "Public Figure" Cases. The following also were found to be post-*Gertz* public figures:[34]

An author who had objected to a critical book review, but who, the court ruled, had voluntarily assumed the role of a spokesperson in opposing new housing in certain areas and therefore had injected herself into a public controversy;[35] a director of an insurance company providing coverage for groups of elderly persons, who also held "a number of philanthropic, educational, and charitable positions";[36] a former close business associate of billionaire recluse Howard Hughes;[37] a high school principal rated as unsuited for his position in a series of newspaper articles on area school administrators;[38] chiropractors who voluntarily appeared on a television broadcast to counter earlier adverse comments about chiropractors;[39] and a track coach (for a "limited range of issues") who became involved in a controversy over recalcitrant black athletes on some college campuses in the 1960s.[40]

Others who fell into this category included: TV entertainer Johnny Carson and his wife (at least under certain circumstances);[41] author, publisher and TV personality, William F. Buckley, Jr.;[42] the publisher of a weekly newspaper in Florida;[43] and a large corporation which brought a $15 million libel suit against the *Washington Star* and others following allegations that a corporation representative had paid two prostitutes to entertain Pentagon officials at a party. The suit against the *Star* was dismissed in 1976 in a summary judgment by District Judge Thomas Flannery on the ground that the newspaper had not printed the story out of actual malice; but litigation continued insofar as the writer of the story was concerned.[44]

Others have included: a belly dancer (but only to facts relating to her professional life);[45] the president of Mobil Oil Corporation, William Tavoulareas, in connection with a *Washington Post* story about Tavoulareas' alleged business dealings with his son (although the son was classified as a private figure in his libel action against the paper);[46] the publisher of *Penthouse* magazine, Bob Guccione;[47] actress Carol Burnett, in her successful libel action against the *National Enquirer;* the star player on a 1961 University of Alabama football team involved in a highly publicized football game incident that was reviewed in 1979 newspaper articles;[48] an attorney who served as one of three trustees governing disbursements of an estate's $14.5 million gift to a university and who voluntarily injected himself into a public controversy concerning designation of the university as recipient of the gift (although the court noted that the attorney was a *limited* public figure—that is, limited to information about that particular controversy);[49] the National Foundation for Cancer Research;[50] an undercover police officer (because his duties were "peculiarly 'governmental' in character and highly charged with the public interest;"[51] an Australian research physician who played a "prominent role in a heated public controversy" over the safety of Bendictin;[52] a head basketball coach who took the job at the time the university was under investigation in connection with its athletic recruitment activities;[53] and a newspaper carrier who involuntarily became involved in a crime.[54]

What about corporations? Are they to be treated as "public figures"? The U.S. District Court for Northern California, in 1977, said that the First Amendment standard for determining liability for libel should be the same whether the plaintiff is a corporation or an individual.[55] This is the thrust of California law which states that a corporation's interest in its reputation is the same as an individual's. When this particular corporation, a debt collecting agency, became the subject of a Federal Trade Commission press release, the court reasoned that this "particular public controversy" made the corporation a "public figure" for a limited range of issues relating to the FTC's complaint and litigation.

In 1985, the Minnesota Supreme Court became the first state supreme court to make a distinction between libel standards as they apply to corporations and the business people who run those corporations. It did so in *Jadwin v. Minneapolis Star and Tribune Co.*[56] If the allegedly defamatory statement involves a matter of public interest or concern, then the corporation is to be treated as a public figure. However, the court ruled that the simple negligence standard applies to the lawsuit by the private individual who sued the newspaper—that person being the sole owner of the corporation.

The newspaper company's attorney said afterward that the "decision gives the media more breathing space in its business coverage but holds coverage of private persons to a higher standard."[57]

The buinessman-plaintiff, Thomas Jadwin, agreed to an out-of-court settlement of $15,000 in late 1988 rather than incur the cost of going to trial again. The case had been remanded for trial a second time.[58]

In the main, courts at both the federal and state levels have struggled with the problem of defining corporations, some holding that corporations should be treated as private figures, while others contend that *Gertz* does not apply to corporations. And when courts decide that corporations are to be treated as public figures, are they public figures for all purposes, limited, or involuntary public figures? Obviously the facts of each case must be closely examined.

Public Figure for All Time? In *Wolston,* discussed earlier, Justice Rehnquist said there had been a flurry of publicity about libel plaintiff Wolston in 1958, but that by the time a book was published in 1974 Wolston had succeeded for the most part in returning to private life. Thus, the Court ruled that Wolston was a private figure.

Wolston did not achieve the kind of national publicity that Victoria Street did in 1931 when she claimed that a group of black youths (the "Scottsboro boys") had raped her. They were tried and convicted. Some 35 years after she had gained national publicity in a case that represented to many people a double standard of justice in the United States, NBC broadcast a documentary about it, *Judge Horton and the Scottsboro Boys.* Street sued and the U.S. District Court ruled that she was no longer a public figure. But even though the libel plaintiff had lived in obscurity for many years prior to the broadcast, a three-judge panel of the Sixth Circuit U.S. Court of Appeals, with one judge dissenting, ruled she was a public figure.[59] The majority said that once a person became a public figure in connection with a particular controversy, that person remains a public figure thereafter for purposes of later commentary or treatment of that controversy. Additionally, the majority believed that Street still had sufficient access to the media to rebut any negative information that might arise from the documentary. Thus, the panel denied the plaintiff any recovery, and she sought a review by the U.S. Supreme Court. Before a review could take place, an out-of-court settlement was reached because NBC attorneys did not want to risk losing the Sixth Circuit decision.[60]

The question, therefore, of whether a person becomes a limited public figure for all time in connection with a particular controversy remains unanswered. Although there are dissimilarities between *Wolston* and *Street v. NBC,* there seem to be enough Supreme Court "signposts" along the way to give clues concerning how the Court might have ruled. Would Victoria Street have been classified by the Supreme Court as a limited public figure at the time of the 1976 broadcast?[61]

WHAT STANDARD OF CARE?

If a story is potentially libelous, a journalist not only has the problem of deciding who is a private figure, but what standard of care is required by the state in which the journalist works or the lawsuit is filed. *Gertz* did not require a state to jettison the actual malice test in a private figure defamation action; it merely gave states that option. But *Gertz* did mandate that states could not impose liability without fault. The question, therefore, is what standard of care (or what degree of fault) have states adopted since *Gertz* in private figure defamation actions?

Reckless Disregard Test

Courts in Colorado, Indiana, and New Jersey continue to apply *Rosenbloom,* or a modified version thereof, to defamation suits filed against the media by private individuals whenever the reports complained of involve "matters of public interest or general public concern."[62] But the decision in Indiana was reached in a lower court; the Colorado Supreme Court rejected the *St. Amant* test of reckless disregard in favor of a less demanding one; and the New Jersey Supreme Court limited the application of the actual malice test to some private defamation lawsuits.

Walker v. Colorado Springs Sun. In the Colorado case, *Walker v. Colorado Springs Sun,* the state supreme court upheld, by a 5–2 vote, a lower court verdict awarding $29,000 in actual damages and $9,900 in punitive damages to a Colorado Springs antique dealer.[63] The *Colorado Springs Sun* had printed an article, an editorial, and several letters to the editor concerning stolen merchandise which the antique dealer allegedly had purchased. The supreme court applied the reckless disregard portion of the actual malice test, rather than a simple negligence test, but in so doing said "reckless disregard" does not require a finding that the person making the statement had serious doubt about the statement's truth. In other words, it rejected the *St. Amant* definition of actual malice. Instead, said the court, reckless disregard, when applied to libel suits brought by private citizens, means "sufficient wanton behavior to indicate an indifference to the consequences."

Aafco v. Northwest Publications, Inc. The Indiana Court of Appeals, Third District, was one of the first courts in the post-*Gertz* era to opt for the reckless disregard test when the story involves matters of public interest. Although one judge dissented, the majority in effect continued the standard announced in the *Rosenbloom* plurality opinion. It did so in *Aafco Heating and Air Conditioning Co. v. Northwest Publications, Inc.*[64]

The lawsuit in *Aafco* stemmed from a series of articles published by the Gary *Post-Tribune* following a fire in which three persons died. Installation of a furnace by the plaintiff was cited in the article, according to the suit, as a possible cause of the blaze.

For the majority, Judge Robert Staton said: (1) a simple negligence standard would require plaintiff to prove only that the publisher failed to exercise "reasonable care"; (2) such a standard assumes that society has a greater interest in protecting "private" reputations; and (3) such a rule would promote self-censorship. The court concluded that the subject matter test (whether the subject is of general public interest) provides both the media and the courts sufficient guidance in those matters which are appropriate for public comment and therefore protected by the constitutional privilege.

Sisler v. Gannett Co., Inc. In its 1986 decision, the New Jersey Supreme Court limited the application of the actual malice test to certain types of private plaintiffs by this holding: "When a private person with sufficient experience, understanding, and knowledge enters into a personal transaction or conducts his personal affairs in a manner that one in his position would reasonably expect implicates legitimate public interest with an attendant risk of publicity, defamatory speech that focuses upon that public interest will not be actionable unless it was published with actual malice."[65]

The court overturned an award of $1.05 million to Mayo Sisler, who had claimed he was libeled by a series of newspaper articles in the *Courier-News* concerning alleged improper loans made by a bank.

The court said that New Jersey fosters and nurtures speech on matters of public concern and that, in contradistinction from federal law, "we do not deem it unfair to favor free speech over the reputational interests of an individual who has voluntarily and knowingly engaged in conduct that one in his position should reasonably know would implicate a legitimate public interest."

The newspaper had argued that Sisler was a public figure, but the state supreme court disagreed. However, in remanding the case for retrial, the court said Sisler would have to show actual malice for the reasons given.

In a product disparagement case before the New Jersey Supreme Court, the court ruled that in such cases the company must prove actual malice to win damages for injury to its business reputation. The decision upheld lower court action in *Dairy Stores Inc. v. Sentinal Publishing Co.* (1986).[66]

The publishing company was sued in May 1981 after it published an article disputing the company's claim that water sold in its stores was clear spring water.

The New Jersey Supreme Court said that the subject of drinking water was a matter of legitimate public interest and that factual statements about it were protected by the common law qualified privilege of fair comment—a privilege that could only be overcome by proof of actual malice. The court also said that the actual malice standard should apply to nonmedia as well as media defendants (in this instance to provide protection for non-government experts who tested the water at the request of the newspaper reporter).

Gross Negligence Test

One state—New York—has adopted the gross negligence standard which offers more protection to the media than an ordinary negligence standard. But as a number of legal experts, including the late Justice Douglas, point out, any negligence standard leaves the press vulnerable to defamation lawsuits.

Dean William Prosser said the difference between gross negligence and ordinary negligence is one of degree, not of kind; that gross negligence is less than reckless disregard, and that it is comparable to extreme departure from the ordinary standard of reasonable care.[67] The extreme departure standard was urged by Justice Harlan in *Curtis Publishing Co. v. Butts* (1967), discussed previously, as the appropriate standard for public figure defamation lawsuits.

Chapadeau v. Utica Observer-Dispatch. New York's highest court held that summary judgment was erroneously denied the *Observer-Dispatch.* The New

York Court of Appeals nevertheless agreed with the appellant school teacher that liability for publishing matters of "legitimate" public interest about a private individual should be governed by a standard of fault other than actual malice.[68] Judge Sol Wachtler, in his unanimous opinion for the court, said that a defamed person, to recover damages, "must establish, by a preponderance of the evidence, that the publisher acted in a grossly irresponsible manner without due consideration for the standards of information gathering and dissemination followed by responsible parties." Elsewhere in his opinion, the judge referred to "grossly irresponsible conduct" as the standard of fault.

Isn't "grossly irresponsible conduct" comparable to the definition of reckless disregard applied by the Colorado Supreme Court in *Walker*? If so, then Colorado's standard of care is similar to New York's.

Ordinary Negligence Test

Courts in 37 states have declared that ordinary negligence, or a standard resembling it, is the one to be used in deciding private person defamation cases against the news media. The terms "mere negligence," "ordinary negligence," "ordinary care," "due care," and "reasonable care" are used to denote the standard of care. Generally, ordinary negligence is predicated on "reasonable care"; that is, the failure of a publisher or broadcaster to exercise reasonable or due care in ascertaining the truth. For example, the Maryland Court of Appeals and the Arizona Supreme Court adopted the standard of negligence set forth in *Restatement (Second) of Torts,* section 580B (Tentative Draft No. 21, April 5, 1975). The *Restatement* provides an organized synthesis of the general common law in the United States as compiled by the American Law Institute. The tentative draft stated:

> One who publishes a false and defamatory communication concerning a private person, or concerning a public official or public figure in relation to a purely private matter not affecting his conduct, fitness or role in his public capacity, is subject to liability, if, but only if, he
>
> (a) knows that the statement is false and that it defames the other,
> (b) acts in reckless disregard of these matters, or
> (c) acts negligently in failing to ascertain . . . [the truth or falsity of statements].

In announcing that an ordinary care test would apply in appropriate cases, the Oklahoma Supreme Court in *Martin v. Griffin Television, Inc.,* quoted an Oklahoma statute (76 O.S. 1971, § 5(a)) which provides, in part, that "everyone is responsible, not only for the result of his willful acts, but also for an injury occasioned to another by his want of ordinary care or skill in the management of his property or person."[69] The court then said that ordinary care is that degree of care which ordinarily prudent persons engaged in the same kind of business usually exercise under similar circumstances, and the failure to exercise such ordinary care would constitute negligence.

Here's what the Kansas Supreme Court said about "ordinary negligence":

> The whole theory of negligence presupposes some uniform standard of behavior for the protection of others from harm. The norm usually is the conduct of the reasonably careful person under the circumstances. Thus ordinary negligence connotes a degree of fault, as that term is generally understood. The mentally competent person, of whatever calling or station, is usually held accountable under that standard.[70]

And the Illinois Supreme Court made this observation:

> Under a standard of ordinary negligence, the question would be, not whether the defendant entertained doubts of the truth of his statement, but rather whether he had reasonable grounds to believe it to be true, and a failure to make a reasonable investigation into the truth of the statement is obviously a relevant factor.[71]

In 30 states and the District of Columbia, decisions announcing ordinary negligence as the standard of care (or fault) have come from the highest courts in those jurisdictions. They are: Alabama, Arizona, Arkansas, California, Delaware, District of Columbia, Florida, Georgia, Hawaii, Illinois, Iowa, Kansas, Kentucky, Maryland, Massachusetts, Michigan, Minnesota, Montana, New Hampshire, New Mexico, Ohio, Oklahoma, Oregon, South Carolina, Tennessee, Texas, Utah, Virginia, Washington, West Virginia, and Wisconsin.[72] The Puerto Rico Supreme Court also has adopted such a standard,[73] and the Pennsylvania and Rhode Island Supreme Courts appear inclined to do so.[74]

Lower courts have used ordinary negligence standards, or minor variations thereof, in Alaska, Connecticut, Louisiana, Mississippi, Missouri, North Carolina, Pennsylvania, and the Virgin Islands.[75] However, Alaska and Louisiana courts, in deciding post-*Gertz* cases, also have used the "actual malice" standard in private figure defamation actions.[76] But it is clear that most states are adopting the ordinary negligence standard (or continuing it in the post-*Gertz* era because they already were committed to it). Nevertheless, an examination of state law is necessary to determine the interplay between press freedoms on the one hand and reputational interests on the other.

In Michigan, for example, the state supreme court announced that the appropriate standard of liability in a private figure defamation action is negligence. It did so in *Rouch v. Enquirer & News* (1986) — a decision that sent shock waves through the state's news media.[77]

What happened is that the plaintiff, David P. Rouch, was "arrested" and taken to jail as a suspect in a sexual assault crime, but no arrest warrant was ever issued and he was never arraigned. The reporter said in an affidavit that he had talked on the telephone with several police officers and had been informed of the details contained in the story (a practice frequently followed by reporters elsewhere).

The trial court, relying on a federal court's interpretation of Michigan common law, ruled that the reporting of arrests is a matter of general public interest and therefore privileged. It granted summary judgment to the defendant. But the

Court of Appeals reversed, saying that the publication of the details of the plaintiff's alleged crime was merely a matter that the public would find interesting and not one "deserving of robust public debate."

The supreme court affirmed the appellate court's ruling, agreeing that details of the alleged crime were merely interesting to the public and not a matter that promoted the public interest. The case was remanded for trial and the plaintiff in 1988 was awarded $1 million in damages. The verdict has been appealed.

Shortly after the supreme court's decision, the newspaper's managing editor, David Smith, said:

> It's a difficult situation for us to have to confront, for journalists to have to confront, in this state. As we interpret this decision, it doesn't allow the newspaper to report until after the arraignment."[78]

After the court's decision, the Michigan legislature amended the libel statute, effective in 1989, by adopting the negligence standard and broadening the term "official proceeding" to include fair and accurate reports of a record journal that's available to the public, a government written or recorded report, and other matters of public record. Thus, the legislature codified the court's adoption of the negligence standard but, in effect, overturned the court's narrow interpretation of what constitutes an official proceeding. Under the new legislation an arrest, even if there is no arraignment, would fall within the meaning of "official proceeding."[79]

In California, the state supreme court examined the scope of Civil Code section 47, subdivision 3, which some lower courts believed had given the news media a broad privilege, sometimes referred to as the "public interest privilege," to make false statements about private individuals if the reports were made without malice. Not so, said the court in *Brown v. Kelly Broadcasting Co. et. al.* (1989).[80]

In his opinion for the court, Justice David N. Eagleson rejected the defendants' contention that 47(3) provided such a privilege by saying:

> [T]he privilege sought by defendants would be so broad that it would apply to almost every defamatory communication. Presumably, the news media generally publish and broadcast only matters that the media believe are of public interest, and the media defendant in every defamation action would therefore argue that the communication was a matter of public interest. . . . Thus, the practical result sought by the news media would be that nearly everything they publish and broadcast would be privileged. A privilege is an exception to a general rule of liability, but under defendants' view of section 47(3), the privilege would be the general rule for the news media and liability would be the exception. We believe the Legislature would have made clear its intention for such a drastic restriction on the common law of defamation, especially because the statute was enacted when strict liability was the standard of fault for defamation actions.[81]

The Iowa Supreme Court adopted a negligence standard in *Jones v. Palmer Communications, Inc.* (1989) that relates to the practice of journalism; that is, a professional standard of care which "ordinarily prudent persons in the same profession usually exercise under similar conditions."[82] The private plaintiff must establish by a preponderance of the evidence, said the court, that this standard of care has been breached.

In Oregon, the state supreme court has ruled in a defamation action that the state Constitution forbids the recovery of punitive damages for conduct based on speech.[83]

Similarly, the Massachusetts Supreme Judicial Court has ruled out the award of punitive damages in defamation suits no matter what the degree of fault. Although it adopted a negligence standard, the court limited recovery to actual damages. As Justice Edward F. Hennessey declared for the court:

> We reject the allowance of punitive damages in this Commonwealth in any defamation action, on any state of proof, whether based on negligence, or reckless or willful conduct. We so hold in recognition that the possibility of excessive and unbridled jury verdicts, grounded on punitive assessment, may impermissibly chill the exercise of First Amendment rights by promoting apprehensive self-censorship.[84]

And in Virginia, where the state supreme court has said that the negligence standard applies to private figure defamation actions, that same court has ruled that where a statement is not clearly libelous (doesn't warn a reasonably prudent editor?), the plaintiff must prove that it was printed with reckless disregard for the truth.[85]

Rationale for Adopting Negligence Standard

What are some of the reasons given by state courts in deciding that an ordinary negligence test should be used in private defamation suits against the news media?

Martin v. Griffin Television, Inc. Balancing of rights was the principal determinant in the opinion written by Justice Robert E. Lavender for a unanimous Oklahoma Supreme Court in *Martin v. Griffin Television, Inc.*[86] In his opinion, Lavender noted that the Colorado Supreme Court had elected in *Walker*, discussed earlier, to continue with the actual malice test if the defamatory matter is of public interest. But Lavender pointed to one of the two dissenting opinions in *Walker* when he wrote:

> There is an additional opinion in *Walker* written by Justice Erickson, which especially concurs in part and dissents in part. That opinion criticizes the adoption by Colorado of *Rosenbloom*. It calls *Rosenbloom* a plurality opinion with little vitality when announced and even less today.
> It faults the majority opinion of *Walker* as not striking a balance between the press and a private citizen. . . .
> *Gertz* was principally concerned with limitations required by the constitution, but gave the states much latitude in their defining standards of liability for news media defamation injurious to a private individual. In its defenestration of the *Ro-*

senbloom test of "general or public interest" for constitutional purposes, the opinion notices the problem of requiring "judges to decide on an ad hoc basis which publications address issues of 'general or public interest' and which do not—to determine, in the words of Mr. Justice Marshall, 'what information is relevant to self-government.' " The opinion continues, "We doubt the wisdom of committing this task to the conscience of judges." *Gertz* examines instead the injured individual. . . .

The Oklahoma Bill of Rights as to liberty of speech and press, Const. Art. II, Sec. 22, provides in part:

> Every person may freely speak, write, or publish his sentiments on all subjects, *being responsible for the abuse of that right;* . . . (Emphasis added.)

Expressly in its constitution, Oklahoma has weighted the right with the responsibility for an abuse of that right. That same responsibility is not expressly found in the federal constitution.

> We, too, must balance the news media rights with that of a private individual. We find, . . . the expressions in *Gertz, supra,* as to the standard of liability to be more parallel with ours and the Oklahoma Constitution. We reject, as did *Gertz,* the *Rosenbloom* test as not achieving a balance or accommodation with these conflicting interests.
> We conclude a reasonable balance between the right of the private individual is best achieved by the negligence test.[87]

Cahill v. Hawaiian Paradise Park. Although the Hawaii Supreme Court used the negligence test in *Cahill*[88] because of a previous decision in *Aku v. Lewis,*[89] it expressly left unresolved the issue of what standard would apply if the alleged defamatory matter concerned a matter of public interest. The resolution of such an issue is not an easy one, as Justice H. Baird Kidwell pointed out for a unanimous court. However, he made this observation:

> The plurality opinion in *Rosenbloom* and the decisions of the Indiana and Colorado courts . . . are founded on the intuitive finding of the Justices,[90] unaided by any empirical evidence, that exposure of the news media to liability for negligence in actions by private individuals for defamatory falsehoods has unduly restrained their freedom of expression. We have not been referred to any instance in which a matter of general or public interest has not been adequately reported because of self-censorship on the part of the news media. We do not have the means to develop empirical evidence to confirm or refute the intuitive findings of the *Rosenbloom* plurality. The nature and scope of the investigation which would be required for this purpose may be more suitable to a legislative resolution of this issue than one achieved by judicial decision. . . . Under these circumstances, we will refrain from announcing at this time any change in the standard of liability to private individuals. . . .

Foster v. Laredo Newspapers, Inc. The Texas Supreme Court adopted the negligence standard in reversing a grant of summary judgment to the defendant.[91] It remanded the case for trial after holding that a county surveyor, serving as a consulting engineer on a flood problem in a subdivision, was not a public official in connection with his consultation activities.

In determining the standard of care that would apply to defamation suits brought by private individuals, the court rejected both the actual malice and gross negligence standards. Justice Sam D. Johnson, in his opinion for the court, wrote that the gross negligence standard "would not provide demonstrably greater protection to the media from self-censorship than a standard of ordinary negligence." Johnson added:

> The distinction between ordinary negligence and gross negligence in the defamation context is not entirely clear, and it is doubtful that the choice of one label rather than the other will significantly affect the evolution of constitutional defamation law. Limitations upon the right of recovery in defamation actions that are deemed necessary to protect publishers and broadcasters from an unreasonable degree of liability will undoubtedly be adopted by the courts regardless which label is used.[92]

GERTZ-RELATED PROBLEMS

From the media's standpoint, major problems are apparent as a result of the *Gertz* decision. The first involves the difficulty of distinguishing between public and private individuals. Media vulnerability to libel suits depends to a considerable extent on whether the person identified in a news story is a public or private figure—a distinction not easy to make in many instances.

Gertz, of course, demonstrates that a person is not a public figure solely by reason of occupation or profession, such as being an attorney. *Firestone* shows that a person involved in a courtroom situation—even a situation that might be "sensational" from a news standpoint—is not necessarily a public figure. The status of a teacher also is dependent on circumstances beyond that of occupation.[93] A businessman or woman is not automatically a public figure.[94] A state employee doing research for the federal government is not a public figure. And so it goes. . . .

Additionally, before a person can be classified as a *limited* public figure (as contrasted with a general public figure), the nature and extent of that person's participation in a *public controversy* becomes crucial. Three factors enter into such a determination: (1) the extent to which participation is voluntary; (2) the extent to which there is access to channels of effective communication in order to counteract false statements; and (3) the prominence of the role played in the public controversy.[95]

Public Interest Requirement?

Another *Gertz* problem is related to the public interest or public concern test. Does *Gertz* apply only when the alleged defamation concerns a matter of public or general interest? If so, then states would be free to adopt any standard of care they wished, even in the absence of fault on the part of a reasonably prudent editor, whenever defamation suits are brought by private individuals against the media if the "public interest" element were absent or missing from the media report that provoked the lawsuit.

Two Supreme Court decisions in the mid-1980s shed light on the public interest question.

Dun & Bradstreet v. Greenmoss Builders, Inc. (1985).[96] A divided U.S. Supreme Court took the position that an erroneous credit report is not a matter of public importance or public concern. It is of private concern only and therefore the *Gertz* rule (that punitive damages cannot be awarded in a private figure's lawsuit unless that person can show actual malice) does not apply. The Court, in a *plurality* opinion by Justice Powell with only Rehnquist and O'Connor joining the opinion, affirmed a Vermont Supreme Court decision that had reinstated a jury award of $50,000 in compensatory damage and $300,000 in punitive damage to Greenmoss Builders. Chief Justice Burger and White joined the judgment of the Court, but did not align themselves with Powell's opinion. Brennan, joined by Marshall, Blackmun, and Stevens, dissented.

This case resulted from an erroneous credit report by Dun & Bradstreet stating that Greenmoss Builders, Inc., had filed for bankruptcy when, in fact, the bankruptcy filing was by a former Greenmoss employee. When the error was discovered, Dun & Bradstreet sent out a correction notice, but the company was not satisfied with the correction and asked for the names of Dun & Bradstreet's subscribers who had received the erroneous credit report. The credit-rating company refused to disclose its subscribers and Greenmoss Builders brought suit.

After the jury verdict, the trial court granted a motion for a new trial because the jury instructions, according to the judge, permitted the award of presumed and punitive damages in violation of *Gertz*. The Vermont Supreme Court found no error in the jury instruction and reinstated the damages, doing so on the ground that the defendant was not part of the media because of its specialized information and its finite audience. Because of its nonmedia status, First Amendment considerations present in *Gertz* did not apply.

But the U.S. Supreme Court rejected the media/nonmedia line of reasoning, holding that the press deserves no more protection than a private figure in a defamation action. Where the Court divided was on the public/private issue. Powell was willing to use such a distinction, which he had rejected in *Rosenbloom* as unworkable, but only as a basis for determining if the *Gertz* safeguards apply and not as a basis for determining liability. When the issue is not of public concern, said Powell, then the First Amendment interests involved in *Gertz* are not as strong. As he put it, certain types of speech "solely in the individual interest of the speaker and its specific business audience" merit less constitutional protection than speech concerning public issues." Because the credit report at issue concerned no public issue and was false, Powell continued, punitive damages could be presumed without a showing of actual malice.

Burger's opinion reflected considerable agreement with Powell's views, while White took the position that *Gertz* should not have been applied to this case either because *Gertz* should be overruled by the Court (a view supported by

Burger) or because the defamatory matter did not deal with a matter of public importance. Thus, White aligned himself with part of Powell's reasoning.

Interestingly, Powell cited court decisions in Wisconsin, Minnesota, Colorado, and Oregon in which *Gertz* was held inapplicable to private figure libel lawsuits against nonmedia defendants. However, contrary results had been reached by the highest courts in Arizona and Maryland.

The dissenters took the position that *Gertz* applies to all defamation cases.

The impact of the *Dun & Bradstreet* decision is considerable. The *National Law Journal,* for example, reported that libel defense lawyers were "in shock" because an entire category of speech (speech not of public concern) is not now protected against the common-law presumption of damages whenever a libel has been committed.[97] Thus, punitive damages can be awarded on the basis of any defamatory falsity, not just *knowing falsity.* And because the Dun and Bradstreet credit reports involved "commercial" speech (which Justice Powell said occupies a subordinate position on the scale of First Amendment values), some analysts believe that advertising may have a difficult time rising to the level of "public concern."[98]

Given the plurality opinion in *Dun & Bradstreet,* any analysis of media liability not only must take into account the status of the individual or corporation involved (public versus private figure) but also the kind of speech involved (public versus private concern). Whether speech is a matter of public concern must be determined, said Powell, by the expression's content, form, and context as revealed by the entire record.[99] Judges can make such decisions in the relative calm of a judicial setting; it's much more difficult given newsroom deadlines.

Philadelphia Newspapers v. Hepps (1986).[100] In this case, the U.S. Supreme Court ruled 5–4 that a private figure libel plaintiff, in an action against a *media defendant* for alleged defamatory statements involving matters of *public concern,* must demonstrate the falsity of such statements. The Court reversed the decision of the Pennsylvania Supreme Court which had reversed the trial court and remanded for a new trial.

The *Philadelphia Inquirer* had published a series of articles whose general theme was that Maurice S. Hepps, a principal stockholder of a corporation that franchises stores that sell beer, soft drinks, and snacks, had links to organized crime and used some of those links to influence the state's governmental processes. The corporation and Hepps sued. The trial judge instructed the jury that plaintiffs bore the burden of proving falsity.

The Court, in an opinion by Justice O'Connor, held that in addition to a showing of fault, the private figure plaintiff cannot recover damages without also showing that the statements at issue are false.

Stevens, joined by Burger, White, and Rehnquist, dissented.

Pennsylvania law, like the common law in at least eight other states (Indiana, Louisiana, Montana, New Jersey, Oklahoma, Tennessee, Texas, and Wisconsin), had placed the burden of proving truth on the defendants. The trial court judge had concluded that such a requirement violated the First Amendment. During the trial, newspaper personnel refused to divulge sources, basing their refusal on the state's shield law (see Chapter 11 for shield law information). The jury ruled in favor of the newspaper. The state supreme court viewed *Gertz* as simply requiring the plaintiff to show fault, not falsity.

O'Connor said that when the plaintiff is a public official or public figure, and the speech at issue is of public concern, the Constitution requires the plaintiff to surmount a much higher barrier before recovering damages from a media defendant than is raised by the common law. When the speech is of public concern, but the plaintiff is a private figure, as in *Gertz,* the Constitution still supplants the standards of the common law (the common law's presumption of fault and damages), but the constitutional requirements are, in at least some of their range, less forbidding than when the plaintiff is a public figure and the speech is of public concern. When the speech is exclusively of private concern, as in *Dun & Bradstreet, Inc. v. Greenmoss Builders,* the constitutional requirements do not necessarily force any change in at least some of the features of the "common-law landscape."

O'Connor did not attempt to specify the quantity of proof of falsity that a private figure plaintiff must present to recover damages. Nor did her opinion for the Court consider what standards would apply if the plaintiff sues a nonmedia defendant. But in his concurring opinion, Brennan reiterated his view that any distinction between a media and a nonmedia defendant is irreconcilable with First Amendment guarantees.

Stevens, in dissent, argued for a return to common law principles in private figure defamation cases—a position previously advocated by Chief Justice Burger and by White (both believing that *Gertz* should be overruled). Stevens agrees that under the Court's prior decisions, public officials and public figures have the burden of proving falsity. Not so when private figures are involved, he said.

"The danger to deliberate defamation by reference to unprovable facts is not merely a speculative or hypothetical concern," he warned.

Stevens also sharply criticized the majority's reliance on what he called "the discredited analysis of the *Rosenbloom* plurality;" that is, reliance on the public interest/public concern test in determining if speech is qualifiedly privileged under the First Amendment. It should be recalled that Justice Marshall, joined by Stewart, wrote a dissenting opinion in *Rosenbloom* in which he expressed concern about courts being involved in the dangerous business of deciding what information is relevant to self-government; that is, what information is of public interest.

Uncertainties of Negligence Standard

Another problem concerns the uncertainties associated with a negligence standard. The late Professor Prosser defined negligence as "conduct which involves an unreasonably great risk of causing damage."[101] Justice Powell, in his opinion for the court in *Gertz,* referred to a "reasonably prudent editor" who had to be warned by the defamatory nature of the words. It would be hard, indeed, to come up with any objective test of such an editor. Prosser describes a "reasonable man" as one of "ordinary prudence, who represents a community ideal of reasonable behavior."[102]

According to Justice Brennan in his plurality opinion for the Court in *Time, Inc. v. Hill,* discussed later, the negligence standard is an elusive one that saddles the press with "the intolerable burden of guessing how a jury might assess the reasonableness of steps taken by . . . the press to verify the accuracy of every reference to a name, picture, or portrait."[103] Such a standard will lead to some media self-censorship because such a standard is close to requiring truth, according to Brennan and others.[104] Chief Justice Burger believed that such a standard would inhibit some editors; but more than that, he did not know the "parameters" of such a standard or test. If judges with the experience of a Brennan or a Burger don't know, how is an editor supposed to know?

Summary Judgment

The negligence standard makes summary judgment more difficult to obtain because questions of fact generally are within the province of the jury, not the judge. The *Meeropols* and *Rosanova* cases demonstrate the value to the news media of being able to gain summary judgment which brings litigation to a quick halt, thereby curtailing large outlays for legal expenses. But in the light of *Wolston* and *Hutchinson,* would the *Meeropols* and *Rosanova* plaintiffs be public figures?

Hutchinson provided an additional hurdle to media defendants obtaining summary judgment. In his opinion for the Court in that case, Chief Justice Burger included a footnote in which he said that proof of actual malice calls a defendant's state of mind into question and "does not readily lend itself to summary disposition."[105]

Under Federal Rules of Civil Procedure, Rule 58 (28 U.S.C.A.), a civil libel suit can be terminated by summary judgment if there is no genuine issue of material fact. This same rule generally is followed elsewhere. But summary judgment, said an Illinois appellate court, is a drastic method of disposing of cases and it should be allowed only when the right of the party to invoke that method is free from doubt.[106] It must not be used to preempt the right to a trial by jury or the right to fully present the factual basis for a case where a material dispute may exist.

A Connecticut court pointed out that "issues of negligence are ordinarily not susceptible of summary judgment but should be resolved by trial in the ordinary manner."[107]

However, about a year after *Hutchinson,* the Wyoming Supreme Court said the use of a motion for summary judgment is not foreclosed by the footnote. It termed summary judgment the "best procedural protection" for press freedom.[108]

The concern expressed by the media about the *Hutchinson* footnote seems to have been largely unnecessary. The footnote has "had little if any impact upon a defendant's chances for prevailing on a motion for summary judgment," according to the Libel Defense Resource Center (LDRC) following a study of 143 summary judgment motions made during 1984–86.[109] Media defendants were successful 76 percent of the time. The success rate is comparable to the center's findings in two earlier studies of 389 summary judgment motions made between 1980–84 when the success rate was 74 percent.

The 1984–86 study found that media defendants prevailed on summary judgment motions in 78 percent of the cases involving public officials or public figures, but were successful in only 58 percent of the cases brought by private figures. This study included summary judgment motions made prior to the Supreme Court's decision in *Anderson v. Liberty Lobby* (see Chapter 5). If anything, said LDRC, the *Anderson* decision is likely to increase the "frequency with which courts grant summary judgment in public figure defamation actions."

In *Anderson,* Justice White referred to the *Hutchinson* footnote, saying that it was included as an acknowledgment "of our reluctance to grant special procedural protections" to libel action defendants beyond the constitutional protections provided in substantive law. But where the factual dispute concerns actual malice, the appropriate summary judgment question will be whether the evidence in the record could support a reasonable jury finding that the plaintiff had shown such malice by clear and convincing evidence.

The importance of summary judgment is demonstrated by the following cases in which *Look* magazine was unable to obtain such judgment while *LIFE* magazine succeeded in quickly terminating a suit against it.

Alioto v. Cowles Communications, Inc. Look magazine published an article on September 23, 1969, entitled "The Web that Links San Francisco Mayor Joseph Alioto and the Mafia." Alioto sought $12.5 million in libel damages and the trial ended in a hung jury. *Look* then filed an affidavit with the U.S. District Court in an unsuccessful effort to ward off a new trial. The affidavit showed that as of July 1, 1971, $75,000 had been spent for legal services which did not include attorney fees. Attorneys estimated that *Look* might end up paying as much as $360,000 to defend against the suit. This cost may have accounted in part for the announcement on September 15, 1971, that *Look* was ceasing publication, although the principal reasons were increases in second-class mailing costs and declining advertising revenue.

Even though the magazine disappeared, Alioto's libel suit did not. A second trial also ended in a hung jury, and Alioto wanted a third trial. At that point the district court dismissed the case—a decision appealed by Mayor Alioto. A three-judge panel of the U.S. Court of Appeals thereupon reversed the district court's action and remanded on the sole issue of actual malice. The Supreme Court declined to review that decision.[110] The third trial also ended in a hung jury, and defendant's motion for dismissal was denied in early 1977 by the U.S. District Court for the Northern District of California. To that time, according to an amicus brief filed by the National Newspaper Association, litigation in this one case had cost Cowles Communications, the publishers of *Look,* nearly $700,000. The chilling effect of such protracted litigation, said the association, "is even more repressive on small newspapers." The fourth trial took place without a jury, and Judge William Schwarzer on May 3, 1977, awarded Alioto $350,000 in damages on the basis that allegations made in the article were in reckless disregard of the truth. The judge also awarded court costs to the plaintiff (estimated at about $50,000).[111] All but $25,000 of the judgment liability reportedly was covered by insurance. In mid-1980, the U.S. Court of Appeals for the Ninth Circuit affirmed the $350,000 libel judgment and the U.S. Supreme Court declined to review that decision.[112]

Cervantes v. Time, Inc. Unlike *Look,* the publishers of *LIFE* obtained summary judgment before trial could commence after an article had been published in a May 1970 issue titled "The Mayor, the Mob and the Lawyer." St. Louis Mayor Alfonso Cervantes had filed suit for $2 million in compensatory and $10 million in punitive damages. *LIFE* and article writer Denny Walsh relied on the defense of truth and the *Times-Sullivan* privilege. Cervantes undertook pretrial discovery, seeking to force Walsh to reveal confidential sources of information within the FBI and U.S. Department of Justice. The U.S. District Court then entered summary judgment for *LIFE* and the writer on the grounds that neither one entertained serious doubts as to the truth of any statement in the article, that neither had knowledge of falsity, and that neither had acted with reckless disregard of the truth.[113] On appeal, the U.S. Court of Appeals affirmed the summary judgment, stating:

> Where, as here, the published materials, objectively considered in the light of all the evidence, must be taken as having been published in good faith, without actual malice and on the basis of careful verification efforts, . . . there is no rule of law or policy consideration of which we are aware that counsels compulsory revelation of news sources. Neither is there any evidence by which a jury could reasonably find liability under the constitutionally required instructions. When these factors conjoin, the proper disposition is to grant the defense motion for summary judgment.[114]

GERTZ-RELATED ADVANTAGES

In reviewing *Gertz* from a media point of view, its positive aspects should not be overlooked. First, and foremost, there is the prohibition against punitive damages except on a showing of actual malice. Second, the plaintiff can recover only for "actual damages" on a showing of negligence (or whatever standard of care is imposed by the state provided the requisite fault is present). This means that competent evidence must be submitted by the plaintiff showing the harm done by the defamatory publication, although evidence of the dollar value of the injury need not be introduced. *Gertz* does not permit the *presumption* of malice or damage because presumed malice would allow liability without fault, and presumed damage would circumvent the "actual damage" requirement. For these reasons, the Oklahoma statutes creating and allowing such presumptions were declared unconstitutional by the state supreme court in *Martin v. Griffin Television, Inc.,* discussed earlier.

In doing away with presumed damages, the U.S. Supreme Court nullified the traditional need for trial courts to distinguish between libel per se and libel per quod (see Chapter 4).

No-Fault Rulings

Gertz requires some kind of fault on the part of the journalist before a defamation plaintiff can collect actual damages. For example, in two Louisiana cases, each involving publication of erroneous information supplied by police officials, intermediate appellate courts gave rulings favoring the defendant newspapers.

Wilson v. Capital City Press. The Court of Appeals for the Third Circuit in *Wilson* noted that plaintiff had been erroneously listed in the *Morning Advocate* as having been arrested in a drug raid.[115] The trial court had awarded plaintiff $3000 damage. Information about the identity of the persons arrested had come from the public relations director of the state police. The appellate court, in a 2–1 split, reversed and gave judgment for the newspaper. The majority, citing the *Gertz* requirement that there must be fault, said, "The Supreme Court did not hold that the printing of an untruth would itself constitute fault. There must be culpability on the part of the publisher." The court then pointed out, "The source was reliable and in a proper position of authority and knowledge that no fault can be attributed" to the reporter or newspaper "for reliance on the information received."

Le Boeuf v. Times Picayune Publishing Corp. After *Wilson,* the Court of Appeals for the Fourth Circuit unanimously affirmed summary judgment for the defendant newspaper.[116] The court held that where the source of a false report about plaintiff was the police information officer, who had based his information on a routine police report, no basis existed for the defamation action because there was no fault by defendant, the Times Picayune Publishing Corp.

PURE OPINION CONSTITUTIONALLY PROTECTED

Developments since *Times-Sullivan* and *Gertz* have profoundly reduced the need of the press to rely on the fair comment and criticism defense accorded under common law or by state statute (a defense discussed in Chapter 4). What has emerged is First Amendment protection for opinion, particularly "pure opinion" as contrasted with a hybrid statement that consists of opinion and facts. But let's go back to the *Times-Sullivan* case and the Supreme Court's determination of an appropriate standard to be applied to defamation actions by public officials when there is a profound "national commitment to the principle that debate on public issues should be uninhibited, robust, and wide open. . . ."[117] The Court decided that under the First and Fourteenth Amendments a qualified privilege had to apply to statements of fact *and of opinion;* otherwise, the wide-open debate on matters of public importance might be inhibited. In his only reference to fair comment, Justice Brennan wrote in a footnote:

Insofar as the proposition means only that the statements about police conduct libeled respondent [Sullivan] by implicitly criticizing his ability to run the Police Department, recovery is also precluded in this case by the doctrine of fair comment. Since the Fourteenth Amendment requires recognition of the conditional privilege for honest mistatements of fact, it follows that a defense of fair comment must be afforded for honest expression of opinion based upon privileged, as well as true, statements of fact. Both defenses are of course defeasible if the public official proves actual malice, as was not done here.[118]

The next development in the emergence of the opinion privilege came in *Gertz* when Justice Powell wrote for the Court:

Under the First Amendment there is no such thing as a false idea. However pernicious an opinion may seem, we depend for its correction not on the conscience of judges and juries but on the competition of other ideas. But there is no constitutional value in false statements of fact. Neither the intentional lie nor the careless error materially advances society's interest in "uninhibited, robust, and wide-open" debate on public issues.[119]

In a footnote, Powell drew attention to Thomas Jefferson's first inaugural speech in which he said that "[I]f there be any among us who would wish to dissolve this Union or change its republican form, let them stand undisturbed as monuments of the safety with which error of opinion may be tolerated where reason is left free to combat it."[120]

On the same day that *Gertz* was announced, the Court also issued an opinion in *Old Dominion Branch No. 496, National Association of Letter Carriers, AFL-CIO v. Austin.*[121] The case came up for review after the Virginia Supreme Court in 1972 upheld the award of $55,000 in damages to each of three nonunion letter carriers.

The awards resulted from comments published in a monthly newsletter issued by the Richmond branch of the National Association of Letter Carriers. Under the heading, "List of Scabs," the newsletter carried the names of the three carriers, and one issue contained the comment that a "SCAB is a traitor to his God, his country, his family, and his class." The state's highest court said that the "fact that plaintiffs elected not to join the union was a private matter and an issue of general or public interest was not involved." Since no conditional privilege existed in this instance, the state's "insulting words" statute applied.

But the U.S. Supreme Court, in a 6–3 decision, reversed the Virginia courts, holding that relevant sections of the National Labor Relations Act and Executive Order 11491 (the latter dealing with federal government/union relationships) required uninhibited, robust, and wide-open debate in labor disputes and organizational attempts by unions; further, that state libel laws could not apply to federal labor laws unless *Times-Sullivan* "actual malice" could be shown.

Justice Powell, joined by Chief Justice Burger and Justice Rehnquist, dissented primarily because the decision extended the *Times-Sullivan* "actual malice" rule to encompass every defamatory statement made in a context that falls within the majority's expansive construction of the phrase 'labor dispute,'" thereby allowing "both unions and employers to defame individual workers with little or no risk of being held acountable for doing so. . . ."

Courts Divided on Interpreting Opinion Privilege

Since Justice Powell wrote those words about a First Amendment opinion privilege, courts have divided on how to interpret such a privilege.

The American Law Institute in its *Restatement (Second) of Torts Section 566* (1977) stated:

> A defamatory communication may consist of a statement in the form of an opinion, but a statement of this nature is actionable only if it implies the allegation of undisclosed defamatory facts as the basis for the opinion.

Previously, Section 566 had interpreted the law as qualifiedly protecting pure opinion, but in the 1977 revision, such opinion is absolutely protected, whereas a "hybrid" statement—a mixture of fact and opinion—is qualifiedly protected. And it makes no difference whether the opinion relates to a matter of public concern or public interest. Nor does it matter, according to *Restatement,* whether the target of the statement is a public official, public figure, or private individual. Likewise, it is irrelevant whether the opinion represents the actual belief of the communicator. Thus, the Institute believes that the common-law fair-comment defense has been supplanted by the opinion privilege rooted in the First Amendment.[122]

Few courts have spoken directly to such an assertion. In fact, since the "no false opinion" dictum by the Supreme Court, the Court has virtually remained silent about how it is to be interpreted or distinguished when fact and opinion intermingle. Nor did the Court use the opinion privilege to resolve cases that arguably involved opinion statements. A case in point is *Hutchinson v. Proxmire,* discussed previously, which resulted from statements by Senator Proxmire about the plaintiff's governmentally funded animal research, described by Proxmire as "nonsense" and "transparent worthlessness." The Court ruled that such statements were not immunized by the Speech and Debate Clause and returned the case to the lower court without any indication that any of the libelous remarks were within the opinion privilege. Proxmire subsequently settled out of court. Even in the *Gertz* case, the Court did not attempt to differentiate between fact and opinion statements, although arguably some of the words complained of might have fallen within the protected realm of "opinion." This was pointed out in an opinion written in support of a per curiam decision in *Ollman v. Evans et al.*[123] Chief Judge Spottswood W. Robinson III of the U.S. Court of Appeals (District of Columbia Circuit) wrote:

> *Gertz* itself involved accusations that the plaintiff had a large police file, held an official position in a Marxist organization advocating violent seizure of government, and was a "Leninist" and a "Communist-fronter." Although the first two observations seem clearly factual, the latter two conceivably could be regarded as expressions of the author's opinion. The [Supreme] Court, however, did not discuss the applicability

of the opinion privilege to these statements. It merely noted that "Leninist" and "Communist-fronter" are "generally considered defamatory. . . ." There was no suggestion that any of the accusations were incapable, as a matter of constitutional law, of being deemed libelous.[124]

Robinson pointed out that in neither *Gertz* nor *Hutchinson* did the Court hold that the statements at issue were not opinion.

Without guidance from the highest court, how have other courts dealt with the opinion privilege? Since the 1977 *Restatement* revision, more than 50 appellate court decisions involving the *Gertz* dictum have been handed down.[125] Not surprisingly, courts interpret and/or apply the privilege differently.

For example, the Ninth Circuit Court of Appeals in *Lewis v. Time*[126] used a "contextual" analysis put forth in an earlier decision.[127] The court said three factors are involved in making a contextual analysis: (1) the words alone are not determinative as to whether they are defamatory; the facts surrounding the publication must also be considered; (2) even apparent statements of fact may assume the character of statements of opinion and thus be privileged, when made in public debate, heated labor dispute (e.g., *National Association of Letter Carriers v. Austin*), or in other circumstances in which efforts are made to persuade audiences by the use of epithets, fiery rhetoric or hyperbole; and (3) an examination of the language itself is necessary. Where the language of the statement is cautiously phrased in terms of "apparency" (e.g., it appears that . . ., in the opinion of . . ., was possibly guilty of . . .), or is of a kind typically generated in a spirited legal dispute in which the judgment, loyalties, and subjective motives of the parties are reciprocally attacked and defended in the media and other public forums, the statement is less likely to be understood as a statement of fact rather than a statement of opinion.[128]

What do courts do analytically when statements are a hybrid of fact and opinion, as is often the case?

In *Ollman,* Chief Judge Robinson discussed the fact-opinion continuum, saying:

> At one end . . . are statements that might . . . be called "pure" opinion. These are expressions which commonly are regarded as incapable of being adjudged "true" or "false" in any objective sense of those terms. Matters of personal taste, aesthetics, literary criticisms, religious beliefs, moral convictions, political views, and social theories would all fall within this class. These are statements of the sort that might be altered by discussion and whose survival as part of society's discourse should be committed to competition in the "market" place of ideas.[129]

He also would include the following at the "pure-opinion" end of the continuum: loosely definable, variously interpretable, generally derogatory remarks frequently flung about in colloquial argument and debate, and metaphorical language when context makes it apparent that a word is being used figuratively or imaginatively without any intention to rely on its literal meaning. The hallmark of the derogatory word used in colloquial debate is that it is divorced

from any specific factual underpinning; it has become an expression of general-
ized criticism or dislike.

But, said the judge, expressions at or near the pure-opinion end of the
continuum probably account for only a small portion of the statements that
become subjects of defamation lawsuits. Most are hybrid statements. They differ
from pure opinion in that most people would regard them as capable of being
denominated "true" or "false." The judge believes that when the "proponent of a
hybrid statement discloses to the reader all pertinent background facts completely and accurately, there is a strong argument . . . for including the hybrid
within the realm of absolute privilege." The same would hold if the reader already knows from personal observation or other sources all of the relevant background facts. But the balance shifts radically, said the judge, when a hybrid
appears without any recitation of the underlying facts, or when those facts are
stated erroneously or incompletely. The false hybrid statement then has the potential "to wreak considerable unjustified damage to reputation."

Robinson said he thought his position was close to that put forth in the
Restatement (§ 566), although he said it was not clear whether the *Restatement*
required *all* of the underlying facts to be reported before the absolute privilege
could be claimed.

Another judge who helped decide *Ollman* differed substantially from Robinson's analysis. Judge George E. MacKinnon noted that the article appeared on
the op-ed page and that readers are likely to assume that such an aritcle is
intended to express opinions. Furthermore, the words must be considered in their
context and not in isolation, he said, noting a Second Circuit statement in 1980 in
Cianci v. New Times Publishing Co.[130] and Comment d of Section 563 in
Restatement (1977). Other courts have agreed, including the Louisiana Supreme
Court in *Mashburn v. Collins.*[131]

In *Mashburn,* the state supreme court reversed the intermediate appellate
court in 1977 and upheld the trial court's grant of summary judgment for defendant. A newspaper columnist had written a column about food served by a
public restaurant, saying:

> T'aint Creole, t'aint Cajun, t'aint French, t'aint Country American, t'aint good
> . . . hideous sauces . . . travesty of pretentious amateurism . . . ghastly concoction.
> . . . Gave a bad taste in one's mouth . . . like bad overcooked broiled fish . . . yel-
> low death on duck. . . . The restaurant as it stands now is a burlesque.

In its decision reversing the court of appeal, the state supreme court used a
mix of the common law (fair comment and criticism) and the First Amendment
opinion privilege, saying:

> It is undisputed that the Maison de Mashburn is a public restaurant, actively engaged
> in advertising and seeking commercial patronage. Thus the establishment was a mat-
> ter of public interest and properly a subject of fair comment under the common law
> and the constitutional privilege. . . . [S]ince . . . the writings complained of were

expressions of opinion rather than statements of fact, they were privileged unless published with knowing or reckless falsity."[132]

Mashburn and *Restatement* (§ 566) (1977) also figured in a West Virginia Supreme Court of Appeals' decision in 1981 in *Havalunch, Inc. v. Mazza.*[133] The court reversed an award of $15,000 in punitive damages against Mary Mazza, a paid reporter for the *Daily Athenaeum,* the student newspaper at West Virginia University. In writing a guide to restaurants, which the reporter said was intended as humorous, Mazza wrote of Havalunch: "Bring a can of Raid if you plan to eat here. . . . You'll regret everything you eat here, especially the BLT's."

In giving the court's opinion, Justice Richard Neely said the article was protected under the doctrine of fair comment and that a jury could not award punitive damages without a showing of actual malice. Havalunch, said the court, was not a "public figure" restaurant like the one in *Mashburn* because it neither solicited reviews nor held itself out "as a place of peculiar interest or culinary quality."

But the court favorably cited *Restatement* (§ 566), in stating that there must be an assertion of a factual charge that would be defamatory if made expressly. Also, said the court, "reasonable latitude" in humor and style is accorded newspaper reporters in writing reviews of restaurants.

Justice Darrell V. McGraw, Jr. disqualified himself from taking part in the decision because he had many "fond memories" of Havalunch while a student at West Virginia University.

In another case, a denial of summary judgment for the defendants was reversed by the Massachusetts Supreme Judicial Court in *Pritsker v. Brudnoy* (1983) because the court said that comments made by WHDH radio talk show host David Brudnoy were protected statements of opinion.[134] A professional restaurant critic, Brudnoy had asserted on his talk show that a particular restaurant's owners "are unconscionably rude and vulgar people" and are "pigs."

Also, the Washington state Court of Appeals unanimously upheld a lower court's decision setting aside a libel verdict against media defendants in *Benjamin v. Cowles Publishing* (1984). The plaintiff, a store owner in a town outside of Spokane, had been awarded $219,493 from *The Spokesman Review,* owned by Cowles, and its managing editor, Chris Peck. Peck had written a column recounting an event at the store where a 13-year-old boy had shoplifted a pack of gum and the store owner had sent a letter to the youth demanding the boy pay the store $100 as a civil penalty under the state's shoplifting law. The last line of the column was: "The question is, who is stealing from whom?"[135] This was constitutionally protected opinion, ruled the three-judge court.

Another case involved William F. Buckley, Jr., owner and editor-in-chief of *National Review,* syndicated newspaper columnist, and public broadcasting personality. He was awarded $7500 punitive damages and $1 nominal damages in U.S. District Court in a libel action filed against Franklin H. Littell, author of *Wild Tongues.* The publisher, Macmillan Company, had been named codefendant but settled out of court.

The trial judge classified Buckley as a public figure and declared that certain statements in the book were made by Littell with knowledge of their falsity, or in reckless disregard of whether they were true or false, and that this had been demonstrated with convincing clarity.[136]

On appeal, however, the Second Circuit court reduced the punitive damages to "the more reasonable figure" of $1000. The U.S. Supreme Court declined to review.

In its 1976 opinion, the three-judge appellate panel concluded that only the author's statement about Buckley's engaging in libelous journalism was constitutionally and tortiously defamatory.[137] Why? Because it purported to be a statement of fact whereas the author's use of such terms as "fascist," "fellow traveler," and "radical right" fell into the category of *ideas* and *opinions* that, by definition, can never be false so as to constitute a false statement. Ideas and opinions, said Judge James L. Oakes for the panel, are matters where the widest latitude for debate in the interests of the First Amendment must be furnished. Another reason given by the judge was the tremendous imprecision of the meaning of such words as "fascist" and "fellow traveler" in the realm of political debate.

Where there was ambiguity in an article stating a fact or an opinion, the California Supreme Court left the resolution of that issue to a jury, doing so in *Good Government Group of Seal Beach v. Superior Court of Los Angeles County* (1979). The U.S. Supreme Court declined to review the case.[138]

The use of the opinion privilege is growing, as more recent cases attest.

In 1987, the U.S. Supreme Court decided not to review Texas court decisions that an editorial statement in the *El Paso Times* about an assistant U.S. attorney were protected under the First Amendment's opinion privilege.[139] The newspaper had accused the attorney, James W. Kerr, Jr., of lying and cheating during his closing arguments in a widely publicized drug conspiracy trial.[140] Kerr filed a defamation suit and a jury awarded him $3.5 million in damages. The trial judge later reduced the amount to $600,000.

On appeal, the Eighth District Court of Appeals threw out the award because it said the article was laced with language typically indicating opinion. Also, it was "replete with rhetorical hyperbole and was featured on the editorial page."

The Texas Supreme Court affirmed the appellate court's decision without writing an opinion.

Similarly, a Los Angeles television critic's column that included a hypothetical conversation involving the producer of a sex education documentary was said by the California Supreme Court to be privileged opinion.[141]

The *Herald Examiner's* critic, Paul Bunzel, had written:

> My impression is that executive producer Walter Baker . . . told his writer-producer . . ., "We've got a hot potato here — let's pour on titillating innuendo and as much bare flesh as we can get away with. Viewers will eat it up!"

Bunzel also condemned the documentary as "hypocritical sleaze."

Baker filed suit and the *Examiner* relied in its defense on the opinion privilege and the state's statutory "fair comment" privilege.

In 1984, the trial court dismissed Baker's complaint, holding that the review was protected opinion, but the Court of Appeal reinstated the suit on the ground that the average reader would interpret the challenged language as fact. In July 1986, the state supreme court dismissed the case, invoking the opinion privilege in doing so. The court said the headline immediately conveyed to the reader that the column was editorial, and that Bunzel's qualifying clause, "My impression is," put the reader on notice that the comments to follow were opinion. Further, Bunzel's use of quotation marks, said the court, were merely a valid exercise of literary style.[142]

The U.S. Supreme Court declined to review the decision.[143]

The Minnesota Court of Appeals, in *Capan v. Daughtery,* ruled that statements quoted in a newspaper, suggesting that the plaintiff was "not dealing with a full deck" and "maybe" has mental problems, were protected by the opinion privilege.[144]

The court cited the Eighth Circuit U.S Court of Appeals' adoption of a multifactor test for determining whether a statement is opinion protected by the First Amendment.[145] The Eighth Circuit previously had relied on a single factor test.

The factors considered by the Eighth Circuit are:[146]

—The precision and specificity of the disputed statement (the more imprecise, the more likely that it is opinion).

—The statement's verifiability (the less verifiable, the more likely it is opinion).

—The literary and social context in which the statement was made (including the entire communication's tone, the use of cautionary language, the category of publication, its style of writing and intended audience).

—The statement's public context (consideration being given to the public or political arena in which the statement was made).

In another case, the First Circuit U.S. Court of Appeals ruled that a newspaper's use of the word "scam" as a jump line for a story continued inside the paper, surmounting an article written in a first-person narrative style concerning the author's experiences with a time-share condominium development owned by the plaintiff, was protected statement of opinion.[147] The court, in *McCabe v. Rattine* (1987), said that the word does not have a precise meaning and therefore is incapable of being proven true or false. Also, the narrative style puts the reader on notice that the author is giving his views concerning a public controversy.

But the opinion privilege defense did not succeed in *Healey v. New England Newspapers, Inc.* The Rhode Island Supreme Court ruled in 1987 that a trial court erred in granting a directed verdict for the defendant newspaper.[148]

The libel suit resulted from publication of an article about a man who collapsed and later died after being refused admission to a meeting chaired by the plaintiff, a physician. The article included statements from the dead person's friends and relatives criticizing the plaintiff's failure to give aid to the stricken man. Those statements, said the the state supreme court, could be read as implying the existence of undisclosed defamatory statements of fact.

Another case involving the opinion privilege is *Brown & Williamson Tobacco Corp. v. Jacobson et al.*[149] The corporation manufactures Viceroy cigarettes and brought suit after a WBBM-TV commentator, Walter Jacobson, said that Viceroy cigarette advertisements encouraged children to smoke by associating smoking with sex, alcohol, and marijuana.[150] A federal district court jury awarded the company $3 million in compensatory damages, $2 million in punitive damages against CBS (the network that owns WBBM-TV), and $50,000 in punitive damages against the commentator. The judge reduced the special damages award to one dollar because the company, he said, had not proved that the broadcast caused any loss of customers or decreased its sales.

CBS appealed, and in its brief it asserted that the verdict resulted "from the court's failure to understand the broadcast as expression of opinion protected by the First Amendment."[151] The company responded by saying that any claim that this "pre-planned libel" was immunized as opinion "is frivolous."[152]

In 1987, a three-judge panel of the Seventh Circuit U.S. Court of Appeals upheld the jury's punitive damages award and restored $1 million of the jury's compensatory damages award. The panel said that it found clear and convincing evidence that the station had acted with actual malice in the broadcast concerning the cigarette advertisements.[153]

The U.S. Supreme Court denied review.[154]

The *Gertz* opinion privilege was cited by the U.S. Supreme Court in 1988 as one reason for the Court's unanimous reversal of a $200,000 award to the Rev. Jerry Falwell against *Hustler* magazine and its publisher for intentional infliction of emotional distress (discussed in Chapter 7). *Hustler* magazine had published an ad parody in which Falwell is purportedly interviewed and reveals an incestuous relationship with his mother.

Letters to the Editor. Newspapers are responsible for what they publish, including letters to the editor. These often express sentiments highly critical of someone or something.

The letter to the editor that follows—with the name withheld by request—led to a lawsuit:

What has happened to our laws? Monday the state attorney's office announced its intention not to prosecute Leroy Hay, Fort Ogden, and Richard Heath, Fort Lauderdale, and the judge fines . . . Hay $5,000 and gives him 5 years probation.

This makes me sick! Catch a crook, pat him on the back and let him go free. I wonder how many laughs they have had on this, at the taxpayers [sic] expense.

No wonder the young people today have no respect for law and order—look at the fine examples you judges and lawyers give them. You twist the laws so the crooks can go free. It makes one wonder who really is the criminal.

It's time, you judges, lawyers, and leaders of our land, to take a good look at yourselves. Who are you really trying to protect, the crook, the innocent or maybe your pocketbooks?

What the courts had to decide in *Hay v. Independent Newspapers* (1984) was whether the letter consisted of pure opinion, or a hybrid containing defamatory facts.[155]

The trial court held that the alleged libelous language was an expression of opinion protected by the First Amendment. On appeal, so did the Florida District Court of Appeal. It made this analysis:

> The complaint alleged that statements contained in the article referred to the appellant as a crook and a criminal. These statements were based in part upon facts disclosed in the article, but the fact that criminal charges had been filed against the appellant was either known or readily available to the reader as a member of the public. Furthermore, the statements were made in a letter to the editor published in a section of the newspaper titled "The Forum, Opinion," and the letter was directed not toward the appellant, but toward the judicial system. Applying the principles . . . set forth, we hold the statement was a pure expression of opinion. . . .[156]

Do you agree with the court's analysis? Interestingly, the court cited an alternative basis for affirming the lower court's dismissal of the complaint; namely, the private figure plaintiff had failed to allege any fault.[157]

Is it not true that almost any *allegation* of criminal behavior is an opinion? That's what the Second Circuit U.S. Court of Appeals said in *Cianci v. New Times Publishing Co.*[158] Nonetheless, such an allegation would not be absolutely protected by the First Amendment as opinion, according to the court. Furthermore, the *Restatement* explicitly recognizes that an allegation of criminal behavior is properly subject to a defamation action.

New York's highest court, in *Rinaldi v. Holt, Rinehart & Winston,* favorably cited a California Supreme Court decision in stating that there is "a critical distinction between opinions which attribute improper motives to public officials and accusations in whatever form that an individual has committed a crime or is personally dishonest."[159] There's no First Amendment protection for false charges of criminal behavior, said the court.

When the writer of a letter to the editor accused a mayor in New Jersey of a "huge coverup" and "a conspiracy" for refusing to reveal the names of property owners delinquent in their tax payments, a majority of the New Jersey Supreme Court concluded that the words were not specific accusations of criminal conduct.[160] Rather, they were merely "rhetoric," criticizing the major "in an identified, isolated instance of his performance in public office." The court continued:

> If letters of this sort were [viewed as] defamatory, newspapers surely would be reluctant to continue publishing strongly worded [opinions]. We are loathe to discourage that robust and uninhibited commentary on public issues that is part of our national heritage.

Editorial Hyperbole

Editorial hyperbole, even when very caustic, also is protected by the common law under the defense of fair comment and criticism and by the constitutional opinion privilege enunciated in *Gertz.*

All of the editorial hyperbole cases have the following in common: (1) the articles or editorials are related to public officials or public figures; (2) they contain expressions of opinion rather than statements purporting to be facts; and (3) there's an absence of actual malice.

Here are several cases where hyperbole was the issue and the defense:

■ The *Palm Beach Post* and *Palm Beach Times* published numerous articles, editorials, and cartoons highly critical of school superintendent Lloyd F. Early. Accusations of incompetence, indecisiveness, and nepotism were made. Early sued and a county court jury awarded him $950,000 in compensatory damages and $50,000 in punitive damages. In 1976 a Court of Appeal reversed and ordered judgment for the defendant.[161] In describing the articles and cartoons, the appellate court said that most of them "can fairly be described as slanted, mean, vicious, and substantially below the level of objectivity that one would expect of responsible journalism. . . ." But, said the court, "there is no evidence called to our attention which clearly and convincingly demonstrates that a single one of the articles was a false statement of fact made with actual malice as defined in the *New York Times* case."

The Florida Supreme Court declined to review the case.[162] Early appealed to the U.S. Supreme Court, saying that the Florida courts had, in effect, "granted an absolute protection to libelous news commentary, no matter how villifying or false," as long as the commentary "can arguably fit within the category of editorial opinion rather than reportorial fact." The U.S. Supreme Court denied review.[163]

■ The U.S. Supreme Court also declined to review the decision in *Pierce v. Capital Cities Communication, Inc.* in which the Third Circuit U.S. Court of Appeals affirmed a U.S. District Court's dismissal of a lawsuit against TV station WPVI.[164] The plaintiff, a public official, had argued that a news report had, in effect, accused him of abusing his public trust, but the Court of Appeals said that "the publication of hyperbole, even if caustic and irritating, cannot by itself support the inference that the [defendant] evidenced actual malice.[165] The court continued:

If reasonable viewers would interpret the statement in the broadcast as editorial hyperbole then the broadcast must be afforded constitutional protection . . . because the hyperbole alone was not evidence of malice against the public figure.

■ But when the U.S. Labor Party claimed in a leaflet that a candidate for the Baltimore, Maryland, City Council had a Nazi Germany SS background, the Maryland Court of Special Appeals rejected the argument that the accusation was mere "rhetorical hyperbole." In upholding the $30,000 in damages, the Court of Special Appeals said there was nothing in the Labor Party's investigation of the candidate that could have formed a basis for the statements in the leaflet, and therefore they must have been made with reckless disregard of the truth.[166]

A statement, said the court, is considered rhetorical hyperbole only when a reader could not possibly understand the statement to be a representation of fact. But in the case before it, the court said the leaflets were distributed to the general public and not to persons familiar with the candidate, and that nothing in the leaflet's content would prevent the general public from understanding the words to have other than their plain meaning.

Both the Maryland Court of Appeals and the U.S. Supreme Court decided not to review the case.

■ When the Dayton, Ohio, *Journal Herald* published an editorial cartoon on August 23, 1984, depicting a car driving by a store front labeled "Ohio Bar Association," and gunmen firing at the store front, it prompted a lawsuit by an Ohio Supreme Court associate justice, James Celebrezze, who was running for re-election. The license plate on the car carried the name "Celebrezze." The cartoon actually was aimed at the feud going on between Ohio Chief Justice Frank Celebrezze — James's brother — and the Ohio Bar Association over that group's endorsement of candidates and other issues. An editorial accompanying the cartoon urged readers to vote against James.

The lawsuit alleged that James had been libeled, that he had been caused emotional distress (see Chapter 7), and that his privacy had been invaded. The trial court said the cartoon was constitutionally protected opinion and granted summary judgment to the newspaper.[167] The Ohio Supreme Court affirmed, stating that even though the newspaper admitted that the cartoon's purpose was to politically embarrass Celebrezze and to prevent him from being re-elected, such a motive did not constitute actual malice. No reasonable person, said the court, could conclude from the cartoon that Celebrezze was being accused of murder or attempted murder. Rather, the cartoon was hyperbole.[168]

Neutral Reportage Protected

In *Edwards v. National Audubon Society,*[169] the U.S. Court of Appeals for the Second Circuit reversed a libel verdict of $61,000 in compensatory damages against *The New York Times* and $1 against a National Audubon Society vice-president. In so doing, the court, in an opinion written by Chief Judge Irving Kaufman, declared that a "right of neutral reportage" existed under the First Amendment — a right that protects the "accurate and disinterested" reporting of defamatory charges made by responsible, prominent organizations, such as the National Audubon Society. Such a right, said Kaufman, protects the journalist who believes, "reasonably and in good faith, that his report accurately conveys the charges made" — even if the journalist believes the charges to be false. Note that knowledge of falsity is the major requisite under the *St. Amant* test.

The case arose out of a *Times* article that quoted an Audubon publication that carried a general charge that some unnamed scientists were being paid to lie concerning the effects of DDT on birds. The *Times* reporter asked for, and was given, the names of five scientists. The reporter was able to contact three of them and two sent extensive research material to the reporter refuting the charges.[170] The story appeared in the August 14, 1972, issue under the headline "Pesticide Spokesmen Accused of 'Lying' on Higher Bird Count." It included the statement about unnamed scientists being paid to lie concerning DDT's effect on birds, the five names supplied by the Audubon Society vice-president, and denials of the charge by the three scientists the reporter had contacted. Libel suits followed. The three scientists were said to be public figures and a jury returned a verdict for the plaintiffs.

On appeal, the *Times* pinpointed the issue as follows: "[It] . . . is nothing less than whether when an organization such as Audubon makes such charges, the *Times* may print them — without concern for the immense burden, costs and the risks resulting." Then, pointing to a practice often followed in public affairs reporting, the *Times* contended: "We think it should be self-evident that if one political figure makes defamatory statements about another — as, for example, candidates for the office of vice-president of the United States — that the press may freely report them . . . *regardless* of the views of the journalists or editors involved as to the truth of the charges."[171]

In reversing and ordering the complaint dismissed, Judge Kaufman said for the court:

> We do not believe that the press may be required under the First Amendment to suppress newsworthy statements merely because it has serious doubts regarding their truth. The public interest in being fully informed about controversies that often rage around sensitive issues demands that the press be afforded the freedom to report such charges without assuming responsibility for them.

What the Second Circuit did was to push protection for the news media beyond the "knowing falsity" qualification of *Times-Sullivan* whenever the news media accurately and disinterestedly report what a responsible or prominent organization (or person) says about an issue of public importance. The precedent established by *Edwards* applies only in the Second Circuit unless adopted by other jurisdictions or unless overruled by the U.S. Supreme Court. The Supreme Court declined to review the decision, but such inaction does not establish *Edwards* as a Supreme Court precedent.

Times attorney Abrams hailed the Second Circuit's decision as a landmark ruling. And the author of a *Journalism Quarterly* article that reviewed the origins and implications of the case, said in the opening paragraph:

> From the viewpoint of the working journalist, the . . . [*Edwards'* decision] may be one of the most significant developments yet in the rapidly changing doctrine of constitutional libel law. The decision . . . is the first unequivocal federal appellate opinion that provides a First Amendment shield for one of the most common forms of public affairs journalism — the report of one public figure's attack on the character or performance of another.[172]

However, New York, which is in the Second Circuit, has expressly rejected

Edwards. In *Hogan v. Herald Co.,* Justice Richard D. Simmons of a lower court wrote:

> The Supreme Court has not adopted *Edwards,* . . . and in our view it is not possible to reconcile it with that court's prior decision in *Gertz.* . . . The unequivocal holding of *Gertz* is that a publisher's immunity is based upon the status of the plaintiff, not the subject matter of the publication. Presumably, all publications of the news media are newsworthy. They are not privileged, however, unless the publisher is free of culpable conduct under the standards stated in *New York Times v. Sullivan, Gertz v. Robert Welch, Inc.,* and, in New York, *Chapadeau v. Utica Observer-Dispatch.*[173]

The New York Court of Appeals affirmed expressly on the opinion of Justice Simmons.[174]

And the Second Circuit itself has not seen fit to accept the neutral reporting privilege in all seemingly appropriate circumstances. In *Cianci v. New Times Publishing Co.,* discussed earlier, the court not only rejected an opinion privilege defense, but also the neutral reportage one. It did so because *New Times* had not reported accusations against Vincent Cianci, mayor of Providence, Rhode Island, in a fair or neutral manner, according to the court.[175] Further, the court said that the neutral reporting privilege does not extend to all "newsworthy" information. Rather, the court seemed to be limiting the privilege to newsworthy accusations by a public official or public figure against another public official or public figure. In *Cianci,* a private figure had made an accusation that the mayor had raped her, according to a *New Times* story. However, the court did not resolve the question of newsworthiness of the accusations. Instead, it remanded the case to the U.S. District Court to allow Cianci an opportunity to prove actual malice.

The Third Circuit U.S. Court of Appeals refused to adopt the neutral reportage privilege when it affirmed a U.S. District Court's summary judgment for defendant CBS in *Dickey v. CBS.*[176] Although the lower court had criticized the "indifference" of CBS's affiliated station WCAU-TV in Philadelphia concerning the truth of charges of "payoffs," the court ruled that Dickey had failed to show that the network entertained serious doubts concerning the truth or falsity of the charge (*St. Amant* test). The Third Circuit declared that a "neutral reporting" privilege is contrary to the *St. Amant* rule in that accurate publication of newsworthy statements would be protected unless the press entertained "serious doubts" as to the truth of such statements.

But the Third Circuit appeared to soften its stand in its affirmance of summary judgment to *Time* magazine in *Medico v. Time* (1981).[177] According to a petition seeking a U.S. Supreme Court review which was denied, the Third Circuit gave some weight to the existence of such a privilege despite its earlier ruling in *Dickey.*

The Tenth Circuit U.S. Court of Appeals said in *Dixson v. Newsweek* that *Edwards* applies only to public figures/public officials, not to private individuals.[178] An award of $45,000 in actual damages against *Newsweek* was affirmed by the Tenth Circuit panel despite the magazine's contention that it reported accurately the statement of airline officials in reporting that some of Frontier

Airlines' schedules were "outright fiction." A Frontier executive also was quoted as saying that certain discharged executives, including plaintiff, were "in jobs they couldn't handle."

The Tenth Circuit panel said that the republication of false defamatory statements is as much a tort as the original publication, adding that the neutral reporting privilege does not apply to private individuals (the defamation plaintiff being classified as a private individual).

In another case, the three-judge Illinois Appellate Court for the Fourth Judicial District applied the "neutral reporting" privilege in affirming summary judgment for defendant newspaper in *Krauss v. Champaign News Gazette*.[179] So, too, did a U.S. District Court in the Tenth Circuit in *Whitaker v. Denver Post*.[180] In the Ninth Circuit, a U.S. District Court in Oregon cited *Edwards* in ruling for the defendant newspaper,[181] and the Arizona Superior Court of Maricopa County did likewise as it issued a directed verdict for the defendant newspaper.[182]

A number of Florida Circuit Courts have recognized the privilege; an Ohio Court of Appeals did so in 1988; and appellate courts in California, the District of Columbia and Georgia appear to have done the same.[183]

Both the Alabama and South Dakota Supreme Courts have refused to adopt or recognize the privilege, and when a Kentucky trial court applied the privilege, the state supreme court reversed and the U.S. Supreme Court denied review.[184]

DE NOVO REVIEW

The emergence of the neutral reporting privilege in some jurisdictions was a bright spot for the news media during an otherwise bleak period that began with *Gertz* and extended through *Firestone, Wolston, Hutchinson, Herbert, Keeton,* and *Calder*. Supreme Court decisions in those cases left little for the press to cheer. But the media won a very important decision when the Court, in a 6–3 decision in *Bose Corporation v. Consumers Union* (1984), held that federal appellate judges must independently review findings of actual malice in cases governed by *Times v. Sullivan*.[185] The importance of such reviews is highlighted by a LDRC study, which showed that 83 percent of all libel verdicts decided by juries between 1980 and 1982 went against the media, but that 71 percent of those were reversed on appeal. Additionally, the 1982 study of 54 then-recent trials in media libel and privacy cases showed that 30 of the damage awards exceeded $100,000. Only seven damage awards were affirmed on appeal, the largest being $400,000. Appellate action still was pending in 19 cases.[186] LDRC also studied 63 libel trials between mid-1982 and mid-1984 and found that plaintiffs prevailed in 54 percent of those trials with an average damage award of slightly more than $2 million. But on appeal, adverse trial judgments were reversed in 68 percent of the cases.[187]

An example is the Tenth Circuit U.S. Court of Appeals' reversal of a $14 million libel judgment won by a former Miss Wyoming against *Penthouse* magazine. The Tenth Circuit panel ruled in *Pring v. Penthouse International* (1983) that the article complained of could reasonably be understood only as "pure fantasy."[188]

During de novo review in *Bose Corporation,* the First Circuit U.S. Court of Appeals applied the actual malice standard in a product disparagement lawsuit brought by a public figure corporation and ruled that *Consumer Reports'* use of "imprecise language" in evaluating plaintiff's stereo loudspeakers was not sufficient to warrant an actual malice finding.[189] The court, therefore, reversed a trial court's award of $210,905. The article in question had claimed that the sound heard through the Bose 901 speaker system "seemed to grow to gigantic proportions and tended to wander about the room."

According to the corporation's petition for review, the appellate court could not set aside the findings of fact in a lawsuit tried without a jury where such findings are not clearly erroneous."

The Supreme Court affirmed with Justice Stevens giving the Court's opinion. It held that appellate judges are not limited by the "clearly erroneous" standard of review prescribed under Rule 52(a) of the Federal Rules of Civil Procedure. This rule provides that "findings of fact shall not be set aside unless clearly erroneous, and due regard shall be given to the opportunity of the trial court to judge the credibility of the witnesses." Stevens said the "clearly erroneous" standard in this rule does not prescribe the standard of review to be applied, and that appellate judges must exercise independent review of both the facts and the law in appropriate cases and determine whether the record establishes actual malice with convincing clarity.

Rehnquist, joined by O'Connor, dissented. He contended that the "clearly erroneous" standard is the only standard of factual review that can be used in connection with the constitutional requirement of actual malice. Except where error is clear, Rehnquist believed the trial court, or trier of fact, is in a better position to make determinations of actual malice than reviewing authorities.

Rehnquist did note that the fact-finding process engaged in by a jury is more suspect than the same process engaged in by a trial judge who makes written findings. "Justifying independent review of facts found by a jury is easier . . .," he wrote.[190]

Justice White also dissented for reasons given by Rehnquist.

The importance of *Bose Corporation* is seen in a 1986 California Supreme Court decision.

A $3.6 million libel judgment against the *San Francisco Examiner* and two reporters was overturned because the court said there was insufficient evidence to show actual malice.

Investigative stories by the two reporters in 1976 had accused two San Francisco homicide investigators and an assistant district attorney of intimidating a witness into giving perjured testimony. The testimony led to conviction of a 19-year-old bank teller for a 1972 Chinatown murder. The jury in *McCoy v. Hearst Corp.* awarded $500,000 in actual damages and $500,000 in punitive damages from the newspaper to each of the plaintiffs and $250,000 in compensatory damages and $10,000 in punitive damages from each of the reporters to each of the plaintiffs.

In an opinion by Chief Justice Rose Bird, the court said the trial court judge was required to independently review all evidence presented on the issue of actual malice and could not delegate this responsibility to the jury.[191] The court chastised the Court of Appeal for the First Appellate District, which had affirmed the trial court's judgment, for upholding the award without independently reviewing the evidence supporting the verdict.

The U.S. Supreme Court declined to review the case with only Justice White voting to hear arguments.[192]

LIBEL INSURANCE

Despite some safeguards against successful libel suits, the risks are considerable. Arthur B. Hanson, general counsel for the American Newspaper Publishers Association (ANPA) in 1974, pointed this out when he spoke at an annual convention of the Pennsylvania Newspaper Publishers Association several months after the *Gertz* decision. Referring to that case, he said that the libel law "has taken a turn for the worse from a newspaper standpoint."[193] He continued, "Today, we are appealing judgments of $750,000 and $214,000. There is no guarantee of success, for they are in the state courts. We have paid out more than $100,000 each in defense costs in two suits successfully defended. . . ."

The director of Mutual Insurance Co. Ltd. in Bermuda told a group of editors in 1983 that since the company was founded in 1963, it had paid $22 million to publishers for the cost of defending against libel suits in 4500 cases and for judgments.[194] The company—one of three libel insurance firms serving news media in the United States—had 2272 libel cases open in 1983 at an estimated liability of $27.5 million. The caseload had climbed at an alarming rate of 200 to 300 new cases annually since 1972, said the director. To meet this wave of litigation, insurers increased their rates and the deductibles media organizations had to pay. Rates doubled in 1985[195] In 1986, National Newspaper Association members saw their libel insurance rates and deductibles nearly doubled.[196] Rates are still going up and some newspapers have been unable to either afford the premiums or the remaining insurers have been unwilling to add new customers. Under such conditions, news media organizations tend to tone down their stories and do fewer investigative ones.

The cost of defending against libel lawsuits can be staggering and some small newspapers have been forced out of business because of such costs. The longest libel trial in American legal history ended May 13, 1982, when a California jury found that *Penthouse* magazine had not libeled La Costa Resort and six other plaintiffs in a 1975 article that made allegations of ties with organized crime.[197] Jurors deliberated for 15 days before returning 14 separate verdicts.

Penthouse publisher Robert Guccione said he spent $6.5 million defending himself and the magazine, and plaintiffs are believed to have spent that much or more.[198]

After former U.S. Sen. Paul Laxalt and McClatchy Newspaper reached an out-of-court settlement of Laxalt's $250 million libel suit against the newspaper chain and the newspaper's $6 million countersuit—with no payment by either party and no retraction—both parties agreed that an arbitration panel of three former judges would decide if Laxalt was entitled to recovery of attorney's fees and costs. Laxalt asked for about $4.3 million in fees and costs. The panel awarded him $647,454.[199]

CBS said it spent $4.5 million defending against retired Gen. William Westmoreland's $125 million libel lawsuit and was described as "battle weary" after the suit was dismissed during the eighth week of the trial.

Media Fighting Back. Spurred by the growing number of lawsuits, megabuck jury awards, skyrocketing insurance costs, and escalating legal expenses, the media are developing a fight-back attitude against frivolous or baseless lawsuits. In addition, there's been a "modest revolution," according to Henry Kaufman, LDRC general counsel, in tort reform legislation. Either by amendment of existing statutes or enactment of new ones, more than half the states are providing the means by which court costs and attorneys' fees can be recovered whenever frivolous or baseless lawsuits, motions, or appeals are filed. In addition to what's happening at the state level, Rule 11 of the Federal Rules of Civil Procedure was amended in 1983 to more effectively deter abuses in the signing of pleadings, motions, and other papers, and to reduce the reluctance of federal judges to impose sanctions, according to Gary B. Pruitt, general counsel for McClatchy Newspapers. The new rule requires mandatory imposition of sanctions under certain circumstances.

Among the early advocates of fighting back was the late W. E. Chilton III, publisher of the *Charleston* (W. Va.) *Gazette.* At the time that he initiated countersuing, he declared:

> I'm sick and tired of being sued by lawyers who have no idea what the First Amendment is about, and bring suits either to harass the newspaper or because they don't know what they're doing or don't have the guts to tell their clients they don't have a case.

The *Gazette*'s decision to fight back probably crystallized in 1981 after five libel suits had been filed against it by a Charleston attorney who was representing several plaintiffs. The newspaper filed a countersuit against the attorney and asked $25,000 in attorneys' fees and compensation for time lost by employees in defending against the libel actions. Ultimately the attorney paid the newspaper $12,500 in an out-of-court settlement.

The impact of the tort reform legislation and the fight-back attitude can best be seen by what happened during one month in 1988:

1. On May 27 the Appellate Division of the New York Supreme Court upheld an award of attorneys' fees and costs to the media defendant in *Stephen L. Mitchell v. The Herald Co.* (publisher of the *Syracuse Journal Herald*). The New York statute limits the maximum recovery to $10,000.
2. On May 11 the King County Superior Court in Washington awarded the *Seattle Times* $41,983 in attorneys' fees and other expenses incurred in its

defense of what the judge said was a frivolous action by plaintiffs in *Rhinehart et al. v. Seattle Times et al.*

3. And on May 2 the Chronicle Broadcasting Co. and a KRON-TV reporter were awarded $220,752 in fees and costs by a San Francisco Superior Court judge who believed that the plaintiffs' libel lawsuit (*Joseph A. Martocchio et al. v. Chronicle Broadcasting Co.*) was frivolous with evidence of bad faith in bringing the lawsuit.

NBC countersued libel plaintiff Lyndon H. LaRouche Jr., an independent presidential candidate who was described as the head of a "political cult" that harassed its critics, and a jury awarded the network $3 million in punitive damages, later reduced to $200,000, and $2,000 in actual damages.

Tort reform legislation and countersuing represent departures from the traditional "American Rule" which, unlike the British practice, ordinarily requires each side to pay its own fees and costs, but the U.S Supreme Court now allows exceptions whenever the losing party has "acted in bad faith, vexatiously, wantonly, or for oppressive reasons."

SUMMARY

Gertz v. Welch, Inc. (1974) returned the development of libel law to the states in cases involving private figures seeking recovery for alleged defamatory statements about them. States can define appropriate standards of care for the news media provided they do not permit the imposition of liability without fault. The defamatory statement must warn a "reasonably prudent editor or broadcaster" of its defamatory potential. Stated another way, the statement must make "substantial danger to reputation apparent." If such fault is present, then the private individual can recover for actual injury; that is, injury to good name or reputation plus out-of-pocket losses. A state cannot, however, permit the imposition of punitive damages unless there is a showing of actual malice as defined by *Times-Sullivan*.

As *Gertz* and its progeny demonstrate, a person becomes a public figure by thrusting himself or herself into a public controversy or by achieving notoriety or lasting fame. Merely being a prominent attorney or being drawn into a court action does not make the person a public figure. The key test seems to be *voluntary* action on a person's part in connection with a public controversy. Therefore, the class of individuals known as public figures is considerably reduced.

An objective test of a person's status was advanced by Judge Edward Tamm in *Waldbaum*. A "general purpose public figure" is a celebrity, or one whose name is a household word. The public follows the ideas and actions of such a person with great interest. Generally, such a person has access to the media if defamed and such a person has assumed the risk that public exposure might bring.

In determining if a person is a limited-issue public figure, the first step is to isolate the public controversy. Newsworthiness alone will not suffice, said Tamm. The public controversy must be a real dispute which affects the general public or some segment of it in an appreciable way. Given such a controversy, then the plaintiff's role in it must not be trivial or tangential. The plaintiff must be trying to influence the outcome or have an impact on its resolution. Also, the alleged defamation must be related to the plaintiff's participation in the controversy.

Concerning the standard of care being imposed by states, most are opting for an ordinary negligence standard. Courts in Colorado, Indiana, and New Jersey are using the *Rosenbloom* public interest test or a modified version thereof. New York has adopted a gross negligence standard.

Supreme courts in 30 states have adopted ordinary negligence standards, or slight variations thereof. Highest courts in Massachusetts and Oregon have ruled out punitive damage awards no matter what degree of fault is found.

Gertz-related problems include: (1) difficulty of distinguishing between public figures and private individuals; (2) uncertainties associated with a negligence standard; (3) increased difficulty of obtaining summary judgment (although this is an added media burden even with the "actual malice" test because that test can figure in any defamation action against the media regardless of the status of the plaintiff) and therefore increased cost of litigation; and (4) exposure of the media to prolonged discovery procedures particularly in connection with any determination of actual malice, including a penetration into the editorial process as countenanced by the *Herbert* decision. *Herbert* denies reporters a "source" privilege; and reporters, in the past, have been willing to go to jail rather than reveal confidential sources (see Chapter 11).

Gertz-related advantages are: (1) punitive damages cannot be awarded without a showing of actual malice; (2) a plaintiff can recover only actual damages, not presumed damages, absent a showing of actual malice; and (3) there must be some degree of fault on the part of the journalist before damages can be awarded.

The public interest/concern test still retains its vitality in defamation lawsuits brought by public officials and public figures even though, in *Wolston,* the U.S. Supreme Court said such a test had been displaced by the status test in private figure defamation actions against the news media.

In *Philadelphia Newspapers v. Hepps,* the Supreme Court ruled that private figure libel plaintiffs must demonstrate falsity if they are suing the news media and the alleged defamatory statements involve matters of public concern.

In *Dun & Bradstreet v. Greenmoss Builders, Inc.,* a divided Court took the position that an erroneous credit report is of private concern only and therefore the protection of *Gertz* does not apply.

The news media thus are in the position of having to determine the status of the individual involved and whether the information to be reported is of public concern before proceeding on the assumption that either *Times-Sullivan* or *Gertz* will provide protection in the event of a defamation lawsuit.

Gertz and a footnote in *Hutchinson* make it more difficult for the news media to gain summary judgment because issues of negligence and "actual malice" — particularly negligence — usually are resolved by trial. However, the Court, in *Anderson v. Liberty Lobby,* seemed to take the sting out of Burger's footnote in *Hutchinson,* and the record shows media defendants often winning on summary judgment motions.

Flowing out of *Times-Sullivan; Old Dominion Branch No. 496, National Association of Letter Carriers;* and *Gertz* is the rule that the Constitution absolutely protects pure opinion, but only conditionally protects hybrid statements (opinion and fact).

According to the *Restatement,* Section 566 (1977), a defamatory communication may consist of a statement in the form of an opinion, but a statement of this nature is actionable only if it implies the allegation of undisclosed defamatory facts as the basis for the opinion.

Allegations of criminal behavior, though falling into the pure opinion realm, are not accorded absolute protection under the pure opinion privilege. Rather, such allegations are subject to defamation actions, according to *Restatement.* Note, however, that other defenses might be used by the media, such as, truth or a conditional privilege under state law (fair and accurate report of a privileged document, such as an arrest warrant).

Editorial hyperbole is protected both by the common law and the federal Constitution's opinion privilege. All hyperbole defenses have in common: (1) the criticism relates to public officials or public figures; (2) it is an expression of opinion that does not purport to be fact; and (3) there's no actual malice.

Several jurisdictions have declared that a "right of neutral reportage" exists under the First Amendment, including the Second Circuit U.S. Court of Appeals, which announced it. Notwithstanding the "knowledge of falsity" requirement in the "actual malice" test, these jurisdictions state that journalists are protected if they accurately and disinterestedly report defamatory charges made by responsible and prominent organizations (or individuals) even if the journalists believe the charges to be false. The Third Circuit said such a "right" is contrary to the *St. Amant* rule. The Tenth Circuit believes that *Edwards* applies only to public figures/public officials, not to private individuals. And New York's highest court has rejected such a privilege.

A case of considerable significance is *Bose Corporation v. Consumers Union* (1984). A 6–3 majority of the Supreme Court said federal appellate judges should review both the facts and the law of appropriate cases in determining if the record establishes actual malice. Previously, such reviews of the facts generally were conducted only when there were indications that findings of fact were "clearly erroneous." The importance of the case is demonstrated by statistics showing that 71 percent of the verdicts that went against the media are reversed on appeal. *Bose Corporation* applies equally to a finding of fact by a trial judge or by a jury. Note that questions of law have always been reviewable.

As costs of litigation skyrocket, and as jury awards against the media reach into the millions of dollars, insurance costs have soared. Litigation expenses reached record heights in a defamation action by La Costa Resort and six other plaintiffs against *Penthouse* magazine and its publisher. The publisher said he spent $6.5 million defending himself and the magazine through the trial stage. And the plaintiffs are believed to have spent a comparable amount!

Because many libel suits are frivolous or baseless, the media are fighting back with countersuits, aided by tort reform legislation (much of it since the mid-1980s).

QUESTIONS IN REVIEW

1. *Gertz* applies to which type of persons: public officials, public figures, or private individuals?
2. What does *Gertz* say about "fault" on the part of the news media?
3. For an individual to be a "public figure," he or she must generally do what or have achieved what?
4. True or False: In most states punitive damages cannot be awarded to a private individual who brings a libel action.
5. If a private individual successfully sues for libel, and if there is no proof of actual malice on the part of news media, what kind of compensation can be awarded in most states?
6. Thus far, three states have elected to stay with *Rosenbloom* as the standard to be followed whenever private individuals file libel suits. Name them.
7. True or False. Most states have adopted a gross negligence standard for private figure defamation suits.
8. *Philadelphia Newspapers v. Hepps* (1986) helps the media defend against private figure defamation suits. Why?
9. In what way, if any, did the public concern test figure in the decisions of the Supreme Court in *Philadelphia Newspapers v. Hepps* and *Dun & Bradstreet v. Greenmoss Builders* (1985)?
10. True or False. It is now virtually impossible for federal appellate judges to review both the facts and the law to determine if actual malice has been established against a media defendant with convincing clarity.
11. True or False. Because of a footnote in *Hutchinson* and subsequent developments, summary judgment is virtually unavailable to the news media whenever private figures file lawsuits against them.

ANSWERS

1. Private individuals.
2. A state can impose liability only if there is fault on the part of the news media.
3. The individual must have voluntarily thrust himself/herself into a public controversy or have achieved pervasive fame or notoriety in the community.
4. False. However, the highest courts in Massachusetts and Oregon have ruled out punitive damages in any libel actions against the news media.
5. Compensation for "actual injury," such as injury to good name or reputation, or for out-of-pocket losses.
6. New Jersey, Colorado, and Indiana.
7. False. Only New York so far.
8. The U.S. Supreme Court ruled that such plaintiffs must show falsity whenever the information published is of public concern.
9. In *Dun & Bradstreet*, the information was of private concern; therefore, the protec-

tion afforded by *Gertz* was not available to the defendant. But in *Philadelphia News-papers,* the published information was of public concern; therefore, the plaintiff (a private figure) had to show falsity.

10. False. *Bose Corporation v. Consumers Union* (1984) mandates independent review whenever there's been a finding of actual malice.
11. False. The media prevail with summary judgment motions in more than half the libel suits filed against them.

ENDNOTES

1. Gertz v. Robert Welch, Inc. 418 U.S. 323, 94 S.Ct. 2997, 41 L.Ed.2d 789.
2. Ibid., 94 S.Ct. at 3025.
3. *The QUILL,* July 1974, p. 11.
4. Gertz v. Welch, Inc., 8 *Med.L.Rptr.* 1769, July 27, 1982.
5. "News Notes," *Media Law Reporter,* March 1, 1983.
6. Time, Inc. v. Mary Alice Firestone, 96 S.Ct. 958, 983.
7. Firestone v. Time, Inc., 271 So.2d 745.
8. Firestone v. Time, Inc., 279 So.2d 389.
9. Firestone v. Time, Inc., 305 So.2d 172 (1974).
10. Time, Inc. v. Firestone, 424 U.S. 448, 96 S.Ct. 958, 47 L.Ed.2d 154.
11. Ibid. 96 S.Ct. at 966–67.
12. Ibid., at 973.
13. Ibid., at 978.
14. Ibid.
15. Ibid., at 983.
16. *Editor & Publisher,* September 16, 1978, p. 11.
17. Gobin v. Globe Publishing Co., 531 P.2d 76 (Kansas Supreme Court, 1975).
18. El Meson Espanol v. NYM Corporation, 389 F.Supp. 357 (Southern District of New York, 1974).
19. George Corbett III v. Register Publishing Co., 356 A.2d 472 (Connecticut Superior Court, New Haven County, 1975).
20. Welch v. Chicago Tribune Co., 340 N.E.2d 539 (Illinois Appellate Court, 1st District, 1975).
21. Peagler and Dodge City Motors, Inc. v. Phoenix Newspapers, Inc., 547 P.2d 1074 (Arizona Court of Appeals, Div. 1, 1976).
22. Bolam v. McGraw-Hill, Inc., 382 N.Y.S.2d 772 (New York County Supreme Court, Appellate Div. 1, 1976).
23. Lawlor v. Gallagher Presidents' Reports, Inc., 394 F.Supp. 721 (Southern District of New York, 1975).
24. Thomas H. Maloney & Sons, Inc. v. E. W. Scripps Co., 334 N.E.2d 494 (Ohio Appeals Court, 1974); cert. denied, 96 S.Ct. 171 (1975).
25. Taskett v. King Broadcasting Co., 546 P.2d 81 (Washington Supreme Court, 1976).
26. Wolston v. Reader's Digest Association, Supplement to 5 *Med.L.Rptr.* 5, July 3, 1979.
27. Gertz v. Welch, Inc., 418 U.S. at 351.
28. Hutchinson v. Proxmire, 443 U.S. 111, 99 S.Ct. 2675, 5 *Med.L.Rptr.* 1279.
29. "News Notes," *Media Law Reporter,* April 8, 1980.
30. Buchanan v. Associated Press, 398 F.Supp. 1196 (District of Columbia, 1975).
31. Rosanova v. Playboy Enterprises, Inc. 411 F.Supp. 410 (1976).
32. Ibid., at 444.
33. Michael and Robert Meeropol v. Louis Nizer and Doubleday & Company, Inc., 381 F.Supp. 29 (1974).
34. As reported by Robert Trager and Harry W. Stonecipher of Southern Illinois University in "*Gertz* and *Firestone*: How Courts Have Construed the 'Public Figure' Criteria"; a paper pre-

sented at the annual convention of the Association for Education in Journalism, College Park, Md., August 1976, pp. 12–14.

35. Guitar v. Westinghouse Electric Corp., 396 F.Supp. 1042 (Southern District of New York, 1975).
36. Davis v. Schuchat, 512 F.2d 731 (District of Columbia Circuit, 1975).
37. Maheu v. Hughes Tool Co., 384 F.Supp. 166 (C.D. Calif., 1974).
38. Kipiloff v. Dunn, 343 A.2d 251 (Maryland Court of Special Appeals, 1975), cert. denied (Case No. 75-1412, 1976).
39. Cera v. Gannett Co., Inc., 365 N.Y.S.2d 99 (Appeals Court, 1975).
40. Vandenburg v. Newsweek, 57 F.2d 1024 (5th Circuit, 1975).
41. Carson v. Allied News Co., 529 F.2d 206 (7th Circuit, 1976).
42. Buckley v. Littell, 394 F. Supp. 918 (Southern District of New York, 1975).
43. Gibson v. Maloney, 263 So.2d 832 (Florida Supreme Court, 1972).
44. Martin-Marietta Corp. v. Evening Star Newspaper Co., 417 F.Supp. 947 (District of Columbia, 1976).
45. James v. Gannett Co., Inc., 366 N.Y.S.2d 737 (Appeals Court, 1975).
46. *Editor & Publisher,* July 31, 1982, p. 28.
47. "News Notes," *Media Law Reporter,* October 12, 1982.
48. Holt v. Cox Enterprises, 10 *Med.L.Rptr.* 1695 (U.S. District Court for Northern District of Georgia, 1984), May 29, 1984.
49. Della-Donna v. Gore Newspapers, 10 *Med.L.Rptr.* 1526 (Florida Circuit Court, 1983), April 24, 1984.
50. National Foundation for Cancer Research v. Council of Better Business Bureaus, 9 *Med.L.Rptr.* 1915 (4th Circuit U.S. Court of Appeals, 1983); cert. denied (No. 82-2153), *Media Law Reporter,* October 11, 1983.
51. Pierce v. Pacific & Southern, 9 *Med.L.Rptr.* 2177 (Georgia Court of Appeals, 1983), October 4, 1983.
52. "News Notes," *Media Law Reporter,* October 4, 1983 (McBride v. Merrell, No. 82–1786, U.S. Court of Appeals for District of Columbia Circuit).
53. Barry v. Time, 10 *Med.L.Rptr.* 1809 (U.S. District Court for Northern California District, 1984), June 26, 1984.
54. Jones v. Gates-Chili News, Inc., 358 N.Y.S.2d 649 (1974).
55. "News Notes," *Media Law Reporter,* March 1, 1977.
56. Jadwin v. Minneapolis Star & Tribune Co., 367 N.W. 2d 476 (1985).
57. *Editor & Publisher,* July 20, 1985, p. 18.
58. "News Notes," *Media Law Reporter,* October 25, 1988.
59. Street v. NBC, 645 F.2d 1227 (6th Circuit, 1981). Judge Peck dissented because he thought Street was a private figure and that the use of a newsworthiness test was contrary to *Gertz.*
60. "News Notes," *Media Law Reporter,* October 13, 1981. Street died on October 17, 1982.
61. If you thought that the Court would most likely classify Street as a private figure, you're in agreement with the writer of an article on the subject (Cynthia Millen), in *Notes,* 8 *Northern Kentucky Law Review* 647, 662 (1981).
62. Walker v. Colorado Springs Sun, Inc., 538 P.2d 450 (1975), cert. denied, 96 S.Ct. 469, 46 L.Ed.2d 399; Aafco Heating and Air Conditioning Co. v. Northwest Publications, Inc., 321 N.E.2d 580 (Ind. Ct. App., 1974), cert. denied, 44 *U.S. Law Week* 3467, February 24, 1976; Sisler v. Gannett Co., Inc., 516 A.2d 1083 (1986), 13 *Med.L.Rptr.* 1577.
63. Ibid.
64. Ibid.
65. Ibid.
66. Dairy Stores, Inc. v. Sentinel Publishing Co., 516 A.2d 220 (1986).
67. William Prosser, *Law of Torts,* 4th ed., Section 34 (1971).
68. Chapadeau v. Utica Observer-Dispatch, 341 N.E.2nd 569, 1 *Med.L.Rptr.* 1693. Judge Jones took no part in the decision.
69. Martin v. Griffin Television, Inc., 549 P.2d 85 (1976).
70. Gobin v. Globe Publishing Co., 531 P.2d 76, 83 (1975).
71. Troman v. Kingsley Wood, 340 N.E.2d 292 (1975).

72. Mead Corporation v. Hicks, 10 *Med.L.Rptr.* 1030 (1983); Peagler v. Phoenix Newspapers, Inc., 114 Ariz. 309, 560 P.2d 1216, 2 *Med.L.Rptr.* 1687 (1977); Dodrill v. Arkansas Democrat Co., 265 Ark. 628, 590 S.W.2d 840, 5 *Med.L.Rptr.* 1633 (1979), cert. denied, 444 U.S. 1076 (1980); Brown v. Kelly Broadcasting Co., 16 *Med.L.Rptr.* 1625 (1989); Gannett Co., Inc. v. Re, 496 A.2d 553 (1985); Phillips v. Evening Star Newspaper Co., 424 A.2d 78, 6 *Med.L.Rptr.* 2191 (U.S. Court of Appeals, District of Columbia Circuit, 1980); Firestone v. Time, Inc. 305 So.2d 172 (1974); Chumley v. Triangle Publications, Inc., 253 Ga. 179, 317 S.E.2d 534 (1984); Cahill v. Hawaiian Paradise Corp., 56 Haw. 522, 543 P.2d 1356 (1975); Troman v. Kingsley Wood, 340 N.E.2d 292 (1975); Jones v. Palmer Communications, Inc., No. 88-371 (1989); Gobin v. Globe Publishing Co., 531 P.2d 76 (1975); McCall v. Courier-Journal, 623 S.W.2d 882, 7 *Med.L.Rptr.* 2118 (1981); Jacron Sales Co. v. Sindorf, 350 A.2d 688 (1976); Stone v. Essex County Newspapers, 330 N.E.2d 161 (1975); Rouch v. Enquirer & News, 398 N.W.2d 245, 13 *Med.L.Rptr.* 2201 (1986); Jadwin v. Minneapolis Star & Tribune Co., 367 N.W.2d 476, 11 *Med.L.Rptr.* 1905 (1985); Madison v. Yunker, 180 Mont. 54, 589 P.2d 126, 4 *Med.L.Rptr.* 1337 (1978); McClusker v. Valley News, 121 N.H. 258, 428 A.2d 493, 7 *Med.L.Rptr.* 1343 (1981); Marchiondo v. Brown, 98 N.M. 394, 649 P.2d 462, 8 *Med.L.Rptr.* 2233 (1982); Embers Supper Club v. Scripps-Howard Broadcasting Co., 10 *Med.L.Rptr.* 1729 (1984), cert. denied, "News Notes," *Media Law Reporter,* June 12, 1984, and Lansdowne v. Beacon Journal Publishing Co., 512 N.E.2d 979, 14 *Med.L.Rptr.* 1801 (1987); Martin v. Griffin Television, Inc. 549 P.2d 85 (1976); Bank of Oregon v. Independent News, Inc., 693 P.2d 35, 11 *Med.L.Rptr.* 1313 (1985); Jones v. Sun Publishing Co., 292 S.E.2d 23 (1982); Memphis Publishing Co. v. Nichols, 529 S.W.2d 412, 4 *Med.L.Rptr.* 1573 (1978); Foster v. Laredo Newspapers, Inc., 541 S.W.2d 809 (1976), cert. denied, 429 U.S. 1123 (1977); Seegmiller v. KSL, 626 P.2d 968, 7 *Med.L.Rptr.* 1012 (1981); Gazette v. Harris, 325 S.E.2d 713, 11 *Med.L.Rptr.* 1609 (1985); Taskett v. King Broadcasting Co., 86 Wash.2d 439, 546 P.2d 81, 1 *Med.L.Rptr.* 1716 (1976); Havalunch, Inc. v. Mazza, 294 S.E.2d 70 (1981); and Denny v. Mertz, 318 N.W.2d 141, 8 *Med.L.Rptr.* 1369 (1982).
73. Torres Silva v. El Mundo, Inc., 106 D.P.R. 415, 3 *Med.L.Rptr.* 1508 (1977).
74. Moyer v. Phillips, 44 *U.S. Law Week* 2046 (1975); and DeCarvalho v. DaSilva, 414 A.2d 806 (1980).
75. Sisemore v. U.S. News & World Report, Inc., 662 F.Supp. 1529, 14 *Med.L.Rptr.* 1590 (U.S. District Court construing Alaska Law (1987)); Corbett v. Register Publishing Co., 356 A.2d 472 (Connecticut Superior Court, New Haven County (1975)); Wilson Jr. v. Capital City Press, 315 So.2d 293 (Louisiana Appeals Court, 3d District (1975)); Brewer v. Memphis Publishing Co., Inc., 626 F.2d 1238, 6 *Med.L.Rptr.* 2025 (U.S. Court of Appeals, 5th Circuit, construing Mississippi law (1980)); Hyde v. City of Columbia, 637 S.W.2d 251 (Missouri Court of Appeals (1982)); Walters v. Sanford Herald, 228 S.E.2d 766, 2 *Med.L.Rptr.* 1959 (North Carolina Court of Appeals (1976)); Rutt v. Bethlehems' Globe Publishing Co., 484 A.2d 72 (Pennsylvania Superior Court (1984)); and Ali v. Daily News Publishing Co., 540 F.Supp. 144, 8 *Med.L.Rptr.* 1844 (U.S. District Court (1982)).
76. See, e.g., Gay v. Williams 5 *Med.L.Rptr.* 1785 (U.S. District Court interpreting Alaska law (1979)), and Le Boeuf v. Times Picayune Publishing Corp., 320 So.2d 430 (4th Circuit Court of Appeals (1976)).
77. Rouch v. Enquirer & News, 398 N.W.2d 245, 13 *Med.L.Rptr.* 2201, 2202, April 21, 1987.
78. *Editor & Publisher,* January 24, 1987, p. 43.
79. *Editor & Publisher,* December 31, 1988, p. 24.
80. Brown v. Kelly Broadcasting Co., 16 *Med.L.Rptr.* 1625, June 6, 1989.
81. Ibid., at 1629.
82. Op. cit., n. 72.
83. Wheeler v. Green, 286 Ore. 99, 593 P.2d 777 (1979).
84. Stone v. Essex County Newspapers, Inc., 330 N.E.2d 161, 169 (1975).
85. *The NEWS Media & The LAW,* Spring 1985, p. 11.
86. Martin v. Griffin Television, Inc., op. cit., note 69.
87. Ibid., at 92.
88. Cahill v. Hawaiian Paradise Park, op. cit., note 72.
89. Aku v. Lewis, op. cit., note 72.

90. Cahill v. Hawaiian Paradise Park, op. cit., note 72, at 1366, in which Justice Kidwell said that the "difference between the provisions of the Indiana and Colorado constitutional provisions as to free speech and press, as compared with the First Amendment, might somewhat explain the preference of these courts for the *Rosenbloom* rule."
91. Foster v. Laredo Newspapers, Inc., op. cit., note 72. Justice Pope dissented, arguing that Foster either was a public official or a public figure at the time the article was written. On rehearing, Justice Reavley, joined by Chief Justice Greenhill, contended that Foster was a public official and *Times-Sullivan* should apply.
92. Ibid., at 819.
93. Johnson v. Board of Junior College District No. 508, 334 N.E.2d 442 (Illinois Appeals Court, 1975).
94. In a study by Robert E. Drechsel and Deborah Moon, "Libel and Business Executives: The Public Figure Problem," *Journalism Quarterly,* Winter 1983, pp. 709, 18 relevant cases were checked and in only eight of them were the business owners or executives found to be public figures.
95. This analysis was provided by Judge Jones in his opinion for a three-judge panel in Bichler v. Union Bank, 9 *Med.L.Rptr.* 2033, 2037 (6th Circuit U.S. Court of Appeals, 1983), September 13, 1983. Judge Wellford dissented.
96. Dun & Bradstreet v. Greenmoss Builders, Inc. (1985), 472 U.S. 749, 11 *Med.L.Rptr.* 2417, 53 *U.S. Law Week* 4866.
97. *Advertising Age,* August 12, 1985, p. 22.
98. Ibid.
99. In making this statement, Powell cited Connick v. Myers, 461 U.S. 138, 147–48 (1983).
100. Philadelphia Newspapers, Inc. v. Hepps, 106 S.Ct. 1558, 12 *Med.L.Rptr.* 1977, May 6, 1986.
101. William Prosser, *Handbook on the Law of Torts,* 2d ed. (1955), p. 119.
102. Ibid., at 124.
103. Time, Inc. v. Hill, 385 U.S. 374, 87 S.Ct. 534, 17 L.Ed.2d 456 (1967).
104. See, for example, dissenting opinion of Associate Justice Horowitz of Washington Supreme Court in Taskett v. King Broadcasting Co., 546 P.2d 81, 104, and dissenting opinion of Justice Brennan in *Gertz,* 418 U.S. at 365, 94 S.Ct. at 3019.
105. Hutchinson v. Proxmire, op. cit., note 28, 5 *Med.L.Rptr.* 1279, 1284; 443 U.S. 111, 120.
106. Welch v. Chicago Tribune Co., op. cit., note 20.
107. Corbett v. Register Publishing Co., op. cit., note 19.
108. "News Notes," *Media Law Reporter,* June 10, 1980.
109. "News Notes," *Media Law Reporter,* January 5, 1988.
110. Alioto v. Cowles Communications, Inc., 519 F.2d 777 (9th Circuit, 1975); cert. denied, 96 S.Ct. 280 (1975).
111. *Time,* May 16, 1978, p. 86.
112. "News Notes," *Media Law Reporter,* January 20, 1981.
113. Cervantes v. Time, Inc., 330 F. Supp. 936, 940 (Eastern District of Missouri, 1970).
114. Cervantes v. Time, Inc., 464 F.2d 986, 995 (8th Circuit, 1972); cert. denied, January 19, 1973.
115. Wilson v. Capital City Press, 315 So.2d 393 (1975).
116. Le Boeuf v. Times Picayune Publishing Corp., 327 So.2d 430 (1976).
117. New York Times v. Sullivan, 376 U.S. at 270.
118. Ibid., at 292, n. 30 (citations omitted).
119. Gertz v. Welch, Inc., 418 U.S. at 339.
120. Ibid., at 340, n. 8.
121. Old Dominion Branch No. 496, National Association of Letter Carriers, AFL-CIO v. Austin, 418 U.S. 264, 94 S.Ct. 2770, 42 *U.S. Law Week* 5105.
122. See, e.g., Notes, "Fact and Opinion After *Gertz v. Robert Welch, Inc.*: The Evolution of a Privilege," 34 *Rutgers Law Review* 81, 98 (1981).
123. Ollman v. Evans et al., 9 *Med.L.Rptr.* 1969, August 23, 1983.
124. Ibid., at 1972. Ultimately the full bench of the District of Columbia U.S. Court of Appeals affirmed a summary judgment grant to the defendants by the trial court and the U.S. Supreme Court denied review (471 U.S. 1129 (1985)).
125. Jerry Chaney, " 'Opinion' dicta now law of libel?", *Media Law Notes,* published by the Law

Division of the Association for Education in Journalism and Mass Communication, Vol. 10, No. 2, February 1983, p.5.

126. Lewis v. Time, 9 *Med.L.Rptr.* 1984, August 23, 1983.
127. Information Control Corp. v. Genesis One Computer Corp., 611 F.2d 781, 783 (1980).
128. Lewis v. Time, op. cit., note 126, at 1987.
129. Ibid., at 1975 (footnotes omitted).
130. Cianci v. New Times Publishing Co., 639 F.2d 54, 60.
131. Mashburn v. Collins, 355 So.2d 879, 2 *Med.L.Rptr.* 1555 (1977). See, also, Golden v. Elmira Star Gazette, 9 *Med.L.Rptr.* 1183 (New York Supreme Court, Ontario County), March 8, 1983; Marchiondo v. New Mexico State Tribune (Marchiondo I), 648 P.2d 321, 8 *Med.L.Rptr.* 1915 (New Mexico Court of Appeals, 1981), cert. quashed, June 29, 1982, and Cole v. Westinghouse Broadcasting, 8 *Med.L.Rptr.* 1828 (Massachusetts Supreme Judicial Court, 1982).
132. Ibid., Mashburn v. Collins, at 1680–81.
133. Havalunch, Inc. v. Mazza, 294 S.E.2d 70.
134. Pritsker v. Brudnoy, 9 *Med.L.Rptr.* 2028, August 30, 1983.
135. Benjamin v. Cowles Publishing, 10 *Med.L.Rptr.* 1970, July 24, 1984.
136. Buckley v. Littell, 394 F.Supp. 918 (Southern District of New York, 1975).
137. Littell v. Buckley, 539 F.2d 882 (1976).
138. Good Government Group of Seal Beach v. Hogard, 441 U.S. 906 (1979).
139. 55 *U.S. Law Week* 3639, March 24, 1987.
140. *The NEWS Media & The LAW,* Fall 1986, p. 13.
141. Baker v. Los Angeles Herald Examiner, 42 Cal.3d 254, 228 Cal.Rptr. 206 (1986), 721 P.2d 87, 55 *U.S. Law Week* 2203, 13 *Med.L.Rptr.* 1159.
142. *The NEWS Media & The LAW,* Winter 1987, p. 24.
143. 55 *U.S. Law Week* 3468, January 13, 1987.
144. Capan v. Daugherty, 13 *Med.L.Rptr.* 2195, April 14, 1987.
145. Janklow v. Newsweek, Inc., 788 F.2d 1300.
146. Op. cit., n. 144, at 2197.
147. McCabe v. Rattine, 13 *Med.L.Rptr.* 2309, May 5, 1987.
148. Healey v. New England Newspapers, Inc., 55 *U.S. Law Week* 2552, April 14, 1987; 13 *Med.L.Rptr.* 2148.
149. "News Notes," *Media Law Reporter,* February 17, 1987.
150. *The NEWS Media & The LAW,* Fall 1986, p. 12.
151. Op. cit., n. 149.
152. Ibid.
153. "News Notes," *Media Law Reporter,* August 25, 1987.
154. "News Notes," *Media Law Reporter,* April 12, 1988.
155. Hay v. Independent Newspapers, 10 *Med.L.Rptr.* 1928 (Florida District Court of Appeal), July 17, 1984.
156. Ibid., at 1929.
157. Ibid., 1930.
158. Cianci v. New Times Publishing Co., 639 F.2d 54, 63.
159. Rinaldi v. Holt, Rinehart & Winston, 42 N.Y.2d 369, 382, cert. denied, 434 U.S. 969 (1977).
160. *Editor & Publisher,* May 15, 1982, p. 15.
161. Early v. Palm Beach Newspapers, 334 So.2d 50 (Florida District Court of Appeal, 1976).
162. Early v. Palm Beach Newspapers, 354 So.2d 351, 3 *Med.L.Rptr.* 2183.
163. 439 U.S. 910 (1978).
164. Pierce v. Capital Cities Communication, Inc., 439 U.S. 861 (1978).
165. 576 F.2d 495 (3d Circuit, 1978).
166. U.S. Labor Party v. Whitman, 47 *U.S. Law Week* 3786.
167. Celebrezze v. Dayton Newspapers Inc., *The NEWS Media & The LAW,* Fall 1988, pp. 38–39.
168. Ibid.
169. "News Notes," *Media Law Reporter,* June 6, 1977.
170. Jack R. Hart, "The Right of Neutral Reportage: Its Origins and Outlook," *Journalism Quarterly,* Summer 1979, p. 229.
171. Ibid.

172. Ibid., p. 227.
173. Hogan v. Herald Co., 446 N.Y.S. 836, 842.
174. 58 N.Y.2d 630, 458 N.Y.S.2d (1982).
175. Cianci v. New Times Publishing Co., 639 F.2d 54, 69 (1980).
176. Dickey v. CBS, "News Notes," *Media Law Reporter,* September 26, 1968.
177. "News Notes," *Media Law Reporter,* July 21, 1981.
178. Dixson v. Newsweek, "News Notes," *Media Law Reporter,* October 4, 1977.
179. Krauss v. Champaign News Gazette, 3 *Med.L.Rptr.* 2507, July 4, 1978.
180. Whitaker v. Denver Post, 4 *Med.L.Rptr.* 1351 (District Court of Wyoming, 1978).
181. Weaver v. Oregonian Publishing Co., 15 *Med.L.Rptr.* 1861, September 27, 1988.
182. Godbehere v. Phoenix Newspaper, 15 *Med.L.Rptr.* 2051, November 1, 1988.
183. El Amin v. Miami Herald, 9 *Med.L.Rptr.* 1079 (Florida 11th Circuit, 1983); Bair v. Palm Beach Newspapers, Inc., 8 *Med.L.Rptr.* 2028 (Florida 15th Circuit, 1983); Smith v. Taylor County Publishing, 8 *Med.L.Rptr.* 1294 (Florida 2d Circuit, 1982); and Wade v. Stocks, 7 *Med.L.Rptr.* 2200 (Florida 3d Circuit, 1981). Also, April v. Reflector-Herald, Inc., 15 *Med.L.Rptr.* 2455 (Ohio Court of Appeals, 1988); Weingarten v. Block, 163 Cal. Rptr. 701 (California Court of Appeal, 1980); Nader v. Toledano, 408 A.2d 31 (District of Columbia Circuit, 1979); and McCracken v. Gainesville Tribune, 246 S.E.2d 360 (Georgia Appeals Court, 1978).
184. WKRG-TV v. Wiley (1986), 13 *Med.L.Rptr.* 1680; Janklow v. Viking Press (1985), 12 *Med.L.Rptr.* 1539; and Courier-Journal v. McCall, 7 *Med.L.Rptr.* 2118, cert. denied, *Media Law Reporter,* May 25, 1982.
185. Bose Corporation v. Consumers Union, 466 U.S 485 (1984), 10 *Med.L.Rptr.* 1625, May 22, 1984.
186. *Editor & Publisher,* May 5, 1984, p. 44.
187. *Editor & Publisher,* September 4, 1982, pp. 16–17.
188. "News Notes," *Media Law Reporter,* October 16, 1984; Pring v. Penthouse International, 8 *Med.L.Rptr.* 2409.
189. 692 F.2d 189, 8 *Med.L.Rptr.* 1069 (1982).
190. Op. cit., n. 185, at 1640–41, n. 2.
191. Hearst Corp. v. McCoy, 52 Cal.3d 835, 231 Cal. Rptr. 518, 727 P.2d 711, 13 *Med.L.Rptr.* 2169.
192. 55 *U.S. Law Week* 3743, May 5, 1987.
193. *Editor & Publisher,* November 2, 1974, p. 11.
194. *Editor & Publisher,* May 14, 1983, p. 11.
195. *Freedom of Information '86–'87,* Society of Professional Journalists, Sigma Delta Chi, p. 6.
196. *Editor & Publisher,* September 20, 1986, p. 14.
197. *Editor & Publisher,* May 22, 1982, p. 26.
198. *Editor & Publisher,* May 29, 1982, p. 28.
199. 15 *Med.L.Rptr.* 1861, September 27, 1988.

7

Privacy

HIGHLIGHTS

■ A law review article in 1890 became the springboard for the emergence of a right of privacy in the United States with the first manifestation being the New York Civil Rights Law passed in 1903.

■ The late William Prosser analyzed the right of privacy and concluded that it involved four torts—intrusion, public disclosure of embarassing private facts, publicity that puts a person in a false light, and appropriation or misappropriation of a person's name or likeness for defendant's advantage.

■ In *Griswold v. Connecticut* (1965), the Supreme Court recognized a constitutional right of privacy for the first time.

■ *Dietemann v. Time, Inc.* (1971) makes it clear that publication is not essential to the intrusion tort.

■ In *Falwell v. Hustler Magazine* (1988), the Supreme Court ruled that public officials and public figures must prove actual malice to succeed with an emotional distress tort if what was published was of public concern.

■ Media disclosure of a rape victim's name, once that name is divulged at a public trial, cannot be punished, the Court ruled in *Cox Broadcasting Corp. v. Cohn* (1975).

■ In *Time, Inc. v. Hill* (1967), Justice Brennan, in a plurality opinion, applied the *Times-Sullivan* "actual malice" rule to a false light invasion of privacy action involving a matter of public interest. Actual malice can overcome the First Amendment qualified privilege in a public figure's false light action, as shown by *Cantrell v. Forest City Publishing Co.* (1974).

Privacy is an expanding legal concept that poses new dangers to mass communicators. With libel suits more difficult to win against the news media, principally because of *Times-Sullivan* and the extension of the actual malice rule to public figures, a seemingly attractive alternative has become invasion of privacy suits. In fact, plaintiffs often bring defamation and invasion of privacy actions simultaneously because defenses which work against the one may be of little or no use against the other.

That the public is greatly concerned about privacy is apparent in a number of ways. The results of a Louis Harris & Associates survey, released in 1979, showed that the American public wants more privacy protection. Three of every four persons who were polled urged a state constitutional guarantee of privacy, and voters in Alaska and California have done just that—adding the right of privacy to other rights listed in those state constitutions.[1] All states have enacted legislation to prevent prying into certain types of records or the release of certain kinds of information. Literature is accumulating on the increasing invasion of privacy as the result of technological developments, including the sharing of stored computer data obtained in various ways and the unauthorized penetration into such stored data. Many of these developments will be reviewed in this and the next chapter, but first, let's examine the emergence of "personality" rights, or protection for one's feelings, as contrasted with the protection of one's reputation from defamatory utterances.

HISTORY OF THE RIGHT OF PRIVACY

That the legal right of privacy is of rather recent origin is reflected in the following comment from Edward L. Godkin, editor of the *New York Evening Post,* who wrote in 1890:

> Privacy is a distinctly modern product, one of the luxuries of civilization, which is not only unsought for but unknown in primitive or barbarous societies. . . . The earliest houses of our Anglo-Saxon ancestors in England . . . consisted of only one large room in which both master and mistress, and retainers, cooked, ate, and slept. The first sign of material progress was the addition of sleepingrooms and afterward of "withdrawingrooms" into which it was possible for the heads of the household to escape from the noise and publicity of the outer hall. One of the greatest attractions of the dwellings of the rich is the provision they make for the segregation of the occupants. . . .[2]

The first case in which relief was granted because of an invasion of privacy is believed to have occurred in Michigan in 1881.[3] And the U.S. Supreme Court, in an 1886 decision, said that the Fourth and Fifth Amendments provide protection against all government invasions of the "sanctity of a man's home and the privacies of life."[4] Two years later Judge Thomas Cooley asserted in a treatise that people have a right "to be let alone."[5] This statement subsequently was subscribed to by various legal experts, including Justice Douglas who wrote in a 1952

Supreme Court decision that the "right to be let alone is indeed the beginning of all freedom."

The principal influence in the emergence of such a right under common law in the United States came in 1890 with publication of what has been termed by Justice Marshall as the most influential law review article yet written. The authors were Samuel D. Warren, an eminent lawyer who became a Boston businessman, and Louis D. Brandeis, a Harvard University law teacher who later distinguished himself as a Supreme Court justice. Both were concerned about the public press prying into the lives of citizens when they wrote the article which included this brief history of individual rights:

> That the individual shall have full protection in person and in property is a principle as old as the common law; but it has been found necessary from time to time to define anew the exact nature and extent of such protection. Political, social, and economic changes entail the recognition of new rights, and the common law, in its eternal youth, grows to meet the demands of society. Thus, in very early times, the law gave a remedy only for physical interference with life and property, for trespasses *vi et armis*. Then the "right to life" served only to protect the subject from battery in various forms; liberty meant freedom from actual restraint; and the right to property secured to the individual his lands and his cattle. Later, there came a recognition of man's spiritual nature, of his feelings and his intellect. Gradually the scope of these legal rights broadened; and now the right to life has come to mean the rights to enjoy life—the right to be left alone; the right to liberty secures the exercise of extensive civil privileges; and the term "property" has grown to comprise every form of possession—intangible, as well as tangible.[6]

Concerning the yellow journalism of their day, the authors said that the press was overstepping the obvious bounds of propriety and decency by publication of gossip and the details of sexual relations—information that could only be procured by "intrusion upon the domestic circle." Yet the complexities of life, they said, have made necessary some retreat from the world. Because of such a need and the refining influences of culture, which make an individual more sensitive to publicity, solitude and privacy have become essential.

The authors then examined the "superficial resemblance" between invasion of privacy and defamation, but concluded that the latter was more material than spiritual. To distinguish the intangible "personality" right of privacy from more tangible rights, they referred to one's personal writings, saying:

> The principle which protects personal writing and all other personal productions, not against theft and physical appropriation, but against publication in any form, is in reality not the principle of private property, but that of an inviolate personality.
>
> If we are correct in this conclusion, the existing law affords a principle which may be invoked to protect the privacy of the individual from invasion either by the too enterprising press, the photographer, or the possessor of any other modern device for recording scenes or sounds. For the protection afforded is not confined by the authorities to those cases where any particular medium or form of expression has been adopted, nor to the products of the intellect. The same protection is afforded to

emotions and sensations expressed in a musical composition or other work of art. . . . The circumstances that a thought or emotion has been recorded in a permanent form renders its identification easier, and hence may be important from the point of view of evidence, but it has no significance as a matter of substantive right. If, then, the decisions indicate a general right to privacy for thoughts, emotions, and sensations, these should receive the same protection, whether expressed in writing, or in conduct, in conversation, in attitudes, or in facial expression.[7]

Brandeis and Warren then asked what limitations should be placed on such a right, and concluded:

1. Such a right would not prohibit publication of a matter of "public or general interest." This is the key phrase in determining if a conditional constitutional privilege extends to defamatory reports by the public news media about public figures and public officials and, as will be shown later, to at least two of four different types of invasion of privacy actions.

    The authors readily admitted that there would be difficulties in applying a public interest test, but said that such difficulties would be no greater than those which existed in other branches of the law. Such a statement seems contemporary because Justice Brennan, in his 1971 plurality opinion in *Rosenbloom,* discussed earlier, announced that the determinant of the conditional constitutional privilege was whether the issue was of "public or general concern," leaving the delineation of the "reach of that term to future cases."[8]

2. Such a right would not extend to those who, in varying degrees, "have renounced the right to live their lives screened from public observation."

3. Such a right would not prohibit the communication of any matter, though private in nature, which is privileged in terms of the law of libel and slander.

4. Such a right would cease upon publication of the facts by the individual, or with his consent.

    However, such a right would *not* be diminished because of the truth of the matter published, since "it is not for injury to the individual's character that redress or prevention is sought, but for injury to the right of privacy." The authors pointed out that the libel law provided sufficient safeguards against injury to reputation. The right of privacy, they wrote, "implies the right not merely to prevent inaccurate portrayal of private life, but to prevent its being depicted at all." As will be shown later, this refers to the "public disclosure" tort.

Following publication of the article, there was no immediate rush to enact privacy statutes or to promote such a right through common law. A conjoining of events helped to spur enactment of laws or the development of case law.

NEW YORK CIVIL RIGHTS LAW

In the 1902 case of *Roberson v. Rochester Folding Box Co.,*[9] the New York Court of Appeals refused in a 4–3 decision to halt the use of a girl's portrait to advertise a brand of flour even though the girl and her parents had not consented. The court held that the law was a practical business system, dealing with what was tangible, and that it did not "undertake to redress psychological injuries." Also, the court ruled that no common-law right of privacy existed.

This decision led to considerable criticism and was instrumental in passage in 1903 of the first binding statutory recognition of the right of privacy in the United States — the New York Civil Rights Law, Section 50, which reads:

> A person, firm or corporation that uses for advertising purposes, or for the purposes of trade, the name, portrait or picture of any living person without having first obtained the written consent of such a person, or if a minor of his or her parent or guardian, is guilty of a misdemeanor.

Section 51 permits an action for injunction and damages.

The New York Civil Rights Law does not mention *privacy* by name. In fact, it falls under what is called the "appropriation" tort — the use of someone's name or likeness for commercial purposes without consent. This tort, aimed at preventing misappropriation of name or likeness, is discussed later in the chapter.

FOUR TORTS, NOT ONE

Because of disagreement whether a right of privacy exists, or confusion as to what the right is, or the rights are, clarifications have been attempted. One of the better known efforts came in an article by the late William Prosser, dean of the University of California Law School at Berkeley, in which he described the right of privacy as four distinct torts, not one. He wrote:

> Today [1960], with something over 300 privacy cases in the books, the holes in the jigsaw puzzle have largely filled in, and some rather definite conclusions are possible.
>
> What has emerged from the decisions is no simple matter. It is not one tort, but a complex of four. The law of privacy comprises four distinct kinds of invasion of four different interests of the plaintiff, which are tied together by the common name, but otherwise have almost nothing in common except that each represents an interference with the right of the plaintiff, in the phrase coined by Judge Cooley, "to be let alone." Without any attempt at exact definition, these four torts may be described as follows:
>
> 1. Intrusion upon the plaintiff's seclusion or solitude, or into his private affairs.
> 2. Public disclosure of embarrassing private facts about the plaintiff.
> 3. Publicity which places the plaintiff in a false light in the public eye.
> 4. Appropriation, for the defendant's advantage, of the plaintiff's name or likeness.[10]

Of the four Prosser torts, three rest on venerable tort doctrine. "Intrusion" expands on the law of trespass; "false light" occupies the same relative position as libel, and "appropriation" follows the reasoning of personal property law, according to the writer of an article in the *Yale Law Journal* who further observed:

> In each category the central injury has long been recognized in law and calling it an injury to "privacy" is a semantic, not a legal, innovation. The public disclosure tort, on the other hand, presents a true conceptual novelty: the idea that mere publication of accurate data about a person might cause him legal injury [a suggestion virtually unheard of prior to the Warren-Brandeis article in 1890].
>
> The false light action protects against injuries to reputation only; and, as with the libel, truth is a defense. It therefore gives the individual no right to control accurate information about himself. Any relationship of the tort action to a concept of privacy is tenuous.
>
> The action for appropriation of name or likeness [as allowed by the New York Civil Rights Law] protects against the publication of true information about the individual, but it concerns only that information on which the individual might have capitalized himself. The injury is a commercial one; the action protects less a right to privacy than a right to publicity. . . . [T]hose who have been utterly unknown before the publication . . . stand to recover least.
>
> The intrusion tort comes closer than false light or appropriation to offering a satisfactory definition of privacy. It protects the individual's right to control access to his immediate surroundings and thus defines privacy as control of physical space. Physical space is an important and well-recognized element of privacy, . . . for example, we most commonly refer to any infringement of privacy as an "invasion. . . ."
>
> The public disclosure tort, by finding legal injury in the mere act of publishing accurate data about a person, protects something which is farther from traditional tort theory, and perhaps closer to a satisfactory concept of privacy. The actual content of a person's privacy is a subjective matter over which people inevitably disagree, but even as they disagree they can share a common concept of how privacy works and what purpose it serves. Scholars who have sought a conceptual definition of privacy have not been unanimous, but a common theme appears in many of their efforts: that privacy reflects a psychological need of the individual to keep some core of personality to himself, outside the notice of society. . . . The public disclosure tort action — which punishes the unjustified exposure through mass publication of the data of an individual's life — contains the only direct recognition which the law has given to that non-libel, non-territorial, non-commercial claim.[11]

Prosser, who did not attempt an exact definition of the public disclosure tort, described it generally as requiring that "something secret, secluded or private pertaining to the plaintiff" be invaded and that the something be publicized, although not requiring that the publication be false, or be for the commercial advantage of the defendant."[12]

Recognition of Privacy Rights

Before examining each of the Prosser torts, a further examination of the emergence of the right of privacy, either by case law or statute, is necessary. As these developments unfold, it is interesting to note that Great Britain does not recognize an invasion of privacy tort. In recommending against a move in that direction, a Parliament-created committee on privacy reported in 1972 that it would be extremely difficult to delineate a right of privacy, and even if this were done the threat to free speech/free press would be too great.[13]

Following New York's enactment of the appropriation tort statutes, the Georgia Supreme Court became the first state court to recognize a common law right of privacy, specifically the appropriation tort. It did so in *Pavesich v. New England Life Insurance Co.* (1905).[14]

Recognition of privacy rights developed slowly at first, and primarily through case law. Only a few states do it through statute. California has a statute similar to New York's but specifies that $300 is the minimum amount recoverable through an appropriations tort. Florida, Georgia, Massachusetts, Nebraska, Oklahoma, Rhode Island, Tennessee, Utah, Virginia, West Virginia, and Wisconsin have statutes, but the Right of Privacy Act in Wisconsin recognizes only three of the Prosser torts (the false-light tort being excluded).[15]

According to a report compiled by the Reporters Committee for Freedom of the Press, published in 1988,[16] the following states and the District of Columbia (either directly through a media case holding or indirectly, as in a nonmedia case, or by statute) recognize all four Prosser torts: Alabama, Arkansas, California, Connecticut, Delaware, Florida, Georgia, Idaho, Illinois, Indiana, Iowa, Kentucky, Louisiana, Maine, Maryland, Michigan, Nevada, New Jersey, New Mexico, New York, Oklahoma, Oregon, Pennsylvania, Rhode Island (the only state to recognize all four torts by statute), South Dakota, Tennessee, Texas, Vermont, and West Virginia.

Six states have recognized all but the false light tort and there are no reported cases to indicate if this tort would be recognized: Arizona, Massachusetts, Mississippi, Missouri, South Carolina, and Wisconsin.

The following states do not recognize the false light tort (and other torts shown in parentheses): Nebraska (public disclosure), New Hampshire (appropriation), North Carolina (public disclosure), Ohio, Utah, and Virginia (public disclosure).

Because there were no reported cases, it is unknown if these states would recognize the following torts: Alaska, public disclosure and false light; Colorado, appropriation; Hawaii, intrusion (although there is a law making the installation or use of hidden cameras illegal), public disclosure, and false light; Minnesota, intrusion, public disclosure, and false light; Montana, public disclosure, and false light; North Dakota, all four torts; Washington, public disclosure; and Wyoming, intrusion and appropriation.

Some states recognize a right of privacy in specified situations. For example, Florida, Georgia, South Carolina, and Wisconsin prohibit by statute the identification of rape victims. But in 1975, the U.S. Supreme Court in *Cox Broadcasting Corp. v. Cohn,* discussed later, ruled that a state—Georgia, in this instance—could not impose sanctions on the accurate publication of information obtained from judicial records that were open to the public, including the names of rape victims. Many states and the federal government protect the identity of juvenile delinquents by closing trials to the public and sealing court records.

Utah is the only state that statutorily gives corporations a right to privacy, but the common law has a long tradition of protecting sensitive commercial information, including, but not limited to, trade secrets.[17] The U.S. Court of Appeals for the District of Columbia Circuit, in deciding in 1984 whether to order the release of confidential commercial information submitted by Mobil Oil Corporation during pretrial discovery, used a balancing test in holding that Mobil has a constitutionally protected privacy interest that outweighed other interests.[18] The three-judge panel made its ruling in a dispute that arose out of a libel action by William Tavoulareas, president of Mobil, and his son, against the *Washington Post*. The *Washington Post* wanted to publish information it had obtained through discovery and the corporation objected to disclosure of some 3800 pages of deposition it had designated as confidential. The panel cited *First National Bank of Boston v. Belotti,* discussed earlier, in which the Supreme Court ruled that corporations have constitutional rights. The specific one in that case was the corporation's right to free speech.

Texas was among those states which gave neither statutory nor common-law recognition to the right of privacy until 1973 when the state supreme court held that "an unwarranted invasion of the right of privacy constitutes a legal injury for which a remedy will be granted."[19] The state's highest court said two lower courts erred in finding that since no right of privacy existed at common law and none had been added by state statute, there could be no recovery. In ordering judgment of $25,000 damages, including $15,000 exemplary damages, in this nonnews media case involving wiretapping, the Texas Supreme Court said:

> The right of privacy has been defined as the right of an individual to be left alone, to live a life of seclusion, to be free from unwarranted publicity. 77 C.J.S. Right of Privacy 8, § 1. A judicially approved definition of the right of privacy is that it is the right to be free from the unwarranted appropriation or exploitation of one's personality, the publicizing of one's private affairs, with which the public has no legitimate concern, or the wrongful intrusion into one's private activities in such manner as to outrage or cause mental suffering, shame or humiliation to a person of ordinary sensibilities. 62 Am.Jur.2d, Privacy, § 1, p. 677, and cases cited.
>
> . . . The right of privacy is generally recognized and a preponderance of authority supports the conclusion that, independently of the common law rights of property contract, reputation and physical integrity, the right exists and an invasion of the right gives rise to a cause of action. . . .
>
> Arguments in support of the right of privacy are summarized in 62 Am.Jur.2d, Privacy, § 4, p. 683, "One of the principal arguments advanced in support of the doctrine of privacy by its original exponents is that the increased complexity and intensity of modern civilization and the development of man's spiritual sensibilities have rendered man more sensitive to publicity and have increased his need of privacy, while the great technological improvements in the means of communication have more and more subjected the intimacies of his private life to exploitation by those who pander to commercialism and to prurient and idle curiosity. A legally enforceable right of privacy is deemed to be a proper protection against this type of encroachment upon the personality of the individual."

Restatement of Torts, § 867, recognized the existence of the right of privacy: "A person who unreasonably and seriously interferes with another's interest in not having his affairs known to others or his likeness exhibited to the public is liable to the other."[20]

Citing such authorities, the Texas Supreme Court reached the conclusion that an unwarranted intrusion of the right of privacy constituted a legal injury for which a remedy could be granted.

THE CONSTITUTION AND PRIVACY

In 1928 Justice Brandeis, coauthor of that famous article on privacy, discussed in a dissenting opinion the constitutional aspects of the tort, saying:

> The makers of our Constitution undertook to secure conditions favorable to the pursuit of happiness. They recognized the significance of man's spiritual nature, of his feelings and of his intellect. They knew that only a part of the pain, pleasure and satisfactions of life are to be found in material things. They sought to protect Americans in their beliefs, their thoughts, their emotions and their sensations. They conferred, as against the government, the right to be let alone—the most comprehensive of rights and the right most valued by civilized man.
>
> To protect that right, every unjustifiable intrusion by government upon the privacy of the individual, whatever the means employed, must be deemed a violation of the Fourth Amendment. . . .[21]

But a majority of the Court did not agree that a right of privacy was constitutionally recognizable. Not then. In 1965, however, Justice Douglas argued that a right to privacy is one of the penumbras stemming from the specific guarantees contained in Bill of Rights amendments. On the constitutional issue of privacy, he wrote, in *Griswold v. Connecticut:*

> The foregoing cases suggest that specific guarantees in the Bill of Rights have penumbras, formed by emanations from those guarantees that help give them life and substance. . . . Various guarantees create zones of privacy. The right of association contained in the penumbra of the First Amendment is one. . . . The Third Amendment in its prohibition against the quartering of soldiers . . . is another facet of that privacy. The Fourth Amendment explicit affirms the "right of the people to be secure in their persons, houses, papers and effects against unreasonable searches and seizures." The Fifth Amendment in its self-incrimination clause enables the citizen to create a zone of privacy which government may not force him to surrender to his detriment. The Ninth Amendment provides: "The enumeration in the Constitution, of certain rights, shall not be construed to deny or disparage others retained by the people."
>
> We have had many controversies over these penumbral rights of "privacy and repose." See, e.g., Breard v. City of Alexandria, . . . Public Utilities Comm. v. Pollak, . . . Monroe v. Pape, . . . Lanza v. State of New York. . . . These cases bear witness that the right of privacy which presses for recognition here is a legitimate one.[22]

To which Justice Stewart, with Black joining him in dissent, commented that in the course of its opinion, the Court referred to no less than six amendments to the Constitution without saying which of the amendments, if any, were infringed by a Connecticut law. Therefore, what provision of the Constitution made the state law invalid? Stewart quoted the Court as saying the right of privacy is "created by several fundamental constitutional guarantees"; but he responded by pointing out that he could find no such general right of privacy in the Bill of Rights, in any other part of the Constitution, or in any case ever before decided by the U.S. Supreme Court.

There no longer is any question that the Supreme Court finds a right to privacy rooted in the Constitution despite the views of Stewart and Black. In *Roe v. Wade* (1973), the Court held that the right to privacy is grounded in the concept of personal liberty guaranteed by the Constitution and encompasses a woman's right to decide whether to terminate her pregnancy.[23] An emotional debate continued for the next 10 years over the abortion issue. Then on June 15, 1983, the Court reaffirmed *Roe* in striking down as unconstitutional an Akron, Ohio, ordinance that had imposed a series of restrictions on having abortions. In giving the Court's opinion, Justice Powell said that the right to choose abortion over childbirth is a fundamental one springing from a woman's constitutional right to privacy.[24] But the issue has not died. The Court agreed in 1989 to review another case involving abortion, and with additional court members appointed by Reagan—an abortion foe—the outcome was in doubt.

In other Supreme Court cases, there emerges additional support that the right to privacy is constitutionally grounded. In *Whalen v. Roe* (1977), the Court considered a New York statute that required information about the dispensing of certain drugs to be filed with the State Health Department.[25] A group of patients who regularly received those drugs claimed the statute violated their constitutional right to privacy. Although the Court upheld the statute, Justice Brennan, in his concurrence, stressed the Court's recognition of an individual's "interest in avoiding disclosure of personal matters." He noted that the "broad dissemination by state officials of such information [such as to the public] . . . would clearly implicate constitutionally protected privacy rights, and would presumably be justified only by a compelling state interest."[26]

In *Nixon v. Administrator of General Services,* discussed later, the Court in 1977 reaffirmed that one element of privacy is the individual's interest in avoiding disclosure of personal matters.[27] The Court indicated that former President Nixon had a constitutional right to avoid disclosure of personal matters in his papers, although it relied mostly on the Fourth Amendment case law and analysis in evaluating the privacy claim. The implication is that the constitutional right to nondisclosure is rooted primarily in the Fourth Amendment, according to the U.S. Court of Appeals for the District of Columbia in its review of these cases.[28]

The above cases show the constitutional basis for the individual's right to privacy and some, but not all, of its dimensions. At least two different interests are involved: the individual's interest in avoiding disclosure of personal matters, and the interest in being free to make certain kinds of important decisions. These interests have been characterized as "confidentiality" and "autonomy." The autonomy branch of privacy protects personal choice in such matters as marriage, procreation, contraception, family relationships, child rearing, and education. Thus, *Roe v. Wade* and the action of the Supreme Court in striking down the Akron ordinance fall into the autonomy category while *Whalen v. Roe* and *Nixon* represent the "confidentiality" interest. Only compelling state interests can overcome these protected rights, Brennan said.

Although prior decisions of the U.S. Supreme Court have recognized a constitutional right of privacy in child rearing, family relationships, procreation, marriage, contraception and abortion, the Court, in *Bowers v. Hardwick* (1986), held that homosexuals do not have such a right to engage in private, consensual sodomy.[29] The 5–4 decision upheld a Georgia statute that makes consensual sodomy a crime. Twenty-three other states have such laws.

In dissent, Justice Blackmun, joined by Brennan, Marshall, and Stevens, argued that this case really involved the long-recognized "right to be let alone"— the "right most valued by civilized men. . . ."

Let's return now to an examination of each of the Prosser common-law torts, particularly as these torts apply to the news media.

INTRUSION TORT

There are various ways of intruding into a person's privacy, the principal ones being trespassing, eavesdropping, and wiretapping. The courts have made it clear that wrongful means used to obtain information—even if that information falls within the protective zone of the First Amendment and the public interest standard—is actionable as an intrusion tort.

Dietemann v. Time, Inc. The 1971 case of *Dietemann v. Time, Inc.* involved two *LIFE* magazine staffers who secretly took photographs and made voice recordings in the plaintiff's home. The $1000 damage award was affirmed by the U.S. appellate court even though the First Amendment was claimed as protection for the way in which the information was obtained. Circuit Judge Shirley M. Hufstedler stated emphatically that the First Amendment "is not a license to trespass, to steal, or to intrude by electronic means into the precincts of another's home or office."[30] The *Dietemann* case illustrates four conditions that relate to the intrusion tort:

1. Surreptitious recording of a person's conversation is actionable.
2. Publication is not essential to the tort.
3. Existence of a technical trespass is immaterial (the *LIFE* staffers gained entry to Dietemann's home on the pretense of seeking medical advice and did not disclose the real purpose of their visit).
4. Proof of special damages is not required.

Not all surreptitious recordings of a person's conversation result in successful lawsuits against "offending" journalists, as will be shown in the next chapter, but certainly the use of such means for obtaining information is fraught with danger, as *Dietemann* shows. So, too, does *Barber v. Time, Inc.,* demonstrate that secretly taking someone's photo or entering a private area without permission is actionable.[31] In this case a reporter and a photographer entered a woman's hospital room without permission and surreptitiously took her picture while she was objecting to any publicity about her illness. She was suffering from a metabolic disorder such that she continued to lose weight even though eating large amounts of food. The article about the illness was not repulsive or unusually intimate, said the court, but she recovered several thousand dollars in damages because of the physical intrusion.

Publication Not Essential

The second of the *Dietemann* "lessons" — that publication is not essential to the intrusion tort — is demonstrated by *Nader v. General Motors Corp.*[32] This case resulted in a $425,000 out-of-court settlement by GM to consumer advocate Ralph Nader — at that time the largest amount ever paid in suits of this type — even though nothing was published about Nader by GM. Nader had claimed that he was shadowed by private detectives after writing a book alleging that GM's Corvair was dangerous to drive, and that acquaintances of his were interviewed in order to compile a dossier on him.

"Unreasonably Intrusive"

"Unreasonably intrusive" is a widely recognized element of this tort law, although the exact phrase may vary slightly from one jurisdiction to another. In the 1930s, for example, the *Restatement of Torts* recognized a right of privacy and, in Section 867, approved a cause of action based on the following circumstances: "A person who *unreasonably* and seriously interferes with another's interest in not having his affairs known to others or his likeness exhibited to the public is liable to others" (emphasis added).

The Kansas Supreme Court said in a 1976 decision that one who intentionally intrudes, physically or otherwise, upon the solitude or seclusion of another, or into his private affairs or concerns, is subject to liability if the intrusion, which must be substantial, would be highly offensive to an ordinary reasonable man.[33]

The Michigan Court of Appeals said the intrusion tort has three elements: (1) existence of a secret and private subject matter, (2) a right possessed by plaintiff to keep the matter private, and (3) information about the subject matter being obtained by some method objectionable to the reasonable man.[34]

Ordinarily a person in public can be photographed for news purposes without that person's permission. But in the case of freelance photographer Ron Galella, his attempts to photograph Jacqueline Kennedy Onassis, widow of assassinated President John F. Kennedy, and her children became so intrusive as to constitute a physical danger to them. In 1973, a federal court took the unusual action of ordering the photographer to stay at least 25 feet away from Jacqueline and her two children. He subsequently was found by the U.S. District Court for the Southern District of New York to be in contempt for violating that order.[35] As part of the settlement subsequently reached, Galella agreed to give up his legal right to ever again photograph Mrs. Onassis or her children and to pay Mrs. Onassis $10,000 for violating the court order.

Another case which demonstrates that publication is not essential to the tort is *Pearson v. Dodd*.[36] Judge J. Skelly Wright of the U.S. Court of Appeals said that whenever a claimed breach of privacy is being analyzed, injuries from intrusion should be kept separate from injuries from publication. Where there is intrusion, he said, the intruder can be held liable no matter what, if anything, is published.

In *Pearson* two former employees of then U.S. Senator Thomas Dodd, neither of whom was a party to the suit, entered the senator's office without authority but with the assistance of two members of Dodd's staff, removed documents from the files, made copies, replaced the originals, and gave the copies to Jack Anderson who then was associated with columnist Drew Pearson. Information gleaned from those documents was published by the defendant journalists. The appellate court emphasized that neither Anderson nor Pearson had trespassed upon Dodd's premises although they were aware that the documents had been removed without authorization. Judge Wright said for the court:

> If we were to hold . . . [Pearson and Anderson] liable for invasion of privacy on these facts, we would establish the proposition that one who received information from an intruder, knowing it has been obtained by improper intrusion, is guilty of a tort. In an untried and developing area of tort law, we are not prepared to go so far.

Wright concluded that since the columnists' role in obtaining the information did not make them liable to Dodd for intrusion, their subsequent publication of the information—itself no invasion of privacy—"could not reach back to render that role tortious."

Common Custom and Usage: a Defense to Intrusion Claim

Journalists in "hot pursuit" of a story frequently enter private property to obtain information or photographs without first obtaining permission. Technically, this constitutes trespass, but the law seems settled that there is no unlawful trespass when peaceable entry is made, without objection, under common custom and usage. Once objection is raised, the "trespasser" should leave. But suppose the owners or occupants of a dwelling are not on the property when the alleged trespass occurs and therefore cannot object to the presence of a "trespasser"? Such a case occurred in *Fletcher v. Florida Publishing Co.* decided by the Florida Supreme Court in 1976 in favor of the publishing company.[37] The U.S. Supreme Court declined to review that decision.

Fletcher v. Florida Publishing Co. The facts show that a 17-year-old girl died in a fire that heavily damaged her home. When the fire marshal arrived to begin an investigation, he and a police sergeant invited newsmen into the building. The fire marshal asked a photographer for the *Florida Times-Union* in Jacksonville to take a photograph of the "silhouette" left on the floor after the girl's body had been removed. The photo subsequently was published in the newspaper. The girl's mother sought to recover damages on three counts: (1) for alleged trespass, (2) for invasion of privacy, and (3) for wrongful intentional infliction of emotional distress arising out of publication of the photograph of the silhouette. According to the suit, the mother, who had gone to New York to visit a friend, first learned of her daughter's death when she saw the story and photograph in the *Times-Union*. The trial court dismissed count 2 and granted final judgment to the newspaper as to counts 1 and 3, but the First District Court of Appeal reversed the grant of summary judgment on count 1 (alleged trespass), stating that *Dietemann* was especially analogous to the case under consideration. The Florida Supreme Court, in a 5–1 decision, quashed the district court's reversal of count 1. In so doing, it quoted approvingly from the dissenting opinion of Judge McCord of the District Court of Appeal, who had said, in part:

> The only photographs taken and published were the fire damage—none were of deceased or injured persons. There is no contention that the particular photograph complained of (the silhouette picture) and the news story were in any way false or inaccurate. There could, therefore, be no recovery under the "false-light" doctrine of invasion of privacy. See *Cantrell v. Forest City Publishing Co.* [discussed later]. . . . Thus, there could be no recovery from the publication if the same photograph had come from a source other than from the news photographer's entry upon the premises. Any recovery in this case must necessarily be based upon trespass. . . . It is my view that the entry in this case was by implied consent.
>
> . . . The fire was a disaster of great public interest and it is clear that the photographer and other members of the news media entered the burned home at the invitation of the investigating officers. (Numerous members of the general public also went through the burned house.) Many affidavits of news editors throughout Florida and the nation and affidavits of Florida law enforcement officials were filed in support of appellee's motion for summary judgment. These affidavits were to the general effect that it has been a long-standing custom and practice throughout the country for representatives of the news media to enter upon private property where disaster of great public interest has occurred—entering in a peaceful manner, without causing any physical damage, and at the invitation of the officers who are investigating the calamity. The affidavits of law enforcement officers indicate that the presence of the news media at such investigations is often helpful to the investigations in developing leads, etc.
>
> The affidavits as to custom and practice do not delineate between various kinds of property where a tragedy occurs. . . . An analysis of the cases on implied consent by custom and usage indicates that they do not rest upon the previous nonobjection to entry by the particular owner of the property in question but rest upon custom and practice generally. Implied consent would, of course, vanish if one were informed not to enter at that time by the owner or possessor or by their direction. But here there was not only no objection to the entry, but *there was an invitation to enter by the officers investigating the fire*. The question of implied consent to news media personnel to enter premises in a circumstance such as this appears to be one of first impression not only in this jurisdiction but elsewhere. This, in itself, tends to indicate that the practice has been accepted by the general public since it is widespread and long-standing. Due to such widespread and long-standing custom, reason and logic sup-

port the application of implied consent to enter the premises in the case before us. It, therefore, was not a trespass. . . . [Emphasis supplied by Florida Supreme Court.][38]

Thus, in *this* case, a practice of long-standing was judged to constitute "implied consent" to enter the property of another in pursuit of a story of great public interest. Note, however, that this is a case of *first impression.* The issues involved generally have not come before the courts before, perhaps, as Judge Guyte P. McCord, Jr. said, because the practice under review has long been accepted by the general public. Note, also, the conditions associated with the decision in this case:

1. Entry was peaceful.
2. No physical damage was caused.
3. An invitation to enter was extended by investigating officers.
4. The owner or possessor of the property was not there to object.

Therefore, within the limits of this case, journalists in Florida have "implied consent" to enter onto someone's property in pursuit of news of great public importance. But if the four conditions are not present, then *Dietemann* most likely states the law insofar as journalists and trespass are concerned.

Compare the results in the Florida Publishing case with a Milwaukee jury's action. The jury awarded $1 each to five persons who said their right to privacy was violated during a raid on their house in which a reporter accompanied police, took photographs of the house during the search for arms believed owned by a convicted felon living there, and later wrote a story about the raid.[39]

The family had brought a $12.7 million lawsuit against the reporter, the publisher of the *Ripon Commonwealth Press,* and Ripon police.

Le Mistral Inc. v. CBS. In 1976, a jury awarded the plaintiff—a Manhattan restaurant—$250,000 in punitive and $1200 in compensatory damages against CBS. A camera crew from network-owned station WCBS-TV entered the mid-Manhattan restaurant that had been accused of health code violations. The crew entered without permission and with "cameras rolling." It was ordered by the management to leave, and the crew left, but the film later was shown on a WCBS-TV newscast.

In pretrial action, the trial judge granted CBS' motion to dismiss the restaurant's defamation suit on the basis of the story being accurate, but the judge refused to dismiss the trespass action, stating:

The right to publish does not include . . . the right to . . . trespass upon the property of these plaintiffs. While the restaurant is a business establishment which by imputation extends an invitation to prospective diners to enter the premises and purchase a meal, that invitation is not extended to others whose business purpose is not the business purpose of the restaurant.

CBS argued unsuccessfully that requiring the press to get prior consent for an interview from those involved in adverse publicity—with respect to information about which the public has a legitimate public interest—would result in an impermissible chilling effect on the First Amendment.

On appeal, the New York Supreme Court, Appellate Division, ordered a new trial on the issue of punitive damages, but allowed the $1200 in compensatory damages to stand.[40] One judge partially dissented on the ground that there was no actual malice on the part of the defendant and therefore punitive damages could not be recovered. But the judges were unanimous in holding that the restaurant was entitled to recover compensatory damage on the basis that a trespass had occurred. *Dietemann* was cited as a precedent.

In another restaurant case, the Iowa Supreme Court reinstated an invasion of privacy action by a woman who claimed that her privacy was invaded when a TV cameraman took pictures of her while she was eating in a pizzeria.[41]

The cameraman for KWWL-TV of Waterloo had permission from the restaurant owners to enter the pizzeria and videotape a story in connection with National Pizza Week. The woman said she objected to being photographed.

A District Court judge dismissed the lawsuit, stating that the woman was in a public building, her likeness was not used for commercial purposes, and the broadcast did not portray her in a false light. But the state's highest court said the plaintiff should have the opportunity to show how the telecast had harmed her. In the past, the high court has held that privacy is invaded when a person's seclusion is unreasonably intruded upon (one of the plaintiff's claims), when there is "unreasonable publicity given to another's private life," or when there is "publicity that unreasonably places another in a false light." The court cited an Alabama case in which a woman successfully sued a newspaper for intrusion after it printed a picture of her with her dress blown up as she was leaving a county fair fun house.

Criminal Trespass Convictions. A number of reporters were arrested in 1979 during an anti-nuclear power demonstration by some 300 persons at a plant site in northeast Oklahoma. An official of the Public Service Company of Oklahoma asked the demonstrators and reporters who had crossed over a fence to leave the company's property, and, when they refused, the sheriff arrested many of them. The journalists were fined $25 each for criminal trespass. On appeal, the fines were upheld by a 2–1 decision of the Oklahoma Court of Criminal Appeals.[42] The majority cited *Dietemann* in saying that the First Amendment is not a license to trespass, although the dissenting justice said the press had a right of reasonable access to newsworthy events. Six of the journalists sought U.S. Supreme Court review of their convictions, with the state in opposition. The First Amendment, said the state, does not grant immunity from arrest and prosecution to journalists who commit illegal acts while attempting to gather news. The Court denied certiorari.[43]

Similarly, eight journalists were arrested near Carlsbad, New Mexico, during a protest at a nuclear waste facility being built by the federal government. Seven of them agreed to pay $50 fines each, but one, Kenneth McCormack, a freelance photographer, decided to fight the criminal trespass charge on the ground that the law does not apply to public lands. He was found guilty. But in 1983 the New Mexico Court of Appeals overturned the conviction, ruling that the criminal trespass law did not apply. However, the court did not deal with McCormack's claim to a First Amendment right to enter the site to cover a newsworthy event.[44]

A different situation developed when two television newsmen attempted to enter what residents of Tega Cay, South Carolina, termed a private community. They were threatened with arrest and detained, but a magistrate refused to sign the trespassing warrants. The newsmen filed suit for $40,000 in damages and an order barring community security officers from interfering with their right of access to what they say is a muncipality.[45]

PUBLIC DISCLOSURE TORT

The public disclosure tort is concerned with the publication of truthful, but private, information of an embarrassing nature about an identifiable individual. This tort can be distinguished from defamation in that "public disclosure" involves truthful information, whereas "defamation" involves false information which injures a person's reputation. To be actionable, the disclosure generally

1. Must be sufficiently widespread to have made it public.
2. Must have resulted in embarrassment sufficient to affect an ordinary reasonable person.
3. Must relate to "private" facts which are not within the realm of "legitimate news."
4. Must not be part of the "public" record.

An early case sheds light on the public disclosure tort and defenses thereto.

Sidis v. FR Publishing Corporation. This case involved a former child prodigy in mathematics, William James Sidis, who had graduated from Harvard at age 16, received considerable publicity at the time, and then disappeared from public view until *New Yorker* magazine published an article which identified him many years later.[46] It detailed personal facts about Sidis' life. He sued, but in 1940 lost in a decision by the U.S. Court of Appeals, even though the court characterized the article as a "ruthless exposure of a once public character, who has since sought and has now been deprived of the seclusion of a private life." The court ruled against Sidis for three reasons: (1) he was a "public figure," albeit an unwilling one, in which there was considerable popular news interest; (2) the article was newsworthy, and (3) the revelations in the article were not so intimate and unwarranted as to outrage the community's notions of decency. The Second Circuit was one of the first, if not the first, to use as a standard "media conduct or behavior that outrages a community's notion of decency." If such conduct, through the publication of shocking, intimate, and objectionable information, reaches the level of community outrage, then the newsworthiness privilege may be lost because of such "unconscionable behavior." The article about Sidis did not reach that level, the court said.

The newsworthiness privilege may also be lost, according to *Restatement (Second) of Torts* (1977), if the publication "becomes a morbid and sensational prying into private lives for its own sake" as determined by community mores.[47] Such a test was used in *Virgil v. Time, Inc.,* discussed later.

Emotional Distress Factor

The intent of the public disclosure tort, according to Brandeis and Warren, was to protect people against emotional harm or distress. The *Restatement (Second) of Torts* (1965) would allow recovery for intentional infliction of emotional distress caused by outrageous behavior, and most jurisdictions that allow public disclosure tort actions follow the *Restatement*. Sidis could not show that the *New Yorker intended* to inflict emotional distress, nor was he able to show the Second Circuit that the community was outraged by the publication.

Emotional distress caused by publishing intimate or shocking details of one's life is often given as a reason, and sometimes the sole reason, for an invasion of privacy action, but courts are reluctant to allow recovery solely or largely on this basis. As the writer of a law review article put it:

> . . . Traditionally, courts were extremely reluctant to compensate plaintiffs for emotional harms except as an adjunct to awards of damages for other injuries that the courts deemed more concrete and easier to value.
>
> Today, . . . the award of damages exclusively for emotional harm remains controversial in tort law. Many states now follow the *Restatement (Second) of Torts* and allow for recovery for the intentional infliction of emotional distress caused by a defendant's outrageous behavior. Nonetheless, sufficient problems of proof and valuation remain that lead courts and commentators alike to tread cautiously in further extending the right to recovery for emotional harm.[48]

A major case involving the emotional distress tort was decided by the U.S. Supreme Court in 1988.

Falwell v. Hustler Magazine

Initially, the Rev. Jerry Falwell, conservative evangelist, was awarded $200,000 in compensatory damage by a federal jury solely on the ground of intentional infliction of emotional distress.

At issue was an advertisement in *Hustler* intended to parody an advertising campaign for Campari Liqueur in which Falwell is purportedly interviewed and "reveals" an incestuous relationship with his mother in an outhouse. At the bottom of the full page ad was this disclaimer: "Ad Parody—Not To Be Taken Seriously," and it was listed in the table of contents as "Fiction; Ad and Personality Parody."

The trial court dismissed Falwell's invasion of privacy claims, and the jury ruled against Falwell on a libel claim. But on Falwell's emotional distress claim, the jury awarded him $100,000 in actual damages and $50,000 in punitive damages from publisher Larry Flynt, and $50,000 in punitive damages from *Hustler* based on its finding of intentional or reckless misconduct by *Hustler* in publishing the parody.

In 1986, a three-judge panel of the U.S. Court of Appeals for the Fourth Circuit upheld the damage awards, noting that four essential elements under Virginia law for a successful action for intentional infliction of emotional distress had been met.[49] The four elements are that the wrongdoer's conduct (1) is intentional or reckless; (2) offends generally accepted standards of decency or morality; (3) is causally connected with plaintiff's emotional distress; and (4) caused severe emotional distress.[50]

In reviewing the four elements, the panel pointed out that publisher Flynt had testified in a deposition that he intended to cause Falwell emotional distress.[51] As for the second element, the panel said that evidence of outrageousness is "quite evident from the language in the parody and in the fact that Flynt republished the parody after the lawsuit was filed." The final elements, said the panel, require the plaintiff to prove that the defendant's conduct "proximately caused severe emotional distress." After reviewing Falwell's testimony, the panel said such testimony would enable a jury to find that Falwell's distress was severe and that it was proximately caused by the publication of the parody.

The jury's finding that the defendant's misconduct was intentional or reckless meets the *New York Times* level of fault required in defamation actions, said the panel, adding that the First Amendment will not shield intentional or reckless misconduct that results in severe emotional distress. The panel also agreed that Falwell's failure to recover for libel did not, as a matter of law, prevent him from recovering for intentional infliction of emotion distress. In support of its position, the panel cited the *en banc* Third Circuit U.S. Court of Appeals' position on this issue.[52]

By a 6–5 vote, the Fourth Circuit court denied Flynt's petition for a rehearing *en banc*.[53]

He then asked the U.S. Supreme Court to review the case. The Court unanimously reversed the award in 1988.[54] In so doing, the Court said that the actual malice rule would apply whenever public officials or public figures sought to recover damages for the tort of intentional infliction of emotional distress. The Court also coupled the public concern test to the actual malice rule, to wit: In order to protect the free flow of ideas and opinions on *matters of public concern,* the First and Fourteenth Amendments prohibit public officials and public figures from recovering damages for this tort without a showing that the publication contains a false statement of fact made with actual malice. Note that in two instances the magazine arguably made it clear that the ad was not to be taken factually.

Chief Justice Rehnquist gave the Court's opinion, noting at the outset that the case presented "a novel question involving First Amendment limitations upon a state's authority to protect its citizens from the intentional infliction of emotional distress." Rehnquist continued:

> We must decide whether a public figure may recover damages for emotional harm caused by the publication of an ad parody offensive to him, and doubtless gross and repugnant in the eyes of most. Respondent would have us find that a state's interest in

protecting public figures from emotional distress is sufficient to deny First Amendment protection to speech that is patently offensive and is intended to inflict emotional injury, even when that speech could not reasonably have been interpreted as stating actual facts about the public figure involved. This we decline to do.[55]

Rehnquist cited a number of cases in reaching the Court's conclusion, among them:

- "The freedom to speak one's mind is not only an aspect of individual liberty . . . but also is essential to the common quest for truth and the vitality of society as a whole." *Bose Corp. v. Consumers Union of United States, Inc.,* 466 U.S. 485, 503-04 (1984).
- The First Amendment recognizes no such thing as a "false" idea. *Gertz v. Welch, Inc.,* 418 U.S. 323, 339 (1974).
- The robust political debate encouraged by the First Amendment is bound to produce speech critical of those in public office or those who are "intimately involved in the resolution of important public questions or, by reason of their fame, shape events in areas of concern to society at large." *Associated Press v. Walker,* 388 U.S. 130, 164 (1967) (Warren, C.J., concurring in the result).
- "Freedoms of expression require 'breathing space.' " *New York Times v. Sullivan,* 376 U.S. 254, 272 (1964).
- "The fact that society may find speech offensive is not a sufficient reason for suppressing it. Indeed, if it is the speaker's opinion that gives offense, that consequence is a reason for according it consitutional protection. For it is a central tenet of the First Amendment that the government must remain neutral in the marketplace of ideas." *FCC v. Pacifica Foundation,* 438 U.S. 726, 745–46 (1978) (see Chapter 12).

Rehnquist also referred to some famous examples of intentionally injurious speech, including political cartoons by Thomas Nast.

Justice White concurred in the judgment and Justice Kennedy took no part in the consideration or decision of this case.

Following the Supreme Court's decision, courts in New Jersey and Ohio used that decision in dismissing suits against media defendants.

The New Jersey case began with the April 25, 1985, edition of the Kean College *Independent* that included a 13-page spoof of the paper. One page consisted of phony ads, including "Whoreline," which parodied "Hotline," a serious ad that appeared regularly in the *Independent.* The "Whoreline" parody listed Ann Walko, a School of Education assistant dean, as one of four college administrators and students who could be called to have "good phone sex."[56] Walko sued the college, the newspaper's adviser, and members of the newspaper staff claiming libel, intentional infliction of emotional distress, and false-light invasion of privacy.

The Superior Court judge said that no reasonable person could conclude that the ad was a statement of fact. Because the ad was not factual, the judge held that it was an expression of opinion absolutely privileged under the state Constitution and the First Amendment.[57] Once the defamation claim had been disposed of, the judge relied on the *Hustler v. Falwell* decision in saying that since the parody was not actionable as defamation, it could not form the basis for recovery for intentional infliction of emotional distress.

As for the false-light claim, since it was based upon a publication that was nondefamatory and absolutely privileged because it was protected by the opinion privilege, the claim could not stand.

Walko was classified as a limited-purpose public figure because the ad parody was related to a controversy concerning loss of funding for "Hotline" and because of her status as a college administrator.

The other case involved a decision of the Ohio Supreme Court in *Celebrezze v. Dayton Newspapers, Inc.,* discussed previously.

Another case which illustrates a plaintiff's inability to maintain a cause of action for intentional infliction of emotional distress once the defamation portion of the action no longer exists is *Ault v. Hustler Magazine* (1986).

In examining the plaintiff's claims, Judge Helen J. Frye of the U.S. District Court for the District of Oregon said:

> Although there appears to be some split in authority (see *Falwell v. Flynt,* 797 F.2d 1270 . . ., in which the Fourth Circuit found a cause of action for intentional infliction of emotional distress independent of the plaintiff's libel claim based on Virginia law), this court finds that the better reasoned cases support dismissing an action for the intentional infliction of emotional distress when the action is based on the same facts which support the plaintiff's defamation claims.[58]

The judge then quoted from a California Court of Appeal opinion in *Grimes v. Carter* (1966), to wit:

> It is elementary that, although the gravamen of a defamation action is injury to reputation, libel or slander also visits upon a plaintiff humiliation, mortification and emotional distress. In circumstances where a plaintiff states a case of libel or slander, such personal distress is a matter which may be taken into account in determining the amount of damages to which the plaintiff is entitled, but it does not give rise to an independent cause of action on the theory of a separate tort.[59]

Case law provides other examples of media defenses—such as newsworthiness—overcoming the emotional distress claim. In *Bridges v. Cape Publications,* a jury awarded plaintiff $1000 compensatory and $9000 punitive damages against a newspaper which published a photograph of the partially nude plaintiff being rushed by police to safety from an apartment where she had been held at gunpoint by her estranged husband. She had been forced to disrobe to prevent her escape. The photograph showed an emotionally distressed plaintiff, holding a small towel to conceal her nudity, being led from the scene by police. Hilda Bridges claimed the publication invaded her privacy and constituted intentional infliction of emotional distress.

On appeal, the award was overturned. A unanimous Florida Court of Appeal (Fifth District) ruled that the photograph was newsworthy.[60] At some point, wrote Judge James Dauksch, the public interest becomes dominant over the individual's right of privacy in an event such as this one. He added: "Just because the story and photograph may be embarrassing or distressful to the plaintiff does not mean the newspaper cannot publish what is otherwise newsworthy." The U.S. Supreme Court denied review.[61]

The emotional distress plea was used by actress Brooke Shields when she unsuccessfully sought an injunction under the New York Civil Rights Law to prevent publication of nude photographs of her taken, with her mother's consent, when she was 10 years old. The U.S. District Court for the Southern District of New York refused to issue an injunction on several grounds and removed interim injunctive relief that had been granted. The court said there already had been substantial dissemination of the photographs, that other nude pictures of her taken by a fashion photographer had been published, and that she had appeared nude in a movie, *Pretty Baby*. On appeal, the state's highest court held that she lacked a cause of action under the Civil Rights Law (the law allowing a cause of action only for misappropriation and, indirectly, false light through ficitionalization).[62]

Briscoe v. Reader's Digest Association (1971). This case began when *Reader's Digest* used Marvin Briscoe's name in an article about truck hijackings, briefly referring to him in connection with a crime he had committed 11 years earlier. Briscoe had served time in prison, and upon being released had resumed his place in society. Following publication of his past misdeed, he brought a lawsuit alleging that (1) the article had placed him in a "false light" (the false light tort involving nondefamatory falsehoods), and that (2) it had disclosed truthful, but embarrassing, private facts about him. Concerning the false light portion of the lawsuit, Briscoe claimed the article falsely implied that his criminal conduct was a recent activity through the use of such words as "today" and "now" near the beginning of the article.

The California Supreme Court did not decide the merits of Briscoe's invasion of privacy claims. Instead, it ruled that Briscoe's complaint stated a cause of action.[63] The court then involved itself in a discussion of such concepts as "hot news," recency, and newsworthiness — the end result being confusion and concern as to how the media could defend against such suits, at least in California.

"Particularly deserving of First Amendment protection," said the court, "are reports of 'hot news' items of possible immediate public concern or interest" — an idea advanced by Justice Harlan of the U.S. Supreme Court in 1967 in the defamation cases of *Curtis Publishing Co. v. Butts* and *Walker v. AP*, discussed previously. The California court went on to observe that in *Hill v. Time, Inc.*, discussed later, the U.S. Supreme Court had cited 22 cases in which the right of privacy gave way to the right of the press to publish matters of public interest; but 17 of these involved events which had occurred quite recently. The court conceded that truthful reports of recent crimes and the names of suspects or offenders would be protected by the First Amendment, but stated that the "identification of the actor in reports of long past crimes usually serves little independent public purpose" with the notable exception of major crimes, such as the Saint Valentine's Day massacre. In connection with public interest, the court suggested that the public's interest in the rehabilitation of former criminals might be paramount.

As for "newsworthiness," the court said that on the basis of the assumed facts "we are convinced that a jury could reasonably find that plaintiff's identity as a former hijacker was not newsworthy." In other words, the incidents of Briscoe's past life were of minimal social value; revelation of one's criminal past is grossly offensive to most people, and Briscoe had not voluntarily consented to publicity.[64]

What threatened to become a journalistic nightmare in California — involving the news media in decisions concerning "hot" news, immediacy, or recency of the events being reported; social value of the information being published; and balancing the public interest in the rehabilitation of criminals against newsworthiness or some other standard — was eased somewhat when the case was moved into the federal courts because of constitutional issues. Judge Lawrence T. Lydick of the U.S. District Court for the Central District of California disposed of the lawsuit by issuing summary judgment for *Reader's Digest* in early 1972. In so doing, Lydick stated the following "conclusions of law":

1. The publication was newsworthy.
2. It was published without malice or recklessness.
3. It was protected by the First Amendment's guarantee of freedom of press; therefore, there could be no recovery for invasion of privacy if the publication was published in a nonmalicious, nonreckless manner.
4. It disclosed no private facts about Briscoe.
5. It did not invade his privacy.

In 1980, the California Supreme Court took the opportunity in *Forsher v. Bugliosi* to distinguish *Briscoe* as an "exception to the more general rule that 'once a man has become a public figure, or news, he remains a matter of legitimate recall to the public mind to the end of his days.' "[65] And even the narrow exception carved out by *Briscoe* against disclosure of long-past criminal activities of rehabilitated or reformed criminals may not stand against the U.S. Supreme Court's ruling in *Cox Broadcasting v. Cohn,* discussed later, that the press cannot be held liable for the accurate publication of official court records open to the public. The conviction of *Briscoe,* of course, is a matter of public court record. The California Supreme Court's reference to *Cox Broadcasting* in *Forsher* shows the limited vitality of its *Briscoe* ruling. However, the social value criterion continues to be used by California courts as one factor in determining newsworthiness.[66]

Public Disclosure of Rape Victim's Name

Cox Broadcasting Corp. v. Cohn (1975).[67] This case stemmed from a broadcast by WSB-TV in Atlanta which identified a 17-year-old girl who had been raped and who had choked to death on her own vomit. The story was aired April

10, 1972, when six youths appeared in court on charges of rape or attempted rape (charges of murder having been dropped). The girl's father brought an action, relying on a state law which prohibited such identification, claiming that his right to privacy had been invaded by the broadcast.

Justice White gave the Court's opinion, in which he said, in part:

> . . . Because the gravamen of the claimed injury is the publication of information, whether true or not, the dissemination of which is embarrassing or otherwise painful to an individual, it is here that claims of privacy most directly confront the constitutional freedoms of speech and press.

Justice White then proceeded to the narrow issue in this case: Can a state impose sanctions on the accurate publication of the name of a rape victim obtained from judicial records maintained in connection with the public prosecution of the six youths—records open to public inspection? The Supreme Court ruled that the state could not impose sanctions in the circumstances of this case—the Court's first ruling in a public disclosure tort case.

White concluded in this way:

> At the very least, the First and Fourteenth Amendments will not allow exposing the press to liability for truthfully publishing information released to the public in official court records. If there are privacy interests to be protected in judicial proceedings [e.g., those involving juvenile delinquents], the States must respond by means which avoid public documentation or other exposure of private information. Their political institutions must weigh the interests in privacy with the interests of the public to know and of the press to publish.[68] Once the true information is disclosed in public court documents open to public inspection, the press cannot be sanctioned for publishing it. In this instance as in others reliance must rest upon the judgment of those who decide what to publish or broadcast.

The *Cox* decision does not answer conclusively whether an accurate report of *any* public record is constitutionally protected in the same way that public court records are. The answer, very likely, is yes—although recency might be a confounding issue, as in *Briscoe.*

Concerning public records in general, Justice White quoted, apparently favorably, from a tentative draft of *Restatement (Second) of Torts,* the following commentary concerning public disclosure:

> [T]here is no liability when the defendant merely gives further publicity to information about the plaintiff which is already public. Thus there is no liability for giving publicity to facts about the plaintiff's life which are matters of public record. . . .[69]

Referring to this tentative draft, White said:

> According to this draft, ascertaining and publishing the contents of public records are simply not within the reach of these kinds of privacy actions.

Thus even the prevailing law of invasion of privacy generally recognizes that interests in privacy fade when the information involved already appears on the public record. . . .

By placing the information in the public domain on the official court records, the State must be presumed to have concluded that the public interest was thereby being served. Public records by their very nature are of interest to those concerned with the administration of government, and a public benefit is performed by the reporting of the true contents of the records by the media. The freedom of the press to publish that information appears to us to be of critical importance to our type of government in which the citizenry is the final judge of the proper conduct of public business. In preserving that form of government the First and Fourteenth Amendments command nothing less than that the States may not impose sanctions for the publication of truthful information contained in official court records open to public inspection.[70]

It should be reiterated that the discussion above falls short of embracing the assumption generally held by the press; that is, accurate reports of *any* public record are protected by the First Amendment. White moves in that direction, but falls back from the broader sweep by limiting the decision to "official court records."

Also deserving of emphasis is the "solution" suggested by Justice White whenever privacy and First Amendment rights collide and privacy rights are deemed to warrant protection. White said:

If there are privacy interests to be protected in judicial proceedings, the States must respond by means which avoid public documentation or other exposure of private information. Their political institutions must weigh the interests in privacy with the interests of the public to know and of the press to publish.

If states seal certain court records or close judicial proceedings to the public, the privacy interests are protected while, at the same time, direct prior restraint of the press from publishing what otherwise would be open to the public is avoided. Such a prior restraint probably would be unconstitutional unless all other measures for protecting the "private information" were first employed and found inadequate. This same solution — which avoids having to choose between two fundamental rights — has been advanced to resolve, or at least reduce, free-press/fair-trial clashes (see Chapter 10). One of the obvious difficulties with White's suggestion vis-à-vis the sealing of court records (and, by extension, other records in which privacy interests are at stake) is the inevitable conflict between privacy and the public's right to know what is happening in the various institutions of government — a right discussed in Chapter 9 in connection with the Freedom of Information Act and sunshine laws.

A dilemma facing state courts was highlighted by Supreme Court action in *Globe Newspapers Co. v. Superior Court* (1982) (also discussed in Chapter 10).[71] A Massachusetts statute that was construed as requiring closure of rape and other sexual assault trials during testimony of victims who are minors was declared unconstitutional by the Court in a 6–3 decision. The press and public cannot be automatically excluded from any type of criminal trial, said the majority.

Although the state's interest in protecting victims from further embarrassment and trauma is compelling, said Justice Brennan in his opinion for the Court, "it does not justify a *mandatory*-closure rule, for it is clear that the circumstances of the particular case may affect the significance of the interest."

One of the questions left unanswered by *Cox*: Can a state impose civil or criminal liability for the publication of truthful information lawfully obtained from either the government or from the news organization's own investigation again was before the U.S. Supreme Court in 1988.

The Court agreed to consider whether a newspaper can be assessed damages for publication of a rape victim's name in a state that makes it unlawful to do so. In 1985, a jury awarded $75,000 damages to a woman who said she suffered emotional distress after the *Florida Star*, a weekly newspaper in Jacksonville, published an accurate story that she had been raped and robbed. The First District Court of Appeal affirmed the decision, stating that the document from which the paper obtained the woman's identity was not a public record even though it had been shown to a reporter by a sheriff's department employee.[72] The state supreme court denied review.[73]

In a 6–3 decision, the U.S. Supreme Court reversed the award of $75,000 in damages in *Florida Star v. B.J.F.,* but did not declare the Florida statute (Sec. 794.03) unconstitutional. The Court, in an opinion by Justice Marshall, ruled that the news media's truthful publication of information lawfully obtained can be punished only if such punishment is "narrowly tailored to a state interest of the highest order."[74]

Justices Brennan, Blackmun, Stevens, and Kennedy joined in the opinion in which Marshall emphasized that the Court's holding is a limited one and does not mean that "truthful publication is automatically constitutionally protected," or that there is no zone of personal privacy within which the state may protect the individual from intrusion. Nor, said Marshall, does it mean that a state may never punish publication of the name of a sex crime victim. As Marshall put it:

> We hold only that where a newspaper publishes truthful information which it has lawfully obtained, punishment may be lawfully imposed, if at all, only when narrowly tailored to a state interest of the highest order, and that no such interest is satisfactorily served [by imposing liability under Sec. 794.03 based on the facts in this case].

The Court rejected the argument by the *Florida Star* that *Cox Newspapers v. Cohn* was controlling. In *Cox,* said Marshall, the name of the rape victim was obtained from open judicial records and a significant interest was served by the press in its role of helping to ensure public openness of trials. "That role is not directly compromised when, as here, the information in question comes from a police report. . . ."

Justice Scalia concurred in part of the opinion and in the judgment. Justice White, joined by Rehnquist and O'Connor, dissented, saying that one result of the Court's decision will be to "obliterate one of the most noteworthy legal inventions of the 20th century: the tort of the publication of private facts" (the public disclosure or a "true" Brandeis-Warren tort).

Whether Justice White's observation that the public disclosure tort is nullified by the Court's decision remains to be seen, but the Court majority seems to have left a window open through which states can provide some protection against the publication of some private facts. That this is so can be seen in the light of another case taken to the Supreme Court in 1988. It involved an invasion of privacy lawsuit filed against the *Los Angeles Times* after it published an article identifying the plaintiff by name as having discovered the body of her murdered roommate. The plaintiff's name was obtained either from the county coroner's office or by interviewing neighbors of the murder victim. The name was included in the public coroner's report about a month after it was published in the newspaper. In its appeal, the newspaper said that where "a state has determined that a particular piece of information should be made public, it cannot punish a newspaper for publishing the same information earlier than the state does so, at least as long as the information was lawfully obtained."[75]

A California Court of Appeal had ruled that a trial should be held to determine if publication of the name was "newsworthy," and the state supreme court denied review.[76]

In its bid to have the U.S. Supreme Court review the lower court decisions, the newspaper's attorneys said:

> In sum, the Court of Appeals gave to a jury broad discretion to second-guess an editorial decision which is made on thousands of occasions each day by the media: whether to report the name of someone involved in a current event.[77]

Additionally, said the newspaper, the newsworthiness standard "is so vague and subjective that it would effectively allow a jury to decide liability solely on the basis of its dislike for what was reported." But the Supreme Court in 1989 decided not to review the case.

Media Defenses to Disclosure Tort

Public record is a major defense whenever a public disclosure tort action is involved — just as it is a defense in defamation actions. This is especially true of public court records. But other defenses are available, including consent (either express or implied), newsworthiness, and public interest.

Consent

Obtaining consent was the procedure followed by the *Greenville* (S.C.) *News* when, on May 20, 1975, it identified a rape victim. The woman signed a statement, witnessed by her father, releasing the newspaper from liability for publishing information in a police report which was not open to public inspection. South Carolina is one of several states which prohibit by statute the publication of the names of rape victims. The statutes cannot, however, prohibit publication of such names when they are divulged at public trial, as the Supreme Court ruled in *Cox Broadcasting*.

If a news source talks freely with a reporter, knowing that person to be a reporter, then such action constitutes implied consent.

Can consent, once given, be revoked? The case of *Virgil v. Time, Inc.* is instructive in this regard and in connection with the defenses of newsworthiness and public interest.[78]

Virgil v. Time, Inc. In 1976, the U.S. Supreme Court let stand a decision of the Ninth Circuit U.S. Court of Appeals which had rejected a move by Time, Inc., to obtain summary judgment against a $12 million privacy suit brought by Virgil.[79]

Briefly, the facts are these: Michael S. Virgil of Newport Beach, California, filed the action because of an article on body surfing published in the February 22, 1971, issue of *Sports Illustrated*. The author of the article included some information that Virgil had willingly provided, such as deliberately burning his hands with cigarettes, or diving headfirst down stairways, to impress girls or to attract attention to himself. In his suit, Virgil said he revoked all consent upon learning that the article would not be confined to his prowess as a surfer. The three-judge panel of the U.S. appellate court agreed that plaintiff could do so, saying:

> Talking freely to a member of the press, knowing the listener to be a member of the press, is not then in itself making public. Such communication can be said to anticipate that what is said will be made public since making public is the function of the press and accordingly such communication can be construed as a consent to publicize. Thus if publicity results it can be said to have been consented to. However, if consent is withdrawn prior to the act of publicizing, the consequent publicity is without consent.

The court noted that Virgil's revocation of consent was not an eleventh-hour change that would unfairly burden a publisher.

Time contended that since Virgil did not deny the truthfulness of the article, its publication was privileged under the First Amendment. The court rejected this, citing *Cox Broadcasting Corp.* in saying the law has not yet gone so far. In *Cox Broadcasting,* according to the appellate court, the Supreme Court "refused to reach . . . [the] broad question 'whether truthful publications may ever be subjected to civil or criminal liability. . . .' It chose instead to . . . [exclude from the protected area of privacy] material to be found in judicial records open to inspection by the public." The court continued:

> To hold that privilege extends to all true statements would seem to deny the existence of "private facts," for if facts be facts—that is, if they be true—they would not (at least to the press) be private, and the press would be free to publicize them to the extent it sees fit. The extent to which areas of privacy continue to exist, then, would appear to be based not on rights bestowed by law but on the taste and discretion of the press. We cannot accept this result. . . .

We conclude that unless it be privileged as newsworthy . . ., the publicizing of private facts is not protected by the First Amendment.

It was to "newsworthiness" that the court next turned. For the court, Circuit Judge Charles M. Merrill said:

The privilege to publicize newsworthy matters is included in the definition of the tort set out in Restatement . . . [Tentative Draft No. 21]. Liability may be imposed for an invasion of privacy only if "the matter publicized is of a kind which . . . is not of legitimate concern to the public." While the Restatement does not so emphasize, we are satisfied that this provision is one of constitutional dimension delimiting the scope of the tort and that the *extent of the privilege thus is controlled by federal rather than state law.* (Emphasis supplied.)

This reads as though the court were opting for extension of the *Rosenbloom* libel standard to the area of privacy, but in a footnote, the three-judge panel commented:

Recent decisions of the Supreme Court . . . serve to emphasize that First Amendment interests may be circumscribed due to competing values which are also of substantial importance to society. . . . More particularly, *Gertz* . . . acknowledged the need to recognize the strength of legitimate state interests in protecting the well-being of its citizens, even in the face of a broad First Amendment challenge. The state's interest in protecting the privacy of its citizens seems to us no less legitimate than the state's interest, upheld in *Gertz,* in protecting its citizens' reputations. Indeed, privacy shares the same underlying purpose invoked by the Court in *Gertz* in upholding the state's interest in the law of libel. . . .

The court cited the *Restatement* in noting that the privilege extends to "voluntary public figures" and to some "involuntary public figures" who, through their own conduct or otherwise, have become "news." It extends to "all matters of the kind customarily regarded as 'news,' " and to "giving information to the public for purposes of education, amusement or enlightenment, where the public may resonably be expected to have a legitimate interest in what is published." But the *Restatement* makes it clear, said the court, that the privilege is not unlimited. It quoted the following comment regarding "legitimate public interest":

In determining what is a matter of legitimate public interest, account must be taken of the customs and conventions of the community; and in the last analysis what is proper becomes a matter of the community mores. The line is to be drawn when the publicity ceases to be the giving of information to which the public is entitled, and becomes a morbid and sensational prying into private lives for its own sake, with which a reasonable member of the public, with decent standards, would say that he had no concern.

The final question addressed by the court was whether the application of the newsworthiness standard presented a question for the jury (rather than the trial judge) to decide. The court concluded that the subject matter (surfing), although not hot news, properly could be regarded as of general public interest. However, the acceptance of that as a matter of law did not necessarily mean that it was in the public interest "to know private facts" about the persons who engaged in that activity.

Thus, among the questions that remained to be answered on remand were whether (and, if so, to what extent) "private" facts concerning Virgil, as a prominent member of the group engaging in body surfing, were matters in which the public had a legitimate interest and whether the identity of Virgil fell within the range of such interest. Such questions are related to concerns expressed by the California Supreme Court in *Briscoe*. In fact, the views of the California court in *Briscoe* are reflected in the *Virgil* opinion even to the extent of the circuit court's observation that the Tentative Draft of Section 652D, *Restatement,* "fairly comports with the requirements established by California law" in *Briscoe*. But state law may not be controlling in a privacy lawsuit, according to the Ninth Circuit, because of a First Amendment privilege to publicize newsworthy matters of legitimate concern to the public. Whenever such a privilege exists, then federal law is controlling.

On remand, the U.S. District Court judge applied the Ninth Circuit's definition of newsworthiness and granted Time's motion for summary judgment. As Judge Gordon Thompson, Jr., said:

> The facts themselves—putting out cigarettes in his [Virgil's] mouth and diving off stairs to impress women, hurting himself in order to collect unemployment so as to have time for body surfing . . ., and eating insects—are not sufficiently offensive to reach the very high level of offensiveness under *Virgil* to lose newsworthiness protection. The Restatement (Second) standard adopted in *Virgil* uses the term "morbid and sensational" and the Ninth Circuit endorsed these terms as "illustrative of the degree of offensiveness which should be present." . . . The above facts are generally unflattering and perhaps embarrassing, but they are simply not offensive to the degree of morbidity or sensationalism . . . [required by the Circuit Court]. . . .
>
> Even if the [Circuit] Court had reached the opposite conclusion that the facts disclosed were highly offensive, Time would still be entitled to summary judgment. For highly offensive facts . . . to be denied protection as newsworthy, the revelation of them must be "for its own sake." *Virgil, supra,* at 1129. Both parties agree that body surfing is a matter of legitimate public interest, and it cannot be doubted that Mike Virgil's unique prowess at the same time is also of legitimate public interest. Any reasonable person reading the *Sports Illustrated* article would have to conclude that the personal facts concerning Mike Virgil were included as a legitimate journalistic attempt to explain Virgil's extremely daring and dangerous style of body surfing. . . . There is no possibility that a juror could conclude that the personal facts were included for any inherent morbid, sensational, or curiosity appeal they might have.[80]

But in a footnote, the district court judge warned that an individual's entire private life does not become fair game for media exploitation under the guise of newsworthiness. The judge said:

> [I]n finding that the facts in this case were revealed in a "legitimate journalistic

attempt to explain Mike Virgil's extremely daring and dangerous style of body surfing" the Court is concluding that there is a rational and at least arguable close relationship between the facts revealed and the activity to be explained. This opinion should not be read as in any way endorsing no-holds-barred rummaging by the media through the private lives of persons engaged in activities of public interest under the pretense of elucidating that activity or the person's participation in it.

Howard v. Des Moines Register & Tribune Co. Public records, legitimate public concern, and newsworthiness were important considerations in the granting and affirming of summary judgment in the *Howard* case.[81] The case resulted from a 1976 *Des Moines Register* story which reported that plaintiff had been involuntarily sterilized while a resident of a county home. Plaintiff conceded that the article about involuntary sterilizations at government-operated homes was newsworthy, but asserted that identification of those sterilized was not. District Judge A.M. Critelli of Polk County dismissed the lawsuit by granting summary judgment to the publishing company, doing so on the basis that the story was newsworthy and not morbid or sensational, or prying for its own sake. The court rejected the public record and waiver of privacy arguments put forth by the newspaper. On appeal, the newspaper asked affirmation on the basis of the grounds rejected by the trial court as well as on the ground of newsworthiness. The Iowa Supreme Court affirmed the granting of summary judgment in 1979 for reasons put forth in Justice Mark McCormick's opinion. The U.S. Supreme Court denied certiorari.

Clearly the newspaper's investigation into abuses at a county home, including forced sterilization, is a matter of legitimate public interest, and is newsworthy by virtually any definition. But did plaintiff's name have to be used? Justice McCormick wrote:

> Assuming, as plaintiff agrees, the newspaper had a right to print an article which documented extrastatutory involuntary sterilizations at the Jasper County Home, the editors also had a right to buttress the force of their evidence by naming names. We do not say it was necessary for them to do so, but we are certain they had a right to treat the identity of victims of involuntary sterilizations as matters of legitimate public concern. . . . Moreover, at a time when it was important to separate fact from rumor, the specificity of the report would strengthen the accuracy of the public perception of the merits of the controversy.
>
> This is a far cry from embarrassing people by exposing their medical conditions or treatment when identity can add nothing to the probity of the account.[82]

As examples of reports of medical conditions or treatments, including identification of the persons involved which added nothing to the probity of the reports, McCormick cited a newspaper publication of an X ray showing a hemostat left in a woman's abdomen after surgery; a story and photograph of a plaintiff who lost weight despite constant eating; and a film of a woman undergoing Ceasarean section.[83] The test, said McCormick, in citing *Virgil,* "is whether revealing identity goes beyond the giving of information and becomes a morbid and sensational prying into private lives for its own sake."[84]

In his partial dissent, joined by three other justices, Justice Arthur A. McGiverin argued that a jury should have determined whether disclosure of the plaintiff's identity was morbid and sensational prying into her life. He also cited the California Supreme Court's statement in *Briscoe* (that "identification of the *actor* in reports of long-past crimes usually serves little independent public purpose") in arguing that his colleagues should have overruled the granting of the summary judgment motion based on newsworthiness.

Oliver Sipple Case. A $15 million invasion of privacy suit was filed by ex-Marine Oliver Sipple who is credited with deflecting the gun of a would-be assassin of President Gerald Ford on September 22, 1975. The suit named several newspapers and claimed that Sipple's brothers and sisters learned of his "homosexual orientation" because of published news reports. As a consequence, they "abandoned the plaintiff," the suit alleged. It also contended that the plaintiff was exposed to contempt and ridicule and suffered great mental anguish, embarrassment, and humiliation.

Undoubtedly there was public interest — legitimate interest — in Sipple as a result of his action which may have saved the President's life. But did that interest extend to his reported homosexuality, particularly since such information had no bearing on the bravery associated with the attempted assassination?

Among the seven newspapers named as codefendants, five were out-of-state papers. A three-judge California Court of Appeal, First Appellate Division, affirmed a lower court's quashing of service of process against the out-of-state newspapers because they did not solicit subscriptions in California, they had only minimal circulation in the state, and they derived only minimal advertising revenue from within the state. The ruling did not affect Sipple's suit against two in-state newspapers and the columnist who had disclosed Sipple's homosexuality. But in 1980 Superior Court Judge Ira Brown dismissed the lawsuit without opinion. Defendant newspapers had argued that the event was intensely newsworthy and that the story contained facts that were already known in the community[85]

On appeal, the Court of Appeal said plaintiff's homosexuality was well known prior to publications of the complained of articles and was therefore in the public domain, and the articles were newsworthy reports concerning matters of legitimate public interest.[86] The state supreme court denied review.[87]

In affirming the trial court's grant of summary judgment, the appellate court favorably cited *Restatement (Second) of Torts* Section 652D, comment d, that the privilege to publicize newsworthy matters is not only accorded by common law, but is one of constitutional dimension based upon the First Amendment.[88] A list of citations included *Cox Broadcasting, Time, Inc. v. Hill,* discussed later, *Virgil, Forsher,* and *Briscoe.* The court then noted that a motion for summary judgment in "First Amendment cases is an approved procedure because unnecessarily protracted litigation would have a chilling effect upon the exercise of First Amendment rights and because speedy resolution of cases involving free speech is desirable."

The state supreme court upheld the lower court's dismissal of the lawsuit principally because of the lower court's finding that Sipple's sexual orientation had been known to many people before newspapers revealed his homosexuality. The case, however, spurred considerable debate among news organizations concerning the right of privacy versus freedom of press.

Sipple died in 1989 at the age of 47. Prior to his death he had received treatment for schizophrenia, alcoholism, and other health problems.

Public Interest, Newsworthiness Defenses

Of the public disclosure cases cited above, *Virgil* and *Howard* involved public interest (or legitimate public interest) as defenses or reasons given by the courts in ruling as they did, and almost all of them involved the newsworthiness test (*Sidis, Briscoe, Virgil, Howard,* and *Sipple*).

Public Interest. The term "public interest" or "legitimate public interest" is crucial in the disposition of many libel and privacy lawsuits because a publication that is in the public interest implicates the First Amendment, rather than just common-law protection.

Wisconsin's right of privacy law, enacted in 1977, stipulates that any relief depends on whether there is "a legitimate public interest in the matter involved." If so, the privacy interest cannot prevail. But how does a journalist know if this element is present in a story being considered for publication? Some decisions will be easier than others, particularly when the stories involve public officials or public figures. But consider news accounts—some of them volunteered by the subjects themselves—concerning mastectomies performed on Betty Ford and Happy Rockefeller, a nonmalignant growth removed from Rosalynn Carter's breast, the publicity given to Joan Kennedy's problems, or reports about the marital difficulties of former Vice-President Spiro Agnew's son. Are such reports of genuine, or legitimate, public interest?

Can "public interest" overcome the public disclosure tort? The answer is not clear. The author of an article in *Yale Law Journal* noted this possibility and then argued against it, contending that a court cannot dispose of the issue by deciding, for example, that the name of an individual is "of legitimate public interest." If the court so decides, then it must balance the resulting First Amendment interest in publication of the name with protection of the privacy of the individual.[89]

The author's reference to disclosure or nondisclosure of the name of an individual relates to a suggestion he made for resolving a First Amendment dilemma conjured by the following example. If a woman suffered from the disease of compulsive overeating, such information could be published as news of public interest, but not her name or photograph since such identification would not be of significant value and would be unlikely to have any effect on the reader's political choices (Meiklejohn's self-governance or "political speech" theory).[90]

Such a suggestion will not gain many followers in the news media although the technique of nonidentification occasionally is used, especially during the early phases of crime stories when suspects are being sought or questioned but no formal charges have been filled, in rape cases, and in cases involving juvenile delinquents.

Newsworthiness. Professor Don Pember of the University of Washington wrote in 1972 that the defense of newsworthiness is the best weapon an editor has in staving off lawsuits. He continued:

> While newsworthiness is an elusive concept to legally define, jurists have granted that American readers have a broad range of tastes and interests. And as long as the press stays within this range of these tastes and interests, it is usually safe.[91]

Newsworthiness, he added, has three basic components: public interest, public figures, and public records. These three components figure in one way or another in virtually all of the cases reviewed in the public disclosure tort section of this book.

Some commentators have argued that the newsworthiness privilege is so broad that it virtually does away with the public disclosure tort.[92] The reason? Virtually all information published by the news media can be defined as newsworthy. If this approach were to become an accepted point of view by the judiciary, then the "true" Warren-Brandeis tort is destroyed. That the tort may be badly frayed at the seams is shown by *McNutt v. New Mexico State Tribune Co., Goldman v. Time, Inc.,* and some of the cases already reviewed.

In *McNutt,* a three-judge court of appeals affirmed a lower court's summary judgment for defendants following publication of the names and addresses of police officers involved in a gun battle with two members, both of whom were killed, of a group known as Black Berets.[93] The court said:

> As to what is "newsworthy," we are impressed with and hereby adopt the definition found in *Jenkins v. Dell Publishing Company, Inc.* 251 F.2d 447 (3rd Cir., 1958):
>
> "For present purposes news need be defined as comprehending no more than relatively current events such as in common experience are likely to be of public interest. . . . A large part of the matter which appears in newspapers and news magazines today is not published or read for the value or importance of the information it conveys. Some readers are attracted by shocking news. Others are titillated by sex in the news. . . . Few newspapers or news magazines would long survive if they did not publish a substantial amount of news on the basis of entertainment value of one kind or another. This may be a disturbing commentary upon our civilization, but it is nonetheless a realistic picture of society which courts shaping new juristic concepts must take into account. In brief, once the character of an item as news is established, it is neither feasible nor desirable for a court to make a distinction between news for information and news for entertainment in determining the extent to which publication is privileged."

In *Goldman,* the U.S. District Court in Northern California ruled in favor of *LIFE* on the basis of newsworthiness. Two Americans traveling abroad had been interviewed and photographed for a *LIFE* article which they claimed invaded their privacy by putting them in a false light by ascribing to them a "despicable set of beliefs, attitudes and ideas and a mode of living which would cause each plaintiff to be shunned and avoided by normal members of society." The judge ruled that the article was newsworthy and that recovery was barred unless plaintiffs could show actual malice. He said:

Plaintiffs take the position that only concrete, specific events can constitute the basis of a story entitled to the protection of newsworthiness. Here, they continue, *LIFE* merely "manufactured" a story . . . to bolster a preconceived idea about youth abroad. Youth, claim the plaintiffs, is simply too broad an issue to qualify as being newsworthy. . . .

We disagree. Certainly discrete events of current interest are entitled to the protection of newsworthiness, but so are matters of more general scope, such as unemployment, the problems of the aged, hospital care, and . . . organized crime.[94]

The judge concluded that the media must necessarily be afforded a great deal of latitude in selecting and presenting news because of the importance of the public's right to know.

This right to know is a part of modern First Amendment theory — one reason why the press should be protected against frivolous or ill-founded tort actions. First Amendment considerations also are reflected in false-light invasion of privacy cases.

FALSE-LIGHT TORT

This tort is related to the defamation tort in the sense that falsity is a key element of both. The difference is that a false-light invasion of privacy tort involves "nondefamatory" falsehoods, whereas libel involves "defamatory" falsehoods. Prosser said the false-light tort differs from the three other privacy torts because the interest protected is reputation with the same overtones of mental distress as in defamation. He even raised the question of whether any false libel could not be redressed upon the alternative ground of this privacy tort.

Time, Inc. v. Hill. In its 1967 decision in *Time, Inc., v. Hill,*[95] the U.S. Supreme Court reversed a $30,000 judgment against *LIFE* magazine and remanded for another trial. In a plurality opinion, Justice Brennan argued for an extension of the conditional privilege in *Times-Sullivan* (actual malice being the condition under which the First Amendment privilege is lost) to protect the news media from invasion of privacy lawsuits resulting from publication of nondefamatory falsehoods. The Court was badly divided in this case — five separate opinions and a 6–3 decision to reverse the $30,000 award to Hill.

The origin of this case goes back to 1952 when James J. Hill and his family were held captives for 20 hours in their home 10 miles outside of Philadelphia by three escaped convicts. Considerable news coverage followed this event and sometime afterward Hill moved his family to Connecticut reportedly to escape publicity. Later, a fictionalized version of the family's ordeal appeared in play and movie form, entitled "The Desperate Hours," which depicted the Hills as being terrorized when, in fact, they were courteously treated. *LIFE* decided to feature the play and even took actors to the family's former home so photographs could be taken for the February 28, 1955, issue. This renewed publicity led to the privacy action, rather than a libel action, because the events reported, although untrue, did not injure the family's good name or reputation. On the contrary, the family was made to appear heroic. In the suit, Hill claimed that *LIFE* had traded on the family's name without consent, thereby violating the Civil Rights Law (the only statutory basis for such a suit in New York).

The first trial in New York ended in a jury award of $50,000 general damages and $25,000 punitive damages, but upon review the New York Court of Appeals ordered a new trial because it thought the award excessive, although it did not dispute the invasion of privacy finding. In its ruling, the court stressed the fictionalization of the event for commercial purposes.

A new trial ended in the award of $30,000 general damages and the case went to the U.S. Supreme Court—the first of its kind involving the news media and a claimed right of privacy. Justice Brennan was joined by Justices Stewart and White in his plurality opinion. Justices Black, Douglas, and Harlan concurred in the result, but not for the reasons given by Brennan. Earlier the *Times-Sullivan* standard had been advanced by *LIFE* attorneys but rejected by the New York courts. Before applying the standard, Brennan, who had authored the famous *Times-Sullivan* opinion in 1964, took note of the following statement by the New York Court of Appeals.

> The free speech which is encouraged and essential to the operation of a healthy government is something quite different from an individual's attempts to enjoin publication of a fictitious biography of him. No public interest is served by protecting the dissemination of the latter. We perceive no constitutional infirmities in this respect.

To which Justice Brennan replied:

> If this is meant to imply that proof of knowing or reckless falsity is not essential to a constitutional application of the statute in these cases, we disagree with the Court of Appeals. We hold that the constitutional protections for speech and press preclude the application of the New York statute to redress false reports of matters of public interest in the absence of proof that the defendant published the report with knowledge of its falsity or in reckless disregard of the truth.

Material and substantial falsification, constituting actual malice, was necessary to overcome First Amendment protection for the *LIFE* article because it contained information of public interest (the opening of a new play), said Brennan.

Justices Black and Douglas would have been even more protective of the news media than the plurality, with Douglas commenting that a fictionalized treatment of the event would be as much in the public domain as a watercolor of the assassination of a public official. Thus, to Douglas, talk of any right of privacy in such a context was irrelevant.

Justice Harlan concurred in part and dissented in part. He argued for a negligence test, rather than the use of the *Times-Sullivan* standard, particularly in a false-light injury of a private individual. The logic he employed in this 1967 opinion would be reflected in his dissenting opinion in the 1971 libel case, *Ro-*

senbloom v. Metromedia, discussed previously, which ultimately a majority of the Court would adopt in *Gertz v. Welch* (1974).

Justice Abe Fortas, joined by Chief Justice Warren and Justice Tom Clark, dissented insofar as remanding for a new trial. In their judgment, the requisite fault existed and no new trial was needed. There is some uncertainty as to whether the fictionalization was such that it reached the *Garrison*-type falsity, but Fortas seemed to be saying that this was so. Fortas would have no hesitancy in applying the *Times-Sullivan* rule to the false-light cases which involved matters of public interest or political personalities, but he did not believe that solicitude for the First Amendment compelled the Court to deny to a state the right to provide a remedy for reckless falsity which injured a private family for no purpose except for dramatic interest and commercial appeal. Brennan, of course, said that the opening of a Broadway play was a matter of public interest.

Although the Court sent the case back to be tried under the libel formula of *Times-Sullivan,* Hill decided not to continue the lawsuit. After twice having the case tried under the state's Civil Rights Law, and then undergoing the cost of appeals — all of this occurring during a span of more than 10 years — he said he could not afford the additional cost that would have been involved. Not until 1974, in *Cantrell v. Forest City Publishing Co.,* discussed later, was an "authoritative" opinion given that Hill could have succeeded in overcoming the knowing or reckless falsity hurdle if he had but persisted with his lawsuit. In an opinion for a near-unanimous court in *Cantrell,* Justice Stewart said that "the jury could have reasonably concluded from the evidence in the *Hill* case that *LIFE* had engaged in knowing falsehood or had recklessly disregarded the truth in stating in the article that 'the story re-enacted' the Hill family's experience. . . ."[96]

The *Hill* case, pockmarked with various opinions by the Supreme Court justices, set off verbal fireworks among legal scholars. Since the decision came four years before *Rosenbloom* and seven years before *Gertz,* would it be applied to libel cases? And because *Hill* involved a matter of public interest, would it make any difference if a private figure was involved? Would *Hill* even be applied, given the plurality opinion by Brennan and the differences among the Court members? These questions seem to have been largely resolved. First, developments in libel law have answered questions about the relationship of *Hill,* if any, to libel law. Second, the majority of jurisdictions that had decided the issue by 1988 have followed the rule put forth in *Hill,* according to the Oklahoma Supreme Court which ruled that a private figure must prove actual malice to win false-light damages.[97] Only three jurisdictions, said the Oklahoma court, have concluded that because of the strong similarity between a false-light claim and a defamation claim, the negligence standard allowed by *Gertz* in private figure actions should replace the actual malice standard put forth in *Hill.* The three jurisdictions to that time were the U.S. Courts of Appeal for the District of Columbia and Fifth Circuits and West Virginia's highest court.[98]

Messner, Inc. v. Warren E. Spahn. About the same time that the *Hill* case was making its way through the courts, another false-light case was being adjudicated, this one also involving fictionalization.

Messner, Inc. v. Warren E. Spahn[99] involved years of litigation and wound up being dismissed in a memorandum decision of the Supreme Court in 1969 after the parties reached an out-of-court settlement.

Spahn, a famous baseball pitcher, filed an action under the New York Civil Rights Law to halt publication of an unauthorized biography. The Supreme Court for the County of New York (a lower court) issued an injunction in 1964 against the book publisher, Messner, Inc., to prevent sale of the book to the public and Spahn was awarded $10,000 in damages. The New York Court of Appeals affirmed, holding that fictionalization of a biography had stripped away First Amendment protection for the book and exposed it to action under the state law, although ordinarily such a biography would not have been included within the meaning of Sections 50–51 because of Spahn's status as a *newsworthy* figure. In its 7–0 decision, the state's highest court said:

> In short, the statute prohibits invasions of privacy for purposes of advertising or trade. Book publication is a trade like any other, except that its intellectual value to society is uniquely great and vital to civilization. To the extent that freedom of the press in the ultimate interest of the public's right to factual knowledge protects the publication of the factual and historical, the publication is exempt from the proscriptions of the statute. Moreover, this exemption extends to . . . secondary uses of the primary news or cultural or historical publications . . . [I]f the publication, however, . . . is neither factual nor historical, the statute applies, and if the subject is a living person his written consent must be obtained.

Messner appealed and the U.S. Supreme Court, in a memorandum decision in 1967, ordered reconsideration in the light of its then-recent *Hill* decision.[100] Accordingly, in a 4–1 opinion later that year, the state's highest court reaffirmed its original determination in the case. The court, in an opinion by Judge Kenneth B. Keating, declared that the requirements of *Times-Sullivan* and *Hill* had been met, noting that the trial court had found "gross errors of fact." The court also noted that the research undertaken by the author of the biography "amounted, primarily, to nothing more than newspaper and magazine clippings, the authenticity of which the author rarely, if ever, attempted to check out."[101]

The lone dissenter, Judge Francis Bergan, urged an alternative action: return the case to the trial court and let a decision rest on the plaintiff's showing of "reckless disregard of the truth" against which, the judge noted, taking a quote from Brennan's opinion in *Hill,* "the constitutional guarantees can tolerate sanctions."

Whether "gross errors of fact" met the *Times-Sullivan* requirement is unknown because of the out-of-court disposition of the case. In fact, between 1967 (*Hill* and *Spahn*) and its *Cantrell v. Forest City Publishing Co.* decision in 1974, the Court had little to say about the right of privacy when balanced against the free press guarantee.[102]

Cantrell v. Forest City Publishing Co. In 1973 a three-judge panel of the U.S. Court of Appeals unanimously reversed a $60,000 invasion of privacy verdict against the *Cleveland Plain Dealer.*[103] In its ruling, the panel showed sympathy for the California Supreme Court's *Briscoe* decision while, at the same time, holding that judgments about newsworthiness must remain primarily a function of the publisher.

The facts in *Cantrell* showed that a reporter and a photographer for the *Plain Dealer,* both off-duty and operating as freelancers, went to Point Pleasant, West Virginia, about five months after 44 persons lost their lives when a bridge over the Ohio River collapsed. Among the victims was Melvin Aaron Cantrell. The journalists did a follow-up magazine supplement feature on the Cantrell family which was published in the August 4, 1968, issue of the *Plain Dealer.*

There was a question of whether the newsmen had been invited into the house. Mrs. Cantrell was not at home at the time, and one of the Cantrell children testified that the newsmen did not ask permission to enter the home nor were they asked to leave; however, none of the children objected to being photographed.

The story, according to the appellate court, contained a number of inaccuracies and implied that Mrs. Cantrell was present in her home when the journalists were there. Five photographs were printed depicting the home as dirty and the children poorly clothed and untidy.

The original complaint had alleged intrusion, unreasonable publicity about the Cantrells' private lives, and false light. In addition, a libel action was filed. The intrusion portion of the complaint was not presented to the jury. On appeal, an effort was made to restore this part of the complaint, but the appellate court rejected such consideration on the ground that "this was not the theory on which the case was tried in the district court."

The court pointed out that the two newsmen "may have been guilty of trespass against the property of the Cantrells," but that the grievance complained of in the action "lies in the claim that the publication of the article, not the physical intrusion [unlike the *Dietemann* case], damaged the plaintiffs."

With the focus shifted to "false light," the appellate court held that actual malice had to be found.

The appellate court therefore reversed on the ground that the jury had not been properly instructed in that it must find "actual malice" in order to award damages. Mrs. Cantrell appealed, and the U.S. Supreme Court, by an 8–1 vote, held that the jury had been properly instructed. It ordered reinstatement of the $60,000 jury award with only Douglas dissenting.

Although the case hinged on the correctness or incorrectness of jury instructions, Justice Stewart's opinion for the Court is instructive in several ways despite the narrow issue on which reversal was based. The Court concluded that there was sufficient evidence to support a finding of reckless falsity against the reporter and the publishing company, but not against the photographer.

As justification for such a conclusion, Stewart said:

There was no dispute during the trial that [Joseph] Eszterhas [the reporter], who did not testify, must have known that a number of the statements in the feature story were untrue. In particular, his article plainly implied that Mrs. Cantrell had been present during his visit to her home and that Eszterhas had observed her "wear(ing) the same mask of non-expression she wore (at her husband's) funeral." These were "calculated falsehoods," and the jury was plainly justified in finding that Eszterhas had portrayed the Cantrells in a false light through knowing or reckless untruth.[104]

The same could not be said of the photographs which were truthful representations.

As for the publishing company, the doctrine of *respondeat superior* was applied in holding that the company was liable for knowing or reckless falsity on the theory that the reporter was acting within the scope of his employment when he performed the acts or acquired the information that resulted in the lawsuit.

Although the knowing or reckless falsity test was applied in *Cantrell,* this case is not definitive in terms of the standard to be applied to false-light privacy claims by private figures. The reason, according to Justice Stewart, is that none of the parties in *Cantrell* objected to the trial judge's jury instruction that knowing or reckless falsity had to be found. Stewart continued:

> Consequently, this case presents no occasion to consider whether a State may constitutionally apply a more relaxed standard of liability for a publisher or broadcaster of false statements injurious to a private individual under a false-light theory of invasion of privacy, or whether the constitutional standard announced in *Time, Inc. v. Hill* applies to all false light cases. Cf. *Gertz v. Welch, Inc.* . . . Rather, the sole question that we need decide is whether the Court of Appeals erred in setting aside the jury's verdict.[105]

As noted earlier, most jurisdictions that have addressed the issue prior to 1988 applied *Hill* to false-light suits although a number of states have even refused to recognize a false-light invasion of privacy action. The states are Missouri, North Carolina, Ohio, Utah, Virginia, and Wisconsin. In addition, it is unknown if these states recognize the tort: Alaska, Arizona, Hawaii, Massachusetts, Minnesota, Mississippi, Montana, and North Dakota.

The North Carolina Supreme Court made such a decision in *Renwick v. News and Observer* (1984), saying, in part:

> Two basic concerns argue against the recognition of a separate tort of false light invasion of privacy. First, any right to recover for a false light invasion of privacy will often either duplicate an existing right of recovery for libel or slander or involve a good deal of overlapping with such rights. Second, the recognition of a separate tort of false light invasion of privacy, to the extent it would allow recovery beyond that permitted in actions for libel and slander, would tend to add to the tension already existing between the First Amendment and the law of torts in cases of this nature.[106]

The court also believed that the conditions which led Warren and Brandeis to argue for an invasion of privacy tort in 1890 — namely, yellow journalism — "have . . . to some extent subsided."

As the court put it:

> . . . Most modern journalists employed in print, television or radio journalism now

receive training in ethics and journalism entirely unheard of during the era of "yellow journalism." As a general rule journalists simply are more responsible and professional today than history tells us they were in that era. Our recognition of these facts is entitled to some weight in deciding the question before us, even though we are completely aware that nothing in the First Amendment mandates that members of the news media be responsible or professional.[107]

But as Justice Louis B. Meyer pointed out in his dissent to that part of the opinion that rejected a false-light tort recognition for North Carolina, the *Restatement (Second) of Torts* Section 652E has significantly tightened the elements necessary to a successful false-light tort action.[108] The *Restatement* provides:

> One who gives publicity to a matter concerning another that places the other before the public in a false light is subject to liability to the other for invasion of his privacy, if (a) the false light in which the other was placed would be highly offensive to a reasonable person, and (b) the actor had knowledge of or acted in reckless disregard as to the falsity of the publicized matter and the false light in which the other would be placed.

The two major hurdles facing a plaintiff in a false-light action, as cited in the *Restatement,* are the "highly offensive" and knowing falsity requirements. Tough hurdles, indeed!

APPROPRIATION OR MISAPPROPRIATION TORT

The leading case in the appropriation tort area — or misappropriation, as it is sometimes called — is *Pavesich v. New England Life Insurance Co.,* in which a Georgia court in 1905 recognized a cause of action for invasion of privacy in connection with the defendant insurance company's use of plaintiff's name in an endorsement without permission.[109] The use of a person's name or likeness for commercial purposes, such as in advertisements, without that person's express or implied consent (and the former is preferable), constitutes an actionable tort. New York and California statutory laws are the most concrete examples of the legal prohibition of appropriation, but virtually all jurisdictions recognize an action for such a wrong. The New York Civil Rights Law Sections 50–51, prohibits such appropriation, and it was under this law that both the *Hill* and *Spahn* cases were brought, the theory being that extensive fictionalization constituted an appropriation for commercial purposes.

Youssoupoff v. CBS, Inc. The use of a person's name or likeness for *news* purposes falls outside the appropriation tort's reach. Generally, stories or programs that have educational or historical value cannot be the basis for an appropriation tort. In New York, such programs fall outside the meaning of Sections 50–51, as demonstrated in *Youssoupoff v. CBS, Inc.,* in which the state's highest court, like the lower Supreme Court for the County of New York, denied summary judgment in 1963 when asked to declare that the CBS program, *If I Should Die,* violated the state statute.[110] The program had recounted the murder in Russia of the infamous Rasputin. Prince Youssoupoff, living in Paris at the time of the suit, admitted killing Rasputin to end his influence over the czarina, but the prince contended that the broadcast was made for the purposes of trade, in violation of Section 50, without his consent. To facilitate the summary judgment motion, the plaintiff accepted CBS's claim of historical accuracy, so truth or falsity was not at issue.

The county court, in denying the motion, said there could be no recovery under the statute for use of a person's name or photograph "in connection with an article of current news or immediate public interest" and that, as a general rule, articles which were not strictly news, but which satisfied an educational need, such as "stories of distant places, tales of historic personages and events, the reproduction of items of past news," were not within the ban of the statute.

Meeropol v. Nizer and Doubleday & Co., Inc. More recently, in *Michael and Robert Meeropol v. Louis Nizer and Doubleday & Co., Inc.,* Judge Harold R. Tyler, Jr. of the U.S. District Court for the Southern District of New York entered summary judgment for the defendants in both the libel and privacy actions brought by the natural children of Julius and Ethel Rosenberg.[111] The Rosenbergs were executed in 1953 for conspiring to transmit atomic bomb information to Russia. Nizer wrote a book, *The Implosion Conspiracy,* about the trial and subsequent events, and the Rosenbergs' sons brought suit. In his 1974 ruling, Judge Tyler disposed of the libel action by applying the actual malice test to certain passages in the book. Concerning the privacy action brought under the Civil Rights Law, the judge said the book dealt with matters of public interest, and that even if the publication were not constitutionally protected, the claim of an invasion of privacy could not be sustained for the following reasons:

1. Members of the family of a deceased person cannot sue for invasion of privacy of the deceased person (48 of the 77 passages complained of referred to the deceased parents).
2. Plaintiffs were not named in the book and therefore cannot recover for the remaining 29 passages. "Nowhere in the book," said the judge, "are they referred to as Meeropol, the name they have used for the last 20 years. This missing element renders the claim for invasion of privacy defective."
3. There was no extreme situation involving abusive, physical intrusion.
4. The state's privacy statute does not apply to a historical account of a newsworthy event or individual unless the account is fictional, and minor fictionalization is not sufficient to support a privacy action.
5. There are no intimate details which would tend to outrage public tolerance—nothing repugnant to one's sense of decency.

The plaintiffs sought to circumvent the limitations of the Civil Rights Law by claiming a new common law right to privacy which they said was established by *Galella v. Onassis,* discussed previously, in which a photographer was enjoined from taking photographs within a certain distance of Jackie Kennedy Onassis even when she or her children were in public. Judge Tyler said that even assuming that *Galella* recognized a right of privacy beyond the statutory grant, the decision was limited to an extreme situation involving abusive, physical intrusion which was not present in *Meeropol.* In fact, said Judge Tyler, the courts in New York have consistently held that an action for invasion of privacy is exclusively statutory.[112]

In a case involving Joe Namath, the professional football quarterback sought $250,000 in compensatory and $2 million in punitive damages from *Sports Illustrated* for a claimed invasion of privacy under the Civil Rights Law. The action stemmed from the unauthorized use of photographs of Namath in connection with the magazine's promotion of itself. The Supreme Court for New York County dismissed the action because (1) the photographs were newsworthy and were used in the promotional ads to establish the news content of *Sports Illustrated,* and (2) the cause of action was deprivation of income from a property right (Namath's testimonials and endorsements having brought him more than $200,000 in 1972), rather than one of invasion of privacy.[113]

Compare the results in *Namath* with the $300,000 award to actress Isabella Adjani in her lawsuit against Time, Inc. Her photograph had been used without permission in an advertising campaign on behalf of *Time* magazine, appearing in such publications as the *New York Times* Sunday magazine and *Women's Wear Daily.*

Time, Inc., and its advertising agency, Young and Rubicam, argued that they did not need the actress's permission to use the photograph because it had previously been used with a news story announcing that she would appear in the movie *Ishtar* with Dustin Hoffman and Warren Beatty. But the U.S. District Court judge, Ronald Lew, rejected this contention, saying that the use of the photo suggested that the actress was endorsing the magazine.[114]

The $300,000 in damages was the judge's estimate of the fair market value for having used Adjani's image. He refused to assess punitive damages, saying that the actions of *Time* and the ad agency were not willful, deliberate, or malicious.

The actress's attorney, Bertram Fields, said he believed that the judge's verdict was the first time that a judgment had been entered against a publication for using one of its own previously published photographs in an advertisement promoting itself.

The case was tried in Los Angeles but the New York Civil Rights Law was controlling.

California, like New York, has legislatively incorporated the appropriation tort into law. Civil Code Section 3344, Subdivision (a), provides, in part, that "any person who knowingly uses another's name, photograph, or likeness, in any manner, for purposes of advertising products, merchandise, goods, or services, or for purposes of solicitation of purchases of products . . . without such person's prior consent . . . shall be liable for any damages sustained by the person . . . injured as a result thereof."

As analyzed by the California Court of Appeal (Second District), in *Eastwood v. Superior Court,* a common-law cause of action for appropriation may be pleaded by alleging (1) the defendant's use of the plaintiff's identity; (2) the appropriation of plaintiff's name or likeness to defendant's advantage, commercially or otherwise; (3) lack of consent; and (4) resulting injury.[115] But to plead the statutory remedy provided by Section 3344, there also must be an allegation of a knowing use of the plaintiff's name, photograph, or likeness for purposes of advertising or solicitation of purchases. Furthermore, Subdivision (d) of Section 3344 provides that the "use of a name, photograph, or likeness in connection with any news . . . shall not constitute a use for purpose of advertising or solicitation."

In *Eastwood,* the appellate court said plaintiff could succeed with his lawsuit if the conditions set forth above are met, if the article complained of is shown to be false, and if the newspaper published it with knowing or reckless falsity (the latter being a requirement for the false-light tort action when a matter of public interest is involved). Having said this, the court ordered a lower court to allow actor Clint Eastwood to amend the commercial appropriation complaint against the *National Enquirer.*

Eastwood had alleged false-light invasion of his privacy and commercial appropriation of his name, photograph, and likeness in connection with the *Enquirer's* publication of an article about the actor in its April 13, 1982, issue, titled "Clint Eastwood in Love Triangle with Tanya Tucker." In his false-light allegation, Eastwood asserted that information in the article was either knowingly false or in reckless disregard of the truth.

Eastwood also alleged that the *Enquirer* made a telecast advertisement in which it featured the actor's name and photograph and prominently mentioned the article. Also, on the cover of the *Enquirer* there appeared a picture of Eastwood and Tucker above the caption "Clint Eastwood in Love Triangle with Tanya Tucker." The *Enquirer* demurred to the second cause of action on the basis that the actor's name and photograph were not used to imply any endorsement of the *Enquirer,* and that they were used in connection with a news account.[116] The lower court sustained the demurrer without leave to amend, but the appellate court ordered that Eastwood be allowed to amend his second cause of action so he could allege knowing or reckless falsity.

The court stated that deliberate fictionalization of a person's personality constitutes commercial exploitation, and becomes actionable when presented to readers as if true when it is known to be false or is recklessly false.[117] Incidentally, the appellate court had no trouble in stating that the "purported romantic involvements of Eastwood with other celebrities" is a matter of public concern; but that alone does not rescue the information about Eastwood from being actionable.[118]

RIGHT OF PUBLICITY

In suing *Sports Illustrated* for invasion of privacy what Joe Namath really was seeking to protect was a right of publicity—a right to make money out of his prominence. The same was true in Adjani's lawsuit against Time, Inc. As the court noted in *Namath,* such a right may fall more properly in the realm of property rights rather than privacy. To a lesser extent the *Spahn* and *Eastwood* cases also involve, in part, the right of publicity. In fact, there is still a question whether appropriation (or misappropriation) and right of publicity involve more than one tort.

Right of publicity cases are of rather recent origin—the first being *Haelan Laboratories, Inc. v. Topps Chewing Gum, Inc.* (1953).[119] But such litigation is "beginning to run rampant" across the United States, an attorney warned in 1984.[120]

The only appropriation or right of publicity case to be decided by the U.S. Supreme Court is *Zacchini v. Scripps-Howard* (1977). In his lawsuit, Hugo Zacchini, the "human cannonball," complained that a Cleveland TV station owned by Scripps-Howard Broadcasting Company had usurped his right when it showed a newsfilm of him being shot from a cannon. The trial court granted Scripps-Howard summary judgment, but the Ohio Court of Appeals reversed, saying that the "total appropriation of a performer's act by videotaping and reshowing without the performer's permission is an invasion of the property right which will give rise to a cause of action for damages based either on conversion [of property] or the invasion of the performer's common law copyright."

In turn, the Ohio Supreme Court reversed by a 6–1 vote.[121] The majority decided the case solely on the common law's sanctions against appropriation, not on the basis of copyright law which is designed to foster and protect literary and artistic expression. The court concluded that the TV station was privileged to report Zacchini's performance in a newscast because the matter was of legitimate public interest.

But the U.S. Supreme Court reversed in a 5–4 decision in 1977.[122] In his opinion for the Court, Justice White said the First Amendment does not immunize the news media's broadcast of a performer's *entire act* without his consent. White noted that Ohio has recognized what may be the strongest case for a "right of publicity"—involving not the appropriation of an entertainer's reputation to enhance the attractiveness of a commercial product, but the appropriation of the very activity by which the entertainer acquired his reputation in the first place. Although stating that entertainment enjoys First Amendment protection, and that entertainment can be important news, the Court majority apparently was swayed by White's view that "neither the public nor . . . [Scripps-Howard] will be deprived of the benefit of petitioner's performance as long as his commercial stake in his act is appropriately recognized."

Justice Powell, joined by Brennan and Marshall, dissented, saying that the "Court's holding that the station's ordinary news report may give rise to substantial liability has disturbing implications, for the decision could lead to a degree of media self-censorship." He recommended a different line of analysis in keeping with the First Amendment, saying:

> . . . Rather than begin with a quantitative analysis of the performer's behavior—is this or is this not his entire act?—we should direct initial attention to the actions of the news media: what use did the station make of the film footage? When a film is used, as here, for a routine portion of a regular news program, I would hold that the First Amendment protects the station from a "right of publicity" or "appropriation" suit, absent a strong showing by the plaintiff that the news broadcast was a subterfuge or cover for private or commercial exploitation.

Justice Stevens dissented because it was unclear if the Ohio Supreme Court had relied on the federal Constitution in deciding the case. He would have remanded for clarification by the state court.

White's opinion applies only to those states with "right of publicity" laws and only to news coverage of an *entire* act or performance. White stressed that states could, if they wished, pass laws immunizing the press from any "right of publicity." However, the rule applied by the majority is the same, White said, as that contained in copyright laws which prevent the media from publishing or broadcasting entire works or performances without compensating the authors or performers.

On remand, the Ohio Supreme Court decided that the state Constitution did not protect the media defendant. It remanded the case for trial and for assessment of damages if liability were established.[123]

Justice White noted that states could pass laws immunizing the press from "right of publicity" lawsuits. But the opposite may be happening. A bill establishing a right of publicity for public figures for a 50-year period following their death was signed into law in Kentucky in 1984. The law recognizes that public figures have property rights in their names and likenesses which are entitled to protection from commercial exploitation. Further, although the traditional right of privacy terminates upon the death of the person asserting it, the state law prohibits the use of the public figure's name or likeness for a period of 50 years from the date of death unless the written consent of the executor or administrator of the estate is first obtained.

Florida, Nebraska, Oklahoma, Utah, and Virginia have enacted similar legislation.

***Price v. Hal Roach Studios, Inc.* (1975).** The right to control publicity about someone who is dead was the principal issue in *Price v. Hal Roach Studios, Inc.* in which the widows of Stan Laurel and Oliver Hardy sued to stop unauthorized use of the actors' names and likenesses and to recover damages for alleged unauthorized use.[124] The U.S. District Court for the Southern District of New York entered a permanent injunction against defendant's continued use of the comedians' names and likenesses and ruled that actual damages could be recovered.

In discussing the case, Judge Charles E. Stewart said that while much confusion is generated by the notion that the right of publicity emanates from the classic right of privacy, the two rights are clearly separable. He wrote, "The protection from intrusion upon an individual's privacy, on the one hand, and protection from appropriation of some element of an individual's personality for commercial exploitation, on the other, are different in theory and in scope." He proceeded to differentiate between them, as follows:

> In New York, there is a statutory right which protects living persons from commercial exploitation of their names and pictures by others without their written consent. This statutory right, however, is deemed a "right of privacy" and is predicated upon the classic right of privacy's theoretical basis which is to prevent injury to feelings. The Second Circuit, in rejecting an argument to restrict one's legal interest in the publication of his picture to such a so-called "right of privacy," stated:
>
> > We think that, in addition to and independent of that right of privacy (which in New York derives from statute), a man has a right in the publicity value of his photographs, i.e., the right to grant the exclusive privilege of publishing his picture. . . . Whether it be labelled a "property" right is immaterial; for here, as often elsewhere, the tag "property" simply symbolizes the fact that courts enforce a claim which has pecuniary worth.[125]

As to the right of publicity terminating upon the death of the individual, the District Court cited *Lugosi v. Universal Pictures Co.* (1972) in which it was stated:

> Bela Lugosi's interest or right in his likeness and appearance as Count Dracula was a property right of such character and substance that it did not terminate with his death but descended to his heirs.[126]

As Judge Stewart pointed out:

> The present case is easier to decide than *Lugosi* since we deal here with actors portraying themselves and developing their own characters rather than fictional characters which have been given a particular interpretation by an actor.

Lugosi v. Universal Pictures. Judge Stewart's differentiation of *Lugosi* from the case he decided proved prophetic because the California Court of Appeal, Second District, reversed the trial court's award of damages to *Lugosi* plaintiffs and the state supreme court in 1979 affirmed. In its affirmance, the supreme court adopted as its own the opinion of Presiding Justice Lester Roth of the Court of Appeal.[127] In essence, the two appellate courts held that the right to exploit name and likeness is personal to the artist and must be exercised by him, if at all, *during his lifetime.*

In a concurring opinion, Justice Stanley Mosk wrote that many actors, including Lon Chaney and John Carradine, have portrayed Count Dracula. Lugosi, either during his lifetime, or his estate, did not own the exclusive right to exploit the fictional character created by author Bram Stoker in 1897, said Mosk, any more than Gregory Peck, or his heirs, possess exclusivity to General MacArthur or George C. Scott to General Patton. Mosk, however, distinguished between merely playing a role, such as in Lugosi's case, and original creation of a figure. He wrote:

> Thus Groucho Marx just being Groucho Marx, with his moustache, cigar, slouch and leer, cannot be exploited by others. Red Skelton's variety of self-devised roles would appear to be protectible, as would the unique personal creations of Abbott and Costello, Laurel and Hardy and others of that genre. Indeed the court in a case brought by the heirs of Stanley Laurel and Oliver Hardy . . . observed: . . . "we deal here with actors portraying themselves and developing their own characters. . . ."[128]

That the law is still unsettled is demonstrated by the following cases:

■ The U.S. Supreme Court declined to review a case involving Elvis Presley's right to publicity after Presley had died. The Court's denial of certiorari came in *Pro Arts, Inc. v. Factors, Etc.*[129] The Second Circuit U.S. Court of Appeals had ruled that Presley's right to publicity was a tangible property right that survived his death and could be assigned and transferred.[130] The Second Circuit panel said that unauthorized publication of a Presley "memorial poster" did not concern a newsworthy event and therefore was not constitutionally privileged.

A few months later, the Sixth Circuit U.S. Court of Appeals reached a different conclusion in *Memphis Development v. Factors, Etc.* (1980), deciding that an entertainer's right to publicity—even when exploited during the person's lifetime—does not survive the person's death and is not inheritable.[131] The U.S. Supreme Court denied certiorari. To overcome this decision, Tennessee passed a law in 1984 that recognizes a descendible right of publicity.

Next, the Second Circuit returned to the fray by striking down a permanent injunction against the sale or distribution of the Presley "memorial poster." Instead, it adopted the Sixth Circuit's view in *Memphis Development* that Tennessee law does not recognize a descendible right of publicity.[132] Then a three-judge panel of the Second Circuit denied a rehearing in a 2–1 vote in 1983.[133] The dissenter, Judge Walter R. Mansfield, said lower Tennessee courts are in dispute on the question of a descendible right of publicity.[134] The Supreme Court again denied review.[135]

But when the laws in other states are applied to the question of a descendible right of publicity for Presley, the results are different. In three separate cases—one in New Jersey and two in New York—U.S. District Courts ruled that the famed singer did have such a right.[136]

And in 1987, the Sixth Circuit U.S. Court of Appeals did an about-face by adopting a Tennessee court's holding that a celebrity's right of publicity is descendible under the state's common law. It did so in *Elvis Presley Enterprises v. Elvisly Tours* (1987).[137] The court explained its change in position by saying:

The Court of Appeals of Tennessee (Middle Section at Nashville) has now declared that a celebrity's right to publicity was and is descendible under the common law of Tennessee. The Tennessee court expressly rejected our holding in *Memphis Development*. In a diversity case we may not reject a ruling on the state law by an appellate court of the state unless there is an indication that the state's highest court would decide otherwise. . . . We can find no indication here that it would.

■ In another case decided by a Second Circuit panel, the court ruled that a musical play which reproduced the appearances and comedic styles of the Marx Brothers did not violate the deceased entertainers' rights of publicity.[138] In applying California law to this diversity action, the panel reversed a U.S. District Court ruling.[139] Whether California recognizes a descendible right is unclear, said the panel in 1982, but it is clear that any such right would not be infringed by an original play using a celebrity's likeness and comedic style.

■ In Georgia, the state supreme court ruled that a person—whether a private or public figure—possesses a descendible right of publicity even if such a right was not exploited during the person's lifetime. The decision in *Martin Luther King Jr. Center for Social Change v. American Heritage Products, Inc.*, halted the unauthorized promotion and sale of a plastic bust of the late Dr. King.[140]

Some courts, as in *Lugosi*, have held that the right of publicity must have been exploited commercially during a person's lifetime for it to be descendible. This was the crucial factor in a dispute over the use of Clyde Beatty's name in conjunction with another circus's name. The Eleventh Circuit U.S. Court of Appeals decided in 1983 that Beatty had exploited this right during his lifetime and the court interpreted *Lugosi* such that California law permits the right to descend in such a circumstance.[141]

■ In a case involving the late mystery writer, Agatha Christie, a U.S. District Court judge for the Southern District of New York said the writer's right of publicity survived her death. The statement came in the combined cases of *Hicks v. Casablanca Records* and *Hicks v. Ballantine Books*. However, Judge Lawrence W. Pierce dismissed the lawsuits in ruling that a fictional account of a true incident in the writer's life cannot be restrained by the writer's heir and assignees.[142]

A book and a motion picture, each entitled "Agatha," presented fictional accounts of the mysterious disappearance of the famous English writer for 11 days in 1926. She simply reappeared and never offered an explanation as to where she had been. Since neither libel nor invasion of privacy survives the death of the individual, the two lawsuits were based on the developing legal doctrine of right of publicity.

■ In *Johnny Carson v. Here's Johnny,* a Sixth Circuit U.S. Court of Appeals ruled 2–1 that a corporation that sold "Here's Johnny" portable toilets violated *Tonight* show host Johnny Carson's right of publicity.[143]

In issuing an injunction, the court said the manufacturer, by using the "Here's Johnny" phrase together with the slogan, "The World's Foremost Commodian," intentionally appropriated Carson's identity for commercial exploitation.

The U.S. District Court for the Eastern District of Michigan had dismissed the complaint because the defendant had not used Carson's name or likeness—a reason supported by the dissenting Circuit Court judge, Cornelia Kennedy, who argued that the phrase, "Here's Johnny," is "more akin to an idea or concept of introducing an individual than an original protectable fixed expression of that idea," and therefore it should not be entitled to right of publicity protection.

"The majority's grant . . . of a publicity right in the phrase 'Here's Johnny' takes this phrase away from the public domain," said Kennedy.[144]

■ A U.S. District Court in California awarded rock star Cher $663,234 in damages ($325,000 exemplary, $200,000 special, and $138,234 general) in a right of publicity lawsuit against Forum International, Ltd., Penthouse International, Ltd., News Group Publications, Inc., and freelance writer Fred Robbins.[145]

The court ruled that the willful and intentional misappropriation by the magazines and the author of Cher's name and likeness, through publication of an interview in a magazine other than *Forum* (the one Cher had expressly designated when she agreed to be interviewed) and through the use of advertisements and cover photographs falsely implying that the entertainer endorsed the magazine or that the interview was "exclusive," violated her right to publicity, the Lanham Act, and the California unfair competition law.

According to trial judge Manuel L. Real: Cher agreed to be interviewed for a cover story in *US Magazine*. Robbins was given the assignment and wrote the interview, but Cher did not approve of it and requested a new interview. *US* agreed. Robbins was aware of this development, but subsequently sold the interview to *Forum* without contacting Cher or seeking her consent, release, or authorization. Penthouse employees coordinate all circulation and advertising efforts of *Forum*. They placed a newspaper advertisement in at least 27 papers, and produced a radio commercial, utilizing Cher's name and/or likeness. The article appeared in the March 1981 issue of *Forum*.

The judge said that *Forum* and *Penthouse* published the cover of the magazine, the article, and advertisements with knowledge of their falsity and with knowledge that their usages were not authorized by Cher. Such actions were a "willful, knowing and intentional misappropriation of Cher's name and likeness, willful and knowing false statements of facts, and a blatant violation and conscious disregard for the rights of Cher."[146]

Robbins also sold the interview to News Group, according to the judge, for use as a two-part series in the weekly tabloid *Star*. The first article appeared March 17, 1981, titled "My Life, My Husband, and My

Many, Many Men." The *Star* heralded the series as an exclusive interview. Neither Robbins nor the *Star* asked Cher's consent for such usage.

The court cited *Lugosi v. Universal Pictures* for saying, "The right of a person to the use of his name and likeness is a right of value upon which plaintiff can capitalize by selling licenses."[147] Further, "A celebrity or other public figure has the right to control the publicity and establish conditions for the use of his or her name and likeness" when voluntarily giving an "exclusive interview" to a particular publication. "Any subsequent usage by the publication, or by a third party who has knowledge of the existence of any such conditions or controls, not in accordance with such delineations, and without the consent of the celebrity, is a wrongful appropriation of the commercial value of the celebrity's identity and right of publicity."[148]

The misrepresentation in the advertisements constituted a violation of the Lanham Act, said the judge.

As for the unfair competition, the California Business and Professional Code (§ 17200) makes unlawful "unfair, deceptive, untrue or misleading advertising." The judge termed as "unfair competition" the acts of Forum, Penthouse, and News Group. He cited *Zacchini v. Scripps-Howard* in saying that no social purpose is served by having defendants get for free some aspect of Cher that has market value for which they would normally pay.[149]

On appeal, the Ninth Circuit U.S. Court of Appeals vacated the $369,000 award against News Group Publications, Inc., publisher of the *Star,* and against Robbins. However, the award of $269,000 against *Forum* was upheld.[150] The Circuit Court, in applying the actual malice test put forth by Justice Brennan in *Time, Inc. v. Hill,* ruled that *Forum* had acted with knowing falsity or reckless disregard in publishing advertisements that allegedly falsely implied Cher's endorsement of the magazine. The court also determined that *Penthouse* had participated with *Forum* in the false advertising and therefore was liable, too.

Cher's lawyers had contended that although the singer could not prevent the *Star* from writing truthful articles about her, she had the right to control where her "exclusive interviews" were published. But the Ninth Circuit said that the *Star's* use of the headline, "Exclusive Series: Cher, My Life, My Husbands, and My Many, Many Men," in connection with the published interview, did not support a finding of knowing or reckless falsity.

On appeal, Cher contended that the Ninth Circuit improperly applied an actual malice test to the *Star.*[151] But the Supreme Court denied review.[152]

Look-Alikes Enjoined. Look-alikes are proliferating in advertisements. Case law will, too. Mrs. Jacqueline Kennedy Onassis succeeded in 1984 in obtaining a preliminary injunction under Section 51 of the New York Civil Rights Law that prohibits a look-alike from "masquerading" as her in an advertisement for Christian Dior clothing. The Supreme Court of New York County ruled that Section 50 of the state law prohibits "any representation" of a person for commercial purposes, including look-alikes.

The advertisement prepared by J. Walter Thompson Co. showed actresses Ruth Gordon and Shari Belafonte, TV personality Gene Shalit, a look-alike for Gen. Charles de Gaulle, and a model, Barbara Reynolds, who was the look-alike for Mrs. Onassis. In her lawsuit, Mrs. Onassis said the advertisement made it appear that she was a photographic model for Christian Dior and that this embarrassed her and infringed on her rights of privacy and publicity.

In granting the temporary injunction, Justice Edward Greenfield pointed out that there is no prohibition against a celebrity being mimicked or impersonated if it is clear that it is not actually the celebrity. But to pass off the look-alike as the actual person is prohibited, said the judge.

Just before the court's ruling, an advertising executive expressed the fear that if Mrs. Onassis won her suit it "would spell an end to satire in advertising and may put look-alikes and their current cottage industry out of business."[153]

The advertising agency contended that the advertisement was satirical or tongue-in-cheek.

Woody Allen was unsuccessful in his claim that his right of publicity had been violated by the use of a "look-alike" in a commercial by a clothing store, but he won summary judgment on his Lanham Act claim that the use of the "look-alike" created the likelihood of consumer confusion.[154]

The lawsuit, *Allen v. Men's World Outlet,* was based in part on New York's Civil Rights Law and on New York's common law of unjust enrichment.[155]

The U.S. District Court judge, in commenting on Allen's Civil Rights Law violation claim, said the "difficulty with this contention is that the statute by its terms extends protection only to the likenesses of *Allen,* and the Men's World photo is a photo of Phil Boroff."[156]

Because of the Lanham Act violation decision, the court did not try to consider the "novel and more interesting argument" that the disclaimer, in small type under the photo, would make it impossible for any reasonable person to find that the ad contained a portrait or picture of Allen.

SUMMARY

The principal influence in the emergence of a right of privacy was an 1890 article by Brandeis and Warren in which they postulated a general right to maintain an inviolate personality which involves one's thoughts, emotions, facial expressions except when the "public or general interest" required exposure, or when the person concerned had (1) renounced the right to live his or her life screened from the public, (2) been involved in matters privileged under the laws of libel, or (3) had given consent.

New York was the first state to enact a "privacy" law which prohibits the use of a person's name or likeness for commercial or trade purposes without that person's consent. Today, most states recognize some kind of privacy rights, either by common law, statute, or by constitution.

The U.S. Supreme Court recognized a right of privacy embedded in the penumbral rights contained in the Bill of Rights, doing so in *Griswold v. Connecticut* (1965). Tension between this constitutional right and the First Amendment can be seen in a number of cases beside *Griswold,* including *Cox Broadcasting Corp. v. Cohn* (1975), *Landmark Communications, Inc. v. Virginia* (1978) (see Chapter 8), and *Globe Newspapers Co. v. Superior Court* (1982). Generally, truthful and accurate information obtained from public judicial records or, in the case of *Landmark Communications,* truthful reports about a confidential judicial proceeding, cannot be prohibited or punished. This includes the divulgence of rape victims' or juvenile delinquents' identity when such information is obtained lawfully.

Because a "right of privacy" is so general, an analysis of case law by Dean Prosser led him to conclude that the law of privacy comprises four torts, not one: intrusion, public disclosure of embarrassing (but truthful) private facts, false light (information false, but not defamatory), and appropriation.

Of the four, the intrusion and appropriation torts are clearest in terms of what the press ought not to do. The media have no basis—constitutional or otherwise—to tortiously intrude upon a person's privacy; that is, when that person is secluded from the eyes and ears of the outside world. But a person or thing in public view generally is fair game for news purposes. Neither can the media use a person's name or likeness for commercial purposes, for example, advertising. The best defense in such instances is consent. Although some states recognize "implied consent" (answering a reporter's questions, posing for a photographer, and so forth), the best defense is to have a printed release form signed by the individual in question (express consent). These forms are available commercially and photographers, as well as newsmen in some circumstances, should use them if there is a suspicion of intrusion or appropriation. The refusal of a person to sign such a release forewarns media representatives of potentially dangerous situations.

And yet the only *absolute* right of privacy, vis-à-vis the press, may be an individual's right to refuse to be interviewed; or the right of those who wish to meet in private for personal or business reasons to exclude the media.[157] Even a person's home may be "invaded" by the press if the public interest is great enough, such as the commission of a crime where there would be great public interest.

The public disclosure tort—disseminating embarassing private, but truthful, information—is one of the principal "uncharted" dangers now confronting the news media in the invasion of privacy realm. This is also the tort about which Brandeis and Warren wrote. It involves the right of persons to shield their private affairs, thoughts, and emotions from an outsider's gaze. Truth is no defense if embarassing private facts are published, just as truth is no defense when wrongful means have been used to obtain information, or when that information is used for commercial purposes without permission.

The danger in connection with the public disclosure tort is the publication of private facts which, when made public, are offensive, or highly offensive, to a reasonable person.

Concerning the tort of intentional infliction of emotional distress, the U.S. Supreme Court ruled in *Falwell v. Hustler Magazine* (1988) that public officials and public figures must show actual malice if what was published was a matter of public concern.

The actual malice requirement also was used in connection with the false-light tort. Constitutional protection was provided for the media in Justice Brennan's plurality opinion for the Court in *Time, Inc. v. Hill* (1967). Plaintiffs bringing false-light actions had to show actual malice if the information that prompted the suit was a matter of public interest—the same First Amendment standard used three years earlier in a defamation case, *Times v. Sullivan*. Both *Hill* and *Times-Sullivan* involved matters of public interest (the opening of a New York play and civil rights). *Cantrell* (1974) left unanswered the question of whether states may impose greater standards of care on the media in connection with the false-light tort whenever publication pertains to private figures, but so far only three jurisdictions have applied the negligence standard to such lawsuits. The majority of those that have addressed this issue have followed *Hill*.

Newsworthiness is a defense to invasion of privacy actions, but it's not easy to define. Clearly it does not encompass everything that the news media make public.

Also involved in media defenses are public interest (and in some jurisdictions this means *legitimate* public interest), public official or public figure status, and/or public records. Combined or separately they help to provide the newsworthiness defense.

In connection with the appropriation or misappropriation tort, which is recognized by statute in 13 states and by case law in most others, newsworthiness and public interest are media defenses. In New York, fictionalization which rises to the level of "actual malice" (as required by *Hill*) constitutes a violation of the Civil Rights Law—the only statutory right of privacy recognized in the state.

Increasingly, a right of publicity, which is similar to, if not the same as, the right protected by the appropriation tort, is being delineated. In *Zacchini v. Scripps-Howard,* the U.S. Supreme Court ruled that the First Amendment does not protect the news media when a performer's entire act is used by the news media without prior consent. However, the ruling came in connection with a state—Ohio—which recognizes the right of publicity.

Whether the right survives to heirs, assignees, or one's estate is not fully resolved. Where an entertainer develops an original character, as Stan Laurel or Oliver Hardy did, courts have held that such a right survives the death of the creators. But where, as in *Lugosi v. Universal Pictures,* the entertainer exploited a fictional character created by someone else, such a right does not survive the entertainer's death.

Here are some danger signs for the news media to consider:

1. Use of methods to obtain information that either are illegal or that a reasonable person would find to be highly objectionable. Trespassing,

stealing, or intruding by electronic means into a home or office is not protected by the First Amendment (*Dietemann*).

2. Unauthorized use of a person's name or likeness for commercial purposes. Gross fictionalization or actual malice is a key element in determining if, say, a biography was written for "commercial purposes."
3. Publication of reports which shock or outrage a community's notions of decency or those of an average person, or which are grossly offensive. Gruesome photographs might be actionable on the grounds of gross offensiveness.
4. Dredging up facts about a person's past except where there's a continuing public interest in those facts.
5. Intentional infliction of emotional distress stemming from actual malice whenever public officials or public figures are involved. Private figures, as in libel, may not have to show actual malice.
6. Knowing or reckless falsity (false-light tort).

QUESTIONS IN REVIEW

1. Judge Thomas Cooley was among the first in America to assert that man has a right _____.
2. Brandeis and Warren wrote an article in 1890 which has been credited with providing the main impetus toward legal recognition of a right to privacy. They would have excluded from such a right matters of _____.
3. True or False: Brandeis and Warren believed that truth was no defense to an invasion of privacy stemming from public disclosure of embarrassing private facts.
4. The first *statutory* recognition of a right to privacy came in the state of _____.
5. A constitutional guarantee of right of privacy was found to exist by the U.S. Supreme Court in which case? In this case, Justice Douglas contended that a right to privacy existed where in the Bill of Rights?
6. Professor Prosser said there are four privacy torts, not one. Name them.
7. The Supreme Court's decision in *Falwell v. Hustler Magazine* (1988) tells prospective plaintiffs that they must overcome which type of hurdle to succeed with their lawsuits if the information made public is of public concern?
8. What case extended the conditional constitutional privilege used in libel cases to "false-light" privacy cases?
9. In *Cantrell,* the U.S. Supreme Court majority applied which test in holding that Mrs. Cantrell was entitled to recover damages?
10. Although public interest is a defense in connection with the public disclosure, false-light, and appropriation torts, it may require a qualification. What is the qualification?
11. Publication is not essential to which of the four Prosser torts?
12. One way to avoid running afoul of the appropriation tort is to obtain _____, which may be either _____ or _____.
13. True or False: *Cox Broadcasting Corp. v. Cohn* makes it clear that a state cannot prevent publication of a rape victim's name if that person's identity is divulged in court records or court proceedings open to the public.
14. Are there likely to be many wrongful acts by the media such as occurred in *Zacchini v. Scripps-Howard*?

ANSWERS

1. To be let alone.
2. Public or general interest.
3. True.
4. New York, even though Sections 50–51 of the Civil Rights Law do not mention privacy by name.
5. *Griswold v. Connecticut.* In a penumbra, or incompletely illuminated area, resulting from more specific rights guaranteed by various amendments in the Bill of Rights.
6. Intrusion, public disclosure, false light, and appropriation.
7. Actual malice test.
8. *Time, Inc. v. Hill.*
9. Actual malice test.
10. The public interest must be *legitimate,* not mere curiosity.
11. Intrusion.
12. Consent — either *express* or *implied.*
13. True.
14. How many "human cannonball" — or two-second acts — can there be?

ENDNOTES

1. Dorothea Wood, "Privacy Concern Prompts State Laws," *FoI Digest,* November/December 1979, p.4.
2. Edward L. Godkin, "The Right of the Citizen: To His Reputation," *Scribner's Magazine,* Vol. 8, July 1890, p. 58.
3. See Beaumont v. Brown, 237 N.W.2d 501, 508 (1975). See also Prosser Torts (4th ed.) § 117, p. 802, *n.* 2.
4. Boyd v. U.S., 116 U.S. 616, 630, 6 S.Ct. 524, 532, 29 L.Ed. 746, 751.
5. Thomas Cooley, *A Treatise on the Law of Torts,* 2d ed. (1888), p. 29.
6. Samuel D. Warren and Louis D. Brandeis, "The Right to Privacy," *Harvard Law Review,* Vol. IV, No. 5 pp. 193 + . Copyright 1890 by the Harvard Law Review Association.
7. Ibid.
8. Rosenbloom v. Metromedia, 403 U.S. 29 at 44–45, 91 S.Ct. at 1820, 29 L.Ed.2d at 312 (1971).
9. Roberson v. Rochester Folding Box Co., 171 N.Y. 538, 64 N.E. 442.
10. William Prosser "Privacy," 48 *California Law Review* 383, 388–89 (1960).
11. Notes, "Privacy in the First Amendment," 82 *The Yale Law Journal* 1462, 1472–75 (1973), reprinted by permission of the Yale Law Journal Company and Fred B. Rothman & Company.
12. Ibid. at 1462.
13. Report of the Committee on Privacy, Command 5, No. 5012 (1972), p. 206.
14. Pavesich v. New England Life Insurance Co., 50 S.E. 68 (1905).
15. Ch. 176, § 5, 1977, codified as Wis. Stat. § 895 (1979).
16. "Photographers & Privacy Case Law in the States," *The NEWS Media & The LAW,* Summer 1988, p. 16.
17. Tavoulareas v. Washington Post, 10 *Med.L.Rptr.* 1129 (District of Columbia Circuit, 1984), January 31, 1984.
18. Ibid., at 1140.
19. Billings v. Atkinson, 489 S.W.2d 858.
20. Ibid., at 859–60.
21. Olmstead v. U.S., 277 U.S. 438, 478, 48 S.Ct. 564, 572, 72 L.Ed. 944, 956.
22. Griswold v. Connecticut, 381 U.S. 479, 85 S.Ct. 1678, 14 L.Ed.2d 510. In this case, the Court reversed the convictions of the defendants who had been found guilty of violating the state's

birth control law. Griswold was executive director of the Planned Parenthood League of Connecticut which gave out information and instructions to married persons on means of preventing conception. The state law prohibited the use of "any drug, medicinal article or instrument for the purpose of preventing conception," and also forbade anyone from aiding or abetting the prevention of conception.

23. Roe v. Wade, 410 U.S. 113, 95 S.Ct. 705 (1973).
24. Justices Rehnquist, White and O'Connor dissented.
25. Whalen v. Roe, 429 U.S. 589 (1977).
26. Ibid., at 606.
27. Nixon v. Administrator of General Services, 433 U.S. 425, 2 *Med.L.Rptr.* 2025 (1977).
28. Tavoulareas v. Washington Post, op. cit., note 17, at 1137.
29. Bowers v. Hardwick, 55 *U.S. Law Week* 1001, July 1, 1986.
30. Dietemann v. Time, Inc., 449 F.2d 245, 249 (9th Circuit).
31. Barber v. Time, Inc., 348 Mo. 1199, 159 S.W.2d 291 (1942).
32. Nader v. General Motors, 25 N.Y.2d 560, 207 N.Y.S.2d 647, 255 N.E.2d 765 (1970).
33. Froelich v. Werbin, 548 P.2d 482.
34. Beaumont v. Brown, op. cit., note 3.
35. Galella v. Onassis, 353 F.Supp.1076 (1982), 8 *Med.L.Rptr.* 1321, April 27, 1982. Earlier consideration of case, 353 F.Supp.196 (1972), 487 F.2d 986 (2d Circuit, 1973).
36. Pearson v. Dodd, 410 F.2d 701 (District of Columbia Circuit, 1968).
37. Fletcher v. Florida Publishing Co., 2 *Med.L.Rptr.* 1088, January 11, 1977. Justice Sundberg dissented on jurisdictional grounds, and Justice England did not participate.
38. Fletcher v. Florida Publishing Co., 319 So.2d 100, 113–14, (1975).
39. *Editor & Publisher,* January 17, 1987, p. 22.
40. CBS v. Le Mistral, Inc., 402 N.Y.S.2d 815 (1978).
41. Stessman v. American Black Hawk Broadcasting Co., 416 N.W.2d 685 (1987).
42. Stahl v. Oklahoma, 665 P.2d 839 (1983), 9 *Med.L.Rptr.* 1945.
43. "News Notes," *Media Law Reporter,* January 24, 1984.
44. *The NEWS Media & The LAW,* September/October 1983, p. 35.
45. Ibid.
46. Sidis v. FR Publishing Corporation, 113 F.2d 806 (2d Circuit, 1940); cert. denied, 311 U.S. 711, 61 S.Ct. 393, 85 L.Ed. 462 (1941).
47. Restatement § 652D, Comment h (1977).
48. Daniel L. Zimmerman, "Requiem for a Heavyweight: A Farewell to Warren and Brandeis' Privacy Tort," 68 *Cornell Law Review* 291, 324. Copyright © 1983 by Cornell University. All rights reserved.
49. *Hustler Magazine v. Falwell,* 797 F.2d 1270, 13 *Med.L.Rptr.* 1145, September 9, 1986.
50. Ibid., at 1148, n. 4.
51. Ibid., at 1149.
52. Chuy v. Philadelphia Eagle Football Club, 595 F.2d 1265 (3d Circuit, 1979), 4 *Med.L.Rptr.* 2537.
53. "News Notes," *Media Law Reporter,* April 7, 1987.
54. Hustler Magazine v. Falwell, 14 *Med.L.Rptr.* 2281, March 15, 1988.
55. Ibid., at 2283.
56. Walko v. Kean College et al., *The NEWS Media & The LAW,* Fall 1988, pp. 38–39.
57. Ibid.
58. Ault v. Hustler Magazine, 13 *Med.L.Rptr.* 1657, December 16, 1986.
59. Grimes v. Carter, 241 Cal.App.2d 694, 702, 50 Cal.Rptr. 808 (1966).
60. Cape Publications v. Bridges, 431 So.2d 988, 8 *Med.L.Rptr.* 2535.
61. 464 U.S. 893 (1983).
62. Shields v. Gross, 9 *Med.L.Rptr.* 1879, August 2, 1983; "News Notes," *Media Law Reporter,* May 3, 1983.
63. Briscoe v. Reader's Digest Association, 93 Cal.Rptr. 886, 483 P.2d 34 (1971), 1 *Med.L.Rptr.* 1845.
64. Ibid., at 38.

65. Forsher v. Bugliosi, 163 Cal.Rptr. 628, 608 P.2d 716 (1980), quoting from Prosser's article in the *California Law Review,* op. cit., n. 10, at 418.
66. E.g., Times Mirror Co. v. Jane Doe, 244 Cal.Rptr. 566, 15 *Med.L.Rptr.* 1129 (1988).
67. Cox Broadcasting Corp. v. Cohn, 420 U.S. 469, 95 S.Ct. 1029 (1975). Justice Rehnquist dissented on jurisdictional grounds.
68. This statement, said Justice White, is not meant to imply anything about constitutional sanctions which might arise from a state's policy of not allowing access by the public and press to various kinds of official records. Ibid., at 1047.
69. American Law Institute, *Restatement (Second) of Torts* § 652D (Tentative Draft No. 13, April 27, 1967).
70. Cox Broadcasting Corp., op. cit., note 67, at 1046.
71. Globe Newspapers Co. v. Superior Court, 102 S.Ct. 2613 (1982).
72. 499 So.2d 883 (1986); rehearing denied, 509 So.2d 1117 (1987).
73. "News Notes," *Media Law Reporter,* December 22, 1987.
74. Florida Star v. B.J.F., "News Notes," *Media Law Reporter,* June 27, 1989.
75. Times Mirror Co. v. Jane Doe, "News Notes," *Media Law Reporter,* August 30, 1988.
76. Op. cit., n. 66.
77. Op. cit., n. 73.
78. Virgil v. Time, Inc., 527 F.2d 1122 (9th Circuit, 1975).
79. Cert. denied May 24, 1976 (Case No. 75–1174). Justices Brennan and Stewart favored the granting of review.
80. Slip opinion No. 71-179-GT, filed December 17, 1976, Southern District of California.
81. Slip opinion No. 120-62059, Robbin Howard v. Des Moines Register & Tribune Co., Sept. 19, 1979.
82. Ibid., p. 26.
83. Banks v. King Features Syndicate, Inc., 30 F.Supp. 352 (Southern District of New York, 1930); Barber v. Time, Inc., 348 Mo. 1199, 159 S.W.2d 291 (1942); Feeney v. Young, 191 App. Div. 501, 191 N.Y.S. 481(1920).
84. Howard v. Des Moines Register, op. cit., note 81, p. 27.
85. "News Notes," *Media Law Reporter,* May 6, 1980.
86. Sipple v. Chronicle Publishing, 10 *Med.L.Rptr.* 1690, May 29, 1984.
87. "State Activities," *Media Law Reporter,* July 10, 1984.
88. Sipple v. Chronicle Publishing, op. cit., note 86, at 1692.
89. *Yale Law Journal,* op. cit., note 11, at 1463.
90. See Chapter 2.
91. Donald Pember, "Newspapers and Privacy: Some Guidelines," 2 *Grassroots Editor* 5 (1972).
92. See, e.g., Harry Kalven, "Privacy in Tort Law — Were Warren and Brandeis Wrong?" 31 *Law & Contemporary Problems* 326, 336 (1966).
93. McNutt v. New Mexico State Tribune Co., 538 P.2d 804 (1975).
94. Goldman v. Time, Inc., 336 F.Supp. 133, 137–38 (1971).
95. Time, Inc. v. Hill, 385 U.S. 374, 87 S.Ct. 534, 17 L.Ed.2d 304 (1967).
96. Cantrell v. Forest City Publishing Co., 419 U.S. 245, 95 S.Ct. 465, 469, 42 L.Ed.2d 419 (1974).
97. Colbert v. World Publishing Co., 747 P.2d 286 (1987), 14 *Med.L.Rptr.* 2188, February 23, 1988.
98. Wood v. Hustler Magazine, Inc., 736 F.2d 1084, 1092, 10 *Med.L.Rptr.* 2113 (5th Circuit, 1984); Dresbach v. Doubleday & Co., 518 F.Supp. 1285, 1288, 7 *Med.L.Rptr.* 2105 (District of Columbia Circuit, 1981); and Crump v. Beckley Newspapers, Inc., 320 S.E.2d 70, 89 (W.Va., 1984).
99. Messner, Inc. v. Warren E. Spahn, 393 U.S. 1046, 89 S.Ct. 676, 21 L.Ed.2d 600 (1967).
100. 387 U.S. 239, 87 S.Ct. 1706, 18 L.Ed.2d 744.
101. 233 N.E.2d at 842.
102. Cantrell v. Forest City Publishing Co., op. cit., note 96.
103. Cantrell v. Forest City Publishing Co., 484 F.2d 150, 153 (6th Circuit).
104. Op cit., n. 96, at 470–71.
105. Ibid., at 469.
106. Renwick v. News and Observer, 10 *Med.L.Rptr.* 1443, 1448, April 10, 1984. Justices Exum and

Meyer concurred in part and dissented in part, and Justice Frye dissented. Justices Meyer and Frye believed that a false-light tort of action should be recognized.

107. Ibid., at 1449.
108. Ibid., at 1451.
109. Pavesich v. New England Life Insurance Co., op. cit., note 14.
110. Youssoupoff v. CBS, Inc., 244 N.Y.S.2d 701; aff'd, 244 N.Y.S.2d 1.
111. Michael and Robert Meeropol v. Louis Nizer and Doubleday & Co., Inc., 381 F.Supp. 29.
112. Ibid., at 38.
113. Namath v. Sports Illustrated, 363 N.Y.S.2d 276 (1975).
114. Adjani v. Time, Inc., *Korea Herald,* April 2, 1988, p. 2.
115. Eastwood v. Superior Court, 149 Cal.App.3d 409 (1983), 10 *Med.L.Rptr.* 1073.
116. Ibid., at 1075.
117. Ibid., at 1080.
118. Ibid., at 1079.
119. 202 F.2d 866 (2d Circuit, 1953), cert. denied, 346 U.S. 816 (1953).
120. "News Notes," *Media Law Reporter,* July 3, 1984. The warning came from John Taylor Williams of Taylor and Dodge, Boston, Mass.
121. Zacchini v. Scripps-Howard Broadcasting, 47 Ohio State 2d 276 (1975).
122. Zacchini v. Scripps-Howard, 433 U.S. 562, 97 S.Ct. 2849 (1977).
123. 3 *Med.L.Rptr* 2444 (1978).
124. Price v. Hal Roach Studios, Inc., 400 F.Supp. 836 (1975).
125. Haelan Laboratories v. Topps Chewing Gum, 202 F.2d at 868.
126. Lugosi v. Universal Pictures Inc., 172 U.S.P.Q. 541, 551.
127. Lugosi v. Universal Pictures, Inc., 5 *Med.L.Rptr.* 2185, January 29, 1980.
128. Ibid., p.2190.
129. Pro Arts, Inc. v. Factors, Etc., "News Notes," *Media Law Reporter,* March 6, 1979.
130. Pro Arts, Inc. v. Factors, Etc., 4 *Med.L.Rptr.* 1144.
131. Memphis Development v. Factors, Etc., *Media Law Reporter,* April 1, 1980.
132. 652 F.2d 278, 7 *Med.L.Rptr.* 1617 (1981).
133. Factors v. Pro Arts, 9 *Med.L.Rptr.* 1110.
134. Ibid., at 1112.
135. "News Notes," *Media Law Reporter,* April 27, 1982.
136. Estate of Presley v. Russen, 513 F.Supp. 1339 (District of New Jersey, 1981); Factors Etc., Inc. v. Creative Card Co., 444 F.Supp. 279, 2 *Med.L.Rptr.* 1290 (Southern District of New York, 1977), aff'd, 579 F.2d 215, 3 *Med.L.Rptr.* 1144 (2d Circuit, 1978), cert. denied 440 U.S. 908 (1979); and Factors Etc., Inc. v. Pro Arts, Inc., 444 F.Supp. 288 (Southern District of New York, 1977), aff'd 579 F.2d 215 (2d Circuit, 1978), cert. denied 440 U.S. 908 (1979).
137. Elvis Presley Enterprises v. Elvisly Tours, 14 *Med.L.Rptr.* 1053.
138. Groucho Marx Productions v. Day and Night Company, 689 F.2d 317, 8 *Med.L.Rptr.* 2201 (2d Circuit, 1982).
139. 7 *Med.L.Rptr.* 2030.
140. Martin Luther King, Jr. Center for Social Change v. American Heritage Products, Inc., 250 Ga. 135, 296 S.E.2d 697, 8 *Med.L.Rptr.* 2377.
141. Acme Circus v. Kuperstock, 9 *Med L.Rptr.* 2138, September 27, 1983.
142. Hicks v. Casablanca Records, 464 F.Supp. 426, 4 *Med.L.Rptr.* 1497 (Southern District of New York, 1978).
143. Carson v. Here's Johnny, 698 F.2d 831, 9 *Med.L.Rptr.* 1153, March 8, 1983.
144. Ibid., at 1159.
145. Cher v. Forum International, 7 *Med.L.Rptr.* 2593 (Central District of California, 1982).
146. Ibid, at 2595.
147. Ibid., at 2596.
148. Ibid.
149. Ibid., at 2598, citing Zacchini, op. cit., note 122, 433 U.S. at 576.
150. 8 *Med.L.Rptr.* 2484.

151. "News Notes," *Media Law Reporter,* May 10, 1983.
152. "News Notes," *Media Law Reporter,* June 21, 1983.
153. *Advertisng Age,* January 25, 1984, p. 79.
154. Lanham Act, Sec. 43(a), 15 USC 1125(a).
155. 15 *Med.L.Rptr.* 1001 (DCSNY), April 5, 1988.
156. Ibid., at 1006.
157. Washington Post Co. and Ben Bagdikian v. Richard Kleindienst, acting U.S. attorney general, and Norman Carlson, director of U.S. Bureau of Prisons, 357 F.Supp. 770, 772 (District of Columbia, 1972).

8

Government and Privacy

HIGHLIGHTS

■ The Privacy Act of 1974 is the federal government's attempt to protect citizens against "excessive and unnecessary" intrusion by government. The law restricts access to government files pertaining to individuals except in eleven instances.

■ Given various government efforts to protect an individual's privacy, numerous confrontations have occurred between the news media and law enforcement agencies which have closed criminal records to news personnel including, in many instances, the police "blotter" and arrest records.

■ Many states impose confidentiality requirements regarding juvenile delinquency proceedings, but in *Smith v. Daily Mail Publishing Co.* (1979), the U.S. Supreme Court said that a state cannot punish truthful publication of a juvenile offender's name if the information were lawfully obtained, except where there's a compelling state interest greater than the one present in the *Smith* case.

■ Many states have enacted privacy legislation aimed at protecting various records from disclosure.

■ Federal and state laws exist, or case law has developed, related to wiretapping, electronic eavesdropping, and undisclosed recording of conversations.

Many of the privacy law developments discussed in the preceding chapter were the result of common law or case law. But there have been significant developments by means of statutory law partly because government, both federal and state, has become one of the principal invaders of the citizenry's right to privacy. The disclosure of extensive eavesdropping, wiretapping, and other spy activities by government agencies has resulted in a spurt of legislation aimed at protecting citizens from such surveillance, or preventing the disclosure of data about citizens contained in government files and in computer storage and retrieval systems that have prolilerated since World War II.

In the mid-1960s, hundreds of U.S. Army intelligence agents were used to spy on various individuals and groups, collecting data for central intelligence files. This activity led Solicitor General Erwin N. Griswold to say to the U.S. Supreme Court in 1972 that "poor judgment" had been shown in creating and conducting this program of surveillance of thousands of citizens. There have been other revelations. The Federal Bureau of Investigation has been revealed as a lawbreaker. Its agents have engaged in such nefarious activities as spying on journalists, civil rights leaders, and on politicians during at least part of the late J. Edgar Hoover's 50-year reign as director. FBI agents maintained telephone taps and electronically eavesdropped on Dr. Martin Luther King, Jr., civil rights leader, in an effort to obtain information to discredit him. King was one of thousands of Americans who were subjected to government agency wiretapping, bugging, physical surveillance, and political espionage. It was revealed that FBI agents engaged in "black bag" capers—burglarizing homes and offices to gain information about those known to be critics or foes of various American presidents or of American foreign policy.

Journalists have been the targets of surveillance, according to a 1975 report by the Senate Select Committee on Intelligence. The Central Intelligence Agency kept syndicated columnist Jack Anderson under close watch after he broke a story in 1971 about President Nixon ordering a "tilt" in American foreign policy away from India and toward Pakistan. Anderson presumably obtained his information by means of a "pipeline" into the highly secret deliberations of the National Security Council. The columnist subsequently filed a $22-million civil suit against Nixon and other government officials and agencies, including the CIA, claiming that they had violated his constitutional rights to free speech and privacy.

But the U.S. District Court for the District of Columbia dismissed the suit in 1978 because Anderson refused to disclose certain confidential news sources.[1] The court earlier had ruled that Anderson was compelled for pretrial discovery purposes to answer certain questions regarding identity of his news sources. Although the judge said that there was "substantial indication" that Anderson could prove "acts of official harassment," the judge nonetheless ruled that the columnist's refusal to disclose his sources precluded an "orderly trial, fair to both sides."

In 1976 a U.S. District Court judge in Washington, D.C., ordered that damages be paid to Morton H. Halperin, a former National Security Council aide, after finding that Halperin's constitutional (Fourth Amendment) rights against unwarranted search had been violated by a wiretap placed on his telephone during a 21-month period from 1969 to 1971. The amount of damages was left unspecified pending filing of a statement by Halperin detailing the damages he believed he had incurred. He asked for $1 million in actual damages and $1 million in punitive damages against former President Nixon, former White House Chief of Staff H.R. Haldeman, and former U.S. Attorney General John Mitchell. In 1977 District Court Judge John Lewis Smith, Jr. ordered the trio to pay $5 in nominal damages to Halperin because the illegal taps had not cost him loss of income or employment. Halperin appealed, saying the damage award was not large enough to deter government officials from engaging in similar illegal acts in the future.

In 1979 the U.S. Court of Appeals for the District of Columbia Circuit affirmed, in part, and reversed, in part. The three-judge panel unanimously reversed Judge Smith's ruling that Nixon and his top aides had not violated the Omnibus Crime Control Act in 1968 that limited warrantless wiretaps to national security matters. The panel was of the opinion that Nixon had not complied with the law when he ordered wiretaps of thirteen government employees and four news reporters, including *New York Times* reporter Hedrick Smith, who filed a separate suit. The court observed that the wiretaps of Halperin continued long after he had left government service.

The panel also ridiculed the token award to Halperin and told the lower court to take into account the emotional distress and mental anguish experienced by the plaintiff. Compensation in cases involving constitutional rights, said the panel, "should not be approached in a niggardly spirit."

The appellate court also rejected Nixon's claim that presidents and former presidents are immune from civil damage suits. "The President," said the panel, "is the elected chief executive of our government, not an omniscient leader cloaked in mystical powers."

Former Secretary of State Henry Kissinger had been named a defendant in the lawsuits by Halperin and Smith, but Judge Smith had ordered Kissinger dropped from the Halperin lawsuit. The appeals court also reversed that part of the decision.

In the *Smith* case, the District Court judge had found for defendants Nixon, Haldeman, and Mitchell, but the appellate court reversed and sent the case back for retrial. Nothing in the record, said the panel, contradicts the reporter's contention that the wiretap was placed on his phone because his stories were embarrassing to the Nixon administration.

In order to collect damages, however, both Smith and Halperin must, according to the appellate court, show that "there was no reasonable national security rationale supporting the wiretapping."

On appeal, the U.S. Supreme Court affirmed the appellate court's ruling in a 1981 decision.[2] The 4–4 decision, which was not accompanied by an opinion, also applied to Smith's lawsuit.

About a year later, the Court, in a 5–4 decision,[3] ruled that a president enjoys absolute immunity from damage lawsuits so long as the alleged illegal conduct is within the outer perimeter of his official duties. The decision came in a case involving the alleged illegal firing of an Air Force civilian worker, Ernest

Fitzgerald, who previously had received $142,000 from Mr. Nixon in return for promising not to take Nixon to trial no matter how the court ruled in this case. The Court chose to review the case anyway.

The decision affected the Halperin and Smith cases, but it did not affect Fitzgerald's litigation against two Nixon aides.

During Nixon's administration, the White House covertly established the infamous plumbers' unit that, among other things, staged break-ins, such as the one at the headquarters of the Democratic National Committee in the Watergate where an unsuccessful attempt was made to bug the telephone. Ultimately it was the Watergate scandal which tumbled Nixon from power. Three years after his resignation and full pardon by successor Gerald Ford for any crimes committed while President, Nixon said on a television show on May 19, 1977, in an interview with David Frost, that burglaries and other crimes are not illegal if ordered by the President. He later recanted, saying the President is not above the law. Against this backdrop of a growing propensity by various government agencies to spy on the people have come some important legislative developments or proposals. For example, President Jimmy Carter asked Congress to approve a plan to halt illegal spying on citizens by government agencies—a plan, he contended, that would successfully resolve the "inherent conflict" between national security and preserving the basic rights to privacy. An administration-supported bill was introduced in the Senate that same day by Senator Edward M. Kennedy. As drafted, it required judicial warrant for any electronic eavesdropping, including national security investigations, and it specifically rejected any inherent power of the President to authorize electronic surveillance without first obtaining a warrant to do so. Ultimately, legislation was enacted that required all national security wiretaps to first have judicial approval. To that end Chief Justice Burger in 1979 named ten federal judges who must rule on requests for such wiretaps and on requests by the FBI for electronic surveillance.

PRIVACY ACT OF 1974

Among the more important legislative developments in connection with the federal government and privacy is enactment of the Privacy Act of 1974. Just before the law went into effect in 1975, President Ford acknowledged that the privacy of Americans is constantly being invaded and that one of the worst offenders is the federal government itself. He said the Privacy Act would give citizens effective protection against "excessive and unnecessary intrusion" by government. He pointed out that the Act prohibits the collection of information concerning the exercise of an individual's First Amendment rights, such as when an individual engages in public protests against government actions.

This Act (Public Law 93-579) is aimed at promoting government respect for the privacy of individuals by regulating the collection, maintenance, use, and dissemination of personal information by federal agencies. In the process, the news media have found it much more difficult to obtain information about identifiable individuals from federal agency records. Partly for this reason the

Office of Management and Budget issued an extensive interpretation of the Act. Generally, a federal agency may not disclose to any other agency or person any information about an individual contained in a Privacy Act record system without the prior written consent of that individual. There are eleven exceptions to this rule of nondisclosure. Information can be released:

1. To officers and employees of the agency which maintains the record who have a need for the record in the performance of their duties.
2. As required under Section 552 whenever an individual asks to examine his record and seeks to purge it of inaccuracies or irrelevancies.
3. For routine use.
4. For Bureau of Census surveys.
5. For nongovernment research projects which do not result in identification of individuals.
6. To the National Archives whenever the record has sufficient historical or other value to warrant its continued preservation.
7. To any government agency in connection with a civil or criminal law enforcement activity "if the activity is authorized by law, and if the head of the agency . . . has made a written request to the agency which maintains the record specifying the particular portion desired and the law enforcement activity for which the record is sought."
8. To a person pursuant to a showing of compelling circumstances affecting the health or safety of an individual.
9. To either House of Congress or any of its committees.
10. To the Comptroller General in the course of the performance of the duties of the General Accounting Office.
11. Pursuant to a court order.

The "routine" use exception was not intended by Congress as a device for circumventing the prohibition in the law against unnecessary invasion of personal privacy interests by unauthorized disclosure of data contained in the estimated 858 data banks and 1.2 billion files maintained by the federal government.[4] Rather, the general rule should prevail; namely, an agency may not disclose to any other agency or person any information pertaining to an individual contained in a Privacy Act record system without prior written consent of that individual.

In addition to the 11 exceptions contained in the Privacy Act, disclosure could be required under the Freedom of Information Act (FOIA) which went into effect in 1967, giving the public for the first time a legal right to know what the federal government is doing. FOIA and the interface between FOIA and the Privacy Act, including conflict between the two laws, are discussed in the next chapter.

Summarized, the principal exceptions to nondisclosure of information under the Privacy Act are:

1. Disclosure pursuant to an FOIA request.

2. Disclosure made in the course of agency activities but on a need-to-know basis.
3. Disclosure for valid law enforcement purposes under a strictly controlled procedure.
4. Disclosure made to the individual who is the subject of the file.[5]

One more exception can be added as the result of a 1987 ruling by the U.S. Court of Appeals for the District of Columbia Circuit.[6] The court said that documents protected by the Privacy Act are discoverable by litigants in pending litigation on a showing of relevancy, not "special need" as a U.S. District Court had required.

In connection with disclosure to individuals, the Office of Management and Budget reported to Congress in 1978 that agencies had received 1,417,214 requests from individuals for access to information being kept in agency files. The agencies complied with 1,355,515 of the requests, either wholly or partially.

The Act entitles any person to see, copy, and request correction of information about them contained in federal files with the exception of files maintained by such agencies as the CIA, FBI, and Secret Service. Any agency refusing such a request must state its reasons and tell the inquiring citizen how to appeal. An individual may seek an injunction ordering compliance with the law and damages can be awarded if an agency's action was "willful, arbitrary or capricious." Federal officials who willfully violate the Act are subject to a maximum fine of $5000, and a person who can prove such a violation can collect actual damages of at least $1000.

There is a two-year statute of limitations and, according to the Seventh Circuit U.S. Court of Appeals, it begins to run when an individual knows or has reason to know of record-keeping errors that allegedly injure that person.[7]

In providing an overview of the effects of the Privacy Act, Professor Gerald L. Grotta of the University of Oklahoma told a seminar on "Secrecy, Government and the Public" that the Act restricts access to an estimated 8,000 kinds of file systems kept by the federal government. Furthermore, this Act and the Fair Credit Reporting Act make it more difficult for the press to obtain certain kinds of information without the permission of the persons who are the objects of the file-keeping activity.[8] Grotta said the press is seeing two hundred years of concern for individual privacy being turned into comprehensive, far-reaching privacy legislation.[9]

PRIVACY PROTECTION STUDY COMMISSION

The Privacy Act established a Privacy Protection Study Commission to make a two-year study to determine if the Act was effective in safeguarding personal privacy and whether Congress should consider similar legislation affecting state and local governments and the private sector.

Jack Landau, former Supreme Court reporter for Newhouse Newspapers and a cofounder of the Reporters Committee for Freedom of the Press, told the Privacy Protection Study Commission in 1976 that government agencies were using the Privacy Act to deny journalists access to records. James E. Donahue of the American Newspaper Publishers Association testified about the ANPA's concern "that the push for privacy not be extended to infringe upon the First Amendment right of the press to gather and disseminate news to the public. . . ."[10]

The Commission in its report to Congress in 1977 made numerous recommendations. Principally, however, the Commission urged self-regulation by the private sector to guard privacy rights.

Some specific legislative recommendations included:

1. Prohibiting employers from requiring workers to take lie detector tests.
2. Denying to employers the arrest records of employees or jobseekers, in most cases.
3. Establishing an independent government unit to monitor computer operations in the private sector.
4. Preventing government agencies from seeing records held by banks, hospitals, and utility companies without a person's consent or a subpoena.
5. Enacting legislation allowing a person to sue for up to $10,000 if an organization gives out information without authorization and if the affected individual can prove a Privacy Act violation. Presently, an individual can recover only provable losses incurred because of such a violation.
6. Requiring an explanation whenever a person is denied credit, and allowing an individual to see any information which a private firm has collected concerning that person.

Law Enforcement Assistance Administration

In conjunction with the Privacy Act came strict regulations from the Law Enforcement Assistance Administration (LEAA) pertaining to records maintained by law enforcement agencies. LEAA came into existence as part of the Omnibus Crime Control Act of 1968. Its chief power stemmed from the estimated $4.5 billion it dispensed to state and local governments to help fight crime. When, in 1975, it issued strict regulations pertaining to the release of information in law enforcement records, it attached a caveat to the allocation of funds to state and local government agencies which previously had received such funds or which were plugged into LEAA-funded information systems, to wit: adopt regulations as stringent as the federal standards on securing the privacy of such records or lose federal funding.[11]

Under the original regulations, only criminal justice and law enforcement agencies could have access to criminal records. The public would be denied access. That meant the press, too. States were given several months to submit plans on compliance. There followed a flurry of action at the state and local level. Some ludicrous situations resulted.

Arrest Records and Police Blotters Closed. During the closing days of its 1975 session, the Oregon Legislature passed H.R. 2579 which was intended to limit access to criminal histories ("rap" sheets) of individuals only to law enforcement agencies and courts. However, reports of arrests, indictments, acquittals and convictions were supposed to remain part of the public record. These exceptions were left out of the bill and the result was a virtual blackout of news about arrests by some law enforcement officials. The jail in Pendleton was jammed with persons arrested for disorderly conduct during the Pendleton Round-Up because police, adhering to an opinion by the state attorney general, could not call anyone to come and bail out those held in jail. This situation ended when the legislature hurriedly was called into special session and repealed the law.[12]

Similarly, the Hawaii state legislature passed a law declaring that all records relating to the questioning, apprehension, detention, or charging of criminal suspects "shall be deemed confidential." Using Act 45 as the fulcrum for decision making, police departments in Honolulu and Oahu refused to release any arrest records until and unless convictions had been obtained. A state judge thereupon enjoined the Honolulu department from refusing access to such records. However, another judge came to a different conclusion, allowing police to keep new arrests confidential. It took almost a year for the legislature to undo Act 45.[13]

Oregon and Hawaii were by no means unique in their haste to conform with LEAA regulations. As one report put it:

> The records keepers were motivated to bar the door by the belief that LEAA money for their police departments or local governments would be snatched away by the federal government if reporters' prying eyes were to peek at the criminal history records.[14]

A wave of protests by the Fourth Estate resulted in amended regulations being published in the *Federal Register* on March 19, 1976, which removed all restrictions on dissemination of criminal history information contained in public court records and conviction data. Furthermore, state and local governments were allowed to decide for themselves how much nonconviction information they would release, and to do so without fear of losing LEAA funds. They had to make this decision in the form of statute, ordinance, or by some other such way, by December 31, 1977. They had to implement a plan by that same date concerning the dissemination and security of criminal records (nonconviction data). As for police blotters, they had to be compiled chronologically and had to be required by law or custom to be made public before the public could have access to them. Reporters can check a chronologically maintained police blotter on a daily basis to see what arrests have been made, but an alphabetical index of arrests or "rap sheet" shows all arrests and police contacts with an individual regardless of whether any convictions resulted.

Although LEAA went out of existence in 1982, it was instrumental in getting states to adopt stricter controls on the release of criminal records. By 1980, 47 states, the District of Columbia, and Puerto Rico had enacted some kind of legislation restricting access to such records. Only North Dakota, South Dakota, and Vermont had no such legislation.

The statutes concerning arrest records mostly deal with the status of such records in the event there is no conviction.

In discussing the closing of arrest, and even conviction, records, J. R. Wiggins, former editor of the *Washington Post* and editor and publisher of the Ellsworth (Maine) *American,* gave these views in a column he wrote for the *Post:*

> Americans are risking their priceless heritage of a relatively open system of criminal justice that protects them against secret arrest, secret trial and secret punishment, by submitting to the enactment of federal and state laws enforcing privacy upon arrest records of persons acquitted, and the files of those who have completed prison sentences, and records of those who have been pardoned.
>
> Twenty-eight states [by 1976] have passed varying laws enforcing some degree of concealment, expungement, or sealing of such records. . . .
>
> The wave of privacy laws being enacted in the states already has brought to two states the reality of secret arrests which Americans have hitherto associated only with fascist and Communist countries. [Wiggins then reviewed the situations in Oregon and Hawaii.] . . .
>
> Aryeh Neier, executive director of the ACLU [American Civil Liberties Union], in his testimony before the Tunney subcommittee [of the Senate Judiciary Committee] . . . made a strong appeal for privacy of both arrest and conviction records. He said that only if the victim of an arrest consents should the fact be made public, and he argued that it violates due process to disseminate to the press conviction records "absent the individual's consent."
>
> If the press discovers the records, it should be free to publish them, in Neier's view—an empty privilege if laws punish all disclosure of the records. In its current solicitation of funds the ACLU states: "ACLU court cases and legislative action seek to open government actions to public view."
>
> The Senate [Tunney] bill and the Oregon, Hawaii and Maine laws seek singular ways to "open government actions to public view" [the ACLU having lobbied for the Oregon law]. Neier offers a Blackstonian opinion that freedom of press consists only of immunity to prior restraint in an age when society, by two centuries of experience, has found that it comprehends (1) the right to get information about government; (2) the right to print without prior restraint; (3) the right to print without fear of punitive punishment; (4) the right to distribute. A press that is deaf and blind, by law, is not able to make effective use of the power of speech.
>
> The state laws already passed, and the agitation launched by ACLU and others, are already, in many practical ways, diminishing the power of the press to fulfill its function as the public's surrogate in the constant scrutiny of the law enforcement process. . . .[15]

In a letter to the *Washington Post,* Neier responded:

> . . . [Wiggins] attacks me for espousing privacy laws. I plead guilty.
>
> As I understand Wiggins's argument, it is this: If any of the nation's half-million police officers once lays his hands on a person and says he is under arrest, the stigma must stick for life. Government, in Wiggins's view, must be sure that the stigma is

never concealed. No matter how mistaken or malicious the policeman's action, the arrest record must be available for circulation to employers, licensers, creditors, insurers, etc.

Discrimination based on government dissemination of arrest records presently injures millions of people. Thus it must always be, in Wiggins's view.

Wiggins says the press has a right to know. That right is the same right as belongs to all citizens. In its right to get access to government information, the press is no more and no less than the surrogate for all the rest of us.

Government must be accountable to us for its actions. But it perverts the idea of accountability to argue that government must disclose to us the details of people's private lives.

Government should not disclose to us medical information on public hospital patients, nor confessions to military chaplains, nor details of individual tax records, nor personnel files of government employees, nor conversations of clients with public defenders, etc.

If a newspaper finds out even such private information, the ACLU defends the right of the press to publish it. But just because such information is gathered by the government does not mean it should be publicly disclosed.

Nor should the government disclose publicly the arrest records without the consent of the arrested person. Of all the records on people gathered by government, arrest records probably have the most devastating impact on their lives.[16]

The dispute continues. An editorial in a 1988 issue of *The NEWS Media & The LAW* began this way:

> When does an arrest record stop being a public record? In seven states, certain types of criminal history data can be sealed or purged either automatically or by court petition after three to 15 years.
>
> In other states, legislation is being considered which would restrict access by non-law enforcement personnel to computerized criminal history repositories. In those states, information which is publicly available in police stations and court dockets — arrest logs and blotters, incident reports, arraignments, adjudications and sentencings — would be sealed from public scrutiny when it is collected in a central location.
>
> In other words, as far as the public record is concerned, the arrest never happened.[17]

The Reporters Committee for Freedom of the Press, which publishes *The NEWS Media & The LAW,* has been in the forefront of a number of access-to-information cases. One of its more recent efforts involved attempts to gain access to "rap sheets" in the FBI's criminal history data base. The *en banc* U.S. Court of Appeals for the District of Columbia Circuit allowed a three-judge panel's ruling to stand that most records or "rap sheets" in the data base are public information under the FOI Act (see Chapter 9).[18] Because much of the information comes from state and local crime records, and because much of that information was public at the time, the court reasserted the principle that there can be no privacy interest in records that have been made public. The government had contended that the release of such data would intrude upon privacy because the rap sheets would make all of the information easily available. But as the appellate court said, the sole consideration for a trial judge is whether the privacy interest has faded because the information is already public. If so, the FBI cannot withhold the information.

As for state laws that prohibit the release of rap sheets, the court said that they are irrelevant to disclosure decisions under the federal FOI Act.

The government appealed.[19] On March 21, 1989, the Supreme Court unanimously ruled that the public and press have no legal right of access to the FBI rap sheets. Such access, said the court in an opinion by Justice Stevens, would be an unwarranted invasion of an individual's right to privacy even though such information generally is available locally. In his opinion, Stevens noted that nearly all of the states severely limit access to such information. Congress permits the FBI to send such information to other law enforcement agencies, banks, local licensing bodies, and to officials in such industries as nuclear power and securities.

Although concurring in the decision, Justice Blackmun expressed concern about the sweeping nature of the decision, saying that a congressional candidate's conviction five years earlier on a tax fraud charge could not be disclosed by the FBI.

Jane Kirtley, executive director of the Reporters Committee for Freedom of the Press, termed the decision "devastating." It closes access to criminal and other information that is important to the public and that once was routinely available, she said.

An additional problem is generated when government information is stored in computers, as are the FBI rap sheets. The FOI Act may not include such stored information, some lawyers contend, since the Act was written when most information was recorded on paper. Some observers have suggested that an electronic freedom of information act may be needed.

Juvenile Delinquency Records and Courts

About half of the states provide for confidentiality of juvenile delinquency hearings, although courts generally have discretionary power to allow entry to such proceedings for those with a direct or proper interest in the case or in the work of such courts.

States that presumptively close such proceedings to the public (that is, the hearings are closed unless an overriding reason exists to open them) are: Alabama, Alaska, Arizona, California, Connecticut, Georgia, Hawaii, Illinois, Kentucky, Massachusetts, Mississippi, Missouri, Nevada, New Hampshire, North Dakota, Oklahoma, Pennsylvania, Rhode Island, South Carolina, Vermont, Washington, West Virginia, Wisconsin, and Wyoming.[20] Although California and Illinois bar the public from attending, the press is permitted to attend. And in 1989 the supreme courts of Arizona and Ohio ruled that the press has a right to attend such proceedings.[21]

States that presumptively open such proceedings to the public and press are: Colorado, Florida, Iowa, Kansas, Michigan, Montana, New Mexico, New York, Ohio, South Dakota, and Tennessee.[22]

States where judges can use their discretion are: Arkansas, Idaho, Indiana, Maryland, Nebraska, Oregon, and Texas.[23]

In Delaware, Maine, Minnesota, and Utah, the seriousness of the charge determines if the proceedings will be open or closed.[24] And in Louisiana, North Carolina, Puerto Rico, and Virginia, the proceedings are closed to public and press unless the minor requests a public hearing.[25]

In New Jersey, the hearings are presumed closed but the press will be admitted when there's no substantial likelihood that specific harm to the juvenile will result.[26] Hearings in the District of Columbia are presumptively closed to the public, but the press has been held to have a proper interest and will be admitted.[27]

Delaware and Montana require juvenile delinquency hearings for certain serious offenses to be open to the general public, but give the court discretion as to the other hearings. California allows public access to juvenile hearings for certain serious offenses, but allows the victim to close such hearings. The general public is excluded from the remaining hearings, although the court has discretion to admit those directly interested in the case or the court. Maine opens hearings for certain serious offenses and closes the remaining one. South Dakota opens all hearings unless the child or his or her representative requests that the hearing be private. Arizona, Connecticut, Nebraska, and New Jersey have not enacted legislation on the matter.

Many courts seal juvenile court records, although there are variations. For example, Georgia requires courts to release the name of repeat offenders.[28] Montana goes further by requiring the release of the names of first-time juvenile felons — a law which one juvenile court judge, Lester Loble of Helena, Montana, claimed had drastically reduced such crimes in his district.[29] Loble's contention was based on the theory that publication of delinquents' names has a deterrent effect. Conversely, social workers usually argue that such publicity hampers rehabilitation of juvenile offenders.

Some states, such as Minnesota and Wisconsin, have statutes which prevent the courts, but not the media, from divulging the names of juvenile offenders.

Oklahoma Publishing Co. v. District Court, Oklahoma County (1977).[30] Some of the problems posed above are seen in a case involving the fatal shooting of a railroad switchman as he stood on the platform of a moving switch engine. The day after the shooting, a 12-year-old boy was taken into custody as a suspect in the killing. His arrest was reported and broadcast; the youth was identified by the initials "L.G.," and his address was given. When he appeared for a hearing on charges filed by the county juvenile bureau, the media used his name, identified his parents, and newspapers and TV stations used photos of him. A closed arraignment hearing was held five days later and on motion of the youth's attorney, the district court judge issued a pretrial order enjoining all news media representatives from disseminating the name or picture of the juvenile in an effort to assure a fair and impartial trial. The *Daily Oklahoman* identified the youth by name two days later and the newspaper sought writs of mandamus and prohibition to prevent the judge from enforcing the pretrial order.

Several issues were involved, but the state supreme court denied the writs partly because the state statute provides that juvenile proceedings are to be held privately unless the judge specifically orders the hearings to be conducted in public (10 0.S. 1971 § 1111). The state statute also provides that juvenile records are not open to inspection by the public unless so ordered by the court (10 0.S. § 1125). The newspaper relied heavily on *Cox Broadcasting,* but the state supreme court held that the statute was sufficiently broad to permit the court to enjoin publication of the name and photograph of the juvenile offender. In so doing, the court adopted as "directives to be utilized in juvenile court proceedings" in Oklahoma the following Kentucky voluntary guidelines that resulted from collaboration between bench, bar, and press:

> (1) News media and judges should work together with confidence in, and respect for, each other; (2) news media should be welcome to attend sessions of the juvenile court, but should not disclose names or identifying data of participants unless authorized by the court; (3) names may be used if alleged juvenile offenders are remanded for criminal prosecution in an adult criminal court; (4) responsibility for developing sound public interest and understanding of the child, the community, and the court must be shared by the judge and the news media; (5) official records may be inspected only with the judge's consent unless prohibited by statute; (6) confidential reports should not be open to inspection except at the express order of the court; (7) the judge, at his discretion, may release the name or other identifying information of a juvenile offender; (8) the Canons of Professional Ethics concerning the release of information in pending judicial proceedings should be adhered to; (9) if an alleged act of delinquency is publicized, news media may be informed of the final disposition of the case; (10) news media should bear in mind that any juvenile matter may ultimately be handled as a criminal case; (11) news media should recognize its [sic] responsibility to report events in a general manner without mentioning names and addresses where some matters are of sufficient public interest and could serve as a deterrent upon others.[31]

The Oklahoma Publishing Co. filed a petition for certiorari with the U.S. Supreme Court, and in 1977 the Court ruled that the pretrial gag order violated the First and Fourteenth Amendments.[32] It therefore reversed the judgment of the Oklahoma Supreme Court. In its per curiam opinion, the Court said it was compelled to reach such a conclusion on the basis of *Cox Broadcasting* and *Nebraska Press Association v. Stuart* (see Chapter 10), the latter decision prohibiting prior restraint of the press by a judge concerning what can be reported from open court.

Two other cases—*Landmark Communications, Inc. v. Virginia* and *Robert K. Smith v. Daily Mail Publishing Co.*—show that a state's attempt to protect the identity of individuals may not stand First Amendment scrutiny.

Landmark Communications, Inc. v. Virginia (1978).[33] The Supreme Court's decisions in *Cox Broadcasting* and *Oklahoma Publishing Co.* figured prominently in the Court's 1978 ruling in *Landmark Communications, Inc.* The Court voted unanimously (7–0) that newspapers cannot be punished for accurately reporting confidential disciplinary proceedings against state judges. The Court struck down a Virginia law which made it a misdemeanor to divulge information about investigations of judges by the state's Judicial Inquiry and Review Commission. The case resulted from the publication of a story in 1975 by the Norfolk *Virginian-Pilot* which named a juvenile court judge who was being investigated by the commission. The state supreme court had upheld the newspaper's conviction on the ground that a clear and present danger was posed by premature disclosure of the commission's proceedings.

Robert K. Smith v. Daily Mail Publishing Co. (1979).[34] The Court affirmed the West Virginia Supreme Court of Appeals' judgment that a state law prohibiting newspapers from publishing the name of any youth charged as a juvenile offender was unconstitutional. The law was silent as to radio-TV divulgence of such information. Justice Rehnquist concurred in the judgment and Justice Powell took no part in the case.

In 1978, a youth was shot and killed in a junior high school and the alleged assailant, a 14-year-old classmate, was identified by eyewitnesses and arrested. Reporters from the *Charleston Daily Mail* and *Charleston Daily Gazette* obtained the assailant's name from witnesses. Initially, the *Daily Mail* did not use the name, but when the *Gazette* published it following use of the boy's name on radio and television, the *Daily Mail* identified the youth. An indictment of both newspapers was issued.

In the opinion written by Chief Justice Burger, the turning point of the case was not prior restraint—the basis on which the state's highest court had found the law to be unconstitutional—but on the conclusion reached in *Cox Broadcasting* and *Landmark Communications;* namely, a state cannot punish truthful publication of information lawfully obtained "except when necessary to further an interest more substantial than is present" in *Smith* (see *Florida Star v. B.J.F.,* Chapter 7).

As in the precedent cases, the decision in *Smith* is a narrow one, said Burger. There was no issue of unlawful press access to confidential judicial proceedings; no privacy issue, and no issue of prejudicial trial publicity.

As pointed out by Burger, many states have statutes concerning confidentiality of juvenile proceedings, but only five at the time of the decision—West Virginia, Colorado, Georgia, New Hampshire, and South Carolina—imposed criminal penalities for publication of the identity of juveniles.

As noted, the *Smith* decision is a narrow one. Just how narrow can be gauged by the Supreme Court's unwillingness to overturn an Illinois Juvenile Court's prior restraint on the publication of the names of two babysitters, ages 12 and 14, accused of sexually abusing three children in their care.[35] Their names and other information about the crime were widely known in the community and one of the names had been placed in a publicly available court file. Nevertheless, the Woodford County Juvenile Court judge issued the gag order. The Bloomington *Daily Pantagraph* and the *Peoria Journal Star* opposed the prior restraint order on First Amendment and state constitutional grounds. The state supreme court denied their request to void the order, and the U.S. Supreme

Court refused to grant a stay in 1984 with Justices Brennan, Marshall, and Blackmun arguing that the media should be allowed to publish any information about the case that was already public.

Similarly, another Juvenile Court judge in January 1985 gagged the media from identifying the 14-year-old brother of a girl found murdered in her bedroom even though area newspapers previously had published information about the case and had identified the suspect.[36] The state supreme court denied media requests to void the gag order.

The Illinois Juvenile Act permits reporters, but not the public, to attend Juvenile Court hearings, but judges also are given the authority to prohibit anyone attending those hearings from disclosing the identity of alleged offenders.

The two Illinois cases can be differentiated from the *Smith* case because of the West Virginia statute that made identification of a juvenile offender a crime, and from the *Oklahoma Publishing Co.* case because the information was made available in *open* court. Illinois juvenile courts are not open to the *public*. Reporters can attend, but the law empowers the judges to prohibit publication of certain information.

However, in 1989 the Illinois Supreme Court ruled that a judge cannot bar publication of the identity of a juvenile defendant when reporters obtain the information using ordinary reporting techniques.[37]

The different results in these cases demonstrate the uncertainty that often confronts reporters when they're covering juvenile court matters.

Federal Courts and Juvenile Delinquents
In a move aimed at avoiding the diversity found at the state level, Congress enacted the Justice and Delinquency Act of 1974 (Public Law 93-415) which establishes a uniform policy for all federal courts regarding juvenile court records. The law requires federal courts to safeguard the records from disclosure and, upon completion of the proceedings, to seal them. Section 5038 states that if a juvenile (anyone under 18) is prosecuted as an adult, the following prohibitions may not be applicable; otherwise, "(1) neither the fingerprints nor a photograph shall be taken without the written consent of the judge; and (2) neither the name nor picture of any juvenile shall be made public by any medium of public information in connection with a juvenile delinquency proceeding."

Fair Information Practices Legislation

From 1974 to 1980, five states funded major privacy commissions, and one—Minnesota—created a permanent commission which continually monitors practices under its Information Practices Act and makes recommendations to the legislature. The other four are Indiana, Iowa, Massachusetts, and New Jersey. During the same period, nine states adopted "Fair Information Practices Acts" that govern government record keeping about individuals and access to those records. The states are Arkansas, California, Connecticut, Indiana, Massachusetts, Minnesota, Ohio, Utah, and Virginia.

A review of these laws was published in the final report in 1980 by the Iowa

Citizens Privacy Task Force which made more than twenty recommendations including enactment of a Fair Information Practices Act.[38] The review gave the following resumé of the laws in the nine states.

Arkansas (**Ark. Stat. Ann. § 16–804**). The Act embodies principles of fair information practices: that there shall be no personal information systems whose existence is secret; that there shall be no unneeded data; that information must be kept accurate and current; that there should be procedures for people to inspect data about themselves and to challenge or correct it; that personal data should not be disseminated without permission for a purpose other than that for which it was collected. The Act creates a state information practices board to oversee state and local government data collection.

California (**Calif. Civil Code § 1798**). The Act gives people the right to see and correct files about themselves. State agencies may release personal information only in limited and lengthily defined circumstances. Agencies must provide (with the forms used to collect personal information) the name of the unit requesting the information, the title, business address, and phone number of the official responsible for the record system, the authority for collecting the information, whether each item is mandatory or voluntary, the consequences of failing to supply all or some of the information, the principal use of the information, any known transfer of the information to another government agency, and the individual's right to review information about himself or herself. The state university system and police are exempted. Invasion of privacy lawsuits are permitted against a person who intentionally discloses information that he or she should have known came from a government agency illegally.

As a result of this Act, at least two state agencies have barred press access to previously public information.

Connecticut (**Conn. Gen. Stat. Ann. § 4–190**). The law prohibits government agencies from disclosing personal data without consent of the subject except to an agency which has a lawful need of the information or to reduce imminent threat of physical injury or as ordered to do so by statute or court. Agencies are required to establish procedures to allow people to contest the accuracy or relevancy of information about them, and to add dissent to the permanent record. Agencies must also adopt regulations which describe the nature and purpose of the agency's personal data systems, the categories of personal and other data kept in these systems, procedures regarding the maintenance of the data, and the uses to be made of the information.

Indiana (**Ind. Code § 4–1–6**). The Act establishes a commission on public records. Agencies are required to publish annual reports on the personal record systems they maintain. The Act is similar to California's in many ways.

Massachusetts (**Mass. Gen. Laws Ann. Chap. 661**). Agencies must establish procedures to allow people to review records about themselves, to contest information in a record, to correct records, to ensure that personal data are not released pursuant to mandatory legal process without notifying the data subject, and to govern access to the records. The law permits civil suits for recovery of damages, and allows recovery of exemplary damages of not less than $100 for each agency violation.

Massachusetts places the responsibility for controlling access to criminal records with the Criminal History Systems Board. The board certifies various law enforcement agencies for access to criminal records. Improper dissemination of criminal records can lead to civil and criminal actions.[39] Individuals may have access to their criminal records and a procedure has been established for correcting false information.

***Minnesota* (Minn. Stat. Ann. § 15.162).** The provisions of this section are similar to the laws in California and Massachusetts. To implement the Act, the commissioner of administration promulgates rules under the Administrative Procedures Act, which applies to state and local agencies. A permanent Privacy Study Commission has been established to monitor practices under the Act and to recommend changes to the legislature.

Under the Information Practices Act, passed in 1974 and amended in 1975, a civil lawsuit is allowed specifically so that an injured person may recover damages, costs, and reasonable attorney fees. In addition, exemplary damages of between $100 and $1000 are permitted for willful violation.

The 1975 amendment provided that data collected by various agencies for the purpose of "legal action" be kept confidential. It was intended to protect the work of the state attorney general. One result was that several police departments closed their records to the press. The St. Paul police refused in late 1975 to allow reporters to look at the complaint forms after the city attorney issued an opinion authorizing such police action. Previously, Minneapolis police had decided not to make public the names of persons who had been arrested.

***Ohio* (Ohio Rev. Code 1347).** This Act creates a Personal Information Control Board. All state and local agencies (except law enforcement) which have personal information systems must file annual statements of the existence and character of the systems with the Board, unless the information is made confidential by statute. Agencies (state and local) must appoint one individual to be responsible for a personal information system; adopt rules to implement the law; inform employees of the law and rules; specify disciplinary measures to be applied to anyone who penalizes a person who brings attention to unauthorized use of the information in the system; tell whether information requested is voluntary or mandatory, and assure necessary accuracy, relevance, timeliness and completeness of the information. The Board adopts rules providing standards for the interconnection or combination of personal information systems; authorizes types of disclosures of information where new programs are developed or public health, safety or welfare is involved; provides standards for security; and supplies standards for the collection of personal information to assure that only necessary and relevant information is gathered.

Personal information may not be released to any others (including federal agencies) without consent of the subject unless the disclosure is consistent with the uses for which the information was collected, or authorized by rule. Agencies must, on request, tell people of personal information about them in a system, allow inspection, and inform of uses (including identity of users). Provision must be made for correcting the record and entering dissents.

Utah (Utah Code Ann. 63–50–1). State agencies must annually file with the secretary of state a listing of all systems containing personal or confidential information with a description of the types of information and the reasons it is kept. Agencies must also provide the title, name and address of the responsible official; policies for retention and disposal; and the procedures by which a person can learn if he or she is the subject of any data in the file, gain access to it, and contest the accuracy, pertinence, or necessity of the information. Agencies must maintain as a public record the purposes and uses of personal information they collect, inform individuals whether requested information is mandatory or voluntary, and the consequences of non-disclosure. No private or confidential information may be used for other than stated purposes without the express consent of the subject. Criminal investigation records are excepted.

Virginia (Va. Code. 2.1–377). Agencies may collect only necessary information and they cannot share information with other agencies unless the same standards of confidentiality will be observed. A list must be maintained of all persons or organizations having regular access, and of the identity of every person, except agency personnel, who had access to the information and their purpose. Agencies must train their personnel in the care and use of personal information. No information on political or religious beliefs, affiliations, or activities may be collected unless explicitly authorized by statute. People must be informed whether the information requested is voluntary or mandatory and the consequences of non-disclosure, and the uses of the information. People may review information about themselves and have corrections made or dissents entered in the record.

Arkansas, Minnesota, Ohio, and Virginia regulate information gathered, used, and disseminated by and at all levels of government within those states. Connecticut, Massachusetts, New Hampshire, North Carolina, and Vermont regulate information gathered, maintained, and disseminated by state agencies. Maryland's Public Information Act was amended in 1978 to provide that state and local governments may maintain only such data about a person "as is relevant and necessary to accomplish a purpose of the governmental entity or agency, executive order of the governor or the chief executive of a local jurisdiction, judicial rule or other legislative mandate."[40] At the same time, the amended act provided for greater access to some investigative, intelligence and security-type records.

In New York, a Personal Privacy Protection Law went into effect in 1984.[41] It is designed to protect the confidentiality of personal information in state agencies. Individuals have the right to see and correct information about themselves in agency files. Agencies can exchange information about individuals if the exchange is "relevant" to the purposes for which it was collected or necessary to accomplish a duty authorized by the statute.

Connecticut, California, Illinois, and Wisconsin, among others, have laws to protect information furnished by subscribers to cable television systems. Confidentiality for personal information furnished to cable systems or used on cable systems for such purposes as ordering items from department stores, banking by cable, and making airline or train reservations places a premium on confidentiality.

Medical Records and Privacy

One of the major dangers to individual rights of privacy stems from computer storage of medical records on millions of Americans and dissemination of such data, according to a report made for the National Bureau of Standards by Professor Alan F. Westin of Columbia University, released in 1977. Titled "Computers, Health Records, and Citizen Rights," the report disclosed that health agencies are creating massive centralized computer systems which are vulnerable to abuse. Blanket release forms are being signed routinely by many Americans which allow insurance companies, potential employers, and others entry to such medical reports.

As for the potential for abuse, Westin cited the establishment of a computer center in Orangeburg, New York, which houses the records of some 400,000 psychiatric patients from five eastern states and the District of Columbia. Although this particular center has established stringent safeguards against the abuse of privacy rights, Westin said that the very existence of such a record center makes some violations almost inevitable.

Because of the growing threat to privacy of medical and health records, the National Commission on the Confidentiality of Health Records was established in 1976 by 17 health and medical agencies and organizations. One of the events which led to the decision to establish the Commission was the burglary of psychiatrist Lewis Fielding's office by the White House "plumbers" to obtain confidential records on Daniel Ellsberg who had made the Pentagon Papers report available to a *New York Times* reporter.

Patients' access to their medical records was one of the issues considered during two days of hearings conducted by the Privacy Protection Study Commission in 1976. Most experts agreed that existing laws had not kept pace with privacy needs as the sheer volume of medical record keeping accelerated through the use of computers. Laws to curb abuses are fast appearing in legislative halls, as are laws and regulations controlling dissemination of information in consumer credit files.

All of the states have statutes making certain medical records confidential, establishing confidentiality for doctor-patient relationships, or otherwise regulating the maintenance and use of such records.

Wiretapping, Electronic Eavesdropping, Recording of Telephone Conversations

Unauthorized wiretapping is a criminal offense in most of the 39 states that have laws dealing with wiretapping. Unauthorized wiretapping was prohibited by Section 522 of the New York Penal Code in 1892. Twenty-two states permit wiretapping for crime-fighting purposes, but states such as California, Illinois, Michigan, and Pennsylvania, have not enacted such wiretap laws although authorized to do so under Title III of the Omnibus Crime Control Act of 1968. They declined to enact such laws because they believed wiretapping or eavesdropping is rather extensive. From 1969 to 1977, nearly 5600 applications were made to federal and state judges for permission to wiretap or bug persons or places in connection with crime investigations. Only 15 requests were rejected. Thus, warrants to tap or bug were being issued routinely.

To prevent abuses, new legislation was enacted by Congress which requires that all national security wiretaps must first have judicial approval from a panel of ten federal judges named by Chief Justice Burger in 1979. Concerning eavesdropping by radio microphones or by microphones wired to amplifiers, a federal regulation in 1966 prohibits the use of any radio device for the purpose of eavesdropping.[42]

The Omnibus Crime Control Act of 1968 provides comprehensive protection against invasion of privacy by modern devices. There are two main classes of offenses, with exclusion for authorized use for official law enforcement purposes and for other use under "color of law" (where a person is a proper party to a communication). The first is unauthorized interception of wire or oral communications, where interception is defined as listening by means of any electronic, mechanical, or other device, with ancillary offenses in connection with attempting to intercept, or procuring another to intercept, and of disclosing and using an intercepted communication. The second class of offenses is related to the manufacture, distribution, possession and advertising of devices for intercepting wire or oral communications where it is known or there is reason to know that "the design of such device renders it primarily useful for the purpose of the surreptitious interception of wire or oral communication." The maximum penalty is a fine of $10,000 or five years' imprisonment, or both, plus confiscation of such devices.

Because of the difficulties of applying that part of the law which states that the outlawed devices must be primarily useful for the purpose of surreptitious interception, Congress chose not to extend the Act to visual surveillance.

One part of the Federal Wiretap Statute (18 U.S.C. § 2511(2)(d)) requires that only one party to a wire or oral conversation needs to give consent for a recording to be made of that conversation, and that one party could be a newsperson who wants to record an interview. However, this qualifier is added: That the communication not be intercepted for the purpose "of committing any criminal or tortious act in violation of the Constitution or laws of the United States or of any State or for the purpose of committing any other injurious act."

The statute did not define "injurious act," but this phase was deleted by a 1986 amendment.[43]

The Federal Communications Commission requires for all interstate telephone calls the use of a beeper device, which produces a short tone signal every 15 seconds, to alert someone being called that a recording is being made. Individual states have various requirements concerning intrastate calls. An article in *Journalism Quarterly* contained this warning:

> In the event Bell Telephone discovers recording equipment being used without a beeper, the subscriber will be warned and will be told to have Bell install the proper equipment by a certain date. If this is not done, Bell has the option either to discontinue service or to notify law enforcement officials, who might then prosecute under state or federal antiwiretapping laws.[44]

The Electronic Communications Privacy Act became law in 1986, making it illegal to intentionally intercept or divulge the contents of any wire, oral or electronic communication.[45] Among its provisions are fines of up to $250,000 and a year in prison for those who, for commercial gain or vandalism, break into any system that stores messages electronically. This provision appears to cover newsroom computer systems. The law also protects satellite transmissions, particularly of network news and sports programming, high frequency cellular telephone conversations, paging devices and electronic mail. The unauthorized interception of scrambled or encryted signals also is punishable, as is interception of signals made for commercial gain or illegal purposes, such as gathering stock information for insider trading. The unauthorized interception of signals for private use, such as by means of backyard satellite antennas, is a misdemeanor punishable by a $500 fine and an injunction against further interception.

The interception of radio broadcasts, including police and fire department communications, amateur and citizens band radios, and marine aeronautical communication systems is not prohibited by the Act.

A number of states now require all parties to consent to the recording of wire or oral conversations. They are California, Delaware, Florida, Hawaii, Illinois, Louisiana, Maryland, Massachusetts, Michigan, Montana, New Hampshire, Pennsylvania, and Washington.[46] Georgia and Oregon follow the federal rule of one-part consent, as do Alabama, New York, North Carolina, and Tennessee.[47]

The unauthorized installation or use of cameras in private places is expressly prohibited by Alabama, Delaware, Georgia, Hawaii, Maine, Michigan, New Hampshire, South Dakota, and Utah.[48]

Trespassing on private property to photograph or observe people there is expressly prohibited by Alabama, Delaware, Georgia, Hawaii, Maine, Michigan, and South Dakota.[49]

CBS News Standards is a notebook issued to network personnel that provides instructions and guidelines on electronic eavesdropping and surreptious recordings. Employees are told that hidden cameras may be used to surreptiously record transactions or events occurring in public places—streets, public parks, and public buildings. There are even limited circumstances when hidden cameras can be used in semipublic places (e.g., restaurants, theaters, and stores), but the legal dangers of so doing may be considerable. Hidden cameras might even be used to film events in private places, specifically a CBS employee's hotel room, office, or home. Where the nature of the place is not clear, CBS advises its employees—consult the network's lawyer.

If a telephone conversation is to be recorded with a non-radio device and with no intent to broadcast the recording, federal law is clear—only one-party consent is needed. But state laws vary, said CBS, so employees are cautioned to consult with the attorneys. If the recorded telephone conversation is to be broadcast, consent of all parties must be obtained prior to the broadcast.

Recording or overhearing oral conversations with radio devices (e.g., a wireless mike) in a public or semipublic place is not prohibited by federal law and consent of the parties to the conversation is not needed *if* one of the parties is the CBS employee or if that employee is within earshot of the conversation. If such a recording is made in a private place, the consent of all parties is required.

The same requirements exist if non-radio devices (such as a miniature tape recorder in an attache case) are used.

The final caution is this: whenever the nature of the place is not absolutely clear, and in the absence of contrary advice from network attorneys, employees are told that they must proceed on the assumption that the place is private. And remember that state laws may impose different limitations.

Greg Walter Case in Pennsylvania. In 1972, Greg Walter, an investigative reporter for the Philadelphia *Bulletin,* was arrested and charged with tape recording telephone conversations between himself and five other persons without their permission or knowledge. Walter, probing police corruption, was found guilty of violating the Pennsylvania "Act of 1957" which states, in part:

> No person shall intercept a communication by telephone or telegraph without permission of the parties to such communication. No person shall install or employ any device for overhearing or recording communications passing through a telephone or telegraph line with intent to intercept a communication in violation of this act. No person shall divulge or use the contents or purport of a communication intercepted in violation of this act.

The Pennsylvania Supreme Court interpreted the statute to require that all parties had to give their consent before any device for overhearing or recording a telephone conversation could be installed or used. Walter was fined $350 in Municipal Court after the judge denied a motion to quash the criminal complaint. Although urged to do so by an assistant district attorney, the judge declined to impose a 15-day jail term. Walter, who could have been sentenced to a year in jail, appealed, and this set in motion a 15-month tug-of-war between Walter's attorney and the district attorney's office. Walter's attorney made it clear that if the case went to trial, top echelon law enforcement officials in Philadelphia and the city's mayor would be subpoenaed in an attempt to show that taping of telephone calls was a common practice. The result: after thousands of pages of testimony, intense legal jousting, and hundreds of hours of conferences, the case was "terminated" by the district attorney which Walter's attorney said was "vindication" of his client and the same as "acquittal after a jury trial."[50] The district attorney called the action a "practical disposition" of the case.

Florida Cases. In *State of Florida v. News-Press Publishing Company* (Fort Myers *News-Press*), a three-judge appellate court in 1977 affirmed a lower court's dismissal of an indictment which had alleged that the publishing company tampered with evidence by destroying tape recordings which were sought in connection with a homicide investigation.[51] A reporter, Fran Williams, had taped a telephone call without the caller's knowledge and then had routinely erased the tape in order to reuse it. Two days later a conversation between two persons in the reporter's car was taped without their knowledge. That tape also was routinely erased for reuse, according to the reporter. One of the reasons cited by the lower court in dismissing the indictment was that the tape recordings were illegal intercepts and therefore inadmissible as evidence. The appellate court agreed that the reporter's tape recording of her telephone conversation with a caller who was unaware that the conversation was being recorded constituted illegal wire intercept. In the opinion by Judge Stephen H. Grimes, the court said:

> The Florida Security of Communications Act was patterned after Title III of the Omnibus Crime Control Act of 1968, 18 U.S.C. Sec. 2510, etc. When first enacted, the Florida act, like its federal counterpart, also contained the following provision:
>
> > "It is not unlawful under this chapter for a person not acting under color of law to intercept a wire or oral communication when such person is a party to the communication or when one of the parties has given prior consent to such interception unless such communication is intercepted for purposes of committing any criminal act." § 934.03(2)(d).
>
> Federal court decisions have interpreted this provision to mean that if one of the parties to a conversation is engaged in recording it, there is no illegal intercept, *U.S. v. Turk,* 526 F.2d 654 (5th Circ. 1976); *Smith v. Wunker,* 356 F.Supp. 44 (S.D. Ohio 1972). However, effective October 1, 1974 (the very day when Ms. Williams made the first tape recording), Section 934.03(2)(d) . . . was amended to read:
>
> > "It is lawful under this chapter for a person to intercept a wire or oral communication when all of the parties to the communication have not given prior consent to such interception."[52]

A different conclusion about the same Florida law was reached in 1977 when Dade County Circuit Court Judge Donald Stone ruled that reporters could not be barred by state law from using tape recorders for in-person interviews without the knowledge and consent of those persons.[53] A suit testing the law was brought by Miami station WCKT after it had provided its reporters with tape recorders that were concealed during reporters' investigation of what ultimately proved to be an award-winning story on "abortions" given to women who were not pregnant. The existence of the recordings that were made at a clinic was divulged by the station after clinic employees denied statements attributed to them. WCKT, joined by the *Miami Herald,* argued that secret tape recordings were necessary to protect the station from lawsuits and to assure accuracy. But in 1977, the Florida Supreme Court ruled that the state law prohibits tape recordings without the consent of the interviewee.[54]

Courts sometimes have problems with the law as demonstrated by an unusual case. The statute that bars unconsented interception of oral communication by one party to a two-party conversation, as interpreted by the state supreme court in *Florida v. Walls* (1978),[55] led a reluctant Florida Fourth District Court of Appeal to suppress as evidence a victim's tape recording of his own murder when that recording was the only evidence in the case.[56] Police found in the victim's office a tape of a conversation between the accused person and the victim arguing over a business deal, then the sound of gunshots, moaning, and an abrupt end of any further sound. The trial court denied a motion to suppress the tape, but the appellate court said it had to vote to suppress because of the interpretation given the statute by the state supreme court. However, the Fourth District court asked the state's highest court to review the case. The state supreme court voted unanimously to allow the tape to be used, saying that a murderer is not entitled to a "reasonable expectation of privacy."

First Amendment Congress's Concern. Given the proliferation of privacy legislation at both the federal and state levels, journalists have been fearful about its impact on the public's right to know and the press's right to report. This concern was manifested at the First Amendment Congress in Williamsburg, Virginia, in 1980, sponsored by national journalism organizations. Out of that meeting came 12 resolutions, one of them related to privacy and the public's right to know. The resolution called on the press to do a better job of convincing the public that "privacy not become a tool misused to shroud the operations and processes of government and the criminal justice system from scrutiny." The press has the duty, said the First Amendment Congress, "to insure that inquiries into matters affecting the private life or concerns of individuals have a compelling public interest." The public must realize that "privacy legislation itself often embodies certain principles of openness vital to individual liberty," such as the right to be "certain no secret dossiers exist anywhere."[57]

SUMMARY

The Privacy Act of 1974, which is aimed at promoting government respect for an individual's privacy by regulating the collection, maintenance, use, and dissemination of personal information contained in any federal agency's files, contains 11 exceptions in addition to disclosures required by the federal Freedom of Information Act. Other principal reasons for disclosure are those made in the course of an agency's activities if revealed on a "need-to-know" basis, those made in connection with valid law enforcement purposes, and to individuals who wish access to their files.

From the standpoint of the press, the Privacy Act has been misconstrued by some government officials to deny reporters information contained in the files of identifiable individuals which should be in the public domain. Even the Privacy Protection Study Commission agreed that some officials "have either misinterpreted or failed to understand" what the Privacy Act requires.

At the same time that the Privacy Act was being used to deny to some journalists information they thought they were entitled to, regulations by the Law Enforcement Assistance Administration (LEAA) were being interpreted by some state and local governments as mandates to close criminal records, including police blotters. A wave of Fourth Estate protests resulted in LEAA removing restrictions concerning the dissemination of criminal history information in public court records and conviction data. However, states still had to make decisions on what criminal justice information should be made or kept public.

Various states and municipalities already have adopted laws or regulations concerning expungement of certain information in arrest and conviction records.

About half of the states provide for confidentiality of juvenile proceedings. Some states require open hearings.

As *Oklahoma Publishing Co.* (1977) and *Smith v. Daily Mail Publishing Co.* (1979) showed, attempts to prevent identification of juveniles involved in crimes may be blocked by the First Amendment. As the Court said in *Smith,* a state cannot punish truthful publication of information lawfully obtained except where there's a compelling state interest.

Five states—Indiana, Iowa, Massachusetts, Minnesota, and New Jersey—funded major privacy commissions during the period 1974–80. During that same period, nine states adopted "Fair Information Practices Acts." They are Arkansas, California, Connecticut, Indiana, Massachusetts, Minnesota, Ohio, Utah, and Virginia. Generally, these acts regulate access to and correction of records kept either by state agencies or, in the case of four of the states, state and local government agencies.

Concerning medical records, all states have statutes pertaining to such records or concerning doctor-patient confidentiality. Seventeen states have statutes regulating credit reporting. And 39 states have laws dealing with wiretapping. Federal law requires only one-party consent to record telephone conversations, but only six states have similar requirements. Thirteen states require all parties to consent.

QUESTIONS IN REVIEW

1. What major federal legislation regulates the collection, maintenance, use, and dissemination of personal information in federal agency files?
2. How many exceptions are there to the general rule that a federal agency may not disclose to any other agency or person any information about an identifiable individual without that individual's prior consent?
3. True or False: Under the Privacy Act of 1974, disclosure of personal information in a

federal agency's file cannot be made even for a valid law enforcement purpose.

4. Which federal organization sought to require state and local governments to declare by law those criminal justice records open to the public?

5. True or False: Federal law requires all parties in a telephone conversation to give their consent before the conversation can be recorded legally. What if the recorded information is to be broadcast?

6. What is the significance of the *Smith v. Daily Mail Publishing Co.* decision by the U.S. Supreme Court?

7. True or False: Most states allow public access to juvenile delinquency proceedings.

ANSWERS

1. Privacy Act of 1974.
2. There are 12 exceptions, including the Freedom of Information Act.
3. False.
4. Law Enforcement Assistance Administration.
5. False. Only one party has to give consent. But don't forget that state law may require all-party consent. If the information is to be broadcast, get all-party consent to record the information.
6. A state cannot punish the truthful publication of information lawfully obtained unless there is a compelling state interest greater than the one present in the *Smith* case.
7. False.

ENDNOTES

1. Anderson v. Nixon, "News Notes," *Media Law Reporter,* April 11, 1978.
2. Halperin v. Nixon, *The NEWS Media & The LAW,* October/November 1981, p. 37. Justice Rehnquist, who served in the Justice Department during the Nixon administration, took no part in the case.
3. Joining Justice Powell's opinion for the Court were Burger, Rehnquist, Stevens, and O'Connor. White, Brennan, Marshall, and Blackmun dissented.
4. James T. O'Reilly, "The Privacy Act of 1974," Freedom of Information Center Report No. 342, September 1975, p. 1.
5. Ibid.
6. Laxalt v. McClatchy Newspapers, 55 *U.S. Law Week* 2404, February 3, 1987.
7. Deliberti v. U.S., 55 *U.S. Law Week* 2592, May 5, 1987.
8. The Fair Credit Reporting Act, passed by Congress in 1971, permits anyone who is the subject of a consumer credit file to have access to that file.
9. Dewey Knudson, "Newsmen Told to Expect New Privacy Laws," *Editor & Publisher,* November 1, 1975, p. 12.
10. *The QUILL,* February 1976, p. 9.
11. Peggy Roberson, "What Are These LEAA Regulations and How Did We Get Into This Mess?" *The QUILL,* July/August 1976, p. 20.
12. Paul Clancy, "Privacy and the First Amendment," Freedom of Information Foundation Series, No. 5, March 1976 (Columbia, Mo.: 1976), p. 7.
13. Ibid., p. 31.
14. Op. cit., n. 11, pp. 19–20.
15. Published in the *Des Moines Register,* March 26, 1976. © *The Washington Post.*
16. Published in the *Des Moines Register,* April 9, 1976, p. 16A. © *The Washington Post.*

17. Editorial, *The NEWS Media & The LAW,* Winter 1988.

18. Reporters Committee for Freedom of the Press et al. v. Department of Justice, 831 F.2d 1124 (District of Columbia Circuit, 1987).

19. "News Notes," *Media Law Reporter,* December 20, 1988.

20. *The NEWS Media & The LAW,* spring 1989, p. 23. Ala. Code Sec. 12-15-65(a) (1986); Alaska Stat. Sec. 47.10.070 (1984); Ariz. Juv. Ct. R. Proc. 19; Conn. Gen. Stat. Sec. 46b-122 (1986); Ga. Code Sec. 15011028 (1985); Hawaii Rev. Stat. Sec. 571-41(b); Ill. Rev. Stat. Ch. 37, Sec. 710-20(6); Ky. Rev. Stat. 610.070(3) (1988); Mass. Gen. Laws Ch. 119, Sec. 65; Miss. Code Sec. 43-21-203(6); Mo. Rev. Stat. Sec. 211.171(5) (1983); Nev. Rev. Stat. Sec. 62.193(1); N.H. Rev. Stat. Sec. 169-B:34; N.D. Cent. Code Sec. 27-20-24; Okla. Stat. Tit. 10, Sec. 1111; Pa. Cons. Stat. Tit. 42, Sec. 6336(d); R.I. Gen. Laws Sec. 14-1-30; S.C. Code Sec. 20-7-755 (1981); Vt. Stat. Tit. 33, Sec. 651(c); Wash. Rev. Code Sec. 13.34.110; W.Va. Code Sec. 49-5-1(d); Wis. Stat. Sec. 48.299; and Wyo. Stat. Sec. 14-6-224(b) (1986).

21. Ibid. Cal. Welf. & Inst. Code, Art. 9, Sec. 346; and Ill. Rev. Stat. Ch. 37, Sec. 701-20(6). Wideman v. Garbarino, No. CV-86-06110-SA (Ariz., 1989); and Ohio ex rel. Fyffe v. Pierce, 531 N.E.2d 673 (Ohio, 1989).

22. Ibid. Colo. Rev. Stat. 19-1-106(2); Fla. Stat. Sec. 39.09(1)(c); Iowa Code, Sec. 232-39; Kan. Stat. Sec. 38-822; Mich. Comp. Laws Sec. 27.3178 (589.17); Mont. Code Sec. 41-5-521(5) (1987); N.M. Stat. Sec. 32-1-31(B) (1986); N.Y. Fam. Ct. Act Sec. 741(b); Ohio R. Juv. Proc. 27; S.D. Comp. Laws Sec. 26-8-32 (1984); and Tenn. Code 37-1-124(d) (1984).

23. Ibid. Ark. Stat. Sec. 9-27-309 (1987); Idaho Code Sec. 1601813 (1984); Ind. Code Sec. 31-6-7-10(b); Md. Rules of Proc. 910(b); Neb. Rev. Stat. 43-277 to 43-282 (1988); Ore. Rev. Stat. 419.498 (1987); and Tex. Fam. Code Tit. 3, Sec. 54.08.

24. Ibid. Del. Code Tit. 10, Sec. 972(a) (1974); Me. Rev. Stat. Tit. 15, Sec. 3307(2); Minn. Stat. Sec. 260.155(1) (1988); and Utah Code Sec. 78-3a-33.

25. Ibid. La. Code Juv. Proc. Art. 14, Sec. 69 (1989); N.C. Gen. Stat. Sec. 7A-629 (1986); P.R. Laws Tit. 34, Sec. 2009; and Va. Code Sec. 16.1-302 (1988).

26. Ibid. N.J. Rules Juv. & Dom. Rel. 5:19-2(a).

27. Ibid. D.C. Code Sec. 16-2316(e).

28. Sec. 24-2432.

29. R.C.M. Sec. 10-633 (1947).

30. Oklahoma Publishing Co. v. District Court, Oklahoma County, 2 *Med.L.Rptr.* 1001.

31. "Guidelines on the Reporting of Juvenile Court Proceedings," 35 Ky.St.B.J. 72 (1971), as reported in 2 *Med.L.Rptr.* 1007.

32. "News Notes," *Media Law Reporter,* March 15, 1977.

33. Landmark Communications, Inc. v. Virginia, 3 *Med.L.Rptr.* 2153. Justices Powell and Brennan did not participate in the decision.

34. Robert K. Smith v. Daily Mail Publishing Co., 443 U.S. 97 (1979). Justice Rehnquist concurred in the result largely because the West Virginia statute did not prohibit radio and television from publicizing the name of the juvenile. But he did not believe that a law which forbade publication of a juvenile's name constituted much of a threat to press freedom.

35. Daily Pantagraph v. Judge Baner, *The NEWS Media & The LAW,* Spring 1985, pp. 15–16.

36. Ibid., Decatur Newspapers v. Judge Bigler, p. 16.

37. In re A Minor Whose Name is Omitted, No. 66013 (Ill., 1989).

38. "Our liberties we prize and our rights we will maintain," Final report of the Iowa Citizens Privacy Task Force, submitted to Governor Robert Ray January 1, 1980, pp. 21–22.

39. Walter Fee, "Privacy and State Action," Freedom of Information Center Report No. 357 (Columbia, Mo.: July, 1976), p. 4.

40. *Access Reports,* June 13, 1978, p. 1. Copyright 1978, Plus Publications, Inc.

41. *FoI Digest,* July/August 1983, p. 3.

42. 31 *Federal Register* 3397.

43. See Boddie v. ABC, 16 *Med.L.Rptr.* 1100, February 21, 1989.

44. Sam G. Riley and Joel M. Wiessler, "Privacy: The Reporter and Telephone and Tape Recorder," *Journalism Quarterly,* Vol. 51, No. 3, Autumn 1974, p. 514.

45. *The NEWS Media & The LAW,* Winter 1987, p. 28.

46. *The First Amendment Handbook,* published by the Reporters Committee for Freedom of the Press (Washington, D.C., 1986), pp. 11–12. Copyright © by the Reporters Committee for Freedom of the Press.
47. Op. cit., n. 44, at 513.
48. Op. cit., n. 46.
49. Ibid.
50. Philadelphia *Bulletin,* August 5, 1973.
51. 2 *Med.L.Rptr.* 1240, February 8, 1977.
52. Ibid., at 1241–42.
53. "Secret Recordings," *The QUILL,* February 1977, p. 8.
54. *FoI Digest,* July/August, 1977, p. 8.
55. Florida v. Wall, 356 So.2d 294 (1978).
56. Inciarrano v. Florida, 447 So.2d 386 (1984).
57. *Editor & Publisher,* March 22, 1980, p. 11.

9

Freedom of Information versus Secrecy

HIGHLIGHTS

■ *U.S. v. Nixon* (1974), in which the Supreme Court denied President Nixon's claim that executive privilege permitted him to withhold Watergate-related tapes from a U.S. District Court judge who had ordered the recordings turned over to the court. In essence, the Supreme Court held that the President does not have an absolute, unqualified privilege.

■ Much information is withheld from the public through government's classification of it as top secret, secret, or confidential. To force the federal government to make more information available to the public, the Freedom of Information Act went into effect in 1967. This Act gives the public a legal right to know what its government is doing. There are, however, nine exemptions to disclosure.

■ The Freedom of Information Act is the federal "open record" law; the Sunshine Act, passed in 1976, is a halfhearted federal open meetings law.

■ All states have enacted open meeting and open record laws.

■ Details are given on how to use the Freedom of Information Act to gain access to government information and how to combat secrecy by governmental bodies.

As the chapters on privacy showed, tension exists between a person's right to privacy and the public's right to know and the press's right to report. Courts and legislatures have served as balancers of these rights. If our system of government rests on an informed citizenry, then obviously the public must be provided with the information necessary for making wise choices. And if this is so, then the news media have the implied—if not explicit—responsibility of providing the necessary information to the public about the operations and performance of government.

But the responsibility does not rest solely on the media. The argument can and has been made that government itself not only should allow public access to, but should facilitate the flow of, information short of endangering national security, the public welfare, or the national interest. But therein lies the rub. Who should make such vital determinations? And what kinds of safeguards should exist against the bureaucracy's inclination to prefer secrecy to exposure? As government at all levels grows in size and power so do concerns about a person's right to privacy and the often conflicting public's right to know.

During the Nixon administration (1969–1974), but by no means limited to that period, concern increased about secrecy in government, the growing use of executive power, the propensity to classify information as secret, and the growing number of incidents of "managed" news and outright deception by the U.S. government officials. This concern was evident during a 1971 inquiry into government information policies and practices undertaken by a House subcommittee. At the opening session, Congressman Ogden R. Reid of New York, a subcommittee member, talked both about the scope of the hearings and their purpose:

> [We] begin today an inquiry into a crisis of truth in government, a study of the improper exercise of the executive power bordering on dereliction. Nothing less than the balance between our coordinate branches of government and the protections set forth in the First Amendment are being threatened. These hearings will focus on the withholding of information by the claim of executive privilege, the misclassification of information, and prior restraint of publication by the executive branch.
>
> These issues raise fundamental constitutional questions, including the right of the public to know what its government is doing and the right of the Congress to have access to information necessary to carry out its legislative function.[1]

A "constitutional crisis in our government" is the way another subcommittee member, Congressman John E. Moss, referred to the issues being investigated.[2]

And in a statement to the subcommittee, Professor Philip Kurland of the University of Chicago Law School told of an English newspaperman, Louis Heren, who made this comparison: "[T]he main difference between the modern American President and a medieval monarch is that there has been a steady increase rather than diminution of his power. In comparative historical terms the United States has been moving steadily backward."[3]

The "crisis" referred to by Congressman Moss is not the doings of one president or of a single administration; rather, it has a long ancestry. It stems from an accretion of power in one branch of government — power that is of questionable legal validity. It is the chief executive who takes a nation to war, with or without a declaration by Congress. Executive orders become substitutes for legislation. Executive privilege and classification of documents help determine the output of information to Congress, and to the people via the press. It is the president who replaces treaties with secret agreements.

EXECUTIVE PRIVILEGE

One of the presidential powers used in the information "battle" is executive privilege, which dates back to 1792 and the administration of President Washington. The House of Representatives had asked the Secretary of War for all papers relating to the ill-fated expedition of Major General St. Clair into the Northwest Territory during which six hundred of his troops were killed by Indians at the headwaters of the Wabash River. Washington called his Cabinet together for consultation, and the Cabinet concluded unanimously "that the Executive ought to communicate such papers as the public good would permit and ought to refuse those the disclosure of which would injure the public."[4] Washington decided the papers should be made available. But in 1796, he refused to comply with a House request to furnish a copy of the instructions pertaining to negotiations on the Jay Treaty. Since then, other Presidents have resorted to the use of this asserted right to conceal information from Congress, the judiciary, and the public.

Any legal basis for the doctrine is tenuous. Proponents of such a privilege claim that the right is constitutionally derived — implicit in the separation of powers and responsibilities of the office; that is, since the President is responsible for the conduct of foreign affairs, he therefore can decide what should or should not be made public in that field of endeavor. Similarly, since he is commander-in-chief, the privilege extends to all information pertaining to national security. Opponents dispute such assertions, arguing that there is neither a constitutional nor a statutory basis for the privilege. Congress, frequently the protagonist along with the press in the struggle to gain information from bureaucrats, has never enacted legislation to provide such a shield for the presidency; and so occasionally the contention shifts to past congressional rules or to the recitation of case histories.

Generally speaking the courts have been reluctant to tackle the legality of privilege for the same practical reason that forestalls a congressional showdown with the executive, even though Congress repeatedly asserts its right to obtain whatever information is necessary to carry out its legislative mission. Who would enforce a court decision against a President who insists on privilege? What congressional agent (sergeant-at-arms?) would wade through Secret Service agents to seize necessary documents or compel testimony by a presidential aide (since the President himself could not be compelled to testify because of the judicially created doctrine of executive immunity)? Who would imprison the President for contempt of Congress or contempt of court?

Watergate Scandal

After President Nixon's reelection in 1971, a series of scandals rocked the White House, including revelations that a so-called plumbers' unit had been formed by aides of the President in an attempt, among other things, to plug leaks of secret government information, such as the Pentagon Papers. In the process, the office of Daniel Ellsberg's psychiatrist was broken into by the F.B.I., it was a later revealed (Ellsberg having admitted making copies of the papers available to the press); a break-in was attempted at the Democratic National Committee headquarters in the Watergate Office Building in Washington, D.C., for the purpose of "bugging" telephones and photographing records; there was disclosure of a White House "enemies list" which contained the names of more than 50 active journalists, and White House approval was given for the wiretapping of telephones of at least four journalists.

In the midst of such incredible developments came the disclosure that tape recordings existed of virtually all conversations which had taken place in the Oval Office of the White House. A confrontation involving executive privilege ensued between Nixon and judicial and legislative branches as efforts were made to determine if the President knew in advance and/or had given prior approval of the Watergate break-in. A grand jury investigation began and some Oval Office tapes were subpoenaed. Claiming immunity under executive privilege, the White House refused an order from U.S. District Judge John Sirica to turn over nine tapes. Judge Sirica's decision was appealed. In 1973 the U.S. Court of Appeals for the District of Columbia upheld Judge Sirica in a 5–2 split.

The central question, said the appellate court, was whether the President may, in his sole discretion, withhold from a grand jury evidence in his possession that is relevant to the grand jury's investigation. Although acknowledging the long-standing judicial recognition of executive privilege, the court majority declared that such a privilege must be weighed against the public interest which, in this case, was overriding. However, the court agreed that the President should be given an opportunity to argue that certain portions of the tapes ought not to be disclosed on the grounds of national security and foreign affairs—a decision that Judge Sirica could make after privately listening to the tapes. Ultimately—and in this instance temporarily avoiding a constitutional crisis—seven of the nine subpoenaed tapes were delivered to the District Court judge for examination prior to portions thereof being turned over to the grand jury. Two of the tapes, the President claimed, did not exist and one of them contained an unexplained 18-minute blank portion.

The confrontation on executive privilege came shortly thereafter. At the request of special Watergate prosecutor Leon Jaworski, a subpoena *duces tecum* was issued by Sirica requiring the President to turn over 64 additional tape recordings or documents so that the judge could determine if they contained information relevant to scheduled trials for seven former Nixon aides who had been indicted on several charges, including obstruction of justice. However, the President claimed executive privilege and sought to have the subpoena quashed. The District Court refused to do so despite the contention by the President's counsel that the judiciary was without authority to review an assertion of executive privilege by the President. The District Court said the judiciary, not the President, was the final arbiter of a claim of executive privilege, a declaration affirmed by the Supreme Court in an 8–0 decision in 1974 that upheld the lower court.[5] This decision would have the effect of bringing about the resignation of Nixon on August 9, 1974, because revelation of the content of the tapes disclosed that he did, despite earlier assertions to the contrary, participate in the attempted cover-up of the Watergate burglary-bugging operation.[6]

U.S. v. Nixon. In giving the Court's opinion, Chief Justice Burger first dealt with the contention that the judiciary could not interfere once the President had asserted a claim of privilege. Not so, said Burger. "Many decisions of this Court . . . have unequivocally reaffirmed the holding of *Marbury v. Madison,* 1 Cranch 137 (1803), that 'it is emphatically the province and duty of the judicial department to say what the law is.' " He went on to say:

> [N]either the doctrine of separation of powers, nor the need for confidentiality of high level communications, without more, can sustain an absolute, unqualified presidential privilege of immunity from judicial process under all circumstances. The President's need for complete candor and objectivity from advisers calls for great deference from the courts. However, when the privilege depends solely on the broad, undifferentiated claim of public interest in the confidentiality of such conversations, a confrontation with other values arises. Absent a claim of need to protect military, diplomatic or sensitive national security secrets, we find it difficult to accept the argument that even the very important interest in confidentiality of presidential communications is significantly diminished by production of such material for *in camera* inspection with all the protection that a District Court will be obliged to provide.
>
> The impediment that an absolute, unqualified privilege would place in the way of the primary constitutional duty of the Judicial Branch to do justice in criminal prosecutions would plainly conflict with the function of the courts under Art. Ill.

In citing a 1972 decision, *Branzburg v. Hayes,* discussed later, in which the Court denied that a constitutional right existed for reporters to refuse to reveal confidential sources of information in criminal matters, the Chief Justice reiterated the concept that the public "has a right to every man's evidence except for those persons protected by a constitutional, common law or statutory privilege."[7] He said:

> We conclude that when the ground for asserting privilege as to subpoenaed materials sought for use in a criminal trial is based only on the generalized interest in confidentiality, it cannot prevail over the fundamental demands of due process of law in the fair administration of criminal justice. The generalized assertion of privilege must yield to the demonstrated, specific need for evidence in a pending criminal case.

Presidential Recordings and Material Preservation Act

Shortly after Nixon resigned to avoid impeachment proceedings, his successor, Gerald Ford, agreed to give the former President private ownership of an estimated 42 million pages of documents, and some 820 reels of tapes which had been recorded in the Oval Office and Nixon's "hideaway" in the Executive Office Building. The agreement in effect gave Nixon the power to preserve or destroy any of these records. Congress thereupon passed the Presidential Recordings and Material Preservation Act[8] which provided that government-employed archivists could sort through the papers and tapes, culling material relating personally to Nixon and his family and returning such material to them. The remainder would be public property. Nixon brought a suit challenging the constitutionality of the law, partly on the basis that public disclosure of some material would violate his personal rights of privacy. In a brief filed by the Justice Department in support of the law, the statement was made that Nixon would "not be a trustworthy custodian, even temporarily," of the presidential material. The brief cited the 18-minute gap in one of the recordings made in the Oval Office as evidence of Nixon's past mishandling of crucial records.

Nixon v. Administrator of General Services. In this case both the U.S. District Court and the U.S. Court of Appeals for the District of Columbia Circuit upheld the constitutionality of the Preservation Act, the latter court by a three-judge unanimous decision in 1976, although the appellate court conceded that Nixon's privacy claim was "the most troublesome" one. Nixon appealed, and the U.S. Supreme Court heard oral arguments in 1977.[9] The major arguments put forth by Nixon's attorneys were: (1) separation of powers, (2) presidential privilege, and (3) Nixon's right to privacy. Concerning the privacy question, a Nixon attorney said the Act constituted a "wholesale invasion of privacy" in violation of the Fourth Amendment. He indicated that Nixon's right to privacy had not been diminished by his tenure in office and that Congress does not have a right to infringe on any person's right to privacy.[10]

U.S. Solicitor General Wade H. McCree argued that Congress has a duty to protect public property; furthermore, that a "reasonable search" is permitted under the Constitution for national security documents comingled with Nixon's private papers. Because Nixon comingled public and private papers, he should not complain, said McCree, that his Fourth Amendment rights were being violated.

The U.S. Supreme Court, by a 7–2 vote, rejected the three major arguments put forth by Nixon in holding that Congress acted within its authority in passing the Preservation Act. Justice Brennan wrote the majority opinion. Chief Justice Burger and Justice Rehnquist dissented. The decision meant that archivists could sift through the tapes and documents to decide which ones should be made public and which concern purely private matters of Nixon and his family and should be kept secret.

By 1988 an estimated 2.7 million documents had been made public along with 12.5 hours of tape recordings despite efforts of Nixon and his aides to keep them from being divulged. Millions of other documents and most of the 4000 hours of taped conversations remain undisclosed.

Some of the Nixon Oval Office tapes were used at the trial which resulted in former presidential aides John Ehrlichman, H. R. Haldeman, and the late John

Mitchell, who was attorney general during these tumultuous times, being found guilty. The U.S. Supreme Court declined to review their convictions, thereby setting the stage for Mitchell and Haldeman to begin serving the 30-month to eight-year prison sentences in connection with their roles in the Watergate cover-up. They entered prison in 1977—the last of the 25 persons imprisoned in connection with the Watergate scandal. Ehrlichman had begun serving his sentence in 1976 pending the outcome of his appeal. Earlier, the Court had let stand his conviction on conspiracy and perjury charges growing out of the 1971 FBI burglary of the office of Ellsberg's psychiatrist.

CLASSIFIED INFORMATION

In addition to executive privilege, another federal government method of controlling the release of information is to classify it into one of three categories permitted by law: top secret, secret, or confidential. The establishment of standards for handling and transmitting classified information has been accomplished by means of executive orders.

There are questions of legality concerning the classification of documents by executive order, in part because the Library of Congress, when it researched the issue, was unable to find any statute which authorizes such presidential action. But the controversy is largely academic. Thousands of government employees annually classify tens of thousands of documents. National archives bulge with "secrets."

A classic example of frustration in attempting to fight bureaucratic censors is afforded by Julius Epstein, a researcher-historian at the Hoover Institution on War, Revolution, and Peace at Stanford University. Epstein had been attempting for many years to gain access to the still-classified records of "Operation Keelhaul." This joint U.S.-British army operation resulted in the forced repatriation of some two million Soviet nationals about the time World War II ended.

In an effort to force disclosure, Epstein filed a suit against the Secretary of the Army in U.S. District Court in which he argued that continued classification of the Keelhaul file could no longer be justified. However, in 1969 the judge upheld the Army, stating that "the circumstances were appropriate for the classification made by the Department of the Army in the interest of the national defense or foreign policy."[11] The judge made that decision without examining a single document in that file, Epstein said, adding that how the court could find as it did without first examining the file "remains a mystery in American judicial history."[12] In 1970 the U.S. Court of Appeals upheld the lower court and in June of that year the U.S. Supreme Court decided not to review the case.[13]

Just what could be so damaging to the nation so many years after the event is hard to imagine. Even more difficult to understand are the estimated 100 million pages of World War II records and documents still classified.

One of the witnesses at the House Government Information Subcommittee hearing in 1971 was William Florence, a federal employee for 43 years before retiring. He had been involved in various ways in the classification of government information and, in his judgment, less than one-half of one percent of the estimated 20 million classified records and documents then in existence warranted secrecy.[14] By the mid-1980s, there were an estimated 100 million classified documents and about 2.6 million workers with access to them.

President Reagan's Actions

Some idea of the concern for national security and the desire of various administrations to stop high-level leaks to the news media is afforded by various actions taken by Ronald Reagan after he became president in 1980.

One of the first things he did was sign into law Executive Order No. 12356, which makes it easier for executive branch officials to classify federal government information.[15] The order, which took effect August 1, 1982, eliminated a Carter administration requirement that officials must weigh the public interest in disclosure when considering classification of information.[16] Among the changes is one that requires classification for at least 30 days if there is reasonable doubt about the need to classify the information. It eliminates the requirement imposed by Carter that classified documents be reviewed every six years. And it creates a new area of classification relating to the vulnerabilities or capabilities of systems, installations, projects, or plans pertaining to the national security. Critics claim that this provision allows a blank check for those in the federal government who want to keep information secret.

In 1983, President Reagan issued a directive, "Safeguarding National Security Information," that provoked a storm of protest from the press, members of Congress, and segments of the public.[17]

The directive required all federal agencies to adopt certain internal procedures to safeguard against unlawful disclosure of classified information. It required thousands of federal employees who have security clearance to sign a pledge not to disclose classified information and to submit to lie detector tests, if asked. An employee who refused to take such a test could be subject to "adverse consequences." Previously federal employees — except for those in the CIA and in certain sections of the Justice and Defense Departments and the National Security Agency — had the right to refuse to submit to such tests without their refusal being held against them or included in their personnel files.

Also, all employees holding Sensitive Compartmented Information clearance (dealing mainly with intelligence sources and methods) were required to get prior clearance for any publication that *might* include classified information.

The order also required federal departments and agencies to adopt appropriate policies to govern the contact between their employees and the news media "to reduce the opportunity for negligent or deliberate disclosure of classified information."

The American Society of Newspaper Editors charged that the directive constituted "peacetime censorship of a scope unparalleled in this country since the adoption of the Bill of Rights. . . ." The Association of American Publishers labeled the directive a prior restraint of "enormous magnitude."[18]

Ultimately, the controversial secrecy pledge requirement became the target of several lawsuits and a rider attached by Congress to the 1988 appropriations bill, signed into law by Reagan on December 22, 1987. It required the President to halt the use of the pledge.

Also in 1983, the Reagan administration announced that all government officials with access to high-level classified information would have to sign a contract requiring them to submit for governmental review any articles or books they write for the general public. They would be bound by the contract for the rest of their lives. These are contracts similar to those required of CIA agents.

The latter directive led Congress to attach a rider to a State Department money-authorization bill ordering the Reagan administration to delay at least until April 15, 1984, enforcement of the directive on prepublication review of the writings of those who have access to certain classified information.[19] This was to give Congress a chance to conduct hearings. Reagan signed the authorization bill and announced that he would delay enforcement of his Executive Order, including the use of lie detector tests, until the White House and congressional leaders could work out a system to guard government secrets and individuals' rights.[20]

Despite the legislation and the President's vow a report prepared by the General Accounting Office (GAO) in 1984 showed that aspects of the President's proposed security program had been in effect for two years.[21] For example, 156,000 employees and officials of the Defense Department already had signed the secrecy contracts. Also, the GAO found a sharp increase in the number of articles and books being reviewed by the Reagan administration.

Even more controversial than Executive Order No. 12356 and the directives, was an unprecedented 48-hour news blackout during the October 1983 invasion by U.S. troops of the Caribbean island of Grenada. Some 400 journalists who wanted to report on the military operation were denied transportation to the island and, in several instances, were prevented from going there by the interception of boats carrying them from nearby islands. The Pentagon gave two major reasons for the ban on journalists going to Grenada at the beginning of the invasion: (1) the necessity for complete secrecy to assure success of the invasion; and (2) the journalists' safety. Both reasons were ridiculed by the press. Journalists have accompanied American military forces in combat in every war since at least the Mexican-American War of 1848. And journalists have received advanced briefings of many, many impending military operations without breaching security. To suggest that they were kept out of Grenada for their own good angered the president of CBS News, Ed Joyce. He termed it "an insult to the men and women who died covering wars."[22] More than 50 journalists were killed during the fighting in Southeast Asia in the 1960s and 1970s, and many others died during the Korean War, World War II and the first World War, including famed correspondent Ernie Pyle who was killed by a sniper on a Pacific island during World War II.

The series of Reagan-directed or -supported restrictions on the flow of information to the press and public, as noted above, led New York attorney Floyd Abrams to charge the Reagan administration with engaging in "a deliberate effort . . . to close off the flow of information about the government to the people."[23]

The Reagan administration, in its prohibition against media access to

Grenada, had been given a model by Britain's example in its war with Argentina over the Falkland islands some 18 months earlier. Strict controls were imposed on the small number of journalists allowed to accompany British forces seeking to wrest control of the island from Argentine forces that earlier had "invaded" the Malvinas, as they called the islands, in the century-old dispute over who owns this small piece of real estate. The British, in effect, "managed" the news during the initial part of their return to the islands, as did the Pentagon during the first two days of operations in Grenada.

After the Grenada invasion, 10 major news media organizations issued a joint statement calling on the Reagan administration to recognize the right of the press to cover U.S. military operations.[24] The "Statement of Principle on Press Access to Military Operations" urged the "highest civilian and military officers of the government" to reaffirm the "historic principle that American journalists, print and broadcast, . . . should be present" when U.S. troops go into combat. The statement followed the organizations' failure to get President Reagan to respond to two letters sent to him by the organizations.

In a move that flabbergasted media attorneys, the publisher of *Hustler* magazine, Larry Flynt, who has a penchant for drawing national publicity to himself, filed a lawsuit in 1983 against Defense Secretary Caspar Weinberger seeking declaratory and injunctive relief against the press coverage prohibitions imposed during the Grenada invasion. In essence, Flynt was claiming a First Amendment right for his reporters to accompany the invasion troops, basing his interpretation of the First Amendment in large part on U.S. Supreme Court decisions in courtroom access cases: *Richmond Newspapers, Inc. v. Virginia* (1980) and *Globe Newspapers, Inc. v. Superior Court* (1982) (see Chapter 10). Even though Jack Landau, executive director of the Reporters Committee for Freedom of the Press, had contended that exclusion of the press from the invasion was a violation of the Constitution,[25] the press wanted no part of Flynt's lawsuit. Said Abrams, after the lawsuit was filed, "Flynt is a clear and present danger to the First Amendment."[26] The lawsuit was described as a "loser" by more than one media attorney. On June 21, 1984, U.S. District Court Judge Oliver Gasch dismissed the lawsuit as moot in view of the government's subsequent voluntary decision to lift the ban and allow unlimited press access to Grenada, said the judge.[27] Further, there was a lack of any "demonstrated probability" that the ban would be imposed again in the foreseeable future under similar circumstances, according to Gasch.

After the Grenada news blackout incident, the press and the Reagan administration attempted in 1985 to devise a pragmatic news pool arrangement for covering military operations like those of Grenada. In April 1986 a test of the arrangement was highly unsatisfactory to the press. Almost everything went wrong. Another test in September, with 12 press representatives being flown secretly to Fort Campbell, Kentucky, to witness a mock invasion proved more sucessful.[28]

The national media pool arrangement was activated by the Pentagon in July 1987 to cover the U.S. Navy's escort of reflagged Kuwaiti oil tankers in the Persian Gulf during the Iran-Iraq war. But it was canceled in mid-1988 because, according to the Pentagon, the media complained that little was happening in the area and pool reporters and photographers were wasting a lot of time and money waiting in hotels to be called aboard ship for interviews or occasional tanker escorts.[29] Three days after the cancellation, the U.S.S. Vincennes fired two surface-to-air missiles at an unarmed Iranian passenger jet, killing all 290 persons aboard. However, it was unlikely that any press pool members would have been aboard the Vincennes at the time.

The Pentagon had no plans to reactivate the regional pool, but a national pool could be called up in secret from Washington to cover military operations should the need arise.

Two other Reagan administration efforts to halt the flow of secret information should be mentioned. One was a memorandum issued in 1986 by national security adviser John Poindexter, who later resigned during the Iran-Contra scandal, involving an attempt by some U.S. officials (with Reagan saying he knew nothing about it) trying to make a deal with Iran to provide ground-to-air missiles (some were provided) either in exchange for Americans being held captive in Lebanon presumably by Iranian sympathizers or for money to be funneled to the Contras who were fighting against the communist government in Nicaruga. The memorandum gave agency heads broad powers to classify government data as "sensitive"—a new classification category that prohibits the dissemination of national security information outside of government. The basis for the issuance of the memorandum was a 1984 presidential order. Its aim is to make it easier to stop the export of technical data that could be used by Eastern bloc nations for military purposes.

The other effort occurred in May 1986 when CIA Director William Casey threatened to seek prosecution of the *Washington Post,* NBC News, *New York Times, Washington Times, Newsweek,* and *Time* magazine under a federal law (19 U.S.C. 798) that forbids the publication of any classified information about U.S. communications intelligence gathering or equipment for doing so. Violators of the 1950 law face a 10-year prison sentence and a fine of up to $10,000. Intent to harm the United States is not required by this statute.[30]

The threat followed publication of articles about the interception of Libyan communications prior to the bombing of a West German discotheque in April 1986, in which two American servicemen were killed, and of the existence of secret equipment used to intercept Soviet communications. The existence of the equipment may have been revealed to the Soviets by an accused Russian spy, Ronald William Pelton, who was scheduled to stand trial shortly after publication of the existence of such equipment.

Ultimately Casey backed away from the threat. Instead, he urged press organizations to contact the CIA for consultation before publishing information about intelligence-gathering techniques. No news organizations have been prosecuted under 19 U.S.C. 798.

With so many efforts being made to keep information secret, and some of those efforts demonstrably having little or nothing to do with national security, the question arises: How do the press and public find out what is happening inside government other than by unauthorized leaks or press releases? One important way is by means of the Freedom of Information Act—the public's legal right to know what the federal government is doing.

FREEDOM OF INFORMATION ACT (FOIA)

An 11-year congressional effort to counteract the withholding of information by means of executive privilege, classification, or just an administrative urge toward secrecy, culminated in passage of the Public Information Act, popularly called the FOI Act, which went into effect July 4, 1967. Previously, under Section 3 of the Administrative Procedure Act—the section replaced by the FOI Act— the burden of showing why information should be made public fell on the person seeking the information. Under the FOI Act (5 U.S.C. 552), which largely resulted from the persistence of Congressman Moss and the House Information Subcommittee that he chaired for many years, the burden was shifted to the bureaucrat. The new philosophy—given the force of law—had become "the public's right to know."

In June 1967 Attorney General Ramsey Clark issued a memorandum explaining the philosophy and key features of FOIA. In the foreword, Clark wrote:

> If Government is to be truly of, by, and for the people, the people must know in detail the activities of government. Nothing so diminishes democracy as secrecy. Self-government, the maximum participation of the citizenry in affairs of state, is meaningful only with an informed public. How can we govern ourselves if we know not how we govern? Never was it more important than in our times of mass society, when government affects each individual in so many ways, that the right of the people to know the actions of their government be secure. . . .
>
> Public Law 89-487 is the product of prolonged deliberation. It reflects the balancing of competing principles. . . . It is not a mere recodification of existing practices in records management and providing individual access to Government documents. Nor is it a mere statement of objectives or an expression of intent.
>
> Rather this statute imposes on the executive branch an affirmative obligation to adopt new standards and practices for publication and availability of information. It leaves no doubt that disclosure is a transcendent goal, yielding only to such compelling considerations as those provided for in the exemptions of the act.

Clark cited the following chief aims of the law:

- Disclosure is the general rule, not the exception.
- All individuals have equal rights of access.
- The burden is on the federal government to justify withholding of documents, not on the requester.
- Individuals improperly denied access to documents have a right to seek injunctive relief in U.S. District Courts.

FOIA Exemptions

The Act, as amended in 1974, lists nine categories of information exempt from disclosure, as follows:

1. Matters (a) specifically authorized by executive order to be kept secret in the interest of national defense or foreign policy, and (b) properly classified pursuant to executive order.
2. Internal personnel rules and practices of an agency.
3. Matters specifically exempt from disclosure by statute.
4. Trade secrets and commercial or financial information obtained from privileged or confidential sources.
5. Intra- or interagency memoranda or letters which would not be available by law to a party other than an agency in litigation with the agency.
6. Personnel and medical files and similar files the disclosure of which would constitute a clearly unwarranted invasion of personal privacy.
7. Law enforcement investigatory records, but only to the extent that disclosure would:
   (a) Interfere with enforcement proceedings
   (b) Deprive a person of a right to a fair trial or impartial adjudication
   (c) Constitute an unwarranted invasion of personal privacy
   (d) Disclose the identity of a confidential source or confidential information obtained from that source
   (e) Disclose investigative techniques and procedures
   (f) Endanger the life or physical safety of law enforcement personnel.
8. Information related to agency regulation or supervision of financial institutions.
9. Geological and geophysical information, including maps concerning wells, and so forth.

FOIA and the Press

During the first four years that the Act was in effect, there were 254,637 requests for information, but only 90 came from the press.[31] Of these, only 12 were "formal requests" in which the press used the FOI Act in an effort to pry out information. Ten came from magazines, two from newspapers, and none from the broadcast media. By mid-1973, the news media had gone to court only three times in an effort to force disclosure of information through FOIA.

This situation prompted Congressman William S. Moorhead, chairman of the House Subcommittee on Foreign Operations and Government Information, to express surprise and to say that the press should be the major user of the law. But the reasons this had not been so became clear largely because of hearings conducted by the subcommittee. The major reason was the time lag involved in requests for information and media's need to have information in a hurry. This, coupled to the "delaying tactics of federal bureaucrats," kept the media from making much use of the law.[32]

FOIA Amended

Various shortcomings in FOIA were spelled out during 41 days of public hearings conducted by the Foreign Operations and Government Information Subcommittee in 1972. The subcommittee issued this general statement:

> The efficient operation of the Freedom of Information Act has been hindered by five years of foot-dragging by the Federal bureaucracy. The widespread reluctance of the bureaucracy to honor the public's legal right to know has been obvious in parts of two administrations. This reluctance has been overcome in a few agencies by continued pressure from appointed officials at the policymaking level and in some other agencies through public hearings and other oversight activities by the Congress.[33]

The committee report concluded with recommendations for major changes in the Act.

Many of the recommendations became law when Congress overrode a veto by President Ford. The amendments accomplished the following:

- Altered that part of the law which required that a request for information be for "identifiable records"; instead, a request for information now must only "reasonably describe" the records being sought.
- Required each agency to issue a schedule of fees for agency search and copying of records. Such fees should recover only the direct costs of search and duplication, not the cost of reviewing the records. As the Conference Committee had reported, ". . . [F]ees should not be used for the purpose of discouraging requests for information or as obstacles to disclosure of requested information."[34]
- Permitted federal courts to make *de novo* (anew) reviews to determine if agencies have wrongfully withheld information from complainants. The amendments specifically authorize District Courts to examine *in camera* (in private) any requested records to determine if they have been properly withheld under one or more of the nine categories of information exempt from forced disclosure. By this action, Congress specifically intended to alter the Supreme Court's decision in *Environmental Protection Agency v. Mink,*[35] under which courts were instructed that they could not review the Executive branch's determination of what could or could not be made public in response to FOIA requests. The House-Senate conferees agreed that while *in camera* examination need not be automatic, "in many situations it will plainly be necessary and appropriate." But before such examination takes place, federal agencies are to be given the opportunity to establish by testimony or detailed affidavits that the documents are clearly exempt from disclosure. It was the *in camera* provision that President Ford chiefly objected to in his veto message. "I simply cannot accept a provision that would risk exposure of our military or intelligence secrets and diplomatic relations," said President Ford, "because of a judicially perceived failure to satisfy a burden of proof." In his judgment, federal judges would lack the expertise to make determination about the classifi-

cation of records, especially those pertaining to national defense, intelligence gathering, and foreign affairs.

The House-Senate conferees anticipated this objection and included this statement in their report:

> . . . [T]he conferees recognize that the Executive departments responsible for national defense and foreign policy matters have unique insights into what adverse affects [sic] might occur as a result of public disclosure of a particular classified record. Accordingly, the conferees expect that Federal courts . . . will accord substantial weight to an agency's affidavit concerning the details of the classified status of the disputed record.

- Modified Subsection (b)(7) Section 552 to make it more difficult for agencies to withhold information under this category of exempt information called "investigatory files."
- Required each agency to provide "any reasonable segregable portion" of any record after that record is purged of information not releasable under one or more of the nine exempt categories.
- Required each agency to determine within 10 work days after receipt of a request for information whether it will comply with the request. If not, the agency must inform the information-seeker of the right of appeal to the agency head. Any such administrative appeal must be decided within 20 work days. If the appeal or the original request is turned down in whole or in part, the agency must inform the information seeker of his/ her right to judicial review. Each of the time limits could be extended 10 days for "unusual circumstances," such as the need to search for and collect information from field offices; the need to gather voluminous amounts of information; or the need to consult with other affected agencies. If an agency becomes a defendant in an FOIA lawsuit, it has 30 days after service in which to answer or otherwise plead to the complaint unless the court permits an exception.
- Called upon U.S. District Courts to give precedence to cases brought under the FOI Act.
- Gave the District Courts the power to assess against the United States reasonable attorney fees and other costs in those cases where complainants have "substantially prevailed." Whenever such court action results, and the court additionally issues a written finding that the circumstances surrounding the withholding of information raise questions whether the agency acted "arbitrarily or capriciously" in the withholding action, the Civil Service Commission can be directed promptly to initiate proceedings to determine whether disciplinary action is warranted against the employee primarily responsible for the withholding. After an investigation, the Commission could make a recommendation to the agency concerned regarding corrective or disciplinary action.

■ Stipulated that each agency must submit annually a report to Congress which would include data showing the number of times the agency did not comply with requests for records and the reasons for such decisions.

FOIA Logjam

Shortly after the amendments went into effect, and because of passage of the Privacy Act of 1974, an avalanche of requests hit federal agencies. In 1975 the Defense Department handled about 44,000 information requests and the Justice Department received more than 30,000. They poured into the FBI at an average daily rate of between 70 and 80. The chief of the FBI's FOI unit asked Congress for a supplemental appropriation of $12 million to reduce the backlog of 8,400 requests involving nearly 10 million pages of files. And in March 1977, Director Clarence Kelley said the "avalanche" of paperwork and "massive waves" of requests required that a task force of 400 agents be assembled in Washington, D.C., from all parts of the country for a six-month period in 1977. The cost of this special effort was put at $6.5 million, while overall FOI cost in fiscal 1977 for the FBI alone was placed at $12 million.

The number of requests for information reached 78 per day in early 1978. The agency was unable to comply with requests within the 10-day period specified by the law, but it did comply with most requests within 30 to 90 days. Because of this situation, the U.S. Court of Appeals for the District of Columbia Circuit ruled in 1976 that the 10-day limitation for agency response to FOI requests did not apply. Instead, the court said the FBI could handle requests on a first-in, first-out basis. According to the court, the reason was: If an agency can show an "exceptional circumstance," and if that agency has exercised "due diligence" in trying to meet its commitments under the law, then additional time can be allowed.

Privacy Act and FOIA

The Privacy Act and the amendments to FOIA were passed by the Senate on the same day, precipating a debate about the impact of the Privacy Act on FOIA, and vice versa. Can the one seriously impede the other? The issue was put into perspective by a law review article which pointed out:

Congress was aware that the Privacy Act would have the practical effect of emasculating the FOIA unless some explicit provision was included allowing the FOIA to remain fully effective. The original House bill contained no exception providing for required FOIA disclosure, and under this version any record covered by the Privacy Act would have been prohibited from FOIA disclosure without the prior written consent of the subject individual. Therefore it would not have been necessary under the House bill to reach the question of whether a FOIA disclosure was required or not, since whenever Privacy Act records would have been the subject of FOIA request, the FOIA would have been effectively nullified. Since Congress ultimately adopted subsection (b)(2) of the Privacy Act, it evidenced a clear intention not to restrict the general policy of disclosure expressed in the FOIA.

Thus Congress provided that when records requested under the FOIA are contained in a Privacy Act record system, the case law interpreting the FOIA exemptions, in addition to determining whether those records are "required" to be disclosed under the FOIA, will necessarily determine whether or not the Privacy Act's restraints on disclosure will operate on that material. In short, if the courts expand required disclosure, the Privacy Act has less material upon which to operate. The agencies, however, have an interest in restricting FOIA disclosure [in an attempt to alleviate the severe administrative burden of compliance brought on by the increasing volume of FOIA requests] and thus they would prefer that as much material as possible be governed exclusively by the Privacy Act. It is in this context that the Privacy Act may have a significant independent influence on judicial interpretations of the FOIA exemptions.[36]

The Supreme Court decided in 1984 to resolve a conflict among the circuit courts and at the same time perhaps clarify the relationship between FOIA and the Privacy Act. The court granted certiorari in two cases in which individuals were barred under the Privacy Act from obtaining their own agency records but sought access to these records by using FOIA.[37] In *U.S. Department of Justice v. Provenzano,* the Justice Department said that records containing Anthony Provenzano's name were exempt from access under a Privacy Act exemption to disclosure. This meant, said the department, that the records also were exempt from FOIA disclosure. Not so, ruled the Third Circuit U.S. Court of Appeals, because the Privacy Act was not intended to have any effect on FOIA.[38] But an opposite conclusion was reached by the Seventh Circuit U.S. Court of Appeals in *Shapiro v. Drug Enforcement Administration.*[39] In a per curiam decision in the combined cases, the Supreme Court said the issues were mooted by passage of the Central Intelligence Information Act in 1984. This Act provides that no agency should rely on any Privacy Act exemption to withhold any record otherwise accessible under FOIA.[40]

Additional Amendments. Given the large number of FOIA information requests, the cost of analyzing the requests, scrutinizing the records, and deciding what information can be released, plus claims by the FBI and CIA that their ability to fight crime or protect national security had been diminished by FOIA requirements, efforts increased to amend the Act in ways favorable to those agencies. In his 1980 State of the Union address, President Carter called for legislation to tighten controls on sensitive intelligence information and to remove "unwarranted restraints on America's ability to collect intelligence." The Justice Department proposed FOIA amendments to Congress in 1980 seeking greater restrictions on the release of certain kinds of information. One result was passage in 1982 of legislation making it a crime to disclose the identity of U.S. spies, as reported in Chapter 3. Another was enactment of the Central Intelligence Information Act that excluded the CIA's "operational files" from FOI disclosure.

When a Ralph Nader lobbying group sought the identity of college researchers who had worked on a CIA mind-control project in the 1950s and 1960s, the U.S. Court of Appeals for the District of Columbia Circuit concluded that the spy agency could keep secret the identities of only those "intelligence sources" who provided the agency with information that could not have been obtained without guaranteeing confidentiality. Clearly, the college researchers would not fall within such a definition. But the U.S. Supreme Court, by a 9–0 vote in 1985 in *CIA v. Sims,* ruled that the CIA has broad discretion to withhold information under the National Security Act.[41] And with only Justices Brennan and Marshall disagreeing, the majority defined "intelligence sources" so broadly as to raise questions of whether or not information that Congress intended for disclosure could be divulged through use of the FOIA. Writing for the majority, Chief Justice Burger said judges should not second-guess the CIA once the agency had determined that a source of information should not be divulged. Thus, as Brennan and Marshall complained, even publicly available sources of CIA information, such as newspapers, books, road maps and telephone books, would not have to be disclosed by the CIA if it did not wish to do so.

Justice Department concerns were dealth with in the closing days of the 99th Congress when the Senate, with House approval, slipped some broad exemptions for law enforcement records and a new fee structure for FOIA requests into a drug enforcement bill that President Reagan signed into law.[42] The FOIA's investigatory records exemption has been broadened to permit secrecy if public access "could reasonably be expected to cause" harm to law enforcement efforts. Prior to passage of the amendments, such records could be withheld only if disclosure "would" harm the agency's law enforcement efforts.[43] In addition, informants' files no longer are disclosable under FOIA except in those instances where the government has "officially confirmed" that a person is an informant. Also, if an investigation is ongoing, an agency now can respond to an FOIA request by stating that it has no responsive documents. Previously, agencies had to acknowledge that they had documents and explain why they were being withheld. Law enforcement agencies had complained that this gave the subjects of investigations valuable information even if no documents were released.[44]

The Federal Trade Commission Improvement Act of 1980 also placed expanded restrictions on disclosure of certain information by the FTC.[45] Previously Section 6(f) of the FTC Act prohibited disclosure of the identity of a business's customers and trade secrets, but the amended act enlarges the prohibition to include "any trade secret or any commercial or financial information which is obtained from any person and which is privileged or confidential." In effect, this language incorporates into the FTC Act Exemption 4 of FOIA.

Case Law and FOIA

As statutory law increases in the areas of privacy and freedom of information, at both the state and federal levels, so does case law. There are hundreds of decisions construing various provisions of FOIA, and the number increases each year. Keeping track of such developments requires special efforts, such as those made by: (1) Freedom of Information Center at Columbia, Missouri, which publishes *FoI Digest* six times a year; (2) *Access Reports/FOI* newsletter, published biweekly by Plus Publications, Inc.; (3) Reporters Committee for Freedom of the Press, which publishes *The NEWS Media & The LAW*; (4) *Media Law*

Reporter, published weekly by the Bureau of National Affairs, Inc.; and (5) numerous freedom of information committees for national or state press organizations.

The decisions of the U.S. Supreme Court interpreting FOIA generally have gone against disclosure. As the Reporters Committee for Freedom of the Press pointed out in 1988, not since a case in 1976 has the Court ordered disclosure of government information.[46]

The 1976 case was *Air Force v. Rose.* In its 5–3 decision, the Court declared that the nine statutory exemptions to disclosing information under FOIA "do not obscure the basic policy that disclosure, not secrecy, is the dominant objective of the Act."[47] Furthermore, said Justice Brennan for the majority, the nine exemptions "must be narrowly construed."

This case stemmed from the Air Force Academy's refusal to grant student editors of *New York University Law Review* access to case summaries involving honor code or ethics code violations. In all but guilty cases, names are deleted from the summaries which are posted on bulletin boards at the Academy. What the editors sought were the summaries in which identifying data had been deleted. The Air Force Academy refused and the student editors brought suit under FOIA. The U.S. District Court granted the Academy summary judgment based on Exemption 2 (internal personnel rules and practices of an agency). The U.S. Court of Appeals for the Second Circuit reversed, holding that Exemption 2 was not applicable; rather, the case summaries fell within Exemption 6 (personnel and medical files and similar files the disclosure of which would constitute a clearly unwarranted invasion of personal privacy). The circuit court held that the Academy had to cooperate with the district court by producing the summaries for *in camera* inspection and in helping to redact them (delete personal references and all other identifying information). The Supreme Court affirmed the Circuit Court's ruling.

In connection with Exemption 2, the Court said the exemption was designed to delineate between trivial matters and more substantial matters in which the public might have a legitimate interest.

As for Exemption 6, Brennan, in his opinion for the Court, said:

> . . . [W]e find nothing in the wording of Exemption 6 or its legislative history to support the . . . [Academy's] claim that Congress created a blanket exemption for personnel files. Judicial interpretation has uniformly reflected the view that no reason would exist for nondisclosure in the absence of a showing of a clearly unwarranted invasion of privacy, whether the documents are filed in "personnel" or "similar" files. . . . Congressional concern for the protection of the kind of confidential personal data usually included in a personnel file is abundantly clear. But Congress also made clear that nonconfidential matter was not to be insulated from disclosure merely because it was stored by the Agency in "personnel" files. Rather, Congress sought to construct an exemption that would require a balancing of the individual's right of privacy against the preservation of the basic purpose of the Freedom of Information Act "to open agency action to the light of public scrutiny." The device adopted to achieve that balance was the limited exemption, where privacy was threatened, for "clearly unwarranted" invasions of personal privacy.

Brennan noted the then-recent congressional action in amending FOIA, such that "any reasonably segregable portion of a record shall be provided to any person requesting such record after deletion of the portions which are exempt," as being consistent with the Court's conclusion. Redaction was the way to eliminate most of the risks of identifiability, he said.

Burger and Blackmun dissented, with Rehnquist agreeing with a part of Burger's dissent when he said the Court's decision requires a virtual reconstruction of the records so information that would be a "clearly unwarranted" invasion of a cadet's personal privacy would be excised. He did not believe the Act contemplated such a reconstruction effort.

Air Force v. Rose is significant because it requires a balancing test whenever Exemptions 2 or 6 are put forward as reasons for nondisclosure. Exemption 2 is to be balanced against matters of "legitimate public interest." And Exemption 6 is to prevail only when there would be a "clearly unwarranted" invasion of personal privacy.

FAA v. Robertson (1975). In a 7–2 decision, the U.S. Supreme Court stated unequivocally that FOIA did not make redundant or repeal the nearly 100 pre-FOIA statutes or parts thereof that restrict public access to specific governing records.

The respondents in *Federal Aviation Administration v. Reuben B. Robertson III,* who were associated with the Center for the Study of Responsive Law, had asked the FAA to make available certain Systems Worthiness Analysis Program reports.[48] The FAA declined, stating that the reports fell under Exemption 3 (material specifically exempt from disclosure by statute). A district court had ruled that the documents should be disclosed; a divided U.S. Court of Appeals had affirmed, but had remanded for consideration of other exemptions which FAA might wish to assert, and the Supreme Court reversed.

Principal points made by Chief Justice Burger in his opinion for the Court:

1. At the time Congress enacted FOIA, it was aware of the numerous existing laws allowing confidentiality and it chose not to repeal them. The Court cannot override that legislative choice.
2. The public interest is served by the free flow of relevant information to the FAA from the airlines. Congress believed that confidentiality of information relevant to safety secured the maximum amount of such information.
3. When Congress amended FOIA, it left Exemption 3 unchanged.

But the following year, Congress attached a rider to the Sunshine Act, discussed later in this chapter, which specifically overrode the *FAA v. Robertson* decision.

Kissinger v. Reporters Committee for Freedom of the Press (1980).[49] Henry Kissinger served as a national security adviser to the President from 1969 to 1975 and was U.S. secretary of state from 1973 to 1977. During these periods, his secretaries monitored his telephone conversations and recorded their contents either by shorthand or tape, the result being some 32,000 pages of transcripts.

In 1976 a *New York Times* columnist, William Safire, sought from the State Department transcripts of Kissinger's telephone conversations made while he was national security adviser. The department turned down the request, saying the records were not agency records subject to FOIA disclosure. Shortly thereafter, Kissinger removed all of the telephone conversation transcripts in his State Department files and donated them by deed to the Library of Congress with restrictions on public access to them. Safire, the Reporters Committee, and one other group thereupon filed FOIA requests for the transcripts. A U.S. District Court judge ordered the State Department to retrieve the records from the Library of Congress and screen out any portions exempt from disclosure under FOIA, but otherwise comply with the FOIA requesters. The order did not apply to the transcripts resulting from the period when Kissinger was national security adviser. The U.S. Court of Appeals for the District of Columbia Circuit affirmed, but stayed release of any of the material pending Supreme Court action. The Supreme Court affirmed in part and reversed in part in an opinion written by Justice Rehnquist. Burger, White, Stewart, and Powell joined in that opinion. Brennan and Stevens filed opinions concurring in part and dissenting in part. Neither Marshall nor Blackmun took part in the decision.

The Court held that the State Department was not improperly withholding records within the meaning of FOIA when it refused to institute action to retrieve records that were improperly taken from the agency. The Court rejected the argument that FOIA permits private actions to recover records wrongfully removed from an agency's custody. The only relief for improper removal of a "record" from an agency, said the Court, was by means of a suit by the attorney general at the behest of the agency's head. In addition, Rehnquist said remedies could be devised for nondisclosed information only if an agency improperly withheld records. Thus, the plaintiff must make such a showing before a remedy can be provided or an agency required to show, in turn, that it is justified in withholding the information. This is quite a hurdle for an FOIA requester.

The Court also noted that two of the FOIA requests came after Kissinger had deeded the documents to the Library of Congress. Since he and the Library were holding the notes under a claim of right, the State Department could not be said to have had possession of the documents at the time the requests were received and therefore was not liable to suit under FOIA. The third request was for notes made while Kissinger was national security adviser and before he became secretary of state. But FOIA does not apply to close personal advisers of the president, the Court noted.

In the dissenting portion of his opinion, Stevens took exception to Kissinger's argument that the State Department summaries were private papers. He wrote:

> . . . As the District Court noted, they were made in the regular course of conducting the agency's business, were the work product of agency personnel and agency

assets, and were maintained in the possession and control of the agency prior to their removal by Dr. Kissinger.

FBI v. Abramson (1982). The Court, by a 5–4 vote, ruled that information used for political purposes, which came from FBI records, is still covered under the investigatory records exemption.[50] The ruling means that not only are the records exempt from disclosure, but information contained therein also is exempt even if later used for investigatory purposes.

The case resulted when summaries, based on FBI records, were prepared for the Nixon White House on 11 opponents of United States involvement in the Vietnam War. Journalist Howard Abramson had received some documents related to the case, but challenged the withholding of a one-page memorandum from FBI Director J. Edgar Hoover to John Ehrlichman and 63 pages of attachments containing some information about the 11 persons.

The Court's ruling overturned a decision of the U.S. Court of Appeals for the District of Columbia Circuit.

Justice White gave the Court's opinion, saying that the case involved a single question: "Whether information originally compiled for law enforcement purposes loses its exemption if summarized in a new document not created for law enforcement purposes." He said Congress clearly intended to protect the information from disclosure, rather than records, even though the language it used refers only to the latter.

In dissent, Justices Blackmun and Brennan said the ruling means that judges considering FOIA cases involving Exemption 7 have to examine agency records to determine if any piece of information contained therein was originally compiled for a law enforcement purpose. If so, it would be exempt from disclosure. Clearly, such a task is formidable.

State Department v. Washington Post (1982). A lower federal court ruling was overturned by the Supreme Court's unanimous decision in this case.[51] At issue was the withholding of government records that would have shown whether two Iranian officials actually were U.S. citizens. To disclose such information about these prominent members of Iran's revolutionary government, said a State Department official in 1980, would be likely to cause a real threat of physical harm to them.

The significance of the ruling is that any federal government record that refers to any identifiable, specific individual falls within the exemption for "personnel, medical, and similar" files and can be withheld from the public if its disclosure would constitute a clearly unwarranted invasion of personal privacy (Exemption 6). The appellate court had ruled that naturalization court records that would show citizenship status are not as highly personal or as intimate in nature as personnel and medical record information; therefore, they were not "similar files." But in the opinion by Justice Rhenquist, "similar files" was given a broader interpretation. Congress intended by it, said Rehnquist, a general restriction on the release of personal files, not just information in the personnel and medical files categories.[52]

Baldridge v. Shapiro (1982). The Court unanimously agreed that lists of addresses compiled by the Census Bureau are exempt from disclosure under both FOIA and the Federal Rules of Civil Procedure.[53] The Court said that Exemption 3 pertains to census information because Congress specifically provided that information furnished to the bureau be treated as confidential.[54] No discretion is allowed, said the Court in reversing the Third Circuit's decision and affirming the Tenth Circuit's.[55]

CIA v. Sims (1985). The court unanimously agreed that the CIA has broad discretion to withhold the identity of its sources of intelligence information from public disclosure.[56] Seven of the nine justices agreed that information the CIA says it needs to perform its statutory duties with respect to foreign intelligence is exempt from disclosure under FOIA. The exemption applies even if the information does not have a bearing on national security or even if the source of the information is a newspaper or magazine of general circulation.

The Court, in an opinion written by Chief Justice Burger, overturned a District of Columbia Circuit Court ruling in which the three-judge panel had adopted a much narrower definition of the "intelligence sources" entitled to exemption from disclosure.

Two organizations—the Public Citizens Health Research Group and the Public Citizen Litigation Group—had filed requests for information under FOIA seeking to learn the names of researchers who had participated in a CIA project, code named MKULTRA, which was designed to develop techniques for controlling human behavior. Some 180 private researchers and 80 institutions participated in this research in the early 1970s. The dispute in this case: Were the names of the researchers "intelligence sources"?

FOIA provides that an agency need not disclose matters that are specifically exempt from disclosure by statute. The CIA based its refusal to disclose on a 1947 statute—the National Security Act—which provides that the CIA director is responsible for protecting intelligence sources and methods from unauthorized disclosure.

Marshall and Brennan agreed with the judgment of the Court, but in an opinion by Marshall, in which Brennan joined, Marshall took the position that the Court majority went too far in protecting the CIA information by establishing "an irrebuttable presumption of secrecy over an expansive array of information." Marshall noted that even publicly available sources of information, such as newspapers, telephone books, and road maps, could be included in a CIA-ordered veil of secrecy.

The research project became a national scandal in the 1970s when congressional investigators disclosed that the project included the testing of biological and chemical substances, often on unwitting subjects, that caused two deaths and some injuries.

Other FOIA Litigation

In addition to the Supreme Court cases cited above, there have been many other noteworthy FOI cases. For example, Michael and Robert Meeropol, the children of Julius and Ethel Rosenberg—the parents having been executed in 1953 for giving A-bomb secrets to the Soviet Union—succeeded in gaining access to some 30,000 pages pertaining to the spy case. The children sought release of the records in the belief that the information would show their parents to have been innocent. Originally, the FBI had wanted a 235-day delay in complying with the children's request and $20,458 in "search fees." The delay was denied by a U.S. District Court judge.[57] The search fees later were waived by the Justice Department because the Rosenberg case "is close to being unique in terms of both current public interest and historical significance." The FBI had to assign nearly one hundred employees to the task of searching its records.

Similarly, the CIA waived search fees of $14,000 in connection with providing 953 pages of information from the Rosenberg files.

The Meeropols subsequently were awarded $195,802 in legal fees—the largest sum awarded to that time in connection with FOIA litigation. A 1974 amendment to FOIA authorizes such payment when a litigant has "substantially prevailed" in a suit against the government.

By means of a FOIA suit, NBC News correspondent Carl Stern compelled the FBI to reveal the existence of its "dirty tricks" program design to harass and disrupt New Left political organizations. In discussing that suit and some of its results, Stern said in a 1975 speech:

> So far, with only occasional exceptions, the courts have been the ally with the news media in ferreting out information to which the press is entitled. Three years ago I came across a document in which FBI agents in the Philadelphia area were being instructed from the main office in Washington to write anonymous letters to college administrators in their area . . . urging the administrator to get tough on local SDS [Students for a Democratic Society] chapters. Whether one approves of SDS or not is hardly the question. The question that immediately popped into my mind was, "On what authority do FBI agents send anonymous letters urging anything?" The subject heading was "Cointelpro new left," "Cointelpro" is an FBI contraction meaning counterintelligence program.
>
> I asked the Justice Department what "Cointelpro" was. They wouldn't tell me. I asked the FBI. They wouldn't tell me. I explained in lengthy correspondence that I wasn't trying to learn the names of agents, or defendants, or informants, or specifics of any actual operations. I was merely trying to find out by what authority a program was operating and what was the nature of that program. Clearly, . . . if citizens cannot even find out what programs their government is operating, then they have no meaningful role in governing themselves.
>
> Well, ultimately I sued the government to get the information, and the courts backed me up. That litigation was the icebreaker that established the legal precedent that citizens have a right—enforceable in court—to learn of such matters.[58]

Ultimately, the Justice Department announced that three FBI officials had been censured because they had "misused their official positions" in the Cointelpro investigations, which involved not only infiltration and attempted disruption of political protest groups but also "black bag" capers, or burglaries, to obtain information about individuals and groups. But when Stern asked that the three be identified, the FBI said the release of the names would serve no purpose other than to embarrass the officials. So the NBC correspondent filed another FOIA lawsuit. In 1983 the U.S. District Court for the District of Columbia ordered the FBI to release the agents' names.[59] The public's interest in learning the names outweighs the trio's privacy interests, said the court, particularly because the three were policy-making executives.

Stern's use of FOIA was more the exception than the rule for journalists. According to a study by the Congressional Research Service, news stories that resulted from FOIA disclosures declined in 1979 and 1980 from the 1975–77 period. Thirty-eight stories resulted from such disclosures in 1978, 22 in 1979, and nine in 1980. Another study by a house subcommittee showed that the news media used FOIA in 439 instances from 1972 to 1984.[60]

The reason for diminished use of the Act is not hard to find. Delays are interminable. The *Washington Post,* for example, originally requested material from the State Department concerning the secretary of state's "emergency fund."[61] When the information request was refused, the newspaper filed an FOIA lawsuit. Litigation proceeded until 1983 when the newspaper informed the State Department that it no longer wanted to pursue its FOIA request despite a favorable Circuit Court ruling. The newspaper was concerned that the Supreme Court might upset the lower court ruling; but more than that, it already had obtained sufficient information from its own sources to publish two stories concerning the emergency fund. So the Supreme Court proceeded to vacate the Circuit Court's judgment and instructed that court to direct the U.S. District Court to dismiss the complaint as moot.

More recently, media organizations have begun to use the FOIA more frequently and some individual reporters are *routinely* using the Act whenever they want information from federal agencies. As one reporter explained, such requests take government officials "off the hook" if information is released pursuant to such a request.

One example of the increased use is provided by the space shuttle Challenger explosion in 1986. At least 15 FOIA suits were filed to gain information about the disaster. In 1988 the Justice Department agreed to the release of information concerning the amount of money paid to the families of four of the astronauts killed in the explosion. Those families received $7.7 million in tax-free annuities.[62]

For anyone wishing to obtain information by using FOIA, a sample request letter was published in the 1986–87 report of the National Freedom of Information Committee of the Society of Professional Journalists, Sigma Delta Chi.[63]

SAMPLE
FOI REQUEST LETTER

Tele. No. (business hours)
Return Address
Date

Name of Public Body
Address

To the FOI Officer:

This request is made under the federal Freedom of Information Act, 5 U.S.C. 552.

Please send me copies of (Here, clearly describe what you want. Include identifying material, such as names, places, and the period of time about which you are inquiring. If you wish, attach news clips, reports, and other documents describing the subject of your research.)

As you know, the FOI Act provides that if portions of a document are exempt from release, the remainder must be segregated and disclosed. Therefore, I will expect you to send me all nonexempt portions of the records which I have requested, and ask that you justify any deletions by reference to specific exemptions of the FOI Act. I reserve the right to appeal your decision to withhold any materials.

I promise to pay reasonable search and duplication fees in connection with this request. However, if you estimate that the total fee will exceed $____, please notify me so that I may authorize expenditure of a greater amount.

(Optional) I am prepared to pay reasonable search and duplication fees in connection with this request. However, if the FOI Act provides for waiver or reduction of fees if disclosure could be considered as "primarily benefiting the general public." I am a journalist (researcher, or scholar) employed by (name of news organization, book publisher, etc.), and intend to use the information I am requesting as the basis for a planned article (broadcast, or book). (Add arguments here in support of fee waiver). Therefore, I ask that you waive all search and duplication fees. If you deny this request, however, and the fees will exceed $____, please notify me of the charges before you fill my request so that I may decide whether to pay the fees or appeal your denial of my request for a waiver.

As I am making this request in the capacity of a journalist (author, or scholar) and this information is of timely value, I will appreciate your communicating with me by telephone, rather than by mail, if you have any questions regarding this request. Thank you for your assistance, and I will look forward to receiving your reply within 10 business days, as required by law.

Very truly yours,

(Signature)

FEDERAL OPEN MEETINGS LAW

FOIA is the federal "open record" law. There also is a legal requirement for many federal agencies and Executive Branch advisory committees to open their meetings to the public.

The "Government in the Sunshine Act" (Pub. L. No. 94-409) went into effect March 12, 1977. Its purpose is stated in the Act's "Declaration of Policy":

> It is hereby declared to be the policy of the United States that the public is entitled to the fullest practicable information regarding the decision-making processes of the Federal Government. It is the purpose of this Act to provide the public with such information while protecting the rights of individuals and the ability of the Government to carry out its responsibilities.

The Sunshine Act opens the meetings of about 50 federal agencies, boards, and commissions with two or more heads or directors, although it does not include executive departments headed by a single cabinet member. Thus, two independent regulatory agencies which have considerable impact on mass communications — the Federal Communications Commission and the Federal Trade Commission — are required to open their meetings to the public except for 10 exemptions to disclosure permitted by the Act. Exemptions 1–4 and 6–8 are similar to those same-numbered exemptions in FOIA. Exemption 5 permits closed meetings when the agency determines that such portion or portions of meetings or the disclosure of such information is likely to "involve accusing any person of a crime, or formally censuring any person."

Exemptions 9 and 10 permit closed meetings when disclosure would:

> **(9)(A)** in the case of an agency which regulates currencies, securities, commodities, or financial institutions, be likely to (*i*) lead to significant financial speculation in currencies, securities, or commodities, or (*ii*) significantly endanger the stability of a financial institution; or
>
> **(B)** in the case of any agency, be likely to significantly frustrate implementation of a proposed agency action, except that subparagraph (B) shall not apply in any instance where the agency has already disclosed to the public the content or nature of its proposed action, or where the agency is required by law to make such disclosure on its own initiative prior to taking final agency action on such proposal; or
>
> **(10)** specifically concern the agency's issuance of subpoena, or the agency's participation in a civil action or proceeding, an action in a foreign court or international tribunal, or an arbitration, or the initiation, conduct, or disposition by the agency of a particular case of formal agency adjudication pursuant to the procedures in section 554 of this title or otherwise involving a determination on the record after opportunity for a hearing.[64]

In signing the Sunshine Act into law, President Ford complained that the definition of what constitutes a meeting was ambiguous. As with FOIA, agency spokespersons generally viewed the Act with foreboding and there was some speculation that decision making might take place in unofficial places prior to a meeting.

Under the Act, modeled on Florida's Sunshine Law, an agency must make a public announcement at least one week before the meeting of the time, place, and subject matter of the meeting, whether it is to be open or closed to the public, and the name and phone number of the official designated by the agency to respond to requests for information about the meeting. There are some limited provisions for changing the time or place of a meeting.

In discussing the relationship of the Sunshine Act to FOIA and personal privacy, Attorney James T. O'Reilly made the following comments in a FOI Center report:

> One of the weaknesses of the Freedom of Information Act, in its initial form, was an unclear intent of Congress regarding the meaning of several exemptions. The congressional intent of Sunshine is very clear; governmental decision making is to be open unless proven to fall under one of the narrow exemptions. . . . Some of the exemptions continue the FOIA intent for balancing legitimate rivalry interests. . . . Overall, the intention toward openness of governmental action is explicit and reinforces that shown in the original and amended FOIA.
>
> . . . Perhaps the strongest impact of Sunshine on the FOIA will come when courts consider the legislative intention of Congress in future FOIA cases. It is remarkable, perhaps even unprecedented, that a statute less than ten years old should have six major Supreme Court interpretations and that the two which most favored withholding of documents—*EPA v. Mink* and *Robertson*—should have been explicitly overruled by the Congress. When a FOIA exemption claim appears to be a borderline matter of government secrecy versus public disclosure in future court proceedings, it seems inevitable that courts reading legislative intentions should give the measure of advantage to pro-disclosure forces.
>
> Except where private interests are affected, interests whose protection of personal and commercial privacy was again protected in Sunshine, the balance will swing heavily in favor of public disclosure.
>
> Finally, the Sunshine judicial review favors a tactic which courts under the FOIA had repeatedly rejected. The agency which denied access under FOIA and lost the case in court could, and did, refuse the same document or type of document to other requesters without effective judicial review. Sunshine provides that an improperly closed meeting can be enjoined by a court, and that the court can issue an injunction against all future agency closings which violate Sunshine procedures. This might be called the "one mistake rule," for future improper closings could evoke a contempt sanction from a federal court against the agency which lost the earlier dispute.[65]

The Sunshine Act appears to be less effective than its sponsors had hoped. An October 1980 special issue of *ACCESS Reports* contained the results of a study that showed almost half of the agencies affected by the Sunshine Act were not opening a majority of their meetings. Most agencies relied on Exemptions 9 and 10 to close meetings. Shortly thereafter, *FoI Digest* reported: "Today, few officials in Washington appear to be taking the act seriously."[66] Not much has changed to the present to alter that appraisal.

Congress and Its "Openness"

Almost from the start, the sessions of the full House and Senate have been open to the public. On rare occasions one or the other House of Congress votes to bar the public and the press from one of its meetings. The Senate, for example, closed its sessions to the public only seven times during the period 1945 to 1970 when it considered such matters as the CIA, missile programs, or the situations in Southeast Asia during the Vietnam War. But congressional committees are a different matter. About 40 percent of all committee meetings take place behind closed doors. Legislation has been introduced to make secret meetings less frequent, including a requirement that explanations must be given each time a committee decides to conduct business in secret; but thus far few committees follow the lead of the Senate Appropriations Committee which requires all of its subcommittees to conduct public sessions under a policy adopted in 1947.

Until the 1970s, broadcasting of House and Senate floor sessions had been barred, although some congressional committees have allowed such coverage at their public hearings. But in 1975, a Joint Committee on Congressional Operations on Congress and Mass Communication reported that "broadcasting of House and Senate floor proceedings seems to be the most practical, immediate, and direct way to enhance public understanding of congressional activities."[67]

In mid-1978 the House allowed live radio broadcasts of regular floor proceedings to begin with broadcasters plugging into the House's public address system to provide live radio coverage on a daily basis.

As for television, Speaker Thomas P. (Tip) O'Neill, Jr. had his way when the House voted 235–150 in 1978 to allow only House employees to control the cameras. Broadcasters and other press groups argued in vain that journalists should control the cameras, but representatives, fearful of being caught in unguarded moments, refused to go along.

Beginning in March 1979, television coverage of floor proceedings has been made available free of charge to commercial, public, and cable television, but only cable TV has made such use of it. About 2,000 cable systems carried the House proceedings in 1986 with six remote-controlled TV cameras used to cover floor debates.

Live, gavel-to-gavel audio coverage of the Senate began on March 12, 1986, and live TV coverage began on June 2 of that year.

Supreme Court and Secrecy

The deliberative process by which the Supreme Court members make up their minds, and the opinions prepared and written prior to their being made public, are shrouded in secrecy. Long-standing rules are designed to prevent premature disclosure in part because such disclosure might give unfair advantage to those in the "know." This would be particularly true whenever a Court decision has economic impact or would influence financial affairs.

Within the past few years court reporters have correctly forecast several decisions by the Court, apparently because of "leaks" from inside sources. An ABC News reporter correctly reported the Court's *Herbert v. Lando* decision on April 16, 1979, two days before the Court announced it. Chief Justice Burger ordered an investigation and a printer at the Government Printing Office was subsequently transferred to another printing job. A reporter for National Public Radio also correctly announced a decision shortly before it was officially announced. And there have been a few other instances of this happening. Generally, however, the internal functioning of the Court on the way to reaching decisions is carefully shielded from public gaze. And members of the press disagree among themselves as to the need for "prematurely" disclosing Court decisions.

Bob Woodward of Watergate reporting fame, and Scott Armstrong teamed up to interview several former associate justices, more than 170 former law clerks of associate justices, and several dozen former employees of the Court and the result, in 1979, was publication of *The Brethren: Inside the Supreme Court.* Because discussions in chamber between justices and law clerks have long been regarded as strictly confidential, the book is another recent example of a breach in the Court's tradition of secrecy.

State Open Meeting, Open Record Laws

All of the states have open meeting and open record laws. Mississippi was the last state to adopt a public record law, doing so in 1983.

There are considerable variations among the state open record laws, along with commonalities. Maryland, for example, exempts relatively few records: personnel files, hospital patient care reports, trade secrets, and library circulation records. The Iowa Code lists 17 types of records that are confidential unless ordered by a court, the lawful custodian or some other authorized person to be disclosed. These include: (1) personal information involving a student; (2) hospital records and medical records; (3) trade secrets; (4) records representing the work of an attorney in regard to litigation or claims made by or against a public body; (5) peace officers' investigative reports except where disclosure is authorized elsewhere in the Iowa Code; (6) reports of governmental bodies that would give advantage to competitors and that are without purpose; (7) appraisals or related information concerning the purchase of real or personal property for public purposes before the project has been publicized; (8) Iowa Development Commission information on current industrial prospects; (9) criminal identification files of law enforcement agencies, although arrest records are public; (10) personal information in confidential personnel records of public bodies, that is, cities, county boards of supervisors, and school districts; (11) personal information in confidential personnel records of the state military department; (12) financial statements given to the Iowa Commerce Commission by a licensed grain dealer or warehouseman or by an applicant for license for either one; (13) library circulation records; (14) the material of a library, museum, or archive contributed by a private person if any limitation is a condition of the contribution; (15) information about the control of disturbances at adult correctional institutions; (16) information directed to the state or local boards or departments of health that identifies a person with a reportable disease; and (17) records of owners of public bonds or obligations as provided for in the Iowa Code or by the issuer of the bonds or obligations.[68]

Similarly, variations in state open meeting laws are considerable. Virtually all of the laws permit executive sessions, but most of the states require that any official action must take place at public sessions.

Unlike federal open record and open meeting laws, some states decree fines and/or jail terms for violators. For example, anyone who violates Michigan's open record law could be fined a maximum of $500 and/or jailed for not more than one year. Minnesota originally did not impose any penalty for violation of its open record law, but established a maximum $100 fine for violation of its open meeting law. But the open record law was amended in 1979 to allow a person to sue for damages, costs, and reasonable attorney fees whenever records are wrongfully withheld. If an agency willfully violates the law, it may be required to pay $100 to $10,000 for each violation, but the government may be awarded costs if a court finds a request for data is frivolous. Florida imposes a maximum $5,000 fine and up to one year in jail for violation of either the open meeting or open record laws. Nebraska permits a fine of not more than $25 for violation of the open meeting law. And Texas law sets a fine of between $100 and $500 and between one and six months in jail for violation of its open meeting statute.

Some penalties have been imposed for violations. In Wisconsin, the state supreme court affirmed a lower court decision to fine a group of public officials $25 each for violation of the open meeting law, even though the violation was said to be unintentional.[69] And in Oklahoma, members of a town council were found guilty in 1979 on three counts of violating the open meeting law and each member was fined $900.[70]

In one of the toughest penalties handed out to date, an Oklahoma court sentenced a local official to a year in jail for repeated violations of the state's open meetings law. A trustee at Wister, Oklahoma, was convicted in September 1986 of repeated failures to post meeting agendas, to keep minutes of meetings and of holding illegal executive sessions.[71] This was the first time that an official had been sentenced to jail for violating that state's open meetings law.

Here are some of the developments in the states concerning open meetings and open records:

Arizona. An amended version of the state's open meeting law went into effect in 1978, making it more difficult for public bodies to hold closed sessions. Advisory committees are included in openness requirements.

Arkansas. Efforts to broaden the definition of public records in the state's FOIA succeeded in 1977. The law was changed to include not only those records required to be kept by law, but also those kept that "constitute a record of performance or lack of performance of official functions which are or should be carried out by a public official or employee, a governmental agency or any other agency wholly or partially supported by public funds or expending public funds."[72] Furthermore, records kept by government agencies are presumed to be public.

The Arkansas Supreme Court boosted openness in these three rulings:

1. It overturned a lower court decision that committees are exempt from the open meeting law because they were not included in the law. Not so, said

the court in 1975. All meetings of committees of public bodies are open to the public.

2. By a 5–2 vote in 1976 the court ruled that governing bodies—in this instance the Eldorado City Council—cannot meet informally, even if a quorum is not present, if the members discuss or act "on any matter on which foreseeable action will be taken."[73] In effect, the state's FOIA was applied to informal meetings whenever action might result.

3. By a unanimous vote in 1977, the court ruled that private organizations which are supported entirely or partly by public funds are subject to the state's FOIA and their meetings must be open in accordance with that law (Ark. Stat. Ann. 12-2805).

California. The Ralph M. Brown Open Meetings Law was amended, effective January 1, 1976, to permit recovery of fees for those who are successful in court action brought under this law. The Brown Act, which opens county and municipal meetings to the public, also was amended to prohibit executive sessions in connection with the hiring or firing of state employees.

The Brown Act was amended again in 1986 to require that agendas be posted and that they include descriptions of items to be discussed. The change resulted after the Los Angeles City Council approved a 10 percent pay hike for itself. The posted agenda had referred to this only as "Item 53." Also, matters not on the agenda can only be considered in "emergency situations" after at least two-thirds of the agency's members agree that there's a need for such action. State courts are given power to void actions taken in violation of the Act.[74]

The open meeting law provides that all meetings of the governing body of a state agency, including student governments at state universities, must be open to the public. However, executive sessions are permitted for a number of reasons.

There also are a number of records exempt from disclosure under the open record law, including most judicial records, agency memoranda and working papers, records pertaining to pending litigation, information which, if released, would constitute an unwarranted invasion of personal privacy, and so forth.

Colorado. The open record law provides that state and local public records can be denied only when the public interest so requires. The state's Sunshine Act requires that all meetings of two or more members of any state body be open to the public. There are no provisions for executive sessions.

Connecticut. In 1975 an open meeting/open record law went into effect. It provides that meetings can be closed if two-thirds of the members present vote for closure. The law also provides that certain records can remain confidential, including labor records, financial and real estate negotiations, certain law enforcement and security records, and documents in pending court cases. Agencies can withhold information when it would be in the public interest to do so, but such a determination can be challenged by appeal to a three-member FOI Commission. The commission teaches citizens what their rights are under openness laws and how to exercise those rights.

District of Columbia. An FOIA was signed into law in 1976 and grants access to all government information except records pertaining to such matters as trade secrets, intra- and interagency memoranda, personal private data, investigatory information, information exempt by statute, test questions, or national defense and foreign policy matters.

Florida. Florida has broad open meeting and open record laws, said by the Society of Professional Journalists' FOI Committee to be "generally well enforced."[75] Two changes in the open record law went into effect in 1983. Personnel files of teachers and other public school employees are open to the public. Evaluation reports of teachers also are available to the public one year after the evaluations are made. Also, complaints against police officers can be inspected after a police agency has completed a preliminary investigation.[76]

There has been considerable litigation in connection with open meetings and open records.

A most unusual case resulted from a ruling by a state trial court that the public be allowed access to all search committees at which official business is conducted, in this instance a University of Florida law school dean-search committee meeting. The state supreme court upheld the ruling. The plaintiffs then sought an award of attorney fees, and as part of a stipulation to dismiss the motion for attorney fees, the university and the plaintiffs' attorneys each agreed to contribute $50,000 to a "Media Access Fund" that will be used for the benefit of the Florida Freedom of Information Clearinghouse, scholarships, lectures and other projects which will increase understanding of the "principles of open government and media law."[77]

Hawaii. A modified version of the Uniform Information Practices Act, drafted by the National Conference of Commissioners on Uniform State Laws in the 1970s, went into effect in 1989. It replaces the Fair Information Practice Act and includes a policy statement that the law is to be construed in favor of disclosure. It lists 16 categories of information which must be made public by state and county governments. There are five exemptions to disclosure: If disclosure would invade privacy (unless the public's interest in disclosure outweighs an individual's privacy interests); litigation records, such as a lawyer's work product; records which, if disclosed, would frustrate "a legitimate government function"; records sealed by law or by order of state or federal courts; and legislative working papers and legislators' personal files.[78]

Requesters who prevail on appeal may be awarded attorney's fees and court costs.

An Office of Information Practices has been established to oversee public access to government information.

Illinois. A comprehensive public record law went into effect in 1984 patterned after the federal FOIA, but including a lengthier list of exemptions. The law requires agencies to respond to information requests within seven work days (up to 14 days in special cases). Among exemptions to disclosure are certain investigatory records, preliminary notes and recommendations by an agency employee, and library circulation records.[79]

Indiana. An "open door" law went into effect in 1977, requiring all state and local governing bodies, including those of advisory agencies, to conduct open meetings. Secret executive sessions are allowed for consideration of such matters as personnel, pending litigation, or that which would invade a person's privacy. However, final action must be taken in public. Violators can be fined between $50 and $500 and be jailed up to 30 days.

The state's public record law was amended in 1983 to cover executive, state, and local legislative and administrative offices. The burden of justifying nondisclosure is shifted to the agency, and an agency is given 24 hours to respond to an information request.[80]

Kansas. The state's open meeting law, although declaring a policy of openness, allows secret executive sessions for any reason when called for by majority vote. An amendment, however, provided that any action taken at an illegally closed meeting can be nullified.

The open record law provides for disclosure except when forbidden by other statutes. Juvenile court records, adoption records, and birth records pertaining to illegitimate children are among the records closed to public gaze.

Kentucky. An open record law passed in 1976 exempts from disclosure only those records pertaining to invasion of personal privacy, trade secrets, or records otherwise prohibited by law from being disclosed. A person denied access to public records can appeal to the state attorney general. Should that fail, injunctive relief can be sought from a circuit court.

Maine. A right-to-know law is on the books which permits the use of recording devices at meetings of state agencies and commissions. The law allows executive sessions by state and local agencies to discuss personnel matters, and for real estate dealings, legal consultations, and labor negotiations. Violators can be fined up to $500 or imprisoned for up to one year, the same penalty that is permissible under the state's open record law.

The open record law provides that most records will be open to the public, and that those persons denied access can appeal to superior court.

Maryland. The state's Public Information Act exempts more than 10 categories of records from disclosure, including law enforcement investigatory files.

State and local open meeting laws are on the books. They allow executive sessions for any reason deemed justifiable by public bodies.

Massachusetts. Massachusetts is one of three states that have created oversight offices to teach citizens about open government and how to exercise their rights. The others are Connecticut and New York. The Division of Public Records in Massachusetts is charged with this responsibility.

Michigan. A new state FOIA went into effect in 1977 which requires public bodies receiving FOI requests to respond within five work days. A considerable number of exemptions exist, including police department operational instructions and manuals. At the beginning of 1977, the state's new open meeting law went into effect. It requires public bodies to open their meetings unless two-thirds of the members vote for closure, which is allowed for such reasons as disciplining public employees or students, real estate transactions, party caucuses, collective bargaining, and matters related to certain government employment activities or procedures.

Minnesota. The open meeting law opens all meetings to the public, including executive sessions. Exempt are a few agencies, specifically the Adult Corrections Commission, Board of Pardons, and the Youth Commission. The attorney general has declared that whenever two or more members of a public body get together, that constitutes a meeting within the meaning of the law. Under the penalty clause, any public official who violates the law can be fined a maximum of $100. Three violations would require the official's removal from office.

The open record law provides that all records not specifically exempt from disclosure should be open to public examination. It was amended in 1979 to permit a person to sue for damages, costs and reasonable attorney fees whenever records are wrongfully withheld. As noted earlier, if a government agency willfully violates the law, it may be required to pay from $100 to $10,000 for each violation. But the government can be awarded costs and attorney fees if a data request is frivolous.

Mississippi. The state's open meeting law went into effect in 1976, and was amended in 1981. It requires the meetings of any public bodies to be open, unless an executive session is declared; and it allows executive sessions for a number of reasons, including, for example, strategy sessions or negotiations concerning prospective litigation.

The state's public record law was passed in 1983. It provides a number of exemptions to disclosure, allows an agency 14 work days in which to respond to requests, and provides for a fine of up to $100 for persons who "willfully and knowingly" deny access to records not exempt from disclosure.

Missouri. In 1982 the legislature passed House Bill No. 1253 to exempt social meetings of public governmental bodies from the provisions of the Sunshine Law. It includes an extensive set of requirements by which the public must be notified of meetings. And it added a section that allows a civil suit against a member of a public body who violates the law. A maximum fine of $100 and reasonable costs and attorney's fees are allowed.

The open records law was amended in 1987 to add a new policy statement that requires liberal construction of the disclosure provisions and narrow construction of exemptions. The Act now applies to boards of universities and colleges that receive public funds. The fine that can be levied for violations of the Act has been increased from $100 to $300. Attorney's fees and costs can be awarded to information seekers. A new fee schedule was included similar to the federal FOIA's; namely, that agencies can charge a reasonable fee for searches and duplication with a fee waiver required if the request is "likely to contribute significantly to public understanding of the operations or activities of the public governmental body and . . . [is] not primarily in the commercial interest of the requester." But five more exemptions were added, bringing the total to 15. The new ones cover testing materials, software codes, bidding specifications, sealed bids, and personnel records.[81]

New Jersey. The state's open meeting law went into effect in 1976 and permits closed sessions whenever public bodies discuss real estate transactions, engage in collective bargaining, or whenever court actions are possible. Certain personnel-related matters are exempt. Advisory board meetings, political caucuses and meetings of the judiciary can be kept closed.

New York. This state created a Committee on Public Records in 1974 to facilitate compliance with open meeting/open record laws and the Personal Privacy Protection Act. The name was changed to the Committee on Open Government. The 11–member committee consists of government officials (including the governor), public representatives, and two representatives of the press.[82] The staff consists of an executive director, who is an attorney, and two secretaries. Since the committee began operations, it has issued more than 3000 advisory opinions. One study showed that 75 percent of the committee's opinions are on the side of disclosure.[83]

The state's FOIA went into effect in 1974 and applies to all state and local government units. It provides for right of access to such records as:

- Adopted statements of policy, and interpretations of such statements, in cluding statistical and factual data used in formulating policy.
- Minutes and votes, including dissenting opinions and votes.
- Internal and external audits of agencies.
- Itemized records of public payrolls.
- Final court orders and opinions, public hearings, police blotters, and booking records.
- Administrative staff manuals and instructions.

Safeguards against invasion of personal privacy are incorporated into the Act which allows access to police blotters and booking records, but not to arrest records. There are other provisions to protect an individual's privacy.

The open meeting law went into effect in 1977 and requires that all meetings of state and local bodies be open unless a majority of the members vote in public to close a session for a specific reason allowed under the law. No action by formal vote can be taken to appropriate public money at a closed session. Executive sessions are permitted only when discussions would imperil public safety or law enforcement, relate to litigation, invade personal privacy, involve collective bargaining for public employees, or real estate transactions. The law was amended in 1979 to include within the definition of an open meeting those meetings at which public business is conducted even though no official action is taken. Also, executive sessions cannot be called to discuss personnel or financial matters. Notices of meetings must be posted in at least one public place and minutes of the meeting must be made public within two weeks after the meeting.

North Carolina. The General Assembly passed a new open meetings law in 1979 that clarifies which public bodies must open their meetings and how the meetings must be conducted.[84]

Changes made in 1986 include the following: Courts can void any action taken in violation of the open meetings law; and members of a public body who knowingly violate the law can be ordered to pay attorney's fees and costs incurred by successful challengers.[85]

North Dakota. An amendment to the state's open meetings law requires advance notice of all meetings, including date, time, location and agenda, according to guidelines issued by the attorney general.

Ohio. A new open meeting law went into effect in 1976. It bans most executive sessions except when certain matters, virtually the same as those included in the Maine law, are to be discussed. The law requires prior announcement of all regular and special meetings and the vote as to who wanted a session closed. All final decisions must be made publicly.

The open record law requires all government unit records to be open to public inspection except for those specifically exempt from disclosure by statute or those records pertaining to medical or mental examinations; or to adoption, parole, and probation proceedings.

The state supreme court broadly interpreted the open record law in early 1976 when it required a police department to make public its jail log. More recently that same court ruled that Ohio public hospital admission and discharge records, which include only patients' names and addresses and facts of admission and discharge, are subject to compulsory disclosure as public records.[86]

A law also was passed that allows a requester of public records to seek a writ of mandamus.[87] The action followed a state supreme court ruling in September 1987 that writs of mandamus were not available to requesters because the open records law permitted them to file civil suits to obtain documents. A writ of mandamus petition receives quick court review and is a relatively inexpensive legal procedure. Civil suits often take years to resolve.

Oklahoma. The state strengthened its Open Meeting Act by requiring public bodies to provide 48 hours notice of special, nonscheduled meeting to those requesting such service.[88] But the agencies can charge up to $18 a year for the notification service. Formerly, public bodies only had to post notices of special meetings.

Oregon. The state's open meeting law permits special meetings, whether open or "executive," to be held provided that at least 24-hour advance notice is given. All such sessions must adhere to the topics cited in such notices. Labor bargaining negotiations are specifically exempt, but generally the intent of the law is to require governing bodies to arrive at decisions openly. However, actions taken in violation of the law specifically are not voided by the law.

State and local records are open to any person, although certain types of records are specifically exempt. They include real estate transactions, personal privacy matters, criminal investigatory files, trade secrets, information pertaining to pending or potential litigation, test and scoring-device information, certain parole and prison records, and memoranda between public bodies. The law states that any exempt records can be opened if it is in the public interest to do so. An arrest and a report of a crime are specifically required by the law to be open to the public, but not criminal investigatory files "unless the public interest requires disclosure. . . ."[89]

Pennsylvania. The state's open record law exempts certain kinds of investigatory files, records pertaining to industrial plant safety and health conditions, or disclosures which might result in loss of federal funds, injure a person's reputation, or endanger a person's security. The state's new Sunshine Law went into effect in 1987, and requires that discussions leading to official actions must be open except for discussion of specific topics, pending lawsuits, and personnel matters.[90]

South Carolina. A Freedom of Information Act was signed into law in 1978, repealing a 1972 act. It permits seven exemptions to disclosure of public records and requires that all meetings of public bodies be open except for five reasons. It was amended in 1987 to prevent a reoccurrence of what happened when the University of South Carolina refused to disclose how much it had paid to Jahan Sadat, the widow of the late Anwar Sadat of Egypt, as a distinguished visiting professor.[91]

Among the major changes: A new policy statement requiring officials to construe the law more favorable to public disclosure; the inclusion of subcommittees and advisory committees in the openness requirements; elimination of closed meetings or sealed records by a three-fourths vote; a requirement that access be granted to records if an agency fails to act within 15 days on a request; the elimination of "straw votes" at closed sessions; a specific notification-of-meetings requirement; and an increase in the time limit for filing lawsuits under the act from 60 days to one year.[92]

Tennessee. The open meeting law, termed the best in the nation in a survey published in 1974, was upheld by the state supreme court after a Memphis judge had ruled that the statutory requirements of "adequate public notice" of meetings was unconstitutionally vague.

The state supreme court again upheld the constitutionality of the law in 1976 in connection with the firing of a teacher at a closed school board meeting. Chief

Justice William H.D. Jones wrote that the state legislature sought to open to the public the meetings of all public bodies having "the authority to make decisions or recommendations on policy or administration affecting the conduct of the business of the people."[93] The court rejected claims that the law was vague or unreasonably broad.

Certain types of records, such as those of the state's Bureau of Criminal Investigation, those involving state or national security, and certain kinds of medical records, are exempt from disclosure. Unless specifically exempt, state and local records are required to be open to public inspection.

Texas. There are 15 types of records specifically exempt from disclosure, and the judiciary is excluded from the provisions of the Access to Public Information statute. Birth and death records, student records, and some types of information exempt under federal FOIA do not have to be disclosed.

The open meeting law applies to state and local government bodies whenever final action is taken or considered, unless those meetings are exempt under law. Exempt meetings are those where the following are discussed: real estate negotiations, certain types of medical files, grand jury sessions, public employee personal matters, school board disciplinary actions, and certain matters relating to pardons and paroles. A bill was signed into law in 1979 which allows the news media to seek a writ of mandamus or an injunction whenever a government body violates the open meeting law.

The open meeting law was amended in 1987 to permit visual as well as audio recordings of government meetings.[94] Also, public bodies must keep a record of closed sessions except where matters under discussion are covered by the attorney-client privilege, but the record can only be made public by court order. Any individual who participates in such a meeting knowing that no record is being kept faces a fine of up to $200. In addition, either minutes or audio recordings must be kept of open meetings.

The new law permits legal action to reverse or void actions taken by agencies that violate the law. Courts are allowed to award attorney's fees and costs.

However, a loophole allows public bodies to receive staff briefings in closed session so long as officials do not discuss public business at such sessions. Also, actions taken at a meeting when the agency provided inadequate notice of the meeting no longer can be voided.

Utah. The state supreme court affirmed a trial court's judgment that the names and salaries of Weber State College employees are subject to disclosure under the state's Information Practices Act. The editor of the college's student newspaper had filed the action in *Redding v. Brady* to compel disclosure.[95]

Virginia. The state's FOIA was amended so that open meeting provisions now apply to all government meetings wherever they are held. The amendment is an effort to prevent government bodies from circumventing the law by conducting meetings outside the state.

Washington. All state and local records are open to the public except those specifically exempt by the statute, such as certain records pertaining to prisoners and parole hearings, medical information, tax reports, real estate transactions, scholastic tests, certain files kept by law enforcement and regulatory agencies, and data identifying welfare recipients.

The Open Public Records Act was amended, effective July 1987. An agency may invoke a privacy exemption only if data requested fall into specific categories and disclosure would be "highly offensive to a reasonable person" and "not of legitimate concern to the public."[96] To protect privacy, agencies may withhold lists of individuals when the lists are requested for commercial purposes, material from personnel files, tax data that individuals are required to file, and law enforcement investigative and intelligence files. Previously, all personal information in governmental files had been exempt.

Seven additional exemptions to disclosure were added, including applications for public employment; business information filed with utilities, the transportation commission, or the attorney general if the provider asks to be notified of any FOI Act requests for the data and a court rules that disclosure would harm the provider; applications from businesses seeking government loans; home addresses and telephone numbers of public employees and of public utility customers; and most information kept by the board of pharmacy on distribution of drug samples by drug manufacturers.

State and local public bodies must conduct open meetings except for discussions relating to real estate transactions, public employee matters, and national or state security matters. Official action can be taken only at open meetings.

Several changes were made in the Open Meetings Act in 1983, including (1) a requirement that interviewing of candidates for vacant elective offices must be conducted in open meetings; (2) a provision requiring open meetings for committees within the governing bodies when the committees are acting on behalf of those bodies, conducting hearings, or taking testimony or public comment; and (3) a section allowing government bodies to meet in executive session to consider negotiations on the performance of publicly-bid contracts when publicity regarding such consideration would cause a likelihood of increased cost.[97]

West Virginia. State and local government meetings are open to the public except for those specifically excluded by other statutes. A majority vote by a governing body permits executive session at any time. In addition, there are eight specified reasons in the statute to permit closed meetings:

- Real estate transactions.
- Certain law enforcement matters.
- Physical or mental health information.
- Certain matters pertaining to licensing or the denial thereof.
- Disciplining of public school students.
- Certain personnel matters.
- Matters adversely affecting a person's reputation.
- Certain state or national security matters.

Government agencies must make public final orders, decisions, and opinions except those withheld for "good cause," a proviso which provides a loophole in the open records law. Other statutes also may exempt official records from disclosure.

Wisconsin. The open meeting law requires state and local governing bodies to meet in open session unless executive sessions are permitted by statute, such as for judicial and quasi-judicial matters, probation and parole consideration, certain types of personnel information that would unduly damage reputations, caucuses by legislative members, employee bargaining sessions, and certain meetings relating to crime detection or prevention.

Under a criminal misdemeanor section of the law, a circuit court judge in late 1976 ordered six members of a village board to pay $651 in legal costs from their own pockets for failing to comply with that part of the law that stipulates that an open meeting, at which official action can be taken, cannot be held for at least twelve hours after a closed meeting.

All state and local records are open to public inspection. State and municipal violators can be fined up to $2000; county violators face fines of $5 for each day of noncompliance.

Combating Secrecy

Within the past few years, press organizations, often in league with journalism schools, have created various kinds of organizations to combat secrecy in government. In many states, freedom of information councils or clearinghouses have been organized, such as in California, Florida, Iowa, and Pennsylvania. Also there is the Freedom of Information Foundation in Columbia, Missouri. These organizations help to educate journalists about open meeting/open record laws and often initiate legal action when they believe "open government" laws are being violated. "Hotlines" have been created, as in Arizona and Texas, and oversight offices have been created by state governments, as in Connecticut, Massachusetts, and New York.

Some practical advice on what journalists or news organizations can or should do when confronted by government secrecy came from 145 city editors who responded to a survey about freedom of information matters:[98]

- Three-fourths of those who replied said their newspapers had standing instructions for reporters on what to do when denied access to records or meetings. Some instructions were elaborate and involved legal warnings. Others were simple, such as this statement from a metro editor: "Basically, I tell them to go in, take a seat and dare them to throw him/her out."[99]
- Reporters need to know the appropriate statutes.
- Officials who vote in secret meetings or closed records should be identified in editorials.
- A box score of closed meetings should be kept and publicized.

- The editor should write to each member of the public body that chose secrecy to inquire if that official still believes secrecy is necessary.
- Pictures of closed doors, behind which public business is being conducted, can be published.

SUMMARY

On the side of "secrecy" are

- Executive privilege.
- Classification of documents as top secret, secret, or confidential.
- Personal privacy considerations, such as those that led to passage of the Privacy Act of 1974.
- A bureaucrat's inclination to shield his/her work from public gaze.

On the side of "disclosure" are

- Systematic "leaking" of information to journalists.
- Instantaneous declassification, such as President Johnson's declassification of a secret document while being interviewed by Walter Cronkite on a February 6, 1970, TV show and in the publication of his memoirs which, like those of many other high public officials, contained classified information.
- Federal FOIA, which went into effect on July 4, 1967, and gave the public its first legal right to know what its government was doing.
- The federal Sunshine Act.
- State open meeting/open record laws.

The federal FOIA, as amended in 1974, provides that disclosure is the general rule, but it exempts nine categories of information from disclosure, including national defense/foreign policy matters, personnel files and practices, internal agency memoranda, investigatory files, and information which would invade a person's privacy. U.S. District Courts can make *in camera* inspections to determine if information is properly being withheld under one of the nine exemptions. Agencies also are required to provide "any reasonable segregable portion" of a record after it has been purged of nondiscloseable information. In addition, agencies are required to respond to a FOI request within 10 work days after receipt of the request; and an administrative appeal (within the agency) must be decided in 20 work days. However, courts have allowed the FBI, CIA, and other agencies to handle requests on a first-in, first-out basis because of "exceptional circumstances" stemming from an avalanche of FOI and Privacy Act requests during the 1970s.

The exemptions used most often by federal agencies tend to be Exemption 7 (investigatory files) and Exemption 5 (intra- and interagency memoranda).

The impact of the Privacy Act on FOIA still is a bit cloudy. Undoubtedly there will be an adverse effect in terms of disclosure, but Congress intended that the general policy of disclosure would guide future adjudications. This is the general policy that came through in the U.S. Supreme Court's 5–3 decision in *Air Force v. Rose* (1976). Furthermore, the Court said FOIA exemptions must be construed narrowly. And the Court ruled that Exemption 6 applies only to "clearly unwarranted" invasions of personal privacy.

About 50 federal agencies—but not the cabinet-member executive departments—are required to open their meetings under the "Government in the Sunshine Act" which went into effect in 1977. There are ten exemptions to openness, seven of which are similar to exemptions contained in FOIA.

Although Congress generally has favored a policy of openness for executive branch operations, its own committees have been far from "open." About 40 percent of all congressional committee meetings are closed to the public. Radio and television coverage of House and Senate floor sessions is allowed.

At the state level, all states now have open record/open meeting laws. But the legal requirements of the various state laws are far from uniform and considerable public business still is transacted behind closed doors.

QUESTIONS IN REVIEW

1. What is executive privilege and what is its legal basis, if any?
2. The Public Information Act, popularly known as the Freedom of Information (FOI) Act, is of historic significance because, for the first time, it gives legal force to a doctrine which the Fourth Estate espoused and helped to popularize, namely
   _____.
3. Which of the following is a requirement under the FOI Act, according to Attorney General Ramsey Clark?
   a. Disclosure is the general rule, not the exception.
   b. All individuals have equal rights to access to information.
   c. The burden rests on the government to justify the withholding of information, not on the person seeking such information.
   d. All of these answers.
   e. None of these answers.
4. Why do the news media not make greater use of the federal FOIA?
5. If there are no "exceptional circumstances," a federal agency has how many work days in which to respond to a FOI request?
6. Which, if any, of the following were included in amendments to the federal FOIA?
   a. Permit courts to make *in camera* inspection of information to determine if it is being legally withheld.
   b. Require agencies to make available "any reasonable segregable portion" of any record otherwise exempt from disclosure.
   c. Modified Exemption 7 to make it more difficult for agencies to withhold information under the "investigatory files" category.
   d. All of these.
   e. None of these.
7. The two exemptions used most often by federal agencies in denying FOI requests tend to be _____ and _____.

8. Two key words were used by a majority of the U.S. Supreme Court in *Air Force v. Rose* whenever courts are balancing FOIA disclosure against invasions of personal privacy. The words are _____.

9. How many exemptions are there to the federal "Government in the Sunshine Act" requirement that federal agencies hold open meetings? Are any of these exemptions comparable to those in FOIA?

10. True or False: In *Kissinger v. Reporters Committee for Freedom of the Press,* the U.S. Supreme Court ordered the State Department to turn over records because they were being improperly withheld from the press.

11. You are the editor of a newspaper and a city council is meeting secretly to discuss city affairs before holding a public meeting where final action is taken. What can you or your newspaper do about the situation, if anything?

ANSWERS

1. Executive privilege is the power claimed by the President not to make information or records available to Congress or to the public. Proponents of this doctrine claim the power is derived from the Constitution. Opponents argue there is no constitutional or statutory basis for the doctrine. The root of the argument goes to "derived" powers versus explicit ones, or implied versus explicit powers. If, for example, the President is charged by the Constitution with the conduct of the nation's foreign affairs, then a derived or implied power would be to conduct such negotiations in secret or to keep highly sensitive information relating to foreign affairs under security wraps.

2. The public's right to know.

3. The best answer is d.

4. Because of long delays in getting information. Even under the amended FOIA, there are long delays. Frequently, journalists will turn to "friendly" or sympathetic sources in government to obtain the desired information.

5. 10 work days. In the event of an administrative appeal, the agency has 20 work days in which to decide whether to grant the request.

6. The best answer is d.

7. Investigatory files and intra- and interagency memoranda.

8. Nondisclosure is permitted if there would be a clearly unwarranted invasion of privacy.

9. There are 10. Yes, seven are comparable.

10. False.

11. First, try friendly persuasion. Telephone or write, asking the council members to cease and desist. If that doesn't work, use the "double whammy" approach—publicize the fact that secret meetings are being held (using a boxscore and photos, if these will help publicize the fact), and bring legal action under your state's open meetings law. Be sure to zero in on those council members who are favoring secrecy.

ENDNOTES

1. Hearings before the House Foreign Operations and Government Information Subcommittee, "U.S. Government Information Policies and Practices—The Pentagon Papers," Part I, June 23, 1971, p. 8.

2. Ibid., p. 20.

3. Ibid., p. 800.

4. Ibid., p. 360. These excerpts from Jefferson's notes of that Cabinet meeting were reported to the subcommittee during testimony of William Rehnquist, then assistant U.S. Attorney General, June 29, 1971.

5. U.S. v. Richard M. Nixon, President of the United States, and Richard M. Nixon, President of the United States, v. U.S., 94 S.Ct. 3090, 41 L.Ed.2d 1039. Justice Rehnquist did not participate in the decision.

6. On June 17, 1972, five men employed directly or indirectly by the Committee to Re-elect the President (Nixon) were arrested inside the Democratic National Committee's offices in the Watergate office building. They were there to photograph documents and to repair a hidden listening device installed during a previous burglary. On September 15, 1972, these men and two others were indicted for conspiracy, burglary, and an unlawful attempt to intercept wire communications. The five, Bernard Barker, Eugenio Martinez, Frank Sturgis, Virgilio Gonzalez, and Howard Hunt entered guilty pleas; the remaining two—James McCord and Gordon Liddy—were found guilty and their convictions were affirmed by the U.S. Court of Appeals in 1975. On March 1, 1974, seven additional individuals, including former Attorney General Mitchell, H.R. Haldeman, and John Ehrlichman, were indicted and four were convicted. On appeal, the U.S. Court of Appeals for the District of Columbia Circuit upheld the convictions of Mitchell, Haldeman, and Ehrlichman, and the verdict against one defendant was reversed. During the trial of the top Nixon aides (Mitchell, Haldeman, and Ehrlichman) the jury heard between 16 and 22 hours of edited tapes which had been recorded in Nixon's Oval Office.

7. Quoting from Branzburg v. Hayes, 408 U.S. 665, 683 (1972). In this and two companion cases the Supreme Court held that there was no constitutional privilege for reporters to refuse to reveal confidential sources and/or information to grand juries investigating criminal matters. The decision came as a disappointment to the news media which had hoped to find in the U.S. Supreme Court a "champion" against forced disclosures. Compare the arguments used in those cases involving the newsmen wth the rationale put forth in the cases involving the president of the United States. If, in "criminal matters," the president cannot successfully assert an absolute claim to privilege, reporters certainly will not be able to do so unless legislation is passed which confers such a privilege.

8. Pub. L. No. 93–526, 88 Stat. 1695, 44 U.S.C. 2107.

9. Case No. 75-1605, argued before the U.S. Supreme Court on April 21, 1977.

10. "News Notes," *Media Law Reporter,* May 3, 1977.

11. Epstein v. Resor, 296 F.Supp. 214 (1969).

12. Hearings, op. cit., note 1, p. 286. This same problem plagued the judiciary in consideration of the Pentagon Papers case.

13. 421 F.2d 930 (9th Circuit, 1970).

14. Hearings, op. cit., note 1, p. 97.

15. Executive Order No. 12356, 8 *Med.L.Rptr.* 1306, April 27, 1982.

16. "News Notes," *Media Law Reporter,* April 13, 1982.

17. Safeguarding National Security Information, 9 *Med.L.Rptr.* 1759, July 5, 1983.

18. "News Notes," *Media Law Reporter,* June 21, 1983.

19. "Congress acts to curb censorship bill," *Editor & Publisher,* December 24, 1983, p. 9.

20. "Reagan backs off on some leak control proposals," *Editor & Publisher,* February 18, 1984, p. 9.

21. *FoI Digest,* May/June 1984, p. 1.

22. "Keeping the Press from the Action," *Time,* November 7, 1983, p. 65.

23. "News Notes," *Media Law Reporter,* April 3, 1984.

24. *Editor & Publisher,* January 14, 1984, p. 18.

25. Jack Landau, "Excluding the press from the Grenada invasion: A violation of the public's constitutional rights," *Editor & Publisher,* December 10, 1983, p. 10.

26. *Editor & Publisher,* December 10, 1983, p. 52.

27. Flynt v. Weinberger, 10 *Med.L.Rptr.* 1978, July 24, 1984.

28. *Freedom of Information 1985–86,* report by the Society of Professional Journalists, Sigma Delta Chi, p. 11.

29. *Editor & Publisher,* July 9, 1988, p. 14.
30. *The NEWS Media & The LAW,* Summer 1986, pp. 4–6.
31. Carole Fader, "The FOl Act and the Media," Freedom of Information Center Report No. 303, May, 1973, p. 1.
32. House Report No. 92-1419, "Administration of the Freedom of Information Act," Committee on Government Operations, September 20, 1972, p. 8.
33. Ibid, pp. 8–9.
34. Conference Committee Report No. 93-1380, "Freedom of Information Act Amendments," 93d Congress, 2d Session, September 25, 1974.
35. Environmental Protection Agency v. Mink, 410 U.S. 73, 93 S.Ct. 287, 35 L.Ed.2d 119. Justice Brennan, joined by Justice Marshall, concurred and dissented to parts of Justice White's opinion for the Court. Justice Douglas dissented. Justice Rehnquist took no part in the consideration or decision of the case.
36. Marc Arnold and Andrew Kisseloff, "An Introduction to the Federal Privacy Act of 1974 and Its Effect on the Freedom of Information Act," *New England Law Review,* Vol. 11, No. 2, Spring 1976, p. 483. Footnotes omitted.
37. "News Notes," *Media Law Reporter,* April 10, 1984.
38. 717 F.2d 799.
39. "News Notes," *Media Law Reporter,* April 10, 1984.
40. Department of Justice v. Provenzano and Shapiro v. Drug Enforcement Agency, 105 S.Ct. 413 (1984). Justice Stevens dissented.
41. CIA v. Sims, 105 S.Ct. 1881 (1985).
42. *The NEWS Media & The LAW,* Fall 1986, pp. 28–29.
43. Ibid., p. 29.
44. Ibid.
45. 15 U.S.C.A. § 46(f) (West Supp., 1981).
46. *The NEWS Media and The LAW,* Summer 1988, p. 21.
47. Department of the Air Force v. Rose, 96 S.Ct. 1504.
48. Federal Aviation Administration v. Reuben B. Robertson III, 422 U.S. 255, 95 S.Ct. 2140. Justices Douglas and Brennan dissented.
49. Kissinger v. Reporters Committee for Freedom of the Press, 445 U.S. 136, 6 *Med.L.Rptr.* 1001
50. *FoI Digest,* May/June 1982, p. 2.
51. "News Notes," *Media Law Reporter,* June 8, 1982.
52. *Editor & Publisher,* May 22, 1982, p. 28.
53. Baldridge v. Shapiro, 50 *U.S. Law Week* 4427.
54. 5 U.S. Code 552(b)(3).
55. 636 F.2d 1210 (3d Circuit, 1980) and 644 F.2d 844 (10th Circuit, 1981).
56. CIA v. Sims, 105 S.Ct. 1881 (1985).
57. *FoI Digest,* Vol. 17, No. 6, November/December 1975, p. 6.
58. "Free Press/Fair Trial: The Role of the News Media in Developing and Advancing Constitutional Processes," an address given on November 4, 1975, in conjunction with the University of Oklahoma College of Law Enrichment Program and published in *Oklahoma Law Review,* Vol. 29, No. 2, Spring 1976, p. 354. Reprinted with permission of *Oklahoma Law Review* © 1976.
59. Stern v. FBI, *The NEWS Media and The LAW,* January/February, 1984, p. 20.
60. "News Notes," *Media Law Reporter,* June 16, 1981, and August 21, 1984.
61. U.S. Department of State v. Washington Post Co., "News Notes," *Media Law Reporter,* November 22, 1983.
62. *The NEWS Media and The LAW,* Spring 1988, pp. 39–40.
63. Elaine English, "Here's How to Use the FOIA," in 1986–87 annual report of the National Freedom of Information Committee of the Society of Professional Journalists, Sigma Delta Chi.
64. 45 *U.S. Law Week* 5.
65. "Government in the Sunshine," Freedom of Information Center Report No. 366, January 1977, pp. 4–5. Footnotes omitted.
66. *FoI Digest,* November/December 1981, p. 2.

67. Report No. 94–539, 94th Congress, 1st Session, by Congressman Jack Brooks of Texas, committee chairman, on October 7, 1975, pp. 2–3. Nine of the 10 committee members approved the substance of the committee recommendations.

68. Iowa Open Meeting Law Handbook, 2nd ed., published by Iowa Freedom of Information Council (Des Moines, 1982), pp. 17–18.

69. *FoI Digest,* November/December 1979, p. 6.

70. Ibid.

71. *The NEWS Media & The LAW,* Winter 1987, p. 39.

72. *Editor & Publisher,* April 30, 1977, p. 42.

73. Eldorado v. Eldorado Broadcasting Co., 2 *Med.L.Rptr.* 1427, 1428, March 15, 1976.

74. *The NEWS Media & The LAW,* Winter 1987, pp. 38–39.

75. The 1976 *Report of the Advancement of Freedom of Information Committee,* Society of Professional Journalists, Sigma Delta Chi, p. 28.

76. *FoI Digest,* May/June 1983, p. 3.

77. "State Activities," *Media Law Reporter,* July 24, 1984.

78. *The NEWS Media & The LAW,* Summer 1988, pp. 40–41.

79. Op. cit., n. 76, p. 8.

80. Ibid., p. 5.

81. *The NEWS Media & The LAW,* Fall 1987, p. 37.

82. Jeanni Atkins, "Oversight Offices Enforce Open Government Statutes," *FoI Digest,* March/April 1984, p.4.

83. Ibid., p.5.

84. *Editor & Publisher,* June 9, 1979, p. 30.

85. *Freedom of Information '86–'87* report, Society of Professional Journalists, Sigma Delta Chi, p. 26.

86. Wooster Daily Record v. Wooster, 4 *Med.L.Rptr.* 1942.

87. *The NEWS Media & The LAW,* Winter 1988, pp. 11–12.

88. Op. cit., n. 81, p. 38.

89. *Press Censorship Newsletter No. VI,* December/January 1974–75, p. 26, published by the Reporters Committee for Freedom of the Press.

90. Op. cit., n. 74, pp. 38–39.

91. *Editor & Publisher,* August 1, 1987, p. 35.

92. Op. cit., n. 81, p. 31.

93. Memphis Publishing Co. v. City of Memphis, 513 S.W.2d 511 (1974).

94. Op. cit., n. 81, p. 38.

95. Redding v. Brady, 5 *Med.L.Rptr.* 2518.

96. Op. cit., n. 81, p. 38.

97. *FoI Digest,* March/April 1983, p. 6.

98. Ernest Morgan, "Informal Methods of Combatting Secrecy in Local Governments," report No. 6, (Columbia, Mo.: Freedom of Information Foundation, 1976).

99. Ibid., p. 5.

10

Free Press versus Fair Trial

HIGHLIGHTS

■ *Sheppard v. Maxwell* (1966). The Supreme Court instructed the judiciary that it must take action to protect an accused person's right to a fair trial short of imposing direct restraints upon the press. If judges fail to take action, such as insulating prospective witnesses from the news media or sequestering the jury, then convictions would be overturned, the Court warned.

■ To help safeguard the right to a fair trial, U.S. Attorney General Katzenbach issued guidelines in 1965 to federal law enforcement officers concerning information that can and cannot be released to the press.

■ Various cases, such as *Bridges v. California* (1941), have established the rule that direct restraints imposed on the press by the judiciary are unconstitutional except when there is a clear and present danger to the administration of justice.

■ *Nebraska Press Association v. Judge Stuart* (1976). The Supreme Court ruled that a judge cannot prevent the news media from reporting or commenting on public judicial proceedings.

■ *Gannett Company v. Judge DePasquale* (1979). The Court ruled that the public (and therefore the press) has no Sixth Amendment right to attend pretrials. Whether this ruling applied to trials was not definitively answered.

■ *Richmond Newspapers, Inc. v. Virginia* (1980). A majority of the Supreme Court said the public and press have a First Amendment right to attend criminal trials. The right is not absolute. Under certain circumstances, and given procedural safeguards, trials can be closed to the public. But there is a presumption that trials will be open.

■ *Press-Enterprise Co. v. Superior Court* (1984). The Supreme Court held that the press and public have a First Amendment right to attend *voir dire* (questioning of prospective jurors) proceedings. And in *Waller v. Georgia* (1984), the Court held that only rarely can a pretrial hearing be closed over defendant's objection.

■ *Press-Enterprise Co. v. Superior Court* (1986). In this second case involving the Press-Enterprise Co. and efforts by a Superior Court judge to deny the newspaper access to a preliminary or pretrial hearing in a criminal case, the U.S. Supreme Court ruled that the press has a qualified First Amendment right to attend these hearings.

■ The issue of cameras in the courtroom was joined as far back as the Lindbergh kidnap case in the 1930s. In *Estes v. Texas* (1965), the Court held that the presence of television cameras at the pretrial hearing and at the opening session of the trial was sufficient reason to reverse Estes's conviction. No isolatable prejudice had to be shown. But in the 1970s, a number of states experimented with cameras in the courtroom. The upshot was a ruling in *Chandler v. Florida* (1981) by the Supreme Court that states can permit cameras in the courtroom provided safeguards are taken. Forty-five states allow such coverage.

Open meeting and open record laws provide the public and press with access to important government information. They constitute legal foundations for the public's right to know. But they also have resulted in clashes between those in government who wish to shield information from public gaze and those who believe such information should be made public. The press frequently is involved in such clashes.

One such area where the clashes have bordered on the spectacular concerns the administration of justice, particularly as the judiciary attempts to assure a fair and impartial trial for persons accused of crimes. Such a trial is guaranteed by the Sixth Amendment to the federal Constitution. But the press, in arguing that it has First Amendment rights to gather information (including the right to shield confidential sources of information in order to better position itself to gather news), has at times found itself barred from courtroom proceedings, or placed under court orders to either reveal some information obtained in confidence or not to reveal information already obtained.

Let's look at a spectacular confrontation.

WILLIAM FARR CASE

The late William T. Farr, reporter for the Los Angeles *Herald-Examiner,* spent 46 days in jail because he ran afoul of a judge's "gag" order aimed at preventing out-of-court statements by lawyers and witnesses connected with the Charles Manson murder trial. Farr found out what a prospective witness purportedly was going to say and the result was a page one story about a bizarre plot to slay movie stars. This upset California Superior Court Judge Charles Older who feared the trial might be contaminated if any jurors, even though sequestered when court was not in session, by chance might see that story while moving to and from the courthouse. Farr was asked to identify who had given him the information, but he refused, and because of the California shield law[1] the judge did not force the issue.

After the trial ended, Farr went to work for the Los Angeles County district attorney. He no longer was a reporter and the shield law no longer protected him, according to Judge Older who again ordered Farr to disclose the source of his information. When Farr refused, he was sentenced to an indefinite jail term for civil contempt. Theoretically, he might have stayed there for life by continuing to defy the judge's order (he was jailed for 46 days), but Justice Douglas of the U.S. Supreme Court intervened and released Farr on his own recognizance "in the interest of justice" pending the outcome of an appeal.[2] Subsequently, a three-judge panel of the California Court of Appeal denied Farr's contention that his open-ended sentence was tantamount to cruel and unusual punishment which is prohibited by the U.S. Constitution. However, an avenue of "escape" was noted by the appellate court. If Farr could not be coerced into disclosing his sources, then any imprisonment beyond the state's five-day limit on imprisonment for contempt would become punitive.[3]

A determination on this question was reached in 1974 by Superior Court Judge William H. Levit. Judge Levit declared that the news profession had established a moral principle to protect the confidentiality of its sources and that Farr's commitment to that principle made it substantially unlikely that further incarceration would result in his compliance with Judge Older's order. By then Farr had rejoined the ranks of the Fourth Estate as a reporter for the *Los Angeles Times.* Since he could not be coerced into compliance, Judge Levit, in his interpretation of the California law, apparently limited Judge Older to imposing a jail term not to exceed five days.

Shortly thereafter, Older imposed the five-day sentence and the $500 fine. Farr appealed on constitutional grounds, and a three-judge panel of the U.S. Court of Appeals in 1975 upheld the sentence and fine. The court said, "Where the case is a notorious one, that burden on the court [of insuring a fair trial] is heavy. We hold that the paramount interest to be protected was that of the power of the court to enforce its duty and obligation in relation to the guarantee of due process."[4] The court added that Farr was not constitutionally protected in his refusal to identify those who violated the proper order of the court. An appeal was taken to the U.S. Supreme Court which denied certiorari in 1976, with only Brennan and Marshall favoring review.[5]

A new move then was made by the reporter's attorney and in 1976 the three-judge California Court of Appeal for the Second District granted Farr's writ of habeas corpus, barring the five-day jail term and $500 fine on the ground that the state's Penal Code (§ 654) precluded multiple punishments or multiple prosecutions (double jeopardy) in connection with the same course of conduct that had led to the 1971 contempt order.[6] A defense committee established on behalf of the beleaguered reporter pointed out that up to that time only one other American journalist ever had served more time in jail than Farr, that person being John Peter Zenger who had been imprisoned for nine months while awaiting trial on a seditious libel charge in 1735.

Meanwhile, Farr came within an eyelash of going through the same ordeal a second time. In 1974 he again was called before a grand jury in Los Angeles that was attempting to determine if any of the six attorneys in the Manson trial had committed perjury when they denied having given Farr the information used in the story about what a prospective witness was going to say. Farr had said he received the information from two of the attorneys, but refused to identify them. Superior Court Judge Raymond Choate then found Farr in contempt of court for refusing to identify the attorneys. Within a week, however, Judge Choate reversed himself and dismissed the contempt conviction on the ground that a 1972 amendment of the California law shielded reporters from being forced to disclose confidential sources when called before grand juries. But a California District Court of Appeal subsequently ruled that the state legislature, by enactment of the amendment, intruded into a judiciary function and that the shield law, as amended, is no barrier to California judges who can, if they wish, order journalists to testify on pain of contempt. Thus the ramifications of the Farr case continued to spread.

Adding to Farr's woes was a $24 million libel lawsuit filed by two of the six attorneys in the Manson trial who claimed their professional reputations were injured by Farr's statement concerning the source of his information. The two lawyers claimed such injury even though Farr had not identified any of the six by name. A Los Angeles Superior Court judge dismissed the lawsuit in 1979 because the plaintiffs, according to the judge, had not brought the case to trial within the five-year statute of limitations.

Not until 1981 did Farr learn from the California Supreme Court that the appeals deadline had passed for the libel lawsuit brought by the two attorneys.[7] This meant that for the first time since Farr was jailed back in 1972 he no longer was under threat of confinement or legal action in connection with his refusal to identify the source of information for a story about what a prospective witness purportedly was going to say!

Perhaps of some consolation to Farr for his ordeal in the California courts was his selection by the Society of Professional Journalists to receive a First

Amendment Award in 1976 for refusing to reveal his sources of information, thereby upholding a principle of long standing among journalists. Farr died on March 4, 1987, at age 52. Of his decision not to reveal, he had this to say:

> There is no need to attach nobility to what I did. All good reporters feel the same way about protecting news sources. . . . I gave a personal and professional promise. I feel I must keep that promise regardless of the consequences.

The *Farr* case is not an isolated clash of interests. Rather, there have been repeated encounters as judges have sought to forestall what they believe is interference by the press in the orderly administration of justice. Conversely, many journalists believe that they are being unconstitutionally prevented from reporting information about crime and justice. The conflict is rooted in the First and Sixth Amendments, the latter requiring that "in all criminal prosecutions, the accused shall enjoy the right to a speedy and public trial, by an impartial jury."

Just when the issue of free press/fair trial emerged is difficult to say, but the famous Lindbergh kidnap case in the 1930s highlighted what was to become an increasingly acrimonious debate between practitioners of law and journalism marked by periodic efforts to restrain the press.

LINDBERGH CASE AND CANON 35

One of the more sordid chapters in American journalism was written after the kidnapping of the 20-month-old son of Charles and Anne Lindbergh on March 1, 1932. Because of the prominence of the father, who had become a national hero after his solo flight across the Atlantic Ocean in the "Spirit of St. Louis," press coverage was extraordinary. The child was found slain, and three years later Bruno Richard Hauptmann was put on trial at Flemington, New Jersey, in a courtroom packed with reporters and photographers. Witnesses, jurors, anyone remotely associated with the trial were fair game for the press. Hauptmann, found guilty and later executed, very likely was deprived of his right to a fair trial in part because of massive publicity accompanying the trial. After the trial, an 18-member Special Committee between the Press, Radio, and Bar was set up to seek "standards of publicity in judicial proceedings and methods of obtaining observance of them." In its 1937 report, the committee characterized the news media's performance before and during the trial as "the most spectacular and depressing example of improper publicity and professional misconduct ever presented to the people of the United States in a criminal trial." But the only tangible result of the study was the adoption of Canon 35 by the American Bar Association (ABA) in 1937. This Canon, as amended in 1952 and 1963, called for a ban on courtroom television and radio broadcasting and photography.

Most states now permit courtroom coverage by means of radio, television, and still photography—a development that will be described later in this chapter.

But first, let's look at some other "notable" cases involving First and Sixth Amendment rights.

Shepherd v. Florida. One such case was *Shepherd v. Florida* (1951)[8] After the arrest of Samuel Shepherd and three other black men in Lake County, Florida, on charges of raping a white girl, a mob gathered at the jail and the four prisoners were transferred elsewhere for safekeeping. In the meantime, the home of Shepherd's parents was destroyed by fire, blacks were forced to flee the community, and the National Guard had to be called to restore order. Various news reports were circulated and one newspaper even published a cartoon picturing four empty electric chairs with the caption, "No Compromise—Supreme Penalty."

In the 1951 majority opinion of the Supreme Court which reversed the convictions, Justice Robert H. Jackson pointed out that newspapers published as a fact, and attributed the information to the sheriff, that the defendants had confessed, even though no confession ever was offered at trial.

Justice Jackson wrote:

> This Court has recently gone a long way to disable a trial judge from dealing with press interference with the trial process.[9] . . . And the Court, by strict construction of an Act of Congress, has held not to be contemptuous any kind of interference unless it takes place in the immediate presence of the court . . . the last place where a well calculated obstruction would be attempted. No doubt this trial judge felt helpless to give the accused any real protection against this out-of-court campaign to convict. But if freedoms of press are so abused as to make fair trial in the locality impossible, the judicial process must be protected by removing the trial to a forum beyond its probable influence. Newspapers, in the enjoyment of their constitutional rights, may not deprive accused persons of their right to a fair trial. These convictions, accompanied by such events, do not meet any civilized conception of due process of law.

Jackson added that this case presented "one of the best examples of one of the worst menaces to American justice."

Irvin v. Dowd. In another decision 10 years later, the Court ruled that the defendant in a sensational murder trial had been deprived of due process of law even though a change of venue had been granted.[10] The defense had asked for a second change of venue and this request was denied. The Indiana Supreme Court had affirmed the conviction in the mass murder case, but the U.S. Supreme Court reversed on the grounds that the barrage of publicity caused eight jurors to believe in the guilt of the accused, even though they said they would be fair and impartial. The Court held that "with such an opinion permeating their minds it would be difficult to say that each (juror) could exclude this preconception of guilt from his deliberations."

Rideau and Estes Cases. Two other fair trial cases led to important decisions by the U.S. Supreme Court. In *Rideau v. Louisiana*[11] in 1963, and *Estes v.*

Texas[12] in 1965, a majority of the Court held that actual prejudice need not be demonstrated in order to show that due process was violated.

Rideau, an accused murderer, bank robber, and kidnapper, was interrogated by the sheriff without benefit of counsel and the event was televised—not once, but three times! The Court held that a change of venue should have been granted and that due process had been denied even without a showing of actual juror prejudice.

Speaking for the Court majority, Justice Stewart said:

> . . . [W]e hold that it was a denial of due process of law to refuse the request for a change of venue, after the people of Calcasieu Parish had been exposed repeatedly and in depth to the spectacle of Rideau personally confessing in detail to the crimes with which he was later to be charged. For anyone who has ever watched television the conclusion cannot be avoided that this spectacle, to the tens of thousands of people who saw and heard it, in a very real sense was Rideau's trial—at which he pleaded guilty to murder. Any subsequent court proceedings in a community so pervasively exposed to such a spectacle could be but a hollow formality.[13]

In the *Estes* case, the defendant's conviction on a swindling charge was reversed because two days of the preliminary hearing and part of the trial were televised.

Media coverage during the two-day pretrial hearing was described by the Court in this way:

> These initial hearings were carried live by both radio and television, and news photography was permitted throughout. The videotapes of these hearings clearly illustrate that the picture presented was not one of judicial serenity and calm to which petitioner was entitled. Indeed, at least 12 cameramen were engaged in the courtroom throughout the hearing taking motion and still pictures and televising the proceedings. Cables and wires were snaked across the courtroom floor, three microphones were on the judges' bench and others were beamed at the jury box and the counsel table. It is conceded that the activities of the television crews and news photographers led to considerable disruption of the hearings.[14]

In stating that no isolatable prejudice had to be shown as a requisite for reversal, the Court said that "at times a procedure employed by the State involves such a probability that prejudice will result that it is deemed lacking in due process." As for the impact of television, the Court had this to say: "Television in its present state and by its very nature, reaches into a variety of areas in which it may cause prejudice to an accused. Still one cannot put his finger on its specific mischief and prove with particularity wherein he was prejudiced."[15]

In effect, what the Court did was to infer prejudice from the circumstances. Facially, therefore, *Estes* stood as a warning to judges not to allow cameras at pretrial hearings and at trials.

SHEPPARD v. MAXWELL

Of the many fair trial cases from the 1930s onward, none was more important than *Sheppard v. Maxwell* (1966). Imagine, if you can, newspapers printing these headlines about a person not even formally accused of a crime:

"Quit Stalling and Bring Him In"
"Why Don't Police Quiz Top Suspect?"
"Why Isn't Sam Sheppard in Jail?"

And in the *Cleveland Press* this headline over a page one editorial:

"Getting Away with Murder"

Even before Dr. Sheppard was convicted of murdering his wife, these typographical pyrotechnics appeared:

"Dr. Sam Faces Quiz at Jail on Marilyn's Fear of Him"
"Sam Called a 'Jekyll-Hyde' by Marilyn; Cousin to Testify"

The cousin was not called as a witness nor was any such testimony introduced at the trial. These headlines were part of newspaper coverage which began with the slaying of the osteopath's wife on July 4, 1954, at the Sheppard home in suburban Cleveland. Louis B. Seltzer, then editor of the *Cleveland Press,* later took "credit" for forcing law enforcement officials to act against Sheppard, who was convicted in 1954 and appealed. The U.S. Supreme Court refused to review the case in 1956, but seven years later, the Court ruled that convictions in state courts could be reviewed by federal district courts in habeas corpus proceedings which require prisoners to be brought before a judge along with information pertaining to reasons for their detention. If the reasons are insufficient, the prisoners can be freed.

Sheppard filed a petition for such a writ against the warden of Ohio State Penitentiary, E. L. Maxwell, and in support he submitted five scrapbooks of news clippings and headlines, principally from the *Cleveland Press* and *Cleveland Plain Dealer,* along with some quotes from Seltzer's book, *The Years Were Good,* in which the editor discussed his role in bringing Sheppard to trial.

In 1964, the chief judge of the U.S. District Court for the southern district of Ohio, Carl Weinman, declared that there had been five separate violations of Sheppard's constitutional rights:

1. Failure to grant a change of venue or a continuance because of newspaper publicity before the trial.
2. Inability to maintain impartial jurors during the trial because of publicity.
3. Failure of the trial judge to disqualify himself although there was some question about his impartiality.

4. Unauthorized communications to the jury during its deliberations.
5. Improper introduction of lie detector testimony.

The State of Ohio appealed and the U.S. Court of Appeals reversed Wein-man's action. This led to a U.S. Supreme Court review of the case. In an 8–1 decision, the Court, in an opinion written by Justice Tom Clark, ruled:

> Since the state trial judge did not fullfill his duty to protect Sheppard from the inherently prejudicial publicity which saturated the community and to control disrup-tive influences in the courtroom, we must reverse the denial of the habeas petition. The case is remanded to the District Court with instructions to issue a writ and order that Sheppard be released from custody unless the State puts him to its charges again within a reasonable time.[16]

The Court Instructs the Judiciary

Sheppard v. Maxwell is a landmark case because trial judges were instructed in what they must do to insure a fair trial. Failure to take safeguards, the Court warned, would lead to reversal of convictions obtained. Judges were told to:

1. Adopt strict rules governing the use of the courtroom by reporters.
2. Limit the number of newspeople in the courtroom "at the first sign that their presence would disrupt the trial."
3. Insulate prospective witnesses from news media.
4. Prohibit "extra-judicial statements by any lawyer, party, witness, or court official which divulged prejudicial matters."
5. Continue a case or transfer it to another county "not so permeated with publicity" whenever there's "reasonable likelihood that prejudicial news prior to trial will prevent a fair trial."
6. Sequester the jury.

The Court said judges must take steps by rule and regulation that will protect their processes, adding:

> Neither prosecutors, counsel for defense, the accused, witnesses, court staff nor en-forcement officers coming under the jurisdiction of the court should be permitted to frustrate its function. Collaboration between counsel and the press as to information affecting the fairness of a criminal trial is not only subject to regulation, but is highly censurable and worthy of disciplinary measures.

Note, however, that the Court avoided direct infringement of First Amend-ment freedoms by instead suggesting "gags" on those who might give information to the press, rather than directly restricting what the press could print. Whether Justice Clark meant, in his opinion for the Court, to suggest that the judiciary should use the power of contempt more freely to curb press interference in the trial process was not clear at the time. Some journalists and judges interpreted the opinion as urging such a course of action. Clark later said that this was not his intent, and that his opinion should not be construed in such a way.

Concerning Sheppard's fate, the writ was issued and the state decided to try him again on the second-degree murder charge. The 16-day trial was marked by tight restrictions, with the number of reporters in the courtroom severely limited. A verdict of innocent was returned on November 16, 1966. Sheppard attempted to put his life together again. He remarried, returned to the practice of osteopathic medicine at a Youngstown, Ohio, hospital, but resigned shortly afterward when he was named in a malpractice suit after a patient died. He was divorced, set up an office in Columbus, turned briefly to professional wrestling, remarried, and died in 1970—the end of a tragic personal story and one that casts a shadow across the news media.

WARREN COMMISSION

On November 22, 1963, President John F. Kennedy was assassinated in Dallas, Texas. Shortly thereafter the Associated Press moved a story which read, in part:

> DALLAS, Tex. (AP)—A 24-year-old man who professed love for Russia was charged today with murder in the death of President Kennedy.
> The charge was filed against Lee Harvey Oswald. Officers said he was the man who hid on the fifth floor of a textbook warehouse and snapped off three quick shots that killed the President and wounded Gov. John B. Connally of Texas.

And United Press International (UPI) moved a story for afternoon papers on November 23 which read, in part:

> DALLAS (UPI)—Lee Harvey Oswald, an avowed Marxist and a Fidel Castro sympathizer, was charged today with the assassination of President Kennedy.
> Manacled, his face cut and bruised, his manner sullen, the 24-year-old political misfit and Marine reject was booked on a murder charge and jailed without bond.
> . . . [D]istrict Attorney Henry Wade said he had 15 witnesses to the assassination. He said investigators had learned from Oswald's Russian-born wife that he had a rifle of the type used to kill the President and had it with him the night before the assassination.
> "I believe we have the evidence to convict him," Wade said.

There were many news reports during the period following the arrest of Oswald until he was slain in the basement of the Dallas Police Department building by Jack Ruby—the first real televised murder. The collective result was to leave no doubt in the minds of most Americans that Oswald was the killer. The question remains: If Ruby had not taken the law into his own hands, could Oswald have received a fair trial anywhere in the United States, let alone in Texas where he would have been tried? No change of venue could have redressed the assault upon his right to a fair trial. Sequestering of a jury would not have safeguarded his rights. He stood convicted in the eyes of most Americans. An assassin "spared" the administrators of justice an ordeal incomparable in the annals of law to that time.

Upon assuming the presidency, Lyndon Johnson appointed a commission headed by Chief Justice Earl Warren to investigate Kennedy's assassination. The Warren Commission, as it became known, issued a report in 1964 which said that neither the press nor the public had a right to be contemporaneously informed by the police or prosecuting authorities of the details of the evidence being accumulated against Oswald. The commission said:

> Undoubtedly the public was interested in these disclosures, but its curiosity should not have been satisfied at the expense of the accused's right to a trial by an impartial jury. The courtroom, not the newspapers or the television screen, is the appropriate forum in our system for the trial of a man accused of crime.

The Commission pointed out that within 24 hours of the assassination more than 300 news media representatives were in Dallas, many of them attempting to crowd onto the third floor of the police department where Oswald was undergoing interrogation.

Concerning the news media and police, the Commission concluded:

> While appreciating the heavy and unique pressures with which the Dallas Police Department was confronted . . ., primary responsibility for having failed to control the press and to check the flow of undigested evidence to the public must be borne by the police department. It was the only agency that could have established orderly and sound operating procedures to control the multitude of newsmen gathered in the police building after the assassination.
>
> The Commission believes, however, that a part of the responsibility for the unfortunate circumstances . . . must be borne by the news media. The crowd of newsmen generally failed to respond properly to the demands of the police. Frequently without permission, news representatives used offices on the third floor, tying up facilities and interfering with normal police operations.
>
> . . . [T]he Commission believes that the news media, as well as police authorities . . . must share responsibility for the failure of law enforcement which occurred in connection with the death of Oswald. On previous occasions, public bodies have voiced the need for the exercise of self-restraint by the news media in periods when the demand for information must be tempered by other fundamental requirements of our society.

Among the recommendations was one that urged representatives of the bar, law enforcement associations, and news media to "work together to establish ethical standards concerning the collection and presentation of information to the public so that there will be no interference with pending criminal investigations, court proceedings, or the right of individuals to a fair trial."

The Commission added that the promulgation of a "code of professional conduct" by the news media to cover future situations would be "welcome evidence that the press had profited by the lesson of Dallas." This recommendation was rejected shortly thereafter by the board of directors of the American Society of Newspaper Editors (ASNE). A voluntary code, the board said, could be "more harmful than the evil complained of" because of restrictions—even self-imposed ones—on freedom of press. But the ABA would act on this recommendation several years later.

KATZENBACH—MITCHELL GUIDELINES

The failure of the news media to act in regard to the Commission's recommendation prompted U.S. Attorney General Nicholas Katzenbach to announce in 1965 rules governing what Justice Department personnel could release to the press at the time a person was arrested for a federal crime. The rules apply to FBI agents, U.S. marshals, U.S. attorneys, U.S. Bureau of Prisons workers, and the U.S. Immigration and Naturalization Service employees.

Katzenbach told the editors that his order placed restraints upon news sources, not on the press. "It is not for us to regulate the conduct or the content of the press," he said, adding: "For my part, I hope we can demonstrate that there is room in our Constitution for both the First Amendment and the Sixth."

Prior to Katzenbach's announcement, the ASNE had approved a committee report calling upon the Fourth Estate to resist vigorously any regulation that might "black out" large areas of crime news.

The Katzenbach guidelines applied only to criminal cases and became operative at the time of arrest or indictment. However, in 1971 Attorney General Mitchell issued another directive which extended the guidelines to federal civil cases and placed the criminal action guidelines in effect from the time a person became the subject of a criminal investigation, rather than from the time of arrest.

Under the guidelines to criminal actions, Justice Department personnel can make public:

- The defendant's name, age, residence, employment, marital status, and similar background information.
- The substance or text of the charge, such as the complaint, indictment, or information.
- The identity of the investigating and arresting agency and the length of the investigation.
- The circumstances immediately surrounding an arrest, including the time and place of arrest, resistance, pursuit, possession and the use of weapons, and a description of any items seized.

In addition, the guidelines state:

Disclosures should include only incontrovertible, factual matters, and should not include subjective observations. . . . [W]here background information or informa-

tion relating to the circumstances of an arrest or investigation would be highly prejudicial or where the release thereof would serve no law enforcement function, such
information should not be made public.

Personnel of the Department shall not volunteer for publication any information
concerning a defendant's prior criminal record, but information drawn from Federal
conviction records may be made available in response to a specific request.[17]

Because releasing certain types of information generally tends to create
dangers of prejudice without serving a significant law enforcement function, the
Justice Department ordered its personnel not to make available the following:

- Observations about a defendant's character.
- Statements, admissions, confessions, or alibis attributable to a defend-
  ant, or the refusal or failure of the accused to make a statement.
- Reference to investigative procedures such as fingerprints, polygraph examinations, ballistic tests, or laboratory tests, or to the refusal by the
  defendant to submit to such tests or examination.
- Statements concerning evidence or arguments in the case.
- Statements concerning the identity, testimony, or credibility of prospective witnesses.
- Any opinion as to the accused's guilt, or the possibility of a plea of guilty
  to the offense charged, or the possibility of a plea to a lesser offense.

Personnel also were instructed not to encourage or assist news media in
photographing or televising a defendant or accused person being held or trans-
ported in federal custody. They were told not to make available photographs of a
defendant unless a law enforcement function would be served thereby. However,
the guidelines do not apply in the case of a fugitive from justice.

The guidelines to civil actions state:

Personnel . . . associated with a civil action shall not during . . . [the Department of
Justice's] investigation or litigation make or participate in making an extrajudicial
statement, other than a quotation from or reference to public records, which a reasonable person would expect to be disseminated by means of public communication if
there is a reasonable likelihood that such dissemination will interfere with a fair trial
and which relates to:

(1) Evidence regarding the occurrence or transaction involved.
(2) The character, credibility, or criminal records of a party, witness, or prospec-
    tive witness.
(3) The performance or results of any examinations or tests or the refusal or
    failure of a party to submit to such.
(4) An opinion as to the merits of the claims or defenses of a party, except as
    required by law or administrative rule.
(5) Any other matter reasonably likely to interfere with a fair trial of the ac-
    tion.[18]

"REARDON COMMITTEE" REPORT

The continuing concern for fair trials and the orderly administration of justice led the ABA to create a study group composed of 12 prominent judges and lawyers with Justice Paul C. Reardon of the Massachusetts Supreme Judicial Court as chairman. The "Reardon Committee" released a report in 1966, and many of the recommendations contained therein were adopted in 1968 by the ABA House of Delegates. The 1966 report sparked the "battle of the century" for American newspapers, according to the annual report of the Freedom of Information Committee of the Associated Press Managing Editors. This report declared that the Reardon Report "would curtail news coverage of the police station and the courts more drastically than anything that's happened to news reporting in this country in many decades."

As adopted by ABA, the standards recommended that lawyers, law enforcement officers, and judges not release information of the type banned under the Katzenbach-Mitchell guidelines. Press representatives reacted most strongly against those standards which called for exclusion of the public, and therefore the press, from any preliminary hearing, bail hearing, or other pretrial hearing in a criminal case if matters might be disclosed that could be inadmissible in evidence at a trial and therefore possibly result in interference with a defendant's right to a fair trial. In addition, the ABA adopted the following standard relating to the exercise of the contempt power:

It is recommended that the contempt power should be used only with considerable caution but should be exercised under the following circumstances:

1. Against a person who, knowing that a criminal trial by jury is in progress or that a jury is being selected for such a trial: (a) disseminates by any means of public communication an extrajudicial statement relating to the defendant or to the issues in the case that goes beyond the public record of the court in the case, that is willfully designed by that person to affect the outcome of the trial, and that seriously threatens to have such an effect; or (b) makes such a statement intending that it be disseminated by any means of public communication.
2. Against a person who knowingly violates a valid judicial order not to disseminate, until completion of the trial or disposition without trial, specified information referred to in the course of the judicial hearing closed pursuant to . . . [ABA-adopted] recommendations.[19]

The controversy unleashed by the report and subsequent adoption of the recommended standards reached such proportions that in 1969 the ABA's Legal Advisory Committee on Fair Trial and Free Press — the successor to the Reardon Committee — published an information manual, *The Rights of Fair Trial and Free Press,* which said, in part:

■ The standards are directed primarily to lawyers, court and law enforcement personnel, and not to the press.

- They specify types of prejudicial information which lawyers participating in the case *should not release,* because such information may not be admissible in court and could influence the outcome of the trial.
- They provide *for the prompt release* from official sources of basic facts about crimes committed and circumstances surrounding them.
- They urge law enforcement agencies to follow the same rules as apply to lawyers with respect to withholding of specified prejudicial information before trials.
- They do not impose restrictions upon the freedom of the media to public information they are able to obtain through their own initiative, or to criticize law enforcement or the courts [Emphasis added].[20]

The controversy did not end and the ABA has moderated its position, doing so through its Adjunct Committee on Fair Trial and Free Press. The committee issued revised standards in 1981 recommending that information be released if it does not pose "a clear and present danger to the fairness of the trial."[21] This standard permits more information to be released than the previous "reasonable likelihood" standard; that is, "reasonable likelihood" that the release of information would interfere with a fair trial.

According to the ABA, the "clear and present danger" test requires four criteria to be met: (1) The restriction advances a legitimate government interest; (2) the public comment poses an extremely serious threat to that interest; (3) the threat is imminent; and (4) the restriction is necessary to protect or advance that legitimate governmental interest.

The committee also placed greater emphasis on First Amendment freedom, as reflected in this commentary:

> . . . [T]he public interest in understanding the workings of the criminal justice system is substantial. Unnecesessarily restrictive information policies are an obstacle to that understanding and ultimately threaten to undermine public confidence.[22]

Standard 8-3.2, pertaining to pretrial proceedings, states that such proceedings should not be closed to the public except where information therefrom would create a clear and present danger to a fair trial and other reasonable alternatives to closure would not work.

And in connection with the exercise of contempt power, Standard 8-4.1 states:

> It is recognized that the contempt power is an extreme measure and its use should be limited to the following circumstances:
> (a) Against a person who, knowing that a criminal trial by jury is in progress or that a jury is being selected for such a trial, disseminates by any means of public communication an extrajudicial statement relating to the defendant or the issues in the case, where that statement:
>
> (i) is beyond the public record of the court;
> (ii) is intended by that person to influence the jury's determination of guilt or innocence; and

(iii) creates a clear and present danger of having that effect.

(b) Against a person who knowingly violates a valid judicial order not to disseminate specified information referred to in a record sealed or a judicial hearing closed pursuant to [other ABA standards]. . . .[23]

More importantly from the press's standpoint, a limited exception to the contempt power is recommended by Standard 8-4.2 for the news media:

A representative of the news media who receives information, through misconduct of others in violation of a valid order . . . shall not be subject to contempt . . . for the further dissemination of that information unless the information is acquired by means of bribery, theft, or fraud.

If this standard had been in place and adhered to at the time Farr's troubles began with Judge Older, a contempt citation would not have been appropriate.

Contempt Power

With courts adopting stricter rules on the release of extrajudicial and pretrial statements, and placing limitations on the press during the hearing and trial phases of cases in accordance with instructions from the U.S. Supreme Court in *Sheppard,* journalists have found themselves dangling at the end of contempt citations. The power of a judge to deal with what he regards as interference in the trial process is well established when the interference takes place in or near the courtroom, such as a disturbance in the courtroom. But what about the judge's contempt power when presumably contemptuous behavior takes place far from the courtroom? The landmark ruling in such situations goes back to 1941 and the U.S. Supreme Court's decision in the combined cases of *Bridges* and the *Times-Mirror Co.*[24]

Bridges v. California and Times-Mirror Co. v. Superior Court

The managing editor of the *Los Angeles Times* was fined $600 for publication of three editorials, one of which concerned two labor union members who had been found guilty of assaulting nonunion truck drivers. The editorial urged the Superior Court judge to deal harshly with the defendants. In the contempt action, the trial judge found an "inherent tendency," and the California Supreme Court a "reasonable tendency" (the standard used by judges in England), on the part of the newspaper to interfere with the orderly administration of justice. But the U.S. Supreme Court reversed the lower courts, stating in part:

It is to be noted at once that we have no direction by the Legislature of California that publications outside the courtroom which comment on a pending case in a specified manner should be punishable. As we said in *Cantwell v. Connecticut,* 310 U.S. 296, 307–308; . . . such a "declaration of the state's policy would weigh heavily in our challenge of the law as infringing constitutional limitations." But as we also said there, the problem is different where "the judgment is based on a common law concept of the most general and undefined nature." . . . For here the Legislature of California has not appraised a particular kind of situation and found a specified kind of danger sufficiently imminent to justify a restriction on a particular kind of utterance.

Then, using a yardstick applied in 1919 by Justice Holmes—the "clear and present danger" doctrine for restricting First Amendment freedoms—the Court commented:

> What finally emerges from the "clear and present danger" cases is a working principle that the substantive evil must be extremely serious and the degree of imminence extremely high before utterances can be punished. . . . For the First Amendment does not speak equivocably. It prohibits any law "abridging the freedom of speech, or of the press." It must be taken as a command of the broadest scope that explicit language, read in context of a liberty-loving society, will allow. . . .
>
> We are aware that although some states have by statute or decision expressly repudiated the power of judges to punish publications as contempts on a finding of mere tendency to interfere with the orderly administration of justice in a pending case, other states have sanctioned the exercise of such a power. . . . But state power in this field was not tested in this Court for more than a century. . . . And this is the first time since 1925 that we have been called upon to determine the constitutionality of a state's exercise of the contempt power in this kind of a situation. Now that such a case is before us, we cannot allow the mere existence of other untested state decisions to destroy the historic constitutional meaning of freedom of speech and of the press.

The Court—in stating that there must be a clear and present danger to the orderly administration of justice before a judge can punish indirect contempt (contempt that takes place outside the courtroom)—concluded unanimously:

> . . . [I]n accordance with what we have said on the "clear and present danger" cases, neither "inherent tendency" nor "reasonable tendency" is enough to justify a restriction of free expression.
>
> We are all of the opinion that, upon any fair construction, their [editors'] influence on the course of justice can be dismissed as negligible, and that the Constitution compels us to set aside the convictions as unpermissible exercise of the state's power.

Craig v. Harney

The decision above was buttressed by the Court's opinion in *Craig v. Harney,* discussed previously, in 1947, a case involving a county court judge at Corpus Christi, Texas, who refused to accept a jury's verdict. An editorial described the judge's action as a "travesty on justice" and the judge promptly sentenced the newspaper publisher, an editorial writer, and a reporter to three days in jail for contempt. In reversing the contempt action, the Supreme Court conceded that the newspaper indulged in "strong language, intemperate language, and, we assume, in unfair comment." But, said the Court: "The vehemence of the language used is not alone the measure of the power to punish for contempt. The fires which it kindles must constitute an imminent, not merely a likely, threat to the administration of justice. The danger must not be remote or even reasonable; it must immediately imperil."

Selected Cases

The effect of *Sheppard* on criminal trials and pretrial hearings was not long in being felt. A few of these cases will be reviewed here and are included because of their notoriety or because of the measures invoked by the judiciary.

Richard Speck Case. Richard Speck was arrested on July 17, 1966, and accused in the slaying of eight student nurses in their hospital dormitory in Chicago. The arrest took place six weeks after the Supreme Court's decision in the *Sheppard* case, 15 months after the Katzenbach guidelines were announced, and about two years after the Warren Commission made its recommendations. Two days before Speck's arrest, Chicago Police Superintendent Orlando Wilson was quoted in Chicago newspapers and by wire services as saying that "he (Speck) is the killer." Using virtually the same words that were used by District Attorney Henry Wade ("I believe we have the evidence to convict him [Oswald]"), Wilson said, "I feel we have enough evidence to convict him."

Resulting criticism prompted Wilson to reply, "I saw no reason for withholding this information." Why? Because Speck's fingerprints were found in the dormitory, the superintendent said, and because the only survivor of the mass murder, who hid under a bed, had identified Speck.

A change of venue was granted and the trial took place in Peoria, Illinois, about 150 miles from the murder scene. The trial judge restricted the number of reporters in the courtroom, limited the number of telephones that could be installed in the building for use by the news media, warned those connected with the case not to discuss it outside the courtroom, and had the jury sequestered. The two-week trial ended in a guilty verdict; and the Illinois Supreme Court rejected a defense counsel contention that Speck had not received a fair trial.

Sirhan Sirhan Case. Following the assassination of U.S. Senator Robert Kennedy in June 1968, Los Angeles Mayor Sam Yorty released notebooks found in the home of the accused, Sirhan Sirhan, which contained a number of statements, including "Kennedy has to be assassinated before June 5, 1968" (the first anniversary of the Arab-Israel six-day war).

On June 7, when Sirhan was indicted, Los Angeles Superior Court Judge Arthur Alarcon prohibited the dissemination of any information about the investigation and prosecution of Sirhan by any attorney, court attaché, public official, grand juror, or law enforcement officer connected with the case.

The judge's "gag" order stirred strong opposition from segments of the California press and the California Freedom of Information Committee which voiced fears that such orders could:

- Deprive the public of its right to be informed of official actions.
- Promote dissemination of false rumors.
- Subordinate the First Amendment and provisions of the California State

Constitution by diluting the right of free speech and forbidding comment even by persons remotely removed from direct connection with the case but who might have helpful information.

■ Put unreasonable emphasis on the rights of the defendant at the expense of other equally important public rights.
■ Provide an undesirable precedent by enunciating principles of secrecy in matters of crime, law enforcement and trials.

Sirhan later was found guilty and sentenced to be executed.

James Earl Ray Case. On July 30, 1968, Judge W. Preston Battle, who presided at the trial of James Earl Ray for the murder of Dr. Martin Luther King, Jr., issued a code of procedures containing various restrictions. The code forbade anyone connected with the case, and all persons employed in the Shelby County, Tennessee, Criminal Courts Building, from participating in interviews or press conferences or from making any extrajudicial statements about the case pertaining to:

■ Guilt or innocence of accused.
■ Any plans relating to preparation or conduct of the trial, including techniques or strategy to be used.
■ Jurors or potential jurors who might be empaneled.
■ Credibility of any information or witness.
■ The treatment, acts, or attitude of the defendant.

The judge also set up a committee of seven lawyers to advise him should any prejudicial pretrial information be released. On September 30, the judge found two Memphis newsmen, a lawyer, and a private detective guilty of contempt of court for violating provisions of the code. He ruled that comments carried in stories written by the two reporters were "extremely prejudicial" and constituted a clear and present danger to empaneling an impartial jury.

Since the contempt citation was based on actions that had not taken place in or near the courtroom, the judge admitted that he was acting at the "frontier of the law," but cited the *Sheppard* decision as the basis for taking such steps.

Charles Manson Case. In one of the strangest cases on record, Charles Manson, later found guilty in the mass slaying of five persons, including actress Sharon Tate, tried to contaminate his own trial in Los Angeles when, on August 4, 1970, he grabbed a newspaper and held it up for the jurors to see. The headline read: MANSON GUILTY, NIXON DECLARES.

A defense attorney had brought the newspaper into the courtroom. He was sentenced to three nights in jail by the presiding judge who stopped the trial and questioned jurors to determine if they had been influenced by the headline. One juror so indicated, but this was not enough for a mistrial, in the judge's opinion.

President Nixon apparently believed it was not necessary to restrain an opinion about Manson's guilt or innocence because the jury was being guarded against outside-the-courtroom contamination. In fact, during a trial that required a six-million-word transcript, the jury was sequestered 197 nights!

Manson appealed his conviction, in part on the ground of prejudicial publicity, but the U.S. Supreme Court let stand the California Supreme Court's decision that Manson had received a fair trial.

Another President—Ronald Reagan—also thrust himself into the due process in connection with the indictment of Marine Corps Lt. Col. Oliver North on charges stemming from the Iran-Contra scandal. On March 28, 1988—shortly after the indictment was handed down—Reagan said on television, in response to a question, that he believed North was a hero and was innocent of the charges. Because of all the publicity surrounding this scandal, it was difficult to empanel a jury in 1989 for North's trial. The jury found North guilty on several of the counts in the indictment and the appeal process was initiated.

Elmer Wayne Henley, Jr., Case. In early 1974 both the prosecution and the defense agreed that Elmer Wayne Henley, Jr., 17, accused of six of 27 murders in Houston, Texas, could not receive a fair trial at that time because of prejudicial publicity. An extended continuance was granted by the District Court judge in Houston who overruled a defense motion to throw out the case on grounds of massive prejudicial publicity. Following the discovery of the murders in August 1973, another defendant in the slayings, David Brooks, reportedly made a statement accusing Henley of killing six of the victims. This statement was published in the *Houston Post* and widely disseminated.

The trial of Henley was moved to San Antonio where, at the time of jury selection, District Court Judge Preston Dial considered barring the press and public from the courtroom to reduce the risk of exposing jurors to possible prejudicial news media reports. When attorneys for several news organizations moved to file a protest, the judge relented and opened the proceedings to the press. Henley was found guilty and sentenced to 594 years in prison (99 years for each of the slayings). But his conviction was overturned in 1978 by the Texas Court of Criminal Appeals. The court said not enough consideration had been given to a request for a change of venue to move the trial from San Antonio. Defense attorneys had claimed that publicity in San Antonio would prejudice jurors. Henley ultimately went to prison, but the question in this case, and in other cases that draw sensational press coverage, persists: Does a change of venue or extended delay of trial overcome the danger of fair trials caused by prejudicial pretrial publicity?

A partial answer came from the U.S. Supreme Court in 1984 in *Patton v. Yount* when the 7–2 majority overturned a ruling by the U.S. Court of Appeals for the Third Circuit.[25] Jon Yount, a Luthersburg, Pennsylvania, high school mathematics teacher, pleaded guilty to the rape and murder of one of his students in 1966. He claimed temporary insanity, was tried and convicted and sentenced to life imprisonment. The state supreme court later reversed the conviction because police had failed to inform Yount of his right to an attorney before he made a confession. Four years later, Yount was tried again and convicted. His attorney, citing pretrial publicity, unsuccessfully sought to have the trial moved outside of

Clearfield County. Instead, the trial judge conducted extensive *voir dire,* or questioning, of prospective jurors before concluding that those selected to decide Yount's fate did not hold preconceived ideas about the defendant's guilt or innocence. The Third Circuit disagreed, ruling that pretrial publicity made a fair trial impossible.

The Supreme Court granted review to consider "the problem of pervasive media publicity that now arises so frequently in the trial of sensational criminal cases." In an opinion for the Court by Justice Powell, the majority held that the trial court did not commit "manifest error" in finding that the jury was impartial.

Powell said jury selection for Yount's second trial did not occur until four years after his first trial — at a time "when prejudicial publicity was greatly diminished and community sentiment had softened."

The relevant question, said Powell, is not whether the community remembered the case, but whether the jurors had fixed opinions such that they could not judge impartially the fate of the defendant. Powell added:

> . . . It is not unusual that one's recollection of the fact that a notorious crime was committed lingers long after the feelings of revulsion that create prejudice have passed. But it is clear the passage of time between a first and a second trial can be a highly relevant fact. In the circumstances of this case, we hold that it clearly rebuts any presumption of partiality or prejudice that existed at the time of the initial trial.[26]

Justice Stevens, joined by Justice Brennan, dissented, commenting that "it is difficult to understand how a neutral observer could conclude that the jury as a whole was impartial."

Thus, extensive *voir dire* and the passage of time were relevant factors for the Court in deciding if a person accused of a sensational crime received a fair trial. For as Powell noted, "time soothes and erases."

The confrontations that characterized press-judiciary relations during the 1960s and 1970s have largely subsided during the 1980s. Although trial judges still issue gag orders, they have extensively used *voir dire,* trial delays, and other "devices" in trying to assure fair trials for accused persons. And they've done this because segments of the news media often publish or broadcast information that constitutes trial by press. Judges have also used their contempt power as demonstrated rather spectacularly in a case involving the *Providence* (R.I.) *Journal* and editor Charles Hauser (see Chapter 3 for details). When the newspaper violated a U.S. District Court judge's order that forbade the publication of information legally obtained by means of the Freedom of Information Act about a reputed mob figure, the judge slapped a $100,000 fine on the newspaper and handed the editor an 18-month suspended jail term. Even though the judge later vacated the order because he believed it was unconstitutional, he was unwilling to rescind the fine or the suspended jail term because, as he put it, the newspaper had chosen to violate his order and communicate such defiance to hundreds of thousands of residents in the newspaper's circulation area. The First Circuit U.S. Court of Appeals reversed the contempt of court decision and the U.S. Supreme Court in

1988 rejected an attempt to reinstate it, doing so on a technicality.

Regardless of the outcome in this case, a judge's power to punish for contempt is awesome.

Voluntary Guidelines

As a way of warding off additional restrictions on the press, and also out of a deepening awareness and concern that Sixth Amendment rights be more fully protected when crime stories are being reported, news representatives in 27 states have joined with state bar associations in promulgating voluntary agreements or guidelines concerning free-press/fair-trial issues. Such agreements are voluntary, do not necessarily represent consensus among journalists in those states, and lack any means of enforcement. What they represent are voluntary efforts to curb abuses. Some guidelines are quite extensive, such as in Nebraska. Others are quite brief. The first such guide was put together in Oregon in 1962. Guidelines also have been adopted in Alabama, Arizona, California, Colorado, Delaware, Georgia, Idaho, Kentucky, Louisiana, Massachusetts, Minnesota, Missouri, Nebraska, New Mexico, New York, North Carolina, North Dakota, Oklahoma, Pennsylvania, South Carolina, South Dakota, Texas, Utah, Virginia, Washington, and Wisconsin.

Guidelines had been adopted in New Jersey in 1972 but were replaced by the New Jersey Supreme Court in 1985. A free-press/fair-trial statement was substituted. According to the court, the reason for the replacement was that some of the earlier guidelines were unenforceable and several U.S. Supreme Court decisions had made other guidelines moot. The statement eases the rules concerning the use of still cameras in the courtroom. There also is general recognition, said a court aide, that there must be an ongoing dialogue among bench, bar, and press representatives to achieve a "wider understanding of the problems and how they can be alleviated."[27]

In California, the "Joint Declaration Regarding News Coverage of Criminal Proceedings" includes these recommendations to journalists:

- Don't call a person brought in for questioning a suspect.
- Don't call a slaying a murder until there's a formal charge.
- Don't say solution when it's just a police accusation or theory.
- Don't let prosecutors, police, or defense attorneys use us as a sounding board for public opinion or personal publicity.[28]

Concerning the impact of the ABA's guidelines on curbing potentially prejudicial information, a survey showed that of 167 stories in a national probability sample of 29 newspapers, 113 (67.7 percent) contained at least one violation of the ABA's guidelines.[29] The guideline violated most frequently (in 35.3 percent of the stories) was the one concerning publication of opinions about an accused person's character, guilt, or innocence. One of the hypotheses put forth for testing was that violations of the guidelines would occur more frequently in states without voluntary guidelines. It was not supported by data. "In fact," said the researchers, "there was a slight tendency for violations to occur more frequently in newspapers from states with press-bar agreements, although the relationship was not significant."[30]

The voluntary guidelines movement may have suffered a setback when a Superior Court judge in Washington was willing to allow access to a pretrial proceeding in a murder case but only if reporters signed an agreement to abide by the voluntary bench-bar-press guidelines worked out in that state in 1966. The media objected on First Amendment grounds, but the state supreme court upheld the order in *Federated Publications v. Swedberg* (1981).[31] The court did so on the grounds that there was no prior restraint and that the order was a reasonable limitation designed to accommodate the interests of the press and the defendant. The U.S. Supreme Court declined to review the case, with only Justices Brennan and Marshall voting to grant certiorari.[32]

Because of Judge Byron Swedberg's order, in essence mandating compliance with a voluntary agreement if reporters wanted to gain access to pretrial proceedings, press representatives in several other states considered withdrawing from voluntary agreements in those states.

Federated Publications hinged on whether there had been prior restraint. The state supreme court said Judge Swedberg imposed no prohibition of publication or other communication of events that took place in the courtroom. This was not the case in *Nebraska Press Association v. Judge Hugh Stuart of the District Court of Lincoln County* (1976).

NEBRASKA PRESS ASSOCIATION CASE

The Supreme Court had been faced with a growing number of gag orders from judges seeking to curb information which they believed would be prejudicial to persons accused of crimes. The Reporters Committee for Freedom of the Press noted that two such orders were issued in 1966, 28 in 1974, and more than 30 in 1975. Some of the orders imposed restraints directly on the press.

The Supreme Court finally acted in *Nebraska Press Association* when it unanimously ruled that a gag order imposed on the press in connection with a sensational murder case was invalid and that the barriers to prior restraints of the press remained high.[33] Those barriers, said Chief Justice Burger in his opinion for the Court, were not overcome with respect to the order that prohibited reporting or commentary on judicial proceedings held in public.

Three justices — Brennan, Marshall, and Stewart — would have gone further by declaring that "resort to prior restraints on the freedom of the press is a constitutionally impermissible method for enforcing" the right to a fair trial. They believed that a broad spectrum of devices are available for ensuring such fairness without resorting to so drastic "an incursion on the equally fundamental . . . constitutional mandate that discussion of public affairs in a free society cannot depend on the preliminary grace of judicial censors."[34]

The facts in *Nebraska Press Association* relate to the murder in 1975 of the six members of the Henry Kellie family in Sutherland, Nebraska. Erwin Charles

Simants was arrested shortly thereafter and arraigned in a Lincoln County court. At the request of the county attorney and Simants' attorney, the judge entered a restrictive order which prohibited those in attendance at the arraignment and preliminary hearing—the latter open to the public—from releasing or authorizing "for public dissemination in any form or manner whatsoever any testimony given or evidence adduced" at those sessions. In addition, the judge's order required members of the press to observe the Nebraska Bar/Press Guidelines, the voluntary standard which stated that the following generally are not appropriate for reporting: confessions, opinions on guilt or innocence of the accused, results of tests or examinations, and so forth.

Simants was bound over to District Court for trial, and Judge Hugh Stuart thereupon entered his own restrictive order, which was to remain in effect until the jury was impaneled. The order specifically prohibited the media from reporting on five subjects:

1. The existence or contents of a confession Simants had made to law enforcement officers, which had been introduced in open court at the arraignment.
2. The fact or nature of statements Simants had made to other persons.
3. The contents of a note he had written the night of the crime.
4. Certain aspects of the medical testimony at the preliminary hearing.
5. The identity of the victims of the alleged sexual assault and the nature of the assault.

The order also prohibited reporting on the exact nature of the order itself! This prohibition would be stayed by Supreme Court Justice Blackmun, but he allowed the rest of the order to remain intact.

In 1975 the Nebraska Supreme Court issued a per curiam opinion upholding the action of the District Court partly on the basis of the clear and present danger doctrine. However, it modified the order so that only three matters were prohibited from being reported: (1) the existence and nature of any confessions or admissions made to law officers; (2) any confessions or admissions made to any third parties, except members of the press, and (3) other facts "strongly implicative" of the guilt of the accused. The Nebraska Press Association appealed.

In his opinion, in which Justices White, Blackmun, Powell, and Rehnquist joined, the Chief Justice reviewed a number of prior restraint cases and reiterated the decision reached in the Pentagon Papers case (see Chapter 3). "The thread running through all of these cases is that prior restraints on speech and publication are the most serious and the least tolerable infringement on First Amendment rights," he wrote. He then cited *Cox Broadcasting Co. v. Cohn,* discussed earlier, saying that "truthful reports of public judicial proceedings have been afforded special protection against subsequent punishment."

As in the Pentagon Papers case, Burger did not rule out the possibility that a prior restraint on the press might be constitutionally tolerated. But before it could pass constitutional muster, courts imposing it presumably must have exhausted other measures aimed at insuring a fair trial. As Burger said, there was no finding that alternative measures (such as those enunciated in *Sheppard*) would not have protected defendant's rights. Furthermore, he cited *Murphy v. Florida* (1975)[35] in saying that pretrial publicity—even pervasive and adverse publicity—does not inevitably lead to an unfair trial. Burger continued:

> The capacity of the jury eventually impaneled to decide the case fairly is influenced by the tone and extent of the publicity, which is in part, and often in large part, shaped by what attorneys, police, and other officials do to precipitate news coverage. The trial judge has a major responsibility. What the judge says about a case, in or out of the courtroom, is likely to appear in newspapers and broadcasts. More important, the measures a judge takes or fails to take to mitigate the effects of pretrial publicity—the measures described in *Sheppard*—may well determine whether the defendant receives a trial consistent with the requirements of due process.

Burger took cognizance of the likelihood of the spread of rumors that could be more damaging than reasonably accurate news accounts. Given such practical problems as those posed by the spread of rumors, the Chief Justice said it was far from clear that prior restraint would have protected Simants' rights. Then, in reviewing settled principles regarding prior restraint, Burger made what appears to be a suggestion to hard-pressed judges, namely, close judicial proceedings to the public. He had preliminary hearing specifically in mind when he wrote:

> To the extent that this order prohibited the reporting of evidence adduced at the open preliminary hearing, it plainly violated settled principles: "there is nothing that proscribes the press from reporting events that transpire in the courtroom." *Sheppard v. Maxwell, supra.* . . . The County Court could not know that closure of the preliminary hearings was an alternative open to it until the Nebraska Supreme Court so construed state law; but once a public hearing had been held, what transpired there could not be subject to prior restraint.

That the specter of prior restraint hovers over Burger's opinion for the Court is demonstrated by his concluding words:

> However difficult it may be, we need not rule out the possibility of showing the kind of threat to fair trial rights that would possess the requisite degree of certainty to justify restraint. This Court has frequently denied that First Amendment rights are absolute and has consistently rejected the proposition that a prior restraint can never be employed.

Nonetheless, the prior restraint was unconstitutional when the facts were arrayed against a three-part test involving: (1) the extent to which the probable publicity threatened the fairness of the forthcoming trial, (2) whether measures short of a prior restraint would have insured a fair trial, and (3) whether the restraint would have reasonably achieved the desired protection of the jury.

Brennan, joined by Stewart and Marshall, disagreed that the courts could impose prior restraints to protect a defendant's rights, saying:

Settled case law concerning the impropriety and constitutional invalidity of prior restraints on the press compels the conclusion that there can be no prohibition on the publication by the press of any information pertaining to pending judicial proceedings or the operation of the criminal justice system, no matter how shabby the means by which the information is obtained. This does not imply, however, any subordination of Sixth Amendments rights, for an accused's right to a fair trial may be adequately assured through methods that do not infringe First Amendment values.

Brennan praised the Nebraska Bar/Press Guidelines as "a commendable acknowledgment by the media that constitutional prerogatives bring enormous responsibilities."

And he concluded with these words," . . . [T]he press may be arrogant, tyrannical, abusive, and sensationalist, just as it may be incisive, probing, and informative. But at least in the context of prior restraints on publication, the decision of what, when, and how to publish is for editors, not judges."

In a separate concurring opinion, Justice Stevens said he subscribed to most of what Brennan said, including the basic thrust that the judiciary can protect a defendant's right to a fair trial without enjoining the press from publishing information in the public domain. He added these reservations:

Whether the same absolute protection would apply no matter how shabby or illegal the means by which the information is obtained, no matter how serious an intrusion on privacy might be involved, no matter how demonstrably false the information might be, no matter how prejudicial it might be to the interests of innocent persons, and no matter how perverse the motivation for publishing it, is a question I would not answer without further argument.

Justice White also came close to adopting Brennan's "absolutist" view, stating that he had grave doubts that gag orders on the press would ever be justifiable.

Justice Powell wrote a brief, concurring opinion in which he stated that anyone seeking such restrictive orders had a "unique burden" to meet; namely, showing that the publicity actually threatened a fair trial. How such a showing could be made before the fact is not entirely clear.

Aftereffects of Nebraska Press Association

Among the aftereffects of the Supreme Court's ruling was *Oklahoma Publishing Co. v. District Court, Oklahoma County* (see Chapter 7). In that case, a trial judge had enjoined the news media from disseminating the name and picture of a juvenile defendant accused of a murder who already had been identified and photographed in connection with an earlier judicial proceeding. The Oklahoma Supreme Court upheld the restrictive order in the interest of the juvenile's possible rehabilitation and subsequent reintegration into society. But the U.S Supreme Court, in a per curiam decision in 1977, reversed on the basis of *Nebraska Press Association* and *Cox Broadcasting,* discussed earlier, the latter holding that state law cannot prevent or punish publication of truthful reports of public court records. Since the juvenile's name already had been publicly disclosed during a court proceeding, the media could not be barred from publishing his name. As the Court said, "The name and picture of the juvenile . . . were 'publicly revealed in connection with the prosecution of the crime' much as the name of the rape victim in *Cox Broadcasting* was placed in the public domain. Under these circumstances, the District Court's order abridges the freedom of the press. . . ."[36]

Other developments in the wake of *Nebraska Press Association* included considerable criticism by the news media of Chief Justice Burger's suggestion that pretrial hearings could be closed to the public. In fact, quite a number of such hearings, and even some trials, were being closed to press and public. Such actions would lead to important Supreme Court decisions concerning public access to pretrial and trial sessions.

Gannett Company v. Judge DePasquale (1979). This case resulted from exclusion of the press by Judge Daniel A. DePasquale of a New York court from a pretrial suppression-of-evidence hearing in a criminal prosecution. The Gannett Company protested the exclusion and the Appellate Division of the New York Supreme Court ruled in 1976 that the exclusion violated the First Amendment in the absence of any (1) findings on the nature and extent of pretrial publicity that would occur in the absence of such a closure order; (2) findings on the availability of alternative protective measures; and (3) determination of the possible effects of the order on First Amendment rights.[37] It therefore vacated the trial judge's order. On appeal, the New York Court of Appeals reversed. The U.S. Supreme Court granted certiorari.

In an opinion by Justice Stewart, the Court affirmed the judgment of New York's highest court and held that the press and public had no constitutional right of access to the pretrial hearing.[38] But Stewart's opinion went beyond the question of exclusion of public and press from pretrial hearings. It declared that the public and press have no constitutional right under the Sixth and Fourteenth Amendments to attend criminal trials. Whether there was a First Amendment right was not decided.

The history of the public trial guarantee, wrote Stewart, demonstrates no more than a common-law rule of open civil and criminal proceedings. Not many common-law rules were elevated to the status of constitutional rights (although the common-law right of trial by jury is specifically included in the Sixth and Seventh Amendments), he said. Nor did the Constitution specifically reject these rules. Although there is no question that the Sixth Amendment "permits and even presumes open trials as a norm," said Stewart, it does not require that they be open. The right to a public trial belongs only to a defendant, not the public, under the Sixth Amendment.

Stewart's opinion was joined by Chief Justice Burger and by Powell, Rehnquist and Stevens. Blackmun filed an opinion concurring in part and dissenting in part, in which Brennan, White, and Marshall joined.

In a separate concurring opinion, Powell wrote, in part:

Although I join the opinion of the Court, I would address the question that it reserves. Because of the importance of the public's having accurate information concerning the operation of its criminal justice system, I would hold explicitly that . . . a Gannett reporter had an interest protected by the First and Fourteenth Amendments in being present at the pretrial suppression hearing. . . .

The right of access to courtroom proceedings . . . is not absolute. It is limited both by the constitutional right of defendants to a fair trial, see, *e.g., Estes v. Texas,* . . . and by the needs of government to obtain just convictions and to preserve the confidentiality of sensitive information and the identity of informants. CF. *Procunier v. Martinez,* 416 U.S. 396, 412–413 (1974); *Houchins v. KQED,* 438 U.S. 1, 34–35 (1978) (Stevens, J., dissenting); *Saxbe v. Washington Post Co.,* [417 U.S. 843, 872–873 (Powell, J., dissenting)].[39]

Powell said that when a defendant requests a closed trial, the trial court should consider whether alternative means are available to protect the fairness of the trial without substantially interfering with the public's interest in prompt access to information about the administration of justice. He concluded with the observation that the procedure followed by Judge DePasquale "fully comported" with that required by the Constitution.

Rehnquist disagreed sharply with Powell's view that the First Amendment guarantees a right of access to courtroom proceedings. Trial courts, said Rehnquist, are free to determine for themselves the question whether to open or close the proceedings. Hopefully, he said, they will decide the question by accommodating competing interests in a judicious manner. "But so far as the Constitution is concerned, the question is for them, not us, to resolve."

Chief Justice Burger wrote to emphasize that the nature of the proceeding involved in the Court's decision was a pretrial hearing, not a trial. Thus, the issue of the public's and press's exclusion from a trial was not presented in the case before the Court.

Blackmun, joined by three other Court members, concurred only in that part of Stewart's opinion related to the issue of mootness; that is, even though the pretrial suppression hearing was completed and the press had, in fact, been excluded, the issue was not moot and the merits of the case should be considered. He also pointed out that the Court had not found, prior to this case, and did not find in this case, any First Amendment right of access to judicial or other government proceedings. He therefore turned to an examination of the public trial provision of the Sixth Amendment.

He agreed that the literal terms of the Sixth Amendment secure the right of a public trial only to the accused, but he then cited a number of cases that came down on the side of openness. He also cited the social values that are secured by public trials, such as public confidence in the system of justice. For these and other reasons he concluded that the Due Process Clause of the Fourteenth Amendment, incorporating the public trial provision of the Sixth Amendment, prohibits the states from excluding the public from a trial or pretrial without first affording full and fair consideration to the public's interests in maintaining an open proceeding. And any exception to the rule of open courts must be narrowly drawn, he said.

An accused person who seeks closure, said Blackmun, should (1) establish an adequate basis to support a finding that there is a substantial probability that irreparable damage to his fair trial will result from conducting the proceeding in public; (2) show a substantial probability that alternatives to closure will not protect adequately his right to a fair trial; and (3) demonstrate that there is substantial probability that closure will be effective in protecting against the perceived harm.

Blackmun continued:

> If, after considering the essential factors, the trial court determines that the accused has carried his burden of establishing that closure is necessary, the Sixth Amendment is no barrier to reasonable restrictions on public access. . . .[40]

Blackmun said the Sixth Amendment also fixes the rights of the press concerning access to pretrial and trial proceedings; namely, the same right of access as the public's. The press is free to report whatever happens in open court.

Blackmun concluded that Judge DePasquale's closure order was not justified by the facts in the case at hand.

Among the cases cited by Blackmun was *In re Oliver* (1948), in which the Court set aside a contempt citation against William Oliver. Oliver had been summarily sentenced to 60 days in jail by a Michigan judge who did not believe that Oliver was telling the truth when he appeared before the judge who was sitting as a one-man grand jury. Oliver was not given a chance to rebut any statements made about him or to call any witnesses.

As Justice Black said for the majority:

> Counsel have not cited and we have been unable to find a single instance of a criminal trial conducted *in camera* in any federal, state or municipal court during the history of this country [although Black noted that a court-martial is an exception]. Nor have we found any record of even one such secret criminal trial in England since abolition of Star Chamber in 1641. . . .[41]

Black concluded by saying that the "law of the land" requires that "no man's life, liberty or property be forfeited . . . until there has been a charge fairly made and fairly tried in a public tribunal."

Reaction to Decision. Within two months of the *Gannett* decision, at least 10 trials were closed to the public by judges citing *Gannett*. Scores of pretrial hearings also were closed. The Reporters Committee for Freedom of the Press and other press organizations monitored these closings and kept a box score of what was happening. As the instances of closures increased, a phenomenon of sorts was witnessed. Chief Justice Burger publicly commented that trial judges were misreading the *Gannett* decision which, in his judgment, applied only to pretrial hearings. Then, in rather quick order, came other public comments about the case from Justices Blackmun, Powell, Stevens, and Brennan. It is very unusual for members of the Supreme Court to publicly comment on Court decisions. The end result was a good deal of confusion concerning *Gannett*. The press generally viewed it as another in a series of anti-press decisions that had flowed from the Court during the nine months preceding the *Gannett* ruling on July 2, 1979.

Meanwhile, state supreme courts were busy addressing the issue of pretrial and/or trial closures. The Arkansas Supreme Court ruled that a trial court erred in holding evidentiary suppression hearings *in camera,* basing its decision on a state law requiring open judicial proceedings.[42] The Pennsylvania Supreme Court decided that closure of pretrial proceedings is not permissible if alternatives, such as jury sequestration, are available to protect a defendant's right to a fair trial.[43] West Virginia's highest court ruled in 1980 that pretrial hearings should be open to the public unless it can be proved that widespread adverse publicity would result.[44] The Maine legislature passed a bill, signed into law in 1980, designed to protect the public's right to attend pretrial criminal proceedings. The public can be excluded only if a court finds a "substantial likelihood" that injury or damage would result to a defendant's right to a fair trial if the proceeding were conducted in public. Connecticut also passed a law making it more difficult to exclude the public from courtroom proceedings.

Most interestingly, New York's highest court, which had upheld the trial judge's pretrial closure order in 1977 in *Gannett v. DePasquale,* returned to the subject in 1979 in another case initiated by Gannett-owned newspapers. But this time the New York Court of Appeals reversed a lower court's pretrial closure order and laid out specific ground rules that would have to be followed if the public and press are to be excluded from such hearings.[45] In referring to the opinion he had authored in the earlier Gannett case, Judge Sol Wachtler said in *Westchester Rockland Newspapers v. Leggett,* "We did not mean to suggest that closure would be necessary or even appropriate in all pretrial proceedings."[46]

FIRST AMENDMENT RIGHT TO ATTEND CRIMINAL TRIALS, PRETRIALS

The upshot to all of the disaffection and uncertainty caused by the *Gannett* decision was another decision—a year to the day that Gannett had been announced—that the press and public have a First Amendment right to attend criminal trials. They cannot be excluded merely upon agreement of the judge and the parties absent any findings that would overcome the presumption of open trial.

Richmond Newspapers v. Virginia

The decision came in *Richmond Newspapers, Inc. v. Virginia* (1980).[47] Seven of the nine Court members agreed that such a First Amendment right exists. Only Justice Rehnquist disagreed. Justice Powell took no part in the case, but his earlier opinions make it clear that he would have agreed with the majority had he participated in the decision.

Richmond Newspapers is a watershed case, in the opinion of Justice Stevens. As he wrote in a concurring opinion:

> Today, . . . the Court unequivocally holds that an arbitrary interference with access to important information is an abridgment of the freedoms of speech and of the press protected by the First Amendment.

Contrast Stevens' assessment of the importance of the Court's decision in *Richmond Newspapers* with Rehnquist's evaluation of the situation a year earlier in his concurring opinion in *Gannett* when he wrote:

> . . . [I]t is clear that this Court repeatedly has held that there is no First Amendment right of access in the public or the press to judicial or other governmental proceedings. . . . [T]his Court emphatically has rejected the proposition advanced in [Powell's concurring opinion in *Gannett*] that the First Amendment is some sort of constitutional "sunshine law" that requires notice, an opportunity to be heard and substantial reasons before a governmental proceeding may be closed to the public and press.

Richmond Newspapers developed when a Virginia trial judge, who had presided over two previous trials that had ended in mistrials, was asked by a murder defendant's attorney to exclude the public and press. The prosecution had no objection and no members of the public, including press representatives, objected at the time. The judge said that a Virginia statute gave him authority to close the courtroom. His reference presumably was to Virginia Code Section 19.2-266, but as the case developed the constitutionality of this statute was not decided by the U.S. Supreme Court. On the same day that the judge closed the trial, two reporters for Richmond Newspapers, Inc., sought a hearing in an attempt to get the closure order vacated. The court allowed the hearing, but rejected a motion to vacate the order. On appeal, the Virginia Supreme Court in effect upheld the trial judge.

Chief Justice Burger announced the judgment of the Court which reversed the Virginia Supreme Court. He wrote a plurality opinion that was joined by Justices White and Stevens. Brennan, joined by Marshall, concurred in the judgment, and wrote a separate opinion. Stewart and Blackmun also concurred in the judgment, but wrote separate opinions. Rehnquist dissented. The various opinions suggest some caution in interpreting *Richmond Newspapers* as expansively as does Stevens, although there's no doubt that the press and public have gained a significant victory in obtaining a right of access under the First Amendment.

In his opinion, Burger distinguished *Gannett* from the case at hand. *Gannett* involved a right of access to pretrial hearings. *Richmond Newspapers* involved a right of access to trials. The decision in Gannett involved Sixth Amendment rights. The issue in *Richmond Newspapers* centered on First Amendment rights. For the first time, said Burger, the Court was asked to decide whether a criminal trial may be closed to the public upon an unopposed request of a defendant, "without any demonstration that closure is required to protect the defendant's superior right to a fair trial, or that some other overriding consideration requires closure." The Court answered with a resounding "No!"

Burger reviewed historical developments and concluded:

> From this unbroken, uncontradicted history, supported by reasons as valid today as in centuries past, we are bound to conclude that a presumption of openness inheres in the very nature of a criminal trial under our system of justice.

Among the antecedent cases cited by Burger for this conclusion were *Craig v. Harney* and Justice Black's opinion for the Court in *In re Oliver*. Furthermore, Burger noted that in *Gannett* both majority and dissenting opinions agreed that open trials were part of the common-law tradition.

In discussing the First Amendment, in conjunction with the Fourteenth, Burger noted that enactment of the Bill of Rights took place against the backdrop of a long history of openness of trials. Furthermore, several decisions of the Court, said Burger, were keyed to the idea of a First Amendment right "to receive information and ideas"[48] and a prohibition against government limiting the amount of information "from which members of the public may draw."[49] What this means in the context of trials, said Burger, is that the First Amendment guarantees of speech and press prohibit government from summarily closing courtroom doors.

Burger then proceeded to distinguish such "right of access" cases as *Saxbe v. Washington Post. Co.* (1974)[50] and *Pell v. Procunier* (1974)[51] from the instant case because those cases concerned penal institutions which, by definition, are not "open" or public places. The *Saxbe* and *Pell* case are discussed in Chapter 11.

In dealing with the State of Virginia's argument that nowhere in the Constitution is the right of the public to attend trials spelled out, Burger pointed out that a number of important rights are not enumerated in that document, including the rights of association and privacy, the right to be presumed innocent, and the right to travel. Even though these fundamental rights are not expressly guaranteed, said Burger, the Court has recognized that they are as indispensable to the enjoyment of rights as those explicitly defined. Therefore, said Burger,

> We hold that the right to attend criminal trials is implicit in the guarantees of the First Amendment; without the freedom to attend such trials, which people have exercised for centuries, important aspects of freedom of speech and "of the press could be eviscerated" [quoting from *Branzburg v. Hayes,* see Chapter 11, 408 U.S. 665, 681 (1972)].

However, the right is not absolute. Assuming that safeguards, such as those enumerated in *Sheppard* and *Nebraska Press Association,* would not ensure fairness for an accused person and based on some kind of findings to support closure (although the procedure was not detailed by which such findings would become apparent), a trial could be closed. As Burger expressed it, "Absent an overriding interest articulated in the findings, the trial of a criminal must be open to the public."

In a footnote, he said that historically both civil and criminal trials have been presumptively open to the public, although civil case trials were not at issue in the case before the Court.[52]

Stevens, in his concurring opinion, agreed that the First Amendment protects the public and press from abridgment of their rights of access to information about the operation of their government including the Judicial Branch, given the absence of any record of justification for closure.

In a brief concurring opinion, White said *Richmond Newspapers* would have been unnecessary had the Court, in *Gannett,* construed the Sixth Amendment to forbid excluding the public from criminal proceedings except in narrowly defined circumstances.

Brennan, joined by Marshall, agreed in a separate opinion that the First Amendment—of itself and as applied to the states through the Fourteenth Amendment—secures to the public an independent right of access to trial proceedings. He did not discuss countervailing interests that might be "sufficiently compelling to reverse this presumption of openness" since they were not at issue in this case. In the main, his opinion seeks to elaborate on his suggested two-model approach as a means of better understanding the protection afforded by the First Amendment (see Chapter 2). Because public access to trials assumes structural importance in our system of government (such as an aid to accurate factfinding), it is protected by the First Amendment, he said.

Brennan went beyond the reach of Burger's opinion in stating that the Virginia statute cited by the trial judge violated the First and Fourteenth Amendments.

Stewart stated unequivocally that the First and Fourteenth Amendments give the press and public a right of access to both criminal and civil trials, but the right is not absolute. Citing *Sheppard,* he said that reasonable limitations can be imposed upon the public and press.

Gannett was in error, said Blackmun in his concurring opinion. He remained convinced that the right to a public trial is where the Constitution explicitly placed it—in the Sixth Amendment. He continued:

> The Court, however, has eschewed the Sixth Amendment route. The plurality turns to other possible constitutional sources and invokes a veritable potpourri of them—the speech clause of the First Amendment, the press clause, the assembly clause, the Ninth Amendment, and a cluster of penumbral guarantees recognized in past decisions. This course is troublesome, but it is the route that has been selected and, at least for now, we must live with it.

Rehnquist, in his dissent, recalled the reasons he had put forth in his concurrence in *Gannett,* and suggested that the Court was smothering the "healthy pluralism" that would ordinarily exist in the 50 states through the ever broadening use of the Supremacy Clause by which the federal Constitution takes precedence over state constitutions and laws.

Significance of Richmond Newspapers. In discussing the effects of this case, James Goodale of a New York law firm, who formerly served as counsel for *The*

New York Times, said it is "absolutely one of the most major decisions of all time" because of the Court's acknowledgment of a right of access.[53] Another attorney referred to it as one of the two or three most important decisions in the whole history of the First Amendment.

"We can expect some limitations on the right of access," said Goodale, but *Richmond Newspapers* means that the right "can't be taken away entirely." He foresaw instances in state courts where both a statutory freedom of information argument and a right of access argument would be asserted whenever attempts are made to shield police blotters, for example, from the public. He also expected *Richmond Newspapers* to have an impact on reporters' privilege cases (discussed in the next chapter), with reporters arguing that the decision upholds their right to gather news.

Whether *Richmond Newspapers* applied to both pretrial and trial proceedings was arguable. In his plurality opinion, Burger specifically emphasized trials and the Court did not specifically overrule *Gannett.* But seven justices who joined in the judgment of the Court did not restrict their views to trials, but included judicial proceedings in the sweep of their logic. Subsequent Court decisions would bear out the more expansive view of *Richmond Newspapers.*

About three months after the *Richmond Newspapers* decision, the Justice Department issued final guidelines for U.S. government attorneys concerning motions to close judicial proceedings. The Guidelines on Open Judicial Proceedings state that the government has a "general overriding affirmative duty" to oppose closure. It should move for, or consent to, closed proceedings only when closure "is plainly essential to the interests of justice."

Globe Newspapers v. Superior Court

The expansive nature of *Richmond Newspapers* is seen in the Court's 6–3 decision in *Globe Newspapers* (1982) in which the Court held unconstitutional a Massachusetts law that required closure of rape and other sexual assault trials during testimony of victims who were minors.[54]

The case stemmed from a 1979 trial of a man accused of raping three girls. The trial judge closed all proceedings, citing the state law. The Boston *Globe's* petition to cover the trial was denied. The state supreme court affirmed the closure order and the newspaper appealed.

Brennan wrote the majority opinion, stating that a mandatory closure rule is unconstitutional. Although the right of access is not absolute, said Brennan, the state's justification in closing the proceeding must be a "weighty one." The safeguarding of the physical and psychological well-being of a minor, Brennan added, must be proved on a case-by-case basis.

Justice O'Connor concurred in the judgment but wrote to state her interpretation of *Richmond Newspapers* (because she was not on the Supreme Court bench at the time of that decision) and the case at hand, namely, that neither case carries any implication of access beyond criminal trials.

Chief Justice Burger, joined by Rehnquist, dissented, arguing that even though the decision is a narrow one, it is a "gross invasion of state authority and a state's duty to protect its citizens. . . ." He said he could not agree with the

Court's "expansive interpretation" of *Richmond Newspapers,* or its "cavalier rejection of the serious interests supporting Massachusetts' mandatory closure rule."

Justice Stevens also dissented, saying that the state supreme court had upheld in the abstract the state statute and that therefore the Court's comments about First Amendment issues involved in the case are "advisory, hypothetical, and, at best, premature." Stevens was not arguing against the applicability of the First Amendment to trials, but only that the case at hand was moot.

It should be emphasized that *Globe Newspapers* produced a majority opinion of the Court whereas *Richmond Newspapers* did not, although seven members did agree with the decision; that is, the press and public have a qualified First Amendment right to attend criminal trials.

Addenda to Gannett Company

The Supreme Court returned to questions left unanswered by its *Gannett Company* decision, doing so in *Press-Enterprise Co. v. Superior Court* (1984)[55] and *Waller v. Georgia* (1984).[56]

Waller v. Georgia. Unlike *Gannett Company, Waller v. Georgia* raised the question of the criminal defendant's right to have a pretrial suppression hearing open to the public. In *Gannett,* the defendant wanted the hearing closed to the public and press. In *Waller,* the prosecution wanted the hearing closed.

Justice Powell gave the opinion for a unanimous Court which held that the defendant's Sixth Amendment right to a public trial extends to pretrial suppression hearings except where the party seeking to close the hearing meets the test laid down in *Press-Enterprise.* As spelled out by Powell, the party seeking closure over the objections of the accused must advance an overriding interest that is likely to be prejudiced by an open hearing; the closure must be no broader than necessary to protect that interest; reasonable alternatives to closure must be considered; and the trial court must make findings adequate to support the closure.

Powell pointed out that suppression hearings often are as important as the trial itself and, in fact, may be the only trial because defendants often plead guilty pursuant to plea bargaining if they lose in their attempt to suppress certain evidence. Thus, the arguments used to justify access to criminal trials apply equally to suppression hearings. Powell also noted that one of the reasons often advanced for closing judicial proceedings—to avoid tainting the jury by pretrial publicity—is largely absent when the defendant makes an informed decision to object to the closing of the proceedings.

In reversing the Georgia Supreme Court, the nation's highest tribunal remanded the case for a decision as to which portions, if any, of a new suppression hearing may be closed to the public in light of conditions present at the time of such a hearing.

Press-Enterprise Co. v. Superior Court. The *Gannett Company* case involved the Sixth Amendment right of a defendant to close a pretrial suppression-of-evidence hearing. The opinion by Justice Stewart mustered support from only three other colleagues. In it, Stewart took the position that the public and press do not have a Sixth Amendment right to attend the pretrial suppression hearing. At the time, Powell argued that there was a First Amendment right of access, and Blackmun, joined by Brennan, White, and Marshall, said there was a Sixth Amendment right of the public and press to attend such hearings.

But in *Press-Enterprise Co.,* the Court unanimously held that the qualified First Amendment right of access to attend criminal trials extended to *voir dire* proceedings by which the jury is selected.

Whether the *voir dire* is a pretrial or trial proceeding was not answered. When the *voir dire* began in a California Superior Court to select jurors to try a man accused of the rape and murder of a teenage girl, the *Press-Enterprise* of Riverside petitioned for the opening of the *voir dire* to the public and press. The state opposed the motion, arguing that the responses of prospective jurors to questions would be less than candid if the press and public were present. The judge allowed access to all but three days of the six-week-long *voir dire*. After the jury was empaneled, the *Press-Enterprise* moved for release of the complete transcript of the *voir dire*. Both the defense counsel and the prosecutor argued that release of the transcript would violate the jurors' rights to privacy. The court denied the motion; the newspaper then sought a writ of mandate from the California Court of Appeal, which was denied, and the state supreme court denied the newspaper's request for a hearing. It should be emphasized that the *Press-Enterprise* argued that the public and press had a First Amendment right to attend the trial and that the trial commenced with the *voir dire* proceedings. Thus, whether the *voir dire* is a pretrial or trial proceeding was not an issue.

In his opinion for the Court, Chief Justice Burger did not bother to make a distinction. It may have been unnecessary because at least a majority of the Court members believed that the public and press have a qualified First or Sixth Amendment right to attend a pretrial suppression hearing (*Gannett Company* involving such a hearing).

The Court held that the guarantees of public criminal trials extend to *voir dire* examinations of prospective jurors. The value of openness, said the Chief Justice, "lies in the fact that people not actually attending trials can have confidence that standards of fairness are being observed. . . . Openness . . . enhances both the basic fairness of the criminal trial and the appearance of fairness so essential to public confidence in the system." There is also a community "therapeutic value," wrote Burger, in that people who are aware that the criminal justice system is functioning are not likely to try to take justice into their own hands. The same arguments used to justify open trials apply to the jury selection process.

The right of access is not absolute, Burger pointed out. He wrote:

The presumption of openness may be overcome only by an overriding interest based on findings that closure is essential to preserve higher values and is narrowly tailored to serve that interest. The interest is to be articulated along with findings specific enough that a reviewing court can determine whether the closure order was properly entered.[57]

Burger pointed out that there were no findings to support the closure of three days of the *voir dire,* nor was any consideration given to alternatives to the denial of access to *voir dire* testimony. Absent such findings and consideration, the trial court could not constitutionally close the *voir dire.*

Justice Blackmun wrote a separate concurring opinion to emphasize that the Court was not deciding prospective jurors' privacy rights.

Justice Stevens, in his concurring opinion, addressed the question of whether the *voir dire* is a part of the trial process. He wrote:

> The constitutional protection for the right of access that the Court upholds today is found in the First Amendment, rather than the public trial provision of the Sixth. If the defendant had advanced a claim that his Sixth Amendment right to a public trial was violated by closure of the *voir dire,* it would be important to determine whether the selection of the jury was a part of the "trial" within the meaning of that Amendment.

Justice Marshall concurred in the judgment, but wrote a separate opinion to stress that the constitutional rights of the public and press to all aspects of criminal trials are not diminished in cases in which "deeply personal matters" are likely to be elicited in *voir dire* proceedings. Only in the most extraordinary circumstances can the juror's responses at *voir dire* be permanently excluded from the "salutory scrutiny of the public and the press."

On remand, the California Supreme Court ruled that the U.S. Supreme Court's decision in *Press-Enterprise Co.* did not warrant repudiation of the earlier state court's determination that the First Amendment does not provide a right of access to pretrial proceedings.[58] The California court said it reached this conclusion in part because the U.S. Supreme Court's decisions in *Press-Enterprise Co.* and *Globe Newspapers,* discussed previously, concerned trials, not pretrials.

The U.S. Supreme Court was not long in responding. In the second *Press-Enterprise* case—this one in 1986 involving once again the Riverside County Superior Court—the Court, in a 7–2 decision, ruled that the press and public have a qualified constitutional right to attend preliminary hearings in criminal cases.[59]

The case arose when the *Press-Enterprise* was barred from attending a 41-day preliminary hearing for Robert Diaz, who was accused of murdering 12 hospital patients by administering massive doses of a heart drug. The California Supreme Court held that the qualified First Amendment right of access to trials did not extend to preliminary hearings (pretrials).[60]

Burger gave the Court's opinion in *Press Enterprise II,* saying that such hearings can be closed only if there is "substantial probability" that an open hearing would produce publicity damaging to a defendant's fair trial rights and if reasonable alternatives to closure would not protect those rights.

The Chief Justice noted that "there has been a tradition of accessibility to preliminary hearings of the type conducted in California." He added that the "near uniform" practice of state and federal courts ever since the 1807 trial of

Aaron Burr for treason "has been to conduct preliminary hearings in open court." Also, because preliminary hearings in California "are sufficiently like a trial," the conclusion is justified that public access is necessary to the proper functioning of the criminal justice system.

Because a qualified First Amendment right of access applies, wrote Burger, the preliminary hearing in California cannot be closed unless specific, on-the-record findings are made demonstrating that closure "is essential to preserving higher values and is narrowly tailored to serve that interest" (quoting from the *Press Enterprise I* decision). "If the interest asserted is the right of the accused to a fair trial," continued Burger, "the preliminary hearing shall be closed only if specific finding are made demonstrating that first, there is a substantial probability that the defendant's right to a fair trial will be prejudiced by publicity that closing would prevent and, second, reasonable alternatives to closure cannot adequately protect the defendant's fair trial rights."

Stevens, joined by Rehnquist, dissented, arguing that if Burger's reasoning were carried to its logical outcome, it could be used to provide public access to secret grand jury proceedings, as well as to other government proceedings. He also contended that the magistrate in the Diaz case had acted correctly in closing the hearing because only the prosecution's evidence was aired and the transcript contained a statement by the magistrate that Diaz is "the most dangerous type of individual there is."

Are Civil Proceedings Open to the Public?

Although mention was made of civil proceedings in *Richmond Newspapers,* that case applied only to criminal proceedings. Justice O'Connor emphasized in her concurring opinion in *Globe Newspapers* that she interpreted the Court's decision in that case and *Richmond Newspapers* as not carrying any implications beyond the context of criminal trials. In *Gannett Company,* Justice Stewart found that for many centuries "both civil and criminal trials have traditionally been open to the public," as did Chief Justice Burger in his plurality opinion in *Richmond Newspapers.* But neither case raised the question of whether the public has a right to attend civil case trials, let alone pretrial proceedings.

The Third Circuit U.S. Court of Appeals interpreted both the common law and the First Amendment as requiring that civil proceedings be presumptively open to the public.[61] It did so in a 1984 ruling that reversed a trial court's decision to close a hearing on a motion for a preliminary injunction in a civil case. The three-judge panel cited the standard used in *Press-Enterprise I* to determine when such proceedings can be closed.

Not all courts are in agreement concerning the right to attend civil proceedings, nor do they concur on whether the right, if it exists, extends to various facets of civil proceedings, such as discovery information, depositions, case files, interrogatories, and so on. In the main, most civil court trials are open. No doubt the U.S. Supreme Court will have to address some of these questions in future litigation, and the media are becoming more inclined to pursue access to such information through litigation, if necessary.

An example is the challenge brought by three Ohio newspapers—the *Cincin-*

nati Post, the *Dayton Daily News,* and the *Columbus Dispatch* — when they were barred from attending a summary jury trial involving an alleged breach of contract in the construction of a nuclear power plant. Such "trials" seek to facilitate pretrial settlements of civil lawsuits and are typically used to lessen the drain on judicial resources. In fact, the "trial" to which the press sought access resulted in a settlement two months later.

When the trial court and Sixth Circuit U.S. Court of Appeals denied access, the newspapers appealed, but the U.S. Supreme Court in 1989 let stand the lower court's ruling that the public has no right to attend such trials.

CAMERAS IN THE COURTROOM

Mention was made earlier in this chapter of Canon 35, and of the *Estes* case (1965) in which Billie Sol Estes's conviction was reversed because of the presence of television cameras at the preliminary hearing and the opening day of the trial. No isolatable prejudice had to be shown, the majority ruled. In effect, what the Court did was to infer prejudice from the circumstances.

At the time, four members of the Court would have barred cameras from the courtroom on Sixth Amendment grounds; that is, the mere presence of cameras creates an inherently prejudicial situation for the defendant. But Justice Harlan, who voted as part of the five-member majority, did not go so far in condemning the use of television at trials. Instead, he favored future experimentation in the states. Justices Stewart, Black, Brennan, and White wanted to leave room for experimentation, and they were anxious not to have the issue resolved on constitutional grounds. Finally, therefore, *Estes* stood as a warning to judges not to allow cameras at pretrial and trial proceedings. That cautionary edict began to erode in the face of developments in electronic communication, in photography, and as a result of experiments in state courts. Television equipment became less obtrusive and needed less light to activate the cameras; still photographers could operate unobtrusively from the back of courtrooms, and a variety of experiments tended to show that the dignity and decorum of courtroom proceedings were not impaired by the presence of such equipment. In all of the experiments, the television equipment was set up in ways to minimize its presence at the proceedings (unlike the *Estes* situation).

The American Bar Association (ABA) had taken the position in Canon 35 of opposing cameras in the courtroom as a result of the Hauptmann trial in 1935. A ban on radio broadcasts was added to the canon in 1941, and television joined the prohibition list in 1963. In 1972 the ABA's House of Delegates adopted Canon 3A(7) in the new Code of Judicial Conduct, which superseded Canon 35, but 3A(7) maintained the recommended ban on what is called "expanded media coverage" — or EMC (namely, still and motion picture coverage, radio broadcasting, and television) — in the courtroom and adjacent areas. There were a few minor exceptions, such as allowing photographic coverage or televising of naturalization ceremonies.

ABA's canons are only recommendations, but only three states—Colorado, Oklahoma, and Texas—had failed to adopt Canon 35 by the 1960s.

ABA's formal opposition to EMC ended in 1982. The reason for the ABA's position change can be found in the EMC experiments conducted in a number of states in the 1970s. Florida experimentally allowed EMC in 1977. In September and October of that year, attention focused on coverage of the sensational Ronny Zamora trial. Zamora had been charged with the murder of an elderly neighbor woman and his defense attorney argued that the teenager was conditioned to kill by watching thousands of television murders. Zamora was convicted after the trial judge limited the defense attorney to showing the specific effect of a particular program on one individual rather than allowing expert testimony on the general effect of television on young viewers. Zamora subsequently filed a $25 million damage suit, later dismissed, against the three major commercial television networks, claiming that violence depicted in television programs showed the youth "how to kill."

Some 27 hours of the murder trial were televised by station WPBT with an average of 100,000 viewers per night in the Miami area. Other stations and national TV networks aired shorter video segments.

In 1979 the Florida Supreme Court decided to allow electronic coverage of all public judicial proceedings on a permanent basis. In reaching that decision, the court unanimously rejected the usual argument against cameras in the courtroom, including those put forth in the *Estes* decision of the U.S. Supreme Court. The court's action would lead to an important decision by the U.S. Supreme Court.

Chandler v. Florida

In 1980 the U.S. Supreme Court agreed to review *Chandler v. Florida.*[62] Two former Miami policemen, convicted of burglarizing a restaurant, had claimed in their appeal that the Florida Supreme Court rules, which permitted electronic coverage of their trial at the judge's discretion even though they objected, deprived them of their right to a fair trial.

A Florida appellate court affirmed their convictions, ruling that no evidence existed to show that they had been harmed by the presence of cameras. The Florida Supreme Court refused to hear the appeal, explaining that it had fully considered the constitutional questions surrounding the issue when it adopted the permanent rules in 1979.

The Supreme Court unanimously (8–0) held that the Constitution does not prohibit a *state* from experimenting with electronic and photographic coverage of the courtroom (federal rules forbid such coverage except for ceremonial purposes).

In his opinion for the Court, Chief Justice Burger made it clear that *Estes* was not being overruled. Instead, he said that "nothing of the 'Roman circus' or 'Yankee Stadium' atmosphere, as in *Estes,* prevailed" in the *Chandler* case. Furthermore, appellants did not attempt to show that the unsequestered jury was exposed to "sensational" coverage, as in *Estes* or in *Sheppard.* Absent a showing of prejudice of constitutional dimensions, said the Chief Justice, "there is no reason for this Court either to endorse or to invalidate Florida's experiment."

Justice Stevens took no part in the decision. Justice Stewart, concurring in the result, and Justice White, concurring in the judgment, believed that the majority, in affirming the convictions, could not do so without overruling *Estes*. As Stewart wrote: "I believe now, as I believed in dissent then, that *Estes* announced a *per se* rule that the Fourteenth Amendment 'prohibits all television cameras from a state courtroom whenever a criminal trial is in progress.' . . . Accordingly, rather than join what seems to me a wholly unsuccessful effort to distinguish that decision, I would now flatly overrule it."

Chief Justice Burger conceded that a reading of Chief Justice Warren's concurring opinion (joined by Justices Douglas and Goldberg) in *Estes* provides some support for the appellants' position that *Estes* is controlling. But Burger made the point that Justice Clark's opinion for the Court was only a plurality opinion (Warren, Douglas, and Goldberg joining in that opinion). Justice Harlan provided the fifth vote necessary to support the judgment, said Burger, but Harlan did not, in Burger's opinion, support a constitutional rule barring photographic, radio, and TV coverage in all cases and under all circumstances.

Among the factors considered by Burger in forming his opinion were:

- Appellants did not attempt to show (and could not show, given the current state of research?) that the mere presence of photographic and recording equipment would so affect the conduct of participants at the trial as to impair fundamental fairness.
- Television technology has changed since 1962 when Estes was tried.
- Safeguards have been built into the experimental programs in various states, and into the Florida program to avoid "some of the most egregious problems envisioned by the six opinions in the *Estes* case."
- States must be free to experiment except when state action infringes on fundamental guarantees.

In one sense, the *Chandler* decision is a narrow one. In this particular case the appellants could not show that their fundamental rights had been harmed, but the door was left open for such attempts in future cases. Clearly, however, the decision gave impetus to the movement toward photographic and electronic coverage of the courtroom. And, significantly, the Court's unwillingness to freeze state experimentation, including Florida's program which does not require the consent of parties at the trial but places discretionary power with the judges, spurred other states to join the movement or modify their guidelines in the direction of Florida's.

Expanded media coverage now is permitted in 45 states either on a permanent basis or experimentally.[63]

States permitting coverage of both trial and appellate courts on a permanent basis, even if the defendant objects, are: Arizona, California, Colorado, Connecticut, Florida, Hawaii, Iowa, Kansas, Kentucky, Massachusetts, Montana,

New Hampshire, New Jersey, New Mexico, Ohio, Tennessee, West Virginia, and Wisconsin.

States allowing coverage of both trial and appellate courts on a permanent basis, but only if the defendant consents, are Alabama (all parties must consent), Alaska (coverage of objecting parties is not allowed), Georgia, Maryland (but only for civil cases), Minnesota, Oklahoma (coverage of objecting defendant is not allowed in civil cases), Rhode Island and Washington (coverage of objecting parties is not allowed).

Experimental trial and appellate court coverage (with any consent requirement shown in parentheses) is taking place in Arkansas (consent of all parties required), Michigan (defendant's consent required), Nevada, North Carolina, and Virginia (defendant's consent required).

Experimental appellate court coverage is allowed by Delaware and Oregon. Permanent appellate court coverage is permitted in Idaho, Illinois, New York, North Dakota, and Vermont.

Louisiana allows permanent appellate court coverage but only with consent of defendants; Maine, experimental EMC in trial courts and the Supreme Court; Nebraska, permanent coverage of its Supreme Court; New York, experimental trial court coverages; North Dakota, experimental trial court coverage; Pennsylvania, experimental coverage of nonjury civil trials with no coverage allowed of objecting parties; Utah, experimental coverage of Supreme Court; Vermont, experimental trial coverage; and Wyoming, permanent coverage of Supreme Court.

Indiana, Mississippi, Missouri, South Carolina, South Dakota, and Texas (audio taping of appellate proceedings permitted) do not allow cameras in the courtroom.

Barriers Still Remain. Despite the *Chandler* decision and the experimentation in photo and electronic coverage of judicial proceedings, some barriers remain. One of them concerns the "reach" of a judge's contempt power. Does it extend to the entire courtroom building and to the sidewalks around the courthouse? To a parking lot next to a courtroom?

In 1973, U.S. District Court Judge Winston E. Arnow at Gainesville, Florida, fined Columbia Broadcasting System, Inc., $500 for criminal contempt when a CBS artist did not, according to the judge, abide by the judge's verbal order banning sketching in or outside the courtroom (the latter from memory) during a trial. The U.S. Fifth Circuit Court of Appeals later voided the ban, but it ordered a different judge to determine if the contempt of court fine should prevail in view of the order being unconstitutional.[64] Thus, the order was illegal but the contempt of court fine could still be upheld.

There are many precedents for a judge controlling the press in the hallway outside the courtroom. For example, the U.S. Fifth Circuit Court of Appeals upheld a fine imposed on a news photographer who violated a standing order of a lower court by taking a picture of a defendant in the hallways.[65] Whether a judge's restrictive order can constitutionally extend to all areas of the courtroom building is arguable. The U.S. Seventh Circuit Court of Appeals upheld a ban on photographers and broadcasters on the floor where the courtroom was located, as well as the first floor entrance to elevators, but it voided that part of the order which attempted to put off-limits the main lobby and an open plaza.[66]

The U.S. Tenth Circuit Court of Appeals was more supportive of restrictions placed on photographers than the Seventh Circuit when it ruled in 1975 that Rule 18 of the U.S. District Court in Leavenworth, Kansas, was not overbroad. That rule not only prohibited the taking of photographs in the courthouse, but in the parking areas and at the entrances and exits of the courthouse.[67] When a photographer persisted in taking photographs of prisoners aboard a bus in the parking lot, despite a warning by marshals, he was arrested and placed in a holding cell where he subsequently relinquished his film to his attorney who surrendered it to marshals. In quoting from *Estes,* the Circuit Court said that Rule 18 is a "reasonable implementation of the due process mandate to preserve . . . an atmosphere essential to 'the most fundamental of all freedoms'—a fair trial."

Compare such an outcome with the 6–1 decision of the Florida Supreme Court in 1976 when it refused to approve a proposed rule of the Criminal Division of the Eleventh Judicial Circuit of Florida which would have banned "broadcasting, televising, recording or taking photographs of any kind . . . on any floor of the Metropolitan Justice Building [Miami] on which proceedings before the Circuit Court . . . are conducted."[68]

SUMMARY

As with previous chapters, this chapter has examined rights in conflict; that is, the right of the public to know what is happening in the nation's courtrooms, the right of the press to gain access to judicial proceedings and records, and the right of an accused person to a fair trial. The tensions between those rights were evident during the Lindbergh kidnap trial of Bruno Richard Hauptmann. One result of that trial was adoption by the ABA of Canon 35, which urged a ban on photographic coverage of trials. The canon later was amended to include radio and television. ABA's opposition to expanded media coverage ended in 1982 after many states had allowed, either on an experimental or a permanent basis, photographic and television coverage of trials.

There are two critical phases in connection with a person's right to a fair trial: the pretrial and the trial stages. An accused person is most vulnerable to prejudicial publicity at the pretrial stage because a jury has not yet been selected and perhaps sequestered. The Katzenbach-Mitchell guidelines, along with the Reardon Committee recommendations which subsequently were adopted by the ABA, are aimed at stemming the flow of prejudicial information at the source. Thus, the Katzenbach-Mitchell guidelines apply to federal law enforcement officers and order them not to release certain kinds of information, such as the existence of a confession, speculation as to the guilt or innocence of the accused, or whether the person in custody refuses to take certain tests. Such guidelines also have been adopted by various states and local police departments.

In 1966 the U.S. Supreme Court in its *Sheppard* decision laid down instructions as to what the judiciary must do to protect the trial process, such as, change the location of trials, insulate witnesses, proscribe extrajudicial statements by anyone connected with the case, sequester juries, and/or limit the number of reporters at the trial. Soon, "gag" orders were being imposed directly on the press, a result neither anticipated nor intended by *Sheppard*. Consequently the U.S. Supreme Court ruled in *Nebraska Press Association v. Stuart* (1976) that such restraints are the least tolerable infringement on First Amendment rights and that the press cannot be barred from reporting what takes place in a courtroom open to the public except in exceedingly rare instances. A court presumably would first have to exhaust all other devices for protecting the fair trial process before resorting to a gag order on the press. One alternative to prior restraint of the press seemed to be Burger's suggestion that where state law permits, pretrial hearings could be closed to press and public alike.

Gannett Company v. DePasquale (1979) not only was directed at the issue of pretrial hearings, but also addressed the question of trial closures as well. The Court held that the public and press do not have a constitutional (Sixth Amendment) right to attend trials, nor do they have a constitutional right to attend pretrial proceedings. But the issue of a First Amendment right to attend *trials* was left unresolved. In his opinion, Justice Stewart had readily agreed that there was a common-law right to attend trials, but such a right had not been incorporated into the Bill of Rights.

Considerable confusion ensued. Trials were closed in various parts of the country. Justices disagreed publicly about the thrust of the *Gannett* decision. The press warned repeatedly about the danger of Star Chamber proceedings.

In 1980—a year after the *Gannett* decision—the Court issued an important decision in *Richmond Newspapers v. Virginia.* Seven members agreed that a First Amendment right exists for the public and press to attend criminal trials. The right is not absolute and it's not entirely clear when the right gives way to the need for closed judicial proceedings (although hearings and fact-finding are prerequisites to a constitutionally valid closure order).

In the view of some observers, this decision will enable journalists to more easily obtain access to government information and meetings that might otherwise be closed.

Flowing out of *Richmond Newspapers* came *Globe Newspapers v. Superior Court* (1982). A majority of the Court agreed that a state cannot, by statute, close all or a portion of a criminal trial; rather, the justification for closure must be done on a case-by-case basis if the qualified First Amendment right of access is to be overcome.

Richmond Newspapers and *Globe Newspapers* did not address questions left by *Gannett Company.* Next the Supreme Court found a qualified First Amendment right to attend *voir dire* proceedings, doing so in *Press-Enterprise Co. v. Superior Court* (1984).

Then, in *Press-Enterprise II* (1986), the Court found a qualified First Amendment right to attend preliminary hearings in criminal cases. But the question of media and public access to civil proceedings remains unaddressed by the Court. Generally, civil cases are tried in open court, but jurisdictions differ over access to various documents and information associated with such cases.

In an effort to reduce tension between First and Sixth Amendment rights, voluntary guidelines have been adopted in 27 states by bench-press-bar groups. The guidelines are unenforceable, although a trial court judge in the state of Washington predicated journalists' access to judicial proceedings on their agreeing in advance to abide by guidelines adopted in that state.

Concerning expanded media coverage of the courtroom, *Estes v. Texas* (1965) resulted in the reversal of a conviction solely because of the presence of cameras at a pretrial hearing and the opening of the trial. But between 1965 and mid-1980, 11 states decided to permit photographic and electronic coverage of the courtroom on a permanent basis with various safeguards for the people involved in the proceedings. A test case, *Chandler v. Florida,* reached the Supreme Court in 1980. Like *Estes* 15 years earlier, *Chandler* involved defendants who did not want cameras present at their trial. But the Florida Supreme Court had adopted rules which allowed such coverage at the discretion of the trial judge.

In *Chandler,* the U.S. Supreme Court unanimously held that the Constitution does not prohibit a state from experimenting with electronic and photographic coverage of trials. In affirming the convictions, the Court chose not to overrule *Estes.* Justices Stewart and White believed this should have been done.

The *Chandler* decision is a narrow one. *Estes* still stands as a warning to judiciary and press alike; no First Amendment right was announced for electronic and photographic coverage of courtroom proceedings and the door was certainly left open for defendants to show that such coverage would harm their Sixth Amendment rights. What the Court did was to allow states, if they wished, to continue or begin expanded media coverage of courtrooms without necessarily jeopardizing convictions obtained in the presence of cameras.

Forty-five states now permit EMC on either a permanent or an experimental basis.

QUESTIONS IN REVIEW

1. What is the Sixth Amendment and why might it "collide" with the First Amendment?
2. One of the chief means of assuring an accused person a fair trial is to grant a change of venue; that is, move a trial beyond the probable influence of prejudicial news reports. Could this have been done in the Lee Harvey Oswald case? What about some other widely publicized criminal cases? Should newspapers report that accused murderers have confessed?
3. The case of *Sheppard v. Maxwell* (1966) is historic for what principal reason?
4. Name at least two specific precautions trial judges are admonished to take to insure a fair trial. Base your answer on *Sheppard v. Maxwell.*
5. What was one of the recommendations of the Warren Commission concerning the news media, bar, and law officers?

6. Name at least two kinds of information that cannot be released by federal officials under the Katzenbach-Mitchell guidelines.
7. *Bridges v. California* and *Times-Mirror Co. v. Superior Court* (1941) established an important precedent, to wit: The only time a judge can deal with out-of-court media interference in the orderly administration of justice (in the absence of legislative direction) is if there is a _____.
8. What is the basic holding of the U.S. Supreme Court in *Nebraska Press Association* in connection with a judge's restrictive order that imposes a prior restraint on the press? Under what conditions might a prior restraint be constitutionally imposed?
9. True or False: The public and press have no constitutional right to attend *pretrial* hearings, according to Justice Stewart's opinion for the Court in *Gannett v. DePasquale* (1979).
10. True or False: Whether or not a First Amendment right existed for the public and press to attend trials was not answered by *Gannett v. DePasquale*.
11. *Richmond Newspapers v. Virginia* (1980) is a landmark case decision because _____.
12. What is the significance of the *Press Enterprise II* decision of the U.S. Supreme Court in 1986?
13. Apart from affirming a lower court's conviction of two defendants, what is the essence of the U.S. Supreme Court's decision in *Chandler v. Florida*?
14. Ordinarily, the Supreme Court's decision in *Press-Enterprise v. Superior Court* (1984) would have been greeted with loud praise from the news media. After all, the Court had found the existence of a qualified First Amendment right of access to *voir dire* proceedings. What question tempers such enthusiasm?

ANSWERS

1. This amendment provides that a person accused of a crime shall have the right to a speedy and public trial by an *impartial* jury. The press, in its enjoyment of First Amendment freedoms (particularly the freedom from prior censorship or restraint), has from time to time published information which endangers a fair trial.
2. The answer in the case of Lee Harvey Oswald is that a change of venue very likely would not have assured him an impartial jury. In your discussion of the issues involved, either with the instructor or with other students, some comment should be directed at the paucity of empirical data concerning the impact of prejudicial news reports on prospective or actual jurors. Also, how practical or feasible is it to "lock up" the jury each night in what may be a three- or four-month-long trial? Do you agree with the press's contention that the reporting of crime news is an important part of the public's right to know; and if you do, how do such reports perform a public service or meet a public need?

   If the advocates of uninhibited crime news reporting use the argument of the public's right to know about the administration of criminal justice, then questions can be generated along these lines:

   ■ Does the public have a right to know everything that government does, even to the detriment of an individual's right?
   ■ Does the public have a right to be contemporaneously informed, or can there be a hiatus between the event and reports of that event?

- Does the public have to be informed about *all* aspects of a criminal case, including information which might be prejudicial?
- What ethical burdens are placed on the press—either by the practitioners themselves or by the public—in the reporting of crime news? Or should there be none in keeping with the notion that the public has a right to know *everything*?

The Code of Ethics adopted in 1975 by the Associated Press Managing Editors Association does not mention any ethical requirements in connection with trial or pretrial coverage. Is such silence deafening?

3. *Sheppard v. Maxwell* is a landmark case because for the first time the U.S. Supreme Court instructed trial judges on what they must do to insure a fair trial.

4. There were six broad instructions: (a) adopt strict rules governing the use of the courtroom by newsmen; (b) limit the number of newsmen in the courtroom if their presence would disrupt the proceedings; (c) insulate prospective witnesses from the media; (d) prohibit prejudicial out-of-court statements by lawyers, witnesses, or court officials; (e) if necessary, continue a case or grant a change of venue, and (f) sequester the jury.

5. Media, bar, and law officials should work together to establish ethical standards to prevent interference with a fair trial.

6. Your answer may have included two of the following: observations about defendant's character; any statements, admissions, or confessions attributable to defendant; references to investigative procedures, such as lie detector or truth serum tests; statements concerning identity, credibility, or testimony of prospective witnesses; and statements concerning evidence or arguments in the case or speculation about the guilt or innocence of the accused.

You might ask yourself this question: When federal law officials refuse to give news reporters information prohibited by the Katzenbach-Mitchell guidelines, aren't they violating the spirit, if not the letter, of the First Amendment which most clearly prohibits the federal government from abridging freedom of press? Isn't the press's freedom being abridged by such a "gag" order? Technically and perhaps constitutionally, the answer is no. The gag order is aimed not at news reporters but at the federal employees. News reporters are free to publish any of the prohibited information, if they can obtain it from other sources.

7. Clear and present danger to the orderly administration of justice.

8. The majority held that except perhaps as a last resort the press constitutionally cannot be prevented from reporting on public record matters or events in the courtroom. Three justices would have gone further and imposed an absolute bar against prior restraint on such reporting no matter what the circumstances, but the majority chose not to take such an absolutist approach. Instead, prior restraint might be tolerable if a judge had tried all other measures available, such as those mentioned in *Sheppard* or by Burger (the possibility of closing pretrial hearings).

9. True.

10. True. Stewart said the press and public did not have a Sixth Amendment right to attend a trial, but the issue of a First Amendment right was specifically reserved for a future case. The Sixth Amendment right is the defendant's, Stewart said.

11. Seven justices (eight if Justice Powell is included—and he should be because of previous opinions) believed that the press and public have a First Amendment right to attend criminal trials and several believed that this right extended to pretrial proceedings. Justice Stevens went farther, saying that the right of access extends to important information.

12. The press and public have a qualified First Amendment right to attend preliminary hearings in criminal cases.
13. States can continue or begin expanded media coverage of judicial proceedings.
14. Is the *voir dire* a part of the trial or is it a pretrial proceeding? If the latter, then the Court recognized a First Amendment right to attend a pretrial proceeding.

ENDNOTES

1. See Chapter 11 for additional information on shield laws.
2. Farr v. Peter J. Pitchess, Sheriff of Los Angeles County, 93 S.Ct. 593. In releasing Farr, Douglas pointed out that he was not judging the merits of the case. Nor, said Douglas, did the fact that the Supreme Court denied certiorari on November 13, 1972 (93 S.Ct. 430) impart any implication or inference concerning the Court's view of the merits of the case.
3. *The QUILL,* February 1974, p. 8.
4. *Editor & Publisher,* April 19, 1975, p. 10.
5. Farr v. Pitchess, 427 U.S. 912, 93 S.Ct. 3000 (1976).
6. In Re: William T. Farr, on Habeas Corpus, No. 49141, decided December 6, 1976; 2 *Med.L.Rptr.* 1392, March 8, 1977.
7. *Editor & Publisher,* December 12, 1981, p. 9.
8. Shepherd v. Florida, 341 U.S. 50, 71 S.Ct. 549, 95 L.Ed. 740 (1951).
9. A reference to the Court's decision in Craig v. Harney, 331 U.S. 367, 67 S.Ct. 1249, 91 L.Ed. 1546 (1946).
10. Irvin v. Dowd, 366 U.S. 717, 81 S.Ct. 1639, 6 L.Ed. 2d 751 (1961).
11. Rideau v. Louisiana, 373 U.S. 723, 83 S.Ct. 1417, 10 L.Ed.2d 663.
12. Estes v. State of Texas, 381 U.S. 532, 85 S.Ct. 1628, 14 L.Ed.2d 543.
13. Rideau v. Louisiana, 373 U.S. at 726, 83 S.Ct. at 1419, 10 L.Ed.2d at 665.
14. Estes v. State of Texas, 381 U.S. at 537, 85 S.Ct. at 1630, 14 L.Ed.2d at 547.
15. Ibid., at 544, 1633, and 551.
16. Sheppard v. Maxwell, 384 U.S. 333, 363, 86 S.Ct. 1507, 1522–23, 16 L.Ed.2d 600, 621 (1966).
17. Order 470–71, *Federal Register,* Vol. 36, No. 212, November 3, 1971, p. 21028.
18. Ibid., pp. 21028–21029.
19. American Bar Association's Legal Advisory Committee on Fair Trial and Free Press, *The Rights of Fair Trial and Free Press,* Chicago, Ill., 1969, Appendix A, pp. 13–14.
20. Ibid., p. 10.
21. *The Rights of Fair Trial and Free Press: The American Bar Association Standards,* Copyright © 1981 by the American Bar Association.
22. Ibid.
23. Ibid.
24. Bridges v. California and Times-Mirror Co. v. Superior Court, 314 U.S. 252, 62 S.Ct. 190, 86 L.Ed. 192 (1941).
25. "News Notes," *Media Law Reporter,* July 3, 1984.
26. Ibid.
27. *Editor & Publisher,* April 13, 1985, p. 22.
28. *Fair Trial/Free Press Voluntary Agreements,* published by the ABA's Legal Advisory Committee on Fair Trial and Free Press (Chicago, 1974), p. 20. © by the American Bar Association.
29. James W. Tankard, Jr., Kent Middleton and Tony Rimmer, "Compliance with American Bar Association Fair Trial-Free Press Guidelines," *Journalism Quarterly,* Autumn 1979, p. 446.
30. Ibid., p. 467.
31. Federated Publications v. Swedberg, 7 *Med.L.Rptr.* 1865, September 29, 1981.
32. "News Notes," *Media Law Reporter,* May 25, 1982.
33. Nebraska Press Association v. Judge Stuart, 427 U.S. 539, 96 S.Ct. 2791, 49 L.E.2d 683, 1 *Med.L.Rptr.* 1064.
34. Ibid., concurring opinion written by Justice Brennan, with Justices Stewart and Marshall joining.

35. Murphy v. Florida, 41 U.S. 794.
36. 45 *U.S. Law Week* 3599, March 8, 1977.
37. 2 *Med.L.Rptr.* 1215, February 1, 1977.
38. Gannett Company v. Judge DePasquale, 443 U.S. 368, 99 S.Ct. 2898, 5 *Med.L.Rptr.* 1337, August 14,1979.
39. Ibid., 5 *Med.L.Rptr.* at 1348.
40. Ibid., at 1369.
41. In re Oliver, 333 U.S. 257, 266, 68 S.Ct. 499, 504.
42. "News Notes," *Media Law Reporter,* December 4, 1979.
43. Commonwealth of Pennsylvania v. Hayes, "News Notes," *Media Law Reporter,* May 13, 1980.
44. *FoI Digest,* May/June 1980, p. 8.
45. *Editor & Publisher,* December 1, 1979, p. 12.
46. Ibid.
47. Richmond Newspapers, Inc. v. Virginia, 448 U.S. 555, 100 S.Ct. 2814 (1980).
48. Kleindienst v. Mandel, 408 U.S. 753, 762 (1972).
49. First National Bank of Boston v. Bellotti, 435 U.S. 765, 783 (1978).
50. Saxbe v. Washington Post Co., 417 U.S. 843.
51. Pell v. Procunier, 417 U.S. 817.
52. Richmond Newspapers v. Virginia, op. cit., note 47.
53. "News Notes," *Media Law Reporter,* July 15, 1980.
54. Globe Newspapers v. Superior Court, 457 U.S. 596, 102 S.Ct. 2613, 73 L.Ed.2d 248, 8 *Med.L.Rptr.* 1689, July 13, 1982.
55. Press-Enterprise Co. v. Superior Court, 104 S.Ct. 819, 10 *Med.L.Rptr.* 1161, February 7, 1984.
56. Waller v. Georgia, 467 U.S. 39, 10 *Med.L.Rptr.* 1714, June 5, 1984.
57. Op. cit., n. 55, at 1164.
58. "News Notes," *Media Law Reporter,* January 22, 1985.
59. Press Enterprise Co. v. Superior Court of Riverside County (Press-Enterprise II), 106 S.Ct. 2735, 10 *Med.L.Rptr.* 1161 (1986).
60. "News Notes," *Media Law Reporter,* October 22, 1985.
61. Publicker Industries v. Cohen, 10 *Med.L.Rptr.* 1777 (3d Circuit, 1984), June 19, 1984.
62. Chandler v. Florida, 449 U.S. 560, 101 S.Ct. 802, 66 L.Ed.2d 740 (1981).
63. *The NEWS Media & The LAW,* Fall 1988, p. 53.
64. U.S. v. Columbia Broadcasting Systems, Inc., 497 F.2d 102 and 497 F.2d 107. Compare action of New Jersey Supreme Court which lifted a ban on sketching in state courtrooms (*The QUILL,* May 1974, p. 10). It did so with the understanding that the new policy would be revoked if the sketching interfered with courtroom decorum. In the CBS case, sketching in the courtroom—but not from memory outside the courtroom—could have been prohibited if, in the trial judge's opinion, such activity would have interfered with the decorum of the courtroom.
65. Seymour v. U.S., 373 F.2d 629 (1967).
66. Dorfman v. Meiszner, 430 F.2d 588 (1970).
67. Mazetti v. U.S. 44 *U.S. Law Week* 2026, July 15, 1975.
68. In re Adoption of Proposed Local Rule 17, 2 *Med.L.Rptr.* 1315, February 22, 1977.

11

Newsgathering Rights

HIGHLIGHTS

■ There arguably is a limited First Amendment right to gather news.

■ This right has not, in cases decided to date, outweighed the Executive branch's determination that travel to certain foreign countries should be prohibited or restricted because of foreign policy or national security considerations.

■ This right is no greater than the general public's when access is sought to prisons or their inmates—*Pell v. Procunier* and *Saxbe v. Washington Post Co.* (1974).

■ The use of subpoenas against journalists and news organizations in the 1960s and early 1970s led to many confrontations between the press and government. The result was a trilogy of cases decided by the U.S. Supreme Court in 1972. In *Branzburg v. Hayes, U.S. v. Caldwell,* and *In re the Matter of Paul Pappas,* an *apparent* majority of the Court said that journalists do not have a First Amendment right against forced disclosure of confidential sources and/or information when summoned before grand juries investigating crimes.

■ Since *Branzburg,* many courts have held that there is a conditional First Amendment privilege for journalists against forced disclosure. The privilege may be less applicable in criminal cases and more applicable in civil cases where journalists are not parties in a lawsuit.

■ Twenty-six states have passed shield laws to protect journalists against forced disclosure of confidential sources.

■ In *Zurcher v. Stanford Daily* (1978), the Supreme Court held that a newspaper office can be searched whenever there is reasonable grounds to believe that criminal evidence is on the premises. The First Amendment does not bar such a search. Various states and Congress subsequently passed legislation to protect newsrooms from unannounced searches except in a few instances.

The two previous chapters examined important issues dealing, in large part, with the right of journalists to have access to important information. The Freedom of Information Act and the federal Sunshine Act, plus the states' open meeting and open record laws, provide the public, and therefore the press, with legal rights of access to government or government-controlled information. Chapter 10 examined the qualified right of public and press to attend criminal trials (*Richmond Newspaper v. Virginia*) and preliminary hearings (*Press-Enterprise II*). Access to the courts for expanded media coverage has taken place in most of the states and there are even a few experiments in such coverage taking place or authorized in the federal courts.

This chapter expands on questions and issues related to access to the news, or newsgathering rights.

Earlier chapters made it clear that the First Amendment provides considerable protection to the news media for making news public *once it has been obtained.* But what role does the First Amendment play in facilitating the acquisition of news or protecting journalists as they seek out the news? The answer, at least until *Richmond Newspapers,* was "very little—if any."

A divided Supreme Court has not been very helpful as some of the issues associated with gathering the news have surfaced. A case in point is the journalists' claim that they have a First Amendment right not to have to reveal confidential sources. Journalists argue that if they can be compelled to reveal confidential sources, these sources will dry up. Consequently, the press and, therefore, the public will be deprived of important information. A Supreme Court decision in a trilogy of cases involving this issue—cases that will be discussed later in this chapter—has done little to clarify the First Amendment claim of journalists. In fact, some uncertainty remains as the legacy of that decision.

In retrospect, it is easy to see the press's use of the First Amendment as a shield to protect its publication rights, but only in the past few years has it begun to voice more shrilly a First Amendment claim related to gathering the news. Thus, when Professor Don Pember of Washington University concluded, after a five-month study of official records pertaining to the nation's formative period, that these records do not suggest that the First Amendment was intended to grant a right to gather news,[1] he was subjected to some editorial "heat" by segments of the press.

About a year after the results of Pember's study were published, along came *Richmond Newspapers* (1980). In its 7–1 decision, the Court held that the public and press have a qualified First Amendment right to attend criminal trials. But recall that Justice Stevens, in a concurring opinion, went far beyond the narrow thrust of the decision, hailing *Richmond Newspapers* as a "watershed case" in terms of *access* to newsworthy information. As he put it:

> Until today the Court has accorded virtually absolute protection to the dissemination of information or ideas, but never before has it squarely held that the acquisition of newsworthy matter is entitled to any constitutional protection whatsoever.[2]

Until *Richmond Newspapers,* the Supreme Court had mixed "emotions" about a First Amendment right of access to news, as *Branzburg v. Hayes* (1972) shows. In that case, and in the two other cases combined with it, Justice White said for an apparent majority (and the reason for the qualifying word—*apparent*—will be explained later) that the "First Amendment does not guarantee the press a constitutional right of special access to information not available to the public generally,"[3] and that "newsmen have no constitutional right of access to the scenes of crime or disaster when the general public is excluded."[4] But the opinion also included the observation that "news gathering is not without its First Amendment protections."[5] White put it this way:

> We do not question the significance of free speech, press, or assembly to the country's welfare. Nor is it suggested that news gathering does not qualify for First Amendment protection; without some protection for seeking out the news, freedom of the press could be eviscerated.[6]

Thus, the Court went on record as believing there is *some* First Amendment protection for news gathering. A host of questions springs from such a statement. What is the extent of the protection? Under what circumstances does the First Amendment right give way? Is the right distinguishable from the public's right of access to information? Unfortunately, there are more questions than answers.

Right to Travel?

One of the first Supreme Court cases dealing with the First Amendment and access to the news involved a reporter for the *Baltimore Afro-American.* William Worthy defied an order in 1956 that prohibited travel to the People's Republic of China. When he returned to the United States, his passport was revoked and the State Department refused to issue him another one. Worthy resorted to legal action, but the U.S. District Court held that the refusal to issue him a passport did not violate his right to travel under the First Amendment. The U.S. Court of Appeals for the District of Columbia Circuit upheld the lower court, saying "freedom of the press bears restrictions. . . . Merely because a newsman has a right to travel does not mean he can go anywhere he wishes."[7] The U.S. Supreme Court denied certiorari.[8]

In another travel-ban case involving a reporter—*Zemel v. Rusk*—the U.S. Supreme Court in 1965 upheld the U.S. State Department's refusal to validate passports for American reporters wishing to visit Cuba, saying that the "right to speak and publish does not carry with it the unrestrained right to gather information."[9] The Court noted that unauthorized entry to such places as the White House can be prohibited. Similarly, the U.S. Court of Appeals in the *Worthy* case had pointed out that freedom of press does not allow journalists to attend conferences of the Supreme Court, sessions of congressional committees, or meetings of the President's cabinet.

A similar case would come to the U.S. Supreme Court in 1981. Former CIA agent Philip Agee, who became a critic of the spy agency after he left it and divulged the names of people he said were U.S. spies (see Chapter 3), had his passport revoked by the State Department — an action upheld by a 7–2 decision of the U.S. Supreme Court in *Haig v. Agee.*[10]

The Court, in an opinion by Chief Justice Burger, held that the department's passport policy, as spelled out in its regulations, is sufficiently "substantial and consistent" to compel the conclusion that Congress has approved it. The regulations authorize revocation of passports for activities abroad that "are causing or are likely to cause serious damage to the national security or foreign policy of the United States." The Court said that Agee's conduct in foreign countries presented a serious danger to American officials abroad and serious danger to the national security.

Using a speech versus action-speech test, the majority said that any restrictions on Agee constitute an inhibition of action, not of speech, because Agee is free to criticize the U.S. government. Justices Brennan and Marshall dissented. According to Floyd Abrams, New York-based attorney, the *Agee* decision is "very dangerous" because it "could significantly interfere with the right of journalists and the public to travel in circumstances where the government opposes such travel."[11]

In 1984, the Court, by a 5–4 vote in *Regan v. Wald,* overturned a unanimous First Circuit U.S. Court of Appeals decision that had struck down a U.S. Treasury Department order forbidding most Americans from spending money on travel to Cuba. The order was part of a general trade embargo on Cuba observed since 1962, with the administration of President Reagan claiming that tourist dollars would aid Cuba in violation of a 1917 Trading with the Enemy Act.[12] The Circuit Court had said that the Treasury Department regulations were illegal and could not be enforced unless a national emergency were declared by Congress.

In his opinion for the Court, Justice Rehnquist said the courts must allow presidents broad powers concerning national security and the conduct of foreign policy. He said there was no difference between the travel restrictions in this instance and the passport restrictions in *Zemel.* The results in both, he said, were justified "by weighty concerns of foreign policy."

Justice Blackmun, joined by Justices Brennan, Marshall, and Powell, dissented on the ground that the majority was ignoring the language and legislative history of congressional action in 1977 that limited to wartime the President's power to impose embargoes. When Congress enacted the International Emergency Economic Powers Act, it "grandfathered" the President's power in effect on July 1, 1977. The First Circuit held that the Treasury Department's regulations were not covered by the grandfather provision, but Rehnquist said that the Court of Appeals had read the provision too narrowly.

In summary, the cases involving travel bans, whether imposed on Americans generally or on journalists specifically, show that the First Amendment has not been persuasive in overcoming those bans. Other considerations, such as foreign policy and national security, outweigh whatever First Amendment rights of access to information may be implicated whenever travel out of the country is involved.

Access to Prisons

In two cases decided in 1974 — *Pell v. Procunier*[13] and *Saxbe v. Washington Post Co.*[14] — the Supreme Court declared that the media have "no constitutional right of access to prisons or their inmates beyond that afforded the general public."[15] On that basis the Court sustained prison regulations that prevented media interviews with inmates other than permitted by regulations.

Then, in 1978, the Court, by a 4–3 vote in *Houchins v. KQED,* reversed the U.S. Court of Appeals' affirmance of a lower court's decision to require a sheriff to give reporters access to jail facilities at reasonable times to interview inmates.[16] However, Justice Stewart, who concurred in the judgment, disassociated himself from the plurality opinion given by Chief Justice Burger. In a separate opinion he argued for a distinction between the access rights of individual members of the public and the broader access needs of reporters so they can more effectively convey information to the general public.[17]

Justice Stevens, joined by Brennan and Powell, dissented. In so doing, he cited the Warren Court decision in *Zemel v. Rusk* in which the Court said: "The right to speak and publish does not carry with it the unrestrained right to gather information."[18] Stevens emphasized the word "unrestrained" — coupled it with the wording in *Branzburg* about there being some First Amendment protection for "seeking out the news" — and concluded that both statements "imply that there is a right to acquire knowledge that derives from protection from the First Amendment."[19] Stevens also interpreted *Pell* to mean that any attempt to *entirely* exclude the public and press from access to information about prison conditions would run afoul of the First Amendment. He, therefore, concluded that "information-gathering is entitled to some measure of constitutional protection."[20] This protection is not for the private benefit of the press, he said, "but to insure that the citizens are fully informed regarding matters of public interest and importance"[21] (the Meiklejohn concept (see Chapter 2) but without Meiklejohn's "absolutism").

Blackmun, who was ill at the time, and Marshall did not participate in the decision, the latter presumably because he once was general counsel for the National Association for the Advancement of Colored People (NAACP), and it was the NAACP which helped KQED bring its action against Sheriff Thomas L. Houchins.

Following the *Houchins* decision, the Supreme Court issued decisions in *Richmond Newspapers* (1980), *Press-Enterprise I,* and *Press-Enterprise II* (discussed in Chapter 10)—each of them expanding on the qualified First Amendment right of the press to attend criminal case proceedings. Apart from a few exceptions, the press's gains in access to courts and court-related information have not expanded to other areas of reporting. This can be seen in the decision of the entire U.S. Court of Appeals for the Third Circuit in the case of *Capital Cities Media v. Chester* (1986).[22] The *en banc* court, with four members dissenting, ruled that the First Amendment does not give the press and public a general right of access to government information. The dissenters disagreed, arguing that *Richmond Newspapers* represented a significant development in the access arena. But the majority said the Supreme Court's decision in *Richmond Newspapers* did not, either expressly or impliedly, overrule *Houchins.* A majority of the Supreme Court members, said the Circuit Court, hold that there is no First Amendment right of press access to government-held information.[23]

In *Capital Cities Media,* a newspaper had sought information from the Pennsylvania Department of Environmental Resources concerning an outbreak of an intestinal illness caused by drinking water. The agency provided some information but refused to supply copies of citizen complaints, attorney-client communications, and memoranda generated by technical personnel. The newspaper then sought to compel disclosure.

The issue was whether the First Amendment requires officials of a state agency either to furnish information relating to an agency investigation to members of the public who request such information or to justify their refusal by demonstrating a compelling state interest which could not be vindicated in a less restrictive manner.

As Judge Walter K. Stapleton put it for the court:

> It is unknown whether the U.S. Supreme Court will apply its analysis of access in the context of judicial proceedings to the context of the executive branch files. Assuming that it is to be so applied, however, under Third Circuit case law and that of the Supreme Court, a party relying on the First Amendment as a source of a right of access to government-held information would normally have to allege and prove that access has traditionally been afforded to the public and that access "plays a significant positive role in the functioning of the particular process in question" (quoting from the Supreme Court's decision in *Press-Enterprise II*).

The access test—access has been traditionally given and plays a significant positive role in the particular process involved in the access issue—was first suggested by Justice Brennan in *Richmond Newspapers.*[24]

But the idea of a press right being grounded in tradition is not new. It suffuses many First Amendment cases. It can be seen in the "common custom and practice" decision of the Florida Supreme Court in *Fletcher v. Florida Publishing Co.* (see Chapter 7)—the custom or practice of news photographers accompanying police or firemen into private dwellings, as when a fire killed a girl. In that case, no one objected to the taking of photographs at the time.

The press is frequently at loggerheads with government officials, public figures, and private figures (as the chapters on privacy showed) concerning access to various places and records. For example, do press representatives have a right to be at the crash sites of airplanes, trains, or cars? What if the crash involves military aircraft? And do they have a *right* of access to a crime scene? Might they not, if granted access, interfere with police investigations? There are repeated confrontations over such instances of access being denied or, in the case of privacy lawsuits, being granted.

Airplane Crash Coverage

Airplane crashes provide examples of the difficulties encountered by the press in trying to gather news or photos.

In California, the Court of Appeal in San Diego ruled that a television cameraman was not falsely imprisoned when he was arrested for refusing to leave the scene of a 1978 air crash that killed 150 people.[25] However, the court limited the circumstances under which disaster coverage may be restricted.

The cameraman, Steve Leiserson of KFMB-TV in San Diego, videotaped at the crash site for 30 minutes before a police sergeant ordered him outside the cordoned area. He moved away, but later returned to the crash site, videotaping the scene again. He was arrested, but released several hours later and the charge subsequently was dismissed. Leiserson sued San Diego and the police sergeant for false imprisonment. At a nonjury trial, a Superior Court judge found that Leiserson had not been falsely imprisoned.

The Court of Appeal opinion interpreted, for the first time, California's statutory right of access for journalists to disaster areas. The law (Penal Code Sec. 409.5) permits police to close disaster areas to unauthorized persons, but states that duly authorized representatives of the news media can enter such areas. However, the trial judge concluded that the police reasonably believed that the crash site might be the scene of a crime. Crime areas, unlike disaster areas, can be closed to public and press alike to allow unhampered investigation for clues and to prevent destruction of evidence.

The Court of Appeal affirmed the lower court's decision, but disagreed that the creation of a separate press area established by police outside the crash area complied with the access statute. "Press representatives must be given unrestricted access to disaster sites unless police . . . reasonably determine that such unrestricted access *will interfere* with emergency operations," said the court.[26] And any such restriction may last only so long as is necessary to prevent actual interference.

Police failed to show either that unrestricted press access would have interfered with the emergency activities, said the court, or that the designated press area was the maximum access possible under the circumstances.

It should be emphasized that not many states provide a statutory right of access to disaster scenes. The question of access is often left to the decision of officials at the scene.

When military planes crash, government regulations presumably are controlling. But the interpretation or application of these regulations often frustrates journalists. For example, police and military officials demanded that photographers and camera crews who had covered three military plane crashes in the fall of 1986 turn over photos and videotapes of the wreckage. In two of the incidents in New York, the photojournalists complied, but those covering a crash in Arizona refused and were detained near the crash scene for two hours.

In the New York case, military public affairs officers and the state police later conceded that they lacked authority under military regulations, or under state or federal law, to make such demands.[27]

The New York State Society of Newspaper Editors protested the film confiscations and the society's president later reported in the society's bulletin on the responses obtained from the Air Force, Army, and state police, stating:

> Military procedures are very specific about what should be done in the wake of a military crash. In cases where classified information could be at risk, military officers must advise members of the press of the fact and warn them that publishing classified information may be a violation of federal law.
>
> But nowhere is anyone authorized to confiscate film or physically bar a member of the press from taking pictures.[28]

In the Arizona incident, an Army public affairs officer was quoted as saying that "at no point in time did I or anyone else from the Army hold or restrain the media, nor did we attempt to confiscate film. I made a request of the media to voluntarily turn over the film."[29]

Police Beat Problems

Police beats offer numerous examples of access problems. Virtually every police department in the United States has rules and regulations governing relationships with the press and press access to crime or accident scenes. But they are far from uniform and even within a department they are not uniformly applied. Personal relationships often play a role in the access equation. Telephone calls from editors to police chiefs (or vice versa) figure prominently in questions of access.

Here are two examples of difficulties encountered by news photographers covering breaking stories:

A *Stuart* (Florida) *News* photographer was acquitted of charges that he resisted a police officer while attempting to take pictures of an automobile accident in which three teenagers were killed.[30] The Martin County judge, Stewart Hershey, granted the motion for acquittal because, he said, the state failed to show that the photographer had interfered with the sheriff's department at the accident scene.

At the time of the arrest, the photographer was attempting to take photographs in a yard near the scene. He initially had been given permission to enter the yard, but the permission later was withdrawn. At that point, said the photographer's attorney, the photographer should have been given the option of moving to a vacant lot where 15 to 20 persons had gathered to watch emergency personnel at work. "Reporters," said the attorney, "have a right to be wherever the pubic has a right to be."[31]

In another incident, photographers at the scene of an arrest inside a convenience store in north Minneapolis were approached by FBI agents who, according to a lawsuit filed by the *Minneapolis Star and Tribune* and WCCO-TV, demanded the cameras of the two photographers, threatening the journalists with arrest if they refused.[32] In the case of the newspaper, the equipment was retrieved only by allowing federal agents to be present at the newspaper when the film was processed. Similarly, a law enforcement officer was present when the unedited videotape was first shown. In both instances, officers feared that undercover agents would be identified.

Exit Polling

This type of polling is done by the news media, especially television, in an effort to determine how voters actually voted. The responses in key precincts then are used to predict the outcome of elections before the polls have closed and the actual vote is known. For various reasons many states have enacted restrictions on such polling, such as limiting how close media pollsters can be to voting areas. In a one-year period beginning in early 1988, such restrictions were overturned by federal courts in Kentucky, Minnesota, and Wyoming, and by other courts in Florida, Georgia, Montana, South Carolina, and Washington.[33] As in Kentucky, judges generally have concluded that excessive restrictions infringe upon the media's right to gather news and violate the First Amendment.

PRIVILEGED STATUS FOR PRESS?

The above situations dramatize the adversarial relationship that frequently exists between the press and government. The press, in effect, becomes the "watchdog" for the people against those in power.

The term *Fourth Estate* signifies virtual branch-of-government status — unofficial to be sure, but indicative of the expectation that the news media will participate in the checks and balances system. To assist the press in carrying out this function, according to some, the First Amendment was adopted with a press clause that specifically protects the press. Justice Stewart has argued, for example, that the Press Clause provides protection for the press as an institution, although Chief Justice Burger disagreed (see Chapter 2). Others contend that the First Amendment gives journalists a privileged status in our society so that they can more effectively fulfill their role. But does this privilege protect the journalist, unlike other citizens, from appearing before grand juries and answering questions relevant to the commission of a crime? Does a privilege exist by which a journalist can protect confidential sources of news? Does the First Amendment shield the news media from newsroom searches in which police seek information or evidence concerning the commission of a crime?

Use of Subpoenas

The adversarial relationship between government and the press occasionally becomes intense, as evidenced by the Democratic party's national convention in Chicago in 1968. While covering the violence associated with that convention, a score of journalists were injured, several seriously, at the hands of Chicago police who seemed to vent on news people either their frustrations in trying to cope with large numbers of anti-Vietnam War demonstrators who frequently goaded police to action, or their dislike of hippie-type dissidents, or both. This was a time when there appeared to be a rising tide of hostility toward the press on the part of public officials and private citizens alike, the hostility demonstrable in several ways.[34] In part, the reaction stemmed from allegations that news reporters had distorted or exaggerated some of the events being reported. Also, some disenchantment probably stemmed from earlier news media coverage of civil rights demonstrations and militant groups, since, like messengers blamed for the bad news they carry, the news media were seen by some as being responsible for, or contributing to, the social malaise being reported.

After the convention, coverage continued of various militant groups, such as the Weathermen faction of Students for a Democratic Society and the Black Panthers. One consequence became manifest when Vice-President Spiro Agnew verbally assaulted the news media in a speech on November 13, 1969. He charged that network TV news often was inaccurate and biased and that the channels of public opinion were being controlled by fewer and fewer people. Another developing theme was that the conservative viewpoint in America was not being adequately presented by the media which allegedly were preoccupied with the shrill voices of dissent.[35]

There was more than just verbal abuse, however. After the Democratic party's convention in 1968, subpoenas were issued in growing numbers as federal attorneys sought to force television network news departments, national news magazines, and some large city newspapers to turn over unused reporters' notes, unused film footage, and file material relating to Weathermen, Black Panthers, and so forth. *Time* magazine was among the first to face legal compulsion pertaining to files about the Weathermen, and its attorneys advised editors to comply. Next came *Newsweek, LIFE,* CBS, and reporters for some large dailies.

Media criticism of the growing use of subpoenas swelled until on February 4, 1970, the Justice Department indicated that henceforth it would temper demands for file material and reporters' notes by entering into negotiations with the affected media; but the media counterattack did not abate. On March 10, NBC President Julian Goodman said:

> Not since 1798 . . . has American journalism been under greater attack. It began with television news. It has moved to newspapers, news magazines and other periodicals. It extends to events the newsman covers, to people he talks to, to confidences he needs, to words he writes and to scenes he photographs. The intent of the attackers doesn't matter, but the effect does. It can limit legitimate news coverage. It can narrow the range of the newsman's sources. It can dry up the flow of information to

the public and reduce the newspaper story or the broadcast report to the level of a handout.[36]

Henceforth, said Goodman, NBC would resist any government actions that "violate the confidence of our sources, that weaken our credibility and that limit our access to information." NBC's policy would be to refuse to turn over any information which had not been broadcast if, by so doing, the network believed its newsgathering operations would be jeopardized.

The controversy continued. On one side it was argued that the administration of justice required the full power to subpoena records and journalists whenever necessary. On the other the press contended that the subpoenas were so broadly worded that they amounted to harassment, intimidation, violation of confidential arrangements between reporters and sources and therefore were in violation of the spirit of the First Amendment.

Attorney General's Guidelines

Against this backdrop, Attorney General John Mitchell laid down five guidelines that he hoped would provide a *modus vivendi* for press and federal attorneys. He did this on August 10, 1970, in a speech to the American Bar Association's House of Delegates. Negotiations with the media were still the rule, but Mitchell said henceforth no Justice Department subpoenas would be issued against the press without his personal approval.

As summarized, the guidelines are:

1. In determining whether to request issuance of a subpoena, the approach must be to weigh any limiting effect on the exercise of First Amendment rights against the public interest to be served by the fair administration of justice.
2. All reasonable attempts should be made to obtain the information from nonpress sources.
3. Negotiations should be attempted in all cases in which a subpoena is contemplated.
4. The attorney general must personally authorize any action leading to a subpoena.
5. In seeking such authorization, the following principles will apply: The information is essential and cannot be obtained elsewhere; subpoenas should be limited to verification of published information under ordinary circumstances; if not, then great caution should be observed when seeking unpublished information or when a claim to confidentiality is made.[37]

Selling of Pentagon Case

This statement by Mitchell helped to calm agitation, at least for a time. But another battle flared after the February 23, 1971, award-winning telecast by CBS of a documentary, *The Selling of the Pentagon,* which dealt with Defense Department expenditures for public relations and propaganda purposes. Vice-President Agnew led a parade of public officials in denouncing the program which he characterized as a "subtle but vicious broadside against the nation's defense establishment." The FCC gave CBS 20 days in which to show how the program met the requirements of the Fairness Doctrine that obligated broadcasters to air different sides of controversial issues.[38] The culmination of the attacks came on April 17 when a House special subcommittee, headed by Congressman Harley Staggers of West Virginia, issued a subpoena ordering the network to deliver to the subcommittee any and all notes, film, sound tape recordings, scripts, names and addresses of all persons appearing in the telecast, and a statement of all disbursements of money made in connection with the program. The sweeping nature of the subpoena was one reason why CBS President Frank Stanton announced that his network would comply only with that portion of the order which demanded film copy and transcript of material actually telecast. Terming the subcommittee's demands unprecedented in the history of the relationship between federal government and press, Stanton declared that no part of the press could constitutionally be required to comply with a subpoena with respect to unpublished material gathered by reporters. Further, argued Stanton, First Amendment protection does not depend upon whether the government believes broadcast journalists are right or wrong in their judgments.

As a showdown loomed in the House, news media spokespersons supported CBS, while ABC and NBC issued statements defending the stand taken by the rival network. The denouement came on July 13, 1971, when, in a rare disavowal of one of its own committees, the House voted 226–181 to return the contempt resolution back to committee, thereby ending further attempts in Congress to punish the network.

After the CBS case, there were many other attempts to use subpoenas against the press. For example, CBS and NBC were served with 121 subpoenas in a 30-month period demanding that they produce various kinds of news material. The editor of the *Los Angeles Times* told a subcommittee of the U.S. Senate's Judiciary Committee that his newspaper had been served with more than 30 subpoenas during a period of several years, threatened with more than 50 others, and that the paper had spent more than $200,000 to defend itself against these subpoenas. A review of the situation led to the issuance of a 193-page report on May 29, 1972, by an 11-member independent task force sponsored by the Twentieth Century Fund. The committee, chaired by Robert Williamson, former chief justice of the Maine Supreme Judicial Court, said: "These subpoenas have raised in the clearest form the central issue: that the government's law enforcement efforts—particularly those directed at political radicals—are taking forms that pose a serious threat to the confidence between journalists and their sources, thus reducing the free flow of information to the public.[39]

Perhaps Justice Douglas capsulized the danger best when, in dissenting to a 5–4 decision that held that reporters cannot refuse to identify confidential sources of information in the absence of protective, or "shield," legislation, he wrote:

> Today's decision is more than a clog upon news gathering. It is a signal to publishers and editors that they exercise caution in how they use whatever information they can

obtain. Without immunity they may be summoned to account for their criticism. Entrenched officers have been quick to crash their powers down upon unfriendly commentators. . . .

The intrusion of government into this domain is symptomatic of the disease of this society. As the years pass the power of government becomes more and more pervasive. It is a power to suffocate both people and causes. Those in power, whatever their politics, want only to perpetuate it. Now that the fences of the law and the tradition that has protected the press are broken down, the people are the victims. The First Amendment, as I read it, was designed precisely to prevent that tragedy.[40]

The pressure continued into 1974 when the president of the American Society of Newspaper Editors, Arthur C. Deck, said that never before had the press lived through such concentrated efforts to restrain it as in the past few years and that "the harassment continues."[41] But with the resignation of Nixon as President in that year, Gerald Ford's move into the White House, and the end of the Vietnam War which removed one of the major causes for dissident movements in the country, relative tranquility returned. This does not mean that the Justice Department ceased issuance of subpoenas. On the contrary, of 53 requests by federal prosecutors for the issuance of subpoenas from May 1975 to November 1976, 42 were approved by the U.S. attorney general.[42] More recently, the Reporters Committee for Freedom of the Press estimated that the use of subpoenas against the news media reached the rate in the early 1980s of about 125 per year.

Justice Department Amends Subpoena Guidelines. In 1980, the Justice Department amended its guidelines on issuance of news media subpoenas. The guidelines were extended specifically to civil proceedings and to subpoenas seeking a journalist's telephone toll call records. The express authorization of the attorney general is required for issuance of a subpoena to a journalist or for seeking telephone records. The original guidelines did not distinguish between civil and criminal litigation. The amended guidelines state that before the attorney general's authorization is sought for issuance of a subpoena in a criminal litigation, the crime must have occurred and the information sought is essential to a successful investigation. In civil cases, the guidelines require that there must exist reasonable grounds, based on nonmedia sources, to believe that the information sought is essential to successful completion of the litigation in a case of substantial importance.

As for telephone records, there must be reasonable grounds to believe that a crime has been committed before the subpoena can be sought. The department also requires negotiations with reporters when such records are sought. An exception is allowed where negotiations "pose a substantial threat to the investigation."[43]

The policy change concerning subpoena guidelines for telephone records resulted in part from the revelation that long-distance telephone calls of three *Philadelphia Bulletin* reporters had been under surveillance for more than a year in connection with an organized crime investigation.[44] Further, the telephone records of the *New York Times'* Atlanta bureau and its bureau chief had been disclosed to authorities under subpoena. The *Times* did not learn of the release of these records until three months after the records were in the hands of authorities.

PRIVILEGE CLAIM OF JOURNALISTS

There are some traditional relationships in society which are legally recognized as privileged, such as conversations between lawyer-client, doctor-patient, priest-confessant, and husband-wife; but the trend is away from such privileged communication situations. Also, journalists have put forth a privilege claim that is unique. They want to shield the source of information. In the other confidential relationships, the parties to the communication are known; only the confidentiality of the information is at stake.

Many lawyers and judges oppose shield legislation for journalists, arguing that due process of law and orderly administration of justice require virtually all citizens to come forth with information when subpoenaed to do so. Failure to do so, they contend, should be punished by fines and/or imprisonment.[45]

Until recently, such punishment has rarely been invoked against the press, perhaps because of the tradition observed by most journalists of refusing to divulge confidential sources of information or the information itself even if such refusal means going to jail. In only four of some 80 cases reported in a 1971 article, did newspersons eventually reveal the identity of confidential sources. The article summarized the history of this tradition in this way:

> The first major American confrontation on the issue of confidential sources, in 1848, sent a Washington correspondent to jail for refusing to tell the Senate his source for publication of a proposed treaty between the United States and Mexico. The court in that case dealt mainly with the right of the Senate to punish contempts of its authority, rather than protection of confidential sources. Additional reported cases in 1874 and 1887 dealt more with questions of anonymous publication than with confidentiality of sources. But these helped to establish the precedent that there is no right under the common law for a reporter to refuse to identify his confidential sources.
>
> In two instances, in 1935 and 1948, judges allowed newsmen to protect their sources on unspecified grounds, without deciding the privilege claim. In several other cases, demands for identification of the sources were dropped on legal grounds which avoided the privilege claims. The only four instances in legal annals in which newsmen did yield to judicial pressure and reveal their sources came in the investigation of a grand jury leak in Hawaii in 1914; during a murder trial in Pennsylvania in 1930; during a 1931 Texas investigation of the alleged beating and kidnapping of two Communist organizers; and during a Minnesota labor dispute in 1961. In all four cases the newsmen were threatened with jail for remaining silent, and in the Pennsylvania and Texas cases, . . . [two journalists] were imprisoned briefly before agreeing to reveal their sources.[46]

The claim of journalists to First Amendment protection to shield confidential sources initially produced results in the courts that were not favorable to journalists. But recent developments offer hope that there is protection under certain conditions. Some of the more notable cases follow.

Garland v. Torre

Actress-singer Judy Garland brought a libel action against CBS in the mid-1950s based on comments reported in Marie Torre's column, "TV-Radio Today," published in the *New York Herald Tribune*.[47] In the column, Miss Torre had attributed certain statements to an unnamed CBS executive. When counsel for Miss Garland took a deposition from Miss Torre, the columnist refused to identify the CBS executive, claiming that to do so would violate a confidence. She still refused to identify the source at a U.S. District Court hearing and was held in criminal contempt and sentenced to 10 days in jail, but she was released on her own recognizance pending appeal.

Until this case, journalists' claim to privilege had been based on the common law, but Miss Torre refused to identify her source of information on First Amendment grounds.

Justice Stewart, then of the Second Circuit Court of Appeals, heard the case in 1958 and agreed with Miss Torre's attorney that compulsory disclosure might abridge press freedom by imposing some limitation upon availability of news. But such freedom, he said, is not absolute. A determination of when curtailment is justified often presents a "delicate and difficult" task which requires a balancing of rights. Concerning the conflicting rights, he agreed that freedom of the press is basic to a free society, but so too are courts armed with the power to discover truth. Further, the concept that it is the duty of a witness to testify has roots as deep in history as the guarantee of a free press. The obligation of a witness to testify and the correlative right of a litigant to obtain judicial compulsion of testimony without question could impinge upon First Amendment freedoms. If so, Stewart added, the court would not hesitate to conclude that freedom of press "must give place under the Constitution to a paramount public interest in the fair administration of justice."[48]

Since the questions asked of Miss Torre went to the heart of Miss Garland's suit, the judge held that the Constitution did not sanction a refusal to answer. If the news source was of doubtful relevancy to the case, or if an attempt was being made to require many disclosures of a newspaper's confidential sources, the judge indicated he would have considered an alternative ruling.

The U.S. Supreme Court declined to review the decision and so, accompanied by considerably publicity, Miss Torre went to jail for 10 days.

Murphy v. Colorado

Another case, marked by the severity of the jail term, involved a reporter for the Colorado Springs *Gazette-Telegraph,* Vi Murphy, who was held in criminal contempt of the state supreme court for refusing to disclose a confidential news source.[49] She was jailed for 30 days after the U.S. Supreme Court decided not to review the case.

State of Oregon v. Buchanan

Annette Buchanan was on the editorial staff of the University of Oregon student newspaper, the *Daily Emerald,* when she wrote a story in 1966 about the use of marijuana.[50] She had interviewed seven students after promising not to reveal their identities. When summoned before a county grand jury, she refused to disclose the names of her informants, was held in contempt of court, and fined $300. The state supreme court upheld the fine although expressing some sympathy for Miss Buchanan's plight. Aided by several journalism groups, Miss Buchanan appealed, but the U.S. Supreme Court refused to review the case.

BRANZBURG TRILOGY OF CASES

In the three previous cases, the newswomen based their refusals to identify sources on the First Amendment. Their attempts failed. Then suddenly, for a few brief months, it seemed that the First Amendment argument might succeed.

Caldwell v. U.S.

Earl Caldwell, a black reporter stationed in San Francisco for *The New York Times,* was subpoenaed in 1970 to appear before a federal grand jury investigating Black Panther activity. He was ordered to bring tape recordings and notes pertaining to interviews with Black Panthers. Not only did he decide not to do so, but he refused to go before the jury. He and the *Times* moved to quash the subpoena which subsequently was modified to omit any mention of documents that Caldwell might have in his possession pertaining to the Panthers. The motion was based principally on the contention that any appearance at a secret grand jury session would destroy Caldwell's relationship with the Panthers and suppress vital First Amendment freedoms by driving a wedge of distrust between him and them. In pressing for qualified, not absolute, privilege, Caldwell and his newspaper argued that only if there were a compelling government interest in the reporter's testimony, which they claimed had not been shown, should he be forced to appear before the jury.

Judge Alfonso J. Zirpoli of the Northern District Court of California ruled that Caldwell had to appear before the grand jury because "it has long been settled 'that the giving of testimony and the attendance upon court or grand jury . . . are public duties which *every person* within the jurisdiction of the government is bound to perform upon being properly summoned.'"[51] But the judge issued a protective order which would have drastically limited the scope of the investigation by (1) not requiring Caldwell to reveal confidential associations, sources or information received, developed, or maintained by him, and (2) not requiring him "to answer questions concerning statements made to him or information given to him by members of the Black Panthers unless such statements or information were given to him for publication or public disclosure. . . ."

Caldwell also would have been permitted to consult with counsel during his appearance before the grand jury to ensure that the court's order was being carried out. Because of this "shield" for the reporter, Zirpoli dismissed the motion to quash. Caldwell still refused to go before the jury, was cited for contempt, and appealed. The *Times,* however, did not join in the appeal although it continued to pay Caldwell's legal expenses because, as managing editor A.M. Rosenthal wrote in a memo to the staff, it believed that when a reporter refuses to authenticate his story, the newspaper must step aside; "otherwise some doubt may be cast upon the integrity of *Times'* news stories."[52]

A month later the newspaper submitted an *amicus curiae* brief considered more conservative than others already on file. *The New York Times'* chief counsel, James Goodale, explained that the newspaper did not want to risk throwing away the entire Zirpoli opinion since it carried the privilege for journalists much further than had any previous court decision. Rather than push for an absolute privilege, the *Times* took the narrower position that a reporter has a conditional privilege which is to be balanced by the government's right to be informed against the reporter's right to gather news.[53]

In the short run, Caldwell seemed to be on the winning track because the Ninth Circuit U.S. Court of Appeals reversed the lower court in a decision which expanded the journalists' privilege and which brought elation to the ranks of the Fourth Estate. Judge Charles Merrill wrote the opinion and stated, in part:

> The case is one of first impression and one in which the news media have shown great interest and have accordingly favored us with briefs as *amici curiae.* As is true with many problems recently confronted by the courts, the case presents vital questions of public policy: questions as to how competing public interests shall be balanced. The issues require us to turn our attention to the underlying conflict between public interests and the nature of such competing interests."[54]

After considering arguments put forth by Caldwell and the government, the judge continued:

> The premise underlying the Government's statement is that First Amendment interests in this area are adequately safeguarded as long as potential news makers do not cease using the media as vehicles for their communication with the public. But the First Amendment means more than that. It exists to preserve an "untrammeled press as a vital source of public information," *Grosjean v. American Press Co.* . . . Its objective is the maximization of the "spectrum of available knowledge," *Griswold v. Connecticut.*
> . . . The need for an untrammeled press takes on special urgency in times of widespread protest and dissent. In such times the First Amendment protections exist to maintain communication with dissenting groups and to provide the public with a wide range of information about the nature of protest and heterodoxy. [See, e.g., *Associated Press v. U.S.* . . . (1945); *Thornhill v. Alabama,* 310 U.S. 88, 102, 60 S.Ct. 736, 84 L. Ed. 1093 (1940).]

Next, the powers of grand juries were reviewed, and the judge said:

> . . . [W]here it has been shown that the public's First Amendment right to be informed would be jeopardized by requiring a journalist to submit to secret grand

jury interrogation, the Government must respond by demonstrating a compelling need for the witness's presence before judicial process properly can issue to require attendance.

We go no further than to announce this general rule. As we noted at the outset, this is a case of first impression. The courts can learn much about the problems in this area as they gain more experience in dealing with them. For the present we lack the omniscience to spell out the details of the Government's burden or the type of proceeding that would accommodate efforts to meet that burden. The fashioning of specific rules and procedures can better be left to the District Court under its retained jurisdiction. . . .

Finally we wish to emphasize what must already be clear: the rule of this case is a narrow one. It is not every news source that is as sensitive as the Black Panther Party has been shown to be respecting the performance of the "establishment" press or the extent to which that performance is open to view. It is not every reporter who so uniquely enjoys the trust and confidence of his sensitive news sources.

In summary, the Circuit Court said this was a case of first impression; the ruling applied only to cases of the Caldwell type, and therefore it was narrowly drawn; and no attempt was being made by the court to detail how the government must meet its burden of showing compelling need for the information possessed by Caldwell.

At this point the government appealed.

Branzburg v. Judge Hayes

Also destined for review by the U.S. Supreme Court were two cases involving the same reporter. The first, *Branzburg v. Judge Hayes,* began with reporter Paul Branzburg of the *Louisville Courier-Journal* writing a story published November 15, 1969, about two unidentified persons in Jefferson County, Kentucky, synthesizing hashish from marijuana. When called before the county grand jury and asked to identify the pair, Branzburg refused on grounds that the Kentucky shield law (shield laws are explained later in this chapter) and the state and U.S. Constitutions justified such refusal. Prior to this case it was generally believed that the Kentucky law granted an absolute privilege to reporters. However the state court of appeals held that the statute did not permit a reporter to refuse to testify about events he personally had observed, including the identity of persons seen by him, although the court conceded that the law did shield the newsman from having to disclose the identity of persons who supplied information.[55] This distinction indicates that reporters in Kentucky should not only observe, but also obtain information from, those at the scene of a story whenever a pledge of confidentiality is given.

The second *Branzburg* case followed publication of a story on January 10, 1971, which described the use of illegal drugs in Frankfort, Kentucky. The newsman reported that he had spent two weeks interviewing several dozen drug users. The Franklin County grand jury ordered the reporter to identify the lawbreakers, but Branzburg moved to have the subpoena quashed because it would entail a drastic "incursion upon First Amendment freedoms in the absence of compelling

Commonwealth interest in requiring . . . [Branzburg's] appearance before the grand jury." Branzburg also argued that he should be excused from any appearance before the jury since once he "is required to go behind the closed doors of the grand jury room, his effectiveness as a reporter in these areas [illegal drugs] is totally destroyed."

As in the *Caldwell* case, a protective order was issued so Branzburg would not have to disclose confidential sources of information, but the order required him to "answer any questions which concern or pertain to any criminal act" actually observed by him. Again, the Kentucky Court of Appeals reaffirmed its earlier interpretation of the state shield law and rejected the reporter's claim to First Amendment privilege. Concerning the U.S. Circuit Court's ruling in the *Caldwell* case, the Kentucky appellate court announced some "misgivings" about that decision because it drastically departed "from the generally recognized rule that the sources of information of a newspaper reporter are not privileged under the First Amendment."

Pappas Case

Another case, which ultimately would be merged with the *Caldwell* and *Branzburg* cases for review by the nation's highest court, involved Paul Pappas, a WTEV television newsman working out of the Providence, Rhode Island, office of a New Bedford, Massachusetts, station. He was called to New Bedford on July 30, 1970, to report on civil disorders taking place there. He went to a Black Panthers' headquarters and was allowed inside on the condition that he not disclose anything except an anticipated police raid which did not materialize. Pappas later was called to testify before the Bristol County grand jury. Claiming a First Amendment privilege, he refused to divulge anything he had witnessed inside the headquarters, but a lower court judge ruled that in the absence of a state shield law the reporter must answer or face contempt charges. Pappas took the case to the state supreme judicial court which affirmed the lower court by stating that the public "has a right to every man's evidence except in exceptional circumstances.[56] This court flatly rejected the U.S. Circuit Court's opinion in *Caldwell v. U.S.,* concluding instead that the obligation of every news reporter, like that of every citizen, is to appear when summoned and to answer relevant and reasonable inquiries.

U.S. Supreme Court Acts

In 1972 the U.S. Supreme Court issued its long-awaited first decision on the claim of journalists to a constitutional privilege against disclosing confidential sources of information or the information itself. By a 5–4 vote, the Court held in the trilogy of cases—*Branzburg v. Hayes, In the Matter of Paul Pappas,* and in *U.S. v. Caldwell*—that freedom of the press is not abridged when journalists are required to appear and to testify before state and federal grand juries.[57]

The Nixon appointees—Chief Justice Burger and Justices Blackmun, Powell and Rehnquist—concurred in the opinion written by Justice White. Justices Douglas, Stewart, Brennan and Marshall dissented. As in the Pentagon Papers case, this decision tended to show the philosophical lineup of the Court, particularly in matters of the so-called law-enforcement type, a classification which includes the *Branzburg* trilogy of cases.

In the decision for the Court, Justice White made the following statements:

1. The sole issue before the Court is the obligation of reporters to respond to subpoenas as other citizens are required to do and to answer questions relevant to an investigation into the commission of a crime.[58]
2. The great weight of authority is that newsmen are not exempt from the normal duty of all citizens. Neither the common law nor constitutional law exempt newsmen from such duty.
3. There is no federal shield law and up to this time the only testimonial privilege has been rooted in the Fifth Amendment. "We are asked to create another by interpreting the First Amendment to grant newsmen a testimonial privilege that other citizens do not enjoy," said Justice White. "This we decline to do."
4. Only when news sources are implicated in crime or possess information relevant to the grand jury's task need they or reporters be concerned about the grand jury's subpoenas. As Justice White observed, "Nothing before us indicates that a large number . . . of *all* confidential news sources fall into either category and would in any way be deterred by our holding that the Constitution does not" exempt newsmen from appearing and furnishing information relevant to the grand jury's task. This is White's answer to the contention that without a testimonial privilege, confidential news sources will dry up with consequent impairment of the public's right to know. As White said, the evidence presented to the Court failed to demonstrate that there would be significant constriction of the flow of news if existing rules were reaffirmed, since these rules had not seriously impeded the development or retention of confidential news sources.
5. There was no evidence in these cases to show that the grand juries were on "fishing" expeditions. If such were the case, White said, a different outcome could be expected. Similarly, harassment of the press by grand juries would not be countenanced by the courts. Such juries are subject to judicial control just as subpoenas, when too broadly drawn, are vulnerable to motions to quash. Grand juries, said White, must operate within the limits of the First and Fifth Amendments.

    In his dissenting opinion, Justice Stewart noted that the judiciary traditionally has imposed virtually no limitations on the grand jury's broad powers to investigate.
6. White raised the question of who would qualify for such a privilege. Pamphleteers? Any one who writes or broadcasts for the public? If so, then the courts would have to determine if the information could be obtained elsewhere and if there were a "compelling need" for such information or testimony. Such difficulties, argued White, would embark the

judiciary on a long journey toward an uncertain destination.

But Stewart retorted, "Better such judgments, however difficult, then the simplistic and stultifying absolutism adopted by the Court in denying any force to the First Amendment in these cases." But Stewart made it clear that he did not favor an absolute privilege for journalists.

7. Congress has the freedom to determine whether a statutory newsman's privilege is necessary, said White, and to fashion one as narrow or as broad as legislators deem necessary. Here, then, was an invitation to lawmakers to resolve the issue by statute, if they wished.

Although bills have been introduced at virtually every congressional session since the *Branzburg* decision, Congress has not chosen to enact statutory protection for journalists against forced disclosure of confidential sources, but 26 states have enacted legislation that either absolutely or qualifiedly shields journalists against forced disclosure.

Justice Stewart, in his dissenting opinion that drew concurrence from Justices Brennan and Marshall, put forth the logic frequently used by the Fourth Estate in pressing a claim to a First Amendment privilege. Stewart wrote:

A corollary of the right to publish must be the right to gather news. . . .

News must not be unnecessarily cut off at its source, for without freedom to acquire information the right to publish would be impermissibly compromised. Accordingly, a right to gather news, of some dimension, must exist. . . .

The right to gather news implies, in turn, a right to a confidential relationship between a reporter and his source. This proposition follows as a matter of simple logic once three factual predicates are recognized: (1) newsmen require informants to gather news; (2) confidentiality . . . is essential to the creation and maintenance of a news-gathering relationship with informants; and (3) the existence of an unbridled subpoena power—the absence of a constitutional right protecting, in any way, a confidential relationship from compulsory process—will either deter sources from divulging information or deter reporters from gathering and publishing information.[59]

Justice Stewart began his dissent with a reference to Justice Powell's concurring opinion. And it is Powell's opinion, coupled to the four dissenting votes (including one by Justice Douglas), that raises the question whether the *Branzburg* trilogy of cases produced majority support for White's opinion, or whether White's opinion mustered only plurality support.

Justice Stewart began his opinion with these words:

The Court's crabbed view of the First Amendment reflects a disturbing insensitivity to the critical role of an independent press in our society. The question whether a reporter has a constitutional right to a confidential relationship with his source is of first impression here, but the principles that should guide our decision are as basic as any to be found in the Constitution. While Mr. Justice Powell's enigmatic concurring opinion gives hope of a more flexible view in the future, the Court in these cases holds that a newsman has no First Amendment right to protect his sources when called before a grand jury. The Court thus invites state and federal authorities to undermine the historic independence of the press by attempting to annex the journalistic profession as an investigative arm of government.[60]

Since Justice Powell's vote proved decisive, here is his brief, "enigmatic" concurring opinion:

I add this brief statement to emphasize what seems to me to be the limited nature of the Court's holding. The Court does not hold that newsmen, subpoenaed to testify before a grand jury, are without constitutional rights with respect to the gathering of news or in safeguarding their sources. Certainly, we do not hold, as suggested in Mr. Justice Stewart's dissenting opinion, that state and federal authorities are free to "annex" the news media as "an investigative arm of government." The solicitude repeatedly shown by this Court for First Amendment freedoms should be sufficient assurance against any such effort. . . .

As indicated in the concluding portion of the opinion, the Court states that no harassment of newsmen will be tolerated. If a newsman believes that the grand jury investigation is not being conducted in good faith he is not without remedy. Indeed, if the newsman is called upon to give information bearing only a remote and tenuous relationship to the subject of the investigation, or if he has some other reason to believe that his testimony implicates confidential source relationships without a legitimate need of law enforcement, he will have access to the court on a motion to quash and an appropriate protective order may be entered. The asserted claim to privilege should be judged on its facts by the striking of a proper balance between freedom of the press and the obligation of all citizens to give relevant testimony with respect to criminal conduct. The balance of these vital constitutional and societal interests on a case-by-case basis accords with the tried and traditional way of adjudicating such questions.

In short, the courts will be available to newsmen under circumstances where legitimate First Amendment interests require protection.[61]

Powell's opinion sparked an ongoing debate. Is there a First Amendment privilege—even a conditional one—by which journalists can shield confidential sources?

At the annual meeting of the American Bar Association's Criminal Justice Section and Young Lawyers Section in 1974, Attorney Curtis E. von Kann, chairman of the Young Lawyers Section's Committee on News Media and the Courts, presided at the session on newsmen's privilege and said of Powell's opinion:

There is then a very brief concurring opinion by Justice Powell . . . in which Justice Powell suggested that a newsman can of course move to quash a subpoena if divulging the confidential source is not outweighed by "a legitimate need of law enforcement." That, of course, is exactly what the newsmen were arguing in this case, and why Justice Powell is on the affirmative side instead of the reversal side is extremely unclear to me and to a number of other people.[62]

Floyd Abrams, an attorney who has represented journalists in subpoena cases, said:

As a result of two years of case law after *Branzburg,* we now have what I consider a qualified First Amendment privilege established in the courts. It is not absolute and it is not absolutely sure that all the courts understand this is the law, but there have been a number of decisions since *Branzburg,* including Court of Appeals decisions in the Second Circuit and in the D.C. Circuit and Supreme Court opinions in Vermont and Virginia. These decisions seem to me likely to continue to issue and to hold that certainly in a rather wide variety of situations newsmen will not be required to disclose confidential sources on the basis of a First Amendment claim of the newsmen that they should not be required to do so.[63]

Abrams cautioned, however, that the Supreme Court's unanimous decision that required President Nixon, under subpoena, to turn over Watergate-related tape recordings (see Chapter 9) might ultimately have an impact on journalists who seek to avoid compliance with subpoenas. "It would be an ultimate and truly supreme irony," said Abrams, "if the final gift of the Nixon administration to the press were a decision which, while striking a dagger into the heart of the President, struck though the President and reached the press as well."

William A. Rusher, publisher of the *National Review,* gave this view of *Branzburg:*

> . . . [T]he Supreme Court held that the First Amendment, in guaranteeing freedom of speech, does not thereby implicitly confer upon a newsman the right to conceal his sources from a state or federal grand jury, if their identity is relevant to an investigation into the commission of a crime. In so holding, the Court rejected the argument that such a newsman's privilege was necessary in order to prevent the threatened exposure of those sources from having a chilling effect on communications to newsmen by persons who desire to remain anonymous.
>
> In *Branzburg,* however, the Court also stressed that the First Amendment required courts, so far as possible, to protect newsmen from harassment — meaning in this case, from unnecessary demands for the exposure of their sources. The majority in *Branzburg* felt, however (and I think this was Justice Powell's point in his enigmatic concurring opinion) that the burden of proof should be on the newsman to show the harassment rather than on the party seeking disclosure. . . .
>
> So as matters now stand, it is up to the newsman, if the identity of his source is otherwise relevant and material, to demonstrate that compulsory disclosure of the source would be an intolerable or at least an unnecessary harassment from which the court should protect him.
>
> Certainly, *Branzburg* was in accordance with the settled tradition of American law. The First Congress, which passed the First Amendment . . ., also made it a crime to commit misprison of felony, which is to say, for a party not involved in a crime to fail to reveal evidence of the commission of that crime. So the First Congress can hardly have thought that the First Amendment implicitly permitted any such withholding, even to newsmen. As a matter of fact, it was not until 1957 [*Garland v. Torre*] that it occurred to any newsman to plead the First Amendment as a ground for not revealing a source.[64]

Rusher was not hostile to the idea of a qualified First Amendment privilege for reporters — qualified in the sense that the reporter's right to be free from forced disclosure would have to be balanced against other rights, such as the

Sixth Amendment rights of an accused person to confront witnesses against him or to subpoena witnesses in his favor. He was, however, opposed to a federal shield law, principally because of the fear that what Congress can give it can also take away. That would be a "dangerous precedent" in relation to press freedom, Rusher said, adding, "I respectfully suggest that we stick by the First Amendment, as presently being interpreted by the courts. It has, for two centuries, provided this country with one of the freest presses in the world. It can do so for another two centuries without the help of Congress."

Decision's Impact on Branzburg, Caldwell, Pappas. Before examining case law developments since the *Branzburg* decision, the ultimate fate of reporters Branzburg, Caldwell, and Pappas should be recounted.

Branzburg took a reporter's job in Michigan prior to the Supreme Court's decision and presumably could be arrested for contempt of court if he returned to Kentucky.

Caldwell refused to go before a specific grand jury and was held in contempt of court. After the Supreme Court's decision, that particular jury no longer existed so he could not go before it and purge himself of contempt. The U.S. district attorney in San Francisco could have subpoenaed Caldwell to appear before another grand jury and the entire process that led to the first contempt citation could have been repeated. The government chose not to do this.

Pappas faced the same situation as Caldwell and the government chose not to call Pappas back before a new grand jury.

CASE LAW SINCE BRANZBURG

A number of cases were affected by the *Branzburg* decision, and there have been a considerable number of decisions by federal and state courts since *Branzburg* concerning a First Amendment privilege for journalists.

One case, *Knops v. Wisconsin,* was being appealed to the Supreme Court at the time the Court was reviewing *Branzburg.* It involved the editor of an "underground" newspaper, Mark Knops.

On August 25, 1970, an explosion ripped through Sterling Hall on the University of Wisconsin campus in Madison, resulting in death to one person and injury to several others. Two days later, the underground newspaper, *Kaleidoscope,* printed a story entitled "The Bombers Tell Who and What Next — Exclusive to the Kaleidoscope." Knops was subpoenaed to appear before a county grand jury. He refused to answers questions about the bombing and an arson at Wisconsin State University in Whitewater by invoking the Fifth Amendment. Immunity from prosecution was promised, but he still refused to answer, basing such refusal on a First Amendment privilege. He was held in contempt and sentenced to five months in jail or until he purged himself of contempt by answering the questions. In 1971, the state supreme court upheld the sentence in a decision that read, in part:

Appellant here does not ask, as did *Caldwell,* that he be allowed to ignore the subpoena entirely. He asks that he be afforded the same prerequisite as the District Court [Zirpoli] afforded to Caldwell before disclosure could be compelled.

Appellant's entire argument rides on the validity of his contention that disclosure will actually result in a diminution of the free flow of news that the public is entitled to read. . . .

In weighing the value which the public derives from receiving this information appellant cites *Bridges v. California* (1941) . . . for the proposition that the framers of the Constitution "intended to give to liberty of the press, as to other liberties, the broadest scope that could be countenanced *in an orderly society."* (Emphasis added.) That may very well have been the intention of the framers. However, in a disorderly society such as we are currently experiencing it may well be appropriate to curtail in a very minor way the free flow of information, if such curtailment will serve the purpose of restoring an atmosphere in which all of our fundamental freedoms can flourish. One exceedingly fundamental freedom which the public is currently doing without is the freedom to walk into public buildings without having to fear for one's life. . . .

The fact situation here is so remote from that in *Caldwell* that even if this court were to accept the premises of the . . . [U.S. Circuit Court's] decision, it would still be inapplicable to this case. Unlike *Caldwell,* the appellant here does not face an unstructured fishing expedition compounded of questions which will meander in and out of his private affairs without apparent purpose or direction.

On the contrary, he faces five very narrow and specific questions, all of which are founded on information which he himself has already volunteered [by publication of a letter purportedly from those responsible for the bombing]. The purpose of these questions is very clear. The need for the answers to them is "overriding," to say the least. The need for these answers is nothing short of the public's need (and right) to protect itself from physical attack by apprehending the perpetrators of such attacks.

We conclude that a weighing of competing values is involved here. The court must consider on the one hand the interest of free flow of information, and on the other, the interest of fair and effective administration of the judicial system. . . . In weighing these conflicting values, we think . . . the appellant is compelled to disclose the information sought.[65]

Prior to completion of his sentence, Knops was released from jail pending the outcome of his appeal to the U.S. Supreme Court. The *Branzburg* decision affected his appeal adversely, but a technicality intervened to keep him from being returned to jail. The county grand jury's term had expired; therefore, Knops could not go back before that jury in order to purge himself of contempt. That is how the case ended, although a newly constituted grand jury could have subpoenaed him and, should he again have refused to answer, another contempt action could have resulted. This did not happen.

Interestingly, the Wisconsin Supreme Court characterized the *Caldwell* case as a fishing expedition, an opinion not shared by a majority of the U.S. Supreme Court when it subsequently decided that case.

Another factor in the Knops case relates to a suggestion made by Professor Zechariah Chafee, Jr., of Harvard that journalists might seek to escape an order to disclose by pleading the Fifth Amendment.[66] This did not work for Knops because when he pleaded the Fifth, he was quickly granted immunity from prosecution. Under such a condition, he could once again be ordered to disclose on pain of contempt for refusal to do so. This would seem a likely course of action for prosecutors whenever journalists seek to evade a disclosure order by pleading the Fifth.

Peter Bridge Case

Peter Bridge, a reporter for the Newark, New Jersey, *Evening News,* was jailed from October 3–24, 1972, for refusing to divulge information to a grand jury. Although he answered more than 50 questions, Bridge refused to answer five questions pertaining to a story he had written about an unidentified man who allegedly offered a public housing official a $10,000 bribe. Bridge unsuccessfully claimed the protection of the New Jersey shield law and the First Amendment, but the state law provides that if a newsman identifies his source in a story — which Bridge had done (the alleged bribery being a second-hand report) — the immunity is waived.[67] The reporter was freed from jail after the grand jury reported there was no basis in fact for the story, therefore there was no need to compel disclosure.

Fresno Bee Case

In November 1974 a Fresno County (California) grand jury indicted a city councilman for allegedly accepting a $4000 bribe. He later was acquitted, but before then Superior Court Judge Denver Peckinpah ordered the transcripts of the grand jury sealed and issued a gag order aimed at preventing anyone associated with the hearings from discussing the case in public. The objective was to prevent potentially prejudicial information from reaching prospective jurors.

On January 12, 1975, the *Fresno Bee* published a story by Joe Rosato and William Patterson purporting to reveal the grand jury proceedings against the councilman. Judge Peckinpah thereupon subpoenaed the reporters and the newspaper's managing editor, George Gruner, and when they refused to reveal their source of information the judge held them in contempt of court. The trio said, however, that their information had not come from anyone subject to the judge's gag order. They also claimed that the state's shield law protected them. This contention was rejected by the judge who, as in the *Farr* case (discussed in Chapter 10), declared that the legislature could not, by enactment of the law, prevent a court from protecting its own processes, or could not infringe upon the judiciary's inherent or implied powers. Another reporter, Jim Bort, also was questioned, and he, too, refused to disclose how the newspaper had gained access to the report.

The "Fresno Four," as the journalists came to be called, were found in contempt a total of 73 times. Eighteen of these contempt citations later were overturned by the California Court of Appeal (Fifth District) in a 2–1 decision, leaving 55 citations intact. The appellate court held that although the newsmen had a limited privilege to shield their sources, this privilege must yield when it conflicts with the duty and power of the court or interferes with the right to a fair trial. By a 6–1 vote, the California Supreme Court declined to intercede and an appeal was taken to the U.S. Supreme Court which, in 1976, decided not to consider the case (over the objection of Justice Douglas).

Meanwhile, Peckinpah had retired from the bench and the case went to Superior Court Judge Hollis Best who proceeded to impose an indeterminate jail term on each of the newsmen. The *Fresno Bee* appealed on the ground that a hearing should have been held by Judge Best to determine if there was any reasonable likelihood that the four would ever reveal their sources even under the duress of imprisonment. If not, then such an open-ended sentence was punitive, not coercive, and perforce had to be limited to five days under state law. Judge Best said the indefinite sentence was coercive and that the journalists could walk out of jail whenever they decided to comply with the order to divulge. And so, on September 3, 1976, the four went to jail.

But 15 days later Judge Best held a hearing at which journalists, including the Fresno Four, testified about the long-standing principle of journalists not to disclose confidential sources. A psychiatrist, called as a witness by the newspaper's attorneys, told the judge that the jailed newsmen would be committing "emotional suicide" if they revealed their source. Judge Best concluded that the four were unlikely to reveal their source because of their commitment to the moral principle. Logically, therefore, an indefinite jail term would be punitive. He therefore sentenced each of the four to serve five days in jail—the maximum punitive sentence allowed. Because they already had served 15 days, they walked from the courtroom free men. Scores of demonstrators outside the Fresno County courthouse, protesting the journalists' imprisonment, also were able to go home.

The Fresno Four and William Farr cases were instrumental in getting California media groups to push for the passage of a state constitutional amendment to protect journalists from forced disclosure of confidential sources and confidential information. The proposed amendment, known as Proposition Five, was approved in 1980. Thus, there now is a constitutional basis for California journalists to refuse to disclose confidential sources and/or information, but whether this will deter state judges from ordering disclosure remains to be seen. A Superior Court judge in Oakland did rule that the amendment violated the fair trial guarantee of the Constitution, but the ruling was rescinded in 1982 when CBS News agreed to submit *60 Minutes* outtakes to the judge, who listened to the audio version of the outtakes in his office.[68]

Lucy Morgan Case

A happier *legal* ending than in the Fresno Four case was recorded for Lucy Ware Morgan because of the Florida Supreme Court's interpretation of the *Branzburg* decision. In 1976, the state's highest court, in a 5–1 decision, quashed a contempt citation against reporter Morgan of the *St. Petersburg Times* who, at one time, had been sentenced to 57 days in jail for contempt of court.[69] The contempt action had resulted from her refusal to disclose the source of information for an article she had written about a sealed grand jury presentment concerning alleged corruption in Dade City. The state supreme court held that reporters have a limited constitutional right to protect the identity of confidential news sources.

As Justice Joseph Hatchett said for the Florida court:

> . . . [The purpose of the contempt proceedings] was to force a newspaper reporter to disclose the source of published information so that the authorities could silence the source. The present case falls squarely within this language in the *Branzburg* plurality opinion [note the court's reference to *Branzburg* as a *plurality* opinion]: "Official harassment of the press undertaken not for purposes of law enforcement but to disrupt a reporter's relationship with his news sources would have no justification."

In quashing the contempt action, Hatchett emphasized that the grand jury that summoned Morgan was not investigating a crime. Furthermore, the Florida law relates only to revealing the testimony of a witness before a grand jury, not to premature disclosure of a grand jury presentment (which is what the reporter revealed).

Interestingly, the state supreme court, which in 1950 had declared that journalists had no constitutional privilege for refusing to reveal confidential sources,[70] moved to its new position by noting that events in the intervening years "suggest that important public interests, as well as private interests, may be served by publication of information the press receives from confidential informants." The court then made this declaration: "The U.S. Supreme Court has now sanctioned the view that the First Amendment affords 'some protection for seeking out the news' [*Branzburg v. Hayes*, 408 U.S. 665, 681]. . . ."

Justice Hatchett based this view on the four dissenting opinions in *Branzburg*, plus the "enigmatic concurring opinion" of Justice Powell, saying:

> Although the plurality opinion rejected even a qualified reportorial privilege . . ., Mr. Justice Powell agreed with the dissenting justices that a reportorial privilege should be recognized in some circumstances. . . . Unlike Mr. Justice Powell, the four dissenting justices would have found the privilege applicable in *Branzburg*, notwithstanding the serious nature of the crimes under investigation.

The Florida court then proceeded to stake out a limited First Amendment privilege for Morgan based on its interpretation of *Branzburg;* its conclusion that there was "harassment of the press," and its view that the Morgan case did not involve a criminal proceeding or a grand jury investigation of a crime (the latter distinguishing the *Branzburg* trilogy of cases from the one under consideration).

Daniel Schorr Case

Veteran CBS reporter Daniel Schorr came into possession of a secret House of Representatives committee report pertaining to CIA activities. Through an intermediary, he made the report available to the *Village Voice*, which published highlights of the report in a 24-page supplement. The case involved an attempt by Schorr to sell the report, although he would not have personally gained from such a sale, having stipulated that the proceeds would go to the Reporters Committee for Freedom of the Press. The Reporters Committee subsequently announced it would accept no payment or gift as a result of publication of the report, and the *Village Voice* later announced that no payment had been made.

As justification for what Schorr did, it was pointed out by various parties, including Schorr himself, that a considerable amount of information in the secret House Intelligence Committee report had been publicized prior to the decision to keep the report secret. At one time it looked as though the House committee was about to release the report, but the House Rules Committee stepped in and blocked such action. That is when Schorr obtained a copy and decided to make it available for publication as a means of getting the information to the public.

Following publication of the report, the House voted 269–115 in 1976 to have its Ethics Committee investigate the leakage of the report. Schorr at first denied having leaked the document to *Village Voice,* but later admitted having done so. He was suspended indefinitely from his CBS News job, although the network continued him on the payroll and provided legal services. In particular, the network pledged that it would fully support Schorr against any attempt to require him to divulge confidential sources.

The Ethics Committee spent $150,000 and interviewed more than 400 persons during a seven-month unsuccessful attempt to identify the person who had given the report to Schorr. It finally subpoenaed Schorr. On September 15, 1976, he appeared before the committee and refused to identify his source, thereby risking a contempt of Congress citation. In his statement to the committee, Schorr said, in part:

> We all build our lives around certain principles, without which our careers lose their meaning.
>
> For some of us—doctors, lawyers, clergymen and journalists—it is an article of faith that we must keep confidential those matters entrusted to us only because of the assurance that they would remain confidential.
>
> For a journalist, the most crucial kind of confidence is the identity of a source of information. To betray a confidential source would mean to dry up many future sources for many future reporters. The reporter and the news organization would be the immediate losers. But I submit the ultimate losers would be the American people and their free institutions.
>
> But, beyond all that, to betray a source would be to betray myself, my career, and my life. It is not as simple as saying that I refuse to do it . . . I cannot do it.

Schorr's statement may have turned the tide. By a narrow margin the Ethics Committee voted against recommending a contempt citation. However, the committee's final report termed Schorr's action "reprehensible."

Before judgment is passed on Schorr, consideration should be given to his previous experiences with those in government. President Nixon had referred to Schorr as an s.o.b. and the CBS correspondent had been included on the infamous White House enemies list. Schorr also was the object of a White House-ordered FBI investigation which involved interviews with friends, employers and members of his family. As a "cover" for the investigation, the White House let it be known that Schorr was being considered for a position with the federal government. It is against this backdrop and the growing revelations about CIA involvement in various domestic and international plots or schemes to use journalists and the media for devious ends that Schorr's actions should be judged.

Schorr resigned from CBS News in 1976 because, as he put it in his letter of resignation, remaining with the network might prove "a source of tension within the organization." As with William Farr and the Fresno Four, he was honored by the Society of Professional Journalists with a First Amendment Award signifying a "strong and continuing effort to preserve and strengthen freedom of press and the First Amendment. . . ."[71]

Myron Farber Case

Myron Farber, a *New York Times* reporter, spent 40 days in jail and the *Times* was fined $285,000 in both civil and criminal contempt of court actions in connection with the trial of Dr. Mario Jascalevich in New Jersey.

In 1976, Farber wrote several articles about a "Doctor X" and the death of five hospital patients. The state put Dr. Jascalevich on trial for murder and defense attorneys sought Farber's notes, plus any other information pertaining to the case in the possession of the *Times*. The trial judge ordered the information turned over to him for *in camera* inspection. Farber refused to comply with the order. The *Times* said it complied with the order, but the judge was not convinced. He imposed a $5000 a day fine on the newspaper for every day it was in violation of the order. He sent Farber to jail.

On September 21, 1978, the New Jersey Supreme Court ruled 5–2 that neither the First Amendment nor the state shield law authorized Farber's refusal. *Branzburg* was controlling in Farber's First Amendment claim, and the state's shield law had to give way to the compulsory process clause of the Sixth Amendment and its counterpart in the New Jersey Constitution, the court declared.[72]

After serving 27 days in jail, Farber was freed pending the outcome of a U.S. Supreme Court hearing, but on October 6, 1978, the Court, in a one-sentence recorded statement, supported by an apparent 7–1 vote, set aside Justice Stewart's order that had temporarily freed Farber. Back to jail went the reporter.

Justices White and Marshall earlier had denied stays in executing the contempt sentences. White did so on the ground that *Branzburg* and *U.S. v. Nixon* were controlling. Marshall did so because he did not believe that four justices could be lined up to bring about review — four being the minimum number necessary for review.

Farber's release came on October 24, 1978 — the same day that a jury found Dr. Jascalevich innocent. Farber's notes and the *Times'* records no longer could make any difference in the outcome of the trial, the judge concluded.

Farber's plight gained considerable publicity and media support, but as in the Schorr case there was a circumstance which tended to cloud the issue. Farber reportedly had signed a contract with a book publisher for $75,000 to write about his investigative work in connection with the hospital deaths. This raised the question of whether a reporter would disclose something in a book for profit, but not disclose the information at a trial where a defendant's life was at stake.

Farber has maintained that his confidential notes would not have altered the verdict in the murder trial. As he said upon release from jail, ". . . I told the court I did not have the material that would establish the innocence or guilt of the defendant. . . ."

In 1982 the New Jersey governor, Brendan Byrne, on his last day in office, pardoned *The New York Times* and Farber of their criminal contempt convictions, and the criminal contempt fine—$101,000—was returned to the newspaper. Farber's book about the case was published in 1982 by Doubleday, titled: *"Somebody Is Lying": The Story of Dr X.*

One of Farber's objections to the procedure by which he was jailed was the absence of any hearing to determine the relevancy of the information being sought. The New Jersey shield law was amended in 1980 to require a criminal defendant's attorney to prove at a special hearing that information sought by subpoena is relevant to the defense and that it cannot be obtained elsewhere. If the judge upholds the subpoena, the information would be submitted to the judge for *in camera* inspection to determine its admissibility as evidence.

The New Jersey shield law amendment pretty well summarizes the evolving First Amendment "limited," or conditional, privilege that has emerged in many jurisdictions. If the information being sought is relevant and material and cannot be obtained elsewhere, then the privilege must yield.

Privilege Recognized

Such a privilege has been recognized by the following U.S. Courts of Appeal in civil or criminal cases: Second, Third, Fourth, Fifth, Eighth, Tenth, and the District of Columbia.[73] A number of state supreme courts also have recognized a qualified First Amendment privilege, such as Connecticut, Florida, Georgia, Idaho, Iowa, Kansas, Massachusetts, Louisiana, New Hampshire, Oklahoma, Vermont, Virginia, and Wisconsin. The Washington Supreme Court has found such a privilege in the common law, as has the Third Circuit. Many lower courts in both the federal and state judiciaries believe a conditional First Amendment privilege exists.

The Third Circuit laid down a three-prong test for overcoming the privilege in a criminal case, *U.S. v. Criden* (1980)—an "Abscam" bribery case in which testimony by *Philadelphia Inquirer* reporter Jan Schaffer was ruled crucial.[74] The test also was adopted by the Second Circuit in another criminal case, *U.S. v. Burke* (1983).[75] To overcome the journalist's privilege, a defendant must show that (1) the information is highly material and relevant; (2) it is necessary or critical to the defense; and (3) it is unobtainable from other sources.

The Wisconsin Supreme Court has ruled that a criminal defendant must show that the information sought will lead to competent relevant material and exculpatory evidence, and show by a preponderance of the evidence that no other reasonable, less obtrusive alternatives are available to obtain such information.[76]

In a civil case, the District of Columbia Circuit used this test:[77] (1) the lawsuit is not frivolous; (2) the information sought is crucial to the case; and (3) alternative sources of information have been exhausted.

The Iowa Supreme Court used this test in *Winegard v. Judge Oxberger* (1977) in deciding that journalists have a conditional First Amendment privilege. But in this instance, reporter Diane Graham of the *Des Moines Tribune* had to disclose sources and/or her notes relating to two articles she had written that were cited in libel and invasion of privacy actions brought against a law firm by a businessman.[78] Once the person seeking the information meets the three conditions, then, the court said, a "compelling state interest" exists for the information. Ultimately, the lawsuit was dismissed by a county district court, thus ending the need for Graham to disclose. In a later case, the Iowa court dropped frivolousness from the test.

In civil cases, the Fifth Circuit and some state courts in Florida use wording slightly different from that used by the District of Columbia Circuit, namely: (1) the information sought is relevant; (2) there is a compelling need for it (this being the Ninth Circuit's "test" in the *Caldwell* case, although the *Caldwell* case involved a grand jury investigation into possible criminal matters); and (3) all alternative sources for discovering the information have been exhaused.[79]

Generally, it is easier for someone seeking information from a journalist to overcome the privilege in a criminal trial, in a grand jury situation, or in a civil libel case where there is a media defendant, than in a civil case where the reporter is not a party in the lawsuit. In a criminal case, for example, a defendant's Sixth Amendment right to compel testimony often is pitted against the newsgatherer's First Amendment interests, as pointed out by the Second, Third, and Ninth Circuits. As for grand jury situations, if Powell's opinion is matched with White's in the *Branzburg* trilogy of cases, it appears that First Amendment protection for journalists in the context of grand jury subpoenas is limited to preventing harassment or nonrelevant inquiries of the journalist.[80] It may not even be recognized. That was the position of the Sixth Circuit U.S. Court of Appeals in 1987 in a case involving WJBK-TV reporter Brad Stone.[81] The court denied a motion for a writ of habeas corpus filed by Stone who had been held in contempt of court for failing to comply with a county grand jury subpoena.

Stone had been subpoenaed and asked to produce videotapes compiled in the course of his reporting on Detroit, Michigan, youth gang activities. The videotaping occurred one month before the murder of a state police officer. Several gang members later told police that the officer's assailants were present during Stone's filming, and other eyewitnesses to the slaying said that they could identify the assailants if shown photographs.

When Stone refused to provide the subpoenaed material he was ruled in civil contempt and ordered jailed, but enforcement was stayed by the Sixth Circuit pending a motion for a writ of habeas corpus. When the federal district court refused to issue a writ, Stone appealed.

The Sixth Circuit panel said that Stone's First Amendment privilege contention "would have us restructure" the U.S. Supreme Court's holding in *Branzburg v. Hayes*.[82] The court rejected Stone's argument that Justice Powell's concurring opinion, when read in conjunction with the majority opinion, requires the government to make a "clear and convincing showing of relevancy, essentiality, and exhaustion of nonmedia sources." Acceptance of such an argument, said the panel, would be tantamount to its substituting, as the holding of *Branzburg,* the dissent for the majority position.

But even if Stone's contention were to be accepted, the panel added, the balancing test he urges would result in a decision for disclosure. Why? Because the government had made a clear and convincing showing that Stone's information is clearly relevant to a specific violation of criminal law, that the information is not available from alternative sources, and that the state has a compelling and overriding interest in obtaining the information.

Stone had included in his arguments that the state's shield law protected him, but the lower court ruled that this law applied to reporters of "newspapers or other publications," not to broadcasters.[83]

Libel Lawsuits and Confidentiality

In libel cases, where journalists are defendants and put forth a privilege claim against disclosure of confidential sources, the claim may not be favored. This is particularly so when libel plaintiffs are seeking to show actual malice. Thus, the Supreme Court allowed the libel plaintiff in *Herbert v. Lando* (see Chapter 6) to penetrate into the editorial process involved in producing a *60 Minutes* segment, and even into the producer's thoughts during discovery despite Lando's argument that such penetration violated his First Amendment rights.

In *Carey v. Hume* (1974), a three-judge panel of the District of Columbia Circuit Court used a balancing test (as Stewart had done in the *Garland v. Torre* case in 1958) and concluded that reporter Britt Hume had to reveal the names of sources who supplied information on which an allegedly defamatory story was based.[84]

The case arose from a story by Hume, then a reporter for columnist Jack Anderson, which alleged that the plaintiff, Edward L. Carey, had removed certain documents from his United Mine Workers office, impliedly to frustrate a government probe into UMW financial matters. The plaintiff then allegedly complained to police that a box, impliedly containing the documents, had been stolen by a burglar. Carey filed a libel suit (which ultimately proved unsuccessful), and Hume claimed that the story was based on eyewitness observations by the plaintiff's coworkers. But he refused to reveal his sources. That was the issue presented to the U.S. Court of Appeals.

In ruling as it did, the panel said that identification of sources is especially important if plaintiffs are to overcome the "actual malice" hurdle imposed by the Supreme Court as a protective device for the news media.

It should be noted that *Garland* continues to have vitality. It was cited by the Supreme Court in *Branzburg* and by many courts since then.

In reaching its decision, the Circuit Court panel favorably cited *Garland.* Thus, the opinion by Justice Stewart, when he was a Circuit Court judge, continues to influence the outcome of privilege claims by journalists. The approach taken in *Garland* was to look at the facts on a case-by-case basis in the course of weighing the need for the journalist's testimony against the claim that forced disclosure will impair the public's right to know because sources of information will dry up. Many courts use this balancing approach in civil lawsuits.

The Idaho Supreme Court took the position in 1977 that there was no First Amendment privilege by which journalists could refuse to disclose confidential sources except in those cases where harassment on a broad scale can be demonstrated — basically the same position taken by the highest courts in Maryland and New Jersey.[85] The Idaho Court took this position by a 3–2 vote in *Caldero v. Tribune Publishing Co.* (1977).[86] The majority stated that *Branzburg* applies to both civil and criminal cases and that *Carey v. Hume* was four-square with the case under consideration. It also quoted favorably from *Garland v. Torre* and, as feared by Attorney Abrams, from *U.S. v. Nixon* (see Chapter 9), in which the U.S. Supreme Court held that President Nixon did not have a privilege — executive or otherwise — to shield Watergate tapes from special prosecutor Leon Jaworski. The Idaho court approvingly quoted Chief Justice Burger in *Nixon,* who said that the public "has a right to every man's evidence, except for those persons protected by a constitutional, common law, or statutory privilege." No statutory privilege existed for journalists in Idaho, said the court, and *Branzburg* showed that there was no constitutional privilege.

The Idaho court's action in affirming the lower court's contempt action meant that reporter James E. Shelledy of the Lewiston *Morning Tribune* faced 30 days in jail for refusing to identify an informant at a pretrial discovery proceeding in connection with an allegedly libelous article he had written. The newspaper undertook an appeal, but the U.S. Supreme Court declined to review the case.

Shelledy did not go to jail. As he said in a speech on February 18, 1978, "Public opposition to my jailing was the very thing that forced the judge to back down at the jail house door."

The absence of any privilege for journalists in Idaho hastened the losing outcome for *Idaho Statesman* reporter Ellen Marks. She was fined $36,000 in 1980 when she refused a judge's order to reveal the location of a mother and her child who were in hiding in a child custody dispute. The child's father had obtained a subpoena to force Marks, who had interviewed the mother, to reveal the whereabouts of the child. Marks refused and was jailed for seven hours for contempt. The judge then terminated the jail sentence and imposed a $500 a day fine, which continued until the child was returned to her father. The Idaho Supreme Court, by a 4–1 vote, ruled in 1983 that the jailing and fine were proper. But in a 1985 decision in *In re Weight,* the state's highest court changed direction, ruling that reporters have a conditional privilege in both criminal and civil cases not to have to disclose confidential sources.

The child custody case is similar to one involving TV personality Phil Donahue. Donahue refused to disclose the whereabouts of a man and his son when asked to do so by the boy's mother. Donahue said that at the time he interviewed the father he had promised not to disclose where they were. The mother's lawsuit, citing Section 700 of the *Restatement (Second) of Torts,* had charged Donahue's production company with conspiracy, negligence, and interference with the parent-child relationship. In 1983 a U.S. District Court jury in Colorado awarded the mother $1.7 million in actual damages and $4.2 million punitive damages. Ultimately the jury award was set aside because of the boy's return to his mother.

Default Judgments. A few courts have taken the position that if journalists refuse to reveal confidential sources when they or their newspapers are defendants in libel lawsuits, then such sources are presumed not to exist and default judgment is made for the plaintiff. This happened to the Twin Falls *Times-News* in Idaho. A state District Court ruled the newspaper in default when it refused to reveal confidential sources. However, the Idaho Supreme Court in 1980 reversed the $1.9 million libel judgment, ruling that the trial court erred in striking the newspaper's pleadings.[87] The supreme court said that at no time during the hearing on a motion for sanctions against the newspaper for its refusal to obey an order to disclose confidential sources, or in its appeal, did the libel plaintiff— an insurance company—show that its inability to discover the confidential sources obstructed its ability to prove the falsity of the publications. The case was remanded with instructions that the newspaper's pleadings be reinstated. Ultimately, the libel action was dismissed by action of the plaintiff on condition that the newspaper waive the $19,000 in costs awarded to the newspaper by the state supreme court.[88]

A case that had some unusual twists started with a $60 million lawsuit filed against the *Los Angeles Daily News* and two of its reporters, Adam Dawson and Arnie Friedman. The action was brought by Jerry Plotkin, who had been one of a number of Americans held hostage by Iranians after the takeover of the American embassy in Teheran. The lawsuit was based on a news article published in 1981, headlined: "Plotkin May Be Questioned in Drug Probe."[89]

When the two reporters refused to reveal confidential news sources, Judge Sara Radin of the California Superior Court in Los Angeles entered a default judgment against the defendants. The newspaper thereupon ordered the reporters to disclose their sources (an action that drew considerable criticism from other journalists). The reporters refused to do so and hired separate attorneys to defend them.

The default judgment subsequently was vacated, although the court stipulated that if no sources were named within 20 days of the order vacating the default judgment, it would be deemed "established as a matter of law" that no sources existed. Subsequently, a deposition was given to Ploktin by the attorney for one of the journalists which identified two sources, both of whom were Drug Enforcement Administration agents. In 1988 Plotkin and the former owners of the *Daily News* reached an out-of-court settlement. The amount of the settlement was not disclosed.[90]

Somewhat later, in an unrelated case, the California Supreme Court ruled that reporters have a qualified privilege in civil cases against having to disclose confidential sources, but that the question of whether the privilege exists in a given situation must be decided on a case-by-case basis. The court distinguished *Branzburg* (involving a criminal matter) from *Herbert v. Lando* (a civil law matter) in the case under review (*Mitchell v. Marin County Superior Court* (1984)) and expressed concern about harassment, embarrassment, or abusive tactics used in discovery proceedings to try to make journalists divulge confidential sources. The scope of the privilege in each case, said the court, will depend on a number of factors, including whether the reporter is a party in the litigation, relevance of the information being sought, whether plaintiff has exhausted all alternative sources of obtaining the needed information, whether the information relates "to a matter of great public importance," and whether the risk of harm to the source is a substantial one if disclosure were ordered.[91] Also, plaintiffs may be required to make a prima facie showing that the alleged defamatory statements are false before disclosure would be required.

In 1980, the New Hampshire Supreme Court addressed the issue of nondisclosure by journalists who are parties in libel lawsuits. In *Downing v. Monitor Publishing Co.,* the court decided that a presumption arises that a defendant has no source when the defendant refuses to disclose confidential sources.[92] As the court said:

> We are aware . . . that most media personnel have refused to obey court orders to disclose, electing to go to jail instead. Confining newsmen to jail in no way aids the plaintiff in proving his case.
>   . . . Therefore, we hold that when a defendant in a libel action, brought by a plaintiff who is required to prove actual malice under *New York Times,* refuses to declare his sources of information upon a valid order of the court, there shall arise a presumption that the defendant had no source. The presumption may be removed by disclosure of the sources a reasonable time before trial.

Clearly, reporters find themselves between the proverbial rock and a hard place when they are asked to give depositions or testimony in libel cases which resulted from something they have reported, but which is based solely on information provided by confidential sources.

What Can Journalists Do?

James Shelledy, who as a reporter for the Lewiston *Morning Tribune* in Idaho came within a whisker of going to jail for 30 days for refusing to identify an informant, had some advice for journalists concering the giving of confidentiality pledges. By then, he was executive editor of the *Morning Tribune.* Reporters should not "grant absolute anonymity to just anyone," he said, "or at the drop of a press card."[93] It is rare that a situation should require a journalist to put himself in a position of going to jail or being fined, he said, suggesting that journalists not "solicit this kind of problem if you don't have to—and usually you don't." Different degrees of anonymity can be offered, including conditional anonymity where the source's identity might be disclosed under certain circumstances, such as to a judge *in camera.*

The *Cleveland Plain Dealer's* response to continuing subpoenas by county prosecutors seeking unpublished information from reporters is adoption of a policy of routine, regular destruction of all notes and other data involved in the reporting process. Executive Editor David L. Hopcraft said he considers the policy to be "preventive medicine," eliminating a legal and personal dilemma for reporters who are ordered to disclose records they still have.[94] What was left undiscussed was the problem such destruction might cause in the event of defamation lawsuits resulting from stories that might be defended on the basis of reporters' notes if those notes had not been destroyed.

SHIELD LAWS

If journalists do not have a First Amendment privilege to protect them from disclosing confidential sources and/or information, or if they have a qualified privilege that quickly gives way to other, "more compelling" interests, can they be given statutory protection? The answer is "yes." Twenty-six states have enacted "shield" laws aimed at protecting journalists from having to disclose confidential sources.

States that absolutely protect journalists from forced disclosure are: Alabama, Arizona, California, Indiana, Kentucky, Maryland, Montana, Nebraska, Nevada, New York, Ohio, Oregon, and Pennsylvania. States which qualifiedly protect journalists from having to disclose confidential sources are: Alaska, Arkansas, Delaware, Illinois, Louisiana, Michigan, Minnesota, New Jersey, New Mexico, North Dakota, Oklahoma, Rhode Island, and Tennessee.[95]

Maryland was the first state to pass a shield law, doing so in 1896. The law was enacted after a reporter for the *Baltimore Sun,* John T. Morris, wrote an article suggesting that certain elected officials and policemen were on the payrolls of illegal gambling establishments. The article contained information virtually identical to testimony given to a grand jury investigating the alleged corruption. Suspecting a leak, the grand jury summoned Morris and demanded to know his source. When he refused, he was jailed. He was released five days later when the grand jury's term expired. The Journalists' Club, alarmed at the prospect of reporters facing jail terms for refusing to disclose confidential sources, persuaded the General Assembly to pass the shield law.[96]

Ten of the states adopted their "privilege" laws after 1970; and, mindful of the Farr case, California in 1971, Indiana and New Mexico in 1973, and Nevada in 1975 amended their laws to protect journalists even after they leave news media jobs.

No matter how often the state shield laws are amended to plug "loopholes," or to make them more "absolute" when they are already thought to be absolute, problems arise when confidentiality issues reach the courts. California has resorted to a constitutional amendment in an attempt to provide absolute protection, but even constitutional amendments may not prevent the judiciary from requiring journalists to disclose because of the separation of powers doctrine contained in the federal and state constitutions. The doctrine means that legislatures cannot encroach on the functions and duties of the judiciary.

No Federal Shield Law. Although many bills have been introduced at various sessions of Congress since the early 1970s, there is no federal shield law and the prospect for passage of such legislation is not promising. The Justice Department opposes such legislation principally because journalists would be able to withhold information from federal grand juries, and because the attorney general has laid down guidelines designed to protect journalists except under conditions in which the information cannot be obtained from any other source and is deemed essential.

Not all journalism groups agree on the extent of the protection that should be afforded by shield legislation. For example, the Reporters Committee for Freedom of the Press, formed as a result of the subpoena issued to *New York Times* reporter Earl Caldwell, wanted a law absolute in its protection. But the American Newspaper Publishers Association, which once sought absolute protection, gave up that position and in 1975 expressed the hope that Congress would provide qualified protection.

Canon 5 of the American Newspaper Guild's Code of Ethics is inflexible in terms of the protection that a news reporter should give to confidential sources and/or information, stating flatly: "The newspaperman shall refuse to reveal confidences or disclose sources of confidential information in court or before judicial investigative bodies, and that the newspaperman's duty to keep confidences shall include those he shared with one employer after he has changed employment." The SPJ,SDX's Code of Ethics, adopted in 1973, states, "Journalists acknowledge the newsman's ethic of protecting confidential sources of information." The Associated Press Managing Editors Association Code of Ethics, adopted in 1975, does not oppose the principle of nondisclosure in order to protect a confidential source, but it does make the following recommendation: "News sources should be disclosed unless there is clear reason not to do so. When it is necessary to protect the confidentiality of a source, the reason should be explained."

Shield Laws and Discovery Proceedings

As pointed out in Chapter 6, discovery is a means of establishing facts in a case and clarifying issues. Plaintiff's attorneys in a defamation lawsuit may, for example, seek to discover defendant's state of mind at the time an allegedly libelous story was published in order to try to establish knowing falsity. Or those same attorneys may seek a reporter's notes or an organization's files pertaining to plaintiff. If the reporter or organization refuses to comply, a court order may be sought to compel such disclosure. In those states having shield laws, the question arises: Does the law protect the journalist or the organization from forced disclosure during discovery proceedings? The results are mixed.

For example, a U.S. District Court judge ruled in late 1979 that a *Philadelphia Inquirer* reporter did not have to disclose confidential sources because of the Pennsylvania shield law.[97] Plaintiff in a libel action had sought such information during a pretrial discovery proceeding.

In Oklahoma, a reporter for the *Daily Oklahoman* was found in contempt of court in 1980 by a Cleveland County district judge and sentenced to 30 days in jail. He had refused to identify confidential news sources and to turn over personal files during a deposition hearing in a libel lawsuit.[98]

In a New Mexico case, a sweeping disclosure order was issued by a trial judge in connection with a libel lawsuit filed by an Albuquerque attorney. Attorneys for William Marchiondo gained the trial court's permission to demand from the *Journal* and *Albuquerque Tribune all* sources of information for any article *ever* published about Marchiondo—even those not alleged to be libelous. In addition, a *Journal* reporter was ordered to surrender to the plaintiff's attorneys *all* documents pertaining to Marchiondo obtained during the previous five years! In 1979, the U.S. Supreme Court refused to hear an appeal by the publishers.[99]

In Illinois, where libel cases are specifically exempt from the state's shield law, an editorial writer, Richard Hargraves, went to jail on July 3, 1984, for 60 hours rather than reveal confidential sources.[100] Working for the *Belleville News-Democrat,* Hargraves wrote an editorial in which he accused a county official of lying. A county judge ordered the journalist to reveal the sources for that information, and when he refused, he was sent to jail for contempt. The Illinois Supreme Court refused to overturn the order, and the U.S. Supreme Court declined to stay the order. Hargraves was freed after two sources voluntarily identified themselves, at which time Hargraves confirmed that they had been his sources.

Breaking Confidentiality Pledge Costly. Two newspapers—the Minneapolis *Star Tribune* and the St. Paul *Pioneer Press*—were ordered to pay $700,000 in damages ($200,00 in actual damages and $250,000 each in punitive damages) to a confidential source who was identified by those newspapers. A jury found that the newspapers had broken an oral contract with Dan Cohen, a public relations executive who had been promised anonymity when he leaked damaging information about a candidate for governor. Editors at both newspapers overruled their reporters in deciding to use Cohen's name. The day the stories appeared, Cohen was fired from his $35,000-a-year job.

During the trial, editors for the newspapers contended that contract law should not control news gathering.

Both newspapers appealed. The Minnesota Court of Appeals upheld the award of actual damages, but threw out the punitive damages award, and in late 1989 the State Supreme Court agreed to hear the case.

Within a few hours of the jury's verdict, the *Star Tribune* faced another problem related to a possible pledge of confidentiality. The publisher ordered all 640,000 copies of the *Sunday Magazine* that ordinarily appears weekly in the newspaper to be recalled from distribution warehouses. The reason: A lawyer identified in one of the magazine stories complained that she had been promised anonymity. The publisher acted after it could not be determined if such a pledge had been given by the free-lance writer of the article, according to the newspaper.

Does the pledge of confidentiality expire at the same time as the information-giver? Bob Woodward of Watergate exposé fame thinks so. In his book, *Veil,* he revealed for the first time that the source for many exclusive stories about controversial intelligence operations by the Central Intelligence Agency was none other than CIA Director William Casey. Casey died before the book was published and Woodward took the position that the confidentiality agreement did not extend to the grave—a position sharply criticized by Casey's widow and others.

NEWSPAPER SEARCH CASE: *ZURCHER v. STANFORD DAILY*

A number of preceding cases, such as *Caldwell v. U.S.* and *Branzburg v. Hayes,* involved the issuance of subpoenas by government units seeking to obtain information. A subpoena can be challenged and the issue taken before a judge who could order the subpoena quashed. Or the parties involved could negotiate on the information being sought and the issue resolved then and there. During the court challenge or the negotiations—in fact, from the moment the subpoena is served—the party being asked to provide information could conceivably destroy the information.

The delays and uncertainties associated with the use of subpoenas can be avoided through the expediency of a search and seizure operation. A search warrant must be issued by a judge, but once signed by the judge, law enforcement officers can search a premise without advance warning. Thus, any dispute over the legality of a search warrant takes place after the search has taken place.

The Fourth Amendment requires that "probable cause" exist for the issuance of such warrant, and the warrant must describe the place to be searched and the "things" to be seized. Generally, however, police do not experience much difficulty in obtaining search warrants.

Prior to *Warden v. Hayden* (1967), search warrants were used against innocent "third parties" only to obtain something that had been stolen, the "tools" used to commit crimes, or contraband, but in *Warden* the Supreme Court held that the Fourth Amendment's ban on unreasonable searches and seizures did not preclude a search of third parties for "mere evidence" of the commission of a crime—in the instant case, blood-stained clothing.[101]

In April 1971 police were called to Stanford University Hospital where a group of demonstrators had occupied administrative offices. During a resulting melee, nine policemen were injured. The *Stanford Daily* published a special issue two days later that included photographs of the disturbance. Police wanted any photographs that might help them identify those who had assaulted the officers, and so they obtained a search warrant. They arrived unannounced at the newspaper office and for about 15 minutes searched the premises, including filing cabinets, desks, and photographic laboratories. Locked drawers and rooms were not opened, but officers had time to read notes and other matter during the search. They did not find anything that would help identify the attackers.

An action under the U.S. Civil Rights Act was brought by the *Stanford Daily* against the Palo Alto police chief and district attorney. It sought an injunction against any further searches and a declaration that the one that had led to the action violated the First, Fourth, and Fourteenth Amendments. In 1972 the U.S. District Court held that the Fourth Amendment prevented the use of a search warrant against any person not suspected of a crime unless there was a showing that a subpoena, if served, might result in destruction or removal of the sought-after material.[102] The court also held that where the innocent third party is a newspaper, the First Amendment requires a "clear showing" that the material would be destroyed or removed and that a restraining order would be futile before a search warrant could be issued.

On appeal, the U.S. Court of Appeals affirmed in a per curiam opinion which adopted the views of the district judge.[103]

The Supreme Court reversed in a 5–3 decision in 1978 in a voting lineup very similar to the one in *Branzburg*.[104] Again, *Zurcher* was a "law-and-order" type case. In giving the Court's opinion, Justice White said that a search may be made of newspaper offices—or any innocent third party's premises—whenever there are reasonable grounds to believe that criminal evidence is on the premises. The warrant must meet the Fourth Amendment's requirements of probable cause, specificity, and reasonableness. And because search warrants are more difficult to obtain, said White, law enforcement officials ordinarily would seek subpoenas unless there were strong reasons to do otherwise.

As for special problems caused by search and seizure when the press is the third party, White discounted the fear, as he had done in *Branzburg,* that confidential sources would disappear or dry up because of police rummaging through newspaper files or desks. Even if the press suppressed news out of fear of warranted searches (the self-censorship or "chilling effect" contention), that still would not make a constitutional difference.[105] When the Fourth Amendment was written, said White, no special provision was inserted to protect the press, and contemporary conditions do not warrant any such innovation. As long as magistrates keep in mind the requirements for issuance of warrants, and do so "with particular exactitude when First Amendment interests would be endangered by the search," nothing more is required. Magistrates can guard against searches that disrupt publication schedules, said White, answering fears that unannounced searches might occur close to presstime, thereby disrupting operations. Furthermore, there have been only a few similar instances since the *Stanford Daily* search, said White. This hardly suggests abuse and, should abuse occur, there will be time to deal with it, he asserted.

As for shield laws and Fifth Amendment claims, which have been used in attempts to combat subpoenas, they are largely irrelevant in determining the legality of search warrants under the Fourth Amendment.

With the door shut on a constitutional privilege shielding the press from third-party search warrants, White again, as in *Branzburg* (when he said shield laws could be passed to protect journalists), indicated that the legislative or executive branches of government could establish protections against possible abuses.

Justice Powell once again provided the fifth vote, as in *Branzburg,* and once again wrote a short, concurring opinion. The tone of the opinion is more solicitous of First Amendment values than White's. Although agreeing with White that the press has no special protection under the Fourth Amendment, nonetheless, said Powell, a magistrate should be cognizant of the values protected by the First Amendment when considering the issuance of a search warrant. In commenting on his concurrence in *Branzburg* and *Zurcher,* Powell notes his rejection of a special procedural exception for the press, but at the same time he wants "recognition of First Amendment concerns within the applicable procedure." In *Branzburg,* he said the courts must be the balancer between competing free press values and society's interest in fighting crime. Magistrates in search warrants cases will have to do the balancing of these competing interests.

Justice Stewart, joined by Marshall, echoed some of the views expressed in his dissent in *Branzburg.* He agreed with the Court's Fourth Amendment analysis, but said the First Amendment bars the use of search warrants against the press unless it can be shown that a subpoena is impracticable. No such showing was made in this case. As in *Branszburg,* Stewart saw the possible disclosure of confidential sources and information resulting from a newspaper search as reducing the flow of information to the public.

In distinguishing *Branzburg* from the instant case, Stewart noted that there was no claim to a privilege to withhold information, only a dispute over which of two methods to use to obtain the information; and, second, there is no opportunity to challenge the warrant until after the search has occurred and the "constitutional protection of the newspaper has been irretrievably invaded."

Although recognizing as "abstract policy" that newspapers should receive no greater protection than doctors or banks, Stewart proceeded to emphasize that the Constitution does not explicitly protect those activities while it does explicitly protect freedom of press.

Justice Stevens dissented solely on Fourth Amendment grounds, arguing for greater safeguards for innocent third parties against searches than afforded by *Warden v. Hayden.*

Justice Brennan took no part in the decision.

Reaction to Decision

For the most part the press reacted loudly and vehemently in condemning the decision. The St. Louis *Post-Dispatch,* for example, termed the decision "a staggering blow to freedom of the press." And the chairman and president of the American Newspaper Publishers Association, Allen H. Neuharth, said the decision "puts a sledgehammer in the hands of those who would batter the American people's First Amendment rights" because it "authorizes harassment and intimidation" of the public's right to know. Neuharth emphasized that he was not urging a complete shield for the press; rather, if a newspaper possesses legitimate evidence, that material can and should be obtained only through the subpoena process . . . not through a search-first-ask-later policy. . . ."[106]

By a 10–1 vote, the National News Council, which ceased operations in July 1984, called for emergency legislation at the state level to provide safeguards against newspaper search "in the absence of reasonable proof that the desired material would otherwise be destroyed or removed from the state." In casting a dissenting vote, council member William Rusher warned that the media run the risk of alienating the public permanently by seeking special privileges and distinguishing the media from the people.

California was the first state to enact legislation prohibiting surprise police searches of newsrooms, doing so effective January 1, 1979. Police must first seek to obtain material via subpoena. If the material is not forthcoming, then a search warrant may be issued. Connecticut passsed a law effective October 1, 1979, which prohibits search of newsrooms unless a news organization or reporter is directly implicated in a crime. To obtain records, authorities first must seek a subpoena. An Illinois law, effective September 19, 1979, permits a newsroom search only if the person who is the object of the requested warrant has committed a crime, or if the things to be seized will be destroyed or removed from the state if the warrant is not issued.

Nebraska, Oregon, Texas, and Washington also quickly responded to *Zurcher* by passing legislation to protect the press against searches. Texas went one step further and passed a bill to strengthen protection for all citizens against searches[107] — the very thing opposed by the U.S. Justice Department when it indicated support for proposed federal legislation providing protection for the news media, but opposing efforts to extend the protection to other groups, such as doctors and lawyers, or to citizens generally.

Within a month of the *Zurcher* decision, 12 bills aimed at offsetting its effects had been introduced in Congress. The Justice Department and Vice-President Walter Mondale had assured the news media that the Carter administration would exercise "administrative restraint" in seeking news media search warrants. On April 2, 1979, President Carter asked Congress to enact new privacy legislation containing protection for the media against searches. The result was passage of the Privacy Protection Act of 1980 that went into effect in 1981.

Privacy Protection Act of 1980

This law requires police at all levels of government — not just federal law officers — to use subpoenas rather than search warrants to obtain a journalist's "work product." "Work product" includes a journalist's notes, article drafts, mental impressions, conclusions, or theories. The Act provides less protection against a search for "documentary materials," including written and printed matter, audio and video tapes, photographs, and film and negatives. "Journalist" is not defined.

If the materials being sought by police have been "prepared, produced, authored or created" for the purpose of "communicating such materials to the public," then police must seek the "work product" by means of subpoena except where there is probable cause to believe that the person holding the material has committed, or is about to commit, a crime related to the material, or there is reason to believe that seizure is necessary to prevent death or serious injury. In the case of documentary materials, additional exceptions exist; namely, that search and seizure also is permitted if there is reason to believe that giving notice of a subpoena would lead to destruction, concealment, or alteration of the materials, or when the materials have not been produced under subpoena and an appellate court has held that such withholding threatens the interests of justice.

The Act does not protect the news media from searches for classified information, restricted data or materials related to the national defense. Thus, the *New York Times* office, for example, probably could be searched for materials such as the Pentagon Papers.

Other Newsroom Searches. From the time of *Zurcher* other newsroom searches have occurred. On May 15, 1980, police in Flint, Michigan, obtained a warrant and searched the offices of the printer of the *Flint Voice*.[108] And on July 26, 1980, police searched the newsroom of KBCI-TV in Boise, Idaho, and seized two videotapes pertaining to rioting at the Idaho State Penitentiary in which two guards were held hostage and 26 inmates were injured. A KBCI-TV reporter had been asked by inmates to come inside the prison and record the activity while they had held the guards hostage.[109] Three newsroom searches took place in 1987 and 1988.[110] The first was by state welfare investigators who, armed with a search warrant, entered the San Jose office of the *Viet Nam Nhat Bao* newspaper and the *Tan Van Magazine* in search of evidence in connection with alleged welfare law violations. A variety of documents and other information was seized, including unpublished manuscripts, letters to the editor, photographs, etc. The publisher later brought a suit against the county and the city of San Jose, alleging violations of the Privacy Protection Act of 1980 and the federal Civil Rights Law.

In the second raid, Riverside County sheriff's deputies seized a videotape of a drug raid from KESQ-TV in Palm Springs. KESQ-TV had been invited to accompany law officers on the raid, but when it took place a suspect shot at deputies and later claimed that he had not heard the officers identify themselves as they entered his house. The station did not sue and the sheriff's department returned the tape and agreed to issue a news release stating that the search and seizure were inconsistent with the Privacy Protection Act, the California shield law and the state's Constitution.

The third raid led to seizure of videotapes from KCBS-TV's bureau in Riverside by San Bernardino County sheriff's deputies. The videotapes were related to the ransacking of an animal research laboratory by animal rights activists. Later, the judge who issued the search warrant ordered the tapes returned and said he had erred in that California law prohibited search warrants from being served on the news media to obtain unpublished information.[111]

SUMMARY

This chapter, like Chapters 9 and 10, deals with the Fourth Estate's claim to a First Amendment right to gather news, including a right or privilege against being forced to divulge confidential sources or records, or having newsrooms searched. Such government actions, the press contends, threaten to dry up its news sources, thereby restricting the flow of information to the public.

Until *Richmond Newspapers,* there was little in the case law to support a First Amendment right to gather news — and a strict reading of *Richmond Newspapers* shows that the right is confined to criminal trials. But Justice Stevens believes that the right extends to the "acquisition of newsworthy matter. . . ."

Certainly, government has been able to restrict the travel of journalists to foreign countries. The power of the Executive branch in foreign policy and national security matters overwhelms whatever First Amendment rights might be implicated in journalists wanting to travel abroad.

Similarly, journalists have no constitutional right of access to prisons or their inmates beyond that accorded to the general public — a theme that runs through most access cases. Thus, if prison authorities restrict visiting hours to two hours daily, that is when journalists can expect to be allowed to visit prisons. But some members of the Supreme Court, in *Houchins v. KQED* (1978), argued that there was *some* First Amendment protection for seeking out the news — as Justice Stewart had argued much earlier in his dissenting opinion in *Branzburg.*

What has emerged from *Richmond Newspapers* and other access-to-the-courts cases is a test first put forth by Justice Brennan; namely, has access been traditionally given and does it play a significant positive role in the particular process being examined? Thus, where the public traditionally has not had access, the press does not have a right of access.

The *Branzburg* trilogy of cases was brought about by a wave of government subpoenas against the press in the late 1960s and early 1970s. The subpoenas led to confrontations between the press and government and a U.S. Supreme Court decision in 1972. In *Branzburg v. Hayes, U.S. v. Caldwell,* and *In re the matter of Paul Pappas,* an apparent majority of the Court declared that the press does not have a First Amendment privilege to refuse to go before grand juries and give testimony except where there is evidence of harassment or the juries are engaged in "fishing expeditions."

Justice Powell's vote, which produced a Court majority, stirred considerable debate. Is his vote an enigma, as Justice Stewart contended? Quite a few courts have read his opinion and coupled it to the four dissenting votes to fashion a conditional or limited First Amendment privilege for journalists not to have to reveal confidential sources either in criminal cases, or in civil cases, or both.

The privilege claim did not prevent William Farr, Peter Bridge, four *Fresno Bee* journalists and Myron Farber from going to jail. It did protect Lucy Ware Morgan.

If there is no First Amendment privilege to protect confidential sources and/or information, shield laws may provide protection. Twenty-six states have such laws. In 13 of them, the protection is supposed to be absolute. However, whenever such laws have been deemed an interference in the judiciary's function of administering a fair and just system of law the laws either have been declared unconstitutional or simply made inoperative for the cases at hand. Even when the voters of a state amend the state constitution, as in California, there is doubt that journalists are absolutely protected against a judge's order to disclose.

There is no federal shield law despite the repeated introduction of bills in Congress to accomplish this. But the U.S. Justice Department now has guidelines related to the issuance of subpoenas for journalists' notes, telephone records, or for journalists to appear before grand juries.

Following the *Zurcher v. Stanford Daily* decision of the Supreme Court in 1978, which upheld the constitutionality of an unannounced search of a "third party" newspaper office, federal legislation was passed to require authorities in most cases to seek a journalist's "work product" by means of subpoenas, rather than search and seizure. A number of states also passed protective legislation.

QUESTIONS IN REVIEW

1. Under the Mitchell guidelines for issuance of Justice Department subpoenas, negotiations with the media continue to be the rule. The issuance of subpoenas has to be approved by whom?

2. Even though CBS was not cited for contempt by the House of Representatives for refusing to produce various information and documents related to "The Selling of the Pentagon," the vote — 226 to 181 — was close. What rationale might be used for defending the position that CBS should have been cited for contempt of Congress? Conversely, why should CBS not have been cited?

3. Journalists first tried to gain protection against forced disclosure under the common law. Failing, they turned to the First Amendment. What case represented the first effort by a journalist to use the First Amendment as a basis for refusing to disclose a confidential source? What did the court decide and what were the principal reasons for the decision?

4. Professor Chafee said that journalists could, if the situation demanded, use the Fifth Amendment; that is, decline to answer on the grounds of self-incrimination. But when Mark Knops invoked the Fifth Amendment, what happened to thwart this protective device?

5. In which state did voters approve a constitutional amendment to protect journalists from forced disclosure of confidential sources and why was it necessary?

6. In *Branzburg,* Justice White said that neither common law nor constitutional law protects journalists from forced disclosure under certain circumstances. But he indicated there was a way that they could be given such protection. How?

7. Justice White indicated in *Branzburg* that there was some protection for journalists when they went before grand juries. To what did he have reference?

8. Insofar as most U.S. Circuit Courts of Appeal are concerned, as well as many state courts, what is the current status of a First Amendment or state constitutional privilege for journalists against having to disclose confidential sources and/or information?

9. On what basis did the Wisconsin Supreme Court hold that Mark Knops could be compelled to testify?

10. In what case did a majority of the Supreme Court hold that a warranted search of a newsroom was constitutionally valid? Under what Fourth Amendment conditions would such a search be unconstitutional?

11. Does *Richmond Newspapers v. Virginia* (1980) grant the press and public a right of access to information? If so, to what kind of information? Be specific.

12. If you were to put forth an access test, what two parts would it contain?

ANSWERS

1. Attorney general.

2. A principal argument for punishing CBS for contempt relates to Congress's need for information to carry out its legislative function. Such an argument is part of the

controversy over executive privilege. If the press can use the argument of the public's right to know in seeking to gain information from reluctant bureaucrats, how can it logically deny information to the people's chosen representatives?

A variety of reasons can be put forth by the press, beginning with the absolutist position that the First Amendment prohibits any interference in the operations of the press, including the threat implicit in subpoenas from congressional committees. If Congress can force the press to reveal its sources of information, then such sources of information may dry up and the net result would be a reduction in the amount of information the public has a right to know. Further, subpoenas represent "threats" against the media and therefore result in a "chilling" effect on First Amendment freedoms. Also, using Justice White's rationale in *Branzburg,* the congressional sub-committee appeared to be on a fishing expedition directed more at punishment for audaciousness than relevancy to remedial legislation. Without protection, therefore, CBS was correct in refusing to provide information other than what was made public during the telecast, according to defenders of CBS's action.

3. *Garland v. Torre.* Circuit Court Judge Stewart balanced the First Amendment claim against the duty of citizens to give testimony and a litigant's right to compel testimony — both included in the broader public interest in fair administration of justice. On balance, the judge tipped the scale in favor of fair administration of justice.

4. He was given immunity from prosecution and then ordered to identify the writer of a letter who claimed "credit" for the bombing of a university building.

5. California. Because courts had ruled that the state's shield statute, as passed by the legislature, violated the state constitution's separation-of-powers clause because it interfered with a function of the judiciary. Any statute designed to protect journalists could run afoul of the same kind of determination; therefore, a constitutional amendment became necessary.

6. Congress could pass shield legislation.

7. The information sought must be relevant to the grand jury's task and the grand jury cannot *harass* newsmen. Judges would protect newsmen in both situations, Justice White said, although skepticism was expressed in dissenting opinions.

8. There is a conditional First Amendment privilege. It is least likely to be recognized in criminal cases and in civil cases, such as libel, where the journalist is a party in the action. It is most likely to be recognized in civil cases where the journalist is a nonparty in the action.

9. In the absence of a state shield law or constitutional immunity against disclosure, Knops could be required to answer the five *specific* questions because of an "overriding" or "compelling" state need for the information. As in *Garland v. Torre*, conflicting rights were balanced and the scale tilted in favor of administration of justice.

10. *Zurcher v. Stanford Daily* (1978). If these elements were absent — probable cause, specificity and reasonableness — then a search warrant would not meet Fourth Amendment requirements.

11. Yes, they have a less-than-absolute right of access to information vis-à-vis a criminal trial. But the extent to which *Richmond Newspapers* goes beyond access to criminal trials is debatable.

12. Has the public traditionally had access to the information or place? Does access — such as to the criminal courts — play a significant positive role in the particular process or activity being examined? Do you know what that significant positive role has been?

ENDNOTES

1. *The Bulletin,* American Society of Newspaper Editors, December/January 1979, p. 6.
2. Richmond Newspapers v. Virginia, op. cit., Chapter 10, note 47.
3. Branzburg v. Hayes, 408 U.S. 665, 684 (1972).
4. Ibid., at 684–685.
5. Ibid., at 707.
6. Ibid., at 681.
7. Worthy v. Herter, 270 F.2d 905 (District of Columbia Circuit, 1959).
8. Worthy v. Herter, 361 U.S. 918, 80 S.Ct. 255.
9. Zemel v. Rusk, 381 U.S. 1, 17, 85 S.Ct. 1271,1281 (1965).
10. Haig v. Agee, 7 *Med.L.Rptr.* 1545, July 21, 1981.
11. "News Notes," *Media Law Reporter,* August 18, 1981.
12. Regan v. Wald, No. 83–436, 52 *U.S. Law Week* 4966.
13. Pell v. Procunier, 417 U.S. 817 (1974).
14. Saxbe v. Washington Post Co., 417 U.S. 843 (1974).
15. Pell, at 834; Saxbe, at 850.
16. Houchins v. KQED (1978), 438 U.S. 1, 3 *Med.L.Rptr.* 2521, July 11, 1978.
17. Ibid., at 2527.
18. Zemel v. Rusk, op. cit., note 9, 381 U.S. 1, 17.
19. Houchins, op cit., note 16, at 2531.
20. Ibid., at 2533.
21. Ibid.
22. Capital Cities Media v. Chester, 55 *U.S. Law Week* 2073, August 5, 1986.
23. Ibid.
24. See Press-Enterprise II, 106 S.Ct. at 2740.
25. *The NEWS Media & The LAW,* Fall 1986, pp. 21–22.
26. Ibid., at 22. Leiserson v. San Diego, 229 Cal.Rptr. 22 (1986).
27. *The NEWS Media & The LAW,* Winter 1987, pp. 2–4.
28. Ibid., at 3.
29. Ibid., at 4.
30. *Editor & Publisher,* March 21, 1987, p. 42.
31. Ibid.
32. "News Notes," *Media Law Reporter,* January 27, 1987.
33. *The NEWS Media & The LAW,* Winter 1989, p. 22.
34. A national poll conducted by CBS early in 1970 showed that 55 percent of those questioned favored peacetime restrictions on the press if the government thought that information to be published was harmful to the national interest. Other indicators of public disaffection included a statement by Chicago Mayor Richard Daley that he had received 60,000 letters in support of police during the demonstrations compared with only 4000 that were critical; a Federal Communications Commission report that hundred of letters critical of TV network news coverage had been received; and an NBC report that 6280 telegrams, phone calls, and letters were received, of which 5200 were critical of NBC convention coverage.
35. The vice-president's criticism of news media continued intermittently into 1972. For example, on March 15, 1972, in a speech at Drake University, Des Moines, Iowa, he said, "I think the national media in particular—by that I mean the networks, national news magazines, the principal newspapers with far flung services—I think they have been oriented too long in one direction. I don't think they're accurately reflecting in every instance the views of conservative people of this country."
36. Sigma Delta Chi Foundation lecture at University of Texas, Austin, Texas, on March 10, 1970. These guidelines later became the principal requirements of Justice Department Order No. 544–73, issued October 16, 1973 (43 *U.S. Law Week* 2232). One of the guidelines in that order was that a news media member could not be subject to questioning "as to any offense which he is suspected of having committed in the course of, or arising out of, the coverage or investigation of a news story."

37. The protection afforded by the guidelines was expanded when U.S. Attorney General Edward Levi announced on November 19, 1975, that henceforth federal attorneys must get his approval before subpoenaing confidential information from *anyone* "engaged in reporting public affairs." This broadened the Justice Department regulation to include authors, documentary film producers, and perhaps representatives of the nontraditional press, rather than just news media representatives.

38. For a more complete definition of the Fairness Doctrine, see Chapter 14.

39. Report by Task Force on Government and the Press, Twentieth Century Fund, entitled *Press Freedoms Under Pressure,* New York, 1972, p. 15.

40. Dissenting opinion in combined cases of Branzburg v. Hayes, In the Matter of Paul Pappas, and U.S. v. Caldwell, 408 U.S. 665, 724–25, 92 S.Ct. 2686, 2693–94, 33 L.Ed.2d 657, 664–65 (1972). Compare Douglas' dissent with disclosure to the Senate Watergate Committee in August 1973, that White House counsel John W. Dean III had prepared a list of "political enemies," which included the names of more than 50 active journalists. The Dean memorandum, prepared August 16, 1971, asked other White House aides "how we maximize the fact of our incumbency in dealing with persons known to be active in opposition to our administration. Stated a bit more bluntly—how we can use the available federal machinery to screw our political enemies."

41. Speech at the 46th annual Georgia Press Institute, Athens, Ga., February 22, 1974.

42. *Editor & Publisher,* January 29, 1977, p. 31.

43. *Editor & Publisher,* December 6, 1980, p. 40.

44. *The NEWS Media & The LAW,* June/July 1981, p. 19.

45. The ABA's House of Delegates, during its midyear meeting February 4–5, 1974, voted 157–122 against shield legislation to protect journalists. The majority agreed that such legislation would create a "privileged class" and that it would be too difficult to clearly and narrowly define those who should be shielded. Cf. such views with the Supreme Court's unanimous decision on July 24, 1974, that President Nixon could not claim executive privilege in refusing to release to a special prosecutor 64 tape recordings that might have relevancy to criminal matters.

46. David Gordon, "The Confidences Newsmen Must Keep," reprinted from *Columbia Journalism Review,* Vol. X, No. 4, November/December 1971, p. 17.

47. Garland v. Torre, 259 F.2d 545 (2d Circuit, 1958); certiorari denied, 358 U.S. 910, 79 S.Ct. 237, 3 L.Ed.2d 231(1958).

48. Ibid., at 548–549.

49. Murphy v. Colorado, not reported; certiorari denied, 365 U.S. 843, 81 S.Ct. 802 (1961).

50. State of Oregon v. Buchanan, 436 P.2d 729, 250 Or. 244 (1968); certiorari denied, 392 U.S. 905 (1968).

51. Application of Caldwell and New York Times for Order Quashing Subpoena, 311 F.Supp. 358 (1970).

52. *Newsweek,* November 30, 1970, p. 87; copyright Newsweek, Inc., 1970, reprinted by permission.

53. Ibid.

54. Caldwell v. U.S., 434 F.2d 1081, 1083 (1970).

55. Branzburg v. Hayes, 461 S.W.2d 345 (1970). This case originally involved Branzburg and Judge Pound of Jefferson County, but he subsequently was replaced by Judge Hayes.

56. In the Matter of Paul Pappas, 266 N.E.2d 297 (1971).

57. Branzburg v. Hayes, 408 U.S. 665, 92 S.Ct. 2646, 33 L.Ed.2d 626, 1 *Med.L.Rptr.* 2617 (1972).

58. Note that the Caldwell, Branzburg, Pappas cases involved investigations by grand juries into possible violations of *criminal* law, unlike the *civil* action suit brought by Mayor Cervantes of St. Louis against *LIFE* Magazine and writer Denny Walsh in which the courts refused to compel Walsh to disclose sources of information.

59. Caldwell v. U.S., op. cit., n. 40, 92 S.Ct. at 2671.

60. Ibid.

61. Ibid.

62. *The Future of "Newsman's Privilege": The Whither and Whether of Disclosure for Newspersons,* a monograph published by the American Bar Association's Section of Criminal Justice (Washington, D.C., 1975), p. 4. Reprinted by permission.

63. Ibid., p.8.
64. Ibid., p. 14.
65. State v. Knops, 183 N.W.2d 93, 49 Wis.2d 647 (1971). Judge Heffernan dissented.
66. Zechariah Chafee, Jr., *Government and Mass Communications,* Vol. II (Chicago: The University of Chicago Press, 1947), pp. 496–97.
67. Rule 37, pertaining to New Jersey's Revised Statutes 2A:84-A21 (supp. 1970), states: "A person waives his right or privilege to refuse to disclose or to prevent another from disclosing a specified matter if he or any other person while the holder thereof has (a) contracted with anyone not to claim the right or privilege or (b) without coercion and with knowledge of his right or privilege made disclosure of any part of the privileged matter or consented to such a disclosure made by anyone."
68. *Editor & Publisher,* February 6, 1982, p. 18.
69. 337 So.2d 951.
70. Clien v. State, 52 So.2d 117.
71. *The QUILL,* December 1976, p. 25.
72. In re Farber, 78 N.J. 259, 394 A.2d 330 (1978), 4 *Med.L.Rptr.* 1360.
73. For citations, see Continental Cablevision v. Storer Broadcasting, 10 *Med.L.Rptr.* 1641 (U.S. District Court, Eastern District of Missouri), May 22, 1984, and Tofani v. Maryland, 9 *Med.L.Rptr.* 2193 (Maryland Court of Appeals, 1983), October 11, 1983.
74. 633 F.2d 346.
75. 9 *Med.L.Rptr.* 1211, March 15, 1983.
76. Wisconsin Green Bay Newspaper v. Circuit Court, 9 *Med.L.Rptr.* 1889, August 19, 1983.
77. U.S. v. Hubbard, 5 *Med.L.Rptr.* 1719 (1979).
78. Winegard v. Judge Oxberger, 158 N.W.2d 847 (1977).
79. Miller v. Transamerica Press, Inc., 621 F.2d 721, 6 *Med.L.Rptr.* 1598 (1980) and Gadsden County Times, Inc. v. Horne, 426 So.2d 1234 (Florida Ist DCA, 1983), 9 *Med.L.Rptr.* 1290.
80. Tofani v. Maryland, op. cit., note 73, at 2197.
81. Storer Communications v. Wayne County Circuit Court, "News Notes," *Media Law Reporter,* February 24, 1987.
82. Ibid.
83. *The NEWS Media & The LAW,* Fall 1986, p. 50.
84. Carey v. Hume, 492 F.2d 631. On May 28, 1974, the Supreme Court denied an application by Hume for a stay of judgment. Justices Brennan, Douglas and Marshall would have granted a stay. A week later the Court dismissed Hume's petition for a writ of certiorari.
85. The Maryland Court of Appeals, in Tofani v. Maryland, 9 *Med.L.Rptr.* 2193, held that the First Amendment does not protect a reporter from having to appear before a grand jury except on a showing that the grand jury is on a fishing expedition or is acting in bad faith. The New Jersey Supreme Court reached the same conclusion in the Farber and Bridge claims to First Amendment protection.
86. Caldero v. Tribune Publishing Co., 2 *Med.L.Rptr.* 1490, March 29, 1977. The court opinion was given by Justice Shephard with a dissenting opinion by Justice Donaldson who noted that *Branzburg* was limited to criminal investigations, not to civil law matters. Donaldson contended that there must be a "compelling interest" which would justify infringement on First Amendment freedoms. Justice Bakes also dissented and, like Donaldson, said there was a limited First Amendment privilege for journalists not to disclose confidential sources.
87. "News Notes," *Media Law Reporter,* September 16, 1980.
88. "News Notes," *Media Law Reporter,* April 6, 1982.
89. "News Notes," *Media Law Reporter,* January 17, 1984.
90. *Editor & Publisher,* October 29, 1988, p. 32.
91. Mitchell v. Marin County Superior Court, 11 *Med.L.Rptr.* 1076, December 18, 1984.
92. "News Notes," *Media Law Reporter,* June 3, 1980.
93. *Editor & Publisher,* March 18, 1978, p. 22.
94. *1981 FOI Committee Report,* p. 17.
95. "Confidential Sources of Information," published by the Reporters Committee for Freedom of the Press as a supplement in *The NEWS Media & The LAW,* Fall 1987, pp. 9–12.

96. The events leading to passage of the state shield law are recounted by the Maryland Court of Appeals in Tofani v. Maryland, 9 *Med.L.Rptr.* 2193, 2194. The court cited an article written by B. Bortz and L. Bortz, " 'Pressing' Out the Wrinkles in Maryland's Shield Law for Journalists," 8 *University of Baltimore Law Review* 461 (1979).

97. Mazella v. Philadelphia Newspapers, Inc., 5 *Med.L.Rptr.* 1983 (Eastern District of New York, 1979), December 11, 1979.

98. *Editor & Publisher,* March 1, 1980, p. 41.

99. *Editor & Publisher,* December 8, 1979, p. 12.

100. *Editor & Publisher,* July 14, 1984, p. 10.

101. Warden v. Hayden, 387 U.S. 294.

102. Zurcher v. Stanford Daily, 355 F.Supp. 124 (N.D. Calif., 1972).

103. Zurcher v. Stanford Daily, 550 F.2d 464 (9th Circuit, 1977).

104. Zurcher v. Stanford Daily, 436 U.S. 547, 98 S.Ct. 1970, 56 L.Ed.2d 552, 3 *Med.L.Rptr.* 2377, June 20, 1978.

105. Ibid., 3 *Med.L.Rptr.* at 2384.

106. As reported in testimony by Jerry W. Friedheim, ANPA general chairman, before the Subcommittee on the Constitution, Senate Judiciary Committee, on July 13, 1978.

107. "States Act to Curb Newsroom Searches," *FoI Digest,* July/August 1979, p. 5.

108. "News Notes," *Media Law Reporter,* August 5, 1980.

109. Ibid.

110. *The NEWS Media & The LAW,* Fall 1988, pp. 4–5.

111. Ibid., at 5.

12

Pornography

HIGHLIGHTS

■ For a long time material was found to be obscene by judging the effect of isolated passages on the most susceptible person. This *Hicklin* test or standard finally gave way as the result of a Supreme Court decision in *Roth v. U.S.* (1957).

■ The *Roth* standard was whether to the average person, applying contemporary community standards, the dominant theme of the material taken as a whole appealed to prurient interest. Later, an additional requirement was added; the material had to be "utterly without redeeming social importance" to be adjudged obscene.

■ But in *Miller v. California* (1973), the Court significantly altered the test of obscenity. It did away with the "utterly without redeeming social importance" requirement. And it also said that material had to be judged by local community, not national, standards.

■ Difficulties of applying *Miller* or other tests or laws in the context of children being exposed to obscene material, or the kind of media involved, are reviewed.

■ The President's Commission on Obscenity and Pornography, appointed by President Johnson, and a later Commission on Pornography, appointed by Attorney General Edwin Meese, reached markedly different conclusions about the effects of pornography and what to do about porno sellers and materials.

■ Indecent materials have some First Amendment protection, but the U.S. Supreme Court upheld the FCC's determination that comedian George Carlin's "seven dirty words" were indecent and could be banned from over-the-air radio and television.

Pornography, like privacy, involves an area of the law still clouded by uncertainties. The reason lies in the difficulty of defining something which may be "obscene" to one person but a work of "art" to another. Justice Stewart capsulized the constitutional dilemma when he pointed out in a 1966 dissenting opinion that the First Amendment protects coarse expression as well as refined, vulgarity as well as elegance. "A book worthless to me," he wrote, "may convey something of value to my neighbor. In a free society to which our Constitution has committed us, it is for each to choose for himself."[1]

Not only are there definitional problems, but other difficulties present themselves in any attempt to control pornography. Can anti-obscenity laws apply equally to adults *and* juveniles? If so, does the fact that an adult wishes to see "pornographic movies," or read "obscene" books, make a difference? Can the law constitutionally distinguish between a person who does not want to be subjected to pornographic literature, such as a patron of the U.S. Postal Service who opens an unmarked envelope which contains "obscene" photographs, and one who requested such photographs? What constitutes commercial exploitation of sex as contrasted with a natural, healthy interest in the subject?

Justice Black, arguing that the "First Amendment forbids any kind . . . of governmental censorship over views as distinguished from conduct," asked "how talk about sex can be placed under . . . censorship . . . without subjecting our society to more dangers than we can anticipate at the moment." It was to avoid such dangers that the First Amendment was adopted, he said, in urging the Court to "recognize that sex at least as much as any other aspect of life is so much a part of society that its discussion should not be made a crime."[2]

At the same-time, Justice Tom Clark demonstrated a growing intolerance of "pornography." He wrote, in a dissenting opinion, of the increasing number of such cases coming before the Supreme Court and of the states' mounting problem of coping with such material.[3] Then, expressing some outrage triggered by frustration, Justice Clark said, "I have 'stomached' past cases for almost 10 years without much outcry. Though I am not known to be a shrinking violet — this book [*Memoirs of a Woman of Pleasure*] is too much even for me."

What Justice Robert Jackson feared would happen in 1948 became a reality. The Supreme Court became the "High Court of Obscenity," representing the last chance to halt or encourage the countless attempts to ban, seize, or otherwise suppress the publication and distribution of books, films, and magazines which local or national censors found offensive. At one time or another, the U.S. Postal Service, state or local review committees, citizens' decency boards, and other organizations, have proscribed such books as Walt Whitman's *Leaves of Grass,* Theodore Dreiser's *An American Tragedy,* John Steinbeck's *The Grapes of Wrath* and *East of Eden,* James Joyce's *Ulysses,* and D.H. Lawrence's *Lady Chatterley's Lover,* to name a few. Films have been banned by government boards. Censors have prohibited the mailing of magazines.

Basically, obscenity is not protected by the First Amendment because it has minimal social value and it is offensive to contemporary moral standards, as the Court said in *Roth v. U.S.,* discussed later.

Early History

Although the advent of the printing press spurred censorship in England, obscenity was not initially within the scope of state prohibition. Rather, censorship by the Star Chamber was aimed primarily at seditious material. The government made no official effort to prohibit dissemination of obscene material. Such material raised moral questions cognizable only in ecclesiastical, not common-law, courts. Not until 1727 was the publication of obscene literature held to constitute an indictable offense.[4]

In the United States, obscenity was the target of both common law and statutory law. By 1792, all 14 states had made blasphemy or profanity, or both, statutory crimes, although they did not specifically outlaw obscenity. Massachusetts made it a crime as early as 1712 for anyone to publish "any filthy, obscene, or profane song, pamphlet, libel or mock sermon." In 1815 the first reported obscenity conviction was obtained under Pennsylvania common law. A similar conviction occurred in Massachusetts in 1821, the same year that Vermont passed the first state law proscribing publication or sale of "lewd and obscene" material. Federal legislation barring importation of such matter first appeared in 1842.

Although obscenity laws were few in number and enforcement lax, according to Justice Brennan, the situation changed significantly after 1870 when federal and state governments became much more active in attempts to suppress obscenity.[5] By the end of the nineteenth century, at least 30 states had some type of general prohibition against dissemination of obscene matter. The federal government had numerous anti-obscenity statutes on the books at the time of the U.S. Supreme Court's landmark decision in *Roth v. U.S.* in 1957.

Hicklin Test. It was the *Roth* decision, discussed later, which finally set aside a century-old legal test of obscenity imported from England—a test that stemmed from *Regina v. Hicklin* (1868).[6] The two-part *Hicklin* standard was whether "the tendency of the matter . . . is to deprave and corrupt those whose minds are open to such immoral influences, and into whose hands a publication of this sort may fall." The result was a determination of obscenity stemming from the effect of "isolated passages" upon the "most susceptible person."

Prior to the *Hicklin* test, a New Yorker, Anthony Comstock, had begun his "war" against obscenity that culminated in passage of the federal Anti-Obscenity Act of 1873. This statute prohibited the mailing of any obscene, lewd, lascivious, or filthy book, pamphlet, picture, paper, letter, writing, print, or other such publication. That statute, now codified as Section 1461 of Title 18 of the United States Code, is still on the books in substantially the same form as when it was originally enacted.

For first offenders the penalty is a $5,000 fine and/or five years in prison. Each subsequent offense can bring a $10,000 fine, or imprisonment for not more than 10 years, or both. There are other federal statutes which prohibit interstate transportation and importation of obscene material. These statutes constitute federal criminal law sanctions against pornography; but for a time there were considerable attempts by the U.S. Post Office in the 1940s to impose administrative sanctions.

Post Office "Censorship"

In 1942 the U.S. Post Office announced rules and policy pertaining to revocation of second-class mailing privileges for publications deemed immoral or not contributing to the public good. During the next 18 months, some 70 publications were denied second-class permits—the second-class postal rate being a tax-subsidized rate authorized by Congress in 1879.

Among the 70 was *Esquire* magazine which lost its second-class permit by order of the postmaster general in 1943. This meant that mailing costs for the magazine would increase about $500,000 annually.[7] *Esquire* brought suit, but lost at the U.S. District Court level. In 1945 the U.S. Court of Appeals for the District of Columbia Circuit reversed, holding that the Post Office Department could not accept periodicals for mailing and then deny them the second-class rate on the ground that they had failed to contribute to the public good.[8] The court rejected the notion that the second-class rate is a privilege. Rather, said the court, the second-class rate is a "highway over which all business must travel" and the "rates charged on this highway must not discriminate between competing businessmen of the same kind."[9]

The government appealed in the name of the postmaster general and the U.S. Supreme Court, in an 8–0 decision in *Hannegan v. Esquire,*[10] affirmed the Circuit Court's judgment. Justice Douglas wrote the Court's opinion and gave the following reasons for rejecting the Post Office's contention that administratively it could deny periodicals a second-class rate on moral or "public good" grounds:

- The Post Office had objected to only a small percentage of *Esquire's* contents, and yet this was the basis for the Post Office's determination that the magazine had a dominantly immoral tone.
- Second-class mail rates need not be open to all types of publications, but restrictions cannot be based on the requirement that applicants must convince the postmaster general that their publications contribute to the public good.[11]

As Professor Patricia Robertus of Bradley University wrote:

The *Esquire* decision marked the end of a short-lived experiment in postal control. It began in April 1942 with the assault on a few borderline girlie magazines and gathered steam. The Post Office became bolder. Initial revocations and denials [of second-class mailing permits] were based on allegations of obscenity; in *Esquire* the charge was simply failure to contribute to the public good.

Justice Douglas . . . noted that to uphold a revocation based on this standard would be to invite similar decisions based on the economic and social views of publications. . . .

Since *Esquire,* the revocation power has been seldom used. . . . In the late 1950s the Department refused to grant its old adversary *Sunshine and Health* a second-class permit, as it had refused since 1933. Among . . . [the reasons] for the denial was the failure of the nudist magazine to contribute to the public good. *Sunshine and Health* appealed . . . and in an unreported decision, the District Court ordered issuance of the permit.[12]

The *Esquire* decision did not mean that the Post Office abandoned its war against smut. During a 12-year period (1957–1969), postal inspectors made more than 100,000 investigations concerning the use of the mails to transmit obscene materials, and federal and state convictions (the latter for the sale of such material) were obtained in nearly 5000 cases.[13] But the power to revoke second-class mailing permits had been curbed. In 1974, the U.S. Supreme Court, in *Hamling v. U.S.,* said the U.S. Postal Service is not authorized to act as censor in granting such mailing permits.[14]

The U.S. Postal Service replaced the Post Office Department under the Postal Reorganization Act of 1970. Instead of a cabinet-level department the Postal Service became an independent entity within the Executive branch of the federal government.

Congress also passed an "anti-pandering" statute in 1968 which allows the Postal Service to order a stop to "pandering advertisements" sent to people who don't want to receive them and the removal of these people's names from the senders' mailing lists. Failure to comply can lead to a Justice Department request for a court order to halt such mailings.

Additionally, forms are available at Postal Service branches to be used by people who do not want to receive sexually explicit material. This form also can be used to ask that the names of these people be removed from the senders' mailing lists.

End of the Hicklin Test. A number of judges began to question the *Hicklin* test, including Judge Learned Hand in 1913 — one of the first to do so.[15] But an especially persuasive opinion came from a U.S. District Court judge, John M. Woolsey, in a 1933 case, *U.S. v. One Book Called "Ulysses."*[16] A U.S. Customs officer had prevented someone from bringing James Joyce's book into the United States. In essence, Judge Woolsey said that any test of obscenity should be based on the dominant effect of the entire book or work, not just isolated passages, on an average person, not on children or abnormal adults (or the most susceptible person). Further, any incidental obscenity should be weighed against the literary or artistic merit of the work being judged.

Woolsey's decision was upheld on appeal.[17] It would be reflected in the language and tone of the U.S. Supreme Court's landmark decision in the combined cases of *Roth v. U.S.* and *Alberts v. State of California* (1957).[18]

Four months prior to the decision in these combined cases, the Supreme Court held in *Butler v. Michigan* that a Michigan law, prohibiting the sale of material that tended to corrupt the morals of minors, was unconstitutional when extended to adults.[19] The law that restricted what adults could read was overly broad, said the Court.

Then came the *Roth* and *Alberts* decisions.

Roth v. U.S., Alberts v. California

In *Roth,* the U.S. Supreme Court upheld the constitutionality of the federal obscenity statute that prohibits the mailing of obscene or otherwise indecent material.[20] In *Alberts* it also upheld the constitutionality of the California law by which Alberts had been convicted. That law did not violate the due process rights of defendants, the Court ruled. The Court split in *Roth* was 6–3, and in *Alberts,* 7–2. In *Roth,* Chief Justice Earl Warren concurred in the result, but not for the reasons given by Justice Brennan, while Justices Harlan, Black, and Douglas dissented. In *Alberts,* Harlan concurred in the Brennan opinion. Black and Douglas dissented.

Briefly, Roth published and sold books, magazines, and photographs in New York. He was convicted by a U.S. District Court jury on four counts of violating the federal obscenity statute. This conviction was affirmed by the U.S. Court of Appeals, and by the Supreme Court.

Alberts conducted a mail order business in Los Angeles. He was convicted by a municipal court judge on a misdemeanor complaint which charged him with lewdly keeping for sale obscene and indecent books and using pandering-type advertisements.[21] He was fined $500, sentenced to 60 days in jail, and placed on probation. The conviction was affirmed by a California Superior Court and by the U.S. Supreme Court.

The significance of *Roth-Alberts* is:

1. The Supreme Court, presented squarely with the issue of whether obscenity is constitutionally protected by the First or Fourteenth Amendment, ruled for the first time that it was not because, as Brennan wrote, it is utterly lacking in "redeeming social importance."
2. The *Hicklin* test was renounced by Brennan, who wrote: "The *Hicklin* test, judging obscenity by the effect of isolated passages upon the most susceptible persons, might well encompass material legitimately treating with sex, and so it must be rejected as unconstitutionally restrictive of the freedom of speech and press."
3. A new standard was enunciated. Henceforth the test for determining if material was obscene would be: "Whether to the average person, applying contemporary community standards, the dominant theme of the material taken as a whole appeals to prurient interest."[22]

Problems of definition are apparent in the standard put forth by Brennan in judging what is or is not obscene.

Warren urged the Court to confine itself to the conduct of the defendants rather than the nature of the materials. Harlan dissented in *Roth* principally on the ground that federal censorship can do far more harm than censorship applied in one or more of the states which, in his view, should have primary responsibility for deciding most obscenity cases. Basically, Harlan believed the states should be permitted considerable leeway in deciding permissible speech and press, or in deciding other legal problems, because they can act as 50 separate social "laboratories" where solutions to common problems can be sought.

Justice Douglas, with Black concurring, dissented principally because thoughts, not actions, were being punished. He noted an earlier California court definition of obscene material, "if it has a substantial tendency to deprave or corrupt its readers by inciting lascivious thoughts or arousing lustful desire,"[23] and then observed:

> By these standards punishment is inflicted for thoughts provoked, not for overt acts nor antisocial conduct. This test cannot be squared with our decisions under the First Amendment. Even the ill-starred *Dennis* case conceded that speech to be punishable must have some relation to action which could be penalized by government.

Jacobellis v. State of Ohio

In *Jacobellis,* which came seven years after *Roth,* six justices in four different opinions reversed the conviction of a Cleveland Heights theater manager who had been fined $2500 for violation of a state statute that prohibited the showing of obscene, lewd, or lascivious films.[24]

In his plurality opinion, Justice Brennan engrafted a corollary onto the *Roth* test; that is, the material must be "utterly without redeeming social importance" to be obscene. He emphasized this by stating categorically that "material dealing with sex in a manner that advocates ideas . . . or that has literary or scientific or artistic value or any other form of social importance, may not be branded as obscenity and denied constitutional protection."

Brennan had used the phrase, "utterly without redeeming social importance," in *Roth,* but he did not include it as a part of the test of obscenity until *Jacobellis.* In *Roth,* obscenity was presumed to be utterly without redeeming social importance, but in *Jacobellis* and afterward, the "utterly without" had to be proved.

In addition to this new requirement, Brennan said that "contemporary community standards" meant national, not local, standards, as he had said in *Roth.* Thus, the film that led to Jacobellis's conviction first had to be found utterly lacking in redeeming social importance as judged by national standards. Only then could a determination be made concerning its appeal to prurient interest and whether it went beyond "normal candor" and became "patently offensive." Since several film critics had praised the movie in question (*Les Amants*), it could not be found obscene when the criterion, "utterly without redeeming social importance," was applied.

Justices Douglas and Black concurred in the reversal for basically the same reasons given in their dissenting opinions in *Roth.* Justice Harlan dissented, principally because he believed the states should take the lead in these cases. Justice Stewart concurred in the reversal and provided his own definition of hard core pornography ("I know it when I see it"). He argued that this should be the only kind punished by criminal law. Chief Justice Warren and Justice Clark dissented, largely because they believed that state courts should play a larger role in interpreting and applying the original *Roth* standard, with the U.S. Supreme Court restricting itself to a review of the record rather than promulgating expanded tests.

Ginzburg, Mishkin and Memoirs Cases

Fourteen opinions "decided" these cases in 1966 as the Court, by a 5–4 decision, affirmed in the *Ginzburg* case one of the heaviest prison sentences handed out in any obscenity case up to that time.

Ginzburg Case. Ralph Ginzburg had been sentenced to five years in prison and fined $28,000 following conviction on 28 counts of violating the federal obscenity statute. According to a majority of the U.S. Supreme Court, the "leer of the sensualist" permeated the advertising used by Ginzburg to promote three publications: *Eros,* a quarterly magazine; *Liaison,* a biweekly newsletter; and a book, *The Housewife's Handbook of Selective Promiscuity.*[25]

Brennan said in his plurality opinion for the Court that as part of the "sordid business of pandering," mailing privileges for *Eros* were sought at Intercourse and Blue Ball, Pennsylvania; but when the post offices at these towns indicated they could not handle the anticipated volume of business, mailing privileges were obtained at Middlesex, New Jersey.

Significantly, the Court did not affirm the conviction on a finding that the publications themselves were obscene—which would have required the tests as announced in *Roth* and *Jacobellis*—but on the basis that Ginzburg, through "pandering" advertisements, had advertised the publications as though they were obscene, thereby leaving himself defenseless. There was no need to apply the *Roth* or *Jacobellis* tests to the content of the publications.

The *Ginzburg* decision, coupled with the Court's 6–3 upholding of the conviction of Edward Mishkin under the New York criminal statute which resulted in a three-year prison sentence and $12,000 fine, sent shock waves through segments of the movie and publishing industries. The "pandering" rule, or the vague "leer of the sensualist" test, was seen by some as a signal from the Court for a crackdown on pornography.

Ginzburg succeeded in obtaining a reduction in sentence to three years, but finally, with all legal moves exhausted, he tore up a copy of the Bill of Rights, and issued a parting statement to newsmen. On February 17, 1972, almost six years after the Supreme Court had affirmed his conviction, he began serving his sentence. Nine months later he was paroled.

Mishkin Case. In the *Mishkin* case,[26] Justice Brennan again delivered the opinion of the Court with Black, Douglas, and Stewart dissenting. A principal argument used by Mishkin and rejected by the Court was that the magazines he published dealt with deviant sexual practices (such as flagellation and lesbianism) and that they therefore did not appeal to the prurient interest of the "average" person. Brennan brusquely swept this argument aside as "being founded on a unrealistic interpretation of the prurient appeal requirement." He said: "Where the material is designed for and primarily disseminated to a clearly deviant sexual group, rather than the public at large, prurient-appeal requirement of the *Roth* test is satisfied if the dominant theme of the material taken as a whole appeals to the prurient interest in sex of the members of that group."

Brennan indicated that the prurient-appeal requirement was adjustable to fit social realities and that it could be applied to the group or groups intended to receive the material in question, rather than to an "average person" in the community.

Memoirs Case. In the *Memoirs* case,[27] the Court by a 6–3 vote reversed a ruling by the Supreme Court for Suffolk County, Massachusetts, that the book, *Memoirs of a Woman of Pleasure,* was obscene. The plurality opinion by Brennan, joined by Chief Justice Warren and Justice Abe Fortas, drew dissent from Justices Clark, Harlan, and White. Black, Douglas, and Stewart agreed that the book was not obscene, but for reasons different from those expressed by Brennan.

Memoirs of a Woman of Pleasure, or *Fanny Hill,* as it also is known, was written by John Cleland around 1749 and was one of the first books to be involved in an obscenity trial in the United States (in Massachusetts in 1821).[28] It again became the target of zealous prosecutors in several states in the 1960s. Although it contained none of the four-letter words which disturb many readers and listeners, it did, as brought out by the prosecutor in Massachusetts, contain descriptions of "20 acts of sexual intercourse, four of them in the presence of others; four acts of lesbianism, two acts of male homosexuality, two acts of flagellation and one of female masturbation."[29]

Brennan's determinative opinion held that the Supreme Judicial Court of Massachusetts, which had affirmed a lower court finding, erred in holding that the book need not be "utterly without redeeming social value" in order to find it obscene. In *Jacobellis,* his opinion had not been a determinative one. A book cannot be proscribed, said Brennan in *Memoirs,* unless it is found to be utterly without such value. He continued:

> This is so even though the book is found to possess the requisite prurient appeal and to be patently offensive.[30] Each of the three federal constitutional criteria is to be applied independently; the social value of the book can neither be weighed against nor canceled by its prurient appeal or patent offensiveness.

As stated by Brennan, the criteria which must be met separately and then coalesce before material can be judged obscene (excluding pandering-type advertisements which obviate the *Roth-Jacobellis* test) were: (a) the dominant theme of the material taken as a whole appeals to prurient interest in sex; (b) the material is patently offensive because it affronts community standards relating to the description or representation of sexual matters; and (c) the material is utterly without redeeming social value.

The latter part of this test is predicated on Professor Meiklejohn's concept of absolute First Amendment protection for "political" speech. Brennan made this clear when he stated in a footnote that "material dealing with sex in a manner that advocates ideas . . . or that has literary or scientific or artistic or any other form of social importance may not be branded as obscenity and denied the constitutional protection."

Justice Black characterized the three-part test of obscenity as "vague and meaningless," and said the "social value" test was more nebulous than the "unknown substance of the Milky Way."[31] Concerning the *Ginzburg* and *Mishkin* cases, Black again urged that a distinction be made between speech and conduct, with the former not subject to government regulation.

Justice Harlan, who had argued against the Court's imposition of standards of obscenity on the states, dissented in *Memoirs* (because the Court was overruling a state determination of obscenity), but joined the majority in upholding the conviction of Mishkin which had occurred in a state court. He dissented in *Ginzburg* on the basis that the federal statute banned only "hard core" pornography and that neither Ginzburg's publications nor his advertising fell within that narrow class. *Memoirs,* he argued, did not fall within the "hard core" definition and therefore could not be barred from the mails, although it could be proscribed by the various states if they so desired.

Concerning the Court's action in the trilogy of cases, Harlan said:

> The central development that emerges from the aftermath of *Roth* . . . is that no stable approach to the obscenity problem has yet been devised by this Court. Two Justices [Black and Douglas] believe that the First and Fourteenth Amendments absolutely protect obscene and nonobscene material alike. Another Justice [Stewart] believes that neither the states nor the federal government may suppress any material save for "hard-core pornography." *Roth* in 1957 stressed prurience and utter lack of redeeming social importance; as *Roth* has been expounded in this case [and in *Ginzburg* and *Mishkin*] . . ., it has undergone significant transformation. The concept of "pandering," emphasized in the separate opinion of the Chief Justice in *Roth,* now emerges as an uncertain gloss or interpretive aid, and the further requisite of "patent offensiveness," has been made explicit as a result of intervening decisions. Given this tangled state of affairs, I feel free to adhere to the principles first set forth in my separate opinion in *Roth.* . . .[32]

Justice White dissented in *Memoirs* principally because he believed that the "social importance" test was relevant "only to determining the predominant prurient interest of the material"; materials should be judged by their predominant theme; and the First Amendment did not prevent a state from treating *Memoirs* as obscene and forbidding its sale.

Justice Clark dissented in *Memoirs* and, like Justice White, urged the Court to return to the original *Roth* standard which did not include the "utterly without" test.

Ginsberg v. State of New York

The conviction of Samuel Ginsberg under a New York state "variable obscenity" statute, which made it unlawful to sell obscene material to minors under age 17 although the same material could legally be sold to those 17 and older, was affirmed by a 6–3 decision of the Court in 1968. Justice Brennan again delivered the Court's opinion with dissent by Black, Douglas and Fortas.[33]

In 1965 a 16-year-old boy bought two "girlie" magazines at Ginsberg's store in Bellmore, Long Island, after being sent there by his mother who wanted to test the New York law. Ginsberg was convicted and placed on probation for one year.

The Court held that to sustain state power in such cases as *Ginsberg* required only that the Court be able to say that it was rational for the legislature to find that exposure to material condemned by the statute is harmful to minors. The Court believed the legislative action was rational.

In concurring, Justice Stewart wrote:

> I think a state may permissibly determine that, at least in some precisely delineated areas, a child—like someone in a captive audience [a reference to a rationale used for imposing more regulation on radio-television than on other media[34]]—is not possessed of that full capacity for individual choice which is the presupposition of First Amendment guarantees. It is only upon such a premise, I should suppose, that a state may deprive children of other rights—the right to marry, for example, or the right to vote—deprivations that would be constitutionally intolerable for adults.[35]

Justice Douglas, joined by Black, dissented for reasons given in earlier dissenting opinions. And Justice Fortas, in questioning why a magazine is obscene when sold to a 16-year-old, but not obscene when sold to a 17-year-old, termed Ginsberg's conviction "a serious invasion of freedom."

In 1969 New York was among 36 states which had laws shielding children from the sale or distribution of material deemed pornographic.[36] Shortly after the *Ginsberg* decision, 14 states either passed or amended their laws to reflect New York's "variable obscenity" feature, although some states placed the protective age limit at 18.

The *Ginsberg* decision left a number of questions unanswered by the Court—questions that remain. Among them: (1) If a state's action in denying juveniles access to material deemed obscene infringes upon an adult's right to obtain such material, is that action unconstitutional? (2) If the infringement is incidental, rather than substantial, can the state's restrictions pass constitutional scrutiny? (3) If the state only proscribes the *sale* of obscene material to juveniles (as in the New York case), can juveniles be barred from *access* to such materials? Lower courts are not in agreement about how to answer the third question.[37]

That juveniles do not enjoy the same constitutional rights as adults is demonstrated by several Supreme Court decisions in addition to *Ginsberg* (see Chapter 3). In the following case, the issue was not obscene speech, but sexually suggestive speech.

By a 7–2 vote, the Supreme Court upheld a school board's suspension of a student who gave a sexually suggestive speech while nominating a fellow student for a school elective office. The Court, in *Bethel School District No. 403 v. Fraser* (1986), emphasized the school's role in inculcating fundamental societal values necessary to maintaining a democratic political system.[38]

The student's speech contained the following comment:

> I know a man who is firm—he's firm in his pants, he's firm in his shirt, his character is firm—but most . . . of all, his belief in you, the students of Bethel, is firm. Jeff Kuhlman is a man who takes his point and pounds it in. . . . He doesn't attack things in spurts—he drives hard, pushing and pushing until finally—he succeeds.

The school suspended the student for three days and removed his name from a list of graduation speakers.

The student successfully sued for damages in U.S. District Court, and the Court of Appeals affirmed, relying heavily on *Tinker v. Des Moines Independent Community School District* (1969). But the Chief Justice, writing for the Court, said that there was a marked distinction between the political message involved in *Tinker* and the sexual content of the speech in the case before the Court. Schools must teach tolerance of divergent political and religious views, said Burger, but they must also teach "consideration of the sensibilities of others." The freedom to advocate unpopular views, he continued, must be balanced against this school interest. The "pervasive sexual innuendo" in the speech was "plainly offensive" to both students and teachers, said Burger, adding that the school's response was justified by society's interest in limiting sexually explicit and vulgar or offensive speech aimed at children.[39]

Justice Marshall and Stevens dissented.

Marshall would have required the school to show that the speech was disruptive. Stevens dissented because he did not believe the student had been given fair notice that his speech was punishable.

Justice Brennan, in a concurring opinion, said that school officials, in the circumstances of this case, could conclude that the speech exceeded permissible limits. He cautioned, however, that the speech might have been protected had it been given under different circumstances.

Stanley v. Georgia

In 1969 the Court ruled for the first time that mere possession of obscene material in the home was not a crime.[40] A Georgia law used to convict Stanley for possession of obscene matter (a "stag" movie) was declared unconstitutional. Justice Marshall gave the Court's opinion and distinguished this case from *Roth* on the ground that *Stanley* involved "mere private possession" contrasted with regulation of commercial distribution of obscene material. As Marshall said, among the people's fundamental rights is the freedom, except in very limited circumstances, from "unwanted" governmental intrusions into one's privacy. Such intrusion resulted when law enforcement officers, while searching Stanley's home for evidence of book-making, found the movie.

LANDMARK DECISION IN MILLER v. CALIFORNIA

The *Roth-Memoirs* test of obscenity underwent a major change in a series of five cases decided simultaneously by the U.S. Supreme Court in 1973. The cases were *Miller v. California,*[41] *Paris Adult Theater I v. Slaton,*[42] *U.S. v. 12 200-ft. Reels of Super 8mm. Film,*[43] *U.S. v. Orito*[44] and *Kaplan v. California.*[45] Separate opinions were written in each of these cases by Chief Justice Burger and, for the first time since Roth, a majority of the Court agreed on substantial changes in the standard for testing obscenity. The effect of the 5–4 decisions is to make it easier—but not easy—for the states to make illegal specific kinds of obscenity.

Dissent was registered in each case by Brennan, Douglas, Marshall, and Stewart because, generally, they feared the decisions would trigger repressive actions against constitutionally protected speech and press.

As a result of the decisions, at least two major changes resulted in the law of obscenity:

1. The Court did away with that part of the Roth standard which had been engrafted by Brennan in his *Memoirs* plurality opinion—the "utterly without redeeming social value" corollary.
2. The Court changed the requirement that allegedly obscene material had to be judged on the basis of a national, rather than a local community, standard. Instead, the Court reinstated the local community standard which, it said, can be determined by local juries.

The Court, however, warned that laws dealing with obscenity must be specific in what is outlawed, otherwise they will be unconstitutional. To provide guidance in what became an exceedingly difficult undertaking, the Chief Justice singled out the laws in Oregon and Hawaii for favorable comment. He also gave some "plain" examples of what could be declared obscene in accordance with the newly announced obscenity test. Henceforth a state could outlaw "patently offensive" representations or descriptions of ultimate sexual acts (actual or simulated, normal or perverted), masturbation, excretory functions, and lewd exhibits of the genitals. There undoubtedly are other kinds of representations or descriptions of sexual acts that can be outlawed which were not mentioned by the Chief Justice.

The test of obscenity that emerges from these decisions marks the first time since *Roth* (1957) that a majority of the Court could agree on the wording. In *Miller,* five Court members agreed that the test of obscenity was (a) whether the average person, applying contemporary community standards, would find that the work, taken as a whole, appeals to prurient interest; (b) whether the work depicts or describes, in a patently offensive way, sexual conduct specifically defined by the applicable state law; and (c) whether the work, taken as a whole, lacks serious literary, artistic, political or scientific value. If the material appeals to prurient interest and is patently offensive, then it must have "serious literary, artistic, political, or scientific value to merit First Amendment protection," Chief Justice Burger said.[46] In *Memoirs,* the material had to be utterly without redeeming social value.

Justice Brennan abandoned his position as stated in *Roth* and subsequent opinions and joined Black and Douglas in the belief that any formulation of what constitutes obscenity will have a suppressive effect on protected expression. He said in his dissenting opinion in *Paris Adult Theater I* that all the states, except Oregon, would have to enact new laws to meet the newly stated criteria of what constitutes obscenity. Burger disagreed with this statement although he declined to speculate on the number of states that would have to redraft their laws to meet the concrete guidelines necessary in any attempt to deal with commercialized "hard core" pornography.

In addition to the changes made in the test of obscenity, the Court declared that the government can (a) act to prevent importation of obscene material even though such material is intended for private, not commercial, use; (b) halt interstate or intrastate transportation of such material no matter what use the purveyor intends to make of it; and (c) act against such material no matter what precautions are taken by the commercial purveyor of such material to prevent juveniles from being exposed to the material. Apparently the only place where obscene material is safe from the reach of the law is when it reaches the privacy of one's home and is for private use only.

Perhaps to guard against overzealous prosecutors, Burger said in *Miller*:

> Under the holdings announced today, no one will be subject to prosecution for the sale or exposure of obscene materials unless these materials depict or describe patently offensive "hard core" sexual conduct specifically defined by the regulating state law, as written or construed. We are satisfied that the specific prerequisites will provide fair notice to a dealer in such material that his public and commercial activities may bring prosecution.[47]

Justice Brennan, joined by Justices Marshall and Stewart, believed that the new formulation would require independent review of every obscenity case by the appellate courts, including the Supreme Court. He felt it would throw upon the highest court the awesome task of making criminal and constitutional law in each case decided by the Court just as Justice Harlan had warned 15 years earlier in *Roth*. Further, Brennan did not agree that the Chief Justice's restriction of the obscenity test to material depicting or describing "conduct" would provide the necessary safeguard for protected speech. As Brennan said, "If the application of the 'physical conduct' test to pictorial material is fraught with difficulty, its application to textual material carries the potential for extraordinary abuse. Surely we have passed the point where the mere written description of sexual conduct is deprived of First Amendment protection."[48]

The Chief Justice attempted to make the following distinction between protected and unprotected speech: "We have directed our holdings, not at thoughts or speech, but at depiction and description of specifically defined sexual conduct that States may regulate within limits designed to prevent infringement of First Amendment rights.[49]

The problem of differentiation is apparent. The Chief Justice said that the decision is not directed at thought or speech; however, the decision permits punishment of "depiction" and "description" of sexual conduct. Words are the means of "describing" sexual conduct. The Chief Justice refers, in a footnote to *Miller*, to the speech-conduct dichotomy, as follows:

> Although we are not presented here with the problem of regulating lewd public conduct itself, the States have greater power to regulate nonverbal, physical conduct than to suppress depictions or descriptions of the same behavior. In *United States v. O'Brien*, . . . a case not dealing with obscenity, the Court held a State regulation of conduct which itself embodied both speech and nonspeech elements to be "sufficiently justified if . . . it furthered an important or substantial government interest;

if the government interest is unrelated to the suppression of free expression; and if
the incidental restriction on alleged First Amendment freedoms is no greater than is
essential to the furtherance of that interest."[50]

Just how any governmental effort to suppress conduct—that is, public exhibition of obscene behavior which presumably would be analogous to O'Brien
burning his draft card (the nonspeech element which was not protected by the
First Amendment)—could be extended to include something that is entirely
speech (pictorial or textual representation of sexual conduct) without there being
suppression of free expression remains to be seen.

This dilemma drew the following response from the Chief Justice:

> The dissenting Justices sound the alarm of repression. But, in our view, to equate the
> free and robust exchange of ideas and political debate with commercial exploitation
> of obscene material demeans the grand conception of the First Amendment and its
> high purposes in the historic struggle for freedom. . . .
> The First Amendment protects works which, taken as a whole, have serious
> literary, artistic, political or scientific value, regardless of whether the government or
> a majority of the people approve of the ideas these works represent. "The protection
> given speech and press was fashioned to assure unfettered interchange of *ideas* for the
> bringing about of political and social changes desired by the people." *Roth v. U.S.*
> . . . But the public portrayal of hard core sexual conduct for its own sake, and for
> the ensuing commercial gain, is a different matter.[51]

Justice Douglas interpreted the First Amendment much differently. He
agreed that "conduct" can be regulated, but not representations—such as words,
drawings, and photographs—of that conduct. Furthermore, he raised the issue
of ex post facto law, which is specifically forbidden by the Constitution. "Ex post
facto" law declares an act to be a crime even though it was not a crime at the time
it was committed. In discussing the new test of obscenity in *Miller,* as well as
those since *Roth,* Douglas said that these are standards written into the Constitution by Supreme Court decisions. "Yet how" he asked, "under these vague tests
can we sustain convictions for the sale of an article prior to the time when some
court has declared it to be obscene?"[52]

Indeed, how? Miller's conviction on a charge of mailing unsolicited sexually
explicit material in violation of a California statute was vacated by the Supreme
Court decision. The case was remanded for further consideration not inconsistent with the majority decision. Thus, a standard not known to Miller at the time
he mailed the material could be used to sustain his conviction. But a majority of
the Court would respond that he was convicted under a tougher standard, *Roth*
and its corollaries, and therefore derives no benefit from *Miller.*

The problem of vagueness persists and resulted in a major change of position on the part of the chief architect of *Roth.* As Brennan wrote:

> . . . [A]fter fifteen years of experimentation and debate I am reluctantly forced
> to the conclusion that none of the available formulas, including the one announced
> today, can reduce the vagueness to a tolerable level while at the same time striking an

acceptable balance between the protections of the First and Fourteenth Amendments, on the one hand, and on the other the asserted state interest in regulating the dissemination of certain sexually oriented materials. Any effort to draw a constitutionally acceptable boundary on state power must resort to such indefinite concepts as "prurient interest, "patent offensiveness," "serious literary value," and the like. The meaning of these concepts necessarily varies with the experience, outlook, and even idiosyncracies of the person defining them.[53]

But Brennan did not go as far as Douglas. To do so, he argued, would be to strip the "states of power to an extent that cannot be justified by the commands of the Constitution, at least so long as there is available an alternative approach that strikes a better balance between the guarantee of free expression and the states' legitimate interest."[54] Since the concept of obscenity "cannot be defined with sufficient specificity and clarity to provide fair notice to those who create and distribute sexually oriented material," Brennan said he would limit state restrictions to material that might fall into the hands of juveniles or unconsenting adults.[55]

Citing such precedents as *Stanley, Ginsberg,* and *Jacobellis,* the Chief Justice noted in *Miller* that sexually explicit material had been thrust upon unwilling recipients. In harmony with Brennan, he wrote:

This Court has recognized that the States have a legitimate interest in prohibiting dissemination or exhibition of obscene material, when the mode of dissemination carries with it a significant danger of offending the sensibilities of unwilling recipients or of exposure to juveniles.

Thus, Justice Douglas stood alone in contending that the First Amendment tolerates no sanctions against material classified as "obscene," even when such material falls into the hands of unconsenting adults or is made available to juveniles.

The effects of the *Miller* decision soon were felt. States were faced with the problem of interpreting *Miller* in terms of existing statutes. In many instances, those laws were not specific enough in detailing what kind of "conduct" could be punished. A few months after the *Miller* decision, 10 states passed new obscenity laws and 18 others were considering similar action.

Part of *Miller* Test Redefined

The Supreme Court returned to the three-part test of obscenity laid down in *Miller* when, in *Pope v. Illinois* (1987), a majority held that the third part of the three-prong test ("lacks serious literary, artistic, political, or scientific value") is "whether a reasonable person would find such value in the material, taken as a whole."[56] Prior to this ruling the third prong had to be measured against a community standards test. Now it's a "reasonable person" requirement. However, the community standards requirement still applies to the first two prongs.

As part of its decision, the Court vacated guilty verdicts against two employees of a Rockford, Illinois, adult bookstore who had been accused of violating the state's obscenity statute and remanded the case to the Illinois Court of Appeals so that it could consider the harmless-error issue (whether the instructions to the jury about the third prong and community standards was harmless error). The vote was 5–4 on the decision to remand, with Justice Blackmun dissenting to that part of the Court's action. He did not believe that a "harmless-error" analysis was appropriate. But he agreed with Justice White, as did three other Court members, that the "reasonable person" standard should be used in considering the third prong of the *Miller* test.[57]

Justices Brennan, Marshall, and Stevens dissented, in part because they do not believe that the sale of magazines to consenting adults can be criminalized.

In one of his first votes in a case involving the First Amendment since joining the Court, Justice Scalia wrote a concurring opinion in which he said, in part:

> Just as there is no use arguing about taste, there is no use litigating about it. For the law courts to decide "What is Beauty" is a novelty even by today's standards.

He urged the Court to re-examine *Miller.*

The Oregon Supreme Court did more than re-examine *Miller.* As a result of *Oregon v. Henry* (1987), *Miller* was jettisoned in that state.[58]

The court, in striking down a state obscenity statute patterned after the federal standard for determining obscenity as established in *Miller,* said that materials that would be considered obscene under *Miller's* three-prong test could not be considered obscene in Oregon because of the state's constitutional guarantee of freedom of expression.

In an opinion by Justice Robert E. Jones, the court said that "obscenity" should never have been excluded from First Amendment protection, adding that the trouble with the U.S. Supreme Court's approach is that it allows government to decide what is socially acceptable expression. That's exactly what the First Amendment was intended to prevent, said the court, adding: "Characterizing expression as 'obscenity' does not deprive it of protection under the Oregon Constitution."[59]

The court reviewed the early American history regarding obscenity and noted that only Massachusetts, among the 13 colonies, had any statutory law on the subject, and then only in the context of pornography being a sacrilegious work. Not until *Roth v. U.S.* (1957) did the U.S. Supreme Court hold that "obscenity" was without First Amendment protection.

The Oregon court did not rule out regulation of this form of expression in the interests of unwilling viewers, captive audiences, minors, and beleaguered neighbors. However, no such issue was presented by the case under review. The court also did not rule out regulation directed against the conduct of producers or participants in the production of sexually explicit material, nor reasonable time, place, and manner regulations of the nuisance aspect of such materials.[60]

Other Supreme Court Decisions
Between the time *Miller* was announced in 1973 and the Court's redefinition of the third prong of the *Miller* test in 1987, a number of other obscenity cases

reached the Court. In two of them, the question of local community, or national, standards by which to test obscenity was raised.

Hamling v. U.S. (1974). The Supreme Court, by a 5–4 split, affirmed the conviction of William L. Hamling and others for conspiring to mail, and then mailing, an obscene advertisement with sexually explicit photographs which were used to promote the sale of a book, *The Illustrated Presidential Report of the Commission on Obscenity and Pornography.*[61] In giving the Court's opinion (with the same lineup of justices as in *Miller*), Justice Rehnquist said about the matter of ex post facto that *Miller* permits the imposition of a lesser burden of proof on the prosecution than did *Memoirs* (by eliminating the "utterly without redeeming social value" test and the national community standard requirement). Therefore, petitioners derived no benefit from the *Miller* formulation. However, Rehnquist pointed out that any appeals in process at the time of *Miller* would receive any benefit flowing from the decisions in *Miller* and the companion cases.

Interestingly, the Court upheld the use of local community standards for interpreting a federal statute even though appellants had argued that a national community standard should be used. Thus, jurors were to determine if material was obscene in federal and state obscenity prosecutions based on local community standards concerning the patent offensiveness of, and prurient interest in, the material.

Concerning the claim of "vagueness" by petitioners Hamling and others, Rehnquist said that the word "obscene," as used in 18 U.S. Code Section 1461, is not merely a descriptive term, but a "legal term of art" which does not change with each indictment. Rather, said Rehnquist:

> It is a term sufficiently definite in legal meaning to give a defendant notice of the charge against him. . . . Since the various component parts of the constitutional definition of obscenity need not be alleged in the indictment in order to establish its sufficiency, the indictment in this case was sufficient to adequately inform petitioners of the charges against them.

Justices Brennan, Douglas, Marshall, and Stewart dissented.

Justice Brennan, joined by Marshall and Stewart, said that the U.S statute, as construed by the Court, "aims at total *suppression* of distribution by mail of sexually oriented materials." Therefore, in his view, it is unconstitutionally broad. He also raised the interesting problem posed by the reversion to local community standards; that is, national distributors of sexually oriented material "will be forced to cope with the community standards of every hamlet into which their goods may wander."[62]

The Court upheld the constitutionality of the anti-obscenity statute when "applied according to the proper standards for judging obscenity." The Court majority, as in *Ginzburg* which involved a violation of the same U.S. law, permitted imprisonment of Hamling for one year on conspiracy charges and three years on the mailing counts in connection with sending out 50,000 one-page illustrated advertisements (also as in *Ginzburg*). The book itself was not judged to be obscene. In addition, Hamling was fined $32,000. One other defendant,

Earl Kemp, drew a prison term totalling three years and several others were fined.

Jenkins v. Georgia

On the same day that the U.S. Supreme Court affirmed the conviction in *Hamling,* a unanimous Court reversed the conviction of Billy Jenkins on a charge of distributing obscene material by showing a film, *Carnal Knowledge,* at a theater in Albany, Georgia.[63]

The state law under which Jenkins was convicted defined obscenity in the way set forth by the Supreme Court's plurality opinion in *Memoirs,* according to Justice Rehnquist who delivered the Court's opinion in *Jenkins.* The law read:

> Material is obscene if considered as a whole applying community standards, its predominant appeal is to prurient interest, that is, a shameful or morbid interest in nudity, sex or excretion, and utterly without redeeming social value and if, in addition, it goes substantially beyond customary limits of candor in describing or representing such matters.[64]

But the film, said Rehnquist, is not obscene under the constitutional standards announced in *Miller,* which provided that no one would be subject to prosecution for the sale or exposure of obscene materials unless they depict or describe patently offensive "hard core" sexual conduct. The "plain examples" cited in *Miller* were recited by Rehnquist who, along with his colleagues, viewed the film and declared that it was not patently offensive. "There is no exhibition whatever of actors' genitals, lewd or otherwise . . .," Rehnquist said. "There are occasional scenes of nudity, but nudity is not enough to make material legally obscene under the *Miller* standards."

The problem of national versus community standards also drew further comment in this case. Rehnquist said for himself and four of his brethren who joined in his opinion, that juries could either be instructed to apply a specific community's standards or the standards of a community which remained unspecified. Further, juries do not have "unbridled discretion" in determining what is patently offensive.

Brennan, Douglas, Marshall, and Stewart concurred in the results, but not for the reasons given by Rehnquist. Brennan, joined by Marshall and Stewart, said the obscenity formulations in *Miller* will require independent appellate review on a case-by-case basis. Then, reiterating a warning given in his dissenting opinion in *Paris Theater I,* Brennan said that it is clear that as long as the *Miller* test remains in effect, "one cannot say with certainty that material is obscene until at least five members of this Court, applying inevitably obscure standards, have pronounced it so."[65]

Splawn v. California. Concerning "pandering obscenity," which proved the downfall of Ralph Ginzburg in a 1966 U.S. Supreme Court decision concerning the way the defendant had advertised three of his publications, the nation's highest tribunal spoke out on the subject again in a 1977 ruling in *Splawn v.*

California.[66] Justice Rehnquist said for a 5–4 majority of the Court that evidence of pandering to prurient interests in the creation, promotion, or dissemination of material is relevant in determining whether the material is obscene. The Court upheld the conviction of a bookseller accused of selling obscene films in violation of California's "pandering law" (Penal Code § 311.2).

Justices Brennan, Stewart, Marshall, and Stevens dissented.

President's Commission on Obscenity

The 18-member President's Commission on Obscenity and Pornography spent $2 million trying to determine the nature and size of the pornography problem, in studying pornography's effects on the public, particularly minors, and in making various recommendations for controlling pornography without infringing upon constitutional guarantees. It estimated that $200 million was being spent annually for X-rated movies, and for pornographic magazines, books, and other forms of erotica. Twelve of the 18 members made these major recommendations:

- Repeal all laws pertaining to the showing or sale of pornography to adults.
- Enact legislation to protect children from pornographic pictures or graphic representations, but not written porn, because the latter is too difficult to define even when intended for children.
- Enact additional laws to protect unwilling persons from the intrusion of certain types of public displays or from pandering-type advertisements sent through the mails.

Not only did Nixon heap scorn upon the report by the President Johnson-appointed Commission, calling it "morally bankrupt," but the U.S. Supreme Court majority virtually ignored the report in its *Miller* decision.

Seeking a "new look" at the findings reported in 1970, President Reagan announced in 1984 the creation of a national commission to study the effects of pornography on society. In announcing that the commission would be set up under Attorney General William French Smith, the President said:

> We think the evidence that has come out since . . . [the 1970 Commission report], plus the tendency of pornography to become increasingly more extreme, shows that it is time to take a new look at this conclusion [that pornography has no significant effect on behavior], and it's time to stop pretending that extreme pornography is a victimless crime.
>
> We consider pornography to be a public problem and we feel it is an issue that demands a second look.

The President said he had seen reports suggesting a causal link between child molestations and pornography and between pornography and sexual violence toward women.

Attorney General's Commission on Pornography

The Attorney General's Commission on Pornography issued a 1960-page report in 1986 that predictably concluded that there is a causal relationship between sexually violent materials and antisocial acts of sexual violence and, for some, unlawful acts of sexual violence.

With two of the 11 Commission members dissenting, the report included this statement:

> The available evidence strongly supports the hypothesis that substantial exposure to sexually violent materials . . . bears a causal relationship to anti-social acts of sexual violence and for some . . . possibly to unlawful acts of sexual violence. . . . The evidence also strongly supports the conclusion that substantial exposure to violent sexually explicit material leads to greater acceptance of the "rape myth" in its broader sense—that women enjoy being physically hurt in sexual context and that as a result a man who forces himself on a woman sexually is in fact merely acceding to the "real" wishes of the woman. . . .

The Commission, formed by Attorney General Edwin Meese a year before issuing its report, made 92 recommendations many of which, if put into effect, would lead to a law enforcement crackdown on many types of pornographic material and tougher enforcement of anti-obscenity laws. But by a 6–5 vote, the Commission decided not to recommend regulation of sexually explicit movies shown on cable television, although it did call for a ban on the showing of obscene materials. It also called for a ban on "dial-a-porn" telephone messages.

The report prompted considerable criticism. The legislative director of the American Civil Liberties Union, Barry Lynn, said that many of the 92 recommendations, if enacted or acted upon, would be unconstitutional. "What they want," he said, "is censorship . . . roving thought police."

About two years after the Commission's report and just before his execution, serial killer Ted Bundy made a videotaped statement in which he linked pornography to incitement to murder—the murders he committed. His statement added fuel to the continuing controversy over the effects of the $8 billion dollar a year smut industry. An ACLU lawyer characterized Bundy's statement as "the final scam of a great con artist." But those opposed to smut saw in Bundy's words a last testament to the evils of pornography.

Child Protection. At the same time that he announced the creation of the national commission, President Reagan also signed into law the Child Protection Act. This Act strengthens the fight of prosecutors against the exploitation of children by increasing the penalties for using children in pornographic materials. The maximum fine for the first offense was increased from $10,000 to $100,000. For subsequent convictions, the maximum fine went from $15,000 to $200,000.[67]

The law also eliminates the need to prove that still or motion pictures related to child pornography are obscene. Earlier, the Supreme Court in *New York v. Ferber* (1982) had removed child pornography from First Amendment protection where state statutes are sufficiently precise so as not to impose curbs on constitutionally protected material.[68]

At the time of the *Ferber* decision, the Court noted that the federal government and 47 states had passed laws related to child pornography and that at least half of them did not require that the material be legally obscene.

In giving the Court's opinion, Justice White made these points:

1. A state's interest in safeguarding the physical and psychological well-being of a minor is "compelling." The Court cited *Globe Newspapers v. Superior Court* and *Ginsberg v. New York,* discussed earlier, among cases where children are given special protection even if that protection infringes on First Amendment values.
2. The *Miller* standard is not a satisfactory solution to the child pornography problem. As White noted, it is irrelevant to a child who has been abused whether the material has literary, artistic, political, or social value.
3. Child pornography as a category of material outside the protection of the First Amendment is not incompatible with the Court's earlier decisions, such as its ruling that "fighting words" are not protected by the First Amendment.

Justice Brennan, joined by Justice Marshall, concurred in the decision, but wondered if there could not be some depictions of children that have substantial literary, artistic, or social value and therefore should be protected by the First Amendment. Justice Stevens, in a separate concurring opinion, believed that whether a specific act of communication is or is not protected by the First Amendment requires consideration of both its content and its context.

Violence Against Women. President Reagan said he believes there is a causal link between pornography and violent sexual attacks on women.

The Indianapolis City Council approved an ordinance April 23, 1984, that defined violent pornography as a form of sexual discrimination. Violators were subject to civil lawsuits. In addition, the city's Equal Opportunity Advisory Board was given the authority to order a halt to allegedly discriminatory actions, such as selling "offensive" books or magazines.

The Indiana Civil Liberties Union opposed the ordinance and challenged its constitutionality. Later that year the U.S. District Court for the Southern District of Indiana declared the ordinance unconstitutional—a ruling affirmed by the Seventh Circuit U.S. Court of Appeals.[69]

When a similar ordinance was passed in 1984 by a narrow vote of the Minneapolis City Council, the mayor vetoed it. However, other ordinances were passed which prohibit the distribution of obscene materials that portray violence against women or the display of sexually explicit material where they can be seen by minors.

Use of Nuisance Laws

Various government units have resorted to nuisance laws in their attempts to regulate pornography. For example, the California Supreme Court, in a 1976 decision involving five cases, cited the U.S. Supreme Court's decision in *Paris Adult Theatre I v. Slaton,* discussed earlier, as authority for the view that states have a legitimate interest in regulating the use of obscene material in local commerce and in all places of public accommodation, including regulation of the exhibition of obscene material to consenting adults.[70] The California court said that a wide variety of cases, both before and after *Paris Adult Theatre I,* have confirmed that exhibitions of obscenity constituted nuisances which may be abated by the courts. Courts in Arizona, Florida, Georgia, Michigan, New Mexico, Ohio, and Tennessee have done so.[71]

Concerning constitutional protection for such exhibitions, the California court said, "It is entirely permissible from a constitutional standpoint to enjoin further exhibition of specific magazines or films which have been fully adjudged to be obscene following a full adversary hearing." However, the court emphasized that abatement proceedings must be directed against specific books, magazines, or movies, rather than against a store, a theater, or a distributor, in order to avoid pervasive, and therefore unconstitutional, prior restraint. Such reasoning was the basis for the court's refusal in these cases to grant a permanent injunction against movie theaters and bookstores adjudged in violation of public nuisance laws, although the court upheld the laws (Penal Code § 370–71 and Civil Code §§ 2479 and 3480). In so doing, the court noted that similar outcomes have been recorded in Alabama, Florida, Georgia, and Louisiana.[72]

Texas Statute Struck Down. The U.S. Supreme Court, in a 5–4 per curiam decision in *Vance v. Universal Amusement* (1980), ruled that a Texas public nuisance statute that authorized the use of injunctions against the future exhibition of unnamed "obscene" motion pictures violated the First Amendment.[73]

The Court affirmed the decision of the U.S. Court of Appeals for the Fifth Circuit.

The statute, said the Court, authorized a prior restraint of indefinite duration of motion pictures that had not been finally adjudicated to be obscene. More narrowly drawn procedures are necessary for the abatement of an ordinary nuisance, said the Court.

Chief Justice Burger and Justices Powell, White and Rehnquist dissented.

Shortly after *Vance,* the Court granted certiorari in *Chateau X v. Andrews* and vacated the judgment of the North Carolina Supreme Court that had upheld a state public nuisance statute.[74] The Court remanded the case for "further consideration in light of" *Vance.*

New York Statute Upheld

The U.S. Supreme Court, in *Arcara v. Cloud Books, Inc.* (1986) decided by a 6–3 vote that the First Amendment does not prohibit New York's closure of an "adult" bookstore under a public health nuisance statute.[75] The statute permits the closure of a business premise for one year when prostitution or lewdness has taken place on the premises. By its action, the Court reversed the New York Court of Appeals.

The case involved a bookstore in which sexually explicit movies and books were available. In his opinion for the Court, Chief Justice Burger noted that a deputy sheriff had "personally observed instances of masturbation, fondling, fellatio by patrons on the premises of the stores, all within the observation of the proprietor."

The New York Court of Appeals had applied the four-part test adopted in *U.S. v. O'Brien* (see Chapter 3) and had decided that the statute failed the test because the statute's closure provision was broader than necessary to achieve the government's purpose of thwarting prostitution. But Burger said that the *O'Brien* test should not have been used because it had no relevance to the statute that was aimed at "nonexpressive activity."

Justice Blackmun, joined by Brennan and Marshall, dissented, saying that while the state has an interest in forbidding public sexual acts, the way to eliminate such acts is by arresting the patron committing them. He cautioned that under the majority's analysis, a state can effectively ban books so long as prohibited conduct (the "nonexpressive activity") occurred on the premises.

In her concurrence, Justice O'Connor cautioned that First Amendment concerns would be implicated if the statute was used "as a pretext for closing down a bookstore because it sold indecent books or because of the perceived secondary effects of having a purveyor of such books in the neighborhood."

Use of Zoning Laws

In 1976 the U.S. Supreme Court, in a 5–4 decision in *Young v. American Mini Theatres, Inc.,* upheld a Detroit ordinance enacted to protect neighborhoods from the spread of "adult" theaters.[76] Rather than confine sex and smut peddlers to only one area, as in Boston's infamous "Combat Zone," the Detroit plan used zoning laws to disperse such establishments. It prohibited adult theaters and bookstores from being within one thousand feet of each other or within one thousand feet of any bar, poolroom, or similar establishment. A three-block strip previously had been the area for much of the city's X-rated entertainment.

In the opinion written by Justice Stevens, the majority held that the First Amendment poses no bar to such zoning schemes. Justices Brennan, Stewart, Marshall, and Blackmun dissented, holding an opposite view concerning the First Amendment's tolerance of such plans.

Officials in many other cities expressed interest in the Detroit plan following the Supreme Court's action.

In 1986, the Court again upheld the constitutionality of a zoning ordinance that prohibited adult movie theaters from locating within a thousand feet of any residential zone, church, park, or school. The effect of the Renton, Washington, ordinance was to concentrate such theaters rather than, as in Detroit, dispersing them. Both methods are constitutional, said Justice Rehnquist for the Court, with only Brennan, joined by Marshall, dissenting.

In giving the Court's opinion in *City of Renton v. Playtime Theatres,* Rehnquist pointed out that "content-neutral" time, place, and manner regulations are acceptable if they serve a substantial government interest and do not unreasonably limit alternative avenues of communication.[77]

". . . [A]s the District Court concluded," wrote Rehnquist, "the Renton ordinance is aimed not at the *content* of the films shown at 'adult motion picture theaters,' but rather at the *secondary effects* of such theaters on the surrounding community." In short, he continued, "the Renton ordinance is completely consistent with our definition of 'content-neutral' speech regulations as those that 'are *justified* without reference to the content of the regulated speech.' " *Virginia Pharmacy Board v. Virginia Citizens Consumer Council, Inc.,* 425 U.S. 748, 771 (1976) (emphasis added by Rehnquist); *Community for Creative Non-Violence,* 468 U.S. 288 (1984); *Heffron v. International Society for Krishna Consciousness, Inc.,* 452 U.S. 640 (1981).[78]

Brennan viewed the purpose of the ordinance differently, saying: "Renton's zoning ordinance selectively imposes limitations on the location of a movie theater based exclusively on the content of the films shown there."[79] He quoted from *Consolidated Edison Co. v. Public Service Commission of New York* (see Chapter 13), to wit: " '[A] constitutionally permissible time, place or manner restriction may not be based upon either the content or subject matter of speech.' "

Rather than speculate as to Renton's motives for adopting the ordinace, said Brennan, the ordinance, like any other content-based restriction on speech, is constitutional only if the city can show that it is precisely drawn to serve a compelling governmental interest. "Only this strict approach," said Brennan, "can insure that cities will not use their zoning power as a pretext for suppressing constitutionally protecting expression."

Search Warrants

Police face uncertainties when they seize allegedly obscene material either with or without a search warrant.

The U.S. Supreme Court unanimously ruled in 1979 that seizure of more than 800 magazines, films, and other objects from an adult bookstore, under an open-ended search warrant, violated the First, Fourth, and Fourteenth Amendments.

In his opinion for the Court in *Lo-Ji Sales v. New York,* Chief Justice Burger noted that the warrant, which authorized the seizure of two films judicially determined to be obscene, was left open to permit a six-hour search of the bookstore and seizure of other objects.[80] The presence of the town justice during the search did not ensure that no items would be seized without probable cause, said Burger, who called the warrant and the entry into the store "reminiscent of the general warrant or writ of assistance" prohibited by the Fourth Amendment.

In a case involving the warrantless screening of films, the Court, in 1980, reversed the judgment of the U.S. Court of Appeals for the Fifth Circuit which had upheld the conviction of two defendants on federal obscenity charges. However, the Supreme Court members could not agree on a rationale in *Walter v. U.S.*[81]

Briefly, what happened is this: a box of films was mistakenly delivered to the wrong firm where employees opened the box, discovered "suggestive drawings" and "explicit descriptions" of the films, and turned them over to the FBI. The FBI screened the films for the purpose of establishing their character.

Justice Stevens, joined by Stewart, accepted the propriety of the FBI's warrantless receipt of the films, but said that the screening was a separate search requiring a warrant. The "unauthorized" exhibition invaded the defendants' constitutionally protected privacy interests. Chief Justice Burger and Justices Blackmun, Powell, and Rehnquist dissented.

Motion Picture Censorship

Censorship has not been confined to books or magazines, but has been used to prevent the showing of motion pictures or to demand that certain acts or scenes in them not be shown. As early as 1915 the Supreme Court declared that the showing of motion pictures was a business unlike that of the Fourth Estate and therefore did not warrant First Amendment protection. As a consequence, motion pictures were heavily censored, either by Hollywood or by city and/or state censorship boards. Not until 1952 did the Court decide that motion pictures were a significant medium for the communication of political and social ideas and, as such, warranted First Amendment protection. This case, *Burstyn v. Wilson,* involved a movie, *The Miracle,* produced by Robert Rossellini. The New York Education Department had issued a license to allow the film to be shown even though its critics had contended it was sacrilegious. However, the department's governing body ordered the license withdrawn and an action was filed in New York courts. The state court upheld the ban, but the Supreme Court, with Justice Tom Clark giving the opinion, unanimously declared the statute unconstitutional.[82] The fact that movies were made for profit, said Clark, did not mean that they forfeited First and Fourteenth Amendment protection. However, this did not mean that obscenity statutes were inapplicable to motion pictures, as Clark pointed out. As a consequence, censorship boards continued to operate, although not with the zeal as in pre-*Burstyn v. Wilson* days.

Freedman v. Maryland. This important 1965 Supreme Court case came about because the operator of a Baltimore theater refused to submit a motion picture to the State Board of Censors before publicly showing it, as required under state law.[83] Freedman was convicted in the Criminal Court of Baltimore; the state's highest court affirmed, but the Supreme Court reversed. In his opinion for the Court, Justice Brennan said the statute's procedural safeguards did not adequately protect against "undue inhibition of protected speech. . . ." Brennan cited three reasons why this was so: (1) if the censor disapproved of a film, the exhibitor had to assume the burden of instituting judicial proceedings; (2) once the board had acted against a film, exhibition of it was prohibited pending judicial review; and (3) the statute provided no assurance of prompt judicial determination of obscenity.

The state's highest court had relied heavily on *Times Film Corp. v. Chicago*[84] in upholding the statute and affirming the conviction, but Brennan said the *only* question decided in *Times Film Corp.* was whether a prior restraint was necessarily unconstitutional "under all circumstances." The Court's answer was "no," but Brennan reiterated that any system of prior restraint, including that imposed on motion pictures, comes to the Court bearing a heavy presumption against its constitutional validity. The requirements of a constitutionally valid prior restraint then were spelled out.

The decision did not preclude a system of censorship. Prior submission, said Brennan, is consistent with the Court's recognition that films differ from other forms of expression, but they could not be subjected to standards drastically different from other media.

Douglas, joined by Black, wrote a concurring opinion — concurring in the results but emphasizing that motion pictures are entitled to the same degree and kind of First Amendment protection as other forms of expression. He urged an end to all forms and types of censorship.

The *Freedman* decision, and others in the prior-restraint area, ultimately led to the demise of the Maryland Board of Censors in 1981.

In the place of municipal and state censor boards is the industry's film rating system designed to protect minors against sex or sex acts that are too explicit. The system, effective in 1968, designated those films with an "X" rating to which persons under age 17 are not admitted.

Censorship of Stage Productions

In 1975 the U.S. Supreme Court ruled for the first time on the issue of stage production censorship.[85] Without deciding whether or not the rock musical *Hair* was obscene, the Court, in a 6–3 decision, reversed lower federal courts which had permitted directors of the Chattanooga, Tennessee, municipal theater board to bar the use of a city-leased theater to Southeastern Promotions, Ltd., which was presenting the road company version of *Hair.* The U.S. District Court, after a three-day hearing, had agreed with a jury verdict that *Hair* was obscene. It concluded that group nudity and simulated sex acts were neither speech nor symbolic speech, but rather conduct, and therefore were not entitled to First Amendment protection. The lower court accordingly denied the promoters' bid for an injunction to compel the board to allow the use of the theater for *Hair.*

Justice Blackmun gave the Supreme Court's opinion and made the following points:

■ The board's action was indistinguishable in its censoring effect from official actions consistently identified as prior restraint. The restraints took a variety of forms, with officials exercising control over different kinds of public places under the authority of particular statutes which had one thing in common: they gave public officials the power to deny the use of a forum in advance of actual expression. The Court has condemned such systems when they were not bounded by precise and clear standards.

■ Prior restraints are not unconstitutional per se, said Blackmun, citing

Times Film Corp. v. Chicago in saying, "We have rejected the contention that the First Amendment's protection 'includes complete and absolute freedom to exhibit, at least once, any and every kind of motion picture . . . even if this film contained the basest type of pornography, or incitement to riot, or forceful overthrow of orderly government. . . .' "[86] However, Blackmun cited such precedents as *Bantam Books,* the Pentagon Papers case, *Organization for a Better Austin,* and *Near* in saying that any system of prior restraint bears a heavy presumption against its constitutional validity. He continued:

We held in *Freedman,* and we reaffirm here, that a system of prior restraint runs afoul of the First Amendment if it lacks certain safeguards: First, the burden of instituting judicial proceedings, and of proving the material is unprotected, must rest on the censor. Second, any restraint prior to judicial review can be imposed only for a specified brief period and only for the purpose of preserving the status quo. Third, a prompt judicial determination must be assured.[87]

In the case at hand, Blackmun said effective judicial review was not obtained until more than five months after use of the theater was denied, and it was the promoters, not the board, who had the burden of obtaining such review. These procedural shortcomings formed the basis for the Court's decision.

In holding as it did, the Court made clear that theater, like motion pictures, was not to be subjected to First Amendment standards drastically different from other media of communication. In citing the Court's decision in 1952 which accorded First Amendment protection to movies (*Burstyn, Inc. v. Wilson*), Blackmun said for the Court:

Each medium of expression . . . must be assessed for First Amendment purposes by standards suited to it, for each may present its own problems. . . . By its nature, theater usually is the acting out — or singing out — of the written word, and frequently mixes speech with live action or conduct. But that is no reason to hold theater subject to drastically different standards.[88]

Justice Douglas agreed with the results but argued that any form of censorship is impermissible no matter what procedural safeguards exist.

Justice White, joined by Chief Justice Burger, dissented because (a) the city's licensing system was not without standards; and (b) the repeated simulated acts of intercourse and the nudity were such that the city officials were not compelled to permit production in a municipal facility.

Justice Rehnquist also dissented, arguing that a community-owned theater is not the same as a city park or city street; that the city, no less than the owner of private property, has the power to preserve the property for the use for which it was lawfully dedicated. "I do not believe fidelity to the First Amendment requires the exaggerated and rigid procedural safeguards which the Court insists upon in this case," he said.

Censorship of Broadcasting

Different media present different First Amendment problems and different regulatory schemes. Broadcasting does not enjoy First Amendment parity with the print media because of its pervasiveness, its unique entry into the privacy of the home, the scarcity of available frequencies such that not everyone can have a license to broadcast, and its accessibility to children. These were points made by the U.S. Supreme Court in *Red Lion Broadcasting Co. v. FCC* (1969) and *FCC v. Pacifica Foundation* (1978) (see Chapter 14).[89]

Because the airwaves are owned by the people, and for other reasons, broadcasting is regulated by the federal government through an independent regulatory agency, the Federal Communications Commission. Its powers (see Chapters 14 and 15), as spelled out in the Federal Communications Act of 1934, as amended, include the authority to license broadcasters and to renew those licenses after stipulated periods of time. It also includes the power to take licenses away, or to fine licensees for failure to adhere to FCC regulations or to abide by the law.

But Section 326 of the 1934 Act specifically prohibits the FCC from exercising "the power of censorship" over radio or television. Further, "no regulation or condition shall be promulgated or fixed by the Commission which shall interfere with the right of free speech by means of radio and television communication."

Section 326 notwithstanding, the FCC imposes a considerable variety of restraints on programming, as one law journal article points out:

> Despite the First Amendment and statutory prohibition of censorship, both the Federal Communications Act and actions taken by the Commission pursuant to its broad range of regulatory power have affected not only the form of broadcasting, but its content as well. Thus, covert sponsorship of broadcast activities—"payola"—is expressly forbidden by statute, as is the airing of rigged quiz shows. Similarly, the Commission has acted to impose sanctions against the broadcasting of obscenity, profanity, defamation, fraudulent contests, illegal lotteries, harmful medical advice, and gambling information.[90]

One of the regulatory areas in which the FCC and the First Amendment have come face to face is obscenity and indecency. The result has been considerable uncertainty on the part of the Commission and the regulated stations.

Obscenity Prohibited

WGLD-FM Case. In 1973 the FCC notified station WGLD-FM of Oak Park, Illinois, that it was liable for a $2000 fine for allegedly violating the criminal obscenity statute (18 U.S.C. 1464) which states that "whoever utters any obscene, indecent, or profane language by means of radio [or television] communication shall be fined not more than $10,000 or imprisoned not more than two years, or both." The fine resulted from a discussion on a sex talk show, "Femme Forum"—one of the so-called topless radio talk shows which proliferated for a time prior to the Commission's crackdown on WGLD-FM.[91] The Commission hoped that imposition of the fine would result in a test case by the station. However, owners of WGLD-FM decided to pay the fine rather than take on the financial burden of challenging the FCC. Earlier, the Commission also had issued a Notice of Apparent Liability to WUHY-FM in Philadelphia, proposing to fine that station for the broadcasting of allegedly obscene and/or indecent language. WUHY-FM likewise elected to pay the fine rather than do battle with the Commission.

In *WGLD*, however, two groups—the Illinois Citizens Committee for Broadcasting and the Illinois Division of the American Civil Liberties Union—filed as representatives of the public an application for remission of the forfeiture and a petition for reconsideration of the decision. Ultimately the case reached the U.S. Court of Appeals (District of Columbia Circuit). A three-judge panel, in an opinion written by Judge Harold Leventhal, upheld the Commission against the claim by the petitioners that they were being deprived of listening alternatives in violation of the First Amendment.[92] In affirming the Commission's action, the panel concluded that

> where a radio call-in show during daytime hours broadcast explicit discussions of ultimate sexual acts in a titillating context, the Commission does not unconstitutionally infringe upon the public's right to listening alternatives when it determines that the broadcast is obscene.[93]

Profanity Forbidden. Concerning profanity, which also is forbidden by Section 1464 of the U.S. Code, the intention of the speaker has been the governing factor. In cases involving language commonly regarded as profane ("hell," "damn," "God damn it," etc.), the test has been whether the utterances were "words importing an imprecation of divine vengeance or implying divine condemnation, so used as to constitute a public nuisance."[94] Complaints of such language, unaccompanied by evidence of the intention of the user, do not normally furnish a basis for Commission action.[95]

The FCC, in noting the definition of obscenity given by the U.S. Supreme Court in *Miller v. California,* discussed previously, pointed out that the Court had never ruled on the meaning of "indecent" or "obscene" as used in Section 1464. It had never made specific reference to the broadcasting of questionable material, in contrast to rulings handed down on obscenity in the print medium or in motion pictures. The FCC was of the opinion that the use of certain language in on-the-spot news coverage might be permissible even when that same language, used gratuitously in a different situation, might be in violation of Section 1464.[96]

FCC Ruling on "Indecency" Upheld

Pacifica Foundation Case. In *Pacifica Foundation, Station WBAI,* the Commission in 1975 issued a declaratory ruling which defined the meaning of "indecent" and distinguished "indecent" from "obscene" material.[97] The ruling came in response to a complaint involving seven words used in an album by comedian George Carlin and played on station WBAI in New York (which is licensed to Pacifica Foundation). The Commission defined, as "indecent," language that describes, in terms patently offensive, as measured by contemporary community standards for the broadcast medium, sexual, or excretory activities and organs, at times of the day when there is a reasonable risk that children may be in the audience. The broadcast of the "seven words you can't say on radio" had drawn a complaint from a man who was driving his car with the radio turned on and whose young son was with him. Just before broadcasting the program on the use of language in American society, the station warned listeners that there might be language offensive to some. However, the Commission found that the seven four-letter words contained in the Carlin monologue were indecent within the stated definition. It then prohibited the seven words from being broadcast.

That order violated Section 326 of the Communications Act, Judge Edward A. Tamm said in 1977 in a 2–1 split opinion by a three-judge panel of the District of Columbia Circuit court.[98]

In the hopes of avoiding the charge that its order was overbroad, the Commission had not prohibited the broadcast of indecent language altogether, but sought to channel it to times when the fewest number of listeners probably would be offended (after 10 P.M.).

But Judge Tamm said that "despite the Commission's professed intentions, the direct effect of its *Order* is to inhibit the free and robust exchange of ideas on a wide range of issues and subjects by means of radio and television communications." Tamm also said,

> In promulgating the *Order* the Commission has ignored both the statute which forbids it to censor radio communications and its own previous decisions and orders which leave the question of programming content to the discretion of the licensee.
>
> The Commission claims that its *Order* does not censor indecent language but rather channels it to certain times of the day. In fact the *Order* is censorship.[99]

Judge Leventhal dissented, in part because protection of children "marks a special enclave in the law of freedoms of publication." Leventhal cited Justice Brennan's dissent in *Paris Adult Theater I* in which Brennan said he favored variable obscenity laws as a means of protecting children from pornography. Leventhal also believed that the FCC had attempted to define "indecent" in terms of the same underlying considerations as those of the Supreme Court when it wrestled with the definition of obscenity in *Miller*. He voiced support of such an effort in the context of protecting children.

The Supreme Court, in a 5–4 decision, reversed the lower court in 1978, holding that the FCC was justified in taking action against the station for the broadcast of the "filthy words" monologue. Justice Stevens, in his opinion for the Court, wrote that the words concededly were not obscene, but that the FCC nonetheless could find them to be patently offensive and "indecent," and therefore prohibited by 18 U.S.C. Section 1464, which bars the broadcast of "any obscene, indecent, or profane language."[100]

As for the 1934 Act's prohibition of censorship of program content (Section 326), the Court said the Commission is barred from editing in advance a proposed broadcast, but that Section 326 has never been construed to deny the agency the power to review the content of completed broadcasts in the performance of its regulatory duties.

The Court did not strip away First Amendment protection for indecent speech. It said there is some constitutional protection for this kind of speech. What the Court emphasized was that content and context are critical elements of any First Amendment analysis. Thus, the content of the monologue was found to be "vulgar," "offensive," and "shocking."[101] The context in which the speech occurred also supported regulation, said the Court, in noting the pervasiveness of broadcasting, its ability to invade the privacy of the home, and the technological scarcity of the available frequencies.

The *Pacifica* decision is to be narrowly construed, said Stevens. The reason is that many variables exist concerning broadcasting, such as the time of day when the messages are transmitted, the content of the program in which the language is used, children's accessibility to the program, and whether the transmission is by radio, television, or closed-circuit cable. As Stevens put it in his concluding sentence: "We simply hold that when the Commission finds that a pig has entered the parlor, the exercise of its regulatory power does not depend on proof that the pig is obscene."

Stewart, joined by Brennan, White, and Marshall, dissented. He argued that 18 U.S.C. 1464 should "be properly read as meaning no more than obscene," and since the monologue concededly was not obscene, the FCC lacked authority to ban it.

In a separate dissent, Brennan, joined by Marshall, sharply criticized the majority for approving censorship of communication solely because of the words contained therein.

Twelve years after the FCC targeted Pacifica Foundation's station WBAI, another Pacifica station—KPFK-FM in Los Angeles—stirred the wrath of the Commission which asked the Justice Department to consider a criminal prosecution of the station on a charge of violating the statutory ban on obscene broadcasts.[102] It also issued written warnings to KPFK-FM and three other stations either because they had broadcast songs with sexually explicit lyrics or because they engaged in "shock radio"—explicit talk about sex reminiscent of "topless radio" which had drawn FCC fire some years earlier. But the Justice Department decided not to prosecute the Pacifica station, saying that it would be difficult to prove criminal intent.

Seven months later—on November 24, 1987—the FCC, by a 4–0 vote, imposed a 6 A.M. to 12 P.M. ban on the broadcast of indecent material—a time period when children were likely to be in the audience. Radio and TV stations could broadcast indecent material from 12 P.M. to 6 A.M. without risking government action.

However, an FCC spokesperson cautioned that the Commission's action did not mean that the seven "dirty words" could be safely broadcast during the "safe period." The Commission itself did not make clear its intentions regarding the broadcast of these and other "dirty" words during the 12 P.M. to 6 A.M. period. Even if it had tried, its efforts would have been academic because Congress, irritated by complaints about "shock radio" and explicit sex talk on television, attached a rider to an appropriations bill prohibiting the broadcast of indecent material at any time. The President signed the measure into law in October 1988.[103] Its constitutionality is expected to be challenged on the basis that indecent material is protected by the Constitution. Obscene material is not. The Commission's approach had been to impose "reasonable" time, place, and manner restrictions on indecency — not to eliminate it entirely. After the Commission followed the congressional mandate by imposing a ban on sexually explicit material, one of the commissioners, Patricia Dennis, expressed the belief that the ban was unconstitutional.

Dial-a-Porn Telephone. In 1984, the FCC adopted a regulation that required so-called "dial-a-porn" telephone services to restrict tape-recorded messages to between 9 P.M. and 8 A.M. or accept only credit card payments. In this way, the Commission reasoned, parents would most likely be in a position to supervise their children's activities.

The American Civil Liberties Union had argued that the only permissible option under the First Amendment was for parents to place locks on their telephones, but the Commission rejected this and several other possible approaches. A test case followed and the Second Circuit U.S. Court of Appeals ruled in 1984 that the regulation violated the First Amendment.

Then, in 1988, Congress banned obscene and indecent "dial-a-porn" messages, and President Reagan signed the measure into law. The ban applied only to interstate and District of Columbia calls and it was scheduled to go into effect July 1, 1988, but Sable Communications of California, Inc., challenged its constitutionality. A U.S. District Court in Los Angeles upheld that part of the law banning "obscene" telephone calls, but ruled that "indecent" messages can't be banned. The decision was appealed and in 1989 the Supreme Court unanimously ruled that the ban on "indecent" messages was unconstitutional. However, the Court upheld the ban on "obscene" messages in affirming the lower court's ruling.

"Indecency" and Cable TV. Cable television is different from over-the-air television in a number of ways, and these differences led the U.S. District Court in Utah to declare a Roy City ordinance, based on a state law, unconstitutional because it inhibited the cablecasting of protected as well as unprotected speech.[104] The ordinance had sought to regulate the transmission of "indecent" material.

A year earlier the Utah legislature had passed another cable indecency act, making it a public nuisance for cable TV to show indecent material and providing for fines up to $1000 for first offenders and $10,000 for repeat offenders.

The statute had defined indecent material as "the visual or verbal depiction or description of human sexual or excretory organs or functions, . . . exposure of genitals, pubic area, buttocks, or the showing of any portion of the female breast below the top of the nipple." The Utah attorney general's office had banned the showing of such material except from midnight to 7 A.M. daily.

A. U.S. District Court in 1985 declared the law unconstitutional.

A Tenth Circuit panel, in *Jones v. Wilkinson,* agreed, saying that the First Amendment prevents government from interfering with cable operators' programming decisions unless the material aired is obscene.[105]

The appellate court's decision was affirmed in a one-sentence ruling by the U.S. Supreme Court in 1987, with only Chief Justice Rehnquist and Justice O'Connor voting to hear arguments in the case.

Ten states had joined Utah in urging the Court to permit regulation of indecent material on cable TV: Arizona, Kansas, Mississippi, Missouri, New Hampshire, New Mexico, Pennsylvania, South Carolina, Washington, and West Virginia.

Similarly, when the City of Miami passed an ordinance that prohibited any distribution of "obscene or indecent" material on cable television, a U.S. District Court found the ordinance overbroad and violative of due process.[106]

The ordinance had been enacted in 1983 and provided that no person, by means of a cable television, could knowingly distribute by wire or cable any obscene or indecent material. The three-prong test in *Miller* was used to define whether material was obscene. Indecent material was defined as a representation or description of a human or excretory organ or function which the average person, applying contemporary community standards, would find to be patently offensive.[107] As the court pointed out, obscene material is not protected by the First Amendment but indecent material is accorded some First Amendment protection. The court declared that the ordinance sweeps within its bounds "indecent" materials without regard for whether such materials may be deserving of such protection. The City of Miami had cited *Pacifica* as the leading case for the regulation of "indecent" speech, particularly the FCC's finding that the Carlin's monologue was "patently offensive" — indecent — and subject to regulation; and the Supreme Court's ruling in the case. But in the Miami case, the District Court noted the Supreme Court's admonition that its decision in *Pacifica* was a narrow one because consideration had to be given to a host of variables, including the "differences between radio, television and perhaps closed-circuit transmission."[108] The U.S. District Court, as in the Roy City case, then noted the differences between over-the-air and cable broadcasting and concluded that *Pacifica* is not controlling; *Miller* is. And *Miller* limits regulation to "obscene" speech. Therefore, reasoned the court, the ordinance's attempt to regulate indecent material exceeded the strict limits of regulation set forth in *Miller*, and such an attempt is unconstitutional.

The due process ground for overturning the ordinance was based on the argument that the city manager was given the power to initiate complaints against licensees, preside at hearings on the complaints, and make determinations on the issues involved — actions which do not comport with the fundamental notion of fairness implicit in due process, said the court.

The Eleventh Circuit U.S. Court of Appeals affirmed the lower court's decision in 1985.

NAB Action

On the self-regulatory front, the Television Board of the National Association of Broadcasters voted 10–4 in 1977 to strengthen the TV Code in connection with both obscenity and violence. Concerning the former, the code was changed from discouraging material which "by law" is considered obscene, profane, and indecent to that which is "generally perceived" to be such.

Ultimately the NAB's guidelines became the target of a court test that led to a U.S. District Court judge saying that the guidelines were tantamount to censorship.[109] After an appeal had been taken to the U.S. Court of Appeals (Ninth Circuit), and then to the U.S. Supreme Court, the entire matter became moot because of developments in another case. The U.S. Department of Justice filed an antitrust action against the NAB because of advertising restrictions in the TV Code and a U.S. District Court judge in Washington, D.C., agreed that the effect of TV Code limitations on the length and number of TV commercials violated antitrust laws. Before additional antitrust action could be taken against other provisions in the code, the NAB announced in 1982 that it was terminating both the Radio and TV Codes.

SUMMARY

Pornography and obscenity have been particularly difficult areas for the courts and legislators. Under the two-part *Hicklin* test, which was used in the United States until the 1950s, the effect of isolated passages on the most susceptible person was the basis for judging whether material was obscene. A change did not fully occur until the Supreme Court's decision in *Roth v. U.S.* (1957). The new standard was whether to the average person, applying contemporary community standards, the dominant theme of the material taken as a whole appealed to prurient interest. Later, an additional requirement was engrafted onto the standard; namely, that the material had to be "utterly without redeeming social importance." Also, material had to be judged by national community standards.

Plurality opinions marked most of the cases decided by the Court from *Roth* in 1957 until *Miller v. California* (1973) — the same period when an avalanche of pornography descended on society.

Prior to *Miller,* these important cases occurred. If a person sold something as though it were obscene, then that person could be convicted for "pandering" obscenity (*Ginzburg v. U.S.* (1966)). It was immaterial whether the content was in fact obscene. In *Ginsberg v. State of New York* (1968), the Court upheld New York's "variable obscenity" statute; that is, a state could forbid the sale of allegedly obscene material to minors even though that same material could be legally sold to adults. And in *Stanley v. Georgia* (1969), the Court held that mere private possession of obscene material, as contrasted with commercial sale or distribution of such material, could not be punished.

A majority of justices finally agreed on a new test of obscenity in the landmark *Miller v. California* (1973) case. The three-pronged test is:

1. Whether the average person, applying contemporary community standards, would find that the work taken as a whole appeals to prurient interest.

2. Whether the work depicts or describes in a patently offensive way, sexual conduct specifically defined by the applicable state law.
3. And whether the work — if it appeals to prurient interest and is patently offensive — lacks serious literary, artistic, political or scientific value.

Further the Court did away with the "utterly without redeeming social value" requirement and said material had to be judged by local, not national, community standards.

In 1987, in *Pope v. Illinois,* the Court held that the third part of the *Miller* test (lacks serious literary, artistic, political, or scientific value) is to be judged by a "reasonable person" finding the specified kind of value in the material "taken as a whole," not by local community standards. However, those standards remain a part of the first two prongs of the *Miller* test.

Three years prior to *Miller,* the President's Commission on Obscenity and Pornography issued a report in which a majority of Commission members urged repeal of all laws that prevent adults from obtaining sexually explicit material. Unhappy with this and other recommendations and conclusions, President Reagan announced in 1984 the creation of another commission to look anew for any causal links. This Commission concluded that there was a causal relationship between sexually violent materials and antisocial acts of sexual violence and, in some instances, unlawful acts of sexual violence.

The use of New York's public health nuisance law to close an adult bookstore was upheld by the U.S. Supreme Court which also has looked favorably on zoning laws in Detroit and Renton, Washington, as a means of controlling the location of adult bookstores, theaters, etc.

The relationship between the First Amendment and censorship attempts against motion pictures, stage productions and television also were reviewed. In *Burstyn v. Wilson* (1952), the Supreme Court included motion pictures within the ambit of the First Amendment for the first time. Later, in *Freedman v. Maryland* (1965), the Court said that a prior restraint of motion pictures faces the same presumption of unconstitutionality as prior restraints of the press. However, the Court noted that the protection accorded the film medium is not as complete as, for example, the print medium's. The *Freedman* Court did not preclude a state requirement that motion pictures must be submitted to a reviewing board before being shown publicly. But procedural safeguards had to be observed. And the burden of instituting judicial proceedings and proving the material obscene fell upon would-be censors. Such procedural requirements virtually wiped out state- or city-mandated censorship requirements for films or stage productions.

As for radio and television, different regulatory measures may constitutionally exist for this medium because of differences between it and other media. This was the essence of the Supreme Court's decision in *Pacifica Foundation* (1978). However, the Court pointed out in that case that just because speech is "indecent" does not mean it lacks First Amendment protection. Content and context have to be considered in any First Amendment analysis.

Using the "context" part of the analysis, courts generally have found that attempts to regulate indecency on cable television fail to meet the safeguards required by the First Amendment for speech in general.

However, in 1988, Congress attached a rider to an appropriations bill banning indecent broadcasts on over-the-air radio and TV stations—a ban signed into law by President Reagan. Whether this ban survives a court test remains to be seen.

And attempts at self-regulation in the broadcast industry, specifically the National Association of Broadcasters' Radio and Television Codes, have not succeeded, ultimately because of antitrust laws.

QUESTIONS IN REVIEW

1. What was the *Hicklin* test of obscenity?
2. What was the *Roth* standard?
3. What is a "variable obscenity" statute?
4. What standard was enunciated in *Miller* (1973), and what did the Supreme Court majority specifically reject or require?
5. True or False: In the case involving the stage production *Hair,* the U.S. Supreme Court in 1975 said that a stage production could be subjected to drastically different First Amendment standards than other forms of expression.
6. True or false. Before Ralph Ginzburg could be found guilty of violating a U.S. anti-obscenity statute, his publications first had to be found obscene.
7. True or false. Indecent radio or TV broadcasts are not protected by the First Amendment. Neither are obscene broadcasts.
8. True or false. The U.S. Supreme Court upheld the FCC's finding that George Carlin's "seven dirty words" were indecent.

ANSWERS

1. The effect of isolated passages on the most susceptible person.
2. Whether to the average person, applying contemporary community standards, the dominant theme of the material taken as a whole appeals to prurient interest.
3. This kind of statute makes it illegal to sell, or make available, obscene material to persons under a certain age. Such statutes are intended to protect juveniles.
4. Basically the Court retained the *Roth* standard, as modified by subsequent cases, but threw out two requirements that had to be met in order to find material obscene; that is, the Court rejected the concept that material had to be "utterly without redeeming social value" (the "social value" test), and that national standards had to be used rather than local community standards. The majority also insisted that state laws must be specific in what is being proscribed. Thus, the law must "spell out" the types of sexual acts/conduct which can be declared unlawful when depicted or described.
5. False.
6. False. Because he advertised his publications as though they were obscene, he left himself defenseless against an obscenity charge.
7. False. True.
8. True. It did so in *FCC v. Pacifica Foundation.*

ENDNOTES

1. Ginzburg v. U.S., 383 U.S. 463, 86 S.Ct. 942, 16 L.Ed.2d 31.
2. Ibid., 383 U.S. at 481–82, 86 S.Ct. at 953, 16 L.Ed.2d at 44–45.
3. Dissenting opinion in A Book Named "John Cleland's Memoirs of a Woman of Pleasure," v. Attorney General of the Commonwealth of Massachusetts, 383 U.S. 413, 441, 86 S.Ct. 975, 989, 16 L.Ed.2d 1, 18 (1966).
4. Ibid., Justice Douglas' dissenting opinion in *Memoirs,* 383 U.S. at 428–30, 86 S.Ct. at 982–83, 16 L.Ed.2d at 11–12.
5. Dissenting opinion in Paris Adult Theater I v. Slaton, 93 S.Ct. 2628, 2658 (1973).
6. L.R.3 Q.B. 360.
7. A paper, "Obscenity in the Mails: Controls on Second-Class Privileges 1942–43," written by Professor Patricia Robertus of Bradley University and presented at the 1975 sessions of the Association for Education in Journalism's Law Division at Ottawa, Canada, p. 29.
8. Ibid., p. 33.
9. Esquire v. Walker, 151 F.2d 49, 51–52.
10. Hannegan v. Esquire, 327 U.S. 146 (1946). Justice Jackson did not participate in the hearing or decision.
11. Robertus, "Obscenity in the Mails," p. 35.
12. Ibid., pp. 36–37.
13. Hearings before Government Activities Subcommittee of Committee on Government Operations, House of Representatives, July 8, 1969, entitled "Use of the Postal Service for the Unsolicited Advertisement of Hard Core Pornographic or Otherwise Obscene Material," p. 4.
14. Hamling v. U.S., 418 U.S. 87, 126, 94 S.Ct. 2887, 2912, 41 L.Ed.2d 590, 625.
15. U.S. v. Kennerly, 209 F. 119 (New York District Court, 1913).
16. U.S. v. One Book Called "Ulysses," 5 F. Supp. 182 (New York District Court, 1933).
17. U.S. v. One Book Called "Ulysses," 72 F.2d 705 (2d Circuit, 1934).
18. Samuel Roth v. U.S. and David S. Alberts v. State of California, 354 U.S. 476, 77 S.Ct. 1304, 1 L.Ed.2d 1498 (1957).
19. Butler v. Michigan, 352 U.S. 380, 77 S.Ct. 524, 1 L.Ed.2d 412 (1957).
20. Anti-Obscenity Act of March 3, 1873.
21. In 1957, the Calilornia Penal Code (§ 311) provided, in part, that a person is guilty of a misdemeanor if he willfully and lewdly "writes, composes, stereotypes, prints, publishes, sells, distributes, keeps for sale, or exhibits any obscene writing, paper or book" or advertises such material.
22. Roth v. U.S., 354 U.S. at 489, 77 S.Ct. at 1311, 1 L.Ed.2d at 1509.
23. People v. Wepplo, 78 Calif. App. 2d Supp. 959, 961, 178 P.2d 853, 855.
24. Jacobellis v. State of Ohio, 378 U.S. 184, 84 S.Ct. 1676, 12 L.Ed.2d 793 (1964).
25. Ginzburg v. U.S., op. cit., note 1.
26. Mishkin v. State of New York, 383 U.S. 502, 86 S.Ct. 958, 16 L.Ed.2d 56.
27. "Memoirs of a Woman . . .," 383 U.S. 413, 86 S.Ct. 975, 16 L.Ed.2d 1.
28. Commonwealth v. Peter Holmes, 17 Mass. 336 (1821).
29. See dissenting opinion of Justice Clark, 383 U.S. 413, 425–26, 86 S.Ct. 975, 990–91.
30. The words "patently offensive" were used in a 1962 Court ruling in Manual Enterprises v. Day, 370 U.S. 478, 82 S.Ct. 1432, 8 L.Ed.2d 639. By a 6–1 decision (two justices not participating) the Court curbed the Postal Service's discretionary power to censor allegedly obscene material.
31. Dissenting opinion in *Ginzburg,* 383 U.S. at 480, 86 S.Ct. at 952, 16 L.Ed.2d at 43. See Meiklejohn concept of what kind of speech should be absolutely protected by the First Amendment, Chapter 2.
32. Dissenting opinion in *Memoirs,* 383 U.S. at 455–56, 86 S.Ct. at 996, 16 L.Ed.2d at 26–27.
33. Ginsberg v. State of New York, 390 U.S. 629, 88 S.Ct. 1274, 20 L.Ed.2d 195.
34. For more complete discussion, see Chapter 14.
35. 390 U.S. at 649–50, 88 S. Ct. at 1285–86, 20 L.Ed.2d at 209–210.
36. State statute citations are included in Appendix B of Ginzburg opinion, 390 U.S. at 647–48, 88 S.Ct. at 1284–85, 20 L.Ed.2d at 208–209.

37. See Notes, "Restricting Adult Access to Material Obscene as to Juveniles," 85 *Michigan Law Review* 7, June 1987, pp. 1681+.
38. Bethel School District No. 403 v. Fraser, 55 *U.S. Law Week* 3086, August 12, 1986.
39. Ibid., at 3087.
40. Stanley v. Georgia, 394 U.S. 557, 89 S.Ct. 1243, 22 L.Ed.2d 542.
41. Miller v. California, 413 U.S. 15, 93 S.Ct. 2607, 37 L.Ed.2d 419.
42. Paris Adult Theater I v. Slaton, 413 U.S. 49, 93 S.Ct. 2628, 37 L.Ed.2d 446.
43. U.S. v. 12 200-Ft. Reels of Super 8mm. Film, 413 U.S. 123, 93 S.Ct. 2665, 37 L.Ed.2d 500.
44. U.S. v. Orito, 413 U.S. 139, 93 S.Ct. 2674, 37 L.Ed.2d 513.
45. Kaplan v. California, 413 U.S. 115, 93 S.Ct. 2680, 37 L.Ed.2d 492.
46. Miller v. California, 413 U.S. at 26, 93 S.Ct. at 2616, 37 L.Ed.2d at 431. Note the shift in emphasis.
47. Ibid., 413 U.S. at 27, 93 S.Ct. at 2616–17, 37 L.Ed.2d at 432–433.
48. Dissenting opinion in Paris Adult Theater I, 93 S.Ct. 2628, 2656.
49. Paris Adult Theater I, 93 S.Ct. at 2641–42.
50. Note 8 in Miller, 93 S.Ct. at 2616.
51. Miller, 93 S.Ct. at 2620–21.
52. Dissenting opinion in Miller, 93 S.Ct. at 2623.
53. Miller v. California, op. cit., note 41, 93 S.Ct. at 2647.
54. Ibid., 93 S.Ct. at 2657.
55. Ibid., at 2662.
56. Pope v. Illinois (1987), 14 *Med.L.Rptr.* 1001, June 2, 1987.
57. Ibid., at 1005.
58. Oregon v. Henry, 55 *U.S. Law Week* 2444, February 24, 1987.
59. Ibid.
60. Ibid., at 2445.
61. Hamling v. U.S., 418 U.S. 87, 94 S.Ct. 2887, 41 L.Ed.2d 590.
62. Ibid., 94 S.Ct. at 2921.
63. Jenkins v. State of Georgia, 418 U.S. 153, 94 S.Ct. 2750, 41 L.Ed.2d 642.
64. Georgia Code Ann. § 26–2101 (b) (1972).
65. Jenkins v. State of Georgia, op. cit., note 63, 94 S.Ct. at 2757.
66. "News Notes," *Media Law Reporter,* June 14, 1977.
67. "Child Pornographers Face Bigger Penalties," *FoI Digest,* May/June 1984, p. 2.
68. New York v. Ferber, 458 U.S. 747, 102 S.Ct. 3348, 73 L.Ed.2d 1113 (1982).
69. Hudnut v. American Booksellers Association, "News Notes," *Media Law Reporter,* September 10, 1986. The U.S. Supreme Court, without comment, upheld the Circuit Court by a 6–3 vote ("News Notes," *Media Law Reporter,* March 4, 1986).
70. People ex rel. Busch v. Projection Room Theater, 550 P.2d 600. Justices Mosk and Tobriner dissented, and Justice Clark dissented in part and concurred in part.
71. Ibid., at 607.
72. Ibid., at 610.
73. Vance v. Universal Amusement, "News Notes," *Media Law Reporter,* April 1, 1980.
74. Chateau X v. Andrews, "News Notes," *Media Law Reporter,* April 8, 1980.
75. Arcara v. Cloud Books, Inc., 55 *U.S. Law Week* 3086, August 12, 1986.
76. Young v. American Mini Theatres, Inc., 427 U.S. 50, 1 *Med.L.Rptr.* 1151, 44 *U.S. Law Week* 4999.
77. City of Renton v. Playtime Theatres, 12 *Med.L.Rptr.* 1721, March 11, 1986.
78. Ibid., at 1723.
79. Ibid., at 1727.
80. Lo-Ji Sales v. New York, 99 S.Ct. 2319, 5 *Med.L.Rptr.* 1177.
81. Walter v. U.S., "News Notes," *Media Law Reporter,* July 1, 1980.
82. Burstyn v. Wilson, 343 U.S. 495, 72 S.Ct. 777, 96 L.Ed. 1098 (1952).
83. Freedman v. Maryland, 380 U.S. 51, 85 S.Ct. 734, 13 L.Ed.2d 649 (1965).
84. Times Film Corp. v. City of Chicago, 365 U.S. 43, 81 S.Ct. 391 (1961).
85. Southeastern Promotions, Ltd. v. Steve Conrad, 95 S.Ct. 1239 (1975).

86. Times Film Corp. v. City of Chicago, op. cit., note 84, 365 U.S. at 46–47.
87. Southeastern Promotions v. Conrad, op. cit., note 85, 95 S.Ct. at 1247.
88. Ibid., at 1246.
89. Red Lion Broadcasting Co. v. FCC, 395 U.S. 363, 89 S.Ct. 1794, 23 L.Ed.2d 37, 1 *Med.L.Rptr.* 2053 (1969), and FCC v. Pacifica Foundation, 438 U.S. 726, 98 S.Ct. 3026, 57 L.Ed.2d 1073, 3 *Med.L.Rptr.* 2553 (1978).
90. "The First Amendment and Regulation of Television News," *Columbia Law Review,* April, 1972, p. 747. Footnotes omitted.
91. *Broadcasting,* April 16, 1973, p. 31. Commissioner Johnson dissented, terming the FCC's action in WGLD-FM "censorship."
92. Illinois Citizens Committee for Broadcasting v. FCC, 515 F.2d 397 (1975).
93. Ibid., at 406.
94. *The FCC and Broadcasting,* FCC brochure, issued January 15, 1974, p. 9.
95. Ibid.
96. Ibid., pp. 8–9.
97. In re Pacifica Foundation, Station WBAI, 56 FCC 2d 94 (1975).
98. Pacifica Foundation v. FCC, 2 *Med.L.Rptr.* 1465, March 29, 1977.
99. Ibid., at 1467–68.
100. FCC v. Pacifica Foundation, 438 U.S. 726, 98 S.Ct. 3026, 57 L.Ed.2d 1073, 3 *Med.L.Rptr.* 2552.
101. Ibid., 438 U.S. at 744, 98 S.Ct. at 3038, 57 L.Ed.2d at 1092.
102. *The NEWS Media & The LAW,* Winter 1987, pp. 31–32.
103. *The NEWS Media & The LAW,* Fall 1988, p. 54.
104. Community Television of Utah v. Roy City, 555 F. Supp. 1164 (1982).
105. Jones v. Wilkinson, 800 F.2d 989; *The NEWS Media & The LAW,* Fall 1986, pp. 43–44.
106. Cruz v. Ferre, 9 *Med.L.Rptr.* 2050 (Southern District of Florida, 1983).
107. Ibid., at 2052.
108. Pacifica, op. cit., note 100, 438 U.S. at 751, 98 S.Ct. at 3041, 57 L.Ed.2d at 1094 (footnote omitted).
109. Writer Guild v. FCC, 45 *U.S. Law Week* 1073, November 16, 1976 (Central District of California).

13

Advertising

HIGHLIGHTS

■ The Federal Trade Commission came into existence in 1914.
Among its duties and responsibilities is the protection of consumers
against false, deceptive, and unfair advertising. Among its weapons
against such advertising are (1) corrective advertising, (2) industrywide ad substantiation orders, and (3) trade regulation rules.

■ Two of these weapons—corrective advertising and industrywide ad
substantiation—did not find favor with the Reagan-appointed
chairman of the FTC Commission, James C. Miller III, who, with
other Reagan appointees, helped to adopt a policy that requires
proof that a "reasonable consumer" has been harmed by deceptive
advertising before the FTC will act. Compare this policy with previous interpretations of the law in which it was held that the tendency of an advertisement to deceive was sufficient to permit FTC
action.

■ In *Valentine v. Chrestensen* (1942), the U.S. Supreme Court ruled
that the First Amendment imposed no restraint on government in
connection with regulation of "purely commercial advertising." But
this doctrine eroded. The main blow came in 1976 in *Virginia State
Board of Pharmacy v. Virginia Citizens Consumer Council, Inc.*
when the Supreme Court ruled that truthful commercial speech is
protected by the First Amendment.

■ In *Bates v. State Bar of Arizona* (1977), a sharply divided Supreme
Court struck down as unconstitutional a rule which prohibited lawyers from advertising. Similar restrictions on other professional
groups soon fell under the weight of *Virginia State Board of Pharmacy* and *Bates*.

■ But even truthful advertising can be banned, as the Supreme Court most recently demonstrated in *Posadas de Puerto Rico Associates v. Tourism Company of Puerto Rico* (1986). A four-part analysis for determining when such bans are legal was put forth by the Court in *Central Hudson Gas & Electric Co. v. Public Service Commission* (1980). What emerges from *Central Hudson* and the Puerto Rico casino cases is the idea of limited First Amendment protection for commercial speech that is not misleading, fraudulent, or related to unlawful activities.

Advertising is a multi-billion dollar industry. Revenue from advertising is the lifeblood of American newspapers (providing about 75 percent of the revenue for the average daily paper). It accounts for at least half of the revenue for many magazines, and it is the sole supporter of commercial radio and television.

Advertising seeks to influence consumers to act or think in certain ways. It is a form of communication that developed in the United States in conjunction with the laissez faire concept that government should intervene as little as possible in the marketplace and only to maintain the marketplace's health and competitiveness. Such a marketplace was deemed vital to the economic system and the public it served.

But revelations that large corporations were "rigging" the marketplace through monopolistic practices led Congress to enact legislation: the Sherman Antitrust Act in 1890 and the Clayton Act in 1914. In connection with the Clayton Act, Congress foresaw the need of a marketplace "police" force and therefore passed the Federal Trade Commission Act (FTCA) a few weeks before the Clayton Act was signed into law. Simply put, the purpose of FTCA at that time was to prevent unfair methods of competition.

ADVERTISING REGULATION

The FTC Act created a five-member Federal Trade Commission and gave it the broad task, as set forth in Section 5 of the Act, of "preventing unfair methods of competition in commerce."

Before examining the FTC's power more closely, it should be pointed out that this agency is not the only government body involved in such regulation. Others include the Alcohol and Tobacco Tax Division of the Internal Revenue Service, the Federal Communications Commission (FCC), Food and Drug Administration (FDA), Securities and Exchange Commission (SEC), and the U.S. Postal Service.

The Alcohol and Tobacco Tax Division is primarily concerned with false and misleading statements in liquor advertisements. The FCC, through a liaison agreement with the FTC, considers instances of unfair or deceptive advertising by broadcast licensees, as brought to its attention by the FTC, at the time of license renewal or in license revocation proceedings. The FDA and FTC also have a liaison agreement by means of which the FDA concentrates on false labeling of drugs while the FTC looks primarily at false advertising of drugs. Additionally, the FDA maintains that it has exclusive jurisdiction over prescription drug advertising while the FTC's responsibility extends to over-the-counter drug ads. SEC has statutory power to regulate advertising related to stocks, bonds, and other securities. And the U.S. Postal Service has authority to halt mail related to false advertising and return it to the sender. But the FTC is the major governmental force for "policing" the marketplace against false, deceptive, and unfair advertising.

Overview of FTC

Probably no other federal agency has undergone such persistent criticism as the FTC. Many studies have been made since its inception, and recommendations concerning it have run the gamut from abolishing it to giving it broad new powers. In response, the FTC in the 1970s sought to bypass slower case-by-case methods with the implementation of new programs and policies, and to tear away the stigma that it only fought trivial battles because it feared political repercussions if it took on blue-chip companies. In fact the agency was buffeted by political pressure in the early 1980s when it considered some controversial rules such as requiring used car dealers to warn prospective buyers what, if anything, was wrong with any cars for sale, or requiring funeral homes to itemize the cost of different services that the homes provide. But following the election of Ronald Reagan as President in 1980, the emphasis of federal regulatory agencies has been toward deregulation with the aim of allowing "marketplace forces" to have their day—a policy expected to continue during President Bush's administration.

Various legislative enactments impose a variety of duties on the FTC, but the policy underlying all of them, according to the agency, is the same: "To prevent the free enterprise system from being stifled or fettered by monopoly or anticompetitive practices and to protect consumers from unfair or deceptive trade practices."[1]

The FTC is actually three distinct entities: (1) the Commission, which has quasi-legislative (rule-making) and quasi-judicial (hearing complaints and issuing edicts) powers; (2) administrative law judges (formerly called hearing examiners) who are independent of the Commission and staff and who conduct hearings into staff-filed complaints; and (3) the staff itself.

Typical Case Flow. Formal FTC complaints develop from staff investigations. The investigations may be initiated by the Commission or from letters sent to the FTC by businessmen or consumers citing alleged illegal practices. These letters are called "applications for complaints" to distinguish them from formal complaints brought by the Commission.

Each application is reviewed to determine whether the practice questioned involves interstate commerce, or whether it may affect interstate commerce, the public interest, and violation of a law administered by the FTC. If it does, an investigation is begun. This may start with correspondence from the Commission requiring the business concerned to file a special report, or with a request of a subpoena for information by the staff of a bureau or regional office.

From the information obtained, the decision is made (1) to close the case (for lack of public interest, or failure to find that a violation has occurred), or (2) to issue a complaint, along with a proposed cease-and-desist order.

Cases can also be settled by "consent order," a formal document signed by the businessman or company involved certifying that the challenged practices will be corrected or discontinued. The public has the opportunity to comment on a proposed consent order and the Commission takes these comments into consideration before the order is finally issued. Violations of consent orders can result in assessment of civil penalties of $10,000 a day for each violation.

Cases which are not settled are litigated before an FTC administrative law judge. Following hearings, either the respondent or the Commission's complaint counsel can appeal the judge's initial decision to the five commissioners.

The Commission hears the argument and announces its decision: to issue a cease-and-desist order or to dismiss some or all of the charges.

If the administrative law judge's initial decision is not appealed, it may be adopted — with or without modifications — by the Commission. FTC staff cannot appeal an adverse decision by the Commission.

If a cease-and-desist order is issued, the respondent has 60 days to appeal the Commission's decision to a U.S. Court of Appeals. Either side may ultimately appeal to the Supreme Court.

Reorganization Urged. In a 1988 speech, Federal Trade Commissioner Terry Calvani called for a major reorganization of the agency.[2] Calvani urged that the power to make law enforcement decisions be taken from the Commission and placed solely in the hands of the agency's general counsel. The general counsel would decide whether to initiate an investigation, issue a complaint, challenge a merger, and exercise the other powers of the Commission with the exception of hearing cases brought on appeal. That would be the Commission's sole duty under the proposal.

Such a reorganization, said Calvani, would solve three problems: constitutionality, perceptions of partiality, and accountability.

The argument about the FTC's alleged unconstitutionality stems from the fact that commissioners do not serve at the pleasure of the President who can only remove them for cause. They are not members of the Executive branch and therefore cannot constitutionally enforce U.S. laws. The problem would be minimized, said Calvani, by vesting most of the Commission's powers in the general counsel appointed by, and serving at the pleasure of, the President.

The perception of a partiality problem arises because commissioners vote to issue an administrative complaint and then review the decision of an administrative law judge who has heard the case stemming from that complaint. Although the commissioners "are scrupulously fair," according to Calvani, there is "at least the perception of unfairness about the process."

Under the proposal, commissioners would only hear appeals from administrative law judges' decisions.

The third problem, accountability, results from the power of the Commission chairman to appoint senior management officials. The senior staff makes law enforcement recommendations based on the chairman's particular philosophical leanings, Calvani said. He added that it was virtually impossible for the majority of the Commission to "impose any enforcement agenda on the agency except with the active consent of the chairman." And yet all of the commissioners are held accountable for the actions or inactions of the agency. Under the proposal, the general counsel would be accountable for any actions or inactions.

Enforcement Methods. Enforcement methods available to the FTC are

1. Publicity.
2. Advisory opinions, by which the FTC responds to a request by an individual or a company concerning the legality of a proposed or planned course of action.
3. Industry guides, which are administrative interpretations intended to show the public how business may be conducted in accordance with FTC administered laws.
4. Trade regulation rules, which implement the substantive requirements of FTC-administered statutes and have the force and effect of law if violated.
5. Letters of voluntary compliance, in which promises are given to the FTC not to engage in a certain practice.
6. Consent orders.
7. Cease-and-desist orders.

The consent order, unlike industry guides and letters of voluntary compliance, has all the force of an order obtained by adjudication, as does a cease-and-desist order, but it avoids the adjudicatory expense and delay associated with cease-and-desist orders. In entering into such an agreement the individual or company does not admit guilt, nor is there any adjudication to determine guilt. Rather, the agreement is for settlement purposes only, although a violation of the consent order can result in civil penalties. Penalties can be included in such an order. Thus, in March 1987 the Commission, by a 4–1 vote, accepted a consent decree under which Sears, Roebuck & Co. and Kellwood Co., a Sears supplier, will pay civil penalties of $200,000 each to settle FTC charges that they misrepresented the amount of down filling in garments made by Kellwood and sold by Sears.[3] The consent decree settled a 1981 FTC court complaint that the companies mislabeled and falsely advertised the down content of the garments.

Commissioner Andrew J. Strenio, Jr. dissented as to the Sears settlement, saying that its terms "are so extreme that Sears appears to be held to a much lower labeling standard than the rest of the industry." He added:

> I am unable to find a rationale for giving Sears special treatment other than the Commission's exhaustion after expending well over a million taxpayer dollars battling a litigant with extensive resources.[4]

But most of the thousands of complaints reaching the agency annually are handled at the informal enforcement level. Only 100 or so are handled at the formal enforcement level (involving cease-and-desist and consent orders).

Commission's Statutory Power. In creating the five-member, independent regulatory agency (independent in the sense that the agency can issue its own rules and regulations and need not defer to Congress for the promulgation of such rules), Congress in 1914 gave the FTC the broad task, as set forth in Section 5 of the Act, of "preventing unfair methods of competition in commerce."[5] Whether this language included false or deceptive advertising, regardless of any impact on competition, was not at first clear. Almost from the beginning the Commission acted as though it did. But in a 1932 decision in *FTC v. Raladam,* the U.S. Supreme Court held that Section 5 applied only to competition.[6] The ruling meant that even if there was false or deceptive advertising adversely affecting the consumer, the FTC could do nothing about it unless an adverse effect on competition could be shown. Such an idea reenforced the laissez-faire concept in place at the time of the Act's passage as reflected by the doctrine of caveat emptor—"let the buyer beware" when entering the marketplace. This decision was instrumental in bringing about passage of the Wheeler–Lea Amendment in 1938 which broadened the FTC's powers by changing Section 5 to read: "Unfair methods of competition in commerce and *unfair or deceptive acts or practices in commerce* are hereby declared unlawful." In addition, Section 12 was added:

> It shall be unlawful for any person, partnership, or corporation to disseminate, or cause to be disseminated, any false advertisement . . . for the purpose of inducing, or which is likely to induce, directly or indirectly, the purchase of food, drugs, devices, or cosmetics. . . .[7] The dissemination or the causing to be disseminated of any false advertisement within the provisions of . . . this section shall be an unfair or deceptive act or practice in commerce within the meaning of Section 5.

In discussing the effect of this amendment, the Third Circuit U.S. Court of Appeals said:

> The change effected by the amendment lay in the fact that the Commission could thenceforth prevent unfair or deceptive acts or practices in commerce which injuriously affect the public interest alone, while under the original act the Commission's power to safeguard the public against unfair trade practices depended upon whether the objectionable acts or practices affected competition.[8]

The Wheeler–Lea Amendment fashioned three major changes:

1. The FTC could protect consumers against deceptive advertising no matter what effect, if any, such advertising had on competition.
2. False advertising of food, drugs, devices, and cosmetics ultimately would be brought within the meaning of Section 5 so that a violation of a final FTC order could result in a suit in federal district court and a maximum

civil penalty (now $10,000). In addition, a criminal misdemeanor charge could result if a product was injurious to health or if there was intent to defraud or mislead.[9] A first offender could be punished by a fine of not more than $5000 or imprisonment for not more than six months, or both.

3. The general rule of "caveat emptor" (let the buyer beware) shifted toward "caveat venditor" — let the seller beware. This is seen most clearly in decisions shortly after enactment of the 1938 amendment whereby the seller's intent,[10] or his knowledge[11] of the advertising's falsity, became immaterial in determining a violation of the law. In the marketplace, standards of deception were to be gauged in terms of what is deceptive to "that vast multitude which includes the ignorant, the unthinking and credulous."[12]

In 1973, as an add-on to the Alaska Pipeline Bill (Public Law 93-153), the Commission was given the power to obtain temporary restraining orders and temporary injunctions to stop the use of deceptive and unfair trade practices. This law increased the civil penalty from $5000 to $10,000 per violation.

Additional powers were conferred upon the FTC in the Magnuson-Moss Warranty/FTC Improvement Act (P.L. 93-637) in 1975. It gave the Commission trade regulation rule-making power (reviewed later in the chapter). Under Title II, the Commission's jurisdiction was extended to practices "affecting" interstate commerce, as well as "in" interstate commerce. This means that the FTC can, if it wishes, reach into the states to act against practices which take place primarily within a state if the practice "affects" interstate commerce. In addition, the Act expanded the Commission's authority to represent itself in court under certain circumstances rather than depend solely on the U.S. attorney general.

False, Deceptive, and Unfair Advertising

Various court decisions have given the Commission broad discretion in determining when it can intervene in the marketplace to protect consumers, but the Commission has been faced with a variety of procedural and legal difficulties. When Section 12 was added, it forbade "false" advertising in connection with food, drugs, devices, or cosmetics. Section 15 defined "false advertisement" as meaning "an advertisement, other than labeling, which is misleading in a material respect. . . ." Furthermore, false advertising is termed an "unfair or deceptive act or practice in or affecting commerce" within the meaning of Section 5.

But what else is an unfair or deceptive act? Congress purposely omitted a definition when writing the law in 1914, and Congress has not provided one since. As one legislator remarked, "Even if all known unfair practices were specifically defined and prohibited, it would be at once necessary to begin over again" because of human inventiveness. He added: "If Congress were to adopt the method of definition, it would undertake an endless task."[13]

The FTC faces more than just definitional problems, as pointed out in a talk given in 1977 by the then director of the FTC's Bureau of Consumer Protection, Albert H. Kramer, entitled: "Marconian Problems, Gutenberg Remedies: Evaluating the Multiple-Sensory-Experience Ad on the Double-Spaced Typewritten Page."

In presenting his own views, not those of the Commission's, Kramer said, in part:

> We regulators, however, need to know communication theory, too. If we are charged with determining whether an advertisement is false or deceptive, we must be able to make that evaluation within the environment in which the ad is presented. Our time-honored environment for resolving disputes is by the written word.
>
> Now, however, the media have changed. The media have left the written word behind in a cloud of dust and have created a new environment of multiple-sensory experience of which the written word is a minor part. A very serious problem arises when regulators evaluate the possible falsity, deception, or unfairness of an ad without considering it in the same "sensory experience" context that the ad sought to instill. Despite all the lessons of communication theory—lessons the advertising technicians have learned very well—we regulators . . . persist in using a relatively ancient method for evaluation . . . [reducing] the total sensory experience of the ad—voices, music, graphics, movement, colors—to the written word.
>
> . . . The futility of this approach is illustrated by health warning messages on cigarette ads, which communication theory experts tell us are seldom noticed.
>
> The reason they are seldom noticed is that advertisers spend a great deal of money to learn how to make them not noticed. They spend their resources creating a sensory experience (the wooden mountain stream, for example) to which the health warning is extraneous. The advertiser tests different ads to determine the most effective presentation of the central message of the ad, and implicitly, the least effective presentation of the "extraneous" health warning.

Technological changes add to the Commission's problems of detection and punishment. Telemarketing fraud is one example.

Commissioner Strenio said in a speech in 1988 that telemarketing frauds currently bilk consumers out of some $1 billion a year—and that estimate, he added, may be on the low side.[14]

Since 1983, the FTC has obtained court judgments for nearly $92 million in redress for victims of such fraud, but because these "scam artists by and large are speedy and skillful when it comes to dissipating their ill-gotten profits," he said, only $35 million of the $92 million has yet been returned or is available for return to consumers.

Television, of course, is one of the marvels of technological development and was uppermost in Kramer's thoughts when he talked about horse-and-buggy solutions in an electronic revolution era.

Television offers new dimensions for deception because movement, sound, and color are combined into one powerful medium. As Circuit Court Judge John Minor Wisdom pointed out in *Carter Products, Inc. v. FTC* (1963):

> Everyone knows that on TV all that glistens is not gold. On a black and white screen, white looks grey and blue looks white; the lily must be painted. Coffee looks like mud. Real ice cream melts much more quickly than the firm but fake sundae. The

plain fact is, except by props and mock-ups some objects cannot be shown on television as the viewer, in his mind's eye, knows the essence of the objects.

The technical limitations of television, driving product manufacturers to the substitution of a mock-up for the genuine article, often has resulted in a collision between truth and salesmanship. "What is truth?" has been asked before. On television truth is relative. Assuming that collisions between truth and salesmanship are avoidable, i.e., that mock-ups are not illegal per se, the basic problem this case presents is: What standards should the Federal Trade Commission and courts work out for television commercials so that advertisers will appear to be telling the truth, consistently with Section 5 . . .[15]

Part of the answer was not long in coming. Colgate-Palmolive Co. had been sponsoring a TV commercial which showed an actor placing "Rapid Shave" cream on what purported to be sandpaper and, moments later, shaving the sandpaper clean with one stroke of the razor. In reality, the "sandpaper" was plexiglass covered with sand. When the shaving cream was tested, the FTC discovered that real sandpaper could not be shaved clean until moisturized for an hour. Thus, the TV commercial was termed a misrepresentation and the FTC issued an order which the Court of Appeals, First Circuit, set aside because, in the court's opinion, the order was so broad that any prop or mock-up would be deceptive. On appeal, the U.S. Supreme Court upheld the FTC's order that the mock-up was materially deceptive, although the Court stated that not all props or mock-ups would fall into such a category. If, for example, mashed potatoes were substituted for ice cream because the latter would melt rapidly under television lights, the way in which they were used would determine whether the deception was material. As the Supreme Court pointed out:

> In the ice cream case the mashed potato prop is not being used for additional proof of the product claim, while the purpose of the Rapid Shave commercial is to give the viewer objective proof of the claims made. If in the ice cream hypothetical, the focus of the commercial becomes the undisclosed potato prop and the viewer is invited, explicitly or by implication, to see for himself the truth of the claims about the ice cream's rich texture and full color, and perhaps compare it to a "rival product," then the commercial has become similar to the one now before us. Clearly, however, a commercial which depicts happy actors delightly eating ice cream that in fact is mashed potatoes or drinking a product appearing to be coffee but which is in fact some other substance is not covered by the present order.[16]

What emerged from this case were these general rules: (1) not all props are deceptive per se; (2) material deception can involve the use of props for a misrepresentation of a product's characteristics; and (3) the undisclosed use of a prop or mock-up at strategic moments in a commercial, such as the substitution of plexiglass for sandpaper in order to substantiate a product claim, is material deception and therefore a violation of Section 5.

Sins of Omission? As advertisers and ad agencies have become more sophisticated in fashioning messages designed to persuade consumers to do something,

. reliance on falsity or deception as a means of selling probably has decreased. But consumers may face a greater problem in terms of what advertisements do not convey, said Lewis A. Engman, FTC chairman in 1974 when he made these comments:

> Sometimes the consumer is provided not with information he wants but only with the information the seller wants him to have.
>
> Sellers, for instance, are not inclined to advertise negative aspects of their products even though those aspects may be of primary concern to the consumer, particularly if they involve considerations of health or safety. . . . We have many laws to protect the consumer from errors of fact in advertising. But we have few laws to protect him from errors of omission, from what he isn't told at all.[17]

The FTC may deal with omissions by means of consent orders which require affirmative disclosure of certain information. Or it may issue guidelines, such as those in 1980 that called upon advertisers to disclose if actors are appearing as consumers in commercials whenever "actual consumers" are not used. Another provision in the guidelines on endorsements and testimonials stipulates that an endorser must have actually used the product if the commercial or ad implies or states such usage.

In terms of deception, it's clear that what an advertiser puts into an advertisement or a commercial, or what is left out, may constitute falsity and/or deception. Through the years the Commission and the courts have had a great deal to say about what constitutes deceptive advertising or deceptive practices. Here are some of those determinations:

1. In determining the likelihood of an advertisement being deceptive, neither actual damage to the public nor actual deception need be shown.[18]
2. The meaning of advertisements, and their tendency or capacity to deceive, are questions to be determined by the Commission and its findings should be upheld by the courts unless arbitrary or clearly wrong.[19]
3. The Commission is required to establish only the tendency or capacity of an advertisement to deceive and not actual deception itself.[20]
4. Misrepresentation of fact is considered deceptive.[21]
5. A totally false statement cannot be qualified or modified.[22] Material falsity is deception.[23]
6. A statement may be deceptive even though literally or technically not construed to be misrepresentative.[24]
7. Ambiguous statements, susceptible of both misleading and truthful interpretations, will be construed against the advertiser.[25]
8. Failure to disclose material facts where the effect is to deceive a substantial segment of the public is equivalent to deception.[26]

New Policy on Deception. When Ronald Reagan became President in 1981, one of his goals was to reduce the federal government regulation of, among other things, the marketplace and, as Chapter 14 will show, radio and television. The person he chose to chair the FTC, James C. Miller III, urged Congress in 1982 to adopt a new definition of consumer deception that would include "reasonable consumers" being misled by "material misrepresentations" to the detriment of the purchasers. Stymied in his effort to get Congress to act, Miller and two other Republican-appointed members of the Commission voted in October 1983 to adopt a new policy statement that requires proof that a "reasonable consumer" has been harmed before an advertiser can be charged with deceptive advertising.[27] Michael Pertschuk and Patricia Bailey voted against adoption of the policy. Almost a year later, Pertschuk, as he was about to leave the Commission, issued a 273-page report highly critical of Miller and the Reagan administration, accusing them of dismantling years of regulatory history. Miller responded with equal vigor, accusing Pertschuk of "half truths, misrepresentations and faulty logic."

What Miller could not achieve by way of the congressional route he essentially achieved by a Republican-controlled Commission. His action led some congressional leaders — mostly Democrats — to attack the action as circumventing the law. Representative John D. Dingell of Michigan, chairman of the House Committee on Energy and Commerce, charged that the policy statement was an attempt to rewrite a 45-year history of law enforcement and that Congress had conferred specific authority on the Commission because it did not believe that the common law was "an acceptable vehicle for modern consumer protection."

The policy statement was used by the Commission majority to reach a decision in March 1984 that a mail order company's advertisement about an automobile fuel-economy device was deceptive. Miller and the two other Republican members of the Commission reached their conclusion on the basis that the claim was "material and likely to mislead consumers acting 'reasonably' under the circumstances."[28] The Democrats on the Commission did so on the basis of the former policy on deception; namely, that an ad claim is unlawful if it has the "tendency or capacity to deceive a substantial number of consumers in a material way." Commissioner Bailey said the Miller formulation had the potential to complicate and delay the prosecution of deceptive advertisers. Pertschuk said the formulation raises the evidentiary level for deception cases.

The importance of the case is that it sets precedent for deciding future deception cases.

Miller left the Commission in 1986 to become Reagan's budget director. He was replaced by Daniel Oliver, another Republican. That Oliver was ideologically in tune with his predecessor is shown in his first major policy statement after he became FTC chairman. He said, in part:

> We don't hold companies liable for every possible reading of their claims. When firms provide useful information to a large audience of consumers, we don't intervene to protect the ever-present small minority who might apply a far-fetched or bizarre interpretation to an ad. We don't concern ourselves with subjective claims or matters of taste. And we don't burden sellers with the requirement that they disclose all material information about the products in their advertisements.[29]

The impact of Miller on some of the "weapons" the FTC had used against false, deceptive, and unfair advertising will be reviewed later in the chapter.

Unfairness Doctrine

According to an FTC official, the Wheeler–Lea Amendment added an entirely new third area to the Commission's authority. It empowered the FTC to attack practices which might not constitute unfair methods of competition in the traditional antitrust sense, or which might not be deceptive or misleading with respect to consumers, but which nevertheless are "unfair" in terms of impact on consumers. By means of this unfairness doctrine, the FTC extended its regulatory function not only to false and deceptive advertising, but to unfair advertising, such as advertisments which make claims that have no "reasonable basis" or have not had sufficient scientific testing.[30]

FTC v. Sperry and Hutchinson. The unfairness doctrine received a major boost from the U.S. Supreme Court in its 7–0 decision in *FTC v. Sperry* and *Hutchinson Co.* (1972), which broadly interpreted the power of the Commission under Section 5.[31] Although the case was remanded to the FTC for further proceedings, the opinion by Justice White served to strengthen greatly the regulatory agency in its efforts to deal with unfair practices absent any effect on competition. The Court said that two major questions were posed concerning Section 5.

> First, does Section 5 empower the Commission to define and proscribe an unfair competitive practice, even though the practice does not infringe either the letter or the spirit of the antitrust laws? Second, does Section 5 empower the Commission to proscribe practices as unfair or deceptive in their effect upon consumers regardless of their nature or quality as competitive practices or their effect on competition? We think the statute, its legislative history and prior cases compel an affirmative answer to both questions.[32]

In addition, the Court said that:

> Legislative and judicial authorities alike convince us that the Federal Trade Commission does not arrogate excessive power to itself if, in measuring a practice against the elusive, but congressionally mandated standard of fairness, it, like a court of equity, considers public values beyond simply those enshrined in the spirit of the antitrust laws."[33]

The Commission has described three factors it considers in determining whether a practice is unfair when it is neither in violation of antitrust laws nor deceptive:

1. Whether the practice, without necessarily having been previously considered unlawful, offends public policy as it has been established by statutes, the common law, or whether, in other words, it is within at least the

penumbra of some common-law, statutory, or other established concept of unfairness;

2. Whether it is immoral, unethical, oppressive or unscrupulous;
3. Whether it causes substantial injury to consumers (or competitors or other businessmen).[34]

After *Sperry and Hutchinson (S & H),* the FTC explored a number of areas in which the unfairness doctrine could be applied, such as: (1) advertising claims implying substantial benefits toward satisfying basic emotional needs or anxieties, such as the need for affection or acceptance, when the advertised product does not in fact offer such benefits; (2) advertising that clearly associates a product with strongly held social values when in fact the product has no significant relationship to such social values; and (3) advertising of products to particularly vulnerable population groups when evaluation of the advertised product requires a mature and sophisticated analysis which the members of the population groups are unable to perform.[35]

The following are two examples of the Commission's use of the unfairness doctrine: (1) A proposed complaint and order from the Commission against Personna razor blades following an FTC determination that distribution of sample blades by means of packets in home-delivered newspapers would be unfair to the public because of hazards to the health and safety of unwary consumers, especially children, handling the newspaper; (2) a Commission consent order by which six major cigarette manufacturers agreed to include in their advertisements danger-to-health warnings on the packages. In the razor blade case, the company discontinued the practice shortly after issuance of the proposed complaint.

The third area, which pertains to vulnerable population groups, was the basis for the FTC's consideration of a ban on certain kinds of television advertising directed at children because they are a particularly vulnerable group. The ramifications of this FTC staff proposal are reviewed later in the chapter.

It should be noted at this point that Chairman Miller, in an appearance before the Senate Commerce Committee in March 1982, called for curbs on the FTC's power to prosecute "unfair" advertising. He did not, however, call for its elimination.[36] A year later he went back to the Senate committee and said a majority of the commissioners supported legislative enactment of a definition of "unfair" acts or practices, and limiting the FTC's "unfairness" jurisdiction to acts or practices likely to cause substantial injury that consumers could not reasonably avoid. Thus, his call for limits on FTC's jurisdiction sounded a bit like the policy statement on deceptive advertising that was adopted at his urging. In fact, he believed that almost anything the agency has done or proposed to do under the fairness jurisdiction could have been done under a deception theory.[37] Meanwhile, most of the ad industry seeks the demise of the unfairness doctrine.

Advertising Agency Responsibility

Advertising agencies at first were considered merely agents for the firms seeking to sell to the public; therefore they were not held responsible if advertisers were found guilty of wrongdoing. But in the late 1940s, the FTC served notice that henceforth it would hold agencies jointly responsible except in situations where they were at the mercy of the advertiser for information.[38] In *Colgate-Palmolive Co. v. FTC,* the U.S. Court of Appeals rejected an advertising agency's plea to be excluded from the FTC's cease-and-desist order.[39] The court said it could see no reason why agencies, "which are now big businesses, should be able to shirk from at least the prima facie responsibility for the conduct in which they participate."

Thus, it now is common practice for the FTC to name as a respondent an agency which prepared allegedly illegal advertisements. The rationale is that the agency contributes to the injury of the consumer and may also enjoy an unfair competitive advantage over agencies that do not use deceptions or falsehoods.

FIRST AMENDMENT AND ADVERTISING

Before examining some novel enforcement methods used by the FTC in the 1970s and, to a diminishing extent, in the 1980s, the relationship of the First Amendment to advertising needs to be explored because of the impact, if any, of the First Amendment on these enforcement methods.

Valentine v. Chrestensen

A starting place is the 1942 decision of the U.S. Supreme Court in *Valentine v. Chrestensen* in which the Court made a distinction between freedom to express political views and freedom to advertise a commercial enterprise. In enunciating a "commercial speech" doctrine, the Court said the Constitution imposes no restraint on government in connection with regulation of "purely commercial advertising."[40]

The genesis of the case was Chrestensen's ownership of a submarine which he planned to exhibit in New York. Handbills were printed to publicize the submarine, but Chrestensen was told that the city's sanitation code prevented their distribution. However, handbills devoted to information or public protest were not banned by the code, so Chrestensen had a protest against the sanitation code printed on one side of the handbill, while the other side advertised the submarine. Again he was prevented from distributing them and he obtained an injunction preventing police commissioner Lewis J. Valentine from any further interference. On appeal, the U.S. Supreme Court unanimously reversed issuance of the injunction, rejecting an argument put forth by the American Civil Liberties Union that it would be impossible to make a philosophically sound distinction between commercial and non-commercial handbills. The Court also characterized the handbills as a willful attempt to circumvent the ordinance. Justice Douglas, who had joined the *Chrestensen* opinion, later would term it "casual, almost offhand"; one that was "ill-conceived."[41]

In 1964, the Court in *Times v. Sullivan* (see Chapter 4) made a distinction between commercial and "informational" advertising. A full-page advertisement appeared in *The New York Times* that was signed by civil rights leaders and that protested certain conditions in Montgomery, Alabama. This led to a libel action, and one of the hurdles the Court had to overcome in even considering the case was that advertising was not protected by the First Amendment. Justice Brennan swept that obstacle aside with these words:

> The publication here was not a "commercial" advertisement in the sense in which the word was used in *Chrestensen*. It communicated information, expressed opinion, recited grievances, protested claimed abuses, and sought financial support on behalf of a movement whose existence and objectives are matters of the highest public interest and concern. . . . That the *Times* was paid for the advertisement is as immaterial in this connection as is the fact that newspapers and books are sold.[42]

The *Valentine v. Chrestensen* decision figured prominently in the Federal Communications Commission (FCC) decision in 1967 that required broadcast stations that carried cigarette commercials to provide a significant amount of time "to this controversial issue of public importance—i.e., that however enjoyable [smoking is made to appear in commercials], such smoking may be a hazard to the smoker's health."

This public health hazard was among the major reasons why courts upheld the FCC's decision when such action was challenged on First Amendment grounds. Later, when Congress banned cigarette and little cigar advertising from radio and television, effective January 1, 1971, the courts again considered the public health menace of cigarette smoking a primary reason for overcoming First Amendment concerns. But another reason often cited was the then-prevailing view that product advertising was less vigorously protected by the First Amendment than other forms of speech.[43]

The constitutionality of the congressional ban was upheld in a 2–1 split of a federal court panel with Circuit Court Judge J. Skelly Wright dissenting. Wright had this to say:

> It would be difficult to argue that there are many who mourn for the Marlboro man or miss the undergrammatical Winston jingles. Most television viewers no doubt agree that cigarette advertising represents the carping hucksterism of Madison Avenue at its very worst. Moreover, overwhelming scientific evidence makes it plain that the Salem girl was in fact a seductive merchant of death—that the real "Marlboro Country" is the graveyard.[44]

But the Constitution, argued Judge Wright, protects more than just "healthy" speech.

Whatever the merits of Wright's views, the U.S. Supreme Court summarily affirmed the legality of the advertising ban in a 7–2 decision in early 1972 with only Douglas and Brennan indicating that the Court should undertake a full-scale review.[45]

Pittsburgh Press v. Pittsburgh Human Relations Commission

In a 5–4 decision, the U.S. Supreme Court, in a narrow holding in *Pittsburgh Press Co. v. Pittsburgh Commission on Human Relations* (1973),[46] ruled that an ordinance which prohibited newspapers from carrying sex-designated advertising columns for certain kinds of job opportunities did not violate the newspaper's First Amendment rights. The Court took the position that the *Pittsburgh Press* advertisements resembled the *Chrestensen,* not the *Sullivan,* advertisement in that they did not express any position, as a matter of social policy, whether certain positions should be filled by certain members of one or the other sex, nor did they criticize the ordinance or the Commission's enforcement practices. They were merely a proposal of possible employment and thus were "classic examples of commercial speech."

The *Pittsburgh Press* had argued that commercial speech should be accorded a higher level of protection than that afforded by *Chrestensen* because the exchange of information is as important in the commercial realm as in any other. Therefore the distinction between commercial and other speech should be abrogated. The majority hedged a bit, with Justice Powell writing:

> Whatever the merits of this contention may be in other contexts, it is unpersuasive in this case. Discrimination in employment is not only commercial activity, it is *illegal* commercial activity under the Ordinance. We have no doubt that a newspaper constitutionally could be forbidden to publish a want ad proposing a sale of narcotics or soliciting prostitutes. Nor would the result be different if the nature of the transaction were indicated by placement under columns captioned "Narcotics for Sale" and "Prostitutes Wanted" rather than stated within the four corners of the advertisement.
>
> The illegality in this case may be less overt, but we see no difference in principle here.[47]

Signs that the *Chrestensen* doctrine was coming apart abound in the dissenting opinions.

Despite the Court's effort to decide only the most narrow question, Chief Justice Burger dissented on the grounds of a "disturbing enlargement" of *Chrestensen.* This launched the Court on a "treacherous path" of defining what layout and organizational decisions of a newspaper are "sufficiently associated" with the "commercial" parts of the newspaper to be constitutionally unprotected and therefore subject to government regulation. Burger believed that the newspaper was clearly within its protected journalistic discretion which, in his view, includes the right to arrange the content of the newspaper, whether news, editorials, or advertisements, as it sees fit. As for the argument posited by the majority that a newspaper could not carry ads that illegally call for such things as prostitutes, the Chief Justice said such a hypothetical situation was not at issue in the present case since there was no "blatant involvement by a newspaper in a criminal transaction."

Justice Douglas also dissented, saying in part:

> Commercial matter as distinguished from news, was held in . . . [*Chrestensen*] not to be subject to First Amendment protection. My views on that issue have changed since 1942. . . . As I have stated on earlier occasions I believe that commercial materials also have First Amendment protection. . . .
>
> I would let any expression in that broad spectrum flourish, unrestrained by

Government, unless it was an integral part of action—the only point which in the Jeffersonian philosophy marks the permissible point of governmental intrusion.[48]

Justice Stewart, joined by Justice Douglas, and in part by Justice Blackmun, dissented principally on traditional grounds of prior restraint. What the Court gave approval to, said Stewart, is a government order dictating to a publisher in advance how he must arrange the layout of the pages in his newspaper. Nothing in *Chrestensen* supports such a decision, he declared. Stewart added that whatever validity the 1942 case has, "it does not stand for the proposition that the advertising pages of a newspaper are outside the protection given the newspaper by the First and Fourteenth Amendments. Any possible doubt on that score was surely laid to rest in . . . [*Times-Sullivan*]."

Stewart concluded with a warning that if government agencies can force a newspaper to print a classified advertisement in a certain way, then there was no reason that he could see which would prevent the government from forcing a newspaper publisher to conform in some other way in order to achieve other goals thought socially desirable. "And if Government can dictate the layout of a newspaper's classified advertising pages today," he said, "what is there to prevent it from dictating the layout of the news pages tomorrow?"

Bigelow v. Commonwealth of Virginia

The next blow to Chrestensen came in 1975 when the Court, by a 7–2 vote, reversed the conviction of a Virginia editor on a charge of publishing an advertisement from a New York abortion referral service that encouraged abortions. Virginia law made it a misdemeanor to encourage abortions. Precedents cited in *Bigelow v. Commonwealth of Virginia*[49] included *Times-Sullivan* and *Pittsburgh Press*.

Although not reaching the conclusion that all truthful commercial speech was protected by the First Amendment, the majority nonetheless moved toward that position by holding that the advertisement contained factual material of public interest. In balancing that interest against the government interest in regulating such speech, the Court held that the advertisement was entitled to First Amendment protection. However, the Court chose not to decide the "precise extent to which the First Amendment permits regulation of advertising that is related to activities the state may legitimately regulate or even prohibit." However, Blackmun did say for the majority that "advertising, like all public expression, may be subject to reasonable regulation that serves a legitimate public interest."[50]

Justice Rehnquist, joined by White, dissented, in part because he could not distinguish the abortion referral advertisement from purely commercial advertising which, he said, is entitled to little constitutional protection. But even assuming that the advertisement was more than purely commercial speech, Rehnquist said he was unable to see why Virginia "does not have a legitimate public interest" in terms of the law it enacted since states "have a strong interest in the prevention of commercial advertising in the health field."[51] He emphasized that the state supreme court had asserted a state interest to prevent commercial exploitation of women who wished to have abortions. And the fact that the advertiser was located in New York (where abortions are legal) did not, according to Rehnquist, diminish that interest.

Virginia Pharmacy Board v. Virginia Citizens Consumer Council

The final blow to *Chrestensen* came in 1976 when the Supreme Court, in a 7–1 decision in *Virginia State Board of Pharmacy v. Virginia Citizens Consumer Council, Inc.,* ruled that truthful commercial speech is protected by the First Amendment.[52]

At issue was a Virginia law which prohibited a licensed pharmacist from advertising or promoting the prices of prescription drugs. A three-judge U.S. District Court had declared that portion of the statute void and had enjoined the pharmacy board from enforcing it. In upholding the lower court, the U.S. Supreme Court was strongly influenced by the public interest test. As Blackmun said for the Court, the "consumer's interest in the free flow of commercial information" may be "as keen, if not keener by far, than his interest in the day's most urgent political debate." Apart from the individual consumer's interest in purely commercial information, "society also may have a strong interest" in the free flow of such information. And an advertisement, even though it is entirely "commercial," may be of "general public interest."

The Court obviously had to limit its ruling. Blackmun did so in this way: "In concluding that commercial speech, like other varieties, is protected, we of course do not hold that it can never be regulated in any way. Some forms of commercial speech regulation are surely permissible." As noted by Blackmun, these could include time, place, and manner restrictions (as with other forms of speech); curbs on false or misleading advertisements; and prohibitions against illegal advertising (such as in *Pittsburgh Press Co.*). The Court, however, declined to rule out constitutional protection for "tasteless and excessive" advertising, saying that such forms of advertising are "nonetheless dissemination of information as to who is producing and selling what product, for what reason, and at what price." Blackmun continued:

> So long as we preserve a predominantly free enterprise economy, the allocation of our resources in large measure will be made through numerous private economic decisions. It is a matter of public interest that those decisions, in the aggregate, be intelligent and well informed. To this end, the free flow of information is indispensable.

Justice Rehnquist dissented, principally because in his view the decision means that it will no longer be possible to prohibit truthful advertising for products that are potentially harmful. "Current prohibitions on television advertising of liquor and cigarettes are prominent in this category," he said, adding that apparently under the Court's holding as long as the advertisements are not deceptive they may no longer be prohibited.

Whether Rehnquist's view is correct remains to be seen. Several liquor advertising ban cases will be reviewed shortly. As for the cigarette advertising ban on radio and television, Blackmun's only reference to it came in a footnote in which he said that inaccurate commercial information may be less tolerable than inaccuracies in news reporting or political commentary because the disseminator is better able to know the truth of the information provided. This condition may also make it "appropriate to require that a commercial message appear in such form, or include such additional information, warnings and disclaimers, as are necessary to prevent its being deceptive." And, added Blackmun, prior restraint might be permissible under such a circumstance.

Aftereffects of Virginia Pharmacy Board

The effects of the Court's ruling in this landmark case were not long in being felt, especially among professional groups, such as lawyers, which traditionally had forbidden their members to advertise. Such policies have come under FTC attack as violations of Section 5 of FTCA. Various courts interpreted *Virginia Pharmacy Board* as requiring state bar associations to allow lawyers to advertise.

Bates v. State Bar of Arizona. In 1977 a sharply divided U.S. Supreme Court overturned an Arizona Supreme Court rule (similar to rules in most other states) prohibiting lawyers from advertising on the ground that to ban truthful advertising concerning the availability of "routine legal services" violates the First Amendment.[53] Justice Blackmun again delivered the Court's opinion with Brennan, White, Marshall, and Stevens concurring. The opinion applied only to routine legal services, Blackmun said, such as uncontested divorces, adoption cases, uncontested bankruptcies.

Within days of the court's decision in *Bates v. State Bar of Arizona* a variety of advertising by lawyers began to appear, including television commercials. Some lawyers believe the profession will lose respect if lawyers are allowed to advertise without any restrictions other than truthfulness. Others contend that advertising will promote more competition and that consumers will benefit as a result.

In 1977 the ABA's House of Delegates amended the ABA Code of Professional Responsibility to permit the advertising of 25 basic facts in the print media or on radio. Then in 1978 it allowed lawyers to use television to solicit business. As a consequence of this action, the Justice Department asked that its antitrust action against ABA be dismissed. Finally, in 1983, the ABA adopted a far less restrictive advertising code which simply prohibits false, deceptive, or misleading statements. The new policy permits lawyers to use any medium and it eliminates virtually all of the prior "do's" and "don'ts."

The U.S. Supreme Court again addressed the matter of restrictions or prohibitions on lawyer advertising in 1982, doing so in *In re: The Matter of R.M.J.*[54] The Court unanimously held that a Missouri Supreme Court rule that limited advertising by lawyers to 10 categories violated the First Amendment in the absence of any showing that the forbidden types of advertising are inherently misleading.

But there still are some restrictions. For example, use of dramatizations, visual displays, and background sounds in lawyers' TV advertising is forbidden in Alabama, Iowa, New Jersey, Ohio, Vermont, and West Virginia.

FTC and Other Professional Societies. In its efforts to promote more competition, the FTC also took actions against other professional societies. Under pressure, the American Dental Association agreed to a consent order in 1979 not to restrict truthful advertising by dentists.[55] Under the interim agreement, a final settlement had to await the outcome of a similar lawsuit against the American Medical Association.

In 1978 an administrative law judge ruled that the AMA violated the FTC Act by conspiring to restrain competition among physicians through restricting their advertising and solicitation of patients. The AMA appealed the ruling to the full Commission which unanimously ruled that the AMA had illegally restrained advertising by member physicians, but the Commission said the AMA could formulate "reasonable ethical guidelines" concerning physicians' advertising and thereby end further FTC action,[56] but the AMA chose otherwise and a final order was issued in 1982 against the AMA forbidding it from prohibiting truthful advertising by its members.[57] A similar order was issued against the American Dental Association that same year.[58] The order followed a 4–4 split vote of the U.S. Supreme Court in *AMA v. FTC* (1982), which upheld the FTC's action that had cleared the way for physicians to advertise in ways not approved by the medical association. The Justice Department had represented the FTC in the case and had cited the need to reverse the effect of what it termed AMA's restraint of trade.

The AMA and other professional societies then went to Congress and lobbied intensely for legislation exempting from FTC regulation professions that already are regulated by state government. Such legislation was passed by the House in 1982 but failed to make it through the Senate.

In the meantime, the Commission ruled that it was illegal for states and professional groups to restrict the advertising of prices for eye examinations and glasses, and it brought pressure on veterinary associations to ease restrictions on advertising by their members.[59] With the handwriting on the wall, the American Institute of Architects voted in 1978 to end its long-standing ban on advertising by its members. Other professional groups have done the same.

Four-Part Test Put Forth. Whenever truthful advertising is banned by a governmental agency, whether state or federal, courts should apply a four-part commercial speech analysis to the restriction. This is the substance of a U.S. Supreme Court action in 1980 in *Central Hudson Gas & Electric Co. v. Public Service Commission* and *Consolidated Edison v. Public Service Commission.*[60] The Court struck down New York Public Service Commission regulations that prohibited electric utility companies from using promotional advertising and that barred them from inserting in customers' bills information that promoted the companies' positions on controversial public policy issues. The New York Court of Appeals had upheld the regulations as valid exercises of the commission's authority. In striking down the ban on the bill inserts, the Court, in an opinion by Justice Powell, said the commission's prohibition of discussion of a controversial issue "strikes at the heart of the freedom to speak." It rejected the state's argument that utility customers are a "captive audience" for the bill inserts, noting that a customer can escape exposure to the message by simply transferring it from the envelope to the wastebasket. Furthermore, the commission's order was not a valid time, place, or manner restriction, nor was it a permissible subject-matter regulation, said Powell, adding that the prohibition was not justified by a compelling state interest.

In the promotional advertising case (*Central Hudson*), the Court, again in an opinion by Justice Powell, applied a four-part commercial speech analysis to the promotional advertising restrictions: (1) whether the expression is protected by the First Amendment; (2) whether the asserted governmental interest is substantial; (3) whether the regulation directly advances the asserted governmental interest; and (4) whether the regulation is more extensive than necessary to serve that interest.[61] The Court recognized the state's substantial interest in fostering energy conservation, but concluded that the state commission's order suppressed speech that in no way impaired the state's attempt to assert that interest.

In another case—this one in California—the state's Public Utilities Commission sought to require Pacific Gas & Electric Co. to include in utility bill mailings literature from a consumer-oriented group called TURN (Toward Utility Rate Normalization). But the U.S. Supreme Court in 1986 ruled that the company could not be compelled to do so.[62] In an opinion by Justice Powell, who was joined by three other justices, the Court said that such compulsion would burden the company's exercise of its own speech rights. Furthermore, Powell criticized the insert plan because it was not content-free (time, place, and manner restrictions or requirements must be content-free).

Marshall concurred in the judgment; White, Rehnquist, and Stevens dissented; and Blackmun did not participate in the case.

Liquor Advertising Bans. The *Central Hudson* four-pronged test would figure in separate cases involving the constitutionality of state laws prohibiting the intrastate advertising of alcoholic beverages.

Justice Rehnquist had dissented in *Virginia Pharmacy Board* principally because he thought that that decision would make it impossible to prohibit truthful advertising of products that are potentially harmful, such as cigarettes and liquor.

In *Lamar Outdoor Advertising, Inc. v. Mississippi State Tax Commission,* a three-judge U.S. Court of Appeals (Fifth Circuit) panel declared unconstitutional Mississippi's regulatory scheme that imposes an absolute prohibition against intrastate liquor advertising in the local media.[63] The panel said, in part, that there had been no showing that the ban directly advanced the state's substantial interest in promoting temperance. The panel said that liquor advertisements in the media constitute commercial speech entitled to First Amendment protection even though the sale of liquor is illegal in certain areas of the state under local option law.

However, the Fifth Circuit voted an *en banc* review of this and a companion case, *Dunagin v. City of Oxford,* and ruled that the regulatory scheme does not violate either the First or Fourteenth Amendments.[64]

The *en banc* court based its conclusion on the four-part *Central Hudson* analysis, but unlike the three-judge panel, it concluded that the advertising ban directly advanced the asserted state interest (part 3). The reason: advertising and consumption of alcoholic beverages are directly linked. The trial judge in *Lamar Outdoor Advertising* had heard testimony from an expert witness who had testified that advertising had only affected brand loyalty and market share, and not overall or individual consumption.[65] The trial court concluded that the commission had not produced concrete scientific evidence to substantiate its position that alcohol advertising artificially stimulates consumption; therefore, the regulation of advertising does little to directly advance the government's interest in promoting temperance.

But the *en banc* court cited the Supreme Court's finding in *Central Hudson* that there is "an immediate connection between advertising and demand for electricity. . . ." The *en banc* court held that there exists sufficient reason to believe that advertising and consumption of alcoholic beverages are linked such that the prohibition directly advances the state's asserted interest and that the restrictions are not more extensive than necessary to serve that interest (part 4).

The state of Mississippi had argued in *Lamar Outdoor Advertising* that the Supreme Court's summary affirmance of the congressional ban on the broadcasting of cigarette commercials (see Chapter 15) was a compelling authority in the case before the *en banc* court. Not so, said the judges. The cigarette commercial ban case has limited precedent-setting value because, according to the Fifth Circuit, (1) it antedated the emergence of the commercial speech doctrine announced in *Virginia Pharmacy Board;* and (2) the Supreme Court expressly limited that case to "the special problems of the electronic broadcast media" — a form of communication "especially subject to regulation in the public interest."[66]

The Supreme Court declined to review the Fifth Circuit's decision.

In 1988, Mississippi ended its 22-year ban on liquor advertising in the state.[67] Advertising in dry counties is still prohibited as is the broadcasting of ads on television before, during, or after cartoon shows aimed at children.

The new law permits Mississippi-based newspapers, television and radio stations, and outdoor billboard companies, to advertise liquor and wine products.

A few days before deciding not to review *Dunagin* and *Lamar Outdoor Advertising,* the Supreme Court had unanimously ruled that federal law preempts Oklahoma from prohibiting cable television system operators within the state from retransmitting any out-of-state signals that contain commercials for alcoholic beverages. The Court did so in *Capital Cities Cable v. Crisp.*[68]

The outcome hinged in large part on FCC rules that encourage cable TV systems to import out-of-state signals (programs), but that prohibit cable operators from deleting or altering any portion of those signals. To comply with the state attorney general's 1980 ruling in deleting commercials for alcoholic beverages from out-of-state signals, cable operators might be compelled either to abandon altogether the carriage of signals that originate outside Oklahoma or run the risk of criminal prosecution. As Justice Brennan said for the Court, such a result would lead to the public being deprived of a wide variety of programming options made possible by cable systems.

Also, in relying on the *Central Hudson* analysis, Brennan noted that Oklahoma has broad power under the Twenty-first Amendment to regulate the importation and use of alcoholic beverages within its borders and that the advertising ban represented only a limited means of furthering the state's goal in promoting temperance. Further, the state's interests are reduced to the extent that it does not enforce the ban against all advertising, such as those appearing in out-of-state publications sold within the state. Said Brennan:

> When this limited interest is measured against the significant interference with the federal objective of ensuring widespread availability of diverse cable services throughout the United States . . . it is clear that the state's interest is not of the same stature as the goals identified in the FCC's ruling and regulations.[69]

A number of questions remain unanswered by the Court's decision in *Capital Cities Cable,* including the one that broadcasting groups hoped would be answered; namely, their contention that governments cannot stop the distribution of truthful advertising for legally available products and services.[70] Also, this situation exists: The state can continue to enforce laws requiring in-state over-the-air TV stations to delete commercials for alcoholic beverages from network signals, but cannot prevent in-state cable systems from importing those commercials from the same networks along with signals from out-of-state network affiliated stations.

Such inconsistency was the reason that U.S. District Court Judge Lee West ruled in 1986 that what was left of the liquor advertising ban was unconstitutional because it had been applied to in-state publications but not to out-of-state ones that circulated in Oklahoma.[71] Therefore, it violated the equal protection under the law requirement. Prior to the ruling, the state had been under a temporary restraining order prohibiting enforcement of the ban.

Additional Advertising Ban Cases. The *Capital Cities Cable* case can be distinguished from other advertising ban cases because of the medium involved and because of special federal agency regulation of that medium. But as with the outcome in the *Lamar Outdoor Advertising* case, governments can ban truthful commercial speech under certain conditions.

Thus, in *Los Angeles City Council v. Taxpayers for Vincent* (1984), the Supreme Court, by a 6–3 vote, upheld Los Angeles' prohibition against the posting of signs, such as billboards and posters, on all public property.[72] The city bans such signs for esthetic reasons.

For the majority, Justice Stevens wrote that the ordinance was not overbroad; there was no hint of bias or censorship (since all signs are prohibited); and it is well established that the state may legitimately use its police powers to advance esthetic values.

Justice Brennan, joined by Justices Marshall and Blackmun, dissented. The forced removal of political campaign signs from utility poles showed a startling insensitivity to the principles of the First Amendment, said Brennan, adding that "esthetic concerns" were insufficient to justify the ban.

In another advertising ban case, the Supreme Court allowed a Nevada Supreme Court decision to stand when it declined to review *Princess Sea Industries v. Nevada* (1982).[73] The Nevada court had upheld the constitutionality of state law that prohibits the advertising of brothels in counties where prostitution is illegal. Such advertising is permitted in counties that have made prostitution legal. Members of the world's oldest profession had argued that the state law unconstitutionally prevented them from truthfully advertising in the state's most populous cities.

And the *Central Hudson* test figured prominently in a unanimous (8–0) Supreme Court decision which struck down as unconstitutional a law stemming from passage of the Comstock Act of 1873. The law banned the mailing of unsolicited advertisements for condoms and other contraceptive devices.

The Court, in *Bolger v. Youngs Drug Products Corporation* (1983), voided 39 U.S. Code 300(e)(2) after applying the *Central Hudson* test.[74] In giving the Court's opinion, Justice Marshall said that the government's asserted interest in shielding persons from receiving mail which they are likely to find offensive "carries little weight."

Casino Advertising Ban Upheld. It was clear by mid-1986, when a casino advertising ban case was decided by the U.S. Supreme Court, that truthful commercial speech was not fully protected by the First Amendment. When there is a "substantial government interest" in banning certain advertising, such as for health reasons, such bans are permitted, regardless of the media being used.

The Court, by a 5–4 decision in *Posadas de Puerto Rico Associates v. Tourism Company of Puerto Rico,* upheld a Puerto Rico statute and regulations that prohibited gambling casinos in the commonwealth from advertising in media circulated on the island.[75]

In his opinion for the Court, Justice Rehnquist, citing *Central Hudson,* made it clear that commerical speech receives a limited form of First Amendment protection so long as it concerns a lawful activity and is not misleading or fraudulent. Also, he said that the "greater power to completely ban casino gambling necessarily includes the lesser power to ban advertising of casino gambling."

The Court decided that the restrictions were narrowly drawn and advanced a substantial government interest "in the health and safety of its citizens."

The commonwealth had argued that there were harmful effects likely from such advertising, such as disruption of moral and cultural patterns, increase in local crime, fostering of prostitution.

The Court agreed that there were "substantial" governmental interests that justified commercial speech restrictions. Furthermore, the Court said that the law dealt only with "pure commercial speech," which is not as fully protected by the First Amendment as, for example, political speech.

Puerto Rico legalized casino gambling in 1948 and, according to its gaming laws, "no gambling room shall be permitted to advertise . . . to the public of Puerto Rico." The casinos can, however, advertise outside of Puerto Rico.

Posados de Puerto Rico Associates, a Texas partnership, obtained a license to operate a casino in Puerto Rico and subsequently was fined several times for violation of the law. It filed a suit in 1982. Ultimately, an appeal was taken to the U.S. Supreme Court with the casino owners arguing that commercial speech that is neither false nor deceptive and does not advertise unlawful activities fulfills an important informational purpose and is entitled to First Amendment protection.

Justice Brennan, joined by Marshall and Blackmun, dissented. He contended that states may regulate commercial speech only to protect against dissemination of false or misleading information. Restrictions on such speech are not justified where "the government seeks to manipulate private behavior by depriving citizens of truthful information concerning lawful activities." Because Puerto Rico permits its residents to patronize casinos, the ad ban does not, in fact, advance substantial government interests, said Brennan.

In a separate dissent, Stevens called the ad restrictions "rather bizarre restraints on speech" that are plainly forbidden by the First Amendment.

Advertising Age commented editorially on this decision by saying, in part: "Although some silver linings appeared in the Court's ruling . . . , the immediate [advertising] industry reaction was gloom, doom and uncertainty over how proposed bans [in Congress] on tobacco and alcohol advertising might be treated by the Court."[76]

A Columbia University Law School professor, Henry Monaghan, believes the Supreme Court's decision in *Posadas de Puerto Rico Associates* strongly reinforces the proposition that there is no constitutional right to advertise harmful things.[77]

When a panel of First Amendment scholars met in 1984 to discuss constitutional protection for commercial speech, they seemed to agree on only one point, namely, that nobody really knows how the Supreme Court will rule on a host of commercial speech issues.[78]

That there are mixed feelings concerning protection for commercial speech is reflected in the statement of Floyd Abrams, New York attorney, who said that the question of providing First Amendment protection to such speech "is one on which I personally have wavered over the years." He continued:

I find it hard to make the argument that the framers of the Constitution intended, or that there is much in the First Amendment, [affording] protection of that sort of speech.[79]

But the risks of not affording that protection, he said, "are greater than the genuine risks of trivializing the First Amendment."

CORRECTIVE ADVERTISING

With First Amendment considerations in mind, let's look at some of the FTC's problems and "solutions" during and after the 1970s.

One problem results from procedural safeguards that are built into the case-by-case approach often taken by the FTC. Delays in bringing cases to a speedy conclusion often led to complaints about agency foot-dragging in dealing with deceptive or unfair advertising.

Responding to the criticism, the FTC decided in 1970 to allocate a larger share of its resources to checking national television advertising for consumer deception.

Concurrent with that decision, the Commission began to issue complaints with proposed orders designed to probe more effective remedies, such as "corrective" advertising.

The first corrective advertising case surfaced on September 30, 1970, when the FTC required — with the consent of the company involved — that a certain percentage of the firm's advertising budget be devoted during a year's time to correcting any false impressions left by previous advertising. However, the company could, if it wished, stop advertising during the year's period, thereby escaping the full thrust of the consent order.

Campbell Soup Case

Corrective advertising was suggested by the FTC staff and adopted by the Commission in part at the urging of a group of law students at George Washington University calling themselves S.O.U.P., Inc. (Students Opposing Unfair Practices). They had petitioned the FTC to require corrective advertising as part of a cease-and-desist order following disclosure that Campbell Soup Co. was using glass marbles to enhance the appearance of its vegetable soup during televised commercials. Not until late 1976 was it revealed that a competitor of Campbell Soup Co. — H.J. Heinz Co. — was behind the much publicized FTC investigation of the soup commercials.[80]

The Commission did not order corrective advertising in the soup case, but it did assert at the time that it had the power to impose such a unique remedy — unique in the sense of requiring corrective advertising in the general media. Prescription drug advertisers previously had been subject to such a requirement, although they could carry out corrective advertising through medical journal ads or by direct mail.

In justifying such a remedy, the FTC believed that it would serve a threefold purpose: (1) dispel residual consumer deception; (2) help to restore competition to its proper level; and (3) deprive false advertisers of ill-gotten gains (such as a disproportionate share of the market), especially since the traditional cease-and-desist order was merely an admonishment to "go and sin no more" and carried no punishment for past "sins."

The frustrations of trying to deal with allegedly deceptive advertising were cited as one reason for the new remedy when Robert Pitofsky, then director of the FTC's Bureau of Consumer Protection, spoke at a convention of the American Association of Advertising Agencies in 1971. He cited these examples:

- It took the FTC 16 years to get the word "liver" out of Carter's Little Liver Pills.
- The FTC began investigating Geritol ads in 1959 and the case wasn't settled until 1976.

The frustrations of such cases, plus the perceived need to deal with "residual consumer deception," led the FTC to implement corrective advertising. In 1971 it issued a consent order (agreed to by the ITT Continental Baking Co., Inc.) which stipulated that if any advertising appeared for Profile bread during a year's period, at least one-fourth of such advertising would have to call attention to the fact that the "bread is not effective for weight reduction," as originally implied.[81] The FTC-approved commercial, which appeared on television, went like this:

> I'd like to clear up any misunderstanding you may have about Profile bread from its advertising or even its name. Does Profile bread have fewer calories than other breads? No, Profile has about the same per ounce as other breads. To be exact, Profile has seven fewer calories per slice. That's because it's sliced thinner. But eating Profile will not cause you to lose weight.[82]

Another corrective ad agreement was reached in May 1972, this time with Ocean Spray Cranberries, Inc. The consent order concerned the food energy in a cranberry juice product

After the Ocean Spray action, the FTC moved against another bread company and subsequently against the makers of various analgesics, but in the latter instance the corrective ad period was placed at two years to make it harder for a company to decide not to advertise at all during the life of the consent order.

Not long after corrective advertising was initiated by the FTC, it came under attack from the advertising industry. Howard Bell, president of the American Advertising Federation, said in 1970 that such a program could lead to a business's possible "self-annihilation," adding:

> Since there are other remedies available to the government today to correct abuses in the marketplace, this kind of punitive remedy maligns business and creates an environment in which it can be neither free nor enterprising. If one wanted to silence advertising in this country and substitute a government information service, I can think of no better way to begin the process.[83]

The trade publication *Advertising Age,* in an editorial entitled "Copout," roundly criticized Ocean Spray Cranberries, Inc., for accepting the corrective ad order, saying that "expediency seems to be winning out over principle these days."[84] The company president earlier had said that "there are times when economics and practicalities dictate that a company compromise on a lawsuit."

Warner-Lambert/Listerine Case. A court test of the legality of a corrective advertisement order resulted when the FTC issued an order requiring Warner-Lambert Co. to include this message in Listerine advertisements until it had spent $10 million: "Contrary to prior advertising, Listerine will not prevent colds or sore throats or lessen their severity."[85]

In *Warner-Lambert Co.* (1975), the Commission said that a "substantial portion of the population will continue to hold this belief about the preventative powers of Listerine well into the 1980s and that this belief plays a material role in purchasing decisions (thereby injuring both consumers and competition)." In view of this, the Commission said that an order "merely requiring cessation of deceptive advertising would not afford the public adequate protection. The lingering false belief must be dispelled, a task which requires corrective advertising."

In 1977, a three-judge panel of the U.S. Court of Appeals for the District of Columbia Circuit voted 2–1 to uphold that part of the FTC order requiring Warner-Lambert to state in its advertisements—if it chooses to advertise—that Listerine is not a cold remedy.[86] But in the opinion written by Judge Wright, the majority said the company need not include in its advertising this portion of the corrective ad order: "Contrary to prior advertising. . . ." In effect, what the court ordered was "affirmative disclosure" (discussed later in the chapter) without a "confessional preamble."

The court said that the "contrary to prior advertising" requirement could serve only two purposes: either to attract attention that a correction follows or to humiliate the advertiser. The court continued:

> The Commission claims only the first purpose for it, and this we think is obviated by the other terms of the order. The second purpose, if it were intended, might be called for in an egregious case of deliberate deception, but this is not one. While we do not decide whether petitioner proffered its cold claims in good faith or bad, the record compiled could support a finding of good faith. On these facts, the confessional preamble to the disclosure is not warranted.[87]

As for the required $10 million expenditure without any time limits, the court held that such a formula "is reasonably related to the violation" found by the Commission.

Warner-Lambert and amici briefs filed by the Association of National Advertisers, Inc., and American Advertising Federation had argued that corrective advertising is not a permissible remedy because of the First Amendment and *Virginia Pharmacy Board.* The majority rejected this contention by noting the Supreme Court's admonition in *Virginia Pharmacy Board* that the First Amendment presents no obstacle to government regulation of false or misleading advertising.

Judge Roger Robb dissented because he did not believe that the FTC had the explicit authority to issue corrective advertising orders. Nor could he find such a grant of power in the legislative history of the FTC Act, as amended, or in the court decisions cited by the majority.

The U.S. Supreme Court denied review, and the makers of Listerine undertook a $10 million advertising campaign which included the disclosure but not the confessional.[88]

Can FTC Require a Correction? All of the corrective advertising mentioned thus far resulted from consent orders issued by the FTC. This means the advertisers voluntarily agreed to do certain things as specified in the orders. But can the Commission compel advertisers to advertise a message against their will? Except in limited circumstances, which were not spelled out, the First Amendment prohibits affirmative orders to advertise, according to a panel of the U.S. Court of Appeals (Seventh Circuit) in *National Commission on Egg Nutrition v. FTC*.[89] The panel ruled that the First Amendment is not violated by an FTC order prohibiting the egg industry trade association from making certain false and misleading claims in its advertising, including the statement that "there is no scientific evidence that eating eggs increases the risk of heart and circulatory disease." The panel used *Virginia Pharmacy Board* for stating that false, deceptive, or misleading advertising is subject to restraints. But the appellate judges did not go along with the FTC's order that the deceptive advertising be replaced with messages stating that increased egg consumption, in the opinion of many experts, increases the risk of heart disease.

The U.S. Supreme Court declined to review the decision[90] and the Commission, by unanimous vote, issued a final order in 1979 prohibiting the national group from advertising that there is no scientific evidence to link egg consumption to a higher risk of heart disease.

Current State of Corrective Advertising. Although corrective advertising still remains a "weapon" that can be used by the Commission, it has been largely unused since President Reagan obtained a Republican majority among the commissioners. The advertising industry has made known its intense dislike of corrective advertising and the business-oriented Republican-dominated Commission has been loathe to use it.

AD SUBSTANTIATION PROGRAM

Another innovative effort to combat deceptive advertising was initiated by the FTC about the same time that the agency resorted to corrective ad orders. This was the advertising substantiation program based on powers contained in Section 6 of FTCA.

Five policy considerations led to the decision to implement the ad substantiation program:

1. Public disclosure of information obtained can assist consumers in making rational choices from among competing claims.
2. The public's information needs are not being met voluntarily.

3. Public disclosure can enhance competition by encouraging competitors to challenge advertising claims which have no basis in fact.
4. Knowledge that documentation, or lack thereof, will be made public will encourage advertisers to have adequate substantiation on hand before claims are made.
5. Since the FTC has limited resources for detecting claims which are not substantiated by adequate proof, making the "documentation" available to the public can help alert consumers, businesspersons, and public interest groups to possible Section 5 violations.[91]

The program's primary goals were education and deterrence; that is, public disclosure of data assists consumers to make rational choices, and disclosure encourages advertisers to have adequate data on hand before making claims.

In its first substantiation action, the FTC asked seven U.S. and foreign automakers to document advertising claims. Then came similar orders to makers of electric shavers, air conditioners, television sets, cough and cold remedies, tires, dentifrices, and detergents. The FTC said that eventually all major industries would be included in such orders. But after the first year of operation, the value of the program stirred some doubts. The seven automakers sent to the FTC hundreds of pages of documentation, much of it so highly technical that private consultants had to be employed to analyze and evaluate that information. In addition, by the time data on 1971 models could be sifted, evaluated, and made available to the public, 1972 models already were in the showrooms.

The program underwent changes to meet some of the criticisms. The Commission decided in 1973 not to seek documentation for each and every advertising claim, but instead to direct substantiation orders at three or four major selling themes of a product's advertising—themes common to the industry. Also, in addition to the technical documentation, companies were requested to submit a narrative summary, in lay language, concerning substantiation of the claims. Then, in 1974, the FTC announced that it was reducing the time frame for responding to substantiation orders from 60 to 30 days and focusing attention on more suspicious claims. The purpose of such changes was to gain quicker action on unsubstantiated claims, although less information would be made available to the public. Instead, summary and backup information would be made public, but not the massive data which had been received in accordance with the first few substantiation orders.

Then, in 1977, the Commission amended its procedural rules to require that advertisers make "timely submissions of advertising substantiation material" or else administrative law judges would exclude the material at trial whenever the material has been offered in defense of the charge that the advertiser lacked a "reasonable basis" for making the advertising claims.[92]

"Reasonable Basis" Standard

In 1972 the FTC withdrew its own complaint against Pfizer, Inc., after trying for two years to get Pfizer to substantiate certain claims about its sunburn lotion, "Un-Burn." The complaint had charged that the company's advertisement falsely implied that scientific tests substantiated the claim that "Un-Burn" anesthetized nerves in the sunburned skin area and stopped pain quickly. Allegations of deception and unfair practice were made, the latter resulting from advertising claims which, according to the FTC, lacked adequate and well-controlled scientific studies or tests. In withdrawing the complaint, the Commission said Pfizer should be held to a "reasonable basis" standard.[93]

The Commission's position was that "failure to possess substantiation amounts to a lack of reasonable basis, which in turn is an unfair act or practice under Section 5."[94] "Reasonable basis" consists of competent and reliable scientific tests or opinions of experts qualified to render judgments in such matters.

New Substantiation Policy Emerges

Shortly after Miller became FTC chairman, he expressed concerns about the ad substantiation program and the "reasonable basis" standard.[95] Surprising, perhaps, was the advertising industry's reaction. Miller was going too fast and too far for the industry.[96] True, the industry objected to the "unfairness" doctrine and wanted it scuttled. For the most part it applauded Miller's initiative to redefine the deception policy, but it thought the chairman was out of bounds when he started urging changes in the fundamental requirement that advertisers have support in hand before advertising claims are made. The upshot was adoption of a "refined" ad substantiation policy in July 1984 that still requires advertisers to have a "reasonable basis" for making objective ad claims.[97] However, it allows the Commission to accept evidence in three instances after advertising claims have been challenged: (1) when deciding whether there is a public interest in proceeding against a company; (2) when assessing whether an advertiser had adequate substantiation before making a claim; and (3) when deciding the need for an order against an advertiser who lacked a reasonable basis before releasing the advertisement in question.[98] Also, the industrywide substantiation orders were to give way to orders against specific companies. Thus, what began in 1971 as a move against the slower case-by-case method had returned substantially to that method 13 years later.

TRADE REGULATION RULES (TRRs)

Under Section 6(g), the Commission has the power "to make rules and regulations for the purpose of carrying out the provisions of" the FTCA. But for 48 years (1914–1962) the power lay dormant, and for 12 years thereafter (until 1974) the question of the FTC's authority to use such power remained in doubt. The issue: Could the powers contained in Section 6 be used to bring about enforcement of Section 5 proceedings?

In *U.S. v. Morton Salt Co.* (1950), the Supreme Court ruled that the FTC Act must be read "as an integrated whole" and that businesses could be required to submit reports under Section 6(b) in order for the FTC to obtain information that could be used to determine compliance with cease-and-desist orders issued under Section 5.[99] But whether this power was tantamount to substantive rule-making power (i.e., the power to specify, prior to any adjudication, what constitutes deceptive or unfair trade practices) remained uncertain through nonuse of the authority. But in 1962 the FTC asserted that Section 6 was not limited merely to investigation and information gathering.

The crucial test of the rule-making power came after the Commission promulgated a trade regulation rule (TRR) which required the posting of octane ratings on gasoline pumps. The rule was attacked in a suit brought by the National Petroleum Refiners Association. In 1972 the U.S. District Court for the District of Columbia nullified the FTC's rule-making power on the ground that the Commission lacked statutory authority.[100] The FTC appealed and it also went to Congress in a move to obtain statutory authority for substantive rule-making. Chairman Miles Kirkpatrick characterized the denial of such authority as a severe blow to the agency's ability to maintain competition and to protect consumers. Without such power, Kirkpatrick said, the FTC would be reduced to case-by-case adjudication, rather than dealing with unfair or deceptive practices on an industry-wide basis.

The FTC's anguish turned to jubilation in 1973 when a three-judge panel of the Court of Appeals for the District of Columbia unanimously upheld the agency's power to issue substantive rules.[101] The petroleum industry appealed but the Supreme Court refused to review the case.[102]

Before a year had passed, Congress enacted the Magnuson-Moss Warranty/FTC Improvement Act, which statutorily gave the agency rule-making power. Prior to this time the FTC's only enforcement method for violation of a TRR was through issuance of a cease-and-desist order. Unless violated, such an order carried no monetary penalties. With passage of the 1975 Act, a TRR violation can result in an immediate court proceeding that could result in one or more consumer "remedies," such as refund of money, return of property, payment of damages, and, to top that off, civil penalties of up to $10,000 for each day of violation.

The importance of the statutory grant of TRR power to the FTC can be judged by this statement in the agency's 1975 annual report:

> By confirming the Commission's authority to issue substantive trade regulation rules, and by empowering the Commission to seek consumer redress and civil penalties for rule violations, the Magnuson-Moss Act made the trade regulation rule the basic building block of the commission's consumer protection programs. The Commission therefore accelerated its efforts to produce enforceable trade regulation rules and also began designing a program to codify into trade regulation rules the definitions of unfair or deceptive conduct previously outlined in litigation, interpretive guides, and trade practice rules.

In a year's period, the Commission proceeded toward the promulgation of TRRs affecting, or related to, credit institutions, prescription eyeglasses, used cars, health spas, vocational schools, mobile homes, hearing aids, cellular plastics, food manufacturers, textile and leather products, and funeral homes.

Despite considerable delays associated with procedural safeguards that must be observed before promulgation of TRRs (a period of three years not being uncommon from the publication of the initial notice of proposed rule-making until the Commission's consideration of whether to promulgate a final rule), there was a decided bias for rule-making over the slower case-by-case adjudicatory method for these reasons:

- Under the civil penalties section, liability for a TRR violation depends either upon actual knowledge of the rule, or upon "knowledge fairly implied from the objective circumstances."[103] By contrast, liability for acts or practices which the Commission previously had found unfair or deceptive depends upon actual knowledge of the prior determination.
- Under the consumer redress section, redress lies for any TRR violation. By contrast, to obtain redress for an act or practice not specifically proscribed by TRR, the FTC would have to satisfy a court that a reasonable person would have known that the act or practice was dishonest or fraudulent.
- Under the redress section, redress for a TRR violation is immediate without any prior administrative adjudication.

This bias toward rule-making existed before the FTC staff proposed a ban on some kinds of television advertising directed at children of a certain age, and before the Commission sought to promulgate a used car "lemon" rule or a funeral home rule. Let's turn first to the *proposed* ban on TV advertising aimed at children of a certain age.

Proposed Ban on TV Advertising Directed at Children

Considerable concern and regulatory activity has swirled around advertising directed at children, and the FTC found itself faced with a serious funding problem and a hostile Congress in 1979 and 1980 as the result of a proposed TRR to ban some kinds of advertising directed at children.

One reason for special protective measures to be considered by the FTC is found in a U.S. Supreme Court decision in *FTC v. R.F. Keppel & Brothers, Inc.* (1934).[104] This case involved the sale of penny candies in "break and take" packs, a form of merchandising which induced children to buy lesser amounts of admittedly inferior candy in the hope of hitting a bonus package containing extra candy and prizes. In sustaining the FTC's conclusion that such a practice was unfair, the court emphasized that children were a special class of consumers "unable to protect themselves."

The FTC reflected the Court's view in *Keppel* when it issued a consent order against Mattel, Inc., requiring the toy manufacturer to cease using any advertising which distorted the performance of its "Hot Wheels" racing car or "Dancerina Doll." The proposed complaint had said the alleged deceptive or unfair advertising "unfairly exploits a consumer group unqualified by age or experience to anticipate or appreciate the possibility that the representations [in TV advertising] may be exaggerated or untrue." The proposed complaint continued,

"Further, respondents unfairly play upon the affection of adults, especially parents and other close relatives, for children, by inducing the purchase of toys and related products through deceptive or unfair claims. . . ."[105] The Commission, in its consent order, required the toymaker to cease doing certain things in its advertising, such as using distorted camera angles, misrepresenting visual perspectives so as to increase the speed or realism of the toys, and other practices—especially, said the FTFC, "taking into consideration the level of knowledge, sophistication, maturity, and experience of such age group or groups."

The law traditionally has afforded children special protection, such as shielding them from pornography or from publicity (in the case of juvenile offenders). More recently the FTC began to consider special protection for children against advertising which exploits their innocence and gullibility and thus destroys their ability to make rational, intelligent purchasing decisions.[106] Prodded by pressure groups, such as Action for Children's Television (ACT), the FTC in 1974 issued a proposed ban on television advertisements which induce children to buy cereals or other prizes. But after nearly three years of soul-searching, spurred on by opposition that surfaced at various proceedings, the Commission decided not to adopt the proposed guide but rather to continue to evaluate the fairness of such advertising on a case-by-case basis. It took this action partly because the "facts available to the Commission at this time do not demonstrate that all premium advertising televised to child audiences is inherently or invariably unfair or deceptive."[107]

The pressure did not abate and, at an ACT-sponsored conference in 1977, the then FTC chairman, Michael Pertschuk, who emphasized that he was speaking for himself and not the Commission, said that television advertising directed at children, especially preschoolers, "may violate the statutory standards of fairness."

In 1978 the FTC released a 346-page staff report on *Television Advertising to Children* with the following TRR recommended by the Bureau of Consumer Protection: (1) Ban all advertising from television shows seen by substantial numbers of children under age eight; (2) ban the advertising of sugary foods that pose a dental health risk from television shows seen by significant numbers of children between the ages of eight and eleven; (3) allow continued television advertising of less "hazardous" sugared foods to the eight-eleven age group but only if the individual food advertisers fund "balancing" dental health and nutritional messages.

Shortly after receiving the staff recommendation, the Commission voted 4–0 to issue the proposed TRR in order to gain "comment on the appropriateness and workability . . . of such a rule as well as other possible remedies" for the alleged harmful effects of television commercials on children. At stake in such rulemaking was an estimated $661 million in spot and network advertising for products most likely to be seriously affected if such a rule were adopted.

The industry's attack upon the proposed rule was both direct and intensive. At one point Congress refused to appropriate money for the agency and there were some payless paydays. Ultimately, the Federal Trade Commission Improvement Act of 1980 was passed which contained a section eliminating, at least through September 1982, the Commission's authority to promulgate a rule based on unfair advertising. Any such rule would have to be based on deceptive advertising. Also, Congress gave itself veto power over any FTC-intended TRRs.

As a result of such pressure and legislative restrictions, the FTC's staff recommended that the Commission terminate the children's advertising rule-making procedure. The staff said that the rule-making record established that although child-oriented television advertising is a legitimate cause for public concern, there did not currently appear to be workable solutions that could be implemented through rule-making. The only effective remedy for the problems associated with advertising directed to children six years and under, said the staff, would be a ban on such advertisements. "Such a ban, as a practical matter, cannot be implemented," the staff concluded. "Because of this there is no need to determine whether or not advertising oriented toward young children is deceptive."[108]

The staff also recommended terminating the rule-making proceeding concerning the advertising of sugared products to children under the age of 12. According to the staff, the evidence was inconclusive as to whether advertising for sugared products adversely affects children's attitudes about nutrition. Also, no accepted scientific methodology existed for determining a specific food's capacity to cause cavities, the staff said.

The Commission voted in 1981 to terminate the rule-making procedure.

Congressional Veto Power "Vetoed." At one time the FTC had considered a proposed rule that would require used car dealers to tell prospective customers about any defects such cars might have. Intense lobbying resulted and a watered-down version of such a TRR finally made it to Congress in 1982 where it was promptly vetoed. The Senate voted 69–27 and the House 286–133 to kill the rule. This was Congress's first exercise of the power it gave itself in 1980 to veto any TRRs it did not like.

Partly as a consequence of such congressional action, the FTC's proposed 1983 fiscal budget reflected a reduction in rule-making resources. As Chairman Miller put it:

> Rule-making will be retained as an enforcement tool but will be used only after careful study shows it to be more effective and efficient than other means.[109]

As an alternative to rule-making, said Miller, the FTC would pursue case-by-case enforcement.

The FTC, by a 3–1 vote in 1982, passed another controversial TRR. This one required funeral homes to provide itemized costs rather than just a "package" cost. Miller cast the only negative vote, and his director of the FTC Consumer Protection Bureau, Timothy J. Muris, was soon at work urging Congress to veto the rule. Congress had 90 work days to decide. Ultimately, it allowed the rule to go into effect on January 1, 1984. The rule also forbids misrepresentation, such as saying or implying that embalming is required by law where such is not the case.

The issue of legislative vetoes was met head-on in 1983 when the U.S. Supreme Court, by a 7–2 vote, struck down such vetoes principally because the Court said they violate the constitutionally required separation of powers doctrine. The decision came in *Immigration and Naturalization Service v. Chadha,* with only Justices White and Rehnquist dissenting.[110]

The full impact of the Court's decision remains to be seen; however, for 50 years Congress inserted legislative veto provisions into many statutes, estimated by Justice White to number nearly 200. Justice Powell was more expansive, saying there were hundreds of such insertions in various statutes. What remains to be seen is how Congress will react to the decision in terms of influencing future regulatory action.

Given the Court's action, the FTC again returned to a used car TRR and passed a rule requiring used-car dealers to put warranty and other information on window stickers. However, the rule does not require dealers to list mechanical defects of the cars being sold. The stickers must: (1) list warranty terms, (2) say whether the consumer should pay for any needed repairs, (3) say whether consumers should seek an independent inspection of the car, (4) give information about service contracts, and (5) warn consumers to get in writing all dealer promises. The rule went into effect in May 1985.

In 1988, the FTC announced that it would undertake a review of the funeral industry rule.

Forty states have passed lemon car laws. The provisions of the laws vary widely. In some instances, arbitration is required when disputes cannot be settled between the parties concerned.

Other TRRs are in place, including mail-order and retail food store advertising rules.

COMPARATIVE ADVERTISING

Comparative advertising, which names competing products when making comparative claims, received a FTC "boost" in 1979 when the Commission unanimously adopted a policy that encourages comparative advertising. As the Commission pointed out:

> Comparative advertising when truthful and nondeceptive, is a source of important information to consumers and assists them in making rational purchase decisions. Comparative advertising encourages product improvement and innovation, and can lead to lower prices in the marketplace. For these reasons, the Commission will continue to scrutinize carefully restraints upon its use.

The Commission's action has resulted in widespread comparative advertising in various media, but especially on television, such that Burger King would claim its burgers were better than either McDonald's or Wendy's in a $20 million advertising campaign. Both Burger King and Wendy's sought court injunctions to stop such advertising. They also filed lawsuits which, ultimately, were settled out-of-court. In recent years, many advertising campaigns have resorted to comparisons of competitors' products.

Subliminal Advertising

Subliminal advertising, like subliminal (below the threshold of consciousness) learning, has been a subject of controversy for many years. Whatever its effectiveness, the Federal Communications Commission announced in 1974 that the use of "subliminal perception is inconsistent with the obligations of a [broadcast] licensee, . . . and broadcasts employing such techniques are contrary to the public interest. Whether effective or not, such broadcasts clearly are intended to be deceptive."

In motion pictures or on television, subliminal advertising, or subliminal suggestion, could take several forms. For example, a picture of popcorn might be inserted as one frame, or several frames, among a series of frames related to, say, the coming attractions at a theater—too few for the audience to be consciously aware of them. The intent of the communicators, of course, would be to stimulate the desire of the audience for popcorn without doing so overtly.

STATE REGULATION

Even before the Federal Trade Commission Act was passed, there was considerable concern about advertising malpractices. A trade journal, *Printers' Ink,* put forth a model statute in 1911 which, if adopted, makes false, deceptive, or misleading advertising punishable as a misdemeanor. Most states have enacted this kind of law.

All of the states, except Alabama, and the District of Columbia have enacted "little FTC Acts" to prevent or deal with deceptive and unfair trade practices. Alabama has established a consumer complaint clearinghouse to facilitate action under existing laws and to recommend new legislation. Fourteen states use the broad language contained in Section 5 of the FTCA: Alaska, Connecticut, Florida, Hawaii, Illinois, Louisiana, Maine, Massachusetts, Montana, North Carolina, South Carolina, Vermont, Washington, and Wisconsin.

Fifteen states itemize deceptive practices but include a catchall clause to reach unlisted forms of deceptions. These states are Colorado, Georgia, Idaho, Indiana, Mississippi, Nevada, New Hampshire, Oklahoma, Oregon, Pennsylvania, Rhode Island, South Dakota, Texas, Virginia, and Wyoming. The remaining states have statutes which reach all forms of fraudulent and deceptive acts and practices, but they may not include unfair acts and practices.

Most of the states authorize investigations through the use of subpoenas, issuance of cease-and-desist orders, and the obtaining of injunctions to halt anticompetitive, deceptive, and sometimes unfair trade practices.

INDUSTRY SELF-REGULATION

Honest businesses are as much victimized by deceptive and false advertising as are consumers because they are put at a competitive disadvantage. Consequently, they have sought ways to bring pressure on those who resort to false and deceptive advertising.

One of the early attempts at self-regulation came in 1915 with the establishment of the National Vigilance Committee which later became the Better Business Bureau. Many other self-regulatory efforts followed, culminating in the most extensive one to date—the National Advertising Review Board (NARB) created jointly in late 1971 by the American Advertising Federation, the American Association of Advertising Agencies, the Association of National Advertisers, and the Council of Better Business Bureaus. A National Advertising Division (NAD) was set up to handle investigations or to initiate complaints. The NAD can dismiss a complaint or find the complaint justified and request modification or withdrawal of the advertisement. An appeal then can be made to the NARB. The board is comprised of 30 advertiser members, 10 advertising agency members, and 10 public or nonindustry members, with five-member panels the mechanism by which the board reviews appeals.

Only complaints involving the truth or accuracy of advertisements are considered by NAD and NARB, although additional kinds of reviews can be authorized. Advertisers who refuse to modify or withdraw untruthful or inaccurate advertisements face the threat of having NAD or NARB turn the matter over to appropriate government agencies.

In addition to NAD and NARB, the National Association of Broadcasters had extensive self-regulatory codes for radio and television for many years (the Radio Code dating back to 1929). These codes emphasized advertising do's and don'ts. Member stations that failed to abide by the Radio or TV Code could lose their right to display the NAB's Seal of Good Practice. A Code Authority, operating from offices in New York, Washington, D.C., and Hollywood, monitored radio and TV commercials for code violations. However, the Justice Department filed an antitrust lawsuit against NAB's TV Code, claiming that code restrictions on commercials, such as the one that limited the number of commercials in a 60-second time segment to two, violated antitrust laws. The upshot was an NAB decision to terminate the two codes in their entirety.

Despite this blow to self-regulatory efforts in the broadcast medium, it should be noted that commercial radio and television networks and most stations are active in maintaining advertising standards, as are many magazines and newspapers. The networks, for example, turn down a great deal of advertising because it is found objectionable for one reason or another.

SUMMARY

The FTC, created by act of Congress in 1914, was given the power under Section 5 to prevent unfair methods of competition in commerce. Whether such power included false advertising that had no relationship to competition remained in doubt until the Wheeler-Lea Amendment of 1938. By this amendment, the FTC was given authority to declare unlawful any unfair or deceptive acts or practices which affected consumers regardless of impact on competition. It was this change in the law that marked the turning point from a philosophy primarily based on the concept of *caveat emptor* ("let the buyer beware") to one of *caveat venditor* ("let the seller beware").

Under the FTC Improvement Act of 1975, the Commission's jurisdiction was extended to practices affecting interstate commerce, rather than only to those in interstate commerce. This means that the FTC can, if it wishes, reach into a state to act against practices in that state if they affect interstate commerce.

Some major developments concerning the FTC's power to deal with deceptive and unfair advertising are summarized in the following paragraphs.

- *Unfairness Doctrine.* The power to deal with unfair practices, even when such practices have no relation to competition, was upheld by the U.S. Supreme Court in the *Sperry & Hutchinson* case (1972). Thus, unfairness to consumers could be the basis for Section 5 actions.

- *Substantive rulemaking power.* The FTC's right to promulgate TRRs was upheld by the courts and statutorily granted by the Improvement Act of 1975. TRRs can expedite complaint proceedings under Section 5. Such rules alert an industry or a trade to deceptive or unfair practices, a violation of which can lead directly to enforcement proceedings via issuance of a consent order or a cease-and-desist order.

  However, what Congress gives it can also take away. In the FTC Improvement Act of 1980, Congress stipulated that the FTC could not use unfairness as the basis for any TRRs at least for a two-year period, including the *proposed* rule which would ban television advertising directed at children under age eight, ban television advertising of heavily sugared products directed at children between the ages of eight and eleven, and impose certain requirements on other kinds of advertising directed at the eight–eleven age group. Given this kind of pressure and restrictions, the FTC staff recommended that the rule-making proceedings related to television advertising directed at children be terminated.

- *Ad substantiation.* This program, implemented in 1971, also was used on an industrywide basis. Its purpose is twofold: education of the public and deterrence of false or deceptive advertising. Problems of coping with voluminous amounts of information, much of it highly technical, and making the information public in time to be of use to consumers led the FTC to redirect ad substantiation toward the more suspicious advertising claims. They also led the FTC to try to make readable summaries of the information available to the public on a faster timetable.

  But under the Reagan-appointed chairman, James C. Miller III, the Commission moved away from industrywide substantiation orders. Instead it requires substantiation on a company-by-company basis.

- *Reasonable basis test.* From the *Pfizer* "Un-Burn" case came a new standard for challenging certain types of advertising claims. In essence, an advertiser must have a reasonable basis for making claims. The failure to possess substantiation, such as competent and reliable scientific tests or opinions of experts qualified to render judgment, is tantamount to an unfair act or practice.
- *Corrective advertising.* This was one of the novel administrative law concepts to emerge in the 1970s. It is a device by which the FTC can deny to an advertiser any ill-gotten gains from deceptive or unfair advertising. By means of a consent order, a company agreed to devote a percentage of its advertising budget for a stipulated period (although the Listerine case was an exception) to corrective advertising in order to dispel residual consumer deception and to make the marketplace more competitive again. The Profile bread case was the first that resulted in a corrective ad order.

But prodded by Miller, the Commission in 1983 adopted a new policy that requires proof that a "reasonable consumer" has been harmed by deceptive advertising before the FTC will act against an advertiser. Miller also called for curbs on the "unfairness" doctrine and dislikes the corrective advertising "weapon." His preference was for the case-by-case approach and only when there is proof that a reasonable consumer has been harmed. His views reflected the Reagan administration's efforts toward deregulation of business and the use of cost/benefit analysis when regulatory efforts are being considered. Miller's departure from the FTC in 1985 to be Reagan's budget director has not affected earlier deregulatory efforts.

Meanwhile, Supreme Court decisions have extended First Amendment protection to truthful commercial speech, unlike the 1942 decision in *Valentine v. Chrestensen*. The landmark ruling came in *Virginia State Board of Pharmacy v. Virginia Citizens Consumer Council, Inc.* (1976). Then in *Bates v. State Bar of Arizona* (1977), a majority of the Supreme Court held that a rule which prohibited an attorney from truthfully advertising routine legal services violated the First Amendment. Since then the FTC has been moving aggressively to end restraints imposed by professional organizations which limit or prevent truthful advertising by members of those organizations.

Truthful advertising can be banned as demonstrated by government prohibitions against tobacco advertising on radio and television, liquor advertising, and casino advertising.

A four-part commercial speech analysis was put forth by the Supreme Court in *Central Hudson Gas & Electric Co.* (1980) to be used whenever the constitutionality of a ban on truthful advertising is being tested. The four parts are: (1) is the advertising protected by the First Amendment; (2) is the asserted government interest in banning the advertising substantial; (3) does the ban directly advance the asserted government interest; and (4) is it narrowly tailored?

In the arena of self-regulation, the advertising industry in 1971 created a

National Advertising Review Board with an investigatory arm (the National Advertising Division) that considers complaints involving the truth or accuracy of advertisements.

Most major media organizations maintain codes or standards by which to accept or reject advertising. However, efforts by the National Association of Broadcasters to use self-regulatory means to maintain advertising standards on radio and television came to an end in 1982 after the Justice Department brought a successful antitrust action against the NAB. As a result, the NAB decided to abandon its self-regulatory codes.

QUESTIONS IN REVIEW

1. The National Advertising Review Board is an industry-created self-regulatory group which basically deals with complaints about two kinds of advertising. What are the two kinds?
2. Originally Section 5 of FTCA pertained only to what kind of unfair methods?
3. What was the purpose of the Wheeler-Lea Amendment?
4. The legal philosophy prior to the Wheeler-Lea Amendment was *caveat emptor* which means _____, but with the amendment the philosophy shifted toward _____, or _____.
5. The undisclosed use of plexiglass as sandpaper in a shaving cream commercial on television was held by the U.S. Supreme Court to constitute what kind of deception?
6. True or False: Because they are only agents, advertising agencies cannot be held responsible for deceptive or unfair advertising.
7. True or False: When an advertiser enters into a consent order he is pleading guilty to the allegations which led to issuance of the order.
8. The landmark case in determining that purely commercial — but truthful — speech is protected by the First Amendment is _____.
9. Give two reasons why the U.S. Supreme Court extended First Amendment protection to purely commercial speech.
10. What were the three reasons given by the FTC for resorting to the use of corrective advertising orders?
11. What is ad substantiation?
12. What weaknesses were initially apparent in the ad substantiation program?
13. What test or standard will the FTC use in determining whether an advertiser has substantiated advertising claims?
14. What policy has been adopted by the Reagan appointees to the FTC as to when the FTC will act against deceptive advertising?
15. Cite a recent Supreme Court case in which a ban on truthful advertising was upheld, regardless of the media being used.

ANSWERS

1. Accuracy and truth.
2. Unfair methods in competition.
3. To extend Section 5 to advertising that was unfair or deceptive to consumers regardless of any impact on competition.

4. "Let the buyer beware." *Caveat venditor* — "let the seller beware."
5. Material deception.
6. False. Some FTC thinking inclines toward the idea that the agency may even have *primary* responsibility because an agency has expertise in such matters.
7. False.
8. *Virginia State Board of Pharmacy v. Virginia Citizens Consumer Council, Inc.* (1976).
9. Free flow of commercial information is in the public interest. Also, consumers may be more interested in purely commercial information than in the day's most important "political speech."
10. To dispel residual consumer deception; to restore competition to its proper level; to deprive advertisers of ill-gotten gains. Such an order adds more sting than the cease-and-desist order or consent order which tells the advertiser to go and sin no more.
11. Ad substantiation is a Section 6(b) order to selected companies in a given industry requiring them to furnish data to support advertising claims.
12. Initially, three major weaknesses were: (a) length of time before the information could be made public; (b) voluminous amounts of information received by the FTC; (c) the highly technical nature of some of the information which made evaluation difficult.
13. A company must have a "reasonable basis" for making advertising claims.
14. The policy requires proof that a "reasonable consumer" has been harmed by deceptive or false advertising before the FTC will act.
15. The most recent one — *Posadas de Puerto Rico Associates v. Tourism Company of Puerto Rico* (1986).

ENDNOTES

1. *Your FTC: What It Is and What It Does,* (Washington, D.C.: U.S. Government Printing Office), p. 8.
2. Speech delivered to the American Law Institute–American Bar Association in San Francisco as reported in *FTC News Notes,* May 16, 1988, p. 1.
3. *FTC News Notes,* March 30, 1987, p. 1.
4. Ibid.
5. Public Law No. 203, 63d Congress, approved September 26, 1914 (38 Statute 717, 15 U.S.C. 41, *et seq.*).
6. FTC v. Raladam, 283 U.S. 643.
7. The term "device" means instruments, apparatus, and contrivances intended (1) for use in the diagnosis, cure, mitigation, treatment, or prevention of human and other animal disease; or (2) to affect the structure or any function of the body of humans or other animals.
8. Scientific Manufacturing Co. v. FTC, 124 F.2d 640, 643–44 (1941).
9. 52 Stat. 114; 15 U.S.C. 54.
10. Gimbel Bros., Inc. v. FTC, 116 F.2d 578 (2d Circuit, 1941).
11. D.D.D. Corp. v. FTC, 125 F.2d 679 (7th Circuit, 1942).
12. Charles of the Ritz Distributors Corp. v. FTC, 143 F.2d 676, 679 (2d Circuit, 1944).
13. H.R. No. 1142, 63d Cong., 2d sess., 18–19 (1914).
14. Speech given to the National Association of Consumer Agency Administrators as reported in *FTC News Notes,* June 13, 1988, p. 1.
15. Carter Products, Inc. v. FTC, 323 F.2d 523, 525–26 (5th Circuit, 1963).
16. Colgate-Palmolive Co. v. FTC, 380 U.S. 374, 85 S.Ct. 1035, 13 L.Ed.2d 904 (1965).
17. Lewis A. Engman, address given at the annual meeting of the Antitrust Law Section of the American Bar Association, Honolulu, Hawaii, August 14, 1974.
18. FTC v. Algoma Lumber Co., 291 U.S. 67, 54 S.Ct. 315, 78 L.Ed. 655 (1934); Montgomery

Ward & Co. v. FTC, 379 F.2d 666, 670 (7th Circuit, 1961); FTC v. Sterling Drug, Inc., 317 F.2d 669, 670 (2d Circuit, 1963); Resort Car Rental System, Inc. v. FTC, 518 F.2d 962, 964 (9th Circuit, 1975).

19. Kalwajtys v. FTC, 237 F.2d 654, 656 (7th Circuit, 1956); cert. denied, 352 U.S. 1025 (1957). Also, Colgate-Palmolive Co. v. FTC, 380 U.S. 374, 85 S.Ct. 1035, 13 L.Ed.2d 904 (1965).

20. Francis J. Charlton and William A. Fawcett, "The FTC and False Advertising," *University of Kansas Law Review,* Vol. 17, June 1969, p. 618.

21. Continental Wax Corp. v. FTC, 330 F.2d 475 (2d Circuit, 1964); Rushing v. FTC. 320 F. 2d 280 (5th Circuit, 1963), cert. denied, 375 U.S. 986 (1964).

22. Bakers Franchise Corp. v. FTC, 302 F. 2d 258 (3d Circuit, 1962).

23. A study of FTC decisions during a 58-year period (through 1973) showed that falsity was equated to deception in 2236 of 3337 decisions, or 67 percent. These results were reported in a paper by Michael T. Brandt and Ivan L. Preston, "The Federal Trade Commission's Use of Evidence to Determine Deception," presented to the Law Division, Association for Education in Journalism, in 1976, p. 11.

24. Kalwajtys v. FTC, op. cit., note 19, 237 F.2d at 656.

25. Murray Space Shop Corp. v. FTC, 304 F.2d 270 (2d Circuit, 1962); Ward Laboratories, Inc. v. FTC, 952 F.2d 952 (2d Circuit, 1960), cert. denied, 364 U.S. 827, 81 S.Ct. 65, 5 L.Ed.2d 55; Resort Car Rental System, Inc., v. FTC, op. cit., note 18, at 964.

26. P. Lorillard Co. v. FTC, 186 F.2d 52, 58 (4th Circuit, 1950); FTC v. Colgate-Palmolive Co., 326 F.2d 517 (Ist Circuit, 1963), reversed, 380 U.S. 374, 393 (1965).

27. The policy statement, released on October 21, 1983, was approved by Miller, David Clanton on his last day on the Commission, and George Douglas.

28. *Advertising Age,* April 2, 1984, p. 6.

29. *FTC News Notes,* November 17, 1986, p. 1.

30. Gerald J. Thain, assistant director for food and drug advertising, FTC's Bureau of Consumer Protection, "Consumer Protection: Advertising—The FTC Response," a speech given July 7, 1971, before the Food and Drug Law Section of the American Bar Association meeting in New York City.

31. FTC v. Sperry and Hutchinson Co., 92 S.Ct. 898 (1972). Justices Powell and Rehnquist took no part in the consideration or decision of this case.

32. Ibid., at 903.

33. Ibid., at 905.

34. Statement of Basis and Purpose of Trade Regulation Rule 406 (Unfair or Deceptive Advertising and Labeling of Cigarettes in Relation to the Health Hazards of Smoking), 29 *Federal Register* 8324, 8355 (1964).

35. Gerald J. Thain, "Regulating Advertising in the 1970s," a speech given before the Federal Bar Association and Bureau of National Affairs conference on new developments in advertising regulation, February 22, 1972.

36. *Advertising Age,* March 22, 1982, p. 3.

37. Ibid.

38. Bristol-Myers Co. v. FTC, 185 F.2d 58 (4th Circuit, 1950). A cease-and-desist order was issued by the FTC against the company, but not against the agency because the FTC thought that Bristol-Myers was very active in preparation of the advertising copy.

39. Colgate-Palmolive Co. v. FTC, op. cit., note 16.

40. Valentine v. Chrestensen, 316 U.S. 52, 62 S.Ct. 920, 86 L.Ed. 1262.

41. Cammarano v. U.S., 358 U.S. 498 (1959), and Dun and Bradstreet, Inc. v. Grove, 404 U.S. 898, 905 (1971).

42. New York Times v. Sullivan, 376 U.S. at 266, 84 S.Ct. at 718.

43. Capital Broadcasting Company v. John Mitchell, U.S. attorney general, 333 F.Supp. 582.

44. Ibid.

45. National Assn. of Broadcasters v. Richard Kleindienst, U.S. Attorney General, and Capital Broadcasting Co. v. Kleindienst, 92 S.Ct. 1290.

46. Pittsburgh Press Co. v. Pittsburgh Commission on Human Relations, 413 U.S. 376, 93 S.Ct. 2553, 37 L.Ed.2d 669.

47. Ibid., at 2560.

48. Ibid., at 2565.
49. Bigelow v. Commonwealth of Virginia, 421 U.S. 809, 95 S.Ct. 2222, 44 L.Ed.2d 600.
50. Ibid., 95 S.Ct. at 2234.
51. Ibid., at 2238.
52. Virginia State Board of Pharmacy v. Virginia Citizens Consumer Council, Inc., 425 U.S. 748, 96 S.Ct. 1817, 48 L.Ed.2d 346 (1976). Justice Stevens took no part in the consideration or decision in this case.
53. John R. Bates and Van O'Steen v. State Bar of Arizona, 433 U.S. 350, 97 S.Ct. 2691, 53 L.Ed.2d 810 (1977).
54. In re The Matter of R.M.J., 7 *Med.L.Rptr.* 2545, February 16, 1982.
55. *FTC News Summary,* May 4, 1979, p. 1.
56. "News Notes," *Media Law Reporter,* November 6, 1979.
57. *FTC News Summary,* June 4, 1982, p. 1.
58. *FTC News Summary,* August 27, 1982, p. 3.
59. *FTC News Summary,* December 29, 1978, p. 1.
60. Central Hudson Gas & Electric Co. v. Public Service Commission of New York, and Consolidated Edison Co. v. Public Service Commission of New York, 447 U.S. 557, 100 S.Ct. 2343, 65 L.Ed.2d 341, 6 *Med.L.Rptr.* 1497 (1980).
61. Ibid.
62. Pacific Gas & Electric Co. v. Public Utilities Commission, 106 S.Ct. 903 (1986).
63. 9 *Med.L.Rptr.* 1449, May 3, 1983.
64. Dunagin v. City of Oxford and Lamar Outdoor Advertising, Inc. v. Mississippi State Tax Commission, 10 *Med.L.Rptr.* 1001, January 3, 1984.
65. Ibid., at 1009.
66. Ibid., at 1007–08, citing Virginia Pharmacy Board, 425 U.S. at 773 and 96 S.Ct. at 1831; Bigelow v. Virginia, 421 U.S. 809, 825 n. 10, 95 S. Ct. 2222, 2234, n. 10.
67. "State Activities," *Media Law Reporter,* June 7, 1988.
68. "News Notes," *Media Law Reporter,* June 26, 1984.
69. Ibid.
70. *Advertising Age,* June 21, 1984, p. 1.
71. *Editor & Publisher,* June 28, 1986, p. 34.
72. 52 *U.S. Law Week* 4594.
73. "News Notes," *Media Law Reporter,* April 27, 1982.
74. "News Notes," *Media law Reporter,* July 12, 1983. Justice Brennan did not participate in the deliberations or decision in this case.
75. Posadas de Puerto Rico Associates v. Tourism Company of Puerto Rico, 106 S.Ct. 2968 (1986).
76. *Advertising Age,* July 7, 1986, p. 1.
77. Prof. Henry Monaghan spoke at a midyear meeting of the American Bar Association's House of Delegates, February 16–17, 1987; "News Notes," *Media Law Reporter,* March 3, 1987.
78. *Editor & Publisher,* September 1, 1984, p. 27.
79. Ibid.
80. *Advertising Age,* December 6, 1976, p. 1. Reprinted with permission. Copyright 1976 by Crain Communications, Inc.
81. Perhaps to forestall any deviousness in compliance with its order, the FTC also stipulated: "In the case of radio and television advertising, such approved advertising is to be disseminated in the same time periods and during the same seasonal periods as other advertising of Profile bread; in the case of print advertising such advertising is to be disseminated in the same print media as other advertising of Profile bread." In the Matter of ITT Continental Baking Co., Inc., 79 FTC 248, 255.
82. Speculation that the corrective advertising increased Profile bread sales was denied by a company official. There was a reduction in the advertising budget during the year the order was in effect and the company shifted from 30- to 60-second spot television commercials because the corrective ads could better be handled in such a time period. See *Broadcasting,* May 1972, p. 33.
83. Speech delivered at the AAF's Tenth District meeting in Dallas, Texas, as reported in the fall 1970 issue of *Linage,* p. 21.
84. *Advertising Age,* May 22, 1972, p. 14.

85. *FTC News Summary,* December 18, 1975.
86. Warner-Lambert Co. v. FTC, 562 F.2d 749 (District of Columbia Circuit, 1977).
87. Ibid.
88. 435 U.S. 950 (1978).
89. National Commission on Egg Nutrition v. FTC, 570 F.2d 157, 3 *Med.L.Rptr.* 2196 (1977).
90. 439 U.S. 821 (1978).
91. Robert Skitol, "What Is an Adequate Substantiation," paper presented at the regional convention in New York City of the American Association of Advertising Agencies, June 5, 1972. At the time, Mr. Skitol was assistant to the director of the FTC's Bureau of Consumer Protection.
92. *FTC News Summary,* June 24, 1977, p. 1.
93. In the Matter of Pfizer, Inc., FTC Docket No. 8819, July 18, 1972.
94. Gerald Thain, "Advertising Regulation: The Contemporary FTC Approach," *Fordham Urban Law Journal,* Spring 1973, p. 390.
95. *FTC News Summary,* November 13, 1981, p. 1.
96. "Why industry wants Miller to slow down," an editorial in *Advertising Age,* March 29, 1982, p. 16.
97. *Advertising Age,* July 30, 1984, p. 1.
98. Ibid., p. 71.
99. U.S. v. Morton Salt Co., 388 U.S. 632 (1950).
100. National Petroleum Refiners Association v. FTC, 340 F.Supp. 1343.
101. 482 F.2d 672.
102. 94 S.Ct. 1475, 39 L.Ed.2d 567 (1974). Justice Stewart would have granted certiorari and Justice Powell took no part in the consideration of the petition or in the decision.
103. Lewis A. Engman, FTC chairman, in speech to the American Bar Association's Antitrust Law Section, Washington, D.C., April 11, 1975.
104. FTC v. R.F. Keppel & Brothers, Inc., 291 U.S. 304, 54 S.Ct. 423, 78 L.Ed.2d 814 (1934).
105. In the Matter of Mattel, Inc., 79 FTC 667, 670 (1971).
106. Gerald Thain, in speech given July 7, 1971, op. cit., note 30.
107. *FTC News Summary,* March 25, 1977, p. 3.
108. *FTC News Summary,* April 10, 1981, p. 1.
109. *FTC News Summary,* March 5, 1982, p. 4.
110. Immigration and Naturalization Service v. Chadha, 51 *U.S. Law Week* 4907.
111. *FTC News Summary,* February 27, 1976, p. 1.

14

Radio and Television

HIGHLIGHTS

■ The Federal Communications Commission, Congress and the courts have used different rationales since enactment of the Communications Act of 1934 to justify regulation of radio and television. They include public ownership of the airwaves, scarcity of over-the-air frequencies, the fiduciary concept, and the "media differences" argument.

■ Section 315 of the Communications Act of 1934, as amended, provides for "equal opportunities" for political candidates once a licensee allows his facilities to be used by a candidate. Many lawsuits have resulted and the FCC has issued extensive regulations in implementing this section.

■ Section 315 also was thought to contain the "Fairness Doctrine" which required broadcasters to air conflicting views on issues of public importance as a guard against one group being able to "monopolize" discussion on a controversial public issue. But the FCC, in carrying out President Reagan's deregulation pledge, repealed the doctrine in 1987 because the Commission said it was chilling broadcasters' First Amendment freedoms.

■ The Supreme Court upheld Section 312(a)(7) as a limited right of access to broadcast facilities for federal candidates for public office in *CBS v. FCC* (1981).

■ The FCC has undertaken deregulation of radio, subscription TV, over-the-air TV and cable TV through rescinding a number of rules.

Advertising and commercial broadcasting are closely related because revenue from the purchase of time by advertisers constitutes virtually the sole support of commercial broadcasting. In fact, some critics contend that commercial television is not an information, but an advertising, medium. Whatever the merits of such criticism, television is relied upon by a great many Americans for information. According to Roper polls, television surpassed newspapers in 1963 as the source of most news for a majority of those polled—a position it has not relinquished since. Its power as an entertainment medium is a communication phenomenon with some prime-time shows drawing 30 to 40 million viewers. In 1977, an estimated 80 million persons watched the final episode of an eight-part "docudrama" based on Alex Haley's best-selling novel, *Roots*. More than 130 million persons watched at least one of the ABC-telecast episodes of *Roots*. On November 22, 1980, an audience estimated at 82 million tuned in to find out who had shot J.R. Ewing in the CBS television series, "Dallas"—the largest single-program audience to that time.

Because of television's power to inform, to entertain, and to sell goods and ideas, it has been the catalyst for continuing debates about how it should be used, who should use it, and how it should be regulated in the "public interest." Some want more regulation of broadcasting; others contend that radio and television already are over regulated.

The first regulatory efforts in broadcasting came with the Radio Act of 1912 which authorized the Secretary of Commerce and Labor to license radio operations. Enforcement presented no immediate problems because there were more frequencies available than license applicants. But that changed rapidly in the early 1920s as more and more stations sought to go on the air. Two federal court decisions resulted in bedlam on the airwaves. One decision in 1923 held that the secretary of commerce could not refuse to renew a license on the ground of licensee interference with other broadcasters.[1] The other decision was in 1926 when a district court judge held that licensees could operate on any frequency they wished no matter what the secretary had ordered.[2] Broadcasters jumped frequency, boosted power, and otherwise operated as they wished. To end the chaos, the Radio Act of 1927 was passed which established the Federal Radio Commission with power to issue licenses, allocate frequencies, and specify operating conditions. The present regulatory law and commission—the Communications Act of 1934 (47 U.S.C. §§ 151–609 (1970)) and the Federal Communications Commission—are direct descendants from the 1927 Act. In fact, some of the language is the same in both acts, including a key phrase in Section 303 which stipulates that the five-member commission (seven members until 1984) shall license and otherwise regulate broadcasters "as the public convenience, interest, or necessity requires."

FEDERAL COMMUNICATIONS COMMISSION

The Federal Communications Commission (FCC) is an independent regulatory agency that licenses about 11,700 operating stations. These include approximately:

- 4900 AM (amplitude modulated) commercial radio stations
- 4100 FM (frequency modulated) commercial radio stations
- 1350 noncommercial FM radio stations
- 550 commercial VHF (very high frequency) television stations
- 510 UHF (ultra high frequency) television stations
- 115 noncommercial (educational) VHF TV stations
- 200 noncommercial UHF TV stations.

In addition, about 8000 cable television systems supply service to more than 48 million subscribers.

Included in this melange, but not subject to licensing, are the three national commercial networks (which have radio and TV networks): National Broadcasting Company (NBC), formed in 1926; Columbia Broadcasting System (CBS), 1927; and American Broadcasting Companies (ABC), created in 1945 out of the so-called Blue network operated by NBC. Until July 1984, each network or group could own no more than five VHF and two UHF stations, and seven AM and seven FM radio stations. This 7-7-7 ownership rule was changed to 12-12-12. Because network-owned stations are licensed by the FCC, and for other reasons discussed later in this chapter, the networks can be subjected to FCC pressure and regulation.

There also is a cable TV news network and a noncommercial, educational network for both radio and television, with the latter consisting of about 260 stations. More than 750 radio stations form the National Public Radio network. Helping to provide services and programs for these networks is the Public Broadcasting Service, which was established by the Corporation for Public Broadcasting (CPB). CPB is a private corporation governed by a bipartisan board appointed by the President with the advice and consent of the Senate. CPB resulted from passage of the Public Broadcasting Act of 1967 and is involved in three major activities: establishment and maintenance of an interconnection service among local public stations, production of national programming, and increasing the support for public stations.

The FCC also has adopted rules governing the licensing and operation of direct broadcast satellites. Eight companies were authorized in 1982 to enter the DBS business. They proposed at that time to build and launch satellites that would offer more than 40 channels for satellite-to-home television, but several companies have since backed out because of doubts about the commercial viability of the service and the huge pricetags for such systems. Existing geostationary communication satellites already provide extensive services to radio and TV stations that are equipped with earth stations to receive satellite signals, and backyard earth stations are increasing at a phenomenal rate. More than 500,000 were in place by 1984, and the number was increasing by an estimated 30,000 a month! As the price of these dishes decrease—many now being obtainable at between $2000 and $3000—purchasers are able to point the receivers skyward and receive clear signals no matter where the homes are located.

In addition, the FCC has authorized low-power TV stations for areas inadequately served by full-power stations. The FCC eventually plans to license about 4000 such stations, but only 450 had been licensed by 1989 to serve rural areas, minority audiences, and small towns. The stations usually have a signal that covers a radius of 15 miles—a small enough area so as not to interfere with signals from other TV stations on the same channel.

Many other technological developments are occurring in telecommunications that occupy the attention of the FCC, such as teletext, videotext and high definition television. The developments have occurred at an accelerated rate and allow for a greater diversity of communication choices. As they occur, there are growing demands for deregulation of radio and television—demands that already have led to significant developments which will be reviewed later in this chapter.

The FCC not only regulates broadcast stations, but it regulates "common carriers" in the communications industry, such as telephone companies. Unlike broadcast stations, these common carriers must provide service to anyone who can pay for it.

In its regulatory activities, the FCC operates in a quasi-legislative, quasi-judicial manner. Similar to the FTC, it is composed of three entities: staff, administrative law judges, and the Commission itself. The judges are independent of the staff and the five-member Commission. They conduct formal hearings and issue interlocutory orders (orders subject to further review). The Commission issues rules and regulations, conducts hearings, and serves an adjudicatory function through findings and the issuance of orders.

Among the FCC's principal tasks are:

1. To issue or renew broadcast licenses in accordance with Section 307 of the 1934 Act.
2. To revoke licenses of stations not operating in the public interest.
3. To otherwise regulate stations in the public interest, convenience, or necessity.

Licensing

From 1934 to 1981, licenses were generally issued for three-year periods, although shorter term license renewals were used occasionally if the FCC had questions about a station's operations. Then, in 1981, Congress passed legislation that permits five-year license periods for television stations and seven-year licenses for radio stations.

A "renewal expectancy" has been included in FCC policy unlike an earlier policy which stated that only "unusually good or unusually poor" performance records of broadcast stations had relevancy when comparative hearings were being conducted at license renewal times. Comparative hearings are necessary when a licensee faces a challenge from a competing group or groups wishing to wrest away the license, usually by promising to provide better programming service to a community. But the FCC now takes the position that where the incumbent licensee has at least a "substantial" record of performance (rather than superior service or programming) a license renewal expectancy is among the factors weighed by the Commission.

License renewal expectancy has long been the rule even though it may not have been the formal policy of the Commission. For example, between 1934 and 1960, only 34 licenses were revoked or not reveiwed. Very few licenses are ever taken away for programming reasons. This situation led a "maverick" FCC commissioner, Nicholas Johnson, who was not reappointed to the Commission by President Nixon when his six-year term expired in 1973, to say to a Senate subcommittee:

> The problem . . . is that in the five and a half years I have been on the Commission, each year, after all the talk is swept away, the fact remains that 2500 licensees come in and ask for a license renewal, and 2500 get a license renewal.
>
> There have been very few exceptions to that general rule. . . .
>
> . . . [FCC staff members] go over the license renewal forms. But after they have been over them, the net result is they all get approved, with exception of some that get letters about minor technical defects, or logging requirements, or antenna towers, and things of that sort. . . .
>
> . . . I don't know of anybody who has lost his license for . . . [programming] reasons. And I cannot believe that all 7500 licensees in America are doing such an all-fired good job that they all deserve to be renewed on that ground, and yet, that is what has happened.[3]

What once was a lengthy license-renewal application form for radio and TV licensees has been reduced — except for a small number of stations randomly selected for more extensive renewal procedure — to a postcard-size form that contains five questions. This action by the Commission in 1981 was part of its efforts to deregulate broadcasting. Among questions dropped from the license renewal application were those related to programming. A challenge was mounted by several public interest groups, including the Black Citizens for a Fair Media, but the Commission's action ultimately was upheld by the U.S. Court of Appeals for the District of Columbia in 1983 and the U.S. Supreme Court declined to review that decision.

Community Ascertainment. Although licensees have rarely lost their licenses because of programming, the FCC has manifested concern about programming in a number of ways. In 1965, for example, the Commission issued its *Policy Statement on Comparative Broadcasting Hearings.*[4] In that policy paper two primary objectives were cited toward which applicants competing for a license had to direct their statements: (1) the best practicable service to the public; and (2) maximum diffusion of media control. Under the first objective, full-time participation in station management, as contrasted with absentee ownership, was of "substantial importance" in determining who would be given the license. Clearly, such management would be in a better position to determine the needs of the community.

At a renewal proceeding, the incumbent licenseholder had to show that the station's programming had adequately served the community's needs and that proposed programming would continue to serve those needs. Those seeking to wrest away the license for themselves had to show that their *proposed* programming would better serve the community. Two issues were immediately apparent: (1) what kind of programming services does a community need?; and (2) what kind of added weight, if any, should the FCC give to a licensee's actual performance when stacked against the mere promises of a contender? The FCC acted on the second of these two with a policy that includes "renewal expectancy." As for ascertaining the kind of programming that serves a community's needs, the FCC said in a 1960 report and statement of policy:

> The major elements usually necessary to meet the public interest, needs and desires of the community in which the station is located . . . have included: (1) opportunity for local self-expression, (2) the development and use of local talent, (3) programs for children, (4) religious programs, (5) educational programs, (6) public affairs programs, (7) editorialization by licensees, (8) political broadcasts, (9) agricultural programs, (10) news programs, (11) weather and market reports, (12) sports programs, (13) service to minority groups, (14) entertainment programming.[5]

A new *Primer on Ascertainment of Community Problems by Broadcast Renewal Applicants* was issued in 1971.[6] It required the applicant to first determine the composition of the community and then consult with a representative cross-section of community leaders and a random sample of members of the general public to ascertain community problems, needs, and interests. Based on the findings, the licensee had to list all the nonfrivolous problems ascertained and propose programming to meet those problems.

As part of a move toward deregulation of broadcasting that began shortly after Ronald Reagan was elected President, the FCC removed the formal ascertainment requirements for new commercial radio stations and commercial radio license-renewal applicants effective in 1981, and it did the same for the 1170 commercial TV stations in 1984. Also eliminated was the need to conduct formal, detailed interviews of community leaders and some audience members in ascertaining community needs.

What licensees now must do on a quarterly basis, is place in their public file a list of five to ten major issues confronting their communities and the programming offered to deal with those issues.

WHDH Case. Programming and media ownership were two factors which entered into a spectacular license renewal case. In 1969, the FCC voted not to renew the license of WHDH-TV in Boston. This decision sent shockwaves through the broadcast industry. The disputed Channel 5 license was valued at $50 million, and the FCC's action raised the specter of other licenses similarly being revoked.

Various legal steps were taken to halt the transfer of the license to a group known as Boston Broadcasters, Inc. (BBI), but the transfer became final in 1972 when the new licensee began operations.[7]

To allay fears stemming from this case, the FCC voted 6–1 for a policy statement under which an incumbent licenseholder would be favored over rivals if the incumbent could show that the station's programming had been "substantially attuned to the needs and interests" of its broadcast area. However, stations not offering "substantial" service still were subject to challenge, as Commissioner Johnson emphasized in his lone dissent.

KHJ-TV License. The "substantial service" concept in the 1970 policy statement was significantly altered several years later when the Commission, by a 3–2 vote,[8] renewed the license of KHJ-TV in Los Angeles. A competing group for Channel 9 had contended, to the satisfaction of a hearing examiner who had the WHDH precedent very much in mind, that KHJ-TV's programming consisted primarily of old movies interspersed with commercials. It also contended that media diversity would be enhanced (in accordance with the Commission's policy statement in 1965 about media ownership diffusion) by awarding the license to the competing group. However, the Commission overruled the examiner's decision in part because the licensee's programming was "within the bounds of *average performance,*" thereby warranting neither a preference nor a demerit, and because the Commission did not believe that renewal proceedings should be used to restructure ownership patterns in the broadcast industry.[9]

A three-judge panel of the U.S. Court of Appeals for the District of Columbia Circuit affirmed the FCC's renewal of KHJ-TV's license in 1975. However, Judge David L. Bazelon, who was not on the panel, issued a statement supporting former Commissioner Johnson's view that the Commission's decision was the worst in Johnson's years with the Commission.[10] Bazelon said the FCC failed to follow its own precedent in ruling that neither applicant was entitled to a preference on the issue of media ownership diversification. He termed that ruling a "miraculous conclusion" in light of RKO's ownership of broadcast properties including KHJ-TV whereas the contender owned no such property. His appraisal presumably was not shared by the U. S. Supreme Court, which, in 1975, denied certiorari.[11]

WESH-TV Case. A three-judge panel of the U.S. Court of Appeals for the District of Columbia Circuit threw a scare into the FCC in 1978 when it reversed a Commission decision to renew the license of Cowles Broadcasting's station WESH-TV in Daytona Beach, Florida. This marked the first time that the District of Columbia Circuit Court had reversed the FCC in a comparative renewal case and the panel did so largely on the ground that the 1934 Act precluded a preference for the licenseholder simply on the basis of incumbency. According to the panel, the FCC gave Cowles a preference merely because it was the "incumbent" licensee. The renewal applicant is entitled to a preference, said the panel, only if its past record is "superior," and even then challengers for the license might prevail because of other criteria used by the Commission (diversification of ownership, integration of ownership with management, and minority participation in the station's operations). If the ruling had remained intact, the number of license challengers once again would have reached staggering numbers.

As a result of the Circuit Court's action, the FCC adopted a new policy in

1981 which the appellate court noted approvingly in July 1982 in affirming the Commission's decision to renew Cowles Broadcasting's license for WESH-TV. The policy is that "renewal expectancy" is a factor to be considered, so a station with a better record creates a greater expectancy that the license will be renewed. In most comparative renewal cases, a "substantial" record of performance would be sufficient to assume license renewal for the incumbent.

WESH-TV's record showed "substantial performance," the FCC said, and this overcame such factors as an illegal move of the station's main studio to Orlando, the involvement of several related companies in a mail fraud case, and the advantage of a competing company for the license in terms of diversification of ownership and management. But the Commission cautioned that its new policy should not be interpreted as ignoring management integration and ownership diversification.

RKO "Revisited." The second time around for RKO General, Inc., proved disastrous. In 1980 the FCC voted 4–3 to strip RKO of its TV station licenses in Boston, New York, and Los Angeles.[12]

The action was taken because of what the Commission termed massive misconduct by RKO and its "parent," General Tire & Rubber Co.[13] over a considerable number of years—misconduct that the FCC said often included an abuse of broadcast facilities which RKO was licensed to operate.

Commission dissenters were Robert E. Lee, James H. Quello, and Abbott Washburn. Quello termed the decision an example of "gross bureaucratic overkill," and said that it represents "the most harsh and unwarranted punishment in the history of communications."[14] There has been, he said, "no judicial finding of guilt" against General Tire, and "the activities investigated did not affect the broadcasting performance of RKO General, nor were the audiences of RKO stations in any way defrauded, deceived, or poorly served."

Total estimated value of RKO's broadcast holdings were put at $400 million.[15] General Tire & Rubber announced it would appeal the "most unfair and discriminatory" decision "ever handed down by a governmental agency."

A three-judge panel for the U.S. Court of Appeals in the District of Columbia Circuit unanimously upheld the FCC's disqualification of RKO as licensee for the Boston station, WNAC-TV[16] It said that the FCC did not abuse its discretion by disqualifying RKO as a renewal applicant for WNAC-TV because of RKO's egregious lack of candor in giving the Commission information relevant to the renewal proceedings. However, the panel said such misconduct could not automatically be applied by the Commission to disqualify RKO from renewal proceedings for its 14 other broadcast licenses, including the stations in New York (WOR-TV) and Los Angeles (KHJ-TV). The court remanded on the matter of licensee disqualification concerning the New York and Los Angeles stations.

The Supreme Court declined to review the remand portion of the Circuit Court's decision and also let stand the ruling that stripped RKO of its license for WNAC-TV.[17]

Ultimately, legislation was passed that allowed RKO to move its New York license to New Jersey—a state which previously did not have a VHF television station. A three-judge panel of the U.S. Court of Appeals in Washington, D.C., upheld the Commission's reallocation of the channel to New Jersey and the issuance of a license to RKO for five years (as stipulated in the legislation). In 1984 the Supreme Court let stand the Circuit Court's decision.

But RKO General's problems continued. In February 1987 the Commission's Mass Media Bureau asked an administrative law judge to declare RKO General an unfit licensee for its 14 radio and TV stations, valued at about $1 billion. In August 1987, Judge Edward J. Kihlmann issued a 75-page decision that denied license renewal. The judge said RKO had overcharged advertisers, lied to the FCC, and destroyed an audit. RKO has appealed the decision.

Network Regulation

Networks are not licensed, but the network-owned and network-affiliated stations are licensed. Therefore, considerable indirect pressure can be exerted on the networks. There also is direct regulation which, in the opinion of some, violates the First Amendment.

At the time of the Radio Act of 1927, networks were just emerging. Few people could foresee their eventual domination of the broadcast industry. In the 1927 legislation, however, Congress alluded to this possibility by reference to "chain broadcasting," defined as the simultaneous broadcasting of an identical program by two or more connected stations. Because of increasing concern over domination of broadcasting by the networks (about 340 of the 660 commercial radio stations were affiliated with national networks by 1939), the FCC issued its chain broadcasting regulations in mid-1941. The regulations struck at the following:

- Contracts requiring stations to be exclusive affiliates of networks.
- Agreements by the networks not to sell programs to other stations in an affiliate's area.
- The 28-day option notice by which a network, having given the prerequisite notice, could require an affiliate to carry a network program during that period called "network optional time."

The third provision hindered stations in the development of local program service, said the FCC as part of its rationale in seeking to limit network ownership of stations.

At the time the rules were promulgated, 18 of the most powerful stations in the nation were owned either by NBC or CBS. NBC brought suit to enjoin enforcement of the regulations, principally on the grounds that its First Amendment rights would be violated and that such regulatory action exceeded the authority granted by Congress. At the heart of the suit was the fundamental question of whether the FCC could be more than a mere traffic officer concerned only with the technical aspects of broadcasting; that is, monitoring stations to be certain they were broadcasting on assigned frequencies at specified power output. NBC argued that FCC authority was limited to serving as traffic controller.

It contended that the FCC could not concern itself with such substantive matters as an affiliate's contractual arrangement with a network, or with territorial exclusivity for an affiliate which a network provided in exchange for a contractual arrangement by which the affiliate agreed to broadcast a certain amount of network programming.

The courts, in holding that the FCC neither exceeded its power under the 1934 Act nor transgressed against the First Amendment, took the position that the Commission was more than just a traffic controller.

In dismissing the *NBC v. FCC* suit, Judge Learned Hand wrote for a three-judge panel of U.S. District Court that Section 303 of the 1934 Act was broad enough to permit a "public interest" in network practices.[18] The Commission, he said, was competent to appraise the effect upon broadcasting of restrictive or monopolistic practices. Concerning the First Amendment argument, Judge Hand conceded that the regulations *indirectly* sought to control what programs the stations could broadcast and that they do "fetter the choice of the stations." The end result of the regulations is coercion, the judge admitted, but he then observed:

> . . . [I]f the public interest in whose name this was being done were other than the interest in free speech itself, we should have a problem under the First Amendment. But that is not the case. The interests which the regulations seek to protect are the very interests which the First Amendment itself protects, i.e., the interests, first, of the "listeners," next, of any licensees who may prefer to be freer of the "networks" than they are, and last, of any future competing "networks." Whether or not the conflict between these interests and those of the "networks" and their "affiliates" has been properly composed, no question of free speech can arise.[19]

In giving pre-eminence to the right of listeners vis-à-vis First Amendment protection, rather than the networks' First Amendment interests, Judge Hand anticipated by a quarter-century one of the basic tenets laid down in *Red Lion,* discussed later, by the U.S. Supreme Court. In that case, the Supreme Court declared that what is crucial under the First Amendment is the right of the public — not the rights of broadcasters — to receive suitable access to social, political, and other ideas. That is the right, declared the Court, which cannot be constitutionally abridged.

NBC appealed and Justice Felix Frankfurter, in delivering the 5–2 opinion of the Supreme Court, dealt with the First Amendment argument by saying:

> The question here is simply whether the Commission, by announcing that it will refuse licenses to persons who engage in specified network practices . . ., is thereby denying such persons the constitutional right of free speech. The right of free speech does not include, however, the right to use the facilities of radio without a license. The licensing system established by Congress . . . was a proper exercise of its power over commerce. The standard it provided for the licensing of stations was the "public interest, convenience, or necessity."
>
> Denial of station license on that ground, if valid under the [1934] Act, is not a denial of free speech.[20]

In upholding the Commission's authority to promulgate the chain broadcasting rules, the Court also said that the FCC may call upon antitrust policies in implementing its public interest mandate.

Antitrust Suit Against the Networks

A reduction in network-controlled or network-produced programming was the aim of a 1974 civil antitrust suit filed against the three commercial TV networks by the Justice Department, which said the suits were filed

> to eliminate restrictive and anticompetitive network practices in the production and procurement of television entertainment programs and to assure that the viewing public, independent program suppliers, and advertisers would no longer be deprived of the benefits of free and open competition.[21]

In 1976 the Justice Department filed a proposed consent judgment that would terminate the suit against NBC after that network accepted broad restrictions for a 10-year period on its production of entertainment programs. However, the agreement was not to take effect until or unless similar results were obtained in connection with the suits against CBS and ABC.

Under the agreement, NBC would:

- Limit its own production of programs to two and one-half hours in prime time, eight hours of daytime, and eleven hours of so-called fringe time weekly.
- Loosen its control over the production of "pilot" programs once fall lineups commenced whereas the common practice is for networks to retain control of such programs in the event that mid-season lineup changes became necessary.
- Eliminate the requirement that independent producers, who lease network studio facilities to film or tape their series, contract for such facilities for more than a year's period.

In addition, two provisions were included in the consent judgment which already were in force as a result of FCC rulemaking: (1) networks are banned from domestic program syndication, and (2) networks cannot have a financial interest in an independent's program being carried on the network.

CBS joined NBC in settling the Justice Department's antitrust complaint, doing so in a proposed consent decree filed in 1980.[22] ABC followed suit shortly afterward.

Because the ABC consent decree allowed that network to produce a greater number of hours of prime-time entertainment programs during the sixth through tenth years of the consent agreement, NBC, with the Department of Justice's tentative approval, asked for similar provisions, doing so in a 1984 motion to modify the decree.

Network Inquiry by FCC Staff

An inquiry into alleged network domination of programming decisions by stations was requested by both the Justice Department and Westinghouse Broadcasting Co. in the mid-1970s — allegations that were denied by the networks. In 1977, Commission Chairman Richard Wiley endorsed such a probe, saying: ". . . It has been almost 20 years since the FCC conducted an overall inquiry and, many people believe, developments since that time warrant a fresh examinaton."

The Commission's Notice of Inquiry specifically invited comments on the following:

- The extent to which clearance of network programming by affiliates is "other than voluntary."
- The likelihood of further expansion of network schedules.
- The adequacy of information provided to affiliates concerning upcoming network programs.
- The extent to which the networks' compensation to affiliates for presenting network programs requires an affiliate to take the majority of its programs from the same network without regard for the merits of the proffered programs.
- The fairness of compensatory payments to affiliates for carrying network programs in light of the powerful economic position of the networks.[23]

According to the staff report, the most important of the Commission's policies affecting the networks' dominance was the spectrum allocation plan adopted in 1952. Under this plan 70 Ultra High Frequency (UHF) channels were added to the 12 Very High Frequency (VHF) channels already earmarked for commercial television. It was this plan that first set aside educational television channels. The staff contended that this plan seriously handicapped the emergence of additional networks.[24] In addition, the staff called for "a systematic and coherent set of ownership policies," terming some of the current ownership rules "capricious and arbitrary" (see Chapter 17 for ownership rules).

In addition, the report also said that many Commission regulations "apparently rest on an inadequate appreciation of the fact that the networks perform substantial and important functions in the wider system of developing and broadcasting television programs." The report continued:

> Television networks are not profit-siphoning intruders into a system of local broadcast stations; they are indispensable organizers of a nationwide system of television broadcasting.[25]

The staff report, of course, provided ammunition for deregulation moves. The partial deregulation of radio and television will be examined later in the chapter, but first let's look at the legal underpinnings of government regulation of broadcasting.

RATIONALE FOR BROADCAST REGULATION

Regulations promulgated by the FCC must pass First Amendment standards because, as clearly established, radio and television enjoy constitutional protection. Section 326 of the 1934 Act specifically forbids the Commission from censoring the content of programs. It states:

> Nothing in this chapter shall be understood or construed to give the Commission the power of censorship over the radio communications or signals transmitted by any radio station, and no regulation or condition shall be promulgated or fixed by the Commission which shall interfere with the right of free speech by means of radio communication.

In *U.S. v. Paramount Pictures, Inc.* (1948), the U.S. Supreme Court said, "We have no doubt that moving pictures, like newspapers and *radio,* are included in the press whose freedom is guaranteed by the First Amendment" (emphasis added).[26] Four years later the same Court said in *Burstyn, Inc. v. Wilson,* discussed earlier, that the First Amendment applies to any "significant medium for the communication of ideas." The Third Circuit U.S. Court of Appeals, in *Rosenbloom v. Metromedia* (1969), stated that "no rational distinction can be made between radio and television on the one hand and the press on the other in affording constitutional protection contemplated by the First Amendment.[27] And yet regulations are imposed upon broadcasters which, if attempted in connection with the print medium, would be unconstitutional. Even the issuance of a license would be intolerable if attempted in connection with a newspaper or magazine.

How can the First Amendment, licensing, and extensive regulation of the broadcast medium coexist?

The main rationales are, or have been, the following: (1) public ownership of the airwaves; (2) scarcity of over-the-air frequencies, hence the need to license and regulate; (3) the "media differences" argument, and (4) the fiduciary concept.

Public "Ownership" Concept

Traditional theory of broadcast regulation begins with the concept that the public "owns" the airwaves. Conversely, newspapers arguably do not use anything that is publicly owned. Since the public "owns" the airwaves, it has the right to say how this valuable resource will be used. This was established when Congress passed the 1934 Act, which stipulates that a licensee must operate in the public convenience, interest, or necessity. Just what constitutes the "public interest" is largely left up to the FCC to define.

At the time the Radio Act of 1927 was being drafted, the senators most involved in choosing the language selected the term "public interest" because (1) it was the statutory standard then in use by the Interstate Commerce Commission for regulating public utilities and railroads, and (2) because the senators couldn't think of anything better.[28]

Scarcity Concept

Another argument used to justify regulation is the "scarcity" concept. The airwaves not only are a valuable publicly owned resource, they are limited. Only so many stations can be accommodated; therefore, those who use this resource can be subjected to regulation. Not so those who use printing presses since, in theory, there's no limit to the number of presses.

But technological developments have knocked the scarcity argument into a cocked hat. For example, the more than 8000 cable systems have drastically altered the scarcity concept. The reasons lie in the different characteristics of the two kinds of broadcasting. "Over-the-air" broadcasting uses a medium — airwaves — which is finite. Only so many signals can be accommodated without interference with other signals. But cable TV does not use the air to transmit signals to subscribers' homes. Like a telephone company, it moves signals by cable and each cable can contain 20, 40, or 60 wires. Each wire represents a different channel. Thus, a veritable cornucopia of programming diversity is *potentially* within reach of every community.

A refocusing on the scarcity argument makes it clear that new technology makes, or threatens to make, such a rationale for regulation obsolete, so new or modified reasons have been advanced for continued regulatory control. Notably these are: (1) the media differences argument, including the contention that television is the most powerful medium of mass communications and therefore more subject to control, and (2) the fiduciary, or proxy, concept.

Media Differences Concept

One approach in the "media differences" argument focuses on the audience. Broadcast messages, unlike their counterpart in newspapers and magazines, are "in the air." Once the radio or television set is turned on, the listener or viewer becomes part of a "captive" audience. The book or newspaper reader not only must make a decision to pick up the book or newspaper, but must actively select the stories or pages to be read. The user of the electronic medium does not make as many "affirmative" decisions, so the theory goes. True, the viewer must decide to turn on the television set, turn it off, or switch channels (and even in these instances someone else could make such choices). But once the person is "tuned in," he or she is more of a "captive" than the print medium user. Concerning such an idea, Chief Justice Burger has said:

> The Commission [FCC] is also entitled to take into account the reality that in a very real sense listeners and viewers constitute a "captive" audience. . . . The "captive" nature of the broadcast audience was recognized as early as 1924, when Commerce Secretary Hoover remarked at the Fourth National Radio Conference that "the radio listener does not have the same option that the reader of publications has — to ignore advertising in which he is not interested — and he may resent its invasion on his set."[29]

A variation of the "media differences" theme is that television is the most powerful medium of mass communications; therefore, it should be subject to more control.[30] The problem with this contention is the lack of empirical evidence. Marshall McLuhan and others have warned that the electronic media, particularly television, threaten society's basic values, but *knowing* this intuitively or philosophically is different from *knowing* this empirically. There are many variables in disentangling cause-effect in something so complex as human communication behavior. Therefore, statements about one medium's power vis-à-vis other media should be regarded with some skepticism.

Fiduciary or Proxy Concept

The fiduciary concept, which reached its zenith in the *Red Lion* case[31], discussed later, is based on the idea that the licensee is only a "trustee," a fiduciary, for the public. Because of this status the First Amendment does not prohibit government from requiring the trustee to do certain things, such as share the frequency with others. In so doing, the licensee functions as the public's proxy. Therefore, he or she can be obligated to give suitable time and attention to matters of public interest without the First Amendment standing in the way.

Concerning the First Amendment's tolerance for any kind of media regulation, Justice Douglas has observed:

> What kind of First Amendment would best serve our needs as we approach the twenty-first century may be an open question. But the old fashioned First Amendment that we have is the Court's only guideline; and one hard and fast principle which it announced is that government shall keep its hands off the press. That principle has served us through days of calm and eras of strife, and I would abide by it until a new First Amendment is adopted. That means, as I view it, that TV and radio, as well as the more conventional methods for disseminating news, are all included in the concept of "press" as used in the First Amendment and therefore are entitled to live under the laissez-faire regime which the First Amendment sanctions.[32]

Especially troubling in the regulatory panoply are those FCC-generated or congressionally mandated doctrines which impinge directly or indirectly on broadcast journalists. Why should such journalists have less First Amendment protection—if indeed they do—than print journalists?

Many broadcast journalists have been particularly agitated by requirements contained in Section 315 of the Communications Act of 1934—the equal-time and Fairness Doctrine section.

EQUAL TIME

The equal-time requirement, referred to in the law as *equal opportunities,* was transferred intact from the Radio Act of 1927 to the 1934 Act. Until 1959, when Congress amended the section to include the Fairness Doctrine, "equal time" was the only provision of Section 315. While reading the law, note that once the section is "activated," the licensee is under legal compulsion to do certain things, but only if it first decides to permit a legally qualified candidate for public office to use its facilities either on a free or a paid basis.

As amended, Section 315 reads:

(a) If any licensee shall permit any person who is a legally qualified candidate for any public office to use a broadcasting station, he shall afford equal opportunities to all other such candidates for that office in the use of such broadcasting station: *Provided,* that such licensee shall have no power of censorship over the material broadcast under the provisions of this section. No obligation is imposed . . . upon any licensee to allow the use of its station by any such candidate. Appearance by a legally qualified candidate on any (1) bonafide newscast, (2) bonafide news interview, (3) bonafide news documentary (if the appearance of the candidate is incidental to the presentation of the subject or subjects covered by the news documentary), or (4) on-the-spot coverage of bonafide news events (including but not limited to political conventions and activities incidental thereto), shall not be deemed to be use of a broadcasting station within the meaning of this subsection. Nothing in the foregoing sentence shall be construed as relieving broadcasters, in connection with the presentation of newscasts, news interviews, news documentaries, and on-the-spot coverage of news events, from the obligation imposed upon them under this chapter to operate in the public interest and to afford reasonable opportunity for the discussion of conflicting views on issues of public importance.

(b) The charges made for the use of any broadcasting station by any person who is a legally qualified candidate for any public office in connection with his campaign for nomination for election, or election, to such office shall not exceed—

(1) during the 45 days preceding the date of a primary or primary runoff election and during the 60 days preceding the date of general or special election in which such person is a candidate, the lowest unit charge of the station for the same class and amount of time for the same period; and

(2) at any other time, the charges made for comparable use of such station by other users thereof.

(c) For the purposes of this section—

(1) the term "broadcast station" includes a community antenna television system; and

(2) the terms "licensee" and "station licensee" when used with respect to a community antenna television system mean the operator of such system.

(d) The Commission shall prescribe appropriate rules and regulations to carry out the provisions of this section.[33]

A 1952 amendment inserted subsection (b). A 1959 amendment incorporated the exemptions pertaining to news and news-type programs and added the Fairness Doctrine in subsection (a). Congress made this change after a perennial candidate, Lar Daly of Chicago, demanded equal time because of an interview with a major candidate on a news-type program. The station refused on the assumption that such programs were exempt from Section 315, a belief dating back to 1927. Daly appealed and to the surprise of many, the FCC ruled in his favor. Since the effect of such a ruling was to discourage stations from allowing major candidates to appear on news or news-type programs, Congress hurriedly amended the law. In so doing, it incorporated the language of the Fairness Doctrine.

Section 315 originally was intended to prevent a licensee from giving exclusive or favored-treatment exposure to a particular candidate. The 1959 amendment, however, made it legal for a licensee's news programs to concentrate on major political contenders to the detriment, except for fairness requirements, of minor party candidates.

Various rules or interpretations have emerged from court or FCC decisions concerning equal-time requirements. For example, a licensee cannot be sued for libel in connection with what a candidate for public office might wish to say because the licensee has no power to censor what is said during an equal-time broadcast. This was the substance of a U.S. Supreme Court decision in 1959 in *Farmers Educational and Cooperative Union v. WDAY Inc.*[34]

Some of the other rules that have been established are:

- *The candidate must be publicly declared.* Senator Eugene J. McCarthy was running for the Democratic party's presidential nomination in 1968 when the three commercial television networks broadcast a "year-ender" interview of President Lyndon Johnson on December 19, 1967. McCarthy attempted to invoke Section 315, but the FCC turned him down on the ground that at the time of the interview President Johnson was not a declared candidate. The Minnesota congressman took his case to the U.S. Court of Appeals, but the FCC's decision was upheld.[35]

- *The time given to all other legally qualified candidates for the same office must be mathematically equal, but it need not be given at exactly the same time.* For example, if one candidate received three minutes of prime time, then all other candidates for that same office would have to be given three minutes of prime time.

- *Licensees are not required to notify candidates about any air time due them under equal opportunities.* Rather, candidates must assert such a right by making requests for equal opportunities directly to a station or network and doing it within one week after the first broadcast that gave rise to the equal-time right.[36]

- *Section 315 does not apply to appearances made on behalf of candidates; that is, by their agents or allies.* It applies only to candidates themselves. In 1970 the FCC adopted the *Zapple* rule, which is known as the quasi-equal opportunities doctrine and is limited to supporters or spokespersons for a candidate.[37] The rule requires that when a licensee sells time to supporters of a candidate who, during a campaign, urge the election of their candidate, discuss the issues, or criticize opponents, then the licensee must afford comparable time to the opponents' spokespersons or supporters. *Zapple* does not require that free time be given to respond to paid-time comments.

- *If a candidate is charged for air time, all other candidates for that office must be charged the same rate for the same amount of time.* The fact that licensees are not required to provide free air time in the first instance benefits the wealthier candidates or parties. Various proposals have been advanced from time to time in an effort to remedy this situation.

- *The mere label, "news-type program," may not protect the station from a demand for equal opportunities.* Congresswoman Shirley Chisholm, D-N.Y., had sought equal time to respond to television appearances by two other party candidates just prior to the June 6, 1972, California primary. The FCC ruled that Senators George McGovern of South Dakota and Hubert Humphrey of Minnesota had been interviewed on news-type programs and therefore ABC and CBS networks and their affiliated stations were exempt under Section 315(a)(2).[38] But on June 3, 1972, the U.S. Court of Appeals for the District of Columbia Circuit, although not specifically ruling on the merits of the case, issued an "interim" relief order which permitted Mrs. Chisholm equal time on the two networks prior to the primary. A delay for the purpose of permitting argument on the merits of the request would have resulted in forfeiture of Mrs. Chisholm's equal-time right, since the primary would have been over by then. The court held that the appearances of McGovern and Humphrey on the television shows were more like debates and consequently were not exempt from the equal opportunities requirement.

■ *If a declared candidate appears on a non-news program, but does not mention his or her candidacy, does Section 315 apply?* Yes, ruled the FCC on June 16, 1972. The candidate is "using" the facilities of the licensee; therefore, all other candidates for that same office must be afforded the same opportunities.

The word "use" has caused considerable difficulty. In an early legislative draft of Section 315, the licensee was to be considered a "common carrier in interstate commerce," much like a telephone company. Such a designation would have had important implications in terms of fairness and access to radio and television. This language was deleted because it was felt that the licensee would lose control over the initial decision whether to permit the use of its facilities by a political candidate. But once a licensee grants the air time to a candidate, either on a paid or free basis and apart from the exceptions already noted, it virtually becomes a common carrier since it cannot censor what a candidate will say and must permit the use of the facilities when legally obligated to do so.

The Commission's 1970 public notice cites numerous rulings that *all* appearances of legally qualified candidates on a television station, except "fleeting" ones, constitute a use of that station's facilities within the meaning of Section 315. Furthermore, the Commission has emphasized that the appearances need not be of a political nature in order to activate equal-time requirements. The only exemption permitted by Congress when it amended Section 315 in 1959 was for certain news-type programs; therefore "nonpolitical" or "entertainment-type" programs are not exempt. The consequences can be amusing, depending on one's point of view.

Comedian Pat Paulsen was declared by the FCC to be a legally qualified candidate for the Republican party's nomination for President in 1972 because he had qualified to be on the New Hampshire ballot.[39] The question arose whether his appearance on a purely entertainment-type program—a Walt Disney series called "The Mouse Factory"—might give rise to equal-time requirements. In deciding that such an appearance would do so, the FCC called attention to a Supreme Court ruling which prohibits licensees from exercising censorship over the material broadcast by candidates, and observed:

> It follows, therefore, that since candidates may broadcast whatever material they desire, a licensee under no circumstances could limit such a candidate to "political uses" only, and any use by a candidate would entitle his opponent to "equal opportunities" unless specifically exempted in Section 315.[40]

Thus, if running for President was a joke, which Paulsen fervently denied, it was a costly one for him in terms of lost opportunities to appear on entertainment-type radio or TV programs.

The *Paulsen* precedent was used to shoot down the proposed telecasting of old Ronald Reagan movies during the period when Reagan and President Ford were jousting for the Republican party presidential nomination. The FCC, in a 5–2 vote in 1976, upheld a staff ruling that the showing of *Cattle Queen of Montana* and *Tennessee Partner* would activate the equal-time requirement if Ford made such a demand. Commissioners Glen Robinson and Benjamin Hooks dissented, saying the Commission has discretion "to follow the dictates of common sense." But the majority agreed that such telecasting would constitute "use" of the station's facilities within the meaning of Section 315 in the same way as the *Paulsen* situation.

Another unusual situation developed when a reporter for a TV station sought election to a town council. The FCC ruled that the Sacramento, California, station would have to give equal time to the reporter's political opponents if the reporter appeared on television. The U.S. Court of Appeals for the District of Columbia Circuit upheld the constitutionality of the FCC's ruling and the Supreme Court denied review in 1988.[41]

Presidential Debates on TV

Until the FCC significantly modified the equal-time rules in 1975, debates by presidential candidates on radio or television were not exempt from Section 315 requirements. The famous televised debates between John F. Kennedy and Richard M. Nixon took place in 1960 only because Congress, through adoption of Senate Joint Resolution 207, temporarily suspended the equal-time requirements so that all other candidates for the presidency, except the two frontrunners, could be denied equal time. Had Congress not acted, the networks would not have carried, on a free basis, the debates. Why? At the time at least 14 other presidential candidates representing little-known political parties were on the ballot in various states, including contenders put forth by the Tax Cut Party, Prohibition Party, Afro-American Unity Party, and American Beat Consensus.

No comparable debates took place until President Ford and Jimmy Carter were pitted against one another in three televised encounters—the first on September 23, 1976 before an audience estimated at 95 million. The debates came about in an unexpected—and controversial—way.

On July 8, 1975, Ford announced that he would seek the Republican party's presidential nomination. CBS then petitioned the FCC to change its 1964 ruling in which it had declared that presidential press conferences were subject to equal-time requirements. On September 25, 1975, the FCC, by 5–2 vote, held that live broadcasting of candidates' *entire* news conferences or press conferences, and, under certain circumstances, candidates' debates, would be exempt from equal-time requirements because they were bonafide news events. The debates had to be nonstudio events initiated by nonbroadcast, independent entities, and broadcast in their entirety. Debates now can be taped, but if so they must be broadcast within 24 hours of the taping. When the League of Women Voters (a nonbroadcast entity) agreed to sponsor the Ford-Carter debates in a nonstudio setting (which caused considerable technical difficulties for the networks), and to exclude minor party candidates, the debates did not activate successful equal-time demands.

However, the cost of "staging" the televised debates was $315,000, according to the League of Women Voters. Because of rules initially put forth by the Federal Election Commission (FEC) on the funding of the 1976 presidential debates, the League at first was prohibited from soliciting funds from business and labor unions to help defray expenses. Thus, the League faced the prospect of paying $91,000 of the costs out of its own treasury. Had not the FEC reversed itself in December 1977 to allow sponsoring organizations to seek funds from corporations and unions to help pay the costs of such debates, the chance of finding future sponsors would have been slim.

The league thus was able to sponsor two televised "debates" between President Reagan and challenger Walter Mondale during the 1984 presidential campaign.

In November 1983 the FCC ruled that broadcasters can stage debates between candidates of their own choosing without activating equal-time requirements. A three-judge U.S. Circuit Court panel in Washington, D.C., upheld the Commission's action in a 1984 decision.

Televised debates took place in 1988 between George Bush and Michael Dukakis, but the League of Women Voters decided not to be a sponsor for several reasons including the candidates' "handlers" virtually dictating the ground rules for the "debates." As the league's president, Nancy Neuman, put it: "It was a charade in debate's clothing, and we wanted nothing to do with it."

Presidential Speeches and FCC Policy

One of the problems perplexing to the FCC is the extent to which a speech by the President, who might also be a candidate, gives rise to equal time for other presidential candidates, or, under the *Zapple* doctrine, comparable time for spokespersons not of the President's party to respond. Also, what should be the regulatory requirement if the President gives a speech when he is not a declared candidate?

In *Fair Broadcasting of Controversial Issues*,[42] the Commission in 1970 declined to extend *Zapple* to presidential broadcasts, saying instead that the Fairness Doctrine was applicable whenever such a broadcast dealt with controversial issues of public importance. The same issue confronted the Commission the following year when it denied requests by the Democratic National Commission (DNC) to compel the three major networks to provide time for the DNC to respond to three separate appearances on radio and television by President Nixon in early 1971. ABC granted DNC's request; the other networks refused. ABC's action led the Republican National Committee (RNC) to seek time to respond to the DNC's broadcast, but the FCC also rejected the RNC's request. Both national committees appealed and the U.S. Court of Appeals upheld the Commission.[43] It endorsed the Commission's policy of not requiring equal time in connection with a presidential address unless the President is a legally qualified candidate and then only if his speech comes under one of the provisions of Section 315. The court agreed that the President may function in a political capacity and as the nonpolitical leader of the nation. Distinguishing between these roles is a burden that "must fall to the Commission" in ruling on requests such as those filed by DNC, the court said.

There has been no resolution of the problem associated with presidential speeches. From time to time a network will refuse to broadcast such a speech in the belief that equal-time requirements will be triggered.

Candidates and Purchase of Broadcast Time

In 1972 the Federal Election Campaign Act (Pub. L. 92-225) went into effect which, among other things, amended Sections 312 and 315 of the 1934 Act. As amended, Section 312 provides, in part, that the Commission may revoke a license "for willful or repeated failure to allow reasonable access to or to permit purchase of reasonable amounts of time for the use of a broadcasting station by a legally qualified candidate for Federal elective office on behalf of his candidacy."

The law requires "reasonable access" on either a paid or a free basis. It also requires broadcasters to sell time to candidates at the lowest unit charge available to any other buyers of time.

As a result of a complaint, the Commission in 1974 issued a public notice stating that reasonable access to prime time is inherently a part of the 1972 law. In addition, said the Commission, in applying an "equal treatment" standard mandated by the law, candidates must be given the opportunity to purchase spot announcements of the same length and type as available to other advertisers.[44]

The importance of the "reasonable access" law can be measured against the fact that candidates spent $59.6 million in 1972 for radio, television, and cable systems time.[45] Of the amount, 62 percent went for TV advertising and 88 percent went for spot announcements. Candidates spent even larger amounts for broadcast time in 1976, 1980, 1984, and 1988 elections.

The refusal of the three commercial television networks to sell a half-hour of time to the Carter/Mondale Presidential Committee in December 1979 violated the reasonable access requirement of Section 312. That was the ruling of a three-judge panel of the U.S. Court of Appeals (District of Columbia Circuit) in *CBS v. FCC* (1980).[46] The court thus affirmed a FCC 4–3 decision that the networks had acted unreasonably in refusing the request.

The networks appealed and the Supreme Court, in a 6–3 vote in 1981, affirmed the decision of the lower court.[47] Chief Justice Burger gave the opinion of the Court. After reviewing the legislative history of Section 312(a)(7), Burger said that the FCC standards that limit right of access to the period after the campaign has begun, as determined by the Commission, and that require broadcasters to evaluate access requests individually, are not arbitrary or capricious. Nor, said the Chief Justice, does the right of access unduly circumscribe broadcaster's editorial discretion. Rather, the law, as defined and applied, constitutes proper balancing of the First Amendment rights of candidates, the public, and broadcasters. In response to the networks' view that neither the First Amendment nor the Communications Act requires broadcasters to accept paid editorial advertisements, Burger responded that the precise responsibilities created by Section 312(a)(7) were not then before the Court. ". . . [We] now hold that 312(a)(7) expanded on those predecessor requirements and granted a new right of access for persons seeking election to federal office."

Opposition to Equal Time

At its 1975 meeting, the American Bar Association's House of Delegates went on record supporting revision or repeal of equal time. The major commercial networks have long urged its demise. Dean Burch, while chairman of the FCC, urged an end to equal time. So did the White House Office of Telecommunications Policy and a number of congressmen. Senator William Proxmire introduced a bill in 1975 that would exempt candidates for President and vice-president from equal-time requirements. Generally, opponents of equal time argue that broadcasters would carry more political programming and better cover political campaigns if equal-time requirements were eliminated. The FCC position was that Congress should decide whether to repeal or revise the doctrine, although Senator John Pastore believed that the Commission's major modification of the equal-time rules in 1975 constituted usurpation of congressional power.

In 1981, the FCC, at the urging of chairman Mark S. Fowler, voted 4–2 to recommend to Congress repeal of Section 315 and the reasonable access portion of Section 312. By that same vote it also urged an end to the Fairness Doctrine and an amendment to the 1934 Act to "establish a presumption that marketplace forces will normally be favored over regulation."[48] Shortly afterward, a coalition of media and consumer groups, called Friends of the Fairness Doctrine, announced opposition to the FCC's action. The coalition charged that the FCC had become "the lobbying arm of the broadcasting industry."[49]

When Dennis R. Patrick became FCC chairman in 1987, replacing Fowler who had headed the Commission for nearly six years, he, too, emphasized the competitiveness of the marketplace as the chief way of enhancing consumer welfare. The process of deregulation was to continue, although at a reduced rate, during the last two years of the Reagan presidency. Unlike Fowler, Patrick faced a Democrat-controlled House and Senate and key committee members increasingly hostile toward some of the deregulatory moves of the FCC. A good deal of that hostility was engendered by the Commission's scuttling of the Fairness Doctrine.

FAIRNESS DOCTRINE

Even though the Fairness Doctrine was included in Section 315 as a result of the 1959 amendment, it was significantly different from the equal-time requirements. Once licensees provide free or paid time to candidates, they become in effect common carriers. In essence, they turn over the use of the facilities to candidates for a stipulated period of time. Under the Fairness Doctrine (except for requirements laid down in 1967 when the personal attack and political editorializing rules were adopted, and except for the *Zapple* corollary to equal time), the licensee had considerable "good faith" discretion in meeting fairness obligations. In fact, the licensee had complete decision-making power concerning the kind of programming necessary to meet fairness obligations.

The Fairness Doctrine was the creation of the FCC as finally endorsed legislatively by Congress—or so it seemed. The Commission said the doctrine was "rooted" in the Radio Act of 1927—not expressly, but impliedly in the "public interest" language of that Act.

One of the earliest statements concerning fairness in broadcasting came in the Commission's *Great Lakes* decision in 1929:

> Insofar as a program consists of discussion of public questions, public interest requires ample play for the free and fair competition of opposing views and the Commission believes that the principle applies to all discussion of issues of public importance.[50]

Fairness also had roots in the FCC policies concerning licensee editorializing. During a 20-year period, the Commission went from a ban on licensee editorializing, to lukewarm endorsement, to outright embrace. The ban was imposed in *Mayflower Broadcasting Corp.*[51] in 1941 on the theory that a broadcast facility ought not be used to support a licensee's partisan ends. But in 1949 the Commission had a change of heart. It adopted a policy statement which discussed the need for radio broadcasting to contribute toward informing the public as part of the public interest requirement in the 1934 Act.[52] Licensees had to provide a reasonable amount of time for news and community public issues, and they had to present different viewpoints concerning controversial issues.

The complete turnabout on editorializing came in 1960 in a report which described licensee programming responsibilities in concrete terms. Editorializing was listed as one of the 14 major elements "usually necessary to meet the public interest, needs, and desires of the community in which the station is located. . . ."[53]

A year earlier Congress had amended Section 315 to exempt news and news-type programs from the equal-time provisions because of the famous Lar Daly case. In so doing, the lawmakers included the Fairness Doctrine:

> Nothing in the foregoing sentence shall be construed as relieving broadcasters, in connection with the presentation of newscasts, news interviews, news documentaries, and on-the-spot coverage of news events, from the obligation imposed upon them

under this Act to operate in the public interest and to afford reasonable opportunity for the discussion of conflicting views on issues of public importance.

No license was ever revoked solely for Fairness Doctrine violations. In some instances, the license renewal period was shortened to one year as a warning to "sin" no more. Generally, the Commission's action in fairness violations was to include a record of the violation in the licensee's file for consideration at license renewal time or simply to request the station to correct the unfairness.

From the time Fowler joined the Commission in 1981 until October 1984 — a period of more than three years — the FCC found only one fairness violation — that one against WTVH-TV in Syracuse, New York, in 1984.

Brandywine-Main Line Radio, Inc. v. FCC. The only FCC refusal to renew a license partly for unfairness reasons occurred in 1970 in a case involving WXUR-AM/FM at Media, Pennsylvania.[54] The stations had been purchased in 1966 by Faith Theological Seminary, headed by Dr. Carl McIntire, to bring the "conservative, fundamentalist" religious viewpoint to the Philadelphia area and to air Dr. McIntire's "Twentieth Century Reformation Hour" — a program carried by several hundred radio stations. License renewal denial was based in part on alleged fairness violations as well as misrepresentation of programming proposals in the renewal application. The U.S. Court of Appeals upheld the Commission's decision to take away the license, but it did so almost entirely on the misrepresentation issue. Judge Tamm, who wrote the decision, said the station had gone "on an independent frolic, broadcasting what it chose in any terms it chose, abusing those who dared differ with its viewpoints."[55] Judge Wright, who concurred, did so only on the misrepresentation issue. Chief Judge Bazelon originally said he would concur, but later dissented for what he said was a prima facie violation of the First Amendment because the station had been ordered off the air. Among the questions most bothersome to him was how a small station with limited resources could monitor all of its programs in order to identify controversial issues or personal attacks. If such a station could not afford to undertake necessary safeguards to abide by Commission rules, the net result would be a "very critical First Amendment question," according to the judge, who proceeded to ask how public access to ideas is enhanced by forcing a station off the air.

Personal Attack, Political Editorializing Rules

As enacted in 1959, the Fairness Doctrine did not confer a right of access to the broadcast medium on any particular individual or group; rather, the only "right" of access was for ideas so that the public would have the benefit of robust, wide-open debate. The licensee could fulfill its obligations under the doctrine without permitting anybody outside of the station to use the facilities. But the personal attack and political editorializing rules, as formalized in 1967 by the Commission, confer a *limited* right of access on certain individuals or groups, just as equal time does.

Through the years the Commission had shown considerable concern for "concretizing" the Fairness Doctrine in certain instances. For example, it made this statement in its 1949 report on editorializing by licensees: ". . . [E]lementary considerations of fairness may dictate that time be allocated to a person or group which has been specifically attacked over the station, where otherwise no such obligation would exist."[56]

FCC guidelines for dealing with personal attack took definite form in a 1962 memorandum opinion concerning renewal of a Florida station's license. In that case, a petition had been filed opposing license renewal on the ground that the licensee had attacked various individuals in the community in a series of editorials. Referring to its 1949 report, the FCC said:

> In appropriate recognition of the serious nature of such attacks, we pointed out that fairness may dictate that "time be allocated" to the person or group attacked. Where, as here, the attacks are of a highly personal nature which impugn the character and honesty of named individuals, the licensee has an affirmative duty to take all appropriate steps to see to it that the persons attacked are afforded the fullest opportunity to respond.

This decision in the *Maypoles* case provided the first Commission definition of "personal attack" and indicated the scope of the licensee's responsibility.[57]

About the same time, the Commission also entered the first stage of a policy decision concerning political editorializing by licensees. During a 1962 gubernatorial campaign in California involving incumbent Pat Brown and contender Richard Nixon, two commentators on KTTV (a Times-Mirror Broadcasting Co. station) aired frequent editorial attacks against Brown. The California State Democratic Committee complained to the FCC, and the Commission, in a telegram to the licensee, stated:

> . . . [F]airness requires that when a broadcast station permits, over its facilities, a commentator or any person other than a candidate, to take a partisan position on the issues, involved in a race for political office and/or to attack one candidate or support another by direct or indirect identification, then it should send a transcript of . . . such program to the . . . candidate immediately and should offer a comparable opportunity for an appropriate spokesman to answer the broadcast.

"Appropriate spokesman" was used because if the candidate himself appeared, then the equal-time provision of Section 315 would come into play.

The formal issuance of the rules by the Commission came in 1967. As amended, the rules are:

§73.123 Personal attacks; political editorials.
(a) When, during the presentation of views on a controversial issue of public importance, an attack is made upon the honesty, character, integrity or like personal qualities of an identified person or group, the licensee shall, within a reasonable time and in no event later than one week after the attack, transmit to the person or group attacked (1) notification of the date, time and identification of the broadcast; (2) a script or tape (or an accurate summary if a script or tape is not available) of the

attack; and (3) an offer of a reasonable opportunity to respond over the licensee's facilities.

(b) The provision of paragraph (a) of this section shall not be applicable (1) to attacks on foreign groups or foreign public figures; (2) to personal attacks which are made by legally qualified candidates, their authorized spokesmen, or those associated with them in the campaign, on other such candidates, their authorized spokesmen, or persons associated with the candidates in the campaign; and (3) to bonafide news-casts, bonafide news interviews, and on-the-spot coverage of a bonafide news event (including commentary or analysis contained in the foregoing programs, but the provisions of paragraph (a) of this section shall be applicable to editorials of the licensee).

. . . (c) Where a licensee, in an editorial, (i) endorses or (ii) opposes a legally qualified candidate or candidates the licensee shall, within 24 hours after the edito-rial, transmit to respectively (i) the other qualified candidate or candidates for the same office or (ii) the candidate opposed in the editorial (1) notification of the date and the time of the editorial; (2) a script or tape of the editorial; and (3) an offer of a reasonable opportunity for a candidate to respond over the licensee's facilities:

Provided, however, that where such editorials are broadcast within 72 hours prior to the day of the election, the licensee shall comply with the provisions of this paragraph sufficiently far in advance of the broadcast to enable the candidate or candidates to have a reasonable opportunity to prepare a response and to present it in a timely fashion.[58]

Networks have opposed the personal attack rules for various reasons. As CBS pointed out, the truth of the attack makes no difference. The right of reply remains vested in the attacked person or group. Furthermore, even if the original broadcast sought to be fair by quoting the attacked person, CBS said that the attacked person would still have a right to reply.[59]

Constitutionality of Fairness Doctrine

Red Lion Broadcasting Co., Inc. v. FCC. Whether the Fairness Doctrine generally, and the personal attack and political editorializing rules specifically, would survive a test of constitutionality was decided in favor of the FCC by court decisions in 1967 and 1969 in the case of *Red Lion Broadcasting Co., Inc. v. FCC.*

On November 27, 1964, Pennsylvania radio station WGCB of the Red Lion Broadcasting Co. carried a 15-minute broadcast by the Reverend Billy James Hargis as part of the minister's "Christian Crusade" series. In discussing a book written by Fred J. Cook, entitled *Goldwater — Extremist on the Right,* Reverend Hargis accused Cook of working for a Communist-affiliated publication and also leveled other charges. Cook demanded free reply time, which the station refused. The FCC then declared that the broadcast constituted a personal attack and that the station had failed to meet its obligation under the Fairness Doctrine by not sending a tape, transcript, or summary of the broadcast to Cook and offering him free time to reply. Such steps were necessary under a Commission decision in 1962 concerning Times-Mirror Broadcasting Co., even though the rules were not formally implemented until 1967.

A U.S. Court of Appeals panel held that the Fairness Doctrine was not unconstitutionally vague and that the broadcaster could not insist upon payment by the party who sought to respond to a personal attack.[60] The Red Lion station appealed.

In the meantime, another case was making its way toward the U.S. Supreme Court and involved a challenge of the political editorializing rules. This case, *U.S. vs. Radio-Television News Directors Association,*[61] was joined with *Red Lion* in the historic ruling by the Supreme Court. Justice White said for a unanimous (8–0) Court in 1969 that the rules were constitutional and that the FCC had the power to promulgate them. In the process of also upholding the constitutionality of the Fairness Doctrine generally, White made these points:

1. The rules enhance, rather than abridge, freedom of speech and press.
2. The FCC was implementing congressional policy and acting in the public interest.
3. The rules fell short of imposing censorship on the licensee's programming — censorship being forbidden by Section 326.
4. Broadcasting, as a new medium, has different characteristics which justify differences in applying First Amendment standards.
5. Personal attack rules are indistinguishable in constitutional principle from Section 315, which had been validated in 1959 by the Court (*Farmers Educational & Cooperative Union v. WDAY*).
6. Those who "are licensed stand no better than those to whom licenses are refused" as far as the First Amendment is concerned. Thus there is nothing in the First Amendment to prevent the government "from requiring a licensee to share his frequency with others and to conduct himself as a proxy or fiduciary with obligations to present those views and voices which are representative of his community." Further, it is the right of the viewers and listeners, not the broadcaster, which is paramount. In this connection, Justice White espoused the Meiklejohn doctrine; that is, it is the right of the public to receive suitable access to social, political, esthetic, moral, and other ideas which is crucial. And it is *this* right which cannot be constitutionally abridged either by Congress or the FCC.
7. As proxies for the entire community, licensees can be obligated to give suitable time and attention to matters of "great public concern" without the First Amendment being violated.

In a nutshell, *Red Lion* allowed the FCC to impose obligations on licensees to present ideas and information about matters of "great public concern" without specifically telling the licensee how to do it. Leaving aside personal attack and political editorializing rules, which allow specific individuals access to a station's facilities, licensees could air those ideas and viewpoints that they chose as long as they were operating in good faith. And they could select whichever spokesperson they desired, or none at all. Under the general Fairness Doctrine, the licensee had a great deal of discretionary power.

Fairness and Broadcast Journalism. Because of Fairness Doctrine criticisms, including the networks' persistent efforts to have the doctrine repealed, the Commission undertook a three-year study of various issues generated by fairness requirements. In 1974, the FCC adopted the new *Fairness Reports*[62] which reaffirmed "the basic validity and soundness of the doctrine in ensuring that broadcasting would continue in a manner consistent with the purposes of the First Amendment and the public interest. . . ."[63]

Concerning the doctrine's alleged inhibitory effect on broadcast journalism the *Report* had this to say:

> In the years since *Red Lion* was decided, we have seen no credible evidence that our policies have in fact had the net effect of reducing rather than enhancing the volume and quality of coverage.[64]

The Commission has always been reluctant to "punish" a licensee for its news programs. Although not condoning such flagrant journalistic malpractices as distortion or suppression of basic factual information, the FCC nonetheless observed that distortions or misrepresentations can occur in perfectly good faith. Therefore, said the Commission, ". . . [W]e do not believe that it would be either useful or appropriate for us to investigate charges of news misrepresentations in the absence of substantial extrinsic evidence or documents that on their face reflect deliberate distortion."[65]

A number of cases, such as the following ones, led the Commission to this position.

Metromedia, Inc. In *Metromedia, Inc.* (1968) a station was accused of altering a videotape to make it appear that an interviewee had responded to an interviewer's question when, in fact, the questioner was not in the studio at the time of that particular question and answer.[66] The Commission informed the licensee that it had the "responsibility for exercising reasonable diligence in preventing the broadcast of false or misleading information," and that it should not permit producers to engage in deliberate distortion. Further, the Commission indicated that the matter would be considered again at license renewal time.

Democratic National Convention TV Coverage. As a result of the turmoil and violence surrounding the Democratic National Convention in Chicago in 1968, thousands of complaints were received by the FCC concerning alleged unfairness on the part of the national television networks. In considering those complaints, the Commission declined to take any action. As it pointed out, the Commission generally refrains from examining the fairness or truthfulness of news coverage, or the news judgment of stations or networks, for fear of acting as a censor. This is not because fairness or truthfulness is unimportant, said the Commission, but because determination of fairness "by a governmental agency is inconsistent with our concept of a free press. . . . We do not sit as a review body of the 'truth' concerning news events."[67]

CBS: Hunger in America. In connection with complaints concerning a CBS documentary, *Hunger in America,* the Commission in 1969 placed the burden of proof upon complainants. Responding to criticisms of the program from some congressmen, the FCC said it would act when there was extrinsic evidence of deliberate misrepresentation, adding:

> And when we refer to appropriate cases involving extrinsic evidence, we do not mean the type of situation, frequently encountered, where a person quoted on a news program complains that he very clearly said something else. The Commission cannot appropriately enter the quagmire of investigating the credibility of the newsmen and the interviewed party in such a type of case.[68]

Since no extrinsic evidence of deliberate misrepresentation was found, even though CBS erroneously reported that a baby had died of malnutrition, the FCC took no further action.

A TV "Staged Pot Party." The Commission also declined to "punish" WBBM-TV of Chicago in another 1969 case that resulted from the televising of a "staged" marijuana "party." Although the FCC said the station had made a mistake in failing to indicate that the event was staged, it decided against any action because to do otherwise might discourage journalistic activity.[69] The licensee also was assured that the incident would not affect license renewal. However, the FCC urged stations to adopt policies which would deal with the "staging" of news events. A mitigating circumstance in the "pot party" episode was that participants in the televised event had previously used the drug.

CBS: The Selling of the Pentagon. Another CBS documentary, *The Selling of the Pentagon,* aired on February 23, 1971, led to a storm of protests, including a denunciation of it by Vice-President Spiro Agnew and other government officials. Despite allegations that a video-tape editing had distorted some of the interviews, the FCC declined to act by virtue of its earlier policy. It said, "Lacking extrinsic evidence or documents that on their face reflect deliberate distortion, we believe that this governmental licensing body cannot properly intervene."[70]

It was *The Selling of the Pentagon* and the network's defiance of a congressional subcommittee's subpoena which very nearly resulted in the House of Representatives voting a contempt citation against CBS President Frank Stanton (see Chapter 11). In the aftermath, several bills were introduced in Congress to punish anyone who was intentionally deceptive in the presentation of broadcast news. One bill, for example, would have imposed a maximum fine of $10,000 and imprisonment of up to one year, or both, plus license revocation, for such deception. The bills, however, made little headway and soon were forgotten.

NBC's Pensions Case. Despite the Commission's avowed reluctance to overrule editorial judgement, it did so in connection with NBC's broadcast of a documentary, *Pensions: The Broken Promise,* on September 12, 1972. A complaint was filed with the FCC by Accuracy in Media (AIM) charging that NBC had presented a one-sided picture of private pension plans. On the same day that the program received the George Foster Peabody Award for excellence, the FCC's Broadcast Bureau notified NBC that the program violated the Fairness Doctrine—a position subsequently upheld by the Commission. NBC rejected the allegation and asserted that the *Pensions* broadcast did not concern a controversial issue of public importance. But the Commission rejected this argument and said it expected prompt compliance with its ruling.

NBC went to court and a three-judge panel of the U.S. Court of Appeals (District of Columbia Circuit), in a 2–1 split, ordered the FCC to vacate its order against NBC and to dismiss AIM's complaint.[71] In the opinion by Judge Harold Leventhal, heavy reliance was placed on the U.S. Supreme Court's decision in *Columbia Broadcasting System v. Democratic National Committee* (1973).[72] In this case Chief Justice Burger had said that journalistic discretion is the keynote to the legislative framework of the Communications Act, adding that no broadcaster can present all colorations of all available public issues. Therefore, choices must be made by those whose mission it is to inform, not by those who must rule. Burger continued:

> For better or worse, editing is what editors are for; and editing is selection and choice of material. That editors—newspaper or broadcast—can and do abuse this power is beyond doubt, but that is not reason to deny the discretion Congress provided. . . .[73]

Therefore, Burger said (and this was the view echoed by the Circuit Court in the *Pensions* case):

> Congress intended to permit private broadcasting to develop with the widest journalistic freedom consistent with its public obligations. . . .
>   The broadcaster, therefore, is allowed significant journalistic discretion in deciding how best to fulfill the Fairness Doctrine obligations, although that discretion is bounded by rules designed to assure that the public interest in fairness is furthered.[74]

The Circuit Court declared that a substantial burden must be overcome by the FCC before it can say there has been an unreasonable exercise of journalistic discretion on the part of licensees. The court did not believe the FCC had overcome that burden in the *Pensions* case. The U.S. Supreme Court declined to review this decision.

The *Pensions* case outcome did not diminish the FCC's interest in licensee fairness as demonstrated by the following:

- Reaffirmation by the Commission in March 1976 of the main features of its 1974 *Fairness Report.*
- A finding in 1976 that eight California radio stations had violated the Fairness Doctrine in connection with spot commercials by Pacific Gas and Electric Co. promoting the construction of nuclear power plants.

The stations were directed to report on how they intended to meet their fairness obligations.

■ The overriding of a licensee's judgment in 1976 that it had presented a significant amount of information on various sides of a controversial issue. This unusual action by the Commission — unusual because the FCC ordinarily does not intrude into the day-to-day editorial decision-making of licensees — came in *Mink v. Radio Station WHAR*.[75] The fairness issue surfaced after Congresswoman Patsy Mink sent an 11-minute tape recording to a number of stations in connection with her sponsorship of antistrip-mining legislation. WHAR(AM) in Clarksburg, West Virginia, declined to air the tape, saying it had previously broadcast information about the strip-mining controversy. But the Commission found no evidence that WHAR had provided any locally originated programs on the subject and said that the licensee was under an affirmative obligation to inform listeners of issues of particular concern to the communities in which the licensee operates. The Commission gave the station 20 days to come up with a proposal on how it intended to meet its fairness obligation.

The Commission emphasized its distaste for intruding into day-to-day editorial decision-making, saying, "Rather, it is the Commission's policy to defer to licensees' journalistic discretion." But this discretion is not absolute, the Commission pointed out, saying that it had previously advised some licensees that certain issues are so critical that it would be unreasonable for a licensee to ignore them completely. The impact of the Commission's ruling in *WHAR* was heightened by the fact that the station's license renewal was pending from the previous year. Therefore the licensee undoubtedly felt great pressure to conform with the Commission's wishes that it originate local programs concerning strip mining.

Opposition to Fairness Doctrine

Opposition to the doctrine increased. The broadcast industry, through the National Association of Broadcasters and CBS and NBC, spearheaded attacks on the Fairness Doctrine. Their arguments, like those of the Commission in defending the efficacy of fairness, were impressive.

At the time networks were under fire because of events associated with the Democratic party's national convention in Chicago in 1968, CBS President Stanton urged the same measure of freedom for broadcast journalists as enjoyed by print journalists, saying:

"Pot Party at a University," "Hunger in America" and our coverage of the Chicago convention and other urban disorders represent legitimate and responsible reporting of serious social problems. As such, they constitute an important contribution to the public interest. And despite government intrusion and threats of intrusion [see Chapter 11], we are determined to continue covering controversial issues as a public service, and exercising our own independent news judgment and enterprise. I, for one, refuse to allow that judgment and enterprise to be affected by official intimidation. To those who say that broadcasters are licensed and, therefore, must submit to greater controls and regulations of content than those imposed upon the print media, I say, in turn, that freedom of the press is not divisible. You cannot have one measure of freedom if journalism is broadcast and another if it is printed.[76]

In 1974, CBS Chairman William S. Paley said of the Fairness Doctrine:

In spite of the fact that the FCC has shown moderation in putting it to use, the very fact that the . . . doctrine confers on a government agency the power to sit in judgment over news broadcasts makes it a tempting device for use by any administration in power to influence the content of broadcast journalism.[77]

Judge Bazelon's change of heart in the WXUR case came primarily as a result of arguments used by NBC President Julian Goodman in opposition to the doctrine. Goodman had said:

Complaints under the . . . doctrine, regardless of their substance, compel the broadcaster to search his files, review reams of broadcast material to show "balance," probe the memories of his newsmen, consult his lawyers and prepare defensive responses. In a minor case affecting NBC, . . . three months of effort and correspondence were involved before the FCC acknowledged that the news judgments we made were within our discretion as journalists.

But the necessary effort and inconvenience this involves is only a small part of the problem. The major part lies in the inhibiting effect this sort of government intrusion can have on independent news investigation and reporting.

A timid broadcaster who has gone through one or two of these experiences may think twice before he tackles a subject of strong controversy—the kind that the public needs most to know about. . . .

There is no censorship in its accepted definition. Nobody is telling anybody else what can or cannot be broadcast. Yet a form of censorship does exist—a censorship after the fact. The peril to the American public is that with time, it can become self-censorship before the fact, inducing caution and blandness. The theoretical advantages of assuring fairness—even if they exist—are certainly not worth the weakening effect on the independence of the press—the strongest instrument democracy has.[78]

Many others joined in the attacks on the Fairness Doctrine. Chairman Burch expressed serious doubts about the "foundations of the doctrine" in a speech in early 1973. Technology's impact on the scarcity rationale and the "chaotic mess" facing the Commission because of the growing number of complaints were chiefly responsible for his doubts.[79] While Nixon was President, the White House Office of Telecommunications Policy issued a call for repeal of the doctrine. Justice Douglas said the doctrine was unconstitutional, and Justice Stewart, who upheld the doctrine's constitutionality in *Red Lion,* later changed his mind.

The FCC voted 4–2 in 1981 to recommend to Congress that it do away with Section 315, including the Fairness Doctrine.

Senator Bob Packwood of Oregon also took up the cudgel with the introduction of the "Freedom of Expression Act of 1983" which would have lifted all content restrictions on broadcasters, including repeal of Section 315. Commission Chairman Fowler actively pursued two goals: deregulation and First Amendment parity for broadcasters (the latter theme also echoed by a prominent newspaper publisher, Arthur Ochs Sulzberger of *The New York Times,* whose company owns broadcast stations). But Fowler linked deregulation to a spectrum fee because he thought that Congress would be more receptive to such a move if broadcasters paid higher fees for using the air waves. The money could be used, for example, to help finance public broadcasting. The trade-off idea went over like a lead balloon. Broadcasters did not want to pay beyond the fee levels already imposed on them.

Senator Packwood's proposed legislation died in the Senate Commerce Committee in 1984, but Fowler did not remain idle. A notice of inquiry into the Fairness Doctrine was issued by the Commission in 1984 and both proponents and opponents of the doctrine squared off through comments to the Commission. Additionally, the Commission announced that it was considering the elimination of the personal attack and political editorializing rules and sought comments on this proposal. It is possible for the Commission to end its own rules without deferring to Congress, but whether it could kill off the Fairness Doctrine without congressional action was debatable.

The Commission drew some unexpected hope from a U.S. Supreme Court decision in 1984 in a case involving the issue of editorializing by public broadcasters. In a 5–4 decision, the Court ruled that public broadcasters had a right to editorialize. In his opinion for the Court, Justice Brennan included two footnotes related to the Fairness Doctrine and the constitutionality of broadcast regulation. The first footnote stated:

> The prevailing rationale for broadcast regulation based on spectrum scarcity has come under increasing criticism in recent years. Critics, including the incumbent chairman of the FCC, charge that with the advent of cable and satellite television technology, communities now have access to such a wide variety of stations that the scarcity doctrine is obsolete. *See, e.g.,* Fowler and Brenner, A Marketplace Approach to Broadcast Regulation, 60 Tex. L. Rev. 207, 221–226 (1982). We are not prepared, however, to reconsider our long-standing approach without some signal from Congress or the FCC that technological developments have advanced so far that some revision of the system of broadcast regulation may be required.[80]

The second footnote stated:

> We note that the FCC, observing that "if any substantial possibility exists that the [Fairness Doctrine] rules have impeded, rather than furthered, First Amendment objectives, repeal may be warranted on that ground alone," has tentatively concluded that the rules, by effectively chilling speech, do not serve the public interest, and has therefore proposed to repeal them. Of course, the Commission may, in the exercise of its discretion, decide to modify or abandon these rules [personal attack, political editorializing], and we express no view on the legality of either course. As we recognized in *Red Lion,* however, were it to be shown by the Commission that the Fairness Doctrine "has the effect of reducing rather than enhancing" speech, we would then be forced to reconsider the constitutional basis of our decision in that case.[81]

A debate ensued concerning significance of these footnotes. Fowler read them as a signal that the Court was ready to reconsider the issues addressed in *Red Lion*.

Concerning the argument that there is a multiplicity of broadcast voices in the United States — more than enough to ensure diversity of views — the Office of Communication of the United Church of Christ and other church groups pointed out that a study of 3926 communities having at least one broadcast station showed that these stations, particularly radio stations, offered the only local communications outlet. And in two-thirds of the communities the radio stations that existed were cross-owned with other existing media. In many of these communities, said the church groups in their 1984 opposition to repeal of the Fairness Doctrine, diversity among media facilities does not exist or is severely limited. Further, the growing concentration of media ownership (see Chapter 16) is another reason cited by various public interest groups that oppose elimination of the doctrine.

Fairness Doctrine Axed

The Fairness Doctrine, but not the equal opportunities requirement in Section 315, nor the personal attack or political editorializing rules, was repealed by a 4–0 vote of the FCC on August 4, 1987 (a decision being challenged in the courts). The doctrine, said the Commission, chilled the First Amendment rights of broadcasters and therefore was unconstitutional.[82] By its action, said Chairman Patrick, the FCC gave broadcasters the same First Amendment rights as the print media.

The FCC could act as it did because of two rulings by the U.S. Court of Appeals for the District of Columbia Circuit. In the first, *TRAC v. FCC* (1986), a three-judge panel said that the Fairness Doctrine had not been incorporated into the Communications Act by virtue of a 1959 amendment.[83] Since it was not law, but FCC policy, the Commission could abolish it.

Then in January 1987, another three-judge panel ruled, in *Meredith Corp. v. FCC,*[84] that the Commission, in light of its publicly expressed doubts about the doctrine, could not avoid consideration of the Meredith Corporation's claim that the doctrine violated the First Amendment. Meredith had brought the court action after the Commission had found that one of Meredith's television stations, WTVH at Syracuse, New York, had violated the doctrine.

The panel voted unanimously to remand *Meredith* to the FCC, instructing the Commission to consider whether enforcement of the doctrine was constitutional or contrary to the public interest. The Commission, said the panel, need not confront the issue of constitutionality "if it concludes that in the light of its 1985 Fairness Report it may not or should not enforce the doctrine because it is contrary to the public interest."[85]

The FCC then called for comments in keeping with the panel's remand and in a 76-page Memorandum Opinion and Order, it concluded that the doctrine was unconstitutional and therefore did not serve the public interest. Repeal of the doctrine was ordered.

In the *TRAC v. FCC* case, the three-judge panel split 2–1 with Judges

Antonin Scalia and Robert H. Bork forming the majority and Judge George E. MacKinnon dissenting. A motion for a rehearing by the *en banc* court was defeated because two of the 11 judges did not vote. Five judges favored a rehearing, but court rules require a majority vote of the active judges before a rehearing can be granted. An attempt to gain a U.S. Supreme Court review was rebuffed when that Court denied certiorari.[86]

After the FCC's action, Chairman Patrick acknowledged that repeal of the doctrine may increase instances of slanted coverage, but said that the "First Amendment does not guarantee a fair press, only a free press."[87]

And Commissioner James Quello stressed that licensees still are required to serve the public interest in their programming. "Our decision in this proceeding," he said, "does not absolve licensees of their public trust responsibilities to present programming that meets the needs of their communities."[88]

Many members of Congress were angered by the Commission's action, believing that the Fairness Doctrine had been legislatively incorporated into Section 315 and that the Commission had exceeded its authority. In an effort to codify the doctrine, the House passed the Fairness in Broadcasting Act of 1987 by a 302–102 vote. The Senate passed it, 59–31. But Reagan vetoed the measure on June 20, 1987.

In his veto message, Reagan said the spectrum scarcity problem had ended and that the *1985 Fairness Doctrine Report* showed that the doctrine is now unnecessary and "in fact inhibits broadcasters from presenting controversial issues . . . and thus defeats its own purpose."

Two influential legislators — Sen. Ernest Hollings and Rep. John Dingell — vowed after the President's veto to tack a fairness requirement on everything coming out of their key committees, but the first attempt to do so failed when a House committee refused to go along with a "rider" attached to an appropriation bill. This was after Reagan threatened to veto the spending bill even if it meant that the government would not be able to operate.

Several bills were introduced in Congress in 1988 to reinstate the Fairness Doctrine, but none was passed.

The FCC by a 3–0 vote in March 1988 refused to reconsider its decision seven months earlier to abolish the doctrine.[89] No alternative to the doctrine will be considered, the Commission said. Instead, the Commission is relying on an "unregulated marketplace of ideas" to accomplish what the Fairness Doctrine was intended to do.

A former FCC chairman, Richard E. Wiley, believes that ultimately the "final chapter over the Fairness Doctrine will be written by the courts."[90]

Other Deregulation Moves

Under Chairman Patrick, the FCC is expected to continue deregulation efforts, especially since George Bush easily won the presidency in 1988 and has espoused many of the policies of his Republican predecessor. The equal-time requirements, along with the personal attack and political editorializing rules, may be targeted for oblivion.

A considerable number of regulations affecting radio, subscription television, commercial over-the-air television, and cable TV already have been eliminated.

Radio

An FCC order in 1981 eliminated (1) the non-entertainment programming guidelines for radio, (2) formal ascertainment requirements for new stations and renewal applicants; (3) commercial limit guidelines, which had stipulated a maximum of 18½ minutes for commercials during a one-hour broadcast period, and (4) the requirement to keep detailed program logs in licensees' public files.

The rationale for this deregulation move went like this: With radio stations proliferating during the past 50 years, the original basis for government regulation—that is, ensuring that the stations provide a broad general service because the airwaves were a "scarce commodity" and stations were few in number—no longer existed.[91] With nearly 9000 AM and FM stations then in existence, the Commission said that radio licensees had found it essential to specialize "to attract an audience so that they may remain financially viable." The acting Commission chairman, Robert E. Lee, said at the time that the "radio industry has developed into a competitive industry in which natural market forces are more effective than Commission regulation in inducing licensees to act in the public interest."[92]

The FCC's action was challenged by the Office of Communication of the United Church of Christ, but a three-judge panel of the U.S. Court of Appeals in Washington, D.C., upheld virtually all of the FCC's action, although it expressed qualms about "blatant commercial excesses" as the result of the decision to remove limitations on commercials.[93]

A number of industry spokespersons claimed that the FCC's "deregulation" effort was more like "re-regulation" or consisted of very little deregulation.[94] Similar complaints have been voiced following the deregulation order affecting commercial television.

Subscription Television

Subscription television (STV) involves the use of over-the-air signals, as in conventional telecasting, only the signals are scrambled. A decoder is used on the subscriber's television set to unscramble the signals. By this system, first-run movies, athletic events, and other programs not available on conventional television can be made available to subscribers. This type of TV came under FCC regulation in 1968 after theater owners complained that they might otherwise lose their audiences.[95] The FCC's jurisdiction over subscription telecasting was upheld by the U.S. Court of Appeals for the District of Columbia Circuit in 1969.[96]

Among the limitations placed on STV were restrictions on feature films, sports events, and series programs. In addition, commercial advertising was prohibited during subscription operations.

In 1982 the FCC eliminated a number of rules, virtually deregulating pay-TV. At the time there were 27 STV stations serving more than one million customers. Another 16 stations had received licenses but had not yet gone into operation.

The scuttled rules had required: (1) a market to have at least four operating commercial TV stations before a STV station could begin operations; (2) a STV station to broadcast at least 28 hours of conventional programming per week; (3) a STV station to ascertain community requirements; and (4) a STV station to lease rather than sell decoders.

The 1982 change means there will be no limit on the number of regular TV stations that can convert to pay-TV.

STV owners still have to acquire an FCC license and their application for licensing still will be judged by the criteria used for other broadcasters.

Television

By a 5–0 vote in 1984, the Commission eliminated rules regulating over-the-air television comparable to those eliminated by its radio deregulation order, namely:

- Non-entertainment programming guidelines. Previously, TV stations had to devote at least five percent of their air time to locally produced programming, at least five percent to news, public affairs and informational programming, and at least 10 percent overall to non-entertainment programming.
- Formal ascertainment requirements for new stations and renewal applicants. However, commercial TV stations still are obligated to provide programming "responsive to the issues" pertaining to their communities and they will have to place an "issues/program" list in their public inspection file on a quarterly basis. However, if a competing TV station is airing programming on a community issue, then the licensee does not have to air programs on that particular issue.
- Limitations on commercials. Previously, TV stations had been limited to 16 minutes of commercials in any hour of broadcasting.
- Detailed or comprehensive logs of all programming aired by a station. Instead of such logs, which had to be open to public inspection, licensees must file the "issues/program" list periodically and report how they are addressing such issues in their programming.

The significance of the TV deregulation order, like the one for radio, has been the subject of considerable debate. Some broadcasters argue that the deregulation order is like the proverbial drop in the bucket; others hail the FCC's move as eliminating considerable paperwork.

Cable TV

Cable TV initially was developed for communities unable to get over-the-air television reception because of terrain or distance problems. Master antennas were built to pick up over-the-air television signals (VHF), amplify them, and carry them by cable over mountains or long distances for a fee.

In the mid-1960s, the FCC began regulating cable TV because it feared that such systems might begin importing distant signals (programs from VHF stations outside the local community) to the detriment of the local over-the-air stations.[97] The FCC's claim to jurisdiction over cable TV regardless of whether the signals were transmitted by airwaves (such as subscription TV) or by cable (as is the case with most systems today) was upheld by the U.S. Supreme Court in 1968 in its *U.S. v. Southwestern Cable Co.* decision.[98] And support for specific FCC regulation of such systems came in *U.S. v. Midwest Video Corp.* (1972)[99] when the Supreme Court, in a plurality opinion, upheld a FCC regulation requiring CATV systems having 3500 or more subscribers to originate their own programs if they carried the signal of any VHF station.

In 1976, the FCC required each cable TV system with 3500 or more subscribers to develop, at a minimum, a 20-channel capacity by 1986, and to make available four of those channels for access by public education, local government, and leased access users. However, the rules were invalidated by the U.S. Court of Appeals (Eighth Circuit) in *Midwest Video Corp. v. FCC*[100] — a decision affirmed by a 6–3 vote of the Supreme Court in 1979.[101] In an opinion by Justice White, the Court said the FCC had exceeded its authority by trying to impose common-carrier obligations on cable operators despite the 1934 Act's Section 3(h) which specifically directs the Commission not to treat persons engaged in broadcasting as common carriers. In a dissenting opinion, Justice Stevens, joined by Justices Brennan and Marshall, said he was unable to distinguish between the regulation that required mandatory origination of programs — a regulation upheld by the Court — and the four-channel access rule that was being struck down by the Court.

In a move to free cable TV from regulations restricting its growth, the FCC by a 4–3 vote in 1980, eliminated the "distant-signal" rule, and the syndicated program exclusivity rule that had permitted VHF stations in the 50 largest markets to force cable TV operators to black out any "imported" show if that show was appearing on local VHF stations.

The Commission said consumers would benefit substantially from elimination of the rules which had restricted competition and denied customers services for which they had been willing to pay.[102] The rescinded rules also had prevented new cable TV services in many communities, thereby restricting diversity and preventing the industry from growing to its fullest potential, according to the Commission. The majority also pointed out that VHF stations had experienced increases in their net profits despite a larger number of CATV stations and, for cable systems with fewer than 1000 subscribers, unlimited signal importations; therefore, a main argument used at the time the rules were adopted no longer existed.

The syndicated program exclusivity rule had authorized a local TV station, which had purchased exclusive exhibition rights to a program, to demand that a local cable system black out or delete that program from distant signals, whether or not the VHF station was simultaneously showing, or planning to show, the program.

Both rules served, in effect, as copyright protection because the courts had refused to restrict cable systems in their use of copyrighted works. But that situation changed with congressional passage of the Copyright Act of 1976 (see

Chapter 17). Included in that act was a compulsory licensing scheme for cable TV which means that cable operators must pay copyright owners a prescribed fee in return for permission to retransmit programs without first having to obtain the copyright owners' permission.

The FCC's action led to lawsuits by the National Association of Broadcasters and the National Football League (NFL). The NAB argued that the Copyright Act barred the FCC from repealing the rules. And the NFL argued that repeal of the distant-signal rule would destroy a congressionally mandated plan to maintain economic balance among NFL teams. Repeal of the rule, said the NFL, would allow all other NFL games to be imported by a cable system into a NFL team's home territory, instead of the two then allowed by NFL contracts. The FCC countered by saying that the Copyright Act allowed for adjustments of the compulsory royalty rates if cable TV rules are altered. Furthermore, the sports blackout rule remained in effect, said the agency, thereby providing protection for the live gate of NFL home teams if tickets to those games are not sold out.[103]

A three-judge panel of the Second Circuit U.S. Court of Appeals ruled in 1981 in *Malrite TV v. FCC* that the Commission had not acted arbitrarily or capriciously in deciding to deregulate cable TV.[104] The NAB and NFL then asked the Supreme Court to review the decision, but the Court declined to do so.[105]

The FCC's deregulation actions prompted state and local governments to move into the "regulatory void." Many of these governments soon were requiring cable systems to provide access channels for the public and government. Even in those communities which did not require such action, cable companies, anxious to win city-bestowed franchises, *voluntarily* offered such channels. A number of states chose to regulate the kind of advertising that cable operators could import into those states, such as liquor advertising—a situation which resulted in a major Supreme Court ruling in 1984 that struck down Oklahoma's law that barred cable systems from carrying wine commercials in signals they retransmitted throughout the state (see Chapter 13). Such state regulatory attempts are preempted by federal law, the Court ruled.

The hodgepodge of state and municipal regulatory requirements led Congress, after much debate, to enact the first major revision of the Communications Act of 1934. The Cable Communications Policy Act was signed into law in 1984. It recognizes the right of cities to grant franchises for cable TV systems, but it limits franchise fees to five percent of the system's gross revenues. By 1986 cable systems were completely freed of local rate regulations. In addition, the law makes it easier for cable operators to renew their franchises because national standards, not local ones, are used. It protects access channels set aside for educational, public and governmental use, and requires operators to provide "lock boxes" for subscribers who wish to prevent their children from watching objectionable shows. The act also requires cable systems to establish affirmative equal employment opportunity programs; regulates the collection and disclosure of information about subscribers collected by the cable system; and prohibits crossownership of cable systems by local TV stations, although crossownership by newspapers is permitted. The theft of cable services is made punishable by up to six months imprisonment and a $1000 fine. Local governments are effectively prohibited from involving themselves in cable programming decisions.

The 1984 Act still leaves regulatory power in the hands of the FCC, and although the Commission has acted to unshackle cable TV to promote its growth, a considerable number of regulations remain. For example, the FCC requires cable systems within a 35-mile radius of a local VHF station to carry that station's programs if the station so requests. Also, cable operators must carry distant broadcast station programs that are defined as "significantly viewed." However, a three-judge panel of the U.S. Court of Appeals (District of Columbia Circuit) decided in 1985 that the "must carry" rule concerning local TV signals violated the First Amendment.

The FCC adopted interim "must carry" rules in an effort to meet the Circuit Court's objections, but those rules also were struck down as unconstitutional and the Supreme Court decided not to review the appellate court's decision.[106] Consequently, the Commission announced in late 1988 that it would recommend to Congress abolition of the rules. This would mean that cable systems would have to pay standard royalty fees if they used any over-the-air signals that had been copyrighted.

A study, released in 1988, showed that cable TV systems were still carrying almost all of the local over-the-air TV station programs even though the FCC rules had been voided.

The FCC also voted in 1988 to reinstate its syndicated exclusivity rule, which the Commission had dropped in 1980.[107]

The 3–0 decision that allows broadcasters to purchase the exclusive rights to air a program in their viewing area drew a sharp reaction from cable TV groups. They charged that the reinstated rule could result in the blacking out of as much as 50 percent of all cable programming in some areas. But the Commission challenged this, saying the blackouts will be unnecessary because cable operators will be free to enter into their own contracts with program owners to obtain exclusive broadcast rights or to negotiate with local stations that have the rights to the programs desired by cable TV systems.

Cable Franchise at Issue. Although cities were given the right to franchise cable TV systems by action of Congress in 1986, the award of exclusive franchises may result in excluded companies claiming that their First Amendment rights have been violated. That was the substance of a U.S. Supreme Court holding in *City of Los Angeles v. Preferred Communications* (1986).[108] However, the Court did not specify what standard should be used to weigh the city's interest against First Amendment claims.

In upholding the U.S. Court of Appeals for the Ninth Circuit, Justice Rehnquist said for the Court that "cable television partakes of some of the aspects of speech and the communication of ideas as do the traditional enterprises of newspapers and book publishers, public speakers and pamphleteers."

In a concurring opinion, Justice Blackmun said that the Court will have to decide in some future case whether the "characteristics of cable television make it sufficiently analogous to another medium to warrant application of an already existing standard or . . . a new analysis."

Earlier, the FCC had told the Court that "the First Amendment does provide protection to person seeking cable television franchises" and, therefore, the refusal of Los Angeles to issue more than one franchise was a possible violation of the First Amendment.[109]

Preferred Communications, which did not bid for the exclusive franchise for the south central area of Los Angeles, sued the city after being denied permission to build a system in that area.

In its brief, the city had argued that the Cable Act of 1984 gave the city the authority to determine the number of cable operators to be franchised in a geographic area. Cable TV is a natural monopoly, said the city in arguing that it acted reasonably by assuming that only one franchisee could successfully operate in south central Los Angeles. Further, said the city, the utility poles to which Preferred sought access are not a public forum.

Preferred contended that the city's restrictions are not content-neutral, and that by upholding the licensing process local government would be permitted to "license the right to speak and (to) assume control over what is said and who speaks on cable."

Children's Programming

Children's programming by TV broadcasters was one of the issues that stalled or delayed broadcast deregulation by Congress. The same kinds of issues that faced the FTC also have faced the FCC with the latter agency being asked by Action for Children's Television to prohibit commercials aimed at children. It declined to do so in 1975 because it feared that such action would reduce funding for children's programming. Instead, the FCC voiced the hope that voluntary regulation might curb abuses to the point where additional federal agency regulation would be unnecessary. But as noted earlier, the TV and Radio Codes ceased to exist because of antitrust actions brought by the U.S. government. So the FCC decided in 1974 to rely upon programming "guidelines," rather than rules, to bring about improvements in the quality and diversity of children's programming. These guidelines also were intended to decrease the amount of advertising on children's programs and to eliminate certain selling practices. But an FCC staff report in 1979 declared that television generally was not in compliance with the guidelines. The report indicated that the best solution was an increase in the number of programming outlets, but in the absence of this, the Commission should institute mandatory programming standards.

The Commission adopted the staff report unanimously, but with reservations, and asked the staff to prepare a rule-making proposal that would contain several options. Five proposals ultimately were made as ways of increasing programming diversity.

The Commission called for public comments on the proposals, but then a period of foot-dragging ensued as the Commission awaited a new chairperson. In March 1982 Chairman Fowler let it be known that formal rule making on children's television was not a priority item for the Commission because, as he has said repeatedly, the Commission does not intend to get into content regulation. Shortly thereafter, ACT filed a lawsuit to force the Commission to take final action on children's TV programming rules. The U.S. Court of Appeals in the District of Columbia subsequently ordered the FCC to complete action on the rule making by the end of 1983. So the Commission, by a 4–1 vote with only Henry Rivera dissenting, adopted a new policy statement stipulating only that commercial broadcasters must continue to offer programming that takes into account children's needs.[110] Chairman Fowler said, "A broadcaster must demonstrate at [license] renewal time that he has paid attention to the specialized needs of children." Rivera's proposal that broadcasters be required to set aside a certain amount of air time for children's programming was rejected.

Peggy Charren, ACT's president, said the FCC action was "another nail in the coffin that . . . Fowler is building for children's television."[111]

In 1984 the FCC eliminated television guidelines for commercials on children's programs,[112] relying on marketplace forces instead. But ACT objected, and in 1987 the U.S. Court of Appeals for the District of Columbia Circuit remanded the case to the Commission for further explanation of the elimination of the commercialization guidelines.[113] The three-judge panel found that the Commission had failed to explain adequately the elimination of the guidelines.

While the Commission was considering how it could better explain its action, the focus of ACT's fight shifted to Congress where, in 1988, both houses approved a bill to limit TV program advertising to 10½ minutes for every hour of children's programming during weekends and 12 minutes per hour during the rest of the week.[114] (Under the rescinded FCC rules it had been 9½ minutes per hour on weekends and 12 minutes during weekdays.) But President Reagan exercised a pocket veto of the bill on November 5, 1988.

Violence on Television

Newton Minow, FCC chairman when he spoke at a NAB convention in 1961, referred to TV programming at that time as a "vast wasteland." In part, violence on television was one reason for his now-famous "wasteland" speech.

Violence on television still remains controversial and has resulted in two widely publicized lawsuits.

The first case stemmed from a NBC telecast on September 10, 1974, of a fictional drama, "Born Innocent," which depicted a teenage girl being "raped" by other females at a reformatory school. Four days later, a San Francisco girl was attacked by three girls and a boy and sexually assaulted in a similar manner. A $9 million damage suit was filed against NBC and its San Francisco outlet, KRON-TV. A state trial judge dismissed the suit on First Amendment grounds and on the basis that the state would not permit the use of a negligence theory to freeze the creative arts. The state Court of Appeals reversed and ordered that a trial be held. The California and U.S. Supreme Courts refused to review that ruling, the latter court by an 8–1 vote. The upshot of this action came on August 7, 1978, when the trial judge ruled that the plaintiff's attorney would have to prove that the network *willfully* sought to incite rape when it televised the program. This was an impossible burden of proof, said the plaintiff's attorney. The judge thereupon dismissed the lawsuit, an action which the plaintiff appealed.

The California Court of Appeals, First Appellate District, affirmed the trial court's action, ruling that the First Amendment bars a negligence action in light of plaintiff conceding that defendants did not encourage violent acts and that therefore there was no incitement.[115] The state Supreme Court declined to review with two justices dissenting, and the U.S. Supreme Court also denied certiorari.[116]

The second case involved a Florida youth, Ronald Zamora, who was convicted in the fall of 1977 of murdering an elderly neighbor woman despite the defense's claim that violence on television had made the youth insane. Subsequently, a $25 million lawsuit was filed against the three commercial television networks. The lawsuit claimed that Zamora, exposed to as many as 50,000 television murders prior to the real murder, had become "voluntarily addicted to . . . and subliminally intoxicated by the prolonged viewing" of such programs.

The networks sought dismissal of the lawsuit in part on First Amendment grounds.

This occurred in 1979 when the U.S. District Court for the Southern District of Florida ruled that the standard of care in Zamora's suit (the television networks allegedly failed to use "ordinary care" to prevent children from being incited and instigated to duplicate violence viewed on television) had no valid basis and would be against public policy. The judge said that imposition of such a "vague and undefined duty" would infringe upon the networks' exercise of their First Amendment rights.[117]

Another case led to a ruling by the Rhode Island Supreme Court that the First Amendment bars a negligence action against NBC by the parents of a 13-year-old boy who hanged himself while trying to imitate a stunt performed on the *Tonight* show.[118] The court said the broadcast could not be considered an "incitement," especially in view of the warnings given by the performer of the stunt against non-professionals attempting such an act. "To permit plaintiffs to recover on the basis of one minor's action would invariably lead to self-censorship by broadcasters in order to remove any matter that may be emulated and lead to a lawsuit," said the court.

ANTILOTTERY LAWS

The 1934 Act specifies in Section 312(a)(6) that a license can be revoked for violation of the U.S. Code prohibiting the broadcast of lottery information. Title 18 of the Code, Section 1304, states that "whoever broadcasts by means of any radio station . . . any advertisement of or information concerning any lottery . . . shall be fined not more than $1000 or imprisoned not more than one year, or both." The law also prohibits publicizing of lotteries via the U.S. mail. Newspapers which publicize them face the loss of their second-class mailing privilege.

A lottery consists of three elements, and all three elements must be present for the definition to apply.

1. *Prize.* Something of value must be offered as an inducement to a person to participate.
2. *Consideration.* The participant must give up something of value, such as money, to take part in the contest.
3. *Chance.* No skill is required in order to have a chance to win a prize.

The FCC believes that in association with a lottery broadcast, pleas to buy tickets; information as to where, how and when to make a purchase or where, how, and when winning tickets will be drawn; and live broadcasts of actual drawings or long lists of winners and prizes constitute violations of Section 1304. In addition, the FCC says that no matter how worthy the purpose of bingo games, raffles, and the like, their promotion by broadcasters appears to be in violation of Section 1304 and FCC regulations.

The antilottery laws were passed before states decided to enter the lottery "business" as a means of increasing state revenue. One result was pressure on Congress to alter the law so publicizing of state lotteries via the mails or by broadcast would be legal.

In 1975 President Gerald Ford signed into law Pub. L. 93-583 (18 U.S.C. 1307) which exempts state-conducted lotteries from certain Criminal Code provisions. Under the law, the transportation, mailing, and broadcast of advertising, information, and materials concerning lotteries authorized by state law are permitted. Stations in states adjacent to those which sanction lotteries also are permitted to publicize those lotteries. The prohibition against the broadcast of information about other lotteries, including foreign lotteries, still continues.

Newspapers in states which conduct lotteries, and newspapers in states adjacent to "lottery" states, were given the go-ahead to publish the same type of lottery information as radio and television by Pub. L. 94-525, passed by Congress in 1975.

SUMMARY

In the Radio Act of 1927 and the Communications Act of 1934, the key phrase pertaining to the licensing and regulation of broadcasting is "public convenience, interest, or necessity." This is the yardstick by which regulation takes place. The rationalization for such regulation, in the face of the First Amendment command that Congress shall not abridge freedom of speech and press, has proceeded along several lines. These include:

- The public owns the airwaves and therefore the use made of this resource can be regulated in the public interest.
- The airwaves are a limited, or scarce, resource which makes their use subject to regulation.
- Listeners and viewers are members of a "captive" audience, unlike the users of the print medium, and therefore the electronic medium is more susceptible to regulation.

- Licensees are fiduciaries or trustees for the public because they use what belongs to the public; therefore, they can be compelled to share their facilities and frequencies with others, or be required to operate in certain ways.
- The broadcast medium, particularly television, is more powerful than other media and therefore subject to more regulation.

Cable television significantly affected the scarcity rationale. For this and other reasons, various critics of government regulation of radio and television have sought to deregulate these media and extend to them the same First Amendment rights as enjoyed by the print media. In the 1980s the FCC took steps to partially deregulate radio, subscription TV, commercial TV, and cable TV.

In addition, the licensing period was extended from three years for both radio and television stations to seven years for radio and five years for television. Also, a "renewal expectancy" factor has been included in FCC's policy on license renewals.

As for networks, the FCC imposed chain broadcasting rules which were upheld by the Supreme Court in *NBC v. FCC* (1943). This case resolved the question of whether the FCC was a mere traffic controller. The courts said otherwise. Since then prime time access rules have been adopted by the FCC; and antitrust suits were filed against the three commercial television networks, with NBC, CBS, and ABC agreeing to limit production of programs and otherwise to loosen controls over program production.

The "equal opportunities" part of Section 315 dates back to the Radio Act of 1927 and constituted the entire section until 1959 when Congress amended that part of the law to exempt news and news-type programs while, at the same time, adding the Fairness Doctrine language. *Equal time* applies only to legally qualified candidates for public office and can be invoked only if the licensee permits a candidate to use its broadcast facilities, either on a paid or a free basis. Once the licensee permits such a use, then all other candidates for that same office have a right to use the station's facilities on an equal basis. In essence, the licensee gives up control of its facilities for that purpose and becomes a common carrier. News and news-type programs are exempt from equal-time; the licensee is not obligated to notify candidates that they qualify for equal time, and the licensee does not have to provide candidates with a script, tape, or summary of what their opponent(s) said.

In a major "reinterpretation" of policy in 1975, the Commission ruled that nonstudio, nonbroadcast entity-sponsored debates by candidates, and live broadcasts of presidential and candidates' news conferences, are exempt from equal-time requirements when broadcast in their entirety. The decision permitted the League of Women Voters to sponsor the Ford-Carter and Carter-Reagan televised debates. In 1983 the FCC ruled that broadcasters also could sponsor such debates without activating equal-time requirements, and that the debates could be taped if broadcast within 24 hours.

If a candidate's supporters or spokespersons are allowed to use a station's facilities, then supporters and spokespersons of all other candidates for that same office must be afforded *comparable*—not equal—time under the *Zapple* corollary.

As for federal candidates, a U.S. Court of Appeals ruled in *CBS v. FCC* (1980) that Section 312(a)(7) of the 1934 Act created an affirmative right of access to broadcast facilities for the candidates—meaning a right independent of any action taken by licensees. This decision followed the networks' turndown of a request to buy television time from the Carter/Mondale Committee.

The Fairness Doctrine was both general and specific. The general part has been scuttled by the FCC, but the specific part remains (for the moment). No station (with the possibile exception of WXUR-AM/FM) ever lost its license solely because of fairness violations.

In 1967, the FCC "concretized" the Fairness Doctrine by formulating personal attack and political editorializing rules. In both instances the licensee is obliged to do certain things whenever the rules come into play. In the case of personal attack on an identifiable person or group (other than on foreigners, political candidates, or those attacks made during a news or news-type program, although an editorial given during such a program is not exempt), the licensee must, within one week, notify the attacked party of the attack, provide a script, tape, or summary of the attack, and offer a *reasonable opportunity* to respond.

Comparable action must be taken by licensees in connection with editorials endorsing or opposing legally qualified candidates. In the event of an attack upon a candidate, that candidate must be notified within 24 hours of the attack, a script or tape of the editorial must be provided, and a *reasonable opportunity* must be afforded the candidate to respond. If the attack is to take place within 72 hours of election day, advance notification of the editorial must be given. Should a licensee endorse a candidate, then all other legally qualified candidates for that office must be notified within 24 hours, provided with a script or tape of what was said, and given a reasonable opportunity to respond. Advance notice is required if the endorsement is to be made within 72 hours of election day.

In 1969 the U.S. Supreme Court in *Red Lion* upheld the constitutionality of the personal attack and political editorializing rules. Justice White said for the unanimous Court that the rules enhanced, rather than abridged, freedom of speech and press; congressional policy was being implemented (the Fairness Doctrine amendment of 1959); censorship was not imposed on licensee's programming; broadcasting has characteristics different from other media and therefore differences are justified in applying First Amendment standards; and licensees are proxies or fiduciaries for the community and, as such, they can be obligated to present views and voices representative of the community, or to air matters of "great public concern."

But two footnotes in an opinion written by Justice Brennan in a 1984 case gave opponents of the Fairness Doctrine, including FCC Chairman Fowler and the NAB, reason to believe that the Supreme Court might be ready to entertain anew the question of the doctrine's constitutionality. This would be done, wrote Brennan, if it could be shown that the doctrine reduces, rather than enhances, speech.

The upshot of these footnotes and two cases decided by the U.S. Court of Appeals for the District of Columbia Circuit was a 4–0 vote of the FCC in 1987 to do away with the doctrine. The equal-time requirements of Section 315 and the two "concrete" rules that had flowed out of the doctrine (personal attack and political editorializing) were not affected by the action. Congressional action to reinstate the doctrine was met by a Reagan veto. Similarly, President Bush has said he'll probably veto any such legislation.

In 1984, the FCC eliminated TV guidelines for commercials on children's programs. The action was challenged by ACT and, on remand, the Commission was asked to explain more fully why it was eliminating the guidelines. Again, Congress was rebuffed in its efforts to override FCC action by another presidential veto.

Concerning violence on television, several lawsuits have unsuccessfully attempted to show a causal relationship between violence on the tube and real-life violence.

QUESTIONS IN REVIEW

1. Which theory or rationale, used to justify regulation of radio-television, is subjected to the most discomfiture by cable television developments?
2. Explain what the "trustee" or "proxy" concept is and why it would "justify" regulatory control of broadcast licensees.
3. The FCC consists of three entities. Name them.
4. True or False: In *NBC v. FCC*—a case involving the constitutionality of the FCC's chain broadcasting rules—the courts upheld the FCC's view that it was more than a mere traffic controller.
5. Radio stations can be licensed for how many years before facing renewal? Television stations?
6. Incumbent licenseholders have an advantage over challengers because of which FCC policy?
7. In deregulating radio and television, the FCC scuttled which rules?
8. Must equal time be equal to the exact minute?
9. True or False: The equal-time provisions of Section 315 apply to supporters and spokesmen of candidates for public office, not just to the candidates themselves.
10. Does equal time apply to entertainment-type programs? News or news-type programs?
11. How could John F. Kennedy and Richard M. Nixon carry out their famous televised debate in 1960 without a host of other presidential candidates being given equal time by the major TV networks?
12. How could the Ford-Carter, Carter-Reagan and Reagan-Mondale televised debates take place without all other candidates for the presidency being afforded equal time?
13. Who and what are not covered by the personal attack rules?
14. Can you think of a good reason why political candidates are not protected by the personal attack rules?
15. What major reason was given by the FCC when it repealed the Fairness Doctrine in 1987?
16. True or false: Congress strongly supported the FCC's repeal of the Fairness Doctrine.

ANSWERS

1. The "scarcity" theory; that is, the airwaves are a limited resource, therefore their use is subject to regulatory control.
2. The public owns the airwaves and the licensee is only granted a privilege (or license) to use what is owned by the people. As the user of what belongs to all of us, the licensee serves as a trustee, proxy, or fiduciary; as such, the trustee can be required to do certain things in the public interest which he/she otherwise might not want to do.
3. Commission, staff, administrative law judges.
4. True.
5. Seven. Five.
6. License renewal expectancy.
7. Formal ascertainment of community problems; non-entertainment programming guidelines; limitations on commercial time during each broadcast hour; the need to keep detailed program logs; and in 1987, the Fairness Doctrine.
8. Yes.
9. False. The *Zapple* corollary applies to supporters and spokespersons of candidates. When invoked, the doctrine provides that "comparable time" must be given to them.
10. Yes, comedian Pat Paulsen discovered that any appearance he made on radio or TV— after he became a legally qualified candidate—could activate the equal-time requirement. News and news-type programs are exempt from equal time, but not from fairness requirements.
11. Congress temporarily suspended the applicable provisions of Section 315.
12. Because the Commission in 1975 "reinterpreted" congressional intent in connection with the 1959 amendment to Section 315 and, as a result, exempted such nonstudio debates, when sponsored by a nonbroadcast entity, *and* presidential news conferences, from equal-time requirements. However, broadcasters now can sponsor such debates.
13. Foreigners, political candidates, news, and news-type programs.
14. Political candidates are afforded a "forum" by means of equal time. In the case of their supporters or spokespersons, the *Zapple* doctrine applies.
15. The Commission said that the doctrine chilled the First Amendment rights of broadcasters.
16. False. Congress tried to enact fairness legislation, but President Reagan vetoed it.

ENDNOTES

1. Hoover v. Intercity Radio Co., 286 F. 1003 (District of Columbia Circuit); appeal dismissed, 266 U.S. 636 (1924).
2. U.S. v. Zenith Radio Corp., 12 F.2d 614 (Northern District of Illinois, 1926).
3. Hearings before Communications Subcommittee of the U.S. Senate Commerce Committee, "Overview of the FCC," 92d Congress, 2d Session, February 1 and 8, 1972, pp. 188–89.
4. *Policy Statement on Comparative Broadcast Hearings,* 1 FCC 2d 393.
5. *Report and Statement of Policy Re: Commission en Banc Programming Inquiry,* 25 F.R. 7291, 7295 (1960).
6. Primer on Ascertainment of Community Problems by Broadcast Renewal Applicants, 27 FCC 2d 650.
7. In re Applications of WHDH, Inc. . . . for license renewal, 33 FCC 2d 432.
8. RKO General, Inc. (KHJ-TV), 16 P.&F. Radio Reg. 2d at 1269–70.
9. RKO General, Inc., 44 FCC 2d 123. Commissioners H. Rex Lee and Johnson dissented and Commissioners Wiley and Hooks did not vote.

10. *Broadcasting,* July 7, 1975, p. 24.
11. Fidelity Television, Inc. v. FCC, 423 U.S. 926, 96 S.Ct. 271, 46 L.Ed.2d 254. Lower court decision, 515 F.2d 684.
12. "News Notes," *Media Law Reporter,* February 12, 1980.
13. "News Notes," *Media Law Reporter,* July 8, 1980.
14. Ibid.
15. *Broadcasting,* June 9, 1980, p. 30.
16. RKO v. FCC, 7 *Med.L.Rptr.* 2313, January 5, 1982.
17. "News Notes," *Media Law Reporter,* June 22, 1982.
18. NBC v. FCC, 47 F.Supp. 940 (1942).
19. Ibid., at 946.
20. NBC v. FCC, 319 U.S. 190, 226–227 (1943). Justices Black and Rutledge took no part in the case. Justice Murphy, joined by Justice Jackson, dissented, principally on the ground that the FCC lacked any power over network contracts with affiliates.
21. Department of Justice news release, November 17, 1976.
22. "News Briefs," *Media Law Reporter,* June 3, 1980.
23. Notice of Inquiry into commercial television network practices and policies regarding the acquisition and distribution of television programming, 62 FCC 2d 548 (1977).
24. "News Briefs," *Media Law Reporter,* October 28, 1980.
25. Ibid.
26. U.S. v. Paramount Pictures, Inc., 334 U.S. 131, 166.
27. Rosenbloom v. Metromedia, 415 F.2d 892, 895; affirmed, 403 U.S. 29 (1971).
28. *The QUILL,* February 1974, p. 12.
29. Combined cases of Columbia Broadcasting System, Inc. v. Democratic National Committee; FCC v. Business Executives' Move for Vietnam Peace; Post-Newsweek Stations, Capital Area, Inc. v. Business Executives' Move for Vietnam Peace; and American Broadcasting Companies, Inc. v. Democratic National Committee, 412 U.S. 94, 128, 93 S.Ct. 2080, 2099, 36 L.Ed. 2d 772, 798 (1973).
30. Capital Broadcasting Co. v. John Mitchell, U.S. Attorney General, 333 F.Supp. 582.
31. Red Lion Broadcasting Co., Inc. v. FCC, 395 U.S. 367, 89 S.Ct. 1794, 23 L.Ed.2d 371 (1969). See Chapter 15 for details.
32. Combined cases, op. cit., note 29; concurring opinion, 93 S.Ct. at 2115.
33. 47 U.S.C.A. 315.
34. Farmers Educational and Co-op Union v. WDAY, Inc., 260 U.S. 525, 79 S.Ct. 1302, 3 L.Ed.2d 1407.
35. 390 F.2d 471 (District of Columbia, 1968).
36. In re: Broadcast Procedure Manual, 37 FCC 2d 286, 290 (1972).
37. Letter to Nicholas Zapple, 23 FCC 2d 707; reaffirmed in In re: Complaint of Committee for the Fair Broadcasting of Controversial Issues, 25 FCC 2d 283 (1970).
38. In re: Complaint of Hon. Shirley Chisholm against ABC and CBS, 35 FCC 2d 572.
39. In re: Request by Walt Disney Productions, Inc., for declaratory ruling with respect to political broadcast equal opportunities, 33 FCC 2d 297 (1972). Also, In re: Request for Review of Pat Paulsen Ruling . . ., 33 FCC 2d 835 (1972).
40. Ibid., 33 FCC 2d at 836.
41. Branch v. FCC, cert. denied, 108 S.Ct. 1220 (1988).
42. *Fair Broadcasting of Controversial Issues,* 25 FCC 2d 283 (1970).
43. DNC v. FCC, and RNC v. FCC, 460 F.2d 891 (District of Columbia Circuit, 1972); cert. denied, October 10, 1972.
44. FCC's *40th Annual Report/Fiscal Year 1974,* Washington, D.C.: U.S. Government Printing Office (1976), pp.19–20.
45. FCC's *39th Annual Report/Fiscal Year 1973,* Washington D.C.: U.S. Government Printing Office (1974), pp. 46–47.
46. CBS v. FCC, 5 *Med.L.Rptr.* 2649, April 29, 1980.
47. CBS v. FCC, 7 *Med.L.Rptr.* 1563, July 21, 1981.
48. "News Notes," *Media Law Reporter,* September 29, 1981.

49. Ibid.
50. F.R.C. *Annual Report* (1929), p. 32.
51. Mayflower Broadcasting Corp., 8 FCC 333.
52. *Report on Editorializing by Broadcast Licensees,* 13 FCC 1.
53. *Report and Statement of Policy Re: Commission en Banc Programming Inquiry,* 25 F.R. 7291, 7295.
54. Brandywine-Main Line Radio, 25 FCC 2d 18 (1970).
55. Brandywine-Main Line Radio, Inc. v. FCC, 473 F.2d 16 (1972).
56. *Report on Editorializing,* op. cit., note 52.
57. *Fairness Doctrine,* a staff report for the Communications Subcommittee of the U.S. Senate Commerce Committee, 90th Cong., 2nd Sess. (1968), p. 38.
58. 47 C.F.R. 73 123 (1971).
59. "Equal Time, Fairness and the Personal Attack Rules: A Comparison," a speech given at the Practicing Law Institute seminar in New York, June 22, 1968, Richard W. Jencks, CBS general counsel.
60. Red Lion Broadcasting Co., Inc. v. FCC, 381 F.2d 908 (District of Columbia Circuit).
61. U.S. v. Radio-Television News Directors Association, 395 U.S. 367, 89 S.Ct. 1794, 23 L.Ed.2d 371, Justice Douglas took no part in the consideration or decision.
62. *Fairness Report,* 48 FCC 2d 1. Commissioner Hooks concurred in part and dissented in part and issued a separate statement. Commissioner Quello concurred and issued a separate statement.
63. FCC's *40th Annual Report,* op. cit., note 44, p. 16.
64. *Fairness Report,* op. cit., note 62, at 7–8.
65. Ibid., at 21.
66. *Metromedia, Inc.,* 14 FCC 2d 194 (1968).
67. Democratic National Convention Television Coverage, 16 FCC 2d 650 (1969).
68. Hunger in America, 20 FCC 2d 143, 151.
69. 18 FCC 2d 124.
70. 30 FCC 2d 150, 152.
71. NBC, Inc. v. FCC, 516 F.2d 1101 (1974). Judge Tamm dissented.
72. Columbia Broadcasting System v. Democratic National Committee (1973), 412 U.S. 94, 93 S.Ct. 2080, 36 L.Ed.2d 772.
73. Ibid., 412 U.S. at 124–25, 93 S.Ct. at 2097.
74. Ibid., at 110–111 and at 2090–91.
75. Mink v. Radio Station WHAR, FCC 76–529, 44 *U.S. Law Week* 2584, June 22, 1976.
76. Frank Stanton, keynote address given at Sigma Delta Chi national convention in Atlanta, Georgia, November 21, 1968.
77. William Paley, address given at the dedication of the Newhouse Communications Center, Syracuse, New York, May 31, 1974.
78. Julian Goodman, " 'Fairness' Today (Censorship Tomorrow?)," an address given at the "Great Issues Forum" at the University of Southern California, October 11, 1972.
79. *Broadcasting,* July 9, 1973, p. 17.
80. FCC v. League of Women Voters, 10 *Med.L.Rptr.* 1937, July 24, 1984. The Court held that Section 399 of the Public Broadcasting Act of 1967 violates the First Amendment. The section (45 U.S.C. § 399) prohibited non-commercial educational broadcasting stations from editorializing if they received money from the Corporation for Public Broadcasting, which is funded by the federal government. Chief Justice Burger and Justices Rehnquist, White and Stevens dissented.
81. Ibid., n. 12 at 1944.
82. "News Notes," *Media Law Reporter,* August 11, 1987.
83. Telecommunications Research and Action Council (TRAC) v. FCC, 13 *Med.L.Rptr.* 1881, February 10, 1987.
84. Meredith Corp. v. FCC, 13 *Med.L.Rptr.* 1993, March 3, 1987.
85. Ibid., at 2002.
86. "News Notes," *Media Law Reporter,* June 23, 1987.

87. Op. cit., n. 82.

88. Ibid.

89. "News Notes," *Media Law Reporter,* April 5, 1988.

90. "News Notes," *Media Law Reporter,* December 1, 1987.

91. *The NEWS Media & The LAW,* June/July 1981, pp. 40–41.

92. Ibid.

93. *Advertising Age,* May 16, 1983, p. 72.

94. See, e.g., "The myth of deregulation," *Broadcasting,* August 15, 1983, pp. 27–28.

95. Fourth Report and Order, 15 FCC 2d 466.

96. National Association of Theatre Owners v. FCC, 420 F.2d 194; cert. denied, 397 U.S. 922 (1970).

97. First Report and Order on Microwave Served CATV, 38 FCC 683; modified, Memorandum and Order, 1 FCC 2d 524 (1965).

98. U.S. v. Southwestern Cable Co., 392 U.S. 155, 88 S.Ct. 1994, 20 L.Ed.2d 1001 (1968).

99. U.S. v. Midwest Video Corp., 406 U.S. 649, 92 S.Ct. 1869, 32 L.Ed.2d 390.

100. Midwest Video Corp. v. FCC, 571 F.2d 1025.

101. FCC v. Midwest Video, 4 *Med.L.Rptr.* 2345, April 17, 1979.

102. "News Briefs," *Media Law Reporter,* July 22, 1980. Dissenters were Robert Lee, James Quello, and Abbott Washburn.

103. Malrite TV v. FCC, 7 *Med.L.Rptr.* 1649, August 4, 1981.

104. Ibid.

105. "News Briefs," *Media Law Reporter,* January 19, 1982.

106. Century Communications v. FCC, 108 S.Ct. 2015 (1988).

107. "News Notes," *Media Law Reporter,* July 7, 1988.

108. City of Los Angeles v. Preferred Communications, 106 S.Ct. 2034 (1985).

109. "News Notes," *Media Law Reporter,* March 18, 1986.

110. "News Briefs," *Media Law Reporter,* January 3, 1984.

111. Ibid.

112. 98 FCC 2d 1076, August 21, 1984.

113. Action for Children's Television v. FCC, 14 *Med.L.Rptr.* 1363, August 18, 1987.

114. "News Notes," *Media Law Reporter,* November 1, 1988.

115. Niemi v. NBC, 7 *Med.L.Rptr.* 2359, January 12, 1982.

116. "News Briefs," *Media Law Reporter,* July 6, 1982.

117. Zamora v. CBS, 5 *Med.L.Rptr.* 2109.

118. DeFilippo v. NBC, *Media Law Reporter,* July 13, 1982.

15

Access to the Media

HIGHLIGHTS

■ In *Tornillo v. Miami Herald* (1973), the Florida Supreme Court upheld the constitutionality of a state statute which gave political candidates, attacked in newspaper columns, a right to reply. But the U.S. Supreme Court declared the law unconstitutional, saying that what goes into a newspaper is a matter for editors to decide, not the government.

■ The FCC applied the Fairness Doctrine to some advertising which involved controversial issues of public importance, doing so in a cigarette smoking case (*Banzhaf*), and in a case involving Alaskan oil development (*Standard Oil* [*ESSO*]). But in 1974 the FCC renounced the *Banzhaf* ruling as it applied to product advertising, although the Fairness Doctrine was still applicable to "advertorials."

■ An FCC decision that broadcasters could follow the general policy of rejecting all "editorial advertisements," if they wished, was upheld by the U.S. Supreme Court in the combined cases of *CBS v. Democratic National Committee* and *FCC v. Business Executives' Move for Vietnam Peace* (1973).

■ The need for opponents of smoking to gain access to the broadcast media to counter commercials for tobacco products has disappeared with legislation that bans such advertising from radio and television. Attempts to ban such advertising from all the media were made in Congress in 1987 and 1988.

Section 315 of the Communications Act of 1934 provides political candidates a right of access to the broadcast media through its equal time provisions, and Section 312 mandates an *affirmative* right of access to broadcast facilities for federal candidates. FCC rules also provide a right of access to respond to personal attacks and political editorializing on radio and television. And prior to 1987, the general Fairness Doctrine provided the public with a right of access to ideas without requiring that any particular individuals or groups be granted access to broadcast facilities. Also, either voluntarily or through compulsion by state or municipal governments, a number of cable TV systems have set aside a number of access channels for educational, governmental or public-use purposes. The Cable Communications Policy Act of 1984 allows franchising authorities to require cable systems to set aside such channels.

But it was Justice White's opinion for a unanimous Court in *Red Lion Broadcasting Co.* v. FCC (see Chapter 14) that precipitated a debate about the public's right of access to the media. The fervor that marked that debate cooled noticeably by the mid-1970s, principally because of decisions by various courts, including the Supreme Court, and because of actions by the FCC. The debate tended to follow two major concerns: whether the public had a right of access to the media (meaning print as well as radio and television), and whether the public could be denied access to the media if they were willing to pay for it.

Advocate of Access

One of the foremost advocates of a public right of access to the media is Jerome Barron of George Washington University Law School. Barron found in *Red Lion* the touchstone for interpreting the First Amendment in terms of the public's rights, rather than the rights of media owners and operators. For nearly a decade, the idea of public access seemed to be gaining momentum, beginning with *Times-Sullivan* in 1964 (a brief notation by Justice Brennan in his opinion for the unanimous Court) and capped by *Red Lion.*

Prior to the Supreme Court's decision in *Red Lion,* Barron wrote an article in which he argued that media-imposed, rather than governmental, censorship is the greater danger to our free society and that some way must be found to permit more diverse views and ideas to be disseminated. He urged a re-examination of First Amendment theory, saying that the constitutional guarantee of free speech can best serve its original purpose only by responding to the present reality of the mass media's repression of ideas. Commercialism is the major reason why conventional media do not convey unorthodox ideas, Barron insisted, and he argued that this failure is demonstrated by the development of new media "to convey unorthodox, unpopular, and new ideas" — most notably the underground press. Monopolistic control (see Chapter 16) is another, he said.

In calling for a reinterpretation of the First Amendment away from the traditional media-oriented one, Barron referred to the First Amendment expansionist views of Professor Alexander Meiklejohn, an "absolutist" in terms of political "speech" being uninhibited so the citizenry would be better informed. It was Meiklejohn who urged a constitutional amendment by which Congress would be given the power "to provide for the intellectual and cultural education of all the citizens of the United States," thereby permitting the fullest participation in the self-governing process.[1] Concerning access to the media, Meiklejohn believed that "what is essential is not that everyone shall speak, but that everything worth saying shall be said." Thus, to him access was idea-oriented and not intended to confer a "right" on any particular individual or group. This same concept undergirded the Fairness Doctrine.

Barron argued that when commercialism predominates among the mass media — as it does now — the First Amendment can be changed, but that this need not be done through amendment. Rather, a right of access can be achieved through congressional statute validated by a "sympathetic court."[2]

Referring to Justice White's opinion in *Red Lion,* Barron provided an "expansionist" interpretation of that opinion by saying:

> *Red Lion* launches the Supreme Court on the path of an affirmative approach to freedom of expression that emphasizes the positive dimension of the First Amendment. In fact, the access-for-ideas rationale practically replaces the original legal justification for broadcast regulation — that broadcasting is a limited access medium.
> . . .
>
> Mr. Justice White says in *Red Lion* that it is not a First Amendment purpose to countenance monopolization of the marketplace of ideas. For this proposition he cites a string of cases, many of them involving print media, particularly newspapers. My point is that *Red Lion* is not just a broadcast case. It is a media case. It represents a look at the First Amendment in the light of new social realities of concentration of ownership and control in a few hands that has been produced by the twin developments of media oligopoly and technological change. It is in the background of these realities that the new First Amendment right of access spoken of by Mr. Justice White should be understood. There's a remarkable sentence in *Red Lion.* It marks the recognition by the Supreme Court of a new constitutional right: "It is the right of the public to receive suitable access to social, political, esthetic, moral, and other ideas and experiences which is crucial here."[3]

Barron concluded:

> . . . [N]ew forms for dialogue are necessary. What I propose is to implant these forms on an existing structure. I would not substitute government control of the media for their present private ownership. What I suggest is that the media be rendered more hospitable as a routine and legal matter to diversity of viewpoint.

Some support was generated for Barron's thesis. At the American Civil Liberties Union (ACLU) biennial national conference in 1968, the conferees went on record as favoring the concept, but two proposals which followed were not approved as policy by the national board of directors.

In a speech on August 11, 1969, before American Bar Association members, FCC Commissioner Kenneth Cox urged that Congress require newspapers to provide free "right of reply" space to persons criticized in print.[4]

The drumming up of support for "access" legislation reached into the White House where, on March 6, 1974, President Nixon announced he would seek enactment of a law giving political candidates the right to reply to false charges in newspapers. The following day, a presidential aide modified Nixon's statement, saying that a right-of-reply law would be sought for public officials and public figures. The scope of such a law was not spelled out, but Nixon had been highly critical of the press's handling of the growing Watergate scandal and had said at the March 6 press conference that former White House aides then under indictment "have been convicted in the press over and over again." His resignation on August 8, 1974, and subsequent acceptance of a presidential pardon for any and all crimes he may have committed during his presidency blunted any additional momentum toward federal right-of-reply legislation.

Opponents of Access

Various arguments have been marshaled to counter the access proponents.

In terms of the monoply charges by Barron, the chairman of CBS, William S. Paley, said there is little overlapping of control of broadcast stations by newspapers: 19 percent of the 934 television stations were owned by newspapers in 1974 and seven percent of the 7500 radio station. Furthermore, of the 8434 stations, two-thirds had no network affiliations. Also, FCC rules limit or prohibit excessive media concentration, particularly in the largest markets (see Chapter 16). Therefore, said Paley,

> The possibility of any major news source consistently distorting or misusing its function in the face of all of these other competing forces for enlightenment is virtually nonexistent. This pluralism constitutes the strongest safeguard that a free society can have against abuses of freedom of the press.[5]

Professor Thomas I. Emerson — no stranger to advocacy of free speech — warned that

> Any effort to solve the broader problems of a monopoly press by forcing newspapers to cover all "newsworthy events" and present all viewpoints under the watchful eyes of petty officials is likely to undermine such independence as the press now shows without achieving any real diversity.[6]

At the same meeting where former FCC Commissioner Cox urged a mandated right of access to the print medium for those subjected to criticism, Clifton Daniel, associate editor of *The New York Times,* said that discrimination is the very essence of the editorial function of newspapers. Because of space limitations only a small portion of the daily flow of news is used by any newspaper.

Any solution concerning access, Daniel argued, should come from the industry itself, since attempts by the judiciary or by legislators to impose such a right would be unconstitutional, in his judgment.[7] He did call attention to the fact that the *Times* and many other newspapers have virtual right-of-reply policies concerning persons or groups that are attacked in print. The *Times* rule is that anyone who is accused or criticized in a controversial or adversary situation should be given an opportunity to comment before publication. However, it should be emphasized that ultimate control over what to print, if anything, remains with the editor. Initially, at least, Barron seemed to be arguing for forced access — both for ideas and in personal-attack situations. At a conference in 1974 at Michigan State University, Barron said:

. . . I sometimes wonder when I read about these strange and demonic beliefs that I'm alleged to hold and how radical and revisionist it all is, I wondered who really is revisionist and radical, particularly in light of the fact that these ideas have been around for a long time. I certainly don't pretend to have invented them.[8]

Among those "ideas" that have been around for a long time, which he singled out, are "retraction statutes." Such statutes, enacted by about half the states, generally eliminate the award of punitive damages in successful libel actions if a fair retraction has been published. In many instances, publishers lobbied for passage of these state laws. But whether a retraction will or will not be published is a decision left to the press. That is the critical distinction between retraction statutes and compulsory publication of a reply or a correction, the hinge that makes forced access to the print medium unconstitutional. Additionally, courts in several states have invalidated such statutes.

The Courts and Access to Print Media

In 1947 the Commission on Freedom of the Press—the so-called Hutchins Commission—made a series of recommendations which produced spontaneous combustion among many editors and publishers. Among its proposals, the Commission suggested that, as an alternative to libel, legislation should be enacted to permit an aggrieved party to obtain a retraction, a restatement of the facts, or be given an opportunity to reply. A legislative "solution" to the access problem was suggested by the Commission. This same idea was included in Justice Brennan's plurality opinion in *Rosenbloom v. Metromedia* (see Chapter 5) when he wrote:

> If States fear that private citizens will not be able to respond adequately to publicity involving them [because of the extension by a plurality of the Court of the *Times-Sullivan* standard to private citizens], the solution lies in the direction of ensuring their ability to respond, rather than in stifling public discussion of matters of public concern.

And in a footnote to the passage above, Brennan pointed out that some states already had adopted retraction statutes or right-of-reply statutes. Before turning to such legislation, however, a quick review of what the courts have done about access vis-à-vis the print medium might be instructive.

Approved Personnel, Inc. v. The Tribune Co. (1965). In this case, the Florida Supreme Court in 1965 said:

> . . . [T]he law seems to be uniformly settled by the great weight of authority through the United States that the newspaper publishing business is a private enterprise and is neither a public utility nor affected with the public interest. The decisions appear to hold that even though a particular newspaper may enjoy virtual monopoly in the area of its publication, this fact is neither usual nor of important significance. The courts have consistently held that in the absence of statutory regula-

tion on the subject, a newspaper may publish or reject commercial advertising tendered to it as its judgment best dictates without incurring liability for advertisements rejected by it.[9]

Office of Communication of United Church of Christ v. FCC (1966). Chief Justice Burger, while an appellate judge in the District of Columbia Circuit, wrote an opinion in *Office of Communication of United Church of Christ v. FCC,* in which he said: "A broadcaster seeks and is granted the free and exclusive use of a limited and valuable part of the public domain; when he accepts that franchise it is burdened by enforceable public obligations. A newspaper can be operated at the whim or caprice of its owners; a broadcast station cannot."[10]

Bloss v. Federated Publications Inc (1968). The Michigan Supreme Court held in this case that a newspaper did not have to accept motion picture advertisements because it is a "purely private business and, therefore, free to contract with and do business with whomsoever the publishers thereof see fit, and conversely, free to refuse to contract with and do business with any parties they choose to reject."[11]

Chicago Joint Board, Amalgamated Clothing Workers v. Chicago Tribune Co. (1969). If courts were going to apply *Red Lion* to newspapers, the chance came in *Chicago Joint Board, Amalgamated Clothing Workers v. Chicago Tribune Co.*[12] U.S. District Court Judge Abraham Marovitz agreed that the newspaper did not have to accept the union's "advertorial" which was critical of a department store's sale of clothing made by nonunion workers. The judge noted that the press is treated with special constitutional regard. And he rejected the union's argument that the newspapers were analogous to the "company town" in *Marsh* (see Chapter 2) or the shopping center in *Logan Valley Plaza* (Chapter 2). Instead, he considered newspapers to be private property.

In commenting on Barron's contention of a right of access for "representative groups" to assure opportunities for minorities to express their views in the marketplace, Judge Marovitz said:

> Under a doctrine of open access, the problems inherent in such line-drawing are obvious. Why limit space to representative groups? Do not non-representative groups or individuals need greater assistance? Are there two sides to every issue or three or an infinite number? Why limit access to the issue-oriented and not to the amateur sports writer or cartoonist? Most important, why limit access to those who can pay, for surely the poor are just as entitled to comment? The mere raising of these questions indicates why such extensive freedom is given to the press. There is scant, if any, middle ground between minor meddling and full abridgement.

The Court of Appeals upheld Judge Marovitz's decision and the Supreme Court denied certiorari.[13] Similarly, another U.S. Court of Appeals upheld a newspaper's refusal to accept an advertorial in a 1971 case.[14]

Forced Access

If access is to be forced on the print medium, it most likely would have to be legislatures that do it and in such a way as to overcome First Amendment obstacles. And for any such "right" to be meaningful *and* constitutional, a change in the Constitution would probably be required.

After the Supreme Court broadened the First Amendment protective shield around the news media in a string of cases that began with *Times-Sullivan* (see Chapter 5) interest quickened on the part of some media critics to find a way or ways to compel the media to grant access or to require the media to correct errors. Attention focused on a rarely used statute in Florida, enacted in 1913, that was specifically applicable to newspapers. The right-of-reply statute, Section 104.38, read:

> If any newspaper in its column assails the personal character of any candidate for nomination or for election in any election, or charges said candidate with malfeasance or misfeasance in office, or otherwise attacks his official record, or gives to another free space for such purpose, such newspaper shall upon request of such candidate immediately publish free of costs any reply he may make thereto in as conspicuous a place and in the same kind of type as the matter that calls for such reply, provided such reply does not take up more space than the matter replied to. Any person or firm failing to comply with the provisions of this statute shall, upon conviction, be guilty of a misdemeanor.

Tornillo Case

In this case (*Tornillo v. Miami Herald*), a candidate for the Florida state legislature, Pat Tornillo, Jr. charged that two *Miami Herald* editorials had assailed his character and that the newspaper had refused him his statutory right by not printing letters he had written in reply. In 1972 Dade County Circuit Court Judge Francis Christie declared the law unconstitutional, agreeing with arguments by the newspaper's attorneys that since a newspaper cannot be prevented from publishing an article, neither can it be compelled to print one.

The Florida Supreme Court, in a 6–1 per curiam decision in 1973, reversed the lower court and upheld the constitutionality of the statute. Relying heavily on *Red Lion* and the Meiklejohn concept of an informed citizenry being paramount in terms of what the First Amendment should protect, as well as the ideas of Professor Barron, who was one of the attorneys representing Tornillo, the court said:

> The statute here under consideration is designed to add to the flow of information and ideas and does not constitute an incursion upon First Amendment rights or a prior restraint, since no *specified paper content is excluded*. There is nothing prohibited but rather it requires, in the interest of full and fair discussion, additional information.
>
> . . . This decision [by the Florida Supreme Court] will encourage rather than impede the wide open and robust dissemination of ideas and counter-thought which the concept of free press both fosters and protects and which is essential to intelligent self-government.[15]

Tornillo provoked considerable concern on the part of newspapers. When the case was argued before the Florida Supreme Court, at least 18 amici curiae briefs were filed — 15 of them by Florida newspapers.

The *Miami Herald* appealed and in 1974 the U.S. Supreme Court unanimously reversed Florida's top court and declared the 61-year-old state law — which had only been used twice during that period — unconstitutional.

Chief Justice Burger, in giving the Court's opinion, said the choice of what goes into a newspaper — whether fair or unfair — constitutes the exercise of editorial judgment and government cannot interfere with that judgment.[16] Although he said that not all future attempts to deal with the access problem would necessarily be unconstitutional, he declared that Florida's "remedy" amounted to governmental coercion which is in conflict with the First Amendment.

"Press responsibility is not mandated by the Constitution." he wrote, "and like many other virtues it cannot be legislated."

Concerning forced access to the media, the Court ignored *Red Lion* (upon which Barron had built much of his access argument), relying instead on the same case used by Tornillo (*Associated Press v. U.S.*) (see Chapter 16), only the Court used it to knock down proponents of access. In that 1945 antitrust decision, the Supreme Court had said that the First Amendment rests on the assumption that "the widest possible dissemination of information from diverse and antagonistic sources is essential to the welfare of the public. . . ."[17] But in reviewing that decision, Chief Justice Burger specifically called attention to the lower court ruling in *Associated Press* which did not compel the wire news service or any of its member newspapers to publish anything which "their 'reason' tells them should not be published."

In reviewing the Supreme Court's decision in *Branzburg v. Hayes* (Chapter 11), Chief Justice Burger emphasized that *Branzburg,* as well as companion cases then before the Court,[18] led to decisions which involved neither an express, nor an implied, command that the press publish what it preferred to withhold.

In citing *Pittsburgh Press Co. v. Human Relations Commission* (see Chapter 13), in which a bare majority of the Court upheld a city ordinance that prohibited help-wanted advertisements from specifying "male" or "female," the Chief Justice recalled the narrowness of the Court's holding in that case by citing the majority's choice of language, to wit:

> Nor . . . does our decision authorize any restrictions whatever, whether of content or layout, on stories or commentary originated by *Pittsburgh Press,* its columnists, or its contributors. On the contrary, we reaffirm unequivocally the protection afforded to editorial judgment and to the free expression of views on these and other issues, however controversial.[19]

Turning to the issues in *Tornillo,* the Chief Justice said:

> We see that beginning with *Associated Press,* . . . the Court has expressed sensitivity as to whether a restriction or requirement constituted the compulsion exerted by government on a newspaper to print that which it would not otherwise print. The

clear implication has been that any such compulsion to publish that which " 'reason' tells them should not be published" is unconstitutional. A responsible press is an undoubtedly desirable goal, but press responsibility is not mandated by the Constitution and like many other virtues it cannot be legislated.

In response to Tornillo's contention that the Florida statute did not restrict the newspaper's right to speak out in any manner it chose, the Court held that such an argument "begs the core question," adding:

> Faced with penalties that would accrue to any newspaper that published news or commentary arguably within the reach of the right of access statute, editors might well conclude that the safe course is to avoid controversy and that, under the operation of the Florida statute, political and electoral coverage would be blunted or reduced. Government enforced right of access inescapably "dampens the vigor and limits the variety of public debate." [*New York Times Co. v. Sullivan,* . . . 376 U.S., at 279.] . . . Even if a newspaper would face no additional costs to comply with a compulsory access law and would not be forced to forego publication of news or opinion by the inclusion of a reply, the Florida statute fails to clear the barriers of the First Amendment because of its intrusion into the function of editors. A newspaper is more than a passive receptacle or conduit for news, comment, and advertising. The choice of material to go into a newspaper, and the decisions made as to limitations on the size of the paper, and content, and treatment of public issues and public officials — whether fair or unfair — constitutes the exercise of editorial control and judgment. It has yet to be demonstrated how governmental regulation of this crucial process can be exercised consistent with First Amendment guarantees of free press as they have evolved to this time.

Tornillo makes it clear that there is to be no forced access into the realm of the print medium, at least not under any plan yet advanced for accomplishing such a goal. And the death of the Fairness Doctrine has virtually ended discussion about a general right of access to the broadcast media — a death anticipated by some.

In a statement at a Federal Trade Commission-sponsored Symposium on Media Concentration in 1978, Professor Monroe E. Price of the UCLA Law School sought to draw out the significance of *Tornillo* and several other similar cases in relation to *Red Lion*. He said:

> There are orphans of the law, and the Fairness Doctrine may fast become one of them. Its finest hour, perhaps, was in 1969, when the Supreme Court, eight to nothing, held the doctrine that the power of Congress and the . . . FCC has been constitutional. But now that the power of Congress and the . . . FCC has been established, there is much more sober reflection about the wisdom of the fairness policy. The signs of orphanness are strong. The missing justice in *Red Lion,* Mr. Justice Douglas, subsequently went out of his way to say that had he participated, he would have held the doctrine unconstitutional. Mr. Justice Stewart has shown signs of a change of mind. And in the famous *Tornillo* case, which everyone but the Court seemed to think revolved around *Red Lion,* the fairness case was not even cited. There is more tumbling around. After its policy of requiring fairness was vindicated,

the Commission started backing away from aggressive access decisions that were outer extensions of the doctrine [e.g., *Banzhaf v. FCC,* and *Friends of the Earth v. FCC,* both discussed later].

. . . What is happening, in terms of First Amendment vibrations, is quite important. Coming almost to the edge of the content regulatory cliff in *Red Lion,* there has been a general retreat. Concerns about concentration, about diversity, about access remain intense, perhaps justifiably so; but something deep inside was suggesting that the progress of the law was moving headlong in an erroneous direction. There is more of a search for alternative approaches. Structure has been identified as a prime candidate for reform, replacing content regulation as a method for achieving First Amendment goals.[20]

The structure approach might include government measures to increase newspaper outlets, broadcast policy aimed at increasing programming competition, or, as suggested by Price, reducing or eliminating restrictions on pay television and ownership of cable television — actions subsequently taken by the FCC.

ADVERTISING AND ACCESS TO RADIO AND TV

Until now we have concentrated primarily on the Fairness Doctrine and its applicability to access without regard for how the controversial issues came to be aired. But advertising and the question of paid or free access to the media raised new and controversial issues for the FCC which, prior to its definitive expression in 1949 that the doctrine existed, had only applied it on one previous occasion to an advertising situation. In a 1946 case, the FCC made a narrow application of fairness to the question of whether a station, which advertised alcoholic beverages, could refuse to accept counter-advertising from a temperance group. The FCC did not deny renewal of the station's license for its failure to provide paid time for the advocates of temperance, but it did invoke the fairness issue by saying that the "advertising of alcoholic beverages can raise substantial issues of public importance."[21]

Cigarette Advertising and Banzhaf Case
The issue of the applicability of the Fairness Doctrine to commercial advertising was not squarely joined until a New York attorney, John P. Banzhaf III, complained to the FCC in 1967 that station WCBS-TV in New York had refused to give him proportional time to rebut cigarette commercials. The station replied that the Fairness Doctrine did not apply to product commercials. Banzhaf, in filing a complaint with the FCC, argued that WCBS-TV was under obligation to "affirmatively endeavor to make its . . . facilities available for the expression of viewpoints held by responsible elements" primarily because "portrayal of youthful and virile-looking or sophisticated persons enjoying cigarettes in interesting and exciting situations deliberately seeks to create the impression . . . that smoking is socially acceptable and desirable, manly, and the necessary part of a rich full life."

The FCC, in considering the case, was mindful of the agitation and concern expressed about the dangers of cigarette smoking, including a 1964 report by a U.S. Surgeon General's committee. The report concluded that cigarette smoking contributed substantially to mortality from certain specific diseases and to the overall death rate and termed it "a health hazard of sufficient importance . . . to warrant remedial action." Additionally, the FTC had announced a proposed regulation to require warnings on cigarette packs to take effect January 1, 1965, plus requiring such warnings in all advertising beginning in July 1965, if the package requirement and voluntary reform did not alter the situation. But the House Commerce Committee began hearings on proposed legislation and prevailed upon the FTC to hold up implementation of the rules.

On June 2, 1967, the FCC in a historic ruling, held that the Fairness Doctrine was applicable to cigarette commercials, stating:

> A station that carries commercials promoting the use of a particular cigarette as attractive and enjoyable is required to provide a significant amount of time to the other side of this controversial issue of public importance—i.e., that however enjoyable, such smoking may be a hazard to the smoker's health.[22]

The FCC, in formulating this decision, relied to some extent on the ruling in *Valentine v. Chrestensen* (see Chapter 13) that product advertising has a weaker claim, if any at all, to First Amendment protection.

The FCC was careful to point out that its ruling applied only to cigarette commercials, that "equal time" for responding to such advertising was not necessary, and that if WCBS-TV could not obtain paid sponsorship for antismoking messages then these would have to be provided without charge in accordance with the *Cullman* rule.[23] The *Cullman* rule (1963) provides that if a licensee broadcasts one viewpoint for the first time on a controversial issue of public importance during a sponsored program, a contrasting view or views must be broadcast even though paid sponsorship cannot be obtained.

With considerable foresight, Commissioner Lee Loevinger, although concurring in the 6–1 *Banzhaf* opinion, doubted that the FCC would be able to rationally distinguish *Banzhaf* from future cases involving hazards to health and life. Commissioner Johnson also concurred, pointing out that he could see no valid reason for excluding other advertising from the "reach" of the Fairness Doctrine. Such advertising should face the same consideration of fairness as any other type of advocacy, he contended.

Although the FCC ruling hit the advertising and broadcasting industries like a bombshell, Banzhaf was not satisfied. He appealed to the U.S. Court of Appeals, District of Columbia Circuit, asking that the FCC's wording—"significant amount of time"—be changed to "substantially equal" time. The NAB and Tobacco Institute also instigated legal action to have the Commission's ruling set aside as unconstitutional.

The appellate court's three-judge panel upheld the FCC's order,[24] but since the Supreme Court had not yet ruled on the constitutionality of the Fairness

Doctrine, the appellate court related the danger of smoking to public health and declared:

> Thus as a public health measure addressed to a unique danger authenticated by official and congressional action, the cigarette ruling is not invalid on account of its unusual particularity. . . . In view of the potentially grave consequences of a decision to [smoke] . . ., we think it was not an abuse of discretion for the Commission to attempt to insure not only that the negative view be heard but that it be heard repeatedly.

On the issue of the First Amendment and the limitation it places on the FCC or any other regulatory agency, the court had considerable difficulty, stating that this issue had to be decided on a case-by-case basis and that in this particular instance the public health concern sustained the FCC ruling.

The Tobacco Institute and the National Broadcasting Co. (NBC) appealed, but the Supreme Court denied certiorari in 1969.[25] Meanwhile, the FCC announced in 1969 that it would consider a rule banning cigarette advertising from radio and television unless Congress intervened. Opposition from the NAB, Tobacco Institute, and other special interest groups was intense (in 1970 the $11-billion tobacco industry spent $205 million for television advertising and $12.4 million for radio advertising). Nevertheless, the regulatory agency decided to ban such advertising after January 1, 1971. Congress then moved into the fray and passed the Public Health Cigarette Smoking Act of 1969, which prohibited cigarette and "little cigar" advertising in the broadcast media on the date set by the FCC. This action led to additional court tests. The NAB filed suit as did owners of six stations. NAB claimed that the ban discriminated against broadcasting and infringed upon freedom of speech. Its purpose in bringing the suit, said NAB, was "to affirm the right of broadcasters to carry advertisements of any legal product, particularly if such advertising is permitted in competing media, such as newspapers and magazines."

In 1971 three judges sitting as a panel of the U.S. District Court in the District of Columbia upheld the constitutionality of the law, with sharp dissent from Circuit Court Judge J. Skelly Wright, sitting by assignment.[26] Both NAB and the station owners appealed and in 1972 the Supreme Court summarily affirmed the legality of the ban in a 7–2 decision. Only Justices Douglas and Brennan indicated that the Court probably should have assumed jurisdiction for a full-scale review.[27]

The FCC changed its position about the uniqueness of its *Banzhaf* ruling as the result of several cases starting with a complaint by Friends of the Earth (FOE) about commercials that promoted more powerful automobile motors and high-test gasoline — products that contributed to air pollution and therefore posed a danger to public health, according to the complaint. But the Commission dismissed the complaint in 1970, citing such reasons as the (1) uniqueness of the *Banzhaf* ruling; (2) the belief that an extension of a cigarette ruling to product advertising generally would undermine the broadcasting system based, as it is, on revenue from such commercials and that this would not be in the public interest; and (3) the complexity of the air pollution problem and the expertise that would be required to deal with it compared with the relative simplicity of the FCC's approach to cigarettes.[28]

FOE appealed and the U.S. Court of Appeals subsequently reversed the FCC's ruling. Before then, the Commission already had begun to modify its view.

In dealing with a complaint against NBC about Chevron commercials which claimed that non-leaded gasoline would minimize air pollution, the FCC in 1971 reaffirmed its earlier position by refusing to apply the Fairness Doctrine to this product advertising case.[29] But in a footnote, the Commission clarified how a product commercial might invoke Fairness Doctrine requirements.

Shortly after its Chevron decision, the FCC used that footnote in upholding a complaint by the Wilderness Society and the FOE that NBC had violated the Fairness Doctrine by broadcasting commercials on behalf of Standard Oil of New Jersey (ESSO) pertaining to Alaskan oil developments. In its ruling, the Commission said:

> In the light of the present controversy over the desirability of developing and transporting Alaskan oil, we are not persuaded by [NBC's] argument that the advertisements are merely "institutional advertising," or that a discussion of an oil company's search for oil and its asserted concern for ecology are not controversial issues of public importance. . . .
>
> It appears, therefore, that . . . [NBC's] determination that such advertisements did not raise Fairness Doctrine obligations was unreasonable.[30]

With this decision—even though the Commission subsequently ruled that NBC had met its fairness obligation because of "continuing programming" on the subject and therefore need not undertake any special programming—the FCC seemed to alter its original position that *Banzhaf* was unique. Until 1974, that is.

Banzhaf Renounced

Any likelihood that there would be widespread application of the Fairness Doctrine to advertising—specifically product advertising—was squelched by the FCC in its 1974 *Fairness Report.* Concerning *Banzhaf,* the Commission rejected it for future cases, saying:

> We do not believe that the underlying purposes of the Fairness Doctrine would be well served by permitting the cigarette case to stand as a Fairness Doctrine precedent. In the absence of some meaningful or substantive discussion, such as that found in . . . "editorial advertisements" . . ., we do not believe that the usual product commercial can realistically be said to inform the public on any side of a controversial issue of public importance. It would be a great mistake to consider standard advertisements, such as those involved in *Banzhaf* and "Friends of the Earth" as though they made a meaningful contribution to public debate. It is a mistake, furthermore, which tends only to divert the attention of broadcasters from their public trustee

responsibilities in aiding the development of an informed public opinion. Accordingly, in the future, we will apply the Fairness Doctrine only to those "commercials" which are devoted in an obvious and meaningful way to the discussion of public issue.[31]

The Commission based its decision on several reasons, the principal one being the Commission's belief that the financial stability of commercial broadcasting would be seriously undermined. Other reasons included: (1) a desire on the part of commissioners to leave the resolution of this issue to Congress, should it wish to act; (2) the likelihood that Commission decisions in this area would interfere with licensees' First Amendment rights; and (3) "counter-advertising" would air only negative aspects of a product while the original commercials, although making products more desirable, had not engaged in any meaningful discussion of controversial issues.

The Commission's decision was challenged in *National Citizens Committee for Broadcasting v. FCC*.[32] The U.S. Court of Appeals for the District of Columbia Circuit rejected the argument that the FCC violated the First Amendment by exempting product commercials from the Fairness Doctrine. In its ruling in 1977, the court, in an opinion by Judge Carl McGowan, said that "application of Fairness Doctrine requirements to commercial advertisements has been fraught with difficulties; remaining faithful to the general principles of the doctrine, the Commission should be allowed to alter the precise contours of the doctrine in a manner it reasonably believes will help resolve those difficulties."[33]

The Supreme Court declined to review the decision.

Although the Commission abandoned its use of the Fairness Doctrine in relation to product advertising, that doctrine still applied (1) to commercials which are in fact editorials, and (2) to institutional advertising whenever such advertising has a substantial and meaningful relationship to a controversial issue of public importance.

The use of the doctrine in relation to "advertorials" is demonstrated by the Commission's finding in 1976 that eight California radio stations had violated the doctrine by carrying Pacific Gas and Electric Co. spot commercials which promoted the idea that construction of a nuclear power plant was necessary. The stations were ordered to report on how they planned to meet their fairness obligations.

In 1977 Texaco commercials activated fairness requirements when the Commission, by a 6–1 vote, upheld a complaint by Energy Action Committee, Inc. against WTOP-TV in Washington.[34] WTOP-TV had broadcast Texaco spot commercials 53 times—commercials which sought to demonstrate the desirability of vertical integration of the oil industry at the very time that Senate hearings were proceeding on bills to force divestiture.

As a consequence of the Commission's decision, Energy Action Committee, Inc., aided by WTOP film crews and editing facilities, prepared four prodivestiture spot announcements which were to be shown by WTOP-TV during a 12-week period. The first one appeared in late July 1977. The tag line on each spot announcement was: 'We'd better break up the oil monopoly, before it breaks us."

FCC and "Editorial" Commercials

In two related cases, the FCC held that broadcasters could follow the general policy of rejecting all "editorial advertisements," if they wished.

The Democratic National Committee (DNC) had asked the FCC to declare that stations could not arbitrarily refuse to sell air time to "responsible entities" for the purpose of soliciting funds and commenting on public issues.[35] The Commission in 1970 turned down DNC's plea. Similarly, the Commission held that WTOP radio in Washington, D.C., could not be required to sell time to Business Executives' Move (BEM) for Vietnam Peace which wished to broadcast anti-Vietnam War announcements.[36]

In a major decision in 1973, the Court upheld the FCC's stand in the combined cases of *CBS v. Democratic National Committee* and *FCC v. Business Executives' Move* (BEM) *for Vietnam Peace.*[37] The essence of that decision by a divided Court was that licensees are not obligated to sell time for advertorials if their general policy is to refuse such advertising.

The Court's reversal of the District of Columbia Circuit Court came in an opinion by Chief Justice Burger which drew complete accord from Rehnquist; partial concurrence from Stewart, White, Blackmun, and Powell; a separate but concurring opinion by Douglas; and outright dissent by Brennan and Marshall.

Among the major points made by the Chief Justice were:

- In evaluating First Amendment claims of *DNC* and *BEM,* great weight must be afforded the decisions of Congress and the experience of the FCC.
- Concerning the discussion of public issues, Congress chose to leave broad journalistic discretion with the licensee because it specifically forbade censorship (§ 326) and it decided against common carrier status for broadcast stations. "Only when the interests of the public are found to outweigh the private journalistic interests of the broadcasters will government power be asserted within the framework of the [1934] Act."
- A licensee's policy against accepting advertorials cannot be examined as an abstract proposition. It must be viewed in the context of his journalistic role—a role which requires considerable licensee discretion and the absence of rigid limitations, especially in light of the fact that every licensee is held accountable for the totality of his performance of the public interest obligation.
- The novel question raised in this case—is the licensee so much a creature of the government that restraint imposed by the licensee is tantamount to government restraint and therefore violative of the First Amendment rights of *DNC* and *BEM*—was answered in the negative by the Chief Justice, principally on the ground that licensees are given wide discretion to operate in the public interest, therefore they are not an instrument of government.
- The interest of the public is foremost in terms of the First Amendment; and the FCC was justified in concluding that the public interest in requiring access to the marketplace of "ideas and experiences" would

scarcely be served by a system so heavily weighted in favor of the financially affluent, or those with access to wealth [*Red Lion,* 395 U.S. at 392]. Even if the Fairness Doctrine or the *Cullman* standard were applied to editorial advertising, the affluent still would determine in large measure the issues to be discussed because the power to initiate such speech would lie with them.

■ The Fairness Doctrine might be jeopardized if applied to editorial advertising because the licensee would experience financial hardship from having to make regular programming time available for those holding views different from the ones expressed by the advertorialists. The result would be the further erosion of journalistic discretion in the coverage of public issues and subordination of the public interest to private whims. This would be so especially since broadcasters would find themselves in the position of being virtually unable to reject advertorials dealing with trivial matters or those already covered by the licensees under the fairness obligation.

■ Congress or the Commission may devise some kind of limited right of access that is both practicable and desirable, Burger said, noting the then on-going Commission inquiry into various aspects of the Fairness Doctrine. He concluded with this observation:

> . . . [T]he history of the Communications Act and the activities of the Commission over a period of 40 years reflect a continuing search for means to achieve reasonable regulation compatible with the First Amendment rights of the public and the licensees. The Commission's pending hearings into the Fairness Doctrine are but one step in this continuing process. At the very best, courts should not freeze this necessarily dynamic process into a constitutional holding.

Justice Brennan, joined by Marshall, dissented, in part because the "exclusionary policy" adopted in DNC and BEM inhibits, rather than furthers, the nation's "profound . . . commitment to the principle that debate on public issues should be uninhibited, robust and wide-open" (*Times-Sullivan,* (see Chapter 5)). Because they thought a station's policy of flatly refusing to accept advertorials would be contrary to the policy announced in *Times-Sullivan,* Brennan and Marshall would have affirmed the appellate court's determination that such a licensee policy would violate the First Amendment.

Brennan also took issue with the Court's position on the Fairness Doctrine vis-à-vis licensee discretion to meet that doctrine. Such a position, said Brennan, is insufficient to satisfy the First Amendment interest of the public since the broadcaster retains almost complete control over the selection of issues and viewpoints to be covered, the manner of presentation and, perhaps most importantly, who shall speak. "Given this doctrinal framework," said Brennan, "I can only conclude that the Fairness Doctrine, standing alone, is insufficient—in theory as well as in practice—to provide the kind of 'uninhibited, robust, and wide-open' exchange of views to which the public is constitutionally entitled."

Later in his opinion, he asserted, ". . . In light of the current dominance of the electronic media as the most effective means of reaching the public, any policy that *absolutely* denies citizens access to the airways necessarily renders even the concept of a 'full and free discussion' practically meaningless." And, he added, that is precisely the policy that the Court upholds in its *DNC-BEM* decision.

Justices Stewart and Douglas were in virtual agreement in terms of major reasons why they opposed forced access for advertorials. Concerning the logic employed to equate the broadcaster to government, such that the broadcaster's control over advertorials would amount to governmental control and therefore, on its face, be unconstitutional, Douglas disputed the validity of any such equation. If the government really were operating the electronic press, he said, it would be prevented by the First Amendment from selecting broadcast content and exercising editorial judgment. It would not be permitted in the name of "fairness" to deny air time to any person or group on the ground that their views had been sufficiently aired. Yet broadcasters perform precisely these functions and enjoy precisely such freedoms under the 1934 Act.

In concurring in the results, Stewart made this important distinction: BEM's spot advertisements were rejected by a single station, while only one network turned down DNC's request for paid air time; yet many broadcasters accept advertising of the BEM and DNC type. This led Stewart to say: "This variation in broadcaster policy reflects the very kind of diversity and competition that best protects the free flow of ideas under a system of broadcasting predicated on private management." It would not be in the public interest, he contended, to force every broadcaster to accept a particular type of advertising.

In a "plug" for greater freedom for broadcasters, Stewart said:

> Those who wrote our First Amendment put their faith in the proposition that a free press is indispensible to a free society. They believed that "fairness" was far too fragile to be left for a government bureaucracy to accomplish. History has many times confirmed the wisdom of their choice.

Concerning the *Red Lion* decision, in which it was decided that the broadcasters' First Amendment rights were "abridgeable," Stewart said that such a decision, whether right or wrong, did not mean that those rights were nonexistent.

Douglas, of course, took the position that television and radio stand in the same protected position under the First Amendment as the print medium does. He commented, "The Court in today's decision by endorsing the Fairness Doctrine sanctions a federal saddle on broadcast licensees that is agreeable to the tradition of nations that never have known freedom of press. . . ."

Total Tobacco Ad Ban Proposed. The controversy over tobacco advertising has moved away from the Fairness Doctrine and into the halls of Congress.

In 1986, President Reagan signed into law a bill banning TV and radio advertising of smokeless tobacco products, such as chewing tobacco and snuff.

The law also requires warning labels about health dangers to be included in print advertising about these products and on the products themselves.

Shortly before the legislation became law, the American Medical Association called for a legislative ban on the advertising and promotion of all tobacco products in any media and, in early 1986, the American Cancer Society endorsed such a ban. Such proposals are opposed by the American Civil Liberties Union and the American Newspaper Publishers Association, among others, on the ground that the First Amendment does not permit the prohibition of truthful advertising that may be lawfully distributed and sold. Interestingly, the chairman of the Federal Trade Commission, Daniel Oliver, also opposed such a ban. At the American Advertising Federation's annual meeting in 1987, he said that the proposed ban represents "an attack on consumer sovereignty itself." He continued:

> We must oppose these efforts to place the government in the position of controlling what we read and see. Informed choice is the essence of our economic system. This is the approach most in accord with the free market, the free press, and free people who collectively must control their own destiny.[38]

Bills were introduced in Congress in 1987 and 1988 to ban all tobacco advertising. Such advertising and promotional activity now exceeds $2 billion a year. Hearings were conducted, and proponents of the ban referred to the Supreme Court's decision in *Posadas de Puerto Rico Associates* (1986) (see Chapter 13) as supporting their view that the advertising of harmful products can be banned. But no final congressional action was taken.

Clearly the focus has shifted from access to the media to rebut tobacco advertising to making such advertising illegal regardless of media.

SUMMARY

The proponents of access to the media saw in the Supreme Court's *Red Lion* decision a means of making all media — not just radio and television — more receptive to demands for access. They construed the First Amendment as protecting the public's right of access to ideas and experiences — a view not inconsistent with some of the language used by Justice White in *Red Lion*. Just how a legislature or court could require access — even limited access — without unconstitutionally weakening freedom of press remained hotly debated until the Supreme Court's decision in *Tornillo*. The Court unanimously declared Florida's limited right-of-reply statute to be unconstitutional because the government (by means of the statute) interfered with editorial judgment. In *Tornillo,* the Court conspicuously did not mention *Red Lion,* thereby leaving unanswered questions about the impact of the Fairness Doctrine on the editorial judgment of broadcast journalists. *Tornillo* makes it clear that there can be no forced access into the print medium, at least by any method yet devised.

As for the Fairness Doctrine and product advertising, the FCC, in an historic ruling in *Banzhaf* (1967), said the doctrine was applicable to cigarette commercials because smoking and its danger to health were controversial issues. The Commission intended to limit the ruling to cigarette commercials because the health issue was considered "unique." A U.S. Court of Appeals subsequently upheld the Commission for these reasons: the ruling did not ban any speech; product advertising is not as rigorously protected by the First Amendment as other kinds of speech; information to the public was increased, not decreased; and the First Amendment stood to gain more than it would lose by any decrease in cigarette advertising.

After Congress banned cigarette and "little cigar" advertising by broadcasters, another case developed in which the claim was put forth that the First Amendment rights of broadcasters were being violated by the ban. A three-judge panel split 2–1 in declaring the law constitutional. The majority relied heavily on the proposition that commercial speech is less vigorously protected than most other forms of speech (a pre-*Virginia Pharmacy Board* decision); the public owns the airwaves (as contrasted with private ownership in the print medium); and licensees are required to operate in the public interest. The decision was summarily affirmed by the U.S. Supreme Court by a 7–2 vote.

In 1974, however, the FCC renounced the *Banzhaf* precedent principally because of the impact it might have on the financial stability of commercial broadcasting. In effect, the Commission ruled that the Fairness Doctrine no longer would be applicable to product advertising. However the Commission said that the doctrine would still apply to "advertorials" or institutional advertising which obviously and meaningfully discuss controversial issues of public importance.

As for paid access to the broadcast medium for the purpose of "advertorializing," the Commission was supported by the U.S. Supreme Court's decision in 1973 in the combined *DNC* and *BEM* cases, to wit: licensees are not obligated to sell time for advertorials if their general policy is to refuse such advertising.

QUESTIONS IN REVIEW

1. Despite some uncertainty concerning the extent to which Professor Barron wanted government to go in mandating public access to the media, he clearly was concerned about the lack of diversity of ideas in a press that is increasingly monopolistic, and he favored some kind of forced access. What arguments can you muster against forced access? Or, if you wish, play the devil's advocate on various sides of the issue.
2. What was the principal reason why the Supreme Court, in its unanimous decision in *Tornillo*, invalidated the Florida right-of-reply statute?
3. True or False: In its *Tornillo* decision, the Supreme Court said its reasoning also applied to broadcasting and therefore overturned *Red Lion*.
4. In what case did the FCC first apply the Fairness Doctrine to commercial speech?
5. What is the *Cullman* rule?
6. Based on the FCC's 1974 policy declaration, does the Fairness Doctrine apply to product advertising?
7. What interest, according to Chief Justice Burger in *DNC-BEM*, can outweigh the First Amendment interest in broad journalistic discretion?

ANSWERS

1. Concerning Barron's forced-access argument, one rejoinder would be that media diversity already exists—more than 1700 daily newspapers; more than 9000 operating radio and TV stations; thousands of weekly newspapers and magazines; a growing number of cable systems, and more. Also, under a forced-access system, who will decide what is to be published? Government bureaucrats? Judges? Do these people have the qualifications and/or experience to make such judgments? As Chief Justice Burger has said, editing is what editors are for.
2. The statute violated the First Amendment because of its intrusion into the function of editors.
3. False. *Red Lion* was mentioned briefly only once; therefore, the impact of *Tornillo* on *Red Lion,* if any, is conjectural.
4. *Banzhaf* case.
5. The FCC-adopted *Cullman* rule provides that if licensees broadcast a sponsored program which for the first time presents one side of a controversial issue, they cannot reject the presentation of other views on the ground that they cannot obtain paid sponsorship for the presentation.
6. No. Only to "advertorials" which obviously and meaningfully discuss controversial issues of public importance.
7. Public interest.

ENDNOTES

1. "Access to the Press—A New First Amendment Right," 80 *Harvard Law Review* 1675–76 (1967). Copyright 1967 by The Harvard Law Review Association. See Meiklejohn, *Political Freedom: The Constitutional Powers of the People,* pp. 25–28 (1960).
2. Ibid., at 1667.
3. Jerome A. Barron, "Access—the Only Choice for the Media," an address given at the eighth annual lecture on Law and the Free Society, December 10, 1969, University of Texas Law School, as reprinted in 48 *Texas Law Review* 766, 769–71 (1970).
4. *FoI Digest,* Vol. 11, No. 3, September/October 1969, p. 4.
5. William S. Paley, " 'Fairness' Today (Censorship Tomorrow?)," an address given at the "Great Issues Forum," University of Southern California, October 11, 1972.
6. *The System of Free Expression* (New York: Random House, 1970), pp. 670–71. Cf., Professor Thomas Emerson's advocacy of the Fairness Doctrine.
7. Clifton Daniel, "Right of Access to Mass Media—Government Obligation to Enforce First Amendment?", an address given at the eighth annual lecture on Law and the Free Society, December 10, 1969, University of Texas Law School, as reprinted in 48 *Texas Law Review* 783.
8. Jerome A. Barron, "Media and the First Amendment 1974, The Changing Patterns of Conflict," Conference Proceedings at Michigan State University, May 3–4, 1974, p. 123.
9. Approved Personnel, Inc. v. The Tribune Co., 177 So.2d 704, 705.
10. Office of Communication of United Church of Christ v. FCC, 359 F.2d 994, 1003 (1966).
11. Bloss v. Federated Publications Inc., 380 Mich. 485, 157 N.W.2d 241 (1968).
12. Chicago Joint Board, Amalgamated Clothing Workers v. Chicago Tribune Co., 307 F.Supp. 422 (1969).
13. 435 F.2d 470 (7th Circuit, 1970); cert. denied, 402 U.S. 973 (1971).
14. Associates & Aldrich Co. v. Times Mirror Co., 440 F.2d 133 (9th Circuit, 1971).
15. Tornillo v. Miami Herald Publishing Co., 287 So.2d 78, 82–86. Justice Boyd cast the dissenting vote, saying, in part, that the extent to which government "limits or adds to that which a publisher must distribute, freedom of speech and freedom of the press are thereby diminished."
16. Miami Herald Publishing Co. v. Tornillo, 418 U.S. 241, 94 S.Ct. 2831. Cf. Burger's view here

with his view in *United Church of Christ,* earlier in this chapter.

17. Associated Press v. U.S., 326 U.S. 1, 20.
18. Branzburg v. Hayes, 408 U.S. 665, 681 (1972).
19. Pittsburgh Press Co. v. Human Relations Commission, see Chapter 13 for fuller discussion.
20. Monroe E. Price, "Taming Red Lion: The First Amendment and Structural Approaches to Media Regulation," published in the *Proceedings of the Symposium on Media Concentration,* Vol. II, December 14–15, 1978, sponsored by the FTC's Bureau of Competition, p. 22. Footnotes omitted.
21. Petition of Sam Morris, 11 FCC 197.
22. 9 FCC 2d 921.
23. 40 FCC 576.
24. Banzhaf v. FCC, 405 F.2d 1082.
25. Tobacco Institute, Inc. v. FCC, 396 U.S. 842, 90 S.Ct. 50; and NBC v. FCC, 396 U.S. 842, 90 S.Ct.51.
26. Capital Broadcasting Co. v. John Mitchell, U.S. attorney general, 333 F.Supp 582.
27. NAB v. Richard G. Kleindienst, U.S. attorney general, and Capital Broadcasting Co. v. Kleindienst, 92 S.Ct. 1290 (1972).
28. Friends of the Earth, 24 FCC 2d 743.
29. National Broadcasting Co. (Chevron Decision), 29 FCC 2d 807.
30. 30 FCC 2d 643, 646 (1971).
31. Fairness Report, op.cit., Chapter 14, note 62, 48 FCC 2d 1, 26.
32. "News Briefs," *Media Law Reporter,* November 22, 1977.
33. Ibid.
34. In re: Complaint of Energy Action, 2 *Med.L.Rptr.* 1622, April 6, 1977.
35. 25 FCC 2d 216 (1970).
36. 25 FCC 2d 242 (1970).
37. CBS v. DNC; FCC v. BEM; Post-Newsweek Stations, Capital Area v. BEM; and ABC v. DNC, 412 U.S. 94, 93 S.Ct. 2080, 36 L.Ed.2d 772.
38. "News Notes," *Media Law Reporter,* March 3, 1987.

16

Antitrust Laws and Media Ownership Concentration

HIGHLIGHTS

■ The trend toward concentration of ownership of the media continues. Not only are independent newspapers rapidly being acquired by publishing groups, but groups are now buying groups.

■ In Associated Press v. U.S. (1945), the U.S. Supreme Court held that the First Amendment was not violated by issuance of an injunction to force the AP to sell its wire service news to a newspaper which was in competition with an AP-member newspaper. The Court declared that the press is not immune from the application of general laws (including antitrust laws).

■ The Newspaper Preservation Act was passed in 1970 to allow competing newspapers to enter into joint operating agreements if one of them was in "economic distress." However, such newspapers must maintain separate editorial and reportorial staffs.

■ A U.S. Court of Appeals ruling in 1977 (*National Citizens Committee for Broadcasting v. FCC*), which would have required divestiture of jointly owned newspaper-broadcast combinations in the same market (except where it could be shown that such cross-ownership was in the public interest), was overturned by the Supreme Court the following year. The Court supported the FCC in requiring divestiture in only "egregious" cases.

■ The FCC made it possible in 1984 for broadcast groups to own more radio and TV stations rather than limit a single company to ownership of seven AM, seven FM and seven TV stations.

The trend in the United States is toward concentration of ownership of the mass media with consequent First Amendment implications. Professor Jerome Barron, for example, has said that if ever there was a self-operating marketplace of ideas — as Justice Oliver Wendell Holmes idealized in 1919 — it has long ceased to exist and that the media somehow must be made more hospitable to the publicizing of diverse viewpoints. At stake, he contends, is the people's right to a diversity of views.

Barron is far from alone in his concern about the possible or actual choking off of diverse views. In its 1947 report the Commission on Freedom of the Press urged that antitrust laws be used, if necessary, to help maintain competition among the larger communications units. The objective of such moves was to provide variety and diversity in mass communications. But the Commission also recognized that large communication units, with the necessary capital and personnel, were needed to provide high-quality service and to launch new communication ventures. Therefore, antitrust laws should be used sparingly in breaking up large concentrations of power; rather, government should invoke the laws to maintain competition among the large units.

How the Commission would view today's situation is impossible to say, but the ever-increasing concentration of ownership probably would have stirred considerable alarm.

Congressmen Morris K. Udall of Arizona and Bob Kastenmeier of Wisconsin introduced a bill in 1977 entitled the "Competition Review Act of 1977."[1] Later that year Udall reintroduced the bill, cosponsored by 25 other congressmen, which would create a Competition Review Commission. The commission would have authority to make studies of various industries and recommend appropriate action to various governmental agencies already concerned with antitrust and monopolistic practices.

At a news conference in June 1977, Udall announced that he was joining the Authors Guild, Inc., in urging Justice Department action under the Clayton Act to slow down or reverse what he called "merger mania" in the book publishing and newspaper industries. As Udall said:

> The disappearance of competition is disturbing anywhere in our economy. Without it, a free market cannot function. And the sad fact is that we have too little competition in too many markets. The result is inflation, inefficiency, lack of innovation, and — when the marketplace no longer provides discipline — a demand for government regulation.
>
> These symptoms are particularly disturbing when they occur in the area of publishing and communications, for they threaten the values that the First Amendment was designed to protect. It is increasingly apparent that competition is disappearing in these fields: independent, hometown publishers are being bought out by chain operators at a record rate. More and more of the independent [book publishing]

houses that brought competition and a willingness to back newcomers in a competitive publishing business are being bought out and swapped around by big conglomerates.[2]

Some weeks earlier, in a speech at the National Press Club, Udall spelled out in more detail his concern about the disappearing independent daily newspaper, saying:

> Today, of the 1500 cities with daily papers—97.5 percent have no local daily newspaper competition. Another disturbing fact, 71 percent of all the daily newspaper circulation is controlled by multiple ownership publishers.
>
> This trend signifies a very real loss to American society—the publisher with roots in the community.
>
> That hometown publisher cared about the profit and loss statement, to be sure. But that publisher carried a passion for the good of the community absent in the corporate board rooms of the big chains.
>
> In my hometown, the Tucson *Daily Citizen,* a good, solid, conservative daily owned for years by the Small family—a family of renowned civic-mindedness and accomplishments—was sold a few months ago to the Gannett chain.
>
> I've nothing against Gannett. They are very successful, they own 73 newspapers, they are based in Rochester, New York. . . .
>
> I do not condemn Gannett for adding to their long list of acquisitions. It is entirely lawful. . . .
>
> What does bother me is that there is an increasingly prevalent pattern here that has disturbing social implications.[3]

Udall went on to discuss concentrations in different industries. Concerning newspaper ownership, he noted that 25 newspaper "chains" control more than half of the daily newspaper circulation in America. At the same time he recognized the need for special caution in connection with any governmental regulation because of First Amendment considerations. As he explained it:

> I am not asking that newspaper chains be outlawed, or publishers prosecuted, or even that coercive federal legislation be enacted. My recommendations are more modest — and they are two:
>
> . . . The time has come for editors and publishers to stop making excuses for the dangerous trend towards corporate news, or wringing their hands about its inevitability. Its dimensions should be faced and discussed. Does technology preclude competition? Is there a shortage of qualified employees that warrants concentration? Editors and journalists should be thinking and speaking out on this issue. We should be finding out what pressures and forces are killing independent publishers as an institution—and what can be done about it.
>
> . . . Second, while I'm no enthusiast for study commissions, the whole area of economic concentration could use one. . . .
>
> My concern about today's trend towards concentration within the publishing and communications industry is not founded on a fear that the big publishers are like William Randolph Hearst Sr., or Col. McCormick in seeking personal political power.

No, today's publishers, with a few notable exceptions . . ., are fair with their coverage and confine their personal political opinions and preferences to the editorial pages.

Today, what the titans of the chains want is profits—not power—just money.

I fear that the quest for profits and higher dividends . . . will transcend their responsibility to maintain an independent and dedicated influence in the community.

As the diversity of the American newspaper is lost—so is the diversity of America.

We can ill afford that loss.[4]

Neither the Competition Review Act of 1977 nor Udall's proposal to create a Competition Review Commission made it through Congress. Now, in the 1990s, the independent daily newspaper is virtually a thing of the past in the United States. It has long warranted "endangered species" classification. As Table 16.1 shows, in 1986 there were 146 groups that owned 1217 of the 1670 daily newspapers, or almost 73 percent of the total. A "group" is defined as a company owning at least two dailies in separate markets. The circulation of group newspapers was 50.5 million, or 80 percent of the total. The groups do even better in the Sunday newspaper business. In 1984 they owned 78 percent of the 772 Sunday newspapers and accounted for 88 percent of total Sunday circulation.

TABLE 16.1. Group Ownership of U.S. Daily Newspapers 1910–1986

Year	Number of Dailies	Circulation 000s	Number of Groups	Group Papers	Group Average
1910	2,202	22,426	13	62	4.7
1930	1,942	39,589	55	311	5.6
1940	1,878	41,132	60	319	5.3
1960	1,763	58,080	109	560	5.1
1970	1,748	62,107	157	879	5.6
1977	1,762	60,977	167	1,047	6.2
1980	1,763	62,223	163	1,115	6.3
1984	1,699	62,611	149	1,136	7.6
1986	1,670	63,100	146	1,217	. . .
1988	1,645	62,800	. . .	. . .	. . .

Source: Editor & Publisher, April 28, 1984, p. 76, and July 9, 1977, pp. 10–11. Also, *Editor & Publisher* Year Books.

The 11 largest groups (Table 16.2) had an aggregate daily circulation of 27.7 million in 1984, or 44 percent of the total daily circulation.

Not only are there very few independent newspapers left in the United States, but the number of cities with competing newspapers is declining—dropping to 50 by 1984. Newspaper closings or mergers have occurred in Cleveland, Dayton, Des Moines, Louisville, Minneapolis, Philadelphia, and St. Louis such that each of these metropolitan areas now has only one major daily newspaper. Other mergers and closures can be expected until only metropolitan areas like New York, Chicago, Detroit, and Los Angeles have competing newspapers—and there are problems in Detroit as noted later in this chapter.

TABLE 16.2. Newspaper Groups by Circulation and Number of Newspapers Owned in 1984

Group Name	Aggregate Daily Circulation	Number of Dailies	Number of Sunday Units
Gannett	4,824,287	85	57
Newhouse	4,240,564	26	20
Knight-Ridder	3,668,117	30	22
Tribune (Chicago)	2,756,000	26	7
Dow Jones	2,555,278	22	10
Times-Mirror (Los Angeles)	2,340,845	7	7
News America	2,087,681	5	3
Scripps-Howard	1,517,000	15	7
Cox	1,379,462	21	4
Thomson	1,305,280	84	41
Hearst	1,055,080	14	41

Source: Editor & Publisher, April 28, 1984, pp. 78–80.

Many groups not only own newspapers but have controlling interests in broadcast stations. For example, the Gannett Company, which owned 90 daily newspapers by 1987, also owned at that time 39 non-daily papers, eight TV stations, 16 radio stations, an outdoor advertising company, and a newspaper magazine. And it published a national daily – USA Today. The Cox group, which has 21 newspapers, also owns five television stations, as does Scripp-Howard. Capital Cities own six television stations, as does Newhouse. Incredible as it may seem, Capital Cities undertook to buy the ABC network in 1985 and needed only FCC approval, which it got, to complete the $3.5 billion deal! ABC already was a conglomerate with the maximum number of VHF-TV stations, three cable TV companies, 10 publishing companies, and motion picture theaters.

By a 5–1 vote in 1979, the FCC approved the merger of Combined Communications Corp. into Gannett Corp. The $270 million transaction – the largest in broadcast history to that time – added two newspapers, seven television stations, and 14 radio stations to Gannett's conglomerate operations.

But even those deals pale by comparison with the FCC approval in May 1989 of a merger of Time, Inc. and Warner Communications, Inc. If Time's $14 billion buyout offer succeeds, the world's largest entertainment and media conglomerates would be created. Time owns *Time, People,* and *Sports Illustrated* magazines, Time-Life books, the Book-of-the-Month Club, two of the largest pay-cable TV networks (Cinemax and HBO), and about 800 cable TV stations. Warner is a major movie and television production company that also has a large cable TV operation. The combined cable ownership would give Time Warner about 10 percent of the 49 million cable TV homes in the United States. Stockholders of both companies must first approve the merger, and before that could happen a fly in the ointment appeared in the shape of a Paramount Communications offer in June 1989 to buy Time, Inc., for $12.2 billion – an offer quickly rejected by Time's management. Paramount Communications also is a major producer of movie and TV programs and is involved in multimedia operations.

The growth of media conglomerates prompted Ben H. Bagdikian, professor of journalism at the University of California at Berkeley, to discuss the dangers inherent and apparent from such concentrations of power. He spoke at a symposium in 1978 sponsored by the FTC, saying, in part:

Today we are looking at a phenomenon that might have surprised even Mr. Hearst. In 1924 he and other chain operators controlled 31 corporations that owned 153 papers, or 8 percent of all dailies. Today there are 167 chains that control 1082 papers, or 61 percent of all papers. It took the first 60 years of this century for chains to control 27 percent of all our papers. It has taken only the last 16 years for chains to reach control of 61 percent of all papers and 75 percent of all daily circulation.

Newspapers are only one medium that influences our culture and our politics. The phenomenon of fewer and fewer people controlling more and more of our public intelligence affects every mass medium in our country. The concentration of control of our newspapers, magazines, broadcasting, books, and movies has reached alarming levels. Fewer than 100 corporate executives have ultimate control of the majority of each medium in the United States. According to the Census of Manufacturers 20 corporations, each with a chief executive officer, control 52 percent of all daily newspaper sales. Twenty corporations control 50 percent of all periodical sales. Twenty corporations control 52 percent of all book sales. Twenty corporations control 76 percent of all record and tape sales. If one counts the three networks and the 10 corporations whose sponsorship dominates prime time, 13 corporations control two-thirds of the audience in television and radio. Seven corporations control 75 percent of movie distribution. These 100 men and women constitute a private Ministry of Information and Culture for the United States.

In fact, there are fewer than 100 corporations because some of them are among the top 20 controllers of more than one medium. For example, 27 percent of all television stations are controlled by newspaper companies. A magazine company, Time, Incorporated, owns magazines, 17 weekly newspapers, five book publishing houses, a film company, and has interests in cable, and records. RCA owns the National Broadcasting Company, a record company, and the book publishing houses of Random House, Ballantine Books, Alfred Knopf, Pantheon, Vintage and Modern Library. The biggest newspaper conglomerate, Times-Mirror, owns the *Los Angeles Times,* the *Dallas Times-Herald, Long Island Newsday* and other papers, four magazines, TV stations, cable systems, 50 percent of a news service and New American Library. CBS is one of three companies with two-thirds of the prime-time audience, owns 20 magazines, three record companies, and the book publishing houses of Holt, Rinehart and Winston, Popular Library, and W.B. Saunders Co.

This really means that when it comes to the mass media that create a major ingredient of our social and political environment, the men and women who control most of it would fit in this room. If that were the case of a government bureaucracy there would be justified alarm among the public and especially among the entrepreneurs who now control our media environment. And I would share their alarm for two reasons: government has police powers to enforce self-serving propagandistic use of our mass media. And even under the best of conditions it is not safe to repose in a small group of human beings, governmental or not, such closely controlled power over the ideas, information, and values that are propagated by our mass media. The small number of private corporations that are increasingly gaining control over our mass media do not have governmental powers. But they are too small a group of fallible human beings to have such unified control. Even if they should be philosopher-saints in their wisdom, this country was founded on the theory that no small group, even philosopher-saints, should have so much power over public information and discourse.

This pattern of control is compounded by two new developments in media ownership. One is the inclusion of journalism and other media companies in large conglomerate corporations that are also in other industries, industries that regularly are reported — or not reported — by the same corporations' media properties [such as General Electric Company's $6.28 billion acquisition of RCA Corp. (including the National Broadcasting Company) in 1986]. A company like ITT, deeply involved with foreign governments and domestic policy, that also controls publishing companies is in a position of direct conflict of interest that we would not condone with government officials or agencies. We know that for many years William Randolph Hearst used his newspapers, magazines, wire services, and movie production companies to urge the United States to declare war on Mexico, not out of a pure instinct for news but because he feared expropriation of his mining properties in Mexico. Today there is greater potential than ever for using journalism as a by-product by large conglomerates who have an explicit desire to influence public opinion and government policy in their favor.

The other new development is a pattern of several traditionally competing media coming under ownership by the same parent corporation. It has always been assumed that a newspaper article might be expanded to a magazine article which could become the basis for a hardcover book which, in turn, could be a paperback, and then, perhaps, a TV series and finally, a movie. At each step of change an author and other enterprises could compete for entry into this array of channels for reaching the public mind and pocketbook. But today several of our media giants own these arrays not only closing off entry points for competition in different media, but influencing the choice of entry at the start on the basis of how a later treatment by the same company will profit.[5]

The concerns expressed by Bagdikian and others led the Newspaper Guild to urge legislation to limit the size of newspaper groups in the United States and Canada. At its 1979 annual convention, the AFL-CIO union said, in part:

> Press analyst Ben Bagdikian has proposed legislation that would put a ceiling on the number of newspapers or the aggregate circulation a single U.S. media company could control. As a First Amendment safeguard, such legislation would not prevent anyone, including a media giant, from establishing a new newspaper; it would simply prevent it from gobbling up any more existing ones. . . .
>
> Congress and Parliament should act, before the last of the fast-dwindling independent dailies disappears from the scene. The Convention urges both national legislatures to enact laws to limit the size of newspaper chains — laws drafted with full consideration for protection of freedom of the press.
>
> There may be those who say freedom of the press makes such a bill impossible. We say that freedom of the press makes it imperative.[6]

The Newspaper Guild has proposed legislation to limit newspaper chains to 30 newspapers or 3 million total circulation. If passed, the legislation would provide for a 15-year divestiture period.

Predictably most media owners or their executives react negatively to views put forth by critics of mass communication conglomerates, although C. K. Mc-Clatchy, editor and chairman of McClatchy Newspapers, is an exception. Mc-Clatchy has warned that concentration of ownership threatens some of the "community values" reflected in family-owned newspapers.[7]

Most newspaper publishers or editors respond to critics of group ownership by saying:

■ Newspaper staffs generally are so independent that they cannot be controlled by a central headquarters (even assuming a desire to control).

■ Instead of group ownership being inherently evil it may be the only way that many newspapers can survive because of high costs and other factors.

■ Traditionally most groups follow a hands-off policy toward newsrooms.[8]

Although most groups may follow a hands-off policy toward the newsroom, an exception was provided by the Panax Corporation and its president, John McGoff. In a statement prepared for a Senate committee, Charles A. Perlik, Jr., president of the Newspaper Guild, said:

"McGoff . . . fired one editor and brought sufficient pressure to force the resignation of another who had refused to run two "must" stories distributed by Panax headquarters in June 1977. One story said President Carter condoned promiscuity among male members of his staff; the other suggested he was grooming his wife, Rosalyn, for vice president. The nature of the articles was indicated by the *Columbia Journalism Review,* which said that the surprising thing was not that two editors preferred leaving their jobs to running such stuff without at least reporting it, or labeling it as opinion, or both but that *any* of Panax's editors could stomach offering them as frontpage news.[9]

Panax, in a public statement, made its governing policy clear—all too clear. "John P. McGoff," it said, "not only has the privilege but the right as principal stockholder, president and chief executive officer of Panax, to distribute whatever news copy he deems appropriate and to demand, if necessary, that such copy be printed."[10]

In the contest between these two conflicting points of view, moral authority may lie with the *Columbia Journalism Review* and the National News Council, which denounced the Panax policy as "regressive,"[11] but McGoff holds all the cards. McGoff is merely invoking the first law of newspaper thermo-dynamics, formulated many years ago by A. J. Liebling: "Freedom of the press is guaranteed only to those who own one."

The fact is there is nothing novel about what McGoff has done; what is novel is the hue and cry about it, touched off by the increased sensitivity to such practices that newspaper monopoly has inspired. As recently as forty years ago all Hearst newspapers marched in formation on orders from San Simeon, not just in the editorials and columns they ran but in their treatment of the most routine news stories. . . . No Hearst editor capable of passing a sanity test would have given so much as a fleeting thought to disregarding an order from headquarters to print a story—any story. It will not take many firings to complete a similar process of natural selection at a chain like Panax today.[12]

Less controversial among the generalizations put forth as editors' or publishers' points of view is the one concerning the difficulty newspapers have with high production costs.

Although the newspaper publishing business can be and is profitable (Gannett's profits were $364.5 million in 1988!), profits flow most readily when there is an absence of newspaper competition. New York City is an example of some very good newspapers not being able to survive the twin forces of rising costs and declining advertising revenue. The result: papers famous in the annals of American journalism no longer exist, including Joseph Pulitzer's *World,* Horace Greeley's *Tribune,* and James Gordon Bennett's *Herald.* Mergers and kill-offs in the 1960s, including the death of the *World Journal Tribune* in 1967, left New York with just three metropolitan daily newspapers. Gradually, competitive newspaper situations have all but been eliminated in most American cities.

In 1977 Loren Ghiglione, publisher of the *Evening News* at Southbridge, Massachusetts, and a member of the now-defunct National News Council, proposed a foundation-funded study of newspaper ownership concentration.

Among the possible responses to group ownership concerns, Ghiglione listed:

1. Tax changes (including possible revision in inheritance tax; the IRS policy of permitting newspapers to set aside profits at special tax advantages to buy more newspapers; and tax incentives to foster other forms of ownership).
2. Limitations on group ownership.
3. Application of antitrust laws.
4. Voluntary efforts on part of newspapers to focus attention on the ownership issue.
5. Establishment of an organization of independent newspaper owners.

Statutory Regulations and Court Decisions

Antitrust laws were among Ghiglione's suggestions. There are two main ones: the Sherman Anti-Trust Act of 1890 and the Clayton Act of 1914.

Sherman Anti-Trust Act of 1890. This Act (26 Stat. 209, 15 U.S.C.A. §§ 1–7) was passed in an effort to control or break up cartels which had developed in several basic industries, such as oil. The Act states that "every contract, combination in the form of a trust or otherwise, or conspiracy, in restraint of trade or commerce among the several states, or with foreign nations, is hereby declared to be illegal." It also forbids, on pain of fine and/or imprisonment, monopolies in trade and commerce, or attempts to bring about such monopolies.

Clayton Act of 1914. This Act (64 Stat. 1125, 15 U.S.C.A. 18 (1964)) was passed about the same time that Congress enacted the Federal Trade Commission Act. In it, Congress declared illegal those acts which "tend to lessen competition or to create a monopoly in any line of commerce." Under the wording of the

Clayton Act, a "tendency" to lessen competition could be the target of antitrust action by the U.S. government. In 1950, the Celler-Kefauver Act was passed and it added Section 7 to the Clayton Act. It stated, in part:

> No corporation engaged in commerce shall acquire, directly or indirectly, the whole or any part of the stock or other share capital . . . of another corporation engaged also in commerce, where in any line of commerce in any section of the country the effect of such acquisition may be substantially to lessen competition, or to tend to create a monopoly.

In the face of such statutory expressions about monopolies and combinations of businesses which might "tend to lessen competition," how has it been possible for the multitude of mergers and cross-ownerships to take place in mass communications? The explanation lies in several different realms. Let's turn first to important court decisions.

Associated Press v. U.S. This case was decided by a 5–3 split of the Supreme Court in 1945, and resulted from a government action seeking an injunction against the Associated Press and others for alleged violation of the Sherman Act.[13] A three-judge panel of the U.S. District Court granted the relief, in part, and the various parties appealed. At issue was the allegation that AP's bylaws constituted an "unreasonable" restraint of trade and commerce. The "unreasonable" standard had been enunciated by the Court in an earlier decision[14] so that only unreasonable restraint of trade could be dealt with under the Sherman Act.

AP's bylaws prohibited AP members from selling news to nonmembers and provided that members could block nonmembers from membership which, perforce, denied AP's news wire services to nonmembers. Thus, the *Chicago Tribune* (an AP member) was able to block the application of the Chicago *Sun* for AP membership—the *Sun* being a competing newspaper. This led the Justice Department to bring its action against the AP and *Chicago Tribune,* alleging a combination and conspiracy in restraint of trade and commerce, and an attempt to monopolize a part of that trade. The District Court agreed with the Justice Department that the bylaws violated the Sherman Act in that they impeded the growth of competing newspapers. It was in his opinion for the District Court that Judge Learned Hand uttered his widely quoted words concerning that which is protected by the First Amendment:

> . . . [N]either exclusively, nor even primarily, are the interests of the newspaper industry conclusive; for that industry serves one of the most vital of all general interests: the dissemination of news from as many different facets and colors as is possible. That interest is closely akin to, if indeed it is not the same as, the interest protected by the First Amendment; it presupposes that right conclusions are more likely to be gathered out of a multitude of tongues than through any kind of authoritative selection. To many this is, and always will be, folly; but we have staked upon it our all.[15]

Among the arguments put forth by AP, the *Chicago Tribune,* and others was that the application of the Sherman Act to the association of publishers constituted an abridgment of the freedom of press clause in the First Amendment.

In his opinion for the Supreme Court, Justice Black said such a contention could be answered by reference to earlier Court decisions, such as *AP v. National Labor Relations Board* (1937)[16] In this case the Court held that the business of Associated Press is not immune from regulation just because it is an agency of the press, nor does the publisher of a newspaper have special immunity because of the First Amendment from the application of general laws (including antitrust laws). But Black chose to respond to such contentions, saying:

> It would be strange indeed . . . if the grave concern for freedom of the press which prompted adoption of the First Amendment should be read as a command that the government was without power to protect that freedom. The First Amendment, far from providing an argument against application of the Sherman Act, here provides powerful reasons to the contrary. That Amendment rests on the assumption that the widest possible dissemination of information from diverse and antagonistic sources is essential to the welfare of the public, that a free press is a condition of a free society. Surely a command that the government itself shall not impede the free flow of ideas does not afford non-governmental combinations a refuge if they impose restraints upon that constitutionally guaranteed freedom. . . . Freedom of the press from governmental interference under the First Amendment does not sanction repression of that freedom by private interests. The First Amendment affords not the slightest support for the contention that a combination to restrain trade in news and views has any constitutional immunity.[17]

Times-Picayune v. U.S. In this 1953 case, the Justice Department was unable to convince the U.S. Supreme Court that "forced combination" advertising in two newspapers, the *Times-Picayune* and the *States,* owned by the same company, violated the Sherman Act.[18] The practice, found to be a violation of the antitrust law by the U.S. District Court in New Orleans, Louisiana, involved advertising contracts by which a classified or local display advertiser had to buy space in both newspapers despite wanting to advertise in only one. The "combination" requirement was seen as detrimental to a competing newspaper, the *New Orleans Item*.

In giving the Court's opinion, Justice Tom Clark noted that the *Item's* local display advertising volume had increased substantially and, therefore, there was no evidence to show a demonstrably deleterious effect on competition. In reversing the District Court, the Supreme Court was careful to point out that it was not ruling on the legality of unit, or "forced combination," advertising in general.

Notwithstanding Justice Clark's assessment of the *Item's* advertising situation, the *Item* was merged five years later with its only competitor. The owner of the combined *New Orleans States Item* is the Times-Picayune Co.

U.S. v. Kansas City Star. In *U.S. v. Kansas City Star* (1957), both civil and criminal antitrust actions were brought by the Justice Department to break up forced combination advertising contracts. The actions also were brought to prevent readers from being compelled to subscribe to three newspapers published by the Kansas City Star Company—the morning *Kansas City Times,* the afternoon *Kansas City Star,* and the *Sunday Star.*[19] This case can be distinguished from *Times-Picayune* along several lines: (1) a competing afternoon newspaper already had gone bankrupt; (2) readers were being forced to accept a combination; and (3) the Kansas City Star Company also owned broadcast property in the Kansas City area and dominated mass communications there.

The company had contended that the three newspapers were, in fact, one, but a District Court jury disagreed. In upholding the jury determination, the U.S. Court of Appeals relied heavily on the views of Justice Black in *Associated Press v. U.S.,* discussed earlier. As the Circuit Court said, "A monopolistic press could attain in tremendous measure the evils sought to be prevented by the Sherman Anti-Trust Act."[20]

The Circuit Court thus upheld fines of $5000 against the company and $2500 against the advertising manager. The civil antitrust action ultimately was settled by consent decree whereby the company agreed to dispose of its broadcast stations and not to acquire any stations in the Kansas City area in the future.

U.S. v. Times-Mirror Company. Section 7 of the Clayton Act was put to the test in *U.S. v. Times-Mirror Company* (1967) following acquisition of the San Bernardino *Sun* and *Telegram* by the company that publishes the *Los Angeles Times.* The U.S. District Court ruled that the $15 million purchase of the Sun Company violated Section 7 of the Clayton Act and it ordered divestiture—a decision affirmed without opinion by the U.S. Supreme Court.[21]

Government antitrust lawyers were highly pleased with the outcome in the *Times-Mirror Company* case. They had prevented a competitor for advertising revenue and circulation from gobbling up one of the chief independent newspapers in Southern California which was located within 50 miles of the *Times.* But the merger mania was not halted by this decision. The Sun Company subsequently was acquired by Gannett Corporation which, as table 16.2 shows, has the largest number of dailies of any "chain." Gannett could acquire the Sun Company because none of its newspapers was in direct competition with the San Bernardino newspapers.

The District Court's decision nonetheless was considered a landmark because it foreclosed on attempts by prosperous metropolitan newspapers to acquire competing newspapers in suburban areas. However, there was nothing in the decision or the laws to prevent the *Los Angeles Times* from publishing a "satellite" edition in suburban areas—an operation undertaken by the *Times* and now rather commonplace in some areas.

JOINT OPERATING AGREEMENTS

In Tucson, Arizona, and 22 other cities in the mid-1960s, agreements had been reached between competing newspapers by which certain joint operations were carried out.

In Tucson, owners of the *Daily Citizen*—an evening newspaper, and the one referred to by Congressman Udall—and the morning *Arizona Star,* reached a joint operating agreement which was to run for 25 years beginning in 1940. Termination date for the agreement later was extended to 1990. Under the agreement, the competing companies formed Tucson Newspapers, Inc., to manage all departments of both newspapers, combining them into one, except for the news and editorial departments. The agreement ended all commercial rivalry between the two newspapers with the result that combined profits before taxes rose from $27,531 in 1940 to $1,727,217 in 1964.

In 1965 the two newspapers merged, although they continued to maintain independent editorial departments. That was when the Justice Department's Antitrust Division acted. It filed a complaint charging an unreasonable restraint of trade or commerce in violation of Section 1 of the Sherman Act, and a monopoly in violation of Section 2 of the Sherman Act. In addition, a Clayton Act (§ 7) violation was alleged.

U.S. v. Citizens Publishing Co. The U.S. District Court, after finding that the joint operating agreement contained provisions which were unlawful per se under Section 1, granted the government's motion for summary judgment. A trial ensued concerning the Section 2 and Section 7 allegations. The result was a finding that the purpose of the joint operating agreement was to monopolize the only newspaper business in Tucson, and the the *Citizen's* acquisition of the *Star's* stock had the effect of continuing in a more permanent form a substantial lessening of competition in violation of the Clayton Act's Section 7. The judge issued a decree ordering submission of a divestiture plan and re-establishment of the *Star* as an independent competitor. The decree also ordered a modification in the joint operating agreement to eliminate price fixing, market control, and profit pooling. However, joint operating agreements were not found to be per se violations of antitrust laws.

The U.S. Supreme Court affirmed the lower court in a 7–1 ruling in *Citizens Publishing Co. v. U.S.* (1969).[22]

In so doing, Justice Douglas said for the majority that the joint operating agreement plainly violated Section 1 of the Sherman Act because of price fixing (the setting of combined advertising rates); pooling of profits (which reduces incentives to compete for circulation and advertising revenues); and because of the agreement not to engage in any other publishing business in the county in which the two newspapers operated. The latter constituted a "division of the field" which, according to Douglas, is banned by the Sherman Act.

Failing Company Defense. The only real defense of the appellants, said Douglas, was the "failing company" defense—a judicially created doctrine whereby mergers are justified if they prevent a business failure.[23]

In rejecting that defense, Douglas wrote:

> There is no indication that the owners of the *Citizen* were contemplating a liquidation. They never sought to sell the *Citizen* and there is no evidence that the joint operating agreement was the last straw at which the *Citizen* grasped. Indeed the

Citizen continued to be a significant threat to the *Star.* How otherwise is one to explain the *Star's* willingness to enter into an agreement to share its profits with the *Citizen?* Would that be true if as now claimed the *Citizen* was on the brink of collapse?[24]

In addition, said Douglas, the "failing company" doctrine would apply in the Tucson situation only if it could be shown that the competitor was the only available purchaser. Preferably, a different purchaser should be found in a failing-newspaper situation who would preserve the competitive system. As Douglas observed:

> So even if we assume, *arguendo,* that in 1940 the then owners of the *Citizen* could not long keep the enterprise afloat, no effort was made to sell the *Citizen;* its properties and franchise were not put in the hands of a broker; and the record is silent on what the market, if any, for the *Citizen* might have been.[25]

Justice Stewart cast the lone dissenting vote principally because the district judge had not resolved the central factual issue concerning the salability of the *Citizen.* The findings failed to support the conclusion by the district judge that the *Citizen* was not a failing company, said Stewart. As for the affirmation of the lower court's judgment by his associates on the bench, Stewart had this to say:

> Prior decisions of this Court have made it clear that a failing company cannot combine with a competitor if its independence could be preserved by sale to an outsider. Today's decision for the first time lays down the blanket rule that the failing company defense is forfeited by a company which cannot show that it made substantial affirmative efforts to sell to a noncompetitor. . . . But proof of unsuccessful efforts to sell the company is not, as a logical, evidentiary matter, the only possible conclusive proof that it was not marketable. In many cases other evidence might make equally clear that any such efforts would surely have been fruitless.[26]

The Court's decision placed in jeopardy the joint operating agreements then in force in the 22 other cities that involved a total of 44 daily newspapers. But Congress came to the rescue.

Newspaper Preservation Act

The Newspaper Preservation Act (15 U.S.C. §§ 1801–1804) was passed in 1970 in response to the situation posed by the "Tucson case" decision. Basically, the Act accomplished two main purposes. It provided that newspapers in "economic distress" could enter into joint operating agreements. Furthermore, existing joint operating agreements were allowable if, at the time the agreement resulted, one of the newspapers was not "financially sound." The effect was to "legitimize" the 22 existing joint operating agreements and to make it possible for newspapers in 37 other cities to contemplate such an operating arrangement because only in those cities were two or more daily newspapers then in competition with one another.

What the Act accomplished whenever there were circumstances of "economic distress" or a lack of financial "soundness" was legal permission for price fixing, profit pooling, and market allocation—the very practices found to be antitrust violations in the Tucson case. It does not, however, exempt "predatory pricing"; that is, lowering a product's price to force a competitor out of business.

The Act requires that any such agreement will preserve the editorial and reportorial independence of newspaper staffs. Also, no more than one of the newspapers entering into such an agreement can be a financially sound newspaper.

As to what constitutes a "failing newspaper," the Act defines it as one that is "in probable danger of financial failure." This wording was selected because it could include all of the then-existing joint operating agreements and thereby shield those agreements from antitrust actions.

21 JOAs Exist

In 1988 there were 21 JOAs (Table 16.3), with a proposed one between the *Detroit News* and *Detroit Free Press* kicking up quite a controversy. But the one between the *Miami News* and the *Miami Herald* ended when the *News* folded on December 31, 1988, after its circulation had dropped from 112,000 in 1966, when the JOA was initiated, to 48,000.

TABLE 16.3. Cities with Joint Operating Agreements

	Population	Began	Partners
Albuquerque, N.M.	357,000	1933	Scripps and Independent
El Paso, Texas	487,000	1936	Scripps and Gannett
Nashville, Tenn.	447,000	1937	Gannett and Independent
Evansville, Ind.	127,000	1938	Scripps and Independent
Tucson, Ariz. (Renewed in 1988)	367,000	1940	Pulitzer and Gannett
Tulsa, Okla.	383,000	1941	Two Independents
Chattanooga, Tenn. (Dissolved in 1966, renewed in 1980)	165,000	1942	Two Independents
Madison, Wis.	167,000	1948	Lee and Independent
Fort Wayne, Ind.	162,000	1950	Knight-Ridder and Independent
Birmingham, Ala	266,000	1950	Scripps and Newhouse
Lincoln, Neb.	183,000	1950	Lee and Independent
Salt Lake City, Utah	148,000	1952	Two Independents
Shreveport, La.	216,000	1953	Gannett and Independent
Knoxville, Tenn.	168,000	1957	Scripps and Persis
Charleston, W.Va.	57,000	1958	Clay and Independent
Pittsburgh, Pa.	388,000	1961	Scripps and Block
Honolulu, Hawaii	369,000	1962	Gannett and Independent
San Francisco, Calif.	733,000	1965	Hearst and Independent
Miami, Fla.	364,000	1966	Knight-Ridder and Cox
Cincinnati, Ohio	357,000	1979	Scripps and Gannett
Seattle, Wash.	479,000	1983	Hearst and Independent

Source: Editor & Publisher, August 13, 1988, p. 15.

Anchorage Case. The first joint operating agreement after passage of the Newspaper Preservation Act permitted the *Anchorage Times* and *Anchorage Daily News* in Alaska to enter into certain joint operations in 1974. In connection with its approval of this joint operation, the Justice Department's Antitrust Division took the position that Congress had two different considerations in mind when it passed the Act and predicated application of the Act on the "probable danger of financial failure." The assistant attorney general in charge of the Antitrust Division said of that phrase:

> First, the test is a more stringent one than the test the Act applies to arrangements already in effect when the Act was passed. . . . On the other hand, Congress intended the "probable danger of financial failure" test to be a "departure" from the usual "failing company" defense . . . The legislative history . . . does not offer precise or quantitative guidelines as to what constitutes "probable danger of financial failure." But with this background we think that a newspaper with a long term history of financial and operating difficulties with profitable operations so remote that the newspaper will, in all likelihood, cease publication may reasonably be said to be in probable danger of financial failure.[27]

This was the rationale which led the Justice Department to approve the joint operating agreement between the two Anchorage newspapers. Such an agreement does not mean, of course, an automatic turnaround in the financial condition of a financially ailing newspaper. The *Anchorage Daily News* made drastic editorial staff reductions in late 1976 in an effort to cut its losses. Whether such action would stave off financial failure was still uncertain a year later. As the November 30, 1977, termination date neared for the joint operating agreement between the *Daily News* and the *Anchorage Times,* the *Times* sought to end the agreement. A U.S. District Court battle ensued, with the *Daily News* claiming that if the agreement was not renewed, the *Daily News* would be unable to continue publication and that the intent of Congress, to provide diverse editorial voices by means of the Newspaper Preservation Act, would be thwarted. The *Times* claimed that if it were compelled to subsidize the losses of the *Daily News* against its wishes, successful newspapers elsewhere would be most reluctant to merge operating departments with failing newspapers, thereby frustrating the purpose of the Preservation Act.

The District Court judge ruled that the *Times* had to continue the operating agreement—a decision which the *Times* said it would appeal. Ultimately the two newspapers decided to end the agreement, doing so in an out-of-court settlement in 1979. The settlement required the *Times* to pay the *News* $750,000 which would be the "financial cornerstone" for a new newspaper operation that would include purchase of new press equipment.[28]

Newspaper Guild v. Edward H. Levi. As in the Anchorage situation, the Preservation Act requires newspapers to obtain written consent of the U.S. attorney general before an agreement can take effect. However, the Act did not make it clear whether the attorney general's approval was required only for those newspapers seeking an "antitrust exemption" for such agreement. Did the Act, for example, require approval for *all* joint operating agreements regardless of antitrust implications? That was the issue raised in *Newspaper Guild v. Edward H. Levi, U.S. Attorney General in 1976.*[29] The Guild and other newspaper unions, such as the International Typographical Union, opposed the Preservation Act in Congress because consolidating production departments of newspapers would, among other results, lead to loss of jobs. When the Justice Department proposed a regulation in connection with the implementation of the Preservation Act—a regulation subsequently adopted—the Newspaper Guild brought a suit seeking to invalidate it. The proposed regulation, as adopted, was explained as follows:

> The Newspaper Preservation Act does not require that all joint newspaper operating arrangements obtain the prior written consent of the Attorney General. The Act and these regulations provide a method for newspapers to obtain the benefit of a limited exemption from the antitrust laws if they desire to do so. Joint newspaper operating arrangements that are put into effect without the prior written consent of the Attorney General remain fully subject to the antitrust laws.[30]

When the proposed regulation was promulgated as an interim regulation, the Guild filed suit, claiming that the regulation contravened Section 4(b) of the Act. The U.S. District Court declared the challenged regulation invalid and enjoined its implementation.[31] The Department of Justice appealed. In a 2–1 split, the U.S. Court of Appeals for the District of Columbia Circuit reversed, thereby upholding the Justice Department's regulation. And the U.S. Supreme Court denied certiorari.[32]

JOA Agreement in Seattle Challenged. In 1982, Attorney General William French Smith approved a joint operating agreement between the *Seattle Times* and the *Seattle Post-Intelligencer.*[33] But before the agreement could take effect, a U.S. District Court judge blocked it on the grounds that the Hearst Corporation might have found a buyer who would have maintained the *Post-Intelligencer's* independence. An appeal was filed and a three-judge panel of the U.S. Court of Appeals for the Ninth Circuit unanimously reversed the lower court.[34] In reinstating the attorney general's original approval, the panel said that the critical question in determining whether a newspaper is "failing" is whether it is "suffering losses which more than likely cannot be reversed" despite reasonable management. The plaintiffs appealed, but the U.S. Supreme Court in 1983 declined to review the case.[35]

Proposed JOA in Detroit. One of the most controversial of proposed JOAs since the Newspaper Preservation Act was passed remained in doubt until late 1989 even though Attorney General Edwin Meese approved it on Aug. 8, 1988, just prior to his resignation taking effect.[36]

The embattled Meese, accused of unethical conduct and conflict of interest in other matters, disregarded the findings of an administrative law judge who had urged him to deny the JOA application of the *Detroit Free Press* and *Detroit News,* and the recommendations of his own Department of Justice Antitrust Division.

The administrative law judge had said that the losses incurred by both newspapers were attributable to their strategies of seeking market dominance. Further, said the judge, the *Free Press* is not dominated by the *News* and is not in a downward spiral. Without proof that the *Free Press* is or probably will be dominated by the *News* and is or probably will be in an downward spiral, it cannot qualify as a failing newspaper, said the judge.

Meese said he accepted as accurate the findings of the administrative law judge, but differed with the judge's conclusion.

The continuing and persistent operating losses of the *Free Press*, "with no prospect of unilaterally reversing the economic condition in the forseeable future," makes it "highly probable," said Meese, that the *Free Press* eventually would fail.

The JOA, scheduled to go into effect August 18, 1988, was temporarily blocked by a U.S. District Court judge for the District of Columbia after a group calling itself Michigan Citizens for an Independent Press brought legal action. The judge said Meese's action may have been "arbitrary and capricious." But the temporary injunction was dissolved on September 17 by another U.S. District Court judge.[37] However, an appeal was taken to the U.S. Court of Appeals for the District of Columbia Circuit and a three-judge panel issued an injunction halting the JOA until a hearing could be conducted. That hearing was held in late 1988 and ultimately the JOA was approved.

Knight-Ridder, the group that owns the *Free Press,* had threatened to shut down the newspaper, with the loss of about 2,000 jobs, if the JOA was not approved. The *Free Press* and *News* have been losing money — about $132 million in the 1980–1987 period (with the *Free Press*'s losses totaling about $70 million). Those losses stemmed primarily from an aggressive circulation battle waged by both newspapers such that the weekly *News* sold for 15 cents while the *Free Press* cost 20 cents — at a time when virtually every other daily newspaper is selling for 25 cents or more per copy.

The fact that the *News* is losing money did not deter Gannett from buying the paper for $717 million in 1985. Such an action raised questions among those who oppose the JOA. The Gannett Company operates very profitably, as does the group owner of the *Free Press*. Isn't it a bit far-fetched to think of either newspaper as financially failing given their ownership? And surely the losses experienced by these two newspapers result in tax write-offs for both conglomerates which could, if they wished, reduce their expenditures by easing up on the "war" the papers have engaged in for some years — apart from a JOA agreement, that is.

There were other interesting aspects of the proposed JOA, including:

- A former Meese adviser was with the public relations firm hired by Knight-Ridder to carry out a lobbying campaign called the most intense in the 17-year history of JOAs.[38]
- Clark Clifford, a former Defense Secretary and presidential adviser, was a Knight-Ridder board member at the time Meese was considering what action to take.[39]
- The *Free Press* and Knight-Ridder's *Miami Herald* canceled editorial car-

toons about Meese (who was in hot water at the time based on allegations made against him on other matters).[40]

At stake in this "battle" was a JOA that one analyst said would be worth nearly $1 billion.[41]

RADIO-TV STATION OWNERSHIP AND CROSS-OWNERSHIP

The trend toward concentration of ownership in the print medium also exists in broadcasting where three commercial networks hold dominant positions, especially in television, and where half of the television stations and 80 percent of the radio stations are owned by companies that also own one or more other media outlets (either broadcast or print). When only the largest markets are considered, group ownership is even more pronounced. Approximately 71 percent of the television stations in the top 100 markets are licensed to group owners with approximately 87 percent of the nation's television households located in those markets. And if just the VHF stations are considered, group ownership accounts for 76 percent of the stations.[42]

If anything, concentration of ownership accelerated with record-breaking sales of TV and radio stations in the mid-1980s. But it was the acquisition of NBC by General Electric, Capital Cities' purchase of ABC, and Ted Turner's efforts to gain control of CBS that spurred some concern in Congress. Three days of hearings were held in April 1987, by the House of Representatives' Energy and Commerce Subcommittee. The subcommittee was considering an amendment to a corporate mergers bill that would require the FCC to review pending acquisitions of large broadcast companies.

Among the witnesses was Fred W. Friendly, former CBS News president and an Edward R. Murrow co-worker, who said, in part:

> Those in Congress, those in the FCC and people like myself who stand idly by are as guilty as the Wall Street traders who have changed something once licensed "in the public interest, convenience and necessity" into a midway of junk entertainment and headline service.

The chief executive officers of the three major networks defended the management of their news divisions and, in the case of NBC, committee members were assured that General Electric, a major defense contractor, would never interfere in the network's news operations.

Meanwhile, the FCC made it easier for stations to be sold or traded by eliminating the rule that stations could not be sold until they had been owned at least three years by the party wishing to sell.

Limitations on Station Ownership

Just prior to FCC proposed rule making in 1970 concerning cross-ownership of newspapers and television stations in the same market, there were 94 such combinations, of which 34 were in the top 50 markets, and 52 in the top 100. In 1975 when the FCC adopted rules banning future cross-ownership in the same city, 79 of those combinations remained intact.[43] Because of a "grandfather" clause, the FCC did not disturb about 70 newspaper-television and 185 newspaper-radio combinations.[44]

The FCC's order forbade the future formation of newspaper-broadcast combinations in the same market and required divestiture within five years in those communities where co-ownership existed of the only daily newspaper and broadcast station having a "city grade signal."[45] The latter rule did not affect 90 percent of the existing combinations.[46] However, the rule led rather quickly to some swapping of broadcast properties. For example, the *Washington Post* and *Detroit News* reached a preliminary agreement in 1977 to swap TV stations. The Washington Post Co. would obtain WWJ-TV in Detroit in exchange for WTOP-TV in the District of Columbia.

Although the FCC long has been aware that concentrated ownership threatened the public interest in having a diversified mass communications media, the Commission observed that stability and continuity of ownership also serve the public interest. Therefore it chose not to order divestiture except "in only the most egregious cases."[47] It took this course because "a mere hoped for gain in diversity" was not adequate cause for disrupting ownership.

An "egregious case" would be one in which a combination owner had an "effective monopoly in the marketplace of ideas" with respect to local community issues.

A public interest group challenged the FCC's order because it did not believe it went far enough in promoting diversity of ownership.

National Citizens Committee for Broadcasting v. FCC. In a surprise ruling in 1977, the U.S. Court of Appeals for the District of Columbia Circuit said that divestiture of jointly owned newspaper-broadcast station combinations in the same market should be required unless such cross-ownership could be shown to be in the public interest.[48] The three-judge panel, with Chief Judge Bazelon writing the opinion, did not disturb that part of the FCC's order which banned future cross-ownership of newspapers and stations in the same market, or that part of the order requiring divestiture within five years in "egregious" cross-ownership cases. In vacating that part of the order which protected the remaining cross-owned combinations, the court turned to the Commission's own policy in reaching an opposite conclusion. As quoted by the court, the FCC's long-standing policy is that "nothing can be more important than insuring that there is a free flow of information from as many divergent sources as possible."[49] But as Judge Bazelon stated:

> The Commission has sought to limit divestiture to cases where the evidence discloses that cross-ownership clearly harms the public interest. . . . We believe precisely the opposite presumption is compelled, and that divestiture is required except in those cases where the evidence clearly discloses that cross-ownership is in the public interest.[50]

An appeal was filed and the U.S. Supreme Court, by an 8–0 vote in 1978, reversed that portion of the Circuit Court's decision requiring the FCC to order divestiture except in those markets where cross-ownership could be shown to be in the public interest. The Court, in an opinion by Justice Marshall, held that the FCC had not acted arbitrarily or capriciously in requiring divestiture in only "egregious" cases.[51] The Court commented favorably upon the Commission's determination that forced divestiture of *all* cross-owned combinations would cause industry disruption and might result in a decline of local media ownership. However, the Court did not rule out challenges to cross-owned monopolies by means of comparative hearings and petitions.

To arguments raised by broadcasters and publishers that their First Amendment rights were being violated by forced divestiture, Marshall cited a string of precedents, such as *Red Lion, Tornillo,* and *DNC,* in pointing out that broadcast and print media have different characteristics that warrant different First Amendment considerations or application.

The FCC set a mid-1980 deadline for the breakup of 16 combinations. Seven "cases" ultimately were resolved by grant of waivers by the FCC, because of changed circumstances, such as entry of competition into the market; six resulted in the sale of one of the units; one successfully contested the FCC's breakup order in court;[52] and two were still in the process of disposition.

Even before its 1975 order establishing the one-to-a-market rule, the FCC had long been on record favoring diversification of control—a fact noted by the Circuit Court in *National Citizens Committee.* For example, the Commission said in its 1965 *Policy Statement on Comparative Renewal Hearings:* "Diversification of control is a public good in a free society, and is additionally desirable where a government licensing system limits access by the public to the use of radio and television facilities."[53]

Media magnate Rupert Murdoch sought ways to sidestep the FCC's ban on cross-ownership of a newspaper and TV station in the same market. Murdoch bought WFXT-TV in Boston, where he already owned the *Boston Herald,* and WNYW-TV in New York, where he owned the *New York Post.* He was granted temporary waivers of the "one-to-a-market" rule by the FCC—the only time the FCC has taken such action. When pressure was exerted on the FCC to scrap the rule, or to waive the rule in Murdoch's situation, Congress inserted a rider into an appropriations bill, passed at the end of 1987, that forbade the Commission from granting any further waivers to Murdoch. Murdoch then asked the FCC to defy Congress by extending the waivers, but the FCC dismissed his petition by a 3–0 vote on January 19, 1988. Murdoch then announced that he would sell the *Post* and put WFXT-TV in a trust. The trust proposal subsequently was approved by the FCC.

In Octber 1988, President Reagan signed into law another appropriations bill that contained a proviso barring the FCC from changing its existing ban on such cross-ownerships.

In addition to the one-to-a-market rule, a number of other restrictions on ownership of radio and TV stations have been adopted by the FCC.

Chain Broadcasting Rules. In 1941 the FCC adopted its chain broadcasting rules to combat the growing power of networks (see Chapter 14).

Multiple-Ownership Rules. The first multiple-ownership rules were adopted in 1943 during the heyday of AM radio broadcasting. The rules prohibited any party from owning or controlling more than one AM radio station in the same area. Twenty-four divestitures were required by the order.[54]

Seven-Station Limitation. In 1953 the Commission imposed the first numerical limitation on the number of stations an individual could control, and its authority to do this was upheld in *U.S. v. Storer Broadcasting* (1956).[55] This part of the multiple-ownership rules was known as "concentration of control" or "seven-station" limitation. A licensee, including a network, was permitted to own a maximum of seven AM and seven FM radio stations, and seven television stations (five VHF and two UHF).

The so-called 7-7-7 rule came to an end in 1984 when the Commission, by a 4–1 vote, decided to change the ownership ceiling to 12-12-12 with all limitations to end in 1990. Commissioner Henry Rivera, the only minority-race member of the Commission, dissented as to 1990 expiration of ownership limitations, but supported the increase in the number of stations that a single company could own; and Commissioner Mimi Wyforth Dawson was in total opposition to the changes. So, too, were many members of Congress, including the Congressional Black and Hispanic Caucuses, and various public interest groups.

Under congressional pressure, the Commission changed the formulation so that a company could own as many as 12 television stations if its share of the market did not exceed 25 percent of the national TV audience—a proposal put forth by Commissioner Dawson in her dissent to the original FCC action. The 12 AM and 12 FM radio portion of the rule remained intact.

Under the new rule, the 1990 expiration date was eliminated. Also, if two of the stations had more than 50 percent minority ownership, the company could own 14 TV stations and the national TV audience could reach 30 percent, provided the additional five percent came from the minority-controlled stations. A similar relaxation of the rule was put into effect if some of the company's stations are UHF rather than VHF.

Duopoly Rules. The second part of the FCC's 1953 ownership rules was known as the "duopoly" rules. These rules generally were intended to limit a licensee to ownership of one television station in the same market, or two radio stations in the same market. But there was no rule barring common ownership of one television station and one radio station in the same market—not until 1970 when the FCC amended the ownership rules to prohibit common ownership of stations in different broadcast services in the same market. Under these rules, which apply only to commercial broadcasters, common ownership of a television station and AM radio station, or AM and FM radio stations, was prohibited.[56] But in 1971 the Commission deleted rules applying to cross-ownership of AM and FM stations in the same market, although it left intact the restrictions against common ownership of VHF TV stations and radio stations in the same market. Applications for common ownership of UHF TV stations and radio stations were to be handled on a case-by-case basis.[57]

In its 1984 action on the 7-7-7 rule, the Commission left intact the rule that prohibits a company from owning a radio and TV station in the same market, but the FCC is considering relaxing this rule.

In 1983 the FCC did away with the cross-ownership rule that prevented TV networks from owning cable TV systems. And the Cable Telecommunications Act of 1984 allows cable systems to be owned by newspapers in the same market but still prohibits cross-ownership of cable systems by local TV stations. Again, the FCC is considering relaxing this rule.

Some states have passed legislation concerning cable TV-newspaper combinations in the same market.[58] Massachusetts forbids newspapers from owning cable TV systems in their major circulation areas. Minnesota also imposes restrictions on such cross-ownership when both are in the same market. In Connecticut, a state regulatory body ruled that a newspaper and cable TV station could not be owned by the same company and ordered divestiture.[59]

Justice Department Activity. The Justice Department has been active in opposing cross-ownership in the same market no matter whether such crossownership was "egregious" or not. There were allegations, as in the antitrust actions against the three networks, that the Department's moves had political overtones. The Department denied such charges and in petitions to the FCC in 1974 urged that licenses not be renewed for newspaper-owned radio-television stations in Des Moines (where the newspaper management denied the existence of joint ownership); St. Louis, Milwaukee, Minneapolis, and later in Salt Lake City. Among the newspapers involved, such as the *Milwaukee Journal* and *St. Louis Post-Dispatch,* were newspapers critical of President Nixon, especially during and after Watergate scandal revelations. Nicholas Johnson, who had left the Commission and returned to his native Iowa by the time of the Justice Department actions, asked why the Department was showing no apparent concern about cross-ownership of such media "giants" as the *Chicago Tribune* and WGN-TV or the Cox-owned media outlets in Atlanta, which were strong supporters of the President. Whatever the merits of Johnson's intimations, the fact remains that the Department, as early as 1970, had urged the FCC to prohibit all cross-ownership of media in the same market.

Ultimately the FCC rejected the Justice Department petitions urging that license renewal hearings be conducted in connection with the newspaper-television station combined ownerships. By 1977 the FCC had renewed the licenses of Cowles Communications, Inc., for KCCI-TV in Des Moines and for stations owned by the management of the *Milwaukee Journal, St. Louis Post-Dispatch* and *Globe Democrat,* and the Salt Lake City *Deseret News.*

Recommendations of FCC Staff

The 600-page final report by an FCC special staff, concerning an inquiry into television networks, contained criticisms of the Commission's ownership policies. Released in 1980, the report said the Commission should adopt and enforce "a systematic and coherent set of ownership policies" vis-à-vis television.[60] The staff took the position that FCC rules limiting the number of communication outlets one firm may own in a single local market, and limiting the number of television stations one firm may own throughout the nation, "are arbitrary and capricious." The Commission should distinguish "those patterns of ownership integration that threaten competition and diversity from those that will not harm these vital interests but, instead, may encourage a more efficient system of television networking," the staff said.

The report, which looked into various aspects of television network practices and regulations affecting the networks, drew criticism from the Justice Department. A department official said, in part, that the staff relied on "theoretical economic analyses with little or no attention paid to factual evidence of market behavior."[61]

Breakup of AT&T

The largest company in the world was broken into smaller units when U.S. District Court Judge Harold Greene signed an order in 1982 that ended a seven-year-old antitrust action by the Justice Department against the telecommunications giant. The consent decree required AT&T to divest itself of its 22 local operating companies within 18 months, but the company was permitted to retain its long-distance telephone service, its manufacturing subsidiary (Western Electric), and its research component (Bell laboratories). The local operating companies subsequently became part of regional entities.

Newspaper publishers succeeded in getting a ban inserted into the consent order that prevented AT&T's entry into electronic publishing for seven years; that is, the generating of news, sports, and other information. It could transmit such information via its long-distance lines or by satellite, but it could not "produce" it.[62] The District Court's judgment was summarily approved in 1983 by a 6–3 vote of the Supreme Court with Chief Justice Burger and Justices Rehnquist and White dissenting. Thirteen states and several of AT&T's competitors had appealed the lower court's judgment, the states arguing that the settlement preempted state regulation of the telephone industry.

The breakup of AT&T and the Bell System was the largest of its kind since Standard Oil was split up by court order in 1911.

NCAA Loses Court Battle

In 1984 the Supreme Court, by a 7–2 vote, ended the National Collegiate Athletic Association's control over televised college football games. Since 1951, the NCAA had negotiated exclusive TV contracts with networks that determined which games would appear on television. Sanctions could be applied against NCAA members that negotiated their own TV contracts, including expulsion from the NCAA.

In giving the Court's opinion, Justice Stevens said the exclusive TV arrangement violated the Sherman Anti-Trust Act by limiting the number of televised games and by forcing networks to pay a higher price than otherwise might be necessary if individual colleges could negotiate their own terms. The ruling still permits the NCAA to represent colleges in negotiating TV contracts, but it allows individual colleges to do the same.

Justices White and Rehnquist dissented.

SUMMARY

The trend toward concentration of media ownership is highlighted by data showing that 80 percent of all daily newspaper circulation is controlled by newspaper groups. These 146 groups own 73 percent of the 1670 dailies in existence in 1986. The same trend is evident throughout the mass communications industry with broadcast groups able to reach three-fourths of the average daily audience in the nation.

The mass media mergers and cross-ownerships have occurred despite the Sherman Anti-Trust Act of 1890, the Clayton Act of 1914, the FTC Act of 1914 (since the FTC is heavily involved in trying to maintain competition in the marketplace), and other antitrust weapons available at various governmental levels.

One reason the antitrust laws have not been used more widely in slowing newspaper ownership concentration is the Newspaper Preservation Act of 1970 which legitimized 22 existing joint operating agreements between newspapers in as many cities. Thirty-seven other pairs of newspapers in as many cities could, at the time the Act was passed, enter into such agreements because newspapers in those cities were in competition with one another. However, the U.S. attorney general first must give his approval; only one of the newspapers can be financially sound and the other must be "in probable danger of financial failure."

In connection with media cross-ownership, the FCC in 1975 issued an order that required divestiture of cross-owned newspaper-television stations or newspaper-radio stations in markets where single ownership of those media existed. The FCC termed them "egregious cases." Some 70 other newspaper-television station combinations, and 185 newspaper-radio combinations would be "grandfathered" by the FCC order. The U.S. Court of Appeals for the District of Columbia Circuit, in *National Citizens Committee for Broadcasting v. FCC,* ruled in a 2–1 split that divestiture is required unless such cross-ownership can be shown to be in the public interest. But the U.S. Supreme Court, in an 8–0 ruling, reversed that part of the lower court's ruling, thus sustaining the policy adopted by the Commission.

Prior to the FCC's 1975 action, various-multiple ownership rules had been promulgated by the Commission, including the 7-7-7 limitation and, the "duopoly" rules. More recently, the FCC has seen fit to alter or eliminate some prohibitions or restrictions on multiple ownership. A company now can own 12 AM and 12 FM radio stations, plus 12 VHF TV stations if the share of the market of those TV stations does not exceed 25 percent. A higher percentage is permitted where the number of stations includes minority-controlled ones.

TV networks now can own cable TV systems and the Cable Telecommunications Act of 1984 allows cable systems to be owned by newspapers even though both serve the same market.

Antitrust action has resulted in the largest common carrier in the world — AT&T — being broken into various units after the Justice Department brought an antitrust action against the telecommunications giant.

Additionally, the NCAA's exclusive control over televised college football games was ended by a 7–2 ruling of the Supreme Court in 1984.

One final comment can be made about the accelerated pace of media ownership concentration. It is this trend which prompted Professor Barron, among others, to see in the courts or lawmaking bodies, or both, ways of making the news media legally more hospitable to a diversity of ideas and views. Professor Thomas I. Emerson would prefer to have government serve as a facilitator for the entry of new and competitive media — an idea also advanced by the Commission on Freedom of the Press in 1947. Many observers doubt that the antitrust laws can be used to bring about any real diversity of ownership and the FCC is not currently inclined to break up existing ownership structures except in clearcut monopoly situations. Against such concerns and the evidence of ownership concentration are the *Red Lion* words of the U.S. Supreme Court.

> It is the right of the viewers and listeners, not the right of the broadcasters, which is paramount. . . . It is the right of the public to receive suitable access to social, political, aesthetic, moral, and other ideas and experiences which is crucial here.

At what point does media ownership become so concentrated that the public's right is imperiled? And who will make such a determination? Or have we, as Professor Barron believes, long ceased to have a marketplace of ideas open to and inviting robust and antagonistic debate on a multitude of ideas? Is Orwell's *1984* — wherein government controls the channels of communication — the real danger, or should our attention be riveted on the possibility that a few giant conglomerates might have the capacity, if not the desire, to influence, shape, and ultimately control what the vast majority of Americans will read or hear via the mass media?

QUESTIONS IN REVIEW

1. In terms of aggregate daily circulation, which newspaper group is the largest?
2. Why doesn't the Sherman Anti-Trust Act of 1890 or the Clayton Act of 1914 prevent joint operating agreements among competing newspapers in the same city when one of these newspapers is experiencing "economic distress" or is in probable danger of failing, even though such agreements restrain trade or commerce?
3. True or False: In *Associated Press v. U.S.* (1945) the U.S. Supreme Court held that the AP's bylaws constituted an "unreasonable" restraint of trade and commerce.
4. True or False: The Newspaper Preservation Act was a direct response by Congress to the U.S. Supreme Court's decision in *Citizens Publishing Co. v. U.S.* (1969) in which the Court held that a joint operating agreement between two competing newspapers violated the antitrust laws.

5. True or False: Editorial departments can be merged legally under Preservation Act joint operating agreements.
6. In its 1975 Order, the FCC said it would only require divestiture in cross-ownership situations when such cross-ownership was _____.
7. The 7-7-7 rule has given way to what limitations on broadcast station ownership?

ANSWERS

1. Gannett.
2. Because of the Newspaper Preservation Act of 1970.
3. True.
4. True.
5. False.
6. "Egregious."
7. To 12-12 and 25 percent; that is, 12 AM and 12 FM radio stations and 12 TV stations if those stations' share of the national TV audience does not exceed 25 percent. Variations in TV station ownership were allowed where UHF, rather than VHF, stations were involved and where stations were minority-controlled.

ENDNOTES

1. Competition Review Act of 1977, H.R. 6098, 95th Cong., 1st Sess.
2. Morris Udall, in *Editor & Publisher,* June 11, 1977, p. 12.
3. Address by Congressman Udall, "No Energy in the East—No Water in the West. How Did It Happen?"
4. Ibid.
5. Ben H. Bagdikian, "Conglomeration, Concentration, and the Flow of Information," *Proceedings of the Symposium on Media Concentration,* Vol. I, December 14–15, 1978, Bureau of Competition, Federal Trade Commission, pp. 7–8.
6. "Time to Draw the Line," a statement adopted at the 46th annual convention of the Newspaper Guild, AFL-CIO, CLC, at Boston, Mass., July 2–6, 1979.
7. *Editor & Publisher,* July 9, 1988, p. 11.
8. *Editor & Publisher,* April 16, 1977.
9. *Columbia Journalism Review,* September/October 1977.
10. National News Council, July 8, 1977.
11. Ibid.
12. Charles A. Perlik, Jr., president, Newspaper Guild, in statement prepared for the U.S. Senate's Select Committee on Small Business, June 1979, pp. 5–6.
13. Associated Press v. U.S., 326 U.S. 1, 65 S.Ct. 1416. Justice Jackson took no part in the consideration or decision, and Chief Justice Stone, and Justices Roberts and Murphy, dissented in part.
14. Standard Oil Co. v. U.S., 221 U.S. 1, 31 S.Ct. 502, 55 L.Ed. 619.
15. 52 F.Supp. 362, 372.
16. AP v. National Labor Relations Board, 301 U.S. 103, 57 S.Ct. 650, 81 L.Ed. 953.
17. AP v. U.S., 326 U.S. at 20; 65 S.Ct. at 1425.
18. Times-Picayune v. U.S., 345 U.S. 594, 73 S.Ct. 872.
19. U.S. v. Kansas City Star, 240 F.2d 648 (8th Circuit, 1957).
20. Ibid., at 666.
21. U.S. v. Times-Mirror Company, 274 F.Supp. 606 (Central District of California, 1967); affd, 390 U.S. 712; 88 S.Ct. 1411 (1968).

22. Citizens Publishing Co. v. U.S., 394 U.S. 131, 89 S.Ct. 927. Justice Fortas took no part in the consideration or decision, and Justice Stewart dissented.

23. The "failing company" doctrine was held to justify mergers in U.S. v. Maryland & Virginia Milk Producers Assn., 167 F.Supp. 799, affd, 362 U.S. 458, 80 S.Ct. 847, 4 L.Ed.2d 890, and in Union Leader Corp. v. Newspapers of New England, 284 F.2d 582.

24. Citizens Publishing Co. v. U.S., op. cit., note 22, 394 U.S. at 137–38, 89 S.Ct. at 930–31.

25. Ibid., at 138; at 931.

26. Ibid., at 143; at 933.

27. Ruth Walden, "Newspaper Failure: An Elusive Concept," a paper presented at the annual convention of the Law Division, Association for Education in Journalism, College Park, Md., 1976, p. 15.

28. *Editor & Publisher,* October 7, 1979, p. 7.

29. Newspaper Guild v. Edward H. Levi, U.S. Attorney General, 539 F.2d 755 (District of Columbia Circuit, 1976). Circuit Judge Tamm dissented.

30. 36 *Fed. Reg.* 20435 (1971).

31. 381 F.Supp. 48 (District of Columbia, 1974).

32. "News Notes," *Media Law Reporter,* March 1, 1977.

33. "News Notes," *Media Law Reporter,* June 29, 1982.

34. Committee for an Independent Post-Intelligencer v. Hearst Corporation, 9 *Med.L.Rptr.* 1489, May 10,1983.

35. "News Notes," *Media Law Reporter,* October 19, 1983.

36. "News Notes," *Media Law Reporter,* August 16, 1988.

37. 15 *Med.L.Rptr.* 1937 and 15 *Med.L.Rptr.* 1943, October 11, 1988.

38. *Editor & Publisher,* August 13, 1988, p. 14.

39. Ibid.

40. Ibid.

41. Ibid.

42. Herbert H. Howard, "The Contemporary Status of Television Group Ownership," *Journalism Quarterly,* Vol. 53, No. 3, Autumn 1976, p. 399.

43. National Citizens Comrnittee for Broadcasting v. FCC, 2 *Med.L.Rptr.* 1405, 1408 n. 11 (U.S. Court of Appeals, District of Columbia Circuit, 1977).

44. 43 *U.S. Law Week* 2340.

45. *Second Report and Order,* 50 FCC 2d 1046 (1974), reconsidered, 53 FCC 2d 589 (1975).

46. National Citizens Committee for Broadcasting v. FCC, op.cit., note 43, at 1407.

47. FCC *Order,* op. cit. note 45, at 1080.

48. National Citizens Committee for Broadcasting v. FCC, op. cit., note 43.

49. Ibid., at 1427.

50. Ibid.

51. FCC v. National Citizens Committee for Broadcasting, 3 *Med.L.Rptr.* 2409, June 27, 1978. Justice Brennan took no part in the case.

52. KCMC, Inc. v. FCC, 5 *Med.L.Rptr.* 1833, November 13, 1979 (U.S. Court of Appeals, 5th Circuit).

53. *Policy Statement on Comparative Renewal Hearings,* 1 FCC 2d 393, 394.

54. 8 *Fed. Reg.* 16065 (1943).

55. U.S. v. Storer Broadcasting, 351 U.S. 192.

56. 22 FCC 2d 306.

57. FCC's *40th Annual Report/Fiscal Year 1974* p. 23.

58. *Editor & Publisher,* March 22, 1980 p. 6.

59. *Editor & Publisher,* February 2, 1980, p. 12.

60. "News Notes," *Media Law Reporter,* October 28, 1980.

61. Ibid.

62. "News Notes," *Media Law Reporter,* August 24, 1982.

17

Copyright and Unfair Competition

HIGHLIGHTS

■ Major changes in copyright law were effected by passage of the 1976 Copyright Act. The law contains a "fair use" section which, for example, allows the news media to use a limited amount of copyrighted material for news purposes without first having to get permission of the copyright holder.

■ An "unfair competition" tort exists to protect against news piracy, as shown by a number of cases.

■ Three major factors often are considered in deciding copyright infringement lawsuits—originality of the work; proof of access to the work, and similarity between the works being compared.

■ By a 5–4 vote in 1984, the Supreme Court ruled that private home videotaping is not an infringement of copyright and that the Sony Corporation's manufacture and sale of Betamax videotape recorders did not constitute contributory infringement.

Copyright is a form of monopoly provided by law to the authors of original literary, dramatic, musical, artistic, and other kinds of intellectual works. The law provides a copyright holder with the exclusive right to determine how or when such a work can be used or reproduced.[1] Except under several circumstances, no part of a copyrighted work can be used by someone else without first obtaining the copyright holder's permission.

The first national copyright law was enacted in 1790 by the First Congress. Since then, there have been four general revisions of the federal copyright act— 1831, 1870, 1909, and 1976.

The 1790 legislation came shortly after ratification of the U.S. Constitution which states in Article I, Section 8, that "Congress shall have the power . . . to promote the progress of science and useful arts, by securing for limited times to authors and inventors the exclusive right to their respective writings and discoveries." At the time, 12 of the 13 original states (Delaware being the exception) had enacted legislation to protect an author's work. These laws, including the 1790 statute, generally were patterned after the first copyright law that had been passed in England in 1709.

The constitutional authorization for copyright is predicated on the belief that the sciences, arts, and other human endeavors will be advanced by encouraging writers and others, through the monopoly that protects their works, to be creative. The protection afforded is for a limited time, whereupon the works become a part of the public domain. The copyright period stipulated in the 1790 legislation was 14 years with right of renewal by the author, if still living, for another 14 years.

Under the Copyright Act of 1909, as amended, the copyright period was 28 years with a proviso that such protection could be renewed for another 28 years. In 1976, President Ford signed a bill which brought about a general revision of the copyright law for the first time since enactment of the 1909 law. Passage of the 1976 Act[2] culminated years of effort to update the 1909 law which, at the time of its passage, could not have anticipated technological changes. Motion pictures and sound recordings had just made their appearance in the early 1900s. Commercial radio and television were hardly dreamed of at the time. There was no way that such a law could take into account developments in computer programming, information storage and retrieval, communication satellites, laser beam technology, and cablecasting.

Between 1924 and 1940 a number of unsuccessful attempts were made to revise the law. After World War II, the United States participated in the development of the new Universal Copyright Convention, becoming a signatory in 1955. In that year, the move for general revision of the 1909 Act was revived and money was appropriated during a three-year period for the Copyright Office to undertake comprehensive studies laying the groundwork for revision. As a result, 35 monographs were published on most of the substantive copyright issues, culminating in a 1961 report by the Register of Copyrights. Thereafter, on and off efforts were made in Congress to bring about the general revision.

THE 1976 COPYRIGHT ACT

The 1976 Act became effective for the most part on January 1, 1978. It provides that a copyrightable work created after that date can be protected during the life of the author plus an additional 50 years. For works created prior to January 1, 1978, the initial 28-year protection remains in effect, but the new law in most instances extends the renewal period to 47 years (for a total of 75 years' protection) instead of a maximum 46 years' protection. These new time periods are a major change which brings the U.S. copyright law into general conformity with international copyright law.

Prior to the 1976 Act, a copyrightable work could be protected under the existing federal statute or by state or common law. Under the new Act, a single system of statutory protection exists for all copyrightable works, whether those works are published or unpublished. Thus, state and common law have been preempted by passage of the federal statute.

Under the new Act, a copyright owner is given the exclusive rights of reproduction, adaptation, publication, performance, and display in connection with any "original works of authorship fixed in any tangible medium of expression, now known or later developed, from which they can be perceived, reproduced, or otherwise communicated, either directly or with the aid of a machine or device." In 17 U.S.C. 102, copyrightable works of authorship may fall into any of the following categories:

- Literary works
- Musical works, including any accompanying words
- Dramatic works, including any accompanying music
- Pantomimes and choreographic works
- Pictorial, graphic, and sculptural works
- Motion pictures and other audiovisual works
- Sound recordings

But the law says, "In no case does copyright protection for an original work of authorship extend to any idea, procedure, process, system, method of operation, concept, principle, or discovery, regardless of the form in which it is described, explained, illustrated, or embodied in such work."

Generally, the following categories of material are not eligible for statutory copyright protection:

- Works that have *not* been fixed in a tangible form of expression. For example: choreographic works which have not been notated or recorded, or improvisational speeches or performances that have not been written or recorded.
- Titles, names, short phrases, and slogans;[3] familiar symbols or designs; mere variations of typographic ornamentation, lettering, or coloring; mere listings of ingredients or contents.
- Ideas, procedures, methods, systems, processes, concepts, principles, discoveries, or devices, as distinguished from a description, explanation, or illustration.
- Works consisting *entirely* of information that is common property and containing no original authorship. For example: standard calendars, height and weight charts, tape measures and rulers, schedules of sporting events, and lists or tables taken from public documents or other common sources.[4]

Included under "common property" are news facts. A news organization can copyright the style of writing, but it cannot copyright news facts. If another news organization can *independently* obtain the facts, it can publish them. Similarly, a photographer can obtain copyright protection for a photograph, but only for the particular arrangement or composition. The same model or subject matter could be used by other photographers to create new compositions.

Copyright Infringement

Section 501 of the 1976 Act states that anyone who violates any of the exclusive rights of the copyright owner is an infringer. Among the remedies available in a civil action are: (1) temporary and final injunctions on such terms as a court may deem reasonable to prevent or restrain infringement of the copyright; (2) impoundment and, after final judgment, destruction or other reasonable disposition of all copies and phonorecords, and the means by which such copies of phonorecords are made, which infringe upon copyright; and (3) recovery of actual damages (plus any profits lost because of infringement). However, a copyright owner may elect at any time before final judgment to recover statutory damages, instead of actual damages. In this case the court may award a sum of not less than $250 and not more than $10,000. Where the copyright owner can show willful infringement, the court has discretionary power to increase the statutory damages to not more than $50,000. Costs and reasonable attorney's fees may be awarded to the prevailing party, at the discretion of the court.

Section 506 provides for criminal sanctions against an infringer. A fine of not more than $10,000 (double the amount permitted under the 1909 Act) and imprisonment of not more than one year, or both, can be imposed. In connection with infringement of sound recordings, the fine, in some cases, can be increased to $25,000 and/or one year in prison, for the first offense. It can be increased to a maximum of $50,000 and/or two years in prison for any subsequent offense. A three-year statute of limitation applies to both criminal proceedings and civil actions. There are special statutory provisions to deal with the importation of copies or phonorecords which infringe upon a copyrighted work.

Section 506(c) provides for a fine of not more than $2500 for anyone who, with fraudulent intent, places on any article a copyright notice or words of the same purport that such person knows to be false.

Factors Considered in Alleged Infringement

Three major factors often are considered in determination of infringement: (1) originality of the copyrighted work; (2) proof of access to the copyrighted work; and/or (3) similarity between the works being compared.

Some courts have held that the copying must be substantial before infringement can be found; but there is disagreement as to what constitutes "substantial." Furthermore, not all courts are willing to apply such a standard.

Access was one of the factors considered in *Senta Marie Runge v. Joyce Lee and Joyce Lee Cosmetics, Inc.*[5] In this case a jury awarded Ms. Runge the following damages resulting from publication of a book about cosmetics: $80,000 compensatory damages against the company for copyright infringement; $25,000 in punitive damages against Ms. Lee for unfair competition; and $20,000 in punitive damages against the company for unfair competition. The district court judge granted Ms. Runge $12,000 in attorney fees, issued a permanent injunction, and ordered the remaining copies of the infringing book impounded and destroyed. These actions were affirmed by the Ninth Circuit U.S. Court of Appeals which considered the factors of access and originality, as well as "circumstantial" evidence.

Concerning "originality," the three-judge panel quoted from an earlier decision of the Ninth Circuit Court, saying: "The author must have created the work by his own skill, labor and judgment, contributing something 'recognizably his own' to prior treatments of the same subject. However, neither great novelty nor superior artistic quality is required" for the work to be copyrightable.[6] The appellate court approvingly quoted one of the district court judge's instructions to the jury, to wit: that there would be no infringement if a subsequent writer "used her own labors, skills or common sources of knowledge open to all men, and the resemblances are accidental or arise from the nature of the subject matter. . . ."

The factors considered by the appellate court in affirming the jury's award of damages were: (1) the defendant had been employed by the plaintiff and in the course of her work had used the book written by the plaintiff (access); (2) the defendant had very little writing experience prior to the publication of the book (one newspaper article that was unrelated to the topic of her book); and (3) the defendant wrote the book in one month. Thus, the issue of infringement was resolved and not alone by a comparison of the two books to determine if there had been unlawful copying of a copyrighted book, but by such considerations as the defendant's demonstrated prior writing ability.

Few cases involve word-by-word copying. Consequently, a similarity test may be used. Some courts have required that any similarity must be "substantial"; but, again, there is no uniformity concerning the meaning of substantial. Evidence of "common errors" in the works being compared also is used in reaching conclusions about similarities.

In determining "substantial similiarity," courts may use a pattern test or an audience test.[7] The pattern test was advocated in 1945 by Professor Zechariah Chafee, Jr., of Harvard University. Using such a test might require the use of experts who would seek to determine if a pattern of appropriation exists, such as an infringement case involving nuclear physics textbooks.[8] The audience, or "ordinary observer," test could be applied by a jury of laypersons. Ultimately, however, the method of analysis will depend on the particular facts of a case. Most likely there will be more than one line of analysis.

In *Universal Pictures Co., Inc. v. Harold Lloyd Corp.,*[9] the Ninth Circuit U.S. Court of Appeals said that complete or substantial identity between the original and the copy is not required, adding that "copying and infringement may exist although the work of the pirate is so cleverly done that no identity of language can be found in the two works."

Copyright Notice

The 1909 Act required, as a mandatory condition of copyright protection, that the published copies of a work bear a copyright notice. Copies of any such work published prior to January 1, 1978, must bear the notice either on the title page or on the reverse side of the title page. If the notice appeared anywhere else, or did not follow one of three forms, copyright protection was lost and the work fell into the public domain. The acceptable forms for published works were

Copyright 1975, by John Doe

Copr. 1975, by John Doe

© John Doe 1975

By adding – © under UCC 1975 John Doe – under the copyright notice, protection is secured in those countries that are signatories of the Universal Copyright Convention.

The date of publication ordinarily is the year in which copies first are placed on sale or publicly distributed by the copyright holder. If the work previously had been registered for copyright in unpublished form, such as a photograph, then the year during which registration occurred should be used in the copyright notice.

Under the 1976 law, the notice need only appear in a location that gives "reasonable notice of a claim of copyright." Omissions or errors will not immediately result in forfeiture of copyright. Corrections can be made within certain time limits. However, there is no liability for infringement caused by copyright notice omission or error. In general, the 1976 Act favors one of the notice forms required under the 1909 Act.

It should be emphasized that both "unpublished" and "published" original works of authorship are protected under the 1976 law.

Copyright Registration

Generally the owner of a copyrightable work will do the following to secure registration of the copyright:

1. Deposit with the Copyright Office two complete copies of the best edition, sound recording, or whatever, of a published work (one copy for an unpublished work).[10]
2. Complete the prescribed form.
3. Pay the required fee which, for most purposes, is $10.

The forms are obtainable from the Register of Copyrights, Library of Congress, Washington, D.C. 20559.

In searching for copyright, a person can examine the Catalog of Copyright Entries, which is divided into parts according to the classes of work registered, such as "Books," "Music," "Motion Pictures," and "Sound Recordings." The catalog entry contains the essential facts concerning a registration, but it is not a verbatim transcript of the registration. A search can be conducted by the public at the Copyright Office in Arlington, Virginia. The office staff will also make a search on advance payment of $10 for each hour or fraction thereof, based on an estimate of the amount of time necessary for the search as provided by the Copyright Office.

"Fair Use" Doctrine

Although the copyright law extends an exclusive right to a copyright owner to reproduce, prepare, distribute, perform, and/or display a copyrighted work, or to authorize any of these activities, some limitations exist. One of these is the "fair use" of a copyrighted work. The 1909 Act did not mention, or make provision for, the fair use of a copyrighted work. Instead, the courts created the doctrine of fair use which, in the opinion of the Second Circuit Court of Appeals, became "the most troublesome in the whole law of copyright. . . ."[11]

The 1976 law contains a "fair use" section, § 107, which states:

> Notwithstanding the provisions of Section 106 [which lists the five exclusive rights of a copyright owner], the fair use of a copyrighted work, including such use by reproduction in copies or phonorecords or by another means specified by that section, for purposes such as criticism, comment, news reporting, teaching (including multiple copies for classroom use), scholarship, or research, is not an infringement of copyright. In determining whether the use made of a work in any particular case is a fair use the factors to be considered shall include—
>
> (1) the purpose and character of the use, including whether such use is of a commercial nature or is for nonprofit educational purposes;
> (2) the nature of the copyrighted work;
> (3) the amount and substantiality of the portion used in relation to the copyrighted work as a whole; and
> (4) the effect of the use upon the potential market for or value of the copyrighted work.

Clearly, an endless variety of situations and uses can arise which could not be detailed in statutory form. In fact, Congress deliberately chose not to freeze the doctrine in statutory form because of rapid technological change. In a report from the Judiciary Committee to the House of Representatives in connection with Senate Bill 22 that ultimately became the statutory revision of the copyright law, Congressman Robert W. Kastenmeier said:

> Beyond a very broad statutory explanation of what fair use is and some of the criteria applicable to it, the courts must be free to adapt the doctrine to particular situations on a case-by-case basis. Section 107 is intended to restate the present judicial doctrine of fair use, not to change, narrow, or enlarge it in any way.[12]

Thus, it is to the judicially created doctrine that one must look to understand the fair use exception to the rights protected by copyright law.

Folsom v. Marsh. The "fair use" doctrine is derived from England. It was used for the first time in the United States in an 1841 case, *Folsom v. Marsh,*[13] involving an abridgement of a biography of George Washington and letters which an author could not have had access to. According to Prof. Kent H. Benjamin:

Justice Story [in *Folsom v. Marsh*] virtually founded fair use by stating that most of the book need not be taken to constitute an infringement, and that the court should ". . . look to the nature and objects of the selections made, the quantity and value of the materials used, and the degree in which the use may prejudice the sale, or diminish the profits, or supersede the objects of the original work . . ." to determine if the use was fair. Without actually using the term "fair use," Justice Story laid the foundation for fair use cases to come.[14]

The doctrine has been applied most often in the fields of science, law, medicine, history, and biography. Only a few cases have occurred in connection with newspapers. Of the newspaper cases, Benjamin wrote:

The most famous is *Chicago Record-Herald Co. v. Tribune Ass'n.*[15] In this case, the *Chicago Record-Herald* had previously declined to purchase a particular news story, but later published an abridged but almost identical version of the story as it appeared in the *Tribune,* a rival newspaper, with a line attributing the story to the *Tribune.* The court held that what the defendant published was infringement because . . . [the newspaper] took the idea but also the arrangement and manner of statement of the *Tribune* story.[16]

The doctrine has been used in a number of cases involving magazine and book publishers, including the following ones.

Conde Nast Publications v. Vogue School of Modeling, Inc. A school of fashion modeling used reproductions of the covers of *Vogue* magazine, without permission, in its promotional brochures. The magazine's publishers sued to halt this practice. The court rejected a fair use defense, saying, "No one is entitled to save time, trouble, and expense by availing himself to another's copyrighted work for the sake of making an unearned profit."[17]

MacDonald v. Du Maurier. In this case, famous author Daphne Du Maurier was sued by another author who alleged that a story and novel she had written was substantially the same as the defendant's novel, *Rebecca.* In ruling in favor of the defendant, the court said that as a general rule the similarity of plots in fictional stories does not necessarily constitute an unfair use.[18]

Rosemont Enterprises, Inc. v. Random House, Inc. Billionaire recluse Howard Hughes attempted unsuccessfully to prevent publication of a biography about him by Random House. As part of an effort to restrict such publicity, Hughes established Rosemont Enterprises which purchased the copyright to articles that had appeared in *Look* magazine on February 9, 23, and March 9, 1954, under the title "The Howard Hughes Story." In granting a preliminary injunction, the U.S. District Court rejected Random House's fair use argument concerning biographies, saying that such a fast-moving biography "can scarcely be said to be scholarly, scientific or educational. . . ."[19] Borrowing from copyrighted sources for nonscholarly purposes said the judge, is severely limited under the doctrine of fair use. But an appellate court disagreed with the lower court, saying that on the facts presented the public interest should prevail over the copyright protection. The court said:

> Whether an author or publisher reaps economic benefits from the sale of biographical work, or whether its publication is motivated in part by a desire for commercial gain, or whether it is designed for the popular market, i.e., the average citizen rather than the college professor, has no bearing on whether a public benefit may be derived from such a work.[20]

Such concerns, the court declared, are irrelevant "to a determination of whether a particular use of copyrighted material in a work which offers some benefit to the public constitutes a fair use. Rather, the public interest should be the primary concern in any fair-use determination.

Time, Inc. v. Bernard Geis Associates. Public interest was a primary consideration in this case.[21] As copyright holder, Time, Inc. had refused to allow the defendant to publish the Zapruder film of the John F. Kennedy assassination. The defendant thereupon published sketches of the photographs. A suit resulted and defendant prevailed, principally because there was considerable interest involved in the assassination and theories about it. The defendant's book, in the court's opinion, would be bought not because of the reproduction of the photos in sketch form but rather for the author's theories about the assassination.

Wainwright Securities v. Wall Street Transcript. In this case, decided by the Second Circuit U.S. Court of Appeals after passage of the 1976 copyright law, a three-judge panel affirmed a District Court's injunction against a weekly newspaper, the *Wall Street Transcript,* enjoining the corporation from publishing abstracts of in-depth research reports by H. C. Wainwright & Co. concerning industrial, financial, utility, and railroad corporations. These reports were used by more than 900 Wainwright clients.[22] The *Transcript* claimed that its summaries of the Wainwright reports constituted important news for the investing public; that they were truthful, of public interest, and therefore the First Amendment should override copyright interests.

The District Court found that the *Transcript's* abstracts did not constitute a fair use because:

1. The takings were "substantial in quality, and . . . quantity."
2. Publication of the abstract probably reduced the value of Wainwright's research reports.
3. The public interest in dissemination is not affected since the *Transcript* is not restrained from researching and preparing its own reports.
4. Such reports could be prepared from original materials.

In its review, the appellate court said the question of First Amendment protection due a news report of a copyrighted research report is "a provocative one." Some day, said Judge Jacob Mishler for the panel, quoting from a law review article written by copyright scholar Melville B. Nimmer, legitimate in-depth news coverage of copyrighted, small-circulation articles dealing with areas of general concern may require courts to distinguish between the doctrine of fair use and "an emerging constitutional limitation on copyright contained in the First Amendment."[23] But *Wainwright Securities* was not such a case, said Judge Mishler, for the following reasons:

> It is . . . axiomatic that "news events" may not be copyrighted [*Time, Inc. v. Bernard Geis Associates,* 293 F.Supp. 130, 143]. . . . But in considering the copyright protection due a report of news events or factual developments, it is important to differentiate between the substance of the information contained in the report, i.e., the event itself, and "the particular form or collocation of words in which the writer has communicated it" [*International News Service v. Associated Press,* 248 U.S. 215, 234, 39 S.Ct. 68, 70 (1918); see *Chicago Record-Herald Co. v. Tribune Ass'n*]. . . . What is protected is the manner of expression, the author's analysis or interpretation of events, the way he structures his material and marshals facts, his choice of words, and the emphasis he gives to particular developments. Thus, the essence of infringement lies not in taking a general theme or in coverage of the reports as events, but in appropriating the "particular expression through similarities of treatment, details, scenes, events and characterization" [*Reyher v. Children's Television Workshop,* 533 F.2d 87, 91 (2nd Circuit, 1976)]. In a parallel manner, the essence or purpose of legitimate journalism is the reporting of objective facts or developments, not the appropriation of the form of expression used by the news source.[24]

According to the appellate court, the *Transcript* did not provide independent analysis or research; it did not solicit comments on the same topics from other financial analysts; and it did not include any criticism, praise, or other reactions by industry officials or investors. "Rather," wrote Judge Mishler "the *Transcript* appropriated almost verbatim the most creative and original aspects of the reports, the financial analyses and predictions, which represent a substantial investment of time, money and labor." The judge concluded by saying that even under a free speech theory, the *Transcript* failed to demonstrate that its use of the Wainwright reports "either was reasonable or pursuant to legitimate news reporting that implicates First Amendment interests."

The U.S. Supreme Court refused to review the appellate court's decision.

Meeropol v. Nizer. Another case which came after enactment of the 1976 copyright law involved a copyright infringement action brought by the sons of Julius and Ethel Rosenberg against Doubleday & Co., publisher of *The Implosion Conspiracy,* Fawcett Publications, Inc., which brought out a paperback version of the book, and the author of the book, Louis Nizer. The Rosenbergs were executed in 1953 after their conviction for conspiracy to transmit information about the atomic bomb to the Soviet Union. Their sons, renamed Michael and Robert Meeropol, alleged that Nizer incorporated into his book substantial portions of copyrighted letters written by their parents without authorization and that this use constituted infringement. They also brought libel and invasion of privacy lawsuits (see Chapter 7). When all counts of the complaint were dismissed against the defendants by the U.S. District Court, the Meeropols appealed. In 1977 the Second Circuit U.S. Court of Appeals affirmed the dismissal of the libel and privacy portion of the complaint. However it reversed and remanded for further proceedings in connection with the copyright infringement allegation.[25]

In the opinion written by Circuit Judge J. Joseph Smith for the three-judge panel, the court disagreed with the lower court's grant of summary judgment which had been given on the basis that there were no genuine issues of fact to be resolved in connection with defendants' fair use defense. Judge Smith wrote:

> Relying on *Rosemont Enterprises, Inc. v. Random House, Inc.* . . ., [the District Court] held that the definition of an historical work for the purpose of the fair use doctrine is a very broad one, and the *The Implosion Conspiracy* fell within this definition [417 F.Supp. 1209]. . . . The fact that the Hughes biography was perhaps not a profound work did not deprive it of the fair use privilege as a book of historical interest. Whether or not an author also has a commercial motive in publishing the work was held irrelevant to the availability of the fair use defense. In *Rosemont,* however, only two direct quotations had been copied. The *Implosion Conspiracy* includes verbatim portions of 28 copyrighted letters. *Rosemont* involved the use of copyrighted statements concerning the actions of a biographical subject, not as here the use of verbatim letters written by the subject. In addition, it appears that the fair use defense was upheld in *Rosemont* at least in part because the court found that the plaintiff there was acting in bad faith seeking to prevent the publication of a legitimate biography of Howard Hughes.
>
> We agree that the mere fact that Nizer's book might be termed a popularized account of the Rosenberg trial lacking substantial scholarship and published for commercial gain, does not, standing alone, deprive Nizer or his publishers of the fair use defense. For a determination whether the fair use defense is applicable on the facts of this case, however, it is relevant whether or not the Rosenberg letters were used primarily for scholarly, historical reasons, or predominantly for commercial exploitation. The purpose and character of the use of the copyrighted material, the nature of the copyrighted work, and amount and substantiality of the work used, and its effect upon the potential market for the copyrighted material are factors which must be evaluated . . . [*Williams & Wilkins Co. v. U.S.,* 487 F.2d 1345, 1353 (Ct. Cl. 1973), *aff'd by an equally divided court,* 420 U.S. 376 (1975) (per curiam)]. If the effect on the market by an infringing work is minimal, for example, far greater use may be privileged than where the market value of the copyrighted material is substantially decreased. Similarly, where use is made of underlying historical facts such use will be entitled to complete freedom but it is otherwise if there is verbatim copying of original, copyrighted material. "The fair use privilege is based on the concept of reasonableness and extensive verbatim copying or paraphrasing of material set down by another can not satisfy that standard" [*Rosemont* . . ., 366 F.2d 310].
>
> A key issue in fair use cases is whether the defendant's work tends to diminish or prejudice the potential sale of plaintiff's work.[26]

The appellate court disagreed with the lower court's holding that Nizer's use of the letters was insubstantial in the sense that the letters did not form a major part of the book. The question, said Judge Smith, should have been left to the trier of fact and appellants should be given the opportunity to introduce evidence on the issues of the purpose of the use of quotations from the letters, and of damages.

The U.S. Supreme Court declined to review the decision.

Harper & Row v. Nation Enterprises. The U.S. Supreme Court agreed in 1984 to review a Second Circuit U.S. Court of Appeals' decision that *The Nation* magazine's use of part of the then-unpublished memoirs of former President Gerald R. Ford did not constitute copyright infringement.[27]

The Nation was accused of infringement by two publishers, Harper & Row and Reader's Digest Association, Inc., owners of publication rights to Ford's memoirs, following publication in its April 3, 1979, issue of a 2500-word article based on a draft of the book which had been obtained by the editor of *The Nation.* The magazine had sought to justify use of some of the material from the manuscript on the basis of the "fair use" doctrine in that the content of the memoirs was "news" and that aspects of the pardon of former President Richard M. Nixon by Ford was "hot news." The U.S. District Court judge for the Southern District of New York disputed the "hot news" claim by pointing out that information about the pardon had previously been made public. Concerning the "fair use" claim, the judge said the article was published for profit; the magazine took what essentially was the heart of the book; and the extensive use of the Nixon pardon material caused an agreement with *Time* magazine and the copyright holders to be aborted, thereby diminishing the value of the copyright. The court therefore ordered *The Nation* to pay $12,500 in damages to the copyright holders.

A three-judge panel of the Second Circuit, by a 2–1 vote, reversed the finding of copyright infringement and the award of damages.[28] In an opinion by Judge Irving Kaufman, the panel ruled that the "paraphrasing of disparate facts" found in the memoirs (with much of the information concerning the pardon having been made public as the result of a U.S. House of Representatives committee hearing) is not an infringement. Furthermore, the panel's majority said that the article contained, at most, 300 words that were copyrightable.

But the U.S. Supreme Court, in a 6–3 decision in 1985, reinstated the $12,500 infringement award, with Justice O'Connor writing the Court's opinion.[29] She termed the article and the act of publishing it "piracy," and pointed out that the unpublished nature of the Ford memoirs tended "to negate a defense of fair use," adding:

> Where an author and publisher have invested extensive resources in creating an original work and are poised to release it to the public, no legitimate aim is served by preempting the right of the first publication.[30]

Although the article may have been newsworthy, as O'Connor indicated, the use of 300 words of direct quotation probably was too much for a "fair use" defense.

Among the dissenters was Justice Brennan who did not believe that the use of 300 words of direct quotation was excessive or inappropriate to *The Nation*'s news reporting purpose. Instead, he feared that the Court's "zealous defense of the copyright owner's prerogative will . . . stifle the broad dissemination of ideas and information copyright is intended to nurture."

CBS v. Roy Export Co. In this case, the U.S. Supreme Court in 1982 let stand a $717,000 jury award against CBS for using clips from several Charlie Chaplin films in a TV program aired shortly after the actor died.[31] The Second Circuit upheld the award because it believed the use of the copyrighted material exceeded fair use, even though there was newsworthy purpose undergirding its use. The jury had believed that the CBS program harmed the marketability of Roy Export's own Chaplin film, *The Gentleman Tramp*. Roy Export owns the Chaplin films copyright.

Zacchini v. Scripps-Howard. The use of a portion of copyrighted material for such purposes as various kinds of criticism, comment, news reporting, teaching, scholarship, or research is not considered an infringement. Sometimes what is done is newsworthy in its entirety. But in those states that recognize a "right of publicity," such as Ohio, neither the fair use defense nor the First Amendment will protect the media if, for example, a performer's *entire* act is televised without the performer's consent. This was the ruling of the U.S. Supreme Court in the "human cannonball" case of *Zacchini v. Scripps-Howard* (1977) (see Chapter 7).[32]

This case involved the videotaping of Hugo Zacchini's entire 15-second act after he had asked a news cameraman for Scripps-Howard Broadcasting Co. not to "film" the act at a county fair. A majority of the Court held that (1) the broadcast of the entire act posed a substantial threat to the economic value of Zacchini's performance; (2) Ohio's decision to provide such protection is no different from the considerations which underlie the patent and copyright laws; and (3) the "right of publicity" does not deprive the public or press of the benefit of the performance as long as the performer is not deprived of the economic benefit of that performance.

Salinger v. Random House, Inc. In 1987 the U.S. Supreme Court decided not to review a Second Circuit U.S. Court of Appeals' decision that literary critic Ian Hamilton's use, in a biography of author J. D. Salinger, of Salinger's unpublished letters is not fair use. The Second Circuit three-judge panel overturned a U.S. District Court's denial of Salinger's request for an injunction restraining publication of the biography.[33]

Hamilton and his publisher, Random House, had told the Supreme Court that the Second Circuit's decision left biographers and historians in a "double bind."[34] On the one hand, "their craft requires them to pursue primary sources, such as unpublished letters, because such documents provide unique insights into the experiences, attitudes, and emotions of their subjects." On the other hand, the Court was told that "the Second Circuit's opinion tells biographers that if, like Ian Hamilton, they discover through their own diligence materials that have not been published generally, they are not at liberty to quote or convey any of the richness of those materials without facing the risk—perhaps the likelihood—of an injunction."[35]

In reaching its decision, the Second Circuit noted the significant amount of the copyrighted expression used in the biography, the unpublished nature of the letters, and the effect Hamilton's use of the letters could have on their potential market.[36]

The panel said that biographers could still use the factual content of letters, but that they had no right to copy the accuracy or the vividness of the letter writer's expression.

The biographer had quoted large portions of unpublished letters donated by their recipients to libraries. When Salinger discovered this, he registered the letters for copyright protection and objected to publication until all of his unpublished materials were deleted. Hamilton then excised many of the direct quotations and paraphrased them. Still dissatisfied, Salinger sued for infringement.

Pacific & Southern Co. v. Duncan. The Supreme Court in 1985 also let stand a ruling that a television "clipping" service violated an Atlanta, Georgia, television station's copyright by videotaping and selling copies of broadcast news stories without station WXIA-TV's permission.[37]

The U.S. Court of Appeals for the Eleventh Circuit had enjoined TV News Clip from copying WXIA-TV stories after rejecting the clipping service's claims that broadcasters were not entitled to unlimited control over news and that such copying was "fair use." A U.S. District Court had refused to issue an injunction.

The copying said the Circuit Court, is not fair use because "profit is . . . [the service's] primary motive" and the service is neither productive nor creative.[38]

Hustler Magazine v. Moral Majority. No infringement was found by a three-judge panel of the Ninth Circuit U.S. Court of Appeals in the Rev. Jerry Falwell's use of a parody advertisement in *Hustler* magazine—the same advertisement that led Falwell to sue the magazine and publisher Larry Flynt for libel and invasion of privacy (see Chapter 7).[39] The 2–1 panel decision in 1986 was that the mailing of more than a million copies of the advertisement, in an effort that raised nearly $1 million to finance Falwell's suit against Flynt and the magazine, constituted fair use. Because the parody was only one page of the 154-page magazine, the court believed that the effect of Falwell's use on the marketability of back issues of that magazine would be inconsequential.

Falwell's lawsuit resulted from publication on the inside front cover of the November 1983 issue of a parody of a Campari Liqueur advertisement. In the real Compari ads, celebrities spoke of their "first time," ostensibly meaning their first taste of the liqueur. But in *Hustler's* parody, Falwell's picture was used along with the text of a fictitious interview in which Falwell describes an incestuous relationship with his mother. At the bottom of the advertisement was this disclaimer: "Ad Parody—Not To Be Taken Seriously," and it was listed in the table of contents as "Fiction; Ad and Personality Parody."[40]

The Circuit Court panel also distinguished between copyrighted material that is "creative" and material that is "informational." The law, said the panel, generally recognizes a greater need to disseminate factual information than to disseminate works of fiction—and *Hustler*'s parody was fiction.

Unfair Competition

Copyright law offers only limited protection to newsgathering organizations which go to considerable expense to gather and disseminate news. The facts pertaining to a news event cannot be copyrighted; only the style in which the facts are "cast." A clever "pirate," however, can copy information gleaned from a competitor, rewrite it, and perhaps escape liability under copyright law. Because of this possibility, and for other reasons, the tort of unfair competition developed. As described by Paul W. Sullivan of the University of Evansville:

> News was to be part of the public domain, but newsgathering offered an opportunity for protection through the English doctrine of "unfair competition." . . . The highly interpretive principle of unfair competition is found in the common law under the category of "Trade-Marks, Trade-Names, and Unfair Competition. . . ."
>
> Unfair competition is a legal wrong for which the courts offer a remedy such as an injunction. The basis for the intervention of a court of equity and the granting of injunctive relief to restrain unfair competition is either "subterfuge, piracy, wrongdoing, or unfair tactics of the competitor." Added to this definition in recent years is "misappropriation."
>
> Unfair competition is a tort governed by the law of the state in which it occurs, . . . and the basis for the common law principle stems from a ruling by the U.S. Supreme Court in the 1918 case of *International News Service [INS] v. Associated Press.*[41] This case has played a part in the decisions of hundreds of other cases made in courts all over the country from 1919 to the present. It has seldom been questioned, never overturned, and was reaffirmed by the Supreme Court in the 1973 case of *Goldstein v. California. INS* is the only case of news piracy ever to have been decided by the Supreme Court on the particulars of that specific problem. Other unfair competition cases that have been heard by the high bench were either limited to procedural errors and technicalities or dealt with different details.[42]

INS v. AP. The U.S. Supreme Court affirmed the protection for news as "quasi-property" against unfair competition in *INS v. AP.*[43] It did so after the Associated Press (AP) had accused the International News Service (INS) of "pirating" news from its wire service for redistribution to INS customers. INS did not deny taking the AP stories from newspapers or from AP bulletin boards since, at the time, it had no way of obtaining news from allied countries during the early days of World War I. The reason: those countries had barred INS reporters because of pro-German editorials and news in Hearst-owned newspapers (William Randolph Hearst was the owner of INS).

INS argued that news is public property once it has happened and that no one can have any property rights in news. Furthermore, news facts can not be copyrighted. The U.S. District Court held for INS. The U.S. Court of Appeals reversed, holding that AP was entitled to an injunction to restrain unfair competition, and the Supreme Court affirmed issuance of the injunction.

Concerning the copyright of news story facts, Justice Mahlon Pitney said for the Supreme Court majority:

> . . . [T]he news element — the information respecting current events contained in the literary production — is not the creation of the writer, but is a report of matters that ordinarily are *public juris;* it is the history of the day. It is not to be supposed that the framers of the Constitution . . . intended to confer upon one who might happen to be the first to report a historic event the exclusive right for any period to spread the knowledge of it.

The Court agreed that news, at least in the circumstances of this case, could be regarded as "quasi" property because of AP's elaborate organization and expenditure of money to acquire and transmit it in exchange for monetary payments from AP members. The Court rejected INS's contention that once the AP stories were transmitted to members, the Associated Press no longer could control the use made of them. As Pitney said:

> The right of the purchaser of a single newspaper to spread knowledge of its contents gratuitously, for any legitimate purpose not unreasonably interfering with complainant's right to make merchandise of it, may be admitted; but to transmit that news for commercial use, in competition with complainant — which is what defendant has done and seeks to justify — is a very different matter. In doing this defendant, by its very act, admits that it is taking material that has been acquired by complainant as a result of organization and the expenditure of labor, skill, and money, and which is salable by complainant for money, and that defendant in appropriating it and selling it as its own is endeavoring to reap where it has not sown, and by disposing of it to newspapers that are competitors of complainant's members is appropriating to itself the harvest of those who have sown. . . . The transaction speaks for itself, and a court of equity ought not to hesitate long in characterizing it as unfair competition in business.

Justice Brandeis wrote the lone dissent, principally because he did not believe that news should be considered as property. "The general rule of law," he said, "is that the noblest of human productions — knowledge, truths ascertained, conceptions, and ideas — become, after voluntary communication to others, free as the air to common use."

Pottstown Daily News Publishing Co. v. Pottstown Broadcasting Co. In a later unfair-competition case, an injunction was granted against radio station WPAZ in Pottstown, Pennsylvania, after the *Pottstown Mercury* complained about the use of its news stories by the station without permission or authorization. The issuance of an injunction was upheld in 1963 by the Pennsylvania Supreme Court.[44]

In both the Pottstown case and the one involving INS and AP, two elements were present: competition between the parties in the lawsuits, and attempts by the defendants to pass off as their own the goods, business, or "property" of the plaintiffs. In the absence of these factors, some courts have held that no unfair competition exists.[45]

The essence of unfair competition between news organizations involving "pirating" of news can be summarized as "bodily appropriation of a statement of fact or a news article, with or without rewriting, but without independent investigation or expense."[46] The critical factor: independent investigation.

Cable Television and Copyright

A complex area of copyright law involves cable-casting. Prior to passage of the 1976 Act, the U.S. Supreme Court had ruled that cable television did not infringe on copyright when it retransmitted a copyrighted over-the-air broadcast. The Court, in a 5–1 decision in 1968, reversed the Second Circuit U.S. Court of Appeals.

In giving the Court's opinion in *Fortnightly Corporation v. United Artists Television, Inc.*[47] Justice Stewart said that cable television serves a function different from over-the-air broadcasting. The latter involves the production and selection of programs. CATV simply retransmits such programs once they have been released to the public without any editing being required. By this logic the Court got around Section 1 of the 1909 Act which gave the copyright owner the exclusive right to control the "public performances" of his work. Because cable systems do not "perform" the programs they receive and carry, they were deemed comparable to a television viewer who receives a copyrighted performance from over-the-air broadcasters. Consequently, any CATV use of such over-the-air copyrighted broadcasts did not make that CATV operator an infringer.

Justice Fortas dissented, partly because he believed the meaning of "perform" was vague. He also thought the Court had indulged in an oversimplification of the function served by CATV, especially when it picks up a signal and carries it beyond the area normally served by the broadcaster of that signal.[48]

The question of infringement when CATV imports distant signals arose in *Teleprompter Corp. v. CBS* and *CBS v. Teleprompter Corp.* (1974).[49] A majority of the Supreme Court held that importation of such signals did not constitute a performance; therefore, a CATV system did not lose its status as a nonperformer or nonbroadcaster as a result of such importations.

In one of the two cases, CBS contended that there were three other differences between *Fortnightly* and the cases then being reviewed. These included:

1. Many CATV systems were originating programs, thereby functioning the same way as over-the-air broadcasters.
2. Teleprompter Corp. sold advertising time on its CATV operations thereby gaining commercially by picking up over-the-air broadcast signals and,

via cable and/or microwave relay towers, retransmitting them to the homes of CATV subscribers.

3. There were interconnections between CATV systems so that one system could relay a program to another system and vice versa, just as network television could relay programs to affiliates and receive material from those stations. Therefore, CBS contended, CATV had crossed over the line and was functioning as a broadcaster.

In discussing these contentions, Justice Stewart, who again gave the opinion of the Court, said:

> The copyright significance of each of these functions—program origination, sale of commercials, and interconnection—suffers from the same logical flaw: in none of these operations is there any nexus with the defendants' reception and rechanneling of the broadcasters' copyrighted materials.

What Stewart meant is that none of CBS's copyrighted material was involved in CATV's origination of programs. Such materials were not transmitted via the systems' interconnections, and advertising was not sold on the basis of the copyrighted programs. Concerning importation of distant signals, the copyright holder argued that if CATV systems are allowed to import and rechannel programs broadcast in other cities, they will dilute or diminish the profitability of later syndication of such programs since viewer appeal diminishes with successive showings in the same market area.

Stewart responded by noting that an advertiser typically pays the broadcasters a fee for each transmission based on an estimate of the number of viewers who will watch a given program. "By extending the range of viewability of a broadcast program," he said, "CATV systems thus do not interfere in any traditional sense with the copyright holders' means of extracting recompense for their creativity or labor." Then in recognition of an anachronistic law, Stewart made this observation:

> These shifts in current business and commercial relationships, while of significance with respect to the organization and growth of the communications industry, simply cannot be controlled by means of litigation based on copyright legislation enacted more than half a century ago, when neither broadcast television nor CATV was yet conceived. Detailed regulation of these relationships, and any ultimate resolution of the many sensitive and important problems in this field, must be left to Congress.

In dissenting, Justice Douglas verbally whiplashed CATV's practice of importing distant signals, saying:

> A CATV that builds an antenna to pick up telecasts in Area B and then transmits it by cable to Area A is *reproducing* the copyright but by theft.
> That is not "encouragement to the production of literary (artistic) works of lasting benefit to the work" that we extolled in *Mazer v. Stein,* 347 U.S. 201, 74 S.Ct. 460, 98 L.Ed. 630. . . .

We are advised by an *amicus* brief of the Motion Picture Association that films from TV telecasts are being imported by CATV into their own markets in competition with the same pictures licensed to TV stations in the area into which the CATV—a nonpaying pirate of the films—imports them. It would be difficult to imagine a more flagrant violation of the Copyright Act. Since the Copyright Act is our only guide to law and justice in this case, it is difficult to see why CATV systems are free of copyright license fees, when they import programs from distant stations and transmit them to their paying customers in a distant market. That result reads the Copyright Act out of existence for CATV.

Compulsory Licensing System. The 1976 Act provides for the payment, under a compulsory licensing system, of certain royalties for the secondary transmission of copyrighted works on cable television systems. The amounts are to be paid to the Register of Copyrights for later distribution to copyright owners by a five-member Copyright Royalty Tribunal (CRT). Appointed by the President, this tribunal determines if certain copyright royalty rates, as established by the 1976 law, are reasonable and, if not, adjusts them. It also determines the distribution of certain statutory royalty fees deposited with the Register of Copyrights.

Compulsory licensing—which means that a copyrighted work can be used without permission as long as certain procedures are followed and royalty fees are paid at stated intervals—is limited to the retransmission of distant non-network programming. All cable systems must make royalty payments.

Compulsory fees paid into the fund stood at about $40 million in 1984. When CRT allocated funds in 1983, various court tests were instituted by dissatisfied claimants, including the National Association of Broadcasters, but in the most recent test, the Second Circuit U.S. Court of Appeals upheld the following CRT distributions: from the basic fund, 67.1 percent to program suppliers, 16.35 percent to sports groups, 5.2 percent to public television, 5 percent to commercial television, 4.5 percent to music claimants, and the remaining 1.85 percent to several other claimants.

The CRT also had required cable systems to pay 3.75 percent of their gross receipts from basic services for each distant signal they added, plus a surcharge for the retransmission of signals formerly subject to the blackout rule. The CRT allocated 95 percent of this fund to program suppliers and nothing to broadcasters. It was this action that led to NAB's challenge.

Controversy over the CRT's allocations and its increase of the rates paid by cable operators led to efforts in 1984 by the chairman of the House Copyright Subcommittee, Congressman Robert Kastenmeier of Wisconsin, to obtain passage of an omnibus copyright bill. Included in the legislative package was relief for some cable operators from the 3.75 percent rate set by the CRT. But attempts to amend the copyright law generated intense lobbying efforts by various special interests groups, such as Hollywood movie producers, broadcasters, the consumer electronics industry, cable operators, and others. Hence, no action was taken.

One of the provisions in Kastenmeier's proposed legislation would have allowed home videotaping of copyrighted TV programs without copyright infringement.

Noncommercial Home Videotaping

In a case of first impression, a U.S. District Court for the Central District of California ruled that the private, noncommercial home-use recording of copyrighted television programs broadcast over the public airwaves does not violate either the 1909 or 1976 Copyright Acts. Such copying is permissible fair use.

The ruling in 1979 came in *Universal City Studios v. Sony Corporation of America*[50] following a five-week trial and three years of litigation. The judge denied plaintiffs' motion for injunctive and declaratory relief and monetary damages.

The plaintiffs, Universal City Studios, Inc. and Walt Disney Productions, Inc., produce and copyright audiovisual materials, some of which are sold for telecast over public airwaves. Sony manufactures and distributes equipment that can record telecasts off-the-air for later viewing.

A Ninth Circuit U.S. Court of Appeals three-judge panel reversed the lower court ruling in 1981, holding that off-air recording for private home use is an illegal infringement.[51] An appeal was taken to the U.S. Supreme Court.

In 1984 the Court, in a 5–4 decision, reversed the Circuit Court panel with Justice Stevens saying for the majority that the sale of video recorders to the general public for noncommercial home use is not a contributory infringement of copyright. Stevens referred to such recordings as "private, noncommercial time-shifting in the home," and said that the plaintiffs had failed to demonstrate that "time-shifting would cause any likelihood of non-minimal harm to the potential market for, or the value of, their copyrighted works."[52]

Stevens added that Congress may have to take a fresh look at this new technology, but that it is not the Court's job "to apply laws that have not yet been written."

Justice Blackmun, joined by Justices Marshall, Powell and Rehnquist, dissented. Such taping of a copyrighted TV program is an infringement if the fair use exemption does not apply, Blackmun contended. As for time-shifting, it could raise the potential for substantial harm, Blackmun wrote, adding that evidence had been presented that demonstrates a substantial adverse effect upon the potential market for copyrighted audiovisual material as a result of "time-shifting." He continued:

> It is my view that the Court's approach alters dramatically the doctrines of fair use and contributory infringement as they have been developed by Congress and the courts.[53]

The decision was a narrow one. It applies only to home videotaping, not to audiotapes, and results from Congress not including videotaping in the 1976 Act.

Off-Air Videotaping for Educational Uses

The Copyright Act of 1976 does not mention off-air videotaping of programs for educational uses. As a consequence, different positions have emerged as to off-air taping and the application of "fair use" to such activity. Educators generally claim that the fair use section permits some taping of copyrighted material, and that the section is applicable to both news and non-news programs. But the Association of Media Producers took the position that the fair use doctrine did not apply to off-air taping, in whole or in part, of copyrighted material distributed to the educational market or when such educational distribution is contemplated by the copyright holder.[54]

After considerable efforts at compromise, the broadcast industry and education groups agreed in 1982 on guidelines that allow limited classroom use of TV programs without infringing upon the rights of performers, writers, and others who "own" the video material. The agreement does not change copyright law, but the National Education Association pointed out that courts are likely to take the guidelines into account because they have been ratified by educators and broadcasters and published by Congress as an expression of congressional intent.

Photocopying

In 1972 a trial judge ruled in *Williams & Wilkins Co. v. U.S.*[55] that the making of single photocopies of magazine articles was sufficient to incur liability because, contrary to what the defendant argued, such "copying" met the definition of "publishing." "Publishing," said the judge, "means disseminating to others, which defendant's libraries [National Institutes of Health and the National Library of Medicine] clearly did when they distributed photocopies to requesters and users." As the judge observed, courts had held "that duplication of a copyrighted work, even to make a single copy, can constitute infringement."

The ruling—that photocopying of an entire article from a journal, even though not for commercial exploitation, constituted an unfair use and therefore infringed upon the copyright—was submitted to the full U.S. Court of Claims since such a decision had important ramifications for libraries, researchers, students, teachers, and so forth, in light of the widespread use of photocopying or xerography.

The full court, by a 4–3 vote, reversed the trial court thereby narrowly vindicating the government's position that the photocopying in question constituted fair use. But the 4–3 decision was limited to photocopying being done by government medical-type libraries. It was not applicable to "dissimilar systems or uses of copyrighted materials by other institutions or enterprises," or in other fields, or as applied to items other than journal articles, or with other significant variables.[56] Thus, considerable uncertainty remained as the residue of *Williams & Wilkins Co.,* particularly since the 1909 Act, as amended, made no mention of the fast-growing technology associated with photocopying. The Supreme Court did nothing to resolve the uncertainty when, by a vote of 4–4, it affirmed in a per curiam decision the U.S. Court of Claims' action and said the entire issue was "preeminently a problem for Congress."[57]

Guidelines for Educational Institutions. In the 1976 Act Congress included in the fair use section reproduction of copyrighted works for teaching purposes (including multiple copies for classroom use), and for other purposes (such as scholarship and research). Section 108 expanded somewhat on how far libraries and archives could go in reproducing copyrighted material. But representatives of teacher and library groups complained that the fair use defense for reproducing certain material was too vague. As a consequence, an ad hoc committee on Copyright Law Revision was established representing some forty education associations. This group hammered out photocopying guidelines with representatives of the Authors League of America and the Association of American Publishers, Inc. The agreement in 1976 became a part of the legislative history of the copyright law and can aid a court in determining congressional intent.[58]

Sound Recordings

The 1976 law retains provisions added to the copyright law in 1972 which protects against the unauthorized duplication of sound recordings. Prior to this amendment, sound recordings were not protected by federal legislation. Once a sound recording was "published" it presumably fell into the public domain. This was part of the rationale put forth in *Goldstein v. California,*[59] in which it was argued that the California penal code (Section 653h), prohibiting unauthorized duplication of sound recordings (commonly referred to as "record piracy"), was invalid. Appellants claimed that the state law conflicted with the U.S. Constitution and the 1909 Act.

Prior to the *Goldstein* ruling by the U.S. Supreme Court, state and federal courts generally had classified sound recordings as unpublished works on the theory that they were not copies of musical compositions. As unpublished works, they could be protected by state law or common law. The Supreme Court held that since sound recordings were not a part of the 1909 Act at the time appellants were accused of violating the California statute, states could not protect those works not specifically enumerated. The new law specifically includes "sound recordings."

In connection with recording rights in music, the new law makes a number of changes, but retains compulsory licensing for the recording of music. Among the changes, the 1976 Act raises the statutory royalty from 2 cents to 2¾ cents or ½ cent per minute of playing time, whichever amount is larger. The rate was subject to review by the Copyright Royalty Tribunal in 1980 and at 10-year intervals thereafter. The so-called jukeboxes, which were exempt from royalty payments under the 1909 Act, lost that exemption under the new law. An $8 per box annual compulsory license fee is required, with periodic review by the Royalty Tribunal. State statutes and common law are not preempted in connection with sound recordings fixed before February 15, 1972. Such laws will be preempted in the year 2047.

Piracy

An act that sharply increased criminal penalties for persons convicted of pirating and counterfeiting records, tapes, and films was signed into law in 1982 by President Reagan. P.L. 97–180 increases the maximum fines and imprisonment terms from $25,000 and two years to $250,000 and five years. Additionally, first-time offenders could be subject to the maximum penalty. The penalties were increased because, according to the Senate Judiciary Committee, pirating and counterfeiting of audio and audiovisual products has grown rapidly in recent years, and existing penalties were regarded as an "insignificant cost of doing business" by criminals involved in such activities.

The Motion Picture Association of America estimated that nearly $700 million a year is stolen from the motion picture industry by "pirates." Videotapes of motion pictures are made from intercepted TV signals and sold commercially around the world. Thriving businesses in such illegal videotaping exist in the United States, the Philippines, Hong Kong and many other places. The MPAA offers a $15,000 reward for information leading to the conviction of pirates.

In addition, the cable TV industry loses an estimated $1.4 billion annually through various forms of thievery.[60] Pay-TV signals sent from ground stations to satellites, or from satellites to ground stations, are illegally intercepted as are signals sent between ground stations. Even when the signals are coded so that TV sets must be equipped with decoders, such decoders or converters can be purchased and used to illegally intercept such copyrighted programs. In addition, cable TV services can be intercepted by illegally tapping into the cables strung from telephone poles.

Many cable systems have mounted advertising campaigns in an attempt to combat piracy. They have offered amnesty periods during which illegal subscribers can convert their reception system into legal ones. In San Diego, for example, a three-month advertising campaign by Cox Cable resulted in the surrender of 14,000 illegal converters and a gain, on an annual basis, of $1.5 million in new-pay subscribers.[61]

New York enacted legislation in 1983 that permits cable operators to seek damages and injunctive relief against persons who knowingly tap into cable service without paying for it.[62] The law also prohibits the sale or distribution of converters or descrambling equipment to anyone other than a telecommunications operator.

Piracy is a major challenge in communication law and technology, and it creates serious problems in areas related to telecommunications. Experts in the computer industry believe that a tremendous amount of piracy is occurring there. One of the problems, however, is uncertainty concerning what is or is not protected by copyright law. For example, Franklin Computer Corporation acknowledged that it had copied 14 operating system programs found in the Apple IIe. When sued by Apple Computer, Inc., Franklin contended that a program embodied in computer hardware was part of the machine and therefore not copyrightable. Franklin won at the U.S. District Court level, but lost when a three-judge panel of the U.S. Court of Appeals for the Third Circuit ruled that programs that control the flow of information through computers can be copyrighted.[63]

In its August 30, 1983, decision, the unanimous panel rejected Franklin's contention that the programs were indistinguishable from the concept of the computer system itself. In stating that the "medium is not the message," the panel took the position that Apple does not seek to copyright the method by which computers are instructed, only the instructions.

Franklin announced it would appeal, but subsequently settled out of court by agreeing to pay Apple corporation $2.5 million in damages.

Subsequently, a new law went into effect that provides 10-year protection to the makers of microchips or semi-conductors of original design. Infringers face a $250,000 penalty for every copyrighted circuit design reproduced without permission. The first registrations of these original designs took place in January 1985, when Intel and Harris Corporations and Motorola, Inc., registered designs with the U.S. Copyright Office.

In 1986, the Third Circuit U.S. Court of Appeals ruled that copyright protection of a computer program extends beyond the program's literal code to its structure, sequence, and organization. Therefore, liability for infringement may be based on a finding of substantial similarity between structures of copyrighted and challenged programs.[64]

Video games also have been ruled copyrightable by the Seventh Circuit U.S. Court of Appeals after Midway Manufacturing, which owns the copyright to Pac-Man, brought suit to prevent Artic International, Inc., from distributing a kit that speeds up the game's action. The Supreme Court denied review.[65]

Midway Manufacturing is a subsidiary of Bally Manufacturing Corporation, which holds the copyright to a number of popular electronic games, including Pac-Man. Bally brought more than 60 lawsuits in 1981 and 1982 against firms it claimed were infringing on the copyright to these games.

The copyright problems associated with new technology were summarized by the Registrar of Copyrights, David Ladd, in a 1984 speech. Ladd said, in part:

> Nowadays a vast new array of technological innovations continues to test our understanding of authorship and copyright and our will to vindicate their values. Authors' and publishers' rights become difficult to enforce as we move away from the print culture and confront a surge of space-age apparatus that enables the broad-based dissemination and simultaneous reception by huge audiences of almost unimaginable quantities of creative works.
>
> In the copyright world there is a prevailing mood of dread that brilliant technologies will overwhelm authorship and copyright. There is danger. But the greater danger is that of despairing, and accepting that result as inevitable. Or of doing nothing to avert it.[66]

Congressional enactment of 10-year protection for computer software designs and stiffer penalties for "pirates"; the first registration of software designs; plus court decisions recognizing copyright protection for video games, computer software, and other technological developments show that something is being done to protect some of the outpourings of human ingenuity.

But not all copyright problems are the result of new technology. Take, for example, a case involving ownership of rights to advertisements created by a newspaper's employees. Do the advertisers who pay for the advertisements own the rights, or do the newspapers?

A Fourth Circuit U.S. Court of Appeals panel ruled 2–1 that newspapers own the rights absent any written agreements.[67]

The panel, in its 1987 ruling, decided that the Copyright Act of 1976 changed the law, which under the 1909 Copyright Act gave ownership of the ads to the advertisers as part of the "work for hire" doctrine.

The decision upheld the ruling of a U.S. District Court following a dispute between two newspapers in Shallotte, N.C. One of the papers, the *Brunswick Free Press*, did not have the capacity to produce its own ads so it copied ads prepared by a competing newspaper, the *Brunswick Beacon*, after deleting the copyright notice.[68]

In dissent, Judge Kenneth K. Hall said that the advertisers who initiated and paid for the ads retain the right to control their use. Congress, he said, did not intend to keep advertisers from reusing at their discretion ads they had paid to have created.

Trademarks, Patents

A trademark is different from copyright in that it protects a sign or brand used in connection with a service or the manufacture or distribution of a particular product. Copyright protects a particular literary style or, in the case of computer software, a particular design by which to "message" information.

A public notice of patent or of trademark must be given, such as a trademark with the words "Registered in the U.S. Patent and Trademark Office," or the symbol ® by the trademark. This notice is required by the Lanham Act as a condition for recovery of damages.

Trademarks are words that can become powerful symbols. The more powerful they are, the more valuable they are. They are protected by the federal trademark statute called the Lanham Act (15 U.S.C. 1125).

One writer described trademarks and their value in this way:

A trademark (brand name) is an indication of the commercial origin of goods. Rights in and to a trademark are dependent on only two things: (1) priority of adoption and use, and (2) continuous occupancy in the marketplace. A trademark serves three basic functions: First, it serves as a base of identification of origin, distinguishing one manufacturer's product from those of competitors. Second, it serves as a guarantee of the consistency of the nature, quality and characteristics of the goods. Third, it serves as an advertising symbol. A trademark should be a good salesman. Without the right to advertise and display the mark, the right to use it would be of little or no value.[69]

Trademarks abound in our commercialized world. Advertisers spend millions of dollars each year to promote their trademarks. Examples are: Coke and Coca-Cola, Ritz, Scrabble, Tabasco, Chevrolet, Ford, Zenith, Dairy Queen, Palmolive, Listerine, *The New York Times,* Babe Ruth candy bar, Eversharp, and on and on and on. . . .

Trademarks go back a long time. As pointed out by Attorney Julius R. Lunsford, Jr., *Colgate* dates from 1806, *Vaseline* from 1879, and *Coca-Cola* from 1886.[70] The guilds during the Middle Ages used them, and there is evidence of them in ancient times.

These marks can be lost by abandonment, whether intentional or not, and by the failure of the trademark owner to take affirmative action to make sure the trademark does not become the common or generic name of the product.[71] Thus, words like aspirin, cellophane, thermos, and escalator have become generic or common words that need not be capitalized when used in publications. In the case of *escalator,* the Otis Elevator Company hurt itself in a trademark case by having used in some of its advertisement a reference to "safe, efficient, economical . . . escalator service." Failure of the company to capitalize the very word that it had registered was deemed proof that the word had become the name of the article. Thus, the registration, issued in 1900, was cancelled in 1950.[72]

An example of affirmative action is afforded by the Coca-Cola Company which began a program in the 1940s and continues to the present. It began by placing advertisements in trade journals to distinguish between a generic meaning of coke and the soft drink: ". . . coke burns out but Coke refreshes."[73] If a publication inadvertently refers to a "coke party"—meaning a party where soft drinks are served—and doesn't capitalize Coke, the company will send a politely worded reminder to that publication that Coke is a registered trademark name.

If a publication or journalist is in doubt whether a word is protected by trademark, the United States Trademark Association can be contacted or reference books can be consulted.[74]

SUMMARY

The Copyright Act of 1976, as with previous copyright laws, provides a monopoly for the creators of literary, dramatic, musical, artistic, and other kinds of intellectual works. Except for "fair use"—which has become a statutory part of the law rather than the creation of the judiciary—the copyright holder has the exclusive right to determine how or when the work he has created will be used or reproduced. The 1976 law does away with common law or state law for works created after January 1, 1978. It provides protection for works from the moment of their creation. The rights to such works are presumed to be owned by the creators who must register the works before seeking judicial remedy against an infringer. For works created after January 1, 1978, copyright protection is provided during the life of the author or creator plus 50 years.

Seven categories of original works can be protected: literary; musical; dramatic; pantomimes and choregraphic; pictorial, graphic, and sculptural; motion pictures and other audiovisual works; and sound recordings.

Fair use takes into consideration four factors:

1. Purpose and character of the use of copyrighted work (such as whether the use is of a commercial nature or for nonprofit educational purposes).
2. The nature of the copyrighted work.
3. The amount of the copyrighted work used in relation to the whole (such that one line from a short poem might be protected whereas the use of one line or one paragraph from a longer work might constitute fair use).

4. The effect of the use upon the potential market or value of the copyrighted work.

The use of a portion of copyrighted material for such purposes as criticism, comment, news reporting, teaching, scholarship, or research is not considered an infringement.

In connection with copyright or unfair competition, it should be noted that news facts cannot be copyrighted; only the style by which the facts are cast into story form. However, the U.S. Supreme Court ruled in *INS v. AP* that the collection and dissemination of news can be protected as "quasi-property" under common law against unfair competition. The critical factor in determining whether there has been "a piracy" or other forms of unfair competition in newsgathering and reporting is whether an independent investigation was made.

Generally three major factors are considered in connection with infringement: originality of the copyrighted work; proof of access to the copyrighted work; and/or similarity between the works being compared. Willful infringement can cost up to $50,000 in damages, plus costs and attorney's fees. Statutory damages of up to $10,000 can be awarded in lieu of actual damages. Under the criminal provisions of the law a first offender can be fined up to $25,000 and sentenced to two years in prison.

The omission of copyright notice, or an incorrect notice, does not result in forfeiture of copyright protection. Only "reasonable" notice must be given.

Cable television stations are subject to a compulsory licensing system whereby they pay certain moneys to the Copyright Royalty Tribunal for programs "imported" into their market. In this way, the cable operators can use copyrighted material without first getting the copyright holder's permission.

New technologies have caused considerable consternation among lawmakers and copyright holders. Videotaping for home use, according to a Supreme Court 5–4 decision in 1984, is not a copyright infringement and those who sell such equipment, such as the Betamax by Sony Corporation, are not in violation of copyright law. Certain off-air videotaping for educational purposes also is allowed, without infringement occurring, under an agreement between audiovisual producers and educators.

Piracy of records, tapes, and motion pictures is a major problem facing producers of these copyrighted materials and Congress passed a law in 1982 that sharply increases the penalty for piracy.

New technology and its impact on copyright can be seen in the Third Circuit's decision that Apple IIe computer software is copyrightable and by passage of a law that affords 10-year protection to original software designs.

Trademarks are different from copyright. They protect a product name or sign, or a company's service. Like patents, they must be registered with the U.S. Patent and Trademark Office and the product or service must carry public notice of the trademark or patent for damages to be recoverable.

Trademarks can be lost through abandonment or the failure of a company to take affirmative action to prevent the word or words from becoming a common or generic name.

QUESTIONS IN REVIEW

1. The Copyright Act of 1976 provides the creator of copyrightable material with protection for what period of time?
2. Even though the owner of copyrighted material is given a "monopoly" concerning the use that can be made of it, there are exceptions. These exceptions are known as the _____ doctrine, as provided for in Section 106 of the new law.
3. Ordinarily a news organization can avoid liability for unfair competition by showing that it conducted an _____ in gathering the information.
4. What three major factors often are considered in determinations of infringement?
5. What action has Congress taken to deal with the pirating or counterfeiting of records, tapes and motion pictures?
6. If names like Coca-Cola, Coke, Vaseline or Anacin are used in a news story, they must be _____.
7. Trademarks do what?

ANSWERS

1. Life plus 50 years.
2. Fair use.
3. Independent investigation.
4. (1) Originality of copyrighted work; (2) proof of access to copyrighted work; and/or (3) similarity between the works being compared.
5. It passed a law in 1982 that increases the fines and imprisonment terms for such a crime to $250,000 and five years.
6. Capitalized.
7. Trademarks protect a sign or brand used in connection with a product or service. If the latter, they may be called "servicemarks."

ENDNOTES

1. In RCA Manufacturing Co. v. Whiteman, 114 F.2d 86, 88 (2d Circuit, 1940), Judge Learned Hand said, "Copyright in any form, whether statutory or at common law, is a monopoly; it consists only in the power to prevent others from reproducing the copyrighted work."
2. 17 U.S.C. 101–118, Pub.L. 94-553, 90 Stat. 2541.
3. Ideas can be protected on the theory that they are literary "property"—the same basis on which an advertising slogan can be protected. However, such protection usually requires that the idea be both "concrete" and "novel," although just what constitutes these qualities is subject to uncertainty. See, for example, Melville B. Nimmer, *Nimmer on Copyright,* Vol. 2 (New York: Matthew Bender & Co., 1973), p. 749.
4. "The Nuts and Bolts of Copyright," Circular R1 (Washington, D.C.: U.S. Government Printing Office), January 1980, p.4.
5. Senta Marie Runge v. Joyce Lee and Joyce Lee Cosmetics, Inc., 441 F.2d 579 (1971).
6. Doran v. Sunset House Dist. Corp., 197 F.Supp. 940, 944 (Southern District of California, 1961); affirmed, 304 F.2d 251 (9th Circuit, 1962).
7. Lanny R. Holbrook, "Copyright Infringement and Fair Use," *University of Cincinnati Law Review,* Vol. 40, No. 3 (1971), p. 539.
8. Ibid., pp. 539–40.

9. Universal Pictures Co., Inc. v. Harold Lloyd Corp., 162 F.2d 354, 360 (1947). Quote from C.J.S. Section 34, p. 176.
10. Photographs need not be individually copyrighted. Instead, the copyright owner can put together a collection of prints, photograph them, and send two copies of the "master" photograph to Register of Copyrights.
11. Dellar v. Samuel Goldwyn, Inc., 104 F.2d 661, 662 (1939).
12. Report No. 94-1476, "Copyright Law Revision," 94th Cong, 2d Sess., September 3, 1976, p. 66.
13. Folsom v. Marsh, 9 Fed. Cas. 342 (C.C.D. Mass.) (No. 4901).
14. Kent H. Benjamin, "The Fair Use Doctrine from Its Inception to Public Law 94-553," a paper presented to the Law Division, Association for Education in Journalism annual convention, in Madison, Wisconsin, August 23-27, 1977, p. 5 (footnotes omitted).
15. Chicago Record-Herald Co. v. Tribune Association, 275 F. 797 (7th Circuit, 1921).
16. Benjamin, "The Fair Use," p. 9.
17. Conde Nast Publications, Inc. v. Vogue School of Fashion Modeling, Inc., 105 F. Supp. 325, 333 (District of Columbia, 1952).
18. MacDonald v. Du Maurier, 75 F.Supp. 655 (S.D.N.Y., 1948).
19. Rosemont Enterprises, Inc. v. Random House, Inc., 256 F.Supp. 55 (Southern District of New York, 1966).
20. 366 F.2d 303 (2d Circuit, 1966); cert. denied, 385 U.S. 1009, 97 S.Ct. 714, 17 L.Ed.2d 546 (1967).
21. Time, Inc. v. Bernard Geis Associates, 293 F.Supp. 130 (Southern District of New York, 1968).
22. Wainwright Securities, Inc. v. Wall Street Transcript Corp. et al., 2 *Med.L.Rptr.* 2153, August 2, 1977.
23. Melville B. Nimmer, "Does Copyright Abridge the First Amendment Guarantees of Free Speech and Press?", 17 *U.C.L.A. Law Review* 1180, 1200 (1970), as quoted at 2 *Med.L.Rptr.* 2155, August 2, 1977.
24. 2 *Med.L.Rptr.* 2155-56, August 2, 1977.
25. Meeropol v. Nizer, 2 *Med.L.Rptr.* 2269, August 30, 1977.
26. Ibid., 2274-75.
27. 501 F.Supp. 848, 6 *Med.L.Rptr.* 2204 (1980).
28. Harper & Row v. Nation, 9 *Med.L.Rptr.* 2489, December 13, 1983. Judge Thomas Meskill dissented.
29. "News Notes," *Media Law Reporter,* May 28, 1985.
30. Ibid.
31. CBS v. Roy Export Co., 672 F.2d 1095 (1982); cert. denied, 102 S.Ct. 60 (1982).
32. Zacchini v. Scripps-Howard, 2 *Med.L.Rptr.* 2089, decided June 28, 1977.
33. Salinger v. Random House, "News Notes," *Media Law Reporter,* February 10, 1987.
34. "News Notes," *Media Law Reporter,* August 18, 1987.
35. Ibid.
36. Op. cit., n. 33.
37. Pacific & Southern Co. v. Duncan, 105 S.Ct. 1867 (1985).
38. *The NEWS Media & The LAW,* Fall 1986, p. 44.
39. Hustler Magazine v. Moral Majority, Inc., 796 F.2d 1148 (1986).
40. *The NEWS Media & The LAW,* Fall 1986, pp. 9-10.
41. International News Service v. Associated Press, 248 U.S. 215, 39 S.Ct. 68, 63 L.Ed. 211.
42. Paul W. Sullivan, "News Piracy: Interpretations of Unfair Competition and the Misappropriation Doctrine," a paper presented at the annual convention of the Association for Education in Journalism, Madison, Wisconsin, August 1977, pp. 2-3. (Except for citations for two cases, other footnotes omitted.)
43. INS v. AP, 248 U.S. 215, 39 S.Ct. 68 (1918).
44. Pottstown Daily News Publishing Co. v. Pottstown Broadcasting Co., 411 Pa. 383, 192 A.2d 657.
45. Sam G. Riley and Jack Shandle, "Commercial Use without Consent: Privacy or Property?" a paper presented at the Association for Education in Journalism convention at San Diego, California, in August 1974, p. 3 (footnotes omitted).

46. INS v. AP, 248 U.S. at 243, 39 S.Ct. at 74.

47. Fortnightly Corporation v. United Artists Television, Inc., 392 U.S. 390, 88 S.Ct. 2084, 20 L.Ed.2d 1176. Justices Douglas, Harlan, and Marshall took no part in either the consideration of the case or in the decision.

48. The FCC asserted regulatory control over CATV in 1972 (37 Fed. Reg. 3252, 36 FCC 2d 141) and was upheld by the U.S. Supreme Court in U.S. v. Southwestern Cable Co., 392 U.S. 157, 88 S.Ct. 1994, 20 L.Ed.2d 1001 (1968), and again in *Fortnightly.*

49. CBS v. Teleprompter Corp., 415 U.S. 394, 94 S.Ct. 1129, 39 L.Ed.2d 415 (1974). Justice Blackmun dissented in part; Justice Douglas, joined by Chief Justice Burger, dissented.

50. Universal City Studios v. Sony Corporation of America, 480 F.Supp. 429 (Central District of California, 1979), 5 *Med.L.Rptr.* 1737, October 30, 1979.

51. 659 F.2d 983 (1981).

52. "News Notes," *Media Law Reporter,* January 24, 1984. Also 52 *U.S. Law Week* 4090.

53. Ibid.

54. "Off-Air Taping, Piracy, and the New Copyright law — A Symposium," *Educational and Industrial Television,* Vol. 10, No. 7, July 1978, p. 33.

55. Williams & Wilkins Co. v. U.S., 172 U.S.P.Q. 670 (Court of Claims).

56. 42 *U.S. Law Week* 2282, December 4, 1973. In his opinion for the court, Judge Davis pointed out that prior to the proliferation of copying machines, copying generally was acceptable, as distinguished from printing, reprinting and publishing.

57. 44 *U.S. Law Week* 3129, August 16, 1975. Justice Blackmun took no part in the consideration or decision of the case.

58. Report No. 94-1476, op. cit., note 12, pp. 68–70.

59. Goldstein v. California, 412 U.S. 546, 93 S.Ct. 2302, 37 L.Ed.2d 163 (1973).

60. *Advertising Age,* June 18, 1984, p. 12.

61. Ibid.

62. "State Activities," *Media Law Reporter,* September 13, 1983.

63. Apple Computer Inc. v. Franklin Computer Corp., No. 82-1582 (3d Circuit, 1983).

64. Whelan Associates, Inc. v. Jaslow Laboratory, Inc. 797 F.2d 1222 (1986).

65. Artic International, Inc. v. Midway (No. 82-1992), *Media Law Reporter,* October 11, 1983. For Seventh Circuit's decision, see 9 *Med.L.Rptr.* 1605.

66. David Ladd, "Securing the Future of Copyright"; remarks before the International Publishers Association in Mexico City, March 13, 1984.

67. Brunswick Beacon v. Schock-Hopchas Publishing, 13 *Med.L.Rptr.* 2030, March 10, 1987.

68. *Editor & Publisher,* March 21, 1987, p. 28.

69. Julius R. Lunsford, Jr., "The Philosophy of Trademark Use — Legal Aspects, History and Guidelines," *Editor & Publisher,* December 3, 1983, p. 11T.

70. Ibid., p. 13T.

71. Lunsford, "Trademark Protection: The Role of the Press," *Editor & Publisher,* December 1, 1984, p. 5T.

72. "The Philosophy of Trademark Use . . .," op. cit., note 69, p. 18T.

73. Ibid., p. 22T.

74. United States Trade Association, 6 East 45th St., New York, N.Y. 10017; *Trade Names Dictionary,* Gale Research Co., Detroit, Mich., and *Standard Directory of Advertisers,* National Register Publishing Co., Inc., Skokie, Ill.

Court Structure, Procedure, and Jurisdiction

There are two main branches of law vis-à-vis court systems and functions: civil and criminal. There are two major classifications of courts: those with original, or "trial court," jurisdiction, and those with appellate jurisdiction. In some instances a court may have both original and appellate jurisdiction. In addition, there are courts of general jurisdiction which handle a wide variety of criminal and civil cases, and courts of specialized jurisdiction which only handle cases involving certain amounts in controversy (small claims courts) or dealing with special subject matter (domestic relations courts).

Criminal law, whether state or federal, involves cases that can lead to forfeiture of life or liberty by means of capital punishment or imprisonment in a penitentiary, and/or result in fines. A criminal misdemeanor involves a lesser offense than does a felony. Consequently, punishment is usually limited to incarceration in a jail or some other comparable penal institution (but not a penitentiary) for no more than one year and/or a fine not to exceed a certain amount.

Under the civil law, someone or something (a person, corporation, or state) usually is claiming that someone or something has caused some kind of injury or damage and seeks, by means of a damage suit, to have such injury redressed. In addition to a damage suit, the plaintiff may also seek a remedy to stop the wrong (or tort) from continuing. In a court that has general jurisdiction, damages could be awarded as a function of the "court of law" while the same judge, sitting as "a court of equity," could issue a restraining order, such as a temporary injunction, to prevent continuation of the wrong or illegal action.

The law that governs a federal or state case, whether criminal or civil, and regardless of the kind of court involved, is found in the constitutions of those states or of the United States (constitutional law), in the statutes (statutory law), or in the common law. The common law, or "case law," is derived from judgments and decrees of courts that go far back in history. Thus, in a sense, common law is judge-made law. Many important legal areas are based on common-law principles, including tort law and contract law. Common law also implements constitutional and statutory law and, in turn, is conditioned by them. The need for "case law" is apparent when judged by the futility of trying to cope, by means of statutory and constitutional law alone, with the multiforms of illegal and harmful situations that can result in complex societies.

Federal Judicial System

Section 1 of Article III of the U.S. Constitution briefly describes how the system is to be set up: "The judicial power of the United States, shall be vested in one supreme court, and in such inferior courts as the Congress may from time to time ordain and establish."

Section 2 of that article addresses itself to the jurisdiction of such a system of courts:

> The judicial power shall extend to all cases, in law and equity, arising under this Constitution, the laws of the United States, and treaties made, or which shall be made, under their authority; to all cases affecting ambassadors, other public ministers and consuls; to all cases of admiralty and maritime jurisdictions; to controversies to which the United States shall be a party; to controversies between two or more States; between a State and citizens of another State; between citizens of different States, between citizens of the same State claiming lands under grants of different States, and between a State, or the citizens thereof, and foreign States, citizens or subjects.
>
> In all cases affecting ambassadors, other public ministers and consuls, and those in which a State shall be party, the supreme court shall have original jurisdiction. In all the other cases before mentioned, the supreme court shall have appellate jurisdiction, both as to law and fact, with such exceptions, and under such regulations as the Congress shall make.

Congress was not long in carrying out the above provisions. The First Congress in 1789 established the federal judicial system at a time when eleven of the thirteen states had ratified the Constitution. It established the Supreme Court comprised of a chief justice and five associate justices; thirteen District Courts as courts of original jurisdiction, and three Circuit Courts, each consisting of one district court judge and two Supreme Court justices who travelled the circuit to hear and adjudicate cases.

Today, by comparison, there are nine members of the Supreme Court—the chief justice of the United States and eight associate justices; 94 District Courts in the 50 states, the District of Columbia, and Puerto Rico, with about 560 judges, and 13 circuit U.S. Courts of Appeal with slightly more than 168 judges (see Fig. A.1). In addition, a Magistrate's Court was created by Congress in 1968 to replace the system of U.S. commissioners then in use. The reason for the change was to reduce the workload on district courts. There are other federal courts, too.

Customs Court. This court hears cases involving the valuation and classification of imported goods.

Court of Customs and Patent Appeals. This court hears appeals from the Customs Court, as well as from the Patent Office and Tariff Commission.

Court of Claims. This court hears cases involving monetary damage suits against the U.S. government brought by private individuals or corporations.

Tax Court. This court hears disputes between taxpayers and the Internal Revenue Service.

Magistrate's Courts. These courts currently consist of about 500 magistrates, of whom a third are full time. These courts are created at the behest of district court judges. Principal functions of the Magistrate's Court are (1) to conduct preliminary hearings and (2) to dispose of minor-type cases under certain circumstances.

Under the Federal Magistrate Act of 1979, magistrates were given authority to dispose of federal criminal misdemeanor cases. They also can try any civil jury or nonjury case if the parties consent.

The preliminary hearing is for the purpose of determining if there is sufficient evidence to hold a person in custody pending further criminal action, such as a grand jury indictment or the filing of an information by a U.S. district attorney. Also, the magistrate can set bond (if the offense charged is a bondable one) and permit the accused to post bond and be free pending further action.

District Courts. These are the "trial courts" in the federal judicial system—courts of original jurisdiction for both criminal and civil cases. In the latter, however, certain conditions may be attached. For example, in a civil action between citizens of two different states (called a "diversity action"), the sum or value involved must exceed $10,000. If the United States is a party in a civil suit and the sum or value is $10,000 or less, the case may be disposed of in the U.S. Court of Claims although the district courts would have concurrent jurisdiction. District Courts also have original jurisdiction in bankruptcy cases, in certain kinds of admiralty and maritime cases, and in those types of cases as Congress, from time to time, might designate. Such mandates have come in the Freedom of Information Act of 1967, the Sherman and Clayton antitrust laws of 1890 and 1914, respectively, and the Copyright Law of 1909 and 1976, to mention a few. U.S. attorneys frequently are required to seek equitable remedies through proceedings initiated in this court. Thus it may sit either as a court of law or a court of equity.

Decisions of District Courts are reviewable directly by the U.S. Supreme Court in certain limited situations, or, more usually, by the intermediate Court of Appeals.

Generally one District Court judge will constitute the court. But in those instances where an "interlocutory" (temporary) injunction is at issue, a three-judge panel is specifically required by a 1910 act of Congress. The powers of a single judge are spelled out in a 1942 statute and by the Supreme Court. Like all federal judges, district judges are appointed by the President subject to confirmation by the Senate. The number of districts in a state depends on the state's population. For example, California has four districts—Northern, Central, Eastern, and Southern; Iowa has two—Northern and Southern. There are eleven district judges in the Northern District of California; there is one each in the Iowa districts.

The reporting of many District Court decisions, in which opinions are filed, is done in a publication known as the *Federal Supplement*. Thus, when a citation such as 52 F.Supp. 362 is given, this means volume 52 of the *Federal Supplement,* p. 362.

Court of Appeals. These courts carry the bulk of appellate reviews in the federal system, deciding 13,127 cases in the year ending June 30, 1983 (excluding cases decided by the then year-old Federal Circuit (see Fig. A.1). By comparison, the Supreme Court will decide 200 to 300 cases a year. One reason for the difference lies in the number of circuit courts. There are 13 circuits, each with a Court of Appeals (the First through the Eleventh Circuits, plus the District of Columbia and Federal Circuits). The smallest circuit (the First) has six judges while the largest, the Ninth Circuit, has 28. More than 20,000 cases may be filed with these appellate courts in a year (Fig. App. A.1).

The Federal Circuit was created in 1983 and consists of 12 judges. Its jurisdiction is set forth in 28 U.S.C.S. 1295, and includes appeals from final decisions of U.S. District Courts in the Canal Zone, Guam, Virgin Islands, and the northern Mariana Islands, plus appeals from final decisions of the U.S. Claims Court, U.S. Court of International Trade, Merit Systems Protection Board, and Board of Patent Interferences. The heads of executive departments or agencies, with the approval of the Attorney General, may refer to this court any final decision by a Board of Contracts.

On the average it takes about four years from the time a case is filed in District Court until it is disposed of at the appellate level. This time-lag persists despite the fact that more cases are being decided at the appellate level without benefit of oral hearings and the absence

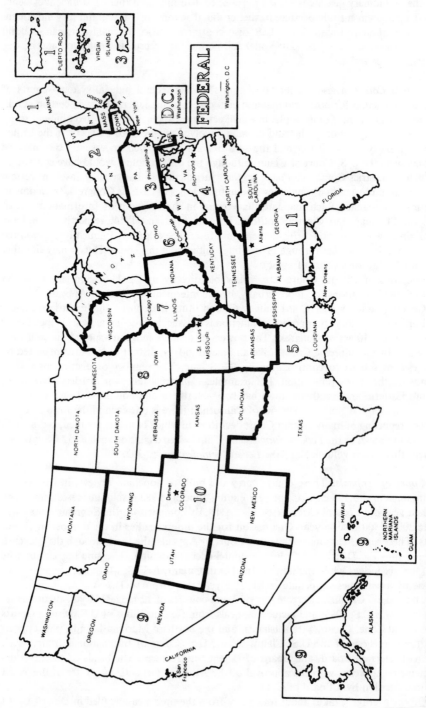

Fig. A.1. The thirteen federal judicial circuits.

of written opinions. When opinions are given, they appear in *Federal Reporter 2nd Series*. Thus, a citation, 480 F.2d 428, means volume 480, page 428, of the *Federal Reporter Second Series*. A citation such as 2 *Med.L.Rptr.* 2763 means volume two, page 2763, of *Media Law Reporter*, a weekly publication of the Bureau of National Affairs.

By far the vast majority of cases handled by the Courts of Appeals stems from appellate jurisdiction, but a small number involves original proceedings. The decisions of numerous administrative agencies, such as the Federal Trade Commission and Federal Communications Commission, are directly reviewable in the District of Columbia Circuit Court of Appeals. Decisions of the District Courts are reviewable for errors. A three-judge panel of a Court of Appeals usually will hear cases and controversies unless a hearing or rehearing before the court *en banc* (all of the judges) is ordered by a majority of the circuit judges of the circuit who are in regular active service. Such *en banc* "sittings" occurred, for example, in the Pentagon Papers cases. But *en banc* hearings are rare. Of the 13,127 cases decided in the year ending in June 1983, only 66 of them were by *en banc* sittings of the circuit courts.

Every case that is filed in, or reaches, a Court of Appeals is first screened by a member of that court who decides if oral arguments are necessary. Such arguments allow the parties in a dispute, such as in a civil matter, or the defense attorney and U.S. district attorney or Justice Department representative, in a criminal matter, to present additional views concerning points raised in briefs which are included at the time of the filing of the case. Furthermore, court members can direct questions to opposing counsel. Whenever a constitutional issue is at stake, a Court of Appeals broadly reviews the initial decision to determine what the Constitution requires.

Supreme Court. The Supreme Court, which since 1869 has consisted of nine members, has original jurisdiction in two classes of cases: those involving U.S. ambassadors and those in which a state is a party. The remainder of its jurisdiction by and large lies in hearing and deciding appeals from cases tried or decided in federal courts or those which usually have been decided by the state supreme courts.

In his review of 1973, Chief Justice Burger noted how the gravity of the issues now facing the Court has changed. From 1803 to 1857, he said, not one act of Congress was declared unconstitutional by the Court, and only 36 state statutes fell into this category. But in 1973 alone, 57 of 177 cases argued before the Court involved claims that city ordinances, state laws, or federal laws violated the U.S. Constitution, and many of these claims were upheld.

Attempts by Congress to delimit the jurisdiction of the Supreme Court, such as in the First Judiciary Act of 1789, must contend with the fact that the Court is the final arbiter as to what the Constitution means. Chief Justice John Marshall declared in an 1803 decision in *Marbury v. Madison* (1 Cranch 137, 2 L.Ed. 60) that the judicial power of the United States (meaning the Supreme Court's power) extended to all cases arising under the Constitution. Through the broad interpretation of the commerce clause, the police power, etc., in the Constitution, many cases have been swept within that ambit and consequently subject to Supreme Court review. If this power of interpretation were not enough, then Congress, by enactment in 1952, considerably expanded the Court's discretionary power of review. Thus, there are two major ways that a case can be brought before the Court: (1) the litigants appeal for review of a lower court decision because they believe they have a right to have their case heard by the court of last resort, or (2) the Court can exercise its discretionary power by means of a writ of certiorari and bring a case up for review.

By far, most cases fall within the latter situation. Thus, the parties may only ask that the Supreme Court review their case; they cannot demand review by right. They ask the Court to consent to review by petitioning for a writ of certiorari. The discretionary power was first given by Congress in 1891 when it also modernized the Courts of Appeals and their circuits.

Concerning which appeals should or should not be granted, the Court follows the so-called rule of four; that is, at least four Court members must agree that the questions or issues contained in the appeal should be carried forward by means of briefs and oral arguments, otherwise the appeal will be dismissed.

Many petitions for writs of certiorari are filed with the Court each year and have contributed substantially to the number of cases being filed with the Court—1234 in 1951; more than 3000 annually now. Most of these cases are disposed of by denying the petitions. Such a denial is not a "holding" of the Court concerning the merits of the case. However, if the Court summarily affirms or dismisses a case, such an action is on the merits.

If a majority of the Court members who take part in the decision of a case agrees on the ultimate disposition of a case, then such agreement will constitute a "holding" by the Court. But the majority might not be in agreement as to why a decision of an inferior court should be affirmed or reversed. If three of the five members, for example, agree on the reasoning, then one member will write the opinion for the Court and the other two most likely will associate themselves with that opinion. But the two who disagreed with the reasoning of the plurality opinion can write separate, but concurring, opinions—concurring in the results. The four who disagree with the decision or holding of the Court register dissent. Such disagreement usually is elaborated upon in a dissenting opinion by one or more of the dissenters.

The *Rosenbloom v. Metromedia* case (see Chapter 5), decided by the Supreme Court in 1971, is an example of a majority of the members agreeing that a radio station should not be held liable for damages because of an error made in a news program (even though the error was clearly libelous). But only three of the five in the majority could agree as to why the court of appeals' decision should be affirmed. Thus, Justice Brennan wrote a plurality opinion and was joined in that opinion by only two other justices who believed that Brennan was correctly interpreting the Constitution insofar as libel suits by private citizens were concerned. Therefore, the Brennan opinion was not a "holding" by the Court. In fact, the plurality opinion was specifically rejected by a majority of the Court in a 1974 case, *Gertz v. Welch.* Similarly, many of the Court's considerations of obscenity cases from *Roth* in 1957 until *Miller* in 1973 could only muster plurality opinions. In some of these cases as many as seven different opinions were written as the justices sought to explain the reasons for their votes.

Under the Court's rules, a tie vote (or Court deadlock) means that the lower court's ruling is affirmed but no precedent is established. A majority vote, of course, establishes precedent.

Per curiam decisions also are given by the Court; that is, an unsigned decision by at least a majority of the Court, such as in the Pentagon Papers cases. A short statement as to the reasons for the Court permitting resumption of publication of the papers was given in the per curiam decision, and then each Court member wrote a separate opinion explaining why *The New York Times* and the *Washington Post* should, or should not, be permitted to publish the classified study.

Court decisions can be of several types. The Court can (1) affirm an inferior court's decision or action; (2) reverse a decision and remand the case to the lower court for dismissal or whatever; (3) return the case to the lower court for proceedings consistent with the views expressed in the Court's opinion; (4) vacate a judgment and remand for further proceedings; and (5) grant or deny applications for stays of judgments.

Court decisions and opinions are recorded in three publications: *United States Reports, Supreme Court Reporter* and *United States Supreme Court Reports,* Lawyers' Edition. A citation such as 94 S.Ct. 2437 (1974) means that the case was decided in 1974 and is reported in volume 94, page 2437, of the *Supreme Court Reporter.*

State Judicial Systems

The federal system is simple compared with the state systems since the latter vary from state to state. Generally the lowest level of courts will have limited jurisdiction in both civil and criminal cases and will be called by such names as magistrate's court, police court, municipal court or justice of the peace court (Fig. A.2).

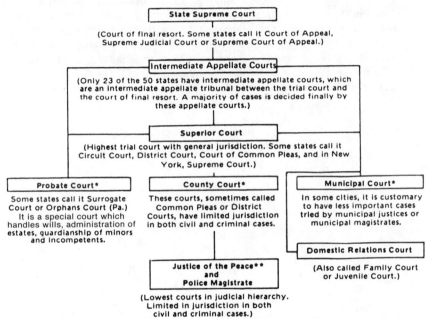

Source: Reprinted by permission of the American Bar Association from its booklet, **Law and the Courts**; copyright, 1974, ABA.

*Courts of special jurisdiction, such as Probate, Family or Juvenile, and so-called inferior courts, such as Common Pleas or Municipal courts, may be separate courts or may be part of the trial court of general jurisdiction.
**Justice of the peace courts do not exist in all states. Their jurisdictions vary greatly from state to state.

Fig. A.2. State judicial system.

These courts deal with a variety of minor offenses, such as public intoxication, speeding, trespassing, illegal parking, etc. They may be empowered to handle civil cases which do not involve a sum of money exceeding a few hundred dollars. If these courts are empowered to impose a jail sentence for a misdemeanor, the length of the sentence will be severely limited.

1. Courts of original jurisdiction. Somewhere above the layer of magistrate or justice of the peace courts will be courts variously designated but which have one thing in common—original jurisdiction for either criminal cases or civil cases, or both. These will be the principal trial courts in the state and will be called by such names as

district court, court of common pleas, circuit court or, as in the state of New York, the supreme court (and each county in that state has such a court with the court of appeals serving as the uppermost appellate court in the state). These courts may handle civil suits usually involving a minimum sum of money. They probably will handle both criminal misdemeanors and felonies (if the two kinds of cases are within the jurisdiction of the same court). In the larger cities, courts of original jurisdiction may be set up to handle civil suits exclusively, or only criminal cases.

2. In the more populated states, an intermediate appellate court structure will exist. In Missouri, for example, courts of appeals sit in Kansas City, Springfield, and St. Louis. Generally they will have appellate jurisdiction only.

3. Each state has a supreme court although it may not be called by that name (as in New York). State constitutions generally indicate the kinds of cases that can be reviewed by the highest court in the state, such as those involving constitutionality of state laws. Usually only civil cases involving a certain amount of money can be appealed to the supreme court, such as in Missouri where the amount must exceed $15,000. Also, any case that involves the state as one of the parties in a suit generally can be reviewed, as can any adjudications at the intermediate appellate level.

Definitions of Legal Terms

Adjudication Giving or pronouncing a judgment or decree; also the judgment given.

Adversary system The system of trial practice in the United States in which each of the opposing, or adversary, parties has full opportunity to present and establish opposing contentions before the court.

Amicus curiae (*a-mi' kus kū' ri-e*) A friend of the court; one who interposes, with the permission of the court, and volunteers information upon some matter of the law.

Appellant The party appealing a decision or judgment, which he considers unfavorable, to a higher court.

Appellate court A court having jurisdiction of appeal and review; not a "trial court."

Appellee The party against whom an appeal is taken.

Arraignment In criminal practice, to bring a prisoner to the bar of the court to answer a criminal charge.

Bail To set at liberty a person arrested or imprisoned, on security being taken, for his appearance on a specified day and place.

Bail bond An obligation signed by the accused, with sureties, to secure his presence in court.

Banc (*bangk*) Bench; the place where a court permanently or regularly sits. A "sitting in banc" is a meeting of all the judges of a court, as distinguished from the sitting of a single judge.

Brief A written or printed document prepared by counsel to file in court, usually setting forth both facts and law in support of his case.

Certiorari (*ser'-shē-ă-răr' ē*) An original writ commanding judges or officers of inferior courts to certify or to return records of proceedings in a cause for judicial review. In effect the issuing of the writ indicates that an appeal of the case will be heard.

Note: Many of the definitions in this appendix were taken, with permission, from a booklet, *The Newsman's Guide to Legalese,* published by the Pennsylvania Bar Association, Harrisburg, Pa.

Change of venue   The removal of suit begun in one county or district to another, for trial.

Common law   Law which derives its authority solely from usages and customs of immemorial antiquity, or from the judgments and decrees of courts. Also called "case law."

Complainant   Synonymous with "plaintiff."

Complaint   The first or initiatory pleading on the part of the complainant, or plaintiff, in a civil action.

Contempt of court   Any act calculated to embarrass, hinder or obstruct a court in the administration of justice, or calculated to lessen its authority or dignity. Contempts are of two kinds: direct and indirect. Direct contempts are those committed in the immediate presence of the court; indirect is the term chiefly used with reference to the failure or refusal to obey a lawful order.

Damages   Pecuniary compensation which may be recovered in the courts by any person who has suffered loss, detriment, or injury to his person, property, or rights, through the unlawful act or negligence of another.

Decree   A decision or order of the court. A final decree is one which fully and finally disposes of the litigation; an interlocutory decree is a provisional or preliminary decree.

Demur (dĭ-*mer'*)   To file a pleading (called a "demurrer"), admitting the truth of the facts in the complaint, or answer, but contending they are legally insufficient.

De novo   Anew, afresh. A "trial de novo" is the retrial of a case.

Dictum, or **obiter dictum**   Statements in a judge's opinion that really are not necessary to the court's decision but often are made in response to some suggestion issuing from the fact situation in the case or by the legal issues involved. Statements characterized as "dicta" do not have precedential value.

Directed verdict   An instruction by the judge to the jury to return a specific verdict.

Diversity action   This is an archaic concept in federal law which permits a resident of one state to sue a resident or corporation of another state in the suing person's home state.

Due process   Law in its regular course of administration through the courts of justice. The guarantee of due process requires that every accused person have the protection of a fair trial.

En banc   All of the judges of the court sitting together to hear a cause (suit, litigation, or action—either civil or criminal).

Enjoin   To require a person, by writ of injunction from a court of equity, to perform or to abstain or desist from some act.

Equitable action   An action which may be brought for the purpose of restraining the threatened infliction of wrongs or injuries and the prevention of threatened illegal action. Such a remedy is not available at common law.

Equity, courts of   Courts which administer a legal remedy according to the system of equity, as distinguished from courts of common law.

Et al. An abbreviation of et alii, meaning "and others."

Ex parte By or for one party; done for, in behalf of or on the application of one party only.

Ex post facto (*eks pōst fak' to*) After the fact; an act or fact occurring after some previous act or fact, and relating thereto.

Fair comment A term used in the law of libel, applying to statements made by a writer in an honest belief of their truth, relating to official act, even though the statements are not true in fact.

Felony A crime of a graver nature than a misdemeanor. Generally, an offense punishable by death or imprisonment in a penitenitiary.

Fiduciary (*fī-dū'-shē-er'-ē*) A term derived from the Roman law, meaning a person holding the character of a trustee, in respect to the trust and confidence involved in it and the scrupulous good faith and candor which it requires.

General demurrer A demurrer which raises the question whether the pleading against which it is directed lacks the definite allegations essential to a cause of action or defense.

Grand jury A jury whose duty is to receive complaints and accusations in criminal cases, hear the evidence and find bills of indictment ("true bills") in cases where they are satisfied a trial ought to be had.

Habeas corpus (*hā' bē-as kor' pus*) "You have the body." The name given a variety of writs whose object is to bring a person before a court or judge. In most common usage, it is directed to the official or person detaining another, commanding him to produce the body of the prisoner or person detained so the court may determine if such person has been denied his liberty without due process of law.

In camera (*in kam'e-ra*) In chambers; in private.

Indictment An accusation in writing, found and presented by a grand jury, charging that a person therein named has done some act, or been guilty of some omission, which, by law, is a crime.

Information An accusation of some criminal offense, in the nature of an indictment, from which it differs only in being presented by a competent public officer instead of a grand jury.

Injunction A mandatory or prohibitive writ issued by a court.

Instruction A direction given by the judge to the jury concerning the law of the case.

Inter alia Among other things or matters.

Interlocutory Provisional; temporary; not final. Refers to orders and decrees of court.

Jurisprudence The philosophy of law, or the science which treats of the principles of positive law and legal relations.

Jury   A certain number of people, selected according to law, and sworn to inquire of certain matters of fact, and declare the truth upon evidence laid before them.

Libel   A method of defamation expressed by print, writing, pictures or signs; in its most general sense, any publication that is injurious to the reputation of another.

Mandamus (*man-dā'mus*)   The name of a writ which issues from a court of superior jurisdiction, directed to an inferior court, commanding the performance of a particular act.

Misdemeanor   Offenses less than felonies; generally those punishable by fine or imprisonment other than in peniteniaries.

Mistrial   An erroneous or invalid trial; a trial which cannot stand in law because of lack of jurisdiction, wrong drawing of jurors or disregard of some other fundamental requisite.

Moot   Unsettled; undecided. A moot point is one not settled by judicial decision.

Nolle prosequi (*nol-ē pros'-e-kwī'*)   A formal entry upon the record by the plaintiff in a civil suit, or the prosecuting officer in a criminal case, by which he declares that he "will not further prosecute" the case.

Nolo contendere (*nō'lō kon-ten'de-rē*)   A pleading, usually by defendants in criminal cases, which literally means, "I will not contest it."

Parties   The persons who are actively concerned in the prosecution or defense of a legal proceeding.

Per curiam   No identifiable member of the court wrote the opinion.

Petit jury   The ordinary jury of twelve (or fewer) persons for the trial of a civil or criminal case; so called to distinguish it from the grand jury.

Plaintiff   A person who brings an action; the party who complains or sues in a personal action and is so named, on the record.

Precedent   A judicial decision that is authority for, or furnishes a rule of law binding on, the disposition of a current case. Precedent cases involve similar facts or raise similar questions of law to the case being decided.

Preliminary hearing   Synonymous with "preliminary examination." This is the hearing given a person charged with crime by a magistrate or judge to determine whether he should be held for trial.

Quasi-judicial   Authority or discretion vested in an officer wherein his acts partake of a judicial character.

Rule of court   An order made by a court having competent jurisdiction. Rules of court are either general or special; the former are the regulations by which the practice of law is governed; the latter are special orders made in particular cases.

Slander Base and defamatory words tending to prejudice another in his reputation, business or means of livelihood. Slander is an oral defamation unlike libel, which is a written or printed defamation.

Special performance An order from a court instructing the subject of the order to carry out an affirmative act.

Stare decisis (*star'-ē de-sī'-sis*) The doctrine that, when a court has once laid down a principle of law as applicable to a certain set of facts, it will adhere to that principle and apply it to future cases where the facts are substantially the same.

Statute The written law in contradistinction to the unwritten law.

Stay A stopping or arresting of a judicial proceeding by order of the court.

Subpoena A process to cause a witness to appear and give testimony before a court or magistrate.

Subpoena duces tecum (*su-pena dū'-sĕ-stē'-kum*) A process by which the court commands a witness to produce certain documents or records in a trial.

Tort An injury or wrong committed, either with or without force, to the person or property of another.

Trial de novo A new trial or retrial in an appellate court in which the whole case is gone into as if no trial had been held in a lower court.

Venue A particular county, city or geographical area in which a court with jurisdiction may hear and determine a case.

Warrant of arrest A writ issued by a magistrate, justice of the peace or other competent authority, to a sheriff or other officer, requiring him to arrest the person therein named and bring him before the magistrate or court to answer to a specified charge.

Writ An order issuing from a court requiring the performance of a specified act, or giving authority and commission to have it done.

Bill of Rights and the Fourteenth Amendment

ARTICLE I

Congress shall make no law respecting an establishment of religion, or prohibiting the free exercise thereof; or abridging the freedom of speech, or of the press; or the right of the people peaceably to assemble, and to petition the government for a redress of grievances.

ARTICLE II

A well regulated Militia, being necessary to the security of a free State, the right of the people to keep and bear Arms, shall not be infringed.

ARTICLE III

No Soldier shall, in time of peace be quartered in any house, without the consent of the Owner, nor in time of war, but in a manner to be prescribed by law.

ARTICLE IV

The right of the people to be secure in their persons, houses, papers, and effects, against unreasonable searches and seizures, shall not be violated, and no Warrants shall issue, but upon probable cause, supported by Oath or affirmation, and particularly the place to be searched, and the persons or things to be seized.

ARTICLE V

No person shall be held to answer for a capital, or otherwise infamous crime, unless on a presentment or indictment of a Grand Jury, except in cases arising in the land or naval forces, or in the Militia, when in actual service in time of War or public danger; nor shall any person be subject for the same offense to be twice put in jeopardy of life or limb; nor shall be compelled in any criminal case to be a witness against himself, nor be deprived of life, liberty, or property, without due process of law; nor shall private property be taken for public use, without just compensation.

ARTICLE VI

In all criminal prosecutions, the accused shall enjoy the right to a speedy and public trial, by an impartial jury of the State and district wherein the crime shall have been committed, which district shall have been previously ascertained by law, and to be informed of the nature and cause of the accusation; to be confronted with the witnesses against him; to have compulsory process for obtaining witnesses in his favor, and to have the Assistance of Counsel for his defense.

ARTICLE VII

In suits at common law, where the value in controversy shall exceed twenty dollars, the right of trial by jury shall be preserved, and no fact tried by a jury, shall be otherwise reexamined in any Court of the United States, than according to the rules of the common law.

ARTICLE VIII

Excessive bail shall not be required, nor excessive fines imposed, nor cruel and unusual punishments inflicted.

ARTICLE IX

The enumeration in the Constitution, of certain rights, shall not be construed to deny or disparage others retained by the people.

ARTICLE X

The powers not delegated to the United States by the Constitution, nor prohibited by it to the States, are reserved to the States respectively, or to the people.

ARTICLE XIV

July 28, 1868

§1. All persons born or naturalized in the United States, and subject to the jurisdiction thereof, are citizens of the United States and of the State wherein they reside. No State shall make or enforce any law which shall abridge the privileges or immunities of citizens of the United States; nor shall any State deprive any person of life, liberty, or property, without due process of law; nor deny to any person within its jurisdiction the equal protection of the laws. . . .

NAME INDEX

SUBJECT INDEX

693

CANISIUS COLLEGE LIBRARY

3 5084 00219 3251

KF 2750 .F7 1990
Francois, William E.
Mass media law and
  regulation

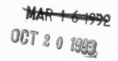

MAR 1 6 1992

OCT 2 0 1993

CANISIUS COLLEGE LIBRARY
BUFFALO, N.Y.

DEMCO